February 18–20, 2013
San Antonio, Texas, USA

**Association for
Computing Machinery**

Advancing Computing as a Science & Profession

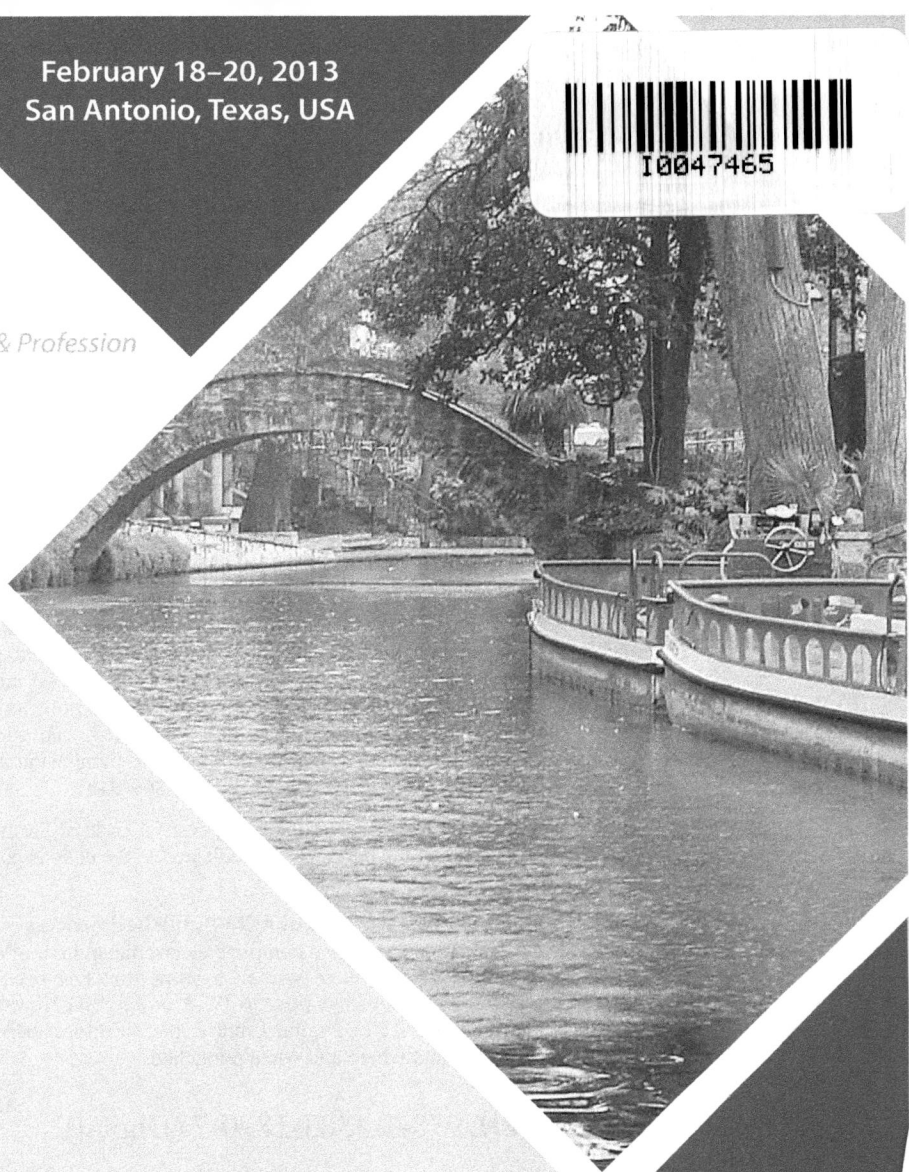

I0047465

CODASPY'13

Proceedings of the Third ACM

Conference on Data and Application Security and Privacy

Sponsored by:
ACM SIGSAC

Supported by:
**The Institute of Cyber Security, Center for Education
& Research in Information Assurance & Security,
and the Cyber Center at Purdue University**

Association for Computing Machinery

Advancing Computing as a Science & Profession

The Association for Computing Machinery
2 Penn Plaza, Suite 701
New York, New York 10121-0701

Notice to Past Authors of ACM-Published Articles

ACM intends to create a complete electronic archive of all articles and/or other material previously published by ACM. If you have written a work that has been previously published by ACM in any journal or conference proceedings prior to 1978, or any SIG Newsletter at any time, and you do NOT want this work to appear in the ACM Digital Library, please inform permissions@acm.org, stating the title of the work, the author(s), and where and when published.

ISBN: 978-1-4503-1890-7 (Digital)

ISBN: 978-1-4503-2089-4 (Print)

Additional copies may be ordered prepaid from:

ACM Order Department
PO Box 30777
New York, NY 10087-0777, USA

Phone: 1-800-342-6626 (USA and Canada)
+1-212-626-0500 (Global)
Fax: +1-212-944-1318
E-mail: acmhelp@acm.org
Hours of Operation: 8:30 am – 4:30 pm ET

Printed in the USA

Foreword

It is our great pleasure to welcome you to the third edition of the *ACM Conference on Data and Application Security and Privacy (CODASPY 2013)*, which follows the successful first and second editions held in February 2011 and 2012. This conference series has been founded to foster novel and exciting research in this arena and to help generate new directions for further research and development. The initial concept came up in a conversation between the two co-founders when both happened to be at the same meeting. This was followed by discussions with a number of fellow cyber security researchers. Their enthusiastic encouragement persuaded us to move ahead with the always daunting task of creating a high-quality conference.

Data and applications that manipulate data are crucial assets in today's information age. With the increasing drive towards availability of data and services anytime and anywhere, security and privacy risks have increased. Vast amounts of privacy-sensitive data are being collected today by organizations for a variety of reasons. Unauthorized disclosure, modification, usage or denial of access to these data and corresponding services may result in high human and financial costs. New applications such as social networking and social computing provide value by aggregating input from numerous individual users and the mobile devices they carry and computing new information of benefit to society and individuals. To achieve efficiency and effectiveness in traditional domains such as healthcare there is a drive to make these records electronic and highly available. The need for organizations to share information effectively is underscored by rapid innovations in the business world that require close collaboration across traditional boundaries. Security and privacy in these and other arenas can be meaningfully achieved only in context of the application domain. Data and applications security and privacy has rapidly expanded as a research field with many important challenges to be addressed.

In response to the call for papers of CODASPY 2013 a total of 107 papers were submitted from Africa, Asia, Australia, Europe, and North America. The program committee selected 24 full-length research papers, which is three more than last year. These papers cover a variety of topics, including privacy of social networks, novel privacy techniques and applications, and access control and security of smart appliances and mobile devices. The program committee also selected nine short papers for presentation. This year for the first time the program also includes a poster paper session presenting exciting work in progress. The program is complemented by keynote speeches by Mike Reiter and by Ronnie Killough, as well as a panel (topic not yet decided at press time).

The organization of a conference like CODASPY requires the collaboration of many individuals. First of all, we would like to thank the authors for submitting to the conference and the keynote speakers for graciously accepting our invitation. We express our gratitude to the program committee members and external reviewers for their efforts in reviewing the papers, engaging in active online discussion during the selection process and providing valuable feedback to authors. We also would like to thank the poster paper track chair, Gabriel Ghinita, and the committee of this track for an excellent job with soliciting and selecting poster papers. Our special thanks go to our local arrangements chair, Suzanne Tanaka, to our Web master and publicity chair, Ram Krishnan, and to Jae Park for assembling the proceedings. Finally, we would like to thank our sponsor, ACM SIGSAC, for their support of this conference.

We hope that you will find this program interesting and that the conference will provide you with a valuable opportunity to interact with other researchers and practitioners from institutions around the world. Enjoy!

Lujo Bauer
CODASPY'13 Program Chair
Carnegie Mellon University, USA

Elisa Bertino
CODASPY'13 General Chair & co-founder
Purdue University, USA

Ravi Sandhu
CODASPY'13 General Chair & co-founder
University of Texas at San Antonio, USA

Table of Contents

Session 8: Short Papers — Access Control and Usage Control for Distributed Systems

Session Chair: Jaehong Park *(University of Texas at San Antonio)*

Session 9: Short Papers — Users and Security Economics

Session Chair: Anna Squicciarini *(Pennsylvania State University)*

Session 10: Cloud and Distributed Computing Security and Privacy

Session Chair: Lujo Bauer *(Carnegie Mellon University)*

Author Index

CODASPY 2013 Conference Organization

General Chairs: Elisa Bertino, *Purdue University, USA*
Ravi Sandhu, *University of Texas at San Antonio, USA*

Program Chair: Lujo Bauer, *Carnegie Mellon University, USA*

Proceedings Chair: Jaehong Park, *University of Texas at San Antonio, USA*

Local Arrangements Chair: Suzanne Tanaka, *University of Texas at San Antonio, USA*

Web Master: Ram Krishnan, *University of Texas at San Antonio, USA*

Publicity Chair: Ram Krishnan, *University of Texas at San Antonio, USA*

Poster Chair: Gabriel Ghinita, *University of Massachusetts at Boston, USA*

Program Committee: Gail-Joon Ahn, *Arizona State University, USA*
Lujo Bauer, *Carnegie Mellon University (chair), USA*
William Enck, *North Carolina State University, USA*
Elena Ferrari, *University of Insubria, Italy*
Philip Fong, *University of Calgary, Canada*
Debin Gao, *Singapore Management University, Singapore*
Gabriel Ghinita, *University of Massachusetts Boston, USA*
Carl Gunter, *University of Illinois at Urbana-Champaign, USA*
Günter Karjoth, *IBM Research – Zurich, Switzerland*
Yongdae Kim, *KAIST, South Korea*
Adam J. Lee, *University of Pittsburgh, USA*
Ninghui Li, *Purdue University, USA*
Peng Liu, *Pennsylvania State University, USA*
Z. Morley Mao, *University of Michigan, USA*
Fabio Martinelli, *National Research Council of Italy, Italy*
Jaehong Park, *University of Texas at San Antonio, USA*
Günther Pernul, *University of Regensburg, Germany*
Alexander Pretschner, *Technische Universität München, Germany*
Mike Reiter, *University of North Carolina at Chapel Hill, USA*
Ahmad-Reza Sadeghi, *Technical University Darmstadt, Germany*
Elaine Shi, *University of Maryland College Park, USA*
Mahesh Tripunitara, *University of Waterloo, Canada*
Jaideep Vaidya, *Rutgers University, USA*
Danfeng Yao, *Virginia Tech, USA*

Poster Committee: Gabriel Ghinita, *University of Massachusetts Boston (chair), USA*
Ali Inan, *Isik University, Turkey*
Ram Krishnan, *University of Texas at San Antonio, USA*
Nabeel Mohamed, *Purdue University, USA*
Ian Molloy, *IBM T.J. Watson Research Center, USA*
Roland Yap, *National University of Singapore, Singapore*

Additional reviewers:

Christian Broser	Alana Libonati
Kevin Butler	Stefan Meier
Robby Cochran	Charles Morisset
Pietro Colombo	Michael Netter
Luca Davi	Dang Nguyen
Alexandra Dmitrienko	Andreas Reisser
Nicholas Farnan	Moritz Riesner
Ludwig Fuchs	Andrea Saracino
William C. Garrison III	Steffen Schulz
Michele Guglielmi	Pouyan Sepehrdad
Cuneyt Gurcan Akcora	Daniele Sgandurra
Sabri Hassan	Ashwin Shashidharan
Nikola Knežević	Michael Weber
Qi Li	Yinqian Zhang

Sponsor:

Supporters:

For Some Eyes Only: Protecting Online Information Sharing

Iulia Ion[§]   Filipe Beato[†]   Srdjan Čapkun[§]   Bart Preneel[†]   Marc Langheinrich[‡]

[§]ETH Zurich
Zurich, Switzerland
{iion,capkuns}@inf.eth.ch

[†]ESAT/ COSIC – KULeuven and iMinds
Leuven, Belgium
{first.lastname}@esat.kuleuven.be

[‡]University of Lugano (USI)
Lugano, Switzerland
marc.langheinrich@usi.ch

ABSTRACT

End-users have become accustomed to the ease with which online systems allow them to exchange messages, pictures, and other files with colleagues, friends, and family. This convenience, however, sometimes comes at the expense of having their data be viewed by a number of unauthorized parties, such as hackers, advertisement companies, other users, or governmental agencies. A number of systems have been proposed to protect data shared online; yet these solutions typically just shift trust to another third party server, are platform specific (e.g., work for Facebook only), or fail to hide that confidential communication is taking place. In this paper, we present a novel system that enables users to exchange data over any web-based sharing platform, while both keeping the communicated data confidential and hiding from a casual observer that an exchange of confidential data is taking place. We provide a proof-of-concept implementation of our system in the form of a publicly available Firefox plugin, and demonstrate the viability of our approach through a performance evaluation.

Categories and Subject Descriptors

C.2.4 [**Computer Systems Organization**]: Computer Communication Networks – Distributed Systems; K.6.5 [**Computer Milieux**]: Management of Computing and Information Systems—*Security and Protection*; E.3 [**Data**]: Data Encryption

General Terms

Security, Privacy, Online Sharing, Steganography, Usability

1. INTRODUCTION

Online sharing platforms enable a new communication paradigm. Users disclose intimate thoughts on Facebook, blog about their political views, upload holiday pictures to Google Plus, and publish their current activities on Twitter. According to estimations by the social media blog 'The

Social Skinny,' over one billion Facebook posts, 175 million Tweets, and 10 years worth of YouTube videos are being uploaded by users every day [48]. This rise in online sharing activity has prompted increasing privacy and security concerns among consumers [29]. By publishing their private information on a range of public or semipublic platforms, consumers get exposed to unauthorized disclosure of their data. Unauthorized access can happen, for instance, if hackers break into user accounts (e.g. the 2009 Google cyber attack [34]), bugs in the access control enforcement system allow unauthorized users to view user data [54], or platform providers grant advertisement companies access without the user's consent for economical reasons [49].

Several solutions have been proposed to protect user data from unauthorized usage. One solution requires the user to encrypt the data before uploading it to the online sharing platform, and to distribute encryption keys to authorized recipients only. For instance, PGP encryption allows users to protect email communication and attachments. However, this approach breaks the ease of sharing data on dedicated platforms such as online social networking sites, which manage users' network of friends and display the data in the browser.

Other solutions displace the trust users put in platform providers by creating sharing systems owned and hosted by users. Such systems require users to run their own web servers or sharing platforms for hosting their data. For example, Diaspora [28] is a private social network that runs on servers owned and operated users. Such approaches, however, force the user to trade the usability of popular data sharing platforms for better privacy protection. This tradeoff might come at the expense of losing the interaction with potentially less privacy-concerned friends. Even apparently successful systems like Diaspora have a much lower user base than popular sharing systems used today. For instance, Diaspora's user base is only 1.9 million [26]; Twitter has 140 million users [53] and Facebook has over 900 million users [30]. To view protected pictures, user's friends would instead of accessing Facebook need to access the user's personal web server, or start using Diaspora or similar services.

Instead, we desire a technical solution that allows users and their friends to have a similar experience on the platforms they normally use for sharing (e.g., Facebook, Flickr), yet be protected from unauthorized usage of their data. Some systems have been proposed that attempt to protect user data from unauthorized usage, while still allowing consumers to use their platform of choice. However, these solutions either require the existence of a trusted third party server to handle user data and encryption keys, are platform specific (e.g., work for Facebook only), or do not hide the fact that confidential data is being exchanged [10, 42, 43, 51].

In this paper, we propose a system that protects user data on web-based social sharing platforms; our system does not require the user to run a dedicated infrastructure or place his trust in another third party, and hides from unauthorized recipients that confidential communications is taking place. In doing so, we are inspired by what Boyd calls *social steganography* [17]: Boyd found that teenagers sometimes post messages on Facebook that seem innocent to parents (e.g, song lyrics), but carry hidden meaning for friends. Similarly, our system allows users to post innocent looking pictures, files, or status updates that will transparently be replaced with real information for selected recipients in the user's network. Note that while *steganography* typically refers to concealing a message or file within another message or file, our system hides a pointer to the protected data, not the data itself.

As a proof of concept, we implemented our system in the form of a plugin for the Firefox browser. Despite the vastly different nature of websites, the underlying HTML elements used to construct user interfaces for uploading text input, pictures, and other documents are the same on all platforms. Our plugin is thus able to support most web-based data-sharing platforms with the help of platform-specific XML-based definition files that allow it to seamlessly replace dummy postings with hidden values.

Contributions. (1) We propose a system for protecting data on online sharing platforms through strong user-side encryption; (2) we introduce a novel mechanism inspired by social steganography techniques to hide the fact that encrypted communication is being transmitted; and (3) we demonstrate the feasibility of our approach through a proof of concept implementation in the form of a publicly available browser plugin.

Outline. First, Section 2 gives an overview of the main idea, presents our threat model and describes the goals of our system. Section 3 defines the components and protocols of our system, and Section 4 presents the security analysis of our protocol. Then, Section 5 presents our implementation approach and performance evaluation. We discuss solutions that make our approach resistant to data-mining techniques for detecting protected messages in Section 6, review related work in Section 7, and conclude in Section 8.

2. A SHORT OVERVIEW

Consider a user who wishes to upload a protected wall post, status update, or a picture to an online social networking (OSN). While the user wants to take advantage of the communication channel offered by the OSN, he also wants to ensure that only a specific set of authorized recipients can access it, keeping the OSN provider and unauthorized parties oblivious. To this end, the user could just post the encrypted version of the content. However, some OSNs impose length limitations or are not able to display encrypted pictures. Thus, our system stores the encrypted data on a different storage service. It then stores a different cleartext, consisting of fake data on the sharing platform. To enable authorized friends to retrieve the encrypted data, our system stores a pointer to its location on a disjoint Internet mapping service.

More specifically, our system performs the following operations. At first, it replaces the user's real posting (i.e., text or a picture) on the OSN with fake data that looks like another genuine message—either automatically or with the user's help. The user's real data is encrypted for a user-defined set of recipients and stored in a user-selectable, public storage service (e.g., Dropbox, or the user's own server), which returns a URL to the encrypted content. Next, in order to keep the storage location private the system applies a pseudo-random function to the posted fake data (our implementation uses a keyed hash function) and computes a lookup-key. In a final step, this lookup-key is then used to store the (encrypted) URL of the encrypted file in another user-selectable, arbitrary URL lookup service (e.g., TinyURL). On the authorized recipient's side, the system performs the reverse operations while the user visits the OSN page. See also Figure 1 for an overview.

Threat model. We consider an attacker who has control over the communication channels used by the user to store and share data. However, we assume that the attacker does not know the secret keys of the users, and cannot control the user computing environments, such as their browsers and computers, and any device used in the protocol.

Goals. Our system should support sharing most data types directly in the browser on a wide range of web-based online sharing platforms. All content published by a user should be kept confidential by means of cryptographic techniques. However, for a good usability, the operations should be simple and the cryptographic techniques transparent. Only authorized recipients should be able to read and verify the integrity of the protected data. Obviously, once a recipient gets access to the protected content, there is no way of preventing this recipient from redistributing it. However, a casual observer should not be able to infer that hidden information is being transmitted.

3. THE SYSTEM

To unlink innocent-looking data stored on the communication platform from the encrypted data secretly exchanged, our system makes use of the following main services:

Online Sharing Platform ($\mathcal{SP}$) is any online communication platform for storing and sharing digital content (e.g., Facebook, Flickr, Gmail). Such platforms usually require registered login, keep and manage the user's list of contacts, and are regularly accessed by the user's friends.

Storage Service (*SS*) allows storing user data in the cloud and accessing this data through a browser (e.g., Dropbox, SugarSync). We assume that *SS* requires users to register before storing data. We assume that each file f stored in *SS* is accessible through a unique URL, which we denote url_f, and that anybody who knows url_f can retrieve the file without authenticating. Nevertheless, only the account owner can modify and delete stored data.

Hashmap Directory (*HD*) is a web-based service that stores short strings mapping (*index, value*) pairs, such as URL shortener services TinyURL or Bit.ly. Given an index, it allows anybody to retrieve the value. The service does not accept duplicate indices and places a restriction on the length of both the index and value strings (e.g., 30–140 characters). We consider that stored entries do not expire and cannot be deleted. We also assume that *HD* accepts any anonymous requests to store and retrieve entries, and does not limit the number of entries one user can make.

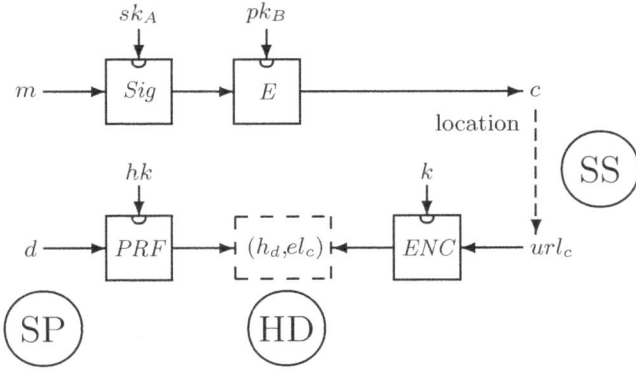

Figure 1: Transmitting a protected message m: After signing and encrypting m, the result c is stored in a publicly accessible URL url_c on storage service SS. Using the fake message d as input to a pseudorandom function, a mapping service HD is then used to store the encrypted link el_c under index h_d.

3.1 Transmitting a Protected Message

In our system, every user U owns a public/private key pair (pk_U, sk_U). Let the users, Alice and Bob who want to exchange protected messages on the platform $\mathcal{SP}$. We assume that Alice and Bob have exchanged and verified their public keys pk_A and pk_B. These keys will be used to encrypt m. We also assume that Alice and Bob have run a key agreement protocol and agreed on two shared keys k_{AB}, a symmetric encryption key, and hk_{AB} a key used to compute a pseudorandom function PRF. We will discuss key management in detail in Section 3.2. In the following, we abbreviate encryption of m with the public key pk_B as $E_{pk_B}(m)$ and decryption using the private key sk_B as $D_{sk_A}(m)$. Furthermore, we abbreviate symmetric encryption using the shared secret key k_{AB} as $ENC_{k_{AB}}(m)$ and decryption as $DEC_{k_{AB}}(m)$.

3.1.1 Send Protected Text

Figure 1 gives an overview of the protocol to exchange a protected message and Figure 2 shows in detail the messages exchanged by the parties. First, to ensure message integrity, Alice signs m with her private key sk_A and obtains $\sigma_m = Sign_{sk_A}(m)$. Then, Alice encrypts (m, σ_m) with Bob's public key pk_B to obtain $c = E_{pk_B}(m, \sigma_m)$.

Next, Alice uploads the ciphertext c to SS. Subsequently, Alice notes the URL url_c under which c can be retrieved. Note that SS allows anyone to access c through the URL url_c without requiring authentication. Next, Alice chooses a dummy text d that looks like a genuine message she wants to transmit to Bob. Alice applies a *pseudo-random function* (PRF) [33] to d using the shared key hk_{AB} and computes $h_d = PRF_{hk_{AB}}(d)$. Note that the result h_d must be an uniformly distributed string, thus a PRF is the appropriate tool to achieve this in the standard model; using random oracles would impose stronger requirements for the building blocks without any benefits. Then she encrypts url_c using a symmetric algorithm to obtain $el_c = ENC_{k_{AB}}(url_c)$. We use symmetric encryption to compute el_c, which produces a ciphertext smaller than public key encryption, because we assume that HD poses a length limitation on the registered content. Finally, Alice registers el_c under the index h_d with

HD and publishes the dummy text d on the online sharing platform $\mathcal{SP}$. Since HD only accepts unique index h_d entries, d must not have been used by Alice to communicate with Bob before, under the same key hk_{AB}.

3.1.2 Read Protected Text

To retrieve the protected message m, Bob follows the reverse steps. He first reads the dummy text d published by Alice on the platform $\mathcal{SP}$. Bob tries to see if there is a hidden message m behind d. To verify this, Bob first computes $h_d = PRF_{hk_{AB}}(d)$, and queries HD to see if there is any value registered under h_d. If no value is registered, Bob concludes that d is a genuine, plaintext message from Alice with no protected content behind it. Otherwise Bob receives the encrypted link el_c from HD and decrypts it to obtain $url_c = DEC_{k_{AB}}(el_c)$. Knowing url_c, Bob retrieves c from SS. Next, Bob decrypts c using his private key sk_B to obtain the initial message $(m, \sigma_m) = D_{sk_B}(c)$. Knowing σ_m, Bob verifies the integrity of the message using pk_A. If the integrity verification fails, Bob concludes that Alice is not the actual sender or that an attacker tampered with c. Otherwise, he considers m a message from Alice.

3.1.3 Send Protected Image or File

Assume that instead of the text m, Alice wants to share a secret file. To transmit, for example, a secret image i, Alice follows the same protocol as for text but with a slight variation. First, Alice encrypts i with pk_B and stores the resulting $c = E_{pk_B}(m, \sigma_i)$ in SS. Next, Alice chooses a dummy image d. Because online sharing platforms often perform image processing techniques such as image compression on uploaded pictures, Alice and Bob cannot use a pseudorandom function on the dummy image; doing so might result in different h_d values on the sender and receiver side. For this reason, Alice chooses a random value w_d and hides it in the image d as a secret watermark using a secret derived from hk_{AB} [38]. She then computes $h_d = PRF_{hk_{AB}}(w_d)$. Finally, as for text, Alice registers the encrypted link el_c under the index h_d with HD, and publishes d on $\mathcal{SP}$.

To receive the protected image i, Bob extracts the secret watermark w_d from the dummy image d, computes $h_d = PRF_{hk_{AB}}(w_d)$, and queries HD to retrieve the encrypted link el_c. He then decrypts el_c to obtain $url_c = D_{k_{AB}}(el_c)$ and retrieves c stored on SS at location url_c. Finally, Bob decrypts c using sk_B, obtains the initial image i and verifies the signature σ_i.

3.1.4 Group Communications

Assume that Alice wants to share m with a group of contacts G, not just with Bob. All recipients in G know that Alice is the sender of the protected message based on information provided by the sharing platform, but they should not find out the identity of other recipients in G. In a straightforward solution, Alice could perform the steps described earlier for each recipient U in G, using shared keys k_{AU} and hk_{AU}. However, this solution results in poor performance for large groups of recepients, because Alice must encrypt the message m for each recipient, and then compute and register different (h_d, el_c) values with HD. To obtain better performance, Alice can encrypt the ciphertext only once, using an anonymous broadcast encryption scheme [9, 41].

Depending on the desired trade-off between protocol security guarantees, on the one hand, and system performance

Alice $(sk_A, pk_B, k_{AB}, hk_{AB})$ SS HD SP **Bob** $(pk_A, sk_B, k_{AB}, hk_{AB})$

m
$\sigma_m = Sign_{sk_A}(m)$
$c = E_{pk_B}(m, \sigma_m)$ $\xrightarrow{\text{Store } c}$ c, url_c
$url_c = $ URL where c is stored $\xleftarrow{url_c\ c}$ c, url_c
Choose dummy text d
$h_d = PRF_{hk_{AB}}(d)$
$el_c = ENC_{k_{AB}}(url_c)$ $\xrightarrow{\text{Register } (h_d, el_c)}$ (h_d, el_c)
$\xrightarrow{\text{Publish } d}$ d

d $\xrightarrow{\text{Read } d}$ d , $h_d = PRF_{hk_{AB}}(d)$
(h_d, el_c) $\xleftarrow{\text{Query index } h_d}$
$\xrightarrow{\hspace{3cm}}$ el_c, $url_c = DEC_{k_{AB}}(el_c)$
el_c
c $\xleftarrow{\text{GET data at } url_c}$
$\xrightarrow{\hspace{3cm}}$ $m, \sigma_m = D_{sk_B}(c)$
c Verify if σ_m holds for pk_A
if not, reject m

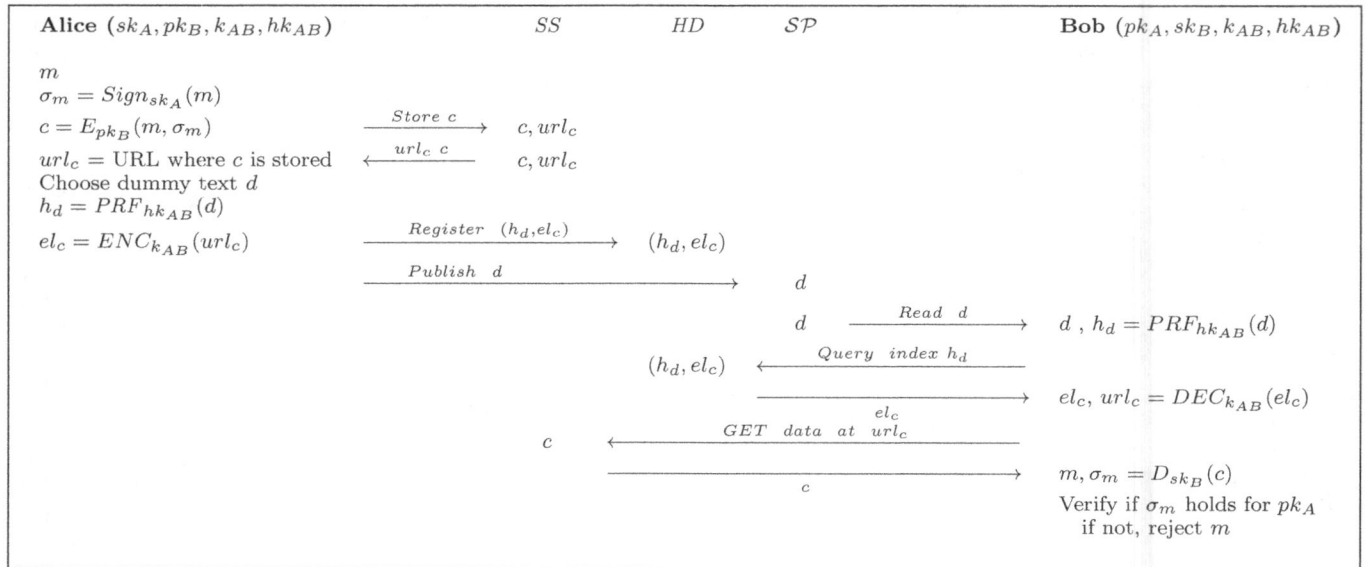

Figure 2: Sending a protected message; (pk_B, sk_B) **is Bob's public/private key pair;** k_{AB} **is a symmetric encryption key and** hk_{AB} **a key for the pseudo-random function** PRF**, both shared by Alice and Bob.**

and scalability, on the other, the shared keys (k_G, hk_G) used by Alice to transmit protected messages to the group G could be (a) the same for all the contacts in a specific group, or (b) different for each contact. Assume Alice shares different keys (k_{AU}, hk_{AU}) with each contact U. To publish protected content, she must compute different h_{dU} and el_{c_U} values for each recipient U and register each (hd_U, el_{c_U}) pair with HD. Note that all el_{c_U} actually decrypt to the same url_c. Maintaining different keys per contact provides stronger security guarantees (e.g., in case some keys are compromised or leaked), but requires creating more HD entries, which ultimately affects performance and increases network traffic.

3.1.5 Access Right Revocation

Assume that Alice shared m with a group G of users that includes Bob. She now wants to remove Bob's access, but have the data available m to other recipients. Note that it might be impossible for Alice to remove or modify a message m already published on SP (e.g., emails that have already reached the recipients' inbox, some forum entries, etc). We distinguish between two cases, depending on whether Alice used different shared keys k_{AU} and hk_{AU} with each recipient U in the group G or group keys k_G and hk_G to transmit m. We assume that Alice stored the ciphertext c at the same location url_c for all recipients. A basic solution to revoke Bob's access to m has Alice simply re-encrypt m to the altered recipient list that excludes Bob, and update the ciphertext c stored on SS. Bob is still in possession of the shared keys k_{AB} and hk_{AB} or the group keys k_G. If he still has access to d (or knows d from a previous access), Bob can find out url_c and therefore retrieve c, by simply following the steps for retrieving a protected message under d. Therefore, Bob could still obtain c, and thus prove the existence of a protected message. However, since c is no longer encrypted with his public key pk_B, Bob cannot decrypt c and find out the content of m.

If Alice is not able to delete d or remove Bob's access

from SP and the $(index, value)$ entries in HD are permanent, she must follow the following steps to impede Bob from proving the existence of m. First, Alice must delete c from SS, thus invalidating url_c and store the ciphertext at a new location url_c'. Furthermore, Alice must establish new keys (k_{AU}', hk_{AU}') or (k_G', hk_G') with the other recipients in G. She should then create new $(h_d' = PRF_{hk_G'}(d)$, $el_c' = ENC_{k_G}(url_c'))$ entries on HD. All entries should point to the same location url_c'. If, however, Alice encrypted and stored the ciphertext c in different locations url_{c_U} for each recipient U, she needs only to remove c_B from url_{c_B} since this operation will not affect other recipients in G.

3.2 Key Management

In this section we consider approaches for contacts to perform key establishment, as well as key revocation. Furthermore, we discuss migrating private keys and contact lists across different personal devices.

3.2.1 Key Establishement

Prior to being able to use the system and exchange protected messages, Alice and Bob must first exchange and verify their public keys pk_A and pk_B. Furthermore, Alice and Bob must agree on the shared keys (k_{AB}, hk_{AB}). Then, Alice adds Bob to her contact list and stores the keys pk_B, k_{AB}, and hk_{AB} locally on her machine. To establish shared secret keys, Alice and Bob must follow the following steps:

1. Exchange public keys. Alice and Bob can exchange pk_A and pk_B over a private channel such as email or by publishing them on a public or semi-public platform such as social networking sites. Publishing the keys over a public platform accessed by her contacts and automatically retrieving them from there offers better scalability than performing one-on-one exchange with each of her contacts. By using multiple SP platforms, one can separate the exchange of cryptographic material from the account used to transmit protected messages, thus hiding clues that encrypted information might be exchanged in the future. Note that this public channel is considered untrusted and might be subject to man-in-the-middle attacks. Alternatively, this could be extended by the mechanism proposed in [14] which converts the OpenPGP Web-of-Trust model into the OSN scenario.

2. Verify public keys. Because a malicious attacker might have mounted a man-in-the-middle attack during step 1, Alice and Bob must make use of a trusted out-of-band channel (e.g., QR codes, GSM network, Bluetooth communications) to verify the fingerprints of pk_A and pk_B. We consider this second channel harder (e.g., the SMS network) or impossible (e.g., direct capturing of QR codes) to compromise. To hide the exchange of public keys from a suspicious observer, Alice and Bob could even resort to the out-of-band channel to perform step 1. If we operate under an honest-but-curious attacker, we might choose to skip or postpone this step to a later stage, for instance, until after the start of the protected communication. This is desirable if, Alice and Bob want to start communicating immediately.

3. Generate shared keys. Having exchanged and verified their public keys, Alice and Bob can run a key establishment protocol over the untrusted Internet channel to obtain the shared keys k_{AB} and hk_{AB}. For example a shared secret key could be obtained using a Sigma Protocol of [40], that is an extended version of the authenticated Diffie-Hellman key agreement protocol. As long as the private keys sk_A and sk_B are not compromised, revocation of k_{AB} and hk_{AB} can take place by merely publishing signed (and possibly encrypted) messages over any agreed-upon Internet communication platform. For example, Alice and Bob could perform the Sigma protocol by transmitting messages on Facebook signed with their private keys sk_A and respectively sk_B to ensure that no attacker interfered during the key agreement protocol.

3.2.2 Key Revocation

If the key k_{AB} gets compromised, an attacker could compute h_d and find out el_c. If, additionally, the attacker also knows hk_{AB}, he can then decrypt el_c to obtain url_c. Because from url_c he can obtain c, the attacker is able to prove the transmission of a protected message. However, as long as he does not know the private key sk_B, he cannot decrypt c to find out the the content of m.

If the shared keys k_{AB} and hk_{AB} get compromised, Alice must re-run the key agreement protocol in step 3 with Bob to obtain new (k'_{AB}, hk'_{AB}) values. If Alice's private key sk_A gets compromised, she must inform her contacts, re-run the key exchange and agreement protocol, and re-encrypt previous content with the new key sk'_A.

3.2.3 Key Migration

Assume Alice has generated her key pair (pk_A, sk_A) on her personal laptop, but now wants to be able to view protected messages on her work desktop as well. To be able to decrypt protected messages on another device, Alice must have (pk_A, sk_A) and the shared secret keys (k_{AU}, hk_{AU}) available on the new device. Therefore, she must securely migrate the secret keys to her work desktop. Note that it suffices for Alice to transfer her key pair (pk_A, sk_A) to the new device through an out-of-band channel, and then synchronize her encrypted contact list and shared keys between several devices by posting encrypted and signed messages in SS or another online storage platform. For weaker protection,

but arguably more usability, instead of her public/private key pair, Alice could carry only a strong passphrase to the new device through a confidential out-of-band channel. The passphrase could then be used in a key derivation function (KDF) to generate a symmetric key. This key is then used to encrypt Alice's sk_A and the keys (k_{AU}, hk_{AU}) (e.g., using a symmetric authenticated encryption, such as AES in CCM-mode [57]), and then decrypt them on the new device.

4. SECURITY ANALYSIS

We analyze the resilience of our system against a number of attacks. We show that none of the services used by our system can find out the content of m or provide its existence, whether they work independently or collaborate. Furthermore, we show that an attacker cannot carry out impersonation attacks and discuss possible approaches to defend our system from traffic analysis attacks.

Sharing Platform. Because Alice published d on $\mathcal{SP}$, $\mathcal{SP}$ knows d. However, $\mathcal{SP}$ does not know the key hk_{AB}. Therefore, it cannot compute $h_d = PRF_{hk_{AB}}(d)$. Consequently, $\mathcal{SP}$ cannot query HD to find out the value el_c registered under the index h_d. Hence, $\mathcal{SP}$ cannot find out m or find out whether there is a hidden message m behind d. However, $\mathcal{SP}$ can erase or alter d, which would result in a denial of service for the communication between Alice and Bob. Under suspicion, $\mathcal{SP}$ might be able to replace d with a previous message transmitted by Alice d', which could hide a protected message m'. In this case, Bob would verify m' as a message originating from Alice, but $\mathcal{SP}$ could not know or choose the value of m'.

Hashmap Directory. HD knows h_d and el_c, but does not know k_{AB}, therefore it cannot decrypt el_c to obtain $url_c = DEC_{k_{AB}}(el_c)$, the location of the ciphertext c. Also, although HD knows h_d, it cannot extract the value of the fake message d (this follows immediately from the properties of a pseudo-random function, $h_d = PRF_{hk_{AB}}(d)$). Furthermore, HD cannot tell if h_d corresponds to any given d because it does not know the key hk_{AB} in the case of text or the key variable for extracting the secret watermark in the case of images. As a result, HD cannot identify m and c corresponding to (h_d, el_c).

Storage Service. SS has access to the encrypted data c, and possibly all other ciphertext stored by Alice. However, since SS does not know the private key sk_U of any authorized recipient, it cannot decrypt c to find out $m = D_{sk_U}(c)$. Furthermore, even though SS knows url_c, it cannot compute $el_c = DEC_{k_{AB}}(url_c)$ because it does not know k_{AB}. Given an entry el_c on HD, SS cannot verify if el_c decrypts url_c. Therefore, SS cannot find out if c is linked to a message d stored by Alice on another platform $\mathcal{SP}$. However, SS can tamper with c, remove it or replace it with a different ciphertext c', previously generated and posted by Alice.

Collusion. We consider that in special circumstances $\mathcal{SP}$, HD, and SS might collude and share user information among themselves or with other parties for profit or legal obligations. We show that, although any attacker with access to d stored on $\mathcal{SP}$ can tell that Alice and Bob are communicating, he cannot tell that there is a hidden message behind d. An attacker cannot link d published on $\mathcal{SP}$ to the ciphertext c stored in SS because he cannot compute h_d.

However, $\mathcal{SP}$, HD, and SS might keep logs, record users' IP addresses and requests, which could be used by an attacker to match requests made by the same user. By matching IP addresses or the timing of the requests, an attacker could conclude that a message d on $\mathcal{SP}$, a ciphertext c on SS and an entry (h_d, el_c) originate from the same user. Thus the attacker might be able to infer the existence of a protected message transmitted with d, though he cannot find out the content of m. We acknowledge that a highly motivated attacker (e.g., governments) might be able to link information across all protocol parties ($\mathcal{SP}/SS/HD$). In practice, however, such attacks may be non-trivial for commercial and/or political reasons, as these parties may be competitors or located in different countries. To avoid such attacks, one could hide IP addresses by running our system on top of Tor [3] and defend against timing attacks by introducing random noise and delay in user requests.

Impersonation attacks. An attacker with read and write access to all messages posted and received by Alice on $\mathcal{SP}$ (e.g., $\mathcal{SP}$ themselves, a hacker who got a hold of Alice's account, or a governmental agency who requests access from $\mathcal{SP}$) could try to create fake messages d and convince Bob that a hidden message m actually comes from Alice. Since the attacker does not know the secret k_{AB} (which is only know by Alice and Bob), he cannot create a valid d, h_d pair. Given a d published by the attacker on Alice's behalf, Bob will query HD for h_d and conclude that there is no hidden message when nothing is returned. If, however, HD is malicious and colludes with the attacker, it could fake an entry by returning a chosen value el_c for any h_d submitted by Bob. However, since HD does not know k_{AB}, it cannot compute a valid el_c that decrypts to an url_c, but could mount a replay attack if in possession of a previous value el'_c posted by Alice for Bob. If SS also colludes and returns a given c' for any request el'_c originating from Bob, the attacker has the chance to deliver a chosen ciphertext c' to Bob. Knowing Bob's public key pk_B, the attacker could compute $E_{pk_B}(m')$. However, the attacker cannot trick Bob to believe this message comes from Alice because he cannot generate a valid signature $\sigma = Sign_{sk_A}(m')$.

5. IMPLEMENTATION

We implement our system as a Firefox plugin, basing our implementation on the Scramble! open source project [11]. Part of our plugin is implemented in Java, therefore the user must have Java Applet support enabled to run our plugin. We use AES-CCM for symmetric (authenticated) encryption, HMAC-SHA-256 as pseudorandom function, and the OpenPGP standard [18] for broadcast encryption. We make use of Dropbox as a Storage Service (SS) and TinyURL as the Hashmap Directory (HD). Ultimately, the user could select from a list of available storage platforms. We use TinyURL because it allows the user to choose a custom short URL to map to. TinyURL could be interchanged with similar URL shortening services, publishing services or online blogs that can store a public list of index-value pairs.

During the first installation for user U, the plugin creates a new Dropbox account with a random username; subsequently it generates an OpenPGP public/private key pair (pk_U, sk_U) and the shared keys k_G and hk_G for his group of friends G. All encrypted user data is later stored in the **Public** folder of the Dropbox account and is accessible through a public URL.

5.1 Sharing Protected Text

The user invokes the plugin while the mouse cursor is inside the input area, e.g., by a mouse right click menu. The plugin extracts the message m typed in by the user in the input field and manipulates the HTML page to replace m with a chosen fake text d. In our implementation, the user must enter d. We discuss approaches on how to automatically generate good fake messages in Section 6.

Support for any Text Input Fields: Websites are becoming richer and more complex, making use of complex Javascript calls and HTML code. As a result, text entry is no longer restricted to just a few HTML elements such as `<input type='text'>` and `<textarea>`.

For example, in Gmail, the input area for composing email messages is in fact an editable `<html>` element within an `<iframe>`. Our plugin can handle special text input types. It identifies the HMTL node containing the entered user input through the `document.popupNode` Firefox API call. It then obtains the inserted text from its `.value` attribute or `.innerHTML`, depending on the HTML node type.

Support for Rich Text Formatting: Web-based sharing platforms increasingly encourage users to edit and annotate documents, and write HTML rich emails and blog entries. As a consequence, separating user-generated content from the page source is becoming more challenging. Our plugin aims to protect user data without loss of website functionality. For example, the email reply together with the initial secret email are tightly coupled with Gmail's specific HTML webpage email header. When clicking the "Send" button, it is crucial to avoid reposting the initial secret message m (which is being displayed on the page, but is unknown to Gmail who only knows d). To achieve this, in our implementation the whole message thread, including the Gmail reply headers and the tags for rich HTML formatting are encrypted, and replaced with a new dummy text.

5.2 Sharing Protected Images

Unlike text input, which can be implemented through a variety of means, file upload in the browser takes place exclusively through an `<input type='file'>` HTML element. When a webpage is loaded, the plugin identifies all `file input` elements and registers `change` event listeners for all of them. Consequently, when the user selects a file to upload, the plugin gets notified first and prompts the user whether to protect the file. Note that this file protection mechanism can be applied to any file type. In our implementation, the plugin retrieves images from different Flickr pages, given a start URL and XPath-based webpage parsing and navigation rules. In a real setting, one might want to be careful about copyright issues.

For watermarking images, we use the DCT-watermark library [32]. Unlike steganography, good image watermarks are resistant to typical image compression, some cropping and scaling techniques. To ensure that only intended recipients can retrieve the watermark from the image, we use a secret derived from the encryption key k to embed and extract the watermark. We noticed that success rate is dependent on the used images. Based on our experiments, to successfully embed a 20-digit long watermark on a random Flickr picture the DCT-watermark library takes an average of 0.3seconds for 595 with 54% success rate. We are not currently aware of other libraries who might perform better. However, a better chosen pool of pictures might lead to better success rates.

Finally, the plugin automatically updates the file selection

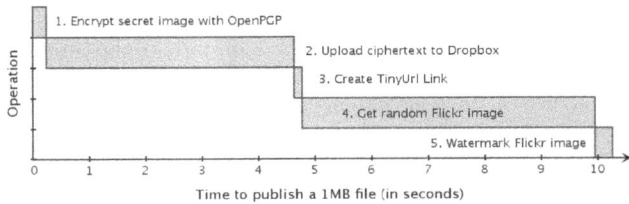

Figure 3: Steps needed to publish a protected file. For optimization, steps could be run in parallel or be precomputed.

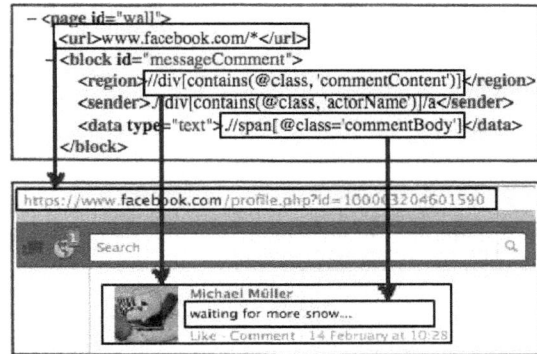

Figure 4: The plugin identifies the dummy messages candidates based on webpage-specific XPath parsing rules.

in the `<input>` field to the watermarked image. For security reasons, websites and Javascript code, including Firefox plugins, are by default not allowed to change the value of a file HTML `<input>` element. To this end, we sign our plugin with a trusted certificate, and request higher security privileges needed.

Unlike text, we display secret images through a pop-up window. For security reasons, images stored locally cannot be embedded in a webpage hosted remotely by simply manipulating the value of the `src` attribute on an HTML `<img>` tag (see the strict origin security policy [2]). This ultimately helps raise more user awareness on data protection levels. Alternatively, decrypted images could be hosted and retrieved from a local web server and displayed in line.

5.3 Extensible Page Parsing Rules

For our implementation to be online sharing platform independent, we make use of simple XML rules that define where and on which pages the browser should expect hidden data. Adding support for one more communication platform comes down to adding the XML specification files. To specify the page structure on a generic form, we make use of XPath queries [59]. XPath is a language used to navigate through elements and attributes in an XML document which uses path expressions to select nodes or node-sets. We use XPath queries to identify (sender, message) pairs on a page. Figure 4 shows an example. The `region` query is used to restrict the search on the page to a single section containing published messages. The execution of the `sender` and `message` subqueries is then restricted to the identified region. Next, the identified sender is matched against contacts from the address book, which can contain email addresses, nicknames and user IDs. To show the universal applicability of our solution, we defined parsing rules for any type of communication over Gmail, Facebook and Twitter. Such XPath-based rules need to be updated if web interfaces change. For the full specifications, see the Appendix.

5.4 Key Management and Distribution

There are two main approaches for end-users to distribute public keys: (1) rely on a mutually trusted certification authority, or (2) manually verify the authenticity by checking the fingerprints of the public keys through an out-of-band channel [37]. However, most everyday users do not have mutually trusted certification authorities (CA) [37]. Furthermore, obtaining certificates from certification authorities is too difficult, expensive and time consuming. It takes even for power users 30 minutes to 4 hours to obtain a certificate from a public CA that performs little to no verification [35].

Therefore, our system perform key exchange and verification through trusted, out-of-band channels.

The plugin makes cryptographic operations, including key generation, management and distribution, transparent to users, thus avoiding the pitfalls of previous systems [58]. The plugin distributes public keys by publishing them on users' Facebook profiles embedded in a QR code image. Our plugin can be easily extended to distribute keys and run key agreement and cryptographic communication protocols over any other platform, by adding external JAR files that are automatically loaded at runtime.

To support key management and verification, we implemented an Android mobile application with two out-of-band key verification methods: SMS and phone-to-phone QR code scanning. The mobile application holds the user's public/private key pair (which is transferred from the computer through a QR code). Furthermore, the plugin can encrypt and sign verified contact keys and upload them to the Dropbox account from where they are synchronized with the browser plugin on other user devices. Finally, the power of the presented solution would not be complete if limited to PCs only. All the functionality of the plugin can be easily ported to a mobile platform, for example in the form of stand-alone mobile applications for different platforms. (Unfortunately, plugin development for Firefox on the Android platform currently lacks Java Applet support.)

5.5 Performance Evaluation

A smooth user experience is essential in the success of any security solution; otherwise users will sacrifice security for usability.

To calculate its performance, we run the plugin on a MacBook Pro laptop with an Intel Core i5 2.4GHz processor and 4GB of memory over a wireless network. The plugin has a memory consumption of 70MB. We measured the time needed to retrieve and display hidden messages on a Facebook page from the time the page is loaded in the browser. Note that only messages with senders in the contact list are candidates for protected communication. Processing a Facebook page with one hidden message (out of two candidates) took on average 0.9s, (N=10, $stdev$=0.2s). Displaying a page with 10 hidden messages (out of 11 candidates) took 6s (N=10, $stdev$=0.6s). On average, retrieving a hidden text message took 0.5s (N=25, $stdev$=0.07s), and processing a message that does not hide any communication took 0.06s (N=25, $stdev$=0.004s). Posting a hidden message took on average 0.67s (N=10, $stdev$=0.1s). Therefore, two users talking over a protected chat message system would experience a delay of approx. 1 second. For our plugin, the time to display a page increases linearly with the number of hidden messages.

Figure 3 displays the time needed to execute each step of our implementation, in order to securely send a 1MB file to 100 contacts who share group shared keys k_G and hk_G. We present here only the extra security steps that must be preformed by our plugin, in comparison to the normal browser experience. The computation intensive tasks, file encryption (1) and image watermarking (5), take very little time compared to network operations, uploading the encrypted file to Dropbox (2) and retrieving a random image from Flickr (4). Note that given the OpenPGP symmetric type of encryption, the encrypted file has approximatively the same size as the initial file. Uploading an encrypted 1MB file to Dropbox took on average 4.4s ($stdev$=0.6s, N=20). Figure 5 shows that the time needed to encrypt a file increases linearly with the number of contacts and file size, but remains relatively low, below 2 seconds for a 100MB file and 500 contacts. Finding and saving a Flickr image took on average 5.2s, of which 3.8s were needed to download and parse the starting webpage. Once the URL was identified, saving an image locally took on average only 0.9s (N=50). Creating a TinyURL mapping the secret watermark to the encrypted Dropbox link took only 0.1s (N=20, $stdev$=0.01s).

While executing all steps sequentially could account for slow browser response time and ultimately poor usability, implementation optimizations can make the process seem instantaneous. For example, a pool of Flickr pictures could be retrieved and stored locally beforehand. Since for files and images the TinyURL index h_d is not a secret derived from a dummy text chosen by the user, but rather from a randomly generated string, even image watermarking could be pre-executed. Similarly, uploading the encrypted file could happen in parallel to other operations and finish after the upload of the watermarked image.

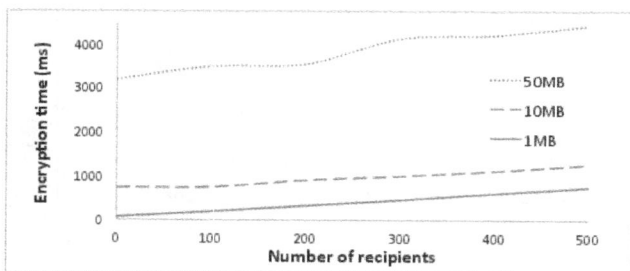

Figure 5: Encryption time increases slowly, remaining bellow one second for a 1MB file shared with 500 contacts.

6. SEMANTICS AND MINING ATTACKS

Suspicion of using our system could cause trouble to users in countries with totalitarian regimes, or simply refusal of service from platform providers with business models exclusively based on targeted advertising. It should therefore be impossible for single or colluding services to tell which users communicate using covert messages. As discussed in Section 3, our solution provides complete data confidentiality against any attacker having access to one or all of $\mathcal{SP}$, HD, SS. However, as data mining and profiling techniques are becoming more advanced and possibly even used by oppressive governments to identify activists, it is crucial to ensure that users cannot be singled out based on semantic analysis of dummy messages and steganographic data. In this section we make a few initial considerations on how dummy messages could be automatically generated.

It should be hard or impossible for an outside observer (e.g., platform provider, governmental agency) to tell with high probability, through mass-targeted or user-targeted mining, that users are protecting their communication. Automatically generated messages must, therefore, be consistent with past user behavior. Ultimately, to ensure less detectability, users can compose the dummy messages themselves. For good usability, however, the plugin should make a good suggestion. Furthermore, it is likely that users are not good at coming up with diverse dummy messages either.

Resistance to machine detection. Previous work on detecting automated posts on Twitter and social networks mainly focused on spam and used simple detection techniques that would not work against our solution. For example, Benvenuto et al. [12] use behavior attributes, such as average hash tags per tweet, number of tweets received, account age, number of followers per number of followees, and fraction of tweets with URLs. Zhang et al. [60] analyze timestamps and observe that humans post messages at random times of the day, whereas bots post at specific minutes of the hour. Since in our system the user would always be the one initiating the posting, such techniques would not be effective to identify dummy messages. Automatic publishing of noise messages, however, should take into account such considerations.

Consistent user behavior. Constantinides et al. [20] have shown that user behavior on social networks follows well defined trends. The authors found that user profiles cluster into four main categories, depending on their usage patterns on Facebook: *Beginner*, *Habitual*, *Outstanding*, and *Expert*. The authors then quantify the likelihood for a certain type of user to engage in a certain activity. For instance, searching for people online, sending private messages and updating profiles are popular among all users, while reporting about products used and commenting about advertising are mostly done by *Expert* users. A plugin user might be easily identified if, for instance, all the public posts on his Facebook wall are about sharing current activities, while all the steganographic messages are TinyURL links (e.g., Scramble! [11]) or sentences from Wikipedia (e.g., FaceCloak [43]).

A solution based on topic models. To make sure dummy text messages are consistent with the previous topics in users' communications, one could use text document analysis techniques, such as constructing and applying topic models [16]. In particular, we propose using the Latent Dirichlet Allocation (LDA), a generative model in which any specific document is viewed as a mixture of topics. Each topic is characterized by a distribution of words. LDAs can be used to learn and define topics from an existing set of documents or communication. Other models consider correlation [15] and hierarchy between topics [19]. Previous work already applied topic models to social networks [46] and images [56].

Possible implementation. To generate valid dummy text messages, one might want to restrict the social network activities identified by Constantinides et al. [20] to those that can be used to transmit a social steganographic message by our plugin: discuss what people do, communicate news or issues, share mood, share links about interesting web sites, report about current activities, and report about brands or products. Based on such predefined types of communication and their expected frequencies, a heuristic could be defined that, for each posting attempt, takes as input a pseudo-random number and determines what kind of dummy text message to generate. In addition, to disguise the usage of steganographic messages the plugin could insert noise communication.

The Machine Learning for Language Toolkit [45] a Java-based software for document classification and topic modeling could be easily integrated with our plugin and used to analyze past user communication. Dummy messages consistent with identified topics could be generated through different means. For instance, the set of keywords in a predicted topic could be used to retrieve sentences from the web through a Google search. Steganographic replies could be generated with the use of online Turing test chats (e.g., Touring Hub [52]), or aggregated among several users and outsourced as tasks to human workers on Mechanical Turk [1].

Good usability. As described above, generating semantically correct sentences, which must be consistent topic-wise with user profiles, is not a trivial task for a computer. The problem becomes even more challenging on long steganographic communication threads, which might be visible to other users, not just to the intended recipients (e.g., public posts on Facebook). Furthermore, the existence of steganographic messages poses usability challenges. More research is needed to find out how well users cope with friends replying to fake posts. Finally, adequate interfaces should help users keep track of the two worlds: the steganographic messages and the hidden message thread.

7. RELATED WORK

Some solutions have been proposed to increase privacy on different online sharing platforms like exclusively on social networks or webmail platforms. However, these solutions either: (1) do not hide that communication is confidential [11, 8], (2) protect only certain kind of data (e.g., profile information or private messages) [43], (3) require the existence of dedicated infrastructure or a trusted third-party, or (4) are restricted to a specific platform. Other solutions propose novel, privacy-friendly architectures meant to replace existing platforms [4, 22, 23, 25, 36]. Instead, our solution enables consumers to keep using current system while protecting their privacy.

While a large body of work has explored privacy-preserving data sharing in an outsourcing scenario (e.g. [6, 39]), these settings differ significantly from ours. They assume the existence of a set of private databases that should be opened up for queries from others without giving complete access to the raw data—a common scenario in business relationships. In contrast, we present a scheme for directly sharing information across a covert channel, without other parties being aware of this fact.

Many research solutions and commercial products have been proposed to encrypt messages and files exchanged over webmail platforms [11, 24, 27, 31, 42, 44]. However, these solutions do not hide that communications are encrypted. Scramble! [11] uses cryptographic mechanisms to enforce access control rules and ensure confidentiality of sensitive information. Our plugin inherits the concept of using OpenPGP for group communication from Scramble!. It can replace encrypted text with a TinyURL link that points to a server storing the ciphertext, but the link and content are public. Furthermore, Scramble! does not offer any support for files, which is a central contribution of our system.

In the context of social networks, Conti et al. [21] propose Virtual Private Social Networks to protect some static user profile information on social networks: name, picture, and current city. The authors do not consider messages and files. The user posts fake information online and distributes his real data unencrypted in an XML file to his friends over email. This data is then matched using regular expressions and automatically replaced by the browser, similar to how our plugin offers extensibility through XPath queries. Yeung et al. [7] also take a decentralized approach. Each user has a trusted server which stores his data, has knowledge of social network specific functionality and applications (e.g., photo tagging, personal wall), and enforces access control rules based on cross-platform specifications. When trying to access data on different platforms, the user's friends are redirected to the trusted server which must handle the access control rules.

FaceCloak [43] is similar to our approach, but limited to Facebook profile data and messages. The secret information is encrypted and stored on a dedicated server, while fake information (e.g., random sentences from Wikipedia) is posted on Facebook. Just like FaceCloak, our system substitutes real information with dummy one. In FaceCloak, the fake information and a key that only the sender and all his contacts know serve to compute the index under which the third-party server stores the ciphertext. In contrast, our solution works solely with currently available services on the Internet and does not require dedicated infrastructure. In addition, our scheme supports per-group communications and file exchange on any platform. Furthermore, by separating the storage service from the Hashmap Directory, we protect against fake data creation in case steganography keys are leaked. This can happen if a malicious user leaks the shared group steganography keys, but the encryption keys of other users (i.e., their private keys) remain uncompromised. If one has control over the FaceCloak server and access to the user's index key, one could swap ciphertexts and create successful plaintext swapping.

StegoWeb [13] is implemented as a browser bookmarklet, i.e., as a simple program that can be executed by clicking on a bookmark in the browser. The user must rely on a trusted third-party server to perform the encryption and data steganalysis. StegoWeb does not use public key cryptography. Instead, for each piece of data shared with each recipient, both the sender and the receiver must enter a shared passphrase. By supporting public key encryption, our solution offers more security and better scalability. Oren and Wool [47] propose a system which increases webmail privacy by hiding the email content with text steganography and then splitting the output into two parts. The user must send the two parts over two different email accounts. This solution requires no key distribution, but protects only against a weak attacker who has access to one of the two webmail servers.

Secretwit [50] uses text and image steganography to transmit secret Twitter messages (e.g., by appending whitespaces at the end of the tweet). The size of messages that can be transmitted purely through steganography is limited, because the size of the hidden data must be much smaller than that of the carrier message. Therefore, an approach purely based on steganography causes a serious limitation on the type and the volume of data users can transmit. For example, picture sharing platforms often compress and resize images, which could not hide a high-quality picture. By transmitting only a pointer to the location of the secret data instead of the data itself, our system poses no limitation on the size and type of protected information. For text, we provide the user with complete freedom on how to compose the dummy messages, thus making it less likely to being identified as unusual communication. Furthermore, our approach is robust against basic image manipulation techniques applied by online sharing platforms.

Adkinson-Orellana et al. [5] encrypt documents stored in Google Docs and enable simultaneous editing of encrypted documents among a group of people by intercepting the HTTP requests for AJAX calls and encrypting/decrypting transmitted document content. This approach requires knowledge of a platform-specific AJAX protocol and does not hide the nature of encrypted communication. However, by dealing with document editing, this work is orthogonal to ours and could be extended to provide a viable solution for group editing of protected data in our system.

8. CONCLUSIONS

While users are lured into storing their personal data online and sharing it with others over an ever wider range of free services (e.g., webmail, social networks, photo sharing platforms), they have little control over which third parties can access their data (e.g., hackers, advertisement companies, governmental agencies). In this paper, we propose a system that allows users to protect data they share online, and hide the fact that confidential information is being exchanged from unauthorized recipients. Our system does not rely on dedicated infrastructure or trusted servers. While the secret data is encrypted and stored in the cloud, dummy data that looks like genuine files or user communication is uploaded on the sharing platform. Users share secret keys which they use to discover the hidden data behind the dummy one. They find out the encrypted location of the secret data through a public indexing service like TinyURL. Our system accounts for easy specification of location of expected hidden messages on HTML paged through simple XML rules based on XPath parsing queries. We provide a proof of concept implementation of our system in the form of a Firefox plugin that focusses on protecting text messages and images.

Our solution does not hide the exchange of communication between two parties, thus leaving such transactional data open to law enforcement agencies. However, an attacker who does not have access to the users' secret keys cannot detect the exchange of confidential communication. Our system preserves most website functionality including text and image display. However, because data is encrypted and not actually stored on the online sharing platform, our solution does cause a loss of functionality on certain types of systems, e.g., Google Spreadsheets. For most online sharing platform functionality though, techniques such as encrypted

search promise to be a viable solution [55]. Further research should investigate techniques to impede websites from sniffing the data while being entered by the user in the browser. One possible solution is to have the plugin disable Javascript which the user types in the message. Furthermore, a future study should evaluate the detectability of image watermarks in different watermarking algorithms. If an attacker can identify users who post watermarked pictures, he might be able to narrow down the consumers who use our system.

While our proof-of-concept implementation deals only with plaintext and image exchange, our solution can be similarly used to implement protected exchange of any data type, including video files and data documents. Further work could implement sharing protected video files through platforms like YouTube. Based on research by Boyd [17], we believe users can cope well with the usage of steganographic messages. However, further research is needed to test the usability of our plugin and devise adequate user interfaces to help them distinguish between regular messages and protected communication. Most importantly, further research should look into having users specify recipient rules for each website or page. The browser should learn users' preferences in terms of when, which data should be protected for which recipients, and automatically apply those data protection policies. Dummy pictures used for watermarking could come from a local folder with user's personal pictures, be automatic repostings of Facebook pictures in which the user was tagged from his friends' profiles, or general photos from public websites (e.g., search queries on Flickr, Google Image Search), possibly corrupted to be harder to match against originals. Finally, future work should investigate techniques to generate sound dummy messages and data.

9. ACKNOWLEDGMENTS

We gratefully acknowledge Jerry Hoff for the initial discussion that helped bootstrap the research of this paper, as well as Elmar Tischhauser, Andreas Pashalidis, Mauro Conti, Kasper Rasmussen, Emiliano De Cristofaro and the anonymous reviewers for their insightful comments and suggestions. We would like to thank Prof. Lujo Bauer for the detailed comments which helped improve the presentation of this work. This work was supported in part by the Research Council K.U.Leuven: GOA TENSE (GOA/11/007), by the Flemish iMinds projects, and by the European Commission through the ICT programme under contract ICT-2007-216676 ECRYPT II. The author Filipe Beato is supported by the FCT doctoral grant SFRH/BD/70311/2010.

10. REFERENCES

[1] MTurk. https://www.mturk.com/.
[2] Strict origin policy. http://kb.mozillazine.org/Security.fileuri.strict_origin_policy. Accessed on August 31, 2012.
[3] Tor. http://www.torproject.org.
[4] 2peer. http://2peer.com. Accessed on Sept. 3, 2012.
[5] L. Adkinson-Orellana, D. A. Rodriguez-Silva, F. J. Gonzalez-Castano, and D. Gonzalez-Martinez. Sharing secure documents in the cloud—a secure layer for Google Docs. In *Proc. of CLOSER 2011*.
[6] R. Agrawal, A. Evfimievski, and R. Srikant. Information sharing across private databases. In *Proc. of ACM SIGMOD*, pages 86–97, June 2003.

[7] C. M. Au Yeung, I. Liccardi, K. Lu, O. Seneviratne, and T. Berners-Lee. Decentralization: The future of online social networking. In *Proc. W3C Workshop on the Future of Social Networking*, January 2009.

[8] R. Baden, A. Bender, N. Spring, B. Bhattacharjee, and D. Starin. Persona: an online social network with user-defined privacy. *SIGCOMM Computing Communication Review*, 39(4):135–146, 2009.

[9] A. Barth, D. Boneh, and B. Waters. Privacy in encrypted content distribution using private broadcast encryption. In *Proc. of Financial Cryptography and Data Security*, pages 52–64, Feb. 2006.

[10] F. Beato, M. Kohlweiss, and K. Wouters. Enforcing access control in social networks. In *Proc. of HotPets 2009*, pages 10–21, August 2009.

[11] F. Beato, M. Kohlweiss, and K. Wouters. Scramble! your social network data. In *Proc. of Privacy Enhancing Technologies*, Waterloo, Canada, July 2011.

[12] F. Benevenuto, G. Magno, T. Rodrigues, and V. Almeida. Detecting spammers on Twitter. In *Proc. of the 7th Annual Collaboration, Electronic Messaging, Anti-Abuse and Spam Conference*, Redmond, 2010.

[13] T. Besenyei, A. M. Foldes, G. G. Gulyas, and S. Imre. StegoWeb: Towards the ideal private web content publishing tool. In *Proc. of SECURWARE 2011*, pages 109–114, August 2011.

[14] P. Bichsel, S. Müller, F.-S. Preiss, D. Sommer, and M. Verdicchio. Security and trust through electronic social network-based interactions. *Computational Science and Engineering, IEEE International Conference on*, 4:1002–1007, 2009.

[15] D. Blei and J. Lafferty. A correlated topic model of science. *Annals of Applied Statistics*, 1:17–35, 2007.

[16] D. M. Blei. Probabilistic topic models. *Communications of the ACM*, 55:77–84, 2012.

[17] D. Boyd and A. Marwick. Social steganography: Privacy in networked publics. In *International Communication Association*, Boston, MA, May 2011.

[18] J. Callas, L. Donnerhacke, H. Finney, D. Shaw, and R. Thayer. OpenPGP Message Format. RFC 4880 (Proposed Standard), November 2007.

[19] J. Chang and D. Blei. Hierarchical relational models for document networks. *Annals of Applied Statistics*, 4(1):124–150, 2010.

[20] E. Constantinides, M. del Carmen Alarcón del Amo, and C. L. Romero. Profiles of social networking sites users in the netherlands. In *Proc. of HTSF 2010*.

[21] M. Conti, A. Hasani, and B. Crispo. Virtual private social networks. In *Proc. of ACM CODASPY 2011*.

[22] E. D. Cristofaro, C. Soriente, G. Tsudik, and A. Williams. Hummingbird: Privacy at the time of twitter. In *IEEE Security and Privacy*, 2012.

[23] L. A. Cutillo, R. Molva, and T. Strufe. Safebook: A privacy-preserving online social network leveraging on real-life trust. *IEEE Communications Magazine*, 47(12):94–101, 2009.

[24] G. D'Angelo, F. Vitali, and S. Zacchiroli. Content cloaking: Preserving privacy with Google Docs and other Web applications. In *Proc. of SAC 2010*, pages 826–830.

[25] Diaspora. `https://joindiaspora.com/`. Accessed on Sept. 3, 2012.

[26] How many users are in the Diaspora network? Data as of Sept. 6, 2012. `https://diasp.eu/stats.html`. Accessed on Sept. 6, 2012.

[27] DocCloak. `http://www.gwebs.com/doccloak.html`. Accessed on Sept. 3, 2012.

[28] J. Dwyer. Four nerds and a cry to arms against Facebook. May 11, 2010. `http://www.nytimes.com/2010/05/12/nyregion/12about.html`. Accessed on Sept. 3, 2012.

[29] Facebook and your privacy: Who sees the data you share on the biggest social network? Consumer Reports magazine, June 2012. `http://www.consumerreports.org/cro/magazine/2012/06/facebook-your-privacy/index.htm`. Accessed on Sept. 6, 2012.

[30] Facebook Newsroom—Key Facts. `http://newsroom.fb.com/content/default.aspx?NewsAreaId=22`. Accessed on Sept. 3, 2012.

[31] FireGPG. `http://getfiregpg.org`. Accessed on Sept. 3, 2012.

[32] C. Gaffga. DCT-watermark: Robust watermarks for color JPEG in java. `https://code.google.com/p/dct-watermark/`. Accessed on Sept 3., 2012.

[33] O. Goldreich, S. Goldwasser, and S. Micali. How to construct random functions. *Journal of the ACM*, 33(4):792–807, August 1986.

[34] A new approach to China. Google Official Blog, `http://googleblog.blogspot.com/2010/01/new-approach-to-china.html`, January 13, 2010.

[35] P. Gutmann. Plug-and-play PKI: a PKI your mother can use. In *Proc. of USENIX Security 2003*, pages 4–4.

[36] S. Jahid, S. Nilizadeh, P. Mittal, N. Borisov, and A. Kapadia. DECENT: a decentralized architecture for enforcing privacy in online social networks. In *Proc. of SESOC 2012*, 2012.

[37] A. Kapadia. A case (study) for usability in secure email communication. *Security Privacy, IEEE*, 5(2):80–84, 2007.

[38] S. Katzenbeisser and F. A. Petitcolas, editors. *Information Hiding Techniques for Steganography and Digital Watermarking*. Artech House, Inc., Norwood, MA, USA, 2000.

[39] L. Kissner and D. Song. Privacy-preserving set operations. In *Proc. of CRYPTO 2005*, pages 241–257.

[40] H. Krawczyk. SIGMA: The 'SIGn-and-MAc' approach to authenticated Diffie-Hellman and its use in the IKE-protocols. In *Proc. of CRYPTO 2003*.

[41] B. Libert, K. G. Paterson, and E. A. Quaglia. Anonymous Broadcast Encryption: Adaptive Security and Efficient Constructions in the Standard Model. In *Proc. of PKC 2012*.

[42] M. M. Lucas and N. Borisov. FlyByNight: mitigating the privacy risks of social networking. In *Proc. of ACM WPES*, October 2008.

[43] W. Luo, Q. Xie, and U. Hengartner. FaceCloak: An architecture for user privacy on social networking sites. In *Proc. of ICCSE 2009*, pages 26–33, August 2009.

[44] MailCloak. `http://www.gwebs.com/mailcloak.html`. Accessed on Sept. 3, 2012.

[45] MALLET. `http://mallet.cs.umass.edu/`. Accessed on August 31, 2012.

[46] A. McCallum, X. Wang, and A. Corrada-Emmanuel. Topic and role discovery in social networks with experiments on enron and academic email. *Journal of Artificial Intelligence Research*, 30:249–272, 2007.

[47] Y. Oren and A. Wool. Perfect privacy for webmail with secret sharing. `http://www.eng.tau.ac.il/~yos/spemail/OrenWool-SPEmail.pdf`. Accessed on Sept. 6, 2012, Feb. 2009.

[48] C. Pring. 100 more social media statistics for 2012. Web Blog "the social skinny". Feb. 13, 2012. `http://thesocialskinny.com/100-more-social-media-statistics-for-2012/`. Accessed on Sept. 6, 2012.

[49] C. Riederer, V. Erramilli, A. Chaintreau, B. Krishnamurthy, and P. Rodriguez. For sale : your data: by : you. In *Proc. of ACM HotNets-X 2011*, pages 13:1–13:6.

[50] SecretTwit. `http://code.google.com/p/secretwit/`. Accessed on Sept. 6, 2012.

[51] A. Tootoonchian, K. K. Gollu, S. Saroiu, Y. Ganjali, and A. Wolman. Lockr: social access control for Web 2.0. In *Proc. of WOSN 2008*, August 2008.

[52] Touring Hub. `http://testing.turinghub.com/`. Accessed on August 31, 2012.

[53] Twitter turns six. Twitter Blog. March 21, 2012. `http://blog.twitter.com/2012/03/twitter-turns-six.html`. Accessed on Sept. 6, 2012.

[54] J. E. Vascellaro. Google discloses privacy glitch. WJS Blogs, March 8, 2009. `http://blogs.wsj.com/digits/2009/03/08/1214/`. Accessed on Sept. 6, 2012.

[55] C. Wang, N. Cao, J. Li, K. Ren, and W. Lou. Secure ranked keyword search over encrypted cloud data. In *Proc. of ICDCS 2010*, June 2010.

[56] Y. Wang and G. Mori. A discriminative latent model of image region and object tag correspondence. In *Proc. of NIPS 2010*.

[57] D. Whiting, R. Housley, and N. Ferguson. Counter with CBC-MAC (CCM). RFC 3610, Sept. 2003.

[58] A. Whitten and J. D. Tygar. Why Johnny can't encrypt: a usability evaluation of PGP 5.0. In *Proc. of USENIX Security 1999*, pages 169–184.

[59] XPath. `http://www.w3schools.com/xpath/`. Accessed on Sept. 6, 2012.

[60] C. M. Zhang and V. Paxson. Detecting and analyzing automated activity on Twitter. In *Proc. of PAM 2011*.

APPENDIX

```xml
<!-- GMAIL -->
<page id="email">
    <url>https://mail.google.com/*</url>
    <block id="mailMessage">
        <region>//div[@class='gs']</region>
        <sender>//div[@class='iw']/span[@class='gD']/@email</sender>
        <data type="text">
            .//*[contains(@class,'ii gt')]//div[not(contains(@class,'gmail_quote'))]/text()
        </data>
    </block>
    <block id="chatMessage">
        <region>//*[contains(@class,'acc')]</region>
        <sender>.//@title</sender>
        <data type="text">.//div[@class='kl']</data>
    </block>
</page>

<pages>
<!-- TWITTER -->
<page id="tweet">
    <url>twitter.com/*</url>
    <block id="twitt">
        <region>//div[@class='tweet-content']</region>
        <sender>.//div[@class='twitt-user-name']</sender>
        <data type="text">.//*[contains(@class,'twitt-text')]</data>
    </block>
</page>
</pages>

<pages>
<!-- FACEBOOK -->
<page id="messages">
    <url>www.facebook.com/messages/</url>
    <block id="message">
        <region>//*[contains(@class,'MessagingMessage')]</region>
        <sender>//strong/a</sender>
        <data type="text">.//*[contains(@class,'uiListItem')]</data>
    </block>
</page>
<page id="wall">
    <url>www.facebook.com/*</url>
    <block id="wallPost">
        <region>//div[@class='mainWrapper']</region>
        <sender>.//div[contains(@class, 'actorName')]/a</sender>
        <data type="text">.//span[@class='messageBody']</data>
    </block>
    <block id="messageComment">
        <region>//div[contains(@class, 'commentContent')]</region>
        <sender>.//div[contains(@class, 'actorName')]/a</sender>
        <data type="text">.//span[@class='commentBody']</data>
    </block>
    <block id="tickerFeedMessage">
        <region>//*[@class='tickerFeedMessage']</region>
        <sender>.//*[contains(@class, 'actorName')]</sender>
        <data type="text">.//span[@class='messageBody']</data>
    </block>
    <block id="chatMessage">
        <region>//*[contains(@class,'fbChatMessageGroup')]</region>
        <sender>.//*[contains(@class,'actorName')]/a</sender>
        <data type="text">
            .//*[contains(@class,'messages')]//div[contains(@class, 'fbChatMessage')]
        </data>
    </block>
</page>
<page id="album">
    <url>www.facebook.com/photo.php*</url>
    <block id="image">
        <region>/html</region>
        <sender>
            //*[contains(@id, 'fbPhotoSnowboxAuthorName') or contains(@id, 'fbPhotoPageAuthorName')]/a
        </sender>
        <data type="img">
            //img[contains(@class, 'spotlight') or contains(@class, 'fbPhotoImage')]/@src
        </data>
    </block>
</page>
</pages>
```

Figure 6: XPath-based webpage parsing rules for Gmail, Twitter, and Facebook

Do Online Social Network Friends Still Threaten My Privacy?

Sebastian Labitzke   Florian Werling   Jens Mittag   Hannes Hartenstein
Steinbuch Centre for Computing & Institute of Telematics
Karlsruhe Institute of Technology (KIT), Germany
sebastian.labitzke@kit.edu, florian.werling@student.kit.edu, jens.mittag@kit.edu,
hannes.hartenstein@kit.edu

ABSTRACT

A user's online social network (OSN) friends commonly share information on their OSN profiles that might also characterize the user him-/herself. Therefore, OSN friends are potentially jeopardizing users' privacy. Previous studies demonstrated that third parties can potentially infer personally identifiable information (PII) based on information shared by users' OSN friends if sufficient information is accessible. However, when considering how privacy settings have been adjusted since then, it is unclear which attributes can still be predicted this way. In this paper, we present an empirical study on PII of Facebook users and their friends. We show that certain pieces of PII can easily be inferred. In contrast, other attributes are rarely made publicly available and/or correlate too little so that not enough information is revealed for intruding user privacy. For this study, we analyzed more than 1.2 million OSN profiles in a compliant manner to investigate the privacy risk due to attribute prediction by third parties. The data shown in this paper provides the basis for acting in a risk aware fashion in OSNs.

Categories and Subject Descriptors

K.4 [**COMPUTERS AND SOCIETY**]: [Privacy]; E.1 [**DATA STRUCTURES**]: [Graphs and networks]

General Terms

Measurement, Human Factors

Keywords

Online Social Networks, Privacy, Facebook, Homophily, Attribute Prediction

1. INTRODUCTION

In recent years, privacy in online social networks (OSNs) has attracted significant media attention. The daily press reported that several companies are crawling OSNs - such

as Facebook - to learn more about the private life of users in general, or of their customers and job applicants, in particular. Some of these reports state that even insurance companies try to gather accessible data of OSNs for risk assessments with respect to specific customers or to acquire new customers[1]. Fortunately, this media attention increased users' risk awareness regarding privacy (cf. Section 2). However, it can be demonstrated that a majority of OSN members is still unduly generous when sharing personally identifiable information (PII). For instance, almost 80 % of Facebook profiles publicly provide at least one piece of actually concealable PII [16]. Even worse, the authors of [21] showed that de facto adjusted privacy settings only match user's expectations of their privacy in 37 % of the time.

Consequently, if third parties are able to access publicly shared friends lists (more than 51 % of friends lists are public), they can extract publicly provided PII and try to predict a user's information that he/she did not make publicly available. This attribute prediction is possible if the information provided within a group of OSN friends correlate strongly. A phenomenon called *homophily* is the basic reason for the fact that attribute values of OSN friends correlate. Homophily means that people who are similar in interests and personal attributes more likely become friends than those with different characteristics [22]. Recent studies have shown that it is possible to predict, for instance, the gender (2008: [26], 2009: [10]). Lewis et al. found correlations of provided favored books, movies, and music [19]. Some others introduced algorithms that can be (ab-)used to infer PII (e.g., [5]). However, recent studies have also shown that the user awareness regarding privacy significantly increased within the past years and users are more restrictive in adjusting privacy settings (see Section 2). Hence, the risk regarding privacy leakage *might be* decreased and it is unclear whether third parties are still able to predict the value of *any* type of attribute in an OSN. The main objective of this paper is to study publicly accessible PII and to quantify corresponding privacy risks with the focus on possible attribute prediction.

In particular, risk quantification is important to develop new privacy tools. The authors of [2] stated that a central point of the model on top of which privacy tools have to be designed is the concept and measure of risk. Previous studies demonstrated that novel privacy tools are needed to further establish privacy risk awareness and to demonstrate privacy implications of PII that already is, or rather is about

---

[1]E.g., http://socialbarrel.com/insurance-companies-watching-you-on-facebook/ [last downloaded 2012-09-14].

to be shared [14]. At the end of this paper, we argue that the findings presented in this paper can lay a foundation to implement innovative privacy applications for OSN users.

This paper provides extensive statistical data, which was uniformly sampled from the entire 950+ million Facebook profiles[2], to quantify the risks regarding attribute prediction by the use of PII provided by OSN friends. The data was sampled in July and August 2012. Note, we implemented a privacy preserving and compliant software to analyze publicly available PII. By applying this software, we do not have access to raw PII that has been published by Facebook users (see Appendix A for a more detailed note on compliant sampling). For the analysis, we utilized the following attacker model: we assume a third party trying to infer users' attributes just based on information that is publicly available to any logged-in user. The attacker is not connected to any user within the network in terms of OSN friendships. With the results, we provide statistical numbers on the measure of interdependences of a user's and his/her friends' PII. Thereby, the identified correlations are based on minimal knowledge a third party can extract from the profiles of users' OSN friends without exploiting sophisticated attack and correlation strategies.

We initially focus on the risk estimation for location attributes and the age of OSN users. Afterwards, we discuss possibilities for third parties to infer other attributes Facebook users provide publicly. Thereby, we identify attributes that are surprisingly predictable, regardless of the fact that they are rarely provided publicly, nowadays. However, we also identify a series of attributes that are infrequently provided publicly and barely correlate. In summary, the contributions of this paper are:

- We present statistical data based on a sample of more than 1.2 million Facebook profiles (see Section 3 for information on sampling, statistical significance and compliance).

- We evaluate the individual risk regarding the attribute prediction by third parties, mainly focused on location attributes and the "year of birth".

- We lay the foundation for future technologies to support users in individual risk assessment with respect to privacy. In this context, we give an outlook on a Facebook privacy application that we are currently implementing on the basis of the findings of this paper.

The paper is structured as follows. Section 2 presents related work with respect to investigations of the publicly shared PII in OSNs and attribute prediction. Section 3 provides the research question, explains the methodology of the empirical study and gives insights into the sample size and its statistical significance, followed by the demonstration of the results in Section 4. Section 5 discusses the results and Section 6 concludes the paper and gives the mentioned outlook on the new privacy tool we are currently developing.

2. RELATED WORK

Previous investigations studied publicly available PII in different OSNs to demonstrate that user privacy is at risk.

---

[2]Status at August 2012; http://newsroom.fb.com/.

Some authors introduced algorithms to demonstrate that attributes are predictable if friends lists are made public and if friends provide enough PII publicly. In the following, we discuss the relationship of these studies to this paper. First, we show the differentiation of the current investigation compared to studies we performed previously. Second, we look at the investigation of publicly available PII in OSNs in general. Afterwards, we focus on those studies that investigated possible attribute prediction in OSNs.

In [16], we demonstrated that a profile of one OSN (e.g. Facebook) and a profile of another OSN (e.g. Xing) - owned by a single user - can easily be linked to each other by third parties, particularly by comparing friends lists. Inter alia, the study resulted in the finding that two profiles are likely to belong to the same physical person if at least four names of friends occur in both corresponding friends lists and, in addition, the user has registered the profiles with similar names. Furthermore, we investigated the amount of publicly available PII in [16] and in [15]. In contrast to the current investigation, the studies were focused on the linkability of several profiles of a single user and the possible gain in information by linking profiles and distributed information of a single user. In the current study, we investigate the risk regarding attribute prediction, i.e., the risk that third parties are able to gain information by analyzing publicly provided PII of users' friends in the same OSN.

In [11], the authors defined the term self-disclosure as the "amount of information shared on a user's profile (...)". Recently, several studies demonstrated which pieces of PII users reveal (especially via Facebook) and which preventive measures they take to hide data from third parties. These studies resulted in findings that changed over time. As early as 2005, Gross and Acquisti investigated the self-disclosure of Facebook users [8]. In 2007 and 2008, an already increased privacy awareness was shown by [17] and [4]. However, in 2008, Krishnamurthy and Wills showed that most users still do not change the default OSN privacy settings [12] and, in 2010, that the default settings of OSNs often permit access to friends lists for anybody [13]. In 2011, we demonstrated that some attributes are rarely provided publicly, but still only between 7 % and 22 % of users (depending on the OSN) hide every actually concealable PII from strangers [16]. Therefore, concerning our current results and those of these related studies, the evolution of user behavior in OSNs and associated risks can be derived (see [16] for a more detailed survey of these studies).

In the following, we present related work with respect to the investigation of potential attribute predictions in OSNs. At first, we present studies that introduced algorithms that can infer users' PII and, therefore, differ from our work in terms of the *methodology* and the *attacker model* utilized for the investigation. Afterwards, we discuss studies that found correlations of provided PII for specific types of attributes. These studies differ mainly in the *type of findings* from the results we present in this paper.

In 2006, the authors of [9] showed that effective privacy protection should include selective hiding of friendship relations. In 2008, experimental results by Xu et al. revealed that PII of most OSN users could be inferred by the use of PII shared by OSN friends [26]. This study focused on the prediction of users' gender in contrast to more sensitive PII. The authors of both papers used a Bayesian network approach for implementing their algorithms. In this context, it has been stated by Gayo-Avello that "all liaisons are dangerous when all your friends are known to us" [5]. He also developed an algorithm to perform attribute prediction. Rao et al. used twitter posts to "classify latent user attributes" [24]. For this, they utilized a model-based and also algorithmic approach to analyze status messages shared by users. Thereby, they focus on a semantic interpretation of the posts, whereas we focus on the similarity of provided attributes. Recently, in 2012, the authors of [7] analyzed algorithms to infer user attributes. They adapted several algorithms to a so called social-attribute network model and evaluated the adaptation. Thereby, they tried to predict attributes of users based on data gathered from the Google+ network[3]. In contrast to these studies, we did not evaluate an algorithm that can be (ab-)used to infer PII under specific conditions. Instead, we quantify the current privacy risk concerning the adequacy of the usage of privacy settings and the actual availability of PII. Therefore, the studies are different in terms of methodology. In addition, unlike Gayo-Avello's study and [24], which both used twitter as the analyzed OSN, we used Facebook where interaction between friends is more common than interaction with strangers. Therefore, attempted attribute prediction on Facebook profiles might be more effective from the perspective of an attacking third party.

Below, we present related studies that show results that mainly differ from the results we present in this paper in terms of the type of their findings or the findings itself. In 2009, Jernigan et al. demonstrated that a prediction of the gender and the sexual orientation is possible [10]. The authors used data recorded by Facebook, proving that with a sufficient amount of available information a user's PII can be inferred. However, we discuss the risk with respect to several other types of attributes based on data that is made publicly available, today. In 2009, according to the studies of Zheleva and Getoor, it was still easy to infer PII even if as much as half of the profiles are private. Their studies present potential attacks to retrieve PII by exploiting friends lists and group memberships ([27], [28]). In contrast to that, we identify a series of attributes that are hard to infer by third parties, nowadays. Lindamood et al. investigated 167,000 profiles on Facebook and showed that it is possible to predict PII by exploiting the social graph [20]. As opposed to concentrating on PII that can be inferred by exploiting information on the social graph, we present findings based on an attacker model that assumes a third party that only accesses shared data of directly connected OSN friends. Therefore, we demonstrate quantifications of risk based on the minimal knowledge a third party can get from OSN profiles and, thus, present a "lower bound" on how much PII can be predicted in OSNs. In 2010, Mislove et al. have asked whether attributes of users in combination with the social graph can be used to predict the attributes of another user in the network [23]. In contrast to this paper, they concentrated their data collection on one group, or rather "sub-network" in Facebook using a member profile of this network. Due to the fact that the visibility of friends lists within such a sub-network was granted by default to everyone in the network, they were able to crawl a large subset of the network members and their attribute values. We discovered that inferring attributes without this

assumption is much harder as a result of rising privacy concerns. The authors of [1] also studied attribute prediction attacks. However, they analyzed the risk regarding attribute prediction focused on third parties that gather their information via the Facebook application programming interface in terms of so called third party Facebook applications. The authors proposed a risk assessment scheme to demonstrate the risk of third party applications to users.

Previous studies mainly invented algorithms to show that attribute prediction poses a risk if enough information is shared by users. In contrast to that, we present a current snapshot of the accessibility of PII from the perspective of a third party. Therefore, we show results of an extensive empirical study on the current situation in Facebook and quantify the actual risks of attribute prediction by third parties.

3. RESEARCH QUESTION AND METHODOLOGY

This paper focuses on the question: *What* do OSN friends tell others about a user and do they still threaten his/her privacy? More than 51 % of Facebook members share their friends lists publicly. Moreover, in [16], we revealed that almost 80 % of Facebook members share at least one piece of actually concealable PII publicly. In contrast, we also demonstrated that some types of attributes are rarely available publicly, e.g., the year of birth is provided in less than two percent of the profiles analyzed in this paper. Hence, the following research question arises:

Is user privacy still at risk with respect to rising user privacy awareness and users' behavior concerning privacy settings? Alternatively, from the attacker's perspective: are attribute values predictable by third parties based on an analysis of publicly available PII of one's OSN friends?

Attacker Model

For the study, we assume the following attacker model: an attacking third party tries to infer users' PII if they provide a public friends list on their Facebook profile. Therefore, the attacker analyzes information provided by a user's friends via the *information* and *favorites pages* in Facebook, regardless of whether the friends are using the recently introduced timeline profile or the old kind of profile pages. The attacking third party has access to any information that is accessible for a logged-in Facebook member. However, the attacker is not connected to any other Facebook member in terms of OSN friendships. An advantage of a study based on this attacker model is that we do not have to involve Facebook users in the study in terms of sending friend requests or messages to them. This also means, we do not utilize more sophisticated attacker models (such as, for instance, those introduced in [3]) or algorithms (e.g., machine learning) to demonstrate the risk for attribute prediction. The risk quantification is consciously based on minimal knowledge a third party can extract from OSN profiles. Thus, the findings present a "lower bound" on how much information is predictable (at low cost), i.e., we present results of the analysis of a big set of statistical data and focus on those probabilities that can be extracted from the data with a minimum of semantic interpretation or combination of findings. Thereby, we provide a foundation for future studies that assume a more sophisticated attacker model.

---

[3]https://plus.google.com

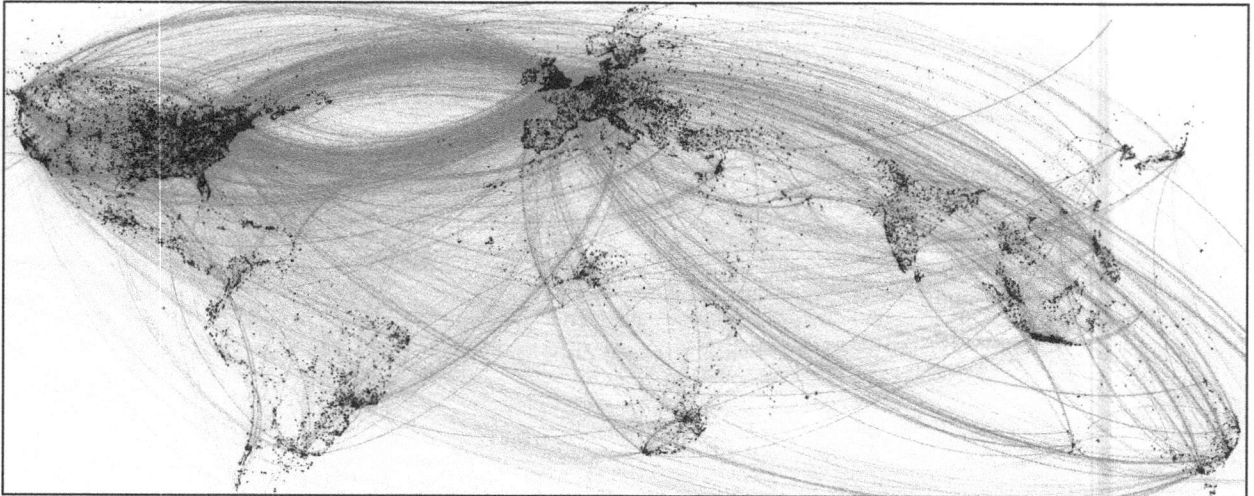

Figure 1: Graph with nodes geo-located with respect to the current cities of those randomly chosen users (α-profiles) and their friends who provided this attribute (381,193 nodes). The edges represent the corresponding friendship relations. Illustration inspired by the visualization of Facebook friendships by Paul Butler (Facebook), Dec. 2010[5]. High resolution version can be downloaded at http://dsn.tm.kit.edu/img/content/fb-kit-2012.jpg

Methodology

In the following, we present the methodology that is used to answer the postulated research question. Furthermore, we present numbers and figures that describe the sampled profiles and indicate its unbiased character, as well as its statistical significance.

For the study, we developed an analysis software that generates random profile identifiers (IDs) and analyzes corresponding Facebook profiles. With the randomly chosen IDs, Facebook profiles were sampled uniformly in the ID space based on an acceptance-rejection sampling [18] as used in [6] (see Appendix A for a note on compliant sampling). If a randomly chosen profile provides a publicly available friends list, every profile linked in this friends list is analyzed by the analysis software as well[6]. Finally, the PII provided by the friends is compared to the PII provided by the owner of the friends list him-/herself. Profiles that did not provide a publicly available friends list were not included in the comparison. After analyzing a profile and corresponding friend profiles, the analysis software discards the raw data (still during runtime, so that the raw data cannot be accessed afterwards), stores the statistical data (that does not reveal which profiles were analyzed), and restarts by generating identifiers until a new profile is found. We refer to the randomly chosen profiles that provided a publicly available friends list as *α-profiles* and to the profiles linked in the corresponding friends list as *friend profiles* in the remainder of this paper.

Table 1 gives an overview of the number of profiles sampled this way. We sampled 12,500 profiles and analyzed their friends lists if provided publicly (6,404 α-profiles were found with a publicly available friends list). With an aver-

Randomly picked profiles	12,500
> Profiles with a public friends list (α-profiles)	*6,404*
Total number of analyzed friend profiles	**1,278,478**
> Average number of friends in an α-profile	*199.64*
Total number of profiles analyzed	**1,290,978**

Table 1: Sample of OSN profiles

age number of almost 200 friends, we compared more than 1.2 million friend profiles to their corresponding α-profile.

In the following, we refer to the city where a Facebook user claims to live as the *current city*[7]. Figure 1 shows a graph with nodes geo-located with respect to the current cities of those users who provided this location information publicly. The graph shows current cities of α-profiles (2,667 α-profiles provided this attribute) and current cities provided by their friends. The distribution matches very well with the overall coverage and relationship visualization published by Facebook in December 2010[5].

4. RESULTS

Based on the described methodology, we analyzed and compared publicly available PII provided by randomly sampled α-profiles and corresponding friend profiles. In the following, the resulting findings are presented. First, we show statistical numbers on the availability of attributes users provide via their information and favorites pages in Facebook. Second, we analyze and discuss the statistical data of certain attribute comparisons in detail.

Not every profile of the 6,404 α-profiles provided the attributes that are focused in this investigation. Hence, we only compare those profiles that provided a particular attribute *and* provided a friends list with a minimum of one friend who also provided this attribute. Table 2 shows the

---

[5]https://www.facebook.com/notes/facebook-engineering/visualizing-friendships/469716398919 [last downloaded 2012-09-14].

[6]Others report that a maximum of only 400 friends can be accessed within a friends list. We did not observe this restriction with the utilized analysis software.

[7]Some other works refer to the attribute *current city* as *current location*. To avoid confusion with mobile locations, we use the term *current city* in the remainder of this paper.

Attributes	A	B	C	D
Friends List	*6,404*	*100 %*	–	–
Personal Attributes				
Gender	5,815	90.8 %	6,345	99.1 %
Current City	2,667	41.7 %	5,900	92.1 %
Hometown	2,316	36.2 %	5,806	90.7 %
Relationship Status	1,362	21.3 %	5,669	88.5 %
University	932	14.6 %	5,201	81.2 %
Employer	784	12.2 %	5,134	80.2 %
School	421	6.5 %	4,715	73.6 %
Year of Birth	117	1.8 %	4,286	66.9 %
Favorites				
Miscellaneous	3,474	54.2 %	6,092	95.1 %
Favorite Music	2,400	37.5 %	5,909	92.3 %
Favorite TV Shows	1,884	29.4 %	5,783	90.3 %
Favorite Movies	1,688	26.4 %	5,736	89.6 %
Interests	1,370	21.4 %	5,613	87.6 %
Favorite Books	1,285	20.1 %	5,572	87.0 %
Activity	1,257	19.6 %	5,632	87.9 %
Favorite Sports Teams	778	12.1 %	5,346	83.5 %
Favorite Sportsmen	721	11.3 %	5,320	83.1 %
Favorite Type of Sport	180	2.8 %	4,082	63.7 %

A: absolute number of α-profiles
B: percent of α-profiles
C: absolute number of analyzed friends lists
D: percent of analyzed friends lists

Table 2: Column A and B: Absolute and relative number of the 6,404 α-profiles that provided the attribute AND shared a friends list, in which a minimum of one friend also provided the attribute. Column C and D: Absolute and relative number of the 6,404 analyzed friends lists that contained a minimum of one profile that shared the attribute.

number of profiles that fulfilled these requirements with respect to specific attributes (columns A and B). Table 2 also provides the number of friends lists, in which a minimum of one friend provided a certain attribute, regardless of whether the friends list owner (the α-profile) provided this attribute or not (columns C and D).[8]

On the one hand, it is indicative that - for some types of attributes - a small number of α-profiles shared an attribute *and* a friends list that contained a minimum of one friend profile that also provided this attribute. For instance, only 6.5 % of the 6,404 α-profiles provided their school and a friends list, in which a minimum of one friend also shared his/her school. On the other hand, multiple times, more than 80 % of all analyzed friends lists contained a minimum of one friend who provided a certain attribute (without consideration of attributes provided by α-profiles, cf. column D). These numbers provide a first indication of the risk that third parties have access to many pieces of PII provided by OSN friends as a basis to predict attributes.

Figure 2 extends the values given in column D even further. In this Figure, we show the ratio of friends lists (y-axis) that contained at least x friend profiles that provided a certain attribute. To give examples, Figure 2 indicates that in about 31 % of the analyzed friends lists a minimum of 175 friends provided the attribute *gender*, the attribute *miscellaneous* is in 20 % of the friends lists provided by 200 or more friend profiles. Each of 20 % of the analyzed friends

[8]The columns B and D provide relative values with regard to the 6,404 α-profiles with a publicly available friends list.

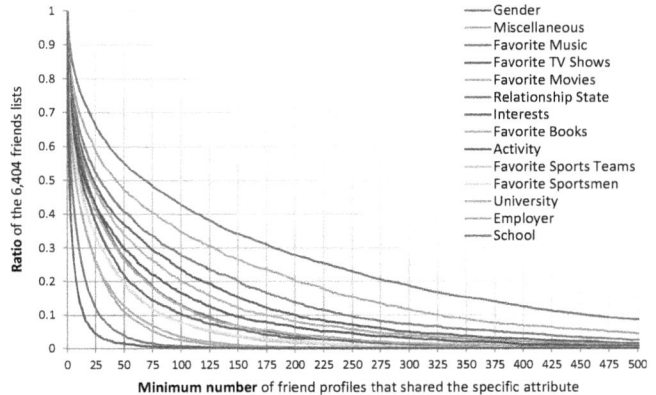

Figure 2: Ratio of the 6,404 analyzed friends lists that contained a minimum of x friend profiles that shared the specific attribute.

lists contained a minimum of 150 profiles that provided the attribute *favorite music*. The risk regarding attribute prediction can be estimated as high, if, in addition to the occurrence of publicly available PII, the attribute values correlate strongly. Moreover, the stronger the attribute values correlate, the less friend profiles that provide a certain attribute are needed to predict PII accurately.

In the following, we show the specific results of attribute comparisons. First, we present observations on the correlation of location attributes provided by α-profiles and their friends. Afterwards, we investigate an attribute that is provided not that often by α-profiles and friend profiles, i.e., the year of birth. However, for this attribute, we found strong correlations within friends lists so that predicting the age attribute of the owner of an α-profile might be feasible as well. The risk regarding attribute prediction for further types of attributes is discussed in Section 4.3.

4.1 Analysis of location attributes

Within the statistical data of the 6,404 profiles with a publicly available friends list, we detected 2,667 α-profiles that provided the current city *and* contained a minimum of one friend in the associated friends lists who also provided this attribute. On average, about 43.5 % of one's OSN friends provide the current city publicly. In the remainder of this paper, we refer to a city provided by an α-profile as the "α-*city*", i.e., the current city a third party might be interested in if not provided. Furthermore, we refer to friend profiles that provided exactly the same current city compared to the corresponding α-profile as "*same-city-friends*".

First, we determine the percentage of analyzed friends lists, in which more same-city-friends can be detected than friends who shared a different current city. Figure 3 provides this result and, moreover, the probability (y-axis) that one of the two, three,... (x-axis) most frequently provided cities represents the current city of the corresponding α-profile, i.e., the α-city. The probability that more friends are same-city-friends than friends in any other provided city is at 56.3 %. Furthermore, the probability that one of the two most frequently provided locations is equal to the α-city is at 72.8 %. For the three most frequently provided cities, this probability is at 80.2 %.

That means, from an attacker's perspective, the most fre-

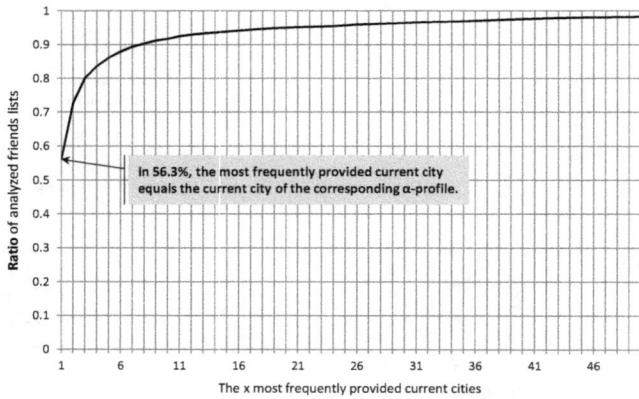

Figure 3: CDF of analyzed friends lists, in which the most, or rather the second, or the third,... (x-axis) most frequently provided current city is equal to the current city of the corresponding α-profile.

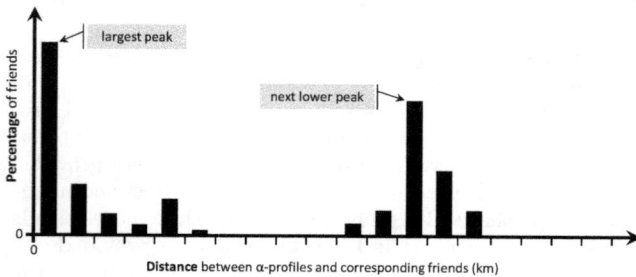

Figure 5: Average percentage of friends (y-axis) who provided a city in specific distances (x-axis) compared to the corresponding α-profile. Additionally, the plot shows the corresponding 0.95 confidence intervals[12].

quently provided city within a friends list can serve as a maximum likelihood estimator[9] for the α-city. In the following, we analyze the geographical spread of friends lists, i.e., how close friends are living around the current city of an α-profile, to further investigate the accuracy of the maximum likelihood estimator.

In the statistical data, we can observe that, on average, 42 different cities are publicly shared within a single friends list (in our sample, the maximum is at 337 different locations). For further investigation, we calculated the air-line distance[10] between any shared city of friend profiles and the corresponding α-city. Afterwards, we counted the number of friends in specific air-line distances to contrast these numbers with the number of same-city-friends, for each of the analyzed friends lists. In the following, we refer to the air-line distance simply as the "*distance*". Figure 4 shows a schematic histogram that represents an exemplary distribution of a single user's friends concerning the distance between provided cities and the α-city. The x-axis shows the distance and the y-axis the percentage of friends in specific distances. In this example, the largest peak represents the peak of same-city-friends.

---

[9]It is most likely that the most frequently provided current city equals the current city of the α-profile (α-city).
[10]Air-line distance: the distance between two provided locations "as the crow flies" (in km; 1 km ≈ 0.62 miles).

We built such a histogram for each of the analyzed friends lists. In turn, these histograms form the basis for Figure 5, which shows the *average* percentage of users' friends whose provided cities are in a specific distance to the users' own cities. In the plot, only those friend profiles were considered that provided this attribute at all. Therefore, 100 % represents the number of those friends only. On the x-axis, the distance between the α-cities and friends' cities is given. The y-axis shows the average percentage of a friends list. The first bar represents the average percentage of same-city-friends. For the sake of legibility, the plots are cut off at a distance of 500 kilometers and the last bar shows the overall value for distances larger than 500 kilometers. The other bars represent bins of ten kilometers distance. Additionally, Figure 5 shows the 0.95 confidence intervals[12]. It can be seen that on average 32.6 % (i.e., an absolute number of about 44 friends) of the friends who provided the current city are same-city-friends, which is 28 percentage points higher compared to other distance bins. However, the standard deviation of the 32.6 % of friends is at 26.9 and, additionally, occasional occurrences of (maybe large) groups of friends that do not live in the α-city are averaged out. Whether

---

[12]Confidence intervals indicate the reliability of statistical values. 0.95 confidence intervals mean that the probability that the actual values of given statistical values are within the specified intervals is at 95 %.

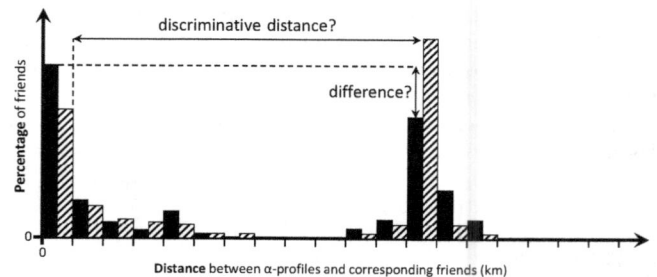

Figure 4: Illustration of an example histogram that shows the percentage of friends of an α-profile who provided a city in specific distances compared to the α-city.

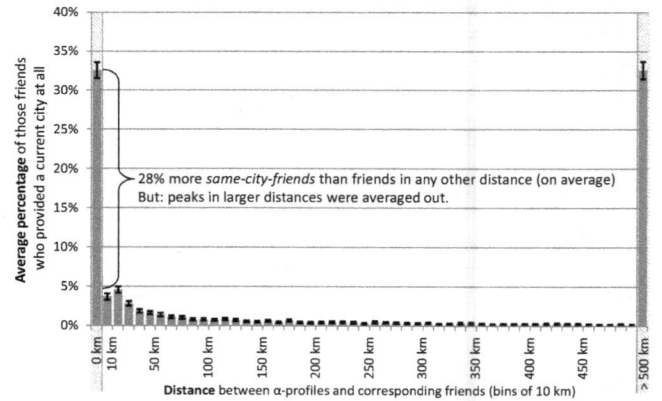

Figure 6: Illustration of how the difference (in percentage points) and the discriminative distance between two peaks is evaluated.

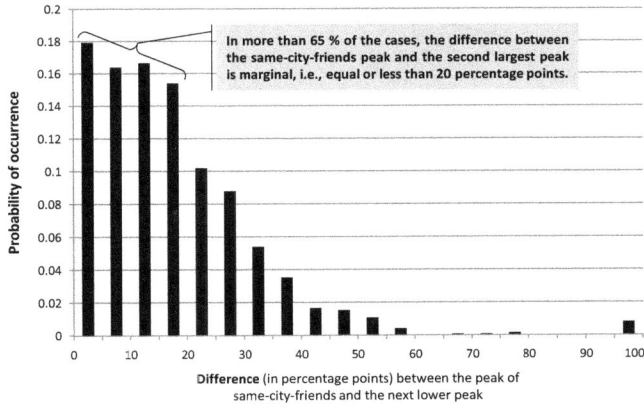

Figure 7: Probability distribution of the differences between the number of same-city-friends and the number of friends that correspond to the second most frequently provided city. The differences are expressed in relative terms w.r.t. the friends list sizes. Only the profiles are considered, in which the same-city-friends yield the highest peak.

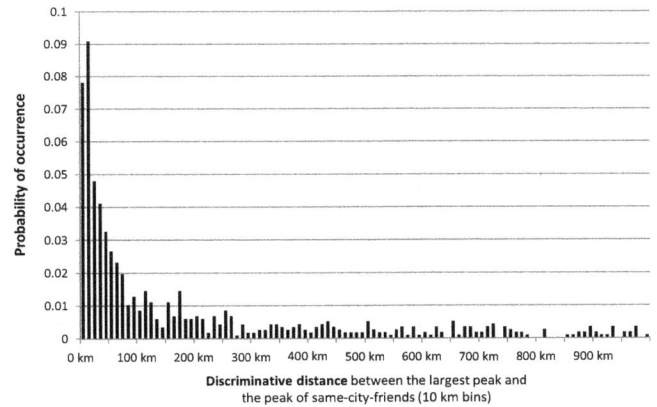

Figure 8: Probability distribution of the discriminative distances between the most frequently provided current city and the α-city. Only the profiles are considered, in which the same-city-friends do not yield the highest peak.

this (negative) distorting effect of averaging is significant is evaluated in the following.

For this purpose, we analyze how the largest peaks actually stand out and apart from other peaks. We assume an attacking third party that picks the most provided current city from a friends list and assumes that this is the α-city he/she tried to predict. Figure 6 shows two schematic histograms, such as the one in Figure 4. The histograms represent two different cases of distributions of friends with respect to the distance between their city and the α-city. The black bars represent the case, in which a city prediction (based on the most frequently provided city) is successful, i.e., the peak at same-city-friends is the largest peak. The striped bars represent the case, in which a city prediction based on the most frequently provided city does not result in the α-city. In the following, we address two questions: 1) how tight was a prediction if it was successful (*difference* between peaks) and 2) if it was not successful, how large was the *discriminative distance* between the predicted city and the α-city.

We start with the first question, i.e., the case that an attack was successful (56.3 % of analyzed friends lists, cf., Figure 3). To answer this question, we calculated the *difference* (in absolute terms) between the number of same-city-friends and the number of friends that correspond to the second most frequently provided city for each friends list (in which the largest peak refers to the same-city-friends). These absolute values are then expressed in relation to the size of each friends list (e.g., if the difference in absolute terms accounts to 10 friends and the friends list size is 100, the difference would be 10 %). The resulting probability distribution of these differences is shown in Figure 7. This figure demonstrates that in more than 65 % of the cases, the difference between the number of same-city-friends and friends in the second most frequently provided city is equal or less than 20 percentage points. Obviously, a correctly predicted city by exploiting the most frequently provided city was often a close decision.

With respect to the second question, i.e., the case that an attack was not successful, we analyze the discriminative distances between every wrong predicted city and the actually provided city of an α-profile. Figure 8 shows these distances on the x-axis (bins of 10 km) and their probability of occurrence on the y-axis. The plot shows that a wrong prediction can result in a city that is very close to the α-city, but also in a city that is located further away. To be precise, in about 30 % of the cases the wrongly predicted city is located less than 50 kilometers away from the α-city.

So far, we have only analyzed whether friends provide exactly the same city. However, the discriminative distances of unsuccessful predictions indicate that not only same-city-friends can be exploited to predict the city of an α-profile. Therefore, we investigate whether other provided locations can be exploited, at least, in order to localize the nearby area of the city of an α-profile. Figure 9 shows the ratio of analyzed friends lists (y-axis), in which the number of

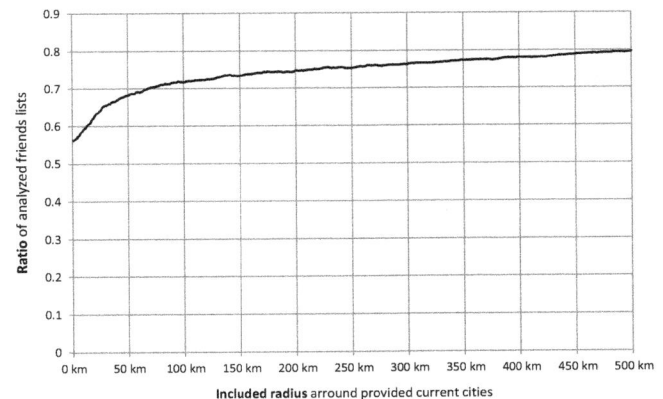

Figure 9: Ratio of analyzed friends lists, in which a city prediction would be successful if the number of friends in an x km radius around provided cities is included in the detection of the most frequently provided city or area, respectively.

same-city-friends plus the number of friends in a specific radius (x-axis) is larger than the number of friends in any other city plus the number of friends in the specific radius around this city. At the x-value of zero kilometers the 56.3 % from Figure 3 can be seen. For instance, at an x-value of 50 km, already 68.2 % of friends lists contained more same-city-friends plus the number of friends in a 50 km radius than friends in any other 50 km radius around a provided city. That means, if an attacking third party is only interested in a prediction of the nearby area of the α-city, the probability of a correct prediction can be increased by exploiting not only the most frequently provided city but also the number of friends in a specific nearby area of cities. However, the larger the included radius around a provided city, the less the increase of the probability of a successful prediction.

Therefore, on the one hand, it is worthwhile to exploit the number of friends in a small nearby area around provided cities if a third party is interested in predicting a user's city. On the other hand, the increase of the probability of a correct prediction diminishes if the radius is more and more increased, which is obvious if we take into account that most people live in the nearby area of their friends.

Since the results regarding the analysis of the *hometown* are very similar to the results regarding users' current city, we show the corresponding plots in the appendix of this paper. These plots have the same structure as Figures 3, 7, 8, and 9, respectively, although the plots in the appendix are based on the statistical data regarding the attribute *hometown*.

In summary, the presented results show that location information could be inferred by exploiting friends' location information and demonstrate a still existing reason to hide OSN friends lists. In particular, the probability that the most frequently provided city is the city of the owner of an α-profile is at 56.3 % (54.1 % for the attribute hometown). Moreover, if an attacking third party considers also the number of friends that provided the current city/hometown in a nearby area of provided cities/hometown and tries to predict the α-city/-hometown based on the number of friends in these areas, the probability of a successful prediction increases to more than 70 % for distance inaccuracy of less than 100 kilometers.

4.2 Analysis of the age distribution

In this section, we present results of the comparisons of the attribute *year of birth*. In contrast to the attribute *current city*, the age, or rather the year of birth is provided very rarely in Facebook profiles. 117 of the 6,404 profiles with a publicly available friends list provided this attribute *and* a friends list containing a minimum of one friend who also provided the age. From a statistical point of view, we could not reach significance by comparing those 117 profiles with their friends.

However, besides the 117 profiles, we found 4,286 profiles that did not provide the year of birth, but provided a friends list, in which at least one friend shared this attribute. On average, about 9.5 friends per friends list shared the year of birth publicly (40,672 friends in total). Hence, we analyzed the interdependence of years of birth within these friends lists by comparing those attribute values among each other.

For this purpose, we took each profile i and extracted the provided ages a_{ij} of corresponding friends ($max(j)$ being the number of friends who provided the age). Next, we

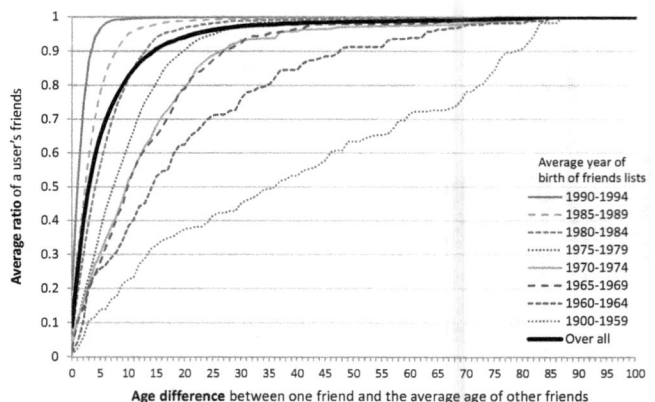

Figure 10: CDF: probability that a randomly chosen OSN friend has a maximum of a specific age difference to the average age of the friends list

calculated the age difference d_{ij} of each friend's age and the average age $\bar{a}_{ij}$ of all other friends of profile i. Afterwards, we calculated the CDF over all d_{ij} of a profile i (with $0 \leq d \leq 100$) and finally computed the average CDF over all profiles, which is shown in Figure 10 (bold curve). Therein, the y-axis provides the average ratio of friends that are a maximum of x years older or younger than the average age of the rest of the friends list. Additionally, Figure 10 shows the results separated by the average year of birth of a friends list (thinner curves; ranges of 5 years; on average 431 friends lists per range). Since just 58 analyzed friends lists have an average year of birth between 1900 and 1959, we added just a single curve that represents this interval for the sake of completeness. Notice that Facebook does not reveal the year of birth of people younger than 18 years. Therefore, 1994 is the average year of birth of the "youngest friends lists" analyzed.

However, the plot shows the probabilities that a friend is not older or younger than a specific number of years (x-value) compared to the average age of the rest of the friends list (for sure, initially, this is only a valid observation for friend profiles that also shared the year of birth). From the perspective of an "attacking" third party, this means that the year of birth of a profile can be predicted on the basis of years of birth provided by other friends of the same friends list with the accuracies given in Figure 10. As an example, if a third party determines the average year of birth of all friends that provided the attribute (except one), the probability that this excepted friend is not older or younger than four years concerning the average age is at 59 %. Moreover, if the average year of birth of the friends list lies between 1990 and 1994, this probability increases to 94 %. Thus, Figure 10 indicates, inter alia, that prediction of the age is more accurate the younger the friends in a friends list are.

Now, we assume that the years of birth of all of a user's friends correlate as strongly as only the years of birth of friend profiles that provided the attribute. If this assumption is true (which is indicated by the strong correlations shown before, but cannot be proven because of the fact that the analysis software had no access to concealed/non-provided years of birth), the prediction of the age of any profile within a friends list would be possible based on the aforementioned results. We are fully aware of the fact that comparisons of the aforementioned 117 α-profiles and their friends cannot result in statistical significant results. However, we compared the year of birth of those α-profiles with the average year of birth of their friends. With these comparisons, we calculated an average age difference of only 3.9 years and 2.4 years for the group of people born between 1990 and 1994. Based on this indicator and the fact that the α-profile is owned by just another person within a group of friends, it can be assumed that his/her age correlates with the ages of his/her friends as strongly as years of birth provided in a friends list itself. Under this assumption, the results demonstrate that if an OSN member shares a publicly available friends list, age prediction poses a risk despite the limited number of users who share their year of birth (about 1.5 %).

4.3 Other Attributes

Figure 11 shows an aggregation of the results concerning several other attributes to show their occurrence and correlation. Every pair of bars in this plot represents the results of comparisons regarding a specific type of attribute (given on the x-axis) and the number of friends who provided the attribute at all. The given relative values (y-axis) are calculated with respect to the number of friends in the friends lists. The grey bars (the right bar in each case) show the average ratio of the friends lists that provided the attribute, the blue bars (left ones) the ratio of the whole friends list that provided exactly the same attribute value as the compared α-profile. Since some of these attributes are rarely provided (cf. Table 2 and Figure 2), the 0.95-confidence interval indicates the accuracy of the given y-values.

As it can be seen, most values of the ratio of friends who shared the same attribute value as the α-profile, are less than 10 %. Exceptions to this are the attributes *gender, relationship state, miscellaneous,* and *interests.* However, the higher values are explainable because of the following reasons. The attributes gender and relationship state can take only a few attribute values (gender: male/female, relationship state: six different values). Therefore, the probability that we found a match between the data of α-profiles and friends is higher than for freely selectable attribute values. The attributes miscellaneous and interest are used by Facebook members to share multiple values and often a large number of single items. For instance, one of the analyzed profiles provided 5,787 items in the category miscellaneous and, on average, people share 16 items (with a high standard deviation of 79.5) in this category. Hence, the probability that one of these items matches one of the items an α-profile shared is relatively high.

However, other attributes are provided rarely within a friends list and are not that often equal compared to the attribute a corresponding α-profile provides. For instance, 19.7 % of friend profiles publish the attribute *university,* but only 2.8 % of all friends of a user share the same attribute value as the user him-/herself. The comparison of the attributes *employer* and *school* resulted in similar low overlaps. Even the comparisons of given favorites resulted in very low overlaps, despite the fact that some users also provide a lot of items in those categories (the most items were provided by a user with 554 shared items within the category *favorite music*). Furthermore, the values that these attributes can take are less dependent among each other than, for instance, the years of birth. Hence, attribute pre-

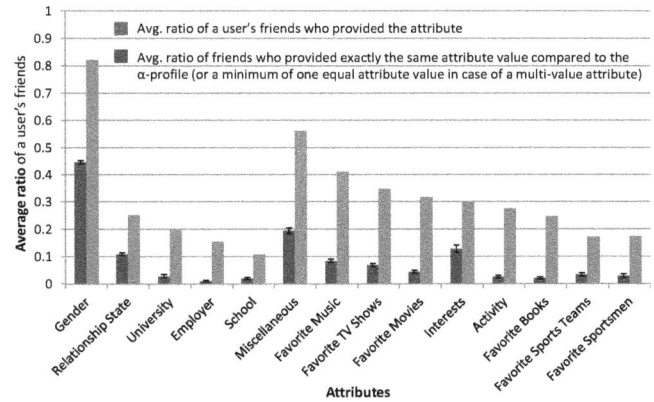

Figure 11: Correlations of other types of attributes provided by compared profiles

diction regarding those attributes might be more inaccurate than the prediction of other attributes. To give a concrete example for this, the prediction of a user's age might be easier than the prediction of his/her favorite music if, on the one hand, friends provide the years of birth 1991, 1992, and 1994 and, on the other hand, the music types *Classical Music, Hip Hop,* and *Jazz.* The reasons for this are the diversity and independency of the values the attribute *favorite music* can take. Therefore, we consider the prediction risk concerning those attributes significantly lower than for the attributes analyzed in Sections 4.1 and 4.2.

In contrast, some of these attributes are rarely provided in general. That means, equal attribute values constitute, for instance, half of the attribute values provided in the whole friends list. Such a pattern might be a sufficient indicator to predict certain pieces of PII by third parties, particularly, if intelligent prediction algorithms are used, or rather if more information - such as more information about the social graph - is exploited by attacking third parties. However, from the perspective of a third party that only analyzes the provided attribute values regarding the attribute that is to be inferred (concerning the presented attacker model), the prediction risk for those attributes can be assumed as significantly lower than for location attributes or the age.

5. LIMITATIONS AND DISCUSSION

In this section, we further discuss the accuracy of attribute prediction in OSNs due to the exploitation of PII shared by OSN friends. We also argue that the presented findings are valuable despite the fact that the statistical data may become outdated in a few years because of changing user awareness and users' behavior in dealing with PII.

Certainly, the probabilities, or rather accuracies, calculated in Section 4 are based on two assumptions: first, the attribute values are not faked by an analyzed OSN user and, second, attribute values of (α-)profiles that provided the attribute correlate with attributes within a corresponding friends lists as strongly as attributes of those (α-)profiles that restricted the access to the attribute from the public.

Let us first assume that the first assumption is not valid, i.e., some OSN friends provided faked PII, which actually seems to be possible. The faked PII mainly deteriorated the calculated accuracies. This is true unless the friends made arrangements and provided similar faked information, which is an even less realistic scenario. Therefore, the provided accuracies represent lower bounds and less faked attributes than in our data would only result in higher accuracies.

As mentioned before, we also make the assumption that correlations are independent of each other, no matter whether an attribute is provided or not. Although, this seems to be an unproven assumption, the detected strong correlations indicate that this assumption is valid. Considering the opposite (the assumption is not valid), the question arises whether an attacking third party cares about some incorrect prediction of attributes. In the end, the information gain by attribute prediction is obviously higher than expected incorrect predictions. Therefore, it seems to be worthwhile for third parties and their businesses to try to predict PII of OSN users.

In this paper, we investigated possibilities and accuracies of attribute prediction based on Facebook profiles. Certainly, this is a restricted perspective if considered that with some side information PII could also be predicted by, for instance, just googling. However, the objective was to investigate the current situation on PII in OSNs. The simple attacker model was utilized to quantify the risk with respect to the behavior and risk awareness of users in OSNs.

In this context, we are also aware of the fact that for risk quantifications not only the accuracies have to be taken into account but also the probability of occurrence that a third party tries to predict PII. Furthermore, the expected "damage" for a user him-/herself has to be considered. Although the daily press reported about the existence of companies that are using (or planning to use) Facebook to gain personal information, the question remains unanswered whether the expected damage of successful attribute prediction is actually significant. In this context, Daniel J. Solove impressively discusses the weakness of users' common "I've nothing to hide" arguments [25].

Finally, we like to argue that the findings are valuable in the future, even if the behavior of users is changing. First, if risk awareness regarding privacy is further increased, the privacy community achieved its main goal, i.e., the demonstration of possible privacy leakages and, thereby, the education of users regarding privacy. Second, compared to previous findings, the results of this paper show the grown risk awareness in the past and laid the foundation for a novel privacy application. Also, if novel privacy tools emerge that are widely deployed and extensively used by OSN members in the future, the presented findings can serve to evaluate the impact of those privacy tools.

6. CONCLUSION AND FUTURE WORK

In this paper, we presented the results of an investigation on the measure of interdependences of personally identifiable information (PII) shared in online social networks (OSNs). The study was focused on location attributes and the users' age. Furthermore, we provided an overview of the correlation of other attributes.

With the location attributes, we have chosen those that are made public by many users and their friends. The observation is that provided location information correlate strongly between an OSN user and his/her friends. For instance, we particularly showed that the most frequently provided location within a friends list provides the current city of the friends list owner with a probability of 56.3 %. Fur-

thermore, if an attacking third party exploits also the number of friends in a nearby area around a provided city, this probability increases significantly. However, even for an attribute that is provided very rarely (the user's age), we could show strong correlations within the friends lists. In particular, we demonstrated that the rarely provided years of birth within a friends list are a strong indicator for the age of other friends and probably the friends list owner him-/herself (e.g., up to 94 % of prediction accuracy concerning an error rate of $+/-$ four years). Therefore, we demonstrated that pieces of PII can still be predicted by third parties, some even with very high accuracy.

In contrast, we discussed the interdependence of other attributes and showed that some are provided rarely and correlate little. Therefore, these results demonstrate that the situation concerning some predictable attributes is not that threatening. Except for the attributes investigated in detail, we consider the accuracy of attribute prediction to be low if attackers just analyze provided values of the targeted attribute in the friends list. On the other hand, we showed that OSN friends still threaten parts of users' privacy and, therefore, no all-clear signal can be given. Attribute prediction still poses a risk, at least, concerning some pieces of PII. The reason for this is not necessarily the availability of an attribute, but also the interdependence of PII shared by the OSN friends. At large, the more information can be accessed publicly the more PII can be predicted. Furthermore, if a third party applies, for instance, pattern learning mechanisms or other intelligent algorithms, OSN friends might reveal a lot more information about a user. Therefore, a strong reasoning for hiding friends lists in publicly accessible OSN areas is still given.

For future work, we already started to develop a Facebook application (Facebook App) that shows a user which information is accessible by third parties and how predictable his/her hidden information is with respect to his/her current privacy settings and the privacy settings of his/her friends. This Facebook App aims at delivering the results of this and former studies to ordinary Facebook users, mapped to their current situation with respect to privacy and attribute prediction. The risk model utilized for the App is based on the findings presented in this paper. In particular, if the user does not provide the App with his/her current city, hometown, and/or age, the App tries to predict these attributes by analyzing PII of those of the user's friends who provide the attribute and permit access for third party Apps used by their friends, which is a default privacy setting in Facebook for certain types of attributes at the time of writing.

7. REFERENCES

[1] S. Ahmadinejad, M. Anwar, and P. Fong. Inference attacks by third-party extensions to social network systems. In *IEEE Int'l Conf. on Pervasive Computing and Communications Workshops (PERCOM Workshops)*, pages 282 –287, 2011.

[2] C. Akcora, B. Carminati, and E. Ferrari. Privacy in social networks: How risky is your social graph? In *IEEE 28th Int'l Conf. on Data Engineering (ICDE)*, pages 9 –19, 2012.

[3] L. Bilge, T. Strufe, D. Balzarotti, and E. Kirda. All your contacts are belong to us: automated identity theft attacks on social networks. In *Proc. of the 18th Int'l Conf. on World Wide Web*, WWW '09, pages 551–560, New York, NY, USA, 2009. ACM.

[4] G. Brown, T. Howe, M. Ihbe, A. Prakash, and K. Borders. Social networks and context-aware spam. In *Proc. of the*

2008 ACM Conf. on Computer Supported Cooperative
Work, pages 403–412, New York, NY, USA, 2008.

[5] D. Gayo Avello. All liaisons are dangerous when all your
friends are known to us. In *Proc. of the 22nd ACM Conf.
on Hypertext and hypermedia*, HT '11, pages 171–180, New
York, NY, USA, 2011. ACM.

[6] M. Gjoka, M. Kurant, C. T. Butts, and A. Markopoulou.
Walking in facebook: a case study of unbiased sampling of
OSNs. In *Proc. of the 29th Conf. on Information
communications*, INFOCOM'10, pages 2498–2506,
Piscataway, NJ, USA, 2010. IEEE Press.

[7] N. Z. Gong, A. Talwalkar, L. Mackey, L. Huang, E. C. R.
Shin, E. Stefanov, E. R. Shi, and D. Song. Jointly
predicting links and inferring attributes using a
social-attribute network (SAN). In *Proc. of the 6th Int'l
ACM Wksp. on Social Network Mining and Analysis
(SNA-KDD'12)*, Beijing, China, 2012.

[8] R. Gross and A. Acquisti. Information revelation and
privacy in online social networks. In *Proc. of the 2005
ACM Wksp. on Privacy in the Electronic Soc.*, WPES,
pages 71–80, New York, NY, USA, 2005. ACM.

[9] J. He, W. W. Chu, and Z. V. Liu. Inferring privacy
information from social networks. In *IEEE Int'l Conf. on
Intelligence and Security Informatics*, 2006.

[10] C. Jernigan and B. F. T. Mistree. Gaydar: Facebook
friendships expose sexual orientation. *First Monday*,
14(10), 2009.

[11] H. Krasnova and N. F. Veltri. Privacy calculus on social
networking sites: Explorative evidence from Germany and
USA. In *Proc. of the 2010 43rd Hawaii Int'l Conf. on
System Sciences*, HICSS '10, pages 1–10, Washington, DC,
USA, 2010. IEEE.

[12] B. Krishnamurthy and C. Wills. Characterizing privacy in
online social networks. In *Proc. of the 1st Wksp. on Online
Social Networks*, WOSP '08, pages 37–42, New York, NY,
USA, 2008. ACM.

[13] B. Krishnamurthy and C. Wills. On the leakage of
personally identifiable information via online social
networks. *SIGCOMM Comput. Com. Rev.*, 40:112–117,
Jan. 2010.

[14] S. Labitzke. Who got all of my personal data? enabling
users to monitor the proliferation of shared personally
identifiable information. In J. Camenisch, B. Crispo,
S. Fischer-Hübner, R. Leenes, and G. Russello, editors,
Privacy and Identity Management for Life, volume 375 of
*IFIP Advances in Information and Communication
Technology*, pages 116–129. Springer Boston, 2012.

[15] S. Labitzke, J. Dinger, and H. Hartenstein. How I and
others can link my various social network profiles as a basis
to reveal my virtual appearance. In *LNI - Proc. of the 4th
DFN Forum Com. Techn., GI-Edition*, 2011.

[16] S. Labitzke, I. Taranu, and H. Hartenstein. What your
friends tell others about you: Low cost linkability of social
network profiles. In *Proc. of the 5th Int'l ACM Wksp. on
Social Network Mining and Analysis (SNA-KDD)*. ACM,
2011.

[17] C. A. C. Lampe, N. Ellison, and C. Steinfield. A familiar
face(book): profile elements as signals in an online social
network. In *Proc. of the SIGCHI Conf. on Human Factors
in Computing Systems*, CHI '07, pages 435–444, New York,
NY, USA, 2007. ACM.

[18] A. Leon-Garcia. *Probability, Statistics, and Random
Processes For Electrical Engineering*. Prentice Hall, 2008.

[19] K. Lewis, M. Gonzalez, and J. Kaufman. Social selection
and peer influence in an online social network. *Proc. of the
National Academy of Sciences*, 109(1):68–72, 2011.

[20] J. Lindamood, R. Heatherly, M. Kantarcioglu, and
B. Thuraisingham. Inferring private information using
social network data. In *Proc. of the 18th Int'l Conf. on
World wide web*, WWW '09, pages 1145–1146, New York,
NY, USA, 2009. ACM.

[21] Y. Liu, K. P. Gummadi, B. Krishnamurthy, and
A. Mislove. Analyzing facebook privacy settings: user
expectations vs. reality. In *Proc. of the 2011 ACM
SIGCOMM Conf. on Internet measurement*, IMC '11,
pages 61–70, New York, NY, USA, 2011. ACM.

[22] M. McPherson, L. Smith-Lovin, and J. M. Cook. Birds of a
feather: Homophily in social networks. *Annual Review of
Sociology*, 27(1):415–444, 2001.

[23] A. Mislove, B. Viswanath, K. P. Gummadi, and
P. Druschel. You are who you know: inferring user profiles
in online social networks. In *Proc. of the third ACM Int'l
Conf. on Web search and data mining*, WSDM '10, page
251–260, New York, NY, USA, 2010. ACM.

[24] D. Rao, D. Yarowsky, A. Shreevats, and M. Gupta.
Classifying latent user attributes in twitter. In *Proc. of the
2nd Int'l Wksp. on Search and mining user-generated
contents*, SMUC '10, pages 37–44, New York, NY, USA,
2010. ACM.

[25] D. J. Solove. 'I've got nothing to hide' and other
misunderstandings of privacy. *San Diego Law Review,
GWU Law School Public Law Research Paper*, 44(289),
2007.

[26] W. Xu, X. Zhou, and L. Li. Inferring privacy information
via social relations. In *Data Engineering Wksp., 2008.
ICDEW 2008. IEEE 24th Int'l Conf. on*, pages 525 –530,
april 2008.

[27] E. Zheleva and L. Getoor. How friendship links and group
memberships affect the privacy of individuals in social
networks. Technical report, University of Maryland, College
Park, 2008.

[28] E. Zheleva and L. Getoor. To join or not to join: the
illusion of privacy in social networks with mixed public and
private user profiles. In *Proc. of the 18th Int'l Conf. on
World wide web*, WWW '09, pages 531–540, New York,
NY, USA, 2009. ACM.

APPENDIX

A. NOTE ON COMPLIANT SAMPLING

A compliant analysis with respect to the German law was
the primary requirement for carrying out this study. In particular, we prevented privacy violations by implementing a
software that analyzes publicly available data of OSN profiles during its runtime and in a fully automated manner.
Furthermore, only calculated statistical data is permanently
stored. This statistical data does not reveal any PII, neither
the profile ID of an OSN profile nor any other connection
to a profile or person, respectively. The raw data provided
in analyzed profiles were discarded by the software immediately subsequent to the analysis process, i.e., we did not
and do not have access to scraped raw data OSN members
published publicly. In [15], we investigate German laws and
privacy acts with regard to concepts for analyzing users'
publicly provided PII.

B. ANALYSIS OF HOMETOWN VALUES

In this appendix, we show four plots that represent the
analysis of the statistical data with respect to the attribute
hometown. For this analysis, we compared the hometowns of
those 2,316 α-profiles that provided the attribute *and* that
provided a friends list with a minimum of one friend who also
provided the hometown. The resulting plots are structured
like the Figures 3, 7, 8, and 9 that represent the results
with respect to the attribute *current city*. Both analysis of
location attributes resulted in very similar findings.

Figure 12 shows that in 54.1 % of the analyzed friends lists
the most frequently provided hometown equals the hometown of the corresponding α-profile. In more than 75 % of

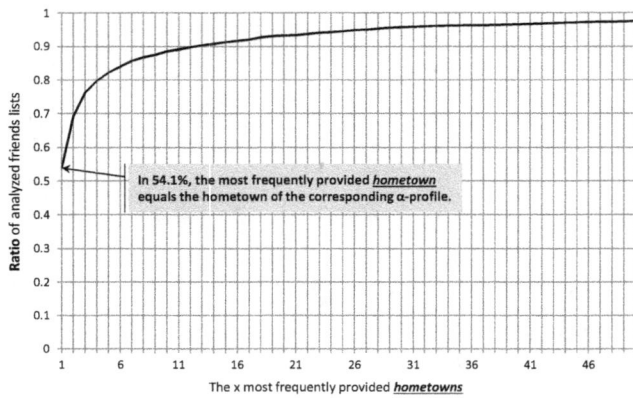

Figure 12: CDF of analyzed friends lists, in which the most, or rather the second, or the third,... (x-axis) most frequently provided *hometown* is equal to the hometown of the corresponding α-profile.

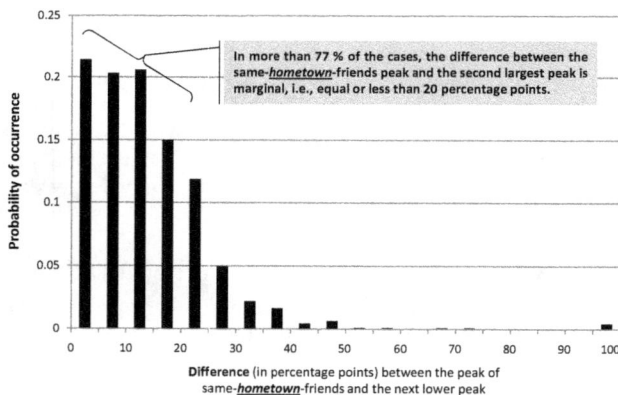

Figure 14: Probability distribution of the discriminative distances between the most frequently provided *hometown* and the hometown of the α-profile. Only the profiles are considered, in which the same-hometown-friends do not yield the highest peak.

the cases, one of the three most frequently provided hometowns equals the one provided by the α-profile. Figure 13 indicates that the difference of the two largest groups of friends who provided a specific hometown is often marginal. For the case of same-hometown-friends, in 77 % of the friends lists the second most frequently provided hometown is provided by a maximum of 20 friends less than the most provided hometown. However, for those friends lists in which the most provided hometown does not equal the hometown provided by the corresponding α-profile, Figure 14 shows that the most frequently provided hometown is often located in the nearby area of the hometown provided by the α-profile. In Figure 15, we show that 66 % of predictions resulted in a correct hometown with a distance inaccuracy of 50 kilometers and more than 70 % for distance inaccuracy of 100 kilometers. For a more detailed explanation of the plots in this appendix, we refer to Section 4.1, in which the corresponding plots are introduced.

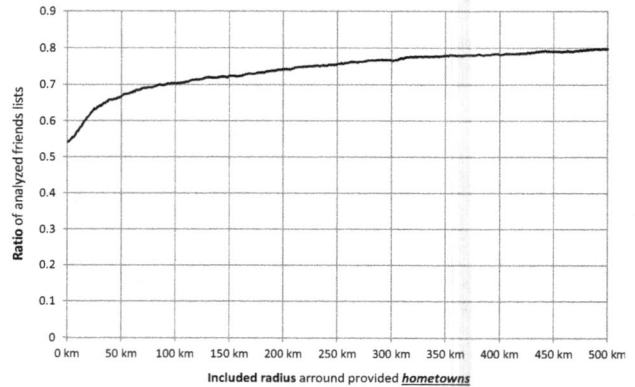

Figure 15: Ratio of analyzed friends lists, in which a *hometown* prediction would be successful if the number of friends in an x km radius around provided hometowns is included in the detection of the most frequently provided hometown or area, respectively.

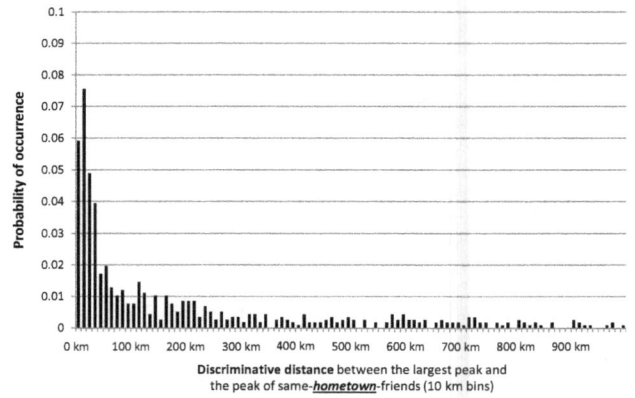

Figure 13: Probability distribution of the differences between the number of same-hometown-friends and number of friends that correspond to the second most frequently provided city. The differences are expressed in relative terms w.r.t. the friends list sizes. Only the profiles are considered, in which the same-*hometown*-friends yield the highest peak.

Geolocation of Data in the Cloud

Mark Gondree
Naval Postgraduate School
1 University Circle
Monterey, CA 93940
mgondree@nps.edu

Zachary N. J. Peterson
Naval Postgraduate School
1 University Circle
Monterey, CA 93940
znpeters@nps.edu

ABSTRACT

We introduce and analyze a general framework for authentically binding data to a location while providing strong assurances against cloud storage providers that (either accidentally or maliciously) attempt to re-locate cloud data. We then evaluate a preliminary solution in this framework that combines constraint-based host geolocation with proofs of data possession, called *constraint-based data geolocation* (CBDG). We evaluate CBDG using a combination of experiments with PlanetLab and real cloud storage services, demonstrating that we can bind fetched data to the location originally hosting it with high precision. We geolocate data hosted on the majority of our PlanetLab targets to regions no larger than 118,000 km^2, and we geolocate data hosted on Amazon S3 to an area no larger than 12,000 km^2, sufficiently small to identify the state or service region.

Categories and Subject Descriptors

D.4.6 [**Security and Protection**]: Cryptographic controls; E.5 [**Files**]: Backup/Recovery; H.3.2 [**Information Storage and Retrieval**]: Information Storage; K.6.5 [**Management of Computing and Information Systems**]: Security and Protection

General Terms

Security, Legal Aspects, Measurement, Experimentation

Keywords

Cloud storage, storage security, data availability, provable data possession, proof of data geolocation

1. INTRODUCTION

Private organizations and governmental agencies with limited storage and IT resources are now outsourcing storage to cloud-based service providers, in an attempt to leverage the manifold benefits associated with cloud services: resource pooling, rapid elasticity, metered service, *etc.* There are legitimate concerns, however, about the implications of using cloud storage services for critical assets. This is especially true in light of recent high-visibility failures, including a massive service outage at Amazon, resulting in the permanent loss of customer data [1, 7]. An Amazon outage in 2008 was due directly to one of its Amazon S3 geographic region centers becoming unreachable for several hours [19].

Increasingly common are cloud service options and service level agreements (SLA) that specify (among other things) the geographic region of a service, at the granularity of a city, state, time zone or political boundary. Geographic region options are provided to help customers achieve a variety of objectives, including performance, continuity and regulatory compliance. For example, a non-U.S. company may want its U.S. customer-serving website located within the continental United States, to improve load time and responsiveness for its target demographic. For contingency planning, a customer may want her data replicated across numerous, geographically distinct locations, for permanence in the face of regional outages or natural disasters. Risk management strategies may be based, in part, on the properties of a specific data center. For example, Amazon GovCloud offers services in a physically separate Amazon service center in Oregon, with specific physical security measures and cleared staff [2, 22]. Further, there are a variety of legal restrictions and protections that may compel a customer to choose to locate data in a specific geographic region. For example, many privacy laws—such as those in Nova Scotia, British Columbia, Australia and soon the EU [16]—require citizens' personal data remain stored within a political border (or, often, that of another nation with comparable protections).

Reliance on a contractual obligation, however, may fail to detect misbehavior (either malicious or accidental) on the part of the service provider. For example, a careless service provider may move client data wholesale, in violation of an SLA, to an overseas data center, to leverage cheaper IT costs. A provider may consolidate data centers or deduplicate client data, undermining those users who are intentionally duplicating data across multiple non-collocated centers for contingency planning. There is concern that the economic incentives for storage providers only align with the goal of preventing reputation-spoiling failures, but do not align with other service characteristics, for which audits, instead, may be appropriate [39]. Indeed, we see these sentiments echoed by potential customers in a variety of sectors. For example, in the United States, the Whitehouse's Federal Cloud Computing Strategy recommends vendors be held accountable for service failures, using active SLA compliance monitoring [27]. Likewise, the US Federal Risk and Authorization Management Program (FedRAMP), which establishes a set of government-wide standards for the use of commercial cloud services, mandates the continuous, active monitoring of services [11].

Verifying that a cloud storage service provider is meeting geographic obligations is a challenging problem, and one that has emerged as a critical issue. Benson *et al.* [6] and Peterson *et al.* [35] each, independently, propose using proofs of data possession and host geolocation to bind cloud data to a specific geographic location. Extending this work, we extract a more generic framework for actively monitoring the geographic location of data in the cloud, using latency-based geolocation techniques to implement data geolocation. We contribute the following:

- We relax the adversarial models and assumptions of previous work, and introduce a generalization of the adversarial model of Peterson *et al.* We show that, against a type of strong, covert adversary, the protocol's soundness is limited relative to the block length, the file size, the bandwidth available to the service provider, and the time period across which an audit is performed.

- We present *constraint-based data geolocation* (CBDG), a data geolocation solution that builds on constraint-based techniques for host geolocation. Our methodology is generic enough to use any distance-latency model, including topology-aware models and those that simulate the overhead of specific storage services. As a preliminary approach, we first explore the effectiveness of a simple linear model.

- We validate CBDG using a proof-of-concept simulation, geolocating targets using large messages on the PlanetLab infrastructure. We use these models to successfully geolocate data stored by Amazon Web Services, both with and without observational landmarks collocated with the storage service.

2. SCOPE

Broadly, the problem we consider is how to actively monitor if a storage service provider is meeting its geographic obligations. As with previous work [6, 35], we note that tracking all copies of data in the cloud is not within the scope of our solution, but instead focus on verifying the location of known data copies. The premise of data geolocation is that a provider may have some (economic) incentive for re-locating data in breach of contract, but assuring that all *copies* exist within some geographic region is outside the scope of our work. In particular, data geolocation may be able to detect (in the context of privacy law) non-compliance, *i.e.* that a host serving citizens' data appears to reside outside the borders of its owners' country in violation of a service provider's geographic obligation; it cannot, however, detect compliance, *i.e.* it cannot "discover" copies of the same data that are held, secretly, at some unknown, remote location. We discuss the relationship between our problem and various outstanding legal questions, similar to these, in Section 8.3.

3. BACKGROUND

To implement data geolocation, we combine two previously orthogonal ideas: host geolocation and cryptographic proofs of data possession. Here, we survey previous work in both areas, and highlight those features we leverage in our work.

3.1 Host Geolocation

Discovering the physical location of a host on the Internet is a natural problem for a variety of applications, has been the focus of recent research, and several commercial products now exist providing these services. In a security context, host geolocation has largely been employed to limit online content and services, such as streaming video or online gambling, to specific geographical regions.

Geolocation of hosts on the Internet is currently achieved through a variety of evidence-gathering practices, including mining data from `whois` databases and DNS records, using Internet topology data and through the manual inspection of Internet artifacts (*e.g.* confirming a webpage is written in Chinese). These methods provide a "best guess" based on a small constellation of heuristic evidence, generously assumed to be non-malicious. The only unspoofable, technical method for bounding location on the Internet, however, is active measurement—*i.e.* delay probes from known landmarks—in conjunction with topological information, *e.g.* from path probing and BGP routing views [20, 26, 29, 33].

To build a topology-based solution, Katz-Bassett *et al.* use `traceroute` and latency measurements along a routing path to infer location. Obtaining latencies between intermediate router hops further constrains the possible location of a target. This approach, and subsequent optimizations [44], underlie current state-of-the-art for Internet host geolocation as used in commercial services. The accuracy of these commercial databases, however, is questionable [23, 36]. A study by Siwpersad *et al.* [40] finds that, in querying more than 1.2M IP addresses, approximately 50% of the results from two popular commercial geolocation databases differ by at least 100 km.

Multiple measurements mitigate variable sources of observed delay, *e.g.* congestion, while transmission and processing delay are assumed to be negligible, relative to propagation time. By using multiple landmarks with known positions, delay measurements allow for multilateration of the target's feasible region. The correlation between delay and distance, however, is not always strong due to Internet peering points, topology, and layer-2 traffic engineering [40]. In particular, Internet delays are known to violate the triangle inequality. This is especially true considering the power of an adversarial node against these types of measurement [18].

In this work, we use constraint-based geolocation (CBG) as described by Gueye *et al.* [20]. CBG utilizes delay-based constraints, measured using a set of landmarks at known locations. Real-world network delays rarely correspond to a simple relationship between great-circle distance and speed of light (a physics-based *baseline*), although such baselines produce conservative, upper-bound models. The CBG *bestline* model attempts to be a more realistic relationship between observed network delay and geographic distance.

In the bestline model, all landmarks measure the delay to all other landmarks. Then, each landmark i builds a linear model from its set of latency-distance observations

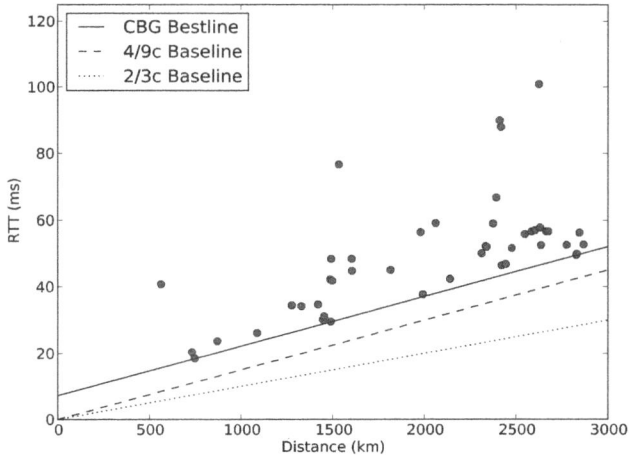

Figure 1: **Example scatter plot of distance *vs.* delay from one node (planetlab1.cs.colorado.edu) to 49 others (see Figure 2), with its CBG bestline and two (previously proposed) baselines for Internet delay:** $\frac{2}{3}c$ **[34] and** $\frac{4}{9}c$ **[26].**

$\{(t_{i,j}, d_{i,j})\}$. This model is characterized by a single line, the CBG bestline (for an example, see Figure 1), defined as the line with non-negative intercept b_i and slope $m_{ij} = (t_{ij} - b_i)/d_{ij}$ closest to that of the baseline slope m,

$$\min_{\substack{b_i \geq 0 \\ m_{ij} \geq m}} \left(\sum_{i \neq j} y - m_{ij}x - b_i \right).$$

Using this model, a landmark can estimate the distance to an unknown target by measuring network delay. Each landmark admits a circular constraint on a target's location, where the circle is centered at the landmark and its radius is equal to the landmark's distance estimation. Define the intersection of these circular constraints to be the target's *feasible region*, a spherical polygon on the surface of the Earth enclosing the target's probable geographical location.

3.2 Provable Data Possession

Provable data possession (PDP) is a class of protocols allowing a client to efficiently audit remote data stores without retrieving the data from the remote server and without requiring the server access the entire file. Recent research has proposed schemes that prove the storage and integrity of remote data [3, 4, 5, 14, 15, 17, 37, 43] and, further, prove the recoverability of the data from incomplete copies [8, 12, 13, 32, 38]. the latter termed a proof of retrievability (POR) scheme. Related, proof of ownership schemes [21] allow a server to challenge a client to prove its ownership of a file before allowing storage or access, typically in the context of client-side de-duplication.

All modern PDP schemes follow a similar four-step protocol: (1) the data owner pre-processes the file to create a small, unforgeable *tag*. Clients may now store their data (and in some cases, the tag) remotely, allowing the client to delete its local copy; (2) At a later time, the client (or an auditor, on the client's behalf) issues a *challenge* to the storage server to ascertain the state of the file; (3) The storage server responds to the challenge with a *proof*, which may require the provider to compute some function of the stored

file, and; (4) Using the proof and the tag, the client *verifies* if the proof is correct; if so, the proof implies the file is stored at the remote server, intact.

Combining the concepts of PDP with Internet geolocation must be done thoughtfully, providing a new and interesting setting for both problems. Naïvely composing latency-based geolocation with provable data possession, *i.e.* applying each technique serially and independently, provides no assurance. Doing so establishes only two, disconnected facts: first, an unmodified copy of the data exists *somewhere* and, second, the responding server exists within some feasible region. We attain no strong binding between the location and the data. In particular, the geolocated server may be acting as a proxy, relaying the PDP challenges to a server at some alternative location.

4. SECURITY MODEL

In their 2010 paper, Gill *et al.* [18] explore the power of an adversarial host to artificially influence its location as inferred by delay- and topology-based geolocation techniques. They find an adversary can manipulate the perceived location of a target by altering the delay observed by each landmark; however, the adversary may only do so by *adding* delay. Assuming that the attacker does not control the environment during model building, this effectively limits the adversary to causing distance overestimation from observed latencies. Since the constrained region size grows in proportion to the amount of delay added by an attacker, Gill *et al.* observe that using additive delay to relocate a target by 3000 km will result in a median feasible region with 10^7 km^2 area, *i.e.* will inflate the feasible region to roughly the size of Europe. These limitations work in our favor. Given that the goal of our work is to place data *within* some boundary, the ability to grow the feasible region to include points far from the true location serves no useful purpose to our adversary. The work of Gill *et al.* indicates that even a sophisticated geolocation adversary, *i.e.* one who has knowledge and control over the network topology, has no significant advantage in undermining the goals of data geolocation. Alternatively, Gill *et al.* demonstrate that relatively small relocations are difficult to perceive: they demonstrate an attack—where an adversary may move less than 1,000 km without detection—that is successful 74% of the time. Thus, as expected, data geolocation has practical limits when the target must be placed within some small, bounded area or when the target exists near the boundary of a geographic obligation.

Assumptions

For latency-based data geolocation, we make the following assumptions: (1) all data are held, jointly, by some set of target data centers whose physical distance from one another is remote enough to be distinguishable (with a high confidence) by latency-based geolocation; (2) the cloud provider does not have a high-bandwidth out-of-band channel between its centers[1]; (3) the auditor controls a set of semi-trusted, geographically distributed landmarks; and (4) the adversary does not control the entire network environment, *i.e.* the Internet. Assumptions (1-3) are explicit, while (4) is im-

---

[1] This assumption—that remote sites are not connected by a private network, of significantly better quality than the Internet—is necessary for delay-based IP geolocation (and our work); we acknowledge, however, that providers renting dark fiber may undermine such an assumption.

plicit, in previous data and host geolocation work [6, 18]. For constraint-based geolocation, we add that (5) during an audit, misbehavior (when detected) has a high probability of being detected by all landmarks. In our model, as long as misbehavior has a high probability of being detected by *some* auditor, then assumption (5) can be satisfied by selecting parameters such that every auditor has a high detection probability. In contrast to previous work: we do not require landmarks to be collocated with the targets; we do not need to assume the locations of all data centers are known in advance; we do not need to restrict data movement to other, known targets; we do not need to build a model of the target by interacting with it; we do not require observing the target during a period in which its behavior is presumed honest or otherwise "normal;" and we do not need to use landmarks (collocated or otherwise) running on infrastructure owned by the target provider. Instead, we build a model of the environment using semi-trusted, geographically dispersed, remote landmarks to geolocate data that may have been relocated to arbitrary, new, and previously unknown locations.

Like Benson *et al.* [6] and our previous work [35] we consider an adversary who may deviate from the protocol during an audit. In particular, Benson *et al.* allow the adversary to fetch blocks from a remote location (in violation of the protocol), when a challenge cannot be satisfied using blocks local to the target. (It is not possible, however, for the storage provider to fool an audit by quickly responding with arbitrary data; per-block authentication protect data authenticity.)

Practical Adversaries

Like Benson *et al.*, we consider economically rational adversaries, under the belief that even untrustworthy providers will avoid transmitting or storing data needlessly, *i.e.* purely for the sake of misbehavior. In Section 7, we describe a stronger form of adversary that is able to misbehave without detection if its bandwidth is large (relative to that of the landmark). It is unlikely, however, that this adversary's misbehavior is economically advantageous. In particular, the target may move portions of an archive to geographically remote locations but, during an audit, it must relocate the data back to the target. For an economically rational adversary, this limited misbehavior can be made punitively expensive.

The most conservative approach to auditing using latency-based constraints is to consider the union of all constraints, rather than the intersection, *i.e.* if even one landmark believes a block is being proxied from a remote location, then the feasible region should expand to include that area. Our assumption that misbehavior, when it occurs, is likely to be detected by all landmarks, allows us to consider the intersection of constraints generated by each landmark's audit. With no additional assumptions, each landmark need only consider the maximum latency observed to produce a constraint. Each landmark might assume that if the majority of blocks appear to be local, then its likely all blocks are local; then, it need only consider the median latency to derive a constraint. A stronger landmark assumption is that, if *any* block appears to be local then all blocks are likely to be local; thus, it need only consider the minimum latency observed. For an economically rational adversary, it may not be advantageous to store fractions of a file across diverse locations. Thus, these become reasonable landmark

assumptions during constraint generation. More generally, a landmark could generate a constraint corresponding to some α confidence interval, such that all landmarks believe, with α confidence, the derived feasible region contains the target. Alternatively, rather than a strict intersection, one might derive the feasible region that the majority of landmarks believe, with α confidence, contains the target. Gill *et al.* propose the constraint radius itself might be an indicator of confidence, and that a threshold-based criteria may be used to accept or reject constraints when generating the feasible region [18].

5. CBDG

We propose *constraint-based data geolocation* (CBDG), a general protocol that binds latency-based geolocation techniques with a probabilistic proof of data possession. We combine these techniques to develop a protocol with the assurances of each, allowing us to place data geographically within a region while proving them to be authentic. In particular, leveraging CBG allows us to detect when target data changes location, arbitrarily. Further, when target data is replicated in multiple places, using enough geographically dispersed observational landmarks has the potential to locate the target at these different positions (or fail to locate the target at any single geographic position).

General Framework

Our techniques are not strongly bound to any particular distance-latency estimate model. Theoretically, pure delay-based models have the advantage that they will always be an overestimation of distance based on the additive delays incurred from both deterministic and stochastic network delays. They are susceptible only to attacks that misplace targets at further distances. Other models that perform better in practice—such as latency models incorporating route and path data—appear susceptible to underestimation in the face of an adversary who controls a portion of the network (as a large cloud provider might). In our work, we consider the CBG bestline model due to its simplicity, for ease of comparison with previous CBG research, and as it is foundational to more sophisticated geolocation models [18, 26, 44]. The bestline model is intended to be an improvement on a pure speed-of-light model, providing the most conservative linear model resembling the baseline while underestimating all observed data.

Our techniques are not strongly bound to any particular proof of possession scheme, either. Initially, we have selected a simple MAC-based PDP scheme [25, 32] in which a file F is broken into blocks $\{m_i\}$ and tagged:

$$T_{i,m_i} = \mathsf{MAC}_k(\mathtt{name}_F||i||m_i).$$

In this scheme, the blocks $\{m_i\}$ and tags $\{T_{i,m_i}\}$ are stored on the remote server. To challenge the server, the client chooses c random indices and requests the corresponding block/tag pairs. To verify, the client recomputes each tag and compares it with the response; the audit's soundness is a function of c.

Using a MAC-based proof scheme has the advantage of requiring no server-side computation and little client-side storage: for each challenge, the server merely retrieves the response from storage; to verify the proof, the client stores only $O(1)$ state, *i.e.* the cryptographic material k. As no cloud *storage* service provides the ability to perform arbitrary computations, *i.e.* to generate complex proofs, using a MAC-based scheme can be immediately implemented given existing cloud infrastructure. The simplicity of a MAC-based PDP scheme, however, comes at a relatively high communication cost. Using a block size of b bytes, at least $c \times b$ bytes must be transferred (at some cost to the client). Some alternative PDP schemes offer $O(1)$ network complexity, but require performing complex server-side cryptographic computations [3, 38]. We comment on the potential complications of using alternative proofs in Section 8.

Protocol Stages

These independent technologies are brought together to create our CBDG protocol:

1. **Model Building:** The landmarks interact, each building a latency-distance estimation model.

2. **Pre-Process and Store:** The data owner splits the file F into blocks, tags each block and stores the block-tag tuple at the target storage service.

3. **Pre-Audit:** The data owner randomly selects c unique challenges and divides them among the landmarks.

4. **Audit:** Each landmark challenges the target. During challenge i, the landmark records the delay t_i associated with the response (m_i, T_{i,m_i}). Using its latency-distance model, the landmark estimates the distance d_i associated with delay t_i. Landmark ℓ uses its set of estimates $\{d_i\}_\ell$ to generate a circular constraint of radius r_ℓ centered at ℓ. Each landmark returns the data $\{(m_i, T_{i,m_i})\}$ and constraint r_ℓ to the data owner.

5. **Verification:** The data owner verifies the proofs $\{(m_i, T_{i,m_i})\}$ received across all landmarks. If all appear valid, the data owner accepts the proof.

6. **Geolocation:** If the proof is accepted, the intersection of all constraints $\{r_\ell\}$ defines the data's feasible region.

The landmark's constraint r_ℓ may be generated from its observations $\{d_i\}_\ell$ in one of various ways, depending on the adversarial model and the desired feasible region accuracy and precision. We discuss some possible choices related to economically rational adversaries in Section 4.

The model building stage is intended to lower-bound the full round-trip time of a challenge and response through the environment. We denote the time to request and receive a single data block as the *data geolocation round-trip time* (DG-RTT). Let DG-RTT$_{\ell,k}$ be the set of DG-RTT observations made by landmark ℓ when contacting landmark k. Landmark ℓ builds a delay-distance model using the min(DG-RTT$_{\ell,k}$) for each k as its data. Assuming the adversary does not control the entire environment during model building, this provides each landmark with data representing the expected minimal latencies between one another.

Protocol *correctness* requires: (a) the verifier accepts all valid provers and (b) the feasible region contains any provers with α confidence. Protocol *soundness* requires: (a) a cheating prover has only negligible advantage in causing the verifier to accept and (b) a prover fetching its data remotely can appear to be storing the data locally, with only limited success. Under the belief that the adversary is economically

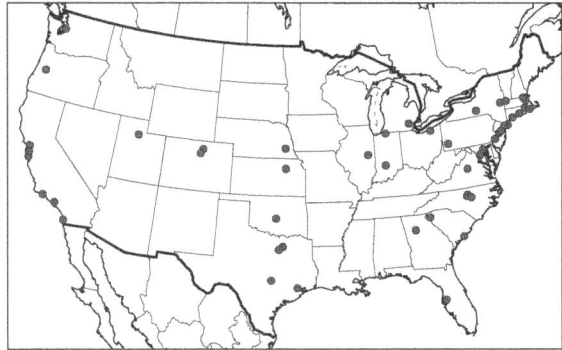

Figure 2: PlanetLab nodes used in experimentation.

rational, that c is chosen so that all landmarks detect misbehavior with a high probability, and that the bestline model underestimates future observations: the landmark can generate the constraint r_ℓ using the minimum (or median) of its d_i estimates, assuming the location of one (or most) blocks can place the location of the entire file with α confidence. We discuss the impact on soundness when weakening these assumptions in Section 7.

We next describe our experiments attempting to validate and assess CBDG. In our analysis, we distinguish between the feasible region's precision and accuracy, as metrics for our protocol's utility. In one sense, if the area encloses the target, then that region is accurate. Gueye *et al.* introduce a different, and heuristic, accuracy metric: the distance of the target from the centroid of the feasible region. Likewise, precision may be related to the area of the feasible region.

6. EXPERIMENTAL RESULTS

To gauge the effectiveness of the proposed techniques, we evaluate them in simulation (on PlanetLab) and in real-world environments (using Amazon S3). We are motivated to discover the simplest, effective data geolocation techniques and our CBDG experimentation follows this motivation. For example, we do not attempt to build a high-fidelity, topology-aware latency-distance model that reflects the provider's overheads: first, that model would likely only be valid in reference to a very weak and specific adversary and, second, the decision to create such a model should be motivated by first exploring much simpler ones. We explore the bestline model, as it is the simplest, non-trivial, conservative delay-based model. We describe the details of our evaluation, next.

Fifty PlanetLab nodes were chosen by hand, based on their geographic diversity and availability (see Figure 2). We choose landmarks in a single country, as we believed this to be a reflection of how CBDG might be deployed: while overseas landmarks may reduce the target's feasible region, particularly for hosts near a border, transferring data internationally during an audit may, in practice, leave it exposed to foreign jurisdictions and subject to divergent (and perhaps conflicting) rules governing protection [31]. While our experimental results are concentrated in the continental United States, we believe our techniques are generalizable to any region where constraint-based geolocation has been demonstrated to be feasible (*e.g.* Western Europe) [20].

On PlanetLab, we utilize a simple TCP challenge-response

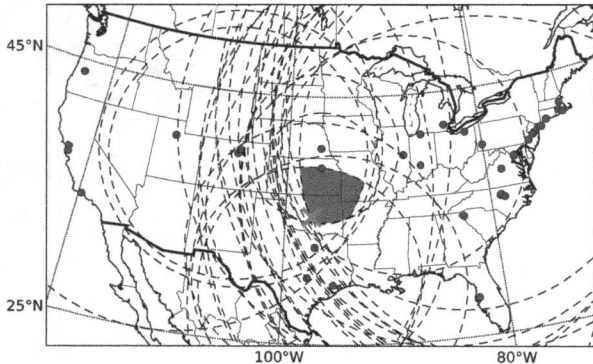

Figure 3: The computed feasible region (grey) for the target data, based our PlanetLab simulation of a CBDG audit, using 32K blocks. The region has area 245,898 km^2 and its centroid is 253 km from the target ($\times$).

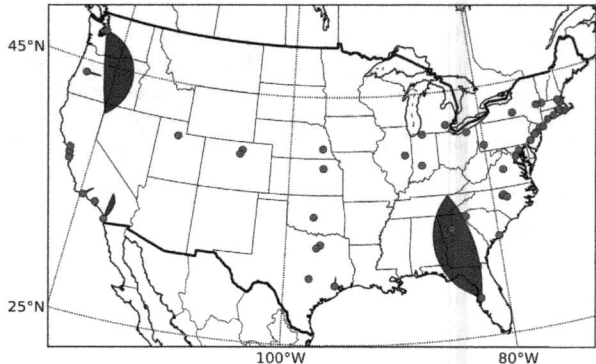

Figure 4: The optimal feasible regions for our selected PlanetLab targets. Note, some regions are so small they are occluded by the target markers.

protocol between landmarks. By using TCP in our measurements, the delay-distance models begin to reflect the protocol overhead associated with interacting with a real cloud storage service provider. As such, our bestline models start to characterize the service behavior of a cloud provider rather than characterize delay artifacts from low-level protocol implementations, such as fragmentation or the maximum transmission unit (artifacts considered by more complicated host geolocation techniques). We do not attempt to model overheads associated with the S3 service or the service infrastructure, e.g. delays from IO latency or load balancing.

In each experiment, nodes serve pseudorandom data generated by the urandom device. This limits any IO delay that might be incurred by reading on-disk data from the set of PlanetLab nodes. These heterogeneous nodes are known to have diverse performance characteristics, whose IO behaviors may not be representative of a real storage provider's IO delays. We acknowledge this simulation may not be appropriate for those providers whose service can become IO bound or otherwise comes with large delays; consider, for example, the seek times associated with random access using tape storage. We believe, however, that imposing a QoS requirement on the provider may be acceptable in many scenarios, and is reasonable to consider as an initial approach.

Our PlanetLab experiments consider data stored in blocks of size 2^n bytes, where $n = 0, \ldots, 15$, (1 to 32K bytes). In our analysis, we often compare the largest of these (4K, 8K, 16K, 32K) to 64 bytes to compare with previous CBG research. Each pairwise DG-RTT interaction is sampled ten times, choosing nodes in random order, to build the set DG-RTT$_{\ell,k}$. Due to intermittent PlanetLab node failures, not all landmarks participated in all measurements or every experiment. In each experiment, we select one distinguished node to be a target, excluding it from the set of landmarks (i.e. during model building), in round-robin fashion.

6.1 Simulated Data Geolocation

We investigate the accuracy and precision of target feasible regions in our PlanetLab simulation. For an example feasible region from these experiments, see Figure 3. For

each experiment, we consider the feasible region generated when participating landmarks act ideally, generating constraints for the target that perfectly reflect its true distance from the landmark. The resulting intersection is the target's *optimal feasible region*. Due to the geographic interrelationship among landmarks some optimal feasible regions are themselves quite large (see Figure 4). This demonstrates that even in the best case, feasible regions are largely a function of landmark placement. We use this optimal behavior as the primary point of comparison for our experiments.

Across all experiments, we see geolocation precision and accuracy that is suboptimal, but relatively similar across block sizes (see Figure 5). In general, accuracy and precision when geolocating with larger block sizes (up to 32K) compare well with that of using CBG-length responses (64 byte blocks). Over 90% of the regions generated during audits on blocks of 32K or smaller have centroids at most 626 km away from their target; over 50% of these regions have centroids no more than 166 km away (see Figure 5(a)). This accuracy is consistent with that of the CBG results of Gueye et al., which claimed an average distance of 78-182 km. The geolocation precision for larger block sizes are similarly favorable. For 32K blocks, 90% of regions are no more than 1,960,510 km^2 in area; 50% are no more than 171,819 km^2 in area (see Figure 5(b)).

6.2 Geolocating Amazon S3

To gauge the usefulness of our techniques in a real-world cloud storage setting, we use our PlanetLab landmarks to geolocate data stored in Amazon's Simple Storage Service (S3) US West-Northern California data center, assumed to be at an unknown location. After interacting with the other landmarks to build a latency-distance model, each PlanetLab landmark fetches a 1GB file in 32K blocks, measuring the DG-RTT of each block request. An HMAC-SHA256 of each block is stored as S3 metadata and returned with each block request. The time to verify the MAC is not considered in the DG-RTT. To ensure our S3 geolocation experiments do not exclusively reflect the utility of collocated landmarks,

(a) CDF of distance from centroid

(b) CDF of feasible region area

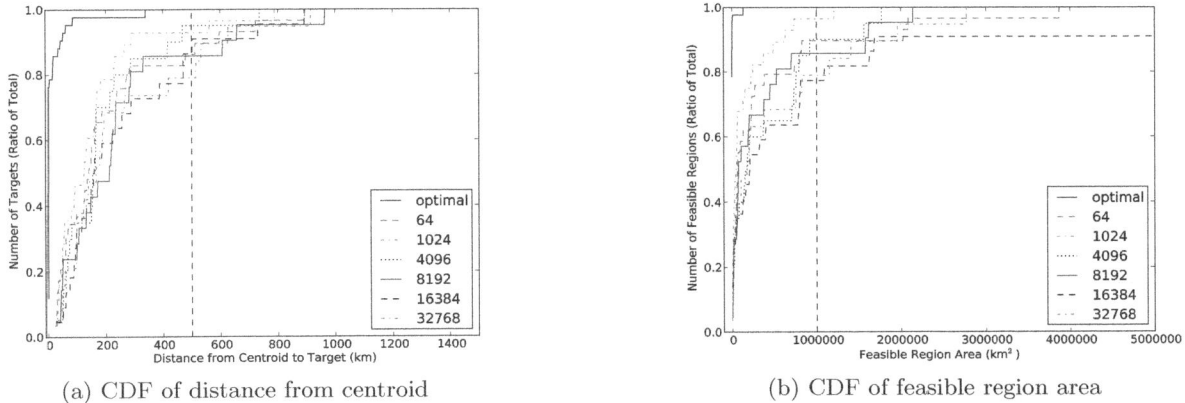

Figure 5: Cumulative distribution functions (CDFs) for feasible region distance and area for 50 PlanetLab nodes over various block sizes.

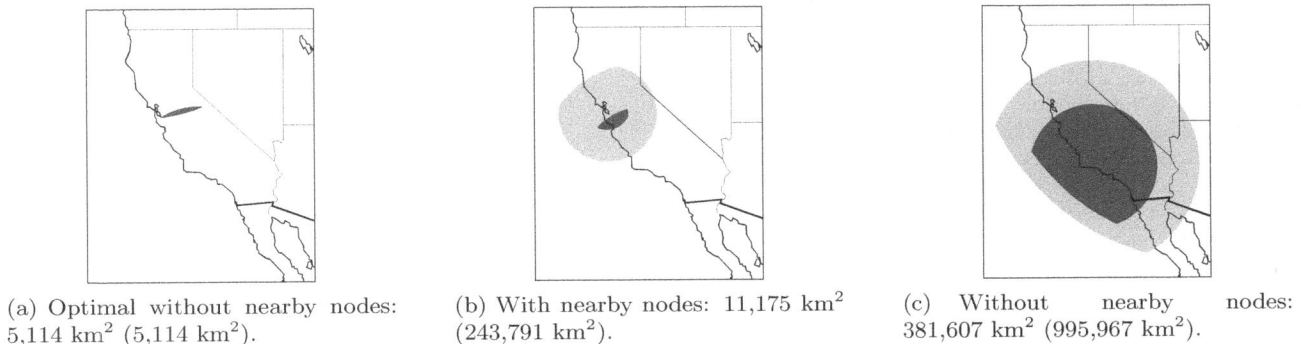

(a) Optimal without nearby nodes: 5,114 km^2 (5,114 km^2).

(b) With nearby nodes: 11,175 km^2 (243,791 km^2).

(c) Without nearby nodes: 381,607 km^2 (995,967 km^2).

Figure 6: Feasible regions for Amazon's S3 Northern California data center using minimum (dark grey) and median (light grey) DG-RTT and optimal measurements. For each, area of the minimum- (median-) derived region is indicated.

we remove all Northern California PlanetLab landmarks[2] and evaluate, separately, the effects of nearby landmarks.

When geolocating S3 data with nearby nodes, we see very high precision at only a small cost in accuracy, i.e. underestimation (see Figure 6(b)). Results compare well with the optimal feasible region (Figure 6(a)). Comparing to the U.S. CBG results of Gueye et al. , this S3 feasible region area is smaller than the majority (approximately 65%) of those experimental results [20]. Since Gueye et al. found European targets generated, on average, smaller feasible regions, this suggests that CBDG may perform equally well in that setting, if it follows the U.S. data set trend.

Unsurprisingly, nearby landmarks contribute significantly in restraining the feasible regions for CBDG. In particular, we see an order of magnitude improvement by including nearby landmarks. We remark that nearby landmarks are substantially different from collocated landmarks, in terms of our model assumptions. Collocated nodes run on the service provider's infrastructure, co-resident with the storage service. Its unclear what assumptions are implicit, when landmarks themselves are under the control of the service provider.

---

[2]Excluding nearby landmarks, the nearest landmark (planetlab1.cs.ucla.edu) is just over 500 km from the target.

7. BEYOND RATIONAL ADVERSARIES

In CBDG, we consider an economically rational adversary, based on the belief that the primary motivation for misbehavior is economic. For these, the cost of misbehavior can be made punitive through regular audit, and certain limited forms of attack are unlikely prima facie. We note that this type of adversary is different from other rational adversaries considered in cryptography. In particular, covert adversaries may misbehave arbitrarily, as long as the probability for detecting misbehavior is negligible. Peterson et al. hypothesize a type of covert attack where the adversary may pre-fetch remote blocks early in the protocol, in anticipation of a future challenge. We expand on this model, as it is potentially applicable to weakening the assumptions of our setting.

We model the protocol as a c-round interactive proof among the target and the landmarks where, each round, some landmark challenges the target. Let r be the number of remote blocks, i.e. those held at some location that is geographically distinct from the target's location. Let time t_i be the time elapsed from the start of the protocol to the end of round i. Thus, the DG-RTT for challenge i is $\Delta t_i = t_i - t_{i-1}$. Let β be the number of blocks that can be moved from remote to local storage, per unit of time. Without loss of generality, we assume this rate of transfer cannot be improved using data compression: either we inflate β to reflect the speed-up as-

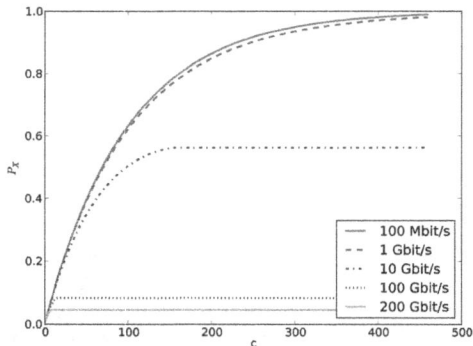

Figure 7: Probability of detecting that no more than 1% of a file is remote before an audit ($r = 1\%$ of n), versus number of challenge rounds (c), for various bandwidths (β); we consider a 1TB file in 4KB blocks, where each challenge round is 50ms.

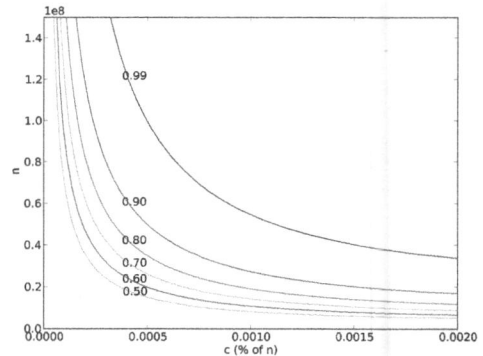

Figure 8: Probability of detecting server misbehavior (P_X) as a function of the number of blocks (n) and the number of challenge rounds (c), for $r = 1\%$ of n; we consider β as a blocks-per-round rate equivalent to the 100Mbit/s bandwidth from Figure 7.

sociated with compressed blocks, or we prevent compression by, say, encrypting all blocks.

Let X be a discrete random variable representing the number of challenged blocks not held local to the target; it is for these blocks that the target will either (i) provide a counterfeit proof that (with a high probability) will be rejected as invalid, or (ii) fetch the data from some geographically remote storage, causing some measurable delay Δt_i during the round. We compute $P_X = P\{X \geq 1\}$, the probability that at least one of the challenged blocks matches a block that is exclusively held at a remote location.

$$
\begin{aligned}
P_X &= P\{X \geq 1\} = 1 - P\{X = 0\} \\
&= 1 - \frac{n-r}{n} \times \frac{n-(r-\beta t_1)-1}{n-1} \times \cdots \\
&= 1 - \prod_{i=0}^{c-1} \frac{n - \delta(r - \beta t_i) - i}{n - i}
\end{aligned}
$$

$$
\text{where} \quad \delta(x) = \begin{cases} x & \text{for } x > 0 \\ 0 & \text{otherwise} \end{cases}
$$

In this model, the time period prior to challenge i may be used to move at most βt_i of the r remote blocks to local storage. Unlike a traditional provable data possession adversary, this model allows the target to "undelete" the blocks that have been locally deleted, at some cost. Letting $\beta = 0$ gives us the soundness of traditional PDP [3]. For $\beta > 0$, the protocol loses the property where querying produces arbitrary soundness amplification. In particular, at the point in the protocol where $\beta t_i > r$, all further queries provide no increase to soundness.

Consider the scenario in which, for any round i, we have $t_i = 1$, i.e. every takes the same "unit of time," during which β blocks can be moved from remote to local storage. This is a scenario where blocks fetched locally from the target yield latencies that are identical, or similar. In this scenario, we have

$$
P_X = 1 - \prod_{i=0}^{c-1} p(i) \quad \text{where} \quad p(i) = \frac{n - \delta(r - i\beta) - i}{n - i}.
$$

For $i \leq r/\beta$ its the case that $p(i-1) \leq p(i)$, and for $i > r/\beta$, we have $p(i) = 1$. Thus, letting $c_0 = \min(c, 1 + \lfloor r/\beta \rfloor)$,

the probability of detecting misbehavior becomes bound by

$$
1 - p(0)^{c_0} \leq P_X \leq 1 - p(c_0 - 1)^{c_0}.
$$

This behavior can be seen in Figure 7, where the protocol's soundness reaches its maximum at some round c_0 and then becomes constant. We use our bounded formulae to show P_X as a function of n and c in Figure 8. The probability of undetected misbehavior, essentially, is characterized as an interaction between the scale of misbehavior, the relative bandwidth available to auditors and providers, and the duration of the audit.

We note that soundness for misbehavior detection degrades as rapidly as the adversary becomes compliant with the geolocation agreement. Thus, auditing may be seen as enforcing correct behavior, rather than detecting slight misbehavior. Our model may be further generalized to allow parallel challenges from landmarks in each round, thus slowing the degradation of soundness across rounds to provide stronger assurance of detection. We do not, however, explore the parallel challenge strategy here. First, such a strategy requires heavyweight assumptions (strict synchronization between landmarks during the protocol). Second, we are interested in worst-case soundness, so we consider the model that most greatly advantages the adversary.

8. DISCUSSION & FUTURE WORK

8.1 CBG Enhancements

Our CBDG framework is relatively general, and may be adapted to incorporate new constraint-based geolocation techniques. Thus, research into CBG improvements and new delay-distance estimation techniques may immediately benefit the problem of data geolocation. We highlight several avenues for constraint-based geolocation research, based on our experiences with CBDG.

In our PlanetLab-based evaluation, we choose a rather arbitrary, convenient set of landmarks in the continental United States. It became clear, however, that landmark selection is an enormous factor affecting the precision of constraint-based geolocation. The reasons for this are many: node responsiveness, quality of network connection, physical location relative to adjacent nodes, etc. Even perfectly predicting landmarks that are geographically distant from the target will generate huge feasible regions: a single East Coast landmark auditing a West Coast target should produce a feasible region encompassing most of North America and parts of Greenland.

We found, in practice, that some landmarks were much more valuable than others. Let a landmark's *influence* be defined as the percentage by which the feasible region's area is reduced when the landmark's constraint is included in the total set of constraints. For those landmarks participating in an experiment, let the optimal feasible region be the region constrained if all participating landmarks provided ideal distance estimates. In this ideal simulation, we find some landmarks—due only to their participation and geographic location—are sometimes very influential. Some, alone, constrain the region by more than 80% (see Figure 9(a)). On average, as might be expected, no single landmark appears strongly influencing when all landmarks behave ideally. In comparison, we see numerous strongly influencing landmarks in our real experiments, including landmarks that (when they influence at all) are strongly influencing on average (see Figure 9(b)). Not only are the constraints from individual landmarks strongly influencing, we find the bestline models themselves are strongly influenced by single landmarks during model building.

We feel that landmark placement for geolocation warrants independent study, with particular attention to both *coverage* (how to place landmarks to geolocate arbitrary targets within some boundary, with high precision) and *robustness* (how to place landmarks so geolocation is precise, despite some of the landmarks failing or under-performing). Related "placement" and visibility problems, *e.g.* the art gallery problem, do not seem to directly apply to our setting.

We feel that constraint-based geolocation might also benefit from improved distance-latency estimate models. The bestline method, in particular, largely ignores a wealth of latency data, and becomes entirely defined by those small set of data points able to bound a line that, by definition, resembles the speed-of-light baseline model. Alternative models might build and utilize sets of linear models, each of which is appropriate for distance predictions on different ranges of latencies: for ranges on which the model has very little data, it might use a very conservative linear estimate; for ranges on which the model has many samples, it might contribute a more aggressive constraint estimate.

8.2 Alternative Proofs of Possession

One drawback of CBDG is the relatively high network overhead required to perform an audit, especially in comparison with recent proof of possession schemes capable of $O(1)$ network communication [3, 38]. In our scheme, the high network complexity is strategic, to relax the computational burden on the target: the server performs only computations related to fetching data blocks. Of course, many web service companies providing cloud storage also provide computation services. For example, Amazon Web Services offers both the Simple Storage Service (S3) and the Elastic Compute Cloud (EC2). Thus, we might develop a collocated PDP service, leveraging more complex data possession proofs in CBDG.

It may be possible to augment latency-based geolocation models with fine-grained measurements of server-based computation delay, to isolate and identify those components of latency associated with cloud storage infrastructure and those induced by server-side cryptographic computations. Such a modeling strategy would necessarily need to focus on tight lower-bounds, since permitting variable latencies from the target or lengthening the audit window will open opportunities for misbehavior from very strong adversaries. This type of latency decomposition has been explored by the storage and network communities, in similar contexts. For example, delay-based techniques have been recently employed to determine if data has been duplicated within a remote data center [9]. We believe such fine-grained decomposition of delays may allow CBDG protocols to utilize more complex proofs of possession schemes—such as those compressing their responses using homomorphic signatures, those with multiple simultaneous challenges, *etc.* For example, PDP audits that measure above a certain (pre-computed) threshold of delay may suggest the target is fetching data from a remote location.

It may also be possible to develop proofs of possession leveraging new assumptions. For example, proofs might constructively leverage un-clonable, tamperproof devices operating on-site at the storage service provider, binding *computation*, rather than data, to a location. Consider a trusted, un-clonable physical device with a GPS receiver at the remote storage server: clients may challenge the server to perform operations on their data using this device, providing an authentic proof of location, albeit under a new and different security model (*e.g.* civilian GPS signals may be spoofed or delayed).

8.3 Data Geolocation in a Legal Context

We previously proposed the concept of *data sovereignty*, with some initial ideas on how it can be attained using data geolocation [35, 24]. In a legal context, the traditional notion of sovereignty is often defined by two rights: a positive right, which allows a legitimate authority exclusive claim to an object, and a negative right, which states that no other authority may lay claim to that object. Legal tests of sovereignty may be applied naturally to tangible objects, such as property or chattel. Applying these historic notions of sovereignty to data stored in the cloud, however, fail both legally and technically, calling into question the appropriateness of the term in the context of this and similar work.

While laws that establish exclusive, positive ownership rights—founded in intellectual property law, data protection law and confidentially law—grant data owners rights similar to that of physical property, we are unable to enjoy traditional notions of sovereignty due to ambiguities in cloud data's jurisdiction, making an owner unable to exclude another party's interest. Consider the US PATRIOT Act, which has been recently used to justify the seizure of data, anywhere in the world, if the data center is owned and operated by a US-based company, irrespective of the data's owner [28]. Further, due to an aging Electronic Communications Privacy Act, data residing in the cloud are currently treated jurisdictionally different than data on privately owned devices. Interestingly, only when the owner of data is a government do historic notions of sovereignty begin to make sense.

Similar limitations arise when using technology to assert positive and negative rights on data stored remotely. While our data geolocation protocol makes a small step towards establishing positive rights (perhaps, through some limited theory of jurisdiction), we know of no technology able to

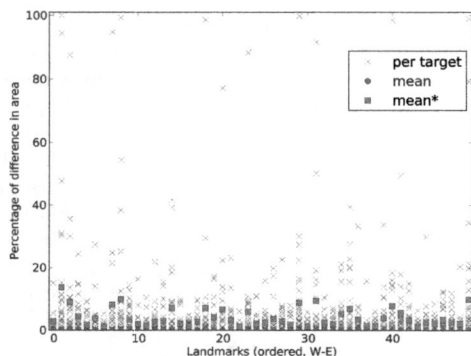

(a) Influence of landmark on optimal feasible regions.

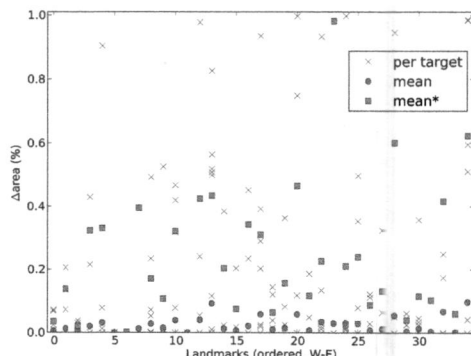

(b) Influence of landmark on measured feasible region.

Figure 9: For each of our PlanetLab landmarks, we plot how much it influenced the actual measured and theoretically optimal feasible regions in our experiments over 4K blocks (Section 6.1). For each, we show the landmark's mean influence and the mean of its non-zero influence (mean*).

track and control the flow of all copies of data in an open system, such as an Internet-based cloud. Indeed, imposing such a technology may be in conflict with the economic benefits of existing cloud models. Cloud providers optimize by leveraging dynamic resource allocation across nodes, moving data and computation to where it is cheapest.

As described in the Introduction, the inertia for organizations to move to cloud-based storage in increasing, but many cloud computing strategies are complicated by a lack of a internationally recognized understanding of data jurisdiction. If these issues are not solved, both legally and technically, cloud storage service providers may be relegated to offering domestic-only services, limiting appeal and increasing costs. We posit one way forward may be an intergovernmental statement of recognition pertaining to cloud services, clarifying which entities have an exclusive jurisdiction over data in transit, storage, and processing. It will be necessary to avoid multiple jurisdictions. To do so, may require readjustments to law enforcement and anti-terrorism efforts (to define minimum requirements for surveillance and seizure of cloud infrastructure), building mutual trust through uniform due process. It is unrealistic to assume that any common understanding of data jurisdiction will be established irrespective of data's physical location. We believe our contributions, and data geolocation in general, provide an important first step in developing methods for establishing the data-location binding, which may be leveraged by future policy. For further reading on the subject, the authors recommend Irion's recent paper on the subject [24].

9. RELATED WORK

Bowers *et al.* propose an approach to verify a cloud storage service provider is replicating data across multiple drives through fine-grained measurements of delay [9]. Their technique, called *Remote Assessment of Fault Tolerance* (RAFT), yields a tool intended to break the common abstraction of the cloud, through an interactive challenge and response protocol, much like CBDG. The idea of having a simple cloud abstraction when we want it, and removing it when we don't, is a powerful one.

The use of semi-trusted landmarks has been at the foundation of many of geolocation solutions [33, 20, 44, 29].

In wireless networks, hidden landmarks (or, "hidden, mobile base stations") have been used in a slightly different model of geolocation that is robust against a small number of colluding adversaries [42]. Recent results in *position-based cryptography* present some interesting positive results in the "bounded storage model" that are secure, even when considering a very strong type of adversary—capable of breaking nearly all previous geolocation strategies—that is able to clone itself at multiple, specific, hidden locations [10]. Interestingly, this adversary does not necessarily undermine CBDG's goal, which is merely to determine that the adversary is inside some bounding area (not to determine its specific position in this area); therefore, we believe our guarantees may be achieved in a weaker model.

Tools to actively monitor real cloud performance or SLA compliance—such as *CloudCmp* [30], *SLAm* [41] or any of various commercial monitoring services—do not yet offer support for checking compliance with respect to data durability or location clauses of an SLA. Most tools do monitor certain QoS metrics potentially relevant to inferring geolocation and data presence, such as up-time and end-to-end response times. Thus, extending support to monitor data geolocation is quite natural. Established commercial SLA monitoring services provide natural partners for outsourcing data audits or for acting as semi-trusted landmarks capable of participating in data geolocation protocols.

10. CONCLUSION

We have proposed and investigated a method for binding data in the cloud to a location, admitting strong assurance to both data integrity and location. Our initial approach using constraint-based geolocation with proofs of data possession appears promising. We attempt to weaken assumptions in previous data geolocation work—*i.e.* those related to collocating landmarks at the target or running observational nodes on adversarial infrastructure—as we believe this to provide stronger assurances, possibly at the cost of precision. We are particularly interested in protocols with higher accuracy and assurances against stronger adversaries. Toward this, combining CBDG with the replica management techniques of Benson *et al.* or more advanced geolocation techniques seems promising. In particular one might leverage collocated landmarks to build a model of service overhead to more accurately simulate landmark-target interactions during model building; our preliminary results using CBDG using TCP-based models are favorable.

11. ACKNOWLEDGEMENTS

The authors would like to thank Andreas Terzis for his assistance with PlanetLab access and Rob Beverly for early discussion about host and data geolocation. Partial support for this work was provided by the National Science Foundation under award No. 1143573.

12. REFERENCES

[1] Amazon Web Services. Summary of the Amazon EC2 and Amazon RDS service disruption in the US east region. Available at `http://aws.amazon.com/message/65648/`.

[2] Amazon Web Services. Overview of security processes, May 2011. Available at `http://aws.amazon.com/security`.

[3] G. Ateniese, R. Burns, R. Curtmola, J. H. amd Lea Kissner, Z. Peterson, and D. Song. Provable data possession at untrusted stores. In *Proceedings of the ACM Conference on Computer and Communications Security*, 2007.

[4] G. Ateniese, S. Kamara, and J. Katz. Proofs of storage from homomorphic identification protocols. In *Proceedings of ASIACRYPT*, 2009.

[5] G. Ateniese, R. D. Pietro, L. V. Mancini, and G. Tsudik. Scalable and efficient provable data possession. In *Proceedings of the International Conference on Security and Privacy in Communication Networks*, 2008.

[6] K. Benson, R. Dowsley, and H. Shacham. Do you know where your cloud files are? In *Proceedings of the ACM Cloud Computing Security Workshop*, 2011.

[7] H. Blodget. Amazon's cloud crash disaster permanently destroyed many customers' data. *Business Insider*, April 4 2011. `http://www.businessinsider.com/amazon-lost-data-2011-4`.

[8] K. D. Bowers, A. Juels, and A. Oprea. Proofs of retrievability: Theory and implementation. In *Proceedings of the ACM Workshop on Cloud Computing Security*, 2009.

[9] K. D. Bowers, M. van Dijk, A. Juels, A. Oprea, and R. L. Rivest. How to tell if your cloud files are vulnerable to drive crashes. In *Proceedings of the ACM Conference on Computer and Communications Security*, 2011.

[10] N. Chandran, V. Goyal, and R. M. R. Ostrovsky. Position based cryptography. In *Proceedings of the International Cryptology Conference*, 2009.

[11] CIO Council. Proposed security assessment & authorization for US government cloud computing, November 2010.

[12] R. Curtmola, O. Khan, and R. Burns. Robust remtoe data checking. In *Proceedings of the ACM International Workshop on Storage Security and Survivability*, 2008.

[13] R. Curtmola, O. Khan, R. Burns, and G. Ateniese. MR-PDP: Multiple-replica provable data possession. In *Proceedings of the International Conference on Distributed Computing Systems*, 2008.

[14] Y. Deswarte, J.-J. Quisquater, and A. Saïdane. Remote integrity checking: How to trust files stored on untrusted servers. In *Proceedings of the Conference on Integrity and Internal Control in Information Systems*, 2003.

[15] C. C. Erway, A. Küpcü, C. Papamanthou, and R. Tamassia. Dynamic provable data possession. In *Proceedings of the ACM Conference on Computer and Communication Security*, 2009.

[16] European Commission. Regulation of the european parliament and of the council on the protection of individuals with regard to the processing of personal data and on the free movement of such data (general data protection regulation). Directive 95/46/EC, 2012.

[17] D. L. G. Filho and P. S. L. M. Barreto. Demonstrating data possession and uncheatable data transfer. Cryptology ePrint Archive, Report 2006/150, 2006.

[18] P. Gill, Y. Ganjali, B. Wong, and D. Lie. Dude, where's that IP? Circumventing measurement-based IP geolocation. In *Proceedings of the USENIX Security Symposium*, 2010.

[19] N. Gohring. Amazon's S3 down for several hours. *PC World*, Feb 15 2008. `http://www.pcworld.com/businesscenter/article/142549/amazons_s3_down_for_several_hours.html`.

[20] B. Gueye, A. Ziviani, M. Crovella, and S. Fdida. Constraint-based geolocation of Internet hosts. *Transactions on Networking*, 14(6), December 2006.

[21] S. Halevi, D. Harnik, B. Pinkas, and A. Shulman-Peleg. Proofs of ownership in remote storage systems. In *Proceedings of the ACM Conference on Computer and Communications Security*, 2011.

[22] D. Harris. Amazon targets US government with GovCloud. *The New York Times*, August 2011. `http://nyti.ms/y6AOZH`.

[23] B. Huffaker, M. Fomenkov, and kc claffy. Geocompare: a comparison of public and commercial geolocation databases. In *Proceedings of the Network Mapping and Measurement Conference (NMC)*, 2011.

[24] K. Irion. Government cloud computing and the policies of data sovereignty, 2011. Available at `http://ssrn.com/abstract=1935859`.

[25] A. Juels and B. S. Kaliski Jr. PORs: Proofs of retrievability for large files. In *Proceedings of the ACM Conference on Computer and Communications Security*, 2007.

[26] E. Katz-Bassett, J. P. John, A. Krishnamurthy, D. Wetherall, T. Anderson, and Y. Chawathe. Towards IP geolocation using delay and topology measurements. In *Proceedings of the Conference on Internet Measurement*, 2006.

[27] V. Kundra. Federal cloud computing strategy, February 2011. Available at `http://www.cio.gov/documents/federal-cloud-computing-strategy.pdf`.

[28] K. E. Kushida, J. Murray, and J. Zysman. Diffusing the cloud: Cloud computing and implications for public policy. *Journal of Industry, Competition and Trade*, 11(3), 2011.

[29] S. Laki, P. Matray, P. Haga, I. Csabai, and G. Vattay. A detailed path-latency model for router geolocation. In *Proceedings of the International Conference on Testbeds and Research Infrastructures for the Development of Networks Communities and Workshops*, 2009.

[30] A. Li, X. Yang, S. Kandula, and M. Zhang. CloudCmp: Comparing public cloud providers. In *Proceedings of the Internet Modeling Conference*, 2010.

[31] Microsoft Corporation. Building confidence in the cloud: A proposal for industry and government action to advance cloud computing. Technical report, Microsoft Corporation, January 2010.

[32] M. Naor and G. N. Rothblum. The complexity of online memory checking. *Journal of the ACM*, 56(1), 2009.

[33] V. N. Padmanabhan and L. Subramanian. An investigation of geographic mapping techniques for Internet hosts. In *Proceedings of the Conference on Applications, Technologies, Architectures, and Protocols for Computer Communications*, 2001.

[34] R. Percacci and A. Vespignani. Scale-free behavior of the internet global performance. *European Physical Journal B*, 32(4), 2003.

[35] Z. N. J. Peterson, M. Gondree, and R. Beverly. A position paper on data sovereignty: The importance of geolocating data in the cloud. In *Proceedings of the USENIX Workshop on Hot Topics in Cloud Computing*, 2010.

[36] I. Poese, S. Uhlig, M. A. Kâafar, B. Donnet, and B. Gueye. Ip geolocation databases: unreliable? *Computer Communication Review*, 41(2), 2011.

[37] T. Schwarz, S.J. and E. L. Miller. Store, forget, and check: Using algebraic signatures to check remotely administered storage. In *Proceedings of the IEEE International Conference on Distributed Computing Systems*, 2006.

[38] H. Shacham and B. Waters. Compact proofs of retrievability. In *Proceedings of ASIACRYPT*, 2008.

[39] M. A. Shah, M. Baker, J. C. Mogul, and R. Swaminathan. Auditing to keep online storage services honest. In *Proceedings of the USENIX workshop on Hot Topics in Operating Systems*, 2007.

[40] S. Siwpersad, B. Gueye, and S. Uhlig. Assessing the geographic resolution of exhaustive tabulation for geolocating internet hosts. In *Passive and Active Network Measurement*, 2008.

[41] J. Sommers, P. Barford, N. Duffield, and A. Ron. Multiobjective monitoring for SLA compliance. *Transaction on Networking*, 18(2), 2010.

[42] S. Čapkun, M. Čagalj, and M. Srivastava. Secure localization with hidden and mobile base stations. In *Proceedings of the IEEE International Conference on Computer Communications*, 2006.

[43] Q. Wang, C. Wang, J. Li, K. Ren, and W. Lou. Enabling public verifiability and data dynamics for storage security in cloud computing. In *Proceedings of the European Symposium on Research in Computer Security*, 2009.

[44] B. Wong, I. Stoyanov, and E. G. Sirer. Octant: A comprehensive framework for the geolocalization of internet hosts. In *Proceedings of the USENIX Networked Systems Design and Implementation*, 2007.

Exploring Dependency for Query Privacy Protection in Location-based Services

Xihui Chen[*]
Interdisciplinary Centre for Security, Reliability and Trust, University of Luxembourg
xihui.chen@uni.lu

Jun Pang
Faculty of Science, Technology and Communication, University of Luxembourg
jun.pang@uni.lu

ABSTRACT

Location-based services have been enduring a fast development for almost fifteen years. Due to the lack of proper privacy protection, especially in the early stage of the development, an enormous amount of user request records have been collected. This exposes potential threats to users' privacy as new contextual information can be extracted from such records. In this paper, we study *query dependency* which can be derived from users' request history, and investigate its impact on users' query privacy.

To achieve our goal, we present an approach to compute the probability for a user to issue a query, by taking into account both user's query dependency and observed requests. We propose new metrics incorporating query dependency for query privacy, and adapt spatial generalisation algorithms in the literature to generate requests satisfying users' privacy requirements expressed in the new metrics. Through experiments, we evaluate the impact of query dependency on query privacy and show that our proposed metrics and algorithms are effective and efficient for practical applications.

Categories and Subject Descriptors

C.2.0 [**Computer-Communication Networks**]: General—*Security and protection*; K.4.1 [**Computers and Society**]: Public Policy Issues—*Privacy*

Keywords

Location based services, dependency, query privacy, anonymity, metrics, generalisation algorithms

1. INTRODUCTION

Location-based services (LBSs) are services customised according to users' locations. In the last fifteen years, LBSs have endured a great growth, especially after GPS-enabled devices such as smartphones became popular. A location-based request contains the issuer's location and a *query* – the type of information of interest,

---

[*]Supported by the National Research Fund, Luxembourg (SE-CLOC 794361).

e.g., where the nearest Chinese restaurants are. In spite of the great convenience brought to users' daily life, LBSs also lead to users' privacy concerns when they send LBS requests. In the literature, two major privacy concerns in LBSs have been studied – *location privacy* and *query privacy* [13] in terms of the types of sensitive information. The former is related to the disclosure of exact locations while query privacy, the focus of our paper, concerns the disclosure of queries.

The basic idea to protect users' query privacy in LBSs is to break the link between user identities and requests [3]. However, in the context of LBSs, removing or replacing identities with pseudonyms has been proved insufficient. With contextual information such as address books, users can still be identified as queries are usually made from fixed locations such as home or offices. In this case, users' spatial and temporal information can serve as *quasi-identifiers*. Anonymisation techniques from other research areas such as sensitive data release [13] are thus introduced, including k-anonymity and its different extensions (e.g., ℓ-diversity and t-closeness [18, 19]). Locations or time are replaced with regions or periods so that a certain number of users share the same quasi-identifier with the real issuer. The calculation of the regions or periods is termed as *generalisation* or *cloaking*. Since in practice LBS providers are usually required to offer immediate responses, throughout the paper, temporal generalisation is out of the scope. A request is called *generalised* if the location is generalised and the user identity is removed.

When the adversary has access to more contextual information, new privacy risks will emerge. For instance, "outlier" attacks are found on existing generalisation algorithms when their implementation is made public [21]. Privacy in LBSs related to context revealing has been recognised as *context-aware privacy* [22] and many types of contextual information have been studied in the literature. For example, Mascetti et al. [4] propose the concept of *historical k-anonymity* which protects against attacks where the adversary can learn a trace of requests issued by the same user.

Our motivations. The first generation of commercial LBSs were launched after the E911 mandate in 1996. From then on, LBSs have evolved from simple single-target finder to diverse, proactive and multi-target services [2]. However, user privacy did not receive fair treatments from the very beginning. This enables LBS providers to accumulate a large amount of users' historical requests. What makes the situation worse is the shift of LBS providers from telecom operators (who were viewed as trusted entities) to open businesses such as Google Latitude, Foursquare, and MyTracks. This increases the risk of potential misuse of the accumulated records. In this paper, we investigate what the adversary can obtain from users' historical requests and how to protect users against potential privacy attacks.

Users tend to have preference in arranging their daily activities [12]. This leads to a repetitive pattern in their requests, e.g., dependency between queries. For instance, a user often posts a check-in of a coffee house after lunch. The fact that users' frequent queries are usually restricted to a small set makes the extraction of query dependency easier and more precise. Users' query dependency can be abused and becomes a potential risk to users' query privacy. We illustrate this by a simple example. Bob issues a request about the nearest night clubs in a 2-anonymous region with Alice being the other user. Suppose the adversary has also learnt that Alice just issued a query about the nearest clinics and Bob queried about bars. As it is not common to ask clubs after clinics compared to bars, the adversary can infer that Bob is more probable to issue the request about night clubs. In this example, even if Alice and Bob share a similar profile, the dependency between queries obviously breaks 2-anonymity for all users in the region who are supposed to be equally likely to issue the request. As far as we know, we are the first to explore *query dependency* for privacy protection in LBSs.

Our contributions. In this paper, we accomplish two tasks – to show the impact of query dependency on users' query privacy and to design new privacy protection mechanisms. For the first task, we model a user's query dependency as a Markov chain and propose a simple method to derive it from the request history (Sect. 4). Then we present an approach from the perspective of the adversary to refine his view on possible issuers based on query dependency (Sect. 5). Our approach also makes use of users' observed requests, a type of dynamic contextual information that keeps changing. For the second task, we propose new query privacy metrics (Sect. 6), which allow users to express their privacy requirements and, more importantly, can take into account query dependency. We then adapt spatial generalisation algorithms in the literature to handle user privacy requirements by designing a method to update users' real-time proabilities of issuing a query (Sect. 7). Through experiments, we show that when the adversary can explore query dependency, query privacy should be carefully addressed and our proposed protection is both effective and efficient in practice (Sect. 8).

2. RELATED WORK

k-anonymity & query privacy. The concept of k-anonymity [25] was originally proposed in the field of database privacy and then introduced for privacy protection in LBSs by Gruteser and Grunwald [13]. Because of its simplicity, k-anonymity has been widely studied in the last decades. For instance, Tan et al. [31] define *information leakage* to quantify location information revealed in spatial cloaking. Xue et al. [32] introduce *location diversity* to ensure that generalised regions contain at least ℓ semantic locations. Kalnis et al. propose a novel cloaking – Hilbert cloak which is the first proved method enforcing reciprocity [17]. However, deeper understanding of k-anonymity reveals its drawbacks in preserving location privacy. Shokri et al. [30] evaluate k-anonymity in different scenarios in terms of the adversary's background knowledge. They conclude that spatial cloaking (e.g., k-anonymity) is only effective for protecting query privacy but not location privacy.

Context-aware privacy analysis. It has been recognised that the effectiveness of spatial cloaking can be compromised when the adversary has access to additional contextual information, e.g., user profiles which have many interpretations in the literature. Shokri et al. [29] use mobility patterns and propose a probabilistic framework to learn users' whereabouts from anonymised and generalised traces. Personal information (e.g., gender, job, salary) is usually available on the Internet, e.g., online social networks such as Face-book and LinkedIn, and can serve as user profiles as well. Shin et al. [27, 28] propose metrics based on k-anonymity by restricting levels of similarity among users in generalised regions in terms of their profiles. Chen and Pang [7] use the same information but obtain probability distributions over users for issuing queries, which allows them to measure query privacy in several new ways.

The contextual information (e.g., mobility pattern, user information) explored in the above papers does not change during their analysis and thus can be considered as *static*. Whereas, in practice, contexts can be *dynamic* as well, e.g., users' whereabouts and observed requests. In the literature, two types of requests have been studied – *associated requests* [4, 3, 8] and *recurrent requests* [23].

Requests are associated once they are recognised as issued by a same (anonymous) user, which can be achieved for example by multi-target tracking techniques [14] or probabilistic reasoning [29]. In this case, the intersection of all requests' anonymity set helps the adversary reduce the number of possible issuers. To handle such privacy threats, Bettini et al. [4, 3] introduce *historical k-anonymity*, which is then extended for continuous LBSs by Dewri et al. [8]. Historical k-anonymity aims to guarantee that associated requests share at least k fixed users in the generalised regions.

Requests are recurrent when they are issued at the same time. For the recurrent requests containing the same query, if they are also from the same region, the protection of spatial cloaking, e.g., k-anonymity, is degraded for query privacy. For instance, in the extreme case, when all users in a region send an identical query, no user has query privacy. Riboni et al. [23] identify the threat and make use of t-closeness to guarantee that the distance between the distribution over the queries from an issuer's generalised region and that of the whole region is below a threshold. Dewri et al. [9] consider a scenario in continuous LBSs which have both associated and recurrent requests . The adversary only learns the regions and time of requests issued by an anonymous user. When recurrent requests are considered, Dewri et al. propose m-invariance to ensure that in addition to k fixed users in the generalised regions, at least m fixed queries are generated from each region.

A short discussion. Associated requests are not always available. Uncertainty of the linkability between requests is inevitable in reality and should be carefully handled. Moreover, the previous research considers queries in historical requests as independent, and ignores users' issuing patterns over queries. Last but not least, we believe both static and dynamic contexts should be taken into account in the analysis of users' privacy in LBSs.

Our work differs from the related papers from the following perspectives: (i) we take into account dependency between successive queries in our privacy analysis; (ii) we infer a user's next query by his probability to issue the query calculated based his observed requests; (iii) we do not assume that a trace of requests are recognised, which makes our work more realistic.

3. PRELIMINARIES

In this section, we first present our formal framework in Sect. 3.1 and then define the adversary model in Sect. 3.2.

3.1 Formal framework

Let $\mathcal{U}$ be the set of all users, who are in fact the potential issuers of LBS requests. We use $\mathcal{L}$ to denote the set of all possible positions where a user can issue a request. The accuracy of any position $\ell \in \mathcal{L}$ is determined by the positioning devices used. We represent time as a totally ordered discrete set $\mathcal{T}$, whose granularity, e.g., minutes or seconds, is decided by LBS providers. The function $whereis : \mathcal{U} \times \mathcal{T} \to \mathcal{L}$ gives the exact position of a user at a given time. Thus, for any time $t \in \mathcal{T}$, users' spatial distribution is $dist_t = \{\langle u, whereis(u,t)\rangle \mid u \in \mathcal{U}\}$. Let $\mathcal{R} \subseteq 2^{\mathcal{L}}$ be the set of all regions with any size that could be included in generalised requests. With $\mathcal{Q}$ being the set of supported queries, an LBS request is in the form of $\langle u, \ell, t, q\rangle \in \mathcal{U} \times \mathcal{L} \times \mathcal{T} \times \mathcal{Q}$. The corresponding generalised request has the form of $\langle r, t, q\rangle$, obtained by the request generalisation function $f : \mathcal{U} \times \mathcal{L} \times \mathcal{T} \times \mathcal{Q} \to \mathcal{R} \times \mathcal{T} \times \mathcal{Q}$ – it removes the issuer's identity and replaces the exact location with a region $r \in \mathcal{R}$. We use function req to obtain the query of a (generalised) request (i.e., $req(\langle u, \ell, t, q\rangle)=q$ and $req(\langle r, t, q\rangle)=q$).

For each user u, we use a sequence to denote the requests that he has issued, i.e., $\mathcal{H}_u = (\langle u, \ell_1, t_1, q_1\rangle, \ldots, \langle u, \ell_n, t_n, q_n\rangle)$ with $t_i < t_{i+1}$ for all $i \in \{1, \ldots, n-1\}$ and $\mathcal{H}_u(i)$ is the ith request in $\mathcal{H}_u$. We call this sequence *user request history*, whose length is denoted as $len(\mathcal{H}_u)$.

After observing a generalised request at time t, the adversary adds it to a sequence, i.e., $\mathcal{O}_t = (\langle r_1, t_1, q_1\rangle, \ldots, \langle r_m, t_m, q_m\rangle)$ $(t_i < t_{i+1}$ for all $i \in \{1, \ldots, m-1\}$ and $t_m < t)$. For the sake of simplicity, we do not consider recurrent queries, i.e., those elements in $\mathcal{O}_t$ with the same time-stamps. Furthermore, for each request in $\mathcal{O}_t$, the adversary calculates its anonymity set, i.e., all those users located in the generalised region. Thus, for each user, the adversary can maintain a sequence of generalised requests, whose anonymity sets contain this user as an element. We call this sequence an *observed request trace* and denote the one for user u up to time t as $\mathcal{O}_{u,t}$. It is obvious that with time passing, a user's observed request trace keeps growing. The length of $\mathcal{O}_{u,t}$ is denoted as $len(\mathcal{O}_{u,t})$. The difference between $\mathcal{H}_u$ and $\mathcal{O}_{u,t}$ is that the adversary is certain about the issuer of each request in $\mathcal{H}_u$ but uncertain about the issuers of the requests in $\mathcal{O}_{u,t}$. Tab. 1 summarises relevant notations used in this paper.

Table 1: Notations

Notations	Description
$\mathcal{Q}$	the set of supported queries
$\mathcal{U}$	the set of users
$\mathcal{L}$	the set of positions
$\mathcal{R}$	the set of regions
$\mathcal{T}$	the set of time granules
$\langle u, \ell, t, q\rangle$	a query q issued by user u at position ℓ at time t
$\langle r, t, q\rangle$	a generalised request by the anonymiser
$\mathcal{O}_{u,t}$	user u's observed request trace up to time t
$\mathcal{H}_u$	user u's request history
$\mathcal{V}^u$	user u's prior vector
$\mathcal{D}^u$	user u's dependency matrix
$p_u(q_i \mid q_j)$	the probability of user u issuing q_i after q_j
$p_u(q_i)$	the priori probability of user u issuing q_i
$p(u \mid \langle r, t, q\rangle)$	the probability of user u issuing the generalised query $\langle r, t, q\rangle$
$dist_t$	user spatial distribution at time t
$u\ell(r,t)$	the set of users located in region r at time t
$req(\langle r, t, q\rangle)$	the query of request $\langle r, t, q\rangle$

3.2 Adversary model

Privacy attacks and countermeasures should be categorised according to the model and aims of the adversary [3]. For query privacy, the aim of the adversary is to associate issuers to their queries. We use the following assumptions to define our adversary model.

Assumption 1. The adversary knows users' spatial distribution $dist_t$ at any time t and the spatial generalisation algorithms. This is now a common assumption used in the literature and it makes a

strong adversary which allows us to analyse users' query privacy in the worst case situations. We have this assumption based on the observation that uses may publish their positions in applications or issue requests at some known places , e.g., home/offices. The availability of $dist_t$ enables the adversary to obtain the set of users located in any region r at time t, which is denoted as $u\ell(r,t)$. This assumption can be relaxed by introducing unidentified users whose positions are not part of the adversary's knowledge [3].

Assumption 2. As we have mentioned, LBS providers have collected users' request history. For each user u, we assume that the adversary has a user u's request history $\mathcal{H}_u$ for a sufficiently long period. Furthermore, the adversary maintains the up-to-date observed request trace $\mathcal{O}_{u,t}$ of every user u. For the sake of simplicity, we assume that $\mathcal{H}_u$ is complete, namely there do not exist any requests that are issued by u during the period but are not included in $\mathcal{H}_u$. To handle incomplete $\mathcal{H}_u$, we can use the approaches such as Gibbs sampling [24] to reconstruct the missing queries similarly to fill missing locations in mobility traces [29].

4. DERIVING QUERY DEPENDENCY

In this section, we present an approach to derive dependency between queries for a user from his request history. *Query dependency* can be used to predict a user's next query based on past queries that he has issued before. There also exists a special situation when a user has no past queries or the past queries have little impact on his future queries. In this case, we need to consider users' *a priori preference* on issuing queries. Both of these two types of information are calculated once and remains unchanged, and thus are classified as static.

4.1 Query dependency

We model query dependency with the assumption that the query that a user will issue next can only be affected by the last query that the user has issued (i.e., the Markov property). For a pair of queries q_i and q_j, the dependency of query q_j on q_i is denoted as the conditional probability $p_u(q_j \mid q_i)$. In other words, it is the probability for user u to issue query q_j after having issued query q_i (without issuing any other queries in between). The query dependency information of user u can thus be expressed as a *dependency matrix* – $\mathcal{D}^u$ of size $|\mathcal{Q}| \times |\mathcal{Q}|$ and $\mathcal{D}^u_{ij} = p_u(q_j \mid q_i)$.

To find dependent queries, we need to identify the successive requests. Intuitively, two requests are successive if there are no other requests between them in the request history. This simply means that $\mathcal{H}_u(i+1)$ is the successive query of $\mathcal{H}_u(i)$ for all $i < len(\mathcal{H}_u)$. All the occurrence of query q_j depending on q_i can be captured by the set of pairs of successive requests $\mathcal{C}_{i,j} = \{(\mathcal{H}_u(k), \mathcal{H}_u(k+1)) \mid req(\mathcal{H}_u(k)) = q_i \wedge req(\mathcal{H}_u(k+1)) = q_j, 0 < k < len(\mathcal{H}_u)\}$. Given a request history $\mathcal{H}_u$, the adversary can derive for a user u the dependency between any pair of queries using the sets $\mathcal{C}_{i,j}$ of successive requests. Furthermore, in this paper we make use of Lidstone's or additive smoothing [20] to ensure that there is no dependency of degree zero for q_j on q_i due to no occurrence of the pair (q_i, q_j) in the request history.

Formally, let λ be the smoothing parameter which is usually set to 1. The dependency $p_u(q_j \mid q_i)$ is calculated as follows:

$$p_u(q_j \mid q_i) = \frac{|\mathcal{C}_{i,j}| + \lambda}{\sum_{q_k \in \mathcal{Q}} |\mathcal{C}_{i,k}| + |\mathcal{Q}| \cdot \lambda}.$$

4.2 A priori preference

There are many cases that a query does not depend on its past queries. For example, users may issue an LBS query for the first time or accidentally for an emergent need. In such cases, the best the adversary can do is to apply users' *a priori* preference to find possible issuers of the query.

We model the *a priori* preference of a user u as a distribution over the set of queries denoted as $\mathcal{V}^u$. The distribution indicates the probability of the user to issue a query. For query $q_i \in \mathcal{Q}$, $\mathcal{V}_i^u = p_u(q_i)$ and $\sum_{q_i \in \mathcal{Q}} p_u(q_i) = 1$.

There are many sources of information reflecting users' *a priori* preference. Users' personal information such as hobbies and occupation have been discussed and shown effective in assessing users' preference [27, 28, 7]. Moreover, a user's request history also reflects his preference. Thus, we estimate a user's *a priori* preference (i.e., $\mathcal{V}^u$) by combining his request history ($\mathcal{H}_u$) and his personal information. For users' personal information, we apply the approach of Chen and Pang [7] where weights are assigned to different types of information as well as their values according to their correlation to a query. Let $\mathcal{P}_u$ be user u's personal information. The preference of user u for query q_i with respect to $\mathcal{P}_u$ is denoted as $p_u(q_i | \mathcal{P}_u)$. Moreover, let $p_u(q_i | \mathcal{H}_u)$ be the likelihood for user u to issue q_i based on his request history, we can use the frequency of the occurrence of the query in the request history to estimate $p_u(q_i | \mathcal{H}_u)$:

$$p_u(q_i | \mathcal{H}_u) = \frac{|\{\mathcal{H}_u(k) \mid req(\mathcal{H}_u(k)) = q_i\}|}{len(\mathcal{H}_u)}.$$

The two distributions evaluate a user's *a priori* preference on next queries from two different perspectives. An agreement between them is needed. This is equivalent to aggregate expert probability judgements [5]. We use *linear opinion pool aggregation* which is empirically effective and has been widely applied in practice [1]. By assigning a weight to each distribution, i.e., $w_\mathcal{P}$ and $w_\mathcal{H}$ with $w_\mathcal{P} + w_\mathcal{H} = 1$, we can calculate $p_u(q_i)$ as follows:

$$p_u(q_i) = w_\mathcal{P} \cdot p_u(q_i | \mathcal{P}_u) + w_\mathcal{H} \cdot p_u(q_i | \mathcal{H}_u).$$

Remark. The way we model users' query dependency and *a priori* preference has some restrictions. For instance, we do not consider the influence of other factors such as time – usually a user's behaviours in weekdays are different from weekends. Our approach can be extended by distinguishing the request history at different time periods. We have also assumed that a query is only dependent on its immediate previous query. This restriction can be lifted by considering, e.g., the last k historical queries. However, deriving such dependency from $\mathcal{H}_u$ might not be as efficient and accurate as the derivation of $\mathcal{D}^u$.

5. QUERY PRIVACY ANALYSIS

In this section, we present an analysis of the possible issuers of a given generalised request from the adversary's point of view by considering both static contexts (query dependency and *a priori* preference) and dynamic contexts (observed request traces). We use a posterior probability distribution over users to represent the results of the analysis. Recall that the trace of observed generalised requests up to time t is denoted by $\mathcal{O}_t$. For a generalised request $\langle r, t, q \rangle$ and a user u, the corresponding posterior probability distributions is defined as $p(u | \langle r, t, q \rangle, \mathcal{O}_t)$. Since the static contexts do not change during the analysis, we do not include them in the definition explicitly.

Through the Bayesian rule we have:

$$\begin{aligned} p(u | \langle r, t, q \rangle, \mathcal{O}_t) &= \frac{p(\langle r, t, q \rangle | u, \mathcal{O}_t)}{p(\langle r, t, q \rangle, \mathcal{O}_t)} \\ &= \frac{p(\langle r, t, q \rangle | u, \mathcal{O}_t) \cdot p(u | \mathcal{O}_t) \cdot p(\mathcal{O}_t)}{\sum_{u'} p(\langle r, t, q \rangle | u', \mathcal{O}_t) \cdot p(u' | \mathcal{O}_t) \cdot p(\mathcal{O}_t)}. \end{aligned}$$

There are three new distributions. The distribution $p(\mathcal{O}_t)$ measures the probability of generating the observed request trace $\mathcal{O}_t$. It is difficult to evaluate its value. Whereas, since it appears in both the numerator and the denominator, we can eliminate it from the formula. The distribution $p(u | \mathcal{O}_t)$ is the probability of user u to issue a request at time t based on the observed requests. As we have no information about the distribution, it is assumed to uniform according to the principle of maximum entropy [15, 16], which leads to $p(u | \mathcal{O}_t) = p(u' | \mathcal{O}_t)$ ($\forall u' \in \mathcal{U}$). Thus, the posterior distribution can be simplified as:

$$p(u | \langle r, t, q \rangle, \mathcal{O}_t) = \frac{p(\langle r, t, q \rangle | u, \mathcal{O}_t)}{\sum_{u' \in \mathcal{U}} p(\langle r, t, q \rangle | u', \mathcal{O}_t)} \qquad (1)$$

The probability $p(\langle r, t, q \rangle | u, \mathcal{O}_t)$ indicates the probability for the user u to issue the generalised request $\langle r, t, q \rangle$ in terms of his observed request trace. As a generalised algorithm (see Sect. 7) always outputs a request with a region including the issuer, only the users located in the region may have issued the request. Thus, for any user u' out of region r at time t, we have $p(\langle r, t, q \rangle | u', \mathcal{O}_t) = 0$ for any $q \in \mathcal{Q}$. Furthermore, because of the independence between users with regard to issuing requests, other users' request history has no influence on the next query of the user. Thus we have $p(\langle r, t, q \rangle | u, \mathcal{O}_t) = p(\langle r, t, q \rangle | u, \mathcal{O}_{u,t})$ for $u \in \mathcal{U}$.

The size of $\mathcal{O}_{u,t}$ is a key factor determining the accuracy and the complexity of the calculation of $p(\langle r, t, q \rangle | u, \mathcal{O}_{u,t})$. Recall that $\mathcal{O}_{u,t}$ consists of all the observed requests that may be issued by user u up to time t. Intuitively, the longer $\mathcal{O}_{u,t}$ is, more computational overhead is required for getting $p(u | \langle r, t, q \rangle, \mathcal{O}_t)$. It is impractical to consider the complete $\mathcal{O}_{u,t}$ during the calculation. Instead, we fix a *history window* which consists of the latest n observed requests of user u (i.e., $n \le len(\mathcal{O}_{u,t})$). Therefore, our problem can be reformulated as to compute $p^n(u | \langle r, t, q \rangle, \mathcal{O}_t)$, indicating the distribution is based on last n observed requests.

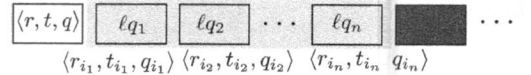

Figure 1: A history window of n observed requests.

In Fig. 1, we show an example of a history window. It has n observed requests, $\langle r_{i_1}, t_{i_1}, q_{i_1} \rangle, \dots, \langle r_{i_n}, t_{i_n}, q_{i_n} \rangle$ with $t_{i_j} > t_{i_{j-1}}$ ($j > 1$). Let $\ell q_j(\mathcal{O}_{u,t})$ be the jth latest observed request in $\mathcal{O}_{u,t}$, whose query is $req(\ell q_j(\mathcal{O}_{u,t})) = q_{i_j}$. In the following discussion, we simply write ℓq_j if $\mathcal{O}_{u,t}$ is clear from the context. It is obvious that ℓq_1 is the latest observed request of user u.

Once $p^n(u | \langle r, t, q \rangle, \mathcal{O}_t)$ is calculated, it is then added into the adversary's knowledge. Therefore, for a past request $\langle r', t', q' \rangle$ in $\mathcal{O}_{u,t}$ ($t' < t$), the adversary has the probability $p(u | \langle r', t', q' \rangle, \mathcal{O}'_t)$. In the sequel, we simply denote it as $p(u | \langle r', t', q' \rangle)$ in cases without any confusion.

The key to calculate the distribution is to determine the user's latest request. Whereas, it is uncertain which is his latest one in the history window. To handle this uncertainty, we distinguish three cases which are depicted in Fig. 2.

1. User u has issued both the last request in the history window (i.e., ℓq_1, see Fig. 2a) and the current request (i.e., $\langle r, t, q \rangle$). Considering query dependence, the probability of this case is

$$p_u(u | \ell q_1) \cdot p_u(q | q_{i_1}).$$

2. User u has issued the current request $\langle r, t, q \rangle$ and his latest request is ℓq_m ($1 < m \le n$) (see Fig. 2b). The probability of ℓq_m being the latest request is the production of

40

(a) The latest request is ℓq_1.

(b) The latest request is $\ell q_m (m \in (1, n])$.

(c) The latest request is not in the history window.

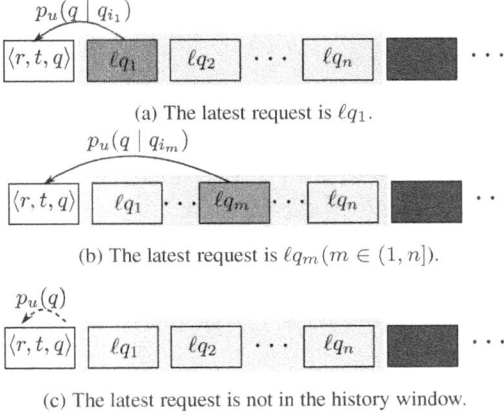

Figure 2: The three cases.

the probability that the last $m - 1$ requests are *not* issued by u and the probability that u has issued ℓq_m, i.e., $p(u \mid \ell q_m) \cdot \prod_{j=1}^{m-1}(1 - p(u \mid \ell q_j))$. Considering query dependence, the probability of this case is

$$p_u(q \mid q_{i_m}) \cdot p(u \mid \ell q_m) \cdot \prod_{j=1}^{m-1}(1 - p(u \mid \ell q_j)).$$

3. User u did not issue any request in the history window (see Fig. 2c). In this case, we suppose that the user issued the current request according to his *a priori* preference, i.e., $p_u(q)$. Based on the probability that the user's latest request is outside of the history window as $\prod_{j=1}^{n}(1 - p(u \mid \ell q_j))$, the probability of this case is

$$p_u(q) \cdot \prod_{j=1}^{n}(1 - p(u \mid \ell q_j)).$$

We sum up the above three probabilities to compute the probability for user u in region r at time t to issue q when a history window of size n is considered:

$$p^n(\langle r, t, q \rangle \mid u, \mathcal{O}_{u,t}) = \qquad (2)$$
$$p(u \mid \ell q_1) \cdot p_u(q \mid req(\ell q_1))$$
$$+ \sum_{m=2}^{n} p(u \mid \ell q_m) \cdot p_u(q \mid req(\ell q_m)) \cdot \prod_{j=1}^{m-1}(1 - p(u \mid \ell q_j))$$
$$+ p_u(q) \cdot \prod_{j=1}^{n}(1 - p(u \mid \ell q_j)).$$

We use the following example with $n = 2$ to show the calculation.

EXAMPLE 1. *Suppose the last two requests are* $\langle r'', t'', q'' \rangle$ *and* $\langle r', t', q' \rangle$ *with* $t'' < t' < t$ *in* $\mathcal{O}_{u,t}$. *Let* $\langle r, t, q \rangle$ *be an observed request. Then for user* u, *the probability that he issues the request is computed as follows:*

$$p^2(\langle r, t, q \rangle \mid u, \mathcal{O}_{u,t}) =$$
$$p_u(q \mid q') \cdot p(u \mid \langle r', t', q' \rangle)$$
$$+ (1 - p(u \mid \langle r', t', q' \rangle)) \cdot p(u \mid \langle r'', t'', q'' \rangle) \cdot p_u(q \mid q'')$$
$$+ (1 - p(u \mid \langle r', t', q' \rangle)) \cdot (1 - p(u \mid \langle r'', t'', q'' \rangle)) \cdot p_u(q).$$

It is clear that the calculation of Eq. 2 combines the static contextual information, i.e., users' *a priori* preference on queries and the dependency between queries, with the dynamic contextual information, i.e., observed request traces.

6. MEASURING QUERY PRIVACY

To protect users' query privacy, we follow the principle that users should be able to express their privacy requirements as it is unlikely to have absolute privacy in the context of spatial anonymisation. In this paper, we consider users' query privacy well-preserved if the spatial generalisation algorithms can generate regions meeting their privacy requirements. The calculation of the probability distribution over users in Sect. 5 provides us a way to measure query privacy through the uncertainty of the adversary. A number of metrics for query privacy are proposed in [7] where it is assumed that the adversary has access to users' profiles. In this paper, we extend two of them, i.e., k-ABS and β-EBA, by taking query dependence into account. The other metrics can be extended similarly.

Query dependent k-ABS. Intuitively, this requirement is satisfied if at least k users are grouped together in the generalised region and they have close posterior probabilities to issue the given request. Let $\| p_1, p_2 \|$ be the distance between two probabilities p_1 and p_2, and ϵ be the maximum distance allowed between users' posterior probabilities. Recall that f is the request generalisation function. Given a history window of size n, the metric *query-dependent k-ABS* can be defined as follows:

DEFINITION 1. *Let* $\langle u, whereis(u, t), t, q \rangle$ *be a request of u and* $\langle r, t, q \rangle$ *be the corresponding generalised request. The issuer u is* query dependent k-approximate beyond suspicious *if*

$$|\{u' \in u\ell(r, t) \mid \| p^n(u \mid \langle r, t, q \rangle, \mathcal{O}_t), p^n(u' \mid \langle r, t, q \rangle, \mathcal{O}_t) \| < \epsilon$$
$$\wedge f(\langle u', whereis(u', t), t, q \rangle) = \langle r, t, q \rangle\}| \geq k$$

Query dependent β-EBA. This metric utilises the notion of entropy from information theory to measure the uncertainty of the adversary about the issuer of a request. Let variable U denote the issuer of request $\langle r, t, q \rangle$ and n be the size of the history window. When query dependency is considered as part of the adversary's knowledge, the adversary's uncertainty of the issuer of $\langle r, t, q \rangle$ can be measured by the following entropy:

$$H^n(U \mid \langle r, t, q \rangle) = - \sum_{u' \in u\ell(r,t)} p^n(u' \mid \langle r, t, q \rangle, \mathcal{O}_t) \cdot$$
$$\log p^n(u' \mid \langle r, t, q \rangle, \mathcal{O}_t).$$

Thus, we can define *query-dependent β-EBA* as follows:

DEFINITION 2. *Let* $\beta > 0$, $\langle u, whereis(u, t), t, q \rangle \in Q$ *be a request and* $\langle r, t, q \rangle$ *the corresponding generalised request. The issuer u is* query-dependent β-entropy based anonymous *if for all* $u' \in u\ell(r, t)$,

$$H^n(U \mid \langle r, t, q \rangle) \geq \beta \ \wedge \ f(\langle u', whereis(u', t), t, q \rangle) = \langle r, t, q \rangle.$$

Remark. When users use these metrics to express their privacy requirements, at least three elements should be provided – a metric, the parameter values of the chosen metric, and the history window's size. However, in practice it is difficult and cumbersome for a user to give exact values to these elements, as this requires them to understand the meaning of each parameter and the corresponding implication on privacy protection. To avoid this situation it is better to provide a list of privacy levels, e.g., from *low* to *very high*. Each level corresponds to a setting of privacy parameters. For example, a user's privacy requirement can be represented as $\langle kABS, high \rangle$, which is then transformed into $\langle kABS, (0.05, 10), 5\rangle$. This ensures that whenever a request is successfully generalised, the region has 10 users with similar posterior probabilities to the issuer's, after taking into account the last 5 observed requests. Furthermore, the distance between two such users' posterior probabilities is bounded by 0.05. In practice, the transformation can be made automatic and embedded in the request generalisation process.

7. AN GENERALISATION ALGORITHM

In this section, we focus on the spatial generalisation procedures, which can generate regions satisfying users' privacy requirements expressed in the metrics as defined in Sect. 6.

Basically, there are two ways to implement generalisation algorithms – *centralised* and *distributed*. A centralised structure relies on a trusted agent, the *anonymiser*, to collect users' requests and anonymise them before sending them to the LBS servers, while in a distributed implementation users cooperate with each other to construct a generalised region [10, 26]. The centralised framework is easy to implement and well-studied in the literature while the distributed framework requires more communication between collaborators and security analysis, e.g., with respect to *insiders*, is not well studied. Because of its simplicity and efficiency, we decide to choose the centralised framework although the trust in the anonymiser is needed. In this centralised structure, users send their positions to the anonymiser, who will generalise a request according to the issuer's privacy requirement.

The two algorithms kABS and uniformDP proposed in [7] protect users' query privacy against the adversary which has users' *a priori* preference on queries as part of his knowledge. The main idea is to compute an anonymity set of users based on the posterior probability of each user to issue the given request. This methodology is generic but the algorithms are designed specially for user profiles, which do not change over time. Whereas, due to query dependency, we need to handle users' observed request traces, which change over time. We start with a brief introduction to the algorithms in [7] and then show how to handle observed request traces.

kABS & uniformDP. The former copes with requirements in terms of k-ABS while the later is a uniform algorithm for the other metrics proposed in [7]. Both algorithms take users' real-time spatial distribution and (static) user a priori preferences as inputs and output a generalised region (if possible). Algorithm kABS first calls a clustering algorithm, i.e., K-means, to cluster users with similar profiles, and then uses existing k-anonymity generalisation algorithms to calculate regions. On the other hand, uniformDP iteratively splits a region into two sub-regions until it is not possible to have a partition such that both of the sub-regions satisfy the issuer's privacy requirement.

Our algorithm. If a request $\langle r, t, q\rangle$ of user u satisfies query-dependent k-ABS, the region r must contain at least another $k-1$ users with posterior probabilities close to $p^n(u \mid \langle r, t, q\rangle, \mathcal{O}_t)$. From Eq. 1, we can see that such users (e.g., u') also have close probabilities to issue the request in terms of their observed requests (i.e., $p^n(\langle r, t, q\rangle \mid u', \mathcal{O}_t)$). Thus, we can apply the idea of the algorithm kABS to find a region with at least k users with similar probability with respects to observed requests.

There are two extensions needed to adapt kABS. First, the probability $p^n(\langle r, t, q\rangle \mid u', \mathcal{O}_t)$ is related to the generalised request, which seems not available before the generalisation. However, an interesting feature of the calculation in Eq. 2 is that for user u, given a time t, for any two regions r and r' such that $whereis(u, t) \in r \cap r'$, we have $p^n(\langle r, t, q\rangle \mid u, \mathcal{O}_t) = p^n(\langle r', t, q\rangle \mid u, \mathcal{O}_t)$. So we can obtain the probability before generalising the request by com-

puting $p^n(\langle r_{ori}, t, q\rangle \mid u, \mathcal{O}_t)$ where r_{ori} is the whole initial region. Second, since observed request traces are part of the computation of users' posterior probabilities, the probability $p^n(\langle r_{ori}, t, q\rangle \mid u, \mathcal{O}_t)$ for all $u \in \mathcal{U}$ has to be updated for any received request. This requires the algorithm to maintain users' status, including their observed request traces (i.e., $\mathcal{O}_{u,t}$) and the corresponding posterior probabilities (i.e., $p(u \mid \langle r, t, q\rangle)$ from the view of the adversary.

Algorithm 1 An algorithm for spatial generalisation.

```
1: FUNCTION: QD-AreaGen
2: INPUT: ⟨u, whereis(u, t), t, q⟩, dis(t), Ot, Ru
3: OUTPUT: A region r that satisfies k-ABS
4:
5:   R'u = transformReq(Ru);
6:   n = getWindowSize(R'u);
7:   M = ∅;
8:   for u' ∈ uℓ(rori, t) do
9:      calculate pⁿ(⟨rori, t, q⟩ | u', Ot);
10:     M = M ∪ {⟨pⁿ(⟨rori, t, q⟩ | u', Ot), u⟩};
11:  end for
12:
13:  if getMetric(Ru) = kABS then
14:     (ϵ, k) = getRequirement(R'u);
15:     r = kABS(u, dis(t), M, ϵ, k);
16:  else if getMetric(Ru) = EBA then
17:     β = getRequirement(R'u);
18:     r = uniformDP(u, dis(t), M, β);
19:  end if
20:
21:  if r ≠ ∅ then
22:     for u' ∈ uℓ(r, t) do
23:        Ou',t = Ou',t ∪ {⟨r, t, q⟩};
24:        p(u' | ⟨r, t, q⟩) = pⁿ(u' | ⟨r, t, q⟩, Ot)
25:     end for
26:  end if
27:  return r
```

In order to find a region satisfying query-dependent β-EBA, we apply the same idea of area splitting – we adapt uniformDP by giving the probabilities $p^n(\langle r_{ori}, t, q\rangle \mid u', \mathcal{O}_t)$ ($u' \in \mathcal{U}$) as input instead of users' *a priori* preference. Similar to the algorithm designed for query-dependent k-ABS, users' status (i.e., observed request traces and the corresponding posterior probabilities) needs to be dynamically updated.

We use Alg. 1 to describe the our spatial generalisation algorithm when query dependency is considered. The algorithm takes a request $\langle u, whereis(u, t), t, q\rangle$ as input and outputs a region r satisfying the requirement R_u based on users' whereabouts $dis(t)$ and observed requests $\mathcal{O}_t$. The user's privacy requirement R_u is first transformed into R'_u by function $transformReq(R_u)$ (line 5) based on a mapping table so R'_u consists of an exact parameter setting that will be used in the generalisation. For requirements using k-ABS and β-EBA, R'_u is of the form of $\langle kABS, (\epsilon, k), n\rangle$ and $\langle EBA, \beta, n\rangle$, respectively. Function $getWindowSize(R'_u)$ returns the size of the history window in R'_u and $getMetric(R'_u)$ gives the type of metric used. Recall that r_{ori} is the whole initial region under our consideration. For the reason discussed above, the probabilities $p^n(\langle r_{ori}, t, q\rangle \mid u', \mathcal{O}_t)$ ($u' \in \mathcal{U}$) is calculated (line 9) and the results are stored in set $\mathcal{M}$.

If query-dependent k-ABS is used, then we call function kABS with a distance parameter (i.e., ϵ) and an anonymity degree (i.e., k), which can be extracted from R'_u (line 14). As our implementation of kABS uses the clustering algorithm K-means, we use ϵ to esti-

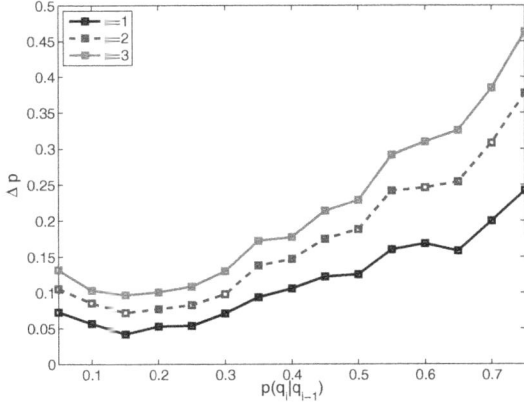

(a) Δp vs. $p(q_i \mid q_{i-1})$ and n.

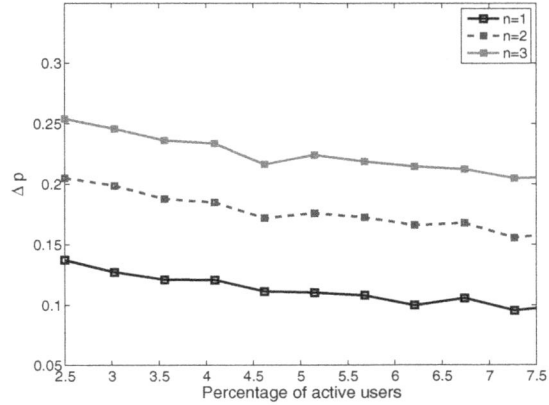

(b) Δp vs. #active users and n.

Figure 3: Impact of query dependency and the number of active users on Δp.

mate the number of clusters (i.e., K). If the privacy requirement is expressed using other metrics, e.g., query dependent β-EBA, uniformDP is called (line 18).

If a valid region is found, then for each user located in it, we need to update his status (line 22-25). First, his observed request sequence is updated (line 23) as they are considered as possible issuers after the generalised request is issued. Second, each user's posterior probability being the issuer is assigned (line 24) which will be used for future requests (line 9).

Note that it is time-consuming to update users' probabilities to issue the request in terms of their observed requests before generalising each request, because it considers all users in the whole area. During implementation, we observe that in each generalisation process, only a small fraction of users are concerned. Thus, for each request, we first calculate a smaller region (e.g., with 100 users) containing the issuer by k-anonymity generalisation algorithms and then execute Alg. 1 on this region. In this way, the computational overhead can be largely reduced.

8. EXPERIMENTAL RESULTS

We conduct experiments to evaluate our work from two aspects. First, we compare issuers' posterior probabilities *with* vs. *without* adding query dependency to the adversary's knowledge. In this way, we illustrate the privacy risks caused by request history and extracted query dependency. Second, we implement and test our algorithm presented in Sect. 7 on a sample dataset to show the effectiveness of our new privacy metrics (see Sect. 6).

To conduct the experiments, we first construct a mobility dataset using the moving object generator [6]. This dataset consists of the positions of 38,500 users travelling in a period with 50 discrete time points. This dataset contains users' spatial distributions. Second, we construct the dataset of users' requests. For a number of active users who would issue requests in the period, we simulate a trace of requests for each active user according to his query dependency matrix and *a priori* preference on queries. Specifically, we assume 6 types of queries for users to choose from. This makes users' *a priori* preference around 17% on average. As our purpose is to evaluate the privacy risk caused by query dependency and the effectiveness of the algorithm, we assume query dependency matrix available and generate it by a random procedure. Users' *a priori* preference is assessed in a similar way. Throughout our experiments, we use one mobility dataset but generate many request

datasets with different number of active users so as to evaluate its influence on query privacy. Our simulation is implemented with Java and run on a Linux laptop with 2.67 Ghz Intel Core (TM) and 4GB memory.

Impact of query dependency on users' posterior probabilities. To measure the privacy risk caused by query dependency, we compare users' posterior probabilities in two attack scenarios when k-anonymity spatial generalisation is used. In one scenario, the adversary only learns users' *a priori* preference while in the other, users' query dependency is added.

Let $p_{pf}(u \mid \langle r, t, q \rangle)$ be the issuer's posterior probability when only user u's *a priori* preference is considered. We use Δp to measure the changes of the posterior probability after query dependency is added, which is defined as follows:

$$\Delta p = \frac{|p_{pf}(u \mid \langle r, t, q \rangle) - p^n(u \mid \langle r, t, q \rangle, \mathcal{O}_t)|}{p_{pf}(u \mid \langle r, t, q \rangle)}.$$

Fig. 3 shows how Δp changes according to (1) different values of history window size n, (2) different strengths of query dependency and (3) the number of active users in the LBS. The results are obtained by a simulation with 8,000 requests. We divide requests into clusters according to the query dependency of the issuers when sending the requests by an interval of 0.05, and use $dep = 0.05x \ (1 \le x \le 20)$ to denote the maximum query dependency allowed in the clusters. For example, if $dep = 0.15$, the issuer of any request in the cluster has a dependency between 0.1 and 0.15. Fig. 3a depicts the average Δp of generalised requests in clusters satisfying k-anonymity with $k = 10$ and with 2.6% of the users being active. Based on the results, we have three observations. First of all, larger history windows lead to big changes in users' posterior probabilities. In our simulation, the average value of Δp increases by 53% and 24% when n grows from 1 to 2 and from 2 to 3, respectively (see Fig. 3a). Second, the average value of Δp increases when query dependency of two successive queries gets stronger (see Fig. 3a). The curves reach their lowest points when dep is about 0.15. This is due to the fact that users' average *a priori* preference on each type of queries ($p_u(q_i)$) is around 17%. The little difference between $p_u(q_i \mid q_{i-1})$ and $p_u(q_i)$ eliminates the influence of query dependency. Third, Δp decreases when there are more active users issuing LBS requests, but the influence becomes smaller with larger history windows. Fig. 3b shows that the average Δp decreases by 30%, 24% and 19% for

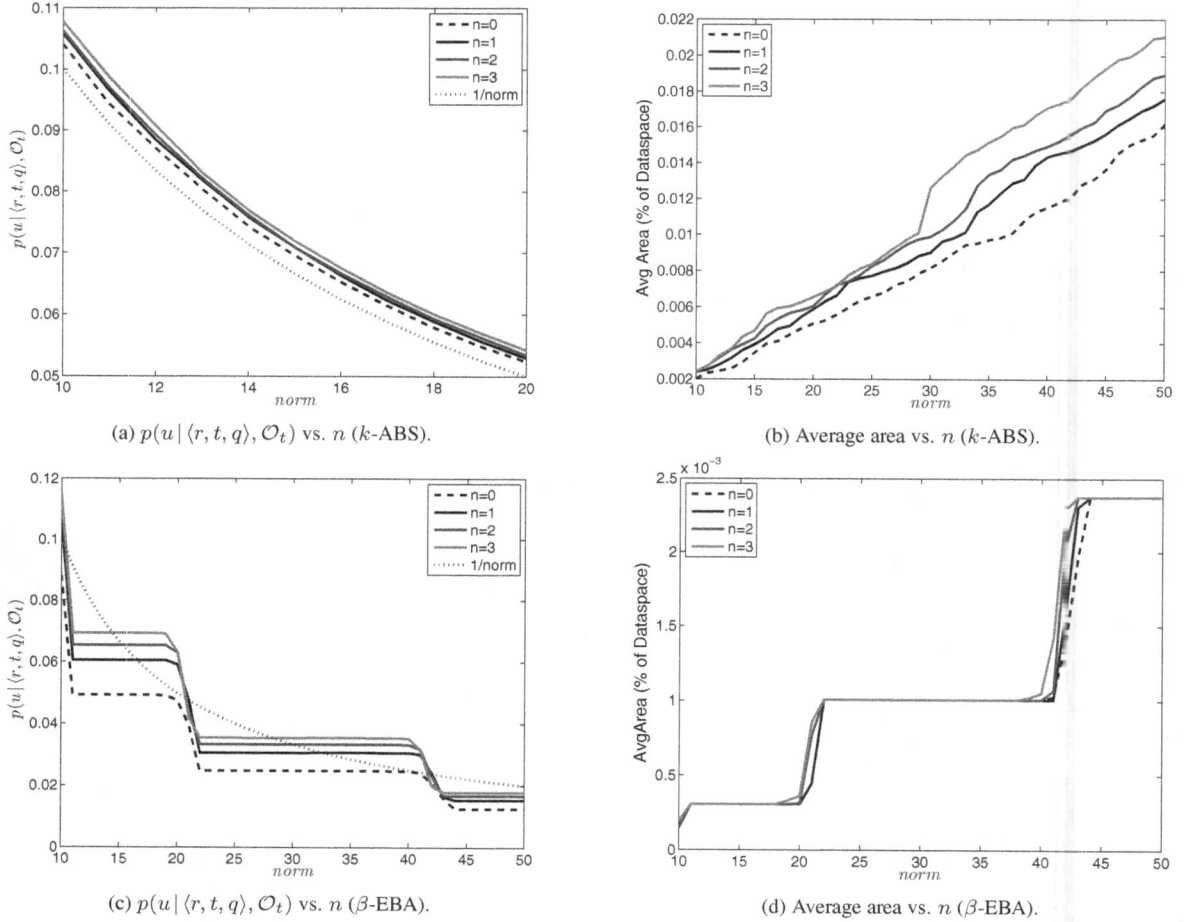

(a) $p(u \mid \langle r, t, q \rangle, \mathcal{O}_t)$ vs. n (k-ABS).

(b) Average area vs. n (k-ABS).

(c) $p(u \mid \langle r, t, q \rangle, \mathcal{O}_t)$ vs. n (β-EBA).

(d) Average area vs. n (β-EBA).

Figure 4: Impact of history window size n.

$n = 1, 2, 3$, respectively, when the percentage of active users increases from 2.5% to 7.5%. This is because more active users in the LBS lead to more observed requests added into users' observed request traces and mixed with users' real requests, while bigger history windows have larger chances to include users' real requests. In general, from Fig. 3, we can conclude that exploring query dependency does greatly decrease the adversary's uncertainty about the real issuers.

Effectiveness of the new privacy metrics. Through experiments, we discuss the features of privacy metrics in terms of (1) area of the generalised regions and (2) issuers' posterior probabilities. We set the percentage of active users to 2.6% and only use the first 1,000 requests after 8,000 requests have been observed. Each number shown in the following discussion is an average of the 1,000 samples. To compare the two metrics presented in Sect. 6, we define a normalised value $norm$: $norm=k$ for query-dependent k-ABS, while $norm=2^\beta$ for query-dependent β-EBA.

From the above discussion, we know that users can have better their query privacy with larger history windows. Fig. 4 shows how issuers' posterior probabilities and the area of generalised regions change according to the normalised value $norm$ and the history window size n. Note that when $n=0$, the generalisation algorithm only considers users' *a priori* preference.

For query-dependent k-ABS, issuers' posterior probabilities are about $\frac{1}{k}$ as the generalised regions have at least k users with simi-

lar posterior probabilities. However, after taking a closer look, we can find that a larger n leads to a larger distance to $\frac{1}{k}$. This is because larger history windows make the issuers' posterior probabilities more different from the others, which in turn makes it more difficult to find users with similar posterior probabilities. This also explains why the corresponding generalised regions become larger with larger history windows as shown in Fig. 4b.

For query-dependent β-EBA, issuers' posterior probabilities can remain almost unchanged in some segments of the curves. The projection of the middle point of such a segment on axis $norm$ has an logarithm of integer, such as 16 and 32 (see in Fig. 4c). Similar to query-dependent k-ABS, larger history windows increase the issuers' posterior probabilities, which leads to smaller entropy. This can be seen from Fig. 4d where the generalised regions of larger n double their sizes earlier than the regions of smaller n.

We can also observe from Fig. 4 that for the same value of $norm$, although the metric β-EBA cannot always ensure issuers' posterior probabilities as close to $\frac{1}{k}$ as k-ABS (see Fig. 4a and Fig. 4c), the corresponding area of generalised regions is about ten times smaller (see Fig. 4b and Fig. 4d). Since bigger regions lead to worse quality of service, this indicates that a balance between privacy protection and quality of services needs to be considered in practice.

The protection of issuers' privacy varies with issuers' query dependency. Fig. 5 plots posterior probabilities and average area of generalised regions for issuers with different levels of query depen-

(a) $p(u \mid \langle r, t, q \rangle, \mathcal{O}_t)$ vs. $p(q_i \mid q_{i-1})$ (k-ABS).

(b) Average area vs. $p(q_i \mid q_{i-1})$ (k-ABS).

(c) $p(u \mid \langle r, t, q \rangle, \mathcal{O}_t)$ vs. $p(q_i \mid q_{i-1})$ (β-EBA).

(d) Average area vs. $p(q_i \mid q_{i-1})$ (β-EBA).

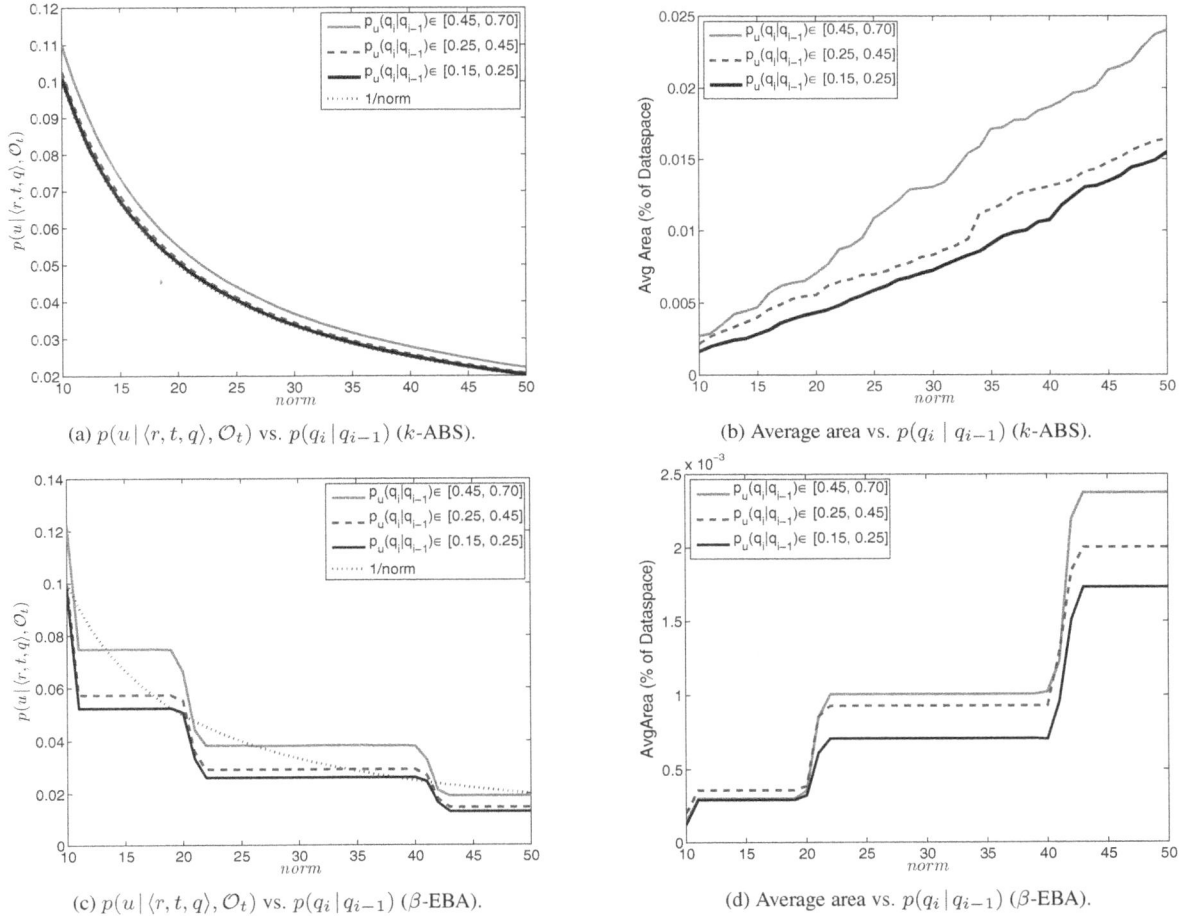

Figure 5: Impact of dependency $p(q_i \mid q_{i-1})$.

dency. The results are collected with the history window size $n=3$. Our general observation is that issuers with larger dependencies have bigger posterior probabilities and larger generalised regions.

Tab. 2 summarises the corresponding average increases (in percentage) for issuers with high (≥ 0.45) and medium ($0.25 - 0.45$) dependencies, when compared with those with low dependencies (≤ 0.25). The table shows that posterior probabilities of the issuers, when β-EBA is used, are more sensitive to the degree of dependency (43.1% increase for high-level dependency), while the generalised regions are more sensitive to dependency (62.9% increase for high-level dependency) when k-ABS is used.

Table 2: Increases in posterior probabilities and average area of generalised regions.

	k-ABS		β-EBA	
	medium	high	medium	high
Posterior Prob.	2.1%	9.5%	11.1%	43.1%
Avg Area	21.3%	62.9%	23.3%	30.1%

Performance of the proposed generalisation algorithm. In Fig. 6, we present the performance of Alg. 1 when dealing with query-dependent privacy metrics (k-ABS and β-EBA). For the sake of comparison, we also show in Fig. 6 the performance of the original

algorithms (k-ABS-ori and β-EBA-ori) in [7]. The computation time recorded is the average time per request based on executions with the same 100 requests.

As discussed in Sect. 7, it is necessary to update the status of each user, i.e., their observed request traces and the corresponding posterior probabilities. This is time-consuming, especially when the initial region is huge and contains a large number of users. In our implementation, we reduce the computation overhead by restricting the size of initial regions. The number of users located in an initial region is fixed as ten times as many as what users require for. For instance, for k-ABS, if $k=10$, then we first call k-anonymity generalisation algorithm to get an initial region with 100 users. As the generalisation algorithm is deterministic, which means for any user in a generalised region, it always returns the same region. Thus, our new algorithm Alg. 1 does not suffer from the "outlier" problem identified in the literature [21].

From Fig. 6, we can see that the computation time increases as $norm$ gets bigger. This is because the algorithm has to consider larger initial regions and more users are involved in the calculation of dependency-based posterior probabilities. For β-EBA, about 20ms are needed when $norm$=50, while k-ABS requires more time (around 35ms) as the K-means clustering algorithm is executed first to find similar users. When compared to the original algorithms, the computation time of Alg. 1 increases by about two times for β-EBA and about four times for k-ABS when $norm$=50.

45

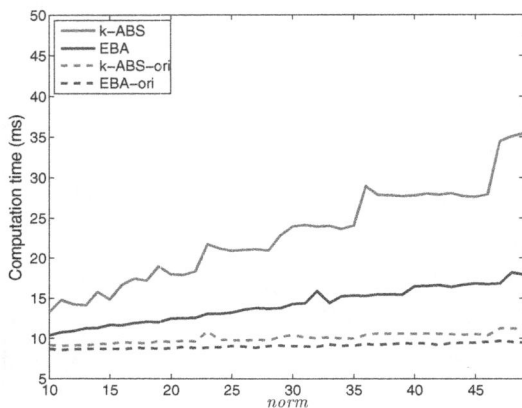

Figure 6: Average computational time (history window $n = 3$).

There are several ways to improve the efficiency of our implementation. For instance, we can use better data structures to main users' status. For practical applications, we can expect that with a powerful anonymiser our algorithm is efficient enough to handle concurrent requests and gives real-time responses to the users.

9. DISCUSSION AND CONCLUSION

In this paper, we have identified a new type of contextual information *query dependency* which has not been studied for query privacy in LBSs. To show its impact on users' query privacy, we presented an analysis, where the adversary explores query dependency to effectively reduce his uncertainty about the real issuers of requests. The analysis also makes use of observed request traces – a dynamic context. To protect query privacy against such an analysis, we first proposed new privacy metrics for users to express their privacy requirements precisely. Then we designed a new spatial generalisation algorithm to compute regions meeting users' privacy requirements. Through experiments, we have shown (1) enabling the adversary to have access users' query dependency does impose risk on query privacy; (2) the proposed metrics is effective to protect users' query privacy and (3) the generalisation algorithm is efficient for practical applications.

In this paper, we modelled query dependency with the Markov property, and ignored other influencing factors. For instance, the time interval between queries can also be explored by the adversary to further refine his view on possible issuers of an observed request. Regular transition time between two places has been studied in spatial and temporal databases as an important pattern in modelling users' mobility profiles [11]. We can expect to find similar patterns of the time intervals between LBS requests. Such temporal patterns can be considered as another support to predict users' behaviour, especially for issuing future requests. Furthermore, it is also useful to determine an appropriate size of history windows as the influence of past queries decreases as time passes.

10. REFERENCES

[1] ARIELY, D., AU, W. T., BENDER, R. H., BUDESCU, D. V., DIETZ, C. B., GU, H., WALLSTEN, T. S., AND ZAUBERMAN, G. The effects of averaging subjective probability estimates between and within judges. *Journal of Experimental Psychology: Applied 6* (2000), 130–147.

[2] BELLAVISTA, P., KÜPPER, A., AND HELAL, S. Location-based services: Back to the future. *IEEE Pervasive Computing 7*, 2 (2008), 85–89.

[3] BETTINI, C., MASCETTI, S., WANG, X. S., FRENI, D., AND JAJODIA, S. Anonymity and historical *k*-anonymity in location-based services. In *Privacy in Location-Based Applications*, vol. 5599 of *LNCS*. Springer, 2009, pp. 1–30.

[4] BETTINI, C., WANG, X. S., AND JAJODIA, S. Protecting privacy against location-based personal identification. In *Proc. 2nd VLDB Workshop on Secure Data Management* (2005), vol. 3674 of *LNCS*, Springer, pp. 185–199.

[5] BOLGER, F., AND WRIGHT, G. Coherence and calibration in expert probability judgement. *Omega 21*, 6 (1993), 629–644.

[6] BRINKHOFF, T. A framework for generating network-based moving objects. *GeoInformatica 6*, 2 (2002), 153–180.

[7] CHEN, X., AND PANG, J. Measuring query privacy in location-based services. In *Proc. 2nd ACM Conference on Data and Application Security and Privacy (CODASPY)* (2012), ACM, pp. 49–60.

[8] DEWRI, R., RAY, I., RAY, I., AND WHITLEY, D. On the formation of historically k-anonymous anonymity sets in a continuous LBS. In *Proc. 6th International Conference on Security and Privacy in Communication Networks (SecureComm)* (2010), vol. 50 of *LNCS*, Springer, pp. 71–88.

[9] DEWRI, R., RAY, I., RAY, I., AND WHITLEY, D. Query *m*-invariance: Preventing query disclosures in continuous location-based services. In *Proc. 11th International Conference on Mobile Data Management (MDM)* (2010), IEEE CS, pp. 95–104.

[10] GHINITA, G., KALNIS, P., AND SKIADOPOULOS, S. PRIVE: anonymous location-based queries in distributed mobile systems. In *Proc. 16th International Conference on World Wide Web (WWW)* (2007), ACM Press, pp. 371–380.

[11] GIANNOTTI, F., NANNI, M., PINELLI, F., AND PEDRESCHI, D. Trajectory pattern mining. In *Proc. 13th ACM International Conference on Knowledge Discovery and Data Mining (KDD)* (2007), ACM, pp. 330–339.

[12] GONZÁLEZ, M. C., HIDALGO, C. A., AND BARABÁSI, A.-L. Understanding individual human mobility patterns. *Nature 453* (2008), 779–782.

[13] GRUTESER, M., AND GRUNWALD, D. Anonymous usage of location-based services through spatial and temporal cloaking. In *Proc. 1st International Conference on Mobile Systems, Applications, and Services (MobSys)* (2003), USENIX Association.

[14] HOH, B., GRUTESER, M., XIONG, H., AND ALRABADY, A. Preserving privacy in GPS traces via uncertainty-aware path cloaking. In *Proc. 14th ACM Conference on Computer and Communications Security (CCS)* (2007), ACM, pp. 161–171.

[15] JAYNES, E. T. Information theory and statistical mechanics. *Physical Review Series II 106*, 4 (1957), 620–630.

[16] JAYNES, E. T. Information theory and statistical mechanics ii. *Physical Review Series II 108*, 2 (1957), 171–190.

[17] KALNIS, P., GHINITA, G., MOURATIDIS, K., AND PAPADIAS, D. Preventing location-based identity inference in anonymous spatial queries. *IEEE Transactions on Knowledge and Data Engineering 19*, 12 (2007), 1719–1733.

[18] LI, N., LI, T., AND VENKATASUBRAMANIAN, S. *t*-closeness: Privacy beyond *k*-anonymity and *l*-diversity. In *Proc. 23rd International Conference on Data Engineering (ICDE)* (2007), IEEE CS, pp. 106–115.

[19] MACHANAVAJJHALA, A., KIFER, D., GEHRKE, J., AND VENKITASUBRAMANIAM, M. ℓ-diversity: Privacy beyond k-anonymity. *ACM Transactions on Knowledge Discovery from Data 1*, 1 (2007).

[20] MANNING, C., AND SCHUÜTZE, H. *Foundations of Statistical Natural Language Processing.* Cambridge, 1999.

[21] MASCETTI, S., BETTINI, C., FRENI, D., AND WANG, X. S. Spatial generalization algorithms for LBS privacy preservation. *Journal of Location Based Services 1*, 3 (2007), 179–207.

[22] RIBONI, D., PARESCHI, L., AND BETTINI, C. Privacy in georeferenced context-aware services: A survey. In *Proc. 1st International Workshop on Privacy in Location-Based Applications (PiLBA)* (2008), vol. 397 of *CEUR Workshop Proceedings*, CEUR.

[23] RIBONI, D., PARESCHI, L., BETTINI, C., AND JAJODIA, S. Preserving anonymity of recurrent location-based queries. In *Proc. 16th International Symposium on Temporal Representation and Reasoning (TIME)* (2009), IEEE CS, pp. 62–69.

[24] ROBERT, C., CELEUX, G., AND DIEBOLT, J. Bayesian estimation of hidden markov chains. *Statics & Probability Letters 16*, 1 (1993), 77–83.

[25] SAMARATI, P. Protecting respondents' identities in microdata release. *IEEE Transactions on Knowledge and Data Engineering 13*, 6 (2001), 1010–1027.

[26] SANTOS, F., HUMBERT, M., SHOKRI, R., AND HUBAUX, J.-P. Collaborative location privacy with rational users. In *Proc. 2nd International Conference on Decision and Game Theory for Security (GameSec)* (2011), vol. 7037 of *LNCS*, Springer, pp. 163–181.

[27] SHIN, H., ATLURI, V., AND VAIDYA, J. A profile anonymization model for privacy in a personalized location based service environment. In *Proc. 9th International Conference on Mobile Data Management (MDM)* (2008), IEEE CS, pp. 73–80.

[28] SHIN, H., ATLURI, V., AND VAIDYA, J. A profile anonymization model for location-based services. *Journal of Computer Security 19*, 5 (2011), 795–833.

[29] SHOKRI, R., THEODORAKOPOULOS, G., BOUDEC, J.-Y. L., AND HUBAUX, J.-P. Quantifying location privacy. In *Proc. 32nd IEEE Symposium on Security and Privacy (S&P)* (2011), IEEE CS, pp. 247–262.

[30] SHOKRI, R., TRONCOSO, C., DÍAZ, C., FREUDIGER, J., AND HUBAUX, J.-P. Unraveling an old cloak: k-anonymity for location privacy. In *Proc. 2010 ACM Workshop on Privacy in the Electronic Society (WPES)* (2010), ACM Press, pp. 115–118.

[31] TAN, K. W., LIN, Y., AND MOURATIDIS, K. Spatial cloaking revisited: Distinguishing information leakage from anonymity. In *Proc. 11th International Symposium on Spatial and Temporal Databases (SSTD)* (2009), vol. 5644 of *LNCS*, Springer, pp. 117–134.

[32] XUE, M., KALNIS, P., AND PUNG, H. K. Location diversity: Enhanced privacy protection in location based services. In *Proc. 4th International Symposium on Location and Context Awareness (LoCA)* (2009), vol. 5561 of *LNCS*, Springer, pp. 70–87.

Expression Rewriting for Optimizing Secure Computation

Florian Kerschbaum
SAP Research
Karlsruhe, Germany
florian.kerschbaum@sap.com

ABSTRACT

In theory secure computation offers a solution for privacy in many collaborative applications. However, in practice poor efficiency of the protocols prevents their use. Hand-crafted protocols are more efficient than those implemented in compilers, but they require significantly more development effort in programming and verification. Recently, Kerschbaum introduced an automatic compiler optimization technique for secure computations that can make compilers as efficient as hand-crafted protocols. This optimization relies on the structure of the secure computation program. The programmer has to implement the program in such a way, such that the optimization can yield the optimal performance. In this paper we present an algorithm that rewrites the program – most notably its expressions – optimizing their efficiency in secure computation protocols. We give a heuristic for whole-program optimization and show the resulting performance gains using examples from the literature.

Categories and Subject Descriptors

D.3.4 [**Programming Languages**]: Processors—*Optimization*; D.4.6 [**Operating Systems**]: Security and Protection—*Cryptographic controls*

General Terms

Security, Programming Languages

Keywords

Secure Two-Party Computation, Programming, Optimization

1. INTRODUCTION

Secure (two-party) computation [39] allows two parties to compute a function f over their joint, private inputs x and y, respectively. No party can infer anything about the other party's input (e.g. y) except what can be inferred from one's own input (e.g. x) and output (e.g. $f(x, y)$). Secure computation has many applications, e.g. in the financial sector, and has been successfully deployed in commercial and industrial settings [8, 9, 27].

Secure computation notoriously suffers from poor efficiency (compared to non-secure computations). Already in 1997 Goldwasser suggested manually optimized, specialized protocols for important problems [17]. We have seen a huge number of manually optimized protocols in the literature and there is growing adoption in industrial practice [8, 9, 27]. Therefore it is foreseeable that this approach will no longer scale.

A number of compilers, e.g. FairPlay [31], and programming environments [5, 7, 14, 19, 21, 38] exist that intend to remedy this problem. Nevertheless, these compilers suffer from worse performance than the manually optimized protocols. A recent automatic compiler optimization for secure computations [24] addresses this problem. Using this technique a compiler is capable of transforming a FairPlay program into a secure computation protocol that is (in many cases) as efficient as a manually optimized one.

However, this optimization technique relies on the structure of the program, such that the programmer has to adapt the program in order to achieve optimal performance. This can be a very complicated task, since the optimization might not be obvious to the programmer. The optimizer may therefore fail to yield an efficient protocol albeit optimization is feasible.

In this paper we consider restructuring the program, such that it is amenable to optimization. We rewrite the program's expressions, such that the optimizer will output a more efficient protocol. We emphasize that the effectiveness of local rewriting can only be judged in the context of the global secure computation. For example, a program can be more efficient as a secure computation, but less efficient as a non-secure computation. Therefore incremental rewriting techniques no longer apply; such as common sub-expression elimination [11], where the effectiveness of each rewriting can be judged independently. Nevertheless, it is generally undecidable to find the optimal program. Hence, we apply a cost-driven heuristic and show its effectiveness using a number of examples drawn from the literature.

In summary, this paper's contributions are

- Expression *rewriting rules* that yield more efficient secure computation protocols.

- A cost-driven *heuristic* to apply these rules, such that the resulting protocol will be at least as efficient as the protocol compiled from the initial program.

- An *evaluation* of examples drawn from the literature to demonstrate the effectiveness of the rewriting rules.

The remainder of this paper is structured as follows. First, we give a motivating example and problem description in Section 2. Then, we briefly describe the secure computation optimization from [24] in Section 3. We explain our rewriting rules in detail in Section 4, before presenting the heuristic applying them in Section 5. In Section 6 evaluate its effectiveness using several examples. We review related work in Section 7 and present our conclusions in 8.

2. PROBLEM STATEMENT

Consider the following secure computation: Alice and Bob, each have n data values a_i and b_i ($0 \leq i < n$), respectively. They want to compute the mean μ and variance σ^2 of the joint $2n$ values.

$$\mu = \frac{1}{2n} \sum_{i=0}^{n-1} (a_i + b_i)$$

$$\sigma^2 = \frac{1}{2n-1} \sum_{i=0}^{n-1} \left((a_i - \mu)^2 + (b_i - \mu)^2 \right)$$

In a single secure computation protocol, e.g. using Yao's garbled circuit protocol [39], this protocol would have $2n$ inputs and 2 outputs. Using the FairPlay compiler [31], the above formulas can be straightforwardly implemented as in Listing 1[1]. Note that the input size n is known to both parties.

Nevertheless, this secure computation protocol is not optimal. Using the ideas of [26] we can construct the following protocol. First, Alice and Bob each locally add their values to an intermediate sum a and b, respectively. Since these intermediate sums can be inferred from one's input and output of the statistics computation, they can simply exchange them and compute (and output) the mean locally as $\mu = \frac{a+b}{2n}$. This constitutes a protocol with identical security in the semi-honest model of secure computation. Similarly, since they now already know the mean, they can sum the square of the differences of their values locally to intermediate sums a' and b', respectively. They again exchange those intermediate sums and compute the variance as $\sigma^2 = \frac{a'+b'}{2n-1}$.

We can implement this protocol in other languages for secure computation, e.g. L1 [38]. We omit depicting the code, since it is straightforward. This protocol is orders of magnitude faster than the FairPlay program. It does not even use one cryptographic operation, such as encryption or oblivious transfer. Furthermore, it reduces the complexity of the secure computation from $O(n^2)$ (computing $2n$ squares for the variance) to $O(1)$ (exchanging two values).

We compared our L1 implementation to an implementation in the framework of [21]. This framework currently yields the most efficient implementations of Yao's protocol [20]. The results are depicted in Figure 1. Even against this best-in-class implementation, the efficiency gain of our optimized protocol is such that its performance bar (dark blue on the left) is barely visible in the figure.

---
[1] The protocol does not run, since multiplication and division have not yet been implemented in FairPlay. This has been fixed in FairPlayMP [5].

```
program Statistics {
const   n          = 20;
type    Elem       = Int <32>;
type    AliceInput = Elem[n];
type    AliceOutput = struct {Elem mean,
                              Elem var2 };

type    BobInput   = Elem[n];
type    BobOutput  = struct {Elem mean,
                             Elem var2 };

type    Input   = struct {AliceInput   alice,
                          BobInput      bob };

type    Output = struct {AliceOutput alice,
                         BobOutput    bob };

function Output main (Input in) {
  var mean, var2;

  mean = 0;
  for (i = 0 to n−1) {
    mean = mean + in.alice[i] + in.bob[i];
  }
  mean = mean / (2 * n);

  var2 = 0;
  for (i = 0 to n−1) {
    var2 = var2 + (in.alice[i]−mean)
                * (in.alice[i]−mean)
                + (in.bob[i]−mean)
                * (in.bob[i]−mean);
  }
  var2 = var2 / (2 * n − 1);

  main.alice.mean = mean;
  main.alice.var2 = var2;
  main.bob.mean = mean;
  main.bob.var2 = var2;
}
}
```

Listing 1: Statistics computation in FairPlay

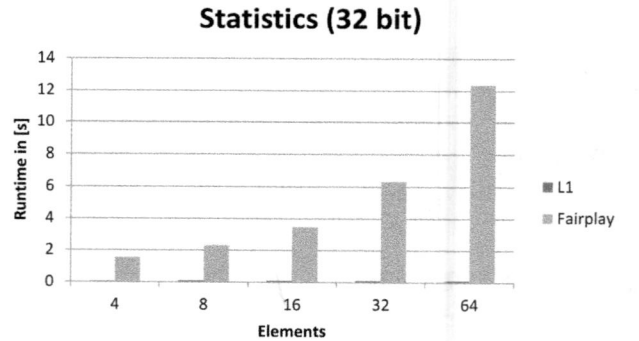

Figure 1: Secure Statistics

This significant performance gain stems from localizing most of the computation. This effect has already been recognized and manually applied in [21]. The compiler optimization technique of [24] can automatically infer parts of the program that can be locally computed. Nevertheless, this algorithm would fail in case of the FairPlay program in Listing 1. The algorithm does not change the structure of the program and since the programmer has not foreseen the necessary structure of localizing the sums, the optimizer is unable to detect it.

We therefore need to rewrite the program, such that the optimizer can be effective. Essentially, we have to untangle the loops, such that values from either Alice or Bob are first summed within their respective sets. Listing 3 in Section 6 displays such a rewritten program.

The optimizer would successfully deduce the efficient protocol from this FairPlay program. The research question of this paper is whether we can automatically rewrite the program from Listing 1 to the program from Listing 3. Furthermore, there are many more examples (see Section 6) which should be also covered. We therefore search for a generic technique that can be applied to many, if not all, secure computation protocols.

3. OPTIMIZATION

3.1 Labels

We only briefly describe the optimization algorithm of [24]. The basic idea is to infer program variables that can always be learnt from input and output. Each variable – whether input, output or intermediary – that is known to a party carries a label. If a variable is known to Alice, it carries the label A; if it is known to Alice and Bob, it carries the label AB.

The optimization of [24] infers labels of variables using epistemic modal logic. Consider the statement in Listing 2. If the variables b and c are known, then so is a. This is

```
a = b + c
```

Listing 2: Simple statement

called forward inference. There is also backward inference. If the variables a and b are known, then so is c, but backward inference is tricky and depends on the operator. For a complete list of inference rules see [24].

3.2 Segmentation

Before applying the inference rules the optimizer transforms the program into an intermediate language. This intermediate language is a loop-free, single static assignment, three operand-code. If all three operands of a statement are known to at least one party, then this statement can be performed locally on that party and no longer needs to be computed in the secure computation protocol.

Using this localization of statements, the optimizer segments the program into possibly several secure computation protocols and local programs. Only the statements that actually need to be performed securely are implemented in a secure computation protocol. Particularly local segments at the beginning and at the end can be commonly exploited. In this paper, we attempt to enable this segmentation, even if the program description as such does not. We therefore extend the optimization technique of [24] by rewriting rules that transform the program into one more amenable to optimization.

3.3 Security

We assume the semi-honest or honest-but-curious model as defined by Goldreich [16]. The adversary in the semi-honest model is assumed to follow the protocol as specified, but may keep a record of the interaction and try to infer as much information as possible. A protocol secure in the semi-honest model ensures that such an adversary learns nothing except what can be inferred from his input and output. This guarantee is captured by Definition 1 of Goldreich using a simulator of the adversary view. The view $VIEW^\Pi(x, y)$ of a party during a protocol Π on this party's input x and the other party's input y is its input x, the outcome of its coin tosses and the messages received during the execution of the protocol.

DEFINITION 1. *We say a protocol Π computing $f(x, y)$ is secure in the* semi-honest *model, if for each party there exist a polynomial-time simulator S given the party's input and output is computationally indistinguishable from the party's view $VIEW^\Pi(x, y)$:*

$$S(x, f(x, y)) \stackrel{c}{\equiv} VIEW^\Pi(x, y)$$

Functions implemented in Yao's garbled circuit protocol [39], e.g. using the FairPlay compiler [31], are always secure in the semi-honest model [30]. In this paper, our rewriting rules also assume the semi-honest model, but do not actually emit a protocol. This protocol is compiled by the optimizer of [24], such that if it preserves semi-honest security, then the optimizations in this paper preserve semi-honest security. All our transformations are performed on the intermediate code of the secure computation protocol. We therefore can omit any further security analysis.

4. REWRITING RULES

4.1 Abstract Syntax Tree

$$
\begin{aligned}
expr &:= bracket|expon|multi|add|compare|simple \\
bracket &:= (expr) \\
expon &:= expr \wedge number|1/number \\
multi &:= expr \cdot |/expr \\
add &:= expr + | - expr \\
compare &:= expr < | <= | == |! = | > | >= expr \\
simple &:= var| - var|number \\
var &:= a|b| \ldots \\
number &:= 0|1|2| \ldots
\end{aligned}
$$

Figure 2: Expression grammar

We consider a language for expressions with the grammar as in Figure 2. For simplicity of the exposition, we consider only one type of operand: fixed-length (e.g. 32 bit), signed fixed-point numbers. Fixed-point numbers are scaled integers where a fixed number of bits is reserved for decimal digits. They can be effectively used to implement division or roots and can be efficiently implemented in secure computation [10]. Each arithmetic operand implements the usual semantics on these numbers. Comparison operations return either 0 for *false* or 1 for *true*.

Instead of representing an expression in the same intermediate language as in [24], we represent it in an abstract syntax tree. The nodes of the tree are the operators $(+, \cdot, \wedge,$ etc.) and the leaves are the simple expressions (numbers and variables). The root of the tree is the last operator to be evaluated. We use the same operator precedence rules as standard programming languages, such as C or Java, indicated by the order of grammar expressions. We resolve bracket expressions into a position in this syntax tree in the usual way. The expression $2 + (3 \cdot 4)$ has an abstract syntax tree with a root operator $+$ whereas the expression $(2+3) \cdot 4$ has an abstract syntax tree with a root operator $\cdot$.

The leaves are assigned labels regarding their origin, i.e. variables input by Alice are assigned label A and variables by Bob are assigned B. Constants (numbers) are assigned label AB, since they are known to both – Alice and Bob. We include the case of public input variables which are also known to Alice and Bob. Only intermediate values can be secret and carry no label.

Forward inference is straightforward. Since in our abstract syntax tree there are no intermediate values, we assign labels to the nodes. For forward inference a node is assigned the intersection of labels of its children.

We only perform a simplified version of backward inference compared to [24]. The rewritten expression is then analyzed in order to further optimize its performance. We named our backward inference *result pruning*. We assume that the final expression result is revealed as an output of the secure computation to both parties. Then each operation at the root of the tree with an operand known to both parties can be pruned. If we encounter such an operation, then we prune it from the tree.

At last, the optimization is performed. A label at a node means that this intermediate value is known to a party and may be computed locally at that party. Nodes with no labels need to be computed using a secure computation protocol.

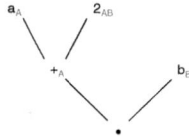

Figure 3: Overview of the basic steps in our cryptographic scheme

We depict abstract syntax trees with the root at the bottom as in the example of Figure 3. It shows the abstract syntax tree – including labels – for the expression $(a + 2) \cdot b$ where Alice has input a and Bob has input b.

4.2 Rule 1: Associative and Commutative Law

For an operator $\oplus$ the associate law holds if and only if

$$a \oplus (b \oplus c) = (a \oplus b) \oplus c$$

The commutative law holds if and only if

$$a \oplus b = b \oplus a$$

Both laws hold for the operators $+$ (addition) and $\cdot$ (multiplication). We can rewrite the operators $-$ (subtraction) and $/$ (division) for labeled, second operands into $+$ and $\cdot$,

respectively. In the expression $a \oplus b$ the second operand is b. An operand is labeled, if it carries one of the labels A, B or AB. We rewrite the operand with its inverse in the operation, i.e. $-b$ or $1/b$. Since inversion is an operation of the neutral element (a constant) which is always labeled AB and the second operand, the inversion operator is assigned the intersection, i.e. the label of the second operand. Therefore we rewrite a labeled operand with a labeled operation. Then we can rewrite the operator of the expression to either $+$ or $\cdot$.

Our *Rule* 1 processes operators for which both – associative and commutative – laws hold in two steps: *merging* and *sorting*. In the merging step, we merge adjacent nodes in the syntax tree into a combined node with three (or more) operands. Due to the associative law we do not change the expression result.

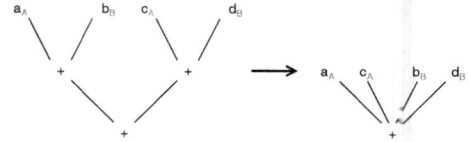

Figure 4: Application of associative and commutative laws

Then, in the sorting step, we sort each child according to its label in the following order of labels AB, A, B and no label. Due to the commutative law we again do not change the expression's result. Figure 4 shows an exemplary application of this rewriting rule.

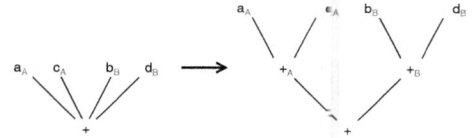

Figure 5: Output of merged and sorted multi-operand operators

When we generate the secure computation protocol, e.g. the 3 operand code of [24] or the circuit description of [31], we create the operands in sequential order of the labels. This means, first public operands (label AB), second Alice's operands (label A), and so on. Finally, we add the operators with different labels, again in order. This ensures that the maximum possible number of operators are assigned the labels of the operands. The only remaining operators in the secure computation are then the ones without label. All other operations are performed locally at one party. Figure 5 shows the generated expression (as an abstract syntax tree) of our example.

4.3 Distributive Law

For a pair $\oplus$, $\odot$ of operators the distributive law holds if and only if

$$(a \oplus b) \odot (a \oplus c) = a \odot (b \oplus c)$$

The distributive law holds for the pairs of operators $+$ or $-$ and $\cdot$ or $/$, respectively.

4.3.1 Rule 2 and 3: Forward

The most straightforward way to apply the distributive law is to reduce the number of operations in case of common sub-expressions. We emphasis that this step does not supersede common sub-expression elimination (CSE) [11]. On the one hand, CSE identifies and optimizes common sub-expressions even in remote parts of the program or protocol whereas our rewriting rule only uses local operands. On the other hand, our rewriting rule actually changes the order of operator evaluation and thereby eliminates the need for temporary storage.

Let e, f, g be sub-expressions with arbitrary labels. Let L be an arbitrary – potentially empty – security label. Let - indicate that there is an empty label and if a sub-expression or operator has no label, then it may carry any label Let e_L be an expression with label L and $\oplus_L$ be an operator with label L. Our *Rule* 2 rewrites the expression

$$(e_L \odot f) \oplus_- (e_L \odot_- g)$$

to

$$e_L \odot_- (f \oplus g)$$

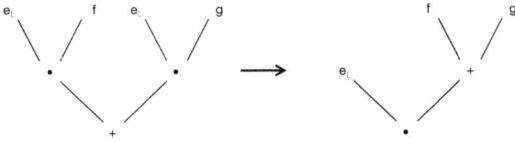

Figure 6: Forward application of distributive law

Note that at least one operator $\odot$ must not carry a label. It is then ensured that the number of operations in the secure computation decreases. Eleven more analogous rewriting rules exist for every position pair of the sub-expression e_L and every combination of unlabeled operators in the initial expression. Figure 6 shows an exemplary transformation of the syntax tree of the first rewriting rule.

We can furthermore create common sub-expressions. This may be useful in combination with our other rewriting techniques, such as the rules for the associative and commutative law. Let L' be a non-empty label, such that L and L' have at least one party in common, i.e. $L \cap L' \neq \varnothing$. Let f^{-1} be the inverse of sub-expression according to operator $\odot$. Then using *Rule* 3 we rewrite the expression

$$e_L \oplus_- (f_{L'} \odot_- g)$$

to

$$((e_L \odot f_{L'}^{-1}) \odot f_{L'}) \oplus_- (f_{L'} \odot g)$$

In a second step we apply the above forward rewriting rule for the distributive law.

$$f_{L'} \odot_- ((e_L \odot f_{L'}^{-1}) \oplus g)$$

On the one hand this rule does not increase performance by itself, but only in combination with other rules. On the other hand, since the operator of the sub-expression $e_L \odot f_{L'}^{-1}$ carries a label, it does not (noticeably) decrease performance

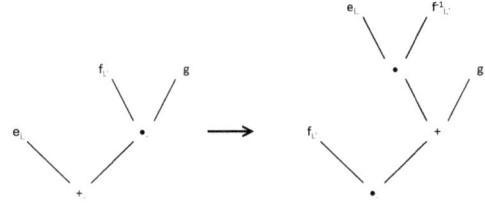

Figure 7: Creation of common sub-expression

either. It only changes the order of the operators – potentially allowing the application of further associate and commutative rewriting rules. We show an example of the combination of both rules in Figure 7.

4.3.2 Rule 4: Backward

A not so obvious way to apply the distributive law is backward. This may seem counter-intuitive at first, since it increases the number of operations. This is an example where the cost of a local computation increases, but due to the higher cost of a secure computation, the overall cost decreases. We therefore need to take precautions, that this optimization yields an improvement in efficiency. If we ensure that the "distributed" operand is labeled, then the number of operations to be performed as secure computations is at least likely to stay constant. Furthermore, if this operand is labeled AB as known to both parties or in combination with the rewriting rules for the associate and commutative laws, it may actually decrease the number of operations in the secure computation protocol.

Again, let L' be a non-empty label. *Rule* 4 rewrites the expression

$$e_{L'} \odot_- (f \oplus_- g)$$

to

$$(e_{L'} \oplus f) \odot_- (e_L \oplus g)$$

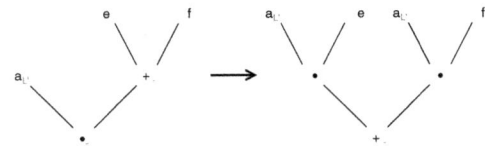

Figure 8: Backward application of distributive law

We show an example in Figure 8. As mentioned above, it is not guaranteed that this rewriting rule decreases the number of operations in the secure computation protocol, but it is possible. We show an example taken from the literature in Section 6.2. We also show how to apply the rewriting rules, such that a performance increase is guaranteed in Section 5.

If this rewriting rule is effective, i.e. it decreases the number of operations in the secure computation, then both operators $\oplus$ must get a label after the rewriting – potentially after applying further rewriting rules. Furthermore, if this is the case, then this rule will not be undone by the forward rewriting rule for the distributive law, since this rule requires at least one operator to be unlabeled.

4.4 Rule 5: Inverse Balancing

For comparison operators there are no algebraic laws that can be used for optimization. Nevertheless, there is one more rewriting rule. Let $\otimes$ be a comparison operator, e.g. $<$. Let $\oplus$ and $\ominus$ be inverse operators. Furthermore, let neither change the result of the comparison. In our language $+$ and $-$ always build such a pair, whereas $\cdot$ and $/$ do not for inequality operators, since multiplication with a negative number inverts the result of the comparison. *Rule* 5 rewrites the expression

$$e \otimes_- f \oplus_- g$$

to

$$e \ominus g \otimes f$$

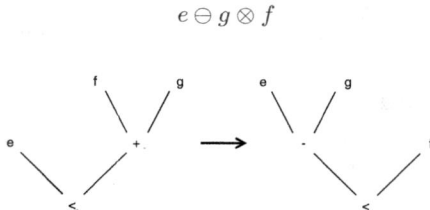

Figure 9: Application of inverse balancing

We also maintain rewriting rules for the other operator $\ominus$, the other operand f and the other side of the comparison in the initial expression. Figure 9 shows an exemplary application of the above rule.

5. ALGORITHM

Even with such a simple language as arithmetic expressions we cannot hope to achieve optimal performance, since the program equivalency problem is recursively unsolvable [11]. We therefore apply a heuristic that results in secure computation protocols which are at least as efficient as the direct compilation of the initial expression. This heuristic considers all rewriting rules iteratively on an incrementally increasing program. Nevertheless, some rewriting rules may even result in less efficient protocols. We therefore need to carefully select the rules to apply. We guide our choice using a cost function for operators. This cost function ensures that the cost of the entire program constantly decreases and only rewriting rules that optimize the whole program (up to the current increment) are considered.

5.1 Cost Function

Predicting the performance of a secure computation protocol is a challenging task. An attempt for comparing homomorphic encryption and garbled circuits (Yao's protocol) has been made been in [37]. Nevertheless the main anticipated benefit of our optimization is to compute more operators locally, although in some cases we might also improve on the type of operators in the secure computation. Local computation is an order of magnitude faster than any secure computation – whether using homomorphic encryption or garbled circuits. This has already been exploited in the manual optimization of [21]. We therefore conclude that the accuracy of our model for comparing operators in the secure computation protocol is of less importance.

We follow the argument of [37] that the performance of a garbled circuit secure computation protocol is linear in the number of gates of the operator. Let λ be the bit length of an operand. Therefore we use the costs as in Table 1 for the operators.

Operator	Cost
Labeled	0
Unlabeled	
Comparison	λ
Addition†	λ
Multiplication†	λ^2
Exponentiation	λ^3

Table 1: Operator costs

There are two distinct cost functions: one for operators cost and one for trees tcost. The operator cost function cost returns the costs as in Table 1. The tree cost function tcost performs a preorder tree traversal and sums the cost of each encountered operator.

5.2 Rewriting

We perform the search for performance-improving rewriting rules using a reverse breadth-first search. The intuition is that in order to judge the effectiveness of a rewriting rule at the root of the tree each sub-tree must be optimal. We visit each sub-tree in order of incrementally increasing height. Then, we apply each of the five possible rewriting rules at the root and perform a subsequent optimization on each sub-tree. This repeated, subsequent optimization is necessary, since a change in the tree, e.g. a change of the order of operators, may have enabled additional rules in the sub-tree.

We emphasize that a rule that causes a cost-reduction cannot be undone by a subsequent rewriting rule. This is also true for the forward and backward rewriting rules for the distributive law due to their choice of labels on the operators. Algorithm 1 depicts the pseudocode for our heuristic. The function toptimize performs the overall optimization whereas the function optimize optimizes a sub-tree. We only keep results of rewriting rules that decrease cost. Therefore our overall heuristic deterministically does not increase cost, i.e. it either improves or maintains cost.

Let there be n nodes in tree and let H_n be the height of tree. Each node is visited at most H_n times. Since $H_n = O(n)$, the worst-case complexity of our heuristic is $O(n^2)$. The expected height of an uniformly randomly chosen tree is $H_n = O(\log n)$ [15]. Therefore the expected average-case complexity of our heuristic is $O(n \log n)$.

6. EXAMPLES

On the one hand, we cannot expect to achieve optimal performance in all cases. On the other hand, our heuristic is not expected to decrease performance. We evaluate its effectiveness using a number of examples from the literature.

6.1 Statistics

Statistics computation is the motivating example from Section 2. We consider the program from Listing 1. We unroll the loops, since they have a fixed number of iterations, and build an abstract syntax tree of expressions for

---

†For multi-operand operators we multiply by the number of unlabeled operators in the expanded tree.

Algorithm 1 Cost-driven heuristic

```
procedure TOPTIMIZE(root)
    for 1 ≤ i ≤ HEIGHT(root) do
        for all t| HEIGHT(t) = i do
            OPTIMIZE(t)
        end for
    end for
end procedure
procedure OPTIMIZE(node)
    for all r ∈ Rules do
        if MATCHES(r, node) then
            new ← COPY(node)
            APPLY(r, new)
            for all c|c ∈ CHILDREN(new) do
                OPTIMIZE(c);
            end for
            if TCOST(new) < TCOST(node) then
                node ← new
            end if
        end if
    end for
end procedure
```

```
program  Statistics {
const  n            = 20;
type   Elem         = Int <32>;
type   AliceInput   = Elem [n];
type   AliceOutput  = struct {Elem mean,
                              Elem var2 };

type   BobInput  = Elem [n];
type   BobOutput = struct {Elem mean,
                           Elem var2 };

type   Input  = struct {AliceInput   alice,
                        BobInput     bob };

type   Output = struct {AliceOutput  alice,
                        BobOutput    bob };

function  Output main (Input in) {
    var meana, meanb, mean, vara, varb, var2;

    meana = 0;
    for (i = 0 to n−1) {
        meana = meana + in.alice[i];
    }

    meanb = 0;
    for (i = 0 to n−1) {
        meanb = meanb + in.bob[i];
    }

    mean = (meana + meanb) / (2 * n);

    vara = 0;
    for (i = 0 to n−1) {
        vara = vara + (in.alice[i]−mean)
                    * (in.alice[i]−mean);
    }

    varb = 0;
    for (i = 0 to n−1) {
        varb = varb + (in.bob[i]−mean)
                    * (in.bob[i]−mean);
    }
    var2 = (vara + varb) / (2 * n − 1);

    main.alice.mean = mean;
    main.alice.var2 = var2;
    main.bob.mean = mean;
    main.bob.var2 = var2;
}
}
```

Listing 3: Rewritten FairPlay program

each output. Then we use our heuristic. First, the addition operators are merged and sorted into one multi-operand addition operator using the rewriting rules for the associative and commutative law (Rule 1). The sorting step leads to the main optimization possible. The division by $2n$ and $2n - 1$, respectively, are pruned using result pruning. No more rewriting rules lead to cost reductions. The generated intermediate code corresponds to the intermediate code of the program in Listing 3. The optimizer can deduce the optimal protocol of exchanging only intermediate sums. Our compiler in this example is as efficient as the manually optimized protocol.

6.2 Joint Economic Lot Size

The joint economic lot size (JELS) is a two-party supply chain optimization following the model of [3]. Using a secure computation protocol has been proposed in [35] and demonstrated as a JavaScript implementation in [36]. We do not give the operations research background in this paper, but refer the reader to [35]. We extend the model by a safety stock s. Alice supplies inputs f_A, h_A and c. Bob supplies inputs f_B, h_B, s and d is a public input known to both. The following formula from [3] is computed securely and output

$$q = \sqrt{2 \cdot d \cdot \frac{f_A + f_B}{d \cdot \frac{h_A}{c} + h_B}} + s.$$

We build the abstract syntax tree for the expression. The backward rewriting rule for the distributive law (Rule 4) is applied to the denominator. This immediately reduces the number of operations in the secure computation by a multiplication, since d is a public variable. This example underpins the necessity for the backward rewriting rule. The term $d \cdot \frac{h_A}{c}$ is labeled using the forward inference algorithm. The resulting expression in the secure computation is

$$q = \sqrt{\frac{a + b}{a' + h_B}} + s$$

where $a = 2 \cdot d \cdot f_A$, $a' = d \cdot \frac{h_A}{c}$ and $b = 2 \cdot d \cdot f_B$. A sim-

ilar computation (without safety stock) has been proposed in [35, 36]. Again, our optimization algorithm is as efficient as the manually optimized protocol.

6.3 XML Transformation

Protocols applicable to XML transformation have been proposed in [23]. A type-safe and therefore provably secure implementation has been shown in [25]. These protocols implement basic string processing operations, such as concatenation, sub-string and find. The protocols are composed of several cryptographic techniques, such as secret sharing, homomorphic encryption, garbled circuits, and oblivious transfer.

The implementation of [25] contains a sub-step where a string length l is compared to a constant. The string length is additively secret shared, i.e. Alice has l_A and Bob has

l_B such that $l = l_A + l_B \pmod{m}$ where the modulus m is public. Then the following expression is evaluated using garbled circuits.

$$l_A + l_B < m$$

Our optimizer will immediately use the inverse balancing rule (Rule 5) to rewrite the expression to

$$l_A < m - l_B$$

saving one secure addition. The manually optimized protocol description of [23] suggests this optimization as well. Nevertheless, due to type safety considerations it cannot be implemented in [25]. Our optimizer is able to remedy this and optimize the type-safe implementation. This example shows that different compiler techniques for security and performance can nicely interact to yield the best-performing, provably secure protocol.

7. RELATED WORK

This work is related to programming environments for secure computation [5, 7, 14, 19, 21, 31, 38], compiler language techniques for secure computation [24, 25, 33], and programming zero-knowledge proofs [1, 2, 32].

Programming environments for secure computation can be coarsely classified into those that implement their own compiler [5, 7, 19, 31] and those that build on top of existing programming languages [14, 21, 38]. The first programming environment – including its own compiler – for secure computation is FairPlay [31]. It implemented Yao's two-party, garbled circuit protocol [39]. It has been later extended to multi-party computations in [5] based on the multi-party version of Yao's protocol [4]. It introduced the SFDL programming language which provided an abstraction of the ideal functionality, i.e. the function computed by the secure protocol. Programs in SFDL are translated into a binary circuit which is interpreted using Yao's protocol.

Secure multi-party computations are also supported by ShareMind [7] based on the information-theoretically secure protocol of [6]. It has its own programming language SecreC [22] and compiler. All these single protocol based environments suffer from very poor performance of the compiled protocols. A first step towards improving performance by mixing protocols in one environment, such as Yao's protocol and homomorphic encryption, was introduced in TASTY [19]. Nevertheless, they restricted themselves to one provably secure composition of [28] and do not perform program-based optimization.

Programming environments as extensions of existing, generic programming languages can implement any protocol, but usually provide built-in support for a few. The first such language is VIFF [14] based on the Python language. It is intended for the protocol of [12]. Similar extensions have been presented for the Java language [21, 38]. The framework of [21] is based on Yao's protocol [39] and currently produces the most efficient protocols. A significant portion of its efficiency gain is based on optimizations by the programmer like manually localizing computations. The L1 language [38] again supports mixed protocol secure computations and outputs its protocols in Java.

The first programming language (domain-specific language) for secure computations was introduced in [33]. It contains a labeling concept similar to ours, but the labels are set by the programmer. We already introduced the first program-based optimization of [24]. It is the first proposal to use programming language techniques to enhance the performance of secure computations. Our work builds on its optimizing algorithm, but removes one of its major problems (for expressions): the dependence on the program structure. There are other optimizations of secure computations, such as the free XOR-technique [29]. This technique optimizes a specific secure computation protocol – Yao's garbled circuits [39] – almost independent of the program. In [25] a type system for mixed protocol secure computation is introduced. It ensures that type-safe programs are protocols secure in the semi-honest model. It provides a security guarantee for the programmer, but does not perform any optimization.

Recently, first in [1] and independently in [32] and later in [2] the authors have proposed compilers for zero-knowledge proofs, which take as input a specification of the statement to be proved. This statement may contain expressions similar to the language considered in this paper and then it is compiled in to a zero-knowledge protocol. The cryptographic implementation of such protocol is either based on Σ-protocols [13] or a pairing-based scheme [18].

Note that optimization of expressions in non-secure programming languages has been considered decades ago, e.g. [11, 34].

8. CONCLUSIONS AND FUTURE WORK

In this paper we consider the automatic optimization of programs compiled into secure computation protocols. We build on the automatic optimization of [24] and present five rewriting rules that restructure expressions in order to yield more efficient protocols. We have successfully applied our optimization algorithm to multiple examples drawn from the literature.

Future work is to extend rewriting rules to conditional statements implementing branches. Furthermore, this work assumes the semi-honest model. Other models which are generally considered more secure, such as the malicious model, should be investigated.

9. REFERENCES

[1] J. B. Almeida, E. Bangerter, M. Barbosa, S. Krenn, A.-R. Sadeghi, and T. Schneider. A certifying compiler for zero-knowledge proofs of knowledge based on σ-protocols. In *ESORICS'10: Proceedings of the 15th European Conference on Research in Computer Security*, 2010.

[2] M. Backes, M. Maffei, and K. Pecina. Automated synthesis of privacy-preserving distributed applications. In *NDSS'12: Proceedings of the 19th Annual Network and Distributed System Security Symposium*, 2012.

[3] A. Banerjee. A joint economic lot-size model for purchaser and vendor. *Decision Sciences*, 17(3), 1986.

[4] D. Beaver, S. Micali, and P. Rogaway. The round complexity of secure protocols. In *STOC'90: Proceedings of the 22nd ACM Symposium on Theory of Computing*, 1990.

[5] A. Ben-David, N. Nisan, and B. Pinkas. Fairplaymp: a system for secure multi-party computation. In *CCS'08: Proceedings of the 15th ACM Conference on Computer and Communications Security*, 2008.

[6] M. Ben-Or, S. Goldwasser, and A. Wigderson. Completeness theorems for non-cryptographic fault-tolerant distributed computation. In *STOC'88: Proceedings of the 20th ACM Symposium on Theory of Computing*, 1988.

[7] D. Bogdanov, S. Laur, and J. Willemson. Sharemind: a framework for fast privacy-preserving computations. In *ESORICS'08: Proceedings of the 13th European Symposium on Research in Computer Security*, 2008.

[8] D. Bogdanov, R. Talviste, and J. Willemson. Deploying secure multi-party computation for financial data analysis. In *FC'12: Proceedings of the 16th International Conference on Financial Cryptography and Data Security*, 2012.

[9] P. Bogetoft, D. L. Christensen, I. Damgård, M. Geisler, T. P. Jakobsen, M. Krøigaard, J. D. Nielsen, J. B. Nielsen, K. Nielsen, J. Pagter, M. I. Schwartzbach, and T. Toft. Secure multiparty computation goes live. In *FC'09: Proceedings of the 13th International Conference on Financial Cryptography and Data Security*, 2009.

[10] O. Catrina and A. Saxena. Secure computation with fixed-point numbers. In *FC'10: Proceedings of the 14th International Conference on Financial Cryptography and Data Security*, 2010.

[11] J. Cocke. Global common subexpression elimination. *SIGPLAN Notices*, 5, 1970.

[12] R. Cramer, I. Damgård, and U. Maurer. Efficient general secure multi-party computation from any linear secret-sharing scheme. In *EUROCRYPT'00: Proceedings of the 19th European Cryptology Conference*, 2000.

[13] R. Cramer, I. Damgård, and B. Schoenmakers. Proofs of partial knowledge and simplified design of witness hiding protocols. In *CRYPTO '94: Proceedings of the 14th International Cryptology Conference*, 1994.

[14] I. Damgård, M. Geisler, M. Krøigaard, and J. B. Nielsen. Asynchronous multiparty computation: theory and implementation. In *PKC'09: Proceedings of the 12th International Conference on Practice and Theory in Public Key Cryptography*, 2009.

[15] L. Devroye. Branching processes in the analysis of the heights of trees. *Acta Informatica*, 24, 1987.

[16] O. Goldreich. *Foundations of Cryptography*, volume 2. Cambridge University Press, 2004.

[17] S. Goldwasser. Multi-party computations: past and present. In *PODC'97: Proceedings of the 16th ACM Symposium on Principles of Distributed Computing*, 1997.

[18] J. Groth and A. Sahai. Efficient non-interactive proof systems for bilinear groups. In *EUROCRYPT'08: Proceedings of the 27th European Cryptology Conference*, 2008.

[19] W. Henecka, S. Kögl, A.-R. Sadeghi, T. Schneider, and I. Wehrenberg. Tasty: tool for automating secure two-party computations. In *CCS'10: Proceedings of the 17th ACM Conference on Computer and Communications Security*, 2010.

[20] Y. Huang, D. Evans, and J. Katz. Private set intersection: Are garbled circuits better than custom protocols? In *Proceedings of the 19th Network and Distributed Security Symposium*, 2012.

[21] Y. Huang, D. Evans, J. Katz, and L. Malka. Faster secure two-party computation using garbled circuits. In *Proceedings of the 20th USENIX Security Symposium*, 2011.

[22] R. Jagomägis. Secrec: a privacy-aware programming language with applications in data mining. Master's thesis, University of Tartu, 2010.

[23] M. Jensen and F. Kerschbaum. Towards privacy-preserving xml transformation. In *ICWS'11: Proceedings of the 9th IEEE International Conference on Web Services*, 2011.

[24] F. Kerschbaum. Automatically optimizing secure computation. In *CCS'11: Proceedings of the 18th ACM Conference on Computer and Communications Security*, 2011.

[25] F. Kerschbaum. A type-system for mixed protocol secure computation. Unpublished manuscript, 2012.

[26] F. Kerschbaum, D. Dahlmeier, A. Schröpfer, and D. Biswas. On the practical importance of communication complexity for secure multi-party computation protocols. In *SAC'09: Proceedings of the 24th ACM Symposium on Applied Computing*, 2009.

[27] F. Kerschbaum, A. Schröpfer, A. Zilli, R. Pibernik, O. Catrina, S. de Hoogh, B. Schoenmakers, S. Cimato, and E. Damiani. Secure collaborative supply chain management. *IEEE Computer*, 44(9), 2011.

[28] V. Kolesnikov, A.-R. Sadeghi, and T. Schneider. Modular design of efficient secure function evaluation protocols. Technical Report Report 2010/079, Cryptology ePrint Archive, 2010.

[29] V. Kolesnikov and T. Schneider. Improved garbled circuit: free xor gates and applications. In *ICALP'08: Proceedings of the 35th International Colloquium on Automata, Languages and Programming, Part II*, 2008.

[30] Y. Lindell and B. Pinkas. A proof of security of yao's protocol for two-party computation. *Journal of Cryptology*, 22(2), 2009.

[31] D. Malkhi, N. Nisan, B. Pinkas, and Y. Sella. Fairplay—a secure two-party computation system. In *Proceedings of the 13th USENIX Security Symposium*, 2004.

[32] S. Meiklejohn, C. C. Erway, A. Küpçü, T. Hinkle, and A. Lysyanskaya. Zkpdl: A language-based system for efficient zero-knowledge proofs and electronic cash. In *Proceedings of the 19th USENIX Security Symposium*, 2010.

[33] J. D. Nielsen and M. I. Schwartzbach. A domain-specific programming language for secure multiparty computation. In *PLAS'07: Proceedings of the ACM Workshop on Programming Languages and Analysis for Security*, 2007.

[34] J. A. Painter. Effectiveness of an optimizing compiler for arithmetic expressions. *SIGPLAN Notices*, 5, 1970.

[35] R. Pibernik, Y. Zhang, F. Kerschbaum, and A. Schröpfer. Secure collaborative supply chain planning and inverse optimization - the jels model. *European Journal of Operational Research*, 208(1), 2011.

[36] A. Schröpfer and F. Kerschbaum. Demo: secure computation in javascript. In *CCS'11: Proceedings of the 18th ACM Conference on Computer and Communications Security*, 2011.

[37] A. Schröpfer and F. Kerschbaum. Forecasting run-times of secure two-party computation. In *QEST'11: Proceedings of the 8th International Conference on Quantitative Evaluation of Systems*, 2011.

[38] A. Schröpfer, F. Kerschbaum, and G. Müller. L1 – an intermediate language for mixed-protocol secure computation. In *COMPSAC'11: Proceedings of the 35th IEEE Computer Software and Applications Conference*, 2011.

[39] A. C. Yao. Protocols for secure computations. In *FOCS'82: Proceedings of the 23rd IEEE Symposium on Foundations of Computer Science*, 1982.

Efficient Discovery of De-identification Policies Through a Risk-Utility Frontier

Weiyi Xia
EECS Dept.
Vanderbilt University
Nashville, TN, USA
weiyi.xia@vanderbilt.edu

Raymond Heatherly
Biomedical Informatics Dept.
Vanderbilt University
Nashville, TN, USA
r.heatherly@vanderbilt.edu

Xiaofeng Ding
Computer Science Dept.
University of South Australia
Mawson Lakes, SA, Australia
Xiaofeng.Ding@unisa.edu.au

Jiuyong Li
Computer Science Dept.
University of South Australia
Mawson Lakes, SA, Australia
Jiuyong.Li@unisa.edu.au

Bradley Malin
Biomedical Informatics Dept.
Vanderbilt University
Nashville, TN, USA
b.malin@vanderbilt.edu

ABSTRACT

Modern information technologies enable organizations to capture large quantities of person-specific data while providing routine services. Many organizations hope, or are legally required, to share such data for secondary purposes (e.g., validation of research findings) in a de-identified manner. In previous work, it was shown de-identification policy alternatives could be modeled on a lattice, which could be searched for policies that met a prespecified risk threshold (e.g., likelihood of re-identification). However, the search was limited in several ways. First, its definition of utility was syntactic - based on the level of the lattice - and not semantic - based on the actual changes induced in the resulting data. Second, the threshold may not be known in advance.

The goal of this work is to build the optimal set of policies that trade-off between privacy risk (R) and utility (U), which we refer to as a R-U frontier. To model this problem, we introduce a semantic definition of utility, based on information theory, that is compatible with the lattice representation of policies. To solve the problem, we initially build a set of policies that define a frontier. We then use a probability-guided heuristic to search the lattice for policies likely to update the frontier. To demonstrate the effectiveness of our approach, we perform an empirical analysis with the Adult dataset of the UCI Machine Learning Repository. We show that our approach can construct a frontier closer to optimal than competitive approaches by searching a smaller number of policies. In addition, we show that a frequently followed de-identification policy (i.e., the Safe Harbor standard of the HIPAA Privacy Rule) is suboptimal in comparison to the frontier discovered by our approach.

Categories and Subject Descriptors

H.2.m [**Information Systems**]: Database Management—*Miscellaneous*; K.4.1 [**Computers and Society**]: Public Policy Issues—*Privacy*

General Terms

Experimentation, Management, Security

Keywords

De-identification, Optimization, Policy, Privacy

1. INTRODUCTION

In the age of big data, organizations from a wide range of domains (e.g., finance, healthcare, homeland security, and social media) will accumulate a substantial quantity of detailed personal data [7, 25]. These large-scale resources will support the development of novel applications and refinement of innovative services. For instance, healthcare facilities are increasingly adopting electronic medical record systems and high-throughput genotyping technologies, which, in turn, have enabled the discovery of personalized treatment regimens [34]. At the same time, there are many pressures to publish person-level data to support information reuse and transparency (e.g., [3, 18, 46]) and adhere to federal requirements (e.g., [29]). While publication enables broad access, there are also concerns that it can violate personal privacy rights [5, 17, 31].

To mitigate privacy threats, various laws and regulations recommend that personal data be de-identified before dissemination (e.g., the EU Data Protection Directive [1] and the US Health Insurance Portability and Accountability Act (HIPAA) [45]). The concept of de-identification is somewhat subjective [35], but is often tied to the notion of re-identification (oftentimes referred to as identity disclosure [21]) risk. While we recognize there are concerns that de-identified data may be re-identified [30], it remains a core principle of privacy regulation [41]. Technically, an organization may adopt various approaches to accomplish de-identification. In this research, we focus on the application of generalization, a common strategy in de-identification policies [12]. The application of such policies has a direct influence on the usability of the resulting data [32]. As a consequence, it is critical that the policy selected for de-identification appropriately balance the competing needs of minimizing risk (R) and maximizing utility (U).

As we recount in the following section, there have been several attempts to achieve this balance. The majority have focused on optimization in the context of anonymization (e.g., k-anonymity [4]), but this is a more rigid formalism than de-identification [28]. Anonymization provides guarantees of protection for each record in a dataset, but de-identification is often a rules-driven policy (e.g., "recode all ages over 90 as 90+"). As such, previous optimization approaches are not as flexible in their policy definitions. To the best of our knowledge, the only work that provides a data structure for such an optimization is the work in [6]. However, their work is limited in several crucial ways. First, it models data utility from a syntactic perspective (e.g., "How many ages are generalized?") as opposed to a semantic perspective (e.g., "How does the generalization of age influence the distribution of patients?"). Second, it does not allow for a complete analysis of the tradeoff between privacy and utility. Rather, it assumes that a privacy risk threshold is known (or can be computed) *a priori*, whereupon it then searches for alternative strategies with risk no greater than the threshold.

As we show in this work, the framework of [6] can be extended to overcome this limitation. To do so, we introduce a semantic utility function and model the de-identification policy search problem as a dual-objective optimization. Thus, our goal is to detect a set of policies that form an R-U frontier, which offers a collection of mutually exclusive de-identification policies. The visualization of such a frontier should provide intuition into the tradeoff between utility and risk for policy alternatives. While the space of possible policies is too large to perform a systematic exhaustive in practical time, we introduce an efficient strategy to navigate the policy space and construct an approximation of the frontier. More specifically, our work has three primary contributions:

- **Problem formalization:** We provide a rigorous definition of the de-identification policy frontier discovery (DPFD) problem. We show how this problem relates to a lattice of policies and measures for re-identification risk and data utility.

- **Search Strategies:** Based on the policy lattice, we develop a novel search strategy, guided by probability-based heuristics, that can construct an approximate frontier efficiently.

- **Empirical Evaluation:** We perform an empirical study on the Adult dataset and demonstrate that our approach is more effective than a competitive search strategy, in terms of the frontier discovered and time required to do so. Moreover, we illustrate how a common health data de-identification policy (i.e., HIPAA Safe Harbor) is suboptimal to the frontier discovered by our policy.

The remainder of this paper is organized as follows. In Section 2, we review related work in optimization strategies for data privacy, with a particular focus on anonymization and statistical disclosure control frameworks. In Section 3, we formalize the DPFD problem and several algorithms for

solving the problem. In Section 4, we present an empirical evaluation of our search strategy. In Section 5, we discuss the contributions and limitations of this work and in Section 6 we offer several conclusions.

2. RELATED WORK

In this section, we review frameworks and strategies for optimizing the search for anonymization and de-identification solutions. This topic is a portion of the broader issue of privacy-preserving data publishing, for which we direct readers to [15] for an excellent survey.

2.1 Search for Anonymization Solutions

Many variations of formal anonymization have been proposed, but the literature primarily focuses on optimization for the k-anonymity protection model [40]. In effect, k-anonymization is a special case of de-identification and thus illustrates the complexity of our problem. k-anonymization dictates that each published record must be equivalent to $k-1$ other published records. This technique is often applied to a quasi-identifier (QI), which is the set of attributes (e.g., date of birth and residential ZIP code) that link a record to a resource containing explicit identifiers (e.g., personal name) [9]. QI attributes have traditionally been formalized as domain generalization hierarchies (DGHs) that can be systematically enumerated [39]. However, the search for the k-anonymous solution which minimizes the total quantity of generalization is an NP-hard problem [2, 27], which has led to a large and growing collection of search strategies [8]. Here, we review the most relevant to our work.

[39] introduced the concept of full-domain generalization in which all values of each attribute are generalized to the same level of the DGH. This paper also proposed greedy heuristics to generate k-anonymous solutions. [33] showed the generalization space maps to a partially ordered lattice and introduced a binary search method, which guarantees the solution is optimal according to a certain cost metric.

By relaxing the constraint of mapping the entire domain to the same level of the DGH, [19] defined the generalization solution space as all arbitrary partitions on the ordered set of values in a single attribute's domain (e.g., age 14 is reported as 10-15 while age 16 is reported as 16-30). Given that the size of the search space is exponential in the size of a QI's domain, exhaustive search strategies are impractical. Thus, [19] proposed a genetic algorithm, to perform a partial search of the generalization space. This work is also notable because it represents QIs and their generalization as bit-strings, a model we adopt in this paper. Since genetic algorithms do not provide a guarantee about the optimality of the solution and are often associated with long runtimes, [16] restructured the space of [19] to a tree and provided a systematic search algorithm using pruning and rearrangement to find an optimal k-anonymization in a practical amount of time. [23] further expanded the solution space to permit arbitrary partitioning of each attribute domain without forcing a total order on it. Based on this partitioning, they proposed a novel method to create a partition enumeration tree and search algorithms to efficiently discover the optimal anonymization solution.

In all the generalization strategies mentioned above, each attribute is generalized independently (i.e., a single-dimension attribute domain). Thus any specific value in each domain is generalized in the same way in every tuple of the dataset. [22] extended this model to a multi-dimensional space by generalizing values of tuples in the dataset. A greedy partitioning strategy was introduced to discover a k-anonymization solution. While flexible (e.g., females with age 14 are expressed as [female, 14] while males with age 14 are expressed as [male, 10-14]), the expansion of the search space provides more generalization options. As a result, the anonymized dataset can be confusing for users because the same value of a QI attribute can be mapped to different values in the same anonymized dataset.

2.2 Search for De-identification Solutions

As mentioned earlier, the work most closely related to ours is that of [6]. The space of possible solutions is modeled as the lattice introduced in [19]. However, the privacy goal is not k-anonymization. Instead, risk is modeled as the expected number of records likely to be re-identified under a certain policy (e.g., HIPAA Safe Harbor).

The lattice is searched for policies that have risk no worse than the prespecified policy. The search process is accomplished through a bisecting search. Our work generalizes and extends this framework. A fundamental difference is that [6] searches for policies with minimum cost that satisfy the predefined risk, whereas in this paper the search is a dual-objective optimization problem.

2.3 Frontiers and Data Privacy

The idea of frontier optimization for privacy protection derives from the Risk-Utility (or R-U) confidentiality map [11] which was first used to assess different statistical disclosure control (SDC) methods based on the optimal tradeoff between risk and utility. [37] introduced a framework that maps SDC methods to an R-U confidentiality map to determine optimal parameterizations for such techniques. Based on this framework, [36] performed an empirical analysis of SDC methods for standard tabular outputs(e.g., swapping, rounding). [42] also adopted the R-U confidentiality map as an optimal criterion for data release. Given its roots in the statistical domain, the R-U confidentiality map was initially applied to protection strategies based on perturbation (e.g., randomization), as opposed to the generalization techniques more commonly found in de-identification.

In the context of data anonymization, the R-U confidentiality map is composed of a set of scattering points mapped from a generalization space instead of a simple curve in previous SDC applications. To explicitly represent the optimal solution curve in the R-U space, the concept of frontier is introduced to the R-U confidentiality framework [24]. It was demonstrated that k-anonymization can be framed as a dual-objective optimization in the R-U space. [24] uses the algorithm in [22] to discover anonymization solutions to map to the R-U space. [26] adopted R-U confidentiality map to transaction data anonymization. [10] also framed k-anonymization as a dual-objective optimization problem. In their framework, the solution space is the lattice structure introduced by [19], which is searched using a genetic algorithm. This approach, however, has several limitations in comparison to the strategy we offer in this paper. In particular, the genetic algorithm is slow and is not clearly guided by the semantics (e.g., risk and utility) of its solutions. By contrast, our algorithm is a combination of systematic and stochastic search and uses several monotonicity cost properties on the lattice to prune large sections from consideration.

3. METHODS

In this section, we present the de-identification policy frontier discovery (DPFD) problem. First, we define a policy search space, a mapping of the policy space to the R-U space, and the formalization of the search problem. Second, we introduce several search algorithms to systematically explore the policy space.

3.1 De-identification Policy

We assume the data to be published is organized in a table for which the explicit identifying attributes (e.g., personal name and Social Security number) have already been suppressed. The remaining attributes of the table constitute the QI and each tuple corresponds to a distinct individual. To de-identify the data, the specific QI values will either i) remain in their specific state or ii) be recoded with more general, but semantically consistent, values.

Different generalization models induce different de-identification polices. In this work, we require a total order in the domain of each QI attribute and apply a *full-subtree generalization* model [22], which means that the values in a domain are mapped to a set of non-overlapping intervals. As such, a mapping function can be defined by the corresponding partition on the domain of a QI attribute.

Formally, a de-identification policy corresponds to the set of domain partitions (Definition 3.1) for each QI attribute (Definition 3.2).

DEFINITION 3.1 (DOMAIN PARTITION). *Let D be a totally ordered domain and p be a set of intervals on D: $p = \{I_1, \ldots, I_l\}$, where l is the number of intervals. p is a partition on D if $\forall i \neq j, I_i \cap I_j = \varnothing$ and $\bigcup_i^l I_i = D$.*

DEFINITION 3.2 (DE-IDENTIFICATION POLICY). *Let $Q = \{Q_1, \ldots, Q_n\}$ be a set of quasi-identifying attributes. Let us assume D_i is the domain of Q_i and p_i is a partition on D_i. The set $\{p_1, \ldots, p_n\}$ is a de-identification policy.*

Figure 1 provides an example of a de-identification policy. The set of QI attributes is {*Age, Gender, ZIP*} and the domains are {1, ..., 10}, {*male, female*}, and {37201, ..., 37229}, respectively. In this policy *Age, Gender*, and *ZIP* are mapped to the aggregated groups: [1-2], [3-6] and [7-10]; [*female*] and [*male*]; and [37201, ..., 37228] and [37229], respectively. This policy is valid because the aggregated groups of values for each QI compose a partition of the corresponding domain. By contrast, a mapping of ages to [1 − 5] and [3 − 10] does not constitute a valid policy because the intervals overlap (i.e., 3, 4, or 5 could be in either interval).

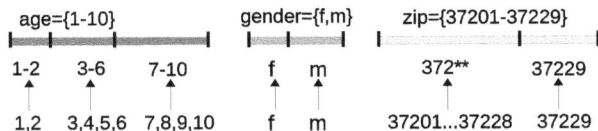

Figure 1: An example of a de-identification policy defined over three quasi-identifying attributes, {*Age, Gender, ZIP*}.

We use the full subtree generalization model because it offers several advantages over alternative models. First, as

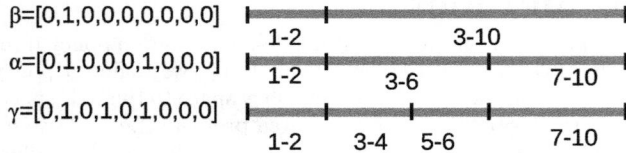

Figure 2: An example of *GLB*. β is a *GLB* of α, while α is a *GLB* of γ.

shown in [6], it enables representation of fine-grained policies, as well as common policies encountered in the real world (e.g., HIPAA Safe Harbor). Second, the set of policies can be structured as a lattice of generalizations which can be systematically searched. Third, it is straightforward to interpret how a policy changes the syntax of the data.

3.2 Policy Space Formalization

3.2.1 Policy Representation

In our model, policies are modeled as bit-strings. To characterize the translation, let n be the number of values in the domain of a QI attribute. After enforcing a total order on the values, they are mapped to a bit-string of size $n-1$. The original domain is represented by a bit-string of 1's, whereas a bit of 0 indicates a demarcation in the partition has been removed to widen an interval[1] (i.e., values have been generalized). For example, the bit-string for *Age* in Figure 1 is $[0, 1, 0, 0, 0, 1, 0, 0, 0]$.

A de-identification policy α is the concatenation of the bit-string for each QI attribute. In the remainder of this paper, we use the term de-identification policy to refer to both the actual policy and its bit-string representation when the meaning is unambiguous. For reference, we use $\alpha[i]$ to represent the value of the ith bit.

3.2.2 Partial Order of Policies

The policy space contains all possible bit-string permutations, which are partially ordered. We use $\prec$ to refer to the ordering on two policies as follows:

DEFINITION 3.3 ($\prec$). *Given policies α and β, we say $\alpha \prec \beta$ if*

$$\forall i(\alpha[i] = 1 \to \beta[i] = 1) \land \exists i(\alpha[i] = 0 \land \beta[i] = 1)$$

By this definition, α is more general than β because we can derive β by making smaller intervals in the partition (i.e., flipping bits from 0 to 1). As an example, Figure 2 depicts three policies for Age. It can be seen that α is the same policy as γ without the demarcation between ages 4 and 5. Similarly, β removes the demarcation between ages 6 and 7. As such, $\beta \prec \alpha \prec \gamma$ and the de-identified data derived from γ will be at least as specific as the data derived from α. We define the *Greatest Lower Bound (GLB)* over the policy space as follows:

DEFINITION 3.4 (GREATEST LOWER BOUND (GLB)). *Policy α is a GLB of policy β, if*

$$\exists i(\alpha[i] = 0 \land \beta[i] = 1 \land \forall j(j \neq i \to \beta[j] = \alpha[j])).$$

---
[1]The final value in the domain is implicit in the partition.

In Figure 2, β is a *GLB* of α while α is a *GLB* of γ.

The most general policy (i.e., all 0's) and the most specific policy (i.e., all 1's), are referred to as *top* and *bottom*, respectively.

3.2.3 Policy Lattice

Based on the partial ordering, the policy space can be structured in a lattice. An example of such a lattice is depicted in Figure 3. The nodes in this lattice are composed of all bit-strings of length n. There is a directed edge from policy α to policy β, if, and only if, α is a *GLB* of β.

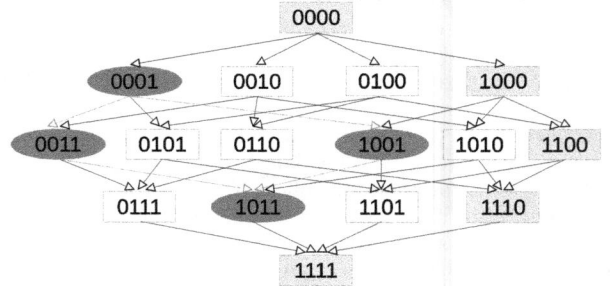

Figure 3: An example of a de-identification policy lattice with five quasi-identifying values. Rectangular nodes depict a maximal chain, while oval nodes represent a sublattice.

In preparation for our policy search algorithms, we define two types of subgraphs over the lattice: 1) chain and 2) sublattice. A chain (Definition 3.5) is a totally ordered subset in the lattice. A maximal chain is one that is not a proper subset of any other chain.

DEFINITION 3.5 (CHAIN). *A sequence of policies C: $\alpha_1 \prec \alpha_2 \prec \cdots \prec \alpha_n$ is a chain if, and only if, $\forall i$, α_i is a GLB of α_{i+1}. The chain is a maximal chain if, and only if, α_1 is top and α_n is bottom.*

In Figure 3, the rectangular nodes (i.e., $[0, 0, 0, 0]$, $[1, 0, 0, 0]$, $[1, 1, 0, 0]$, $[1, 1, 1, 0]$, $[1, 1, 1, 1]$) constitute a maximal chain.

A sublattice (Definition 3.6) is a subgraph *i*) bounded by an upper node and lower node on some chain and *ii*) contains every node in the set of all chains between them. Any two policies with a chain between them can define a sublattice.

DEFINITION 3.6 (SUBLATTICE). *Given policies α and β, if $\alpha \prec \beta$, then the set $\{p|\alpha \prec p \land p \prec \beta\}$ is a sublattice. This set is referred to as sublattice (α, β), where α and β are the upper and lower policies of the sublattice, respectively.*

An example of a sublattice is shown in the oval nodes of Figure 3. Here *sublattice*($[0, 0, 0, 1]$, $[1, 0, 1, 1]$) defines the set $\{[0, 0, 0, 1], [0, 0, 1, 1], [1, 0, 0, 1], [1, 0, 1, 1]\}$.

3.3 Policy Frontier Search Problem

3.3.1 Risk and Utility Measurement

To map a policy to the R-U space, we assess its risk and utility with respect to the data under consideration for dissemination. To enable an efficient search, it is crucial to ensure the order of risk and utility scores are consistent with the natural partial order in the policy space. This notion is formalized through the following order homomorphisms:

DEFINITION 3.7 (RISK ORDER HOMOMORPHISM). *Given a policy lattice S and a data table T, a risk function $R_T(\alpha)$ satisfies a risk order homomorphism if $\forall \alpha, \beta \in S, \alpha \prec \beta \to R_T(\alpha) \leq R_T(\beta)$.*

DEFINITION 3.8 (UTILITY ORDER HOMOMORPHISM). *Given policy lattice S and a data table T, an information loss function $U_T(\alpha)$ satisfies a utility order homomorphism if $\forall \alpha, \beta \in S, \alpha \prec \beta \to U_T(\alpha) \geq U_T(\beta)$,*

3.4 Policy Frontier

By applying risk and utility functions that satisfy their respective homomorphisms, each policy in the lattice is mapped into the R-U space to be searched for frontier policies.

To define a *frontier*, we introduce the notion of a strictly dominated relationship:

DEFINITION 3.9 (STRICTLY DOMINATED). *Given policies α and β and a data table T, α is strictly dominated by β if*

$$(R_T(\beta) \leqslant R_T(\alpha)) \wedge (U_T(\beta) \leqslant U_T(\alpha))$$

and

$$(R_T(\beta) < R_T(\alpha)) \vee (U_T(\beta) < U_T(\alpha)).$$

Informally, policy β *strictly dominates* policy α if both risk and utility values of β are *no greater than* the corresponding values of α and at least one value of β is strictly less that of α. The dominated relationship defines a partial order in the R-U space. Based on this partial order, the frontier corresponds to the set of policies for which we have found no dominating policies:

DEFINITION 3.10 (FRONTIER). *Given a policy lattice S, the frontier is the non-dominated set of policies $\{\alpha | \alpha \in S \wedge \nexists \beta (\beta \in S \wedge \beta$ strictly dominates $\alpha)\}$.*

The goal of the de-identification policy frontier discovery (DPFD) problem is to find all frontier policies in a lattice.

3.5 Search Algorithms

The size of a typical policy lattice is too large for an exhaustive, systematic search. Thus, we developed two heuristic approaches: 1) Random Chain Search and 2) Heuristic Sublattice Search.

3.5.1 Random Chain

The first strategy is called the Random Chain Search (RCS) and is shown in Algorithm 1.

The process begins by assigning an arbitrary non-dominated set of policies in the lattice to the frontier, which is accomplished through *InitializeFrontier*().[2] Next, we iteratively select maximal random chains, via the *selectRandomChain*(), and update the frontier with policies on the chains. This process iterates until n policies have been searched. Updating the frontier is accomplished through the function *updateFrontier*(f,α), which attempts to revise the frontier f with each policy α in the chain. If the frontier does not contain policies that dominate α, it is inserted into the frontier. The frontier then drops all policies dominated by α. As an example of this function, consider Figure 4(a).

---

[2] The initial frontier may affect the performance of the search; however, this issue is outside the scope of this paper.

Algorithm 1 Random Chain Search (*RCS*)

Input: n, the maximum number of policies to estimate; L, the length of a policy; T, a dataset
Output: f, the frontier policies
1: $i \leftarrow 0$
2: $f \leftarrow$ InitializeFrontier() {This function returns a non-dominated set of policies, including *top* and *bottom*.}
3: **while** $i < n$ **do**
4:     $c \leftarrow$ selectRandomChain() {This function begins at *bottom*. It iteratively selects a policy at random from the GLB, to which it proceeds until it reaches *top*. It returns all the policies selected.}
5:     **for all** α in c **do**
6:        $f \leftarrow$ updateFrontier(f,α)
7:     **end for**
8:     $i \leftarrow i + L$ {L is the number of policies on the chain}
9: **end while**
10: **return** f

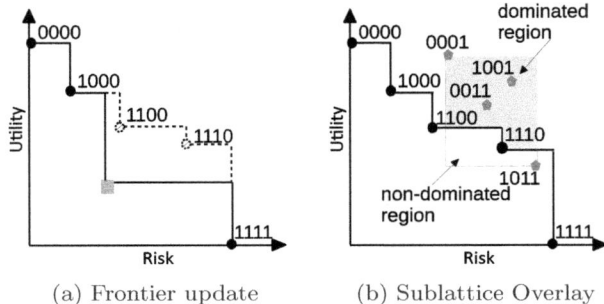

(a) Frontier update   (b) Sublattice Overlay

Figure 4: An example of updating the frontier in the R-U space using policies from Figure 3. The current frontier is composed of policies mapped to the stair-step curve. In 4(a), the policy mapped to the square will be added to the frontier because it dominates policies currently on the frontier (i.e., [1, 1, 0, 0] and [1, 1, 1, 0]), which will be removed. In 4(b), the rectangle represents the bounding region of the R-U mapping of policies in sublattice ([0, 0, 0, 1], [1, 0, 1, 1])

3.5.2 Sublattice Heuristic Search

The RCS algorithm is naïve in that it assumes all regions of the lattice are equally likely to update the frontier. However, this is not the case, and we suspect sublattices can be compared to the frontier to search more efficiently. Consider, given a frontier f, we can draw a stair-step curve in the R-U space that connects all policies on the frontier. An example of such a curve is depicted in Figures 4(a) and 4(b). It is clear that any policy mapped to the region above the curve will be dominated by at least one policy on the frontier. Additionally, any policy mapped to the region below the frontier will always update the frontier. Thus, this curve divides the R-U space into two regions: 1) dominated and 2) non-dominated.

Given *sublattice*(α, β), it can be proven that the risk and utility values of policies in the sublattice are bounded in a rectangle defined by the risk and utility values of policies α and β, which we call the *bounding region*. In other words, all policies in the sublattice will have risk in the range $[R_T(\alpha),$ $R_T(\beta)]$ and utility in the range $[U_T(\beta), U_T(\alpha)]$.[3] For example, in Figure 3, all policies in $sublattice([0, 0, 0, 1], [1, 0,$ $1, 1])$ are mapped to the rectangular area bounded by the R-U mapping of the *top* and *bottom* policies of the frontier in Figure 4(b).

To leverage this fact from a probabilistic perspective, we assume that the policies in a sublattice are uniformly distributed in the bounding rectangle. This implies the probability that a policy in a sublattice updates the frontier is the proportion of the lattice's bounding rectangle which falls below the curve of the frontier. Formally, imagine policies on the frontier f are mapped to a set of R-U points that are ordered increasingly by risk $\{(r_0, u_0), \ldots, (r_h, u_h)\}$, where h is the number of polices on the frontier. Now, given *sublattice*(α, β), let us assume the policies α and β are mapped to points (r_α, u_α) and (r_β, u_β), respectively.

We compute the area of the bounding region as $(r_\beta - r_\alpha)$ $\times (u_\alpha - u_\beta)$. If we draw a line parallel to the y-axis at each point of the frontier in the R-U space, then the area of the non-dominated region is composed of the resulting rectangles. More specifically, if $r_i < r_\alpha < r_{i+1}$ and $r_j < r_\beta$ $< r_{j+1}$, then the area of the non-dominated region is

$$ND(s, f) = \sum_{k=i}^{j} \max(0, \quad (u_k - u_\beta) \times$$
$$(\min(r_\beta, r_{k+1}) - \max(r_k, r_\alpha)))$$

Finally, the probability that a policy in the sublattice can update the frontier is computed as:

$$H(s, f) = \frac{ND(s, f)}{(r_\beta - r_\alpha) \times (u_t - u_\beta)} \qquad (1)$$

For example, in Figure 4(b), the probability that any policy in *sublattice*$([0, 0, 0, 1], [1, 0, 1, 1])$ can update the frontier is the ratio between the area below the step curve in the rectangle (*non-dominated region*) and the entire rectangle (*bounding region*).

Based on this observation, we introduce a second search algorithm called the Sublattice Heuristic Search (SHS). The steps of the process are shown in Algorithm 2, which we describe here.

As in RCS, this algorithm begins with a call to *intializeFrontier*(), which instantiates the frontier f as a non-dominated policy set. Next, the algorithm instantiates a list to maintain memory of which policies (or sections of the lattice) have been pruned due to dominance by the frontier. At this point, the algorithm iteratively selects a sublattice (details in the Appendix) and tailors its process depending on the following conditions:

- **Condition 1:** If the entire bounding region of a sublattice is in the dominated region of the frontier, the sublattice is pruned.

- **Condition 2:** If the entire bounding region of a sublattice is in the non-dominated region of the frontier, we search a random maximal chain of the sublattice. Though any of the policies in the sublattice can improve the current frontier, they may dominate one another. Moreover, the entire sublattice can contain a

---

[3] A proof sketch for this claim is as follows. Any policy γ in sublattice(α, β) satisfies $\alpha \prec \gamma \prec \beta$ and $R_T(\alpha)$ and $U_T(\alpha)$ satisfies the order homomorphisms. Thus, $R_T(\alpha) \leqslant R_T(\gamma)$ $\leqslant R_T(\beta)$ and $U_T(\alpha) \geqslant U_T(\gamma) \geqslant U_T(\beta)$.

Algorithm 2 Sublattice Heuristic Search (*SHS*)

Input: n, the maximal number of polices to assess; TH, the threshold for searching a sublattice; L, the length of a policy; T, a dataset
Output: f, list of frontier policies of the searched policies
1: $i \leftarrow 0$
2: $f \leftarrow$ initializeFrontier()
3: *prunedlist* $\leftarrow \emptyset$
4: **while** $i < n$ **do**
5:    *sublattice* $\leftarrow$ generateRandomSublattice(*prunedlist*)
6:    $p \leftarrow H(sublattice, f)$ {Equation 1}
7:    **if** $p \geq TH$ **then**
8:       $c \leftarrow$ selectRandomChain(*sublattice*)
9:       **for all** α in c **do**
10:          $f \leftarrow$ updateFrontier(f, α)
11:       **end for**
12:       $i \leftarrow i + $ length(c)
13:    **else**
14:       **if** $p = 0$ **then**
15:          *prunedlist.append*(*sublattice*)
16:       **end if**
17:       $i \leftarrow i + 2$
18:    **end if**
19: **end while**
20: **return** f

---

substantial number of policies, which would make a complete search infeasible. By contrast, a maximal chain is the maximal set of policies in the sublattice that can be guaranteed to be on the new frontier.

- **Condition 3:** If neither of the previous conditions are satisfied, we use the update probability to determine if the sublattice is worth further searching. Specifically, if the update probability is greater than a threshold, we search a maximal chain of the sublattice, selected at random. Otherwise, no search is initiated.

4. EXPERIMENTS

4.1 Evaluation Framework

4.1.1 Real World Policy: HIPAA Safe Harbor

To perform a comparison with an existing rules-based de-identification policy, we compare our frontier to the Safe Harbor policy of the HIPAA Privacy Rule. This policy enumerates eighteen specific attributes that must be generalized or suppressed from a dataset before it is considered de-identified. Of importance to this study, we focus on Safe Harbor's perspective of demographics. For such features, it states that 1) all ZIP codes must be rolled back to their initial three characters and that codes with populations of less than 20,000 individuals must be grouped into a single code and 2) all ages over 90 must be recoded as a single group of 90+. Safe Harbor does not prevent the dissemination of gender or ethnicity, but we include these features because they are common demographics, which could be generalized in favor of age and geocodes [13].

4.1.2 Evaluation Dataset

For evaluation, we use the *Adult* dataset from the UCI Machine Learning Repository [14]. This dataset consists of

32,561 tuples without missing values. There are fourteen fields included in this dataset, but many (e.g., *occupation*) are related to economic analysis and are not considered for comparison with Safe Harbor or other de-identification policies. Thus, we use the demographics {*Age, Gender, Race*} as the QI attributes.

To enable a comparison with Safe Harbor, we synthesize and append an additional attribute, which corresponds to 5-digit ZIP codes. To do so, we combine the available demographics data from *Adult* with demographic information obtained from the US Census Bureau's 2000 Census Tables PCT12A-G [44] to provide each tuple with a valid Tennessee 5-digit ZIP code. Additionally, since the *Age* field in *Adult* appears to have aggregated all ages 90 and above to be [90+], we use the 2000 Census Tables to disaggregate these ages into years 90 through 120. This disaggregation affects 43 tuples.

4.1.3 Risk Computation

To compute risk, we adopt the disclosure measure in [6], which is based on the distinguishability metric proposed by [43]. This measure assumes a tuple in the generalized dataset contributes an amount of risk inversely proportional to the size of the population group that matches its QI values. Again, the population information is based on the PCT12A-G Census tables.

For example, imagine a record in the Adult dataset is [39, male, white, 37203]. This record is unique in the dataset, but the census tables show there are 5 people in the region with the same demographics. As a result, this record contributes a risk of 0.2. Further details on this risk computation can be found in [6].

The disclosure risk of the entire generalized dataset corresponds to the sum of the risk of each record. To ensure the risk score for a dataset is normalized between [0, 1], we divide this sum by the risk value for the original dataset. This dataset has no generalization and constitutes the maximum risk for all policies in the lattice. Given a dataset D, a population P, the formal definition of the risk for generalized dataset D' is:

$$risk(D', P) = \frac{\sum_{d' \in D'} \left(\frac{1}{g(d')} \right)}{max(risk)} \quad (2)$$

$$max(risk) = \sum_{d \in D} \left(\frac{1}{g(d)} \right), \quad (3)$$

where $g(d')$ is the size of the population group in P with the set of quasi-identifiers of record $d \in D'$. [6] demonstrated this risk measurement satisfies the order homomorphism.

4.1.4 Utility Computation

To compute utility we use an information loss measure. In particular, we use KL-divergence to measure the loss incurred by a generalized dataset with respect to its original form. This measure satisfies the order homomorphism constraint.[4] Formally, the KL-divergence is computed as:

$$D_{KL}(P \parallel Q) = \sum_i P(i) \ln \frac{P(i)}{Q(i)} \quad (4)$$

---

[4]The proof of this homomorphism is withheld due to space constraints.

where $P(i)$ and $Q(i)$ are the probability distributions of the quasi-identifying values in the original and de-identified datasets, respectively.

While $P(i)$ is computed from the frequency of quasi-identifying values in the original dataset, $Q(i)$ is an approximation. Specifically, $Q(i)$ is based on the assumption that if several values are generalized to a single group, then the corresponding records are uniformly distributed across the group. For example, imagine the quasi-identifier set is {*Age, Gender*} and there is a record in the generalized dataset [*Age* = [1-2], *Gender* = [male, female]] with a frequency of m. Then, each possible value (i.e., [1, male], [1, female], [2, male], and [2, female]) is assigned a frequency of $m/4$. Following [20], we use the standard convention that $\ln 0 = 0$. Based on this definition, the information loss measure is in the range of [0, 1] and there is no need for normalization.

4.2 Results

4.2.1 Efficiency of the Search Strategies

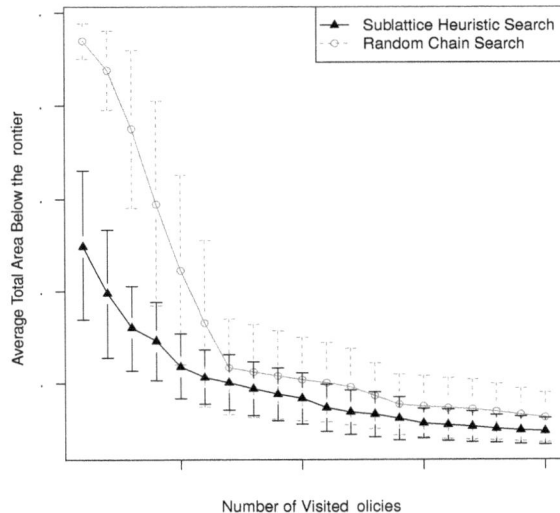

Figure 5: The efficiency of search strategies on the Adult dataset as a function of number of policies searched.

To conduct experiments on efficiency, we provide a search budget of 14,780 total policies to search. This value represents 20 maximal chain searches (i.e., the policy lattice is composed of 739 levels).

First, we evaluated the efficiency of the search algorithms. We assessed the progress of the algorithms over 20 complete runs. There is minimal variance in actual time to completion between the algorithms, but a significant difference in *how quickly* the algorithms converge a high-quality frontiers.

To illustrate this finding, we established checkpoints during the runtime of the experiments. At each checkpoint (e.g., every 100 policies examined), the current average area under the frontier was determined (i.e., smaller areas illustrate better frontiers). The result (mean and the standard deviation) of this evaluation is depicted in Figure 5. The result shows that the SHS method dominates the RCS. In particular, after computing 100 policies, the average result of the sublattice search is 28% better than the average result of the random chain search. This result indicates that the

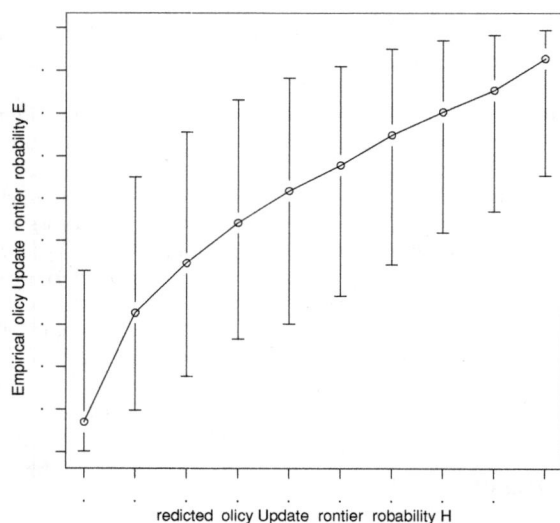

Figure 6: An empirical evaluation of the sublattice heuristic H().

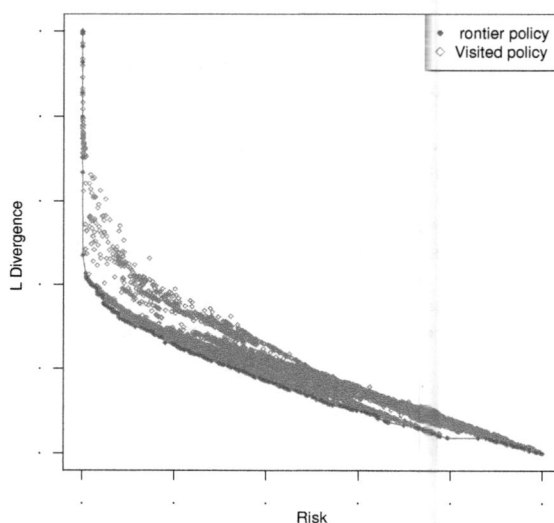

Figure 7: Policies searched and frontier discovered through one run of the SHS algorithm.

SHS method is particularly efficient when a quick solution is needed.

Next, we evaluated the effect of the sublattice heuristic (i.e., area under the frontier) upon searching. In this experiment, we initialized the frontier to a random maximal chain and subsequently generated 24240 random sublattices. For each sublattice, we applied $H()$ to predict the probability that searching a random chain through the sublattice yields frontier updates. We then picked a random chain and computed the empirical probability $E()$ of a policy in a random chain in the sublattice updating the frontier in terms of the ratio of the number of policies that actually updated the frontier and the total number of policies in the searched chain. Finally, we analyze the correlation between the predicted probability $H()$ and the empirical probability $E()$.

We first run a linear regression over the aggregated set of $H()$ and $E()$ values. In particular, we partition the sublattices into 10 groups based on the value of $H()$ (e.g., lattices with $H() \in [0, 0.1]$ are placed in the first group). The representative $H()$ value of each group is assigned to the upper bound of the interval. For the set of lattices in each group, the average and confidence interval of the ratio of number of policies that update the frontier to the total number of policies are computed. The results are depicted in Figure 6, where the mean of the actual update ratio clearly increases with the predicted frontier probability. This result suggests that the driving intuition behind the SHS heuristic was reasonable with respect to the *Adult* dataset.

To further demonstrate the relationship between the probabilities $H()$ and $E()$, we ran a linear regression and a correlation test on the set of values. The Pearson's product-moment correlation coefficient of $H()$ and $E()$ is 0.8643536, with a p-value of 2.2×10^{-16}. This result indicates that the actual probability a policy in the path of a sublattice will improve the current frontier is positively correlated with the estimated probability based on our heuristic.

4.2.2 Quality of Frontier Policies

Next, we evaluated the quality of search results. The re-

sults in the previous experiments indicated that SHS is a superior search strategy to RCS, so we continue our evaluation using only SHS.

For illustration, Figure 7 shows the policies the SHS algorithm visit and the frontier constructed. Again, the algorithm visited 14,780 policies, which resulted in a frontier composed of 796 policies. Approximately 750 of the policies on the frontier represent unique R-U values.

We then compared the frontier policies returned by SHS to the Safe Harbor de-identification policy. Figure 8 indicates that within the *Adult* dataset, 24 out of 796 policies (i.e., the green squares on the frontier) strictly dominate the Safe Harbor policy. The average Euclidean distance between each of these 24 policies and Safe Harbor policy in the R-space is 0.025. This indicates that Safe Harbor policy is very near in the $[0, 1] \times [0, 1]$ R-U space.

After investigating the policies which dominated Safe Harbor, we found that 23 of the policies were from one chain of the same sublattice. This observation indicates that the frontier policies found by SHS can provide a user with highly related policies which should be useful in practice. We show examples of policies that dominate Safe Harbor in Figure 9. [5] Here, we illustrate through two policies (A and B), the actual semantic differences proposed by our discovered policies. We note that for brevity, we abbreviate the enumeration of ZIP code generalizations in both Policies A and B. We further note that Policy A is one policy in the previously mentioned group of 23 along the same chain, while Policy B is the lone unrelated policy. While each policy generalizes *Age* and *ZIP* to different levels, the primary difference is the generalization of Race and Gender. Where Policy A generalizes "Black or African American" with all other races, it leaves Gender unmodified. Policy B, however, generalizes "Black or African American alone" with "Asian", "American Indian and Alaska Native alone", and "Native Hawaiian and Other Pacific Islander alone", while "Some other race

---

[5] The three-digit with an "XX" suffix is a convention used in Census 2000 for a large land area with no sufficient information to determine the five-digit codes.

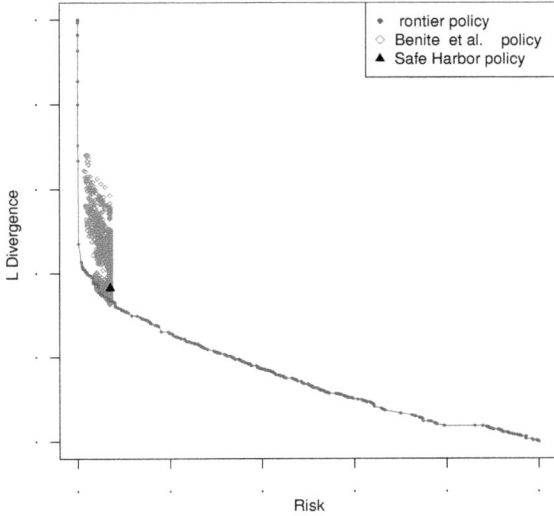

(a) Complete R-U space

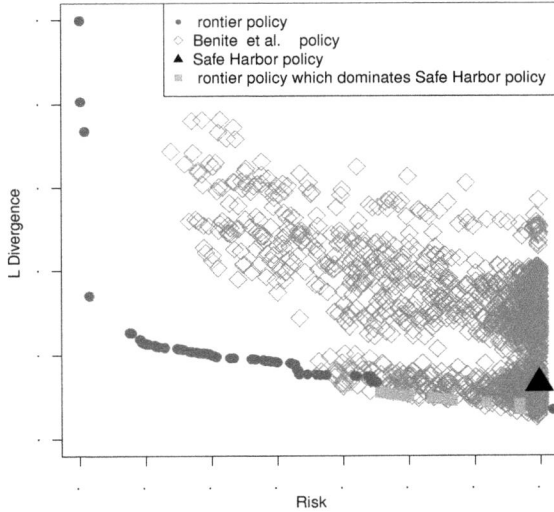

(b) Zoom of risk smaller than 0.08

Figure 8: Comparison of the SHS frontier, Safe Harbor, and policies discovered by the algorithm in [6].

Figure 9: Examples of two policies (upper and middle) discovered by SHS that strictly dominate Safe Harbor (lower).

tion policy frontier discovery (DPFD) as a dual-objective optimization. We demonstrated how to map the space of policy alternatives to a Risk-Utility (R-U) metric space for each given dataset, where a frontier represents a set of non-dominating policy tradeoffs. Given the complexity of the discovery task, we introduced a probability-driven heuristic search algorithm, whose effectiveness over an existing competitor strategy was verified through an empirical evaluation. We demonstrated that the heuristic enabled efficient construction of a frontier, but further showed that, for a dataset representative of the demographics of Tennessee, a common de-identification policy for health information is suboptimal to the frontier.

Although we cannot guarantee discovery of the optimal frontier, we believe there are several major benefits of our research. First, the fact that the policies in our frontier can dominate a broadly-adopted mainstream de-identification policy suggests that our approximate frontier is useful. We believe that a healthcare organization willing to follow the Safe Harbor policy can justify the use of an alternative on our frontier when it dominates in both risk and information loss. Second, we believe that our approach could be useful for assisting policy makers to reason about what might constitute a different de-identification standard. The visualization of the trade-off between privacy risk and information loss should assist in such decision making. For instance, our approach can demonstrate how small changes in risk (or information loss) could lead to significant gains in information loss (or risk). Third, we provide the visualization of R-U frontier to address the alternative policy set navigation issue in previous de-identification policy discovery methods such as [6]. A user can easily locate a policy that satisfies their R-U tradeoff preference through navigating the frontier.

alone" is generalized with "Two or more races". While these policies differ greatly from that suggested by Safe Harbor, it is worth mentioning that these policies – again – strictly dominate Safe Harbor.

Additionally, we compared our algorithm to the method of Benitez et al. [6]. It can see in Figure 8(b) that [6] returns *only* policies with risk not greater than Safe Harbor, while our method returns the "best" alternatives discovered.

Indeed, while [6] yields 500 policies which dominate the Safe Harbor policy, 98% of these are dominated by the 24 policies we return as a part of our discovered frontier.

5. DISCUSSION

5.1 Main Findings and Implications

In this work, we formalized the problem of de-identifica-

5.2 Limitations and Next Steps

Despite its merits, there are several limitations of the work that we wish to highlight. First, our framework requires a complete ordering of the domain of QI attributes and a structuring of all policy alternatives in a lattice. Yet, some data publishers may want to measure the information loss or risk in a function that does not satisfy this limitation. At this time, it is unclear how partial orders of a domain could be explored through a systematic search. One concern in particular is that partial orders may violate the homomorphism requirement of the risk and information loss functions.

Second, our study uses specific risk and utility measures, which may not be desirable in all cases. For instance, our risk measure assumes each record contributes a risk proportional to its group size (e.g., an individual in a group size of one contributes an equal amount of risk as two individuals in a group size of two). This is not necessarily the case and alternative risk measures may be more appropriate for modeling [38]. Similarly, our utility is based on an information theoretic measure which characterizes the distance between the distribution of QI values in the original and de-identified dataset. It thus neglects the relationship between the QI attributes and additional information that may be disclosed (e.g., the diagnoses for a patient). We adopted this perspective because regulation (e.g., the HIPAA Privacy Rule) does not address this issue. We recognize that models exist for characterizing such a relationship (e.g., mutual information measures) and believe they are worth considering in the future.

Third, it is possible that our dataset is not properly representative. In our analysis, we analyzed demographics in Tennessee, but not other states or smaller locales (e.g., counties). To further evaluate the effectiveness of our approaches, we plan on performing empirical studies with additional populations in the US and abroad.

Finally, as mentioned earlier, our search algorithm does not provide any guarantees with respect to the optimal solution. We believe a fruitful research direction is in the definition of approximation algorithms for the discovery of the frontier. Such approximation strategies have been addressed for certain anonymization [2] problems and it is possible that similar approaches may be appropriate for de-identification.

6. CONCLUSIONS

Organizations that must publish person-specific data for secondary use applications need to make a tradeoff between privacy risks (R) and utility (U). To provide a guideline for data publishers to make this tradeoff, we 1) added a semantic utility metric to an alternative de-identification policy discovery framework, 2) mapped each policy to a two-dimensional R-U space, and 3) formalized the frontier search problem. To solve the problem, we build a set of policies that define a frontier in the R-U space through a heuristic search with a probabilistic basis. We demonstrated that our approach dominates a baseline approach in terms of the quality of the frontier obtained within a fixed number of searched policies.

Our empirical study on the Adult dataset, supplemented with population statistics from of the state of Tennessee showed that our method can efficiently find a frontier in the R-U space which dominates the commonly applied HIPAA Safe Harbor policy (i.e., less risk and more utility). We believe that the frontier can be used as a tool to assist data managers make informed decisions about the relationships between risk and utility when sharing data. Our frontier policy framework is highly generalizable in the sense that the risk and utility measures can be any function, provided 1)

they satisfy certain order homomorphisms and 2) the policy space can be structured for a systematic search.

In future research, we anticipate investigating if other heuristic (or approximation) strategies could be invoked to discover better frontiers and assess if similar results are obtained through the study of other geographic locales.

7. ACKNOWLEDGMENTS

The authors would like to thank Jonathan Haines and Dan Roden for valuable discussions and feedback during the formulation of this project. This research was sponsored, in part, by grants from the Australian Research Council (DP110103142), National Institutes of Health (R01LM009989, U01HG006378, and U01HG006385), and the National Science Foundation (CCF-0424422).

8. REFERENCES

[1] Directive 95/46/EC of the european parliament and of the council of 24 October 1995 on the protection of individuals with regard to the processing of personal data and on the free movement of such data, 1995.

[2] G. Aggarwal, T. Feder, K. Kenthapadi, R. Motwani, R. Panigrahy, D. Thomas, and A. Zhu. Anonymizing tables. In *Proceedings of the 10th International Conference on Database Theory*, pages 246–258, 2005.

[3] P. Arzberger, P. Schroeder, A. Beaulieu, et al. Science and government. An international framework to promote access to data. *Science*, 303(5665):1777–1778, 2004.

[4] R. J. Bayardo and R. Agrawal. Data privacy through optimal k-anonymization. In *Proceedings of the 21st International Conference on Data Engineering*, pages 217–228, 2005.

[5] F. Belanger, J. Hiller, and W. Smith. Trustworthiness in electronic commerce: the role of privacy, security, and site attributes. *Journal of Strategic Information Systems*, 11:245–270, 2002.

[6] K. Benitez, G. Loukides, and B. Malin. Beyond safe harbor: automatic discovery of health information de-identification policy alternatives. In *Proceedings of the 1st ACM International Health Informatics Symposium*, pages 163–172, 2010.

[7] J. Bughlin, M. Chui, and J. Manyika. Clouds, big data, and smart assets: ten tech-enabled business trends to watch. *McKinsey Quarterly*, August 2010.

[8] V. Ciriani, S. D. C. di Vimercati, S. Foresti, and P. Samarati. k-anonymity. In *Secure Data Management in Decentralized Systems*, pages 323–353. 2007.

[9] T. Dalenius. Finding a needle in a haystack or identifying anonymous census records. *Journal of Official Statistics*, 2:329–336, 1986.

[10] R. Dewri, I. Ray, I. Ray, and D. Whitley. On the optimal selection of k in the k-anonymity problem. In *Proceedings of the 24th IEEE International Conference on Data Engineering*, pages 1364–1366, 2008.

[11] G. T. Duncan, S. A. Keller-Mcnulty, and S. L. Stokes. Disclosure risk vs. data utility: The R-U confidentiality map. Technical Report 121, National Institute for Statistical Science, Research Triangle Park, NC, December 2001.

[12] K. El Emam. Heuristics for de-identifying health data. *IEEE Security and Privacy*, 6(4):58–61, 2008.

[13] K. El Emam, L. Arbuckle, G. Koru, et al. De-identification methods for open health data: the case of the Heritage Health Prize claims dataset. *Journal of Medical Internet Research*, 14(1):e33, 2012.

[14] A. Frank and A. Asuncion. UCI machine learning repository, 2012.

[15] B. C. M. Fung, K. Wang, R. Chen, and P. S. Yu. Privacy-preserving data publishing: A survey of recent developments. *ACM Computing Surveys*, 42(4):14, 2010.

[16] B. C. M. Fung, K. Wang, and P. S. Yu. Top-down specialization for information and privacy preservation. In *Proceedings of the 21st International Conference on Data Engineering*, pages 205–216, 2005.

[17] D. Hallinan, M. Friedewald, and P. McCarthy. Citizens' perceptions of data protection and privacy in europe. *Computer Law and Security Review*, 28:263–272, 2012.

[18] I. Hrynaszkiewicz, M. L. Norton, A. J. Vickers, and D. G. Altman. Preparing raw clinical data for publication: guidance for journal editors, authors, and peer reviewers. *BMJ*, 340:c181, 2010.

[19] V. S. Iyengar. Transforming data to satisfy privacy constraints. In *Proceedings of the 8th ACM SIGKDD International Conference on Knowledge Discovery and Data Mining*, pages 279–288, 2002.

[20] D. Kifer and J. Gehrke. Injecting utility into anonymized datasets. In *Proceedings of the ACM SIGMOD International Conference on Management of Data*, pages 217–228, 2006.

[21] D. Lambert. Measures of disclosure risk and harm. *Journal of Official Statistics*, 9:313–331, 1993.

[22] K. LeFevre, D. J. DeWitt, and R. Ramakrishnan. Mondrian multidimensional *k*-anonymity. In *Proceedings of the 22nd IEEE International Conference on Data Engineering*, page 25, 2006.

[23] T. Li and N. Li. Towards optimal k-anonymization. *Data Knowl. Eng.*, 65(1):22–39, Apr. 2008.

[24] T. Li and N. Li. On the tradeoff between privacy and utility in data publishing. In *Proceedings of the 15th ACM SIGKDD International Conference on Knowledge Discovery and Data Mining*, pages 517–526, 2009.

[25] S. Lohr. The age of big data. *New York Times*, February 11 2012.

[26] G. Loukides, A. Gkoulalas-Divanis, and J. Shao. On balancing disclosure risk and data utility in transaction data sharing using R-U confidentiality map. *Joint UNECE/Eurostat Work Session on Statistical Data Confidentiality*, page 19, 2011.

[27] A. Meyerson and R. Williams. On the complexity of optimal *k*-anonymity. In *Proceedings of the 23rd ACM Symposium on Principles of Database Systems*, pages 223–228, 2004.

[28] A. Narayanan and V. Shmatikov. Myths and fallacies of "personally identifiable information". *Communications of the ACM*, 53(6):24–26, 2010.

[29] National Institutes of Health. Policy for sharing of data obtained in NIH supported or conducted genome-wide association studies. NOT-OD-07-088, Aug 2002.

[30] P. Ohm. Broken promises of privacy: responding to the surprising failure of anonymization. *UCLA Law Review*, 57:1701–1777, 2010.

[31] J. S. Olson, J. Grudin, and E. Horvitz. A study of preferences for sharing and privacy. In *Proceedings of the CHI'05 Extended Abstracts on Human Factors in Computing Systems*, pages 1985–1988, 2005.

[32] V. Rastogi, D. Suciu, and S. Hong. The boundary between privacy and utility in data publishing. In *Proceedings of the 33rd International Conference on Very Large Data Bases*, pages 531–542, 2007.

[33] P. Samarati and L. Sweeney. Protecting privacy when disclosing information: *k*-anonymity and its enforcement through generalization and suppression. Technical Report SRI-CSL-98-04, SRI Computer Science Laboratory, 1998.

[34] J. Schildcrout, J. Denny, E. Bowton, et al. Optimizing drug outcomes through pharmacogenetics: a case for preemptive genotyping. *Clinical Pharmacology and Therapeutics*, 92(2):235–242, 2012.

[35] P. Schwartz and D. Solove. The PII problem: Privacy and a new concept of personally identifiable information. *New York University Law Review*, 86:1814–1894, 2011.

[36] N. Shlomo. Statistical disclosure control methods for census frequency tables. *International Statistical Review*, 75(2):199–217, 2007.

[37] N. Shlomo and C. Young. Statistical disclosure control methods through a risk-utility framework. In *Proceedings of the 2006 CENEX-SDC project international conference on Privacy in Statistical Databases*, PSD'06, pages 68–81, Berlin, Heidelberg, 2006. Springer-Verlag.

[38] C. Skinner and M. Elliot. A measure of disclosure risk for microdata. *Journal of the Royal Statistical Society*, 64:855–867, 2002.

[39] L. Sweeney. Achieving *k*-anonymity privacy protection using generalization and suppression. *International Journal on Uncertainty, Fuzziness and Knowledge-based Systems*, 10:571–588, 2002.

[40] L. Sweeney. *k*-anonymity: a model for protecting privacy. *International Journal on Uncertainty, Fuzziness and Knowledge-based Systems*, 10(5):557–570, 2002.

[41] O. Tene and J. Polonetsky. Privacy in the age of big data. *Stanford Law Review Online*, 64:63–69, 2012.

[42] M. Trottini and S. E. Fienberg. Modelling user uncertainty for disclosure risk and data utility. *International Journal of Uncertainty, Fuzziness and Knowledge-Based Systems*, 10(5):511–527, Oct. 2002.

[43] T. M. Truta, F. Fotouhi, and D. Barth-Jones. Disclosure risk measures for microdata. In *Proceedings of the 15th International Conference on Scientific and Statistical Database Management*, pages 15–22, 2003.

[44] U.S. Census Bureau. American fact finder website: `http://www.americanfactfinder.gov`, 2012.

[45] U.S. Department of Health & Human Services. Standards for privacy of individually identifiable

health information, final rule, 45 CFR, pt 160-164, Aug 2002.

[46] M. Walport and P. Brest. Sharing research data to improve public health. *Lancet*, 377(9765):537–539, 2011.

APPENDIX

Appendix: Generating Sublattices for SHS

To ensure new regions in the lattice are explored, the SHS algorithm systematically generates sublattices which do not overlap with the list of pruned regions.

A Constraint Satisfaction Formulation

Given a list of pruned sublattices, we define the problem of generating the next sublattice to consider as a constraint satisfaction problem.

Based on the definition of a sublattice, each policy in a sublattice is bounded by the upper policy α and the lower policy β will have a set of bits in common. In particular,

$$\forall \gamma(\alpha_i \in sublattice(\alpha, \beta) \rightarrow$$

$$\forall j(\alpha[j] = 1 \rightarrow \gamma[j] = 1) \wedge \forall j(\beta[j] = 0 \rightarrow \gamma[j] = 0))$$

Now, let us assume $\{a_1, a_2, \ldots, a_{n_2}\}$ and $\{b_1, b_2, \ldots, b_{n_1}\}$ are the sets of bits set to 0 and 1 in all policies of the sublattice, respectively. For reference, assume B is a bit-string that represents a policy. A $sublattice(\alpha, \beta)$ can then be represented as a conjunction clause:

$$B[b_1] = 1 \wedge \cdots \wedge B[b_{n_1}] = 1 \wedge B[a_1] = 0 \wedge \cdots \wedge B[a_{n_2}] = 0.$$

A sufficient condition for a sublattice to not to have any overlap with another sublattice is:

$$\neg(B[b_1] = 1 \wedge \cdots \wedge B[b_{n_1}] = 1 \wedge B[a_1] = 0 \wedge \cdots \wedge B[a_{n_2}] = 0)$$

This condition is equivalent to:

$$B[b_1] = 0 \vee \cdots \vee B[b_{n_1}] = 0 \vee B[a_1] = 1 \vee \cdots \vee B[a_{n_2}] = 1.$$

and is precisely the constraint defined by $sublattice(\alpha, \beta)$. For example, all policies in $sublattice([0, 0, 0, 0, 1], [1, 0, 1, 0, 1])$ satisfy $B[4] = 1 \wedge B[1] = 0 \wedge B[3] = 0$ As a result, the corresponding constraint clause is $B[4] = 0 \vee B[1] = 1 \vee B[3] = 1$.

Searching for Sublattices

Algorithm 3 summarizes the search process for non-overlapping lattices. Given a set of pruned sublattices, each one defines a clause. The conjunction of the set of clauses is the constraint which the new sublattice should satisfy. We assume the set of clauses is $C = \{c_0, \ldots, c_m\}$, and each clause is a disjunction set of literals $c_i = \{l_i^0, \ldots, l_i^{n_i}\}$. If this constraint set is satisfiable, we can find a set of literals $S = \{s_0, \ldots, s_{n_s}\}$, such that $s_0 \wedge \cdots \wedge s_{n_s} \rightarrow c_0 \wedge \cdots \wedge c_m$.

We use a depth-first search to find a set of literals for which the conjunction satisfies the aforementioned requirement. We begin by randomly selecting a literal l from the clause with the least number of literals. We check each clause and if $l \rightarrow c_0 \wedge \cdots \wedge c_m$, then it is deemed a solution; otherwise, we add l to $path$, which keeps the solution set S, and keep searching.

In each iteration, we add a random literal from the clause with the least number of literals in the unsatisfied constraint

---

Algorithm 3 Search Non-overlapping Lattices (*SNL*)

Input: *Constraints*, a list of clauses defined by the set of pruned sublattice
Output: *path*, a list of literals that defines a solution sublattice

```
1:  path ← ∅
2:  Stack ← ∅
3:  root ← shortestclause(Constraints)
4:  push(Stack,root)
5:  while Stack ≠ ∅ do
6:      clause ← pop(Stack)
7:      if clause ≠ ∅ then
8:          literal ← randomliteral(clause)
9:          remove(clause,literal)
10:         push(Stack,clause)
11:         if Conflict(literal,path)= TRUE then
12:             continue
13:         else
14:             push(path, literal)
15:             unsatisfied ← unsatisfied(Constraints, path)
16:             if unsatisfied = ∅ then
17:                 return path
18:             else
19:                 clause ← shortestclause(unsatisfied)
20:                 push(Stack,clause)
21:             end if
22:         end if
23:     else
24:         if path ≠ ∅ then
25:             pop(path)
26:         end if
27:     end if
28: end while
29: return path
```

---

clause by the current *path* to expand the path. Selecting the clause with the least number of literals is a greedy strategy.

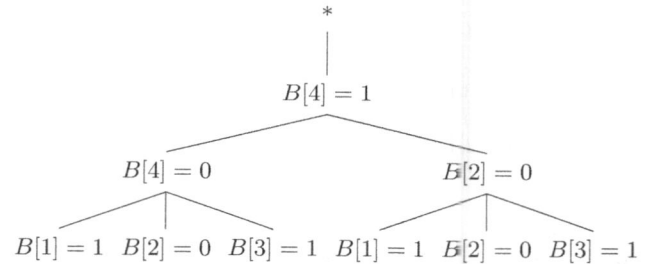

Figure 10: The search tree of the constraint satisfaction problem defined by the pruned lattice set.

The process is relatively straightforward. Instead of proceeding through all of the details for the algorithm, we present an simple example. Assume the constraint set is:

$$(B[4] = 1) \wedge (B[2] = 0 \vee B[4] = 0) \wedge$$
$$(B[1] = 1 \vee B[2] = 0 \vee B[3] = 1)$$

Then, the complete search tree is depicted in Figure 10. $Path = \{B[4] = 1, B[2] = 0\}$ is a possible solution.

Data Usage Control Enforcement in Distributed Systems

Florian Kelbert
Technische Universität München
Garching bei München, Germany
kelbert@cs.tum.edu

Alexander Pretschner
Technische Universität München
Garching bei München, Germany
pretschner@cs.tum.edu

ABSTRACT

Distributed usage control is concerned with how data may or may not be used in distributed system environments after initial access has been granted. If data flows through a distributed system, there exist multiple copies of the data on different client machines. Usage constraints then have to be enforced for all these clients. We extend a generic model for intra-system data flow tracking—that has been designed and used to track the existence of copies of data on single clients—to the cross-system case. When transferring, i.e., copying, data from one machine to another, our model makes it possible to (1) transfer usage control policies along with the data to the end of local enforcement at the receiving end, and (2) to be aware of the existence of copies of the data in the distributed system. As one example, we concretize "transfer of data" to the Transmission Control Protocol (TCP). Based on this concretized model, we develop a distributed usage control enforcement infrastructure that generically and application-independently extends the scope of usage control enforcement to any system receiving usage-controlled data. We instantiate and implement our work for OpenBSD and evaluate its security and performance.

Categories and Subject Descriptors

D.4.6 [**Security and Protection**]: Information flow controls; D.4.6 [**Security and Protection**]: Access controls

General Terms

Security

Keywords

Distributed Usage Control; Policy Enforcement; Security and Privacy; Sticky Policies; Data Flow Tracking

1. INTRODUCTION

Distributed usage control [26, 30] has been proposed with the goal of overcoming one shortcoming of access control

models: loss of control over data once it has been released. Usage control is therefore concerned with what must or must not happen to data *after* access to it has been granted and is particularly interesting in distributed system environments [16, 18]. While traditional access control mechanisms are deployed at the data provider's site, *distributed* usage control requirements must be enforced at the data consumer's site.

Such requirements are expressed in usage control policies by the data provider [11, 17, 34]. Example policies include "only process my data with application X," "do not redistribute my data to company Y," and "delete my data after thirty days." In a distributed setting, these policies must be enforced at *all systems* that store, process, and distribute data. Since data can easily be redistributed in today's internet, it is particularly challenging to make sure that a policy is enforced even after data has been transferred to another system. This paper's subject is the problem of building a usage control infrastructure that ensures that if data is transferred, respective policies are transferred along with the data, and that they will be enforced at the receiving end.

1.1 Motivating Example

Consider a company in which confidential digital business reports are repeatedly handled by several cooperating employees of the finance department for means of creation, modification, approval, and reading. Although the company deployed state-of-the-art security mechanisms such as encrypted and access controlled shared file servers, Public-Key Infrastructures, and secured web services, a data breach happened recently: an employee sent business reports to a server outside the company. While the employees, including Alice and Bob, should be able to do their work as usual, the CEO does not want such incidents to happen ever again.

The CEO thus decides to equip all servers and client machines with a usage control infrastructure and to deploy a policy stating that "business reports may not leave the financial department." Now, once Alice tries to access a business report on the shared file sever, the file server's usage control infrastructure determines whether also Alice has such an infrastructure in place and, if so, allows the access. Our infrastructure will then also transfer the usage policy and enforce it on Alice's machine. Similarly, Alice would then only be able to share the report with Bob if he has the corresponding infrastructure in place. This way, the CEO can be sure that the business reports are not leaked—be the attempt intentional or inadvertent. Note that in general the CEO may also provide more complex policies consisting of additional rules such as "only use with application X," "delete after 30 days," or "do not modify."

1.2 Realization of Usage Control

Within one computer system, data exists in different representations (e.g., file, pixmap, Java object) at different system layers (operating system, window manager, Java virtual machine). Therefore, the flow of data must be tracked at and across different system layers. It has been shown how usage control requirements can be enforced at each of these layers [28]. To this end, a generic data flow model [10, 29] as well as a generic enforcement infrastructure have been proposed and instantiated at several system layers [33]. By combining the instantiations of the data flow model and the enforcement infrastructures of each single layer, policies can be enforced at and across different layers *of one system* [33].

These instantiations of the data flow model do not take into account the fundamentally distributed nature of data usage control enforcement [10, 29, 33]. Other proposed models and implementations do not consider data flow tracking and/or fix data provider and data consumer beforehand [2, 12, 18, 20, 21]. Despite being the natural way of data dissemination in today's internet, generic and application-independent data dissemination in the context of usage control has, to our knowledge, not yet been investigated.

We address this shortcoming by extending a generic data flow model for intra-system data flow tracking to the case of cross-system data flow tracking. We use this model to develop a Data Distribution Infrastructure (DDI). As one example, we concretize the data flow model for internet communication using the Transmission Control Protocol (TCP) and instantiate both the concretized model and the DDI at the operating system layer. This allows for generic, transparent, and application-independent cross-system data flow tracking, transferring usage control policies along with to-be-controlled data, and extending the scope of usage control enforcement to any system receiving data.

Big Picture. If usage control requirements are to be enforced within a single system, a *Local Enforcement Infrastructure* (LEI) must be deployed on that system. The task of the LEI is to (i) track the flow of data within and across several system layers, (ii) take usage control policy decisions, and (iii) enforce these decisions. Several LEIs have been described and implemented [7, 10, 18, 29, 33, 44]. For distributed systems, an additional *Data Distribution Infrastructure* (DDI) is needed. Its task is to (i) track the flow of data across different connected systems, (ii) transfer the corresponding policies along with the data, and (iii) trigger the receiving LEI to take care of local enforcement. The DDI thus provides additional functionalities for usage control enforcement in distributed system environments. The subject of this paper is the development of a generic DDI and its integration with generic LEIs as depicted in Fig. 1. Because the DDI transfers policies but is not responsible for local enforcement, the content of any specific usage control policy is irrelevant from the DDI's perspective. As a consequence, in this paper, we do not provide any concrete examples of policies (see [7, 10, 18, 29, 33, 44] for various LEIs).

1.3 Organization

We organize our work along six steps as follows:
Step A: Generic data flow model, §2.1. In order to enforce usage control policies on all representations of a particular data item, the flow of that data must be tracked both within one system and across systems. We recap a generic

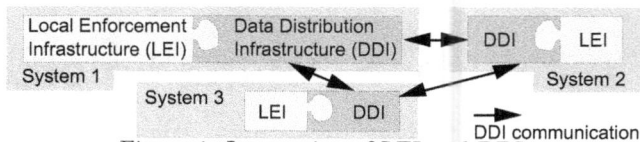

Figure 1: Integration of LEI and DDI.

data flow model, a transition system that has been designed to allow for data flow tracking within single systems.
Step B: Cross-system data flows, §2.2. We extend the data flow model from step A to the cross-system case.
Step C: Concretization, §3. As one example, we concretize the model of step B for TCP; we identify TCP-related actions and describe how they change the data flow state.
Step D: DDI, §4. We develop a Data Distribution Infrastructure (DDI) that allows for transparent and application-independent cross-system data flow tracking and that transfers policies along with data to be controlled. Using this infrastructure, the scope of policy enforcement can be extended to any system receiving usage controlled data.
Step E: Integration with LEI, §4. We integrate our DDI with a Local Enforcement Infrastructure (LEI) for single independent systems, thus combining cross-system and intra-system data flow tracking and policy enforcement.
Step F: Instantiation, §5. We instantiate and implement both the concretized model and the integrated infrastructure for the OpenBSD operating system.

We evaluate our work in §6. In §7, we discuss the limitations of our work and point to future work. §8 puts our work in context. §9 concludes.

1.4 Contribution and Assumptions

In sum, we tackle the following **research problem**. If data usage is to be controlled across system boundaries, then policies need to be (1) transferred together with data when data is transmitted and (2) enforced at the receiving end. Current instantiations and implementations of usage control models do not consider generic data flows in-between different connected systems but rather focus on one single machine. Other solutions fix data provider and data consumer beforehand, therefore not catering to the complexity of today's internet environment, where data may be arbitrarily redistributed by any data possessor.

Our **solution** is a model for cross-system data flow tracking and its concretization for TCP. We develop and deploy a DDI, realizing application-independent cross-system data flow tracking and the sticky policy paradigm for usage control. We instantiate our concepts for the OpenBSD operating system and evaluate our work. A demo video is available at http://www22.cs.tum.edu/index.php?id=64.

We see our **contribution** in the development of a generic usage control enforcement model for distributed systems. We are not aware of usage control solutions that generically, transparently, and application-independently (1) track the flow of data both within one system and in-between different connected systems, and (2) extend the scope of policy enforcement to any system receiving usage-controlled data.

An implementation of the system connected to a smart metering system has been published as a short demo paper before [13]. In contrast, the present paper describes the underlying theory and evaluates and discusses the approach.

Assumptions. To reduce complexity, we assume a static network structure: the same IP address may not be assigned to more than one host over time. Policy considerations such as policy specification, policy translation, and policy evolution are out of the scope of this work; they are discussed in [17,34,35]. We assume an initial policy to be deployed and assume that the receiving end of a data transfer is equipped with a usage control enforcement infrastructure. Policies are assumed to be formulated in terms of system calls as described in [17,33]. We discuss these assumptions in §6-§8.

Attacker Model. As motivated in §1.1, we consider non-privileged end users on both local and remote systems to be a threat w.r.t. sensitive data. Attempts to use usage controlled data without respecting the corresponding policy may be either intentional or inadvertent.

2. APPLICATION-INDEPENDENT CROSS-SYSTEM DATA FLOW TRACKING

To extend the scope of usage control to other systems over the network, data flow between the communicating systems must be tracked. We recap a generic data flow model in §2.1 and provide an extension in §2.2 that allows for tracking both cross-system and intra-system data flows.

2.1 Generic Data Flow Model

Step A. The data flow model presented in [10,29] allows to overapproximate the existence of data item copies in a system by capturing the flow of data within this system. To this end, the distinction between abstract data (e.g., picture) and data representations (e.g., file or database entry), so-called containers, is made: containers are entities that may contain data. The data flow model is a transition system: states capture which data is stored in which container; state transitions are initiated by actions related to data flow and change the mapping between data and containers (i.e., which containers potentially contain which data).

Formally, the model is a tuple $(D, C, F, \Sigma, \sigma_i, P, A, \varrho)$; D is the set of data items whose usage is restricted by a policy, C is the set of containers, and F is the set of identifiers that are used to identify containers. $P \subseteq C$ are all possible principals in the system; principals may have read sensitive data (which is why they are considered a subset of C) and they can, as opposed to other containers, invoke actions from the set of all possible actions A. $\Sigma = (C \to \mathbb{P}(D)) \times (C \to \mathbb{P}(C)) \times (P \times F \to C)$ are all possible states of the system; σ_i is the initial state. A state therefore consists of three mappings: (1) A storage function $s : C \to \mathbb{P}(D)$ capturing which data is potentially stored in which container. (2) An alias function $l : C \to \mathbb{P}(C)$ capturing that some containers may implicitly get updated whenever other containers do: If $c_2 \in l(c_1)$ for $c_1, c_2 \in C$, then any data written into c_1 is immediately propagated to c_2. (3) A naming function $f : P \times F \to C$ capturing the mapping from principal-relative identifiers to containers. $f(p, n)$ thus returns the container that can be accessed by principal $p \in P$ via identifier $n \in F$.

Actions A change the system state; these changes are described by relation $\varrho \subseteq \Sigma \times P \times A \times \Sigma$. Additional notation for specifying state changes is needed. For any mapping $m : S \to T$ and an element $x \in X \subseteq S$, define $m[x \leftarrow expr]_{x \in X} = m'$ with $m' : S \to T$ such that $m'(y) = expr$ if $y \in X$ and $m'(y) = m(y)$ if $y \notin X$.

Multiple updates for disjoint sets are combined by function composition $\circ$. The replacements are done simultaneously and atomically; the semicolon is syntactic sugar:
$$m[x_1 \leftarrow expr_{x_1}; \ldots; x_n \leftarrow expr_{x_n}]_{x_1 \in X_1, \ldots, x_n \in X_n} =$$
$$m[x_n \leftarrow expr_{x_n}]_{x_n \in X_n} \circ \ldots \circ m[x_1 \leftarrow expr_{x_1}]_{x_1 \in X_1}$$

Function f^- returns the set of all names for a given container: $\forall c \in C : f^-(c) = \{(p, n) \in P \times F \mid f(p, n) = c\}$

The described model was originally designed to model the flow of data within one system. In §2.2 we provide an extended model to allow for both intra-system and cross-system data flow tracking from a global point of view.

2.2 Cross-system Data Flow Tracking for IP

All major application-level protocols (e.g., HTTP, FTP, SMB, SSH, DNS) in today's internet build on the Internet Protocol (IP) which transfers data packets between internet hosts in a best-effort manner. Protocols at the transport layer bridge the gap between IP (host-to-host communication) and application-layer protocols (end-to-end application communication) by delivering the data packets addressed to a particular host to the correct process running on that host.

Step B. On the basis of the model of step A we provide a model that allows for both intra-system and cross-system data flow tracking from a global point of view. Our model supports any protocol building on IP and is applicable to all unicast internet-based communication.

Hosts. Since we investigate cross-system data flows, we need to introduce the concept of hosts. In real-world systems, multiple IP addresses may be assigned to the same host, which is why we define a host as a set of IP addresses. We consider all IP addresses to be globally unique: no IP address may be assigned to more than one host over time. Exceptionally, each host can refer to itself by using several reserved IP addresses. For IPv4, these are all IP addresses starting with "127.", while in IPv6 the single address "::1" is reserved. We refer to any of these addresses as *localhost* (*lo*). We consider *lo* to be a reserved value within *IPAddr* where *IPAddr* is the set of all IP addresses. The set of hosts $H \subseteq \mathbb{P}(IPAddr \setminus \{lo\})$ is defined such that

$$\forall h_x, h_y \in H : h_x \neq \varnothing \wedge h_y \neq \varnothing \wedge (h_x \cap h_y \neq \varnothing \Rightarrow h_x = h_y)$$

Therefore, each host $h_z \in H$ is identified by its set of globally unique IP addresses. Note that $\forall h_z \in H : lo \notin h_z$. Additionally, we define *Port* as the set of network ports.

Principals. Principals P are processes. They are also containers ($P \subseteq C$) because their memory is a possible location for data. Each process runs on exactly one host, while a host can run multiple processes at the same time. Each process $p \in P$ is assigned a host-relative process ID (PID). Thus, the set of principals P is defined as $P = H \times PID$. Function $h : P \to H$ returns for each process $p \in P$ its host $h_p \in H$. In order to model the fact that a network communication endpoint (i.e., a network socket) bound to IP address $lo \in IPAddr$ is only able to communicate with processes running on the same host, we define $\forall p \in P, \forall a \in h(p) \setminus \{lo\} : scope(p, lo) = \{q \in P \mid h(p) = h(q)\}$ and $scope(p, a) = P$ as the set of all processes that can communicate with process p via p's network socket that is bound to IP address a.

Containers. We consider both network sockets (C_S) and the runtime memory of each process (i.e., the processes themselves) as containers: $C_S \cup P \subseteq C$.

Identifiers. Network socket containers are identified by process-relative file descriptors $e \in F_S$, which are only valid for the process that created the socket. For network communication, processes refer to other processes' sockets using an IP address and a port. Yet, this is not sufficient to uniquely identify a socket, since a process may use the same IP address and port for different communications. For this reason, a socket is identified by the IP address and port of the caller and the IP address and port of the receiver, called *local socket name* and *remote socket name*, respectively. Note that the remote socket is not necessarily on a different machine. Hence, the set of identifiers F is $F = F_S \cup (F_N \times F_N)$ with $F_N = (IPAddr \times Port)$.

Actions. We consider all system calls related to IP networking and writing to and reading from file descriptors as actions. System calls are provided by the operating system kernel and may be invoked by user-space processes to access resources, communicate, retrieve system information, and the like. Actions (system calls) are performed by principals (processes) and may change the system's data flow state as defined by ϱ (cf. §3).

The presented model allows for intra-system and cross-system data flow tracking for any unicast communication method building upon IP. As one example, §3 concretizes this extended generic data flow model for TCP.G

3. CROSS-SYSTEM DATA FLOW TRACKING FOR TCP

Since IP does not provide means for end-to-end application communication, different protocols at the transport layer bridge the gap between IP and the corresponding application-layer protocol. The most well-known protocols at this layer are the User Datagram Protocol (UDP) and the Transmission Control Protocol (TCP). While UDP is a connectionless protocol (no dedicated connection is established between the communication partners and no delivery guarantees are provided), TCP is a connection-based protocol providing reliable data delivery. Using TCP, a client and a server process establish a full-duplex connection before exchanging data. Two network sockets exist, each allowing for sending and receiving data on one end of the connection.

We model and realize cross-system data flow tracking at the level of TCP. Before we model the protocol in detail in terms of ϱ in §3.1-§3.3, let us provide a high-level overview of TCP-related system calls (cf. Fig. 2): First, both client and server create a communication endpoint, called socket, (system call *socket*) and bind a name, i.e. an IP address and a port, to it (*bind*). The server then marks its socket as passive (*listen*) and waits for incoming connections (*accept*). The client then initiates a connection to the server's passive and listening socket (*connect*). Once *accept* and *connect* return, the TCP communication channel has transparently been set up by the underlying operating systems. The processes may then exchange any kind of information by writing to and reading from the network sockets using a variety of system calls (e.g., *write*, *read*). Finally, the communication channel is torn down (*shutdown*, *close*, *exit*).

Step C. We concretize the cross-system data flow model for TCP networking at the layer of the operating system. At this layer, TCP-relevant actions are system calls [10,21]. Since most application layer protocols rely on TCP, our con-

cretization supports a variety of internet protocols, including web browsing, e-mail, and file transfer. In order to model the data flow according to our model (cf. §2.2), we need to define the transitions ϱ for TCP-related system calls.

3.1 Connection Establishment

socket. First, each communication partner must execute the *socket* system call. With parameter SOCK_STREAM *socket* creates a new unconnected socket for connection-based communication (i.e., TCP) on top of IP. *socket* returns a file descriptor $e \in F_S$ that identifies the newly created socket container $c \in C_S$ for the calling process $p \in P$:

$$
\begin{aligned}
&\forall s \in [C \to \mathbb{P}(D)], \forall l \in [C \to \mathbb{P}(C)], \forall f \in [P \times F \to C], \\
&\forall p \in P, \forall e \in F_S, \forall c \in C_S : \\
&((s,l,f), p, socket(e,c), (s,l,f[(p,e) \leftarrow c])) \in \varrho.
\end{aligned}
$$

bind, listen. After creating a socket, each communication partner $p \in P$ must *bind* the local socket name to its socket. *bind* is especially important for the server process, because it will be waiting for incoming connections and its socket name must therefore be fixed and known. The server process then marks its socket as passive using system call *listen*. A listening socket may neither initiate connections nor be part of an actual communication channel. *bind* and *listen* do not change the data flow state.

accept. The server process then performs an *accept* system call on the passive and listening socket. *accept* does not return until an actual connection establishment request to that socket has been made. We discuss the *accept* response and the respective state transition shortly.

connect. The client process then initializes the actual connection establishment by issuing system call *connect*. Parameters are file descriptor $e \in F_S$ of the client's socket, as well as IP address $a_S \in IPAddr$ and port $x_S \in Port$ of the server's listening socket. If the client's socket has not been bound explicitly before, *connect* does an implicit call to *bind*. *connect* returns successfully, once the connection to (a_S, x_S) has been established. Parameters $a_c = h(p)$ and $x_c \in Port$ correspond to the local socket name of the client's connected socket. This information is retrievable from the operating system via e once the connection has been established:

$$
\begin{aligned}
&\forall s \in [C \to \mathbb{P}(D)], \forall l \in [C \to \mathbb{P}(C)], \forall f \in [P \times F \to C], \\
&\forall p \in P, \forall e \in F_S, \forall a_S \in IPAddr, \forall a_C \in h(p), \\
&\forall x_S, x_C \in Port : \\
&((s,l,f), p, connect(e, a_S, x_S, a_C, x_C), (s, l, \\
&f[(q, ((a_C, x_C), (a_S, x_S))) \leftarrow f(p,e)]_{q \in scope(p, a_C)})) \in \varrho.
\end{aligned}
$$

The establishment of the communication channel is modeled along with the *accept* response at the server's side as follows. Note that our model assumes that *connect* always returns before *accept*; we cater to this assumption in §5.1.

accept (cont.). Once the server's *accept* returns, a new communication channel has been established by the operating systems. For this purpose, a new socket has been created and connected to the remote (client's) socket that requested the connection establishment. Output parameters of *accept* are a socket file descriptor $e \in F_S$ referring to the newly created socket container $c \in C_S$ and the local socket name $(a_C, x_C) \in F_N$ of the client's connected socket. $(a_S, x_S) \in h(p) \times Port$ refers to the local socket name that can be retrieved from the operating system via e.

Connection establishment finally is modeled by bidirectionally aliasing the server's and client's socket containers:

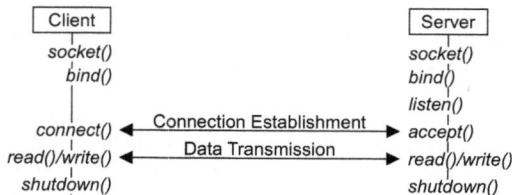

Figure 2: Sequence of TCP-related system calls.

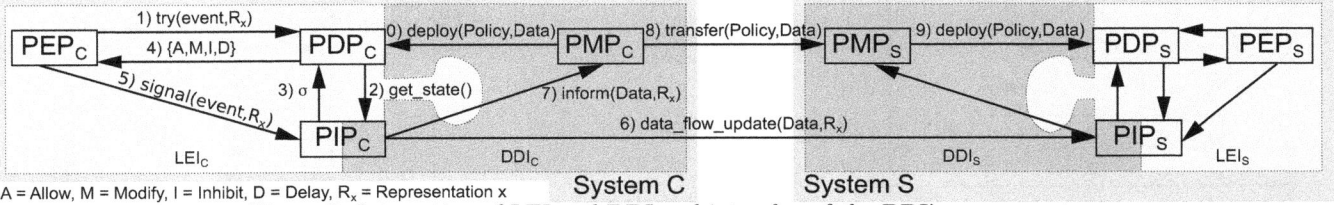

Figure 3: Integration of LEI and DDI and interplay of the DDI's components.

A = Allow, M = Modify, I = Inhibit, D = Delay, R_x = Representation x

$$\forall s \in [C \to \mathbb{P}(D)], \forall l \in [C \to \mathbb{P}(C)], \forall f \in [P \times F \to C],$$
$$\forall p \in P, \forall e \in F_S, \forall c \in C_S,$$
$$\forall a_S \in h(p), \forall a_C \in IPAddr, \forall x_S, x_C \in Port :$$
$$((s, l, f), p, accept(e, a_C, x_C, a_S, x_S, c), (s,$$
$$l[c \leftarrow f(p, ((a_C, x_C), (a_S, x_S)))];$$
$$f(p, ((a_C, x_C), (a_S, x_S))) \leftarrow c],$$
$$f[(p, e) \leftarrow c;$$
$$(q, ((a_S, x_S), (a_C, x_C))) \leftarrow c]_{q \in scope(p, a_S)})) \in \varrho.$$

3.2 Data Transmission

Once the TCP connection has been established, the corresponding processes may write to and read from the communication channel. Modelling sending and receiving of data then corresponds to writing to and reading from any other file descriptor as described in [10]. For completeness, we cite the corresponding state changes for system calls *write* and *read*; l^* denotes the reflexive transitive closure of function l.[1] Other system calls for sending are *sendmsg*, *pwritev*, *pwrite*, *writev*, *send*, *sendto*; system calls for reading are *recvmsg*, *preadv*, *pread*, *readv*, *recv*, *recvfrom*. Their state transitions are analogous: when writing, (potentially) all knowledge of the process flows into the socket container and recursively into all aliased containers. When reading, (potentially) all knowledge from the socket container flows into the reading process and recursively into all aliased containers:

$$\forall s \in [C \to \mathbb{P}(D)], \forall l \in [C \to \mathbb{P}(C)], \forall f \in [P \times F \to C],$$
$$\forall p \in P, \forall e \in F_S :$$
$$((s, l, f), p, write(e), (s[t \leftarrow s(t) \cup s(p)]_{t \in l^*(f(p,e))}, l, f)) \in \varrho.$$

$$\forall s \in [C \to \mathbb{P}(D)], \forall l \in [C \to \mathbb{P}(C)], \forall f \in [P \times F \to C],$$
$$\forall p \in P, \forall e \in F_S :$$
$$((s, l, f), p, read(e), ($$
$$s[t \leftarrow s(t) \cup s(f(p, e))]_{t \in l^*(p)}, l, f)) \in \varrho.$$

3.3 Connection Teardown

After data transmission the connection is shut down. System calls *shutdown*, *close*, and *exit* cause a (potentially partial) connection teardown.

shutdown. Using the *shutdown* system call, process $p \in P$ may shut down all or part of the connection constituted by the socket identified by file descriptor $e \in F_S$. Parameter SHUT_RD disallows further receptions, SHUT_WR disallows further transmission, and SHUT_RDWR forbids further receptions and transmissions. In terms of the data flow model, this has the following implications: In case of SHUT_RD, the socket container is emptied and all aliases to it are deleted. In case of SHUT_WR, all aliases from the socket container are deleted. In case of SHUT_RDWR, the

socket container is emptied and all aliases to and from it are deleted; additionally, all its identifiers of type $F_N \times F_N$ are deleted. We use the reserved value $nil \in C$ to refer to non-existing containers.

$$\forall s \in [C \to \mathbb{P}(D)], \forall l \in [C \to \mathbb{P}(C)], \forall f \in [P \times F \to C],$$
$$\forall p \in P, \forall e \in F_S :$$
$$((s, l, f), p, shutdown(e, SHUT\_RD), (s[f(p, e) \leftarrow \varnothing],$$
$$l[c \leftarrow l(c) \setminus \{f(p, e)\}]_{c \in C}, f)) \in \varrho.$$

$$\forall s \in [C \to \mathbb{P}(D)], \forall l \in [C \to \mathbb{P}(C)], \forall f \in [P \times F \to C],$$
$$\forall p \in P, \forall e \in F_S :$$
$$((s, l, f), p, shutdown(e, SHUT\_WR), (s,$$
$$l[f(p, e) \leftarrow \varnothing], f)) \in \varrho.$$

$$\forall s \in [C \to \mathbb{P}(D)], \forall l \in [C \to \mathbb{P}(C)], \forall f \in [P \times F \to C],$$
$$\forall p \in P, \forall e \in F_S :$$
$$((s, l, f), p, shutdown(e, SHUT\_RDWR), (s[f(p, e) \leftarrow \varnothing],$$
$$l[f(p, e) \leftarrow \varnothing; c \leftarrow l(c) \setminus \{f(p, e)\}]_{c \in C},$$
$$f[x \leftarrow nil]_{x \in \{(q, n) \in f^-(f(p,e)) | n \in F_N \times F_N\}})) \in \varrho.$$

close, exit. Process $p \in P$ may close a file descriptor $e \in F_S$ using system call *close*. The behaviour of *close* is modeled as described in [10] by mapping identifier (p, e) to nil. Yet, if (p, e) is the last remaining file descriptor for socket $c = f(p, e)$ (i.e., $P \times F_S \cap f^-(f(p, e)) = \{(p, e)\}$), the connection is implicitly shut down by the operating system. In this case, we model an implicit *shutdown* with parameter SHUT_RDWR. When a process exits (system call *exit*), all of its file descriptors and TCP connections are closed alike.

We have concretized the cross-system data flow model by defining transition relation ϱ for TCP-related system calls. It enables us to know which data is—due to over-approximations induced by the semantics of the write system call: potentially—stored on which system whenever data has been transferred via TCP. In §4 we develop a usage control enforcement infrastructure; §5 will show how this technical infrastructure uses the presented cross-system data flow model.

4. A DISTRIBUTED ENFORCEMENT INFRASTRUCTURE

Step D. In order to practically extend the scope of usage control enforcement to the system that receives usage-controlled data, we develop a Data Distribution Infrastructure (DDI, Fig. 3) to (1) track cross-system data flows as modeled in §2.2 and §3, (2) transfer policies along with the to-be controlled data, and (3) deploy the policy at the receiving end where the respective local enforcement infrastructure is responsible for its local enforcement. The main components are a distribution-enhanced Policy Information Point (PIP), which implements ϱ as defined in §3, and a

---

[1] $\forall a \in C : l^*(a)$ is the smallest set satisfying
$l^*(a) = \{a\} \cup \{b \in C \mid b \in l(a) \vee (\exists c \in l(a) \wedge b \in l^*(c))\}$.

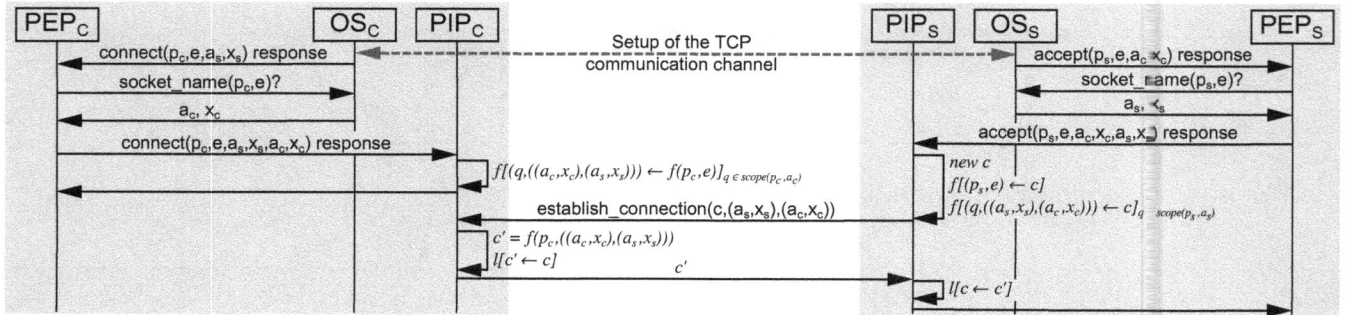

Figure 4: Connection establishment according to §3.1 and §5.1.

Policy Management Point (PMP). The infrastructure is distributed in that its components must be deployed on any system that is expected to enforce usage control policies. Each PIP holds the data flow state of the system on which it is deployed. The PMP manages all usage control policies for data entering, leaving, and residing in the system on which it is deployed. Both the PIP and the PMP are able to communicate with their respective counterparts on other systems. Thus they allow for the exchange of information regarding cross-system data flows and usage policies when data flows between systems take place. We provide more details of our infrastructure when presenting its instantiation in §5. At this point we assume that the receiving system has the necessary infrastructure in place; this is discussed in §6.

Step E. We integrate the DDI into a Local Enforcement Infrastructure (LEI) for single independent systems [10, 33]. The main components of the latter are a Policy Enforcement Point (PEP), a Policy Decision Point (PDP), and a local Policy Information Point (PIP). Fig. 3 shows an instantiation of the integrated infrastructure for two operating system instances, C and S.

Initially, the PMP of system C deploys a usage control policy (Fig. 3, step 0) for some specified data. From this point onward, the LEI monitors the corresponding data, tracks its local copies—including any derivations even after operations such as compression or encryption—, and enforces the policy upon every usage of that data as follows: The PEP is tailored to one system layer (in our case the operating system); its task is to intercept attempted and actual events within this layer (system calls). The PEP temporarily blocks the execution of these events and signals them to the PDP (step 1). The PDP decides for each event whether it conforms to the deployed usage control policy. In order to take this decision, the PDP queries the PIP for additional information about the data flow state (steps 2,3) and then decides, on the grounds of this information and the usage control policy, whether to allow, inhibit, delay, or modify the event in question [31]. The PDP returns the decision to the PEP (step 4) which enforces it. If an actual event happened, the PEP signals the event to the PIP (step 5) that then updates the system's data flow state accordingly. [10] describes how the state evolves for intra-system data flow system calls and thus also how any modifications to the data are tracked.

If a TCP-related system call happens on system C (analogous for system S), it is intercepted and evaluated by the components of LEI_C (PEP_C, PDP_C). The PIP_C component of DDI_C, which implements the transition relation ϱ described in §3, then communicates the fact that the system call happened as well as the relevant parameters to PIP_S (step 6), thus realizing cross-system data flow tracking.

Upon data transmission, PIP_C additionally informs PMP_C (step 7). PMP_C then transfers the respective usage control policies to PMP_S (step 8), thereby realizing the sticky policy paradigm. PMP_S eventually deploys the policy on system S (step 9). Details for steps 6 through 9 are provided in §5.

5. INSTANTIATION

Step F. To show the usefulness of our approach, we instantiate the concretized cross-system data flow model (§3) and the integrated enforcement infrastructure (§4) for the OpenBSD operating system. As explained in §4, all usage control enforcement components are deployed on each operating system instance. While the PEP must be deployed locally, this is not inevitable for PDP, PIP, and PMP. However, deploying PDP and PIP remotely would lead to communication overhead and thus to higher system response times and lower performance. This is because system calls happen frequently and usage control decisions must be taken for each. Hence, we chose to deploy all components locally. PIPs keep the data flow state of their local system. The work presented here extends the knowledge of local PIPs with information about data that has been communicated to or from other PIPs. The product of the *storage*, *alias*, and *naming* functions (cf. §2.1) of all PIPs corresponds to the system's global data flow state.

Systrace [36] has been used to implement the PEP; it allows to intercept, observe, modify, and prohibit system calls both before and after their execution by the kernel. Using systrace, no modifications to the operating system itself are needed; details are provided in [10, 36]. While LEIs at the operating system layer have been built before [7, 10, 44], our DDI implementation complements this work for TCP-based data flows and policy enforcement on multiple machines. We will now look into the crucial parts of the implementation.

5.1 Connection Establishment

If two communicating processes, p_S and p_C (server and client), run on the same host, the local PIP tracks the data flow through the local TCP connection. In contrast, if p_S and p_C run on two different hosts (cf. Fig. 4), the PIPs of the two DDIs must communicate the fact of connection establishment. As soon as the TCP communication channel has been set up by the underlying operating systems, both the server's *accept* and the client's *connect* return and are intercepted by the corresponding PEPs. On the server side, PEP_S then asks OS_S for the assigned local socket name (a_s, x_s) and notifies PIP_S that the event happened. PIP_S then creates a new socket container c and assigns the corresponding identifiers as described in §3.1 by updating naming function f. PIP_S then communicates the socket's ID (c),

76

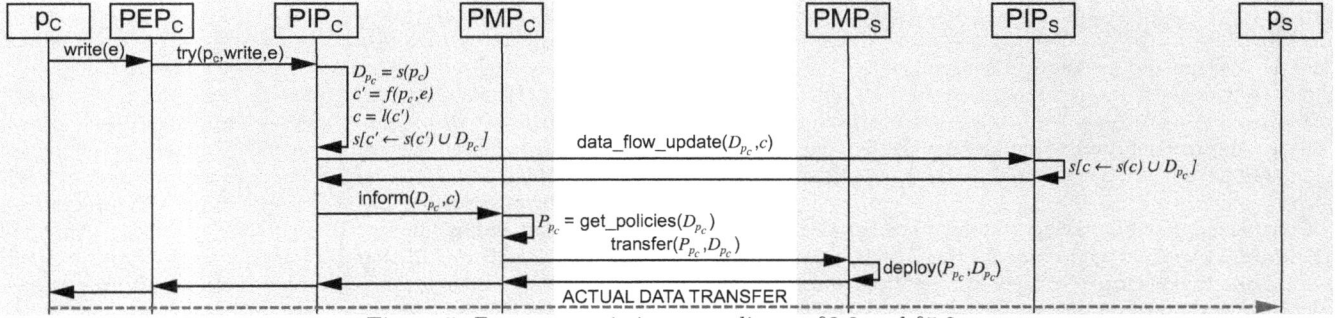

Figure 5: Data transmission according to §3.2 and §5.2.

its local socket name (a_s, x_s), and its remote socket name (a_c, x_c) to PIP_C. If this remote procedure call (*establish_connection()*) is about to be handled by PIP_C before the corresponding client's *connect* response, it is put on hold until the client's *connect* returned. Similarly, upon return of the client's *connect*, PEP_C asks OS_C for the assigned local socket name (a_c, x_c) and notifies PIP_C, which then assigns the corresponding identifiers according to §3.1 by updating naming function f. From the information sent by PIP_S, PIP_C can then identify the client's socket container (c') and create the alias to the server's socket container (c) by updating the alias function l as described in §3.1. PIP_C replies to PIP_S with the ID of the client socket container (c') and PIP_S then creates the second alias from c to c'.

5.2 Data Transmission

After connection establishment, p_S and p_C may cause cross-system data flows by writing to the TCP channel. If p_C (analogous for p_S) executes sytem call *write* (or any equivalent, cf. §3.2) on a file descriptor referring to a TCP channel to p_S, PIP_C and PIP_S realize cross-system data flow tracking, while PMP_C and PMP_S implement the sticky policy paradigm as follows (cf. Fig. 3 steps 6-9 and Fig. 5)[2]:

When p_C's *write* is intercepted and temporarily blocked by PEP_C, PIP_C is informed and updates its storage function s according to §3.2. PIP_C then performs a call to PIP_S conveying the information that the set of abstract data items D_{p_c} (i.e., all data read by p_C) is going to be transmitted to the aliased socket container c (*data_flow_update()*). PIP_S therefore updates its storage function s according to §3.2. PIP_C then informs PMP_C about the transmission of D_{p_c} to socket container c (*inform()*), and PMP_C performs a call to PMP_S, transferring the set of usage control policies P_{p_c} that apply to any of the data items in D_{p_c} (*transfer()*). PMP_S then deploys the policies on system S. On success, p_C's *write* is unblocked and the actual data transfer succeeds. While they are conceptually different, our implementation bundles the two remote procedure calls (*data_flow_update()*, *transfer()*) for performance reasons.

As soon as p_S reads from the aliased socket container c, PDP_S and PIP_S are already aware of the cross-system data flow and the corresponding policies, therefore extending usage control to system S. Note that PIP_C's data flow state may change in-between two *write* system calls of p_C (e.g., if p_C reads additional data). In this case the remote communication (i.e., *data_flow_update()*, *transfer()*) needs to be repeated upon the next *write* system call.

---

[2]We assume that PDP_C decided to allow the *write*; otherwise no cross-system data flow (tracking) would happen.

5.3 Connection Teardown

If a TCP connection between two processes on different hosts is torn down, this fact is communicated between the corresponding PIPs; parameters are the connection's identifiers (local socket name and remote socket name) and the type of connection teardown. Each PIP is then responsible for updating its state according to §3.3.

Note. By its very nature TCP communication is limited to two communication partners. Thus all considerations in §3-§5 are limited to a client and a server system. For distributed scenarios with a larger number of systems our infrastructure and its features apply transitively.

6. EVALUATION

6.1 Provided Guarantees

If the presented integrated infrastructure (LEI and DDI) is in place and not tampered with, the CEO (cf. §1.1) can now be sure that all copies and derivations of business reports are accompanied with the usage control policy he specified (duty of the DDI), and that employees can use the business reports only in accordance with the policy (duty of the LEI). As described in §2-§5, the CEO's policy is always transferred along with the business reports and enforced on any receiving system—as long as TCP is used as the transport layer. Via intra-system and cross-system data flow tracking at the level of system calls, all copies and derivations of the business reports are detected and protected on both local and remote systems. While our DDI realizes cross-system data flow tracking and the sticky policy paradigm, the LEI is responsible for intra-system data flow tracking, policy decisions and policy enforcement.

Assume that the CEO has defined a weaker policy that permits Alice to share business reports with the PR department after blackening certain parts of the report. Our system would make sure that if Alice sends the report to Charlie, (1) Alice's LEI blackens the corresponding parts and (2) Alice's DDI would send the policy along with the modified report to Charlie. Charlie's usage control infrastructure would work identically. A further recipient outside of the company would then get the report from Charlie only after blackening further details. Different semantics of this kind of requirements are discussed in [35]. In other words, using our system, enforcement of usage control requirements is not restricted to the initial data provider and the initial data consumer, but rather to all (transitive) consumers of a data item, as long as they are equipped with LEI and DDI.

We obviously assume that the receiving system has the necessary distributed usage control infrastructure in place.

Our current instantiation gives some kind of weak assurance for this fact by (1) detecting whether usage controlled data is transmitted to another system and (2) disallowing the data transfer if the receiving system does not follow the infrastructure's protocol. We are aware that this only constitutes an interim solution while more sophisticated solutions are being developed, since attackers could easily circumvent such a solution (cf. §6.2).

Considering the increasing amount of sensitive digital information in various environments (e.g., businesses, governmental institutions, car to car communication, smart meters, cyber-physical systems) as well as the increasing number of embedded and integrated devices (e.g., phones, tablets, cars, smart meters), we are convinced that within (semi-)closed environments such usage control solutions can and will become reality. For this, users must not have administrative privileges on their computing devices and there must not be means to modify underlying hard- and software. In contrast, in completely open environments it is unclear whether such technologies can become reality, since trusted computing technologies would be needed to assure the existence of a usage control infrastructure on a remote machine.

6.2 Attack Vectors

While we are aware that a security analysis cannot be exhausting, the purpose of this section is to understand the attack surface and vulnerabilities in our work. We consider two attacker models: non-privileged end users (root users cannot be controlled but only observed [25]) and a man-in-the-middle between the two communicating systems. Goals of the attackers (w.r.t. usage control in general and our infrastructure in particular) may be to (1) use usage-controlled data without respecting the applicable policies or (2) render the usage control infrastructure useless or unusable.

Assumptions. Since our work focuses on the distributed aspect of usage control, we assume that usage control policies are enforced once they have been deployed locally. By tackling usage control at the operating system layer, we must assume that the operating system and the underlying hardware are not vulnerable and that the user does not have root privileges, since a root user could easily switch off the usage control infrastructure. The latter assumption could be avoided by exploiting trusted computing technologies to assure that the usage control infrastructure, the operating system, as well as underlying hardware are in a proper state and that they cannot be modified in an unwanted way (i.e. by disabling the enforcement infrastructure), cf. §8.

Non-TCP Communication. Since our implementation investigates usage control at the TCP-layer, data could unrestrictedly be redistributed using other transport layer protocols, e.g. by tunneling TCP via UDP [23] or by redistributing data via non-TCP application-layer protocols such as DNS. Additionally, users can share usage controlled data using protocols such as USB or Bluetooth. These attacks can be addressed by disallowing any non-TCP data flows. Since this is unlikely to be accepted in real world scenarios, usage control must be extended to support these protocols. Our model for cross-system data flow tracking has been developed for unicast communication using the Internet Protocol (IP); in this paper TCP serves as just one example.

Portable media. In general, users have the possibility to save usage controlled data to portable media, physically removable hard disks, or the like. Such attacks can be prevented by inhibiting all attempts to save usage-controlled data to portable media or by mediating all corresponding actions through encryption tools such as TrueCrypt [42].

Fool Infrastructure. If data is sent, the DDIs of the communicating systems exchange information about cross-system data flows and usage control policies. A malicious user could set up fake usage control components, particularly the distributed parts of PIP and PMP, pretending to have an enforcement infrastructure in place. An honest infrastructure will then be fooled into thinking that the remote enforcement infrastructure is in place while it actually isn't. The malicious user would then receive usage controlled data without having an enforcement infrastructure in place. Certificates cannot eliminate this attack but introduce means for liability. Trusted computing technologies would be needed to defend against such attacks, cf. §8.

Man-in-the-Middle (MitM) Attack. A MitM attack can be performed both on the actual data transfer and on the DDI's communication.

Considering the actual data transfer, a MitM could sniff or modify the usage controlled data, and hence use the sniffed data without having a usage control infrastructure in place. Means to protect the data transfer exist, e.g. TLS [6], IPSec [14], tcpcrypt [3]. While TLS is commonly used for security-critical internet applications, it comes with the drawback that it must be supported by both the application-layer protocol and the corresponding applications. For non-TLS applications, tcpcrypt and IPSec can be integrated, since they are transparent to the application layer while providing similar guarantees in terms of confidentiality.

A MitM could also attack the DDI's communication by (1) inserting, dropping, or changing usage control policies or information regarding cross-system data flow (e.g., dropping messages between the PIPs) or by (2) changing the mapping between policies and data. Similarly, techniques like IPSec or tcpcrypt may be used to transparently secure this communication without interference with our infrastructure.

(Distributed) Denial-of-Service ((D)DoS) Attack. (D)DoS attacks may be mounted both by the local user and by a remote user by causing high amounts of system calls. While a local user could mount such an attack by issuing any kind of system calls, a remote user could do so by sending (potentially from different sources) messages to open ports that then result in system calls for the corresponding process. Such attacks may lead to high system response times and in the worst case render the usage controlled system unusable. Since in this case no data usage is possible at all (all system calls are handled sequentially by the same PEP), soundness of the infrastructure (i.e., no non-controlled usage of data) is not compromised by such an attack. Of course, availability of data can then no longer be guaranteed.

6.3 Performance

Influencing Factors. Hardware as well as system and network load will impact measurement results; in our case network interfaces and bandwidth are particularly important. The amount of system calls plays a significant role, since we intercept the security-relevant ones and take usage control decisions at each. This amount is given by the applications used for performance measurements, i.e. client and server process. Another influencing factor is the time

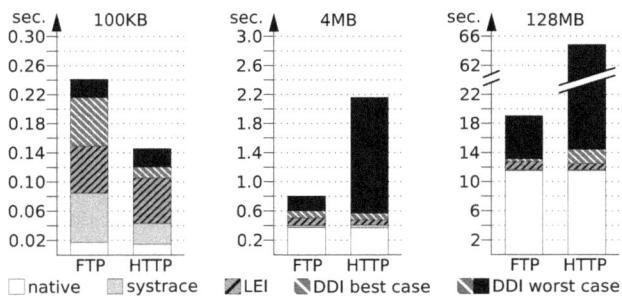

Figure 6: Performance measurement results.
Legend: □ native, ▨ systrace, ▧ LEI, ◩ DDI best case, ◼ DDI worst case.

number of syscalls	FTP Server: vsftpd			HTTP Server: Apache		
	100KB	4MB	128MB	100KB	4MB	128MB
write()	43	139	4107	22	996	32740
total	148	358	8294	52	1523	49139
performance overhead factor w.r.t. native execution						
best case	11.66	0.61	0.14	7.29	0.53	0.25
worst case	13.15	1.16	0.65	9.01	4.90	4.65

Table 2: Number of system calls and performance overhead for transferring files in OpenBSD 4.9.

needed for policy evaluation, which heavily depends on the complexity of the policies that must be evaluated[3].

Test Setup. For testing the performance of cross-system data flow tracking, policy transfer, and policy deployment (being the crucial parts of the presented DDI), we transferred files of sizes 100KB, 4MB, and 128MB between a client process and a server process using HTTP and FTP—two of the most popular protocols for transferring data on today's internet. Both server and client run the integrated infrastructure consisting of (1) systrace for intercepting system calls, (2) a LEI for intra-system data flow tracking and policy enforcement (§4, step E, [10]), and (3) our DDI as instantiated in §5.

We ran our tests on two dedicated computers[4] that were linked via a 100Mbit switch. No services other than the enforcement infrastructure and the applications needed for testing run on the machines. For file transfers via HTTP and FTP we used `Apache 2.2.15` and `vsftpd 2.3.2` as server, respectively. In both cases `wget 1.12` was used as client application. The time of data transfer was measured by invoking `wget` with the `time` command. Each test was repeated ten times; the observed standard deviation was negligible.

Since policy evaluations in the PDP are not subject of this paper, we deployed a policy that constantly evaluated to *allow*. Also, our evaluation does not focus on other overhead introduced by the LEI, since the overhead of such infrastructures has been discussed before [7,10,44].

Results. Fig. 6 and Table 1 show the results of our performance evaluation. The overhead stems from (1) systrace (□), (2) the LEI for tracking intra-system flows at the level of the operating system (▧), and (3) the overhead induced by this paper's DDI in the best case (◩) and in the worst case (the induced overhead being the sum of ◩ and ◼ : ◩◼).

Time for file transfer in seconds	native □	systrace ▨	LEI ▧	DDI best case ◩	DDI worst case ◩◼
FTP 100KB	0.017	0.084	0.148	0.215	0.240
HTTP 100KB	0.014	0.043	0.105	0.120	0.145
FTP 4MB	0.369	0.397	0.499	0.597	0.800
HTTP 4MB	0.365	0.402	0.474	0.560	2.153
FTP 128MB	11.454	11.601	12.672	13.063	18.987
HTTP 128MB	11.463	11.602	12.426	14.394	64.816

Table 1: Detailed performance measurement results.

We differentiate the overhead of the DDI in a best case and a worst case scenario for the following reason: As described in §5.2, it may happen that the data flow state changes

---

[3]These are all policies referring to some data being stored in some container being a parameter of the system call.
[4]Each Athlon 64 X2 3800+, 4GB RAM, Gigabyte GA-K8NF-9 mainboard, Gigabit LAN; clean OpenBSD 4.9.

in-between two *write* system calls, e.g. if the corresponding process reads additional sensitive data. In this case the communication between the remote PIPs and PMPs must be repeated in order to update the data flow state of the receiving system and to transfer policies that have not been transferred before. In the worst case this communication must be repeated upon every *write*, while in the best case the PMPs and PIPs must communicate upon the initial *write* only.

In the **best case** the accumulated overhead induced by the integrated infrastructure ranges from a factor of 0.14 to 11.66 w.r.t. native execution (□) (cf. Table 2). For transferring small files (100KB), we observe that the accumulated overhead is higher for FTP than for HTTP. This is because FTP operates on two TCP channels, a data channel and a control channel, and our DDI monitors both. Operating on two TCP channels also results in `vsftpd` issuing much more system calls for transferring the same file of 100KB than `Apache` (cf. Table 2). On the other hand, we observe that for the 128MB test case, the overhead induced by our DDI is higher for HTTP than for FTP. There are two reasons for this: First, the overhead for establishing and monitoring the FTP control channel is negligible for larger files. Second, `Apache` issues eight times more *write* system calls than `vsftpd` for transferring the same file (cf. Table 2). Since the DDI has to re-evaluate the data flow state upon every *write* in order to decide whether the PIPs and PMPs need to communicate, this leads to a higher overhead for HTTP.

In the **worst case**, the accumulated overhead ranges between factors of 0.65 to 13.15 w.r.t. native execution (cf. Table 2). Since in this case the PMPs and PIPs must communicate upon every *write*, the amount of *write* system calls determines the induced overhead. Again, since `Apache` issues much more *write* system calls for transferring large files, the accumulated worst case overhead is higher for HTTP.

In sum, large parts of the performance overhead induced by our infrastructure depends on the amount of system calls issued by the server process. For this reason, the performance overhead depends on the implementation of a protocol rather than the protocol itself. Also, we observed that the performance overhead is smaller when transferring larger files (cf. Table 2). Reasons for this are the bootstrapping process of the file transfer, which has smaller performance impact for large files, as well as the one-time policy transfer and data flow tracking in our best case scenario.

While we did not take into account other protocols or other implementations of HTTP/FTP, we are confident that our measurement results are close to best and worse case scenarios for other protocols and implementations as well. We base our confidence on two facts: First, the internal handling of buffers and system calls of `vsftpd` and `Apache` is quite different: While `vsftpd` operates with little *write* system calls on large buffers (4107 *writes* for 128MB), `Apache` operates with many *writes* on small buffers (32740 *writes* for 128MB). Second, HTTP and FTP are quite different from a technical perspective, since FTP operates on two TCP channels. Considering these differences and the fact that performance overheads for our best case scenario are similar[5], we are confident that our results are representative. Considering the difference in performance between our best case and worse case scenario, we are convinced that our best case results are close to real-world data usage scenarios, since (1) real world applications do not read additional data while sending data over the network and (2) usage control policies are rather long-lived and thus they usually do not have to be resend upon data transfer. Of course, additional overhead would be introduced by securing our infrastructure with IPSec [9], tcpcrypt [3], or remote attestation [15, 25, 38].

While we measured performance overheads of factors between 0.14 and 13.15 w.r.t. native execution (the worst case overhead is thus one order of magnitude), we contextualize these measurements in order to give an impression whether such overheads are acceptable. In case of a one-time transfer of 100KB, our measurements resulted in performance overheads between factors of 7.29 and 13.15. Considering that the transfer of a single file may then take 240ms instead of 17ms, such an overhead is likely to be acceptable in *user-interactive* workflows where such transfers happen occasionally. In contrast, when large amounts of small files are transferred in a sequence, e.g. 100 files of 100KB, a total transfer time of 24s instead of 1.7s is likely not to be acceptable in *user-interactive* applications. For transferring larger files in the best case scenario, performance overhead factors of 0.14 (FTP 128MB) to 0.61 (FTP 4MB) w.r.t. native execution are likely to be acceptable. In general, acceptability of performance overheads depends on the specific context. Note that we did not optimize performance of our prototype; the results thus show an upper bound for solutions like ours.

7. LIMITATIONS & FUTURE WORK

In our solution we focused on locally enforceable policies, meaning that the local information flow state is sufficient to take usage control decisions. We plan to extend our work to support usage control policies that refer to the global information flow state, therefore being able to enforce policies like "this data item must not reside in more than three systems," "not more than five instances of this process may be run at the same time," or "access that data only four times."

In this work we assumed a static network structure. Since technologies such as DHCP and network address translation (NAT) are in widespread use in today's internet, we plan to extend our work to this dynamic dimension.

Although our implementation supports most internet applications by realizing cross-system data flow tracking at the level of TCP, other important usage control applications like multimedia streaming and Voice over IP are not covered. This is because such applications use UDP as transport layer, as low-latency delivery is preferred to the guarantees provided by TCP. We thus plan to instantiate our model for UDP and/or tackle the problem of usage control at the level of IP. This way, we are also able to address some "non-TCP communication" attacks described in §6.2. This necessitates the definition of state transitions ϱ for UDP/IP and adjustment of the infrastructure to cope with the unreliability of

UDP/IP. Multimedia streaming then also motivates to investigate multicast communication in usage control.

At the level of system call interposition, processes are considered black boxes that might write any of their knowledge into a TCP channel. By tainting the communication channel once usage-controlled data is (potentially) sent, all further data transmitted on the same channel is considered tainted as well. In order to overcome these overapproximations in an application-independent manner, we plan to (1) apply declassification techniques to our proposed solution and (2) bring in knowledge about the application-level protocol.

Our solution does not cover side channels such as timing attacks or power monitoring. Moreover, we did not put excessive effort into securing the prototypically implemented infrastructure. Solutions to this have been proposed and implemented; we give an overview in §8.

8. RELATED WORK

Application-dependent distributed usage control. Some distributed usage control concepts [12, 18] are application(-protocol) dependent by integrating the PEP into the application and incorporating policies into the application protocol. These solutions fix data provider and data consumer beforehand, thus not catering to bidirectional data flows and redistribution of data as usual in today's internet. [5, 21, 22] realize usage control for grid computational services by making the grid user deploy her application together with the policy. The application is monitored at the level of the Java Virtual Machine, whereby system calls are considered as security-relevant actions. Their approach is different from ours in that the policy is defined for the application instead of data. Since this approach does not consider data flow, cooperating applications could circumvent the usage control policy, which is not possible with our solution due to intra-system and cross-system data flow tracking.

Sticky Policies. In terms of sticking policies to data, the back channel model [4] is close to our approach. In this approach, on each system the communication between PEP and PDP is mediated through an application independent PEP (AIPEP). Once data is sent to another system, the AIPEP is responsible for sending the sticky policy to the AIPEP of the receiving system. The model differs from ours, since it was one of our goals to integrate seamlessly into an existing infrastructure for independent systems. Furthermore, we are not aware of corresponding implementations.

Trustworthiness of security mechanisms. As usage control is naturally distributed and policies must be enforced at the data consumer's site, the latter must implement at least the PEP. In order to convincingly spread distributed usage control mechanisms, any remotely deployed component must "behave in a 'good' manner and this manner [must be verifiable] by the policy stakeholder" [45]. To this end, solutions leveraging the Trusted Platform Module (TPM) have been proposed [25, 37, 39, 45]. Their basic idea is to verify the integrity of crucial system components (e.g., BIOS, Bootloader, Operating System, usage control infrastructure) before their execution and verify their integrity by comparing the measurements to a set of known "good" values. [2, 16] propose to send data that is to be controlled only to data consumers that persuade the data provider of having usage control mechanisms deployed.

Digital Rights Management (DRM). DRM [1, 8, 19, 24, 41] refers to concepts and techniques that aim at con-

---
[5]100KB: 11.66 FTP overhead vs. 7.29 HTTP overhead; 4MB: 0.61 vs. 0.53; 128MB: 0.14 vs. 0.25; cf. Table 2.

trolling the usage and distribution of copyrighted, usually read-only, digital information at the data consumer's site. DRM can therefore be considered a specialization of usage control [32] that largely focuses on payment-based dissemination [26]; end users are not considered content providers: DRM does not provide means to protect their valuable (personal) information. While some solutions [1] work with central servers for storing keys, such a central component is not needed in our approach. Also, DRM solutions [1, 24] are tailored to specific file types and rely on specific applications to enforce digital licenses. Instead, our approach is independent of particular file types and applications.

Detective enforcement. The work presented in this paper enforces policies in a preventive manner: it is made sure that policies are adhered to. Enforcement can also be detective [27]: if a policy violation is detected, then various measures can be taken; prevention is thus replaced by accountability [43]. Our infrastructure can also be used for detective enforcement: rather than preventing Alice from forwarding the original business report to Charlie, the fact that she *did not* blacken certain parts before forwarding can be stored. A different approach is taken by Seneviratne [40] who directly embeds information accountability into HTTP. Different to our work, this approach is limited to one particular application-layer protocol and does not implement preventive enforcement mechanisms but rather gives users the opportunity to figure out how their data was misused and to take appropriate action.

9. CONCLUSIONS

Today's highly distributed computing environments lack mechanisms when it comes to enforcing restrictions on the usage of data after its release. This is relevant for both privacy and the protection of intellectual property or secrets. To fill this gap, we have extended a model that allows for intra-system data flow tracking to the cross-system case. We have concretized the model for tracking all TCP data flows at the level of the operating system by considering networking-related system calls as security-relevant actions. We based our work on a previously implemented infrastructure that can detect local *intra-system* data flows. In order to extend this infrastructure to the enforcement of usage control policies in *distributed* systems, we developed a distributed infrastructure for transparently and application-independently tracking *cross-system* data flows as well. In addition to tracking data flows to remote systems, this infrastructure takes care of transferring policies along with the data to be controlled. By integrating this infrastructure with an existing infrastructure for single independent systems, we manage to track data both within and across systems and enforce usage control policies at all systems processing usage controlled data. We instantiated and evaluated the data flow model and the enforcement infrastructure for the OpenBSD operating system. Our measurement results yielded overheads between factors of 0.14 and one order of magnitude w.r.t. native execution in a best case and a worst case scenario, respectively. We conclude that acceptability of such overheads depends on the specific context.

With an infrastructure like ours, it is now possible to not only track and control the local flow of data in-between different representations (files, pixmaps, Java objects, etc.) on one machine, but also across several machines. We believe that this constitutes a further step towards the represen-

tation-independent protection of data in today's company intranets as well as cloud-based systems on the internet.

Acknowledgment. The work described was funded by a Google Focused Research Award on Cloud Computing.

10. REFERENCES

[1] Adobe Systems Incorporated. Adobe Content Server, http://www.adobe.com/products/content-server.html, 2012.

[2] A. Berthold, M. Alam, R. Breu, M. Hafner, A. Pretschner, J.-P. Seifert, and X. Zhang. A Technical Architecture for Enforcing Usage Control Requirements in Service-Oriented Architectures. In *Proc. of the 2007 ACM Workshop on Secure Web Services*, pages 18–25, 2007.

[3] A. Bittau, M. Hamburg, M. Handley, D. Mazières, and D. Boneh. The case for ubiquitous transport-level encryption. In *Proc. 19th USENIX Conference on Security*, 2010.

[4] D. W. Chadwick and S. F. Lievens. Enforcing "Sticky" Security Policies throughout a Distributed Application. In *Proc. of the 2008 Workshop on Middleware Security*, pages 1–6, 2008.

[5] M. Colombo, F. Martinelli, P. Mori, and A. Lazouski. On Usage Control for GRID Services. In *International Joint Conference on Computational Sciences and Optimization*, pages 47–51, Apr. 2009.

[6] T. Dierks and E. Rescorla. RFC 5246: The Transport Layer Security (TLS) Protocol Version 1.2, 2008.

[7] D. Feth and A. Pretschner. Flexible Data-Driven Security for Android. In *2012 IEEE Sixth International Conference on Software Security and Reliability*, pages 41–50, June 2012.

[8] D. Geer. Digital Rights Technology Sparks Interoperability Concerns. *IEEE Computer*, 37(12):20–22, 2004.

[9] G. Hadjichristofi, I. Davis, N.J., and S. Midkiff. IPSec Overhead in Wireline and Wireless Networks for Web and Email Applications. In *Proc. of the 2003 IEEE International Performance, Computing, and Communications Conference*, pages 543–547, 2003.

[10] M. Harvan and A. Pretschner. State-Based Usage Control Enforcement with Data Flow Tracking using System Call Interposition. In *Proc. 2009 Third International Conference on Network and System Security*, pages 373–380, 2009.

[11] M. Hilty, A. Pretschner, D. Basin, C. Schaefer, and T. Walter. A Policy Language for Distributed Usage Control. *Proc. 12th European Symp. on Research in Computer Security*, pages 531–546, 2007.

[12] B. Katt, X. Zhang, R. Breu, M. Hafner, and J.-P. Seifert. A General Obligation Model and Continuity-Enhanced Policy Enforcement Engine for Usage Control. In *Proc. 13th ACM Symposium on Access Control Models and Technologies*, pages 123–132, 2008.

[13] F. Kelbert and A. Pretschner. Towards a Policy Enforcement Infrastructure for Distributed Usage Control. In *Proc. 17th ACM Symposium on Access Control Models and Technologies*, pages 119–122, 2012.

[14] S. Kent and K. Seo. RFC 4301: Security Architecture for the Internet Protocol, 2005.

[15] C. Kil, E. Sezer, A. Azab, P. Ning, and X. Zhang. Remote Attestation to Dynamic System Properties: Towards Providing Complete System Integrity Evidence. In *IEEE/IFIP Intl. Conf. on Dependable Systems Networks*, pages 115–124, July 2009.

[16] P. Kumari, F. Kelbert, and A. Pretschner. Data Protection in Heterogeneous Distributed Systems: A Smart Meter Example. In *INFORMATIK 2011 - Dependable Software for Critical Infrastructures*, 2011.

[17] P. Kumari and A. Pretschner. Deriving Implementation-level Policies for Usage Control Enforcement. In *Proc. 2nd ACM Conf. on Data and Application Security and Privacy*, pages 83–94, 2012.

[18] P. Kumari, A. Pretschner, J. Peschla, and J.-M. Kuhn. Distributed Data Usage Control for Web Applications: A Social Network Implementation. *Proc. 1st ACM Conference on Data and Application Security and Privacy*, pages 85–96, 2011.

[19] Q. Liu, R. Safavi-Naini, and N. P. Sheppard. Digital Rights Management for Content Distribution. In *Proc. Australasian Information Security Workshop Conference*, volume 21, pages 49–58, 2003.

[20] E. Lovat and A. Pretschner. Data-centric Multi-layer Usage Control Enforcement: A Social Network Example. In *Proc. 16th ACM Symposium on Access Control Models and Technologies*, pages 151–152, 2011.

[21] F. Martinelli and P. Mori. On Usage Control for GRID Systems. *Future Generation Computer Systems*, 26(7):1032–1042, July 2010.

[22] F. Martinelli, P. Mori, and A. Vaccarelli. Towards Continuous Usage Control on Grid Computational Services. In *Joint Intl. Conference on Autonomic and Autonomous Systems and Intl. Conference on Networking and Services*, 2005.

[23] D. Meekins. UDP Tunnel - Tunnel TCP data through UDP messages, http://code.google.com/p/udptunnel/, 2009-2011.

[24] Microsoft Corporation. Architecture of Windows Media Rights Manager, http://www.microsoft.com/windows/windowsmedia/howto/articles/drmarchitecture.aspx, 2004.

[25] R. Neisse, D. Holling, and A. Pretschner. Implementing Trust in Cloud Infrastructures. *Proc. 11th IEEE/ACM International Conference on Cluster Cloud and Grid Computing*, 2011.

[26] J. Park and R. Sandhu. Towards Usage Control Models: Beyond Traditional Access Control. In *Proc. 7th ACM Symposium on Access Control Models and Technologies*, pages 57–64, 2002.

[27] D. Povey. Optimistic Security: A New Access Control Paradigm. In *Proc. Workshop on New Security Paradigms*, pages 40–45, 1999.

[28] A. Pretschner. An Overview of Distributed Usage Control. In *Knowledge Engineering: Principles and Techniques Conference*, pages 25–33, 2009.

[29] A. Pretschner, M. Büchler, M. Harvan, C. Schaefer, and T. Walter. Usage Control Enforcement with Data Flow Tracking for X11. In *Proc. 5th Intl. Workshop on Security and Trust Management*, pages 124–137, 2009.

[30] A. Pretschner, M. Hilty, and D. Basin. Distributed Usage Control. *Communications of the ACM*, 49(9):39–44, 2006.

[31] A. Pretschner, M. Hilty, D. Basin, C. Schaefer, and T. Walter. Mechanisms for Usage Control. In *Proc. 2008 ACM Symposium on Information, Computer and Communications Security*, pages 240–244, 2008.

[32] A. Pretschner, M. Hilty, F. Schütz, C. Schaefer, and T. Walter. Usage Control Enforcement: Present and Future. *IEEE Security & Privacy*, 6(4):44–53, 2008.

[33] A. Pretschner, E. Lovat, and M. Büchler. Representation-Independent Data Usage Control. In *Data Privacy Management and Autonomous Spontaneus Security*, volume 7122 of *Lecture Notes in Computer Science*, pages 122–140. 2012.

[34] A. Pretschner, J. Rüesch, C. Schaefer, and T. Walter. Formal Analyses of Usage Control Policies. *Proc. 2009 International Conference on Availability, Reliability and Security*, pages 98–105, 2009.

[35] A. Pretschner, F. Schütz, C. Schaefer, and T. Walter. Policy Evolution in Distributed Usage Control. *Electron. Notes Theor. Comput. Sci.*, 244:109–123, Aug. 2009.

[36] N. Provos. Improving Host Security with System Call Policies. In *Proc. 12th USENIX Security Symp.*, 2003.

[37] R. Sailer, T. Jaeger, X. Zhang, and L. van Doorn. Attestation-based Policy Enforcement for Remote Access. In *Proc. 11th ACM Conference on Computer and Communications Security*, pages 308–317, 2004.

[38] R. Sailer, X. Zhang, T. Jaeger, and L. van Doorn. Design and Implementation of a TCG-based Integrity Measurement Architecture. In *Proceedings of the 13th USENIX Security Symposium*, 2004.

[39] R. Sandhu and X. Zhang. Peer-to-peer Access Control Architecture Using Trusted Computing Technology. In *Proc. 10th ACM Symposium on Access Control Models and Technologies*, pages 147–158, 2005.

[40] O. W. Seneviratne. Augmenting the Web with Accountability. In *Proc. 21st Intl. Conf. Companion on World Wide Web*, pages 185–190, 2012.

[41] S. Subramanya and B. K. Yi. Digital Rights Management. *IEEE Potentials*, (April):31–34, 2006.

[42] TrueCrypt Foundation. TrueCrypt, http://www.truecrypt.org/, 2004-2012.

[43] D. J. Weitzner, H. Abelson, T. Berners-Lee, J. Feigenbaum, J. Hendler, and G. J. Sussman. Information Accountability. *Commun. ACM*, 51(6):82–87, June 2008.

[44] T. Wüchner and A. Pretschner. Data Loss Prevention Based on Data-Driven Usage Control. In *Proc. 23rd IEEE Intl. Symposium on Software Reliability Engineering*, Nov. 2012.

[45] X. Zhang, J.-P. Seifert, and R. Sandhu. Security Enforcement Model for Distributed Usage Control. *IEEE Intl. Conf. on Sensor Networks, Ubiquitous, and Trustworthy Computing*, pages 10–18, 2008.

The Usability of TrueCrypt, or
How I Learned to Stop Whining and Fix an Interface

Sumeet Gujrati
Kansas State University
Manhattan, KS, USA
sgujrati@ksu.edu

Eugene Vasserman
Kansas State University
Manhattan, KS, USA
eyv@ksu.edu

ABSTRACT

Non-use or incorrect use of security software is one major reason for privacy breaches of all scales. The problem is compounded by software, security policies, and user interfaces that are difficult to use and understand. Using widely accepted user interface analysis methods, we examine a popular free and open source disk encryption software package, and find that it is far from accessible to ordinary users. Using rigorous interface design principles, we derive several concrete changes that would make the software easier to use, and construct a new interface to test our theories. We evaluate the two interfaces through a randomized user study in a controlled laboratory setting, and determine that the new interface is significantly easier to understand and faster to use, especially for novice computer users. We observe not only measurable speed-ups of common tasks, but also improved user-reported ease of use ratings. Several of our design choices turn out to have been misguided, making some tasks more difficult in our modified interface, but fortunately our alterations are mutually independent, i.e. reverting some components to their original design does not nullify the benefit of other modifications. Our experience shows that even simple, intuitive, and logically consistent modifications to complex interfaces have dramatic positive usability effects, and can be easily applied to different pieces of security software in order to reduce the impediment to uptake by novice users.

Categories and Subject Descriptors

D.2.2 [**Design Tools and Techniques**]: User interfaces; D.4.6 [**Security and Protection**]: Access controls; H.1.2 [**Information Systems**]: Human factors

Keywords

Security; Usability; Software design; User interfaces

1. INTRODUCTION

There are numerous examples of private information leaks which could have been prevented by keeping data encrypted when not in use. In 2006, a single laptop theft from a Veterans Affairs data

analyst resulted in the loss of unencrypted data affecting 26.5 million people [2]. The costs are staggering: the agency estimated that it will cost between $100 million to $500 million to prevent and fix possible monetary losses from this information incident. Liu and Kuhn [15] discuss the consequences of sensitive data loss for companies which can substantially harm a company's competitiveness and reputation and could also invite lawsuits. However, media theft does not have to lead to data exposure if the data is protected through file or disk encryption. While corporations are slowly learning this lesson, home users are far behind. Many do not even realize the risk of storing information unencrypted on their own computers, but more and more users are storing their private information this way given the increased usage of paperless billing and online banking. Since more and more sensitive transactions are performed electronically, the consequences of private information leaks due to personal computer theft are becoming more severe. Many security tools, including whole disk encryption, are available for end-users, but their uptake is very limited. Possible reasons include lack of awareness, difficulty of managing security settings, and costs of purchasing security products. The latter is increasingly unlikely, as many operating systems, including Linux, Windows 7, Mac OS (10.4 and later) have included disk encryption technologies. Even earlier, application-level encryption has been available for free as part of many open-source projects. In terms of awareness, many users underestimate their own security risks [19] and therefore may find the overhead, complexity, or product cost to be unjustifiable. However, there is another major reason that needs attention — usability of security — as many technologies are too hard to understand and configure, or are simply too inconvenient, e.g. due to repeated password entry. Users either stop using them or compromise their security by using them incorrectly.

In this paper, we carry out a usability case study of TrueCrypt [3], a popular, mature, and free disk encryption tool. Our goal is to improve the user experience, especially for new users, *without sacrificing any security options or functionality* originally available in TrueCrypt for advanced users, i.e. we would like to make the software accessible for novice users without reducing its utility for advanced users. Our broader goal is to show that the amount of work required to vastly improve the usability of a piece of software, even when dealing with external code, is far from prohibitive. We derive some general guidelines for developers to quickly evaluate their software for common usability flaws, and would allow significant usability improvements in only a few hours of developer time. In short, the reward of performing a quick usability analysis far outweighs the time and programming cost.

We chose TrueCrypt because it is free and open source, it is cross-platform, available for Windows, Mac, and Linux, and its popularity — its download count is more than 23 million [4]. We evaluate usability of TrueCrypt[1] for two main tasks, which must be performed by every new user of the software who intends to use file containers: *creating* an encrypted file container and *opening* that file container. We identify three factors which may prevent correct usage of the software or cause sufficient frustration to make users abandon TrueCrypt: 1) a non-intuitive user interface, 2) terminology unfamiliar to novice users, and 3) a lack of logic or consistency in the sequence of steps required to perform certain tasks. The contributions of our work are four-fold:

- We evaluate TrueCrypt's original user interface using a *cognitive walkthrough*, and find it to be very difficult to learn or understand for non-expert users.[2] We caution that however successful this approach is, it is not a replacement for a full user study, as some of our seemingly straightforward changes lead to surprising outcomes, but the ease of the cognitive walkthrough, the accuracy of resulting predictions, and the scale of measurable usability improvements suggest that all security software would benefit from this inexpensive and quick exercise.

- We modify the main TrueCrypt user interface and the installer to incorporate a post-installation quick-start wizard and streamline the process of initially creating and using file containers. We also overhaul the visual appearance and rewrite the terminology used throughout the application. We rigorously ensure that we retain all security functionality after these modifications — the security-sensitive operations of the back-end logic are unaffected. Our redesigned interface is available for download and modification,[3] and can be applied as a patch to the existing TrueCrypt source code distribution.[4]

- We evaluate the usability improvements resulting from our modifications through a randomized, single-blind user study, and objectively compare the speed and success rates of several common tasks, as well as subjective user-reported usability ratings. We find a significant improvement to core functionality, and yet observe that some of our changes make some tasks *more difficult* to perform. We can therefore show, at a high granularity, which changes to which TrueCrypt interface components are beneficial, and which are detrimental to usability.

- Through this experience, we demonstrate that a few hours of time analyzing the user interface of software at the design phase, development phase, or even immediately before release, can vastly improve the usability of the software. The payoff is high even when using external, never-before-seen code, as well as feature-frozen code. We find that usability can be improved **without sacrificing features** of the final product. We further note that developers do not need to be experts in user interface design to carry out this exercise.

The rest of the paper is organized as follows. Section 2 discusses preliminaries and prior work. Section 3 presents specific hypotheses about the ease of certain critical tasks within the old interface, and describes our design process to develop the new interface. Section 4 details the experimental results comparing the two interfaces. Section 5 discusses suggestions for developers to improve the usability of their software for novice users. Finally, we conclude in Section 6.

---

[1] Version 7.0a, the latest available at the beginning of the study
[2] We suspect even security experts may have some trouble
[3] http://www.cis.ksu.edu/~eyv/projects/truecrypt/
[4] We have contacted TrueCrypt's authors, offering our improvements for incorporation into the official binary distribution.

2. BACKGROUND AND RELATED WORK

Our subject of the study in this paper is TrueCrypt. As of version 5.0, it implements whole-disk encryption (on Windows), but its original (and still widely-used) purpose is creation and use of encrypted virtual volumes, or file containers, to store sensitive information on non-encrypted disks. A TrueCrypt file container is an ordinary file, mounted like a disk using TrueCrypt's virtual disk driver (on Windows) or the loopback or userfs filesystems on Linux, Mac OS, and BSD derivatives. The container is encrypted using choice of several algorithms, and ultimately protected by a user-chosen password. Unlike whole disk encryption, which generally only requires the user to enter a password once at boot time, containers are used as needed, and users are prompted for passwords every time the container is opened, potentially creating a conflict between security and usability, in which the latter almost always triumphs [6, 10, 24]. (Hidden container creation and use, a more advanced function, is left for future work.)

In 1999, Whitten and Tygar [27] proposed a definition of usable security and discussed it in the context of PGP 5.5. Since then, researchers have evaluated usability of many security tools and studied user's behavior, perception, and mental models related to security. Frequently, usability studies attempt to understand user' *mental models*: Chiasson and van Oorschot discuss the usability of two password managers [8]; Asgharpour, Liu, and Camp demonstrate that, for a variety of security risks, security experts and non-experts have differing mental models [7]; Motiee, Hawkey, and Beznosov analyze users' knowledge, behavior, motivations and challenges in using security software [18] and find that achieving this understanding is challenging due to the limitations of current research methodologies; Raja, Hawkey, and Beznosov study users' mental models of the Microsoft Windows Vista operating system firewall, and how users' models and understanding of the firewall's settings evolved after working with both the Vista firewall interface and authors' prototype interface [21]. These studies show that the mental models of experts and non-experts differ significantly. Inducing correct mental models is challenging when users lack a detailed understanding of the internals of a security mechanism. However, not everyone can be an expert, and users should not be required to be experts just to use personal security technologies.

Less often, *cognitive walkthroughs* are used as a tool to extract potential usability issues, such as Herzog and Shahmehri's result regarding personal firewalls [12]. We argue that cognitive walkthroughs can be an invaluable tool for developers as they are easier and faster to carry out for non-experts in usability and user modeling, and produce a high payoff in a short amount of time.

The concern about usability of security software has been gaining traction, from Whitten and Tygar's seminal report on the problem of usable security [27], to more recent work from Adams and Sasse [5] and Clark et al. [9]. However, these results have not been put into practice. Based on our experience, we derive four high-level, easy to follow guidelines for software developers, listed in Section 5. Incorporating these suggestions throughout the development process should greatly improve the usability of the resulting software, even if no usability specialists are consulted.

2.1 Cognitive Walkthrough

There are two main methods for evaluating usability of a software which influence our work: *cognitive walkthrough* and *user testing*. The *cognitive walkthrough* is a usability evaluation and improvement method in which an evaluator, a usability expert and knowledgeable in the domain of the software to be tested, uses the software as if he or she is a novice user, and identifies interface issues such as confusing terminology or tasks which are difficult to perform [20,

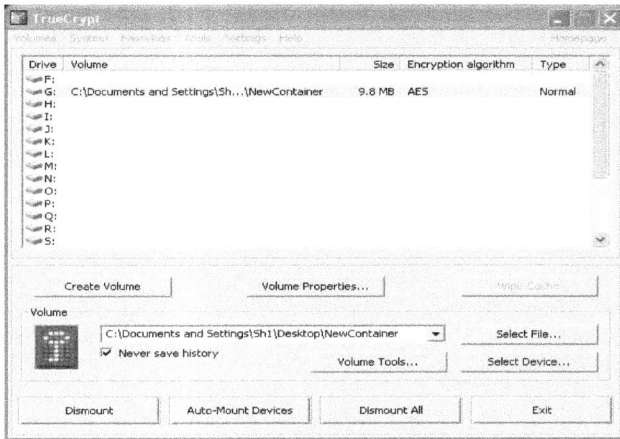

(a) TrueCrypt's interface

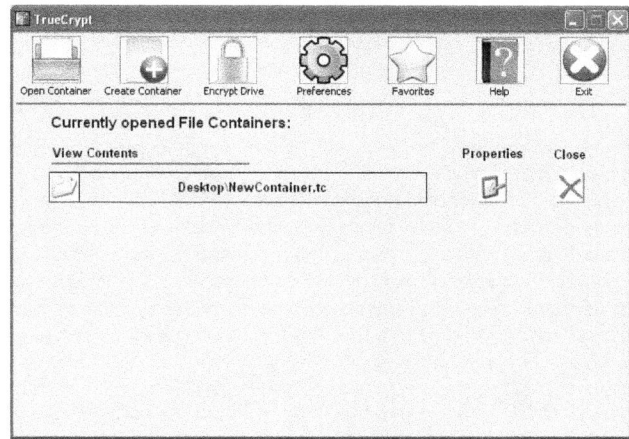

(b) Our modified interface

Figure 1: Main window of TrueCrypt's interface (a) and our modifications (b). Notice the terminology and non-intuitive visuals of the old interface.

22, 26]. This method is more appropriate for software which a user is expected to learn through "discovery," i.e. jumping in and using it rather than studying a manual. At each step of the walkthrough, the following four properties should hold [26]:

P1: The user should be able to achieve the right effect.

P2: The user should be able to notice that the correct action is available.

P3: The user should be able to associate the correct action with the effect he or she is trying to achieve.

P4: If the user performs the correct action, he or she should be able to see that progress is being made towards solution.

Lewis et al. report that this method has the advantages of relatively low cost and speedy results (almost 50% issues can be revealed), but is not a substitute for full user tests, which should still be conducted when the software is deemed ready [13]. Due to the length of user tests, at least one cognitive walkthrough should take place first.

2.2 User Testing

A *user test* is performed either in an environment similar to where the software is meant to be used, or in a controlled environment [11, 23]. Each user is given a set of tasks, and user performance is observed and recorded. The outcome of each task is evaluated, and the results are compiled and analyzed to identify major usability issues. Users may be asked to think aloud. Lewis proposed the "think aloud" protocol to gather user data by asking users to speak up while they perform various tasks [14], e.g. a user may say "starting" when beginning a new task, and "done" when completing it. Pre- and post-study questionnaires are also useful for collecting users' opinions and experiences regarding the software. Unstructured comments, however, are qualitative rather than quantitative, and hence should be used with great caution when analyzing results.

Due to the unique risks involved when using security software, the measures of usability of security are somewhat different. Whitten and Tygar report on the problem of usable security and propose a four point working definition [27] — security software is usable if the people who are *the expected user base*:

- are reliably made aware of the tasks they need to perform to be secure;
- can determine how to successfully perform those tasks;
- do not make dangerous errors; and

- are sufficiently comfortable with the interface to continue using it.

They additionally derive five properties of usable security, listed below. In Section 4.3, we test TrueCrypt's original interface and our modifications against these properties in addition to empirically measuring user performance in several common security-critical tasks.

S1 — Barn door property: If a user creates an insecure environment, the damage may already be done, even if the security error is quickly reversed. For example, leaving a laptop unprotected, someone may retrieve private information from it and there is no way to later determine conclusively whether this occurred.

S2 — Weakest link property: The available functionality of some application software, such as word processors and photo editing software, can be discovered by attempting to use it, essentially through random exploration of the interface. Mistakes do not lead to critical failures. This is not true with security software, since if a user makes a mistake, the damage may be irreversible — see the **barn door property**. Users of security software should be guided through its correct use, so the chance of failure to correctly complete a security task, especially while believing that the task was completed successfully, is minimized.

S3 — Unmotivated user property: Security is usually a secondary goal. People do not want to spend time managing information security policies; instead they want to use their applications. Security should function in the background, unobtrusively. If security obstructs user workflow, they will likely disable or bypass security controls. User interfaces designed for security should not assume that users will be motivated to read manuals or even dialog box text in order to use security correctly.

S4 — Abstraction property: Security policies usually involve abstract rules which specify whether to grant access to a resource. Creating, managing, and reasoning about such policies is too difficult for untrained users — one of the reasons that many users avoid using security software.

S5 — Lack of feedback property: In order to prevent dangerous errors, it is important to provide a feedback of current state of security to the user. Since this is generally a multi-variable, complex metric, it is difficult to summarize and adequately display.

3. DESIGN

In this section, we describe the results of our cognitive walkthrough of TrueCrypt's interface, our rapid prototype of a modified interface and installer, and reimplementation of full TrueCrypt interface and installer. In Section 4 we present the results of an empirical user study to validate or disprove our hypotheses regarding the effectiveness and impediments of specific components of the TrueCrypt user interface. We also discuss the technical challenges in moving from the rapid prototype to a full TrueCrypt interface implementation without sacrificing any security functionality.

3.1 Cognitive Walkthrough of TrueCrypt

As mentioned in [22, 26], prerequisites to the cognitive walkthrough include a general description of the users of the system, a specific description of representative tasks to be performed with the system, and a list of the correct actions required to complete each of these tasks. In the case of TrueCrypt, anyone who owns or uses a computer is a potential user of the system, and the representative tasks include installing TrueCrypt, creating a file container, opening and closing the container, and working with files within and outside of the container. Our cognitive walkthrough focuses on finding usability issues in these tasks. We conclude that TrueCrypt's user interface presents serious usability roadblocks even for experienced computer users. We classify the discovered issues into three categories, which drive some of our suggestions to software developers in 5:

1. **Non-intuitive visuals:** The main window of TrueCrypt, shown every time the software is run, including for the first time, appears overloaded with visual controls — see Fig. 1(a). This violates properties **P1**, **P2**, and **P3** of the cognitive walkthrough rules in Section 2.1. Compare to our modifications in Fig. 1(b) for a cleaner, more discoverable, and more visually pleasing alternative. In the original interface, users see a list of drive letters, a menu bar, and buttons whose functionality is not clear, especially for first-time use. In many places, clicking "help" opens a browser and leads the user to TrueCrypt's website, loading the relevant section of a user guide rather than offering quick tips about the nature of the controls.

2. **Terminology:** The terminology used in the main window, dialog boxes, and menus is likely familiar to expert computer users, but terms such as "Volume" "Mount," "Dismount," and "Device" are almost certainly unknown to inexperienced users, violating properties **P1**, **P2**, and **P3**. Furthermore, controls are displayed without sufficient context, preventing users from inferring their functionality without understanding the labels, violating **P3**. For instance, "Select File," "Select Device," and "Volume Tools" appear near each other, but "Volume Tools" is only relevant once a volume has been selected. This button (which actually acts as a pop-up menu) is never disabled ("grayed out"). There is no button or control using the specific language "Create file container" (violation of **P2** and **P3**), although this action is the first thing a new user is likely to need. "Create Volume" seems to imply creation, and is easily discoverable, but experimental results (in Section 4) support our hypothesis that "Volume" and "Container," while used interchangeably in TrueCrypt, are understood differently by users in practice.

3. **Illogical Flow of Tasks:** Creating a file container requires the user to make several choices, such as file container name, location, size, password, partitioning scheme, and encryption algorithm. TrueCrypt provides a Volume Creation Wizard (used to create file containers) to guide users through this process (Fig. 2), but the wizard itself seems to exhibit many usability issues, mostly due to option overload for novices (advanced options are shown to everyone). Other problems include illogical order of steps and its consequences. All these items are violations of property **P4**.

The Volume Creation Wizard is particularly troubling. The 5 steps needed to complete this task are shown in Fig. 2 (compare to our *one-step process* in Fig. 3). First, the wizard title of "Volume Creation Wizard" presents a terminology issue. The "Select File" option on the "Volume Location" screen (Fig. 2(a)) is misleading, implying that the user should select an existing file rather than enter the name of a *new file* to be created (see Suggestion 2 regarding the misuse of native controls in Section 5). If an existing file is selected and "Next" is pressed on this screen, it displays an overly lengthy warning message stating that the file already exists and will be replaced. If this warning is ignored, the wizard presents another warning when "Format" button is pressed in step 5 (Fig. 2(e)). It is unlikely that users expect this behavior or know to return to step 1 to fix it.

Instead of initially gathering essential information, such as file container location (Fig. 2(a)), size (Fig. 2(c)), and password (Fig. 2(d)), these options are scattered throughout the process, with each step collecting one piece of crucial information. Moreover, several advanced options, such as encryption algorithm (Fig. 2(b)) and filesystem options (Fig. 2(e)) are inter-spaced with more essential options throughout the process. While the wizard uses "sane" defaults, a novice user may not realize that changing these defaults is optional. All screens contain a large amount of help text, but it is difficult to understand, and its sheer volume makes it unlikely to actually assist the user with his or her choices.

It is not even clear when the wizard has finished. Immediately before container creation in step 5 (Fig. 2(e)), the user is instructed to "Move your mouse as randomly as possible within this window." This collects entropy and refreshes the "Random Pool" display continuously, but never indicates when there is "enough." The last screen of the wizard, while indicating successful container creation, has a "Next" button as well as an "Exit" button (Fig. 2(f)). If only one container is to be created, users should exit the wizard. However, users have spent many steps pressing "Next" to continue, so their first instinct may be to press "Next" (selected by default), which will guide them through the wizard *again* to create a new container. This leads to an immediate impression that container creation must be restarted for some unknown reason, likely leading to user frustration, even when it later becomes clear that the process does not need to be repeated.

3.2 Rapid Prototype

To test our hypothesis about the usability of TrueCrypt, we developed a rapid prototype of a new interface and installer addressing the above issues, and compared the speed with which users can create and use containers using the two interfaces. The new installer asks the user to launch a quick-start wizard to create file container immediately after installation is complete, removing the need to discover this action in the main TrueCrypt window. The next section describes our move from the rapid prototype to a full TrueCrypt-compatible interface implementation.

3.3 Implementation

Our cognitive walkthrough discovered many usability issues in TrueCrypt's interface, which we aim to rectify by updating TrueCrypt's source code. Integrating our changes into the TrueCrypt

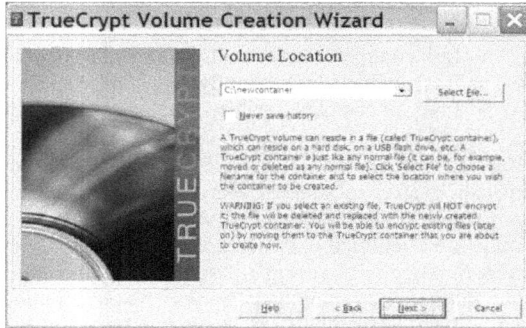

(a) Step 1: File selection screen

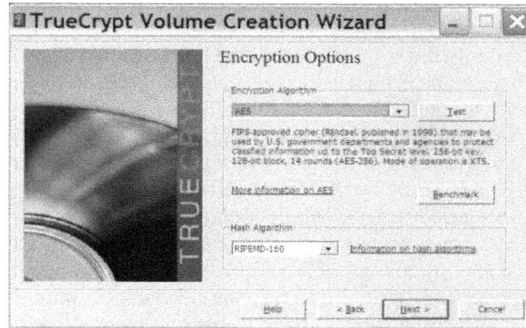

(b) Step 2: Encryption options screen

(c) Step 3: Container size screen

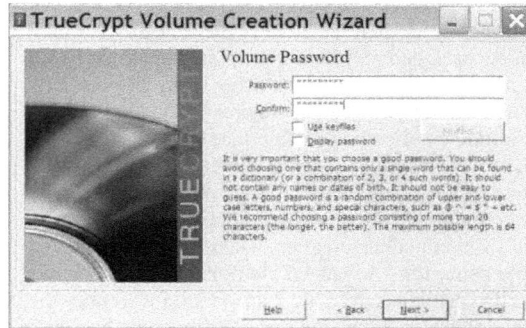

(d) Step 4: Container password screen

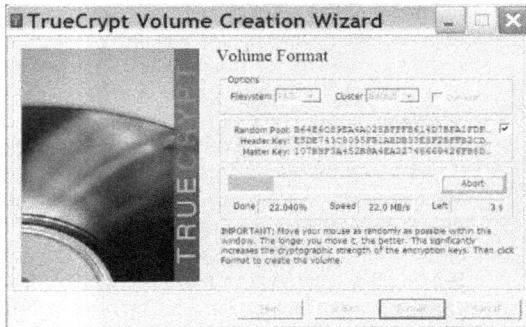

(e) Step 5: Container filesystem options screen

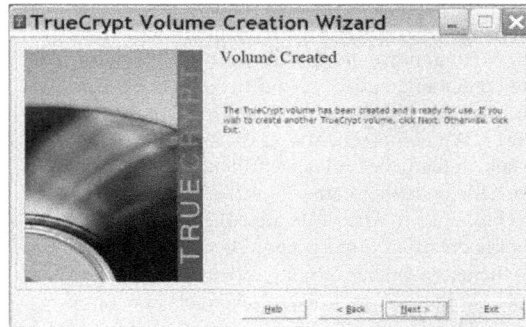

(f) Finish screen

Figure 2: The 5 steps of file container creation wizard in TrueCrypt's interface.

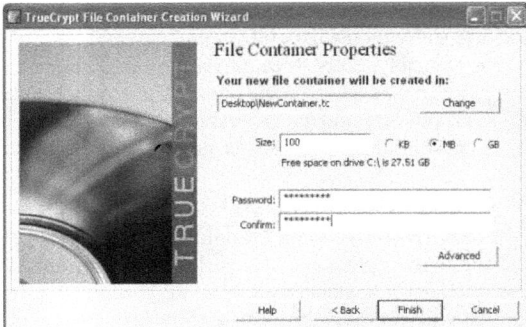

(a) Combined required options screen

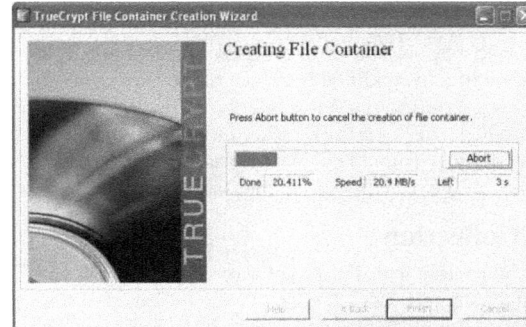

(b) Finish screen

Figure 3: The *single-step* file container creation wizard in our modified interface. The first screen is replaced with the second when a user selects "Finish."

code-base proved to be a larger challenge than initially expected. The Microsoft Visual Studio-compatible source distribution of True-Crypt contains six separate projects: Boot, Crypto, Driver, Format, Mount, and Setup, with the last three containing functionality which we need to modify i.e. the main window, file container creation wizard, and installer. Our goal is to make minimal necessary changes, supporting file container-related operation and installation with a quick-start wizard, *without sacrificing any options or functionality originally available in TrueCrypt*. This is particularly challenging, as UI code is interspersed with cryptographic logic and other operations in the TrueCrypt source, meaning that any of the more than 10K lines of code may control the UI. Fig. 1(b) shows main window of our modified interface. We ensured that our change set is minimal and does not sacrifice any prior functionality by separating UI functions from "back-end" logic, and verifying that our new interface makes identical back-end calls when compared to the original TrueCrypt interface. For areas of the code where a clean separation of UI code from the back-end may destroy original functionality, we hide old interface elements instead of removing them. For instance, the drive list which appears in the main window of the old interface (Fig. 1(a)) is still functional in the new interface (Fig. 1(b)), but not visible. In fact, we still use this list to assign letters to various file containers, ensuring that we maintain all original back-end calls.

The new file container creation wizard supports all options provided by the old file container creation wizard,[5] with advanced options available using the "Advanced" button. This interface is more intuitive and visually discoverable than the original (notice the terminology and visuals), replacing the menu bar text-only lists with icons and text labels — clicking them displays appropriate dialog boxes to select further action.[6] We also remove a large number of redundant elements (e.g. buttons with identical functionality as some menu options) to improve the appeal of the main window. The steps for the file container creation wizard (which is now automatically launched when the installer completes) in the new interface are shown in Fig. 3. All non-essential options are grouped together and available when clicking the "Advanced" button in Fig. 3(a). We populate a default file container name "NewContainer" and save it on the Desktop (Fig. 3(a)) in case users are confused regarding file selection versus file creation. Finally, upon successful completion, the wizard asks the user whether or not to open the newly-created file container. While the vast majority of changes saw a positive result, two independent design choices caused trouble for users in the modified interface. In fact, in both cases we had inadvertently violated property **P3** of cognitive walkthrough rules, but had not realized this until after analyzing user study results.

4. EVALUATION

This section describes our empirical evaluation, comparing True-Crypt's interface with our modified interface for several common tasks. Each user was exposed to a single interface only. We measure the speed with which users perform tasks, including whether or not they are successfully completed. We also asked users for their subjective opinion of the usability of the interfaces.

4.1 Data Collection

Users' entire interaction with TrueCrypt was recorded, along with audio, using screen capture software (users were informed of this). Users were asked to "think aloud," and especially to indicate when they started their tasks, finished, or were stuck. Time to complete

---

[5]With the exception of "Never save history," which requires longer to implement using native controls for platform-specific reasons.
[6]Some of these visuals are not yet fully implemented

individual tasks was recovered from these recordings, along with the following outcomes:

- Task completed successfully with no errors or hints.
- Task completed successfully with hints from the experimenter.
- Task not completed successfully or irrecoverable error.

Recruitment. 60 users were selected randomly from over 400 responses to an email sent to the graduate and undergraduate student population between 18 and 65 years old. Users selected for the study were required to own a computer, but no other constraints were imposed on the sample. Users were then randomly split into two groups: *Treatment* and *Control*. Not all users arrived at the scheduled time, yielding a final count of 25 and 29 for *Control* and *Treatment* groups, respectively. Although selection was random (no information other than email address was collected before participation), *Control* users were 80% male with an age range of 18 to 42, while *Treatment* was 48% female with ages between 18 and 32. However, gender distribution shows no statistically significant effect on the outcome of the study ($p > 0.1$). The vast majority of users had completed high school and were in the process of getting a bachelor's degree. *Control* users were asked to perform tasks using the original TrueCrypt interface on a Windows XP laptop with no Internet connectivity. Users in the *Treatment* group were asked to complete the same tasks using an interface incorporating our modifications, using the same computer. Users were compensated $10 at the end of the user study. Each user test has three phases:

- **Introduction:** Users were asked a series of questions regarding their knowledge of computer security, the steps they take to protect their personal data, and the risk of personal data loss if their computers are stolen. They were further introduced, at a very abstract level, to the concept of disk encryption software.
- **Data Collection:** The experimenter asked users to perform 9 tasks, one by one, using TrueCrypt. These tasks are designed to include file container-related operations, and can be grouped into three categories: *Installation and Setup*, *Using a Container*, and *Exiting*. Installation and Setup involved running the TrueCrypt installer and then using TrueCrypt to create a file container. Using a Container consisted of opening a file container, moving files into the container to secure them, and creating files securely within the container. Exiting required users to securely close a file container, such that opening it again required knowledge of the password. Each task is goal- rather than step-oriented, e.g. the experimenter asked the user to "create a secure file container" rather than specifying the list of steps required to do so.
- **Debrief:** Users were informed about the goals of the study, and asked several questions related to their experience with TrueCrypt and its interface, the ease or difficulty level of performing the tasks, and suggestions for improvement.

4.2 Results

Users' responses to an introductory questionnaire provided insight into their practices of securing private information and their knowledge of disk encryption. Of all participating users, 81% reported storing private information on their computers. *Everyone* reported using online banking. The vast majority (92%) were aware of the consequences of private information leaks, but all believed that using antivirus and/or login passwords keeps their private information secure in case their computer is physically stolen. 93% were unaware of the concept of disk encryption software.

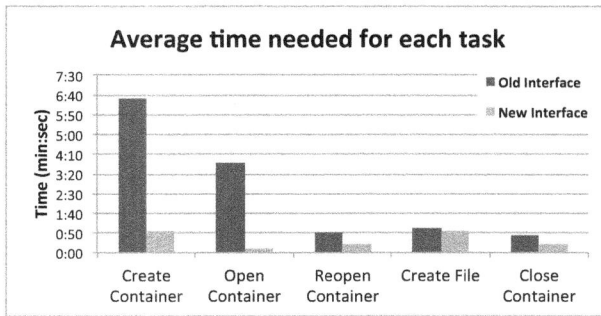

(a) Time required to perform various tasks. All differences statistically significant except "Reopen Container" and "Create File."

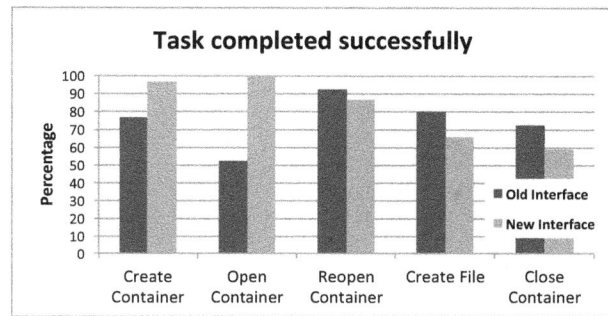

(b) Percentage of successfully-completed tasks.

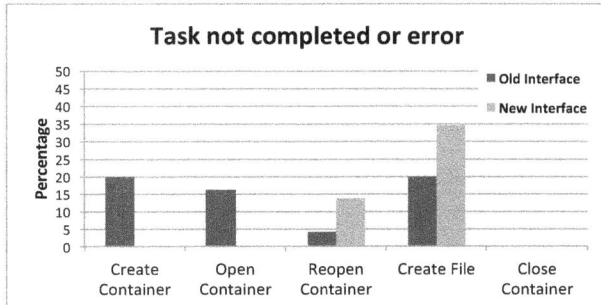

(c) Percentage of tasks not completed or completed with errors.

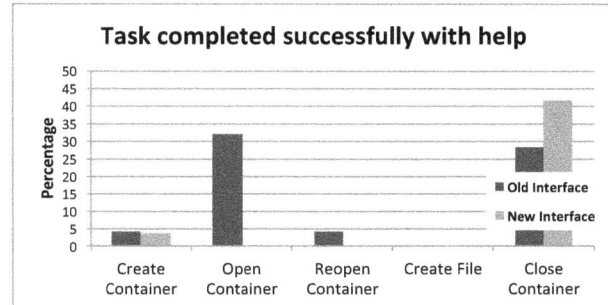

(d) Percentage of tasks successfully completed with hints.

Figure 4: Comparison of user performance when using the old and new interfaces in terms of task time (a) and success rates (b)–(d).

Create Container is the second step of *Installation and Setup* tasks, the first of which — installing TrueCrypt — is trivial. Creating a new file container ("volume") shows a significant difference in the mean time to completion between the *Control* and *Treatment* groups. While it took 6.5 minutes, on average, to perform this task using unmodified TrueCrypt, only 1 minute was required with our modifications (Fig. 4(a)). These differences are statistically significant ($p < 0.001$).[7] Error rates also dropped drastically when using our modified interface: while 76% of *Control* users successfully performed this task (Fig. 4(b)), 20% failed (Fig. 4(c)), and remaining users required some hint from the experimenter (Fig. 4(d)); in the modified interface, these rates changed to 97%, 0%, and 3% respectively.

Users encountered difficulties in discovering how to create file containers, in separating the required options from advanced options, and in creating a new file container rather than selecting an existing file and subsequently overwriting it. *Control* users struggled to find a button or menu option to create a container. The menu item and button refers to a "volume" rather than a "container," and users eventually discovered the creation wizard by trial and error, usually by noticing the word "create." This supports our initial suspicion that the old interface uses non-intuitive visuals and terminology, making it difficult to determine the correct steps to complete some actions. Before tasks were assigned, all users were informed that the overall goal of is to protect a file already present on the Desktop, called "private.doc." Possibly for this reason, 52% of *Control* users selected "private.doc" in the new file container selection screen in Fig. 2(a), and ignored the warning that this will overwrite the existing file

rather than encrypt it. When clicking "Format" at the end of the wizard (Fig. 2(e)), another warning was triggered, and 54% of users eventually made their way back to the file selection screen in Fig. 2(a). After thoroughly examining the help text on that screen, they generally typed a new file name rather then selecting an existing file. The remaining 46% returned to the screen in Fig. 2(a), read the text, but proceeded to override all warnings and destroy the file. *All* options in "Encryption Options" (Fig. 2(b)) and "Volume Format" (Fig. 2(e)) wizard steps are meant for advanced users. Almost all users in the *Control* group tried to explore these screens, but ultimately admitted a lack of understanding of the options. Users were also seen to move the mouse on the screen Fig. 2(e) until interrupted by the experimenter. Most of these design issues were raised during our cognitive walkthrough (Section 3.1).

Open Container, the first step in the *Using a Container* group, involves opening the file container created in previous task. While *Treatment* users completed this quickly, needing only 9 seconds on average (Fig. 4(a)), with a success rate of 100% (Fig. 4(b)), *Control* users took an average of 3.78 minutes (Fig. 4(a)) with 52% ultimately succeeding (Fig. 4(b)). Of the remaining *Control* users, 32% succeeded with hints from the experimenter (Fig. 4(d)) and 16% did not perform the task correctly (Fig. 4(c)). The difference is statistically significant ($p < 0.001$), again confirming our assertion of non-intuitive visuals and difficult terminology in the old interface. Users reported not being familiar with the term "Mount," stumbled upon it (to open a file container) by trial and error, increasing the required time to perform the task. In the new interface, the file container creation wizard asks the user whether to open the file container; all *Treatment* users opted to open the file container, reducing task time.

Given the time and success percentage improvement for the modified interface, offering to automatically open the container appears

---

[7]All *p*-values calculated using *t*-test (confirmed using Mann-Whitney-U) over average completion time, including success and failure.

to be a valuable option to offer in the installer in order to ease the user into the correct workflow of the software. All *Treatment* users successfully opened the file container for the first time, since they did not need to remember the name and location — the creation wizard itself asks to open the newly created file container on completion. Surprisingly, this appeared to be a bad design choice, as it caused users to forget the container name and location (see below). In the future, we plan to allow full control of the file container name and location to ease recall. However, the "Select File" language should not be used as it caused irreversible destruction of important data.

Reopen Container, in the task group *Using a Container*, required the user to complete the "Open Container" task. The container was opened automatically by the creation wizard for users of the new interface, so for them this task was new, while users of the original interface had to repeat a previously-completed task. The average time was 53 seconds in the original, and 22 seconds in the modified interfaces, respectively (Fig. 4(a)). Not surprisingly, this difference is not statistically significant ($p > 0.1$). The failure rate was 4% using the original interface, and 14% with the modified interface (Fig. 4(c)). Surprisingly, the higher failure rate in the new interface was due to the pre-populated default file container name and location (Fig. 3(a)). While this window contains bolded text "Your new file container will be created in:," which users appeared not to notice or read, so when asked to reopen the container, they had forgotten the location, but since the file container was stored on the desktop by default, they noticed it and clicked on it. In retrospect, we realize this is a violation of property **P3** of cognitive walkthrough rules.

Create File, yet another part of *Using a Container* group, asked users to securely create a file within the container and only within the container. It is considered successful if the user either creates a new file directly in the container and edits it afterward, or opens a word processor, then saves the file into the file container. 20% of *Control* and 35% of *Treatment* failed to perform this task (Fig. 4(c)). *These tasks relate to the operating system and word processor rather than TrueCrypt*, and the time difference is not statistically significant ($p > 0.5$). The only notable exception is the task to open a file which is within the container ($p < 0.001$). While it is not immediately clear why overall success rates should be so much lower in the new interface, as this task is mainly a function of the operating system and word processor rather than TrueCrypt. We observe that this is due to another misguided design decision: in the new interface, we removed the association between drive letters and container names from the main window. Users therefore did not realize that a particular drive letter (generally E:) contained the mounted TrueCrypt volume and the files within that volume, which is another violation of property **P3** of cognitive walkthrough rules.

Close Container, belonging to the *Exiting* group, requires the user to *securely* close the file container, i.e. unmount the volume and clear the container password from TrueCrypt memory. The average time to perform this task was 45 seconds for the old, and 21 seconds for the new interface (Fig. 4(a)), which is statistically significant ($p < 0.05$). Everyone succeeded in this task: the old interface saw success rates of 72% (Fig. 4(b)) and the other 28% succeeded with hints (Fig. 4(d)). In the new interface, 59% succeed (Fig. 4(b)), and 41% succeeded with hints (Fig. 4(d)). Users who required hints usually clicked the window close button in the main TrueCrypt window, assuming that the file container was securely closed. This action actually minimizes the main window (for both the old and new interface), and does not close the file container. This behavior may have to be altered in the future, and we plan to differentiate between "minimize" and "exit" explicitly. *Control*

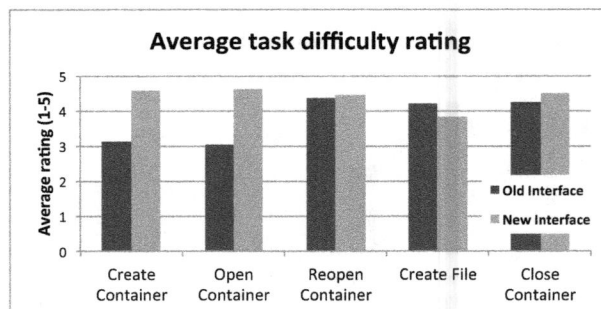

Figure 5: Comparison of average ratings (1 – 5, very difficult to very easy, respectively) for various tasks in the old and new interfaces. The first two differences are statistically significant.

users who struggled to open the container determined that since "Mount" is used to open it, "Dismount" should be used to close it.

4.3 Discussion

Recall the properties of usable security in Section 2.2. Neither our modified interface nor the original satisfies the **barn door property**: if a user leaves a file container open, anyone can retrieve the information stored in it. The interface, in this case, cannot do anything significant to prevent information leaks except for closing the file container if no activity is detected for a considerable amount of time (this option is available in TrueCrypt preferences). However, the user may not always want this, as a major security usability comment was the reluctance to repeatedly type a password.

There are two tasks for which the chances of false completion are higher (see **weakest link property**). The first is to provide file container location in the old interface (Fig. 2(a)). Users may select an existing file and destroy it, which the *Control* users did. Note that TrueCrypt does *not* suffer from the **lack of feedback property**, as the repercussions of selecting a file are made very clear. However, users did not understand the importance of these messages. The new interface eliminated chances of this error by 1) changing the terminology, and 2) pre-populating the new file name (Fig. 3(a)). A second task where false completion is likely is in closing the file container, when a user may assume that the file container is closed, but in reality, it is left open. Both the old and new interfaces exhibit this problem, likely due to users' prior experience with the window close, or "X" button in Microsoft operating systems.

The **unmotivated user property** is very significant in case of TrueCrypt. We suspected that the interface has sufficiently many design flaws to cause users to abandon TrueCrypt entirely. Results discussed above confirm that the modified interface is better accepted by users: 40% of the *Control* group said that they will not use TrueCrypt. Many cited poor interface design as a major reason. Another 33%, while performing poorly, reported that they would use TrueCrypt. In contrast, only 10% of *Treatment* said they will not use TrueCrypt — these are the users who had trouble finding the file container location. Fig. 5 shows the average subjective rating for the ease of various tasks in the original and modified interfaces on a 5-point Likert scale (1 being very difficult and 5 being very easy). Note that the new interface is either equivalent or superior compared to the old interface, except for the task "Create File," due to a design error discussed above. Given the difficulty in getting users to accurately report on their own activities, opinions, and moods, it is not surprising that, even given the vast differences in success rates and task times for the two interfaces, most user ratings do not differ significantly between *Control* and *Treatment* groups

$(p > 0.05)$. However, the two tasks we identified as the most difficult, namely "Create Container" (average 4.6 vs. 3.04) and "Open Container" (4.6 vs. 3.12), were both rated significantly easier in the new interface $(p < 0.001)$.

Neither the **abstraction** nor the **lack of feedback** properties are significant in the context of our work. They are related to specifying and managing policies and providing feedback regarding the current state of security, respectively. In the next section, we discuss the four suggestions to user interface developers which may help build the interface more usable.

5. SUGGESTIONS FOR DEVELOPERS

In this section we outline, in broad strokes, not only the interface mistakes present in TrueCrypt, but mistakes likely to appear in many pieces of software, including security- and mission-critical systems. Note that these are not rules, but rather guidelines which should hold in the vast majority of cases. Exceptions should be carefully thought out and experts should be consulted before making UI design decisions which may give the user a feeling of non-intuitive user interface and may impede the correct use of the software. We ourselves inadvertently violated one of these suggestions, and the negative impact is evident from the results, as discussed below. Suggestions refer to the rules of cognitive walkthroughs and of usable security in Section 2, which we reference for completeness, but developers need not know those rules to benefit from the suggestions. In other words, *the suggestions are usable by themselves*, without much additional material, although referring to platform UI guidelines is always advisable.

- **Suggestion 1 — Do not use unknown terminology:** The effects of using unknown terminology in a user interface are little studied in the context of usable security. Our results highlight the important relationship between terminology and usability of security software. For instance, changing the terms "Mount", "Dismount" and "Volume" to "Open", "Close", and "File Container" improved the usability of TrueCrypt's interface. We suggest that developers get rid of unknown terms or minimize their use, and instead use intuitive terms, even when they may not be the correct technical terms. If a more intuitive term can not be found in lieu of an unknown term, such as the name of an encryption algorithm, then developers should try to separate that term from the main workflow of the task, as discussed in Suggestion 3 below. (See **P1**, **P2**, **P3** and **S3**.)

- **Suggestion 2 — Do not misuse native UI controls:** Users are most likely to be familiar with the behavior of a native control in the context of a user interface. For example, clicking a "Command Button" control, such as "OK" or "Cancel", the user can initiate an immediate action. The label and/or icon on it indicates the action it performs when clicked, and the user should be able to determine the action without any external reference. The Microsoft user experience interaction guidelines for command buttons [1] further states that adding an ellipsis (...) at the end of the button label indicates that the command needs additional information (including confirmation). The command button is not designed as a substitute of displaying a pop up menu, or to indicate an action which it does not perform. For example, the behaviors of "Volume Tools..." button in Fig. 1(a) which displays a pop up menu, and "Select File..." button in Fig. 2(a) which requires entering a new file name (or it will overwrite the selected file) are not typical command button behaviors, and confused users.

We ourselves inadvertently violated this suggestion in the modified interface by replacing the drive letter and opened container association (which was visible in the original interface, in Fig. 1(a)) in the main window of modified interface with a command button marked with an open folder icon (Fig. 1(b)). However the command button icon suggested the action of opening a folder, and failed to convey to the user "which drive" or "which path" it is opening. Note that the text label next to the open folder icon is the path where the file container is saved, not the path which the folder command button opens. In this case, the icon on the button does not indicate the complete action it performs. Since two concepts are being conveyed: 1) the drive letter of the TrueCrypt container, and 2) the path to the TrueCrypt file, a single control/label proved insufficient. We suggest that developers refer to the user interface design guidelines of the specific control if unsure about its correct usage. (See **P1**, **P3**, **P4**, **S2** and **S3**.)

- **Suggestion 3 — Separate required and optional input parameters:** There are times when optional input parameters to a task are unknown to novice users, such as the names of encryption algorithms, and displaying these choices may impede successful completion of tasks. We suggest that those parameters should be given some reasonable default values (as TrueCrypt does) and be separated from the main workflow (which TrueCrypt does *not* do — see Figs. 2(b) and 2(e)). Advanced users are likely to understand those parameter and can change them by launching an optional input screen. This suggestion is similar to multiple interfaces (one personalized and the other is the full set of functions), as proposed in [17] as a solution to some of the difficulties in designing complex software. It is also important to gather required input ahead of time, using as few screens as possible. The impact of doing this is evident from the modified file container creation wizard (Fig. 3), which reduced the number of steps to create a container from 5 to 1. There are occasions when some of the required parameters are also unknown to the user. In those cases, we suggest providing sufficient but small help messages, such as tool tips, as we have observed that users do not read lengthy help messages and/or do not understand them. (See **S3**.)

- **Suggestion 4 — Display the consequences of an action immediately (Immediacy of consequences):** Immediate versus delayed consequences have mostly been studied in the context of behavioral learning. In the context of user interfaces, the consequences of an action such as clicking a button, if displayed immediately after performing the action, affect the user's behavior (in terms of ability to rectify the action if performed incorrectly) more positively than if displayed at a later point of time. In one such study, Meson and Redmon examine the effects of immediate versus delayed visual feedback on the accuracy of identifying errors (signals) in sample stimuli [16]. The results suggest that the accuracy of signal detection is greater under immediate feedback than delayed feedback. [25] presents a study which aims to understand spatial proximity of access control information and the item that the information describes. The results reveal that placing the access-control policy directly under the object that the policy describes (such as photo and album thumbnail) improves users' ability to notice errors in setting access-control policies without negatively impacting other non-access-control tasks than placing it on the sidebar, or on a separate settings page.

TrueCrypt's original file container creation wizard performs poorly in this regard: as discussed in Section 3.1, if an existing file is selected and "Next" button is pressed in step 1 (Fig. 2(a)), the wizard displays an overly lengthy warning message stating that the file already exists and will be replaced. If this warning is ignored, the wizard presents another warning when "Format" is pressed in step 5 (Fig. 2(e)). It is unlikely that users expect this behavior or know to return to step 1 to fix it. We suggest the developers to thoroughly analyze the action performed by each control and its consequences, and provide options to the users to rectify a potential problem (if needed) immediately rather than delaying. (See **P4** and **S2**.)

Overall, applying these suggestions along with carefully chosen controls, their proper placement and grouping in the interface, and understandable labels will produce more intuitive, discoverable, and more usable software.

6. CONCLUSION

As security professionals, we strive to develop security tools which provide strong protection against vulnerabilities. These tools fail in practice if they are unusable. Based on the findings of our cognitive walkthrough, we suspected that TrueCrypt's user interface is unnecessarily complex and has serious usability issues. Using the existing code base of TrueCrypt, we systematically developed a minimal interface without sacrificing any options or functionality originally available, and evaluated the two interfaces using a medium-scale single-blind randomized user study. We found that that the new interface is considerably easier and faster to use, especially for non-technical users. We observed statistically significant improvements in average time to completion of common tasks. Surprisingly, some of our design decisions made some tasks more difficult to perform in the new interface, but our modifications are such that they can be reverted back to their original design without sacrificing other, clearly beneficial changes.

Based on the results of evaluation of the two interfaces, we found that non-intuitive user interfaces, terminology unfamiliar to novice users, and a lack of logic or consistency in the sequence of steps required to perform certain tasks are roadblocks to the usability of software. These factors may impede potential users from using the software correctly or may cause sufficient frustration to make them stop using the software. In this work, we restricted our focus to tasks related to file containers. More work is needed to integrate other features of TrueCrypt, such as whole-disk encryption and more advanced options.

7. ACKNOWLEDGMENTS

The authors would like to thank Dan Li for valuable advice on statistical analysis and user surveys.

8. REFERENCES

[1] Command Button Guidelines, accessed on August 29th, 2012. [online] http://msdn.microsoft.com/en-us/library/windows/desktop/aa511453.aspx.

[2] Veterans affairs data theft, accessed on July 9th, 2012. [online] http://epic.org/privacy/vatheft/.

[3] TrueCrypt, accessed on June 19th, 2012. [online] http://www.truecrypt.org/.

[4] TrueCrypt download statistics, accessed on June 19th, 2012. [online] http://www.truecrypt.org/statistics.

[5] Anne Adams and M. Angela Sasse. Users are not the enemy. *Commun. ACM*, 42(12), 1999.

[6] Ross Anderson. Why cryptosystems fail. n *In Proceedings of the ACM Conference on Computer and Communications Security (CCS)*, December 1993.

[7] Farzaneh Asgharpour, Debin Liu, and L. Jean Camp. Mental models of security risks. In *Financial Cryptography*, volume 4886 of *Lecture Notes in Computer Science*, 2007.

[8] Sonia Chiasson and Paul C. van Oorschot. A usability study and critique of two password managers. In *Proceedings of the USENIX Security Symposium*, 2006.

[9] Sandy Clark, Travis Goodspeed, Perry Metzger, Zachary Wasserman, Kevin Xu, and Matt Blaze. Why (special agent) Johnny (still) can't encrypt: A security analysis of the APCO project 25 two-way radio system. In *Proceedings of the USENIX conference on Security*, 2011.

[10] Don Davis. Compliance defects in public key cryptography. In *Proceedings of the USENIX Security Symposium*, July 1996.

[11] Joseph S. Dumas. The human-computer interaction handbook. chapter User-based evaluations, pages 1093–1117. 2003.

[12] Almut Herzog and Nahid Shahmehri. Usability and security of personal firewalls. In *New Approaches for Security, Privacy and Trust in Complex Environments*, 2007.

[13] Clayton Lewis, Peter G. Polson, Cathleen Wharton, and John Rieman. Testing a walkthrough methodology for theory-based design of walk-up-and-use interfaces. In *Proceedings of the SIGCHI conference on Human factors in computing systems: Empowering people*, pages 235–242, 1990.

[14] Clayton H. Lewis. Using the "thinking aloud" method in cognitive interface design. Technical Report RC-9265, IBM, 1982.

[15] Simon Liu and Rick Kuhn. Data loss prevention. *IT Professional*, 12(2), 2010.

[16] Matthew A. Mason and William K. Redmon. Effects of immediate versus delayed feedback on error detection accuracy in a quality control simulation. *Journal of Organizational Behavior Management*, 13(1):49–83, 1993.

[17] Joanna McGrenere. *The Design and Evaluation of Multiple Interfaces: A Solution for Complex Software*. PhD thesis, The University of Toronto, 2002.

[18] Sara Motiee, Kirstie Hawkey, and Konstantin Beznosov. The challenges of understanding users' security-related knowledge, behaviour, and motivations. In *In Proceedings of Symposium on Usable Privacy and Security (SOUPS)* July 2010.

[19] Bryant Paul, Michael B. Salwen, and Michel Dupagne. The third-person effect: A meta-analysis of the perceptual hypothesis. *Mass Communication & Society*, 3(1):57–85, 2000.

[20] Peter G. Polson, Clayton Lewis, John Rieman, and Cathleen Wharton. Cognitive walkthroughs: a method for theory-based evaluation of user interfaces. *International Journal of Man-Machine Studies*, 36(5):741 – 773, 1992.

[21] Fahimeh Raja, Kirstie Hawkey, and Konstantin Beznosov. Revealing hidden context: improving mental models of personal firewall users. In *In Proceedings of Symposium on Usable Privacy and Security (SOUPS)*, 2009.

[22] John Rieman, Marita Franzke, and David Redmiles. Usability evaluation with the cognitive walkthrough. In *Conference companion on Human factors in computing systems*, pages 387–388, 1995.

[23] Jeffrey Rubin. *Handbook of usability testing: how to plan, design and conduct effective tests*. Wiley, 2004.

[24] M. Angela Sasse and Ivan Flechais. *Security and Usability*, pages 13–30. O'Reilly Media, 2005.

[25] Kami Vaniea, Lujo Bauer, Lorrie F. Cranor, and Michael K. Reiter. Out of sight, out of mind: Effects of displaying access-control information near the item it controls. In *In Proceedings of the Tenth Annual Conference on Privacy, Security and Trust*, July 2012.

[26] Cathleen Wharton, John Rieman, Clayton Lewis, and Peter Polson. *The cognitive walkthrough method: A practitioners guide*. John Wiley & Sons, Inc., 1994.

[27] Alma Whitten and J. D. Tygar. Why Johnny can't encrypt; a usability evaluation of PGP 5.0. In *Proceedings of the USENIX Security Symposium*, pages 169–184, 1999.

Privacy by Design: A Formal Framework for the Analysis of Architectural Choices

Daniel Le Métayer
Inria, University of Lyon
CITI, Domaine Scientifique de la Doua
6, avenue des Arts
69621 Villeurbanne, France
Daniel.Le-Metayer@inria.fr

ABSTRACT

The privacy by design approach has already been applied in different areas. We believe that the next challenge in this area today is to go beyond individual cases and to provide methodologies to explore the design space in a systematic way. As a first step in this direction, we focus in this paper on the data minimization principle and consider different options using decentralized architectures in which actors do not necessarily trust each other. We propose a framework to express the parameters to be taken into account (the service to be performed, the actors involved, their respective requirements, etc.) and an inference system to derive properties such as the possibility for an actor to detect potential errors (or frauds) in the computation of a variable. This inference system can be used in the design phase to check if an architecture meets the requirements of the parties or to point out conflicting requirements.

Categories and Subject Descriptors

K.6 [**Management of Computing and Information Systems**]: Security and Protection; K.4.1 [**Computers and Society**]: Public Policy Issues—*privacy*

General Terms

Privacy

Keywords

privacy, design, architecture, methodology, formal, model

1. MOTIVATION

The privacy by design approach is often praised by lawyers as well as computer scientists as an essential step towards a better privacy protection [28, 46]. The general philosophy of privacy by design is that privacy should not be treated as an afterthought but rather as a first-class requirement during the design of a system. The approach has been applied

in different areas such as smart metering [18, 33, 48], electronic traffic pricing [2, 22, 45]), ubiquitous computing [28] or location based services [14, 25, 26]. More generally, it is possible to identify a number of core principles that are widely accepted and can form a basis for privacy by design. For example, the Organization for Economic Co-operation and Development (OECD) has put forward principles [44] such as the consent, limitation of use, data quality, security and accountability. These principles, which were themselves inspired by the fair information practices initially proposed by a U.S. government advisory committee in the seventies, are also in line with the European Directive 95/46/EC on data protection.

One must admit however that the take-up of privacy by design in the industry is still rather limited. This situation is partly due to legal and economic reasons: as long as the law does not impose binding commitments, ICT providers and data collectors do not have sufficient incentives to invest into privacy by design [31]. The situation on the legal side might change in Europe though because the regulation proposed by the European Commission in January 2012 (to replace the European Directive 95/46/EC) includes binding commitments on privacy by design[1].

But the reasons for the lack of adoption of privacy by design are not only legal and economic [7]: even though computer scientists have devised a wide range of privacy enhancing tools [15, 19, 47], no general methodology is available to integrate them in a consistent way to meet a set of privacy requirements. Indeed, privacy by design goes beyond the use of privacy enhancing tools : it has to do with the general requirements of a system and the definition of its architecture. As such, privacy by design is a matter of choice: multiple options are generally available to achieve a given set of functionalities, some of them being privacy friendly, others less. Therefore, it is necessary to have a clear view of the overall system, the actors involved, what they need to know and the information flows between them, in order to ensure that a given choice of tools is consistent with the privacy requirements.

The next challenge in this area is thus to go beyond individual cases and to establish sound foundations and methodologies for privacy by design [20, 51]. As a first step in this direction, we focus in this paper on the data minimization principle which stipulates that the collection should be limited to the pieces of data strictly necessary for the purpose,

---

[1]http://ec.europa.eu/justice/newsroom/data-protection/news/120125-en.htm

and we provide a framework to reason about the choices of architecture and their impact in terms of privacy. The first strategic choices are the allocation of the computation tasks to the nodes of the architecture and the types of communications between the nodes. For example, data can be encrypted or hashed, either to protect their confidentiality or to provide guarantees with respect to their correctness or origin. The main benefit of a centralized architecture for the "central" actor is that he can trust the result because he keeps full control over its computation [43]. As we can see from the examples in Section 2, the loss of control by a single actor in decentralized architectures can be offset by extra requirements ensuring that errors (or frauds) can be detected *a posteriori*.

In this paper, we focus on the investigation of the architectural choices based on these criteria, especially the decentralization and error detection requirements. In order to help the designer grasp the combination of possible options, we propose a framework to express the parameters to be taken into account (the service to be performed, the actors involved, their respective requirements, etc.) and an inference system to derive properties such as the possibility for an actor to detect potential errors (or frauds) in the computation of a variable. This inference system can be used in the design phase to check if an architecture meets the requirements of the parties or to point out conflicting requirements.

The rest of the paper is organized as follows. Section 2 presents, as a motivating example, different architectural choices for electronic traffic pricing systems. Section 3 introduces our formal framework and establishes the correctness of our inference system. This framework is applied to the motivating example in Section 4. Section 5 discusses related work. Section 6 concludes the paper and outlines directions for further work.

2. MOTIVATING EXAMPLE

Electronic Traffic Pricing (ETP) makes it possible to replace flat road tax schemes by systems in which the fee to be paid by the drivers depends on a variety of parameters related to their actual usage of the roads such as, for example, the type of roads they have used, the time of use, the traffic conditions, weather conditions, etc. These systems can be used to provide incentives for drivers to avoid using congested roads during peak hours and thus contributing to reduce traffic jams and pollution. For this reason, there are more and more initiatives around the world to deploy this kind of system on sections of roads, in urban areas, or even at the level of entire countries such as the Netherlands. These systems have obvious benefits, but they can also represent new risks for privacy. In this section, we review different architectural choices for ETP and analyze their impact in terms of privacy.

2.1 First option (centralized)

The first and maybe most natural option is the centralized architecture. This option relies on the idea that the on board equipment (OBE) of each vehicle includes a device to get its geographical position (e.g. GPS) and communication means (e.g. GSM) to send all location data to the server of the traffic pricing authority. The server computes the fee due for each car and the authority periodically sends the bill to the driver (e.g. every quarter). In addition, in order to make

it possible to detect potential misbehaviors from the drivers (e.g. drivers tampering with their GPS device or turning it off), the authority is allowed to perform sporadic spot checks (similar to existing speed limitation spot checks).

This option is rather secure for the traffic pricing authority but it is highly intrusive for the drivers because the authority becomes aware of all the whereabouts of all the vehicles. This solution had originally been chosen by the Dutch government but it has triggered a lot of protests, precisely for this reason, and the project has been suspended.

2.2 Second option (secure OBE)

A first alternative is to avoid the disclosure of any location information, which is possible if the computation of the fee can be performed by the OBE. In this case, the only data sent by the vehicles is the fee due at the end of each period (e.g. quarter). However, for this option to be acceptable for the pricing authority, the computation of the fee should be performed by a trusted device (e.g. a smart card). In addition, for the same reasons as above, the authority should be able to conduct spot checks. These spot checks are a bit more sophisticated than in the first option though, because it is necessary to communicate with the car to check that the observed location has been correctly provided as input to the OBE[2].

This solution is excellent with respect to data minimization but it requires more expensive OBEs. In addition, it is necessary to provide a solution to update the fee calculation software securely (because the fees are likely to evolve during the life time of the equipment).

2.3 Third option (commitments)

A possibility to avoid the drawbacks of the previous solution is to resort to a *commitment scheme* [22]. Commitment schemes provide two key guarantees: (1) a commitment γ about a value η is such that η cannot be discovered (or "opened") by the receiver without the help of the sender and (2) it binds the sender (it is not feasible for the sender to find another value η' consistent with γ). In this solution, the OBE sends commitments to the location data to the server of the pricing authority. Like in the previous option, it performs the computation of the fee and sends it to the operator at the end of each period. The authority can initiate a verification protocol after each spot check. This protocol leads to the disclosure of partial sums of the fee to allow the authority to check that the observed position has been correctly taken into account in the computation of the global fee.

In contrast with the previous option, no secure device is required in this solution: the confidence of the authority relies on the commitment scheme and the possibility to conduct spot checks. This solution offers a high level of privacy protection to the drivers. It still leads to non minimal disclosures of data during spot checks and it can be improved using homomorphic commitments [2] (which allow for the verification of partial sums without any disclosure of the actual values).

2.4 Need for reasoned decisions

Other solutions are possible for privacy friendly ETP such as the protocol proposed in [45] based on anonymous com-

---

[2]Even if the OBE is secure, its result might be wrong if the location values provided as inputs have been tampered with.

munications and commitments to anonymous tags. The goal of this section is not to provide a comprehensive survey on privacy in ETP but to illustrate the fact that, to provide a given service, a wide variety of design choices may be available, relying on the same building blocks (commitments, spot checks and secure computation here) and leading to more or less privacy friendly solutions. One of the most important challenges for the development of privacy by design is therefore to be able to provide tools to help designers facing this combination of possibilities and to ensure they can make the best choices in terms of privacy following a rigorous and reasoned approach.

3. FORMAL FRAMEWORK

In order to be able to reason about architectural choices, it is necessary to integrate into a single framework all the parameters that can have an impact on the architecture and its properties. The first parameter is obviously the service to be provided by the system under design. The second parameter is the set of actors involved and their respective requirements. These requirements can express the need for an actor to get access to a given information or to ensure that another actor cannot get access to the information. Other requirements are related to the possibility for an actor to challenge the provider of the information to detect potential errors ("detectability" in the sequel). Obviously, architectural choices also depend on the functionalities of the available components (e.g. encryption, commitments, secure computation, etc.) and the associated guarantees. In the following subsections, we present successively our framework for the specification of the architectures and the requirements of the actors (Subsection 3.1), the associated trace based semantics (Subsection 3.2) and an inference system that can be used for the verification of detectability (Subsection 3.3).

3.1 Architectures

The starting point of the design phase is the identification of the set Ω of actors involved and the specification of the service to be delivered. We assume in a first stage that the service is defined as a set of equations Σ defined on variables in Var with values in Val and we write $X =_\Sigma F(Y_1, \ldots Y_2)$ an equation in Σ. $Dep(X)$ denotes the set of variables on which X depend (involved in the equations that contribute to the definition of X) and In the set of terminal variables (variables that do not appear in the left hand side of any equation). By convention, terminal variables are the inputs of the system provided by a specific actor called the *environment*. For example, variables representing the actual locations of the vehicles in the ETP use case are terminal variables. To illustrate our approach, we use the following set of operations (or basic blocks) in this paper :

$$Op \;=\; \{Compute, Send, Commit, Open, Get\}$$

Based on this set of operations, the domain of architectures

is defined as follows:

$$
\begin{aligned}
Arch &= (\overline{Comp} \times \overline{Send} \times \overline{Commit} \times \\
&\quad \overline{Means} \times \overline{Trusted}) \\
\overline{Comp} &= \Omega \to Vars \\
\overline{Send} &= (\Omega \times \Omega) \to Vars \\
\overline{Commit} &= (\Omega \times \Omega) \to Vars \\
\overline{Means} &= \mathcal{P}((\overline{Open} \times \overline{Get})) \\
\overline{Open} &= (\Omega \times \Omega) \to Vars \\
\overline{Get} &= \Omega \to Vars \\
\overline{Trusted} &= Vars \\
Vars &= \mathcal{P}(Var)
\end{aligned}
$$

An architecture (C, S, K, M, T) defines the sets of variables which can be computed (C), sent (S), commited (K), spot checked or opened after a commitment (M), or trusted (T). A variable is trusted if the correctness of the computation of the equation defining it in Σ can be assumed. In practice, a trusted variable could be computed by a secure element such as a smart card or a secure OBE as discussed in Section 2. *Means* is defined as a powerset because the sets of spot checked or opened variables cannot be fixed once for all, they can be chosen randomly by the actors allowed to perform these operations[3]. We consider only *consistent* architectures here, i.e. architectures such that an actor cannot both receive and compute a variable, or compute it and spot check it, etc.

We call a *context* a set of tuples made of the sets of variables which can be respectively received, opened or spot checked by an actor in a run:

$$Context = \mathcal{P}(Vars \times Vars \times Vars)$$

The function VC returns, for each architecture and actor, the associated valid context:

$$VC \;\in\; (Arch \times \Omega) \to Context$$

$$
\begin{aligned}
VC((C,S,K,M,T),A) = \{(R,O,G)| \\
R = \{X | \exists B \in \Omega, X \in S(B,A)\} \\
\wedge \;\exists (F_O, F_G) \in M \\
O = \{X | \exists B \in \Omega, X \in F_O(B,A)\} \\
G = F_G(A)\}
\end{aligned}
$$

The intuition behind this definition is that, for a given architecture $\mathcal{A}$ and actor A, the operations available to A for collecting information is characterized by $VC(\mathcal{A}, A)$. In other words, each run of A must be covered by an element (R, O, G) of $VC(\mathcal{A}, A)$: all variables received, opened or spot checked by A should belong respectively to R, O and G. The role of the function VC is therefore to extract, for a given actor, the set of operations (context) authorized by the architecture.

A first way to express the requirements of the actors is to use constraints on the components of the architecture. For example, if (C, S, K, M, T) denotes the architecture, the fact that an actor A does not want to disclose the value of a variable X to an actor B, neither in clear nor as a commitment, can be expressed as $X \notin S(A,B) \cup K(A,B)$. If A

---

[3]In the same way as car drivers cannot generally predict if and where their speed will be checked by a radar.

wants to restrict spot checks to variables $\{X_1, \ldots, X_n\}$ and to limit them to 1 in a run, the constraint can be expressed as $\forall(F_O, F_G) \in M, F_G(B) \subseteq \{X_1, \ldots, X_n\} \wedge Card(F_G(B)) \leq 1$. Constraints on the side of the controller can be expressed in the same way. For example, the fact that A wants to compute himself the value of X is expressed as $X \in C(A)$. We show in the following sections how to express detectability properties.

3.2 Semantics

In order to be able to reason about the correctness of an architecture with respect to detectability requirements, it is necessary to define the semantics of the operations. We first define the domains of global traces and local traces (respectively $\overline{\Theta}$ and Θ).

$$\overline{\Theta} = \Omega \to \Theta$$
$$\Theta = Seq(Event)$$
$$Event = \{O_A^B(X,V) | A \in \Omega, B \in \Omega, X \in Var,$$
$$V \in Val, O \in \{Send, Commit, Open\}\}$$
$$\cup \{O_A(X,V) | A \in \Omega, X \in Var, V \in Val,$$
$$O \in \{Compute, Get\}\}$$

A local trace is a sequence of events associated with a given actor, each event corresponding to the occurrence of an operation involving this actor. $Send_A^B(X,V)$, $Commit_A^B(X,V)$ and $Open_A^B(X,V)$ are events denoting respectively the communication of the value V of the variable X from B to A, the commitment of B (towards A) to the value V of X, and the opening of the commitment by A. Note that the value V which appears in $Commit_A^B(X,V)$ is not revealed to A; in contrast, $Open_A^B(X,V)$ discloses to A a value V to which B is commited (i.e. for which B has previously issued a $Commit_A^B(X,V)$ event).

The state of an actor is defined as a function in

$$St = Var \to Val_\perp$$

where $Val_\perp$ is the domain of values extended with $\perp$, which denotes the undefined value, and values of type "Commitment", which are written symbolically as $\Xi(V)$. As explained above, $\Xi(V)$ does not provide any information about V itself. If Σ is a state, $Extend(\Sigma)$ defines the extension of Σ in which all commited values are disclosed:

$$Extend(\Sigma)(X) = if\ \Sigma(X) = \Xi(V)\ then\ V\ else\ \Sigma(X)$$

The intuition behind Σ is that it reveals all the information present in the state of an actor (including commited values that the actor himself does not know). By abuse of notation, we also write $\perp$ the error state.

The state of an actor A after the execution of the operations in a trace σ is defined by $S_A(\sigma, \eta_0)$, where η_0 stands for the initial state. By abuse of notation, we write $S_A(\sigma)$ for $S_A(\sigma, \emptyset)$ in the sequel, with $\emptyset$ the empty environment.

$$S_A(\langle\rangle, \eta) = \eta$$
$$S_A(e.\sigma, \eta) = S_A(\sigma, T_A(e, \eta))$$

$$T_A(Compute_A(X,V), \eta) = \eta[V/X]$$
$$T_A(Send_A^B(X,V), \eta) = \eta[V/X]$$
$$T_A(Send_B^A(X,V), \eta) = \eta$$
$$T_A(Commit_A^B(X,V), \eta) = \eta[\Xi(V)/X]$$
$$T_A(Commit_B^A(X,V), \eta) = \eta$$
$$T_A(Open_A^B(X,V), \eta) = \eta[V/X]\ if\ \eta(X) = \Xi(V)$$
$$= \perp\ otherwise$$
$$T_A(Open_B^A(X,V), \eta) = \eta$$
$$T_A(Get_A(X,V), \eta) = \eta[V/X]$$

The expression $\eta[V/X]$ denotes a state similar to η except that V is bound to X. Note that the value discovered through an $Open$ operation must be consistent with the commitment received previously ($\eta(X) = \Xi(V)$); otherwise the resulting state is $\perp$.

3.3 Detectability

The requirements on the possibility (or impossibility) for an actor to have access to a given variable (either by default, or sporadically through a spot check or the opening of a commitment) can be verified by simple static reasoning (akin to flow analysis) based on the definition of the architecture. The situation is much more complex for the possibility to detect a potential error (or fraud) in the computation of a variable. Indeed, because an actor may not control entirely the computation of a variable, he can generally not be sure that the value of this variable in his environment is correct. To be able to reason about the possibility for an actor to detect errors, we introduce an inference system and we establish its correctness with respect to the semantics defined in the previous subsection.

The inference system is made of the following three rules:

(R1) If $X =_\Sigma F(Y_1, \ldots, Y_n)$ and $X \in T$ then

$$\frac{\forall i \in \{1, \ldots, n\}, U_i \vdash_T Y_i}{\bigcup_{i=1}^{n} U_i \vdash_T X}$$

(R2) If $X =_\Sigma F(Y_1, \ldots, Y_n)$ and $X \notin T$ and $R' \cup O' \cup G' = \{X, Y_1, \ldots, Y_n\}$ then

$$\frac{\forall i \in \{1, \ldots, n\}, U_i \vdash_T Y_i}{U \vdash_T X}$$

with $U = \{(R \cup R', O \cup O', G \cup G') | (R, O, G) \in \bigcup_{i=1}^{n} U_i\}$

(R3) If $X \in In$ then $U \vdash_T X$

The intuition behind these rules is as follows:

- Rule R1 corresponds to the case of a trusted variable ($X \in T$). As stated in Section 3.1, a trusted variable is a variable such that the computation of the associated equation can be assumed to be correct. Therefore it is sufficient to be able to check the variables $Y_1, \ldots, Y_n$ used to compute X.

- The motivation for rule R2 is similar except that X cannot be trusted. Therefore, it must be possible in addition to check that the equation $X =_\Sigma F(Y_1, \ldots, Y_n)$ itself is satisfied. To this aim, it is necessary to be able to collect the values of all variables involved, hence the definitions of R', O', G' and U: the variables $X, Y_1, \ldots, Y_n$ are split up into the sets R', O' and G' which are added to the respective sets R, O and G in the context of the conclusion of the rule.

- Rule R3 deals with terminal variables (elements of In as introduced in Subsection 3.1). By assumption, these variables are the genuine values provided by the environment. Therefore they can be trusted in any context.

Before stating the correctness of this inference system, we need to introduce some properties on traces.

Definition 1. If $A \in \Omega$, $\sigma \in \Theta$, $U \in Context$, $Complete_A(U, \sigma)$ holds if and only if $\forall (R, O, G) \in U$,

$$\forall X \in R, \exists V \in Val, \exists B \in \Omega, Send_A^B(X, V) \in \sigma \text{ and}$$

$$\forall X \in O, \exists V \in Val, \exists B \in \Omega, Commit_A^B(X, V) \in \sigma$$

By abuse of notation, we use the symbol $\in$ to denote membership to a sequence. A trace σ is complete with respect to a context U if all the variables that can be sent or committed have actually been sent or committed. Hence, completeness here means that all communications which are at the initiative of the sender have occured.

Definition 2. If $\eta \in St$, $\eta' \in St$ and $X \in Var$, $Incorrect(\eta, \eta', X)$ holds if and only if

$$Extend(\eta)(X) \neq \bot \ \wedge \ Extend(\eta)(X) \neq Eval(X, \eta')$$

A variable X is incorrect in a state η if it has a value (or a commited value[4]) that is different from the value derived from the equations in Σ, with η' defining the values of the terminal variables. Note that the incorrectness of a variable X in a state η may remain unknown from the actor A in this state η (because A may not know the values of the terminal variables). $Eval(X, \eta)$ defines the correct value of a variable X assuming that the input variables are defined by η:

Definition 3. If $X \in Var$ and $\eta \in St$, $Eval(X, \eta) =$ if $X =_\Sigma (Y_1, \ldots, Y_n)$ then $F(Eval(Y_1, \eta), \ldots, Eval(X_n, \eta))$ else $\eta(X)$

We can now introduce the function $Detect$ which defines what we mean by "being able to detect any error in the computation of variable".

Definition 4. If $A \in \Omega, \sigma \in \Theta, \eta \in St, X \in Var$ and

---

[4]Because the function $Extend$ extends a state with the commited values.

$U \in Context$, $Detect_A^U(\sigma, \eta, X)$ holds if and only if

$$\exists Z \in Dep(X), Z =_\Sigma (Z_1, \ldots, Z_n), \exists (R, O, G) \in U,$$
$$\exists Y_1, \ldots, Y_m \in G, \exists Y_1', \ldots, Y_{m'}' \in O,$$
$$E(Y_1) = \ldots = E(Y_m) = E(Y_1') = \ldots E(Y_{m'}') = \bot$$
$$\wedge \ \sigma' = \sigma. Get(Y_1, \eta(Y_1)) \ldots Get(Y_m, \eta(Y_m)).$$
$$Open(Y_1', V_1) \ldots Open(Y_{m'}', V_{m'})$$
$$\text{with } Commit_A^{B_i}(Y_i', V_i) \in \sigma$$
$$\Rightarrow$$
$$E'(Z) \neq F(E'(Z_1), \ldots, E'(Z_n))$$
$$\text{with } E = S_A(\sigma) \text{ and } E' = S_A(\sigma')$$

The intuition behind the definition of $Detect_A^U(\sigma, \eta, X)$ is that, in order to be able to detect an error in the value of X, A should be able to apply Get and $Open$ operations allowed in the context U (definition of σ') to reach a state E' in which he has the proof of an inconsistency in the values of variables $Z, Z_1, \ldots, Z_n$. This inconsistency ($E'(Z) \neq F(E'(Z_1), \ldots, E'(Z_n))$) reveals an error in the value of X itself because $Z \in Dep(X)$ (which means that the value of X depends on the value of Z).

We can now state the correctness property of our inference system:

THEOREM 1. $\forall (C, S, K, M, T) \in Arch, \forall A \in \Omega, \forall X \in Var, \forall U \in Context, U = VC((C, S, K, M, T), A),$

$$\text{if } U \vdash_T X \text{ then}$$
$$\forall \sigma \in \Theta, \forall \eta \in St,$$
$$Complete_A(U, \sigma) \wedge Incorrect(S_A(\sigma), \eta, X) \Rightarrow$$
$$Detect_A^U(\sigma, \eta, X)$$

The correctness property states that if U is a valid context for an actor A in an architecture (C, S, K, M, T) and we can derive $U \vdash_T X$, then it must be the case that A can detect any error in the computation of X. In other words, any complete trace can be extended by A into a trace leading to an inconsistent state (with respect to the equations of Σ).

The correctness of Theorem 1 can be proved by induction on the derivation tree of statements $U \vdash_T X$ considering each rule in turn [29].

4. APPLICATION

In this section, we illustrate the framework presented in the previous section with the ETP case study described in Section 2. In order to instantiate the framework to a given application, we need to define the service to be delivered, the set of actors involved and their respective requirements. We assume that the ETP service is the computation of the fee due by each driver for a given period of time, for example a quarter. This service can be defined by the following system of equations Σ:

$$Q \ =_\Sigma \ M_1 + M_2 + M_3$$
$$M_i \ =_\Sigma \ D_{i,1} + \ldots D_{i,31}$$
$$D_{i,j} \ =_\Sigma \ H_{i,j,1} + \ldots H_{i,j,144}$$
$$H_{i,j,k} \ =_\Sigma \ F(P_{i,j,k})$$
$$P_{i,j,k} \ =_\Sigma \ A_{i,j,k}$$

Variables $Q, M_i, D_{i,i}, H_{i,j,k}$ represent the fees due for, respectively, a quarter, a month, a day and a ten minutes slot. $P_{i,j,k}$ are the position variables used to compute the fees whereas $A_{i,j,k}$ denote the actual (genuine) positions of the vehicle. In general, it is useful to distinguish different occurrences of variables to account for potential discrepencies resulting from frauds or errors occuring during their communication. It is necessary to distinguish between $A_{i,j,k}$ and $P_{i,j,k}$ here because the former is an environment variable whereas the latter is under the control of the OBE. Similar distinctions could have been introduced between the other variables to account for potential communication errors, but we choose to limit the number of variables for the sake of conciseness.

We consider three actors here, namely the driver δ, the pricing authority α and the environment ϵ: $\Omega = \{\delta, \alpha, \epsilon\}$. Let us denote by $\mathcal{A} = (C, S, K, M, T)$ the architecture to be defined. The first requirement of the pricing authority, which is to be met in all scenarios, is that it should be able to detect any error in the computation of the fee Q:

$$VC(\mathcal{A}, \alpha) \vdash_T Q$$

A first scenario corresponds to the additional requirement that the pricing authority receives all position data $P_{i,j,k}$ and performs all computations.

$$P_{i,j,k} \in S(\delta, \alpha) \wedge \{H_{i,j,k}, D_{i,j}, M_i, Q\} \in C(\alpha)$$

By convention, non quantified indexes are implictly quantified over their respective ranges ($i \in [1..3], j \in [1, 31], k \in [1, 144]$). There are several cases in which these requirements can conflict with the requirements of the driver: the first and obvious case is when the driver does not accept to disclose any location data ($\forall i, j, k, P_{i,j,k} \notin S(\delta, \alpha)$) or not all of them. But it is also the case if the driver does not accept spot checks ($\forall (O, G) \in M, G = \emptyset$) because it is then impossible to establish $VC(\mathcal{A}, \alpha) \vdash_T Q$. The reason is that the authority is not able to detect an error in the last equation of Σ: $P_{i,j,k} = A_{i,j,k}$. If this requirement is relaxed, for example into $\forall (O, G) \in M, G \subseteq \{A_{i,j,k}\} \wedge Card(G) \leq 1$, which allows for one single spot check in a quarter, the conflict disappears and the inference system allows us to prove $VC(\mathcal{A}_1, \alpha) \vdash_{T_1} Q$ with $\mathcal{A}_1 = (C_1, S_1, K_1, M_1, T_1)$ defined as follows:

$$
\begin{aligned}
C_1(\alpha) &= \{Q, M_i, D_{i,j}, H_{i,j,k}\} \\
S_1(\delta, \alpha) &= \{P_{i,j,k}\} \\
M_1 &= \{(O, G_{i,j,k}) | G_{i,j,k}(\alpha) = \{A_{i,j,k}\}\} \\
T_1 &= \{Q, M_i, D_{i,j}, H_{i,j,k}\}
\end{aligned}
$$

By convention, all other sets are empty. This architecture corresponds to the first option of Section 2 (centralized solution) and it is easy to check that $U_1 \vdash_{T_1} Q$ with $U_1 = VC(\mathcal{A}_1, \alpha)$ can be derived through the application of rules R2 and R3 (Subsection 3.3) on the system of equations Σ defining Q.

Let us consider now another scenario in which the driver does not accept that any location data is disclosed to the pricing authority but the OBE is equipped with a secure component for the computation of the fee. If the driver imposes the same constraint as above on spot checks, we get the architecture $\mathcal{A}_2 = (C_2, S_2, K_2, M_2, T_2)$ defined as

follows:

$$
\begin{aligned}
C_2(\delta) &= \{Q, M_i, D_{i,j}, H_{i,j,k}\} \\
S_2(\delta, \alpha) &= \{Q\} \\
M_2 &= \{(O, G_{i,j,k}) | G_{i,j,k}(\alpha) = \{A_{i,j,k}\}\} \\
T_2 &= \{Q, M_i, D_{i,j}, H_{i,j,k}\}
\end{aligned}
$$

However, this architecture does not satisfy $VC(\mathcal{A}_2, \alpha) \vdash_{T_2} Q$ because it is impossible to prove $U \vdash_{T_2} P_{i,j,k}$ for any valid context U. The reason is that, even if it can conduct spot checks, the authority does not have any means to detect that the genuine location data have been provided as inputs to the secure component (that is to say that $P_{i,j,k} = A_{i,j,k}$). To check this, the authority must be able, after a spot check of a position $A_{i,j,k}$, to get also the corresponding value $P_{i,j,k}$. This observation leads to the architecture $\mathcal{A}'_2 = (C'_2, S'_2, K'_2, M'_2, T'_2)$ which satisfies $VC(\mathcal{A}_2, \alpha) \vdash_{T'_2} Q$:

$$
\begin{aligned}
C'_2(\delta) &= \{Q, M_i, D_{i,j}, H_{i,j,k}\} \\
S'_2(\delta, \alpha) &= \{Q\} \\
M'_2 &= \{(O, G_{i,j,k}) | G_{i,j,k}(\alpha) = \{P_{i,j,k}, A_{i,j,k}\}\} \\
T'_2 &= \{Q, M_i, D_{i,j}, H_{i,j,k}\}
\end{aligned}
$$

The proof of $U'_2 \vdash_{T'_2} Q$ with $U'_2 = VC(\mathcal{A}'_2, \alpha)$ can be derived by the application of rule R3 to get $U'_2 \vdash_{T'_2} A_{i,j,k}$, followed by the application of rule R2 to prove $U'_2 \vdash_{T'_2} P_{i,j,k}$ and the application of rule R1 to derive successively $U'_2 \vdash_{T'_2} H_{i,j,k}$, $U'_2 \vdash_{T'_2} D_{i,j}$, $U'_2 \vdash_{T'_2} M_i$ and $U'_2 \vdash_{T'_2} Q$.

The above architecture corresponds to option 2 in Section 2. The third option, which is based on commitments[5], can be defined as $\mathcal{A}_3 = (C_3, S_3, K_3, M_3, T_3)$ with:

$$
\begin{aligned}
C_3(\delta) &= \{Q, M_i, D_{i,j}, H_{i,j,k}\} \\
S_3(\delta, \alpha) &= \{Q\} \\
M_3 &= \{(O_{i,j,k}, G_{i,j,k}) | O_{i,j,k}(\delta, \alpha) = \\
&\quad \{P_{i,j,k}, H_{i,j,k'}, D_{i,j'}, M_{i'}| \\
&\quad i' \in [1..3], j' \in [1, 31], k' \in [1, 144]\} \wedge \\
&\quad G_{i,j,k}(\alpha) = \{A_{i,j,k}\}\}
\end{aligned}
$$

In this case, the only information that the authority can get by spot checks is, as in $\mathcal{A}_1$, one position of the vehicle ($\{A_{i,j,k}\}$) per quarter. As in $\mathcal{A}'_2$, all computations are done by the OBE. However, in contrast with $\mathcal{A}'_2$, no trust assumption is made here ($T_3 = \emptyset$). Detectability comes from the possibility to disclose commitments after a spot check: the intuition behind $O_{i,j,k}(\delta, \alpha)$ is that all variables contributing to the computation of the part of the fee in which $\{A_{i,j,k}\}$ is involved must be disclosed for the authority to be able to check that they have been correctly included in the computation of the quarterly fee Q.

5. RELATED WORK

Privacy by design has been strongly advocated by the Information and Privacy Commissioner of Ontario [8, 9] and it has been praised by a number of academic lawyers as an essential step towards a better privacy protection [46].

On the technological front, privacy enhancing technologies (PETs) have been an active research topic in computer sci-

---

[5] For the sake of the example, we consider the version with commitment trees here, i.e. commitments on location data and on partial sums.

ence during the last decades [15, 19, 47] and a variety of techniques have been proposed (including anonymizers, identity management systems, privacy proxies, encryption mechanisms, filters, anonymous credentials, commitment schemes, sanitization techniques, etc.). As discussed in Section 1 and Section 2, these techniques have been applied in a variety of areas[6], but on a case by case basis and "privacy by design" is generally not addressed from a general perspective. As pointed out in [20], privacy by design "requires the development of generalizable methodologies that build upon the principle of data minimization". The goal of this paper is precisely to propose a formal framework to address this need.

As far as formal models for privacy are concerned, previous work in this area can be classified into three main categories:

- *Language based approaches:* a number of languages and logics have been proposed to express privacy policies [1, 3, 4, 5, 11, 12, 13, 21, 23, 30, 24, 35, 38, 53]. These languages may target citizens, businesses or organizations; they can be used to express individual privacy policies, corporate rules or legal rules. Not all of them are endowed with a formal semantics though. When it is the case (e.g. [1, 3, 4, 5, 30, 21, 35, 38, 53]), they can be used to verify consistency properties or to check if a system complies with a privacy policy. These verifications can be performed either *a priori*, through static verification techniques, on the fly, using monitoring, or *a posteriori* in the context of audits or accountability procedures. The policies expressed in these languages are usually more fine-grained than the properties considered here and they tend to be more complete with respect to privacy (e.g. including notions of obligations or data deletion). In contrast with the framework proposed here, they do not provide ways to reason about architectural choices, in particular about the relationship between trust requirements and decentralization, which is the heart of this paper.

- *Decentralized security models*: the decentralized label model [42] makes it possible to reason about information flows between principals that do not trust each other. Labels are used to express confidentiality requirements on the data. They define, for each principal, the authorized readers of their data. The model can be extended to include the authorized writers in order to express integrity constraints. The decentralized label model has been applied to the Jif programming language [42]: labels can be associated with variables and checked by static analysis. They can also be used to split Jif programs securely, i.e. to derive a distributed implementation that statisfies all policies of the principals [54]. Labels have also been used in Fabric, another extension of Jif with support for secure distributed programming [36]. The decentralized label model could be used to express certain aspects of our framework, such as the $\overline{Send}$ component of our architectures, but it is not suitable to reason about detectability properties.

- *Privacy metrics*: notions such as k-anonymity [34, 49], l-diversity [37] or ϵ-differential privacy [16, 17] have been proposed as ways to measure the level of privacy provided by an algorithm. Methods [17, 40, 39] have been proposed to design algorithms achieving these privacy metrics (e.g. through the deletion of values, generalization or the introduction of noise) or to verify that a system achieves a given level of privacy [50]. These contributions on privacy metrics are complementary to the work described in this paper. We have followed a logical (or qualitative) approach here, proving that a given privacy property is met (or not) by an architecture. As suggested in the next section, an avenue for further research would be to cope with quantitative reasoning as well, using inference systems to derive properties expressed in terms of privacy metrics.

6. DISCUSSION AND FURTHER WORK

The framework presented in this paper has been applied to the verification of architectures for electronic traffic payment systems and smart metering. The tool, which is implemented in Haskell, provides different modes of use: fully automatic, assisted and manual. In all cases, the first task of the user is to define the fixed parameters of the problem, as specified in Section 3 (the service defined as a set of equations and the requirements of the actors defined as constraints on sets of variables). In the fully automatic mode, the user just requests the proof of detectability of a given variable X for an actor A. The tool then looks for all architectures meeting the constraints that can lead to a proof of X by the inference system defined in Section 3. In the assisted mode, the same principle applies but the search is limited to the application of a rule (R1, R2 or R3) proposed by the user. In the manual mode, the user provides not only the rule to apply but also the variable to check. The rationale for the use of these modes is the following: when the designer is able to define sufficiently constraining requirements (either because he already has a good intuition about the appropriate architecture or because the constraints imposed by the actors are strong enough), he can use the fully automatic mode to confirm his intuition or to check that the constraints can be met. The other modes can be used either if the initial constraints are too loose[7] or in "debugging mode" to understand why the system fails to find a proof for a given variable. In general, the designer should strive to express from the start all obvious constraints or to use in a first stage the tool in assisted mode to better understand the options investigated by the system and possibly refine iteratively his initial set of constraints.

We would like to emphasize that several conditions have to be met for the above tool and the overall approach to be applicable:

- First, it must be possible to define the service to be provided by the system as the result of a computation involving the input data (e.g. the computation of a

---

[6]For example, ubiquitous systems in [28], smart metering in [18, 33, 48], pay as you drive in [22, 2, 45], or location privacy in [14, 25, 26].

---

[7]The response time of the automatic mode can become unacceptable in such cases because the worst case complexity of the search (when no constraint at all are imposed on the architecture) is exponential in terms of the number of variables involved in the definition of the services (because the system may have to explore all possible contexts).

fee in ETP or smart metering, or the computation of a test to decide whether a given ad should be sent to an internet user). This definition plays a pivotal rôle in the analysis of acceptable architectures. Thus the approach does not help in situations such as social networks where the service is just the display of the data (and its access based on a given privacy policy).

- In addition, the framework proposed here does not provide off-the-shelf solutions nor answers to broad questions such as: "What is the best architecture to solve this problem?". It provides answers to specific questions such as "Given this service to be delivered, this set of constraints from the actors involved and this set of available operations (building blocks), what are the acceptable architectures or is this architecture acceptable?". In addition, it is necessary to be able to provide a formal characterization of all the aforementioned parameters. Section 3 presents such a formalization for ETP systems, given a set of available operations and we suggest below how other operations could be dealt with.

- In this paper, we have considered only one of the privacy by design principles, namely data minimization; other principles such as, for example, transparency or accountability [52] are also of upmost importance and require further research.

Beyond this framework, the goal of this paper is to put forward a formal approach to privacy by design [32] which can be used as a foundation for a systematic exploration of the design space and the justification of architectural choices. A systematic method is needed for at least two reasons: first, privacy is a very complex issue, which may sometimes conflict (or seem to conflict) with other requirements. Secondly, a wide variety of Privacy Enhancing Technologies (PETs) are available and many more will be proposed in the future. Tools are thus badly needed to allow designers to master this complexity and to take decisions based on rigorous grounds. Before giving up on privacy on the pretext of apparently conflicting requirements, all options must be considered and the controller should be in a position to prove that no other solution can meet the functional constraints while collecting less personal data. This requirement is also in line with the accountability principle of the draft regulation published by the European Commission in January 2012[8].

The framework introduced in Section 3 is a first step in this direction and an illustration of a more general approach. For example, the definition of architectures is based on the set of operations or buiding blocks available. In this paper, we have chosen a set of operations useful to investigate a class of solutions for ETP. The same set of operations can be applied to other application areas such as smart metering. But other techniques can be included as well in the set of operations and the corresponding sets added to architectures and contexts. The condition to be able to integrate a new operation in the framework is to be able to express the relevant properties as inference rules. For example, in order to include homomorphic commitments into the framework, we need to extend architectures with an additional set K_F

[8]http://ec.europa.eu/justice/newsroom/data-protection/news/120125-en.htm, Art. 22

(for variables that are commited using an homomorphic encryption algorithm for operation F), extend valid contexts to include this set K_F and add the following rule:

(R4) If $X =_\Sigma F(Y_1, \ldots, Y_n)$, $X \notin T$ and $\{X, Y_1, \ldots, Y_n\} \subseteq K_F$

$$\frac{\forall i \in \{1, \ldots, n\}, U_i \vdash_T Y_i}{\bigcup_{i=1}^{n} U_i \vdash_T X}$$

This rule expresses the fact that if all the variables involved are commited using an homomorphic scheme, the only requirement is to be able to detect an error in the computation of the variables $Y_1, \ldots, Y_n$ because the validity of the equation $X =_\Sigma F(Y_1, \ldots, Y_n)$ can be checked directly on the commitments.

Other straightforward enhancements to the formalism are possible, at the price of extra administration burden, such as the distinction between nodes and actors or the introduction of constraints on the physical architecture (such as, for example, the possibility to implement a given computation on a given node or to have a communication link between two nodes). It would also be possible to consider a richer input language to express services and to provide an abstraction function to extract (from specifications in this richer language) the equations used here to express the dependencies between variables.

A complementary extension would be the introduction of an inference system to reason about the knowledge of the actors in a more abstract way than done in Section 3. In this paper, we decided to focus on the detectability constraint because it has received less attention so far, but the possibility for an actor to know a given information (beyond the fact that he may receive or not a given set of variables) is obviously at the heart of privacy protection. Inference systems to prove knowledge properties (akin to epistemic logic [6, 10, 41]) can be defined independently of the detectability system introduced in Section 3 and used to check additional constraints. Such an inference system typically includes rules to prove that, from a given set of knowledge, an actor can derive a new knowledge.

Another interesting problem for the future would be the analysis of the specification of the service itself. In this paper, we have taken this specification for granted and considered that all variables involved in a definition were really necessary. There may be cases where this assumption does not hold though, and it would be interesting to be able to detect this situation and to transform the initial specification into an equivalent, but less "personal data consuming" solution. This kind of analysis is reminiscent of *strictness analysis* in functional languages [27] and inspiration can be taken in this area.

Last but not least, in this paper, we have followed a "logical" (or qualitative) approach, as opposed to a quantitative approach to privacy. An avenue for further research in this area would be to study the integration of quantitative measures of privacy (such as differential privacy) into the framework.

7. ACKNOWLEDGMENTS

The author would like to thank the reviewers for their valuable comments and suggestions to improve the paper. The final version of this paper has benefited substantially from their comments. Many thanks are due also to Gustavo

Grieco for his implementation of the tool sketched in this paper.

8. REFERENCES

[1] M. Backes, M. Dürmuth, and G. Karjoth. Unification in privacy policy evaluation - translating EPAL into Prolog. In *POLICY*, pages 185–188, 2004.

[2] J. Balasch, A. Rial, C. Troncoso, B. Preneel, I. Verbauwhede, and C. Geuens. PrETP: Privacy-preserving electronic toll pricing. In *USENIX Security Symposium*, pages 63–78, 2010.

[3] A. Barth, A. Datta, J. C. Mitchell, and H. Nissenbaum. Privacy and contextual integrity: Framework and applications. In *IEEE Symposium on Security and Privacy*, pages 184–198, 2006.

[4] A. Barth, J. C. Mitchell, A. Datta, and S. Sundaram. Privacy and utility in business processes. In *CSF*, pages 279–294, 2007.

[5] M. Y. Becker, A. Malkis, and L. Bussard. A practical generic privacy language. In *ICISS*, pages 125–139, 2010.

[6] M. Burrows, M. Abadi, and R. M. Needham. A logic of authentication. *ACM Trans. Comput. Syst.*, 8(1):18–36, 1990.

[7] L. Bygrave. Privacy-enhancing technologies - caught between a rock and the hard place. *Privacy Law and Policy Reporter*, 9, 2002.

[8] A. Cavoukian. *Privacy and radical pragmatism: change the paradigm*. White Paper, Information and Privacy Commissioner of Ontario, Canada, 2008.

[9] A. Cavoukian. *Privacy by design. The 7 foundational principles*. White Paper, Information and Privacy Commissioner of Ontario, Canada, 2009.

[10] R. Chadha, S. Delaune, and S. Kremer. Epistemic logic for the applied pi calculus. In *FMOODS/FORTE*, pages 182–197, 2009.

[11] O. Chowdhury, H. Chen, J. Niu, N. Li, and E. Bertino. On XACML's adequacy to specify and to enforce HIPAA. In *USENIX Workshop on Health Security and Privacy*, 2012.

[12] L. Cranor, B. Dobbs, S. Egelman, G. Hogben, J. Humphrey, M. Langheinrich, M. Marchiori, M. Presler-Marshall, J. Reagle, M. Schunter, D. A. Stampley, and R. Wenning. *The Platform for Privacy Preferences 1.1 (P3P1.1) Specification*. W3C, 2006.

[13] L. Cranor, M. Langheinrich, and M. Marchiori. *A P3P Preference Exchange Language 1.0 (APPEL1.0)*. W3C, 2002.

[14] M. L. Damiani, E. Bertino, and C. Silvestri. The probe framework for the personalized cloaking of private locations. *Transactions on Data Privacy*, 3(2):123–148, 2010.

[15] Y. Deswarte and C. A. Melchor. Current and future privacy enhancing technologies for the internet. *Annals of Telecommunications*, 61(3):399–417, 2006.

[16] C. Dwork. Differential privacy. In *ICALP (2)*, pages 1–12, 2006.

[17] C. Dwork. A firm foundation for private data analysis. *Commun. ACM*, 54(1):86–95, 2011.

[18] F. D. Garcia and B. Jacobs. Privacy-friendly energy-metering via homomorphic encryption. In *STM'10 Proceedings of the 6th international conference on Security and trust management*, pages 226–238. Springer, 2010.

[19] I. Goldberg. Privacy-enhancing technologies for the internet iii: ten years later. In *Digital Privacy: Theory, Technologies, and Practices*, pages 84–89. TeX Users Group, December 2007.

[20] S. Gürses, C. Troncoso, and C. Diaz. Engineering privacy by design. In *Conference on Computers, Privacy and Data Protection (CPDP 2011)*, 2011.

[21] M. Jafari, P. W. L. Fong, R. Safavi-Naini, K. Barker, and N. P. Sheppard. Towards defining semantic foundations for purpose-based privacy policies. In *CODASPY*, pages 213–224, 2011.

[22] W. D. Jonge and B. Jacobs. Privacy-friendly electronic traffic pricing via commits. In *Proceedings of the Workshop of Formal Aspects of Securiy and Trust*, pages 132–137. Springer, LNCS 5491, 2009.

[23] G. Karjoth, M. Schunter, and E. V. Herreweghen. Translating privacy practices into privacy promises -how to promise what you can keep. In *POLICY*, pages 135–146, 2003.

[24] G. Karjoth, M. Schunter, E. V. Herreweghen, and M. Waidner. Amending P3P for clearer privacy promises. In *DEXA Workshops*, pages 445–449, 2003.

[25] E. Kosta, J. Zibuschka, T. Scherner, and J. Dumortier. Legal considerations on privacy-enhancing location based services using PRIME technology. *Computer Law and Security Report*, 4:139–146, 2008.

[26] J. Krumm. A survey of computational location privacy. *Pers Ubiquit Comput*, 13:391–399, 2008.

[27] T.-M. Kuo and P. Mishra. Strictness analysis: A new perspective based on type inference. In *FPCA*, pages 260–272, 1989.

[28] M. Langheinrich. Privacy by design - principles of privacy aware ubiquitous systems. In *Proceedings of the Ubicomp Conference*, pages 273–291. Springer, LNCS 2201, 2001.

[29] D. Le Métayer. *Privacy by Design: a Formal Framework for the Analysis of Architectural Choices (extended version)*. INRIA Research Report (to appear).

[30] D. Le Métayer. A formal privacy management framework. In *FAST (Formal Aspects of Security and Trust)*, pages 161–176. Springer, LNCS 5491, 2009.

[31] D. Le Métayer. Privacy by design: a matter of choice. In *Data Protection in a Profiled World*, pages 323–334. Springer, 2010.

[32] D. Le Métayer. Formal methods a link between software code and legal rules. In *SEFM (Software Engineering and Formal Methods)*, pages 3–18. Springer, LNCS 7041, 2011.

[33] M. LeMay, G. Gross, C. A. Gunter, and S. Garg. Unified architecture for large-scale attested metering. In *HICSS*, page 115, 2007.

[34] N. Li, W. H. Qardaji, and D. Su. Provably private data anonymization: Or, k-anonymity meets differential privacy. *CoRR*, abs/1101.2604, 2011.

[35] N. Li, T. Yu, and A. I. Antón. A semantics based approach to privacy languages. *Comput. Syst. Sci. Eng.*, 21(5), 2006.

[36] J. Liu, M. D. George, K. Vikram, X. Qi, L. Waye, and A. C. Myers. Fabric: a platform for secure distributed computation and storage. In *SOSP*, pages 321–334, 2009.

[37] A. Machanavajjhala, J. Gehrke, D. Kifer, and M. Venkitasubramaniam. l-diversity: Privacy beyond k-anonymity. In *ICDE*, page 24, 2006.

[38] M. J. May, C. A. Gunter, and I. Lee. Privacy APIs: Access control techniques to analyze and verify legal privacy policies. In *CSFW*, pages 85–97, 2006.

[39] F. McSherry. Privacy integrated queries: an extensible platform for privacy-preserving data analysis. *Commun. ACM*, 53(9):89–97, 2010.

[40] F. McSherry and K. Talwar. Mechanism design via differential privacy. In *FOCS*, pages 94–103, 2007.

[41] J.-J. C. Meyer and W. van der Hoek. *Epistemic Logic for Computer Science and Artificial Intelligence*.

[42] A. C. Myers and B. Liskov. Protecting privacy using the decentralized label model. *ACM Trans. Softw. Eng. Methodol.*, 9(4):410–442, 2000.

[43] A. Narayanan, V. Toubiana, S. Barocas, H. Nissenbaum, and D. Boneh. A critical look at decentralized personal data architectures. *CoRR*, abs/1202.4503, 2012.

[44] OECD. *OECD guidelines on the protection of privacy and transborder flows of personal data, Organization for Economic Co-operation and Development*. OECD, 1980.

[45] R. A. Popa, H. Balakrishnan, and A. J. Blumberg. Vpriv: Protecting privacy in location-based vehicular services. In *USENIX Security Symposium*, pages 335–350, 2009.

[46] Y. Poullet. About the e-privacy directive, towards a third generation of data protection legislations. In *Data Protection in a Profile World*, pages 3–29. Springer, 2010.

[47] A. Rezgui, A. Bouguettaya, and M. Y. Eltoweissy. Privacy on the web: facts, challenges, and solutions. *IEEE Security and Privacy*, pages 40–49, 2003.

[48] A. Rial and G. Danezis. Privacy-preserving smart metering. In *Proceedings of the 2011 ACM Workshop on Privacy in the Electronic Society, WPES 2011*. ACM, 2011.

[49] L. Sweeney. k-anonymity: A model for protecting privacy. *International Journal of Uncertainty, Fuzziness and Knowledge-Based Systems*, 10(5):557–570, 2002.

[50] M. C. Tschantz, D. K. Kaynar, and A. Datta. Formal verification of differential privacy for interactive systems. *CoRR*, abs/1101.2819, 2011.

[51] M. C. Tschantz and J. M. Wing. Formal methods for privacy. In *FM*, pages 1–15, 2009.

[52] D. J. Weitzner, H. Abelson, T. Berners-Lee, J. Feigenbaum, J. A. Hendler, and G. J. Sussman. Information accountability. *Commun. ACM*, 51(6):82–87, 2008.

[53] T. Yu, N. Li, and A. I. Antón. A formal semantics for P3P. In *SWS*, pages 1–8, 2004.

[54] S. Zdancewic, L. Zheng, N. Nystrom, and A. C. Myers. Secure program partitioning. *ACM Trans. Comput. Syst.*, 20(3):283–328, 2002.

Comparative Eye Tracking of Experts and Novices in Web Single Sign-on

Majid Arianezhad
School of Engineering Science
Simon Fraser University
Burnaby, B.C., Canada
arianezhad@sfu.ca

Timothy Kelley
Indiana University Bloomington
107 S. Indiana Ave.
Bloomington, IN, 47405
kelleyt@indiana.edu

L. Jean Camp
Indiana University Bloomington
107 S. Indiana Ave.
Bloomington, IN, 47405
ljcamp@indiana.edu

Douglas Stebila
Science and Engineering Faculty
Queensland University of Technology
Brisbane, Queensland, Australia
stebila@qut.edu.au

ABSTRACT

Security indicators in web browsers alert users to the presence of a secure connection between their computer and a web server; many studies have shown that such indicators are largely ignored by users in general. In other areas of computer security, research has shown that technical expertise can decrease user susceptibility to attacks.

In this work, we examine whether computer or security expertise affects use of web browser security indicators. Our study takes place in the context of web-based single sign-on, in which a user can use credentials from a single identity provider to login to many relying websites; single sign-on is a more complex, and hence more difficult, security task for users. In our study, we used eye trackers and surveyed participants to examine the cues individuals use and those they report using, respectively.

Our results show that users with security expertise are more likely to self-report looking at security indicators, and eye-tracking data shows they have longer gaze duration at security indicators than those without security expertise. However, computer expertise alone is not correlated with recorded use of security indicators. In survey questions, neither experts nor novices demonstrate a good understanding of the security consequences of web-based single sign-on.

Categories and Subject Descriptors

C2.0 [**Computer-communication networks**]: General—*security and protection*; H.1.2 [**Information Systems Models and Principles**]: User/Machine Systems—*human factors*

Keywords

HTTPS; security indicators; single sign-on; web browsers; usability; eye-tracking; experts

1. INTRODUCTION

Web browsers employ certain security indicators—such as the presence of the lock icon, the use of "https" and domain name in the location bar, or certificate information—to help users make decisions regarding potential online threats, particularly related to the security of the web communications transmitted over the Secure Sockets Layer (SSL) / Transport Layer Security (TLS) protocol. Despite having been present in browsers for more than 15 years, many studies have demonstrated, using both self-reported usage and eye-tracking data, that security indicators are largely ineffective at communicating security information to users.

In other areas of security research, such as phishing, technical expertise has been shown to be a mitigating factor in user susceptibility to online attacks.

Recently, the nature of user authentication on the web has changed. While user authentication was originally site-centric—users had different usernames and passwords for each web site—the use of *single sign-on authentication* has allowed users to use their credentials from a single *identity provider* to log in to multiple sites, which are called *relying parties*. Single sign-on can provide several benefits to users: most notably, they do not need to remember as many username/password combinations, and they do not need to register for new accounts at each site. On the other hand, there is a single point of failure (the identity provider), and users may have less control over their personal information.

Single sign-on systems are of growing importance within organizations and corporations. On the public Internet, several end-user single sign-on systems are currently available, both proprietary, such as ones provided by social networking sites like Facebook and Google, and open, such as the distributed standard OpenID. As of October 2012, one industry study reported that 54% of logins using social networking single-sign on used Facebook's system [9].

Web-based single sign-on typically involves authentication via redirection from the relying party to the identity provider; the user authenticates to the identity provider, and then the browser is redirected back to the relying party with authentication tokens which the relying party can use in a back-channel to obtain the user's profile information from the identity provider. Because of the redirection, information flow is much less clear than the traditional login process and may place a substantial cognitive burden on users.

In this work, we explore two related themes. First, we examine whether users with higher technical expertise make better use of security indicators in web browsers. Second, we examine to what extent users employing single sign-on make use of security indicators in web browsers and their degree of understanding of the flow of information in single sign-on. Our study employs eye-trackers to obtain data on actual user behaviour, using both Facebook and OpenID as single sign-on identity providers.

Our goal is to provide answers to the following questions:

- Do users look for security indicators when using single sign-on in web browsers?
- Does the behaviour of users with respect to security indicators differ between novices and those with computer or security expertise?
- To what extent do users understand the flow of information and risks involved in single sign-on? Do novices and experts have different understandings?

Approach. Our study involved 19 participants who completed a variety of online tasks involving both Facebook and OpenID for single sign-on and then filled out a survey. The surveys were used to compare reported behaviour to observed behaviour. Because eye-tracking is time-intensive, data-intensive, and often perceived as invasive, relatively small sample sizes are common.

While completing online tasks, participants' gazes were recorded using eye-tracking equipment. The online tasks included a variety of social networking tasks, such as rating an item on a movie website, sharing an item onto a social networking profile, and using a social networking account to login to other websites. Participants were asked to use their own Facebook account, but were provided with an alternative account upon request; for tasks involving OpenID, participants used a provided account.

The survey had three sections of questions: demographics, technological expertise, and single sign-on. Using answers from the technological experience section, we classified participants as either (a) novice, (b) computer experts, or (c) computer and security experts.

Results. After classifying users' expertise, we examined a variety of user behaviours and responses within the context of expertise. Here are some of the results of our analysis:

- Security experts have higher self-reported use of security indicators than non-security experts, and this is confirmed with eye-tracking data, both in terms of gaze duration and number of fixations at security indicators.
- Users with only computer expertise, not security expertise, have no more frequent self-reported or actual use of security indicators than novices.
- In general, users have a poor understanding of the flow of information during single sign-on. They do not understand the flow of credentials and profile information between the browser, the identity provider, and the relying party. They cannot correctly say whether relying parties learn the password for their account at the identity provider; computer experts are somewhat

better than computer novices at this, though surprisingly we cannot say the same for security experts.

- Users do not always realize that they are using single sign-on, especially when doing so within the context of a single organization whose services are distributed across multiple internal web servers.
- Users *do* understand that, after logging in to a relying party via an identity provider, they need to logout of the identity provider when terminating their session at a public computer.

Outline. Section 2 reviews background on single sign-on, security indicators, and expertise in security usability. In Section 3, we present our detailed methodology. Analysis and discussion is presented in Section 4. Additional discussion, including study limitations, appears in Section 5, and Section 6 concludes. The study tasks and statistical analysis methodology appear in the appendices. The full survey and statistical methodology have been omitted due to space constraints, but appear in the full version.[1]

2. BACKGROUND

2.1 Single sign-on

Single sign-on (SSO) protocols allow a user with an account at an *identity provider* to identify herself to a third-party service, called a *relying party*.

Only recently has single sign-on seen widespread implementation on the public Internet. OpenID [10] is a standard for federated authentication in which anyone can setup an identity provider and anyone can be a relying party, with no formal relationships required between relying parties and identity providers. Several commercial OpenID providers exist, and many webmail services act as OpenID providers, but at present relatively few relying parties exist.

Closely related to single sign-on is the notion of delegated authorisation, such as in the OAuth protocol [1], where a user can delegate authority to a third party to access a particular resource on a server. For example, in August 2009, the popular microblogging site Twitter started requiring OAuth for all delegated authorisation.

In December 2008 the social networking site Facebook started offering a feature called "Facebook Connect" in which third party websites can allow users to login using their Facebook credentials rather than having to register for a separate account; this proprietary single sign-on service is built in part on the OAuth protocol.

For OpenID, Facebook Connect, and OAuth, single sign-on works via a sequence of redirects between webpages:

1. The user is on the website of a relying party, such as the movie review site Rotten Tomatoes.
2. The user clicks the "Login with Facebook" button on Rotten Tomatoes.
3. The user is redirected from Rotten Tomatoes to a Facebook login screen.
4. The user enters their Facebook username and password on the Facebook login screen and clicks "Submit".
5. Facebook verifies the credentials and asks the user to authorise the release of certain profile information.
6. The user consents to the release of profile information and then is redirected back to Rotten Tomatoes.

---

[1]http://eprints.qut.edu.au/55714

Figure 1: Web browser security indicators. Google Chrome 17.0, Microsoft Internet Explorer 9.0.5, Microsoft Internet Explorer 9.0.5 with an extended validation certificate, and Mozilla Firefox 10.0.2

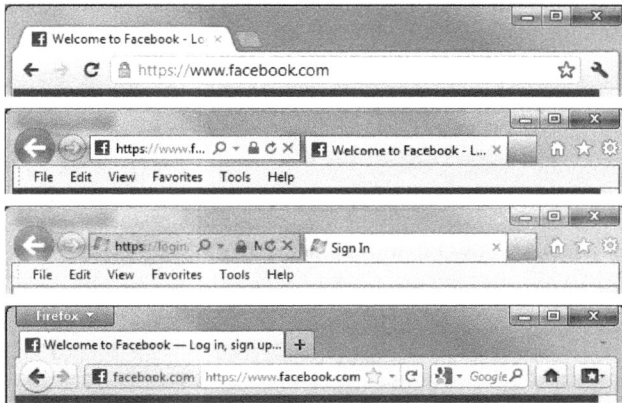

The redirect includes cryptographic tokens that Rotten Tomatoes uses to subsequently request profile information from Facebook for that user.

Sun et al. [18] performed the first usability study of single sign-on protocols on the web. Participants using OpenID performed single sign-on related tasks using the existing browser interface and a proposed browser interface. They also surveyed attitudes towards single sign-on and comprehension of the risks and functionality of single sign-on.

2.2 Security indicators in web browsers

The Secure Sockets Layer (SSL) / Transport Layer Security (TLS) protocol provides encryption and authentication of communication on the Internet. The combination of SSL/TLS with web content delivered over the Hypertext Transport Protocol (HTTP) is jointly referred to as HTTPS. Authentication is performed using public key certificates a certificate authority (CA) who has verified that a given public key belongs to the legitimate owner of the given domain name and, in the case of extended validation certificates, that the key belongs to that real-world entity or business. Multiple CAs exist, and today's popular web browsers typically trust upwards of 650 CAs [5].

Web browsers use several user interface elements, called *security indicators*, help users judge the security of a connection. Typically, these include the display of the protocol name (https) and domain name in the location bar, a lock icon, and additional colouring or elements for extended validation certificates. These security indicators are displayed within the browser *chrome*, the portions of the window controlled by the browser, as opposed to the *content* portion of the window that displays the HTML page. With several different major web browsers, different computing platforms, and frequent releases of new versions, the placement and semantics of security indicators in web browsers is inconsistent. Notably, Mozilla Firefox versions 4–13 did not display a lock icon to indicate the use of HTTPS, but it returned in version 14, after completion of our study. The indicators for each browser in our study are shown in Figure 1.

Research in the usability of security in web browsers traces its origins to the work of Friedman et al. [6] who conducted in-depth interviews to understand how users evaluate security of web sites. They collected types of evidence that users employed to decide if a website was secure: these included the above security indicators provided by the web browser chrome, as well as non-chrome indicators such as the type of information requested, the type of the site, the quality of the site, and statements within the page about security.

Several subsequent works have investigated the extent to which users and websites employ these and other security indicators. Whalen and Inkpen [20] used eye-tracking equipment and interviews to analyse how users interact with security indicators: most looked at the lock icon, though few made use of its interactive capabilities to display certificate information; less than half looked for the the use of HTTPS in the location bar. Notably, no participants gazed at security indicators prior to being "primed" for security.

Certificate authorities, in conjunction with browser manufacturers introduced *extended validation (EV) certificates* in 2007; CAs would perform more extensive identity validation checks on parties (in exchange for more money), and browser manufacturers would introduce user interface elements, such as colouring the location bar green, to convey the purportedly greater trustworthiness of sites with EV certificates. Sobey et al. [14] analysed the relative effectiveness of the indicators of Mozilla Firefox 3 and their own modification; users did not generally notice the EV indicators in the standard Firefox 3, but their own modification was more successful. However, no major browser currently employs an interface similar to their modification.

Schechter et al. [12] observed that users continue to login to websites when security indicators have been removed, even when security warnings are presented. Sunshine et al. [19] tested the effectiveness of various SSL security warnings; some designs were more effective than others, but in all cases a large proportion of users clicked through warnings.

Several works [11, 15, 16] have raised questions about the extent to which this insecure behaviour can be explained by the artificial study environment. Complicating factors may include: participants using artificial credentials may feel less motivation to protect them; participants being "task focused"; and participants trusting that performing these operations in a study at a university means there is no risk.

2.3 Experts versus non-experts

Early research by Friedman et al. [6] observed that users from a high-technology neighbourhood were better able to describe the security indicators associated with an encrypted channel compared to users from a less technical neighbourhood. Sobey et al. [14] found that expert users were better able to identify extended validation certificate security indicators in web browsers. Sunshine et al. [19] in their research on the effectiveness of SSL warnings briefly consider whether technical expertise influences ability to identify warnings; they observed that experts made slightly better decisions than non-experts in some specific situations.

A real-life phishing attack performed by Jagatic et al. [7] on students at Indiana University found that students majoring in technical fields were roughly half as likely to fall for spear phishing emails as students in non-technical fields. Wright and Marett [21] confirmed that individuals with high self-reported computer self-efficacy or web experience, or participants who had high scores on a security awareness evaluation, were less susceptible to phishing attacks.

3. METHODOLOGY

In this study, we observed the behaviour of study participants while performing certain social networking tasks; our observation equipment included eye-tracking devices to record where the participant's gaze was during the tasks. After the online tasks, participants completed a survey.

Participants were recruited via email and personal contacts; we aimed to recruit approximately 50% of participants as people we believed might end up classified as being security or computer experts and 50% as novices. Participants received a $15 gift card for participating, and could withdraw from the study at any time while still receiving the full value gift card, although no participants did. The study was conducted in a small computer lab at an off-campus university building. Descriptions of the study indicated to participants that we wanted to observe their of social media; we omitted any references to security in the study description or instructions. The study was approved by the Human Ethics committee of the Queensland University of Technology and by the Institutional Review Board (IRB) of Indiana University.

3.1 Eye-tracker calibration

After signing the study consent sheet, participants were seated at a desktop PC running Microsoft Windows 7, with a widescreen 19" monitor (a trial version of this study run earlier noted that some eye-tracking systems perform poorly on small monitors). The PC was equipped with the Mirametrix S2 Eye Tracker, placed just below the monitor. This eye-tracking device has a data rate of 60 Hz with binocular tracking. The accuracy range of the device is 0.5 to 1 degree and the drift range is less than 0.3 degrees.

The device manufacturer's 9-point calibration routine was run. Accuracy varied by participant: participants without astigmatisms had average error of 40 to 50 pixels. Relying solely on manufacturer calibration had two drawbacks. First, the distance between some security indicators was less than 50 pixels, so it would be difficult to distinguish gazes at nearby indicators. Second, reported error for the device was averaged over the 9 calibration points, but subjects had differing inaccuracies: some users had small errors for points close to the centre of the screen but large errors for points near the edge of the screen, and vice versa.

As a result, we designed a secondary calibration phase in which we showed users additional calibration points which corresponded to points of interest for our study, for example the point at which the lock icon would appear when logging at a certain stage. We identified these points for each of the browsers in our study and prepared calibration videos. Participants were given a choice of web browser: Google Chrome 17.0, Microsoft Internet Explorer 9.0.5, or Mozilla Firefox 10.0.2 (the most recent versions of the browsers at the time of the study). We then showed users the secondary calibration video and directed users to gaze at the points in our calibration videos. This secondary calibration was done twice: before Facebook tasks and before OpenID tasks.

This secondary calibration phase allowed us to identify what the eye-tracker recorded for points of interest of our study, and compare those recorded points with points of gaze during the online tasks to determine whether participants gazed at our points of interest. Since the device's precision error was substantially lower than its accuracy error, this allowed us to obtain higher accuracy. We deemed a participant to have gazed at a security indicator while it was on screen if there was a fixation whose recorded distance to an indicator was within the average, plus two standard deviations, of the distances recorded for that point of interest during secondary calibration; two standard deviations ensured that all gazes recorded during secondary calibration would be accepted as valid, whereas one standard deviation would have missed some of the calibration gazes.

3.2 Online tasks

After calibration, participants were instructed to begin the online tasks. Prior to the participant's arrival, we randomly decided whether the participant would be assigned to complete tasks involving Facebook first or tasks involving OpenID first. In this explanation, we will proceed for a participant who was assigned Facebook tasks first; the Facebook and OpenID descriptions below would be swapped for participants assigned to completed the OpenID tasks first.

Facebook. The participant was given the list of Facebook tasks as in the appendix. In summary: in task F1, the participant was asked to navigate to the movie rating site Rotten Tomatoes, login with their Facebook account, and rate a movie; in task F2, they were asked to post a story about a movie from Rotten Tomatoes to their Facebook profile and then log out "as if you were walking away from a public computer"; in task F3, they were asked to visit a blog on LiveJournal and post a comment on a story using their Facebook account, then log out; in task F4, they were asked to share something from Amazon on to their Facebook profile; finally in task F5 they were asked to log out, go back to Facebook, log in, and then log out one last time.

Each Facebook logins resulted in a pop-up window being displayed in the centre of the screen as shown in Figure 2. Participants were asked to use their own Facebook account if they had one, however they were instructed that they could request alternative credentials to use instead of their own. After logging in to Facebook, participants were asked to grant the relying party access to certain personal information. In the statistical analysis, we analyzed the login portion and the personal information grant portion of the tasks separately.

We did not alter the behaviour or code of any of the websites used in this portion of the study. Although the front page of facebook.com is not delivered over HTTP, HTTPS is used to display the login page when Facebook single sign-on is accessed via a secondary website, so HTTPS security indicators were present during Facebook single sign-on login; no extended validation indicator was displayed as Facebook does not have an EV certificate. After logging in to Facebook, an additional page was displayed asking the user to share profile information with the relying party, security indicators may or may not be present on this screen depending on whether users have enabled Facebook's "Secure browsing" setting.

OpenID. The participant was next given the list of OpenID tasks as in the appendix. In contrast with the Facebook tasks, participants were not asked to use their own credentials. Instead, they were given credentials (an identity URL and password) for the OpenID provider we set up for this study.[2] In task O1, the participant was asked to visit a blog on LiveJournal and post a comment on a story using the provided OpenID account; in task O2 they were asked to visit

---

[2] http://barnraiser.org/prairie

Figure 2: Login screen for Facebook single sign-on from Rotten Tomatoes in task F1 in Microsoft Internet Explorer 9.0.5.

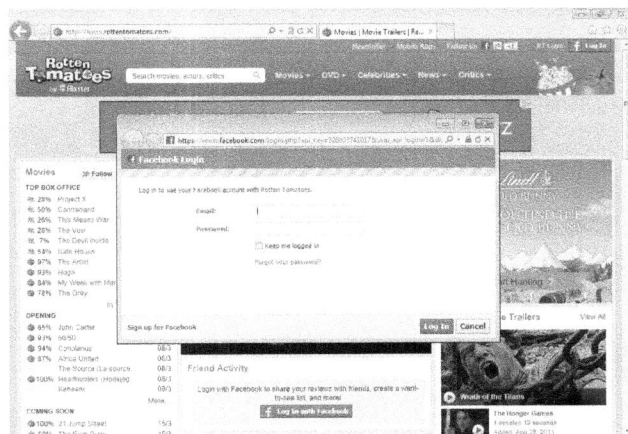

a blog on BlogSpot and post a comment on a story, again using the provided OpenID account. Our OpenID provider operated entirely over HTTP, so no security indicators were ever present during interaction with our provider.

3.3 Survey

After completing the above online tasks, participants were given a 39-question survey to complete online. There were three components to the survey: (1) participant general demographic information, (2) information to assess the participant's computer and security expertise, and (3) information pertaining to their understanding of single sign-on and their behaviour in the online tasks. Some of our questions were based on questions in existing survey instruments: section 2 included questions on technology expertise from Egelman [4] and Sotirakopoulos [16]; section 3 included questions on single sign-on comprehension from Sun et al. [18].

Some of the questions in our survey tried to identify which security indicators users use when signing in to websites. Where possible, we designed the sequence of questions in our survey to avoid priming participant responses: for example, in question 32 we asked the free-form question "How do you decide if it is safe to enter your username and password on a particular website?", but not until question 38, several screens later, did we explicitly list various security indicators and ask users to indicate which ones they used.

Upon completion of the online tasks and survey, participants were given a debriefing sheet with tips on using social networking sites, specifically Facebook, more securely. For participants that used their own Facebook account during the study, we offered to help them remove artifacts of the study from their account, including posts added to their wall/timeline and apps/websites linked to their account.

3.4 Classifying expertise

We used survey answers to classify participants on two dimensions: computer expertise and security expertise.

Computer expertise.
In the city and country in which we conducted our study,

most people are indeed highly proficient at using computers. For example, no participants in our study answered below 3 on our 5-point Likert scale question (#9) where 1 was "I often ask others for help with the computer" and 5 was "Others often ask my for help with the computer". Thus, our rating of computer expertise was relative within this context. In particular, participants were assigned points for computer expertise as follows:

- 0.5: "Yes" to #8 "Do you use a computer daily for work?"
- 0.2–1.0: Answer to #9 "Rate yourself on this scale: 1— I often ask others for help with the computer ...5— Others often ask me for help with the computer"
- 1.0: "Yes" to #12 "Do you have a degree in an IT-related field?"
- 0.5 each: "Yes" to #13 "Have you ever... designed a website ... created a database ... written a computer program?"

The maximum possible score was 4.0. Participants with scores $\geq$ 2.5 were classified as computer experts.

Security expertise.
We used answers from the following questions to assign points for security expertise as follows:

- 0.5 each: "Yes" to #13 "Have you ever... used SSH ... configured a firewall?"
- 1.0: "Yes" to #20 "Have you ever taken or taught a course on computer security?"
- 1.0: "Yes" to #21 "Have you attended a computer security conference in the past year?"
- 1.0: "Yes" to #22 "Is computer security one of your primary job responsibilities?"
- 0.5: "Yes" to #24 "Do you have an up-to-date virus scanner on your computer?"

The maximum possible score was 4.5. Participants with scores $\geq$ 2.5 were classified as security experts.

While the survey included several security-related free-form questions (#18 "If you know, please describe what a 'security certificate' is in the context of the Internet.", #19 "If you know, please describe what is meant by 'phishing'."), we explicitly did not use answers to these free-form questions in deciding security expertise. Instead, we used answers to the free-form questions to cross-check validity of the security expertise score above. Points for the free-form answers were as follows, up to 1 point for each question:

- #18 "If you know, please describe what a 'security certificate' is in the context of the Internet."
  - 0.5: Mentioned SSL or HTTPS.
  - 0.5: Mentioned use to secure communication or demonstrate trust of a website.
  - 0.5: Mentioned ownership of a public key.
- #19 "If you know, please describe what is meant by 'phishing'."
  - 0.5: Mentioned stealing user information.
  - 0.5: Mentioned fake email or fake website.

3.5 Eye-tracking data

During our analysis, we found that using eye-tracking data to answer the question "did the user look at this point?" is somewhat difficult. Users have a lot of eye movement during web browsing tasks, and may fixate near a point for just a fraction of a second; how long does the gaze need to be in order to "count" as having looked at that point? We will consider both the number of fixations over a security indicator and the duration of gazes at security indicators.

3.6 Statistical analysis

We analyzed the eye-tracking data using Bayesian two-way analysis of variance and cross-validated our results using standard null-hypothesis testing. We examined mean gaze duration per fixation, mean number of fixations, and mean total gaze duration per task. The full methodology is in Appendix B; our source code is available online.[3]

4. RESULTS AND DISCUSSION

Our study had 19 participants overall but our eye-tracking equipment failed to record data for 1 of them.

During the online tasks, two participants requested to use alternative Facebook credentials rather than their own.

Note that based on survey question #33, few participants found the online tasks difficult, with no more than 3–4 participants (out of 19) rating any task "hard" or "very hard".

4.1 Participant demographics

Our participant pool consisted of 3 females and 16 males, with an average age of 26 and an age range of 18–39. Although our participants' gender and age distributions do not match that of the general population, several previous studies on Internet security suggest that gender and age do not affect participant security behaviour [3][16, §4.3, §5.2].

In terms of education, 1 participant had completed at most high school, 8 had studied some of or completed an undergraduate degree, and 10 had some postgraduate education. For those with some university education, 9 responded that they studied in a subject area related to information technology, 4 were in a subject area not related to IT, and 5 gave no answer. Only 5 of our 19 participants had English as a first language, but no participant appeared to have any trouble understanding instructions during the experiment.

All participants indicated that they had a Facebook account, and 17 had used their Facebook account at least once in the past month. Four participants with Facebook accounts reported having previously used their Facebook account to sign in to another website. No participant indicated that they had an OpenID account. However, given that many major webmail services are also OpenID providers, it is likely that many of the participants did indeed have an OpenID account but did not realize it.

In terms of web browser usage, during the study 9 participants chose to use Google Chrome, 2 chose to use Microsoft Internet Explorer, and 8 chose to use Mozilla Firefox. All but one user reported using one of the available browsers as their primary web browser.

4.2 Classifying expertise

Based on the methodology of Section 3.4, we classified participants on their expertise.

- *novices*: 9 participants had computer and security expertise scores < 2.5
- *computer experts*: 4 participants had computer expertise scores ≥ 2.5
- *security and computer experts*: 6 participants had computer and security expertise scores ≥ 2.5

---
[3]http://eprints.qut.edu.au/55714

Table 1: Use of security indicators. Average total gaze duration (seconds) and average number of fixations on security indicators by task and classification for login and personal information grant dialog boxes.

Task	Security experts /6		Computer experts /3		Novices /9	
	dur.	# fix.	dur.	# fix.	dur.	# fix.
F1: Rotten Tomatoes / Facebook						
Login	1.788	2.667	0.679	1.000	0.794	1.556
Personal info	0.282	0.500	0.170	0.333	0.064	0.111
F3: LiveJournal / Facebook						
Login	0.110	0.167	0	0	0	0
Personal info	0.058	0.167	0.016	0.333	0	0
F4: Amazon / Facebook						
Login	0.036	0.167	0.186	0.333	0.274	0.556
Personal info	1.188	2.167	0.701	1.667	0.617	1.444
O1: LiveJournal / OpenID						
Login	0	0	0.455	1.000	0.142	0.444
Personal info	0.225	0.333	0.099	0.333	0.194	0.444
O2: BlogSpot / OpenID						
Login	0.126	0.333	0	0	0.049	0.111
Personal info	0.479	0.833	0	0	0.029	0.111

No participants had high security expertise but low computer expertise. As a result, from here on we use "*security expert*" to mean "security and computer expert"; "*non-security experts*" includes both novices and computer experts who were not security experts.

To assess the validity of our security expertise questions, we included some free-form questions (#18, #19) in our survey, and scored participants on their answers to those questions as described in Section 3.4. We then compared the score on free-form answers to the classification based on the non-free-form answers. The mean score on free-form answers by the 6 security experts was 1.0, while the mean score by the 13 security non-experts was 0.423. The difference in means was statistically significant (Mann-Whitney $U = 62, n_1 = 6, n_2 = 13, p = 0.0398$). We argue this provides evidence for the validity of our security expertise classification.

4.3 Use of security indicators

4.3.1 Eye-tracking evidence

As reported in Table 1, the majority of users in all expertise classifications did have a gaze point near the https or domain name security indicators. We now explore in detail the extent to which task and expertise affected number and duration of gazes.

Number of fixations.

Expertise effects. When we examine the overall mean number of fixations between different expertise groups, we find that, while there appear to be differences between the groups in terms of number of fixations—with security experts having a higher mean number of fixations—those differences fall within our uncertainty measures and cannot be considered credibly different (Figure 3).

Task effects. However, when we examine the data by task, a different story emerges. When we consider all of the Facebook tasks and compare them with the OpenID tasks we observe that while a mean difference of 0.0 is to the left of the distribution, it is fully within our 95% highest density interval, meaning that we cannot credibly conclude that the

Figure 3: Differences in mean number of fixations based on expertise.

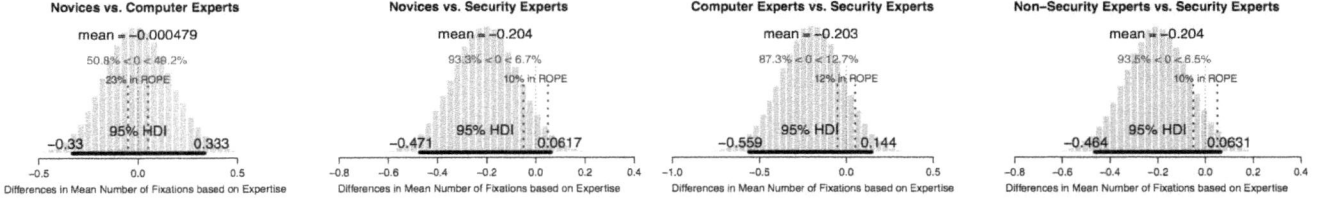

mean number of fixations differs in terms of task groups (Figure 4).

However, we note that Task F1 login and Task F4 personal information grant have noticeable and credible differences in terms of the mean number of fixations they receive. Furthermore, when we remove those tasks from consideration, any differences between Facebook tasks and OpenID tasks disappear (Figure 4).

Cross validation. These results correspond to our standard two factor ANOVA analysis looking at expertise (factor A) and task (factor B). Only factor B was found to be statistically significant ($p = 5.85e\text{-}06$). Neither factor A nor the interaction were found to be statistically significant. When we use Tukey's Honestly Significant Difference (Tukey HSD) to investigate the results, we find that only tasks F1 and F4 have any significant differences compared to the other tasks, supporting our initial Bayesian analysis.

These results demonstrate that users checked security indicators more during their initial login to Facebook, as well as when being asked to confirm sharing personal data on Amazon, but that overall number of gazes did not change for the OpenID login tasks[4].

Gaze duration.

The number of fixations gives us a picture of what tasks subjects consider important, but it does not give us the full picture. We also want to know the length of consideration each subject gives to each fixation and the total time they spend gazing at security indicators. We analyzed mean gaze duration per fixation in two ways: First we look at a more fine grained model of expertise while only considering if the task is from Facebook or OpenID, then we look at a fine grained model of individual tasks, but treat subjects as either having security expertise (security experts) or not (non-security experts).

Expertise effects. Looking at our fine grained model of expertise, we find that security experts, on average, gaze longer than novices[5]. However, our results suggest a bit of uncertainty: the mean difference of 0.0 falls outside our 95% HDI, but the 95% HDI includes part of the ROPE (Figure 5). A similar situation arises when we compare security experts with non-security experts. No mean difference lies outside our 95% HDI, but part of the ROPE is contained within the 95% HDI. We find no credible difference between security experts and computer experts, nor between novices and computer experts.

Cross validation. When we cross-validate we find that

the results of our Bayesian analysis are confirmed using a two factor ANOVA considering expertise (factor A) and task type (factor B). We find that expertise is an important factor. However, when we use Tukey's HSD to examine the paired comparisons, we find that only the difference between security experts and novices is significant ($p = 0.061$), roughly corresponding to our Bayesian results.

When we compare security experts to those without security expertise (non-security experts)[6], the cross validation is stronger than our Bayesian results. The log transformation of the data gives us approximately normal data. This allowed us to use a Welch two sample t-test to compare the results due to differences in group variances. We found that differences between the groups were statistically significant ($\mu = -0.2858$, 95% CI $= -0.50284292, -0.06874345$, $t(99.869) = -2.6124$, $p = 0.01038$), confirming that security experts gaze longer than non-security experts.

Task effects. When we consider gaze durations per fixation based on specific expertise, and analyze the general task type differences we find there is no credible difference between Facebook and OpenID in terms of mean log(duration), meaning that subjects gaze for roughly the same amount of time during Facebook tasks and OpenID tasks.

However, when we consider our fine grained task model to see if any tasks receive more time per fixation based on expertise, we find that participants of all expertise levels gazed somewhat longer at security indicators during the login portion of task F1 and the personal information grant portion of task F4, but the difference in average gaze duration during these tasks compared to other tasks fall within our uncertainty measures and cannot be considered credibly different.

Cross validation. With a two factor ANOVA test, we did find an statistically significant effect for task on mean per fixation duration. However, in the post-hoc analysis, the only truly significant differences were between task F3 and all other tasks. Looking at the data, this is due to an outlier effect, rather than any true artifact. No other tasks had any significant differences in mean per fixation durations.

Total duration. Having both the number of fixations and mean per duration of fixation, we also wanted to examine differences between expertise (factor A) and tasks (factor B) on the total fixation duration per task, rather than per fixation. Due to difficulty of specifying an accurate sampling distribution, we analyzed total duration using standard NHST techniques.

We find that task has a significant effect on total gaze duration, but there is still too much uncertainty about the effect of expertise to make a strong claim that it has an effect Table 2). When we look at post-hoc Tukey HSD analysis we

---

[4]Recall that OpenID login in our study occurred over HTTP, so no SSL security indicators were present. However, we still analyzed whether participants gazed at where those indicators would have been.

[5]Recall that "novices" excludes computer experts.

[6]Recall that "non-security experts" includes both novices and computer experts who are not security experts.

Figure 4: Differences in mean number of fixations based on task. In the charts, Task 1 refers to the login portion of the Facebook F1 task on Rotten Tomatoes, and Task 6 refers to personal information grant portion of the Facebook F4 task on Amazon.

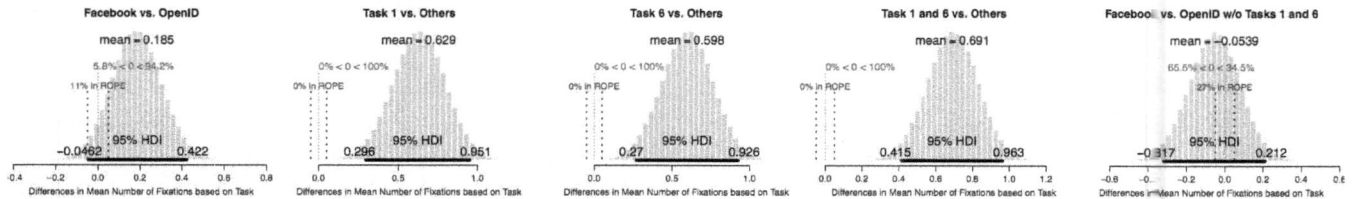

Figure 5: Differences in mean log(duration) based on expertise.

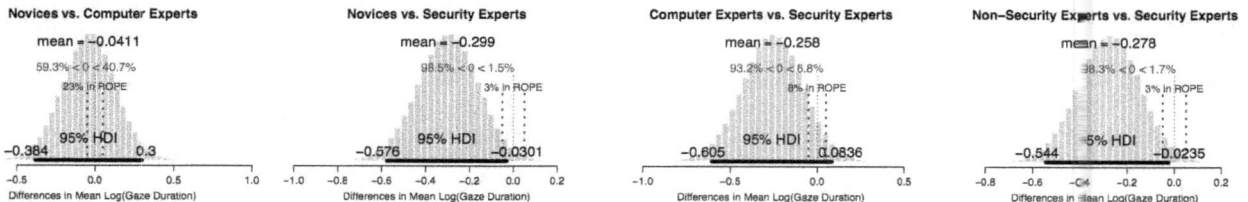

Table 2: Two-way ANOVA analysis of mean total gaze duration per task.

	Df	Sum Sq	Mean Sq	F value	Pr($>$ F)
A (Expertise)	2	2.60	1.3018	2.193	0.116
B (Task)	9	24.49	2.7213	4.584	2.9e-05
A:B	18	7.29	0.4048	0.682	0.824
Residuals	130	77.18	0.5937		

find that the only two tasks that are significantly different from the mean are tasks F1 and F4, which makes sense, given that they receive more fixations total (Figure 4).

Discussion. It is difficult to directly compare our rates of security indicator usage with those of Whalen and Inkpen [20], since they simply reported the number of participants for which they "verified" that the user checked the indicator. In Table 1 we report the proportion of participants that gazed at security indicators, but we see from the average duration of these gazes that the time spent looking at security indicators varies significantly. As a result, we cannot say whether our participants' observed use of security indicators matches or disagrees with that of Whalen and Inkpen. This does highlight the open issue of how to report and compare usage of security indicators from eye-tracking data.

Unlike Whalen and Inkpen, who reported observing no fixations before priming their participants for security, we do observe fixations without any security priming. However, the nature of the fixations focuses primarily on tasks F1 (initial Facebook login) and F4 (share information with Amazon). The first represents the first time a subject logs in, while the second represents interacting with a commercial website. It appears that, aside from these tasks, subjects give only cursory attention to security indicators, supporting Whalen and Inkpen's results that without security priming, subjects will not pay attention to security indicators.

On the other hand, our results seem to suggest that most users, regardless of security experience, are aware of security indicators and consult them in tasks they view as risky. This is an encouraging result, but, our experimental design

does not allow us to determine the effects of the security indicators on decision making.

4.3.2 Self-reported use

Next, we compared self-reported use of indicators versus gaze duration. Recall that survey questions #32 and #38 asked subjects to report which security indicators they used to decide if it is safe to enter their username and password; in question #32, it was a free-form question, whereas in the later question #38 subjects were presented with a list of indicators and asked to check the ones that they looked for.

In the free-form question #32, only 4 subjects' responses mentioned one of the three accepted SSL security indicators (https, lock icon in browser, certificate); all 4 of these subjects were classified as security experts. (We emphasize that the classification in Section 3.4 of subjects as security experts did not depend on question #32 or question #38.)

In contrast, when presented with a list of security indicators in question #38, many more users reported using security indicators (Table 3). When prompted, participants self-report much higher use of security indicators.

To analyze this data, we assigned each user a score between 0 and 3, with one point for each of "https", "lock icon in the browser", and "certificate", which are the only security indicators presented in the browser chrome. In particular, we omitted "lock icon in the page": as an element of the web page content, a lock icon on the page is not a trusted user interface element [17]. All but 3 participants reported looking for at least one of these three security indicators. The average score for security experts was 2.5, whereas the average score for security non-experts was approximately half that at 1.38, with the difference in these averages being statistically significant (Mann-Whitney $U = 62, n_1 = 6, n_2 = 13, p = 0.0408$). In contrast, the average score for computer experts was 1.8 compared to 1.67 for computer non-experts; the difference was not statistically significant (Mann-Whitney $U = 50.5, n_1 = 9, n_2 = 10, p = 0.6722$).

We then compared the self-reported use of security indicators with eye-tracking data. Of the 4 users that self-reported use of security indicators in free-form question #32,

Table 3: Self-reported use of security indicators.

Indicator	Security experts /6	Computer experts /4	Novices /9
https	6	1	6
lock icon on the page	2	1	5
certificate	4	1	6
website privacy statements	2	3	4
type of website	6	2	6
professional-looking site	2	1	3
lock icon in browser	5	1	3

Other security indicators reported: "brand", "lack of ads", "firewall", "anti-virus safe browsing feature" ($\times 2$).

2 did gaze for security indicators and 2 did not. To analyze self-reported use of security indicators in prompted question #38, we used the security indicator score computed in the previous paragraph and compared it with security indicator gaze duration during Facebook login in task F1. The correlation was quite low and not statistically significant (Spearman rank correlation coefficient $\rho = 0.188, P = 0.4546$).

4.4 Understanding of single sign-on

To determine participants' understanding of single sign-on, we considered participants' successful completion of logout tasks and their responses to survey questions related to the flow of information in single sign-on.

We asked participants questions about their previous use of single sign-on. Nine of 19 participants had heard of single sign-on, all of whom provided a reasonably correct definition (question #27); 4 were security experts, 2 were computer experts, and 3 were novices. Thirteen of 19 participants reported having "previously experienced using a single username and password to access different systems" (question #28). Of the 7 who responded "No" to that question, we have reason to believe as least 6 of them had in fact used single sign-on systems before, as they were or had been students at a university that the authors know uses single sign-on for a variety of services. This suggests that in today's web-based environment, users and system administrators do not have the same view of what constitutes "different systems".

4.4.1 Logout

We directed the participants to log out several times: during Facebook tasks F2, F3, and F5, the participants were instructed to "Log out of the web browser as if you were walking away from a public computer. (Do not log out of Windows, however.)" Subsequently in task F5, they were asked to "Go back to the Facebook site and log in." and then "Log out of Facebook." All participants completed the last part of task F5—"Log out of Facebook". Participants' behaviour at earlier tasks is more interesting; we focus on the first logout at task F2.

The participant is actually logged in to two websites during task F2: Rotten Tomatoes and Facebook. Rotten Tomatoes appears to make use of Facebook's single sign-on API for logout: users that log out via the link on Rotten Tomatoes are also logged out of Facebook. This is not a required feature of the Facebook single sign-on API, and users do not know a priori if dual logout will occur.

For task F2, we recorded whether users explicitly logged out of Rotten Tomatoes website and whether they explicitly logged of Facebook (Table 4). Overall, 14 of 19 users successfully logged out of either Rotten Tomatoes or Facebook,

Table 4: Participant logout actions on Rotten Tomatoes and Facebook in task F2.

Classification	Logout of			
	RT&FB	RT only	FB only	none
Security experts /6	3	0	1	2
Computer experts /4	3	0	0	1
Novices /9	3	3	1	2

Table 5: Mental models of single sign-on.

Classification	Correct drawing	#34 Does Rotten Tomatoes know your Facebook p.w.?		
		Yes (wrong)	No (correct)	Don't Know
Security experts /6	3	3	3	0
Computer experts /4	0	0	3	1
Novices /9	5	1	4	4

with 11 actually visiting Facebook to logout or check that they were logged out. There was no significant difference between the behaviour of experts and novices.

We did not specify any logout task for OpenID, although our OpenID provider did have a logout function. Curiously, one participant did return—unprompted—to the URL for the OpenID provider to logout after task O2.

Discussion. The participants seemed to demonstrate conservative logout behaviour, in that when using a single sign-on service such as Facebook on a public computer and when directed to logout upon completion of their work, they logged out of both the relying party and the identity provider, and in particular all participants logged out of Facebook at the completion of the study.

4.4.2 Mental model

Several survey questions provide insight into participants' mental models of single sign-on, including the drawing exercise after question #33 and questions about password and profile information.

For the drawing exercise, we used the same methodology as Sun et al. [18] for assessing the correctness of the mental model expressed in the drawing. As reported in Table 5, security experts did not do significantly better than security non-experts at answering this question.

Question #34 tested participants' understanding of the flow of information during single sign-on: it aksed if they believed that the relying parties, such as Rotten Tomatoes, learned their password for the identity provider Facebook. Table 5 reports the results: security experts did not do better than security non-experts, in fact they did worse.

5. ADDITIONAL DISCUSSION

In this section we discuss some additional observations.

5.1 Preference for single sign-on

When asked in question #37 if they would use their Facebook or OpenID account to login to third-party websites in the future, only 11% of participants responded "yes"; 42% chose "depends", and 47% chose "no". Contrast this with the results of Sun et al. [18], where they asked participants whether they would in the future prefer to use single sign-on in the form of OpenID (3%), in the form of Sun et al.'s identity-enhanced browser (9%), it "depends" on the type of site (36%, of which 30% preferred the ID-enhanced browser and 6% preferred OpenID), or not use single sign-on at all (29%). Our participants were substantially less inclined to use single sign-on than Sun et al.'s participants; since our participants only had the option of using traditional single sign-on as opposed to Sun et al.'s ID-enhanced browser, they did demonstrate a slightly more favourable response than Sun et al.'s participants did to OpenID.

5.2 Nature of task and risk

The Facebook and OpenID tasks involved different levels of risk: in the Facebook tasks, most participants used their own accounts despite having the option to use manufactured accounts, whereas in the OpenID tasks all participants were instructed to use manufactured accounts. However we noticed no significant difference in number of fixations or gaze duration between OpenID and Facebook tasks.

However, we did notice a difference between certain Facebook tasks. As noted in Section 4.3.1, participants of all expertise levels paid more attention to security indicators during their initial Facebook login, and when they granted Amazon, the only e-commerce site in our study, personal information. The difference in security behaviour depending on the nature of the site is interesting and we believe merits further study in future work.

5.3 Study limitations and mitigations

It is well known that there are limitations to the ability of laboratory usability studies to reflect real-world environments [11, 15, 16]. We consciously made several study design choices aligned with recommendations previous work to try to reduce the impact of the study environment.

Setting. The setting of a study and the demeanour of the person running the study can have an effect on study participants. Individuals participating in a study—particular a security study—at a university can be of the frame of mind that "this is being run at a university, nothing can go wrong". Our ethics restrictions did not permit us to disassociate the study with the university, but we did take some measures to attempt to mitigate these factors. Our study took place in a university building a few blocks from the main campus, in an office tower in the city's central business district. The person running the study was a Master's student, casually dressed in shorts and a t-shirt.

In terms of the electronic "setting" of the study, we tried to match the participants' natural computing environment to some extent. Participants were given a choice of browser. All had previous experience using Facebook, so that single sign-on mechanism was not entirely foreign. One unavoidable unnatural characteristic was the use of eye-tracking equipment and the required calibration stage, though the device itself is relatively unobtrusive, and requires no further user attention once calibration is complete.

Demand characteristics refer to the "tendency for research subjects to guess the reason for a study, and then to attempt to confirm the experimenter's apparent hypothesis" [11]. All materials that our participants saw before and during the online tasks described the study as being interested in 'participants' use of social networking and social media', with no mention of security or privacy. Mentions of security only began in the survey, after completion of the online tasks.

Task focus is a risk in security usability studies: participants in studies are often highly motivated to complete the given tasks. Some previous studies [12] gave participants tasks to complete and then analyzed whether the participants completed these tasks even when security indicators or site authentication images were removed; participants who so completed the tasks were deemed to have not paid attention to indicators. Patrick [11] criticizes that approach due to task-focused participants being motivated to complete the tasks they have been given. As a result, we did not artificially remove any security indicators during our study, instead relying on eye-tracking data to assess participant attention to security indicators, both on tasks where security indicators were naturally present (single sign-on with Facebook which uses HTTPS), and naturally absent (single sign-on with our OpenID provider which designed to use only HTTP). Moreover, our participants were promised that they would receive the full value of their compensation regardless of whether they completed the tasks or not. Nonetheless, in the informal discussions we had with participants upon completion of the survey, some participants reported task focus affecting their decisions.

Use of credentials. Schechter et al. [12] confirmed that study participants who use their own account credentials, rather than provided credentials, behave more securely. As a result, we asked participants to use their own credentials for Facebook tasks; we provided participants with alternative Facebook credentials if asked, which 2 participants did.

6. CONCLUSIONS

With ever more websites that users need accounts for, and with the growing popularity of social networking, the use of web-based single sign-on systems is likely to increase. With multiple parties involved—the user's browser, the identity provider, and many relying parties—users may have a hard time understanding what happens with their credentials and personal information, and what conditions should be satisfied for them to believe that a connection is secure or that it is safe to enter their username and password.

We examined users' use of security indicators in web-based single sign-on using Facebook and OpenID by employing eye-tracking equipment and surveyed users on their perception of information flow in single sign-on to determine if users with technical experts behave more securely than novices. Our survey tool for classifying users as computer or security experts adapts existing tools and is cross-validated against other questions in our survey.

We found that users with security expertise did look at web browser security indicators more than those without security expertise; but computer expertise alone was not a predictor. Our participants—security experts and novices alike—in general had very poor understandings of the flow of information and trust in web-based single sign-on.

Future work directly related to the study includes examining the proportion of users that logout without being directed to do so and examining the generalizability of the results to others demographics.

Important future work in this area includes the study of long-term trends. As users continue to use the Internet more and more and as their general computer proficiency advances, do they make better or worse use of security indicators? With the recent popularity of social networking, it seems plausible that web-based single sign-on will become far more prevalent in the coming years, and it will be interesting to see if and how users' understanding of web-based single sign-on improves as frequency of use increases.

7. ACKNOWLEDGEMENTS

This research was performed while M.A. was a student at the Queensland University of Technology. The authors acknowledge helpful discussions with Tom Busey and Sonia Chiasson and programming assistance from Reza Ahli Araghi.

8. REFERENCES

[1] The OAuth 1.0 protocol, April 2010. RFC 5849.

[2] L. F. Cranor, editor. *Proc. 7th Symposium on Usable Privacy and Security (SOUPS) 2011*. ACM, 2011.

[3] R. Dhamija, J. D. Tygar, and M. Hearst. Why phishing works. In *Proc. SIGCHI Conference on Human Factors in Computing Systems (CHI) 2006*, pages 581–590. ACM, 2006.

[4] S. Egelman. *Trust me: Design patterns for constructing trustworthy trust indicators*. PhD thesis, Carnegie Mellon University, April 2009.

[5] Electronic Frontier Foundation. The EFF SSL Observatory, 2010.

[6] B. Friedman, D. Hurley, D. C. Howe, E. W. Felten, and H. Nissenbaum. Users' conceptions of web security: a comparative study. In *Proc. CHI '02 Extended Abstracts on Human Factors in Computing Systems*, pages 746–747. ACM, 2002.

[7] T. N. Jagatic, N. A. Johnson, M. Jakobsson, and F. Menczer. Social phishing. *Communications of the ACM*, 50(10):94–100, October 2007.

[8] J. Kruschke. *Doing Bayesian Data Analysis: A Tutorial with R and BUGS*. Academic Press, 1st edition, 2010.

[9] M. Olson. Janrain social login and social sharing trends across the web for Q3 2012, October 2012.

[10] OpenID Foundation. Specifications, 2010.

[11] A. Patrick. Commentary on research on new security indicators, March 2007.

[12] S. E. Schechter, R. Dhamija, A. Ozment, and I. Fischer. The emperor's new security indicators: An evaluation of website authentication and the effect of role playing on usability studies. In *Proc. IEEE Symposium on Security and Privacy (S&P) 2007*, pages 51–65. IEEE Press, 2007.

[13] A. Smith and G. Roberts. Bayesian computation via the Gibbs sampler and related Markov Chain Monte Carlo methods. *J. Royal Statistical Society. Series B (Methodological)*, 55(1):3–23, 1993.

[14] J. Sobey, R. Biddle, P. van Oorschot, and A. S. Patrick. Exploring user reactions to new browser cues for extended validation certificates. In S. Jajodia and J. Lopez, editors, *Proc. 13th European Symposium on Research in Computer Security (ESORICS) 2008*, volume 5283 of *LNCS*, pages 411–427. Springer, 2008.

[15] A. Sotirakopoulos, K. Hawkey, and K. Beznosov. "I did it because I trusted you": Challenges with the study environment biasing participant behaviours. In *SOUPS Usable Security Experiment Reports (USER) Workshop*, 2010.

[16] A. Sotirakopoulos, K. Hawkey, and K. Beznosov. On the challenges in usable security lab studies: Lessons learned from replicating a study on SSL warnings. In Cranor [2].

[17] D. Stebila. Reinforcing bad behaviour: the misuse of security indicators on popular websites. In *Proc. 22nd Australasian Conf. on Computer-Human Interaction (OzCHI) 2010*, pages 248–251. ACM, 2010.

[18] S.-T. Sun, E. Pospisil, I. Muslukhov, N. Dindar, K. Hawkey, and K. Beznosov. What makes users refuse web single sign-on?: an empirical investigation of OpenID. In Cranor [2], pages 4:1–4:20.

[19] J. Sunshine, S. Egelman, H. Almuhimedi, N. Atri, and L. F. Cranor. Crying wolf: An empirical study of SSL warning effectiveness. In *Proc. 18th USENIX Security Symposium*, 2009.

[20] T. Whalen and K. M. Inkpen. Gathering evidence: use of visual security cues in web browsers. In K. M. Inkpen and M. van de Panne, editors, *Proc. Graphics Interface 2005*, volume 112 of *Graphics Interface*, pages 137–144. Canadian Human-Computer Communications Society, 2005.

[21] R. T. Wright and K. Marett. The influence of experiential and dispositional factors in phishing: An empirical investigation of the deceived. *J. Management Info. Sys.*, 27(1):273–303, July 2010.

APPENDIX

A. ONLINE TASKS INSTRUCTIONS

[As noted in Section 3.2, participants were randomly given either the Facebook tasks first or the OpenID tasks first.]

A.1 Study Tasks—Facebook

Task F1—Rotten Tomatoes
1. RottenTomatoes.com is a movie information and review website. It allows users to login using their Facebook account. Please use your Facebook account to sign in to the Rotten Tomatoes website.
2. Please pick a movie on Rotten Tomatoes, rate it.

Task F2—Rotten Tomatoes
1. Please post a story about a movie from Rotten Tomatoes on your Facebook profile.
2. Log out of the web browser as if you were walking away from a public computer. (Do not log out of Windows, however.)

Task F3—LiveJournal
1. LiveJournal is a blogging and community site. It allows users to post comments using their Facebook account. Please visit the blog at the address "[omitted from paper]" and post a comment on a story using your Facebook account.
2. Log out of the web browser as if you were walking away from a public computer. (Do not log out of Windows, however.)

Task F4—Amazon
1. Amazon.com is an online shopping website. It allows users to post items from Amazon onto their Facebook profile. Please visit Amazon, find an item, and share it to your Facebook profile.

Task F5—Facebook
1. Log out of the web browser as if you were walking away from a public computer. (Do not log out of Windows, however.)
2. Go back to the Facebook site and log in.
3. Log out of Facebook.

A.2 Study Tasks—OpenID

For these tasks, you will be using a different account to login to websites. Here are the credentials you should use:
- Identity URL: [omitted]
- Password: [omitted]

Task O1—LiveJournal
- LiveJournal is a blogging and community site. It allows users to post comments using their OpenID account. Please visit the blog at the address "[omitted]" and post a comment on a story using your OpenID account.

Task O2—BlogSpot
- BlogSpot is another blogging and community site. It allows users to post comments using their OpenID account. Please visit the blog at the address "[omitted]" and post a comment on a story using your OpenID account.

B. BAYESIAN MODELS

We analyzed the recorded eye-tracking data using Bayesian two-way analysis of variance and standard null-hypothesis testing. We examined mean gaze duration per fixation, mean number of fixations, and mean total gaze duration per task. After examining the initial data, we found that a log transform of the mean gaze duration per fixation would transform the data into a normal distribution, rendering it more amenable to standard null-hypothesis testing.

For all of our analysis we at looked two nominal predictors: *expertise* and *task*. While our experiment design is within-subjects, due to the nature of data collection, there are tasks where subjects may not fixate at all, leading to missing data points for groups of subjects. This is fine for number of fixations and total fixation duration per task, where we can record a 0 for number of fixations, or total fixation duration, respectively. However, for mean gaze duration per fixation, it makes analyzing the task factor difficult, as a task with no fixations has an undefinded mean fixation duration. To address this issue, we looked at two situations:

1. 3 levels of expertise: novice, computer expert, and security expert; but 2 levels of task: Facebook or OpenID.
2. 2 levels of expertise: security non-expert, and security expert; but 7 levels of task.

The analysis in condition 1 demonstrated no credible difference between novices and computer experts in terms of mean gaze duration, providing support for the validity of the analysis in condition 2.

For our statistical analysis we used R with JAGS, through the library rjags. We also used the library coin to faciliate the use of the Mann-Whitney Rank Sum Test during our cross-validation.

B.1 Bayesian model definitions

We used two different Bayesian ANOVA models using two nominal predictors of mean log-fixation duration and mean number of fixations. We evaluated the Bayesian model for the conditions in Section B and each of the duration models had the same parameters, but evaluated under different factor conditions. We looked at individual factors as well as interactions between factors [8]: $y = \beta_0 + \vec{\beta_1}\vec{x_1} + \vec{\beta_2}\vec{x_2} + \vec{\beta}_{1\times2}\vec{x}_{1\times2}$ where the each dot product of the vectors β_i and x_j sums to 0. This allows us to understand how each factor relates to the baseline β_0.

The hierarchical model used for the mean log duration analysis (Figure 6) has the same structure between conditions 1 and 2, but has different levels j and k, depending on the condition. The model for mean number of fixations has the same overall structure, but takes its sample values from a Poisson distribution.

We use skeptical priors, informed by the data to reduce the need for long burn-in times. Our priors are based on the means of the data, but use larger standard deviations than what are observed. For example, we calculate the shape and rate parameters by using the observed standard deviation of the entire dataset as the mode and standard deviation of the gamma distribution. This gives a prior distribution that is based on the data, but is broad enough to avoid an overly biased assumption.

We assume all of the data comes from the same overarching distribution, but, as the data is integrated, the posterior will reveal any differences based on the factors being investigated. This is akin to standard NHST in that we can evaluate the differences between the distributions, and if those differences are credibly different than 0.0, we can conclude that, given the data, we can be reasonably certain that the groups differ. In order to get a good estimation of the desired distribution, we sample the model through a Markov Chain Monte Carlo (MCMC) process.

B.2 MCMC features

The goal of the hierarchical model is to describe a Markov Chain Monte Carlo process to recover the correct distributions of the factors under consideration by sampling from the given state space. When a long enough chain of samples is considered, it can recover the features of a given equilibrium distribution [13]. However, given the nature of the sampling, there can be correlations between samples at time t and $t-1$. We also need to be certain that the MCMC process is sampling from the correct distribution.

In order to address these issues we use multiple sample chains, each with a period of time to adapt and burn-in the MCMC sample. Because our prior assumptions are initialized in an informed way, our burn-in and adaption phases need not be too long, but we use 12000 steps to adapt each MCMC sample chain, and 15000 steps to burn the chain in to the correct distribution [13].

Once the MCMC is in place to sample the distribution, we save a total of 250000 samples. However, we only take 1 out

Figure 6: Hierarchical Bayesian Model for mean log(duration) of fixations. μ_0 and τ_0 represent the baseline mean and precision of the normal distribution representing the log transformed duration data as a whole. S_k and R_k are the shape and rate parameters of the gamma distributions of σ_β, which are used to calculate τ_β. τ_β is the precision $(1/\sigma_\beta^2)$ of the normal distributions used to model the deflections β_1 and β_2. β_{1j} represents factor 1 (experience), across levels j. β_{2k} represents factor 2 (task), across levels k. L_{σ_y} and H_{σ_y} represent the low and high values for the uniform distribution describing τ_y. τ_y is the precision of the normal distribution with mean μ_i. This final normal is generated for each data point according to the equation given in the figure. The sample data point y_i is taken from this final distribution. This illustration shows the prior distributions, which are adjusted by the data before the final samples are made.

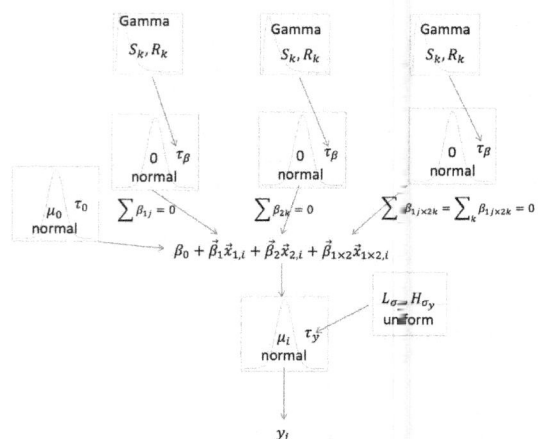

of every 75 samples to reduce autocorrelation. Thus, each one of our 25 chains has a length of 7.5e05. This lets us perform convergence analysis to ensure that the chains in fact, converge to an equilibrium distribution [13]. After these assurances that our Bayesian analysis is robust, we also cross-validated our results with standard null-hypothesis testing.

B.3 Standard null-hypothesis testing

Since Bayesian analysis is not yet standard, we compared the Bayesian results with standard null-hypothesis testing using a two-way analysis of variance with interactions between expertise and task. We corrected for the unbalanced nature of the results using Tukey's Honest Significant Difference. We performed analogous ANOVA comparisons on all of the Bayesian analysis to test agreement.

JStill: Mostly Static Detection of Obfuscated Malicious JavaScript Code

Wei Xu
Department of Computer
Science and Engineering
Pennsylvania State University
University Park, PA
wxx104@cse.psu.edu

Fangfang Zhang
Department of Computer
Science and Engineering
Pennsylvania State University
University Park, PA
fuz104@cse.psu.edu

Sencun Zhu
Department of Computer
Science and Engineering
Pennsylvania State University
University Park, PA
szhu@cse.psu.edu

ABSTRACT

The dynamic features of the JavaScript language not only promote various means for users to interact with websites through Web browsers, but also pose serious security threats to both users and websites. On top of this, obfuscation has become a popular technique among malicious JavaScript code that tries to hide its malicious purpose and to evade the detection of anti-virus software. To defend against obfuscated malicious JavaScript code, in this paper we propose a mostly static approach called *JStill*. JStill captures some essential characteristics of obfuscated malicious code by function invocation based analysis. It also leverages the combination of static analysis and lightweight runtime inspection so that it can not only detect, but also prevent the execution of the obfuscated malicious JavaScript code in browsers. Our evaluation based on real-world malicious JavaScript samples as well as Alexa top 50,000 websites demonstrates high detection accuracy (all in our experiment) and low false positives of JStill. Meanwhile, JStill only incurs negligible performance overhead, making it a practical solution to preventing obfuscated malicious JavaScript code.

Categories and Subject Descriptors

K.6.5 [**Management of Computing and Information Systems**]: Security and Protection

General Terms

Security

Keywords

JavaScript, Obfuscation, Static Detection

1. INTRODUCTION

JavaScript based attacks have been reported as top Internet security threats in recent years [20] [14]. To defend against the malicious JavaScript code behind these attacks,

most of the users rely on the protection provided by anti-virus software. Unfortunately, the effectiveness of static signature based anti-virus software is often thwarted by obfuscation techniques. In fact, malicious JavaScript code has been increasingly applying obfuscation techniques to evade the detection of anti-virus software and to hide its malicious intent. For example, many previously known ActiveX based attacks now adopt obfuscation to hide their exploits [24]. Besides, a similar trend has also been reported in [10, 7].

The popularity of obfuscation among malicious JavaScript code is caused by the following reasons. First, signature-based detection systems, e.g., anti-virus software, can be effectively evaded by obfuscation. For example, by applying encoding-based obfuscation on 100 known malicious samples, we demonstrated that all these obfuscated samples can successfully evade the detection of all popular anti-virus software listed in VirusTotal. Second, the dynamic features of JavaScript language, such as dynamic code generation and run-time evaluation, facilitate the creation of obfuscation routines. For instance, dynamic generation combined with a string manipulation process can easily generate an obfuscation function in JavaScript (e.g., [1]).

Many approaches have been proposed to detect malicious JavaScript code. Some of these approaches [9, 19, 17] focus on detecting obfuscated malicious JavaScript code, whereas the others [10, 23, 22, 12, 7] treat obfuscation as one of the features of malicious JavaScript code. To detect obfuscated malicious JavaScript code, these approaches either adopt machine learning techniques using features extracted from various representation levels (e.g., source code, lexical token, AST), or they perform runtime analysis. Machine learning based approaches can achieve high throughput, and they can also achieve high accuracy with a large set of features. However, they do not capture the essential characteristics of obfuscated malicious JavaScript code, thus easy to be evaded. On the other hand, runtime analysis can expose the deobfuscation behavior, but the performance penalty incurred by runtime analysis prevents it from being used in online or large-scale scenarios.

In this work, we propose JStill, a mostly static obfuscated malicious JavaScript detector. The design of JStill is inspired by the following observation: *obfuscated malicious JavaScript code has to be deobfuscated prior to fulfilling its malicious intent, and in JavaScript, the deobfuscation process has to invoke certain functions.* Based on this observation, JStill analyzes function invocations and identifies the ones that can be potentially involved in obfuscated malicious JavaScript code. Although the analysis is fully static, JStill also leverages certain runtime operations of a browser because static approaches are limited in inspecting JavaScript code. In runtime, JStill intercepts and examines the *suspicious function invocations before they are executed*. Note that JStill does not rely on the dynamic behavior of suspicious JavaScript code. The combination of static analysis and runtime inspection has been proposed in the literatures [21, 12, 23, 6]. In this work, JStill strikes the balance between these two components such that the requirements on both performance and accuracy can be met. Because JStill has a runtime component, it can not only detect obfuscated malicious JavaScript code, but also prevent detected malicious code from being executed in a browser. Moreover, we will show that the integration of JStill in a browser requires very few modifications and causes very small (negligible) performance impact.

In our evaluation of JStill, we use Alexa [5] top 50,000 web sites as the benign sample set (to test false positives), and over 30,000 obfuscated malicious JavaScript samples as malicious sample set (to test false negatives) . The evaluation results show that JStill has a small number of false positives and negligible false negatives. The performance overhead incurred by a prototype implementation of JStill only increases the average Web page loading time by 4.9%, which makes it an efficient scheme for detecting obfuscated malicious code.

1.1 Contributions

Our paper makes the following contributions:

- **Mostly static detection of obfuscated malicious code** We propose JStill, a lightweight, mostly static approach to detect obfuscated malicious JavaScript code, most of which can evade the detection of state-of-art anti-virus software. *JStill can not only detect, but also prevent the execution of obfuscated malicious JavaScript code on a user's Web browser.*

- **Function invocation based analysis** We present a function invocation based analysis technique that leverages the combination of static analysis and runtime inspection. Our analysis is based on three different aspects of function invocations so that it can effectively distinguish malicious obfuscated JavaScript code from benign code.

- **Evaluation** We implement a prototype of JStill in a commodity browser and evaluate its detection effectiveness. Our evaluation uses a large number of real-world samples, and its results demonstrate that JStill has a very low false positive rate and negligible false negative rate.

- **Realtime protection system** We also measure the performance overhead of JStill in terms of averaged increased webpage loading time. The results indicate the performance overhead incurred by JStill is very small, making it a practical intrusion prevention system (IPS).

1.2 Paper Organization

The rest of the paper is organized as follows. Section 2 introduces the background of JavaScript obfuscation. Section 3 provides an overview of JStill. Section 4 elaborates the design. Section 5 presents the evaluation results, followed by discussion in Section 6. Section 7 reviews the related work and Section 8 concludes the paper.

2. BACKGROUND ON JAVASCRIPT OBFUSCATION

2.1 JavaScript Obfuscation

JavaScript obfuscation is to "make modifications to the program, changing the names of variables, functions, and members, making the program much harder to understand ... " [11]. Note that obfuscation is different from minification, which "removes the comments and unnecessary whitespace from a program" [11] to reduce the code size.

Both benign and malicious JavaScript code have been observed adopting obfuscation techniques; hence, obfuscation does not imply maliciousness. However, their purposes of obfuscation are different. Benign JavaScript code mainly leverages obfuscation to protect code privacy or intellectual property. This purpose requires obfuscated code to be human unreadable and without downgrading the execution performance. Malicious JavaScript code exploits obfuscation to hide its malicious intent; therefore, the obfuscated code aims to evade static inspection. Normally, execution performance is not a concern for attackers. In fact, attackers often apply multiple obfuscation to better hide their malicious intent. For example, a drive-by download attack in Figure 1 is concealed by two levels of obfuscation.

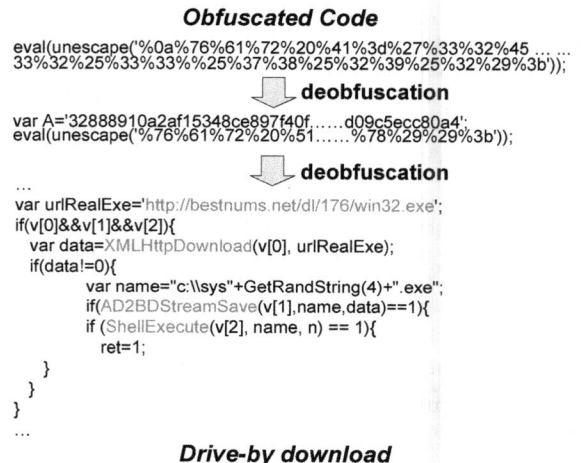

Figure 1: A real-world obfuscated drive-by download example

2.2 Obfuscation Techniques and Tools

The goal of this work is to detect obfuscated malicious JavaScript code. It is important to understand the obfuscation techniques adopted by malicious JavaScript code. To this end, we conducted a survey study. We randomly selected 100 (out of 510) known malicious JavaScript samples and manually examined the obfuscation techniques adopted by these samples. We summarized the techniques into the following five categories. Note that this categorization is by no means an exhaustive list, but it includes most of the basic building blocks that can be combined to generate more complicated obfuscation techniques as shown in [16].

Data Obfuscation, in which a variable or a constant is converted into the computational results of one or several variables or constants, e.g., string splitting and JavaScript keyword substitution. 47% of samples adopt this technique.
ASCII/Unicode/Hexadecimal Encoding, in which malicious JavaScript code is encoded into escaped ASCII char-

acters/unicode/hexadecimal representations. 32% of samples adopt this technique.

Customized Encoding Functions, in which malicious JavaScript code is obfuscated by a customized encoding function. Meanwhile, a corresponding customized decoding function is also attached to decode the obfuscated code at runtime. 23% of samples adopt this technique.

Standard Encryption and Decryption, in which the malicious JavaScript code is encrypted and decrypted for execution using standard cryptographic functions. 3% of samples adopt this technique.

Logical Structure Obfuscation, in which the execution paths of malicious JavaScript code is changed without affecting the original semantics, e.g., inserting some instructions that are independent of the functionality of the malicious code, adding/changing conditional branches, etc. 11% of samples adopt this technique.

Our results show that 71% of examined malicious samples employ obfuscation techniques (counting multiple obfuscation as one). Data Obfuscation appears to be the most popular technique. However, an in-depth analysis shows that most of the samples that adopt data obfuscation also adopt other obfuscation techniques such as encoding or encryption based obfuscation. In fact, 40% of the obfuscated malicious samples apply multiple obfuscation to further hide their malicious purposes. Figure 1 shows an example of multiple obfuscation. The first level is ASCII encoding obfuscation, and the second level is customized encoding function obfuscation.

More importantly, we notice two common operations among these obfuscation techniques. The first one is the recovery of the clear-text version of malicious code from an encoded string or other objects on the Web page. A similar observation has also been reported in [10]. Since JavaScript code is delivered as text, the code can be manipulated as text; meanwhile, any text can also be potentially executed as JavaScript code. This flexibility is leveraged extensively in obfuscated malicious JavaScript code because: 1) it is easier to manipulate or obfuscate text than code; 2) attackers can potentially hide code anywhere in a Web page as text. The second common operation is the execution of the recovered malicious code has to involve dynamic generation and runtime evaluation functions. However, the existence of these common operations does not always mean attacks because they are also heavily used in benign JavaScript code [25].

As part of the survey, we also investigated the obfuscation techniques adopted by the top 10 most popular JavaScript obfuscation tools[2](Appendix B). We notice that 7 out of 10 tools use both encoding/encryption based obfuscation and data obfuscation. The other 3 tools use only data obfuscation. To study the effectiveness of evading anti-virus software by data obfuscation and by encoding/encryption based obfuscation, we applied both types of obfuscation techniques on the 100 known malicious samples, respectively. We submitted the obfuscated samples to the 20 highest ranked anti-virus software [5]. The average detection rate on obfuscated samples using data obfuscation is 45.7% (Appendix D), whereas the detection rate on samples using encoding/encryption obfuscation is 0. Apparently, data obfuscation can not evade the detection of anti-virus software as effectively as encoding/encryption obfuscation. Therefore, our approach focuses on the detection of encoding/encryption based obfuscated malicious code.

2.3 Dynamic Generation and Runtime Evaluation

Dynamic generation (D-Gen) and runtime evaluation (R-Eval) functions play an important role in obfuscated malicious JavaScript code. D-Gen functions can generate JavaScript code from text in runtime, and R-Eval functions can evaluate a text string as code. These two features provide a means of transforming text to code in JavaScript, and this transformation is a typical operation in the deobfuscation of obfuscated malicious JavaScript code as we discussed above. Therefore, these two features are widely exploited in malicious JavaScript obfuscation. In the example of Figure 1, the obfuscation leverages the "`eval`" function to dynamically generate the deobfuscated code.

On the other hand, D-Gen and R-Eval functions are also commonly used features in benign JavaScript code [25]. In the case of conditional loading, an external JavaScript code is loaded using dynamic generation only when certain condition is met. This can avoid unnecessary bandwidth consumption. Another example is including runtime generated information in JavaScript code to increase the flexibility in programming. When JavaScript code contains information that can only be obtained during runtime from either user input or client-server interaction, it will leverage runtime evaluation. Therefore, the adoption of D-Gen and R-Eval functions does not always imply the existence of obfuscated malicious code.

3. OVERVIEW

This section gives an overview on the design of JStill.

3.1 Function Invocation Based Analysis

As we mentioned before, the basic observation in the design of JStill is that either the deobfuscation or the execution of obfuscated malicious JavaScript code has to involve function invocations. To leverage this observation, we first categorize functions in JavaScript into the following types: [1] 1) JavaScript native functions (e.g., `eval`), 2) JavaScript built-in functions (e.g., `unescape`, `string.fromCharCode`), 3) DOM methods (e.g., `document.write`, `window.setTimeout`) and 4) user-defined functions. Since both obfuscated malicious JavaScript code and benign JavaScript code invoke these four types of functions, the challenge here is how to distinguish function invocations in obfuscated malicious code from that in benign code.

To this end, JStill captures the essential difference between obfuscated malicious invocations and benign invocations from the following three aspects.

Function arguments. We notice that for some language-defined functions that are often used in deobfuscation, e.g., the D-Gen and R-Eval functions, malicious invocations of these functions often hide their arguments from the static perspective, e.g., using the output of another function as arguments. This is necessary for obfuscated malicious code because the arguments of these function invocations often contain part or all of the malicious code. Exposing these arguments will increase the chance of being detected by static inspections. For other language-defined functions used in deobfuscation, e.g., `unescape`, we noticed that the outputs of these functions are often used as or in the arguments of D-Gen and R-Eval functions. This is because in obfuscated

---

[1]the first three types of functions, which can also be collectively called language-defined functions.

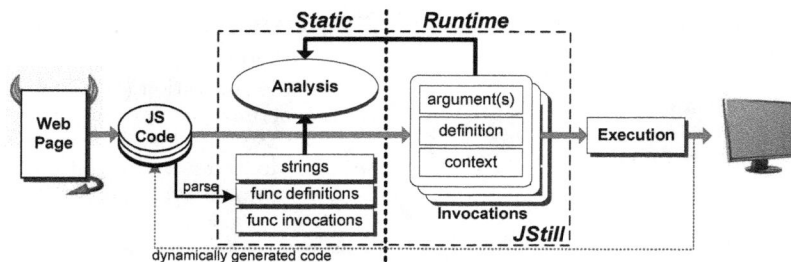

Figure 2: Overview of JStill

malicious JavaScript code, functions like `unescape` can decode the obfuscated string, which will later be generated or evaluated as code.

Function definition. In benign code, a user-defined function is normally first defined before it is invoked. However, in many cases of obfuscated malicious code, a malicious function's definition is either entirely or partially obfuscated in order to hide the semantics of the malicious code. Therefore, when the malicious function is invoked later, it would appear undefined from the static point of view, even though its definition has already been evaluated by a JavaScript engine. In addition to obfuscated malicious code, a coding bug can also cause invocations of undefined functions. The only difference here is that in a coding bug, the function is indeed undefined before its invocation.

Note that hiding definitions of user-defined functions is very rare in benign JavaScript code. As we mentioned before, the purpose of obfuscation for benign JavaScript code is mainly for intellectual property protection. Since JavaScript is delivered in source form, not as compiled machine code, its source code cannot be protected as much as in other languages. An instrumented browser can reveal the source JavaScript code to people who are interested, no matter what obfuscation is applied on that code. Therefore, rather than hiding the source code, most benign obfuscation focuses on reducing the interpretability of the source code to make it hard for human to understand the logic of the code. To this end, benign code favors randomization and substitution based obfuscation techniques. Another reason that benign code normally does not adopt dynamic generation based obfuscation is the concern with extra performance overhead, which is an important factor to evaluate the coding quality of a website.

The context of a function invocation. A context means what function is actually invoked. Based on our analysis of obfuscated malicious JavaScript code, we observed the disguise in invoking language-defined functions, in order to evade detection that leverages invocation patterns of language-defined functions.

Figure 3 lists two common disguise techniques. In part (a) of Figure 3, `eval()` function is assigned to an object a, which is later invoked as `eval()`. In part (b), the properties of a window object are traversed to look for the "document" keyword, which is assigned to object b, whereas object c actually contains the string "write" after the execution of "`unescape()`", so together the last statement actually invokes "`document.write()`". In these examples, static analysis may be able to trace back to the language-defined functions that are actually invoked, but it is neither reliable nor efficient. If the statement "`a = eval;`" in part

```
a = eval;
a('alert("test")');
```

```
for(b in window){
    if(b.length == 8){
        if(b[0] == 'd'){
            break;
        }
    }
}
c = unescape("%77%72%69%74%65");
this[b][c]('test'+'</I>');
```

(a)   (b)

Figure 3: Examples of disguised invocations of language-defined functions

(a) is escaped and evaluated in runtime using "`eval (unescape("%61%3D%65%76%61%6C")`)", static analysis will not detect that "`eval`" has been assigned to "a" unless it has access to the runtime generated code.

3.2 System Overview

To detect obfuscated malicious JavaScript code, JStill uses static analysis to examine function invocations from the above three aspects: *function definition, content of arguments* and *context of invocation*. As illustrated in Figure 2, the static analysis first parses JavaScript code and logs information such as strings, function definitions and function invocations based on the parsing results. JStill leverages the static information about function definitions and invocations by comparing it with the runtime information about function definitions and invocations. This comparison can reveal what functions are statically undefined as well as what function definitions are hidden by obfuscation. The information about string is used by JStill in the analysis of hidden arguments, which will be discussed later.

Meanwhile, since static analysis itself is insufficient to discern coding bugs from obfuscated malicious code, or to identify disguised function invocations, JStill also leverages its runtime component to assist static analysis. In runtime, JStill hooks the invocations of selected language-defined functions in a browser. In this way, it can examine the suspicious arguments just before the execution since the arguments are in clear-format at this stage. JStill can also spot disguised invocations of these hooked functions. Because no matter what disguise is applied, the invocation will always be handled by the hooked functions such that JStill has an opportunity to check if the invoked function in the code is actually the hooked function.

Since JStill detects obfuscated malicious JavaScript code from three aspects, it consists of three detection criterions: 1) disguised invocations of language-defined functions, 2) obfuscated function definitions, 3) obfuscated malicious arguments. JStill raises an alarm if at least one criterion is

120

met. Note that the design of JStill does not rely on any unique specification in a browser's implementation. Therefore, JStill can be implemented compatibly in any Web browser.

4. THE DESIGN OF JSTILL

In this section, we explicate the design of JStill, particularly the technical challenges and their solutions in enforcing the three detection criterions.

4.1 Identification of Disguised Function Invocations

To identify a disguised function invocation, two pieces of information are necessary: 1) what function is actually invoked in an invocation; 2) what function appears to be invoked in an invocation.

To gather the information about what function is actually invoked, static approaches, such as tracing back to the actual function being invoked, are either unreliable or infeasible. Therefore, JStill leverages runtime inspection to identify the function that is actually invoked. More specifically, JStill hooks the implementation of language-defined functions that are mostly likely to be disguised in obfuscated malicious JavaScript code. These functions include but not limited to D-Gen and R-Eval functions (e.g., the functions disguised in Figure 3, "eval" and "document.write"), and functions that are commonly used in string manipulations (e.g., "unescape", etc.). These functions are mostly likely to be disguised because their prevalence in obfuscated malicious code makes them (part of) the widely used detection signatures in static inspections. When one of these hooked functions is invoked by a function invocation, JStill can identify the hooked function as the actually invoked function.

However, hooking a function's implementation cannot reveal what function appears to be invoked. Many of these functions (e.g., DOM based functions) are not implemented within the JavaScript engine; the invocations of these function are actually wrapped by a component (e.g., XPConnect in Firefox) that allows JavaScript code to invoke these functions without revealing the function name in the invocation (e.g., "a" in Figure 3(a)).

To address this issue and obtain the information about what function appears to be invoked, JStill marks all the statically identified invocations of a hooked function (not only from source code, but also from dynamically generated code). As a result, when a hooked function is invoked during runtime, JStill can check if this invocation has been marked; any unmarked invocation in this case indicates this invocation is disguised from the static perspective.

The marking scheme must cover all the statically identifiable invocations of hooked functions to eliminate false positive in disguised invocation detection, but identification of function invocations in JavaScript is not a trivial task. Since function in JavaScript is merely a special type of object, it can be assigned as variables, stored as properties in other objects or as elements in arrays. In other words, a function definition can be passed as a value from one object to another object. For example, Figure 4 lists different means by which "function addition()" is passed to various objects (or properties) and gets invoked. In all four cases, the last statement actually invokes "addition(2, 3);". In invocation 1, function "addition" is passed to an array element, e.g., "arr[0]". In invocation 2, it is passed to an object's (including other function object's) property, e.g., "obj.func2".

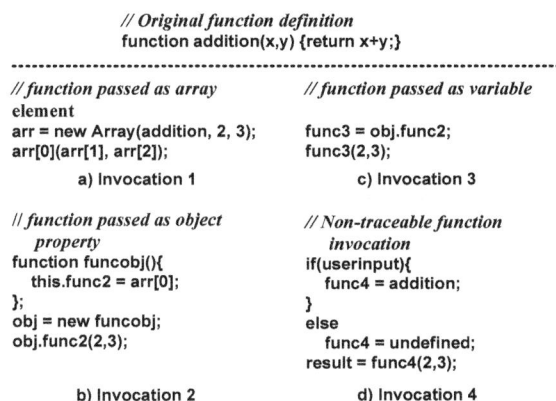

```
// Original function definition
function addition(x,y) {return x+y;}
```

// function passed as array element	// function passed as variable
`arr = new Array(addition, 2, 3);` `arr[0](arr[1], arr[2]);`	`func3 = obj.func2;` `func3(2,3);`
a) Invocation 1	**c) Invocation 3**

// function passed as object property
`function funcobj(){`
`    this.func2 = arr[0];`
`};`
`obj = new funcobj;`
`obj.func2(2,3);`
	// Non-traceable function invocation
	`if(userinput){`
	`    func4 = addition;`
	`}`
	`else`
	`    func4 = undefined;`
	`result = func4(2,3);`

b) Invocation 2	**d) Invocation 4**

Figure 4: Example of legitimate function invocations in JavaScript

After that, it is passed to a variable and gets invoked by a variable's name, e.g., "func3" in both invocation 3 and 4.

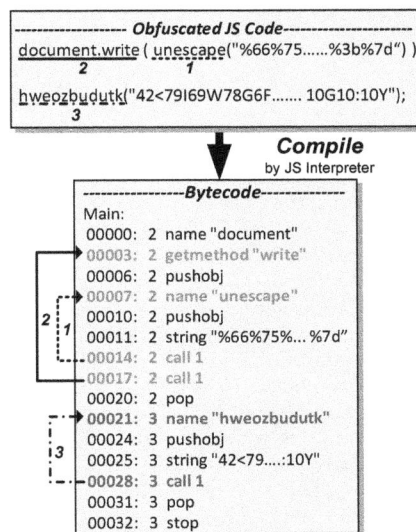

Figure 5: Identify function invocations via bytecode

To identify all the function invocations despite the flexibility in the syntax of JavaScript, necessary syntactic information needs to be parsed from the source code. To this end, JStill leverages the bytecode that is compiled from source code, an example of which is shown in Figure 5. From bytecode in Figure 5, it is clear that there exist three function invocations (the three bytecode "call" marked by different colors). To leverage the bytecode to identify function invocations, JStill needs to understand the structured syntactic information offered by bytecode. The information is organized as a set of 3-tuples. As illustrated in Figure 5, each line of bytecode is a 3-tuple that represents a sequence number, a line number and a bytecode instruction, respectively.

When marking a function invocation for runtime inspection, JStill needs to make sure that the mark cannot be bypassed by malicious code. Meanwhile, it also tries to avoid modification on the source code to prevent unwanted impact on the runtime behavior of the code. As a result, JStill actually marks invocations by logging the locations of these invocation instructions. In this way, when a hooked function is actually invoked, JStill can determine whether the invocation is disguised by checking if the location of instruction for this invocation is marked. An unmarked bytecode will indicate a disguised invocation of a hooked function.

The same approach however cannot be applied on user-defined functions because these functions are not implemented in the browser and hence cannot be hooked. To identify disguised invocations of user-defined functions, JStill leverages the object hierarchy in JavaScript. Every user-defined function is a property of its parent object. When a user-defined function is invoked, JStill can identify what property this invocation actually uses. If the property's name and the caller in the invocation do not match, it means the invocation is disguised.

Note that bytecode, as an intermediate interpretation of JavaScript source code, has different forms in various browsers (e.g., Firefox, Safari and IE). However, it is not indispensable to a browser's implementation (e.g., Chrome's JavaScript engine V8 escapes bytecode) or to JStill. The reason to use bytecode generated by a JavaScript engine rather than parsing the source code by JStill itself is that commodity JavaScript engines such as SpiderMonkey are highly optimized and robust facing malformed JavaScript code.

4.2 Detection of Obfuscated Function Definitions

As we discussed in the overview section, the second aspect in JStill's analysis of invocation is function definition. Since an obfuscated definition of a user-defined function is an indication of obfuscated malicious JavaScript code, we will discuss how to detect obfuscated function definition in this section.

A function definition can be obfuscated by either hiding the entire function definition or a part of the function body. When the entire function definition is hidden, the definition cannot be observed in the process of parsing the source code. Hence, an invocation of this function would appear statically undefined. However, a coding bug may appear the same way. Therefore, to provide a more accurate detection of obfuscated function definition, JStill checks every invocation to see whether the invoked function is actually defined or not. If the actually invoked function is defined only in runtime and the definition is hidden from static perspectives, it is an obfuscated function definition.

To examine whether a function has been defined or not, JStill checks all the function definitions it logs in parsing JavaScript code (both source code and dynamically generated JavaScript code). In this process, JStill uses both function names and the object hierarchy to match a function definition, since function name based definition match can cause inaccuracy due to different JavaScript contexts. For example, functions with the same name can be defined within different objects. Therefore, to accurately match a function definition, information about where the function is defined also needs to be checked. Such information can be obtained by checking the object hierarchy of a function definition. Therefore, object hierarchy is also logged together with function definition during the course of parsing.

To identify obfuscated function definitions, JStill checks every function definition identified in runtime-generated code. If a function definition is generated from obfuscated arguments (the detection of which will be discussed in the next

Section) of D-Gen and R-Eval functions, it is an obfuscated definition.

A function definition can also be partially obfuscated, i.e., only part of the function body is hidden. In this case, the function must contain code that is dynamically generated using obfuscated arguments. Therefore, partially obfuscated function definition can be identified via the detection of obfuscated arguments within a function body. Specifically, JStill marks the invocations of D-Gen and R-Eval functions within a function body in parsing. When the marked invocations are detected as containing obfuscated arguments in JStill, partial obfuscation in the function body can also be detected.

Another practical issue is that there exist cases in which the function definition of an invocation cannot be determined statically. For example, in invocation 4 of Figure 4, the value of the variable "userinput" cannot be determined statically, so the actual definition of "func4" remains unknown from the static viewpoint. To solve this issue, JStill leverages the result from identification of disguised invocations such that it can determine which function definition is actually invoked before checking definition obfuscation.

4.3 Detection of Obfuscated Malicious Arguments in D-Gen and R-Eval Functions

D-Gen and R-Eval functions used in obfuscated malicious code often obfuscate their arguments, as we mentioned in Overview. Since these functions can transform text to JavaScript code, their arguments are hidden in the form of the outputs of string manipulation functions. These functions can be either language-defined or user-defined. In the example of Figure 5, the argument of document.write is the output of unescape. Moreover, the trace from the output of a string manipulation function to the arguments of D-Gen and R-Eval functions can be obfuscated as well. For the code in Figure 5, an attacker can change the first statement to "document.write(s);", where "s" is a string that actually equals to "unescape("%66...%7d")" except this equivalence is disguised by other statements crafted by attackers.

Hooking D-Gen and R-Eval functions provides an opportunity to examine the content of arguments, but the content itself does not shed any light on whether it has been obfuscated. Besides, patterns that show a resemblance to the obfuscated malicious code in Figure 5 have been observed in benign JavaScript code as well , e.g., "document.write('<scr' + 'ipt src="' + urlStart + ".2mdn.net/" + iframeScript-File + '">');". In view of this, detection of obfuscated arguments in D-Gen and R-Eval functions is a challenging problem.

To solve the problem, JStill introduces an obfuscated malicious argument (OMA) metric for all the arguments of dynamic generation and runtime evaluation functions. This metric indicates the possibility that an argument is used in obfuscated malicious code. The main purpose of applying obfuscation on malicious arguments is to hide the content of the malicious arguments; hence, the malicious arguments, or most of the arguments must not be observed from the source code. In benign code, the arguments do not need to be hidden, but often need to be dynamically assembled (or concatenated), since some parts of the benign arguments depend on user input or environment variables. In other words, in benign JavaScript code, most (if not all) of the content of the arguments can be found in the Web page (including URLs). Based on this observation, JStill defines the OMA metric as *the percentage of an argument that can be found in the Web page.* For arguments with a low value on this metric, it is highly likely that they are obfuscated malicious code.

Since only the arguments that generate JavaScript code are potentially involved with obfuscated malicious code, other arguments can be excluded from examination to improve performance. For example, JStill rules out the invocations of D-Gen and R-Eval functions which create new HTML elements that are neither a script tag nor containing any event handler, because these arguments will not introduce new JavaScript code. Besides, arguments that create script tags used for dynamic inclusions (e.g., `<script src="a.js">`) are also excluded from this examination, because the dynamically included code will be analyzed by JStill later.

To calculate the metric of an argument, e.g., a string, JStill logs all the string variables from the parsed source code and the values of some environment variables that are commonly used in benign JavaScript code, such as window.location.href, navigator.userAgent, element IDs, etc. The details on the calculation of the metric will be explained in Section 4.4.

JavaScript provides many functions that can be used for D-Gen and R-Eval. Appendix C lists the functions that JStill hooks in Firefox. We realize that this list is browser specific (e.g., Firefox in this work), but the design of JStill is not exclusive to a certain browser. We will further discuss the discrepancy caused by different browsers in Section 6.

4.4 Obfuscated Malicious Argument Metric

OMA metric measures the possibility of an argument being used in obfuscated malicious JavaScript code. Given a set of strings and the content of an argument, the metric is calculated as the largest percentage of the argument's content that can be found as the combination of the strings or substrings from the set.

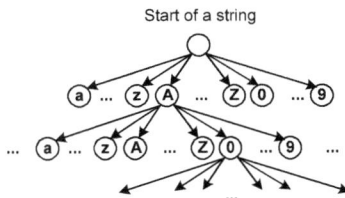

Figure 6: A Search Tree for Basic Strings

In benign JavaScript code, not only the strings, but also their substrings may be used in the composition of benign arguments. Therefore, the logged strings in the set are first divided into basic strings, which are substrings consisting of consecutive letters and numbers with a minimal length of 2 characters. This is because benign code mostly uses substrings that are divided by symbol separators, such as query content divided by questions mark in a URL, or cookie id after an equal sign.

Given a set of basic strings (let the size of the set be p, the average length of the strings in the set be m), the first calculation step is to find which basic strings are substrings of the argument (with size n). A brute-force algorithm has a complexity of $O(pmn)$. This will cause a significant performance penalty when p and n are large numbers. In fact, p is usually large due to the large number of strings defined in JavaScript code.

To avoid the performance penalty, we propose a search tree based algorithm. As illustrated in Figure 6, each inter-

nal node can have at most 62 children, which are mapped to the characters set (a-z,A-Z,0-9). This tree has p leaf nodes and an average depth of m. Based on this tree, JStill can accomplish the first step using the Substring Identification Algorithm (Appendix A.1)

Given the set of matched basic strings, the next step is to find a subset so that the combination of strings in this subset matches the largest percentage of the argument. This problem reduces to the knapsack problem, which is NP-Complete, so we propose an approximate, the Metric Calculation Algorithm (Appendix A.2) that leverages the following greedy heuristic: always using the longest matched and non-overlapping substring. In practice, this algorithm works very well, because the overlapped substrings are not very common.

The time complexity of the Substring Identification Algorithm (Appendix A.1) is $O(mn)$, and the time complexity of the Metric Calculation Algorithm (Appendix A.2) is $O(qn)$, where q is the number of matched substring set output by the Substring Identification Algorithm.

4.5 Whitelisting

As the most popular client-side language in Web development, JavaScript has many libraries and widgets. Most of these libraries are frequently used in many websites and are known to be benign, e.g., JQuery. Therefore, it is only a waste of resource to examine these known benign libraries in JStill.

To save the resource and to improve performance, we propose a whitelist mechanism in JStill. For a known JavaScript library that is often included as an external file, its hash value is computed and stored in JStill. During the examination, the hash value of every fetched external JavaScript file will be compared with the stored hash values. A match in the comparison will exempt the external file from further inspection. The same whitelist scheme can also be applied to web pages when JStill resides in a Web proxy and inspects all the incoming Web contents going through the proxy. When an http request hits the cache in the proxy, the requested Web page must have been examined by JStill; hence, JStill need not inspect the page again.

4.6 Prevention of Malicious Obfuscated JavaScript Code

The runtime inspection component can not only be used in the detection of obfuscated malicious JavaScript code, but also in prevention of the execution of detected malicious code in a browser.

```
<script>
...
flag = mal_ob();/* ob() is malicious obfuscated function */
if (typeof flag == "function") {
    benign();   /* the following is benign code */
    ...
}
...
</script>
```

Figure 7: An example of disrupting benign execution

For obfuscated malicious code that uses invocations of D-Gen and R-Eval functions, since JStill intercepts the arguments of the invocations, it can replace the malicious content with NULL and continue the execution. For obfuscated malicious code that uses user-defined functions, the same approach may disrupt the normal execution of the benign JavaScript code in some cases. Since the basic interpretation unit in most JavaScript engines is a code segment enclosed by "<script>" tags, disabling a detected malicious function will lead to the following benign code in the segment being skipped. For example, as illustrated in Figure 7, if the detected obfuscated function invocation "mal_ob()" is disabled or commented out, the rest of the benign JavaScript code will not be executed because the type of "flag" will be "undefined".

JStill tries to prevent the malicious code from being executed while keeping the execution of benign JavaScript intact. Therefore, JStill substitutes the invocation of a detected malicious user-defined function with an invocation of a NULL function, which does nothing except returning a NULL. In this way, when a user's browser renders the web pages, these NULL function invocations will reduce the possibility of interrupting the execution of benign JavaScript code.

One concern regarding this substitution-based prevention scheme is that the false positives in obfuscation detection may cause loss of functionalities in the Web pages. However, based on our evaluation, which will be described in Section 5, normally this is not a big issue even a false positive occurs.

5. EVALUATION

In this section, based on a prototype implementation, we evaluate JStill in terms of (1) detection effectiveness and (2) performance overhead. The prototype of JStill is implemented in Firefox (version 3.6), which uses a rendering engine Gecko (1.9.2) and a JavaScript engine SpiderMonkey (version 1.8). The implementation adds 1.1 KLOC into the source code of Firefox. We also automate the process of rendering a Web page from the instrumented Firefox using Python scripts such that the browser can check against either a list of URLs or a directory of offline Web pages.

5.1 Evaluation Setting

The prototype of JStill is tested in Ubuntu 8.0, which runs a Pentium 4 3.4 GHz single-core CPU, 1 GB RAM, 160 GB 7200 RPM hard drive and 100 Mbps ethernet interface.

Sample Collection We collect both benign and malicious samples from the real world. The benign sample set consists of Web pages crawled from Alexa [5] top 50,000 websites. The malicious samples are collected from VirusTotal (flagged by $\geq$ 5 AV vendors). There are two sets of malicious samples. The first set contains 2,327 samples, among which 1,499 samples include obfuscated malicious JavaScript code (identified by manual examination). The second set contains 10,501 samples. Since these samples have already been detected by AV vendors, to better evaluate the effectiveness of JStill in detecting obfuscated malicious code, we apply 3 JavaScript obfuscation tools on each sample in the second set. This process generates another 31,505 obfuscated malicious samples.

Table 1: False Positives and False Negatives in Malicious Obfuscation Detection

Obfuscation Metric Threshold	FP	FN
1	2.19%	0%
0.9	1.90%	0%
0.8	1.89%	0.13%
0.7	1.75%	0.53%

5.2 Detection Effectiveness

Table 1 shows the overall detection accuracy of JStill in the evaluation using both benign and malicious sample sets. Each row in Table 1 corresponds to a different obfuscated malicious argument (OMA) metric threshold used in evaluation. Note that OMA metric is the only adjustable detection criterion in JStill, the other two criterions are obfuscated function definitions and disguised invocations of language-defined functions. The purpose of choosing different values is to understand how detection accuracy (i.e., FP and FN)is affected by the threshold of OMA metric.

One insight from the results in Table 1 is that the OMA threshold leads to a trade-off between false positive rate and false negative rate. When the threshold is low (e.g., 0.5), the false positive rate is also low (1.63%). This is because some arguments of benign invocations of D-Gen and R-Eval functions contain strings that cannot be found in Web pages; thus, these arguments have relatively low OMA metric values. However, when JStill adopts a low threshold on obfuscation metric, these arguments may not cause false positives, hence the false positive rate is low.

On the other hand, when the threshold is high (e.g., 1.0), the false negative rate becomes low (0%). A high threshold means that an argument can be considered as benign only when a large portion of the argument can be found in the Web page. Attackers can increase the OMA metric of some malicious arguments (e.g., by only obfuscating part of the malicious content and leaving the rest of the arguments in plaintext) and cause false negatives by surpassing the threshold. However, this becomes very hard when the threshold is set high, because passing a high threshold requires most of the arguments not being obfuscated, in which case the chance of malicious code being detected by signature-based approaches also increases. Note that JStill is not designed to replace the signature-based schemes, but instead they are complementary to each other.

Table 2: Composition of False Positives

Cause of False Positives	%
Obfuscated arguments of D-Gen and R-Eval functions	95.89%
Disguised invocations of language-defined function	0.46%
Obfuscated function definitions	3.65%

False Positives Table 2 lists the false positives incurred on each detection criterion of JStill. Most of the false positives are caused by obfuscated arguments of D-Gen and R-Eval functions. There are two main causes of the non-negligible false positives. The first cause is that information generated at runtime(e.g., random number, user inputs) takes a large portion in the arguments of the R-Eval functions. Given the fact that the arguments of R-Eval functions are JavaScript code and a large portion of the code cannot be observed in any static perspective, this case is very similar to that of obfuscated malicious code.

The second cause is that some benign Web pages actually adopt encoding-based obfuscation on some parts of their JavaScript code. One example is the Web page retrieved by the URL "www.360buy.com". In this Web page, the argument of an invocation to "eval" is encoded using a customized encoding function. Meanwhile, a decoding function is also observed as part of the code. After decoding, the execution of "eval" evaluates a large body of JavaScript code, which is actually a JQuery library. Given the open-source nature of JQuery, the purpose of this obfuscation is not clear. Indeed, when benign code adopts the same obfuscation techniques as malicious code, the problem of differentiating one from the other is probably undecidable. We believe this problem may only be solved by observing the runtime behavior, which, however, is not an efficient approach to be deployed in any large-scale or realtime scenarios, not to mention the challenge in traversing all execution paths.

One concern regarding the false positives is the possibility of interrupting user's browsing experience. However, in reality this normally is not a big concern. This is because: 1) the prevention scheme in JStill does not hinder the execution of the rest of the code; 2) Most of the false positives only affect a single function invocation in a Web page. Considering the popularity of tools such as NoScript, nullifying a single JavaScript function invocation would probably not affect user's browsing experience.

It is also worth noting that we implicitly assumed that none of the 50,000 Web pages as well as their linked .js files is malicious in our evaluation. To verify whether it is the case, we will have to resort to a dynamic analysis approach (e.g., [8]). However, if some of these Websites are indeed malicious, the false positive rate of JStill will only be lower.

False Negative The analysis of JStill's false negative rate is based on the examination of both obfuscated malicious sample sets. The overall false negative rate is listed in the third column in Table 1.

Since false negative rate is related to the threshold of the OMA metric, when the threshold is high (e.g., 1), the overall false negative is 0. That is to say JStill can detect all the malicious obfuscated JavaScript code in our malicious sample set when the threshold is set to 1. When the threshold is low (e.g., 0.7), false negatives start to happen in the first set of malicious samples. These false negatives are incurred on the criterion using the OMA metric. Most of the samples causing false negatives obfuscate only a part of the malicious arguments in D-Gen and R-Eval invocations. As we discussed before, this will also increase the chance of being detected by signature-based approaches. In fact, these samples are detected by multiple AV vendors. There is no false negatives in the second set even when the threshold of OMA metric is low. This means JStill can effectively detect obfuscated malicious code that is generated by JavaScript obfuscation tools.

5.3 Comparison with Other Techniques

Although there are many works on malicious JavaScript code detection, these works either detect general malicious JavaScript (e.g., Prophiler [7],JSAND [10]) or focus on specific malicious JavaScript (e.g., Nozzle [22], Zozzle [12]). Therefore, they are not comparable with JStill. However, several other works also focus on the detection of obfuscated (malicious) JavaScript code, so in Table 3 we compare them with JStill in terms of detection effectiveness. Further discussions on the difference between JStill and these schemes can be found in the related work section.

Table 3: Comparison with Existing Approaches on Detection of Obfuscated (Malicious) JavaScript Code

Approach	FP	FN
NoFus [17]	1%	5%
[18]	12.13%	3.84%
JStill	1.75%	0.53%

5.4 Performance Overhead

In our evaluation, performance overhead is measured in

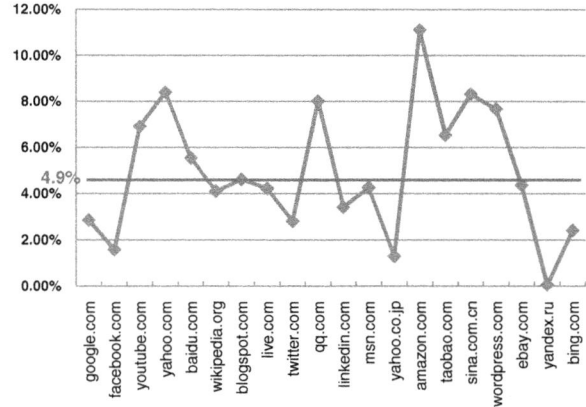

Figure 8: Average Performance Overhead for Top 20 Websites

terms of *the average increased loading time* for Web pages. To factor out the random fluctuations in network latency, JStill automatically visits the same website 20 times. Meanwhile, the option of caching visited Web pages is also disabled in the instrumented browser to make sure the Web pages are retrieved from the Web server instead of being loaded from the local cache. To calculate the overhead in loading time, the same evaluation is preformed again using an non-instrumented Firefox, and the difference between the results from two evaluations is the performance overhead. Figure 8 lists the average performance overhead in loading time for Alexa top 20 websites. The overall average performance overhead is 4.9%, which makes JStill a practical realtime detection tool.

6. DISCUSSION AND FUTURE WORK

Minification v.s. Obfuscation Minification in JavaScript works by removing the comments and unnecessary whitespace from the code. Its purpose is to reduce the size of code, not to hide the code. Although the readability of minified code may be reduced as a result, it is different from obfuscation. As discussed in [11], some obfuscation tools may include minification as one of the steps, but they in addition modify the JavaScript code so that the logic of the code can be concealed.

In this work, we focus on obfuscation, not minification, because minification will not help attackers hide the malicious JavaScript code from inspection.

Discrepancy in Browsers Different Web browsers may render Web pages differently, parse and interpret JavaScript code differently according to their implementations. One practical concern is that the discrepancy in browser implementations will affect the detection effectiveness of JStill. For example, scripted browser detection and conditional comments can cause different scripts being executed in different Web browsers. Since JStill is based on static analysis, even if a part of script is not executed because of scripted browser detection, it is still parsed and examined by JStill. For conditional comments, we acknowledge that the IE-targeted scripts cannot be observed by an implementation of JStill on Firefox. However, as we mentioned, the design of JStill does not rely on any unique feature from Firefox. JSTILL can also be implemented on other Web browsers. In this work, we choose Firefox as the platform because it is the most popular open source browser [3, 4].

Other Evading Techniques JStill is designed to detect obfuscated malicious JavaScript code that hides the malicious code from static analysis, because this is the most effective way of evading static inspection and the most prevalent choice among the observed malicious JavaScript code. However, we do realize that there exist other forms of obfuscation, e.g., variable and function name randomization or substitution, etc. One common characteristic among these simple forms of obfuscation is that the semantics of the malicious code is not hidden. Although they may be able to evade some signature-based detection systems, they cannot evade an effective static detection tool that captures the unchangeable parts in malicious code. These unchangeable parts include exploited vulnerabilities (e.g., an ActiveX object), language-defined functions (e.g., "eval") or the location of a malicious payload (e.g., "http://foo.com/malware.exe"). Therefore, in this work, we focus on the obfuscation that actually hides the malicious code (or part of the code), and we believe JStill is a nice complement to other detection approaches, e.g., signature-based approaches and dynamic analysis based schemes.

Other Scripting Languages Malicious obfuscation is also seen in other scripting languages (e.g., VBScript, JScript) that are supported by specific browsers (e.g., IE). Some of these languages such as JScript are derived from the same ECMAScript standard as JavaScript. Therefore, the design principle of JStill can be applied to detect malicious obfuscated code in these languages. For other languages such as VBScript, despite the difference in syntax and language features, we believe the general idea of JStill, such as function invocation based analysis and the combination of static and runtime analysis can still shed some light in the new context.

7. RELATED WORK

JStill is the only approach that leverages both bytecode representation and runtime of JavaScript code. Figure 9 shows how JStill differs from existing approaches based on the representation level of JavaScript code used in each approach. It also illustrates the objective of a related approach, focusing on detection obfuscation or malicious JavaScript.

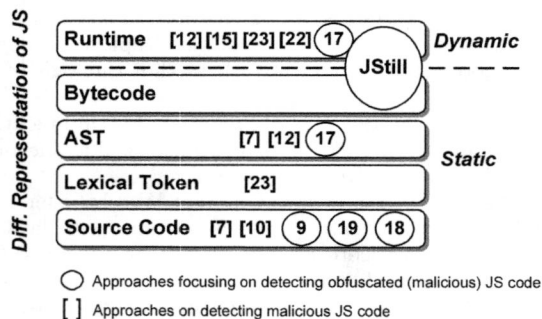

Figure 9: Comparison of JStill with other approaches

Obfuscated (Malicious) Javascript Detection. Figure 9 lists the four approaches that focus on the detection of obfuscated (malicious) JavaScript code. The one closest to JStill is NoFus [17]. NoFus is a follow-up of Zozzle [12], and it also leverages an AST based static classifier. NoFus detects if a piece of JavaScript code has been obfuscated for

any purpose, and it also distinguishes benign obfuscated JavaScript and malicious JavaScript. NoFuS achieves a false positive rate of 1% and a false negative rate of 5%. JStill is different from NoFuS in the following aspects: 1) instead of AST representation, JStill leverages the bytecode representation, which contains more semantic information. 2) JStill focuses on detecting obfuscated malicious JavaScript code, instead of detecting obfuscation. 3) JStill achieves a comparable false positive rate, and a much lower false negative rate.

Likarish *et al.* [19] also leveraged classification techniques to detect obfuscated malicious JavaScript code. The features they applied on their classifier include length of the code, number of strings in the code, percentage of whitespace, etc. Choi *et al.* [9] proposed an approach to detecting the obfuscated strings in malicious JavaScript code based on the characteristics of obfuscated string objects, such as excessive usage of specific characters and excessive length of the string. Kim *et al.* [18] proposed an entropy-based system to detect obfuscated malicious JavaScript. JStill is different from these three approaches in: 1) JStill leverages function invocation based analysis, which captures the difference between obfuscated malicious JavaScript code and other JavaScript code. 2) Both false positives and false negatives rates of JStill is lower than those reported.

Malicious JavaScript Detection. Figure 9 also lists six approaches for detection of malicious JavaScript code. Curtsinger *et al.* [12] proposed Zozzle, a JavaScript malware detection system that also combines both static and dynamic analysis. As the precedent of NoFus [17], Zozzle is also based on machine learning using features extracted from AST of JavaScript code. Because Zozzle is trained using samples collected by Nozzle [22], it is more effective in classifying malware with heap spray and shellcode instead of obfuscated malicious code. There exist similarities between the purpose of the runtime component in JStill and in their work, since both components provide view of dynamically generated code. However, JStill also compares the information parsed from dynamically generated code with the information obtained from static analysis. Ratanaworabhan *et al.* [22] proposed a runtime approach to detecting heap spray attacks. Their approach monitors a browser's heap to identify structured x86 code (e.g., NOPs) that are often exploited by a heap spray attack. In JStill, the runtime inspection is lightweight and only focuses on accessing dynamically generated code and identifying JavaScript invocations. Cova *et al.* [10] proposed a detection scheme for malicious JavaScript code. Their scheme detects the obfuscated malicious JavaScript code by extracting features such as ratio of string definitions and string uses, length of dynamic code generation during the execution. These features, however, can be evaded by obfuscation techniques that manifest differently. Instead, JStill relies on more fundamental characteristics of obfuscation that cannot be easily evaded by "crafted" obfuscation. Hallaraker *et al.* [15] proposed an auditing system to examine the execution of JavaScript code on the client-side. To detect malicious JavaScript code, the audited code is compared with policies that specify the suspicious activities. Egele *et al.* [13] proposed an approach to detecting drive-by download by identifying JavaScript code that contains shellcode through x86 instruction emulation. Rieck *et al.* [23] proposed a system for detection and prevention of drive-by-download attacks using the combination of static and dynamic analysis. The static analysis in their work focuses on features extracted from lexical tokens, and the dynamic analysis leverages a JavaScript sandbox such that it can reveal the runtime behavior of JavaScript code. In JStill, the analysis is mostly static, and the purpose of a runtime component is to provide access to dynamically generated and evaluated code.

8. CONCLUSIONS

This paper presents JStill, a mostly static approach to detect obfuscated malicious JavaScript code. JStill focuses on three aspects of function invocation analysis to provides efficient and effective detection and prevention of obfuscated malicious JavaScript code. It leverages the comparison of information obtained from both static analysis and runtime inspection. An evaluation has demonstrated the detection effectiveness of JStill as well as the low performance overhead. We see JStill as a good and practical complementary approach to existing signature-based detection systems. We also believe the design of JStill can shed some light on other obfuscation detection problems.

9. ACKNOWLEDGMENTS

We thank the reviewers for their valuable comments and suggestions. This work was partially supported by NSF CAREER 0643906.

10. REFERENCES

[1] Online JavaScript Obfuscator. http://www.daftlogic.com/projects-online-javascript-obfuscator.htm.

[2] Javascript obfuscators review. http://javascript-reference.info/javascript-obfuscators-review.htm, 2006.

[3] Browser statistics. http://www.w3schools.com/browsers/browsers_stats.asp, 2011.

[4] Browser stats. http://upsdell.com/BrowserNews/stat.htm, 2011.

[5] ALEXA. Alexa top global sites. http://www.alexa.com/topsites, 2010.

[6] BALZAROTTI, D., COVA, M., FELMETSGER, V., JOVANOVIC, N., KIRDA, E., KRUEGEL, C., AND VIGNA, G. Saner: Composing static and dynamic analysis to validate sanitization in web applications. In Proceedings of the 2008 IEEE Symposium on Security and Privacy (Washington, DC, USA, 2008), IEEE Computer Society, pp. 387–401.

[7] CANALI, D., COVA, M., VIGNA, G., AND KRUEGEL, C. Prophiler: a fast filter for the large-scale detection of malicious web pages. In Proceedings of the 20th international conference on World wide web (New York, NY, USA, 2011), WWW '11, ACM, pp. 197–206.

[8] CHENETTE, S. ToorConX: The Ultimate Deobfuscator. http://securitylabs.websense.com/content/Blogs/3198.aspx#, 2010.

[9] CHOI, Y., KIM, T., CHOI, S., AND LEE, C. Automatic detection for javascript obfuscation attacks in web pages through string pattern analysis. In Proceedings of the 1st International Conference on Future Generation Information Technology (Berlin, Heidelberg, 2009), FGIT '09, Springer-Verlag, pp. 160–172.

[10] COVA, M., KRUEGEL, C., AND VIGNA, G. Detection and analysis of drive-by-download attacks and malicious javascript code. In Proceedings of the 19th international conference on World wide web (New York, NY, USA, 2010), WWW '10, ACM, pp. 281–290.

[11] CROCKFORD, D. Minification v obfuscation. http://yuiblog.com/blog/2006/03/06/minification-v-obfuscation/, 2006.

[12] CURTSINGER, C., LIVSHITS, B., ZORN, B., AND SEIFERT, C. Zozzle: Fast and precise in-browser javascript malware detection. In Proceedings of the 20th conference on USENIX security symposium (2011), USENIX Association.

[13] EGELE, M., WURZINGER, P., KRUEGEL, C., AND KIRDA, E. Defending browsers against drive-by downloads: Mitigating heap-spraying code injection attacks. In Proceedings of the 6th International Conference on Detection of Intrusions and Malware, and Vulnerability Assessment (Berlin, Heidelberg, 2009), DIMVA '09, Springer-Verlag, pp. 88–106.

[14] FOSSI, M., JOHNSON, E., AND MACK, T. Symantec global internet security threat report. Tech. rep., Symantec, 2009.

[15] HALLARAKER, O., AND VIGNA, G. Detecting malicious javascript code in mozilla. In Proceedings of the 10th IEEE International Conference on Engineering of Complex Computer Systems (Washington, DC, USA, 2005), ICECCS '05, IEEE Computer Society, pp. 85–94.

[16] HOWARD, F. Malware with your mocha? obfuscation and anti emulation tricks in malicious javascript. Tech. rep., Sophos, 2010.

[17] KAPLAN, S., LIVSHITS, B., ZORN, B., SIEFERT, C., AND CURTSINGER, C. "nofus: Automatically detecting" + string.fromcharcode(32) +"obfuscated ".tolowercase() + "javascript code". Tech. rep., Microsoft Research, 2011.

[18] KIM, B.-I., IM, C.-T., AND JUNG, H.-C. Suspicious malicious web site detection with strength analysis of a javascript obfuscation. In International Journal of Advanced Science and Technology (2011).

[19] LIKARISH, P., JUNG, E., AND JO, I. Obfuscated malicious javascript detection using classification techniques. In Proceedings of the 4th International Conference on Malicious and Unwanted Software (Oct 2009), MALWARE '09, pp. 47–54.

[20] PERCOCO, N. J. Global security report 2010 analysis of investigations and penetration tests. Tech. rep., SpiderLabs, 2010.

[21] RABEK, J. C., KHAZAN, R. I., LEWANDOWSKI, S. M., AND CUNNINGHAM, R. K. Detection of injected, dynamically generated, and obfuscated malicious code. In Proceedings of the 2003 ACM workshop on Rapid malcode (New York, NY, USA, 2003), WORM '03, ACM, pp. 76–82.

[22] RATANAWORABHAN, P., LIVSHITS, B., AND ZORN, B. Nozzle: a defense against heap-spraying code injection attacks. In Proceedings of the 18th conference on USENIX security symposium (Berkeley, CA, USA, 2009), USENIX Association, pp. 169–186.

[23] RIECK, K., KRUEGER, T., AND DEWALD, A. Cujo: efficient detection and prevention of drive-by-download attacks. In Proceedings of the 26th Annual Computer Security Applications Conference (New York, NY, USA, 2010), ACSAC '10, ACM, pp. 31–39.

[24] SYMANTEC. ActiveX file overwrite delete vulnerabilities. http://www.symantec.com/connect/blogs/activex-file-overwritedelete-vulnerabilities-continued, 2008.

[25] YUE, C., AND WANG, H. Characterizing insecure javascript practices on the web. In Proceedings of the 18th international conference on World wide web (New York, NY, USA, 2009), WWW '09, ACM, pp. 961–970.

APPENDIX

A. ALGORITHMS

Algorithm 1 Substring Identification

Input: Basic strings set $S = s_1, ..., s_p$ in tree S_T, Argument string arg

Output: Subset of basic strings C

1: $C \leftarrow \emptyset$
2: $T \leftarrow S_T$
3: $i \leftarrow 0$
4: searchtree(T, i)
5: **while** $i < length(arg)$ **do**
6:     search level 1 of tree T for key $arg[i]$
7:     **if** key $arg[i]$ is found on node j **then**
8:         **if** node j is leaf **then**
9:             $C \leftarrow s$ ($s \in S$ $s :=$ path from root to j)
10:        **else**
11:           $T_j :=$ subtree from node j
12:           searchtree$(T_j, i \leftarrow i + 1)$
13:        **end if**
14:     **end if**
15:     $i \leftarrow i + 1$
16: **end while**

Algorithm 2 Metric Calculation

Input: Substrings set $S = s_1, ..., s_q$, argument string arg

Output: max percentage max_p

1: $max_p \leftarrow 0$
2: **while** $S \neq \emptyset$ **do**
3:     find the longest substring s_i in S
4:     $max_p \leftarrow max_p + length(s_i)/length(arg)$
5:     $S \leftarrow S - \{s_i\}$
6: **end while**

B. JAVASCRIPT OBFUSCATION TOOLS

Table 4: JavaScript Obfuscation Tools

Tools	Techniques
Thicket	D, A, S
Jasob	D
JS Obfuscator	D, A
Stunnix	D, A
JCE Pro	D, A
ScrEnc	D, A, C
Shane	D, A
Dean	D, A
Jammer	D
JSCrunch Pro	D

D:Data Obfuscation
A:ASCII/Unicode/Hexadecimal encoding
C:Customized Encoding Functions
S:Standard Encryption and Decryption
*Encoding/encryption based obfuscation includes A,C,S

C. D-GEN AND R-EVAL FUNCTION HOOKED BY JSTILL

Table 5: D-Gen and R-Eval Function hooked by JStill

Function Name	Description
document.write	dynamic code generation
document.writeln	dynamic code generation
window.setTimeout	evaluate the 1st argument as code
window.setInterval	evaluate the 1st argument as code
eval	evaluate the argument as code

D. EVADING EFFECTIVENESS

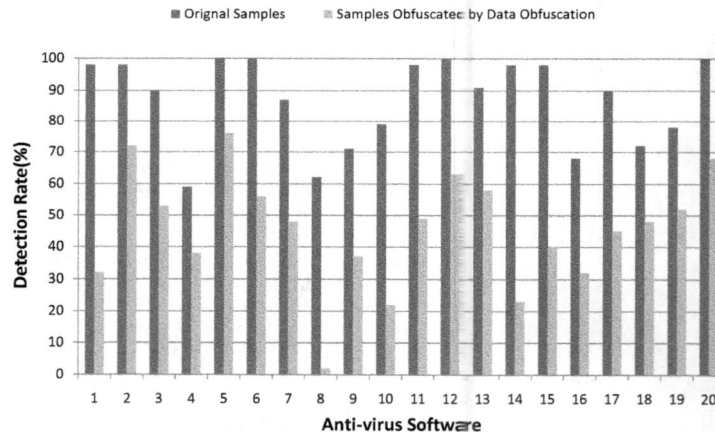

Figure 10: The Detection Rate of 20 Anti-Virus Software on Samples Obfuscated by Data Obfuscation

TamperProof: A Server-Agnostic Defense for Parameter Tampering Attacks on Web Applications

Nazari Skrupsky
University of Illinois at Chicago

Prithvi Bisht
University of Illinois at Chicago

Timothy Hinrichs
University of Illinois at Chicago

V. N. Venkatakrishnan
University of Illinois at Chicago

Lenore Zuck
University of Illinois at Chicago

ABSTRACT

Parameter tampering attacks are dangerous to a web application whose server performs weaker data sanitization than its client. This paper presents TAMPERPROOF, a methodology and tool that offers a novel and efficient mechanism to protect Web applications from parameter tampering attacks. TAMPERPROOF is an online defense deployed in a trusted environment between the client and server and requires no access to, or knowledge of, the server side codebase, making it effective for both new and legacy applications. The paper reports on experiments that demonstrate TAMPERPROOF's power in efficiently preventing all known parameter tampering vulnerabilities on ten different applications.

Categories and Subject Descriptors

D.4.6 [**Security and Protection**]: Verification
; K.4.4 [**Electronic Commerce**]: Security
; K.6.5 [**Security and Protection**]: Unauthorized access

General Terms

Languages, Security

Keywords

Parameter Tampering; Prevention

1. INTRODUCTION

Interactive processing and validation of user input are increasingly becoming the de-facto standard for Web applications. With the advent of client-side scripting there has been a rapid transition in recent years to validate user input in the browser itself, before it is submitted to the server. This client-side validation offers numerous advantages, among which are faster response time for users and reduction of load on servers. Yet, client-side validation exposes new vulnerabilities as malicious clients can circumvent

it and supply invalid data to the server. A server that accepts such invalid data is vulnerable to *parameter tampering* attacks.

Several recent studies [5, 6, 18, 3] have presented automated techniques to *detect* parameter tampering and have uncovered parameter tampering vulnerabilities in both open source and commercial websites, most notably in websites for banking and on-line shopping, as well as those accepting payments through third party cashiers (such as `PayPal` and `AmazonPayments`.) These vulnerabilities enable takeovers of accounts and allow a malicious user to perform unauthorized financial transactions.

Defense against parameter tampering attacks for new applications is conceptually straightforward: Ensure that the input validation of the server is at least as strong as that of the client. Legacy applications are more challenging since manually editing source code to ensure the server's validation is as strong as the client's is error prone, expensive, and must be performed each time the code is modified. We therefore seek automated solutions to defend against parameter-tampering attacks for both new and legacy applications.

A major hurdle to an automated solution is that for most web applications the client's code changes from one HTTP request to the next. Each time the server receives a request, it responds with a client program that is generated based on the data the server received, the server's session state, and the database state. Each time a server protected against parameter tampering receives an HTTP request, it must therefore not only perform validation on the data it receives but also determine which of the potentially infinitely many possible clients sent the data so as to perform the proper validation.

The existing defense literature has focused on preventing popular attacks on web applications such as SQL injection, Cross-site scripting, etc., and does not address challenges posed by parameter tampering vulnerabilities. A large body of work exists for preventing client-side cheating in online games e.g., [4, 10]. These techniques cannot be applied to web application setup: unlike game clients which have fixed code, web forms are dynamically generated based on server-side state. Other relevant works include Guha et al., [11] and Ripley [17]. The work in [11] computes a model of expected flow of requests by analyzing client side code of web applications. As with the case of online game client code, properties such as the sequence of requests do not change over time and hence this technique cannot be applied to prevent parameter tampering attacks. Ripley [17] relies on executing another copy of the client code in a trusted environment to detect tampering attempts from the actual client. Ripley seems to require complex engineering in keeping replicated client executions in sync. As it does not analyze client-side validation it may fail to prevent certain class of parameter tampering attacks (See Section 7). Given the severity of parameter tampering vulnerabilities, further research is warranted to prevent them.

The goal of this work is to offer an efficient defense against parameter tampering attacks that addresses the challenges above. We describe TAMPERPROOF, a transparent, automatic solution for the *prevention* of parameter tampering attacks. TAMPERPROOF protects both legacy and new applications without requiring access to, knowledge of, or changes to existing code. TAMPERPROOF is deployed in a trusted environment between client and server and intercepts all communication between them. We demonstrate that the overheads of TAMPERPROOF are similar to those of a standard web proxy. (For a live demonstration, see the anonymous website [2].)

This paper makes the following contributions:

- A method to determine the validation that ought to be performed on the server for any given HTTP request;

- Design and implementation of a tool for preventing parameter tampering attacks;

- A study of resiliency and efficiency issues of the method to ensure robustness of the defense and acceptable overheads;

- An evaluation over a large corpus of medium to large web applications.

The rest of the paper is organized as follows. Section 2 provides an overview of parameter tampering attacks and uses a simple web application to illustrate challenges in preventing them. Section 3 provides an overview of TAMPERPROOF. Section 4 elaborates on TAMPERPROOF's design and discusses challenges that were addressed to ensure security and acceptable performance. Section 5 describes implementation of TAMPERPROOF and our experiences in evaluating it over a large corpus of vulnerable web applications. Section 6 is a discussion of Web 2.0 applications. We compare TAMPERPROOF to relevant literature in Section 7 and conclude in Section 8.

2. BACKGROUND

A Running Example. Figure 1 shows three forms that are part of a typical online purchase process. (This example is based on a real-world parameter tampering exploit found on a shopping website, which was reported in [5].) The Shopping Cart form (first on the left) shows two products selected by a user for purchase and solicits a quantity for each product, a credit card to be charged (displayed in a drop down list of previously used cards) and any special delivery instructions. When the user submits this form, the client-side JavaScript verifies that the specified quantities for the selected products are positive and delivery instructions contain 30 characters or less. If any of these conditions are violated, the JavaScript code cancels the submission and prompts the user to correct the mistakes; otherwise, the user inputs $quantity_1$, $quantity_2$, `card` and `delivery` are sent to the server. The server then computes the total cost of

the requested products and generates the Shipping Details form. This form asks the user where and how the products should be shipped. When the user submits this form her shipping information is sent to the server, who computes the shipping cost, adds it to the total cost and generates a (read-only) Confirmation form. Once the user confirms her purchase by submitting the Confirmation form, the server places her order and the transaction is complete.

Basic Parameter Tampering Attack. Suppose the server-side code that processes the shopping cart submission fails to check if the values of the inputs $quantity_1$ and $quantity_2$ are positive numbers. In this form, a malicious user can bypass client side restrictions (by disabling JavaScript) and submit a negative number for one or both products. It is possible that submitting a negative number for both products would result in the user's account being credited; however, that attack will likely be thwarted because of differences in credit card transactions on the banking server responsible for debit and credit operations. However, if a negative quantity is submitted for one product and a positive quantity is submitted for the other product so that the resulting total is positive, the negative quantity acts as a discount on the total price. For instance, in Figure 1, if the values for $quantity_1$ and $quantity_2$ were -4 and 1 respectively, the end result would be an unauthorized "discount" of $400.

Negative Parameter Tampering Attack. Now suppose that the web application is designed to give all employees a 10% reduction in their total costs. One (poor) way to implement this feature is to include on every employee form a hidden field $ediscount = 1$ that when present causes the server to subtract 10% from the total price. A malicious user (non-employee) can launch a negative parameter tampering attack to gain the employee discount by modifying her form to include $ediscount = 1$ (a field not originally present on the form).

Tampering based Sequencing Attack. Finally consider the sequence of forms the server intends the user to navigate: the Shopping Cart, the Shipping Details, and the Confirmation. If the server does not force the user to follow this sequence, it is vulnerable to a *sequencing* attack, wherein the user can skip one or more steps in the above sequence. For example, a malicious user could manually submit the Confirmation form and choose the products, quantities, shipping costs, and total cost. This attack (a generalization of the attack on quantities described earlier) enables a malicious user to drive the total cost to a value close to zero.

2.1 Challenges in Preventing Parameter Tampering Attacks

To prevent parameter tampering attacks in legacy applications, one must augment the server-side input validation such that it is as strong as the corresponding client-side validation. In our running example, parameter tampering vulnerability of the parameter `quantity` can be patched by checking and rejecting negative values of the parameter `quantity`. Intuitively, this check can be performed after the form is submitted and before the parameter `quantity` is used. More specifically, the following check must be performed before `quantity` field is used in any server-side computation: exit if ($quantity < 0$ AND $op ==$ "purchase")

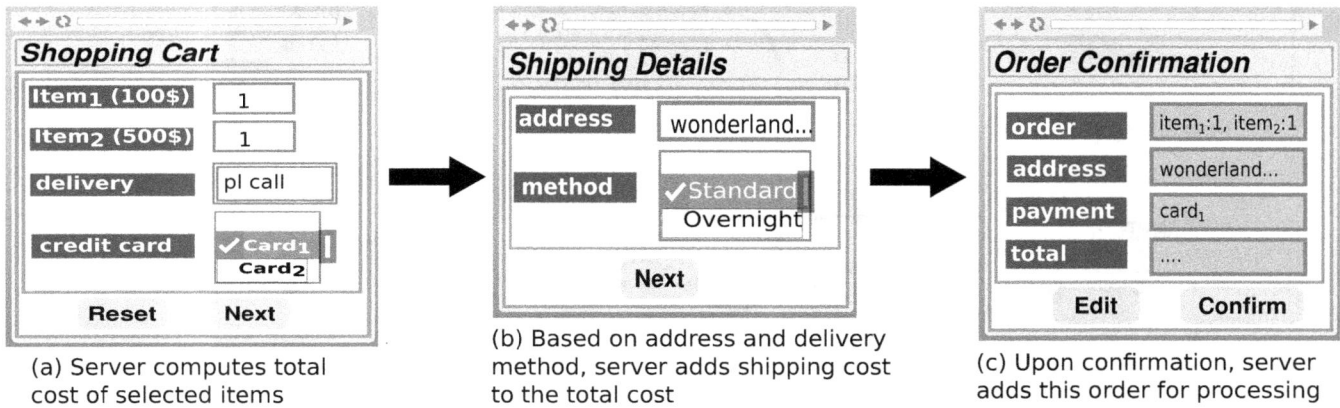

(a) Server computes total cost of selected items

(b) Based on address and delivery method, server adds shipping cost to the total cost

(c) Upon confirmation, server adds this order for processing

Figure 1: Web forms in a typical order processing functionality: (a) first form solicits items to be purchased, delivery instructions and credit card to be charged, (b) second form solicits shipping address and shipping method, and (c) third form seeks user confirmation, displaying all order details in a read-only manner.

i.e., forbid execution if value of the parameter `quantity` is negative and the requested operation is "purchase".

The process of generating and enforcing the above checks (intuitively the patch) faces two main challenges: (a) as web forms may change over time, this computation must factor in dynamism in form generation (challenge C_1), and (b) as parameter tampering vulnerabilities may only be present in specific executions of the server-side code, patches should *only* be triggered in applicable executions (challenge C_2). We discuss these challenges in detail below.

Challenge 1: Factoring in Dynamism in Form Generation (C_1). Perhaps the biggest challenge for generating correct patches stems from the dynamic nature of web applications. Quite frequently, web applications use server-side state (database, files, etc.) to create web forms. In our running example, the `card` drop down menu is populated from a database that stores credit cards used by a user in the past. As the server-side state changes, such form fields change and in turn may imply a different set of constraints. In our running example, if the user makes use of a new credit card say `card3`, the constraint implied by the drop down menu changes from $\boxed{\texttt{card} \in \{card_1, card_2\}}$ to $\boxed{\texttt{card} \in \{card_1, card_2, card_3\}}$. In general, a form field may encode state information that is different across user sessions but could also change within a session over time (for example, different users will likely have different credit cards, but even a single user may use new cards during the lifetime of a session). Consequently, the challenge is in computing patches that also evolve with changes in server-side state.

Challenge 2: Patching Only Vulnerable Server-side Executions (C_2). A parameter tampering vulnerability may be specific to certain executions of the server-side code. It is possible that some or all of the other executions either don't use the vulnerable parameter (and hence aren't vulnerable) or use it in security insensitive operations. Hence even when a patch is computed, it is necessary to compute the exact conditions that must be met to enforce the patch. In the running example the server-side execution may only use parameter `quantity` when the requested operation is purchase. Intuitively, such conditions identify vulnerable executions of the server code and hence when

to enforce missing checks (or patch) e.g., before requiring `quantity` field to have positive values, the patch must ensure that the requested operation is purchase. Without the knowledge of vulnerable executions, a patch may result in false positives e.g., by always demanding a positive value for the parameter `quantity`. The key challenge is in finding mechanisms that can identify vulnerable executions of the server to precisely enforce patches.

3. OVERVIEW

3.1 Problem Description

The above discussion illustrates the basic nature of parameter tampering attacks. We now formalize these attacks as violations of constraints the server intended to impose on the submission and processing of user inputs.

DEFINITION 1 (INPUT). *We define an* input *received by a server from a client as a set of field name/value pairs:*
$$\mathcal{I} = \{\langle \mathcal{N}_1, \mathcal{V}_1 \rangle, \langle \mathcal{N}_2, \mathcal{V}_2 \rangle, \ldots, \langle \mathcal{N}_n, \mathcal{V}_n \rangle\}$$

A server receives a sequence

$$\mathcal{I}_1, \quad \mathcal{I}_2, \quad \mathcal{I}_3, \quad \ldots, \quad \mathcal{I}_k, \ldots$$

of such inputs, and each time a new input arrives the server must decide whether or not the sequence up to that point in time constitutes an attack on the server and accept or reject the new input accordingly.

Intuitively, a malicious user can launch an attack in three conceptually separate ways: tamper with the field *names* in the inputs, tamper with the field *values* in the inputs, or tamper with the *order* in which inputs arrive. Each type of attack violates a constraint the server intended to enforce on its inputs—a constraint defined by the form used to submit each input (if one exists). Thus, we associate with every input $\mathcal{I}$ the form $\mathcal{F}_{\mathcal{I}}$ used to submit it. Below we describe the three constraints corresponding to each attack: the Field Constraints, the Value Constraints, and the Sequencing constraints, respectively.

Field Constraints. Field Constraints dictate which field names an input is allowed to include. The Field Constraints for input $\mathcal{I}$ are usually implicit in the form $\mathcal{F}_{\mathcal{I}}$ be-

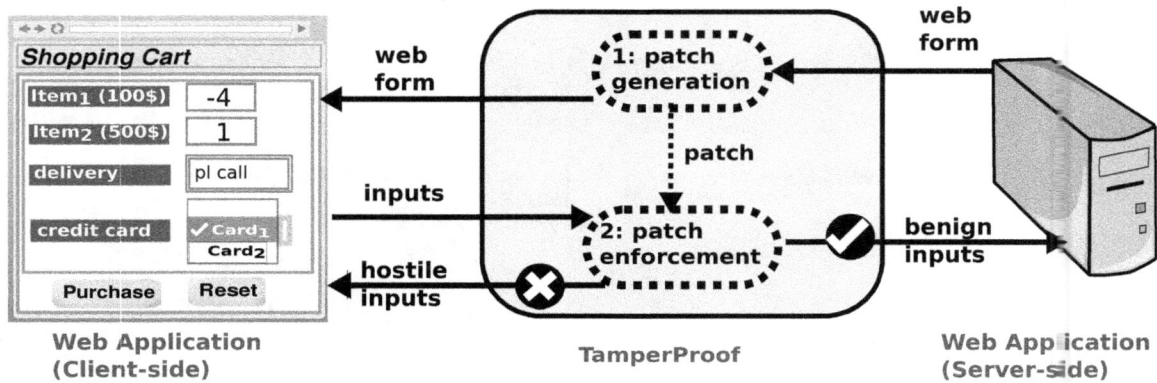

Figure 2: Overview of TAMPERPROOF: **Per form patch generation and enforcement: 1) Each form is analyzed to generate a patch, and 2) form submissions conforming to this patch are submitted to the server for further processing; otherwise rejected and sent to the client.**

cause the only field names the form submits are those included in it.

> Given a form $\mathcal{F}$ and input $\mathcal{I}$, we say that $\mathcal{I}$ satisfies the Field Constraints of $\mathcal{F}$ if the set of field names in $\mathcal{I}$ is a subset of fields present in $\mathcal{F}$.

Enforcing Field Constraints on our running example prevents the employee discount attack.

Value Constraints. Value constraints dictate which data values can be assigned to which field names in an input. The Value Constraints for input $\mathcal{I}$ are enforced by form $\mathcal{F}_{\mathcal{I}}$ either through its JavaScript (e.g., the product quantities in the Shopping Cart form) or its HTML (e.g., the length restriction on the delivery instructions).

> Given a form $\mathcal{F}$ and input $\mathcal{I}$, we say that $\mathcal{I}$ satisfies the Value Constraints of $\mathcal{F}$ if when $\mathcal{I}$'s values are inserted into $\mathcal{F}$'s fields, the form allows the input to be submitted to the server.

Enforcing Value Constraints in our running example prevents the product quantity attack described earlier.

Sequencing Constraints. These constraints ensure that inputs are sent to the server in a plausible order. By plausible we mean that at the time input $\mathcal{I}$ is submitted, form $\mathcal{F}_{\mathcal{I}}$ has already been generated by the server. This simple condition ensures that many of the server's intended sequence of requests are respected. If the server intends for form A to precede form B, then it is likely that form B will only be generated in response to the inputs from form A.

> We say input sequence $\mathcal{I}_1, \mathcal{I}_2, \ldots$ satisfies the Sequencing Constraints if for every input $\mathcal{I}_j$, $\mathcal{F}_{\mathcal{I}_j}$ was generated before $\mathcal{I}_j$ was submitted.

Enforcing the Sequencing Constraints prevents the sequencing attack in our running example where the Confirmation form is submitted before the Shipping Details form. The only way to generate the Confirmation form is by submitting the Shipping Details form and thus at the time the attacker submits the Confirmation form's inputs, that form has not yet been generated.

3.2 Approach Overview

The key idea in our approach is to dynamically infer and enforce Sequencing, Field, and Value constraints on each input submitted to the server. This avoids the precision issues associated with static analysis and learning approaches. Dynamic approaches come at the cost of some performance, and we develop techniques to improve performance in Section 4.2.

Once constraints are learnt, they are placed as patches (i.e., filters) at a web application proxies that enforce these constraints on incoming inputs from clients. Enforcing these patches in a proxy simplifies our implementation and has the added benefit that our approach is applicable regardless of the platform used to implement the server.

To infer and enforce constraints on server inputs, our approach uses the following ideas.

Enforcing Sequencing Constraints. To enforce these constraints, we ensure that every non-malicious input is mapped to the form used to submit the input. To implement this idea, we dynamically instrument every form generated by the server to include a hidden field with that form's identifier. Any input that arrives at the server without such an identifier (or with a spurious identifier) is rejected. Further, each such identifier is used only once i.e., a form's identifier expires when the form is submitted with inputs that satisfy client-side validation.

Enforcing Field and Value Constraints. To enforce these constraints, we verify that every non-malicious input could have been submitted by the form associated with that input (as described above). To implement this idea, we dynamically analyze each form generated by the server to extract the constraints enforced by HTML and JavaScript and record which form identifier corresponds to which constraints. Any input that arrives at the server and does not satisfy the constraints corresponding to the form used to submit the input, is rejected.

The above observations are developed in our approach and the tool TAMPERPROOF that prevents parameter tampering attacks in existing applications. In essence, TAMPERPROOF generates *a per form patch* by analyzing client side code of each form generated by a web application and then uses it to forbid parameter tampering attempts when the form is submitted. Figure 2 presents a functional overview of these two steps, which we discuss in more detail below.

1. Patch Generation. In the first step, TAMPERPROOF intercepts web pages being sent to a client and locates any web forms in them. In each form TAMPERPROOF inserts a (randomly generated) unique form identifier, which for brevity we call the patchID. TAMPERPROOF then extracts the Field and Value constraints enforced by this form and associates them with the patchID. More precisely, TAMPERPROOF first analyzes the HTML to extract the Field constraints as well as a few Value constraints. It also analyzes JavaScript (using standard symbolic evaluation techniques e.g., [15, 5]) to extract the remaining Value constraints. Intuitively the combination of the patchID, the Field, and the Value constraints represents the patch for this form.

For the Shopping Cart form in our running example, the Field constraints TAMPERPROOF extracts is a simple set of field names: $\{quantity_1, quantity_2, card, delivery\}$. The Value constraints are captured by the formula:

$$\bigwedge \begin{array}{l} quantity_1 \geq 0 \wedge quantity_2 \geq 0 \\ delivery \in [\texttt{a} - \texttt{zA} - \texttt{Z}]* \\ card \in (card_1 \mid card_2) \end{array}$$

Note that the permitted credit card selections depend on the application's backend database, which means that if the user requests the Shopping Cart form twice her credit card options may be different each time. Because patch generation is performed each time a form is generated, the Value constraints will always properly reflect the user's actual options at the time she submits her data. As the patches are generated for each web form (which capture the server-side state at the time of their generation and hence the most up-to-date constraints), the above mechanism effectively addresses the challenge posed by dynamism in form generation (challenge $\mathcal{C}_1$).

We also note that the patchID is a nonce similar to *tokens* used in Cross-site request forgery (XSRF) prevention solutions such as [13, 12]. Such tokens are used to identify and reject unsolicited HTTP requests. patchID is used for a different purpose – to associate each generated web form with its submission. We discuss implications of similarities between patchID and XSRF tokens in Section 7.

2. Patch Enforcement. In the second step, TAMPERPROOF intercepts form submissions before they reach the server. TAMPERPROOF checks that the supplied patchID exists (thus preventing sequencing attacks) and that the supplied inputs satisfy the Field and Value constraints extracted in the previous step. A form submission is rejected if it fails any of these checks; otherwise, it is forwarded to the server for normal processing.

The following two form submissions show values assigned to various fields in the Shopping Cart form. TAMPERPROOF forwards the first submission to the server because it satisfies all the Field and Value constraints, but it rejects the second submission because $quantity_1$ is negative, violating the Value constraints.

1. $\{quantity_1 \rightarrow 1, quantity_2 \rightarrow 1, delivery \rightarrow ``call",$
   $card \rightarrow card_2\}$
2. $\{quantity_1 \rightarrow -1, quantity_2 \rightarrow 1, delivery \rightarrow ``",$
   $card \rightarrow card_1\}$

The addition of patchID in forms, affords TAMPERPROOF an effective mechanism to tie web forms (and constraints they imply) with their submissions (and hence constraints they must satisfy). This mechanism enables TAMPERPROOF to precisely check constraints specific to a web form that tampered form submissions will fail to satisfy, thus providing an effective mechanism to safeguard *only* the vulnerable executions of server code (challenge $\mathcal{C}_2$).

4. SECURITY AND PERFORMANCE

The practical effectiveness of TAMPERPROOF depends crucially on it being secure against attacks and it performing well enough for real-world web applications.

4.1 Security

The previous section gave a conceptual description of what a patch for a form is, how it is generated, and how it is enforced. In this section we expand on these ideas to ensure that TAMPERPROOF is robust against a series of attacks that attempt to violate the Field, Value, and Sequencing constraints of the application as well as the mechanisms TAMPERPROOF uses to enforce those constraints.

The key insight is that inserting a patchID into a form gives a malicious user another field to tamper with. For TAMPERPROOF to be secure, it must ensure that a form's patchID field is itself tamperproof. Tampering with a patchID is useful because different forms have different constraints, and some constraints are more permissive (i.e., weaker) than others: weaker constraints reject fewer inputs and hence are better for attackers. By submitting a patchID for a form with weaker constraints, an attacker can try to fool TAMPERPROOF into accepting data that violate the constraints on her actual form.

It turns out that making a form's patchID tamperproof only requires expanding our notion of a patch to include one additional piece of information about each form: the URL to which that form submits its data. Thus, the patch generation phase must extract the target URL for each form and tie it to the form's patchID, and the patch enforcement phase becomes the following sequence of checks.

1. patchID exists
2. server has a record of patchID
3. the data fields are a subset of those for patchID
4. the URL is the same as that for patchID
5. the data satisfies the constraints for patchID

If any of the above check fails, TAMPERPROOF rejects the submission as a parameter tampering attack; otherwise, it forwards the submission to the web application as usual and deletes the patchID entry from memory. Below we describe how this enforcement algorithm defends against attacks.

Basic parameter tampering. Basic parameter tampering attacks are those where an attacker submits data to the server that violate the form's Value constraints. In our running example, a submission where $quantity_1$ is negative (to obtain an unauthorized discount) constitutes a basic parameter tampering attack. TAMPERPROOF rejects such an attack at Check 5.

Negative parameter tampering. Negative parameter tampering attacks are those that violate the form's Field constraints (the set of permitted field names). In our running example, a non-employee submission that includes the `ediscount` field (to gain a 10% discount), would constitute a negative parameter tampering attack. TAMPERPROOF rejects such attacks at Check 3.

Sequencing attacks. A sequencing attack is one that violates the form's Sequencing Constraints. In our running example, submitting the Order Confirmation form before the Shipping Details form constitutes a sequencing attack. TAMPERPROOF rejects such attacks at Checks 1 and 2 because the out-of-order submission could not have been submitted from a properly generated form, all of which have patchIDs.

Replay. Replay attacks are those where two different submissions include the same patchID. TAMPERPROOF rejects such attacks with high probability because once it receives the first submission, it deletes that patchID from memory, and hence unless the patchID was regenerated (a low probability event) the second submission will be rejected because the patchID does not exist.

patchID Spoofing. patchID spoofing attacks are those where the attacker generates a brand new patchID, attempting to forge a valid submission. TAMPERPROOF rejects such attacks with high probability because patchIDs are randomly generated and are therefore unpredictable for an attacker (i.e., Check 2 fails). This defense has the added benefit of protecting against cross-site request forgery attacks (XSRF), since the patchID is effectively a one-time use XSRF token (i.e., Check 1 fails for XSRF attacks).

patchID Swapping. patchID swapping attacks are those where a malicious user has two legitimate forms, A and B, and then submits data for form A using the patchID from form B. In our running example, a user could request a Shopping Cart form and a Shipping Details form. Then she could choose her own shipping costs by submitting the Shopping Cart form with the field `shippingCosts` and the Shipping form's patchID.

For patchID swapping attacks, TAMPERPROOF either identifies the request as an attack and rejects it or forwards the request on to the application because the attacker could have generated exactly the same request without any tampering. The cases where the attack is rejected are simple: (i) the request includes fields that form B does not (and hence Check 3 fails), (ii) the request's URL differs from that of form B (and hence Check 4 fails), (iii) the data submitted violates B's constraints (and hence Check 5 fails). Note however that if the request is not rejected, this "attack" uses exactly the same fields and URL as form B, and satisfies the constraints on form B. The attacker can therefore generate exactly the same request without any parameter tampering by simply filling out form B directly. TAMPERPROOF therefore should and does forward the request on to the application. In our running example, if a user attempts to skip the Shipping Details form by supplying too low (or high) a shipping cost, she fails, but if she supplies exactly the right shipping costs, she succeeds.

If, however, the attacker cannot legitimately checkout form B, she can fool TAMPERPROOF into treating her submission of form A as if it came from B—a form the attacker may not be permitted to submit. (Of course, the server itself still treats the submission as if it came from A.) For example, suppose there are two versions of a single form: one displayed to authenticated users with less stringent client-side

validation and one to the general public with more stringent validation. If an authenticated user leaks her form's patchID before she submits it, an attacker can convince TAMPERPROOF to apply the less stringent validation to her submission, even if she is an unauthenticated user. The effectiveness of TAMPERPROOF's defense therefore relies on the secrecy of "active" patchIDs, i.e., patchIDs of forms that have been sent to client but have yet not been submitted. Admittedly, requiring patchIDs be kept secret is a limitation of TAMPERPROOF; however, it is no more a limitation than today's mainstream defense against XSRF attacks: embedding tokens into web pages. If the secrecy of patchIDs proves to be a practical limitation of TAMPERPROOF's effectiveness, then so too the insertion of XSRF tokens will prove ineffective against XSRF attacks—something that today's web development community deems unlikely.

4.2 Efficiency

The other practical concern for TAMPERPROOF is whether or not it is sufficiently efficient to be deployed on real-world web applications. Here there are two main metrics of interest: the time required for the server to generate a single page (latency) and the number of requests the server can support per second (throughput). Below we describe the ways in which TAMPERPROOF has been designed to minimize its impact on both these metrics. (Another relevant metric is that of scalability: how easy it is to improve latency and/or throughput by adding hardware to the system. We do not discuss scalability below because the only techniques needed to scale TAMPERPROOF are straightforward adaptations of traditional web optimization techniques for load balancing.)

Latency. Latency reflects how a single user perceives the performance of a web application: it is the amount of time required for the web server to generate the results of a single HTTP request. TAMPERPROOF incurs some overhead for all HTTP requests because it uses a proxy, but the main overheads are when the server generates a web form or processes a web form submission.

For web form generation, TAMPERPROOF must analyze the HTML produced by the server (to extract the patch) as well as add a patchID to each form. The key insight to avoiding high latencies is that there is a (sometimes significant) window of time from when the user requests a form to when the user submits the form for processing. The only thing that must be done before the form is sent to the user is that its patchID must be inserted. The rest of the analysis can take place on the server while the user is filling out the form. For each form request, TAMPERPROOF returns the form after inserting a patchID and spawns another thread to do the patch extraction. Thus its latency overhead is the cost of inserting patchIDs, which is no more than the overhead of proxy-based XSRF prevention solutions [11, 12].

Throughput. Of course, the server must still analyze the HTML page to extract the expected fields, the target URL, and the constraints for each form—analysis that can significantly reduce a server's throughput (requests handled per second). The dominating cost in this analysis is extracting the constraints from the JavaScript embedded in each page (e.g., the quantity of each product must be positive).

Fortunately, not all of the JavaScript appearing in a form needs to be analyzed. TAMPERPROOF begins by isolating the JavaScript that effects form submissions into what we call the page's JavaScript signature (the code run when the user submits the form). The JavaScript signature implicitly represents the set of constraints that are enforced by the form. Once that signature is identified, TAMPERPROOF applies symbolic execution to extract the constraints (see e.g., [5, 15] for details), a process that can be expensive because it may result in analyzing all possible code paths.

The key insight to reducing the overheads of JavaScript analysis is that in many web applications, much of the JavaScript is the same across web pages. More to the point, it is common that the JavaScript code for constraint checking is the same across many different pages (even if those pages differ significantly in terms of their HTML). In our running example, a profile page might allow a logged-in user to change her personal information. The JavaScript validation code will be the same regardless of which user is logged in, but the HTML constraints for each page may differ substantially, e.g., each user has her own list of previously used shipping addresses. This means that caching the results of JavaScript analysis can greatly improve throughput.

To this end, TAMPERPROOF caches the results of JavaScript analysis. Each time it generates the JavaScript signature for a page, it canonicalizes that signature (e.g., alphabetizing the list of function definitions) and checks to see if that canonicalized signature is in the cache. If so, it uses the constraints from the cache; otherwise, it performs JavaScript analysis and adds a new entry to the cache. To avoid memory problems stemming from web applications with many distinct JavaScript signatures, TAMPERPROOF limits the size of the cache (to a value chosen by the web developer), keeps counters representing the relative frequency with which cache entries are used, and replaces the most infrequently used cache entry when the cache becomes full. By adjusting the cache size, the developer can balance the needs of high-throughput and low-memory consumption.

Algorithm 1 TAMPERPROOF-TOUSER(html)

1: html := add-patchids(html)
2: fork(analyzeClient,html)
3: **return** html

Algorithm 2 ANALYZECLIENT(html)

1: **for all** forms f in html **do**
2:     js := javascript-signature(html)
3:     id := find-patchID (html)
4:     ⟨url, fields, constraints⟩ := codeAnalysis(html,js)
5:     patches[id] = ⟨url, fields, constraints⟩

4.3 Implementation Details

Algorithms 1, 2, and 3 describe TAMPERPROOF in more detail. TAMPERPROOF-TOUSER (Algorithm 1) runs whenever the proxy forwards a web page generated by the server to the user. It embeds patchIDs into all the forms and links on that page, forks off a thread to analyze that page, and returns the modified page, which is then returned to the user. ANALYZECLIENT (Algorithm 2) is the code that is run between a form request and the corresponding form submission: it extracts the patch for that form. TAMPERPROOF-FROMUSER (Algorithm 3) runs every time the user submits a request to the server. When the user

---

Algorithm 3 TAMPERPROOF-FROMUSER(request)

1: **if** request.url $\notin$ Entries **then**
2:     id := request.data['patchID']
3:     **if** id $\notin$ patches.keys() **then return** error
4:     wait until patches[id] is non-empty
5:     ⟨url, fields, constraints⟩ := patches[id]
6:     **if** request.data.keys() $\not\subseteq$ fields **then return** error
7:     **if** !sat(request.data,constraints) **then return** error
8:     patches.delete(id)
9: **return** request

---

requests one of the entry pages (landing pages for web applications), TAMPERPROOF simply forwards it to the server as such requests could be made directly and thus may not legitimately have patchIDs. For a non-entry page, TAMPERPROOF either identifies a parameter tampering attack or returns the original request, which is then forwarded to the server.

TAMPERPROOF maintains two global variables shared by all of these algorithms: *patches* and a cache for JavaScript constraints (not shown). *patches* is a hash table keyed on patchIDs that stores the patch for each active patchID. All three algorithms access *patches*. TAMPERPROOF-FROMUSER uses *patches* to check if submitted data satisfies the necessary constraints; ANALYZECLIENT stores a new patch in *patches*. TAMPERPROOF-TOUSER implicitly updates *patches* so that all of the patchIDs added to an outgoing webpage have (empty) entries in *patches* to ensure TAMPERPROOF knows those patchIDs are valid.

The cache for JavaScript constraints (not shown) is a hash table keyed on JavaScript signatures that stores the constraints corresponding to those signatures. ANALYZECLIENT is the only one to manipulate that cache. When ANALYZECLIENT is invoked, it extracts the JavaScript signature from the webpage and relies on another routine CODEANALYSIS to do the actual analysis. That routine first consults the JavaScript cache to see if the constraints for the JavaScript have already been extracted and if so simply adds those constraints to the result of the HTML constraint extraction; otherwise, it extracts the constraints from the JavaScript and updates the cache.

5. EVALUATION

Implementation. We implemented TAMPERPROOF by extending NoForge [13] (a server-side proxy for preventing XSRF attacks) with 600 lines of PHP and 200 lines of Perl to include the algorithms TAMPERPROOF-TOUSER and TAMPERPROOF-FROMUSER described in Section 4.3. Checking that an input's data satisfies a form's Value constraints is performed by a Perl script created to check exactly those constraints. The code to generate the Perl script for a given set of constraints is 1K lines of Lisp code. The implementation of ANALYZECLIENT is 5K lines of JavaScript code and 2K lines of Java code.

Applications. Our test suite is comprised of 10 medium to large PHP web applications that contained 49 parameter tampering vulnerabilities. These applications were previously evaluated [6]. Table 1 provides background information on these applications: lines of code, number of files, and functionality. The test suite was deployed on a virtual machine (2.4 GHz Intel dual core, 2.0 GB RAM) running

Application	Size (LOC)	Files	Use	Exploits (Patched /Total)
DcpPortal	144.7k	484	Contnt Mgmt	32/32
Landshop	15.4k	158	Real Estate	3/3
MyBloggie	9.4k	59	Blog	6/6
Newspro	5.0k	26	News Mgmt	1/1
OpenDB	100.2k	300	Media Mgmt	1/1
PHPNews	6.4k	21	News Mgmt	1/1
PHPNuke	249.6k	2217	Contnt Mgmt	1/1
SnipeGallery	9.1k	54	Img Mgmt	2/2
SPHPBlog	26.5k	113	Blog	1/1
OpenIT	146.1k	455	Support	1/1

Table 1: Applications & Attack Results

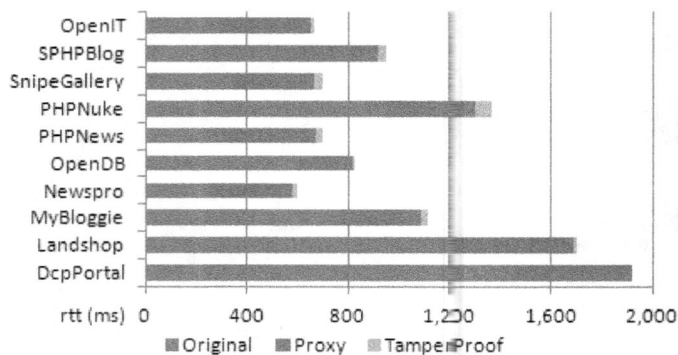

Figure 3: TAMPERPROOF: Incurred at most 4.8% overhead in round trip times.

Ubuntu 9.10 with the LAMP application stack and was connected via a local area network to the client (2.45Ghz Intel quad core, 4.0 GB RAM) running Windows XP.

5.1 Effectiveness

For evaluating the effectiveness of TAMPERPROOF in preventing parameter tampering exploits, we developed a `wget`-based shell script to generate HTTP requests to vulnerable web forms. The exact parameters needed to exploit each web form were manually provided to this automated script. This script was also manually given session cookies for forms that could only be accessed in authenticated sessions.

To test the correctness of our automated shell script, we tested each vulnerable web form without deploying TAMPER-PROOF. Each form with tampered parameters that was successfully submitted and processed by the server confirmed the existence of a vulnerability as well as proper implementation of the shell script. We then deployed TAMPERPROOF and re-tested all of these applications. The result of this testing is summarized in the 5th column of Table 1, which shows the number of exploits that were prevented along with total number of known exploits for each form. As shown by this table, TAMPERPROOF was able to defend 100% of the known exploits. Below we discuss several exploits that represent the common types of vulnerabilities encountered in our test suite. The details of most of the tested exploits are available on the supplemental website [2].

Tampering HTML Controls. The OpenDB application is vulnerable to script injection through a tampered select input field. The root cause of this vulnerability is the server's failure to ensure that the submitted input belongs to one of the select box options available to the client. TAMPERPROOF detects inputs that are outside their allowed value range and also prevents attacks that involve tampering with other types of form fields including hidden fields, checkboxes, radio buttons, and text fields.

Tampering JavaScript Validation. The DcpPortal application fails to replicate the JavaScript validations on the server, allowing attackers to bypass a regular expression check and avoid mandatory fields during submission of a registration form. TAMPERPROOF captures JavaScript validation during constraint extraction and is therefore able to generate the appropriate patch to prevent such attacks.

Sequencing Attack. The PHPNuke application is susceptible to a sequencing attack that bypasses a CAPTCHA verification during the registration process. The application uses a hidden field in the form to control a user's registration progress. By tampering with this field, the CAPTCHA page can be skipped without affecting the registration process otherwise. TAMPERPROOF is able to prevent such sequencing attacks by rejecting tampered hidden field values.

Security of TAMPERPROOF. We also tested that the TAMPERPROOF solution itself could not be tampered with. To this end, we intercepted form submission in one of the applications from the test suite and conducted the following three attacks: (a) removed patchID, (b) replaced patchID in a form submission with a patchID from a prior submission, and (c) checked out two forms and swapped their patchIDs. The first two attacks were rejected as TAMPERPROOF either failed to find a patchID with the submitted form or the supplied patchID did not match any of the active patchIDs.

To test whether TAMPERPROOF protects again patchID swapping, we constructed a sample application that generated two forms, A and B, with the same fields: name and age. Form B forbids submission of empty values for both name and age, whereas form A forbids submissions where age is empty, i.e., validation for A is weaker than B.

In two separate browser windows we accessed the two forms. We then submitted form B with an empty name and the patchID for A, a submission that B would normally disallow. TAMPERPROOF forwarded this request to the server, despite the fact that we tampered with the patchID. Though this seems like a successful attack, the submission could just as easily have been created by filling out form A. Hence, had TAMPERPROOF rejected the submission, it would have also stopped a user from legitimately filling out form A.

The results from this experiment indicate that TAMPER-PROOF allows requests that could be created without parameter tampering, but no more.

False Positives and False Negatives. TAMPER-PROOF is guaranteed to not produce false negatives because the client code analysis engine used by TAMPERPROOF precisely models constraints implied by HTML code but conservatively approximates those implied by JavaScript. More specifically, this JavaScript engine conservatively assumes that all JavaScript event handlers relevant to validation were launched (which may not be the case in actual form submissions.) This enables TAMPERPROOF patches to be complete with respect to the HTML and JavaScript validation embedded in a form and subsequently enables it to prevent exploitation of all parameter tampering vulnerabilities.

False positives, on the other hand, may arise for the following reasons: (a) the JavaScript validation approximation computes stronger constraints than are actually enforced in the form or (b) the client JavaScript dynamically modifies the form, e.g., creates new input fields causing TAMPER-PROOF to signal a negative parameter tampering attack. We tested TAMPERPROOF for false positives by submitting a wide variety of inputs, e.g., where optional fields were empty. TAMPERPROOF did not reject any valid submissions and in our evaluation was free of false positives.

One seemingly additional case for false positives occurs when the server sanitizes and accepts malicious inputs that are rejected by client. Since TAMPERPROOF rejects inputs the server can safely handle, it may seem to be a false positive; however, the only way to submit such inputs is via parameter tampering, and hence only impacts malicious users.

5.2 Performance

Latency. Since TAMPERPROOF performs additional processing both when a server sends a form to a user and when the user submits data to the server, we measured the overheads introduced by TAMPERPROOF for a combination of these events: the round-trip time (RTT). The RTT for a form is the sum of (a) the time from when a user requests a form to when she receives a response and (b) the time from when she submits form data to when she receives a reply. The time spent in filling out the form is *not* included.

For this experiment, we used an off-the-shelf, academic-grade proxy that includes XSRF protection. We deployed both the client and server on a LAN, simulating the worst-case scenario where network latencies are minimal and therefore RTT is almost entirely server performance. We then measured the RTT for forms from each of our applications.

Figure 3 shows the results. For each application, we measured the RTTs for the original application, the application with a server-side proxy with XSRF protection (but without TAMPERPROOF), and the application with the server-side proxy and TAMPERPROOF. The original application's RTTs are the blue portions of Figure 3; the overheads caused by the XSRF proxy without TAMPERPROOF are the red portions; the overheads caused by TAMPERPROOF are the green portions.

From the results, we observe that the bulk of the overhead is introduced by the XSRF proxy (32%-126%) and that the additional overhead for TAMPERPROOF is merely 0%-4.8%. This means that if an organization deploys an XSRF proxy defense, there is little added cost in deploying TAMPERPROOF. That said, the combined overhead of the XSRF defense and TAMPERPROOF is dominated by the cost of augmenting a form an XSRF tokens/a patchID. Table 2 Column 3 shows that this cost ranges from 170ms to 240 ms, which amounts to 15%-75% higher latency than the original application. The main conclusion we take away from these experiments is that a high-performance XSRF proxy (e.g., one built using an industrial-grade proxy with access to the byte stream) could be adapted to produce a high-performance version of TAMPERPROOF with little additional overhead.

Throughput. To understand the computational load added to a server by TAMPERPROOF (which influences throughput), we measured the processing times of TAMPERPROOF's internal components. For each application, Table 2 breaks down the processing times of the three core components:

Application	Patch Formu. Compl.	Processing Time (s)		
		form updt.	const extra. (w/ cache)	patch valid.
DcpPortal	187	0.22	14.68 (0.50)	0.01
Landshop	20	0.24	0.41 (0.41)	0.01
MyBloggie	37	0.22	5.66 (0.39)	0.01
Newspro	6	0.17	0.36 (0.36)	0.01
OpenDB	26	0.22	0.52 (0.52)	0.01
PHPNews	3	0.17	0.31 (0.31)	0.01
PHPNuke	11	0.18	1.15 (0.50)	0.01
SnipeGallery	11	0.16	1.47 (0.33)	0.01
SPHPBlog	37	0.18	2.41 (0.38)	0.01
OpenIT	17	0.22	0.64 (0.64)	0.01

Table 2: TAMPERPROOF: **Other Evaluation Results**

augmenting the form with patchID (Column 3), extracting constraints with and without a caching strategy (Column 4), and validating inputs (Column 5).

The form augmentation component averaged 197ms, though we think this component can be further optimized. The formula extractor component consumed the most time during processing. In our experience, HTML constraints were extracted at a constant time of about 300-600ms, whereas JavaScript constraints were extracted in time proportional to the formula size (Column 2) and ranged between 0.31s and 14.6s. To help save time on the costly JavaScript analysis, we implemented the caching strategy described in §4.2 to reuse the analysis of frequently appearing JavaScript code. We noticed that caching reduces the server load by as much as an order of magnitude. Column 4 shows caching improved times within parenthesis. This is an important savings because it improves the server's throughput (responses the server can generate per second). Input validation was the fastest component with an average time of 10ms.

Even with our caching strategy in place, constraint extraction dominates over all other components of TAMPERPROOF. But recall that this processing happens while the user is filling out the form (as explained in §4.3). To illustrate, Figure 4 depicts the timeline for when a client requests a form, receives the form, submits the form, and receives a reply. The timeline demonstrates that the time when the user is filling out the form is relatively long, which allows constraint extraction to occur without negatively impacting the user experience. Furthermore, when constraint extraction is expensive, it often means the form's constraints are complex, making it unlikely that users will quickly submit the form.

6. DISCUSSION: AJAX

TAMPERPROOF does not currently address applications written for Web 2.0 or Web 3.0 or those that dynamically alter the client code of a web form, e.g., by employing JavaScript. However, TAMPERPROOF can be used to safeguard many of the applications that have recently been shown vulnerable to parameter tampering attacks (e.g., [3, 18, 6, 5]). Here we discuss how to enhance TAMPERPROOF to properly handle a common feature of Web 2.0 web applications: Asynchronous JavaScript and XML (AJAX) requests.

Currently, a web page utilizing AJAX is problematic for TAMPERPROOF because every AJAX request the page sends

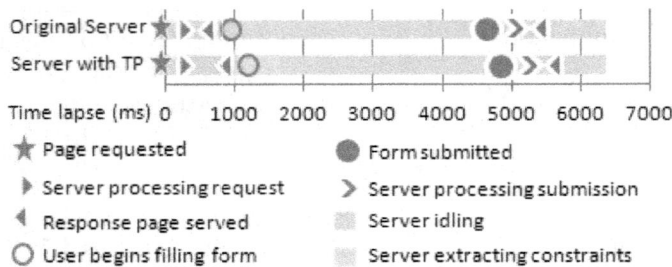

Figure 4: TAMPERPROOF: **Timeline depicting actual delays experienced by end users (most expensive analysis coincides with user filling out the form).**

to the server is rejected since it includes no patchID. One avenue for enhancing TAMPERPROOF to cope with AJAX would be expanding its instrumentation of outgoing HTML pages to ensure that all AJAX requests include the patchID. This fix alone does not suffice since TAMPERPROOF currently expires a patchID as soon as it receives an HTTP request that includes it. Without changing the patchID expiration policy, the first AJAX request would be properly validated and processed, but all future AJAX requests (as well as the user's ultimate submission) would be rejected as having an expired patchID.

Currently TAMPERPROOF expires patchIDs so that replay attacks are not possible. If an attacker gains access to an old patchID (e.g., in a caching proxy server), she would be able to fool TAMPERPROOF into running the same validations that were in place when the original user requested the web page, even if those validations are no longer the right ones. To properly address AJAX, TAMPERPROOF must allow multiple requests to use the same patchID. To do this while avoiding the problem of replay attacks, we could delay the expiration of a patchID to the first non-AJAX HTTP submission, thereby allowing AJAX submissions until the form itself has been submitted. This expiration policy enables AJAX clients to function properly; however, it also enlarges TAMPERPROOF's attack surface. In the non-AJAX expiration policy, the attacker can submit at most one attack for each patchID (assuming the legitimate user does not submit first), but the AJAX expiration policy allows the attacker to submit as many (AJAX) attacks as possible from the time the user requests the form to the time she submits it. Thus whereas the non-AJAX expiration policy only allows for attacks with a *single* HTTP request, the AJAX expiration policy allows for attacks comprised of *multiple* HTTP-requests.

While this enlarged attack surface is worrisome, it is important to keep in mind what a successful attack requires. First, the attacker must learn the patchID in the usually small window of time between when a legitimate user requests a form and when she submits it. Second, TAMPERPROOF still performs validation on incoming data, so the attacker must find a patchID whose validation is weaker than the validation on forms she has legitimate access to, or there is no point to the attack. Third, the attack does not fool the underlying application into acting as though the request came from the patchID's legitimate owner—it only fools TAMPERPROOF into checking a different set of constraints. Overall, allowing limited AJAX replay attacks

may be a reasonable tradeoff for enabling TAMPERPROOF to properly address Web 2.0 applications.

7. RELATED WORK

Detecting and preventing malicious behavior from clients executing in untrusted environment is a topic of active research. Recently several works [5, 6, 18, 3] have reported severe parameter tampering vulnerabilities in open source applications and commercial websites. These works focus on learning the validations being performed at client and server and generate exploits by comparing them. While preventing attacks that exploit these vulnerabilities (the goal of TAMPERPROOF) is not the focus of the above work, the goals and techniques of that work is worth discussion.

The main difference between tools that detect parameter tampering vulnerabilities and tools that prevent parameter tampering attacks is that false positives (and to a lesser extent false negatives) for detection tools are less serious than for prevention tools. If a detection tool mistakenly signals that a particular input constitutes a parameter tampering attack, the developer/tester using the tool can simply ignore the false positive, but if a prevention tool mistakenly signals that a particular input is an attack and that input is rejected, a real user is prevented from legitimately using the application as it was designed.

The need for high precision results is especially problematic when analyzing web application code, which has significant technical challenges in extracting the constraints that ought to be added to the server's input validation defenses. A web application's code routinely generates code (HTML and to a lesser extent JavaScript), the results of which must be analyzed to extract the constraints imposed by the client. Moreover, the constraints imposed are sometimes dependent on the database, e.g., the client includes a drop-down list populated with credit cards the user has registered with the application (implicitly requiring the user to select one of the entries already present in the database). Finally, the web application code that runs when the user submits a web page may be completely separate from the code that generates that page, thereby requiring analysis that links the page-generation code to the page-submission code. While techniques for addressing these issues have been developed for detection tools, we were not convinced they were sufficiently robust to meet the high standards for precision required of a prevention tool.

TAMPERPROOF was designed as an online tool that analyzes each web page as it is generated. It avoids the problem of analyzing code-generating-code because it only analyzes the output. It avoids the problem of database-dependent constraints (embedded in HTML and non-AJAX JavaScript) because the database constraints have already been incorporated into the HTML and JavaScript that TAMPERPROOF analyzes. TAMPERPROOF addresses the problem of linking page-generation and page-submission code quite directly by using a patchID. Overall, this online approach is only susceptible to false positives to the extent that the HTML/JavaScript analysis is inaccurate.

Taming Online Game Clients. A conceptually closely related line of work [10, 4] aims to curb client-side cheating in online games by constructing a model of proper client behavior against which actual clients are compared. The client codebases of online games are often separate from server and do not evolve over time as web applications do when changes in server-side state often alters HTML and JavaScript. Analyzing web application client offline would require understanding of how the server generates the client and approaches for online game clients do not directly apply to web applications. Instead of this complicated offline analysis, TAMPERPROOF analyzes the client online (i.e., as soon as the server generates the client).

Taming Web Application Clients. Similar efforts have been made to curb malicious client behavior in web applications. Guha et al., [11] compute a model of the expected flow of requests from the client portion JavaScript) of Ajax web applications. Requests that violate the expected flow are rejected. This solution is applicable to web applications that serve static server-side content. It is vulnerable to a class of mimicry attacks that may arise due to imprecisions in static analysis. In contrast, TAMPERPROOF tackles the problem for dynamically generated server-side content. In addition, being a runtime method, it is more precise, at the cost of modest performance overheads.

Ripley. Ripley [17] executes a copy of client side code in a trusted environment to identify differences in outputs of the two clients as malicious behavior. Apart from limitations mentioned in the [17], Ripley requires substantial and careful engineering. Moreover, Ripley requires all "relevant" client events (application specific concept) be transmitted to the server. When the number and frequency of relevant events becomes too high, Ripley becomes impractical (e.g., an online game where all mouse-movement events are relevant.) Finally, Ripley makes no attempt to extract the intended validation encoded in the client which is the main goal of TAMPERPROOF. Consider a simple web form with two fields `beginDate` and `endDate` (associated JavaScript event handler `endDate` is later than `beginDate`). A malicious user can violate the constraint by entering the `endDate` before `beginDate`, as the event handler is only invoked when former is entered. While TAMPERPROOF correctly extracts and enforces the constraint, both actual client and Ripley will accept these malicious inputs.

Bypass-Shield. Bypass-Shield [14] is a direct competitor to TAMPERPROOF: a defense against parameter-tampering attacks deployed in a proxy. There are two main differences between Bypass-Shield and TAMPERPROOF: the class of applications they handle and the manner in which they check whether incoming data satisfies the appropriate constraints. Bypass-Shield employs two distinct phases of deployment: (i) an offline phase where a web crawler searches for web forms and records the constraints each one enforces and (ii) an online phase where the proxy validates incoming data against those constraints. Because all of the form constraints are extracted in an offline approach, Bypass-Shield does not properly deal with forms generated dynamically based on the backend database (e.g. in our running example, the form's drop-down list includes credit card numbers pulled from the database). In contrast, TAMPERPROOF does properly deal with dynamically generated forms because it extracts form constraints each time a form is generated.

Secondly, to validate incoming data against constraints, Bypass-Shield uses a fragment of the original JavaScript on the page; in contrast, TAMPERPROOF extracts a logical representation of the constraints the JavaScript enforces. Bypass-Shield's description in [14] leaves unanswered several basic questions. First, how is the JavaScript code for

validating data identified, i.e., how do they separate validation code from non-validation code, and what happens if non-validation code is interleaved within validation code? Second, even the simplest validation code usually queries the browser's DOM to access the data it is validating; does Bypass-Shield simulate the DOM, or is the JavaScript code rewritten to take the data submitted in the HTTP request as inputs? Third, how does Bypass-Shield cope with the fact that the same data can be validated by JavaScript in multiple ways depending on the order in which the user entered that data (which can happen if the validation is performed in event handlers)? Overall, it is unclear whether this approach is closer to Ripley, attempting to perfectly replicate the data validation behavior of the client (discussed above), or to TAMPERPROOF, which attempts to extract the validation semantics of the JavaScript code and enforce exactly that.

Cross-site Request Forgery Prevention. Both XSRF prevention [13, 12] and TAMPERPROOF augment web forms and check certain properties when they are submitted. The XSRF prevention solutions typically intercept HTTP responses to augment web forms with tokens and intercept HTTP requests to validate tokens. While XSRF prevention solutions disambiguate origin of an HTTP request, TAMPERPROOF checks *semantic* aspects of an HTTP request.

Our instrumentation of forms with patchID is similar to token-based XSRF defenses. Such XSRF defenses obviously fail to prevent parameter tampering attacks, but they can protect against some sequencing attacks, depending on how the XSRF tokens are generated. If the XSRF token is the same for all forms and pages for a user's session, then it does not protect against sequencing attacks (same token can be used in submitting forms that bypass steps in desired sequence) and is therefore strictly weaker than TAMPERPROOF. But if the XSRF token is unique for each form, then it protects against those sequencing attacks that do not violate Value or Field constraints (e.g., tampering hidden fields indicating next step in the sequence). In this sense, TAMPERPROOF offers robust defense against parameter tampering and a certain class of sequencing attacks while also subsuming the protection offered by existing XSRF defenses.

Ensuring Security-by-Construction. Developing secure web applications in a ground up fashion is an exciting area of research and may eliminate vulnerabilities such as parameter tampering. The works in [8, 9, 7] aim to avoid mismatches in logic in various layers of a web application and enforce information flow confidentiality / integrity properties. Although such efforts can eliminate security vulnerabilities in new applications, they are not applicable to existing web applications. TAMPERPROOF is applicable to both new and existing web application that produce clients written in HTML and JavaScript and is independent of the language(s) and architecture used on the server.

Frameworks. To the best of our knowledge, none of the existing Web development frameworks effectively support prevention of parameter tampering in newly developed web applications. Ruby on Rails with the SimpleForm plugin [16] allows a developer to write the constraints that data should satisfy on the server, and enforces those constraints on the client. However, it only supports a handful of built-in validation routines and fails to factor in constraints encoded in HTML form fields that depend on server-side state.

Another related work is Open Web Application Security

Project (OWASP) AppSensor [1]. This project offers recommendations on avoiding parameter tampering vulnerabilities by incorporating detection points and actions in web applications. When compared to TAMPERPROOF, it does not offer automated prevention of parameter tampering attacks and like frameworks is suitable for freshly written applications.

8. CONCLUSION

We presented TAMPERPROOF, an approach to generating per-form patches for preventing parameter tampering exploits. TAMPERPROOF was evaluated on several medium to large applications demonstrating it to be both effective and efficient. As TAMPERPROOF does not require any changes or analysis of server-side source code, it can be deployed in existing proxies and defend any server-side technology or platform. By offering a robust protection that treats the server as a black box, TAMPERPROOF offers an attractive option to protect web applications from parameter tampering attacks.

9. REFERENCES

[1] Open Web Application Security Project (OWASP) AppSensor. https://www.owasp.org/index.php/Category:OWASP_AppSensor_Project.

[2] TAMPERPROOF demo site. http://secwebapps.com, 2012.

[3] ALKHALAF, M., BULTAN, T., CHOUDHARY, S. R., FAZZINI, M., ORSO, A., AND KRUEGEL, C. ViewPoints: Differential String Analysis for Discovering Client and Server-Side Input Validation Inconsistencies. In *ISSTA'12: Proceedings of the 2011 International Symposium on Software Testing and Analysis* (Minneapolis, MN, USA, 2012).

[4] BETHEA, D., COCHRAN, R., AND REITER, M. Server-side Verification of Client Behavior in Online Games. In *NDSS'10: Proceedings of the 17th Annual Network and Distributed System Security Symposium* (San Diego, CA, USA, 2010).

[5] BISHT, P., HINRICHS, T., SKRUPSKY, N., BOBROWICZ, R., AND VENKATAKRISHNAN, V. NoTamper: Automatic Blackbox Detection of Parameter Tampering Opportunities in Web Applications. In *CCS'10: Proceedings of the 17th ACM Conference on Computer and Communications Security* (Chicago, IL, USA, 2010).

[6] BISHT, P., HINRICHS, T., SKRUPSKY, N., AND VENKATAKRISHNAN, V. WAPTEC: Whitebox Analysis of Web Applications for Parameter Tampering Exploit Construction. In *CCS'11: Proceedings of the 18th ACM Conference on Computer and Communications Security* (Chicago, IL, USA, 2011).

[7] CHONG, S., LIU, J., MYERS, A. C., QI, X., VIKRAM, K., ZHENG, L., AND ZHENG, X. Secure Web Application via Automatic Partitioning. *SIGOPS Oper. Syst. Rev. 41*, 6 (2007), 31–44.

[8] COOPER, E., LINDLEY, S., WADLER, P., AND YALLOP, J. Links: Web Programming Without Tiers. In *FMCO'06: Proceedings of the International Symposium on Formal Methods for Components and Objects* (Amsterdam, The Netherlands, 2006).

[9] CORCORAN, B. J., SWAMY, N., AND HICKS, M. Cross-tier, Label-based Security Enforcement for Web Applications. In *SIGMOD'09: Proceedings of the ACM SIGMOD International Conference on Management of Data* (Providence, RI, USA, 2009).

[10] GIFFIN, J. T., JHA, S., AND MILLER, B. P. Detecting Manipulated Remote Call Streams. In *Security'02: Proceedings of the 11th USENIX Security Symposium* (Berkeley, CA, USA, 2002).

[11] GUHA, A., KRISHNAMURTHI, S., AND JIM, T. Using Static Analysis for Ajax Intrusion Detection. In *WWW'09: Proceedings of the 18th International Conference on World Wide Web* (Madrid, Spain, 2009).

[12] JOHNS, M., AND WINTER, J. RequestRodeo: Client Side Protection against Session Riding. In *OWASP'06: Proceedings of the OWASP Europe 2006 Conference* (Leuven, Belgium, 2006).

[13] JOVANOVIC, N., KIRDA, E., AND KRUEGEL, C. Preventing Cross-site Request Forgery Attacks. In *SecureComm'06: Proceedings of the Second IEEE Conference on Security and Privacy in Communications Networks* (Baltimore, MD, USA, 2006).

[14] MOUELHI, T., TRAON, Y. L., ABGRALL, E., BAUDRY, B., AND GOMBAULT, S. Tailored shielding and bypass testing of web applications. In *ICST* (2011), IEEE Computer Society, pp. 210–219.

[15] SAXENA, P., AKHAWE, D., HANNA, S., MAO, F., MCCAMANT, S., AND SONG, D. A Symbolic Execution Framework for JavaScript. In *SP'10: Proceedings of the 31st IEEE Symposium on Security and Privacy* (Oakland, CA, USA, 2010).

[16] Simpleform website. http://blog.plataformatec.com.br/2010/06/simpleform-forms-made-easy/, 2011.

[17] VIKRAM, K., PRATEEK, A., AND LIVSHITS, B. Ripley: Automatically Securing Distributed Web Applications Through Replicated Execution. In *CCS'09: Proceedings of the 16th Conference on Computer and Communications Security* (Chicago, IL, USA, 2009).

[18] WANG, R., CHEN, S., WANG, X., AND QADEER, S. How to Shop for Free Online – Security Analysis of Cashier-as-a-Service Based Web Stores. In *Oakland'11: Proceedings of the 2011 IEEE Symposium on Security and Privacy* (Oakland, CA, USA, 2011).

Cross-Layer Detection of Malicious Websites

Li Xu
Dept. of Computer Science
UT San Antonio
lxu@cs.utsa.edu

Zhenxin Zhan
Dept. of Computer Science
UT San Antonio
zzhan@cs.utsa.edu

Shouhuai Xu
Dept. of Computer Science
UT San Antonio
shxu@cs.utsa.edu

Keying Ye
Dept. of Management Science
and Statistics
UT San Antonio
keying.ye@utsa.edu

ABSTRACT

Web threats pose the most significant cyber threat. Websites have been developed or manipulated by attackers for use as attack tools. Existing malicious website detection techniques can be classified into the categories of static and dynamic detection approaches, which respectively aim to detect malicious websites by analyzing web contents, and analyzing run-time behaviors using honeypots. However, existing malicious website detection approaches have technical and computational limitations to detect sophisticated attacks and analyze massive collected data. The main objective of this research is to minimize the limitations of malicious website detection. This paper presents a novel cross-layer malicious website detection approach which analyzes network-layer traffic and application-layer website contents simultaneously. Detailed data collection and performance evaluation methods are also presented. Evaluation based on data collected during 37 days shows that the computing time of the cross-layer detection is 50 times faster than the dynamic approach while detection can be almost as effective as the dynamic approach. Experimental results indicate that the cross-layer detection outperforms existing malicious website detection techniques.

Categories and Subject Descriptors

K.6.5 [**MANAGEMENT OF COMPUTING AND INFORMA- TION SYSTEMS**]: Security and Protection—*Invasive software*

Keywords

Malicious URL, Cross-layer detection, static analysis, dynamic analysis, hybrid analysis

1. INTRODUCTION

Malicious websites have become a severe cyber threat because they can cause the automatic download and execution of malware in browsers, and thus compromise vulnerable computers [33]. The phenomenon of malicious websites will persevere in the future because we cannot prevent websites from being compromised or abused. For example, Sophos Corporation has identified the percentage of malicious code that is hosted on hacked sites as 90% [38]. Often the malicious code is implanted using SQL injection methods and shows up in the form of an embedded file. In addition, stolen ftp credentials allow hackers to have direct access to files, where they can implant malicious code directly into the body of a web page or again as an embedded file reference. Yet another powerful adversarial technique is obfuscation [37], which is very difficult to cope with. These attacks are attractive to hackers because the hackers can exploit them to better hide the malicious nature of these embedded links from the defenders.

Existing approaches to detect malicious websites can be classified into two categories:

- The *static* approach aims to detect malicious websites by analyzing their URLs [26, 27] or their contents [39]. This approach is very efficient and can scale up to deal with the huge population of websites in cyberspace. This approach however has limited success in coping with the aforesaid sophisticated attacks, and can cause high false-negative rates by classifying malicious websites as benign ones.

- The *dynamic* approach aims to detect malicious websites by analyzing their run-time behaviors using Client Honeypots or their like [17, 18, 19, 29, 40]. This approach is very effective. However, it is resource-consuming because it runs or emulates the browser and possibly the operating system [2], and thus cannot scale up to deal with the large number of websites in cyberspace.

How can we achieve the best of the static and dynamic approaches simultaneously? A simple solution is to run a front-end static analysis tool that aims to rapidly detect suspicious websites, which are then examined by a back-end dynamic analysis tool. However, the effectiveness of this approach is fundamentally limited by the assumption that the front-end static analysis tool has a very low false-negative rate; otherwise, many malicious websites will not be examined by the back-end dynamic analysis tool. Unfortunately, static analysis tools often incur high false-negative rates, especially when malicious websites are equipped with the aforesaid sophisticated techniques. In this paper, we propose a novel technique by which we can simultaneously achieve almost the same effectiveness of the dynamic approach and the efficiency of the static approach. The core idea is to exploit the network-layer or cross-layer information that somehow exposes the nature of malicious websites from a different perspective.

1.1 Our Contributions

We propose an analysis of the corresponding network-layer traffic between the browser and the web server by incorporating the static analysis of website contents. The insight of this approach is that the network-layer may expose useful information about malicious websites from a different perspective. The cross-layer detection is further coupled with the trick of statically tracing redirects, which are embedded into the websites to hide the actual websites that disseminate malwares. That is, the redirection URLs are not obtained via dynamic analysis, but obtained by slightly extending the static analysis method. This allows us to consider not only redirection related features of the present website, but also the redirection website contents.

Evaluation of our approach is based on real data that was collected during the span of 37 days. We found that cross-layer detection can be almost as effective as the dynamic approach and almost as efficient as the static approach, where effectiveness is measured via the vector of (detection accuracy, false-negative rate, false-positive rate). For example, using the dynamic approach as effectiveness base, our data-aggregation cross-layer classifier achieved (99.178%, 2.284%, 0.422%), while the application-layer classifier only achieved (96.394%, 6.096%, 2.933%). Moreover, the XOR-aggregation cross-layer classifier can achieve (99.986%, 0.054%, 0.003%), while subjecting only 0.014% of the websites to the dynamic approach. We also discuss the deployment issues of the cross-layer detection approach. Since performance experiments in Section 4.4 show that cross-layer detection can be 50 times faster than the dynamic approach when processing a batch of URLs, the cross-layer detection approach is very suitable for deployment as a service. Moreover, cross-layer detection incurs no more than 4.9 seconds for processing an individual URL, whereas the dynamic approach takes 20 seconds to process a URL on average. This means that cross-layer detection would be acceptable for real-time detection.

1.2 Related Work

Both industry and academia are actively seeking effective solutions to the problem of malicious websites. Industry has mainly offered their proprietary blacklists of malicious websites, such as Google's Safe Browsing [15] and Mcafee's SiteAdvisor [21]. Effectiveness of the blacklist approach is fundamentally limited by the frequency at which the blacklists are updated and disseminated. This justifies why we advocate pursuing light-weight real-time detection, which is the goal of the present paper.

Researchers have used logistic regression to study phishing URLs [11], which does not consider the issue of redirection. On the other hand, redirection has been used as an indicator of web spams [1, 30, 34, 41]. Kurt et al. [39] presented a system for scalably detecting spam contents. Ma et al. [26, 27] studied how to detect phishing and spams based on URLs themselves.

In terms of detecting malicious websites that may host malwares, Choi et al. [4] investigated the detection of malicious URLs, and Canali et al. [2] presented the design and implementation of a static detection tool called Prophiler. However, these studies did not consider the usefulness of cross-layer detection. On the other hand, the back-end system for deeper analysis is also an active research topic [3, 6, 28, 42], because attackers have been attempting to circumvent dynamic analysis [24, 36].

The rest of the paper is organized as follows. Section 2 describes our cross-layer data collection and analysis methodology. Section 3 investigates two single-layer detection systems. Section 4 presents our cross-layer detection systems. Section 5 explores the deployment of cross-layer detection systems. Section 6 discusses the limitation of the present study and future research directions. Section 7 concludes the present paper.

2. METHODOLOGY

We now describe the methodology underlying our study, including data collection, data pre-processing, evaluation metrics and data analysis methods. The methodology is general enough to accommodate single-layer analyses, but will be extended slightly to accommodate extra ideas that are specific to cross-layer analyses.

2.1 Data Collection

In order to facilitate cross-layer analysis and detection, we need an automated system to collect both the application-layer website contents and the corresponding network-layer traffic. The architecture of our automated data collection system is depicted in Figure 1. At a high level, the data collection system is centered on a crawler. The crawler takes a list of URLs as input, automatically fetches the website contents by launching HTTP requests and tracks the redirects that are identified from the website contents (elaborated below). The crawler also uses the URLs, including the input URL and the detected redirection URLs, to query the DNS, Whois, and Geographic services. This collects information about the registration dates of websites and the geographic locations of the URL owners/registrants. The application-layer website contents and the corresponding network-layer IP packets are recorded separately (where the IP packets are caused by application-layer activities), but are indexed by the input URLs to facilitate cross-layer analysis.

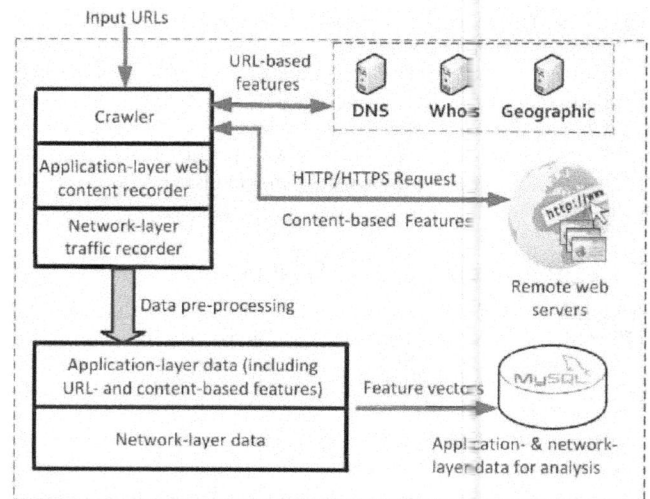

Figure 1: Data collection system architecture.

As mentioned above, the data collection system proactively tracks redirects by analyzing the website contents in a static fashion. Specifically, it considers the following four types of redirects. The first type is the server side redirects, which are initiated either by server rules (i.e., .htaccess file) or by server side page code such as PHP. These redirects often utilize HTTP 300 level status codes. The second type is JavaScript-based redirects. The third type is the refresh Meta tag and the HTTP refresh header, which allow the URLs of the redirection pages to be specified. The fourth type is the embedded file redirects. Some examples of this type are the following: `<script src='badsite.php'> </script>`,

```
<iframe src='badsite.php'/>,
```
and `<img src='badsite.php'/>`.

The input URLs may consist of malicious and benign websites. A URL is malicious if the corresponding website content is malicious or any of its redirects leads to a URL that corresponds to malicious content; otherwise, it is benign. In this paper, the terms *malicious URLs* and *malicious websites* are used interchangeably. In our experimental system for training and testing detection models, malicious URLs are initially obtained from the following blacklists: `compuweb.com/url-domain-bl.txt`, `malware.com.br`, `malwaredomainlist.com`, `zeustracker.abuse.ch` and `spyeyetracker.abuse.ch`. Since some of the blacklisted URLs are not accessible or malicious any more, we use the high-interactive client honeypot called Capture-HPC version 3.0 [17] to identify the subset of URLs that are still accessible and malicious. We emphasize that our experiments were based on Capture-HPC, which is assumed to offer the ground truth. This is a practical choice because we cannot manually analyze the large number of websites. Even if we could, manual analysis might still be error-prone. Note that any dynamic analysis system (e.g., another client honeypot system) can be used instead in a plug-and-play fashion. Pursuing a client honeypot that truly offers the ground truth is an orthogonal research problem. The benign URLs are obtained from `alexa.com`, which lists the top 2,088 websites that are supposed to be well protected. The data was collected for a period of 37 days between 12/07/2011 and 01/12/2012, with the input URLs updated daily.

2.2 Data Pre-Processing

Each input URL has an associated application-layer raw feature vector. The features record information such as HTTP header fields, information returned by DNS, Whois and Geographic services, information about JavaScript functions that are called in the JavaScript code embedded into the website content, and information about redirects (e.g., redirection method, whether or not a redirect points to a different domain, and the number of redirection hops). Since different URLs may lead to different numbers of redirection hops, the raw feature vectors may not have the same number of features. In order to facilitate analysis, we use a pre-processing step to aggregate multiple-hop information into some *artificial* single-hop information. Specifically, for numerical data, we aggregate them by using their average instead; for boolean data, we aggregate them by taking the OR operation; for nominal data, we only consider the final destination URL of the redirection chain. For example, suppose the features of interest are: (`Content-Length`, "Does JavaScript function `eval()` exist in the code?", `Country`). Suppose an input URL is redirected twice to reach the final destination URL, and the raw feature vectors corresponding to the input, first redirect, and second redirect URLs are (100, FALSE, US), (200, FALSE, UK), and (300, TRUE, RUSSIA), respectively. We aggregate the three raw features into a single feature (200, TRUE, RUSSIA). After the pre-processing step, the application-layer data have 105 features, some of which will be elaborated below.

Each input URL has an associated network-layer raw feature vector. The features are extracted from the corresponding PCAP (Packet CAPture) files that are recorded when the crawler accesses the URLs. There are 19 network-layer features that are derived from the IP, UDP/TCP or flow level, where a flow is uniquely identified by a tuple (source IP, source port number, destination IP, destination port number, protocol).

Each URL is also associated with a cross-layer feature vector, which is simply the concatenation of its associated application-layer and network-layer feature vectors.

2.3 Data Description

The resulting data has 105 application-layer features of 4 subclasses and 19 network-layer features of 3 sub-classes. Throughout the paper, "average" means the average over the 37-day data.

2.3.1 Application-Layer Features

Feature based on the URL lexical information.

We defined 15 features based on the URL lexical information, 3 of which are elaborated below.
(A1): `URL_Length`. URLs include the following parts: protocol, domain name or plain IP address, optional port, directory file. When using HTTP Get to request information from a server, there will be an additional part consisting of a question mark followed by a list of "$key = value$" pairs. In order to make malicious URLs hard to blacklist, malicious URLs often include automatically and dynamically generated long random character strings. Our data showed that the average length of benign URLs is 18.23 characters, whereas the average length of malicious URLs is 25.11 characters.
(A2): `Number_of_special_characters_in_URL`. This is the number of special characters (e.g., ?, -, _, =, %) that appear in a URL. Our data showed that benign URLs used on average 2.93 special characters, whereas malicious URLs used on average 3.36 special characters.
(A3): `Presence_of_IP_address_in_URL`. This feature indicates whether an IP address is presented as the domain name in a URL. Some websites use IP addresses instead of domain names in the URL because the IP addresses represent the compromised computers that actually do not have registered domain names. This explains why this feature may be indicative of malicious URLs. This feature has been used in [2].

Features based on the HTTP header information.

We defined 15 features based on the HTTP header information, 4 of which are elaborated below.
(A4): `Charset`. This is the encoding charset of the URL in question (e.g., iso-8859-1). It hints at the language a website uses and the ethnicity of the targeted users of the website. It is also indicative of the nationality of the webpage.
(A5): `HTTPHeader_server`. This is the server field in the http response head. It gives the software information at the server side, such as the webserver type/name and its version. Our data showed that the Top 3 webservers that were abused to host malicious websites are Apache, Microsoft IIS, and nginx, which respectively correspond to 322, 97, and 44 malicious websites on average. On the other hand, Apache, Microsoft IIS, and nginx were abused to host 879, 253, and 357 benign websites on average.
(A6): `HTTPHeader_cacheControl`. Four cache control strategies are identified in the websites of our data: no-cache, private, public, and cache with max-age. The average numbers of benign websites that use these strategies are respectively 444, 276, 67, and 397, whereas the average numbers of malicious websites that use these strategies are respectively 99, 46, 0.5, and 23.
(A7): `HTTPHeader_content_length`. This feature indicates the content-length field of a HTTP header. For malicious URLs, the value of this field may be manipulated so that it does not match the actual length of the content.

Features based on the host information (include DNS, Whois data).

We defined 7 features based on the host information, 5 of which are elaborated below.

(A8-A9): `Whois_regDate` and `Updated_date`. These two features are closely related to each other. They indicate the dates the webserver was registered and updated with the Whois service, respectively. Our data showed that on average, malicious websites were registered in 2004, whereas benign websites were registered in 2002. We also observed that on average, malicious websites were updated in 2009, one year earlier than the average update date of 2010 for benign websites .

(A10-A11): `Whois_country` and `Whois_stateProv`. These two features respectively indicate the counter and the location where the website was registered. These two features, together with the aforementioned `charset` feature, can be indicative of the locations of websites. Our data showed that the average numbers of benign websites registered in US, NL, and AU are respectively 618, 523, and 302, whereas the average numbers of malicious websites registered in US, NL, and AU are respectively 152, 177, and 98.

(A12): `Within_domain`. This feature indicates whether or not the destination URL and the original URL are in the same domain. Redirection has been widely used by both benign and malicious websites. From our data, we found that malicious websites are more often redirected to exploit servers that reside in different domains. Specifically, we found that 21.7% of malicious websites redirect to different domains, whereas 16.1% of benign websites redirect to different domains.

Features based on web content information (including HTML and Script source code).

We defined 68 content-based features, 7 of which are described as follows.

(A13): `Number_of_redirect`. This is the total number of redirects embedded into an input URL. It is indicative of malicious URLs because our data showed that on average, malicious URLs have 0.67 redirects whereas benign URLs have 0.43 redirects. Note that this feature is unique at the application layer because it cannot be precisely obtained at the network layer, which cannot tell a redirect from a normal link.

(A14): `Number_of_embedded_external_URLs`. This feature counts the number of URLs that are embedded into the input URL and use external resources (e.g., image, voice and video). This feature can be indicative of malicious URLs because external URLs are often abused by attackers to import malicious content to hacked URLs.

(A15): `Content_length_valid`. This feature checks the consistency between the `HTTPHeader_content_Length` feature value (i.e., the value of the content length field in HTTP header) and the actual length of web content. It is relevant because the content length field could be a negative number, which may cause buffer overflow attacks. This feature has been used in [4].

(A16): `Number_of_long_strings`. This feature counts the number of long strings used in the JavaScript code that is embedded into the input URL. A string is considered long if its length is greater than 50. Because attackers try to encode some shell code into a string and then use heap-overflow to execute that shell code, this feature can be indicative of malicious URLs as suggested in [2]. Our data showed that the average `Number_of_long_strings` is 0.88 for malicious URLs and 0.43 for benign URLs.

(A17-A18): `Number_of_iframe` and `number_of_small_size_iframe`. These two features respectively count how many iframe and small size iframes are present in a webpage. If any iframe contains malicious code, the URL is malicious. A small size

iframe is even more harmful because it imports malicious content that is invisible to the users.

(A19): `Number_of_suspicious_JS_functions`. This feature [14] indicates whether or not the JavaScript code is obfuscated. In the script block and imported JavaScript files, we check for suspicious JavaScript functions such as `eval()`, `escape()`, and `unescape()`. JavaScript functions are often used by attackers to obfuscate their code and bypass static analysis. For example, `eval()` can be used to dynamically execute a long string at runtime, where the string can be the concatenation of many dynamic pieces of obfuscated substrings at runtime; this makes the obfuscated substrings hard to detect by static analysis.

2.3.2 Network-Layer Features

Features based on remote server attributes.

(N1): `Tcp_conversation_exchange`. This is the total number of TCP packets sent to the remote server by the crawler. Malicious websites often use rich web resources that may cause multiple HTTP requests sent to the webserver. Our data showed the average `Tcp_conversation_exchange` is 73.72 for malicious websites and 693.38 for benign websites.

(N2): `Dist_remote_TCP_port`. This is the total number of distinct TCP ports that the remote webserver used during the conversation with the crawler. Our data showed that benign websites often use the standard http port 80, whereas malicious websites often use some of the other ports. Our data showed the average `Dist_remote_TCP_port` is 1.98 for malicious websites and 1.99 for benign websites.

(N3): `Remote_ips`. This is the number of distinct remote IP addresses connected by the crawler, not including the DNS server IP addresses. Multiple remote IP addresses can be caused by redirection, internal and external resources that are embedded into the webpage corresponding to the input URL. Our data showed the average `Remote_ips` is 2.15 for malicious websites and 2.40 for benign websites.

Features based on crawler-server communication.

(N4): `App_bytes`. This is the number of Bytes of the application-layer data sent by the crawler to the remote webserver, not including the data sent to the DNS servers. Malicious URLs often cause the crawler to initiate multiple requests to remote servers, such as multiple redirections, iframes, and external links to other domain names. Our data showed the average `App_bytes` is 36818 bytes for malicious websites and 53959 bytes for benign websites.

(N5): `UDP_packets`. This is the number of UDP packets generated during the entire lifecycle when the crawler visits a URL, not including the DNS packets. Benign websites running an online streaming application (such as video, audio and internet phone) will generate numerous UDP packets, whereas malicious websites often exhibit numerous TCP packets. Our data showed the average `UDP_packets` for both benign and malicious URLs are 0 because the crawler does not download any video/audio stream from the sever.

(N6): `TCP_urg_packets`. This is the number of urgent TCP packets with the URG (urgent) flag set. Some attacks abuse this flag to bypass the IDS or firewall systems that are not properly set up. If a packet has the URGENT POINTER field set, but the URG flag is not set, this constitutes a protocol anomaly and usually indicates a malicious activity that involves transmission of malformed TCP/IP datagrams. Our data showed the average `TCP_urg_packets` is 0.0003 for malicious websites and 0.001 for benign websites.

(N7): `Source_app_packets`. This is the number of packets send by the crawler to remote servers. Our data showed the average `source_app_packets` is 130.65 for malicious websites and 35.44 for benign websites.

(N8): `Remote_app_packets`. This is the number of packets sent by the remote webserver(s) to the crawler. This feature is unique to the network layer. Our data showed the average value of this feature is 100.47 for malicious websites and 38.28 for benign websites.

(N9): `Source_app_bytes`. This is the volume (in bytes) of the crawler-to-webserver communications. Our data showed that the average application payload volumes of benign websites and malicious websites are about 146 bytes and 269 bytes, respectively.

(N10): `Remote_app_bytes`. This is the volume (in bytes) of data from the webserver(s) to the crawler, which is similar to feature `Source_app_byte`. Our data showed the average value of this feature is 36527 bytes for malicious websites and 49761 bytes for benign websites.

(N11): `Duration`. This is the the duration of time, starting from the point the crawler was fed with an input URL to the point the webpage was successfully obtained by the crawler or an error returned by the webserver. This feature is indicative of malicious websites because visiting malicious URLs may cause the crawler to send multiple DNS queries and multiple connections to multiple web servers, which could lead to a high volume of communications. Our data showed that visiting benign websites caused 0.793 seconds duration time on average, whereas visiting malicious websites caused 2.05 seconds duration time on average.

(N12): `Avg_local_pkt_rate`. This is the average rate of IP packets (packets per second) that are sent from the crawler to the remote webserver(s) with respect to an input URL, which equals `source_app_packets/duration`. This feature measures the packet sending speed of the crawler, which is related to the richness of webpage resources. Webpages containing rich resources often cause the crawler to send a large volume of data to the server. Our data showed the average `Avg_local_pkt_rate` is 63.73 for malicious websites and 44.69 for benign websites.

(N13): `Avg_remote_pkt_rate`. This is the average IP packet rate (in packets per second) of packets sent from the remote server to the crawler. When multiple remote IP addresses are involved (e.g., because of redirection or because the webpage uses external links), we amortize the number of packets, despite the fact that some remote IP addresses may send more packets than others back to the crawler. Websites containing malicious code or contents can cause large volume communications between the remote server(s) and the crawler. Our data showed the average `Avg_remote_pkt_rate` is 63.73 for malicious websites and is 48.27 for benign websites.

(N14): `App_packets`. This is the total number of IP packets generated for obtaining the content corresponding to an input URL, including redirects and DNS queries. It measures the data exchange volume between the crawler and the remote webserver(s). Our data showed the average value of this feature is 63.73 for malicious websites and 48.27 for benign websites.

Features based on crawler-DNS flows.

(N15): `DNS_query_times`. This is the number of DNS queries sent by the crawler. Because of redirection, visiting malicious URLs often causes the crawler to send multiple DNS queries and to connect multiple remote webservers. Our data showed the average value of this feature is 13.30 for malicious websites and 7.36 for benign websites.

(N16): `DNS_response_time`. This is the response time of DNS servers. Benign URLs often have longer lifetimes and their domain names are more likely cached at local DNS servers. As a result, the average value of this feature may be shorter for benign URLs. Our data showed the average value of this feature is 13.29 ms for malicious websites and is 7.36 ms for benign websites.

Features based on aggregated values.

(N17): `Iat_flow`. This is the accumulated inter-arrival time between consecutive flows. Given two consecutive flows, the inter-arrival time is the difference between the timestamps of the first packet in each flow. Our data showed the average `Iat_flow` is 1358.4 for malicious websites and 512.99 for benign websites.

(N18): `Flow_number`. This is the number of flows generated during the entire lifecycle for the crawler to download the web content corresponding to an input URL, including the recursive queries to DNS and recursive access to redirects. It includes both TCP flows and UDP flows, and is a more general way to measure the communications between the crawler and the remote webservers. Each resource in the webpage may generate a new flow. This feature is also unique to the network layer. Our data showed the average `Flow_number` is 19.48 for malicious websites and 4.91 for benign websites.

(N19): `Flow_duration`. This is the accumulated duration of each basic flow. Different from feature `Duration`, this feature indicates the linear process time of visiting a URL. Our data showed the average `Flow_duration` is 22285.43 for malicious websites and 13191 for benign websites.

2.4 Effectiveness Metrics

In order to compare different detection models (or methods, or algorithms), we consider three effectiveness metrics: *detection accuracy*, *false-negative rate*, and *false-positive rate*. Suppose we are given a detection model (e.g., J48 classifier or decision tree), which may be learned from the training data. Suppose we are given test data that consists of d_1 malicious URLs and d_2 benign URLs. Suppose further that the detection model correctly detects d_1' of the d_1 malicious URLs and d_2' of the d_2 benign URLs. The detection accuracy is defined as $\frac{d_1'+d_2'}{d_1+d_2}$. The false-negative rate is defined as $\frac{d_1-d_1'}{d_1}$. The false-positive rate is defined as $\frac{d_2-d_2'}{d_2}$. A good detection model achieves high effectiveness (i.e., high detection accuracy, low false-positive and low false-negative rate).

2.5 Data Analysis Methods

In order to identify the better detection model, we consider four popular machine learning algorithms: Naive Bayes, Logistic regression, Support Vector Machine (SVM) and J48. Naive Bayes classifier is a probabilistic classifier based on Bayes' rule [23]. Logistic regression classifier [25] is a type of linear classifier, where the domain of the target variable is 0, 1. SVM classifier aims to find an maximum-margin hyperplane for separating different classes in the training data [5]. We use the SMO (Sequential Minimal-Optimization) algorithm in our experiment with polynomial kernel function [32]. J48 classifier is an implementation of C4.5 decision trees [35] for binary classification. These algorithms have been implemented in the Weka toolbox [12], which also resolves issues such as missing feature data and conversion of strings to numbers.

In order to know whether using a few features is as powerful as using all features and which features are more indicative of malicious websites, we consider the following three feature selection methods. The first method is Principle Component Analysis (PCA), which transforms a set of feature vectors to a set of shorter feature vectors [12]. The second feature selection method is called "CfsSubsetEval with best-first search method" in the Weka toolbox [12], or `Subset` for short. It essentially computes the features' prediction power according to their contributions [13]. It outputs a subset of features, which are substantially correlated with the class but have low inter-feature correlations. The third feature selection method is called "`InfoGainAttributeEval` with ranker search method" in the Weka toolbox [12], or `InfoGain` for short. Its evaluation algorithm essentially computes the information gain ratio (or more intuitively the importance of each feature) with respect to the class. Its selection algorithm ranks features based on their information gains [7]. It outputs the ranks of all features in the order of decreasing importance.

3. SINGLE-LAYER DETECTION OF MALICIOUS WEBSITES

In this section, we investigate two kinds of single-layer detection systems. One uses the application-layer information only, and corresponds to the traditional static approach. The other uses the network-layer information only, which is newly introduced in the present paper. The latter was motivated by our insight that the network layer may expose useful information about malicious websites from a different perspective. At each layer, we report the results obtained by using the methodology described in Section 2.

The application-layer and network-layer effectiveness results averaged over the 37 days are described in Table 1. For application-layer detection, we make two observations.

- J48 classifier is significantly more effective than the other three detection models, whether feature selection is used or not. However, J48 classifiers may incur somewhat high false-negative rates.

- Feature selection will significantly hurt detection effectiveness, which is true even for J48 classifiers. This means that conducting feature selection at the application layer does not appear to be a good choice.

For network-layer detection, we observe the following:

- J48 classifier is significantly more effective than the other three detection models, whether feature selection is used or not. Note that although Naive Bayes incurs a lower false-negative rate, it has a very low detection accuracy. Similar to what we observed at the application layer, J48 classifier also produces high false-negative rates, meaning that network-layer analysis alone is not sufficient.

- Overall, feature selection hurts detection effectiveness. This also means that conducting feature selection at the network layer is not a good approach.

By comparing the application layer and the network layer, we observed two interesting phenomena. First, each single-layer detection method has some inherent limitation. Specifically, since we were somewhat surprised by the high false-negative and false-positive rates of the single-layer detection methods, we wanted to know whether they are caused by some outliers (extremely high rates for some days), or are persistent over the 37 days. By looking into the data in detail, we found that the false-negative and false-positive rates are reasonably persistent. This means that single-layer detection has an inherent weakness.

Second, we observe that network-layer detection is only slightly less effective than application-layer detection. This confirms our original insight that the network-layer traffic data can expose useful information about malicious websites. Although network-layer detection alone is not sufficient, this paved the way for exploring

the utility of cross-layer detection of malicious websites, which is explored in Section 4.

4. CROSS-LAYER DETECTION OF MALICIOUS WEBSITE

Having shown that network-layer traffic information can give approximately the same detection effectiveness as the application layer, we now show how cross-layer detection can achieve much better detection effectiveness. Given the pre-processed feature vectors at the application and network layers, we extend the preceding methodology slightly to accommodate extra ideas that are specific to cross-layer detection.

- Data-aggregation cross-layer detection: For a given URL, we obtain its cross-layer feature vector by concatenating its application-layer feature vector and its network-layer feature vector. The resultant feature vectors are then treated as the pre-processed data in the methodology described in Section 2 for further analysis.

- OR-aggregation cross-layer detection: For a given URL, if either the application-layer detection model or the network-layer detection model says the URL is malicious, then the cross-layer detection model says the URL is malicious; otherwise, the cross-layer detection model says the URL is benign. This explains why we call this approach OR-aggregation.

- AND-aggregation cross-layer detection: For a given URL, if both the application-layer detection model and the network-layer detection model say the URL is malicious, then the cross-layer detection model says the URL is malicious; otherwise, the cross-layer detection model says the URL is benign. This explains why we call this approach AND-aggregation.

- XOR-aggregation cross-layer detection: For a given URL, if both the application-layer detection model and the network-layer detection model say the URL is malicious, then the cross-layer detection model says the URL is malicious; if both the application-layer detection model and the network-layer detection model say the URL is benign, then the cross-layer detection model says the URL is benign. Otherwise, the cross-layer detection model resorts to the dynamic approach. That is, if the dynamic approach says the URL is malicious, then the cross-layer detection model says the URL is malicious; otherwise, the cross-layer detection model says the URL is benign. We call this approach XOR-aggregation because it is in the spirit of the XOR operation.

We stress that the XOR-aggregation cross-layer detection model resides in between the above three cross-layer detection models and the dynamic approach because it partly relies on the dynamic approach. XOR-aggregation cross-layer detection is practical *only when* it rarely invokes the dynamic approach.

4.1 Overall Effectiveness of Cross-Layer Detection

The effectiveness of cross-layer detection models, averaged over the 37 days, is described in Table 2, from which we make six observations discussed in the rest of this section.

First, data-aggregation cross-layer J48 classifier without using feature selection achieves (99.178%, 2.284%, 0.422%)-effectiveness, which is significantly better than the application-layer J48 classifier that achieves (96.394%, 6.096%, 2.933%)-effectiveness, and is significantly better than the network-layer J48 classifier that achieves

Feature selection?	Naive Bayes			Logistic			SVM			J48		
	Acc (%)	FN (%)	FP (%)	Acc (%)	FN (%)	FP (%)	Acc (%)	FN (%)	FP (%)	Acc (%)	FN (%)	FP (%)
application-layer average detection effectiveness												
none	51.260	11.029	59.275	90.551	22.990	5.692	85.659	55.504	3.068	96.394	6.096	2.933
PCA	67.757	9.998	38.477	91.495	20.526	5.166	89.460	30.031	5.189	95.668	9.537	2.896
Subset	77.962	35.311	18.162	86.864	37.895	6.283	84.688	51.671	5.279	93.581	15.075	3.999
InfoGain	71.702	19.675	30.664	84.895	43.857	7.097	83.733	52.071	6.363	94.737	12.148	3.390
network-layer average detection effectiveness												
none	51.767	0.796	61.645	90.126	21.531	6.630	86.919	24.449	9.986	95.161	9.127	3.676
PCA	67.766	4.017	40.278	87.454	30.651	7.520	85.851	32.957	9.346	89.907	22.587	6.604
Subset	70.188	0.625	38.035	88.141	25.629	8.061	86.534	25.397	10.188	92.415	14.580	5.658
InfoGain	55.533	0.824	56.801	86.756	29.783	8.647	82.822	40.875	10.560	92.853	15.442	4.852

Table 1: Single-layer average effectiveness (Acc: detection accuracy; FN: false negative rate; FP: false positive rate)

(95.161%, 9.127%, 3.676%)-effectiveness. In other words, cross-layer detection can achieve significantly higher effectiveness than the single-layer detection models. This further confirms our motivational insight that the network-layer can expose useful information about malicious websites from a different perspective. This phenomenon can be explained by the low correlation between the application-layer feature vectors and the network-layer feature vectors of the respective URLs. We plot the correlation coefficients in Figure 2, which shows the absence of any correlation because the correlation coefficients fall into the interval of $(-0.4, 0.16]$. This implies that the application layer and the network layer expose different kinds of perspectives of malicious websites, and can be exploited to construct more effective detection models.

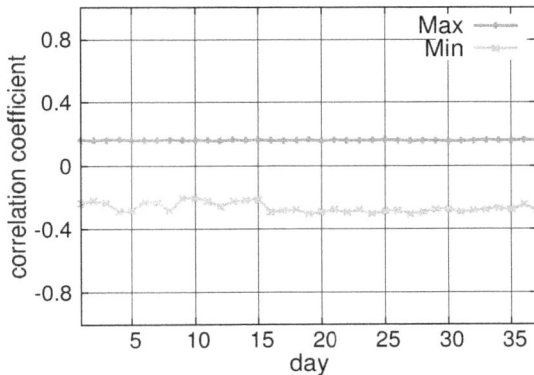

Figure 2: The max and min correlation coefficients between application-layer and network-layer feature vectors.

Second, J48 classifier is significantly better than the other three classifiers, with or without feature selection. Since the above comparison is based on the average over 37 days, we wanted to know whether or not J48 classifier is consistently more effective than the other three classifiers. For this purpose, we looked into the data and found that J48 classifier is almost always more effective than the other three classifiers. Therefore, we recommend to use J48 classifier and will focus on J48 classifier in the rest of the paper.

Third, looking into the day-by-day effectiveness of cross-layer detection models with respect to the InfoGain feature selection algorithm, we found the effect of feature selection to be persistent over the 37 days, especially for the XOR-aggregation cross-layer detection model. This further confirms that feature selection can be adopted in practice.

Fourth, the OR-aggregation cross-layer J48 classifier can achieve significantly lower false-negative rate than the data-aggregation cross-layer J48 classifier, at the price of a lower detection accuracy and a higher false-positive rate. On the other hand, the AND-aggregation

cross-layer J48 classifier can achieve a significantly lower false-negative rate than the data-aggregation cross-layer J48 classifier, at the price of a lower detection accuracy and a higher false-negative rate. This phenomenon can be explained by using the definitions of the effectiveness metrics as follows. For a fixed population of d_1 malicious URLs and d_2 benign URLs, a lower false-negative rate $\frac{d_1-d_1'}{d_1}$ implies a higher d_1'. Since the detection accuracy $\frac{d_1'+d_2'}{d_1+d_2}$ slightly decreases when compared with the data-aggregation cross-layer detection, d_2' must decrease. This means that the false-positive rate $\frac{d_2-d_2'}{d_2}$ increases. In a similar fashion, we can deduce that an increase in false-positive rate can lead to a decrease in the false-negative rate. Thus, cross-layer classifiers offer a spectrum of deployment possibilities, depending on security needs (e.g., a preference for lower false-negative rate or lower false-positive rate). In Section 5, we will explore the deployment issues of the cross-layer detection models.

Fifth, feature selection still hurts cross-layer detection effectiveness, but to a much lesser degree than without feature selection. Indeed, the data-aggregation cross-layer J48 classifier with feature selection is significantly better than the single-layer J48 classifier without using feature selection. Moreover, the data-aggregation cross-layer J48 classifier with feature selection offers very high detection accuracy and very low false-positive rate, the OR-aggregation cross-layer J48 classifier with feature selection offers reasonably high detection accuracy and reasonably low false-negative rate, and the AND-aggregation cross-layer J48 classifier with feature selection offers reasonably high detection accuracy and extremely low false-positive rate. When compared with data-aggregation cross-layer detection, OR-aggregation cross-layer detection has a lower false-negative rate, but a lower detection accuracy and a higher false-positive rate. This can be explained as before.

Sixth and lastly, XOR-aggregation cross-layer detection can achie-

ve almost the same effectiveness as the dynamic approach. For example, it achieves (99.986%, 0.054%, 0.003%) effectiveness without using feature selection, while only losing 100-99.086=0.014% accuracy to the dynamic approach. This means that the J48 classifier with XOR-aggregation can be appropriate for real-world deployment. Also, note that the false-negative rate of the XOR-aggregation J48 classifier equals the false-negative rate of the OR-aggregation J48 classifier. This is because all of the malicious websites which are mistakenly classified as benign by the OR-aggregation J48 classifier are necessarily mistakenly classified as benign by the XOR-aggregation J48 classifier. For a similar reason, we see why the false-positive rate of the XOR-aggregation J48 classifier equals the false-positive rate of the AND-aggregation J48 classifier.

4.2 Which Features Are Indicative?

Identifying the features that are most indicative of malicious web-

Layer	Feature selection?	Naive Bayes			Logistic			SVM			J48		
		Acc (%)	FN (%)	FP (%)	Acc (%)	FN (%)	FP (%)	Acc (%)	FN (%)	FP (%)	Acc (%)	FN (%)	FP (%)
Cross-layer (data-aggregation)	none	55.245	7.961	55.104	96.861	7.945	1.781	94.568	21.227	1.112	99.178	2.284	0.422
	PCA	72.084	4.124	34.659	97.582	5.740	1.481	96.014	9.330	2.492	98.807	3.007	0.692
	Subset	80.396	1.402	24.729	94.568	13.662	3.129	93.296	15.575	4.244	98.335	4.245	0.945
	InfoGain	73.146	1.342	34.069	90.703	22.267	5.693	88.297	26.562	7.571	97.365	6.052	1.685
Cross-layer (OR-aggregation)	none	40.286	0.162	76.437	91.565	6.116	9.104	88.517	7.858	12.542	97.101	0.054	3.708
	PCA	41.582	0.212	74.707	90.039	7.992	10.529	88.342	19.301	9.919	94.251	1.279	7.010
	Subset	57.666	0.065	54.162	88.493	11.460	11.554	86.958	14.154	12.770	94.263	2.615	6.622
	InfoGain	45.276	0.150	70.051	87.342	12.075	12.851	85.266	18.144	13.802	95.129	1.621	5.794
Cross-layer (AND-aggregation)	none	79.097	8.262	24.502	92.528	33.536	0.202	90.335	44.216	0.142	97.888	9.781	0.003
	PCA	79.918	12.428	22.355	90.437	43.244	0.192	85.642	66.755	0.005	94.524	24.998	0.037
	Subset	88.188	17.355	10.246	88.984	49.660	0.300	86.738	60.510	0.205	95.448	20.508	0.111
	InfoGain	83.719	14.269	16.888	87.625	55.774	0.293	84.313	71.175	0.265	95.496	20.685	0.023
Cross-layer (XOR-aggregation)	none	80.861	0.162	24.502	98.510	6.116	0.202	98.186	7.858	0.142	99.986	0.054	0.003
	PCA	82.552	0.212	22.355	98.103	7.992	0.192	96.052	19.301	0.005	99.693	1.279	0.037
	Subset	91.990	0.065	10.246	97.275	11.460	0.300	96.754	14.154	0.205	99.346	2.615	0.111
	InfoGain	86.803	0.150	16.888	97.140	12.075	0.293	95.822	18.144	0.265	99.630	1.621	0.023

Table 2: Cross-layer average effectiveness (Acc: detection accuracy; FN: false-negative rate; FP: false-positive rate). In the XOR-aggregation cross-layer detection, the portions of websites queried in the dynamic approach (i.e., the websites for which the application-layer and cross-layer detection models have different opinions) with respect to the four machine learning algorithms are respectively: without using feature selection, (19.139%, 1.49%, 1.814%, 0.014%); using PCA feature selection, (17.448%, 1.897%, 3.948%, 0.307%); using Subset feature selection, (8.01%, 2.725%, 3.246%, 0.654%); using InfoGain feature section, (13.197%, 2.86%, 4.178%, 0.37%). Therefore, J48 classifier is appropriate for XOR-aggregation.

sites is important because it can deepen our understanding of malicious websites. Principal Components Analysis (PCA) has been widely applied to obtain unsupervised feature selections by using linear dimensionality reduction techniques. However, the PCA-based feature selection method is not appropriate to discover indications of malicious websites. Therefore, this research has focused on Subset and InfoGain.

The Subset feature selection algorithm.

This algorithm selects a subset of features with low correlation while achieving high detection accuracy. Over the 37 days, this algorithm selected 15 to 16 (median: 16) features for the data-aggregation cross-layer detection, and 15 to 21 (median: 18) features for both the OR-aggregation and the AND-aggregation. Since this algorithm selects at least 15 features daily, space limitation does not allow us to discuss the features in detail. Nevertheless, we will identify the few features that are also most commonly selected by the InfoGain algorithm.

The InfoGain feature selection algorithm.

This algorithm ranks the contributions of individual features. For each of the three specific cross-layer J48 classifiers and for each of the 37 days, we used this algorithm to select the 5 most contributive application-layer features and the 4 most contributive network-layer features, which together led to the detection effectiveness described in Table 2. The five most contributive application-layer features are (in descending order): (A1): URL_Length; (A5): HTTPHead_server; (A8): Whois_regDate; (A6): HTTPHead_cacheControl; (A11): Whois_stateProv. The four most contributive network-layer features are (in descending order): (N11): Duration; (N9): Source_app_byte; (N13): Avg_remote_pkt_rate; (N2): Dist_remote_TCP_port.

Intuitively, these features are indicative of malicious websites because during the compromise of browsers, extra communications may be incurred for connecting to the redirection websites while involving more remote TCP ports. We observed that most of the HTTP connections with large (N11): Duration time are caused by slow HTTP responses. This is seemingly because malicious websites usually employ dynamic DNS and Fast-Flush service net-work techniques to better hide from detection. This would also explain why malicious websites often lead to larger values of (N2): Dist_remote_TCP_port. We also observed that malicious websites often have longer DNS query time (1.33 seconds on average) than benign websites (0.28 seconds on average). This can be because the DNS information of benign websites is often cached in local DNS servers, meaning there is no need to launch recursive or iterative DNS queries. Moreover, we observe that malicious websites often incur smaller (N13): Avg_remote_pkt_rate because the average volume of malicious website contents is often smaller than the average volume of benign website contents. Our datasets show that the average volume of malicious website contents is about 36.6% of the average volume of benign website contents.

The most commonly selected features.

Now we discuss the features that are most commonly selected by both feature selection algorithms. On each of the 37 days, the Subset feature selection algorithm selected the aforesaid 15-21 features of the 124 features. Overall, many more features are selected by this algorithm over the 37 days. However, only 5 features were selected every day, where 4 features are from the application layer and 1 feature is from the network layer. Specifically, these features are: (A1): URL_Length; (A5): HTTPHead_server; (A2): Number_of_special_characters_in_URL; (A13): Number_of_redirects; (N1): Duration. These features are indicative of malicious websites because visiting malicious URLs may cause the crawler to send multiple DNS queries and to connect to multiple web servers, which could lead to a high volume of communications.

The InfoGain feature selection algorithm selected the aforesaid 15-16 features out of the 124 application-layer and network-layer features. Overall, only 17 of the 124 features were ever selected, where 6 features are from the application layer and the other 11 features are from the network layer. Three of the aforesaid features were selected every day: (A1): URL_Length, (N1): Duration, (N9): Source_app_byte. As mentioned in the description of the InfoGain feature selection algorithm, (N1): Duration represents one important feature of a malicious web page. As for the (N9): Source_app_byte feature, intuitively,

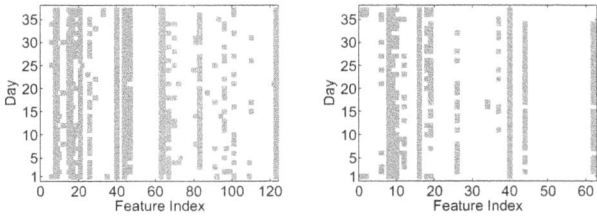

(a) `Subset` feature selection (b) `InfoGain` feature selection

Figure 3: Selected features during the 37 days (features 1-19 correspond to the network-layer features, and features 20-124 correspond to the application-layer features).

malicious web pages that contain rich content (usually phishing contents) can cause multiple HTTP requests.

Overall, the features most commonly selected by the two feature selection algorithms are the aforementioned (**A1**): `URL_Length`, (**A5**): `HTTPHead_server` and (**N1**): `Duration`. This further confirms the power of cross-layer detection. These features are indicative of malicious websites as explained before.

4.3   How Did the Network Layer Help Out?

Previously, we observed the overall effectiveness of cross-layer detection, which at a high level can be attributed to the fact that the network-layer data has a low correlation with the application-layer data (i.e., the network-layer data does expose extra information about websites). Now we give a deeper characterization of the specific contributions of the network-layer information that leads to the correct classification of URLs.

Cross-layer aggregation method	Average correction of FN	Average correction of FP
Data-aggregation	79.59	13.91
OR-aggregation	126.16	N/A
AND-aggregation	N/A	16.23
XOR-aggregation	126.16	16.32

Table 3: Breakdown of the average mis-classifications that were corrected by the network-layer classifiers, where N/A means that the network-layer cannot help (see text for explanation).

Table 3 summarizes the average number of "corrections" made through the network-layer classifiers, where the average is taken over the 37 days. The mis-classifications by the application-layer classifiers are either false-negative (i.e., the application-layer classifiers missed some malicious URLs) or false-positive (i.e., the application-layer classifiers wrongly accused some benign URLs). Note that for OR-aggregation, the network-layer classifiers cannot help correct the FP mistakes made by the application-layer classifiers because the benign URLs are always classified as malicious as long as one classifier (in this case, the application-layer one) says they are malicious. Similarly, for AND-aggregation, the network-layer classifiers cannot help correct the FN mistakes made by the application-layer classifiers because (i) the malicious URLs are always classified as benign unless both kinds of classifiers think they are malicious and (ii) the application-layer classifier already says they are benign. We observe that the contributions of the network-layer classifiers for XOR-aggregation in terms of correcting both FP and FN (126.16 and 16.32, respectively) are strictly more significant than the contributions of the network-layer information for

data-aggregation (79.59 and 13.91, correspondingly). This explains why XOR-aggregation is more effective than data-aggregation.

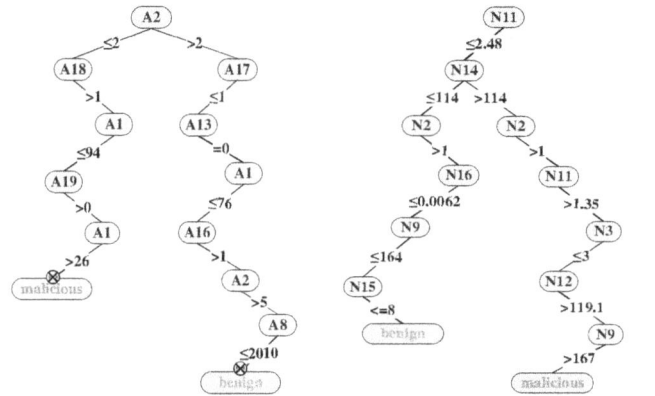

(a) Two mis-classification examples by application-layer classifier (b) Network-layer corrections of the two application-layer mis-classifications

Figure 4: Portions of the application-layer and network-layer classifiers corresponding to the two URLs.

In what follows we examine two example URLs that were mis-classified by the application-layer classifier but corrected through the network-layer classifier. The two examples are among the URLs on the first day data, where one example corresponds to the FP mistake (i.e., the application-layer classifier mis-classified a benign URL as malicious) and the other example corresponds to the FN mistake (i.e., the application-layer classifier mis-classified a malicious URL as benign). The portion of the application-layer classifier corresponding to the two example URLs are highlighted in Figure 4(a), which involves the following features (in the order of their appearances on the paths):

(**A2**)	`Number_of_special_char`
(**A18**)	`Number_of_small_size_iframe`
(**A1**)	`URL_length`
(**A19**)	`Number_of_suspicious_JavaScript_functions`
(**A17**)	`Number_iframe`
(**A13**)	`number_of_redirect`
(**A16**)	`Number_of_long_strings`
(**A8**)	`register_date`

The portions of the network-layer classified corresponding to the two URLs are highlighted in Figure 4(b), which involves the following features (in the order of their appearances on the paths):

(**N11**)	`Duration`
(**N14**)	`App_packets`
(**N2**)	`Dist_remote_TCP_port`
(**N16**)	`DNS_response_time`
(**N9**)	`Avg_local_pkt_rate`
(**N15**)	`DNS_query_times`
(**N3**)	`Remote_ips`
(**N12**)	`Source_app_bytes`

Note that some features can, and indeed often, appear multiple times on a single path.

For the FP mistake made by the application-layer classifier, the feature values are **A2**=0 (no special characters in URL), **A18**=2 (two small iframes), **A1**=61 (medium URL length) and **A19**=4 (four suspicious JavaScript functions), which lead to the left-hand path in Figure 4(a). The application-layer mis-classification may be attributed to **A18**=2 and **A19**=4, while noting that benign websites also use the `eval()` function to dynamically generate code according to certain information about the browser/user and use obfuscation to hide/protect JavaScript source code. On the other hand, the relevant network-layer feature values are $N11$=0.89 seconds (close to 0.793 second, the average of benign URLs), $N14$=79 (close to 63.73, the average of malicious URLs), $N2$=5 (not indicative because it is almost equally close to the averages of both benign URLs and malicious URLs), $N16$=13.11ms (close to 13.29, the average of malicious URLs), $N9$=113 (close to 146, the average of benign URLs), $N15$=6 (close to 7.36, the average of benign URLs). We observe that the three network-layer features, namely $N11$, $N9$ and $N15$, played a more important role in correctly classifying the URL.

For the FN mistake made by the application-layer classifier, $A2$=7 (close to 3.36, the average of malicious URLs), $A17$=0 (indicating benign URL because there are no iframes), $A13$=0 (indicating benign URL because there are no redirects), $A1$=22 (close to 18.23, the average of malicious URLs), $A16$=2 (close to 0.88, the average of malicious URLs), and $A8$=2007 (indicating benign URL because the domain name has been registered for multiple years). The above suggests that $A17$, $A13$ and $A8$ played a bigger role in causing the mis-classification. On the other hand, the relevant network feature values are $N11$=2.13 (close to 2.05, the average of malicious URLs), $N14$=342 (close to 63.73, the average of malicious URLs), $N2$=7 (not very indicative because the respective averages of benign URLs and malicious URLs are about the same), $N3$=3 (close to 2.40, the average of benign URLs), $N12$=289 bytes (relatively close to 63.73, the average of malicious URLs), and $N9$=423 (relatively close to 269, the average of malicious URLs). The above suggests that the network-layer classifier can correct the mistake made by the application-layer classifier because of features $N11$, $N14$, $N12$ and $N9$.

4.4 Performance Evaluation

As discussed in the Introduction, we aim to make our system as fast and scalable as the static approach while achieving as high an effectiveness as the dynamic approach. In the preceding, we have demonstrated that cross-layer J48 classifiers (indeed, all of the cross-layer detection models we investigated) are almost as effective as the dynamic approach. In what follows we report that the cross-layer J48 classifiers are much faster than the dynamic approach and almost as efficient as the static approach.

The time spent on running our system consists of three parts: the time spent for collecting application-layer and network-layer data, the time spent for training the cross-layer J48 classifiers, and the time spent for using the J48 classifiers to classify websites. Since the training of cross-layer J48 classifiers is conducted periodically (e.g., once a day in our experiments), this time is not a significant factor and can be omitted. Nevertheless, we report that the time spent for learning data-aggregation cross-layer J48 classifiers is typically less than 10 seconds on a modest computer when the training dataset has thousands of feature vectors. The training time spent for learning OR-aggregation, AND-aggregation, or XOR-aggregation cross-layer J48 classifiers is about the same. Therefore, we will focus on the time spent for collecting the application-layer and network-layer data corresponding to a given URL and the time spent for classifying the given URL. These two metrics are the most important because they ultimately determine whether the cross-layer J48 classifiers can be deployed for the purpose of real-time detection.

In the afore-reported effectiveness experiments, the cross-layer J48 classifiers and the Capture-HPC client honeypot (as an example of the dynamic approach) were tested on different computers with different hardware configurations. Therefore, we cannot simply measure and compare their respective time complexities. In order to have a fair comparison, we conducted extra experiments by using two computers with the same configuration. One computer ran our cross-layer J48 classifiers and the other computer ran the Capture-HPC client honeypot. The hardware of the two computers is Intel Xeon X3320 4 cores CPU and 8GB memory. We used Capture-HPC version 3.0.0 and VMWare Server version 1.0.6. The Host OS is Windows Server 2008 and the Guest OS is Windows XP sp3. Our crawler was written in JAVA 1.6 and ran on top of Debian 6.0. We used IPTABLES [20] and a modified version of TCPDUMP [22] to parallelize the data collection system. The application-layer features were directly obtained by each crawler instance, but the network-layer features were extracted from the network traffic collected by the TCPDUMP software on the local host. IPTABLES were configured to log network flow information with respect to different processes, which correspond to different crawler instances. Since our crawler is light-weight, we ran 50 instances concurrently in our experiments, whereas we ran 5 guest Operating Systems to parallelize the Capture-HPC. Experimental results indicated that more guest Operating Systems make the system unstable. Both computers used network cards with 100Mbps network cable.

Data-aggregation cross-layer J48 classifier	
Total data collection time	4 min
Total classification time	302 ms
Total time	≈ 4 min
Capture-HPC	
Total time	199min

Table 4: Measured performance comparison between the data-aggregation cross-layer J48 classifier and the dynamic approach (the Capture-HPC client honeypot) with 3,062 input URLs (1,562 malicious URLs + 1,500 Benign URLs)

Table 4 describes the performance of the cross-layer J48 classifier and of the Capture-HPC client honeypot. It took the data-aggregation cross-layer J48 classifier about 4 minutes to process the 3,062 input URLs, whereas it took the Capture-HPC 199 minutes to process the same 3,062 URLs. In other words, the cross-layer detection approach can be about 50 times faster than the dynamic approach, while achieving about the same detection effectiveness.

The preceding conclusion that the cross-layer detection approach is faster than the dynamic approach was based on batch processing of 3,062 URLs. To compare processing times for individual URLs, we approximately broke down the performance as follows, where *approximation* is caused by the concurrent executions of the respective systems. Specifically, the time for the data-aggregation cross-layer J48 classifier to determine whether a given website is malicious or not is calculated as $240/(3062/50) \approx 3.92$ seconds because each crawler actually processed 3062/50 URLs on average. Among the 3.92 seconds, on average 2.73 seconds were actually spent on downloading the website content, which means that 1.19 seconds were spent for feature extractions, etc. Similarly, the time for Capture-HPC to determine whether a given website is malicious or not is $(199 \times 60)/(3062/5) = 19.5$ seconds because 5 Capture-HPC instances ran concurrently. The reason why Capture-HPC is slow is because Capture-HPC spent much time on receiving all the diagnostic results caused by visiting URLs in the virtual machine and reverting the virtual machine back to a clean snapshot whenever a URL was deemed to be malicious. Moreover, the XOR-aggregation cross-layer J48 classifier without feature selection would only incur the dynamic approach to analyze, on average, about $5.04\% \times 3062 \approx 154$ websites. This means that even for XOR-aggregation, the processing time per URL is no more than $3.92 + 19.5 \times 154/3062 \approx 4.9$ seconds. Therefore, we conclude that even if the cross-layer detection system runs within each individual computer, rather than a third-party server, it is about 4 times faster than the dynamic approach. In any case, 4 seconds waiting time is arguably acceptable, especially since we can let the browser start displaying the portions of website content that have no security concerns. This is reasonable because the same idea has been used to give users the illusion that website contents are displayed almost instantly, but actually it takes a few seconds to display the entire website contents. On the other hand, waiting for 19.5 seconds for the dynamic approach to test whether a website is malicious or not is not reasonable, which perhaps explains why the dynamic approach, while powerful, is not used for real-time detection in practice.

5. DEPLOYMENT

Cross-layer detection offers a spectrum of deployment options. It can be deployed as a stand-alone solution because it is highly effective as analyzed before. Moreover, it can be deployed as a light-weight front-end detection system of a bigger solution (see Figure 5), which aims at detecting as many malicious websites as possible while scaling up to a large population of websites. For this purpose, the data-aggregation and the OR-aggregation method would be efficient. Moreover, the XOR-aggregation is particularly effective and should be deployed when it only incurs the back-end dynamic approach occasionally.

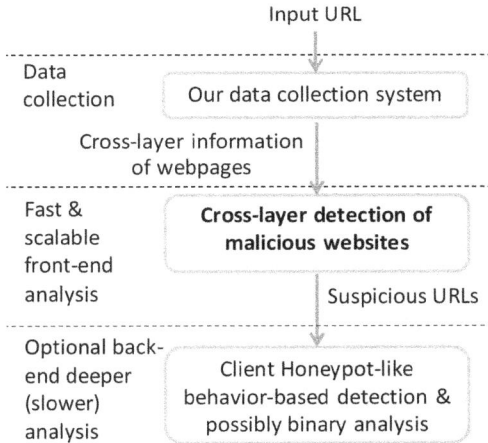

Figure 5: Example deployment of the cross-layer detection system as the front-end of a bigger solution because XOR-aggregation J48 classifiers achieve extremely high detection accuracy, extremely low false-negative and false-positive rates.

There are several ways to deploy the physical components of the cross-layer detection service. Recall that our system has three components: application-layer data collector (i.e., crawler), network-layer traffic recorder, and cross-layer data correlator. The crawler takes URLs as input, fetches the corresponding website contents, and conducts a light-weight analysis to identify the redirects that are embedded into the website contents. The traffic recorder collects the network traffic corresponding to the crawler's activities in fetching the website contents. The cross-layer data correlator relates the application-layer website contents to the corresponding network-layer traffic via the input URLs. These components may or may not be deployed on the same physical computer, as the following scenarios demonstrate.

First, we can deploy the stand-alone cross-layer detection system as a web browser plug-in. In this case, the detection system can test whether the website is malicious or not before the browser actually displays the website content. If it is malicious, the browser can take appropriate actions according to a pre-determined policy (e.g., warning the user that the website is malicious). The plug-in should collect the network-layer traffic corresponding to the application-layer website content of the given URL. The plug-in also may act as the network-layer traffic collector and the cross-layer correlator. Moreover, network-traffic could be collected at some routers or gateways, from which the plug-in can obtain the traffic corresponding to the application-layer website content.

Second, we can deploy the cross-layer detection system as an online service. This service may be accessed by web browsers via the proxy or gateway technique. Specifically, when a user browser points to a URL, the corresponding website will be analyzed by the cross-layer detection service, which will then communicate the outcome back to the browser. The browser can take appropriate actions based on its pre-determined policy (e.g., displaying the website or not).

Third, we can deploy the cross-layer detection system at the website hosting server itself. The website hosting service vendor might have the incentive for proactively examining whether the websites it hosts have been compromised, because this might enhance the reputation of the vendor. In this case, the vendor can deploy it as a front-end to a bigger detection system, or deploy it as a stand-alone system.

6. SUGGESTIONS FOR FUTURE WORK

A key limitation of the present study is that, as pointed out in [24, 36], the (back-end) dynamic approach itself may have its own non-zero false-negative and false-positive rates. While studying the dynamic approach is an orthogonal issue, we suggest a future study on the impact of false-negatives and false-positives incurred in the dynamic approach, with an emphasis on Capture-HPC.

Another problem of interest for future work is to learn to what extent the effectiveness of cross-layer detection systems can be improved by incorporating new techniques such as those described in [6, 8, 16, 31].

Our cross-layer detection system provides a best-effort capability by statistically tracking the redirects that are embedded into the website contents. It is difficult to statistically detect obfuscated JavaScript-based redirects [10, 9]. Even though the effectiveness of our cross-layer detection system is almost as good as the dynamic approach, it would be useful in future work to determine the impact of progress made in the direction of detecting obfuscated JavaScript-based redirects. This is an important issue because, although our collected data hints that JavaScript-based redirection is widely used by malicious websites, it appears that JavaScript obfuscation may not have been widely used because our system can effectively detect the malicious URLs (almost as effectively as the dynamic approach which is capable of dealing with redirects). However, this may not remain true if in the future such redirects may be more widely exploited by the adversary. Fortunately, any progress in dealing with obfuscated redirects can be adopted by our system in a plug-and-play fashion.

7. CONCLUSIONS

We presented a novel approach to detecting malicious websites based on the insight that network-layer traffic data may expose useful information about websites, which may be exploited to attain cross-layer detection of malicious websites. Experimental results showed that cross-layer detection can achieve almost the same detection effectiveness, but about 50 times faster than, the dynamic approach based on client honeypot systems. Moreover, the cross-layer detection systems can also be deployed to detect malicious websites in real time because the average time for processing a website is approximately 4.9 seconds, which could be improved with some engineering optimization.

8. ACKNOWLEDGMENTS

This work was supported in part by the U.S. Air Force Office of Scientific Research (AFOSR) under Grant No. AFOSR-FA9550-09-1-0165. We thank Ninghui Li for his guidance and the anonymous reviewers for their constructive comments.

9. REFERENCES

[1] A. A. Benczur, K. Csalogany, T. Sarlos, and M. Uher. SpamRank - fully automatic link spam detection. In *AIRWeb'05*, 2005.

[2] D. Canali, M. Cova, G. Vigna, and C. Kruegel. Prophiler: a fast filter for the large-scale detection of malicious web pages. In *WWW'11*, pages 197–206. ACM, 2011.

[3] K. Z. Chen, G. Gu, J. Nazario, X. Han, and J. Zhuge. WebPatrol: Automated collection and replay of web-based malware scenarios. In *ASIACCS'11*, pages 186–195, 2011.

[4] H. Choi, B. B. Zhu, and H. Lee. Detecting malicious web links and identifying their attack types. In *WebApps'11*, pages 11–11, 2011.

[5] C. Cortes and V. Vapnik. Support-vector networks. In *Machine Learning*, pages 273–297, 1995.

[6] M. Cova, C. Kruegel, and G. Vigna. Detection and analysis of drive-by-download attacks and malicious javascript code. In *WWW'10*, pages 281–290, 2010.

[7] T. M. Cover and J. A. Thomas. *Elements of Information Theory*. Wiley-Interscience, New York, NY, USA, 1991.

[8] C. Curtsinger, B. Livshits, B. Zorn, and C. Seifert. ZOZZLE: Fast and precise in-browser javascript malware detection. In *USENIX Security*, 2011.

[9] A. Dewald, T. Holz, and F. C. Freiling. Adsandbox: Sandboxing javascript to fight malicious websites. In *SAC'10*, pages 1859–1864, 2010.

[10] B. Feinstein and D. Peck. Caffeine Monkey: Automated collection, detection and analysis of malicious javascript. In *Black Hat'07*, 2007.

[11] S. Garera, N. Provos, M. Chew, and A. D. Rubin. A framework for detection and measurement of phishing attacks. In *WORM'07*, pages 1–8, 2007.

[12] M. Hall, E. Frank, G. Holmes, B. Pfahringer, P. Reutemann, and I. H. Witten. The weka data mining software: an update. *SIGKDD Explor. Newsl.*, pages 10–18, 2009.

[13] M. A. Hall. *Correlation-based Feature Subset Selection for Machine Learning*. PhD thesis, University of Waikato, Hamilton, New Zealand, 1998.

[14] Y.-T. Hou, Y. Chang, T. Chen, C.-S. Laih, and C.-M. Chen. Malicious web content detection by machine learning. *Expert Syst. Appl.*, pages 55–60, January 2010.

[15] Google Safe Browsing API. http://goo.gl/tsXz2.

[16] The Ultimate Deobfuscator. http://goo.gl/KVM8w.

[17] Capture - Honeypot Client (Capture-HPC). http://goo.gl/u7qJz.

[18] Know your enemy: Malicious web servers. http://goo.gl/tfxQl.

[19] Know your enemy: Behind the scenes of malicious web servers. http://goo.gl/MNfTY.

[20] netfilter - iptables. http://goo.gl/bfh6F.

[21] McAfee SiteAdvisor. http://goo.gl/cfjC.

[22] Tcpdump & libcap. http://goo.gl/vt2W.

[23] G. H. John and P. Langley. Estimating continuous distributions in Bayesian classifiers. *UAI*, pages 338–345, 1995.

[24] A. Kapravelos, M. Cova, C. Kruegel, and G. Vigna. Escape from monkey island: Evading high-interaction honeyclients. In *DIMVA'11*, 2011.

[25] S. le Cessie and J. van Houwelingen. Ridge estimators in logistic regression. *Applied Statistics*, pages 191–201, 1992.

[26] J. Ma, L. K. Saul, S. Savage, and G. M. Voelker. Beyond blacklists: Learning to detect malicious web sites from suspicious urls. In *KDD'09*, pages 1245–1254, 2009.

[27] J. Ma, L. K. Saul, S. Savage, and G. M. Voelker. Identifying suspicious urls: an application of large-scale online learning. In *ICML'09*, pages 681–688, 2009.

[28] T. F. Mario Heiderich and T. Holz. IceShield: Detection and mitigation of malicious websites with a frozen DOM. In *RAID'11*, pages 281–300, 2011.

[29] J. Nazario. PhoneyC: a virtual client honeypot. In *LEET'09*, 2009.

[30] Y. Niu, Y. min Wang, H. Chen, M. Ma, and F. Hsu. A quantitative study of forum spamming using contextbased analysis. In *NDSS'07*, 2007.

[31] W. Palant. JavaScript Deobfuscator. http://goo.gl/u80Va.

[32] J. C. Platt. Fast training of support vector machines using sequential minimal optimization. In *Advances in Kernel Methods*, pages 185–208. MIT Press, 1999.

[33] N. Provos, P. Mavrommatis, M. A. Rajab and F. Monrose. All your iframes point to us. In *USENIX Security*, 2008.

[34] Z. Qian, Z. M. Mao, Y. Xie, and F. Yu. On network-level clusters for spam detection. In *NDSS'10*, 2010.

[35] R. Quinlan. *C4.5: Programs for Machine Learning*. Morgan Kaufmann Publishers Inc., San Mateo, CA, 1993.

[36] M. Rajab, L. Ballard, N. Jagpal, P. Mavrommatis, D. Nojiri, N. Provos, and L. Schmidt. Trends in circumventing web-malware detection. Technical report. Google, 2011.

[37] K. Rieck, T. Krueger, and A. Dewald. Cujo: efficient detection and prevention of drive-by-download attacks. In *ACSAC'10*, pages 31–39, 2010.

[38] Sophos Corporation. Security Threat Report Update 07/2008. http://goo.gl/pg8HE.

[39] K. Thomas, C. Grier, J. Ma, V. Paxson, and D. Song. Design and evaluation of a real-time url spam filtering service. In *S&P'11*, 2011.

[40] Y.-M. Wang, D. Beck, X. Jiang, and R. Roussev. Automated web patrol with strider honeymonkeys: Finding web sites that exploit browser vulnerabilities. In *NDSS'06*, 2006.

[41] C. Whittaker, B. Ryner, and M. Nazif. Large-scale automatic classification of phishing pages. In *NDSS'10*, 2010.

[42] J. Zhang, C. Seifert, J. W. Stokes, and W. Lee. ARROW: Generating signatures to detect drive-by downloads. In *WWW'11*, pages 187–196, 2011.

A File Provenance System

Salmin Sultana
Purdue University
ssultana@purdue.edu

Elisa Bertino
Purdue University
bertino@cs.purdue.edu

ABSTRACT

A file provenance system supports the automatic collection and management of provenance i.e. the complete processing history of a data object. File system level provenance provides functionality unavailable in the existing provenance systems. In this paper, we discuss the design objectives for a flexible and efficient file provenance system and then propose the design of such a system, called FiPS. We design FiPS as a thin stackable file system for capturing provenance in a portable manner. FiPS can capture provenance at various degrees of granularity, can transform provenance records into secure information, and can direct the resulting provenance data to various persistent storage systems.

Categories and Subject Descriptors

C.5 [**Computer System Implementation**]: General

General Terms

Reliability, Security

Keywords

Data Provenance, Operating Systems, File System

1. INTRODUCTION

Provenance refers to the history of ownership and the actions performed on a data object. Provenance has been widely used in the scientific and grid computing domains in order to document workflows, data generation, and processing. For scientific experiments, provenance contains input datasets, experimental procedures, parameters, etc. information which are sufficient to enable reproduction and validation of results [1]. A number of domain specific provenance systems, such as Chimera [2], ESSW [3] have been developed for various experimental systems. They capture provenance for scientific data and record provenance at the semantic level of application. Other application level provenance systems capture provenance at the level of business objects, lines of source code or other units with semantic meaning to the application. The fundamental problem with domain-specific approaches is that the data object and the provenance are managed by two separate data management systems (i.e. data by file system and provenance by database

system) [5]. Consequently, data and provenance do not remain tightly coupled and thus the provenance may not completely reflect the data processing history. Moreover, the application specific provenance systems require the users to manually track provenance by building appropriate provenance collection tools. In this context, it has been suggested that the provenance collection should be a responsibility of the operating system (OS) that can also generate system level provenance meta data [5].

In this paper, we propose the design of a *file provenance system*, named as FiPS, which is a file system that not only manages files but also transparently captures, stores and manages the file provenance. FiPS autonomically collects sufficient metadata in order to recreate a file i.e. to re-enact the series of actions that generated the content of the file. We design FiPS as a thin layer operating between the *Virtual File System* (VFS) and the underlying file system. In contrast to a system-call based provenance approach [5], we intercept file system calls passed through the VFS layer and then generate provenance records. System call level approaches often fail to see how a system call activity is translated into multiple actions in the lower layers of the OS. Memory-mapped I/O can only be traced at the file system level. In addition, server-side operations of network file system (NFS) are performed directly in the kernel, not through system calls.

To make the provenance system useful, we also incorporate *flexibility* and *security* into our design. To be flexible, FiPS allows provenance to be captured based on fine-grained conditions. This feature also helps capture and store only desired information, making the solution efficient in space and time. To be *secure*, FiPS can apply appropriate security function on a file provenance in order to protect it from unauthorized access. The system can also write provenance to a local or networked storage. Our implementation is still a work in progress. To layer FiPS on top of any conventional file system, we implement our functionalities on the stackable wrapper file system *Wrapfs* [6]. We use in-kernel Berkeley DB [4] to manage granularity and security policies.

2. DESIGN OBJECTIVES

Based on the features of the existing file system provenance solutions and their limitations, we outline the following design goals required to build a robust file provenance system:

Portability: The file provenance system should capture provenance for any file system, without modifying the OS or the provenanced file system. FiPS is designed as a stackable filesystem and thus can be layered on top of any conventional file system. In addition, FiPS is to be implemented as a kernel module which requires no kernel modification in order to collect provenance.

Efficiency: It is essential that provenance capture and management do not add too much overhead to the file system operations with respect to space and time. The provenance system should provide fast, high-throughput provenance operations in order to avoid impacting operating system and application performance. The system must record enough provenance metadata to serve the desired purpose but not any unintended information. Hence, it should distinguish between data objects that are required to be provenanced and data objects that are not. On the other hand, capturing provenance information by intercepting system calls often misses information about how a system call activity is translated into multiple actions in the lower layers of the OS. Also NFS servers cannot work with system call level logging since they operate directly in kernel, not through system calls. Finally, it is more natural to manage file system provenance in terms of file system instead of system calls. We design FiPS as a thin layer between the Virtual File System (VFS) and any other file system which results in space and time efficiency.

Flexibility: Traditionally provenance-aware file systems collect a specific detail of the provenanced objects which in some cases are inadequate. On the other hand, PASS captures a good amount of information for each provenanced object which results in a huge volume of provenance records when integrated with an end-to-end provenance solution. To be productive, the provenance system should be flexible by supporting a wide range of fine grained policies on provenance collection. The policies should allow one to specify the granularity of provenance information to be captured based on applications, users, file names, attributes, etc.

Security: The system must capture and store provenance in a way so that the information is kept secure against attacks and subversion. Besides, the provenance information may require access control to be protected from unauthorized user access. Our in-kernel system design provides stronger security. Moreover, we incorporate security policies used to apply appropriate security mechanisms (e.g. encryption, signature) while sending provenance to persistent storage.

Redundancy Elimination: Recording provenance for file system operations may result in large amount of data which are difficult to store, manage and query efficiently and effectively. Hence, mechanisms for provenance pruning or compression should be provided, e.g., for replacing a part of the provenance graph with the end result of the modification.

Queries on Provenance: Collecting data provenance is not useful unless the provenance can be accessed and utilized easily. Hence, the file provenance system must provide support for a structured storage of provenance which in turn will facilitate provenance queries. The management system should also respond quickly to the relationship queries leading to the generation of ancestry or descendancy graphs.

3. FIPS - THE PROPOSED PROVENANCE FRAMEWORK

FiPS is designed to collect and store provenance for the data objects at a file granularity. However, the provenance can be tracked easily at finer or coarser granularities by defining the granularity policies accordingly. We define the *provenance of a data object (file) as the documented history of the actors, process, operations, inter-process/operation communications, input/output data, the hardware and OS environment related to the creation and modification of the object.* The complete provenance of a data object form a directed acyclic graph (DAG), referred to as the *provenance graph.*

We design FiPS as a stackable file system [6] that can work on top of any underlying file system. Figure 1(a) shows how FiPS is placed between the *Virtual File System* (VFS) and any other file system. In a traditional file system, the system calls related to file operations invoke VFS calls which in turn invoke underlying file system procedures. When integrated, FiPS intercepts the VFS calls, extract arguments and other necessary information from kernel data structures, and translates them into in-memory provenance records. While recording the provenance metadata for a data object, the level of details to be stored is determined according to the associated granularity policy. At the end, FiPS sends the in-memory provenance records to a persistent storage, either to a local disk or to a remote server.

Figure 1(b) shows the detailed architecture of the FiPS layer. The key components are: the provenance *logger* which records the provenance metadata and translates them into in-memory provenance records, and the provenance *writer* that stores in-memory records into persistent storage. To control the granularity and security of provenance, the components act upon two databases: the *granularity policy DB* and the *security policy DB*, respectively. Below, we briefly discuss the components and the policy databases:

Logger: The role of a logger is to record provenance data or VFS calls and then to ensure that these records are passed to the destination file system for attachment to the appropriate files. FiPS supports multiple *logger* threads where the intercepted VFS calls pertaining to an application/process will be handled by one *logger*. Such a design will increase the speed of the provenance tracking for simultaneous processes and make it easier to deal with the granularity policies.

As in PASS, all files and processes in our system are considered provenanced kernel objects. The logger generates a provenance record for each provenance related VFS call and stores the record in an intermediate storage. This intermediate storage may be a buffer or in-kernel Berkeley Database (KBDB). The metadata to be captured in the provenance record may vary depending on the associated granularity policy. For example, a provenance record may include a subset of Process ID, input files, User ID, command line, kernel version, etc. information. In addition, granularity policies may specify when the system should not capture provenance (e.g. for a particular application, file, etc.) or when the intermediate results should not be recorded, etc. Unlike PASS, our system can distinguish between provenanced and non-provenanced file systems and does not retain provenance in memory for non-provenanced files.

Granularity Policy DB: This database stores the granularity policies which determine how much information has to be captured as provenance. The policies may be associated with a process, application, user, file or file attributes. The policy database may be populated with policies during

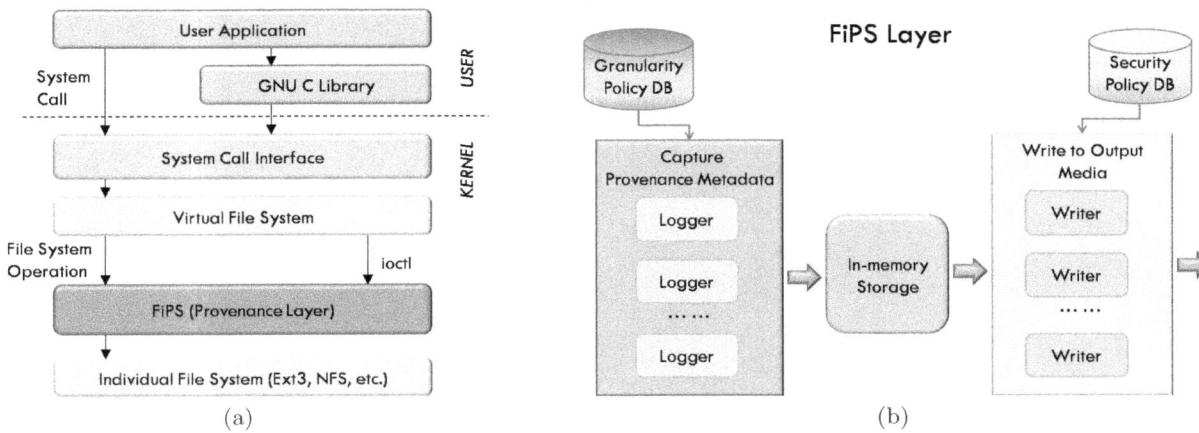

Figure 1: (a) FiPS as a stackable file system. (b) Architecture of the FiPS layer.

the OS start or with application specific policies when the application executes.

We design this database as an in-kernel Berkeley DB. The policy database has the *object* and the unique *object ID* (e.g. file and inode) as the key and a 4 or 8 byte value containing the policy bits as the data. The policy bits include: (i) OBJECT - specifies the object for which the policy is defined; (ii) ATTRIBUTES - the set of attributes of the respective objective, used to check the condition in the policy; (iii) ACTION - specifies the action taken if the condition is satisfied. The actions include *capture-all, no-capture, capture-set, no-intermediate-data*, etc.

Security Policy DB: This database, also designed as a KBDB, stores security policies which are applied to the in-memory provenance records when they are stored in a persistent storage. The design of the database is similar to the granularity policy DB with a difference in the taken actions. The actions here include applicable security mechanisms, such as *encryption, signature*, etc.

Writer: A writer writes out the in-memory provenance records to the persistent storage. The output media may be a regular file on local disk, a raw device or a socket. When writing to a socket, the writer connects to a TCP socket at a remote location and sends the provenance over the network. This is particularly useful when storing provenance in a remote NFS server. To ensure desired security for the provenance, the writer first finds out the security policy associated with the provenanced data object, performs the security action and then writes the secure provenance to the destination storage. The system activates multiple writers to fasten the performance.

In addition, we include a *redactor* which compresses and prunes long term history for older files. The redactor may be a user level or a system process. Provenance pruning/compression may be managed by the system wide retention policies or user-specified policies for a file, a group of files, or a directory. The redactor periodically examines the file system and uses the policies to decide when and which files can be left to carry on with a compressed provenance graph. This approach allows users to indicate the files for which it is required to keep detailed provenance and versioning information.

4. CONCLUSION

We present the modular design of a low-overhead and flexible file provenance system (FiPS) that collects provenance by operating below the VFS layer. Unlike system call tracing, FiPS can handle memory mapped I/O and NFS server operations easily. FiPS incorporates granularity policies which provides flexibility in provenance capturing and security policies to ensure the desired security. Currently, we are implementing the system which is bringing forth various design and implementation issues. In future, we plan to extend the system to collect provenance at virtual machine monitors.

5. ACKNOWLEDGMENTS

The work reported in this paper has been partially funded by NSF under Award 1111512 "Privacy-Enhanced Secure Data Provenance".

6. REFERENCES

[1] P. Buneman, S. Khanna, and W.-c. Tan. Why and where: A characterization of data provenance. *ICDT*, 1973:316–330, 2001.

[2] I. Foster, J. Vöckler, M. Wilde, and Y. Zhao. Chimera: A virtual data system for representing, querying, and automating data derivation. In *Proc. of the Conference on Scientific and Statistical Database Management (SSDBM)*, pages 37–46, 2002.

[3] G. Janée, J. Mathena, and J. Frew. A data model and architecture for long-term preservation. In *Proc. of the conference on Digital libraries*, pages 134–144, 2008.

[4] A. Kashyap. File system extensibility and reliability using an in-kernel database. Technical Report FSL-04-06, Master's Thesis, Stony Brook University, 2004.

[5] K.-K. Muniswamy-Reddy, D. Holland, U. Braun, and M. Seltzer. Provenance-aware storage systems. In *Proc. of the USENIX Annual Technical Conference*, 2006.

[6] E. Zadok and I. Badulescu. A stackable file system interface for linux. Technical Report CUCS-021-98, Columbia University, 1998.

Enhancing Performance of Searchable Encryption in Cloud Computing

Razvan Rughinis
"POLITEHNICA" University of Bucharest, Romania
razvan.rughinis@cs.pub.ro

ABSTRACT

Predicate evaluation on encrypted data is a challenge that modern cryptography is starting to address. The advantages of constructing logical primitives that are able to operate on encrypted data are numerous, such as allowing untrusted parties to take decisions without actually having access to the plaintext. Systems that offer these methods are grouped under the name of searchable encryption systems. One of the challenges that searchable encryption faces today is related to computational and bandwidth costs, because the mathematical operations involved are expensive. Recent algorithms such as Hidden Vector Encryption exhibit improved efficiency, but for large scale systems the optimizations are often not enough. Many problems that can be solved using searchable encryption are embarrassingly parallel. Using a prototype, we show that parallel solutions offer sufficient cost reduction so that large scale applications become feasible.

Keywords

Searchable encryption, Hidden Vector Encryption, performance evaluation, parallel

Categories and Subject Descriptors

E.3 [**Data encryption**]: Public key cryptosystems

1. INTRODUCTION

Present day security demands have encouraged the development of new cryptographic primitives that can perform queries on encrypted data. Such primitives are known by the name of searchable encryption, as they do not require decryption of the data for search. Most systems are based on public-key cryptography, although symmetric systems have also been built.

Searchable encryption usage scenarios are summarized in Fig. 1, where the data transferred from a *Sender* to a *Receiver* must be filtered at an untrusted cloud gateway server. The gateway has to make a decision based on the encrypted contents, without actually decrypting data. For example, say John (the receiver) receives an e-mail from a business partner (the sender). The e-mail is encrypted using John's public key. He wants to automatically redirect messages that contain certain words in the title to another e-mail account, but the server is unable to perform this check on the e-mail without John's secret key, and he is unwilling to share it because it would be a clear violation of security guidelines. The solution is to give the server a predicate, encrypted with the secret key, that

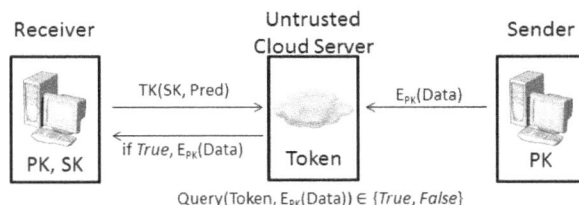

Figure 1: Searchable Encryption Example

the server can later use to perform checks on the encrypted e-mails without actually deciphering them.

Searchable encryption systems use a ciphertext that is composed of two parts, the encrypted index I and the encrypted message M [4]. Searchable encryption predicates are built to test parts of I without actually decrypting it, while M is used to carry the payload data. When predicates evaluate to true, the message is decrypted. If the evaluation fails, no information about the message is revealed.

Current searchable encryption primitives support various conditions or their conjunctive variants [4] [1]. Equality tests check if a value in the index matches the value in the predicate. Range tests check if a value in the index is in an interval specified by the predicate. Finally, subset tests check if a value in the index is contained in a subset of values specified in the predicate.

Hidden Vector Encryption, or HVE for short, is a form of searchable encryption introduced in [4]. It supports conjunctive equality, range or subset predicates. HVE uses bilinear maps based on groups of composite order. The required mathematical operations include exponentiations with large integers, thus making the algorithms costly. Because the costs scale poorly, parallelism is an attractive solution to achieve acceptable performance. This owes to the fact that predicate evaluation on large sets of encrypted data is inherently an embarrassingly parallel problem.

In this paper we assess the performance of the HVE query algorithm on single and multiple processor machines. We argue that the former are unable to cope with multiple queries over a short time span. The latter can exploit the nature of problems involving HVE to obtain good speedup rates and thus make HVE implementations feasible in practice.

The rest of the paper is organized as follows: Section 2 gives an overview of sequential and parallel HVE, followed by the experimental evaluation results in Section 3. Finally, Section 4 concludes the paper and highlights directions for future work.

2. PARALLELIZING HVE

Hidden Vector Encryption (HVE) [4] is a searchable encryption system that supports predicates in the form of conjunctive equality,

attribute:	1	0	1	1	0
predicate:	1	0	*	1	0

(a) Match

attribute:	1	0	1	1	0
predicate:	*	0	0	1	*

(b) Non-Match

Figure 2: Predicate evaluation on ciphertexts with HVE

range and subset queries. Compared to earlier solutions ([1, 3]), HVE yields ciphertexts with considerably smaller length. Search on ciphertexts can be performed with respect to a number of *index attributes*. HVE represents an attribute as a bit vector (each element has value 0 or 1), and the search predicate as a *pattern* vector where each element can be 0, 1 or '*' that signifies a wildcard (or "don't care") value. A predicate evaluates to $True$ for a ciphertext C if the attribute vector I used to encrypt C has the same values as the pattern vector of the predicate in all positions that are not '*' in the latter. Figure 2 illustrates the two cases of *Match* and *Non-Match* for HVE.

HVE is built on top of a symmetrical bilinear map of composite order [2], which is a function $e : \mathbb{G} \times \mathbb{G} \to \mathbb{G}_T$ such that $\forall a, b \in G$ and $\forall u, v \in \mathbb{Z}$ it holds that $e(a^u, b^v) = e(a, b)^{uv}$. $\mathbb{G}$ and $\mathbb{G}_T$ are cyclic multiplicative groups of composite order $N = P \cdot Q$ where P and Q are large primes of equal bit length. We denote by $\mathbb{G}_p$, $\mathbb{G}_q$ the subgroups of $\mathbb{G}$ of orders P and Q, respectively. Let l denote the HVE *length*, which is the number of bits that form the attribute, and consequently the search predicate. HVE consists of four phases:

Setup. The user generates the public (PK) and secret (SK) key pair. The user keeps SK to itself, and shares the public key PK. SK consists of the following randomly generated elements:

$$SK = (g_q \in \mathbb{G}_q, \quad a \in \mathbb{Z}_p, \quad \forall i \in [1..l] : u_i, h_i, w_i, g, v \in \mathbb{G}_p)$$

To generate PK, the user first chooses at random elements $R_{u,i}, R_{h,i}, R_{w,i} \in \mathbb{G}_q, \forall i \in [1..l]$ and $R_v \in \mathbb{G}_q$. Next, PK is determined as:

$$PK = (g_q, \quad V = vR_v, \quad A = e(g, v)^a,$$

$$\forall i \in [1..l] : U_i = u_i R_{u,i}, \quad H_i = h_i R_{h,i}, \quad W_i = w_i R_{w,i})$$

Encryption is executed by remote users. Encryption uses PK and takes as parameters the index attribute I and the payload message $M \in \mathbb{G}_T$. The following random elements are generated: $Z, Z_{i,1}, Z_{i,2} \in \mathbb{G}_g$ and $s \in \mathbb{Z}_n$. Then, the ciphertext is created as

$$C = (C' = MA^s, \quad C_0 = V^s Z,$$

$$\forall i \in [1..l] : C_{i,1} = (U_i^{I_i} H_i)^s Z_{i,1}, \quad C_{i,2} = W_i^s Z_{i,2})$$

Token Generation. Using SK, and given a search predicate encoded as pattern vector I_*, the user generates a search token TK as follows: let J be the set of all indices i where $I_*[i] \neq *$. The user randomly generates $r_{i,1}$ and $r_{i,2} \in \mathbb{Z}_p, \forall i \in J$. Then

$$TK = (I_*, K_0 = g^a \prod_{i \in J} (u_i^{I_*[i]} h_i)^{r_{i,1}} w_i^{r_{i,2}},$$

$$\forall i \in [1..l] : K_{i,1} = v^{r_{i,1}}, \quad K_{i,2} = v^{r_{i,2}})$$

Query is executed at the server, and evaluates if the predicate represented by TK holds for ciphertext C. The server attempts to determine the value of M as

$$M = C' / (e(C_0, K_0) / \prod_{i \in J} e(C_{i,1}, K_{i,1}) e(C_{i,2}, K_{i,2})$$

Table 1: Parallel test results (20-bit attributes, 1200-bit keys)

CPU count	Average Execution Time per Request	Speedup
1	2.976	1
8	0.392	7.58
16	0.187	15.85
32	0.097	30.61

If the index I based on which C was computed satisfies TK, then the actual value of M is returned, otherwise a special number which is not in the valid message domain (denoted by $\perp$) is obtained.

The recent growth of cloud computing platforms has lowered the costs of running complex services. The most significant improvement is exhibited by parallel applications, because they can be deployed over multiple nodes. Serial algorithms that are too expensive to run on a single processor can become feasible when deployed in a cloud computing environment. One example is HVE, where the mathematical algorithms include exponentiations with big integers. Serial implementations of HVE are unable to execute the mathematical steps and also ensure good response times and scalability. Parallel solutions are thus required.

The typical usage scenario for HVE is highly parallel on the server side. Because there are no dependencies between messages, whether they originate from the same remote users or not, they can be allocated to empty processing units as soon as they arrive. Before processing, all units need to have the token information. Because tokens are rarely expected to change, it is safe to assume that they will be propagated before processing begins. After token evaluation is done, depending on the results, the processing unit can send the required information to a specialized component without the other units even knowing about it.

3. EXPERIMENTAL EVALUATION

We implemented a C++ prototype of the HVE system presented in [4]. The Gnu MP library[1] is used for operations with large numbers and the Pairing-Based Cryptography library[2] from Stanford University is used for bilinear map operations. Throughout the experimental evaluation, we focus on the query operation. The setup phase is not included in the plots because it can be computed offline and thus does not impact the real time operation of the server. The encryption and token generation phases are performed at the client and do not impact the scalability of the system. The experimental testbed consisted of a cluster with 8 machines, each having an Intel Xeon E5405 2GHz CPU with 4 cores and 16GB of RAM, running Red Hat Enterprise Linux and using a network connection of 10Gbps. For the parallel tests we use Open MPI 1.6.

To assess the scalability of the system, we varied key length, attribute length and number of queries both in a serial and parallel setting. Tests included 256 or 384 dispatched requests and the total time that the server took to answer all requests was measured. Attribute lengths varied between 10-bit and 20-bit to showcase the influence of attribute size in total running time. Key length varied between 1024, 1100, 1200 and 1300. Longer key sizes lead to better security guarantees. The 1024 key length is sufficient for compliance with current security guidelines, but as computing power increases longer key lengths will become a necessity.

---

[1] Available online at http://gmplib.org/

[2] Available online at http://crypto.stanford.edu/pbc/

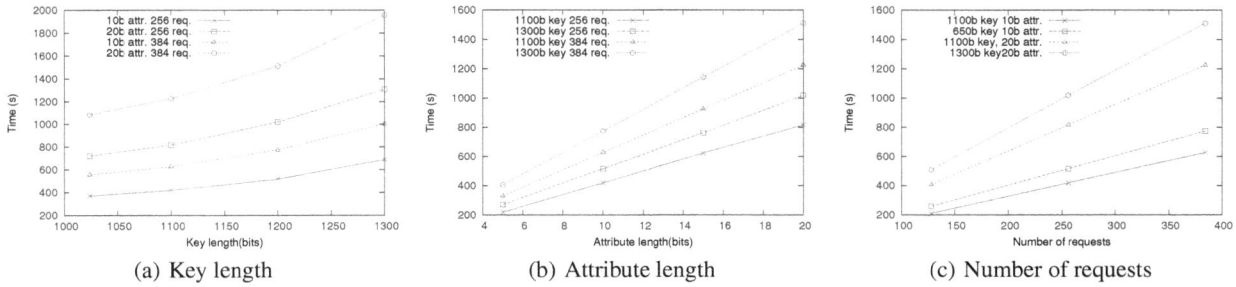

| (a) Key length | (b) Attribute length | (c) Number of requests |

Figure 3: Serial execution time

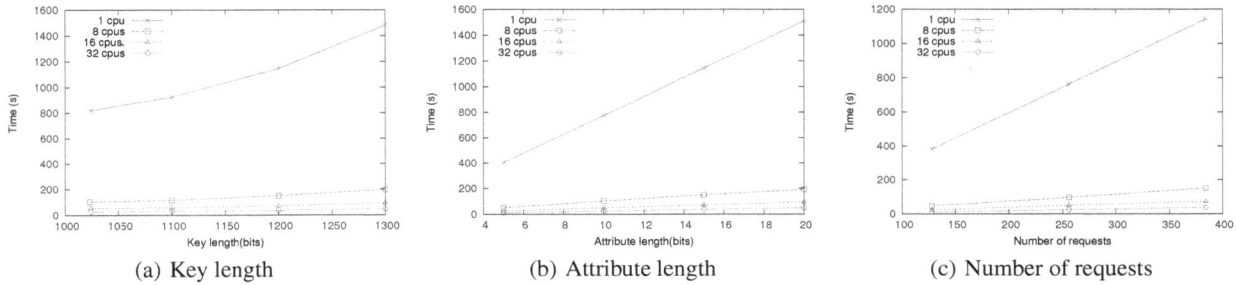

| (a) Key length | (b) Attribute length | (c) Number of requests |

Figure 4: Parallel execution time

Figure 3(a) shows that by increasing the key length, performance is severely impacted. A 30% increase in the key length leads to an approximately 100% increase in execution time. The absolute times are also unacceptable, as large scale systems are expected to receive multiple requests per second. In the best case, a 10-bit attribute and 1024-bit key length serial system can handle approximately one request per second. In an actual implementation, such a system would be unable to handle all requests in real time.

Attribute length has a linear impact on execution time (Figure 3(b)). Although for small attribute size values the serial system leads to acceptable execution times, for applications that require larger attribute sizes the times are unacceptable. Increasing the number of requests leads to an expected linear increase in execution time (Figure 3(c)).

For the parallel tests the same execution parameters were used. The tests were ran on 1, 8, 16 and 32 CPUs. The algorithm simply dispatched each new request to a free cpu. Because there are no dependencies between requests, this leads to a near-optimal speedup as can be seen in Table 1. In Figures 4(a), 4(b), 4(c) the default values for variables not represented on the Ox axis are 384 requests, 15-bit attribute size and 1200-bit key size. Parallel execution leads to acceptable execution times, i.e. 37.33 seconds processing time for 384 requests with a 15-bit attribute size and 1200-bit key size with 32 CPUs. In other words, approximately 10 requests can be handled per second, which is a significant improvement over the serial case.

4. CONCLUSION

We showed that HVE based serial implementations are not efficient enough to ensure scalability. To make HVE feasible, parallel solutions need to be explored. Because most problems that involve searchable encryption are embarrassingly parallel, the speedup is close to optimal values and is strictly related to the load distribu-

tion algorithm and not to the HVE algorithms themselves. Future work can explore optimizations that improve the running time of serial execution or practical applications that benefit from the improved efficiency that parallel solutions offer.

5. ACKNOWLEDGEMENTS

In completing this project I have benefited from the constant support of Marian Barbu and Sergiu Costea, for which I am grateful.

6. REFERENCES

[1] D. Boneh, G. D. Crescenzo, R. Ostrovsky, and G. Persiano. Public key encryption with keyword search. In *EUROCRYPT 2004, volume 3027 of LNCS*, 2003.

[2] D. Boneh, E.-J. Goh, and K. Nissim. Evaluating 2-dnf formulas on ciphertexts. In *Proceedings of the Second international conference on Theory of Cryptography*, pages 325–341, 2005.

[3] D. Boneh, A. Sahai, and B. Waters. Fully collusion resistant traitor tracing with short ciphertexts and private keys. In *EUROCRYPT 2006, volume 4004 of LNCS*, pages 573–592, 2006.

[4] D. Boneh and B. Waters. Conjunctive, subset, and range queries on encrypted data. In *Proceedings of the 4th conference on Theory of cryptography*, pages 535–554, 2007.

A Fine-grained Access Control Model for Key-value Systems

Dr. Devdatta Kulkarni *
devdattakulkarni@gmail.com

ABSTRACT

In this paper we present K-VAC – a key-value access control model for modern non-relational data stores. This model supports specification and enforcement of access control policies at different levels of resource hierarchy, such as a column family, a row, or a column. The policies can be based on *contents* of the key-value store and they may also include context information. Through a case-study example we demonstrate the capabilities of this system.

Categories and Subject Descriptors

D.4.6 [**Security and Protection**]: Access controls

Keywords

Non-relational systems; Cassandra; Access control

1. INTRODUCTION

Modern Internet-scale applications are using key-value stores as their back end data systems. Several such systems have been built including, Cassandra, MongoDB, HBase. Such systems provide several advantages over traditional databases, such as ease of evolution due to schema-less data model, scalability, relaxation of data consistency requirements, and so on. Given such advantages, it would not be incorrect to assume that such systems would be used in more large scale distributed applications in the future.

The access control capabilities of such systems are currently limited. Specifically, they do not support complex access control requirements, such as restricting users' access to certain keys or values, or restricting access based on context conditions or user roles. This can represent a barrier for their wide-spread adoption, especially in fields such as health-care which put premium on stringent access control and audit requirements from the underlying data stores.

The focus of this paper is on the issues related to building fine-grained access control models and systems for key-value stores. Specifically, we argue that an access control model for such systems needs to support three key requirements, hierarchical access control, content-based access control, and context-based access control.

---

*Author affiliation: Rackspace. This work has been done independently and is not related to author's work at Rackspace.

Hierarchical access control refers to the ability of the access control system to be able to specify access control policies for data at different levels of hierarchy within a key-value store. We should be able to specify access control policies at the granularity of the entire key-value store, or a grouping of some rows, or on a specific row, or a specific column. *Content-based access control* is the ability of the system to restrict access to resources based on the *values* of certain keys or their attributes within a key-value store. Finally, in certain situations the permissions granted to a user may need to be constrained based on context conditions, such as a user's location, or who a user is co-located with, or time, using *context-based access control* mechanisms.

2. ACCESS CONTROL REQUIREMENTS

Consider a patient information system built using a key-value data store. Such a system stores information about patients, doctors, and nurses. The information associated with patients may include, medications, the attending doctor, and the reports created by the doctor. The information associated with doctors and nurses may include, current patients and work hours. One piece of information that may be associated with all three is their location, which may correspond to a room or a ward. We consider the following access control requirements for such a system [1]. A doctor can access all medical information of only those patients who are currently assigned to him or her (R1). A patient's medications can only be accessed by the patient's nurse (R2). A nurse is allowed to access a patient's medications only during work hours (R3). A nurse can access information of only those patients corresponding to the ward in which the nurse is currently present (R4). A nurse can access a doctor's patient reports only while the nurse and the doctor are present in the patient's room (R5).

We now describe how such an application can be built using Cassandra,[1] which we use as a representative key-value system in this paper. In Cassandra, data is stored in a *Keyspace*. A keyspace may contain one or more *Column Families*. Within a column family, data items are stored in the form of key-value pairs. Each data item is made up of a unique element (the row key) and number of attributes (columns). Using Cassandra, the patient information system can be modeled as follows. We define a keyspace named PI and three column families (c.f.) as follows.

[Patient c.f.:] id, medications, doctor, report, location.
[Nurse c.f.:] id, patients, work_hours, location.

---

[1] http://cassandra.apache.org/

[Doctor c.f.:] id, patients, work_hours, location.

The *id* attribute is the row key in each of the column families. The other attributes are represented as columns in that column family. The *patients* column in the *Nurse* and the *Doctor* column families may have multiple values. These are the *ids* from the *Patient* column family.

Let us consider how the access control requirements R1 to R5 can be realized in the above Cassandra data model. For R1, we need that a doctor should be able to access rows in the *Patient c.f.* for only those patients whose ids are present in the *patients* column corresponding to that doctor's row in the *Doctor c.f.*. This means that we need to be able to restrict access to specific rows within a column family based on the contents of columns in a different column family. For R2, we need that the *medications* column in the *Patient c.f.* for a patient can be accessed only by a nurse whose *patients* column contains that patient's id. This means we need to be able to restrict access to a specific column within a column family. For R3-R5, we need to be able to express context-based access control requirements. For R3, we need to restrict access based on the time of the day, for R4 and R5, the access needs to be restricted based on the locations of nurses, doctors, and patients.

Based on the above an access control model for key-value systems needs to support the following. First, the model needs the ability to specify access control policies at different levels of data model hierarchy. Policies may need to be specified at the level of a row or a column. Second, the model needs to support specifying policies that are based on *contents* of a row or a column. Third, policies also need to be based on context information, such as a person's location, or a person's co-location with other person, or time.

3. KEY-VALUE ACCESS CONTROL MODEL

To address the above requirements, we have developed a key-value access control model (K-VAC). An access control policy in K-VAC is defined as the following *k-vac expression*:
<permission_type, resource_expression, constraint_expression>
The access specified in *permission_type* is granted to the user on the resource specified in the *resource_expression* only if the constraint specified in the *constraint_expression* is true. A *permission_type* can be one of *read row, read column, write row,* or *write column*. A *resource_expression* identifies the resource on which the access control policy is specified. A resource can be a column family, a row, or a column.

A *resource_expression* is specified in the following format: */keyspace/column_family(id=value)/column*. The specification *(id=value)* is optional. When specified, it acts as a filter predicate on the column family to select only the row with the id equal to the specified value. We support three different mechanisms for specifying the value in the filter predicate. First, a value can be specified literally. For example, selecting row for the patient named John is specified as: */PI/Patient(id=John)/*. Second, a value can be specified to be obtained by querying a column. For example, selecting the row for the doctor attending the patient John is specified as: */PI/Doctor(id=/PI/Patient(id=John)/doctor)/*. Third, a value can be specified as a *parameterized variable*, which is bound at runtime. For example, selecting the row for a doctor who is attending a patient whose name is provided at runtime is specified as:
/PI/Doctor(id=/PI/Patient(id=$patient_name)/doctor)/.
Here *patient_name* is a parameterized variable.

A *constraint_expression* consists of logical conditions over resources defined in the system. It is specified as follows: *constraint_expression := **cond** operand_1 operator operand_2*. Currently we support the following operators: *in, equal, and, or, minus*. An operand can be a *resource_expression, current_time*, an integer, or a string.

We now show how the various access control requirements identified in Section 2 can be specified using k-vac expressions. Policies are specified in XML in the K-VAC system. Here we use a pseudo notation. The terms that appear in **bold** in the examples below correspond to XML elements in the policy specification. The following k-vac expression is used to specify R1. **read row** */PI/Patient*,
cond */PI/Patient(id=$n)/id* **in** */PI/Doctor(id=user.id)/patients*
The resource on which the policy is specified is the row of the *Patient* column family. The *constraint_expression* specifies that a doctor can read a patient's records if that patient's id appears in the *patients* column in that row of the *Doctor* column family whose id attribute matches the id of the user who is requesting the access. In our system, each user making a request is mapped to a runtime object called *user* with the id attribute set to the identity of that user.

The k-vac expression shown below is used to specify R2. Read access to a patient's *medications* column is granted to a nurse if that patient's id appears in the *patients* column of the nurse who is requesting the access.
read column */PI/Patient/medications*
cond */PI/Patient(id=$n)/id* **in** */PI/Nurse(id=user.id)/patients*
The k-vac expression shown below is used to specify R3. A nurse is granted access to a patient's *medications* column only if current time is within her work hours. *current_time* is evaluated at runtime to get the current time.
read column */PI/Patient/medications*
cond *current_time* **in** */PI/Nurse(id=user.id)/work_hours*
The following k-vac expression is used to specify R4. A nurse is granted read access to a patient's row if the values of the *location* column for that nurse and that patient match.
read row */PI/Patient/* **cond** */PI/Patient(id=$n)/location*
equal */PI/Nurse(id=user.id)/location*
The k-vac expression shown below is used to specify R5. A nurse is granted read access to a patient's report if the value of the *location* column for the nurse matches that of the patient and that of the patient's doctor.
read column */PI/Patient/report* **cond**
/PI/Nurse(id=user.id)/location **equal** */PI/Patient(id=$n)/location*
and */PI/Nurse(id=user.id)/location*
equal */PI/Doctor(id=/PI/Patient(id=$n)/doctor)/location*

4. IMPLEMENTATION AND EVALUATION

In implementing the K-VAC system we investigated two approaches in the design space. One approach consisted of implementing the K-VAC layer within the key-value store itself. The advantage of this approach is that an application need not be aware of the K-VAC layer. We modified Cassandra's implementation to perform access control based on K-VAC using this approach.[2] The second approach was to implement K-VAC outside a key-value store as a library. This approach requires no change to the key-value store. Also, the library can be interfaced with different key-value stores. However, an application needs to be interfaced to the key-value store through the library. We implemented

---

[2]https://github.com/devdattakulkarni/Cassandra-KVAC

162

Num. of Queries to c.f.s	K-VAC Library Median (ms)	Cassandra-KVAC Median (ms)
1	48	48
2	71	54
5	75 (R5 orig.)	57
10	84	68
20	133	107
40	169	142

Table 1: Policy evaluation performance

K-VAC as a library[3] and implemented its bindings for Cassandra, HBase, and MongoDB. Apart from patient information system, we have also implemented a social information sharing application with K-VAC for access control.

The core part of K-VAC policy evaluation is queries to the underlying key-value store. Our evaluation of the two design approaches consisted of finding out how does policy enforcement performance varies as the number of queries to column families increase. To evaluate this we ran a single node Cassandra cluster on a Intel Core 2 Duo CPU T64002.00GHz Laptop with 4.00 GB RAM and 288 GB disk. We used the patient information system for this evaluation. We created three column families corresponding to *Patient*, *Nurse*, and *Doctor*. Each column family was populated with 10K rows, each consisting of one column. In order to measure the worst case performance we took following steps. We set the *keys_cached* and *rows_cached* parameters for the three column families to zero. We did not add secondary indexes to any columns in the system. We restarted the Cassandra server for each run of the experiment to eliminate OS-level caching of the row data in memory.

In Table 1 we present median values (across five runs) for querying data from Cassandra with different number of queries to column families as part of policy evaluation. We implemented R3, R4, and R5 for evaluating performance for one, two, and five queries respectively. For evaluating performance for ten, twenty, and forty queries, we used R5 with the k-vac expression modified with additional *and* clauses.

We see that even with forty queries the policy evaluation time is less than a quarter of a second for both designs in the worst case. Second, the design where K-VAC is implemented within Cassandra is marginally better than the library based design. The performance numbers with no data in the system were similar. The baseline performance of querying a single row having one column with no other data in the system and no access control checks was 44 milliseconds (ms).

By the structure of a *constraint_expression* it is clear that the data model will have bearing on the policy evaluation performance. To test this we considered an alternate data model for the patient information system. Specifically, we defined a de-normalized model in which we stored the information about a patients attending nurse and doctor in the *Patient* column family itself. Specifically, we added columns *doc_loc*, *nurse*, *nurse_loc* to the *Patient* column family to represent the location of the attending doctor and the identity and location of the attending nurse for a patient. With this change we remodeled R5 as follows:

read column */PI/Patient/report*
cond */PI/Patient(id=$n)/nurse_loc* **equal**
/PI/Patient(id=$n)/location **and** */PI/Patient(id=$n)/nurse_loc*

---

equal */PI/Patient(id=$n)/doc_loc* **and** */PI/Patient(id=$n)/nurse*
equal *user.id* We wanted to measure the best case performance for this setting so we turned on row and key caching. We also added secondary indexes to all the columns that are queried in the above policy. With policy enforcement done in the K-VAC library the median policy evaluation time was 49 ms. For comparison, we ran *R5 orig.* (marked in Table 1) with row and key caching turned on and also with secondary indexes. The policy evaluation took 58 ms.

An optimization that can possibly improve performance is to cache values of columns that are queried on different branches of a policy's expression tree (e.g.: the *nurse_loc* column above). Our current policy interpreter does not support this as it interprets each node of the expression tree as it is encountered, without first analyzing the whole tree.

5. RELATED WORK

In Cassandra access control policies can be specified at the level of a keyspace or a column family. Accumulo [4] is a key-value store that supports cell-based access control policies where a cell represents a row and a column combination. In K-VAC, access control policies can be specified at the level of a keyspace, a column family, a row, or a column and can be based on their *contents*. The need for content-based access control is well-known [3]. K-VAC provides mechanisms to address this requirement for key-value systems. The format of *resource_expressions* and its use within access control policy specification is reminiscent of the use of XPath in specifying access control policies for XML documents [2]. Our motivation to use this format was driven by the need to succinctly identify resources within the hierarchical data model of key-value stores.

6. CONCLUSION

In this paper we have presented K-VAC, a fine-grained access control model for non-relational key-value systems. This model supports specification of access control policies at the level of a keyspace, a column family, rows and columns. The policies can be based on contents within the system and may include context information. Through a case-study example we have presented the capabilities of the K-VAC system. Our future work consists of extending K-VAC to accommodate relaxed consistency of data that is used within content-based policy enforcement in a key-value system.

7. REFERENCES

[1] M. Evered and S. Bögeholz. A Case Study in Access Control Requirements for a Health Information System. In *ACSW Frontiers '04: Proceedings of the Second Workshop on Australasian Information Security, Data Mining and Web Intelligence, and Software Internationalization*, pages 53–61, 2004.

[2] I. Fundulaki and M. Marx. Specifying Access Control Policies for XML Documents with XPath. In *Proceedings of the ninth ACM symposium on Access control models and technologies*, SACMAT '04, pages 61–69, New York, NY, USA, 2004. ACM.

[3] L. Giuri and P. Iglio. Role Templates for Content-based Access Control. In *RBAC '97: Proceedings of the Second ACM Workshop on Role Based Access Control*, pages 153–159, 1997.

[4] http://accumulo.apache.org/.

Emulating Internet Topology Snapshots in Deterlab

[Extended Abstract]

Graciela Perera, Nathan Miller,
John Mela
Youngstown State University
gcperera@ysu.edu, {ndmiller,
jnmela}@student.ysu.edu

Michael P. McGarry
Department of Electrical and
Computer Engineering
University of Texas at El Paso
mpmcgarry@utep.edu

Jaime C. Acosta
U.S. Army Research Laboratory
White Sands Missile Range, NM
jaime.c.acosta.civ@mail.mil

ABSTRACT

Investigating the Internet's topology is one component towards developing mechanisms that can protect the communication infrastructure underlying our critical systems and applications. We study the feasibility of capturing and fitting Internet's topology snapshots to an emulated environment called Deterlab. Physical limitations on Deterlab include the number of nodes available (i.e., about 400) and the number of interfaces (i.e., 4) to interconnect them. For example, one Internet's topology snapshot at the Autonomous Systems (AS) level has about 100 nodes with 5 nodes requiring more than 4 interfaces. In this paper, we present a short summary of the Internet's topology snapshots collected and propose a solution on how we can represent the snapshots in Deterlab and overcome the limitation of nodes requiring more than four interfaces. Preliminary results show that all paths from snapshots are maintained if a node requiring more than four interfaces had no more than four other nodes requiring four interfaces. Also, we constructed a proof of concept that captures the main idea of using then snapshots in a security experiment in Deterlab. The topology shows a Multiple Origin Autonomous System (MOAS) conflict for 10 nodes. It is scalable to larger topologies in Deterlab because we have automated the topology creation and protocol configuration.

Categories and Subject Descriptors

C.2.1 [**Network Architecture and Design**]: Network topology;
C.4 [**Performance of Systems**]: Measurement techniques;

Keywords

Testbed, Internet topology, vulnerability analysis

1. INTRODUCTION

In 2011, the Kapersky Security Bulletin reported over 2.5 trillion attempted network attacks across the globe [10]. Many financial and other critical systems depend on the communication infrastructure provided by the Internet [1]. As a result, it is of utmost importance to protect the Internet's infrastructure through network security measures. The Internet's infrastructure connects large, mid-size, and small networks that include Internet Service Providers (ISP), content providers like Google, Facebook, and customers. Each of these networks or Autonomous Systems (AS) are independently administered and maintained by a single entity. Constructing flexible models of the Internet's network topologies at the AS-level is crucial for identifying, measuring, and

mitigating security flaws. For example, ASes use the Border Gateway Protocol (BGP) for interconnection and while common mistakes and vulnerabilities are well documented in BGP, many are unresolved and have affects for large and small content providers [8]. Deterlab can provide the means to study these vulnerabilities and potential solutions [4]. Before we can study these vulnerabilities we need to use topologies that capture real paths towards large and small content providers. For the sake of tractability in analysis and in the emulation, it is necessary to have a manageable network topology size while maintaining a model with enough fidelity to represent the Internet's topology snapshots with respect to valid routes towards content providers. Capturing the Internet's topology is a challenging and open problem. We use the method proposed Gill, et al. [6] of collecting Internet's topology snapshots and investigate an approach to representing them in Deterlab. In this paper, we present a short summary of the Internet's topology snapshots collected and propose a solution on how we can represent the snapshots in Deterlab and overcome the limitation of nodes requiring more than 4 interfaces. The fidelity of our solution in Deterlab is based on the conservation in the routes towards content providers.

The contributions of this study are important because they enhance the versatility of the Deterlab emulation environment as an Internet security experimentation tool. Representing the Internet's topology snapshots in a network emulation environment, like Deterlab, is a necessary step in the evaluation of the security vulnerabilities of inter-domain routing [8]. Our work makes three contributions: 1) we have collected recent Internet topology snapshots following the method proposed by Gill et al. in [6] and obtained the same conclusions, 2) we developed an automated solution to represent our snapshots and overcome Deterlab limitations 3) we implemented a scalable Multiple Origin Autonomous System (MOAS) conflict and tested with 10 nodes.

The remainder of this paper is organized as follows. Section II describes the related work. Section III summarizes the results obtained from the collection of Internet's topology snapshots showing the need for our solution in Deterlab. Section IV describes the solution on how to implement snapshots in Deterlab and explains briefly the MOAS conflict. Finally, section V presents conclusions and future work.

2. RELATED WORK

Previous work from [3] with respect to Deterlab, create topologies using a generator or by constructing a subgraph from large datasets collected via well-known repositories. The work in [3] constructed topologies from repositories that may or not include paths leading towards content providers.

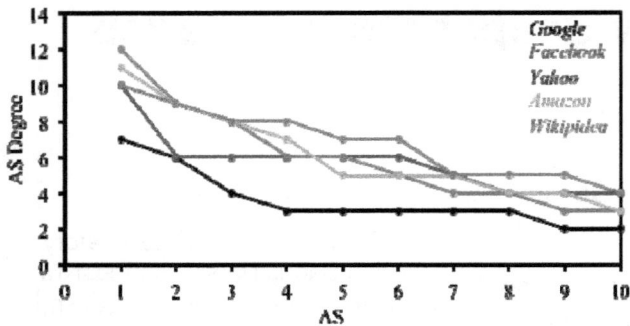

Figure 1. Ranked AS degree for various providers

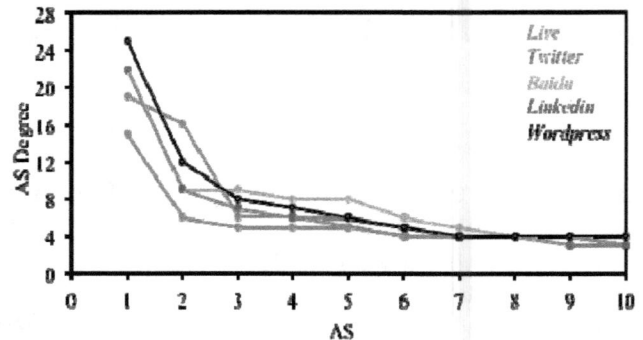

Figure 2. Ranked AS degree for various providers

They focus on a general scale-down approach whereas we use the paths from the snapshots involving large and small content providers.

On the other hand, the authors in [2] propose scale down approach that includes some of the path preserving properties. We consider the degree of nodes as it directly affects how nodes are connected in Deterlab. For example, authors in [7] include node degree as a metric because it is a popular way to characterize nodes connectivity for the Internet's topology. Although, there are other important metrics in [7] to consider, we will include these in our future work to determine the fidelity of experiments. We based are approach on the work presented in [2], which only considers static topologies. Our solution differs from [2] because it includes switching elements and nodes that can be configured with different routing protocols. This could potentially enable paths to change during experimentation as traffic is generated from end systems towards a content provider. An open research question is how to determine the router configuration that best represents interesting dynamic paths used for attacks.

3. SNAPSHOT COLLECTION

The snapshots used to construct the topologies in Deterlab were derived from the data collected by [5], which only has paths towards content providers. They used an active measurement platform called Deep Internet Performance Zoom (DipZoom), which allows the use of public traceroute servers from different geographically located vantage points all over the world. Each snapshot represents the collection of ASes found from 50 geographically distributed public traceroute servers around world. From these servers, traceroutes were issued to major content providers. We used the same 10 top content providers and 10 small ones used by [5]. Due to the difficulty in discovering the commercial agreements, the authors in [5] determined the different ASes using data supplied by the Cooperative Association for Internet Data Analysis (CAIDA), BGP Looking Glass, and Whois database available by the various ICANN regional Internet registries. Thus, the snapshots used, represent downward paths between servers around the world and content providers. The snapshots contain over 100 nodes and with node degrees of over 20. We used the data collected from [5] as they were able to parse traceroute data to identify the ASes that were traversed on the paths. We show in figures 1 and 2 respectively the degree for the top ranked ASes for popular content providers. Each content provider corresponds to a snapshot, thus comparing the degree of the top ranked ASes per content provider snapshot. These figures

show that there are roughly 5 or more nodes in each snapshot connected to more than four other nodes. This requires more than four interfaces in their representation in Deterlab. We also did the same analysis for unpopular and well-known content providers. We found the same problem presented with an even larger number of nodes requiring more interfaces than just four.

4. SNAPSHOTS IN DETERLAB

The snapshot collected in the previous section must be converted into a valid network topology for a Deterlab experiment. A Deterlab experiment consists of a file in network simulator (NS) format and the node configuration. We illustrate the use of our solution in a MOAS conflict with ten nodes or ASes. The NS files and protocol configuration are automated so that experiments can easily scale to larger size shapshots.

4.1 Deterlab Solution

The NS file specifies the experiment's topology and other attributes regarding network behavior such as delay, link bandwidth, node type, etc. We use the Perl programming language to traverse through each node and translate into nodes and links in the topology. When Perl encounters a node of degree higher than four, a switch is created for the node, its neighbors are added to the switch, and the node itself is also added to the switch. We call a node with degree higher than four a *high degree node* because they require a higher number of interfaces not available in Deterlab. Thus, the switch provides linkage between the *high* degree node and each neighbor as though it were directly linked to them. We use software at each node to configure the network protocol. If a neighbor is a high degree node, it cannot be added to the switch. It must be directly linked. This limits the application of the switched solution. For any high degree node, it can have three or less neighbors, which themselves are high degree nodes. Visually, it is easy to see why a high degree node can only support three high degree node neighbors. One link must be used for the switch. Three links remain for neighbors, which themselves are high degree nodes. It may seem intuitive to simply add all neighbors of a high degree node to its switch, but this may result in inconsistencies in the paths. Suppose we have a topology consisting of two high degree nodes (HighDegree1 and HighDegree2). If we add HighDegree1's high degree neighbor (HighDegree2) to HighDegree1's switch, HighDegree1 will be removed from the path towards HighDegree2. We have NS files that will specify an experiment and add switches to high degree nodes. All files were configured to run on Deterlab.

The fidelity of the solution relies that we configured at each node the protocol that will route the data between each node or AS from the snapshot. The protocol should be able to offer the same paths as the original snapshot. (BGP) is the routing protocol used to route between ASes and is not a default feature of Deterlab. We use the Quagga software suite to implement BGP on each node of the snapshot. We construct a small topology and apply the switched solution to a topology shown in figure 3. High degree nodes are named High Degree 1, 2, 3, and other nodes to represent the ASes towards the ContentProvider node. The BGP configurations require the name and IP address of each network interface. At a bare minimum, the configuration files require IP and AS number information about each node and its neighbors. We aggregate the IP addresses and interface names from each running node in the experiment. We use Perl to parse this information and create Quagga configuration files based on connectivity of the original graph. The result is a Deterlab experiment with BGP routing configure such that the routes towards the content providers in the snapshot are conserve and available.

4.1.1 Evaluation

The evaluation of our method was based on validating that all paths from the snapshots were available in our Deterlab solution. We extracted the BGP tables as they contain the routing information of each node or the path a packet will take to reach a specified destination. We used a Perl script to aggregate the BGP tables from each node in Deterlab. After aggregating and eliminating repetitions, we find 1) all nodes in the snapshots are represented in the testbed, and 2) all paths for the snapshots tested existed in the BGP tables extracted from Deterlab. This was only true when a node in the snapshot requiring more than four interfaces had no more than four neighbor nodes requiring four interfaces.

4.2 MOAS in Deterlab

To prove the usefulness of our solution we constructed a small scale BGP topology in the Deterlab that was produced by our solution. The BGP configuration was done with the GNU Zebra and BGPd software packages in Quagga. Results were gathered using tcpdump, BGP debug output, and routing table dumps of the participating BGP nodes. Additionally, the SEER GUI was used to generate legitimate web traffic for the verification of the routing of traffic flows. Our intent is to introduce false duplicate path advertisements in order to determine their effects on the BGP Best Path Selection process. Routing policies were not considered and default metric values were used for path advertisements.

The results gathered indicate false advertisements can have a negative impact on the BGP Best Path Selection process. This is only true if certain conditions are met. In order to construct an experiment to test this theory; we constructed two separate topologies. Both topologies introduce a node appropriately named RogueAS which represents a misconfigured or compromised AS. The ultimate destination is a content provider. The results indicate that with no other metrics properly configured, BGP selected the best path to be whichever advertisement was the oldest or first received. Since no weight, local preference, or M.E.D. metrics were configured; the oldest (first received) path will be considered the best path. The implications of this result are that

both RogueAS and the originating AS were both likely to be considered the best path to Google. In the second example, two additional nodes were introduced in front of RogueAS in order to lengthen the overall path of the false advertisement. After the topology was configured and BGP converged, the resulting effects of false path advertisements were negligible. The longest length AS path advertised by RogueAS resulted in the selection favoring the path advertised by originating AS. This is a direct result from RogueAS path being advertised and having a longer length than that advertised by originating AS. Since the path to the same network advertised by RogueAS is longer, BGP will consistently choose the originating AS as the best path to Google. The results obtained through both experiments indicate that if no other metrics are configured; paths of equal lengths negatively affect the BGP Best Path Selection process.

5. CONCLUSIONS

We successfully found a solution to represent Internet's topology snapshot in Deterlab. Also, we constructed a proof of concept for our solution by implementing a Multiple Origin Autonomous System (MOAS) conflict for 10 nodes. It is scalable to larger topologies in Deterlab because we have automated the topology creation and protocol configuration.

6. REFERENCES

[1] T. Benzel, B. Braden, T. Faber, J. Mirkovic, S. Schwab, K. Sollins, and J. Wroclawski, "Current Developments in DETER Cybersecurity Testbed Technology," Cybersecurity Applications & Technology Conference for Homeland Security, 2009.

[2] G. Carl, and G. Kesidi, "Large-scale testing of the Internet's Border Gateway Protocol (BGP) via topological scale-down," ACM Transactions on Modeling and Computer Simulation, vol. 18, no. 3, July 2008.

[3] G. Carl, G. Kesidis, B. Madan, and S. Phoha, "Preliminary BGP Multiple-Origin Autonomous Aystems (MOAS) Experiments on the DETER Testbed. DETER Community Workshop on Cyber Security Experimentation, June 2006, Arlington, VA.

[4] DETERLab, URL: http://www.isi.deterlab.net/

[5] A. Drivere, and G. Perera, "A First Step towards Evaluating the Impact of Wide Area Deployments on the Internet," 16th Annual International Conference on Mobile Computing and Networking, September 2010, Chicago, IL.

[6] P. Gill, M. Arlitt, M. Li Z., and A. Mahanti, "The Flattening Internet Topology: Natural Evolution, unsightly Barnacles or Contrived Collapse?" 2008, University of Calgary, Calgary, AB, Canada.

[7] P. Mahadevan , D. Krioukov , M. Fomenkov , X. Dimitropoulos , K. C. Claffy , and A. Vahdat, "The Internet AS-level Topology: Three Data Sources and One Definitive Metric," SIGCOMM, 2006.

[8] S. Murphy. BGP Security Vulnerabilities Analysis. IETF draft-ietf-idr-bgp-vuln-00, February 2002.

[9] R. Oliveira, M. Lad, and L. Zhang, "Understanding the Challenges in Securing Internet Routing," IEEE FIST Workshop, July 2009.

[10] http://www.securelist.com/en/analysis/204792216/Kaspersky _SecurityBulletin_Statistics_2011#11

Persea: A Sybil-Resistant Social DHT

Mahdi N. Al-Ameen
The University of Texas at Arlington
Arlington, TX, USA
mahdi.al-ameen@mavs.uta.edu

Matthew Wright
The University of Texas at Arlington
Arlington, TX, USA
mwright@cse.uta.edu

ABSTRACT

P2P systems are inherently vulnerable to Sybil attacks, in which an attacker can have a large number of identities and use them to control a substantial fraction of the system. We propose Persea, a novel P2P system that is more robust against Sybil attacks than prior approaches. Persea derives its Sybil resistance by assigning IDs through a bootstrap tree, the graph of how nodes have joined the system through invitations. More specifically, a node joins Persea when it gets an invitation from an existing node in the system. The inviting node assigns a node ID to the joining node and gives it a chunk of node IDs for further distribution. For each chunk of ID space, the attacker needs to socially engineer a connection to another node already in the system. This hierarchical distribution of node IDs confines a large attacker botnet to a considerably smaller region of the ID space than in a normal P2P system. Persea uses a replication mechanism in which each (key,value) pair is stored in nodes that are evenly spaced over the network. Thus, even if a given region is occupied by attackers, the desired (key,value) pair can be retrieved from other regions. We compare our results with Kad, Whanau, and X-Vine and show that Persea is a better solution against Sybil attacks.

Categories and Subject Descriptors

C.2.4 [**Communication Networks**]: Distributed Systems-Distributed applications

Keywords

Sybil attack, security, social DHT

1. INTRODUCTION

Peer-to-peer (P2P) systems are highly susceptible to Sybil attacks, in which an attacker creates a large number of pseudonymous entities and use them to gain a disproportionately large influence over the system [1, 2]. Such attacks have been shown to be quite problematic in *structured* P2P systems in which nodes are placed into a distributed hash table (DHT) like Kademlia [8], which is widely used in file-sharing systems.

Recent research has focused on leveraging information from social networks to make the system robust against Sybil attackers, resulting in several decentralized approaches [6, 7,

13]. In these defenses, it is often required that the social network be *fast-mixing*, meaning that a random walk in the honest part of the network approaches the unifrom distribution in a small number of steps. However, a recent study shows that the mixing times of real-world social networks may not be as fast as what these approaches assume [10]. Further, Viswanath et al. have shown that a number of Sybil defenses are ineffective for these slower-mixing, highly *modular* social networks [12].

Contributions. In this paper, we propose a new Sybil-resistant DHT called Persea that addresses these problems and provides better Sybil resistance than the state of the art. The Persea approach offers a number of important advantages over existing schemes:

- A Sybil attacker is limited to isolated regions of the ID space.
- Our system does not depend on the assumption that the social networks are fast-mixing, making Persea more dependable in real-world scenarios.
- Building a bootstrap tree is more realistic than assuming that the clients have access to lists of social network connections from a system like Facebook; such lists may also bear little resemblence to social connections inside the P2P system.
- Although we test it with a DHT routing table design similar to Kademlia, which is widely used, it can be adapted to other DHT routing tables.
- IDs are certified, making attacks based on ID forging impossible outside of attacker-controlled ID ranges.

Our simulation results show that Persea performs much better than Kad [3] in terms of lookup success-rates, e.g. with 100% success compared to just 59.3% when the ratio of attack edges to honest nodes is 0.15. In Whānau [6,7] and X-Vine [9], the success rates are less than 100% for similar scenarios.

2. SYSTEM DESIGN

In this section, we describe the design of Persea. We begin with a brief attack model. We then overview the system and address ID space allocation, ID certification, and key replication. Persea uses the routing table organization and lookup mechanism of Kademlia [8].

Attack Model. A link between an honest node and a malicious node is called an *attack edge*, and it represents a successful act of social engineering to cause the user to accept the malicious node as a social connection [7, 13]. In Persea, creating an attack edge means obtaining an invitation to join the network as a child of the inviting node in the

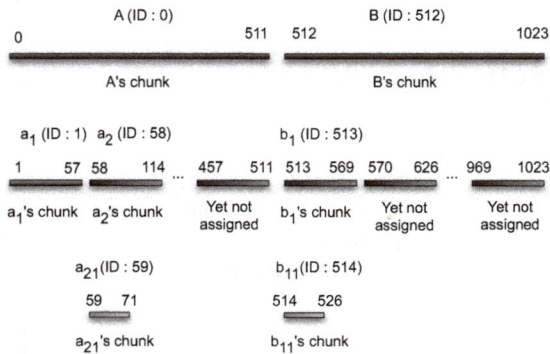

Figure 1: Hierarchical Distribution of Node IDs

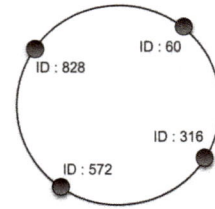

Figure 2: Evenly spaced target nodes

bootstrap tree. When an attacker joins the network, it gets a chunk of node IDs for further distribution and may invite more attacker nodes to join the network. During lookup, when the attacker gets a request to return the value associated with the search-key, it simply drops the message and does not reply as part of a denial of service attack.

2.1 Design Overview

Persea consists of two layers: the bootstrap layer and the DHT layer. In this paper, an *edge* refers to a link between two nodes in the DHT layer. The bootstrap network and DHT are simultaneously built starting with a set of bootstrap nodes. The bootstrap nodes are the initiators of the system. They are connected to each other in both the social network and the DHT. Node IDs in the DHT are assigned to the bootstrap nodes such that they are evenly spaced over the circular ID space. Thus, the ID space of the DHT is divided into one region for each bootstrap node.

A new peer must join the Persea system through an invitation from an existing node in the network. In general, it is expected that a node that is invited is socially known to the inviting peer. When a node is invited, it not only becomes a part of the bootstrap network but also gets a node ID in DHT layer. The new node gets a chunk of node IDs that it can use to invite more nodes for joining the network. ID assignments and chunk allocations are put into certificates signed by the parent nodes, and certificates are stored in the DHT itself to allow for reliable distributed checking of the chain of certificates all the way up to the boostrap nodes.

The number of nodes that a peer can invite is limited by the number of node IDs in its chunk. Thus, there is an incentive for peers to only invite other peers based on actual social connections and to limit the size of each chunk that it gives out so that it does not run out of node IDs. In this way, Persea offers some resilience against social engineering. We would also leverage the user interface to warn users during the invitation process to not invite strangers.

The DHT layer of Persea is based on Kademlia [8], a DHT that is widely adopted for the BitTorrent file-sharing P2P system. The main difference in Persea is that IDs are replicated evenly around the ID space for greater resiliency given our ID distribution scheme.

2.2 Hierarchical ID Space

We now describe how node IDs are distributed in Persea. Each bootstrap node has a contiguous range of node IDs

called a *chunk*, which includes the bootstrap node's ID. A bootstrap node divides its chunk of node IDs into sub-chunks based on the *chunk-factor*, a system parameter.

When a bootstrap node invites a peer to join the system, it assigns a node ID to the joining node from one of its sub-chunks and also assigns the new node control over the rest of the sub-chunk for further distribution. The newly joined node becomes the authority for distributing node IDs from the given sub-chunk. Thus, once the joining node becomes a part of the system, it can invite more nodes to join the system. Based on the invitation-relationship among peers, a *bootstrap tree* is formed in which an inviter node is the parent of its invited peers. If we have more than one bootstrap node, then we would have a forest of trees, where each bootstrap node is the root of each tree. The chunk-factor and size of the ID space define the maximum possible height and width of a tree. This mechanism has the advantage that even if a bot compromises a node and leverages it to add a large number of malicious nodes to the system, they will be still confined in a particular region of ID space.

We briefly explain the mechanism with an example illustrated in Figure 1. Let A and B be two bootstrap nodes that initiate building the system. If we consider a b-bit ID space, then the total number of IDs in the DHT n_{max} would be 2^b. In this example, we consider a 10-bit ID space, so $n_{max} = 2^{10}$. If Z is the number of bootstrap nodes, $\lfloor \frac{n_{max}}{Z} \rfloor$ represents the number of node IDs that each bootstrap node has in its chunk (with a small difference for the bootstrap node with the highest ID). In this example, both node A and node B have 512 node IDs. The lowest node ID in a chunk is assigned to the bootstrap node itself and the remaining node IDs are for further distribution to the newly joined nodes. In this example, node A's ID is 0 and the interval $[1, 511]$ is its chunk of IDs for further distribution.

Each node divides its chunk into sub-chunks based on the chunk-factor. Let n_c be the number of node IDs in a chunk and n_s represent the number of node IDs in each of its sub-chunks (except the last sub-chunk). In a chunk, the lowest ID is assigned to the owner node and the remaining node IDs are for further distribution. Thus $n_c - 1$ represents the number of node IDs in a chunk available for distribution by the owner node. If the chunk-factor is c_f $(0 \leq c_f \leq 1)$ then n_s would be $\lfloor (n_c - 1)^{c_f} \rfloor$. So, the number of sub-chunks that can be created from a chunk is $\lfloor \frac{n_c-1}{n_s} \rfloor + 1$. This also represents the maximum number of nodes that can be invited by a node having chunk of size n_c.

Let $c_f = 0.65$ in this example. Node A divides its chunk into nine sub-chunks where each sub-chunk (except the last one) accommodates 57 node IDs and the last sub-chunk has 55 IDs. Node a_1 joins the network after getting an invitation from node A and node A assigns a sub-chunk to node a_1. The lowest node ID in this sub-chunk is 1, which is assigned as the node ID of node a_1 and the interval $[2, 57]$ represents the remaining node IDs of the sub-chunk that are for further distribution by node a_1. As the chunk space becomes smaller with a deeper tree, a large ID space and appropriate selection of the chunk factor is critical for large systems.

In Persea, we assume that each node knows the value of Z, b and c_f. Thus, if an inviter node intends to assign a node ID to the joining node out of its chunk, the joining node can easily verify it, because any node in Persea can calculate the chunk distribution.

2.3 Replication Mechanism

We describe our replication mechanism in this section, which is the key difference between the Persea DHT layer and Kademlia [8].

When the initiator intends to store or retrieve a (key, value) pair in Persea, it calculates the node ID of the target nodes as follows. Assume a b-bit ID space, such that $n_{max} = 2^b$. We virtually divide the ID space into R regions where each region (except the last one) accommodates at most $D = \lfloor \frac{n_{max}}{R} \rfloor$ IDs, and the last region has $n_{max} - D \times (R - 1)$ IDs. The interval $[r, r + D - 1]$ for $0 \leq r < R - 1$ represents the node IDs that are in the rth region; the last region spans $[D \times (R-1), n_{max} - 1]$. A node ID i is replicated to each other region by taking $(i + D \times r)$ mod n for $1 \leq r < R$. In other words, the information is replicated evenly around the ID space to R locations.

In Figure 2, we show an example of key replication for a 10-bit ID space and $R = 4$, where the key of the (key, value) pair to be stored is 60. The target nodes are evenly spaced around the circular ID space.

3. SIMULATION AND RESULTS

We evaluate Persea in simulations for the social network dataset of wiki-Vote (7, 115 nodes, 103, 689 edges) [4,5] and soc-Epinions1 (75, 879 nodes, 508, 837 edges) [11]. In our experiments, the nodes in these datasets are considered to be honest and attacker nodes are dynamically added to the network. We use n to refer to the number of honest nodes and g to denote the number of attack edges.

We compare our results with other DHTs: Kad [3], Whanau [6, 7], and X-Vine [9]. We simulate Kad to get the lookup success-rate for varying attack edges. The results show that Persea performs much better than Kad in terms of lookup success-rate (see Figure 3). For Whanau and X-Vine, we compare our results with the results reported in [6,7,9].

Whanau: The network size used in [6] is comparable to our wiki-Vote dataset. Our simulation results show that for $g/n = 0.15$ the lookup success rate in Persea is 100%, which is higher than that reported in [6]. For higher values of g/n up to one, the lookup success rate in [6] is no better than Persea. Moreover, Whanau is built upon one-hop DHT routing mechanism and has high maintenance overheads [9].

X-Vine: For different network sizes, the maximum value of g/n considered in [9] is no greater than 0.1. For this value of g/n the maximum probability of success reported in [9] is less than one. But in Persea for higher value of g/n, which is 0.15 we find that the percentage of successful lookup is 100% for wiki-Vote and 99% for soc-Epinoins1 dataset. In topologies with 100, 000 nodes, X-Vine requires 10-15 hops for routing. In Persea, the average hop-count per lookup is only 3.58 for a topology of 75, 879 nodes (soc-Epinions1)

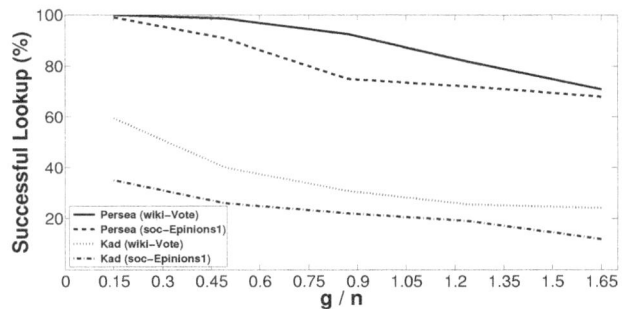

Figure 3: Comparison between Persea and Kad

and we extrapolate that it would remain less than four hops for 100, 000 nodes.

4. FUTURE WORK

We would implement Persea in larger networks and our future experiments would include detail performance and overhead analysis for varying system parameters. Also, we would perform theoretical analysis of Persea to find the probability of lookup failure for varying attack edges.

5. ACKNOWLEDGEMENT

This material is based upon work supported by the National Science Foundation under Grant No. CNS-1117866 and CAREER Grant No. 0954133.

6. REFERENCES

[1] T. Cholez, I. Chrisment, and O. Festor. Evaluation of Sybil attacks protection schemes in KAD. In *AIMS: Scalability of Networks and Services*, 2009.

[2] J. R. Douceur. The Sybil attack. In *IPTPS*, 2002.

[3] H. J. Kang, E. Chan-Tin, N. J. Hopper, and Y. Kim. Why Kad lookup fails. In *P2P*, 2009.

[4] J. Leskovec, D. Huttenlocher, and J. Kleinberg. Predicting positive and negative links in online social networks. In *WWW*, 2010.

[5] J. Leskovec, D. Huttenlocher, and J. Kleinberg. Signed networks in social media. In *CHI*, 2010.

[6] C. Lesniewski-Laas. A Sybil-proof one-hop DHT. In *Workshop on Social Network Systems*, 2008.

[7] C. Lesniewski-Laas and M. F. Kaashoek. Whānau: A Sybil-proof distributed hash table. In *NSDI*, 2010.

[8] P. Maymounkov and D. Mazieres. Kademlia: A peer-to-peer information sytem based on the XOR metric. In *IPTPS*, 2002.

[9] P. Mittal, M. Caesar, and N. Borisov. X-Vine: Secure and pseudonymous routing in DHTs using social networks. In *NDSS*, 2012.

[10] A. Mohaisen, A. Yun, and Y. Kim. Measuring the mixing time of social graphs. In *IMC*, 2010.

[11] M. Richardson, R. Agrawal, and P. Domingos. Trust management for the semantic web. In *ISWC*, 2003.

[12] B. Viswanath, A. Post, K. P. Gummadi, and A. Mislove. An analysis of social network-based Sybil defenses. In *ACM SIGCOMM*, 2010.

[13] H. Yu, P. B. Gibbons, M. Kaminsky, and F. Xiao. SybilLimit: A near-optimal social network defense against Sybil attacks. In *IEEE S&P*, 2008.

A Study of User Password Strategy for Multiple Accounts

S M Taiabul Haque
Department of CSE
University of Texas at Arlington
Arlington,TX USA 76019
eresh03@gmail.com

Matthew Wright
Department of CSE
University of Texas at Arlington
Arlington,TX USA 76019
mwright@cse.uta.edu

Shannon Scielzo
Department of Psychology
University of Texas at Arlington
Arlington,TX USA 76019
scielzo@uta.edu

ABSTRACT

Despite advances in biometrics and other technologies, passwords remain the most commonly used means of authentication in computer systems. Users maintain different security levels for different passwords. In this study, we examine the degree of similarity among passwords of different security levels of a user. We conducted a laboratory experiment with 80 students from the University of Texas at Arlington (UTA). We asked the subjects to construct new passwords for websites of different security levels. We collected the lower-level passwords (e.g., passwords for online news sites) constructed by the subjects, combined them with a comprehensive wordlist, and performed dictionary attacks on their constructed passwords from the higher-level sites (e.g., banking websites). We could successfully crack almost one-third of their constructed passwords from the higher-level sites with this method. This suggests that, if a user's lower-level password is leaked, it can be used effectively by an attacker to crack some of the user's higher-level passwords.

Categories and Subject Descriptors

D.4.6 [**Security and Protection**]: Authentication; H.1.2 [**User/Machine Systems**]: Human factors

General Terms

Security, Human Factors

Keywords

Security; usability; passwords; laboratory experiment

1. INTRODUCTION

Password-based authentication is considered to be the most popular method of user authentication, mainly because of its simplicity and cost effectiveness. However, it is by no means a panacea as far as usability is concerned. As formulated by Wiedenbeck et al., a good password, with its associated character of being an easy-to-remember and a hard-to-guess sequence of characters, presents a conflict [6]. Naturally, words that are easy to recollect from memory are short single words found in dictionaries, or slight variations of them. A tendency to choose such words as passwords makes them susceptible to dictionary attacks.

The password management problem is aggravated by the fact that users need to maintain multiple accounts that require passwords. In a large-scale study, Florêncio et al. reported that Internet users, on average, maintain 25 password-protected accounts [2]. An average user is not expected to be sufficiently equipped on a cognitive level to deal with 25 different passwords. In fact, Adams and Sasse reported that a typical user can be expected to cope with at most four or five passwords effectively [1]. Due to this cognitive capacity constraint, users reuse passwords across different sites, with little or no modification.

Many studies have been conducted for understanding the password habits of users. Researchers from industry periodically gather large-scale data about passwords and publish many insightful lists[1]. The study of Florêncio et al. from Microsoft Research involved half a million users and revealed many interesting findings about different user password habits [2]. Academic researchers, on the other hand, use various novel methods and laboratory studies to observe more closely a particular password behavior (e.g., password reuse habit) of a sample population. Shay et al. capitalized on the opportunity of a Carnegie Mellon University (CMU) password policy change [5], while Gaw et al. gathered feedbacks from users after they had made actual login attempts in different websites [3]. Although these papers have reported about password reuse, our work attempts to look at finer-grained aspects of reuse – how similar are passwords to one another across sites, and how do they vary with perceived security level.

Our study was inspired by the work of Notoatmodjo et al., where they confirmed that users mentally group their accounts and tend to make stronger passwords for accounts that they consider more important [4]. Users have different levels of incentive to protect their different accounts. In this study, we examined how vulnerable the higher-level passwords (Webmail or banking account passwords) of a specific user would become if the lower-level passwords (online news account or weather portal passwords) of that user could be compromised. Our results showed that almost one-third of the higher-level passwords of the participants could be cracked by using the lower-level passwords and a comprehensive worldlist. This demonstrated that the knowledge of a password of a lower-level account seems to increase the chance to crack higher-level account based on similarity to the lower-level password.

---

[1]SplashData recently published its annual list of the most common passwords used on the Internet. The list can be found at http://splashdata.com/press/PR121023.htm.

2. METHODOLOGY

We conducted a laboratory experiment with 80 UTA students. Although a larger number of participants could have been drawn from an online study, we preferred a laboratory study because our pilot study (N=12) showed that a laboratory study would produce more consistent responses. Students were assigned partial course credits in exchange for their participation. The complete study was approved by the local Institutional Review Board (IRB).

In our study, we considered online banking accounts and accounts in all kinds of merchant sites like Amazon.com or Ebay.com to be financial accounts. Webmail accounts and social networking accounts were considered as identity accounts. Users are always concerned about the security of financial accounts because it is always important for them to keep their hard-earned money safe. Users also have a lot of incentives to protect the security of identity accounts, because they build long term reputations of trust in their professional and personal lives through identity accounts.

On the other hand, users create accounts in some websites only to customize the contents of those sites. No significant interaction with other users or financial transaction happens through these accounts. Online news websites and search portals belong to this category. Users do not have much incentive to protect the security of these content accounts.

It is unlikely that all of the password-protected accounts of an individual user belong to one of the categories of identity, financial, or content sites as mentioned above. In our study, we considered users' accounts in all kinds of little recognized websites as *sketchy* accounts. It includes unfamiliar sites that claim to have various kinds of deals, little known online forums or content provider sites. Users have the least incentive to protect the security of these accounts.

We designed a PHP script that prompted the users to create passwords for their new accounts in eight different websites of these four different categories:

- Financial website : Chase.com and Wellsfargo.com

- Identity website : Yahoomail.com and Facebook.com

- Content website : Nytimes.com and Weather.com

- *Sketchy* website : Dreamdeals.com and Justchill.com (hypothetically constructed sites)

We selected Chase.com and Wellsfargo.com as representatives of banking/financial websites because these two banks should be familiar to the participant students due to the prevalence of their ATMs on campus. Facebook.com and Yahoomail.com were selected as identity websites, mainly because of their popularity as a social networking site and a Webmail site, respectively. For content websites, we selected Nytimes.com and Weather.com because these two sites readily present a clear distinction between identity sites and content sites, without any requirement of explicitly labeling them as content sites.

We did not want to give the participants any clue about our experimental motive because we expected the participants to spontaneously construct new passwords, exactly in the same way as they do in real life. Therefore, for all the six real sites, we designed the interfaces such that they would look similar to the original sites. For the two hypothetical unfamiliar sketchy sites, we gave their interfaces a very informal appearance.

2.1 Password Construction

For ethical and security reasons, we explicitly told the participants not to provide any of their existing passwords. For each website, we provided a brief introduction and presented a real-life scenario. For example, for Weather.com, the participants were presented with the following scenario:

> Weather.com provides the latest weather forecasts, maps, and alerts. You want Weather.com to show weather for your local city when you go to the site. To do that, you need to register an account on Weather.com so that you can customize your location. Imagine that you are registering a new account on Weather.com. You have reached the final step of registering your new account, and you need to input a password. Proceed to the next page to input your new password.

As they proceeded, the password construction page for Weather.com appeared.

2.2 Password Policy

For the six real websites, we enforced the same password policies as they are enforced in those sites, which we discovered by attempting to create accounts in those sites. For the two hypothetical sites, we required that the passwords provided by the participants be at least five characters long. As with the original sites, participants were also required to retype their passwords in a second box, which prevented them from typing some random characters as their passwords.

In this way, we implicitly tried to trigger the real life password creation mechanisms of users for websites of different security levels. In designing the interfaces and providing the introduction for each site, we were careful about not revealing to the participants that our main objective is to categorize their constructed passwords based on financial, identity, content or *sketchy* websites.

3. RESULTS

We collected the passwords that were constructed by the participants and grouped together the passwords of the same category. We analyzed each group separately to find out the frequencies of using capital letters, digits and special characters. We also calculated the lengths of the passwords. As expected, the length and the frequency values decreased as the security levels of the sites decreased. Figures 1 and 2 summarize our analysis.

Next, we tried to crack the financial and identity (higher-level) passwords of a participant by using the participant's content and sketchy (lower-level) passwords. For cracking purposes, we used the John The Ripper (JTR) password cracker. We combined the "wordlist" mode of JTR with the "single crack" mode.

The "wordlist" mode cracking is basically a dictionary attack where every word in a wordlist is tried against the candidate password until a match is found. If word mangling rules are enabled, each word in the wordlist is modified or mangled to generate other possible combinations. The "single crack" mode is the default cracking mode of JTR where a large number of word mangling rules are applied to a small dictionary to perform a dictionary attack. As the default set of word mangling rules is very small in the "wordlist" mode, we modified the configuration file of JTR so that it

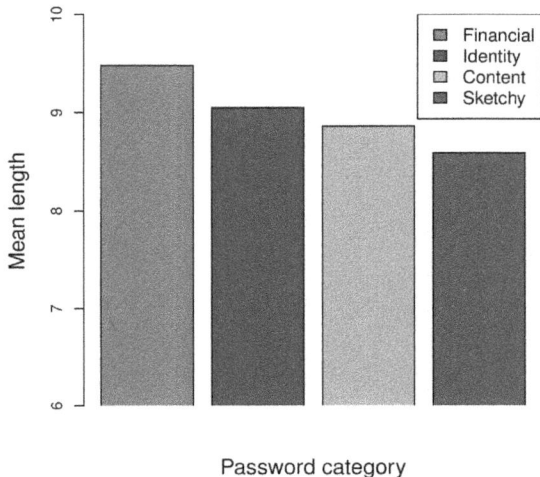

Figure 1: A comparison of mean lengths.

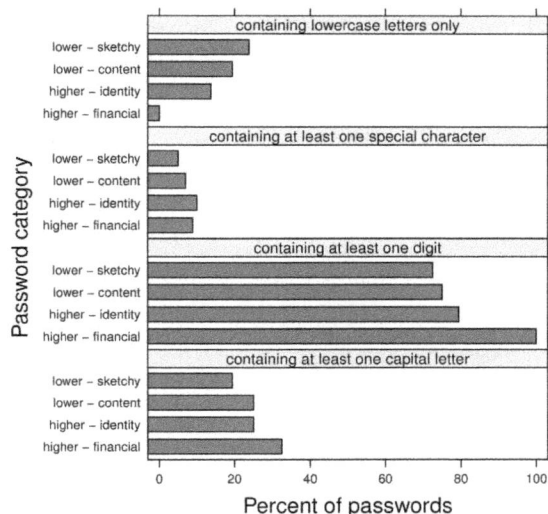

Figure 2: A comparison among passwords of different category.

is possible to apply the large set of word mangling rules of the "single crack" mode while performing cracking in the "wordlist" mode.

For each participant, we combined the participant's four lower-level passwords with the Cain & Abel wordlist and tried to crack four higher-level passwords of that participant in our modified "wordlist" mode. Among the 320 higher-level passwords, we could successfully crack 33.1% (106) of passwords with this method.

We also tried to crack the four higher-level passwords of a participant by using the four lower-level passwords only, without using any wordlist. We could successfully crack 19.1% (61) of higher-level passwords this time. This demonstrates that passwords used at a higher security level have a strong degree of syntactic similarity with the passwords used at a lower level.

4. DISCUSSION AND FUTURE WORK

We do not dispute the fact that our experimental setting was artificial. However, we tried our best to achieve realism in our experiment. For each website, we presented a real-life scenario to the participants and the scenario was created in such a way that it would resemble a real-world application as much as possible. Although our sample size was not large, it can be considered as a reasonable one, compared to the sample sizes of [3], [4], and [6], which were also laboratory experiments among students. Finally, we note that the presence of an observer may, if anything, motivate users to create stronger passwords than they might otherwise.

Our cracking methodology through JTR relied only on syntactic similarity. Through word mangling rules, it modified the lower-level passwords in various ways to guess the higher-level passwords. The semantic similarity was not considered at all. For example, multiple passwords of a user can be inspired from a common source (e.g., music, film, sports etc.). If one of the passwords of a user is related with a personally meaningful word (e.g., the name of the pet), it is probable that another password of that user is also inspired

by a similar thing (e.g., the color of the pet). Our cracking methodology did not leverage these kinds of semantic similarity. We believe that, by exploiting the semantic similarity, a larger percentage of higher level passwords can be cracked. We leave this as a future work.

In addition to asking the participants to construct new passwords, we had them answer a survey regarding their password behaviors for websites of different security levels. We plan to thoroughly review the responses of the survey and report in greater detail how users manage a range of passwords for websites of different security levels.

5. REFERENCES

[1] A. Adams and M. A. Sasse. Users are not the enemy. *Commun. ACM*, 42(12):40–46, 1999.

[2] D. Florêncio and C. Herley. A large-scale study of web password habits. In *Proceedings of the 16th international conference on World Wide Web*, pages 657–666, May 2007.

[3] S. Gaw and E. W. Felten. Password management strategies for online accounts. In *Proceedings of the second symposium on Usable privacy and security*, pages 44–55, July 2006.

[4] G. Notoatmodjo and C. Thomborson. Passwords and perceptions. In *Proceedings of the Seventh Australasian Conference on Information Security - Volume 98*, pages 71–78, January 2009.

[5] R. Shay, S. Komanduri, P. G. Kelley, P. G. Leon, M. L. Mazurek, L. Bauer, N. Christin, and L. F. Cranor. Encountering stronger password requirements: user attitudes and behaviors. In *Proceedings of the Sixth Symposium on Usable Privacy and Security*, July 2010.

[6] S. Wiedenbeck, J. Waters, J.-C. Birget, A. Brodskiy, and N. Memon. Authentication using graphical passwords: effects of tolerance and image choice. In *Proceedings of the 2005 symposium on Usable privacy and security*, pages 1–12, July 2005.

Authenticating Spatial Skyline Queries with Low Communication Overhead

Hans Lo and Gabriel Ghinita
Dept. of Computer Science
University of Massachusetts, Boston
{hlo, gghinita}@cs.umb.edu

ABSTRACT

With the emergence of cloud computing and location-based services, owners of spatial data (e.g., collections of geo-tagged photos, social network location check-ins, etc.) have the option to outsource services such as storage and query processing to a cloud service provider. However, providers of such services are not trusted to properly execute queries, so clients must be given assurance that the results are trustworthy. Therefore, authentication of database queries is needed to ensure correctness and completeness of the results provided by the cloud provider. One type of spatial query that is prominent in practice is the spatial skyline query (SSQ), which allows clients to retrieve results according to specific preferences. In this paper, we propose a solution for authenticating spatial skyline queries that focuses on reducing communication cost compared to existing solutions (MR-Trees). By using a flexible partitioning of the domain coupled with an efficient heuristic, we obtain communication costs that are up to three times lower than existing state-of-the-art.

Categories and Subject Descriptors

H.2.7 **[Database management]**: Database Administration-*security, integrity, and protection*

Keywords

Skyline Queries, Authentication

1. INTRODUCTION

Outsourced database services allow Data Owners (DO) to use a powerful computing infrastructure of a Service Provider (SP) in a flexible and cost-effective fashion. The SP stores data and processes queries from clients, without the DO having to purchase and maintain expensive hardware and software resources. Clients receive results to their queries directly from the SP. However, SPs may not always be trusted, so clients need to be provided assurance that the results to their queries are trustworthy. To that extent, query authentication is necessary to prove to the clients that the results returned by the SP are correct and complete.

Figure 1 outlines the procedure of query authentication. When the DO stores the outsourced data at the SP, it also provides the SP with an authentication dataset signature (ADS) that is computed once by the DO for each dataset instance. In order to verify a query, the SP computes in addition to the results a special *verification object (VO)* which is sent to the client with the query results. The VO typically contains cryptographic hashes that allow the client to verify the ADS and thus ensure that the results received are correct and complete.

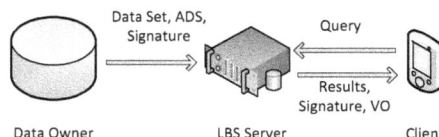

Figure 1: Authenticated Query Processing

One very popular type of query that clients ask are spatial skyline queries (SSQ). Given a set of data points (typically within a two- or three- dimensional spatial domain), and a set Q of query points submitted by the client, the SSQ returns the maximal set of data points R such that no other data point exists which is closer to all the query points in Q than any of the points in the set R.

Formally, the spatial skyline query is defined as follows (we adopt the definition introduced by Shahabi et al. in [1]):

Definition (Spatial Dominance). *Let the set P contain points in the d-dimensional space $\mathbb{R}^d$, and $D(., .)$ be a distance metric defined in $\mathbb{R}^d$ where $D(., .)$ obeys the triangle inequality. Given a set of d-dimensional query points $Q=\{q_1, \ldots, q_n\}$ and the two points p and p' in $\mathbb{R}^d$, p spatially dominates p' with respect to Q iff we have $D(p, q_i) \leq D(p', q_i)$ for all $q_i \in Q$ and $D(p, q_j) < D(p', q_j)$ for some $q_j \in Q$.*

In other words, p spatially dominates p' iff every query point q_i is closer to p than to p' or at the same distance from p and p'. Figure 2 shows a set of four two-dimensional points and two query points q_1 and q_2. With Euclidean distance metric, the point p spatially dominates the point p' as both q_1 and q_2 are closer to p than to p'.

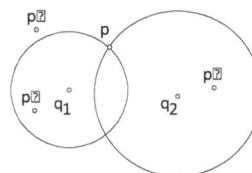

Figure 2: Spatial skyline example

Definition (Spatial Skyline Query). *Given set P of data points and set Q of query points, the spatial skyline of P with respect to Q is the set of points in P which are not spatially dominated by any other point of P. The point $p \in P$ is in the spatial skyline of P with respect to Q iff for any point $p' \in P$ there is a query point $q_i \in Q$ for which we have $D(p, q_i) \leq D(p', q_i)$.*

That is, p is in the spatial skyline iff we have:

$$\forall p' \in P, p' \neq p, \exists q_i \in Q \text{ s.t. } D(p, q_i) \leq D(p', q_i)$$

Figure 2 shows how p' is inside the dominance region of p because p is closer to both q_1 and q_2 than p'.

Currently, the predominant technique used to verify queries relies on an authenticated, hierarchical spatial data structure called Merkle R-Tree (MR-Tree), as described in [2]. Figure 3 shows how authentication is done for a sample dataset indexed by a R-tree [3]. Each leaf node in the MR-tree is identical to that of the R-tree, which stores pointers to actual data objects. The hash digest of a leaf node is obtained by hashing the concatenation of the binary representations of all objects in the node. Each internal node contains a number of entries in the form (ptr_i, MBR_i, H_i), where ptr_i, MBR_i, and H_i are the pointer, the minimum bounding rectangle (MBR), and the digest of the i-th child, respectively. The digest of an internal node summarizes the MBRs and digests of all children nodes (e.g., $H1$ and $H2$ in Figure 3). The VO contains the digests that border the query result in the MR-Tree, and thus allows the client to verify the authenticity of the result.

Note that, due to the large number of digests that are being sent to the client, the VO can grow large. Our objective is to authenticate the result set for a SSQ while reducing communication cost.

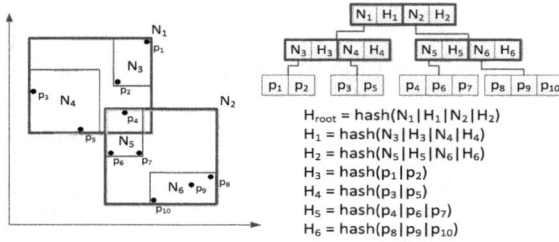

Figure 3: Illustration of MR-Tree

2. PROPOSED SOLUTION

Our solution relies on the observation that only part of the search space is required for authenticating the SSQ, and if this area is captured accurately in the VO, significant costs can be obtained compared to MR-Trees. The area that needs to be authenticated is determined by the relative locations of the query points and the data points. In general, the shape of this space is irregular, as it consists of a set of possibly intersecting circles. In the rest of the paper, we consider a two-dimensional space (most practical case), but our results can be extended to three dimensions as well.

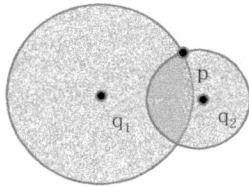

Figure 4: Area that must be verified for SSQ result

In Figure 4, p dominates any point that is outside the shaded areas, which are obtained by drawing circles centered at all query points, with radius given by the distance from p to the respective query point. We use a grid to divide up the spatial domain, and multiple VOs are created, where each VO covers a square region of the grid and is signed by the data owner so that the clients can use them to authenticate results. Using different sizes of squares, we can achieve different levels of granularity. Smaller squares result in more verification objects that need to be signed, but allows for capturing the required area more precisely. Having more levels of granularity allows for an optimal number of verification objects, but results in a larger number of signatures.

Figure 5 shows two examples of how the region not dominated by p can be covered by verification objects. In the first example, the region is covered by a single large VO, while in the second case there are three smaller VOs.

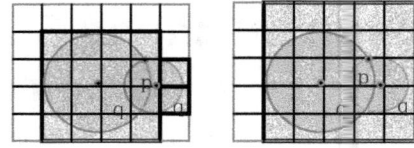

Figure 5: Covering the required area with VOs

Our aim is to calculate the set of VOs that need to be sent to the client while minimizing communication cost. The problem is modeled as a painting problem, where we try to cover the space that needs to be authenticated with as few VOs as possible. One VO can be thought of as a *brush* that covers an area. The brush size is the length of the square represented by the verification object, and it can paint on a particular position of a grid. For example, a *size-2* brush can be painted at the position *(0,0)* of a grid, which would mean that the squares *(0,0)*, *(0,1)*, *(1,0)*, and *(1,1)* have been covered by a single verification object.

The choice of brushes is an element in the solution search space, and is stored in a min-heap. Each element has a set of brush instances to represent the set of VOs chosen so far, as well as a set of coordinate squares representing the grid part still to be painted, which we call the *search region (SR)*. An entry that has an empty SR is a solution to the problem. The value of an entry in the min-heap is the cost of the VO plus the result of a heuristic metric to determine the cost of the SR.

```
Algorithm Compute_VO_Set(Region R, Threshold T)
01. H ← new minheap
02. H.push(h(R, ∅), R, ∅)
03. While(1):
04.   entry ← H.pop()
05.   If entry.SR = ∅
06.     return entry.VO
07.   For each brush size b:
08.     If b ≤ smallest(entry.VO) AND b/entry.SF > T
09.       For each placement of VO V that intersects entry.SR:
10.         newSR ← enty.SR-V
11.         newVO ← entry.VO
12.         H.push(h(newSR, newVO), newSR, newVO)
```

We assume a uniform distribution of data points in the search region, so we express the cost of a single VO as $(V + n\rho)$, where V is a constant cost associated with each verification object (i.e., the size of the signature), n represents the number of grid cells that the VO covers, and ρ is the cost of verifying all the points in a grid cell. For example a 3x3 square will have a cost of $V + 9\rho$.

The algorithm *Compute_VO_Set* starts with the search region as the entire domain covered by the SSQ result (e.g., the set of intersecting circles shown in Figure 4), and an empty set of VOs as the only entry in the min-heap. In each iteration of the while loop, the top entry of the min-heap is removed and examined. If this entry is a solution (SR is empty) then the algorithm returns the result. Otherwise, it examines every possible placement of a verification object (i.e., brush) instance that intersects the SR for this entry. For each of these possibilities, a new entry is created and pushed into the min-heap after calculating its cost value as the cost of the new VO plus the heuristic cost of the newly-obtained SR. As an example, Figure 6 shows two possible placements of verification objects for a 4x4 brush size.

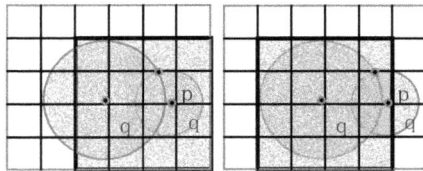

Figure 6: Choices of placing a VO brush instance

The while loop (line 3) continues to execute until a complete solution is popped from the heap, i.e., an element where the associated SR is empty. The quality of the solution (i.e., whether it is optimal or not in terms of communication cost) and the time taken to reach it depend on the search method employed. If an exhaustive search is used to examine all possibilities, then the solution will be optimal, but the performance will suffer as there are exponentially-many combinations of verification objects with respect to the set of possible brush sizes and placements. In order to achieve reasonable performance, we remove from the set of partial solutions cases where the brush size is far smaller than the SR of the corresponding heap element.

Specifically, our heuristic uses an *irregularity measure I*, which quantifies the number of rectangular connected components c in the SR region. The I value captures how "irregular" the shape of the SR is: if the SR is a square shape, then a low I value is obtained. For instance, in Figure 7, even though both shaded regions have the same number of grid cells, the left region has a low irregularity, whereas the one on the right has high irregularity. We quantify I by counting the number of "turns" the SR border makes along its perimeter.

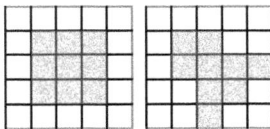

Figure 7: Shapes of different irregularity

Denote the number of cells left uncovered in the SR by n, and let V and ρ be the values from the cost formula introduced above. Then we use as a cost metric for a partial solution the value

$$I(V*c + n*\rho)$$

The heuristic assumes that each connected component needs at least one VO, and that each cell in the grid that needs verified is covered by some verification object. Next, we show the experimental results obtained for the proposed heuristic.

3. EXPERIMENTS

We implemented a Python prototype of the proposed heuristic to find VO sets with low communication cost. We use the Sequoia data set from R-Tree Portal (www.rtreeportal.org) which has 62K points. The experiments were run on a 2.8Ghz Intel Core Duo processor with 4GB of RAM. As a benchmark for comparison, we use an MR-Tree [2] that has a maximum fill factor of *100*. For each test we ran *20* queries using randomly selected query points. The maximum MBR of Q is *0.3%* of the entire data domain, and the query points are chosen in a way that follows the distribution of points in the data set. We assume RSA signatures with a 1024-bit modulus, 256 bytes hashes (SHA-1), and 8-byte data points.

We also benchmark against a baseline method where the entire set of brush instances are *1x1* grid cells in size. This would guarantee that the smallest number of data points is returned in the VO, but the client would have to check many signatures.

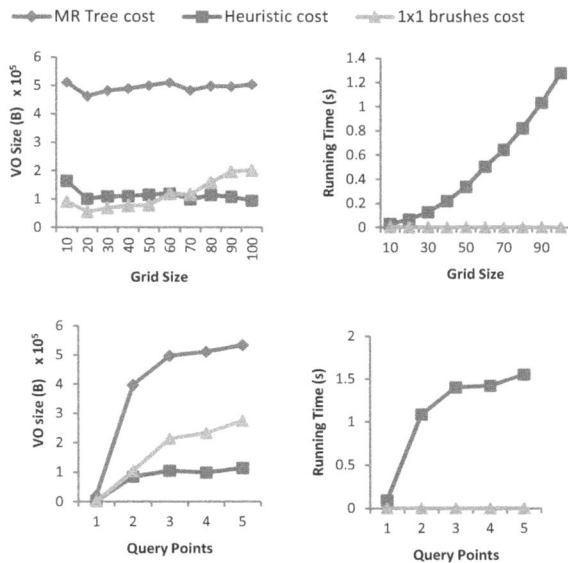

Figure 8: Experimental results

Figure 8 shows that both the proposed heuristic as well as the baseline benchmark clearly outperform the MR-Tree method, due to their increased flexibility in selecting the areas covered by the VOs. The communication cost incurred by our method is as much as five times lower than MR-trees. Also, in many cases we outperform the *1x1* baseline, which, although it minimizes the number of sent data points, it may generate a larger number of signatures that consume bandwidth. The proposed method is relatively robust to the grid size, with a slight improvement for finer-grained grids. Note that, the advantage of the proposed method increases with the number of query points, due to the fact that the resulting SSQ result area becomes more irregular (intersections of many circles), therefore our heuristic that factors in irregularity has larger gains compared to competitors. The time incurred by our heuristic is also acceptable, with sub-second processing times in most cases, and 1.5 seconds in the worst-case.

4. CONCLUSION

We proposed a novel method for generation of VOs in the case of spatial skyline queries. Our method achieves superior communication cost compared to existing state-of-the-art thanks to a flexible technique of splitting and authenticating the search region. Note that, minimizing communication cost is essential for cases where network bandwidth is slow and expensive, such as mobile devices that are prevalent in location-based applications. In future work, we plan to extend our methods to non-spatial skyline queries, and also to investigate alternate heuristics that focus on reducing computation cost as well.

REFERENCES

[1] M. Sharifzadeh and C. Shahabi. 2006. The spatial skyline queries. In *Proceedings of the 32nd international conference on Very large data bases* (VLDB '06), 751-762.

[2] X. Lin, J. Xu, and H. Hu. 2011. Authentication of location-based skyline queries. In *Proceedings of the 20th ACM international conference on Information and knowledge management* (CIKM '11), 1583-1588.

[3] A. Guttman. 1984. R-trees: a dynamic index structure for spatial searching. *SIGMOD Rec.* 14, 2 (June 1984), 47-57.

An Efficient Certificateless Cryptography Scheme without Pairing

Seung-Hyun Seo, Mohamed Nabeel, Xiaoyu Ding, Elisa Bertino
Purdue University
305 N. University Street
West Lafayette, IN, 47907
{seo29, nabeel, ding55, bertino}@purdue.edu

abstract
ABSTRACT

We propose a mediated certificateless encryption scheme without pairing operations. Mediated certificateless public key encryption (mCL-PKE) solves the key escrow problem in identity based encryption and certificate revocation problem in public key cryptography. However, existing mCL-PKE schemes are either inefficient because of the use of expensive pairing operations or vulnerable against partial decryption attacks. In order to address the performance and security issues, in this poster, we propose a novel mCL-PKE scheme. We implement our mCL-PKE scheme and a recent scheme, and evaluate the security and performance. Our results show that our algorithms are efficient and practical.

Categories and Subject Descriptors

E.3 [**Data**]: Data Encryption—*Public key cryptosystems*

Keywords

Key Management, Certificateless cryptography, Confidentiality, Access Control

1. INTRODUCTION

Key management plays a fundamental role in building secure outsourced systems. Earlier systems utilized symmetric keys [7]. Even though key derivation-based approaches [8] reduce the number of keys to be managed, symmetric key based mechanisms in general have the problem of high costs for key management. In order to reduce the overhead of key management, an alternative is to use a public key cryptosystem. However, a traditional public key cryptosystem requires a trusted Certificate Authority (CA) to issue digital certificates that bind users to their associated public keys. Because the CA has to generate its own signature on each user's public key and manage each user's certificate, the overall certificate management is very expensive and complex. To address such shortcoming, Identity-Based Public Key Cryptosystems (IB-PKC) were introduced. However, such cryptosystems suffer from the key escrow problem as the key generation server learns the private keys of all users. Recently, Attribute Based Encryption (ABE) has been proposed that allows one to encrypt each data item only once based on the access control policy applicable to the data. However, in addition to the key escrow problem, ABE has

boilerplate
Copyright is held by the author/owner(s).
CODASPY'13, February 18–20, 2013, San Antonio, Texas, USA.
ACM 978-1-4503-1890-7/13/02.

the revocation problem as the private keys given to existing users should be updated whenever a user is revoked. In order to address the key escrow problem in IB-PKC, Al-Riyami and Paterson introduced a new cryptosystem called Certificateless Public Key Cryptography (CL-PKC) [1].

Lei et al. [5] then proposed the CL-PRE (Certificateless Proxy Re-Encryption) scheme for secure data sharing in public cloud environments. Although their scheme is based on the CL-PKC to solve the key escrow problem and certificate management, it relies on pairing operations. Despite recent advances in implementation techniques, the computational costs required for pairing are still considerably high compared to the costs of standard operations such as modular exponentiation in finite fields. Moreover, their scheme only achieves Chosen Plaintext Attack (CPA) security. As pointed out in [2], CPA security is often not sufficient to guarantee security in general protocol settings. For example, CPA is not sufficient for many applications such as encrypted email forwarding and secure data sharing that require security against Chosen Ciphertext Attack (CCA).

In this poster, we address the shortcomings of such previous approaches and propose a novel mediated Certificateless Public Key Encryption (mCL-PKE) scheme that does not utilize pairing operations. Since most CL-PKC schemes are based on bilinear pairings, they are computationally expensive. Our scheme reduces the computational overhead by using a pairing-free approach. Further, the computation costs for decryption at the users are reduced as a semi-trusted security mediator (SEM) partially decrypts the encrypted data before decryption by the users. The security mediator acts as a policy enforcement point as well and supports instantaneous revocation of compromised or malicious users. In section 3, we show that our scheme is more efficient than the pairing based scheme proposed by Lei et al. [5].

The remainder of this paper is organized as follows: Section 2 introduces our mCL-PKE scheme without pairing. Section 3 reports and discusses results from the experimental evaluation of our scheme and its comparison with other schemes. Finally, Section 4 concludes the poster.

2. MCL-PKE WITHOUT PAIRINGS

In this section, we present the mediated Certificateless Public Key Encryption (mCL-PKE) scheme.

mCL-PKE is a 7-tuple mCL-PKE=(SetUp, SetPrivateKey, SetPublicKey, SEM-KeyExtract, Encrypt, SEM-Decrypt, USER-Decrypt). The description of each algorithm is as follows.

SetUp: It takes a security parameter k as input and returns system parameters **params** and a secret master key **mk**. We assume that **params** are publicly available to all users.

SetPrivateKey: It takes **params** and an identity (ID) as input and outputs the user's (the owner of ID) secret value SK_{ID}. Each user runs this algorithm.

SetPublicKey: It takes **params** and a user's secret value SK_{ID} as input and returns the user's public key PK_{ID}. Each user runs this algorithm.

SEM-KeyExtract: Each user registers its own identity and public key to KGC. After KGC verifies the user's knowledge of the private key corresponding to its public key, KGC takes **params**, **mk** and user identity ID as input and generates a SEM-key corresponding to ID required during decryption time by the SEM. KGC runs this algorithm for each user, and we assume that the SEM-key is distributed securely to the SEM.

Encrypt: It takes **params**, a user's identity ID, a user's public key PK_{ID}, and a message M as inputs and returns either a ciphertext C_{ID} or a special symbol $\perp$ meaning an encryption failure. Any entity can run this algorithm.

SEM-Decrypt: It takes **params**, a SEM-key, and a ciphertext C_{ID} as input, and then returns either a partial decrypted message C'_{ID} for the user or a special symbol $\perp$ meaning an decryption failure. Only SEM runs this algorithm using SEM-key.

USER-Decrypt: It takes **params**, a user's private key SK_{ID}, the partial decrypted message C'_{ID} by SEM as input and returns either a fully decrypted message M or a special symbol $\perp$ meaning an decryption failure. Only the user can run this algorithm using its own private key and the partial decrypted message by SEM.

Now we provide details of the above algorithms.

SetUp: KGC takes as input a security parameter k to generate two primes p and q such that $q|p-1$. It then performs the following steps:

1. Pick a generator g of $\mathbb{Z}_p^*$ with order q.

2. Select $x \in \mathbb{Z}_q^*$ uniformly at random and compute $y = g^x$.

3. Choose cryptographic hash functions $H_1 : \{0,1\}^* \times \mathbb{Z}_p^* \to \mathbb{Z}_q^*$, $H_2 : \{0,1\}^* \times \mathbb{Z}_p^* \times \mathbb{Z}_p^* \to \mathbb{Z}_q^*$, $H_3 : \{0,1\}^* \to \mathbb{Z}_q^*$, $H_4 : \mathbb{Z}_p^* \to \{0,1\}^{n+k_0}$, $H_5 : \mathbb{Z}_p^* \to \{0,1\}^{n+k_0}$, and $H_6 : \mathbb{Z}_p^* \times \{0,1\}^{n+k_0} \times \mathbb{Z}_p^* \times \{0,1\}^{n+k_0} \to \mathbb{Z}_q^*$, where n, k_0 are the bit-length of a plaintext and a random bit string, respectively.

The system parameters *params* are $(p, q, n, k_0, g, y, H_1, H_2, H_3, H_4, H_5, H_6)$. The master key of KGC is x. The plaintext space is $\mathsf{M} = \{0,1\}^n$ and the ciphertext space is $\mathsf{C} = \mathbb{Z}_p^* \times \{0,1\}^{n+k_0} \times \mathbb{Z}_q^*$

SetPrivateKey: The entity **A** chooses $z_A \in \mathbb{Z}_q^*$ uniformly at random as the private key of **A**.

SetPublicKey: The entity **A** computes $U_A = g^{z_A}$.

SEM-KeyExtract: KGC selects $s_0, s_1 \in \mathbb{Z}_q^*$ and computes $w_0 = g^{s_0}$, $w_1 = g^{s_1}$, $d_0 = s_0 + xH_1(ID_A, w_0)$, $d_1 = s_1 + xH_2(ID_A, w_0, w_1)$. KGC sets d_0 as the SEM-key for **A**. After **A** proves the knowledge of the secret value z_A such that $U_A = g^{z_A}$, KGC sets (U_A, w_0, w_1, d_1) as the **A**'s public keys.

Encrypt: To encrypt a plaintext $M \in \{0,1\}^n$ for the entity **A** with identity ID_A and public keys (U_A, w_0, w_1, d_1), it performs the following steps:

1. Check whether $g^{d_1} = w_1 \cdot y^{H_2(ID_A, w_0, w_1)}$.
   If the verification fails, the encryption algorithm is aborted.

2. Choose $\sigma \in \{0,1\}^{k_0}$ and compute $r = H_3(M, \sigma, ID_A, U_A)$.

3. Compute $C_1 = g^r$.

4. Compute $C_2 = (M||\sigma) \oplus H_4(U_A{}^r) \oplus H_5(w_0^r \cdot y^{H_1(ID_A, w_0) \cdot r})$.

5. Compute $C_3 = H_6(U_A, (M||\sigma) \oplus H_4(U_A^r), C_1, C_2)$.

Output the ciphertext $C = (C_1, C_2, C_3)$.

In Step 1, an entity who wants to encrypt a message can verify the validity of receiver's public key. Steps 2-5 are the encryption steps.

SEM-Decrypt: Given the ciphertext $C = (C_1, C_2, C_3)$, an identity ID_A, **A**'s public keys (U_A, w_0, w_1, d_1), SEM performs the following steps using the SEM-key d_0:

1. Check that ID_A is a legitimate user whose key has not been revoked.

2. Compute $C_1{}^{d_0}$.
   $C_1{}^{d_0} = g^{r \cdot d_0} = g^{r \cdot (s_0 + xH_1(ID_A, w_0))}$
   $= g^{r \cdot s_0} \cdot g^{r \cdot xH_1(ID_A, w_0)} = w_0{}^r \cdot y^{r \cdot H_1(ID_A, w_0)}$

3. Compute $C_2 \oplus H_5(C_1^{d_0})$
   $C_2 \oplus H_5(C_1^{d_0})$
   $= (M||\sigma) \oplus H_4(U_A^r) \oplus H_5(w_0^r \cdot y^{H_1(ID_A, w_0) \cdot r}) \oplus H_5(C_1^{d_0})$
   $= (M||\sigma) \oplus H_4(U_A^r) \oplus H_5(w_0^r \cdot y^{H_1(ID_A, w_0) \cdot r}) \oplus H_5(w_0^r \cdot y^{H_1(ID_A, w_0) \cdot r})$
   $= (M||\sigma) \oplus H_4(U_A^r)$

4. Check whether $C_3 = H_6(U_A, C_2 \oplus H_5(C_1^{d_0}), C_1, C_2)$.

If the verification at Step 2 succeeds, SEM sends C_1 and $C_2' = (M||\sigma) \oplus H_4(U_A^r)$ to **A**. Otherwise, it aborts SEM-Decrypt.

In Step 1, SEM ascertains whether the user's identification information is valid. In Step 2 SEM performs the partial decryption of the ciphertext C using SEM-key. In Step 3, SEM computes token information that is needed for the complete decryption by the USER-Decrypt algorithm. After SEM finishes executing the partial decryption and the token generation, it performs the validity checking for the ciphertext C in Step 4. In order to prevent partial decryption attacks, Step 4 is required.

USER-Decrypt: Given C_1 and C_2' from the SEM, **A** performs the following steps using its private key z_A:

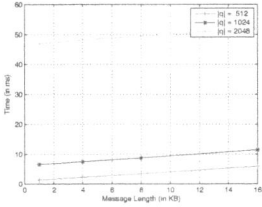

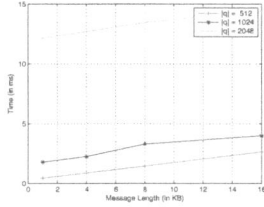

(a) mCL-PKE Encryption   (b) mCL-PKE Decryption   (c) Encryption Comparison   (d) Decryption Comparison

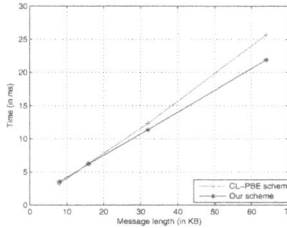

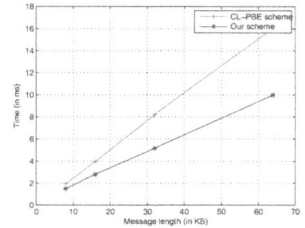

1. Compute $C_1{}^{z_A}$
   $$C_1{}^{z_A} = g^{r \cdot z_A} = g^{z_A \cdot r} = U_A{}^r$$

2. Parse M' and σ' from $M'||\sigma' = H_4(C_1{}^{z_A}) \oplus C_2'$

3. Compute $r' = H_3(M', \sigma', ID_A, U_A)$ and $g^{r'}$

4. Check whether $g^{r'} = C_1$

If the verification succeeds then the fully decrypted message $M' = M$ is returned. Otherwise, the USER-Decrypt is aborted.

In Steps 1 and 2, **A** fully decrypts C_2' using its own private key z_A. In Step 3, **A** computes a value which is then used at Step 4 to determine whether the decryption is successful.

3. EXPERIMENTAL RESULTS

In this section, we first present the experimental results for our mCL-PKE scheme. Then we compare our approach with a recent pairing-based scheme proposed by Lei et al.[5].

The experiments were performed on a machine running 32 bits GNU Linux kernel version 3.2.0-30 with an Intel®Core™i5-2430 CPU @ 2.40GHZ and 8 GBytes memory. Our prototype system is implemented in C/C++. We use V. Shoup's NTL library [9] version 5.5.2 for big number calculation and field arithmetic. The NTL library is compiled along with the GMP library [4] in order to improve the performance of computations involving large numbers. We construct the hash function required for the mCL-PKE scheme based on MD5 [3] version 1.6.

Figure 1a shows the time required to perform the encryption operation in the mCL-PKE scheme for different message sizes. Since our scheme does not use pairing operations, it performs encryption efficiently. As can be seen from the graph, the encryption time increases linearly as the message size increases. As the bit length of q increases, the cost increases non-linearly since the encryption algorithm performs exponentiation operations. As in Figure 1b, a similar observation applies to the SEM decryption and user decryption.

We have also implemented Lei et al.[5]'s certificateless proxy re-encryption scheme based on pairing. According to the results reported in their paper, proxy-encryption takes 7-8ms to encrypt a message with length 3K bits. We reimplemented their scheme using the PBC-library [6]. Our implementation of their scheme is actually more efficient and the time for encrypting a message of 8K Bytes is about 3ms. We then compared our scheme with their scheme for encryption. Even with the improved implementation, as shown in Figure 1c, our encryption algorithm is more efficient than their algorithm for message sizes above 16K bytes. A similar observation applies to the decryption algorithm. This observation is consistent with the fact that our scheme uses an efficient hash function and XOR operations to perform encryption and decryption whereas their scheme uses more expensive constructs.

4. CONCLUSIONS

In this poster, we proposed a mediated certificateless public key encryption scheme without pairing operations called mCL-PKE. Our mCL-PKE solves the key escrow problem and revocation problem. As our experimental results show, our mCL-PKE scheme is efficient. We plan to extend certificateless cryptography to support group scenarios.

ACKNOWLEDGEMENTS

The work reported in this paper has been partially funded by the US Department of Energy under the project "Cryptographic Key Management Systems" through a subcontract by Sypris Electronics.

5. REFERENCES

[1] S. Al-Riyami and K. Paterson. Certificateless public key cryptography. In C.-S. Laih, editor, *ASIACRYPT '03*, volume 2894, pages 452–473. 2003.

[2] R. Canetti and S. Hohenberger. Chosen-ciphertext secure proxy re-encryption. In *CCS '07*, pages 185–194, 2007.

[3] L. P. Deutsch. MD5 hash function. http://sourceforge.net/projects/libmd5-rfc/files/.

[4] The gnu multiple precision arithmetic library. http://gmplib.org/.

[5] X. W. Lei Xu and X. Zhang. CL-PKE: a certificateless proxy re-encryption scheme for secure data sharing with public cloud. In *CCS '12*.

[6] B. Lynn. Pairing-based cryptography. http://crypto.stanford.edu/pbc.

[7] G. Miklau and D. Suciu. Controlling access to published data using cryptography. In *VLDB '03*, pages 898–909. VLDB Endowment, 2003.

[8] M. Nabeel, N. Shang, and E. Bertino. Privacy preserving policy based content sharing in public clouds. *TKDE*, 2012.

[9] V. Shoup. NTL library for doing number theory. http://www.shoup.net/ntl/.

Fast, Scalable Detection of "Piggybacked" Mobile Applications

Wu Zhou, Yajin Zhou, Michael Grace,
and Xuxian Jiang
North Carolina State University
Raleigh, NC, USA
{wzhou2, yajin_zhou,mcgrace,
xjiang4}@ncsu.edu

Shihong Zou
Beijing Univ. of Posts & Telecommunications
Beijing, China
zoush@bupt.edu.cn

ABSTRACT

Mobile applications (or apps) are rapidly growing in number and variety. These apps provide useful features, but also bring certain privacy and security risks. For example, malicious authors may attach destructive payloads to legitimate apps to create so-called "piggybacked" apps and advertise them in various app markets to infect unsuspecting users. To detect them, existing approaches typically employ pair-wise comparison, which unfortunately has limited scalability. In this paper, we present a fast and scalable approach to detect these apps in existing Android markets. Based on the fact that the attached payload is not an integral part of a given app's primary functionality, we propose a module decoupling technique to partition an app's code into primary and non-primary modules. Also, noticing that piggybacked apps share the same primary modules as the original apps, we develop a feature fingerprint technique to extract various semantic features (from primary modules) and convert them into feature vectors. We then construct a metric space and propose a linearithmic search algorithm (with $O(n \log n)$ time complexity) to efficiently and scalably detect piggybacked apps. We have implemented a prototype and used it to study $84,767$ apps collected from various Android markets in 2011. Our results show that the processing of these apps takes less than nine hours on a single machine. In addition, among these markets, piggybacked apps range from 0.97% to 2.7% (the official Android Market has 1%). Further investigation shows that they are mainly used to steal ad revenue from the original developers and implant malicious payloads (e.g., for remote bot control). These results demonstrate the effectiveness and scalability of our approach.

Categories and Subject Descriptors

C.4 [**Performance of Systems**]: Measurement techniques; K.6.5 [**Management of Computing and Information Systems**]: Security and protection – *Invasive software*

General Terms

Security; Algorithms; Measurement

Keywords

Mobile Application; Smartphone Security; App Repackaging; Piggybacked Application

1. INTRODUCTION

With the wide adoption of smartphones and mobile devices, mobile applications (or apps) are rapidly growing in number and variety. Recent statistics [6] show that since January 2012, Google's Android Market is home to more than $400,000$ apps for users to browse and download. What is more, the number is increasing at an astonishing rate: each month will see more than $20,000$ apps being published [6]. The convenience and functionality these apps offer greatly extend the capability and reach of mobile devices. Unfortunately, along with the above benefits, there are undesirable privacy risks and security issues associated with these mobile apps. For example, malware authors may piggyback destructive payloads on known good apps and then advertise the *piggybacked apps* in various app markets to infect unsuspecting users. For ease of presentation, we use the term *carrier* to refer to the original app being piggybacked and the term *rider* to denote the additional code injected into the original app. Notice that piggybacked apps are a special kind of repackaged apps [26, 44], which are created by modifying and re-signing legitimate apps for distribution. The distinction however is that piggybacked apps involve injecting (new) rider code into the original apps while repackaged apps may only make minor modifications, including tweaking resource files or replacing constant strings for new language support.

With the inclusion of new rider code, piggybacked apps pose greater security threats than other kinds of repackaged apps. In fact, a number of security alerts have been issued about the presence of piggybacked apps in various app markets. Specifically, these piggybacked apps embed malicious rider code into popular carrier apps, such as games and utility programs. Once installed, the rider code could perform a variety of malicious actions, such as sending text messages to premium numbers [32] and converting the infected phones into bots [31].

Recognizing these threats, researchers have explored different ways to detect them. The App Genome Project [26] and DroidMOSS [44] are two representative examples. They are designed to detect repackaged apps in general among third-party app markets – by assuming that apps in the official Android Market are original. This assumption is intuitive and reasonable in some aspect, but it prevents them from detecting repackaged apps in the official Android Market, where repackaged apps are also found in considerable amount [28]. In addition, while App Genome Project does not disclose its detection methodology, DroidMOSS uses a fuzzy hashing technique to generate app fingerprints based on their instruction sequences and then applies *pair-wise comparison* to detect repackaged apps. Pair-wise comparison does not scale to the large amount of apps available in modern marketplaces.

In this paper, we propose a fast and scalable approach called *Pig-*

gyApp to effectively detect piggybacked apps in existing Android markets, including both official and unofficial ones. PiggyApp meets the need for scalability and timeliness by accommodating the fast influx of a large number of apps in existing marketplaces, which dwarfs earlier approaches. Moreover, our system eliminates the previous assumption by considering apps from different marketplaces in the same manner, which uniquely enables the detection of piggybacked apps in the official Android Market (now part of Google Play).

Our approach is based on two main observations. First, in a piggybacked app, the rider code is relatively independent and does not tightly interweave, if any, with the primary functionality of the host app. Therefore, we propose a technique called *module decoupling* to effectively partition the app code into primary and non-primary modules. Each app has one unique primary module, which mainly implements the advertised functionality. Meanwhile, it may have a number of non-primary modules that are relatively standalone. Various support routines or libraries, advertisement packages, and mobile payment frameworks – as well as embedded rider code – fall in this category.

Second, a piggybacked app typically shares the same primary module as the original carrier app. Accordingly, we propose another technique called *feature fingerprinting* to extract certain semantic features (e.g., the requested permissions and used Android APIs) embodied in the primary module. To facilitate this comparison and meet our scalability requirements, we represent them as feature vectors, organize these feature vectors into a metric space, and then propose a linearithmic search algorithm (with $O(n \log n)$ time complexity – compared to the previous $O(n^2)$ complexity of pair-wise comparison) to detect piggybacked apps. From these piggybacked apps, we further derive the corresponding rider code and perform a systematic study about its functionality and purpose.

We have implemented a proof-of-concept prototype and used it to detect piggybacked apps in multiple Android markets worldwide, including the official market and six alternative ones: two from the US, two from Eastern Europe and two from China. Our study includes $84,767$ apps and $68,187$ of them come from the official Android Market. These apps are collected by taking a snapshot of the available apps on these marketplaces in the first week of March 2011. By running our system on a standalone desktop machine (with 4 cores and 8G memory), it takes less than 9 hours to process all of these apps, which meets our scalability and timeliness requirements. The results show that 1.0% apps in the official Android Market are piggybacked. For the rest alternative ones, the piggybacked apps vary from 0.97% to 2.7%. By analyzing the rider code, we find that its main purposes are to embed ad libraries to steal the generated ad revenue from the original developers or to implant malicious payloads to compromise users' phones.

The rest of this paper is organized as follows: We describe the system design in Section 2, followed by its prototyping and evaluation results in Section 3. After that, we discuss the system's limitations and suggest possible improvements in Section 4. Lastly, we describe related work in Section 5 and conclude in Section 6.

2. DESIGN

In Figure 1, we show the overall architecture of our system. While piggybacked apps leverage carrier apps to entice users into downloading and installing them, the main purpose is to execute the attached rider code unnoticed. Notice that the rider code is relatively independent and should not closely interweave, if any, with the primary functionality of the carrier app. Accordingly, we propose *module decoupling* to first isolate the primary modules

from existing apps. Moreover, as piggybacked apps still share the same primary module code base as the originals, we then propose to mainly compare primary modules to infer the piggybacking relationship between two apps.

In our system design, there are three competing goals: *scalability*, *accuracy*, and *efficiency*. Scalability is needed to accommodate the large number of apps in existing markets; accuracy requires our system to effectively detect piggybacked apps with few false positives and negatives; and efficiency imposes the need for our system to handle existing apps in a timely and resource-efficient manner. Specifically, to meet the scalability requirement, our system must improve upon the $O(n^2)$ time complexity of pair-wise comparison in existing systems [44]. To this end, we develop a *feature fingerprinting* technique that extracts semantic features from the primary module, including requested permissions and used Android APIs, and represents them as feature vectors. These feature vectors are used to construct a metric space from which we can efficiently identify similar apps using a linearithmic search algorithm ($O(n \log n)$ time complexity). By further examining the signing certificates and other non-primary modules of similar apps, we can effectively detect piggybacked apps as well as the related rider code.

In this work, we assume that piggybacking mainly occurs by adding Java code to a legitimate app, instead of native code. There are two main reasons: first, compared to native code, Java code is typically a more vulnerable target for piggybacking. A number of tools [9, 40] have been developed and can be readily misused for this purpose. Second, existing apps are still primarily written in Java, instead of C, which results in much less native code in existing apps. Considering the dataset used in this study, we find that only 5% of all apps contain native code. In addition, we assume that legitimate app developers do not disclose their private keys (for app signing) to others. Therefore, piggybacked apps will not share the same certificates as the original apps. Next, we detail each essential component in our system.

2.1 Module Decoupling

An Android app is typically composed of multiple relatively independent modules. The primary module implements the main functionality, which is advertised to attract user downloads. Other non-primary modules may serve the primary module with support routines and utility libraries, but could also be completely independent (such as ad libraries). Within each module, either primary or non-primary, the code is tightly coupled or organized; between modules, the code is loosely coupled or even not related. (Some standalone apps may only contain one module – the primary module.) Without the access to the app's source code, we resort to program comprehension techniques [5] to decouple internal modules within an app.

For a given app, our module decoupling process takes as input its `classes.dex` file and works in two main steps. First, based on the Dalvik bytecode, we build a program dependency graph (PDG). Within the graph, the node represents a Java class package that contains a number of Java class files declared within it. An edge connects two class packages if there exists an interaction or a dependency between these two packages. A weight is assigned to an edge to indicate how close these two class packages are connected. In our system, the edge essentially captures the following interaction or dependency relationship: class inheritance, package homogeny[1], method calls, and member field references. Each of this relationship in general represents certain degree of coupling

---
[1] Two packages are homogeneous if they form a parent-child relation or share the same parent.

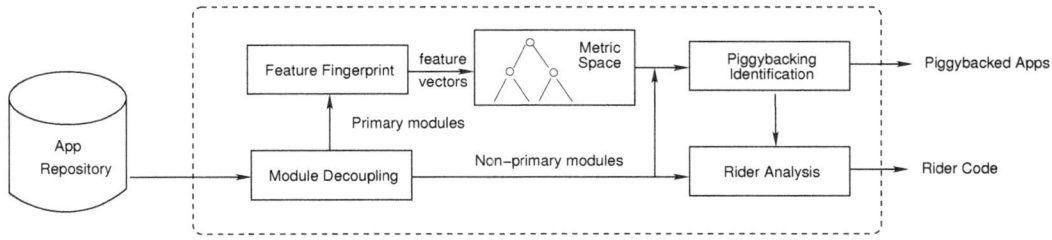

Figure 1: The overall system architecture

and our system will collect it and assign a weight. As the class inheritance relationship shows tighter coupling between two classes, we accordingly assign a higher weight to the edge than others that may simply indicate a single method call. Between two class packages, we use two cumulative weight values to unidirectionally sum all the edge weights from one to another.

Second, based on this program dependency graph, we use an agglomerative clustering algorithm (Algorithm 1) to group these class packages into different modules. To begin with, we initialize a number of singleton clusters one for each class package in the graph. After that, we repeat the process of checking whether any two clusters can be merged and, if they can, merging the pair of clusters that have the largest cumulative weight values. Otherwise, we report the resulting set of clusters as the modules contained in the app. Note the merge_able condition (line 2) in the algorithm examines the remaining largest cumulative weight values between any cluster pair. In our prototype, we empirically choose a cut-off value (Section 3).

Algorithm 1 Agglomerative clustering
___
Input: `Program dependency graph (PDG) of an app`
Output: `A list of primary and non-primary modules`

```
1: clusters = create_singleton_clusters(PDG)
2: while merge_able(clusters) do
3:    compute_coupling_between_each_pair(clusters)
4:    (c1, c2) ← select_the_most_coupled_pair(clusters)
5:    clusters ← merge(c1, c2, clusters)
6: end while
7: return clusters
```

In Figure 2, we show an example run of the clustering algorithm on a piggybacked app (MD5: 09105460be466d0c024c37df8997b061). Initially, it has six modules com.rechild.advancedtaskkiller, com.google.ads, com.google.ads.util, org.json, com.android.root, and jackpal.androidterm. The figure shows the cumulative weight values between each pair. After the run, our algorithm effectively merges com.google.ads and com.google.ads.util and reports five remaining clusters as standalone modules.

Among the reported modules, we then determine which one is the primary module. In particular, we leverage the information in the AndroidManifest.xml file that declares various components of an app, including its activities, services, receivers, and content providers. Specifically, it specifies concrete classes that will be invoked to handle certain events or actions. A special one is ACTION.MAIN that represents the main entry point of the app. Accordingly, we choose the module that contains this class as a candidate for the primary module. Meanwhile, notice that the primary module tends to provide the main interface for users to interact with. Therefore, we also select the module with classes that handle most activities as the primary module candidate. If

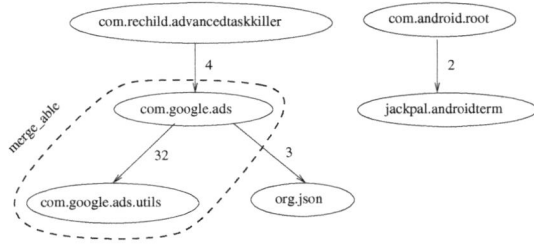

Figure 2: An example module decoupling run

there are multiple candidates, we choose the most similar one by calculating the similarity of the module name against the app name in the manifest file. In our experiments, we do not encounter any piggybacked apps that change the app name to a completely unrelated one.

2.2 Feature Fingerprint and Representation

After module decoupling, we then generate feature fingerprints for the primary module. More specifically, feature fingerprints are supposed to distinguish the functionality of one primary module from another. To this end, we extract various semantic features such as the requested permissions, the Android API calls used, involved intent types (which represent the way for inter-component or inter-process communication), the use of native code or external classes, as well as the authorship information (from the developer certificates in the META-INFO directory). The intuition is that it is rare for two different modules to be coincidentally the same in all the above items. Notice that we include the developer information to exclude different apps authored by the same developer as there is no such need.

With the collected features, we then represent them into a vector where 0 and 1 respectively represent the absence and presence of certain feature in the primary module. After that, we organize these feature vectors (each representing an app) into a metric space and transform the problem of detecting piggybacked apps into a nearest neighbor searching problem. A naive approach for nearest neighbor searching is to perform pair-wise comparison and choose the one with the smallest distance. Considering the number of apps in current app markets, this approach is not scalable with its $O(n^2)$ complexity. That is also the main reason why we choose to construct a metric space from the extracted feature vectors. By exploiting its triangle inequality property [43], we can effectively prune irrelevant portion during the search and achieve an $O(n \log n)$ time complexity, thus accommodating the scalability challenge.

In the metric space construction, we use the following Jaccard distance between the primary module features of two apps as the

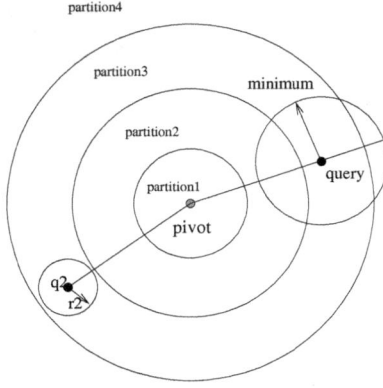

Figure 3: Triangle inequality-based VPT pruning

distance metric:

$$Jaccard(F_A, F_B) = \frac{|F_A \cup F_B| - |F_A \cap F_B|}{|F_A \cup F_B|} \quad (1)$$

where F_A and F_B represent the feature vector of primary module A and B respectively. Recall that they are vectors of binary values (0 or 1) to indicate whether one specific API call, permission, intent type or any external code loading behaviors occur in the module code. Formula 1 essentially calculates the ratio of disjoint features over the union of features present in these two modules to characterize how different they are. As shown in [41], the Jaccard distance satisfies the property of the triangle inequality that is being exploited to prune the irrelevant part of the search space.

In our system, we use a Vantage Point Tree (VPT) [43] to construct the metric space. Specifically, we first select a primary module as the root pivot P, measure the Jaccard distances between P and all the rest of the modules, sort these modules in an ascending order of their distances to the pivot, and then divide them into a fixed number N of balanced partitions, represented as P_i, i = 1,2,...N. At the pivot, the distance range associated with each partition P_i is recorded, represented as $P_i.MIN$ and $P_i.MAX$. For each partition of the pivot, we will repeat this partitioning procedure to reduce its size to a manageable level.

To elaborate how the triangle inequality property enables efficient search pruning in the constructed VPT tree, we present in Figure 3 the partitions as concentric circles based on their distance ranges to the pivot. For an app query, suppose we discovered another app nearest_neighbor with the minimum distance to query. The search space is then reduced to locate another app, say test, whose distance to query is smaller than minimum. Due to the triangle inequality property in Jaccard distance, we have:

$$distance(query, test) > |distance(query, pivot) \\ - distance(pivot, test)| \quad (2)$$

If |distance(query, pivot) - distance(pivot, test)| > minimum holds for any app test inside a partition, we can safely ignore this partition during the search. Thus we can use the following pruning conditions to skip any irrelevant partition P_i because it is not possible to find a shorter distance than minimum:

$$minimum < distance(pivot, query) - P_i.MAX \quad (3)$$

$$minimum < P_i.MIN - distance(pivot, query) \quad (4)$$

In Algorithm 2, we outline how nearest neighbor search works in VPT. It has two inputs: the query app query and the current

---

Algorithm 2 Nearest Neighbor Search in VPT: nearestNeighborSearch(query, currentNode)

```
 1:  if currentNode is a leaf node then
 2:      for each app in this leaf node do
 3:          if app and query not from the same author then
 4:              if minimum > distance(app, query) then
 5:                  minimum = distance(app, query)
 6:                  nearest_neighbor = app
 7:              end if
 8:          end if
 9:      end for
10:  end if

11:  if currentNode is a pivot node then
12:      if pivot and query not from the same author then
13:          if minimum > distance(pivot, query) then
14:              minimum = distance(pivot, query)
15:              nearest_neighbor = pivot
16:          end if
17:      end if
18:      for each partition P_i of this pivot code do
19:          if minimum< distance(pivot, query)-P_i.MAX or
                  minimum< P_i.MIN-distance(pivot, query) then
20:              continue
21:          end if
22:          nearestNeighborSearch(query, P_i)
23:      end for
24:  end if
```

root VPT node currentNode. During the search, we maintain two global variables, i.e., nearest_neighbor and the current minimum distance. If we reach a leaf node (lines 1 to 10), the algorithm simply computes the distances between the query app and each app stored in this leaf node. If any distance is smaller than current minimum value and they are also from different developers, we locate a closer distance and accordingly update minimum and nearest_neighbor (lines 4 to 7). If we hit a pivot node (lines 11 to 24), the same procedure will be applied to the pivot app. Moreover, we will further examine each partition of this pivot node (line 18). If any of the pruning conditions in Formula 3 and Formula 4 are satisfied (line 19), this partition can be safely skipped; otherwise the nearest neighbor searching procedure will be recursively invoked on this partition (line 22). To speed up the search, we can also initialize the minimum to a small number that indicates the acceptable level for piggybacking detection. This is possible because our previous module decoupling technique only retains primary modules for comparison while removing other non-essential ones (i.e., non-primary modules) as noise. Also, instead of only returning one nearest_neighbor, we can adjust the algorithm to report a list of apps that fall in a range of distance with the query app. In either case, the algorithm has the time complexity of $O(n \log n)$.

2.3 Piggybacking Identification and Rider Analysis

By iterating through each app collected from an app market, our algorithm effectively reports a list of related apps which share similar primary modules and thus are candidates for piggybacked apps. To identify the exact piggybacking relationship, we take into account non-primary modules of related apps. Specifically, for each reported pair A and B, we match their non-primary modules.

If the non-primary modules of an app A are a strict sub-set of B, any non-primary modules in B, but not in A, will be considered part of the rider code. Accordingly, we label the app with the rider code as the piggybacked app, and the other as the corresponding carrier app. If both apps have non-matched modules standing out, we choose to report them as a piggybacked pair, as we are not able to determine which one is piggybacked.

Besides determining the piggybacking relationship, we are also interested in what functionality is implemented in the rider code. While manual analysis in general cannot be avoided, our investigation shows that the same rider code may be injected into multiple piggybacked apps. Accordingly, we elect to cluster the detected rider code and group them for correlation. By doing so, we are able to identify several clusters whose members are very similar to each other. In our prototype, we choose to reuse the previous algorithm and build another VPT tree (Section 2.2) *only* for these identified riders. Our experience shows that the number of rider-related non-primary modules is one magnitude smaller than that of apps, which allows us to select a smaller distance (as the range parameter). As to be shown in Section 3.5, such clustering quickly exposes several clusters with the same rider code piggybacking on a number of carrier apps.

3. PROTOTYPING AND EVALUATION

We have implemented a prototype of PiggyApp in Linux. In our prototype, the first component – module decoupling (Section 2.1) – is implemented by extending the open source Dalvik disassembler `baksmali` [3] (with an additional 1926 lines of Java code) to generate the program dependency graph (PDG) and then isolate primary modules from other non-primary modules. When generating the graph, we assign weights 10, 10, 2, 1 to edges representing class inheritance, package homogeny, method calls, and member field references, respectively. The cut-off value for the `merge_able` condition (Algorithm 1) is empirically set to 5, which works well in practice (Section 3.2).

The second component – feature fingerprint and representation (Section 2.2) – extracts the semantic features of 32,011 APIs, 136 permissions, 122 intent types, 180 content provider features, and 2 additional code loading features, which essentially condense each app into a feature vector of length 32,451. These feature vectors are then organized into a Vantage Point Tree (VPT) that is implemented in 2,731 lines of C code. For search efficiency, we set the number of partitions at each pivot node to 3. To strike a good balance between accuracy and efficiency, we select Jaccard distance 0.15 for the similarity measurement of two primary modules. We will detail how we choose this Jaccard distance in Section 3.3.

The third component – piggybacking identification and rider analysis (Section 2.3) – is implemented in 611 lines of Python code. Basically, it scans the list of candidate app pairs reported from the second component, fetches the non-primary modules of related apps, determines the piggybacked apps, and exposes the rider code. In our implementation, we re-target the second component to organize the rider code with one exception: no author information is needed to constrain the nearest neighbor search.

To evaluate the scalability and efficacy of our system, we use it to detect piggybacked apps in a dataset with 84,767 apps collected from seven different app marketplaces. In the following, we first present our evaluation setup and then assess the accuracy of our module decoupling technique. After that, we determine the Jaccard distance for similarity measurement and report the detection results, including the analysis of uncovered rider code. Finally, we report the performance overhead.

Table 1: The dataset for PiggyApp evaluation (†: the number in parenthesis shows the percentage of apps that are also hosted in the official Android Market.)

Marketplace	Total Number of Apps
slideme (US1)	3108 (29.8%†)
freewarelovers (US2)	3188 (13.2%†)
eoemarket (CN1)	8261 (30%†)
goapk (CN2)	4334 (13.5%†)
softportal (EE1)	2305 (19.6%†)
proandroid (EE2)	1710 (20.2%†)
Official Android Market	68187

3.1 Evaluation Setup

In Table 1, we summarize the collected apps in our dataset. Basically, our crawler takes a snapshot of the available apps from seven different Android marketplaces in the first week of March, 2011. In total, the dataset contains 84,767 distinct apps: 68,187 of them appear in the official Android Market [25] and the rest come from other six popular third-party marketplaces: two in the US, two in China, and two in Eastern Europe. We highlight that we analyzed all these 84,767 apps in this data set, which is made possible by our scalable analysis framework. Earlier systems such as DroidMOSS [44] employ pairwise comparison, which is not scalable and can only work on limited samples (e.g., 200 in [44]).

For each app in our dataset, our system extracts 32,451 semantic features and presents them in a vector. In total, our system produces 84,767 feature vectors. To understand the distribution of each app pair distance, we randomly select 2,000 and 4,000 samples and measure their distances with all other apps in the dataset. The results are shown in Figure 4 (with the y-axis in the log-scale). As expected, most apps are not similar to each other, which is reflected by the fact that a majority of distances (around 99.4%) are larger than 0.8 (the largest possible distance is 1). Also, there are a small fraction (0.06%) of apps whose distances fall below distance 0.2, suggesting most piggybacked apps are located in this range (Section 3.4). This distribution is helpful to create a balanced VPT tree and leads to efficient nearest neighbor search.

3.2 Module Decoupling Accuracy

Module decoupling is an essential component, which affects both the accuracy and efficiency of our system. To concretely evaluate its effectiveness, we randomly choose 200 samples from our dataset, apply the module decoupling algorithm (Algorithm 1), and then manually verify the decoupling results. As with the module decoupling process, verification involves two main aspects. The first one is to determine whether these apps are decoupled into the correct modules. Our results show that 193 apps (96.5%) are correctly decoupled. The second aspect is to determine whether primary modules are correctly labeled. For the correctly decoupled 193 apps, our system identifies 178 primary modules (92.2%). We further examine the 15 mis-labeled apps and find that most cases, especially game- and social network-related apps, use feature-rich engines or libraries (e.g., Scoreloop [30] and Openfeint [38]) for GUI rendering, user interaction, and virtual currency support. They are generally considered as the main functionality of an app, but are implemented as supporting frameworks and shared among related apps. As these mis-labeled cases are rare and usually come from a limited number of special-purpose SDKs, we choose to apply a quick patch to our prototype by using a short white-list.

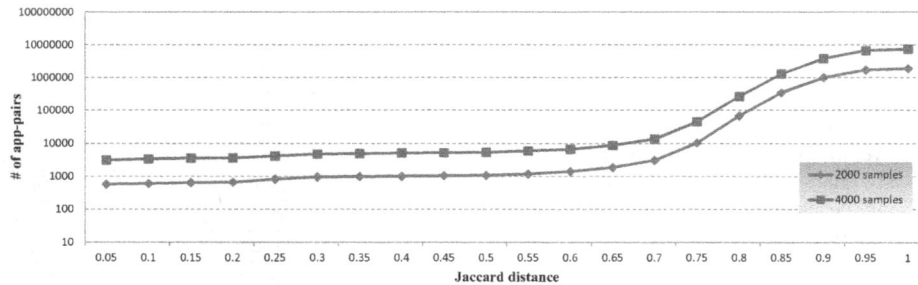

Figure 4: The cumulative distribution of pair-wise Jaccard distances

Table 2: Determining the right Jaccard distance

Jaccard Distance	0.05	0.1	0.15	0.2	0.25	0.3
True Positives	28	38	39	39	39	39
False Positives	0	0	2	2	4	4

3.3 Jaccard Distance Trade-Off

Next we present our experiments to determine the proper Jaccard distance in our study. As it measures the overlapped semantic features, our feature fingerprint is by design robust to existing code obfuscation techniques [2]. Moreover, it provides a "tuning knob" to adjust the trade-off between accuracy and efficiency. Specifically, a larger distance will likely tolerate more disjoint features between two apps, which has the benefit of reducing false negatives but at the cost of increasing false positives. A smaller distance leads to more false positives but less false negatives. As a general rule of thumb, if two apps have a Jaccard distance greater than 0.3, we consider the possibility of having a piggybacking relationship to be very low.

In our study, we aim to achieve a lower threshold to improve the search efficiency while still obtaining sufficient accuracy. To this end, we choose 4,000 random samples and use a series of Jaccard distances to measure their accuracy. Specifically, for each distance, we calculate the true positives and false positives by examining each reported pair (as candidate piggybacked apps). The results are shown in Table 2. The experiments clearly indicate the Jaccard distance 0.15 as the threshold. In particular, the larger distances (> 0.15) detect two more pairs, but they are false positives. We also do not want to choose smaller distances because we still detect more true positives as we move closer to 0.15 threshold. This result is consistent with an earlier measurement reported in Figure 4.

We want to emphasize that the Jaccard distance threshold provides a desirable way to balance between efficiency and accuracy. Based on the resources available to scrutinize candidate piggybacked apps, we can adjust the distance accordingly. For a smaller dataset with less than 10,000 apps, we might choose to use a larger distance so as to catch as many piggybacked apps as possible. For a larger dataset with hundreds of thousands of apps, we might want to use a smaller distance to accurately return a high-density set that contains true piggybacked apps. In our above series of experiments, when we use the distance 0.15, our system reports 41 candidate pairs within 630 seconds and the distance of 0.05 returns 28 within 227 seconds.

3.4 Piggybacking Detection

From the previous section, we have empirically chosen 0.15 as the optimal Jaccard distance threshold. In this section, we apply it to our dataset and present our detection results. Overall, our system detects 1,094 (1.3%) piggybacked apps in our dataset. For these repackaged apps, we further obtain the corresponding carrier apps and then classify them based on their sources. The results are shown in Table 3.

Table 3: Piggybacking detection results

App Marketplace	# Piggybacked Apps	Piggyback Rate	# Carrier Apps
Slideme (US1)	49	1.6%	32
Freewarelovers (US2)	31	0.97%	52
Eoemarket (CN1)	224	2.7%	98
Goapk (CN2)	83	1.9%	108
Softportal (EE2)	39	1.7%	26
Proandroid (EE1)	32	1.9%	15
Official Android Market	683	1.0%	298

In the table, the second column shows the number of piggybacked apps in each market and the third column contains the ratio of piggybacked apps to the number of apps we collected from each market. Due to the large number of apps it hosts, the official Android Market contains the largest number of piggybacked apps, but its piggyback rate is one of the lowest. The fourth column reports the number of carrier apps that have been chosen for piggybacking, which in general reflects which market is of interest to piggybacking authors in order to find popular apps to piggyback on. Our results show that game, wallpaper, and electronic book apps are among the most popular targets. Notice that the numbers in the carrier apps column are smaller than those in the piggybacked apps column. The reason is that the same carrier apps may be piggybacked multiple times to include different rider code (one concrete example is shown in the next section).

Interestingly, when examining these piggybacked apps inside the official Android Market, we find that 513 out of 683 (75%) are actually based on carrier apps also located in the official market. This clearly indicates the need for the official Android Market to adopt a rigorous policing to detect and potentially remove them. Also, notice that the remaining 170 piggyback on apps from third-party markets. This may sound counter-intuitive at first glance, but it is actually reasonable for two reasons: first, the official Android Market may not always be accessible or convenient to users outside the US, which partially explains the popularity of third-party markets in China; second, by choosing popular apps in third-party markets and uploading piggybacked apps into the official one, the app repackagers could reach more users for download and thus potentially maximize their impact.

To further measure the false negative rate, we study a list of 77 apps that were known to be piggybacked in our dataset (before our system was designed). PiggyApp correctly identifies 73 of them and misses four, indicating a false negative rate of 5.2%. Our manual analysis shows that these four failing cases are due to our module decoupling implementation, which incorrectly labels certain non-primary modules as primary and thus results in unnecessarily large Jaccard distances of related pairs.

3.5 Rider Analysis

After detecting these piggybacked apps, it is also interesting to find out answers to the following questions: what are the purposes

Table 4: The statistics of piggybacked ad libraries

Ad Library	Module Name	# Piggybacked Apps
admob	com.admob.android.ads	724
wooboo	com.wooboo.adlib_android	321
youmi	net.youmi.android	197
adwhirl	com.adwhirl	173
google/ads	com.google.ads	170
zestadz	com.zestadz.android	101
millennialmedia	com.millennialmedia.android	97
urbanairship	com.urbanairship.push	85
mobclix	com.mobclix.android.sdk	45
wiyun	com.wiyun.ad	36
mobclick	com.mobclick.android	26
greystripe	com.greystripe.android.sdk	26
madhouse	com.madhouse.android.ads	5

Table 5: The statistics of piggybacked malicious payloads

Malware Family	Module Name	# Piggybacked Apps
Geinimi	com.geinimi	6
ADRD	com.xxx.yyy	1
Pjapps	com.android.main	8
DDream	com.android.root	10
BgServ	com.mms.bg	1

behind these piggybacked apps? What rider code is injected into carrier apps? Are there (additional) permissions the rider code asks for? If there are, what are they? To answer these questions, we perform a further analysis on these piggybacked apps. As it is not feasible to examine every single piggybacked app, we choose to use cluster analysis to group and correlate the rider code.

The clustering analysis is motivated from our detailed investigation of these piggybacked apps. Specifically, when analyzing specific samples, we observe two common characteristics: first, many piggybacked apps share similar or even the same rider code; second, the same carrier apps are found piggybacked with different rider code. Our clustering analysis helps identify both of them.

In particular, to identify these common carrier apps, we simply count the number of each carrier app that occurs in the set of identified app pairs. One such example is a popular game app named com.appspot.swisscodemonkey.steam, which has been piggybacked on at least six times: four of them are variants of the Pjapps malicious payload [31], one is the ADRD malicious payload [4], and the other is an ad library named wooboo [33].

To locate the related rider code, we again apply our feature fingerprint technique to fetch the feature vectors of the rider code (there are 2067 of them present in 1094 different piggybacked apps) and apply the same nearest neighbor search algorithm (Algorithm 2). In this case, instead of choosing the previous threshold 0.15, we select 0.2 to loosely group rider code. As a result, we identify 16 clusters (ranging in size from 5 to 724). For each cluster, we randomly choose some samples for manual investigation. By doing so, we significantly reduce the time and effort needed to analyze them. From the analysis, it becomes evident the inclusion of rider code mainly serves two purposes. The first one is to inject various ad libraries with the intention to collect ad revenue or steal it from the original developers. The second one is to enclose malicious payloads to directly control compromised phones or steal personal information on the phones. In the next two sections, we examine these two purposes in more detail.

3.5.1 Collecting Ad Revenue

In the first purpose, the piggybacked apps are used to insert additional ad libraries, which help the repackagers, instead of the original developers, to collect ad revenues (generated from users' views or clicks). As most of existing apps are free, developers want to monetize by including ad libraries and there are a variety of them [24, 29, 33], which are provided as standalone packages for simple reuse. Many of them require little or no change on the original code. Examples include admob [24] and mobclix [29]. Such convenience also makes it easy for repackagers to integrate

them into popular apps as their carriers. Among the detected 1,094 piggybacked apps, 1,068 (97.6%) fall in this category. In Table 4, we show 13 top ad libraries in the rider code.

In the table, the first column shows the library name, the second column contains its detailed module name, while the third column counts the number of piggybacked apps that have it embedded. Among these 13 ad libraries, admob tops the list by being present in 724 carrier apps in our dataset. These ad libraries naturally request their own permissions for the provided functionality, some of which may not be requested by the carrier apps. It turns out that all these ad libraries ask for the INTERNET permission, 9 of them request the LOCATION permission, 5 need READ_PHONE_STATE, 1 demands CALL_PHONE, 1 uses ACCESS_WIFI_STATE, and 1 makes use of ACCESS_NETWORK_STATE. On average, these modules ask for 2.3 permissions.

3.5.2 Injecting Malicious Payloads

In the second purpose, repackagers implant malicious payloads into chosen carrier apps. In our dataset, we discover 5 different malicious rider payloads embedded in 26 different carrier apps that are present in various app markets. These malware are all listed in the yearly report of Android malware [39]. In Table 5, we show the list of detected malicious rider payloads. In the following, we choose representative samples and present our analysis.

Geinimi [27] is one of the earliest Android malware discovered in the wild that piggybacks on legitimate apps to perform malicious activities on the background. Our system identifies 6 piggybacked apps that have similar Geinimi code embedded (two different variants with 96% of their code in common). Both variants add their own activity, which once triggered invokes the embedded malicious code, including the bootstrap of a new service. These variants also add a new receiver to register for callbacks when certain events such as SMS_RECEIVED and BOOT_COMPLETED happen. By doing so, the malware can immediately run once the system boots or when a short message is received. To accomplish all these tasks, Geinimi needs 17 different permissions.

Compared to Geinimi, ADRD [4] is less complicated. Based on our analysis, the rider code is composed of four new receivers, which listen on the system boot completion event BOOT_COMPLETED, phone state change PHONE_STATE, network connection state change CONNECTIVITY
_CHANGE and its own alarm timer com.lz.myservicestart. It also defines a new service that will send device-specific information to a remote server and receive instructions from it. In the piggybacked app, the main entry point remains the same as in the carrier apps. In our dataset, we only find one ADRD-piggybacked app with a new module named com.xxx.yyy. Overall, ADRD demands 7 different permissions.

Pjapps [31] is another malicious rider embedded in a number of carrier apps. In our dataset, there are 8 of them. All the related rider code share the same class package named com.android.main. In essence, it adds two new receivers and one more service. The internal mechanism of these new components works similar to that of ADRD. In total, Pjapps requests 9 permissions.

`DroidDream` [28] was reported in the official Android Market and our dataset contains 10 infected apps. Similarly, all of its rider code share a common module named `com.android.root`. As with `Geinimi`, it adds its own activity and starts a new service to set up an alarm timer, which in return triggers another service to launch one root exploit to elevate its privilege. With the root exploit, `DroidDream` requests fewer permissions, but can essentially do whatever it wants on the compromised devices.

The last piece of malicious rider code is from the `BgServ` malware, which injects one module named `com.mms.bg` into carrier apps to transport device-specific information (via short messages) to a remote party. One interesting thing about this payload is that it leverages an open source project hosted at Google code projects [1]. For its wrongdoings, BgServ asks for 9 permissions.

Overall, these malicious payloads all request more permissions than original carrier apps, which imply that the request for a bulk of permissions may be an indicator for potentially suspicious apps.

3.6 Performance

In this section, we report the performance measurement of our system. Our test runs on a Ubuntu Server 10.04 Linux machine with an four-core Intel Xeon CPU (2.67HZ) and 8G memory. Our current prototype runs on a single thread, which leaves room for future improvement to take advantage of multiple threads for speed-up.

In our test, we run the module decoupling and feature extraction separately, which is easily parallelized. Each app, depending on its complexity, takes from 0.167 to 5.492 seconds to process. On average, it takes 0.952 seconds to process one app. Our module decoupling task of all these 84,767 apps takes 5 hours and 36 minutes in total. The construction of the VPT tree requires 126 seconds. Based on the VPT tree, given a single app, our algorithm takes between 0.00001 seconds and 0.576 seconds to find its nearest neighbor with 0.133 seconds on average. To iterate the apps in our dataset to locate possible piggybacked apps, it takes 3 hours and 15 minutes in total. The memory footprint seems small as only 127M main memory is used.

When streamlining the processing of these components, it takes less than nine hours to analyze our dataset with 84,767 apps from seven different Android markets. As mentioned earlier, improvements exist to better parallelize various components so that we can further reduce the processing time.

4. DISCUSSION

Our prototype demonstrates promising results by allowing for fast and scalable detection of piggybacked apps. In this section, we examine possible limitations in the current prototype and discuss future improvements.

First, to infer piggybacking relationship, we extract semantic features based on primary modules of existing apps. These semantic features are mainly based on the Android APIs, requested permissions, and various intents, etc. Though these features satisfy our current needs, they are still limited in a number of ways. To improve the system, we could extend these semantic features to include syntactic instruction sequences [44] or control-flow graphs. The addition will be helpful to better characterize and identify a particular app. Meanwhile, our core prototype remains intact as we can easily expand feature vectors to accommodate them and reuse the same VPT tree for construction and lookup.

Second, our current prototype largely depends on the existence of authentic carrier apps in order to detect piggybacked apps. Unfortunately, due to the variety, scale, and dynamic nature of existing app markets, it is not possible to build a centralized repository having every app in existence; our current collection is far from complete. For example, there are cases where we can infer a potential piggybacking relationship but can not determine which one is actually piggybacked (Section 2). Also, our collection is comprised of only free apps and does not include paid apps, which are sold for their features and will likely be attractive targets for piggybacking. This also indicates the need to continuously expand our current data set with more comprehensive samples.

Finally, our current prototype basically serializes the execution of different components. As mentioned earlier, for improved performance, there is a need to re-engineer our prototype for a parallel version. Fortunately, the overall system design of PiggyApp is parallelizable in nature and does not require complete revamp.

5. RELATED WORK

Software similarity measurement and searching The first category of related work includes prior efforts in effectively measuring software similarity and detecting plagiarized code [12, 23, 34, 44]. Among all these works, DroidMOSS [44] is a closely related one to measure the similarity of mobile apps. PiggyApp differs from it in three aspects: First, DroidMOSS detects repackaged apps while PiggyApp focuses on piggybacked apps. As mentioned earlier, piggybacked apps are a subset of repackaged ones but pose greater security threats. Second, our system overcomes the scalability limitation from the pair-wise comparison in DroidMOSS. Specifically, by proposing a new distance metric design and the associated nearest neighbor search algorithm, our system achieves better detection efficiency and scalability (with $O(n \log n)$ complexity, instead of $O(n^2)$), and enables a large scale evaluation instead of sampling based study. Third, for app comparison, DroidMOSS depends on syntactic instruction sequences of entire apps while PiggyApp extracts semantic features *only* from their primary modules, which leads to better accuracy and efficiency. DNADroid [12] uses program dependency graph (PDG) to characterize Android app and compares PDGs between methods in app pair, showing resistance to several evasion techniques. But it also applies pair-wise comparison as DroidMOSS, therefore lacking the scalability as presented in PiggyApp.

Smit [23] leverages a similar Vantage Point Tree but for large scale malware indexing and queries. In particular, by focusing on detecting malware variants, it does not have the need to further decouple internal modules, which is essential for our system. Similarly, BitShred [34] focuses on large-scale malware triage analysis by using feature hashing techniques to dramatically reduce the dimensions in the constructed malware feature space. After reduction, pair-wise comparison is still necessary to infer similar malware families. In comparison, PiggyApp focuses on a different problem, i.e., piggybacking detection among existing mobile apps, which necessitates module decoupling-like techniques to partition apps into primary and non-primary modules. Also, our linearithmic nearest neighbor search algorithm avoids the need of performing pair-wise comparison.

Program comprehension As our system centers on module decoupling to identify piggybacking relationships, we also consider the second category of related work from existing program comprehension techniques. Specifically, module decoupling has been an important tool to comprehend and manage large-scale legacy software that may not be well understood or easily maintained. To reduce a given large system into smaller and more manageable units, different techniques have been proposed in two general subcategories. The first one concerns different clustering techniques, which use a variety of software metrics to group smaller units of code into larger modules [5,36]. Our module decoupling technique is based on one such clustering method – agglomerative clustering. In particular, our system initially considers Java class packages as the smallest unit and then infers different kinds of program dependencies as metrics to merge them. The second one is concept analysis [35, 42], which in general uses functions as the smallest unit and employs lattice theory to group functions that have some specific common attributes. We consider function-level granularity may not be appropriate for our purpose and thus have not explored it further.

Mobile app security and analysis The third category covers a variety of projects [11, 15–17, 19–22, 37, 45–47] that have been undertaken to analyze or improve mobile security. Specifically, they can be loosely classified into two groups. The first group of projects analyze a single app from various perspectives to identify possible security and privacy problems. For example, both TaintDroid [15] and PiOS [14] focus on the privacy leak problem, and respectively use dynamic taint analysis and static data flow analysis to infer potential privacy leaks. DroidRanger [47] instead combines both static permission analysis and dynamic footprint monitoring to detect malicious applications in existing Android marketplaces. SCanDroid [19] examines an app's manifest file to automatically extract a data flow policy, and then checks whether the data flows in the app are consistent with the extracted specification. Stowaway [17] studies a set of 940 apps and finds that about one-third are not following the principle of least privilege. Enck *et al.* [16] crafted a byte code decompiler to study 1, 100 popular Android apps for characterization. All these tools use static analysis, or dynamic analysis, or both techniques to infer some specific security or privacy properties for individual mobile app. In contrast, PiggyApp uses feature vectors, rather than more expensive and complicated static or dynamic analysis techniques, to enable the rapid comparison of *pairs* of apps.

The second group is more closely related to PiggyApp, as it involves the interactions between apps. For example, one line of research [10, 11, 13, 18, 21, 37] studies the security risks causes by inter-application interaction. Among them, both ComDroid [11] and Saint [37] examine the interfaces third-party apps export in order to uncover possible unintended consequences. Woodpecker [21] focuses on a similar "capability leak" problem in Android firmware apps preloaded on the device. Numerous solutions to this problem have been proposed. For example, Saint [37] further extends the Android framework to enforce a user-configurable inter-application policy. Felt *et al.* [18] proposes a mechanism called IPC Inspection that allows the framework to inspect the complete call chain that leads to a request for a dangerous feature. QUIRE [13] addresses the same permission delegation problem by proposing IPC call chain tracking to identify the provenance of these IPC requests and then enforce security checks. Bugiel et al. [10] use a runtime monitor to regulate communications between apps, to protect Android against confused deputy and colluding apps attacks. While PiggyApp is concerned with the relationship between apps and the interfaces they export, it differs substantially from these systems in that it does not attempt to model the flow of information or control through an app; PiggyApp is concerned with the similarity between two apps, not what they do or whether they may be tricked into doing something inappropriate.

Another line of research [7,8] focuses more broadly on entire app markets. For example, Stratus [7] explores the security problem of the whole app ecosystem composed of multiple markets, each of which has its own security policy, and proposes a new app installation method to retain the original single-market security semantics (e.g., kill switches or developer name consistency). While its focus is markedly different from ours, both directly concern the issues that face app marketplaces today. Barrera *et al.* [8] uses a self-organization map to analyze 1,100 popular Android apps and identifies common usage patterns of permissions shared by different apps. Our approach also employs clustering techniques and extracts certain semantic features from the set of permissions an app requests. However, Barrera *et al.* uses them to visualize the relationships (in terms of requested permissions) among popular apps. PiggyApp instead makes use of them to build a VPT tree for efficient piggybacking detection.

6. CONCLUSION

In this paper, we present PiggyApp, a system for fast and scalable detection of piggybacked apps in existing Android markets. Based on the observation that in a piggybacked app, the added rider code is loosely coupled with the primary functionality (or module) of the original app, we develop a module decoupling technique to effectively locate the primary module for comparison. To avoid pair-wise comparison, we further propose a scalable approach to extract semantic features from the decoupled primary modules and organize them in a metric space, which allows for fast and efficient search (with $O(n \log n)$ complexity). We have implemented a prototype and used it to detect piggybacked apps in a dataset collected from seven different markets. Our results show that 0.97% to 2.7% of apps hosted in these markets, including the official Android Market, are piggybacked. Based on these results, we further analyze rider code and find that it mainly serves two purposes: stealing ad revenue and implanting malicious payloads. These results call for a rigorous vetting process for their detection.

Acknowledgements The authors would like to thank the anonymous reviewers for their insightful comments that helped improve the presentation of this paper. We also want to thank Chiachih Wu, Minh Q. Tran, Lei Wu and Kunal Patel for the helpful discussion. This work was supported in part by the US National Science Foundation (NSF) under Grants 0855297, 0855036, 0910767, and 0952640. Any opinions, findings, and conclusions or recommendations expressed in this material are those of the authors and do not necessarily reflect the views of the NSF.

7. REFERENCES

[1] MMSBG: An Open-Source Project. https://code.google.com/p/mmsbg. Online; accessed at Dec 1, 2011.

[2] ProGuard | Android Developers. http://developer.android.com/guide/developing/tools/proguard.html. Online; accessed at Dec 1, 2011.

[3] Smali - An Assembler/Disassembler for Android's dex Format. http://code.google.com/p/smali/. Online; accessed at Dec 1, 2011.

[4] AndroidCommunity. [ALERT] New Trojan Called Hong Tou Tou Lurking. http://androidcommunity.com/android-trojan-alert-hong-tou-tou-20110216/. Online; accessed at Dec 1, 2011.

[5] Nicolas Anquetil, Cédric Fourrier, and Timothy C. Lethbridge. Experiments with Clustering as a Software Remodularization Method. In *Proceedings of the Sixth Working Conference on Reverse Engineering*, WCRE '99, pages 235–, Washington, DC, USA, 1999. IEEE Computer Society.

[6] AppBrain. Number of Available Android Applications. http://www.appbrain.com/stats/number-of-android-apps. Online; accessed at Dec 1, 2011.

[7] David Barrera, William Enck, and Paul Oorschot. Seeding a Security-Enhancing Infrastructure for Multi-market Application Ecosystems. Technical report, School of Computer Science, Carleton University, http://www.scs.carleton.ca/shared/research/tech_reports/2010/TR-11-06%20Barrera.pdf. Online; accessed at Dec 1, 2011.

[8] David Barrera, H. Güneş Kayacik, Paul C. van Oorschot, and Anil Somayaji. A Methodology for Empirical Analysis of Permission-Based Security Models and Its Application to Android. In *Proceedings of the 17th ACM Conference on Computer and Communications Security*, CCS '10, 2010.

[9] Joany Boutet. Malicious Android Applications: Risks and Exploitation - A Spyware Story about Android Application and Reverse Engineering. http://www.sans.org/reading_room/whitepapers/malicious/malicious-android-applications_risks-exploitation_33578. Online; accessed at Dec 1, 2011.

[10] Sven Bugiel, Lucas Davi, Alexandra Dmitrienko, Thomas Fischer, Ahmad-Reza Sadeghi, and Bhargava Shastry. Towards Taming Privilege-Escalation Attacks on Android. In *19th Annual Network & Distributed System Security Symposium (NDSS)*, Feb 2012.

[11] Erika Chin, Adrienne Felt, Kate Greenwood, and David Wagner. Analyzing Inter-Application Communication in Android. In *Proceedings of the 9th Annual International Conference on Mobile Systems, Applications, and Services*, MobiSys 2011, 2011.

[12] Jonathan Crussell, Clint Gibler, and Hao Chen. Attack of the Clones: Detecting Cloned Applications on Android Markets. In Sara Foresti, Moti Yung, and Fabio Martinelli, editors, *Computer Security âĂŞ ESORICS 2012*, volume 7459 of *Lecture Notes in Computer Science*, pages 37–54. Springer Berlin Heidelberg, 2012.

[13] Michael Dietz, Shashi Shekhar, Yuliy Pisetsky, Anhei Shu, and Dan Wallach. QUIRE: Lightweight Provenance for Smart Phone Operating Systems. In *Proceedings of the 20th USENIX Security Symposium*, USENIX Security '11, San Francisco, CA, 2011.

[14] Manuel Egele, Christopher Kruegel, Engin Kirda, and Giovanni Vigna. PiOS: Detecting Privacy Leaks in iOS Applications. In *Proceedings of the 18th Annual Network and Distributed System Security Symposium*, NDSS '11, February 2011.

[15] William Enck, Peter Gilbert, Byung-gon Chun, Landon Cox, Jaeyeon Jung, Patrick McDaniel, and Anmol Sheth. TaintDroid: An Information-Flow Tracking System for Realtime Privacy Monitoring on Smartphones. In *Proceedings of the 9th USENIX Symposium on Operating Systems Design and Implementation*, USENIX OSDI '11, 2011.

[16] William Enck, Damien Octeau, Patrick McDaniel, and Swarat Chaudhuri. A Study of Android Application Security. In *Proceedings of the 20th USENIX Security Symposium*, USENIX Security '11, San Francisco, CA, 2011.

[17] Adrienne Felt, Erika Chin, Steve Hanna, Dawn Song, and David Wagner. Android Permissions Demystified. In *Proceedings of the 18th ACM Conference on Computer and Communications Security*, CCS' 11, 2011.

[18] Adrienne Felt, Helen Wang, Alexander Moschhuk, Steve Hanna, and Erika Chin. Permission Re-Delegation: Attacks and Defense. In *Proceedings of the 20th USENIX Security Symposium*, USENIX Security '11, San Francisco, CA, 2011.

[19] Adam Fuchs, Avik Chaudhuri, and Jeffrey Foster. SCanDroid: Automated Security Certification of Android Applications. http://www.cs.umd.edu/~avik/projects/scandroidascaa/paper.pdf. Online; accessed at Dec 1, 2011.

[20] Michael Grace, Wu Zhou, Xuxian Jiang, and Ahmad-Reza Sadeghi. Unsafe Exposure Analysis of Mobile In-App Advertisements. In *Proceedings of the 5th ACM Conference on Security and Privacy in Wireless and Mobile Networks*, 2012.

[21] Michael Grace, Yajin Zhou, Zhi Wang, and Xuxian Jiang. Systematic Detection of Capability Leaks in Stock Android Smartphones. In *Proceedings of the 19th Annual Network and Distributed System Security Symposium*, NDSS '12, February 2012.

[22] Michael Grace, Yajin Zhou, Qiang Zhang, Shihong Zou, and Xuxian Jiang. RiskRanker: Scalable and Accurate Zero-day Android Malware Detection. In *10th International Conference on Mobile Systems, Applications and Services*, June 2012.

[23] Xin Hu, Tzi-cker Chiueh, and Kang G. Shin. Large-Scale Malware Indexing using Function-Call Graphs. In *Proceedings of the 16th ACM conference on Computer and communications security*, CCS '09, pages 511–620, New York, NY, USA, 2009. ACM.

[24] Google Inc. Admob for Android Developers. http://developer.admob.com/wiki/Android.

[25] Google Inc. Android Market. https://market.android.com/. Online; accessed at Dec 1, 2011.

[26] Lookout Inc. App Genome Report: February 2011. https://www.mylookout.com/appgenome/. Online; accessed at Dec 1, 2011.

[27] Lookout Inc. Security Alert: Geinimi, Sophisticated New Android Trojan Found in Wild. http://blog.mylookout.com/2010/12/geinimi_trojan/. Online; accessed at Dec 1, 2011.

[28] Lookout Inc. Update: Security Alert: DroidDream Malware Found in Official Android Market. http://blog.mylookout.com/2011/03/security-alert-malware-found-in_official-android-market-droiddream/. Online; accessed at Dec 1, 2011.

[29] MobClix Inc. Mobclix SDK Integration Guide. http://support.mobclix.com/attachments/token/lvbgrqsfpjgvgxb/?name=Detailed_Start_Guide_for_Android.pdf. Online; accessed at Dec 1, 2011.

[30] Scoreloop Inc. Scoreloop : Cross Platform Mobile Gaming SDK for Virtual Currency, Social Games and Distribution. http://www.scoreloop.com/developers/.

[31] Symantec Inc. Android Threats Getting Steamy. http://www.symantec.com/connect/blogs/android-threats-getting-steamy. Online; accessed at Dec 1, 2011.

[32] Symantec Inc. Android.Basebridge: Technical Details. http://www.symantec.com/security_response/writeup.jsp?docid=2011-060915-4938-99&tabid=2. Online; accessed at Dec 1, 2011.

[33] Wooboo Inc. How to Add Wooboo Advertisement SDK into Android. http://admin.wooboo.com.cn:9001/cbFiles/down/1272545843644.swf.

[34] Jiyong Jang, David Brumley, and Shobha Venkataraman. BitShred: Feature Hashing Malware for Scalable Triage and Semantic Analysis. In *Proceedings of the 18th ACM conference on Computer and communications security*, CCS '11, pages 309–320, New York, NY, USA, 2011. ACM.

[35] Christian Lindig and Gregor Snelting. Assessing Modular Structure of Legacy Code based on Mathematical Concept Analysis. In *Proceedings of the 19th international conference on Software engineering*, ICSE '97, pages 349–359, New York, NY, USA, 1997. ACM.

[36] S. Mancoridis, B. S. Mitchell, C. Rorres, Y. Chen, and E. R. Gansner. Using Automatic Clustering to Produce High-Level System Organizations of Source Code. In *Proceedings of the 6th International Workshop on Program Comprehension*, IWPC '98, pages 45–, Washington, DC, USA, 1998. IEEE Computer Society.

[37] Machigar Ongtang, Stephen McLaughlin, William Enck, and Patrick McDaniel. Semantically Rich Application-Centric Security in Android. In *Proceedings of the 2009 Annual Computer Security Applications Conference*, ACSAC '09, 2009.

[38] OpenFeint. OpenFeint Developers - Mobile Open Source Social SDK & Tools for iOS & Android. `http://openfeint.com/developers`. Online; accessed at Dec 1, 2011.

[39] Paolo Passeri. One Year of Android Malware (Full List)). `http://paulsparrows.wordpress.com/2011/08/11/one-year-of-android-malware-full-list/`. Online; accessed at Dec 1, 2011.

[40] Google Code Project. Android-apktool - Tool for Reengineering Android apk Files. `http://code.google.com/p/android-apktool/`. Online; accessed at Dec 1, 2011.

[41] Helmuth Spaeth. *Cluster Analysis Algorithms for Data Reduction and Classification of Objects*. J. Wiley and Sons, 1980.

[42] Paolo Tonella. Concept Analysis for Module Restructuring. *IEEE Trans. Softw. Eng.*, 27:351–363, April 2001.

[43] Peter N. Yianilos. Data Structures and Algorithms for Nearest Neighbor Search in General Metric Spaces. In *Proceedings of the fourth annual ACM-SIAM Symposium on Discrete algorithms*, SODA '93, pages 311–321, Philadelphia, PA, USA, 1993. Society for Industrial and Applied Mathematics.

[44] Wu Zhou, Yajin Zhou, Xuxian Jiang, and Peng Ning. DroidMOSS: Detecting Repackaged Smartphone Applications in Third-Party Android Marketplaces. In *Proceedings of the 2nd ACM Conference on Data and Application Security and Privacy*, CODASPY '12, February 2012.

[45] Yajin Zhou and Xuxian Jiang. Dissecting Android Malware: Characterization and Evolution. In *Proceedings of the 33rd IEEE Symposium on Security and Privacy*, 2012.

[46] Yajin Zhou and Xuxian Jiang. Detecting Passive Content Leaks and Pollution in Android Applications. In *Proceedings of the 20th Annual Symposium on Network and Distributed System Security*, 2013.

[47] Yajin Zhou, Zhi Wang, Wu Zhou, and Xuxian Jiang. Hey, You, Get off of My Market: Detecting Malicious Apps in Official and Alternative Android Markets. In *Proceedings of the 19th Annual Network and Distributed System Security Symposium*, NDSS '12, February 2012.

Sweetening Android Lemon Markets: Measuring and Combating Malware in Application Marketplaces

Timothy Vidas
Carnegie Mellon University
Pittsburgh, PA
tvidas@cmu.edu

Nicolas Christin
Carnegie Mellon University
Pittsburgh, PA
nicolasc@andrew.cmu.edu

ABSTRACT

Application marketplaces are the main software distribution mechanism for modern mobile devices but are also emerging as a viable alternative to brick-and-mortar stores for personal computers. While most application marketplaces require applications to be cryptographically signed by their developers, in Android marketplaces, self-signed certificates are common, thereby offering very limited authentication properties. As a result, there have been reports of malware being distributed through application "repackaging." We provide a quantitative assessment of this phenomenon by collecting 41,057 applications from 194 alternative Android application markets in October 2011, in addition to a sample of 35,423 applications from the official Android market, Google Play. We observe that certain alternative markets almost exclusively distribute repackaged applications containing malware. To remedy this situation we propose a simple verification protocol, and discuss a proof-of-concept implementation, AppIntegrity. AppIntegrity strengthens the authentication properties offered in application marketplaces, thereby making it more difficult for miscreants to repackage apps, while presenting very little computational or communication overhead, and being deployable without requiring significant changes to the Android platform.

Categories and Subject Descriptors

C.2.0 [**Computer-Communication Networks**]: Security and Protection; C.4 [**Performance of Systems**]: Measurement Techniques; D.4.6 [**Operating Systems**]: Security and Protection

Keywords

Android, Software Marketplace, Malware, Smartphones, Repackaging

1. INTRODUCTION

Online application stores or "markets" are becoming an increasingly important vector of software distribution. For instance, Apple's flagship MacOS X operating system is, since version 10.7,
only distributed through the Apple App Store, thereby entirely forgoing the traditional distribution channel – packaged optical media sold in brick-and-mortar stores. Likewise, the Google Chrome Web Store is a consolidated place to download all extensions to the Chrome browser.

While their importance is growing, for personal computers application markets are a relatively recent development,[1] and still merely represent one of several alternatives. On the other hand, application markets have been the primary (if not the only, for most users) means of acquiring and installing software on advanced mobile devices such as smartphones and tablets.

"Official" application markets for mobile devices, such as Google Play or the Apple App Store act as a centralized software distribution point for a given platform, and allow users to find, download and install applications through a single interface.

Besides official markets, a large number of third-party (or *alternative*) markets exist. Users may rely on these alternative markets, for a variety of reasons, including the unavailability of the official market in a particular country, name-brand recognition (e.g., Amazon's Appstore), or to freely obtain applications that require payment in the official market. Some markets are also locale specific, where existing applications are modified and redistributed for localization purposes. For instance, popular applications may be translated in languages that they do not natively support.

Markets adopt several techniques to provide users with confidence that they are downloading safe applications. First, usually, applications must be cryptographically signed so that their providers are authenticated. Second, markets enforce policies to deal with malicious applications. Some markets (e.g., Apple AppStore) vet applications prior to publication [11]. Others, such as Google Play, allow relatively unmoderated publication, but react to identified malware by removing it both from the market and from all (connected) devices that have already installed the malicious application [32].

Unfortunately, these techniques fall short of providing strong security guarantees. When application signatures are certified by the market proprietor (e.g., Amazon and Apple markets), the user has to completely trust the market proprietor to manage and secure the certificates. The fact that existing centralized vetting systems have shown to be imperfect in keeping malware at bay [7, 8, 9] seems to indicate that the security guarantees provided by such centralized systems are relatively weak.

In Google Play, the security guarantees are even weaker. Certificates are typically self-signed and, thus, are not bound to any particular identity. Almost anybody can upload applications into the market; and it may take time to realize that some harmful applica-

---

[1]The AppStore first appeared on MacOS 10.6.6 in Jan 2011.

tions have been uploaded. Worse, some of the third-party Android markets may not police malware at all. In fact, it may even be in a market's best interest *not* to do so, as the market operators could enjoy revenue from infected applications.

In other words, existing authentication mechanisms for market applications appear insufficient. For instance, grafting viruses onto pirated software is certainly not a new attack; yet, the lack of proper authentication allows miscreants to use such techniques to distribute malware through application markets.

In this paper, we focus on Android application markets, and present two main contributions. First, through measurement experiments, we evaluate to which extent existing markets for Android devices facilitate malware installation. We build crawling mechanisms that identify a large number (195) of existing Android application markets, and gather a total of 76,480 applications from these markets, including Google Play (35,423 applications). From this application corpus, we show that *application repackaging*, in which miscreants disseminate malware posing as legitimate, well-known applications, presents a significant threat. By analyzing signing strategies used in alternative marketplaces, we show that some malicious markets extensively reuse certificates to provide valid signatures on maliciously repackaged applications.

Second, we propose a simple authentication protocol for market applications, that can be immediately deployed on Android, piggybacks on the naming conventions used for Android packages and applications, and would make it significantly more difficult for an attacker to perform application repackaging.

The remainder of this paper has the following structure. We first discuss application repackaging techniques in section 2. In section 3, we describe our measurements on the incidence of malware in current Android marketplaces, and show the threats posed by application repackaging. Then, in section 4, we provide a novel application authentication mechanism and present a proof-of-concept mobile application, AppIntegrity, which implements such a verification mechanism. We provide a security analysis of our mechanism in section 5, outline its limitations, and propose extensions to overcome these limitations. We discuss related work in section 6. Finally, we conclude with a discussion and directions for future work in section 7.

2. APPLICATION REPACKAGING IN ANDROID

We next summarize how application repackaging is performed in Android. To do so, we first describe the contents of an Android application, before turning to repackaging mechanics.

2.1 Android applications

In Android, applications are usually written in Java (although some have "native" C calls), and are distributed as APK (Android package) files. Those APK files are in fact Zip archives, which contain compiled Java classes (in Dalvik DEX format), application resources, and an `AndroidManifest.xml` binary XML file containing application metadata. The APK also contains a public key and its associated X.509 certificate, bundled as a PKCS#7 message in DER format.

Naming conventions. When creating a new project, the Android developer documentation dictates that a full "Java-language-style" package name be used, and that developers "should use Internet domain ownership as the basis for package names (in reverse) [4]." This creates package names such as `com.google.maps` for the mobile Google Maps application. To avoid name conflicts, package names must be unique across the entire universe of applica-

tions. Using reversed domain names theoretically limits potential namespace conflicts to a developer's own domain.

Signing applications. All Android applications must be cryptographically signed by the developer; an Android device will not install an application that is not signed. Typical Java tools, such as `keytool` and `jarsigner`, may be used to create a unique keypair and sign the mobile application.

In Android, the only key distribution mechanism used consists in bundling developer's public key with the application. Further, Android has no requirement for a keypair to be certified by a Certificate Authority (CA). In fact, we observed that more than 99% of the 76,480 applications we gathered as part of this study (see section 3) use self-signed certificates.

In other words, the primary purpose of the keypair is to distinguish between application authors, but not to provide any stronger security properties. In practice, keypairs are also used to 1) ensure that applications allowed to automatically update are signed by the same key as the previous version, 2) potentially allow applications signed by the same key to share resources, 3) grant or deny permissions to a family of applications signed by the same key, and 4) to remove all applications signed with the same key from the Android market and potentially from all connected devices when one of these applications is flagged as malware [32].

On the other hand, due to the absence of any certification authority or PKI, signatures on Android do not provide any assurance about the identity of the signer. Shortly stated, Android ensures that the Facebook application is correctly signed by somebody, but cannot prove the Facebook company actually signed the Facebook application.

2.2 Application Repackaging

An existing application redistributed with a different signing key, often with functionality not present in the original version, is said to be *repackaged*. Some, all, or none, of the application's existing functionality can be preserved in the repackaged version.

Applications can be repackaged for many reasons other than to distribute malware. For instance, a repackager may simply wish to add advertising to an existing application to profit from somebody else's application. Application repackaging falls broadly in two classes: spoofing and grafting.

Spoofing. Mobile applications can simply be published under false pretenses, *spoofing* little or none of the features a legitimate application would possess. To deceive the user, a malicious program may advertise to be an existing application, or a nonexistent application that may plausibly exist, yet provide none of the expected functionality. As previously shown in peer-to-peer networks [15] and search-engine result poisoning [23,27], this type of attack could flood a market with enough false positives to attract users.

As an example, in July 2011, the legitimate Netflix application only supported specific devices and versions of Android. Unsupported devices could not locate and install the official application in the market. In October 2011, a fake version of the Netflix application was published in the official Android Market, claimed to "support" all devices, and thus appeared to owners of devices that could not download the legitimate application. The fake application displayed a plausible login screen, but then simply stole service credentials. Once credentials were entered, the application uninstalled itself [10].

Grafting. To achieve the desired functionality of a legitimate application, an attacker may elect to graft malware onto an existing application, and subsequently republish the modified application.

The attacker starts by downloading and extracting an existing application. To do so, she unzips the APK archive to extract the application components (class files and manifest).

Then, she adds malware to the application, and repackages it. Adding malware may require to reverse the DEX-formatted Java classes. While not entirely straightforward, tools such as `undx` [31], `baksmali`, `dedexer`, or `ded` [18] can often successfully decompile `.dex` files to source code. DEX can also be converted to a typical Java jar collection of classes using the `dex2jar` utility, at which point a typical Java decompiler can be used.

In the quite common case in which the `.dex` file does not need to be fully reversed to source code, much of the disassembly and repackaging process can be automated. For instance, `apktool` [3] can unpack and repackage an existing `.apk` with two commands. `apktool` has several side effects that result in non-required changes to the repackaged `.apk`. For instance, some files may be compressed in the repackaged application regardless of whether or not original file was compressed. With automatic compression the repackaged file may actually be smaller than the original despite the addition of malicious code. These side effects may be undesirable for an attacker that wishes for the application to remain as similar as possible to the original application.

In addition to the class files, the attacker may need to modify the `AndroidManifest.xml`, since this is where application-level permissions are specified. This can be done using a tool such as AXMLPrinter2 [5]. For instance, the malware to be added to the existing application may require the `INTERNET` or `SEND_SMS` permissions, even if the permission is not specified in the original application.

Last, prior to publishing the "new" application to one or more markets, the attacker must cryptographically sign the application. The signing can easily be performed with standard Java tools, e.g., using `jarsigner`. Since Android uses self-signed certificates, such signatures will pass installation-time checks.

3. MEASURING THE PREVALENCE OF MALWARE IN MARKETS

Each market may have different policies for policing applications. Google maintains a reactive policy in the official Android market, but alternative markets may have a less effective policing policy or no policy at all. To demonstrate the threat of application repackaging we investigated the presence of repackaged applications in existing markets. In this section we discuss our measurement methodology to create a corpus of alternative market applications, how we created a corpus of official market applications, and a description of the resulting corpora.

3.1 Collecting applications in alternative marketplaces

In order to create a corpus of applications from alternative markets, we first conducted an experiment to observe alternative distribution mechanisms.

We identified 194 alternative marketplaces by popularity based on search engine results. First we created a list of candidate site seeded with search results for "alternative market android","third party android market","free android applications","android app store", and simply "android market." We then expanded the list of candidates to include the same strings translated to all 63 languages currently supported by Google Translate. We manually inspected search results to prune candidate sites that did not actually deliver mobile applications (many only offer meta-data, directing an interested user to then download the application from the official mar-

ket). During manual inspection of search results, we appended obvious links to other marketplaces to the list of markets. Perhaps the most important observation from the search results inspection is that, unlike the official market, applications from some alternative markets can currently be downloaded using common, unauthenticated HTTP methods. In many cases the URL for applications is highly predictable and can facilitate complete coverage, as in `http://yadroid.com/?download=n` where n is between 1 and 2696.

While an Android application is a Zip archive packaged in a certain way (see section 2), there is no guarantee that a given marketplace delivers applications to the device in this form. In fact, we observed many other methods. For example, one site delivers applications as expected, but the file extension is ".ipa" instead of ".apk." Similarly other sites also deliver the application archive as expected but with no file extension all, and are instead accessed by a URL such as `http://yadroid.com/?download=260`. Yet others will "double package" the application for delivery, resulting in a Zip (or other) archive that contains a Zip file that is an application.

We performed recursive decompression of archives, and tested each file we eventually obtained to determine whether it was a ZIP file that contained the `AndroidManifest.xml` binary XML file. If so, we classified it as a valid Android application.

Corpus size. We used the above described collection and pruning process to collect 41,057 applications from 194 alternative markets in October 2011. The identification of markets and subsequent downloading of applications is biased by popularity, both by using search results to identify marketplaces, and by the likelihood that popular applications are made easier to locate by each marketplace interface.

3.2 Collecting applications from the official Android market

The official Android market, on Google Play, is intended to only be accessed directly from Android devices. Even when "installing" an application using the online interface at `market.android.com`, a signal is pushed directly to a device associated with logged-in user.

Even though the Android framework is open source, many software components found on Android devices are proprietary, including the Google Play software. We created a protocol-compatible tool that facilitates granular access to applications in the official market. We designed the tool iteratively by reverse-engineering the market components found on an Android device, observing network traffic during a market transaction, and by inspecting server responses after manually adjusting protocol parameters.

The official market protocol requires authentication and a device identifier. To authenticate to the service, we created a new user using an actual smartphone, and extracted the device identifier from the device. The username, password, device identifier, and SDK version are used to establish a market session. This session is similar to the session status that would occur when opening the *Play Store*[2] application, the official client, on an Android device.

Once a session is established the server is queried for a list of application categories (e.g., Finance, Education, Medical). Much like the official client, server results vary depending on several parameters. By manipulating these parameters, a client can obtain different results to mimic views present in the official client such as "Featured" or "Top Free" in any category. For example, ap-

---

[2]Or *Market* application on older devices.

plications can be ordered by any of POPULAR, NEWEST, FEATURED, NONE; or the field can be omitted.

In addition to mimicking the capabilities of an official client, we are able to manipulate additional parameters, such as the wireless carrier associated with this client. A physical device is typically associated with a single carrier and the official client simply utilizes the carrier associated with the device. We can enumerate sets of carriers impersonating devices on several networks by altering the Mobile Country Code (MCC) and Mobile Network Code (MNC) as defined in ITU E.212. For example the United States has MCC's 310-316, and MNC 260 specifies T-Mobile. We can iterate 310012, 310410, 310120, and 310260 to impersonate devices from Verizon, AT&T, Sprint and T-Mobile, respectively.

The ability to impersonate devices from various networks is important for coverage as some applications may only be made available to customers on certain networks. Likewise, certain applications only exist for certain types of device hardware, geographic region, and software versions of Android. Any particular combination of market parameters will currently return a maximum of 800 results, so that it is not possible to simply iteratively collect all applications in the entire market.

The actual applications are not downloaded through the existing market session. Market query results contain meta-data about applications. Some of this meta-data is available in the official client such as the title, cost, and review ratings. Other meta-data is not visually displayed, such as the application's AssetID. The AssetID is needed to download applications independent of the existing market session. The AssetID is approximately 20 ASCII digits long and must be precisely specified in order to download the application.

When attempting to download too many applications over a period of time a the server may not permit further downloads, temporarily blocking connections. We observed that HTTP 503 errors precede such blacklisting, and accordingly implemented a back-off procedure.

Corpus size. To create our corpus, we collected free applications from each application category as accessible from the United States on four carriers: Verizon, AT&T, Sprint and T-Mobile. We additionally iterated through known Android and SDK versions, eventually collecting 35,423 applications in October 2011. Because we collected by category, the 35,423 collected applications are biased by popularity in each category. Furthermore, due to the complexity of automating the payment protocol, we only collected free applications.

3.3 Results

We next discuss the prevalence of malware in the marketplaces we have measured. From our collected corpora, we identify known malware attributable to each marketplace. We also offer particular measurements (e.g., on certificate reuse) from the corpus to inform discussion of the protocol provided in section 4.

To determine a lower bound on malware present in each market, we scanned each file with multiple antivirus products, through the VirusTotal interface [1].[3] VirusTotal is a service that offers file scanning through 42 different antivirus products by vendors such as Symantec, McAfee, Kaspersky, and TrendMicro. Despite the large number of antivirus products being used, malware detection in this manner remains a very conservative lower bound as mobile malware detection is less mature than desktop malware detection. Some reports show that many mobile anti-virus detection rates are

---

[3]Due to limitations to the VirusTotal interface, applications larger than 20 MB were not scanned.

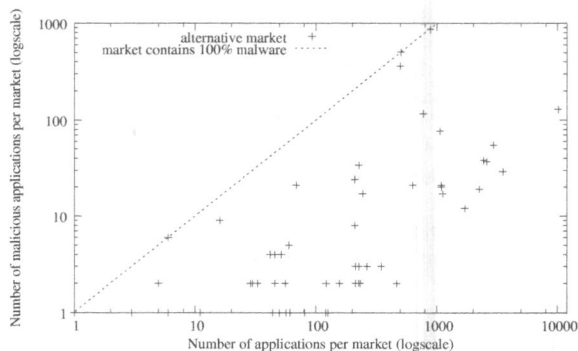

Figure 1: Alternative Market Malware: Total applications and detected malware per market. Each point corresponds to one measured market. Points closer to the dashed line deliver higher percentages of malware.

very low: between 0% and 32% [28]. It is highly unlikely that any so-called "zero-day" malware would ever be detected under this procedure. Therefore, the actual delivery of malware from marketplaces is quite likely a larger problem than we show.

Some alternative markets appear to be completely absent of malware, but a few markets distribute malware almost exclusively. In the scatterplot shown in Figure 1, each market we crawled corresponds to one point, whose x-coordinate denotes the total number of applications in that market, and whose y-coordinate denotes the number of applications detected as malicious in this market. The dashed line in Figure 1 represents the threshold where *every* application sampled from a market would be detected as malicious (and hence, no point can be above that line). Several points approach this line, demonstrating that our naive sampling identified a number of markets which almost exclusively distribute malicious applications. Particularly preoccupying is the case of the markets in the top right corner of the graph. Not only do these markets have very high percentage of infected applications, but they also provide a large number of applications.

We can further use this data to attempt to exhaustively classify all Android malware as repackaged or some other type of malware. After eliminating "potentially unwanted programs" detected by anti-virus, such as spyware, we can concisely catalog all existing malware as of November 2011. We observed 55 different families of malware, 40 of which (or 73%) (such as those enumerated in [20] and more exhaustively in [37]) employ some type of repackaging or spoofing. We note that many early Android malware families as well as the most recent employ some type of repackaging.

As another datapoint, in [37], the authors use a combination of package name comparison to applications found in the official market and manual analysis to classify repackaged applications. They similarly find that 86% of unique samples in their Android malware corpus are repackaged. The reported number is different from our observation for two reasons: First, in [37] the described corpus is entirely comprised of malware samples, many of which belong to the same family leading to a non-uniform distribution across malware families. Second, the definition of *repackaged* in [37] is slightly different and does not include the category we term *spoofed* in section 2.2.

We next look at possible indicators of malware distribution strategies. We first measured the number of applications which provide package names that form valid domains. To do so, we parse each package name with the Perl module `Data::Validate::Domain`. We find that 83% percent of the applications originating from the official marketplace have package names that, when reversed, represent a well-formed domain, following Google's suggestions (see section 2) for package naming conventions. Interestingly, applications from alternative markets exhibit a slightly higher rate at 86%. This seems to indicate that exotic naming conventions are not indicative of malware. On the contrary, we found that, in markets with the highest percentage of malicious applications. applications tend to comply *more* with the proposed standard naming conventions. In hindsight, this does not come as a surprise: malicious applications designers have incentives to make their applications "blend in" as much as possible.

Figure 2 shows the distribution of application sizes for the official and alternative Android markets. Approximately 40% of all applications are greater than 1 MB. Alternative market applications are generally slightly larger than those in the official market, but the size distribution between the market types is clearly similar.

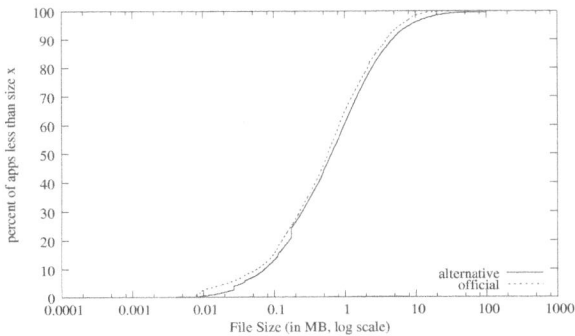

Figure 2: Application Sizes: CDT of market applications

Finally, we attempt to characterize which signing strategies are being used in alternative marketeplaces. The lack of a PKI and general lack of proper certificate validation does not encourage adoption of best practices. Indeed the near-ubiquitous use of self-signing certificates enables the publisher to adopt a number of different signing strategies. For instance a publisher could use the same certificate to sign every application they publish, or could use a different certificate for each version of each application. Shortly stated, certificates do not provide any guarantee on the application integrity, or origin, and patterns of certificate misuse may be evidence of application repackaging.

We observed heavy re-use of signing certifications in our collection. Indeed, only 52% of certificates from the official market were unique. The distribution of certificates is not uniform, as some certificates are used as many as 693 times, while others are only used once. In alternative markets, the signing strategies vary drastically. Some markets exhibit distributions similar to the official market, while others use a single signing certificate.

Figure 3 plots, for each market among the 64 markets that distribute the most applications, the highest percentage of applications in the market that are signed using the same signing certificate. We overlay the plot with a line showing the corresponding percentage of malware in the same markets. Strikingly, almost all the alternate marketplaces with high percentage of malware appear to significantly re-use signing certificates. Calculating the Pearson correlation coefficient between the percentage of malware, and the percentage of certificate reuse, across all markets yields $\rho \approx 0.64$. In the seediest markets with close to 100% known malware, *all* appli-

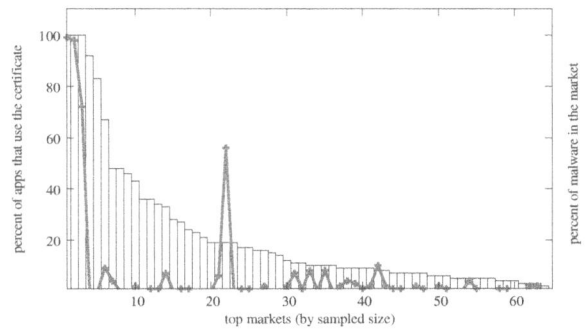

Figure 3: Certificate Reuse in Alternative Markets: Percentage of apps which share the same certificate (bars) overlaid with the percentage of malware (line plot). Each point corresponds to one measured market. Markets are ranked by decreasing reuse of certificates. Only the top 64 markets (in number of applications) are presented.

cations are signed using the same signing certificate. In this case, the remaining applications to make up the 100% are quite likely malware that is not yet detected by anti-virus.

In sum, these results provide clear evidence that malware in alternative markets is a problem we cannot neglect. As a point of comparison, in the official market, we discovered 119 applications containing malware, or 0.003% of all applications we surveyed. While certainly very low, this number needs to be taken with caution: these are the applications that were detected by anti-viruses as being malicious, and are therefore a strict lower bound on the total amount of malware actually present in the official Android market.

4. TOWARD APPLICATION VERIFICATION

Regardless of application vetting policies, it is possible that an application can be repackaged and published into marketplaces that users will frequent. Yet users have no way of knowing if an application claiming a particular origin is in fact created by the assumed author. Here we present a very simple protocol for end-to-end application verification, and discuss an example implementation. The idea behind the protocol is that, while not a panacea against all attacks (see section 7), it raises the bar that attackers have to clear to be able to carry out spoofing attacks, while being essentially freely deployable with the current Android infrastructure.

In the context of this paper, verification means that the application is *authenticated*, and that, as a result, its *integrity* against repackaging by third-parties is guaranteed.

4.1 Protocol

Prior to publishing, an application must be cryptographically signed. This signing makes use of the private key of a keypair generated by the developer. The existence of a keypair provides developers and users with the primitives required to perform other PKCS actions. In particular, the protocol described below takes advantage of the well-known ability to verify a signature. That is for a keypair: secret signing key ssk and public verification key pvk, that the signing of data d results in signed data sd:

$$sd = sign_{ssk}(d) .$$

Furthermore, that signed data can be verified using only the associated public key:

$$verify_{pvk}(sd) = true \, .$$

It is assumed that the ssk is selected uniformly at random from the set of all possible keys, and that without the ssk it is computationally infeasible create an sd' that can be verified.

If the developer makes the pvk widely available, it can be used to locally verify signed applications. In order to deter developer impersonation in repackaged applications, the pvk should *not* be published via the marketplace from which the application is obtained. If this were permitted, unscrupulous persons could simply continue to repackage applications and provide new pvk' keys along with new applications when published. Instead we propose that the author's pvk be stored in a predefined location on the author's web server or use methods similar to Domain Key Identified Mail (DKIM) [25] to provide the pvk via DNS (or both). In both cases the verification is tied closely to the DNS controlled by the publisher. Again, to deter repackaging, this DNS location must not be specified in a hidden manifest, but must be closely coupled to information presented to the user. As mentioned in section 2, application package namespaces "should use Internet domain ownership as the basis... (in reverse)." Therefore, by reversing the package name, a URL can be constructed to locate the pvk.

If developers honor the direction to name packages appropriately (83% of applications in the official market already conform to this convention), the pvk can be unambiguously located relative to the URL corresponding to the package name. Suppose that, by convention, the pvk is stored in a file `android.cert` at the root of the domain. For instance, an application with the package name `com.facebook.katana` would be signed using an ssk that has an associated pvk available at `http://facebook.com/android.cert`. The use of domain ownership for key publishing permits the use of self-signed certificates making this protocol immediately deployable. The use of CA's and other PKI infrastructures remain (at this point) optional.

Propagating key information via DNS has certain performance benefits compared to storing the public verification key on a webserver, which must serve the key to every mobile device at verification time. Both methods are however susceptible to various attacks discussed in section 5.

By decoupling cryptographic signing from the distribution mechanism, the application can be verified independent of how an application is obtained. Applications obtained via unmoderated file sharing forums, will still bear a package name plausible to the user (e.g., `com.facebook.katana`), and the device will attempt to verify the application with the legitimate Facebook pvk. If the application had been repackaged, the verification will fail. If the verification succeeds, it was signed by the owner of the `facebook.com` domain.

Application verification should take place as part of the installation process. Install-time verification can prevent undesirable applications from ever executing on the mobile device. Figure 4 shows a timing diagram of the entire verification process. As previously described, the publisher's keypair is created orthogonal to verification. First a user locates an application in some mobile marketplace and the application is downloaded to the mobile device via whatever mechanism the marketplace supports. Once the entire application is downloaded, the embedded signatures can be checked to be well-formed (locally on the mobile device). Next the package name is extracted from the application and reversed in order to determine the location of the pvk. The pvk is retrieved from the publisher's server (or from DNS). The application is then verified using the pvk. If the verification succeeds the application is installed us-

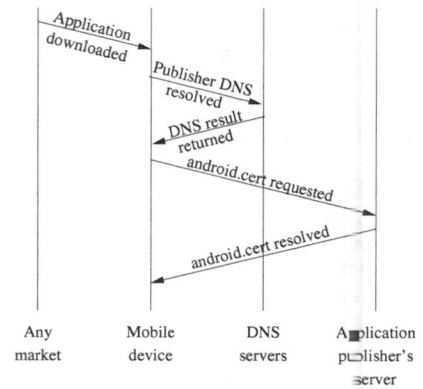

Figure 4: Verification protocol: Network Diagram

ing the typical platform installation process. If verification fails, the application is not installed. Of course, when applications fail verification the protocol could be modified to permit the user to install the application anyway, or to upload the file to a security team for analysis.

Publishers may need to update to a new, legitimate keypair resulting in a new pvk becoming available. Similarly, if a publisher's ssk is compromised a repackaged application may be installed with an pvk that is thought to be valid at install time, but was later found to be compromised. For these reasons, application verification may also be performed periodically or on-demand. Similar to the end result of failed verification at install time, a failed verification in this case would likely result in the uninstallation of an application.

A verification process such as described here is independent to any vetting process imposed by a market policy. The cryptographic verification simply demonstrates that an application is what the publisher intended to provide to the consumer. It makes no attempt to determine if the behavior of an application is malicious.

With this protocol, the end-device is able to verify that the application is exactly what the publisher intended for the user. In the physical world, in addition to the trusting integrity of the store, there is some independent binding to the creator of the software. This binding takes many forms such as product packaging, branding, holographic CDs, and other anti-piracy technologies. The protocol we propose, called AppIntegrity, enables similar binding to take place on modern application markets, creating a way to bind a website owner to a particular application.

Publishers currently do not make the pvk available, as a consequence it is not possible to fully test the mitigation capabilities of AppIntegrity. However, our measurements (by domain validity checks and manual malware analysis) and the repackaging classification techniques in [37] suggest that AppIntegrity may see great success in mitigating current malware.

4.2 Implementation

The protocol described in section 4.1, is realized in proof-of-concept applications designed to run on any computer and as an Android application, which, mirroring the name of the proposed protocol, we call AppIntegrity as well. Android's architecture permits the entirety of an application to be observed by other applications. Accordingly, AppIntegrity registers a handler for the PACKAGE_ADDED[4] intent that performs verification whenever new ap-

---

[4]Note that this isn't exactly the same as the described protocol, since the application is technically already installed by the time the PACKAGE_ADDED intent is broadcast. This intent is the nearest

Algorithm	Official	Alternative
MD5withRSA	9.784%	7.553%
SHA1withDSA	2.662%	2.743%
SHA1withRSA	87.458%	87.157%
SHA256withRSA	0.091%	2.543%
MD2withRSA	0.005%	0.004%

Table 1: Signing Algorithms Observed in Markets.

plications are downloaded. Since most publishers have not made public keys available, a failed verification results in giving the user the choice to uninstall the application.

AppIntegrity takes advantage of several Android features:

1. Application package names are intended to be unique and based upon domain ownership of the developer.

2. Android applications have read access to other applications. While each application can store data in a private area, the application itself may be read by other applications. Thus a verification program has the ability to obtain package name and signature information from other applications.

3. Android applications are written in Java which has extensive cryptographic libraries that can be used to verify signatures.

4. The Android documentation specifies RSA when generating a private key. The use of RSA in key creation results in a SHA1withRSA (see Figure 5) signature, which is compatible with the existing specification for DKIM (DKIM is defined to use RSA-SHA-1 or RSA-SHA-256 for signing and verification). As seen in Table 1 the majority of applications we observed use one of the two DKIM compatible algorithms.

```
$ keytool -printcert -file CERT.RSA
Owner: CN=First Last, OU=Unk, O=Unk, L=City, ST=State, C=US
Issuer: CN=First Last, OU=Unk, O=Unk, L=City, ST=State, C=US
Serial number: 4d895f96
Valid from: Tue Mar 22 22:48:54 EDT 2011 until: Sat Aug 07 22:48:54 EDT 2038
Certificate fingerprints:
  MD5:  07:E4:51:41:E8:80:92:97:F9:6F:AF:BF:57:2F:28:2A
  SHA1: D5:A0:3D:A4:E5:0F:D7:9E:B3:53:95:83:8C:CA:AB:A5:EB:E2:C4:29
  Signature algorithm name: SHA1withRSA
  Version: 3
```

Figure 5: Android Signing Key: Keytool output for signing key.

Future implementation could take many forms. To fully realize the protocol shown in Figure 4, the Android framework needs minor modification to the install process. Either verification must be built into the package installation process or a new intent needs to be broadcast post-download prior to package install. Meanwhile, the proof-of-concept application may be downloaded from the authors website[5]. Device carriers or manufactures may choose to install a verification application in such a way that the user can't uninstall it, forcing verification to occur.

4.3 Performance Evaluation

Minimal network overhead is crucial as many carriers now have limited data plans. Currently, a typical RSA key found in the official market averages 922 bytes (0.0008 MB). Given the current distribution of application sizes (as shown in Figure 2), the additional network overhead introduced by verification is marginal. Figure 6

---

to the desired functionality that a typical, unprivileged application can achieve.

[5]www.ece.cmu.edu/ tvidas/tools.html

is scaled to show the only appreciable overhead introduced by obtaining the certificate. As seen in the Figure 6, less than 4% of applications would exhibit significant overhead relative to downloading the application. The applications in question are simply so small that the additional 922 bytes is significant, however it is extremely likely that the user is already downloading many other [24], larger applications further reducing any concerns of network performance degradation.

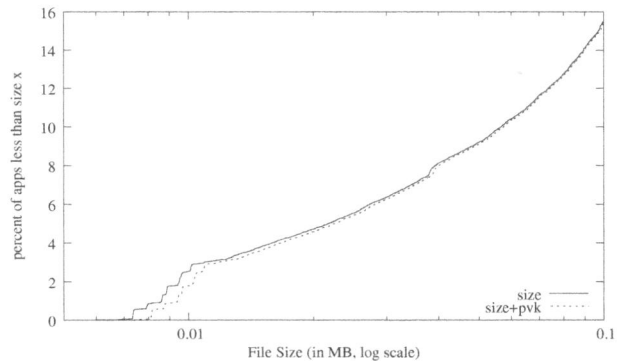

Figure 6: Size Overhead: Less than 4% of applications would exhibit appreciable overhead (plot magnified from official market plot in Figure 2).

Similarly, processor use directly affects battery life on mobile devices [11], and as such, excessive resource use could hinder adoption. Since devices already perform cryptographic signature verification the additional verification is not significantly different. Currently a manifest (different that the `AndroidManifest.xml`) is stored in a special `META-INF` directory along with the public keys in the `.apk`. The device currently verifies the signatures stored in the manifest using the embedded public key. With our proposed protocol the same key would be obtained dynamically, but the cryptographic operations would remain the same.

To encourage adoption, public keys could still be included in the `.apk` files, and actually both keys (which may be identical) could be used to verify the application. This additional verification would result in a linear increase in processing time as each `.apk` component is verified twice. If the protocol is integrated into the Android package installer, there would effectively be no additional overhead over the existing installer.

The lightweight cryptographic verification of AppIntegrity will likely outperform other types of "fingerprint" or "signature"(not cryptographic signature) based security solutions. In particular, anti-virus, symbolic execution, anomaly detection [14], static analysis [29, 30] would all likely require extensive processor and/or memory requirement which are not desirable on a resource-constrained mobile device.

Since little or no modification is required to to the Android framework, there is negligible network and processing overhead, and there is no additional burden to implement a PKI, AppIntegrity can be deployed to Android with little cost.

5. SECURITY ANALYSIS

The primary benefit of AppIntegrity is the ability to verify the integrity of a published application independent of how the application is obtained. Under the current model, an attacker needs only to succeed in getting malware onto a device. Typically this is achieved by publishing a malicious application to a marketplace and allowing users to locate and install the application. AppIntegrity significantly increases the effort required for a successful attack. Under this new model, the attacker must also either obtain the original publisher's secret signing key, be in control of the publisher's web server, or commit a man-in-the-middle (MitM) attack on the publisher's DNS records and/or web server. In all cases the attacker must now conduct two successful attacks, and the secondary attack requires more effort than application repackaging.

Man-in-the-middle attacks that target the mobile device may be more difficult to conduct than such an attack on a traditional computer. Modern smartphones and tablets can communicate over several medium. A successful MitM attack on the client will either need to predict the specific media that will be used, or will need to conduct simultaneous MitM attacks on all nearby WIFI, 2G, 3G and 4G networks.

The official market enforces unique package names, which incidentally lightly deters the republication of repackaged applications back to the market. An application with exactly the same package name may not be published. In order to republish in the official market, some existing malware, such as DroidDreamLight2, uses capitalization differently in package names. For example, `com.gb.CompassLeveler` vs `com.gb.compassleveler`. Since DNS does not preserve case, the AppIntegrity verification would resolve to the legitimate key, and fail.

5.1 Limitations

AppIntegrity would benefit from a few minor design changes to the Android platform: permitting additional privilege to the verification software, enabling actions to perform prior to application install and clearly displaying package name information to users prior to install. The proposed protocol does make several assumptions about the user, and if the user is deceived the effectiveness of AppIntegrity suffers.

Domain name deception. Once a user has located a particular application that they are interested in installing, the installation interface must clearly display the package name (or derived domain) to the user. The user may or may not recognize the application name, package name, developer, etc. Even when the user does recognize the application name and developer, it is up to the user to detect *typosquatting*, the intentional registration of domain misspellings [26]. For example, if the user installs a repackaged Google maps look-alike that has a package name `com.g00gle.maps` the certificate will be retrieved from `maps.g00gle.com` and will cryptographically verify. Without an external validation service for URLs (e.g., PKI, reputation system), such attacks will remain possible.

Domain recognition. Similarly, many users recognize names such as Google, Facebook, etc but the vast majority of applications are created by less recognizable publishers. One may argue that as an application becomes popular, users are more likely to recognize the publisher (and associated domain). However, the problem of unrecognized publishers remains. AppIntegrity provides a foundation that could be used to create additional protocols or services to help solve this problem. For instance, AppIntegrity would provide assurance that a given publisher produced a certain application, and an external vetting service could assist in confirming that this publisher is reputable.

To address both domain name deception and domain recognition, one could reasonably imagine such a service building upon Perspectives [35], with notaries voting on the reputation of a given publisher. Such an architecture is already deployed as a Firefox browser add-on (Convergence, [33]), and the same functionality could be implemented on Android devices.

Lack of Privilege. The current AppIntegrity application could be uninstalled by a user or potentially by malware. A previously mentioned, a manufacturer or wireless carrier could install AppIntegrity in a way that makes user uninstallation difficult. Ideally, verification services would be built into Android itself. However, as with most mobile device security properties, *rooting* or *jailbreaking* the device undermines this added security.

Prior Infection. Devices that are already infected with malware that has elevated (root) privileges are subject to other attack classes, such as drawing over the existing user interface. In these situations, AppIntegrity only assists in preventing malware from entering the device, and is subject to all the same issues as typical software.

5.2 Keeping Private Keys Private

As with most PKCS structures, the cryptographic properties provided by the keypair require the private key to remain secret, known only to the owner. Any other party that knows a user's private key can impersonate that user. For these reasons, users typically create their own cryptographic keypair. Contrary to this convention, Amazon's Appstore (one of the commercially-backed Android markets) supplies an account-unique key to the publisher [2]. In this model, Amazon could impersonate any application publisher, and a security breach of the Amazon market would result in all keypairs being compromised. We encourage developers to exercise the option to request the use of a non-assigned key for application signing.[6] As stated in section 4.1, to enable legitimate verification, public keys should not be stored alongside applications in a marketplace.

Similarly, smartphone or tablet users that have "rooted" their device often install entire new operating system images known as "custom ROMs." These ROMs are created and made available by enterprising developers such as the Android Open Source Project (AOSP). The developers of these ROMs may chose to publicly publish associated private keys. Since the private keys are widely available, no identity can be bound to anything signed by the key. Malware, such as jsmshider [6], may take advantage of this cryptography faux-pas.

Under a model that encourages self-signed certificates, such as the current Android model, the burden of securing the private key falls solely on the publisher. Application publishers that do not properly secure their secret signing key risk others using their identity to publish applications. Under the protocol outlined in section 4.1, loss of the private key would allow an attacker to modify an application and have the modified application successfully verify.

6. RELATED WORK

Spoofing attacks similar to the Netflix malware were theorized by Felt et al. in [21]. Felt et al.'s work [21] predates the recent Netflix spoofing malware which very closely mimics the Facebook attack described in the paper. Additionally Felt et al. also provide a survey of much of the mobile malware discovered from 2009 to 2011 in [20].

In [34], Vidas et al. observe application repackaging as one type of an "unprivileged attack." The class of unprivileged attacks is one part of a greater taxonomy targeting Android devices. Vidas et al. also observe that malware is often present in alternative ("black") markets and such applications often "offer no additional value to the consumer." These observations are confirmed in our alternative

---

[6]Developers may request to use a non-Amazon key by submitting a request through the Amazon AppStore Developer Portal

market corpus discussed in section 3. Burguera et al. also cite the repackaging and distribution in alternative markets as evidence for the need of their primary contribution in [12], which is a system for crowd-based behavioral malware detection. Both Vidas et al. and Burguera et al. observe that applications are signed and the current signing process in no way inhibits repackaging and republication of applications.

Zhou et al. conducted alternative market research focusing on four alternative marketplaces [38], and have found a significantly smaller percentage of malware than we observed. Different from Zhou et al.'s study, we investigate a larger number of application marketplaces, and look at possible indicators of suspicious markets (e.g., extensive reuse of identical signing certificates). In another difference, Zhou et al. present a new tool for re-actively detecting malware on found in markets, where AppIntegrity strives to proactively prevent the installation of software signed by those other than the originator. In another work, Zhou et al. focus on detecting repackaging in six alternative marketplaces [36]. The repackaging found in these six marketplaces was prodominately performed in order to redirect ad revenue, but in a few cases the authors observed malicious payloads.

In [37], Zhou et al. describe a malware collection consisting entirely of Android samples. The authors provide measurement of the malware collection and describe the "evolution" of malware by studying related samples chronologically. The authors also find a large amount of application repackaging and provide measurements of activation mechanisms, secondary payloads, and permission used by malicious applications.

Chen et al. [13] use application metadata to identify web applications which the authors then provide a means of app isolation. Chen et al. reference the Chrome Web Store which allows "verified apps." The procedure for obtaining the "verified" icon in the store is to pay a $5 fee and the application developer must verify domain ownership via Google's "webmaster tools." The term "verified" is used differently here, as the verification is proven to the market which then assures the consumer. The additional assurance provided by proving domain ownership is likely useful as a means to increase application use and market reputation, but is somewhat orthogonal to the end-to-end integrity provided by AppIntegrity.

Enck et al. describe a lightweight application certification service, Kirin [19]. This service forces applications to pass several rules at install-time, such as the absence of permission combinations the rule creator deemed dangerous. AppIntegrity could possibly be implemented as a feature of Kirin, or independently as described above, in addition to Kirin.

AppIntegrity focuses on ensuring end-to-end integrity for applications, and makes no attempt to analyze the inner workings of an applications or otherwise protect the user from applications that are malicious from origin. For this reason it makes sense to pair AppIntegrity with taint tracking systems such as TaintDroid [17] or PiOS [16] in order to detect privacy leaks. Similarly, Hornyack et. al have retrofitted Android [22] in a way that permits executing existing applications in a safe way.

7. DISCUSSION AND FUTURE WORK

AppIntegrity does not require any changes to the current developer build process for Android. The application structure and cryptographic signing are used in exactly the same manner as currently employed. Similarly, AppIntegrity is designed to make use of the self-signed keys widely used by Android developers. As shown by the reference implementation provided for Android, AppIntegrity can be immediately adopted without the need of a large PKI system.

If an entity desires the added value of a trusted third party verifying developer entities, a PKI can be applied in addition to the protocol described in section 4.1. Again, Android has features that facilitate this, as applications can be signed by multiple keys, allowing for an application to be signed by a market proprietor in addition to the developer. Additional signing by the market proprietor is akin to physical store reputation, in both cases the market is certifying that the software obtained from the market is legitimate. Of course, a more traditional PKI model could be imposed where a developer key is signed by a third party who also maintains a registry of developer public keys.

We hope that developers elect to publish their public keys as we describe in section 4.1. In order to encourage adoption, we hope that Google will adjust the Android developer documentation and effectively make public key publication part of the standard developer account setup.

AppIntegrity is still compatible with alternative markets. Applications that are republished via alternative markets can be downloaded and verified by a user who can be confident that the installed software is what the developer intended for delivery. Similarly, AppIntegrity would be compatible with "private markets" given that the devices that have the private markets provisioned have network access to protected domain spaces. Consider a "secure Android" under development by a government entity, as long as devices can access the government network (via VPN for example), certificates can still be retrieved from the appropriate URLs and verification can be performed.

Even though our reference implementation and related discussions largely focus on Android, AppIntegrity can leverage existing application signing for many mobile platforms, and indeed application delivery mechanisms for traditional PCs. The most common mobile consumer platforms: Android, iOS, and Symbian all already use application signing in some way, and can benefit from a verification system like AppIntegrity.

Throughout this text we have framed the use of AppIntegrity on terminal devices, such as smartphones. Additional verifiers could be used to embody trust in other ways. For example, a third party could monitor all the public keys found in applications and resolve and verify these keys with the keys found the applications respective domains. The third party could provide a "verified" seal similar to services for websites available today. Similarly a market might proactively and/or periodically verify applications that are submitted for publication.

AppIntegrity relies upon public keys being readily available and bound to an entity via domain ownership. The availability of these keys could complement other application market functions such as application revocation. Currently when malware is identified in Google Play, both the publisher and the consumer are at the mercy of Google to remotely uninstall applications from infected devices. By extending our presented protocol to verify applications prior to execution, disabling of malware can be performed by either the market proprietor (e.g. Google) or by the domain owner (e.g. the publisher).

8. CONCLUSION

Application markets are now commonplace for mobile devices. We have shown that not all markets are created equal: quite the opposite, in fact, as some distribute malware almost exclusively. Most of this malware is *repackaged* in some way giving victims something desirable to execute.

By analyzing signing certificate strategies we observed that markets that deliver the highest percentage of malware are also those that reuse signing keys the most, unilaterally across the marketplace in fact.

In order to mitigate the threat of repackaging, we present an end-to-end verification protocol, AppIntegrity, that facilitates cryptographic verification between the software creator and the end consumer. The protocol is realized in reference implementations for PC and Android devices, but is applicable to other mobile frameworks and application markets.

The cost of adoption for AppIntegrity is very low. The minimal network and local resource use is ideal for the constrained environment of mobile devices. Furthermore, the end-to-end protocol can be used with existing official and alternative markets alike.

Relating to Android in particular, AppIntegrity requires no changes to the existing Android development process. Minimal changes to the Android framework could enhance the ability for AppIntegrity protect users, but even when used with the current version of Android, AppIntegrity can provide added safety by rapidly uninstalling unverified applications, and providing building blocks for future protocols and services. By binding public keys based on domain ownership, AppIntegrity has the ability to leverage PKCS without the need for a complicated PKI, further contributing to making AppIntegrity rapidly deployable.

Acknowledgments

This work is supported in part by CyLab at Carnegie Mellon University under grant DAAD19-02-1-0389 from the Army Research Office, and by the National Science Foundation under IGERT award DGE-0903659. The authors wish to thank the proprietors of VirusTotal for access to VirusTotal's resources and the anonymous reviewers for their comments.

9. REFERENCES

[1] Virustotal. http://www.virustotal.com.

[2] Amazon appstore frequently asked questions. https://developer.amazon.com/help/faq.html, Oct. 2011.

[3] android-apktool: a tool to reverse engineer Android apk files, 2011. https://code.google.com/p/android-apktool/.

[4] Android developer guide 4.0 r1. http://developer.android.com/guide/topics/manifest/manifest-element.html, Oct. 2011.

[5] android4me: J2ME port of Google's Android, 2011. https://code.google.com/p/android4me/downloads/list.

[6] Security alert: Malware found targeting custom roms. http://blog.mylookout.com/2011/06/security-alert-malware-found-targeting-custom-roms-jsmshider/, June 2011.

[7] ASRAR, I. Could sexy space be the birth of the sms botnet? http://www.symantec.com/connect/blogs/could-sexy-space-be-birth-sms-botnet, July 2009.

[8] ASRAR, I. A touch of mobile threat déjà vu. http://www.symantec.com/connect/blogs/touch-mobile-threat-deja-vu, Feb. 2010.

[9] ASRAR, I. Will sms bring you free vouchers? http://www.symantec.com/connect/blogs/will-sms-bring-you-free-vouchers, Apr. 2010.

[10] ASRAR, I. Will your next tv manual ask you to run a scan instead of adjusting the antenna? http://www.symantec.com/connect/blogs/will-your-next-tv-manual-ask-you-run-scan-instead-adjusting-antenna, Oct. 2011.

[11] BECHER, M., FREILING, F., HOFFMANN, J., HOLZ, T., UELLENBECK, S., AND WOLF, C. Mobile security catching up? revealing the nuts and bolts of the security of mobile devices. In *Proc. IEEE Symp. on Security and Privacy* (2011), IEEE, pp. 96–111.

[12] BURGUERA, I., ZURUTUZA, U., AND NADJM-TEHRANI, S. Crowdroid: behavior-based malware detection system for android. In *Proc. ACM work. Security and privacy in smartphones and mobile devices* (2011), ACM, pp. 15–26.

[13] CHEN, E., BAU, J., REIS, C., BARTH, A., AND JACKSON, C. App isolation: get the security of multiple browsers with just one. In *Proc. ACM CCS* (2011), ACM, pp. 227–238.

[14] CHENG, J., WONG, S., YANG, H., AND LU, S. Smartsiren: virus detection and alert for smartphones. In *Proc. ACM MobiSys* (2007), pp. 258–271.

[15] CHRISTIN, N., WEIGEND, A., AND CHUANG, J. Content availability, pollution and poisoning in file sharing peer-to-peer networks. In *Proceedings of the 6th ACM conference on Electronic commerce* (2005), ACM, pp. 68–77.

[16] EGELE, M., KRUEGEL, C., KIRDA, E., AND VIGNA, G. PiOS: Detecting privacy leaks in iOS applications. In *Proceedings of the Network and Distributed System Security Symposium* (2011).

[17] ENCK, W., GILBERT, P., CHUN, B., COX, L., JUNG, J., MCDANIEL, P., AND SHETH, A. TaintDroid: an Information-Flow tracking system for realtime privacy monitoring on smartphones. In *OSDI 2010* (Vancouver, BC, Canada).

[18] ENCK, W., OCTEAU, D., MCDANIEL, P. AND CHAUDHURI, S. A study of android application security. In *Proc. of the 20th USENIX Security Symposium* (2011).

[19] ENCK, W., ONGTANG, M., AND MCDANIEL, P. On lightweight mobile phone application certification. In *Proc. ACM CCS* (Chicago, IL), pp. 235–245.

[20] FELT, A., FINIFTER, M., CHIN, E., HANNA, S., AND WAGNER, D. A survey of mobile malware in the wild. In *Proc. ACM work. Security and privacy in smartphones and mobile devices* (2011), ACM, pp. 3–14.

[21] FELT, A., AND WAGNER, D. Phishing on mobile devices. In *IEEE Workshop on Web 2.0 Security and Privacy* (2011).

[22] HORNYACK, P., HAN, S., JUNG, J., SCHECHTER, S., AND WETHERALL, D. These aren't the droids you're looking for: retrofitting android to protect data from imperious applications. In *Proc. ACM CCS* (Chicago, IL, 2011), ACM, pp. 639–652.

[23] JOHN, J., YU, F., XIE, Y., ABADI, M., AND KRISHNAMURTHY, A. deSEO: Combating search-result poisoning. In *Proceedings of USENIX Security 2011* (San Francisco, CA, Aug. 2011).

[24] KELLEY, P., CONSOLVO, S., CRANOR, L., JUNG, J., SADEH, N., AND WETHERALL, D. An conundrum of permissions: Installing applications on an android smartphone. In *the Workshop on Usable Security* (2012).

[25] LEIBA, B., AND FENTON, J. Domainkeys identified mail (dkim): Using digital signatures for domain verification. In *Proceedings of the Fourth Conference on Email and Anti-Spam (CEAS)* (2007), Citeseer.

[26] MOORE, T., AND EDELMAN, B. Measuring the perpetrators and funders of typosquatting. *Financial Cryptography and Data Security* (2010), 175–191.

[27] MOORE, T., LEONTIADIS, N., AND CHRISTIN, N. Fashion crimes: trending-term exploitation on the web. In *Proc. ACM CCS* (Chicago, IL, 2011), pp. 455–466.

[28] PILZ, H., AND SCHINDLER, S. Are free android virus scanners any good? Tech. rep., Nov. 2011.

[29] SCHMIDT, A., BYE, R., SCHMIDT, H., CLAUSEN, J., KIRAZ, O., YUKSEL, K., CAMTEPE, S., AND ALBAYRAK, S. Static analysis of executables for collaborative malware detection on android. In *Proc. IEEE ICC* (2009), IEEE, pp. 1–5.

[30] SCHMIDT, A., CLAUSEN, J., CAMTEPE, A., AND ALBAYRAK, S. Detecting symbian os malware through static function call analysis. In *Proc. MALWARE* (2009), IEEE, pp. 15–22.

[31] SCHÖNEFELD, M. Reconstructing dalvik applications. *CANSECWEST 2009* (Mar. 2009).

[32] SCHWARTS, M. Google removes malware apps from android market. `http://www.informationweek.com/news/security/client/229700298`, June 2011.

[33] THOUGHTCRIME LABS. Convergence: An agile, distributed and secure stratefy for replacing certificate authorities. `http://convergence.io`.

[34] VIDAS, T., VOTIPKA, D., AND CHRISTIN, N. All your droid are belong to us: A survey of current android attacks. In *Proceedings of the 5th USENIX Workshop on Offensive technologies* (2011), USENIX Association.

[35] WENDLANDT, D., ANDERSEN, D., AND PERRIG, A. Perspectives: Improving SSH-style host authentication with multi-path probing. In *USENIX Annual Technical Conference* (2008), pp. 321–334.

[36] ZHOU, W. ZHOU Y. JIANG, X., AND NING, P. Detecting repackaged smartphone applications in third-party android marketplaces. In *Proc. 3rd ACM Conference on Data and Application Security and Privacy* (2012).

[37] ZHOU, Y., AND JIANG, X. Dissecting android malware: Characterization and evolution. In *Proc. IEEE Symp. on Security and Privacy* (2012).

[38] ZHOU, Y., WANG, Z., ZHOU, W., AND JIANG, X. Hey, you, get off of my market: Detecting malicious apps in official and alternative android markets. In *NDSS* (2012).

AppsPlayground: Automatic Security Analysis of Smartphone Applications

Vaibhav Rastogi, Yan Chen, and William Enck[†]
Northwestern University, [†]North Carolina State University
vrastogi@u.northwestern.edu, ychen@northwestern.edu, enck@cs.ncsu.edu

ABSTRACT

Today's smartphone application markets host an ever increasing number of applications. The sheer number of applications makes their review a daunting task. We propose AppsPlayground for Android, a framework that automates the analysis smartphone applications. AppsPlayground integrates multiple components comprising different detection and automatic exploration techniques for this purpose. We evaluated the system using multiple large scale and small scale experiments involving real benign and malicious applications. Our evaluation shows that AppsPlayground is quite effective at automatically detecting privacy leaks and malicious functionality in applications.

Categories and Subject Descriptors

D.4.6 [**Operating Systems**]: Security and Protection—*Invasive software (e.g., viruses, worms, Trojan horses)*; D.2.5 [**Software Engineering**]: Testing and Debugging

General Terms

Security

Keywords

Dynamic analysis, Android, malware, privacy leakage

1. INTRODUCTION

Mobile devices such as smartphones have gained great popularity in response to vast repositories of applications. Most of these applications are created by unknown developers who may not operate in the users' best interests, leading to malware [14, 16] and frequent exposure of privacy sensitive information such as phone identifiers and location [6, 7, 8].

Recently, researchers have proposed both static and dynamic security analysis techniques for smartphone applications. While static analysis approaches such as those used

by PiOS [6] and Enck et al. [8] scale to large numbers of applications, they do not capture runtime environment context such as configuration variables and user input. More importantly, code may be obfuscated to thwart static analysis, either intentionally or unintentionally (such as stripping symbol information of native binaries to reduce size).

On the other hand, TaintDroid [7] uses dynamic analysis to capture runtime environment context. However, the researchers had to manually navigate the user interfaces of each analyzed application to sufficiently exercise dangerous functionality. More recently, DroidScope [30] used dynamic analysis for malware forensics. Large-scale dynamic analysis however requires more than what has been proposed earlier – a fast analysis system and strategies to provide automatic code coverage.

In this paper, we propose *AppsPlayground*, referred to as simply *Playground* for brevity, a framework for automated dynamic security analysis of Android applications. Playground is meant to analyze applications for both malware, i.e., apps that have a malicous intent, and grayware, i.e., apps that are not malicious but may still be annoying, for example, by leaking private information for a legitimate purpose but without user's awareness. From this point on, for the sake of conciseness, we will not particularly distinguish between malware and grayware and refer to them both as malware. An automatic dynamic analysis framework needs to possess not only detection techniques for identifying malicious or annoying functionality but also automatic exploration techniques to explore the application code as much as possible. Furthermore, the dynamic analysis environment needs to appear as real (in this case, a real smartphone) to the app as possible, lest a malicious app can easily detect the special environment and not show any malicious behavior.

In Playground, solutions to all the above requirements are integrated together in a modular manner. We use multiple detection techniques, ranging from taint tracing to kernel-level system call monitoring. For taint-tracing, we are able to seamlessly integrate and reuse TaintDroid [7], an already available taint-tracing engine with very good performance for Android into the rest of our system. In order to deal with root attacks in Android, we describe vulnerability conditions in Android as succint signatures in terms of system calls and kernel-level data structures. These signatures may easily be incorporated into a dynamic analysis.

For automatic exploration, we find that the nature of Android imposes non-conventional requirements on the exploration techniques that need to be used. Application code can be triggered by several kinds of system events and so such events need to be simulated. Moreover, most of the apps in Android provide GUI, which requires sophisticated GUI exploration schemes. Trivial approaches for GUI exploration such as fuzz testing have their advantages in their simplicity and, if designed properly, have the ability to eventually exhaustively explore a finite state space. They however take more time and are sometimes insufficient because application user interfaces have complex requirements such as login credentials for Internet services. Therefore, we also need to intelligently drive the user interface to exercise code implementing interesting and dangerous functionality. Our heuristic-based intelligent execution technique is able to avoid redundant exploration and is able to use contextual information to fill editable text boxes meaningfully.

To demonstrate the practical advantage of Playground, we evaluated 3,968 from the official Android Market (now Google Play). We identified exposures of privacy sensitive information in 946 applications, flagged by the taint-tracing engine. Of these, 844 applications leaked phone identifiers (such as phone number and IMEI), and 212 applications leaked geographic location. We note that detecting privacy violations still requires manual confirmation, as TaintDroid only identifies that information has left the device over the network interface, and not privacy violations. For further validation, we also tested the applications used in the TaintDroid study. Playground's findings almost completely coincided with the findings manually made by the TaintDroid authors on the much smaller set of thirty applications they evaluated. Furthermore, we also evaluated Playground on known malware samples, falling under diverse categories of root attacks and SMS trojans, and were able to detect the malicious nature of all of them.

Finally, to evaluate the performance of automatic GUI exploration, we compare our system with GUIRipper [19], a system that automatically generates test cases based on windowing elements in traditional desktop GUIs. To the best of our knowledge, this is the only system, apart from fuzz-testing, available in the literature for GUI exploration. It lacks advanced techniques such as filling in contextual data in text boxes and repeatedly exercising GUI widgets to achieve better code coverage, both of which we have found are often critical requirements when testing Android applications. Our comparison with an Android port of this system shows our technique to achieve a mean 30% improvement in terms of code coverage.

To summarize, this paper makes the following contributions.

- We propose AppsPlayground (or simply, Playground), a modular framework for scalable dynamic analysis of Android application.

- We identify the key requirements for automatically exploring Android applications. We use automatic system event triggering and propose and develop a new intelligent execution technique that can use contextual information to provide meaningful textual input.

- We describe vulnerability conditions for known vulnerabilities in Android as succint signatures that may be used in dynamic analysis. These vulnerability conditions are necessary for a system compromise.

- We implement the AppsPlayground framework for Android and evaluate 3,968 applications from the official Android app Market. Our analysis identified exposures of privacy sensitive information in 946 applica-

tions. Moreover, we were able to confirm the malicious nature of already known malware samples using this framework.

The remainder of this paper proceeds as follows. Section 2 provides relevant background in Android and Section 3 gives an overview of Playground. Sections 4, 5 and 6 provide detailed discussion of the techniques incorporated into Playground. Section 7 discusses the implementation of Playground. Section 8 describes our measurements with Playground. Section 9 discusses the effectiveness of the automatic exploration techniques employed. Section 10 presents related work and Section 11 concludes.

2. ANDROID BACKGROUND

Android is a widely popular and open source operating system designed for smartphones and other mobile devices. While Android is based on Linux, it defines an entirely new middleware and GUI environment in which applications execute. Applications are mostly written in Java, which is compiled to Dalvik bytecode, which runs in a virtual machine similar to the Java virtual machine. Apart from Java, Android also allows parts of apps to be coded in native code.

Every Android application runs as an unprivileged user with Linux UIDs effectively being used to provide application sandboxes. Android applications are composed of *components*. There are four component types: *activity*, *service*, *broadcast receiver*, and *content provider*. The user interface is defined by one or more activity components. Services are meant to run in background while content providers manage access to data. Broadcast Receivers are registered with system services and can receive system events, such as reboot completed, or an SMS received, and so on. Once a broadcast receiver is registered to receive a system event, the code specified in the broadcast receiver is run whenever the system event is triggered.[1] Most system events are guarded by permissions, which the app must declare and get approved for at installation time.

For automatic exploration, it is necessary to understand the GUI features in Android. Each activity corresponds to a screen displayed to the user. This screen is functionally equivalent to a traditional GUI window, the only difference being that only one screen is shown at a time (with minor exceptions), whereas traditional GUIs can typically display multiple windows.

An application's GUI consists of several activities that invoke one another and possibly return results. At any point in time, only one activity has input focus and processing. This activity is referred to as the *active* activity. When one activity invokes another, the former is paused and the new activity is pushed to the top of the activity stack and made active. Once an activity has completed its work, it terminates, optionally returning a value, and the next activity on the stack is made active. Note that activities are not limited to invoking activities within the same application. A sequence of related activities on the stack is called a *task*.

The activity GUI layout is commonly defined in XML but may also be defined programmatically. As in traditional GUIs, an Android window consists of widgets, which are are referred to as *views* in Android terminology. The Android library supplies several useful views which may either

---

[1]This may sometimes not hold due to, for example, abort of a broadcast.

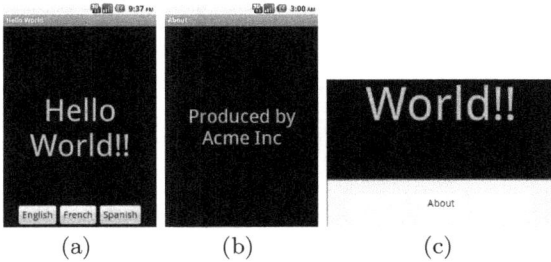

Figure 1: A simple application with three windows. Window (a) invokes window (c) which invokes window (b). (c) shows only the lower half of the screen emphasizing the menu window.

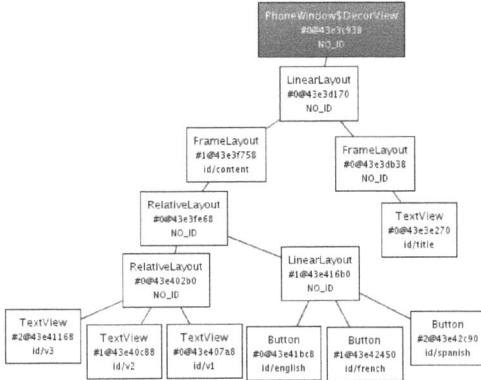

Figure 2: The GUI hierarchy for the window in Figure 1(a)

be standalone (e.g., buttons) or act as containers for other views. In addition to the window layout, an activity can define a menu that appears when the user presses the physical "Menu" button on the phone.

Example. Figure 1 shows a simple example application. The application consists of two activities, "Hello World" and "About" (Figures 1(a) and 1(b), respectively). The "Hello World" activity has three buttons which bring up the "Hello World!!" message in three different languages. The "About" activity is non interactive. There is a menu attached to the "Hello World" activity, which we model as a separate window. After opening this menu, one may click on the only option (named "About") to go to the "About" activity. Figure 2 depicts the GUI hierarchy of the window in Figure 1(a).

3. APPSPLAYGROUND OVERVIEW

This section gives a broad view of Playground. We begin with describing the overall architecture of Playground followed by the different components involved in brief.

3.1 Overall Architecture

We seek to design a general framework for automatic dynamic analysis for smartphone applications. Playground is built as a virtual machine environment. Specifically, it repurposes the Android emulator, available with the Android SDK, for the dynamic analysis environement. Built on Qemu [1], the emulator emulates an ARM machine and provides support for a few features available on a real phone, such as telephony.

A virtualized environment is essential to providing scalability required for malware analysis. For example, every

analysis can use a fresh snapshot of the environment without affecting the analyses of other samples; this is not feasible when using real devices. However, different from a few past approaches [30], we do not employ virtual machine introspection, a technique in which the virtual machine (VM) guest is run unmodified and any analysis tools run outside the VM, analyzing its physical memory to get information from inside the virtual machine. This approach while complicated, allows the analysis tools to be strictly more privileged than the analyzed environment.

In the case of Android however, apps typically run as unprivileged users and hence introspection is not actually required. Even for known attacks that try to get root privileges, signatures may be developed for identifying the attack and safely recording it before the privilege escalation actually completes. For apps requiring root (through su), these arguments do not apply; however, the number of such apps is low and the number of rooted devices is also significantly smaller. Furthermore, the complexity of introspection also hinders in the retrieval of GUI information or sending events from outside the emulator.

Figure 3 shows the architecture of Playground. Playground has several components comprising multiple detection techniques, multiple automatic exploration techniques, and techniques to make analysis environment appear like a real phone. All these components work independently of each other and integrate together in a plugin-able manner. We next briefly discuss the components listed in the figure.

3.2 Playground Components

Detection techniques are the components that actually provide the detection of a possibly malicious functionality while a sample is being tested. The detection techniques that we include are taint tracing for information leakage detection, based on TaintDroid; sensitive API monitoring, such as monitoring for the SMS API; and kernel-level monitoring for detection of root exploits. Disguise techniques are those that make the environment appear like a real device; these include the use of realistic phone identifiers, keeping realistic data in phone databases, and so on.

Automatic exploration techniques help in automatically increasing code coverage of the application code. Without automatic code coverage, it is likely that much of the code in an application will not be executed. Playground simulates events, such as location change and sms received, to trigger code in event receivers (primarily broadcast receivers). To explore the app GUI, we use fuzz testing and intelligent black-box execution. Since fuzz testing simply sends in a stream of random inputs, it may be described as a random walk on the state space. Given the ability to restart from the start state any number of times, it can eventually explore any finite connected state space. Applications that do not need any meaningful text to be filled in have a small state space consisting of screen taps and drags. Fuzz testing can deal with such applications quite well without any knowledge of their interaction model. On the other hand if some meaningful texts such as login credentials are required, fuzz testing cannot enter in the right input, and fails. For such cases, we need intelligent execution, which heuristically determines what data has to be entered in. Furthermore, since fuzz testing is random, it may sometimes fail to explore some states. Intelligent exploration however deterministically explores states that it can model.

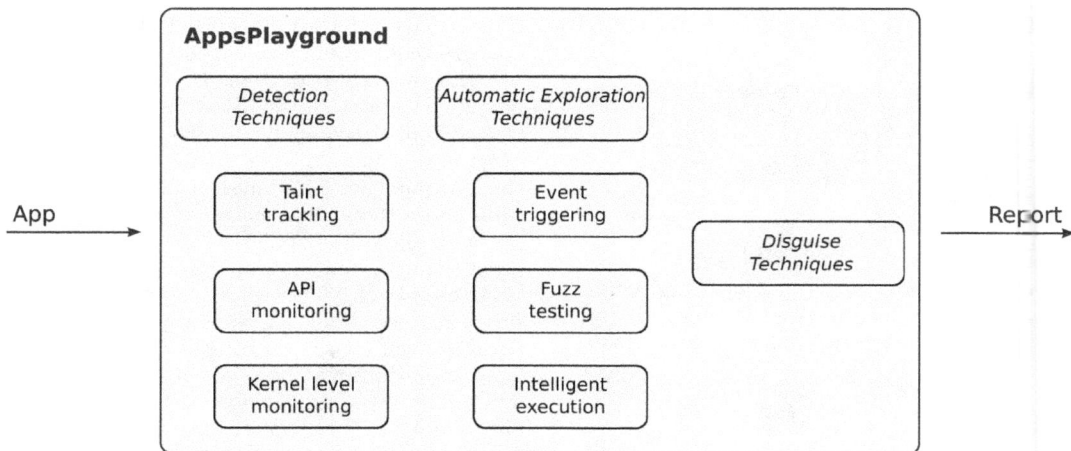

Figure 3: Architectural overview of AppsPlayground analysis framework

Intelligently driving the user interface of smartphone applications presents several challenges:

- *Modeling the GUI.* In order to intelligently exercise the user interfaces of applications, a representation of the program flow must be abstracted from the GUI. The closeness of this approximation to the actual program flow determines the completeness of the automation algorithms.

- *Efficient exploration strategy.* Even simple applications can have a very large (if not infinite) number of unique program states based on user input (e.g., a counter). Practical testing of applications requires an efficient exploration strategy with the ability to effectively discover distinct and useful states and remove redundant states.

- *Context determination.* Applications often have text fields that require special values. Leaving them empty or filling in garbage can limit application exploration. A few real world examples follow.

  - *Login credentials.* Unless a correct username and password is supplied in the correct fields, the exploration of the application will be seriously limited.

  - *Cities and zip codes.* Application functionality depending on zip codes and cities entered in input fields will likely fail in the presence of random input.

  - *Duplicate input fields.* Applications occasionally require the user to enter the same information in two text fields for consistency checks, e.g., passwords, PINs, and Email addresses.

  - *Input format.* Fields such as Email addresses and phone numbers are occasionally required to be entered in a specific format before the application will accept the input.

  - *Dates.* A future date may not work when a past date is expected. An application which asks for date of birth may not move forward if a date is in the past but is one that does not indicate the user is now over 13.

In all these cases, Playground must infer from the context present around text fields what should be filled in. We note in most cases, these inputs are validated by remote servers and so even symbolic execution cannot help determine correct values for them.

4. DETECTION TECHNIQUES

In this section we discuss the various detection techniques that are included in Playground. Other techniques may be included as needed.

Taint tracing.

Playground uses taint tracing to track privacy-sensitive information leakage. We have integrated a slightly modified version of TaintDroid [7], an open-source, high-performance taint-tracing system for Android. We note that TaintDroid works only for Dalvik bytecode only. Native code taint-tracing would likely require dynamic binary instrumentation or VM instrospection. We currently do not use such methods for native code taint-tracing; these methods result in a typical slowdown of 10x to 30x for the code and hence are not very attractive from the performance perspective.

Sensitive API monitoring.

Playground monitors a few system APIs for detecting possibly malicious functionality. The SMS API is one of the most exploited API in Android. Malicious apps use it to send text messages to premium rate numbers without user's awareness. Playground can record the destination and content of the SMS messages sent by an app. Similarly, Playground monitors the Java reflection API to record method calls and field accesses through reflection as some of these may be indicative of obfuscated codes typical in malware. Playground also monitors dynamic bytecode loading and can inform the analyst of which bytecodes (contained in a .dex file) were loaded. We note that monitoring reflection and bytecode loading APIs is done for application code only. Framework code is trusted and so need not be monitored. The differentiation is done on the basis of class loaders; in Android the class loaders for application code are always different from the class loader that loads the framework code.

Kernel-level monitoring.

We also provide kernel-level tracking to identify known

root-exploits. Our method of identification of root exploits is based on vulnerability conditions and is thus immune to code polymorphism. We observe that known root exploits such as rageagainstthecage, exploid, and gingerbreak, all have signatures that can easily be used in dynamic analysis without raising too many false alarms:

- Rageagainstthecage/Zimperlich. These attacks fork RLIMIT_NPROC (the maximum allowable) number of processes for a UID (the UID associated with the malicious app) and then make zygote (a system daemon) spawn another process for that user. The zygote daemon typically uses setuid system call to change the UID to the app's uid. However, since this UID already has as many processes as are allowed, setuid fails, and the app gets a process with root privileges. We observe that this attack can be detected simply by monitoring if the number of processes for a user comes close to the maximum allowed.

- Exploid (CVE-2009-1185). This exploit is based on a vulnerability in the init, in which init does not check the origin of NETLINK messages. Untrusted code may thus be registered and get called later. For this vulnerability to happen, a neccessary condition is that the app code must send a NETLINK message later. We can use this as our signature.

- Gingerbreak (CVE-2011-1823). This exploits a vulnerability in the vold daemon in Android, again requiring untrusted code to send NETLINK messages to vold. Hence our signature here is similar to that for exploid.

We note that the above three are representative examples. In general we can encode conditions for any vulnerability in code; the checks will be inserted in the crtical path that leads to the given vulnerability. We note that the OS used for analysis need not actually be vulnerable for the vulnerability conditions to get triggered. Hence, attacks for vulnerabilities in multiple versions of Android may be detected on the same version. Moreover, attacks that would normally not succeed in the emulator may also be detected.

5. DISGUISE TECHNIQUES

Playground adopts a number of measures to make the analysis environment appear realistic. It provides real-looking phone identifiers to the app. These identifiers include the phone number, IMEI, IMSI, Android ID and so on. We also modify the build.prop (a file that contains several properties about the system) properties to match a real device. In a similar vein, we can also modify identifiers that relate to Qemu and other virtualization-related features.

Furthermore, we provide realistic data on the device, such as contacts, SMS, pictures, files on SDCard, and so on. We also provide additional libraries such as the Google Maps library, which is available on real devices. In addition Google apps (a set of Google proprietary apps available on a majority of Android devices) may also be provided though we do not provide them at this moment. Data from sensors such as GPS is also made to appear realistic. Currently, we do not support all sensors. Support for microphones is partial while we do not have any support for accelerometers.

We note that evasion of virtualized environments has long been an issue. Even if the above problems are fixed, there will always be evasion techniques based on timing (virtual devices run slower) and Qemu fingerprinting, for example [22]. These problems are general to all dynamic analysis systems.

6. AUTOMATIC EXPLORATION TECHNIQUES

We discuss here the techniques used for automatic exploration in Playground. The next two subsections describe event triggering and intelligent execution. Fuzz testing being almost a trivial technique is skipped from discussion here. Currently, Playground does not use any symbolic execution, which appears to be a good option for state space exploration of an app. We note that there are presently no effective symbolic execution solutions for interactive applications such as those involving GUI. Even projects developed around symbolic execution use random walks or fuzz testing to explore the GUI parts of the applications [25]. Symbolic execution can however be used to make event triggering better. For example, SMS messages received from only certain numbers may trigger some code in the application; symbolic execution could be used to construct the right kinds of messages here. We plan to include symbolic execution into Playground as a future work.

6.1 Event Triggering

Several API elements in Android are event based. Applications may register some code to be triggered whenever an event happens. There are specific events raised by the system when, for example, an SMS is received, the device location changes, the system completes a reboot, a call is received or is hung up, and so on. Sensitive events are guarded by permissions, which an app must declare statically and get approved for at the time of installation. Many malicious applications have been found to register for specific events [32].

Based on the permissions declared by the application, we raise specific events in the system. For example, if an application contains the BOOT_COMPLETED permission, Playground artificially raises the reboot completed event (note that we use VM snapshots only; booting the VM will be much more time consuming). This triggers the app's code that was registered with this event. However, artificially raising important events may cause system inconsistencies as well. This happened with the reboot completed event. We correct some of the framework code so that it would react to this event only once. Other events are handled similarly.

6.2 Intelligent Execution

Playground intelligently drives the user interface of a smartphone application by dynamically defining and exploring a model created from window and widget features. We extract features from displayed user interfaces to iteratively define a model that approximates the application's logic. For example, when an application launches, it displays a window with one or more buttons. When a button is selected, a new window appears. The transitions between windows are captured by this model. Note that this approach is based on the intuition that smartphone applications are highly interactive and that the resulting model provides a good approximation of the application's logic states.

Figure 4 presents an overview of the intelligent execution module. For every iteration, Playground checks if focus has changed to a different window. To avoid redundant exploration, a window equivalence module uses heuristics to determine if the newly displayed window is similar to previ-

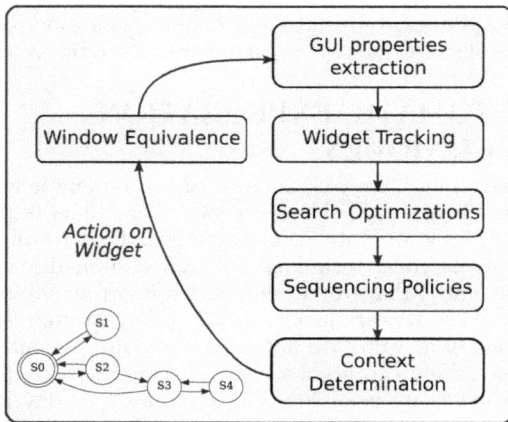

Figure 4: Overview of the intelligent execution module of Playground

ously viewed windows. If so, the window is merged with an existing state. Playground then extracts features relevant to driving the GUI. These include widgets containing texts, editable text fields, buttons, scroll containers and so on. It then creates associations between the current features and those retrieved earlier using widget tracking (why this is needed is discussed below). A few search optimizations are applied next to prune the search space. Next, Playground uses sequencing policies to determine the next GUI action (such as select a button, scroll down, fill text fields). Text fields are filled using heuristics defined by the context determination module. The current iteration is completed with the performance of an action. The rest of this section describes the various modules shown in Figure 4 in greater detail.

Widget Tracking

When navigating windows, widgets may disappear and later reappear. Failure to identify a widget when it reappears may result in concluding identical states or events to be different and hence redundant exploration. For example, consider a window with buttons A and B. Upon pressing button A, the window closes. To complete the exploration, the window is re-opened. The problem would be trivial if the each widget has a unique identifier. This is unfortunately not true for Android.

Playground tracks widgets similar to the way a human user might. We have identified the following widget properties for widget tracking. (1) *Text associated with a widget.* Widgets often have some text associated with them which is made visible to the user, e.g., a text label on a button. In many conditions, this text is sufficient to uniquely identify the widget. However, not all widgets have associated text. Additionally, multiple widgets may have the same text. (2) *Image associated with a widget.* GUI layouts often use widgets containing an image. In such cases, the image can uniquely identify the widget.[2] (3) *Position within the window.* Combined with the previous previous, the location of the widget on the screen is a useful indicator. Finally, (4) *Position in the GUI hierarchy.* Widgets often have fixed chains of ascendents. A button, for example, will always

---

[2]We modified Android framework for exporting image identifiers which could be hashes of images, their resource names, and so on.

have the same chain of ascendents in a window. The user perceives this in terms of the relative positioning of widgets.

Sequencing Policies

Each window can contain many widgets that allow input events. In addition to buttons, a window can contain editable text boxes, check boxes, spinners, etc. The result of selecting a button can be directly influenced by interaction with other widgets. Check-boxes can enable/disable other widgets. Finally, scrollable container widgets hide other widgets from the user. Exercising every possible sequence of widget interaction is infeasible. So, we have to arrange the order of event execution in the most meaningful way.

The sequence of interaction with widgets in a window requires consideration. Based on observation, we classify GUI input events into two groups: (*a*) those that input parameters or variables into the app, such as inputting text into an editable text box or a spinner, and (*b*) those that provide actions, such as buttons. First, widgets that accept input variables should be acted upon before action widgets. Second, widgets that are contained within a scrollable container are acted upon before scrolling the container. Third, contents of the scrollable container and the container itself are exercised before acting upon widgets outside the container, except when this is in conflict with the first rule. This design choice follows the intuition that the widgets outside the scrollable widget (if present) are often the control buttons such as "OK", "Submit", and "Cancel".

Note that the choice of these policies has important ramifications. If the behavior of a widget depends on another widget, Playground may not be able to trigger the entire set of behaviors. While we discuss this problem within a single window, it is easy to see such problems would also arise across windows.

Search Optimizations

For the sake of practicality, we heuristically prune redundant navigation paths where possible. For items organized as a list or a grid, we explore the items up to a threshold. In addition to reducing exploration time, a threshold is sometimes necessary to achieve program termination. For example, an Android list may dynamically expand and thereby go infinitely deep. We also put a threshold on the number of times the same widget may be interacted with (interacting with the same widget more than once may be required to completely explore the states that this widget leads to).

Window Equivalence

When exploring an application, a window is often invoked several times with different parameters. For example, consider an address book application. One window displays a list of contacts. When a contact is selected, an "edit contact" window is opened. On selecting different contacts, the resulting window will be similar, but not identical. Similar windows often correspond to the same application functionality and underlying code. Playground reduces the search space by annotating such equivalent windows.

Playground uses window equivalence heuristics to determine if the current window state is sufficiently similar to a previously visited window state. For our Android implementation, we leverage the correspondence between activity components and window design. That is, our heuristic classifies all windows belonging to the same activity component as equivalent. GUI Ripper [19] also used window titles to determine window equivalence.

Context Determination

As previously discussed, applications often have text fields that must be filled with appropriate values to lead them to the right states. Playground searches for keywords in the hints and the widget IDs[3] associated with editable text boxes and in the visible text labels next to them. For example, the string "Email" may appear immediately to the left of a text box, indicating that it should be filled in with an Email address.

Determining the keyword rules requires empirical investigation. We analyzed the string resources of over 500 Android applications to determine which strings application developers use for particular fields. To do this, we first extracted all of the strings an application's string resource file. We then converted the strings into a canonical form (lowercase, de-hyphenated). Next, we sorted the strings of all applications by frequency. The result was used to manually classify the strings into various semantic buckets, e.g. email, name, and phone. Finally we coded keyword rules for each semantic bucket. Our final specification included rules for email, address, date, phone number, password, username, cancel, and ok, among several others. The approach of automatically filling in text fields has also been used for web form completion [11, 23]. These techniques are more sophisticated and include self-learning. We plan to integrate these techniques into Playground.

Our strategy for addressing account sign-up and sign-in follows from the keyword rules approach for context determination. Sometimes, an application requiring sign-in will also include a window to sign-up for the service. The sign-up window will contain text input fields for Email, username, and password. By identifying these fields, Playground can automatically sign up for an account if a sign up option is available from within the app. Currently, Playground always uses the same Email address, username, and password; subsequent tests of an application will automatically sign in by filling in the same credentials. In future, Playground may also be able to identify if it could not successfully log in. A human tester can then create an account which Playground can use to automatically test at least future versions of the application.

7. IMPLEMENTATION

We have implemented the Playground analysis framework. The implementation is done over the standard Android emulator that comes with the Android SDK. We modify the Android source code to integrate TaintDroid and to insert hooks for API level monitoring. Kernel modifications are made to provide kernel-level monitoring. Furthermore, disguise measures are implemented by changing the appropriate identifiers and data, either directly in the Android source code or by adding files on the disk images and changing the content of the standard databases (such as contacts). Minor changes were required to the Android source for doing event triggering and fuzz testing. Intelligent execution interfaces with the window manager in Android to retrieve window and widget properties from the system. We use the ViewServer/HierarchyViewer for the interface. Changes are

[3]Developers often tend to give descriptive IDs to widgets which often convey the purpose of those widgets

Table 1: Private Information Leaks Detected

Number of applications	3968
Information type	Number of applications leaking
GPS	212
Android ID (AID)	581
IMEI	329
IMSI	91
Phone number	63
ICC-ID	3
WiFi MAC address	4
All types	946
At least one ID	844
At least one non-AID ID	442
GPS with at least one ID	120

made to the code of many standard widgets so that required widget properties may be retrieved. We further modified related code to make retrieval of properties faster than in the original code.

Apart from the guest (Android) side, Playground also has a host side, written in over 3,000 lines of Java code. The host side implements the algorithms for intelligent execution, and also handles the dispatch of apps to multiple emulators for parallel testing and the logging of information received from the detection techniques running inside the emulator.

8. FINDINGS

To show the effectiveness of Playground, we conduct some small-scale and a large-scale experiment. Our first experiment tries to automatically derive the results obtained in the TaintDroid paper. The second experiment is conducted on a set of 3,968 apps downloaded from the Android Market in November 2010. Finally, we also test Playground on real, known malware to evaluate the effectiveness of Playground at detecting malware.

For taint tracing in our experiments, we tracked device identifiers and location information leaks. By device identifiers we mean any strings that may be used to identify a particular device. Android ID is an identifier on Android available to any app without requesting any special permission. IMEI is an identifier available on all GSM phones. IMSI is associated with the SIM card and identifies a user on the cellular network. The ICC-ID is also specific to a SIM card. Access to IMEI, IMSI, ICC-ID, and WiFi Mac address requires special permissions.

8.1 Small-Scale Validation

To validate the effectiveness of Playground in helping discover privacy leaks, we used Playground to drive the same set of applications as that studied in the original TaintDroid paper. The TaintDroid researchers had to manually explore the applications but we attempt to achieve the same detection automatically here. Out of thirty total applications, we had to exclude nine because they were now obsolete and non functional or would not run properly on the Android emulator. Of the rest we were able to reproduce the exact findings from the manual tests conducted by the TaintDroid authors except in two cases (Wisdom Quotes Lite, Traffic Jam) where location leaks were not detected. In one other case (Babble) however, we detected an additional location leak which was not found in the original TaintDroid experiments. Such discrepancies are possible due to non deterministic behavior of applications which has been witnessed by others also [9]. Moreover, we also detected several leaks of Android ID which was not being tracked in the TaintDroid paper. This experiment thus conclusively establishes the effectiveness of Playground at automatically detecting privacy leaks.

8.2 Large Scale Measurements

We used Playground to drive 3,968 applications. Our findings are summarized in Table 1. We detected 946 applications to be leaking information to Internet, which is 23.8% of total number of applications we evaluate. This is because many free applications likely include third party ads and/or analytics libraries which track unique users based on these identifiers. Among the identifiers, Android ID is the one with least risk, as it can be changed at any time. Other identifiers are permanently associated with either the device or the SIM card. We find that in 52.3% of applications leaking an identifier, there is at least one non Android ID identifier. In 56.7% of instances of location leaks, both an ID and the location information is leaked out. In these cases, the applications can uniquely track the location history of the users. We also found 63 phone number leaks. Since phone numbers are often found on social networking profiles, the privacy implications of tracking are more significant than those of other identifiers.

Analysis of Results: We would like to know the final destinations of information leaks; if the leaks are to advertisement/analytics networks or to developer's own servers. Usually, the applications from a single creator[4] may share the same set of servers. If applications from multiple creators leak the information to a single destination domain, it is most likely the domain belongs an advertisement/analytics network, or a domain related to third-party libraries used by the applications. We found a total of 392 unique domains. Of these 29 domains relate to at least two creators. These are more likely to be advertisement/analytics networks. The rest of the domains come from single creators and hence are very likely to be domains used by the developers.

In Table 2, we show the domains that are related to a large number of unique applications. We also show what information has been leaked to this domain. For example, we find in 98.1% of leaks to data.flurry.com, the Android ID has been leaked. We find most of these are advertisement/analytics networks. localwireless.com and playgamesite.com are however developer sites. We note that AdMob is known to track users on the basis of hashed device identifiers. TaintDroid does not propagate taint through cryptographic hash functions and hence it appears, that none of the identifiers were sent to AdMob.

8.3 Analyses on Known Malware

We also analyzed known malware to confirm that Playground is able to detect malware in the wild. We considered three malware samples, FakePlayer, DroidDream, and DroidKungfu. The first one is an SMS trojan that sends SMS messages to premium numbers. The other two are root exploits. Detailed information about the samples may be found in Table 3. Following is our experience of analyzing these malware samples with Playground.

----

[4]We obtained the creator information from the Android Market

FakePlayer.

This malware sample installs as a movie player. On starting the application, the an activity came up momentarily and then closed. On checking the logging done by Playground, we found that this app had sent three text messages to short numbers 3353, 3354, and 3353 in sequence. Each message contained text "798657". The SMS destinations being short would make it highly suspicious that this sample is malware.

DroidDream.

On starting the application inside Playground, we did not experience anything suspicious; rather the app crashed. On disassembling the app's code and examining it, it turned out that the app would get stuck on the "phoning home" behavior. Apparently, it tries to connect to a remote server sending private information about the phone, including IMEI and IMSI numbers, but failed when we tested because the remote server did not respond. We removed this "phoning home" behavior (which is a single method call with the name of postUrl()), and tested the modified app again. It turns out that this time app did execute the rageagainstthecage exploit. We could see several running processes with this app's UID and finally could also see a root process; the privilege escalation had completed. Next, we checked the logs collected by Playground. The logs showed a huge number of forks and exceeding of a threshold number of processes. The logs thus give sufficient evidence of the rageagainstthecage attack having being attempted.

DroidKungFu.

On launching this app inside Playground, the only thing we observed was the "phoning home" behavior, which is quite well documented. The app sent the IMEI, Android version, and phone model out of the phone. While IMEI was explicitly marked to be taint-traced; the Android version and phone model appeared as plain text in the logs as being sent out of the phone. We however did not observe any attempt to gain root privileges. On looking deeper into the code, we found that the root exploits were not executed due to some condition checks, which looked for the existence of /system/xbin/su and some version checks. Changing either the analysis environment or the app code would allow us to see the attacks being executed. This is a general problem in dynamic analysis that sometimes the environment conditions may not match. Symbolic execution may be of help here.

9. EFFECTIVENESS OF AUTOMATIC EXPLORATION

In this section we evaluate and discuss the effectiveness of automatic exploration. For this, we augmented the Dalvik VM to report code coverage in terms of the number of instructions executed. Next we compare our system with GUI Ripper and then provide a discussion where we include our experience on automatic exploration.

9.1 Comparison with GUI Ripper

We compare our system with GUI Ripper [19]. We ported it to Android based on the information available in Memon et al. [19]. Playground is essentially a superset of GUI Ripper. This meant that we simply remove some of the functionality of Playground (such as context determination and

Table 2: Most common leaking domains. The percentages indicate the proportion of apps which leak the corresponding information.

	# uniq apps	# uniq creators	Android_id	IMEI	IMSI	Phone #	Location
data.flurry.com	265	180	98.1%	2.2%	0	0	14.0%
mobclix.com	152	71	95.4%	68.4%	0	0	12.5%
Google related domains	63	58	0	0	0	0	96.8%
localwireless.com	58	1	0	0	100%	0	24.1%
admob.com	51	27	0	0	0	0	90.1%
ad.qwapi.com	45	26	97.8%	2.2%	0	0	13.3%
playgamesite.com	29	2	0	100%	0	0	0
ade.wooboo.com.cn	21	8	100%	0	0	100%	4.7%

Table 3: Malware samples used for testing anti-malware tools

Family	Package name	SHA-1 code	Date found	Remarks
Fakeplayer	org.me.androidapplication1	1e993b0632d5bc6f0741 0ee31e41dd316435d997	08/2010	SMS trojan
DroidDream	com.droiddream. bowlingtime	72adcf43e5f945ca9f72 064b81dc0062007f0fbf	03/2011	Root exploit
DroidKungFu	com.sansec	4bf050f089a0d44d6865 ff74b75cb7f1706fdcaa	05/2011	Root exploit

repeatedly exercising widgets) to get a GUI Ripper configuration.

For Playground, we observed a code coverage mean of 33%. We observed 27% mean code coverage GUI Ripper. The low coverage is expected because both the systems treat the application as a black-box. In fact, low coverage is one of the most limiting factors in dynamic analysis. It is also true that many applications may not give close-to-100% coverage. There may be several reasons for this. Applications may have dead code or code which executes only under special circumstances such as special device configurations and so on.

To get a comparison between Playground and GUI Ripper, we (a) disregard instructions executed by simply starting the application (since these instructions are trivially executed without the need of any navigation), and (b) calculate the *percent difference* between Playground and GUI Ripper. Since, we are interested in the cases when Playground performs better (or worse) than the other approaches, we do not use the absolute value of the difference, i.e., we use $C(x,y) = \frac{(x-y)}{(x+y)/2}$. Moreover, because GUI Ripper does not include fuzz testing, we use coverage results from only the intelligent execution component for Playground. Using this metric, our measurements indicate Playground's intelligent component improves by a 31% in mean over GUI Ripper. We plot this difference against the number of applications in Figure 5. For applications on the positive side, Playground does better. Some applications lie on the negative side. This is likely because of non-determinism in applications because of which a run of GUI Ripper may be able to execute more code in an application than a different run of Playground. Such non deterministic behavior has been encountered earlier also [9].

9.2 Discussion

While event triggering is undoubtedly needed, it was not clear to us before the experiments how fuzz testing and intelligent execution would help and compare with each other. First, we found that the code coverage at simply launching the applications is only 16% while our automatic exploration

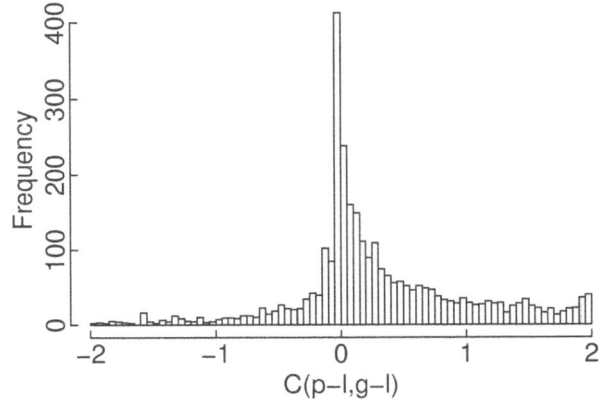

Figure 5: Percentage difference in code coverage between Playground and GUI Ripper

techniques of fuzz testing and intelligent execution nearly double the code coverage. Second, intelligent execution cannot work in cases that it does not model; this applies to all the custom-made widgets and, in the current implementation, to web-based GUI, which may also be embedded in apps and which is not handled currently (the process would be similar to handling normal GUI but in a different environment). In such cases, fuzz testing was found help, filling up the limitations of intelligent execution.

Intelligent execution was primarily useful in cases where user credentials or some meaningful information was required. In fact, for automatic login, we found that in several cases we had received emails on the email account we used for testing from several services. Playground had automatically created accounts with these services. In particular, we found emails from 34 different services. Some of these are popular social networking, cloud and media services such as Pandora, Dropbox, Last.fm, and Kik Messenger. Most of these related to account registrations while a few were received on supplying email address alone. We note that account registration for most applications is done through web sites. Playground currently cannot work with web pages. Moreover, many account registration routines also have captcha tests. However, once registered, Playground can easily use these credentials for subsequent navigation. A few situations were also related to providing other meaningful inputs such as a city name or a zipcode. For example, the Weather.com app asks for this in the absence of consent to location data access. Exploration is quite stunted if this is not provided.

Intelligent execution is thus specially useful for complex apps, such as those for social networking. In these cases, fuzz testing is usually stuck at the beginning only due to need of login or similar things. It is however, usually after login only, that there is access to the user's databases, files, location and other sensor information.

10. RELATED WORK

Dynamic Malware Analysis. Given we are trying to run applications and detect security and privacy breaches, our work naturally falls into the category traditionally known as dynamic malware analysis. For Android two works are quite comparable to our work. DroidScope [30] is a malware analysis framework for Android applications. It is however different from our work in that while we aim to detect malicious or unwanted functionality on a large scale (in thousands of apps), they aim at malware forensics, to provide accurate analysis of apps that are known to be malware. Their analysis does not provide automatic exploration and requires significant manual effort to understand the working of the malware.

Google Bouncer is a tool that screens applications uploaded to the Google Play market for malware. This tool appears to be similar to Playground in that it needs to provide automatic exploration and detection techniques. It is however a closed, proprietary tool and not much is known about it. Researchers [20, 28] have however found that it is poor at disguising techniques and many of the common identifiers may be used to identify the virtual environment.

Strider HoneyMonkey [27] loads webpages in the browser, automatically clicks dialog boxes to allow installation of any binary and then detect if it is malware. CWSandbox [29] and Botlab [12] study malware behavior in monitored environments. All the above works have little or even no interaction with the malware executables being studied. Playground however is designed to work with highly interactive applications. These applications are different from the traditional malware in that the former's execution is primarily driven by interaction.

Driving Applications. Any dynamic program analysis approach may be classified as either a black-box or a white-box approach depending on whether it meaningfully uses the program code to do the analysis. For our automatic exploration, we decided to stick to the black-box (or a somewhat gray-box) approach which is far simpler than the white-box paradigms. Approaches like model checking [5] and symbolic and concolic execution [15, 26] would fall into the white-box space. We plan to include symbolic execution in the future in Playground. Zheng et al. [31] also propose a framework for automatic UI exploration of Android apps. It is a grey-box technique as some static analysis is involved. We can improve our approach by including similar static analysis to guide the dynamic exploration. However, as they also note static analysis is insufficient to analyze all aspects of the UI. Our black-box, yet sophisticated dynamic exploration techniques can help to cover such aspects.

GUI Testing. Automatic GUI testing has for long been an intriguing area in software engineering, specifically because of the complexity of event interactions that are possible. Much of the commercially available tools are directed towards capture-playback [4] or towards programmatic descriptions of input and output event sequences [2, 24]. These however do not provide completely automatic solutions to GUI testing. Our task at GUI exploration is obviously very different from what these tools can accomplish. Privacy Oracle [13] however uses capture-playback to its advantage for multiple runs along same paths on application GUI but with slightly perturbed inputs.

GUI testing is often accomplished as model based testing [3], involving coming up with a finite state machine model of the event space that the app provides and subsequent generation and execution of test cases based on that model. Given a model, automatic techniques may be used to come up with test cases [17, 21].

Memon et al. automatically deduce GUI models by exploring the GUI [18, 19]. We face a similar problem of automatically generating an abstract state machine by exploring the application UI. However, we model much more accurately window transitions without assuming a directed-acyclic-graph organization amongst windows (in Android, for example, cycles are possible). More importantly, Memon et al. do not provide abilities to fill contextual text input and do not talk about modules such as widget tracking and sequencing policies which we found crucial for black-box exploration. These advantages do show up in Section 9.

Hu and Neamtiu [10] have discover GUI bugs in Android applications. They fuzz applications and monitor the system logs to discover bugs. Playground can complement their work by driving applications automatically.

11. CONCLUSION AND FUTURE WORK

In this paper we proposed AppsPlayground, a tool automatic dynamic analysis of smartphone applications. We integrated a number of detection, exploration, and disguise techniques to come up with an effective analysis environment that may be used to evaluate Android applications on a large scale.

The future directions for Playground include including symbolic execution for systematic exploration of the applications' state space and to make Playground even more stealthy by enhancing the disguise techniques.

Acknowledgements

We would like to thank Zhichun Li for his extensive comments through the major part of this project. We are grateful to Patrick Traynor for helpful comments during the writing of the paper. We would further like to extend our thanks to the anonymous reviewers and our shepherd, Debin Gao, for valuable comments and suggestions for improving the paper.

References

[1] Qemu. http://www.qemu.org.

[2] Abbot. http://abbot.sourceforge.net/.

[3] Larry Apfelbaum and John Doyle. Model Based Testing. In *Software Quality Week Conference*, pages 296–300, 1997. URL http://citeseerx.ist.psu.edu/viewdoc/summary?doi=10.1.1.86.1342.

[4] AutoIt. http://www.autoitscript.com/site/autoit/.

[5] Edmund M. Clarke, Orna Grumberg, and Doron A. Peled. *Model Checking*. The MIT Press, January 1999. ISBN 0262032708. URL http://www.worldcat.org/isbn/0262032708.

[6] Manuel Egele, Christopher Kruegel, Engin Kirda, and Giovanni Vigna. PiOS: Detecting Privacy Leaks in iOS Applications. In *ISOC Network and Distributed System Security Symposium (NDSS)*, February 2011.

[7] William Enck, Peter Gilbert, Byung-Gon Chun, Landon P. Cox, Jaeyeon Jung, Patrick McDaniel, and Anmol N. Sheth. TaintDroid: An Information-Flow Tracking System for Realtime Privacy Monitoring on Smartphones. In *Proceedings of the 9th USENIX Symposium on Operating Systems Design and Implementation (OSDI)*, Vancouver, BC, October 2010.

[8] William Enck, Damien Octeau, Patrick McDaniel, and Swarat Chaudhuri. A Study of Android Application Security. In *Proceedings of the 20th USENIX Security Symposium*, San Francisco, CA, August 2011.

[9] P. Hornyack, S. Han, J. Jung, S. Schechter, and D. Wetherall. "These aren't the Droids you're looking for": Retrofitting Android to protect data from imperious applications. In *Proceedings of the 18th ACM Conference on Computer and Communications Security (CCS 2011)*, 2011.

[10] Cuixiong Hu and Iulian Neamtiu. Automating gui testing for android applications. In *Proceeding of the 6th international workshop on Automation of software test*, 2011.

[11] Y.W. Huang, S.K. Huang, T.P. Lin, and C.H. Tsai. Web application security assessment by fault injection and behavior monitoring. In *Proceedings of the 12th international conference on World Wide Web*, pages 148–159, 2003.

[12] John P. John, Alexander Moshchuk, Steven D. Gribble, and Arvind Krishnamurthy. Studying spamming botnets using Botlab. In *Proceedings of the 6th USENIX symposium on Networked systems design and implementation*, pages 291–306, Berkeley, CA, USA, 2009. USENIX Association. URL http://portal.acm.org/citation.cfm?id=1558977.1558997.

[13] Jaeyeon Jung, Anmol Sheth, Ben Greenstein, David Wetherall, Gabriel Maganis, and Tadayoshi Kohno. Privacy oracle: a system for finding application leaks with black box differential testing. In *CCS '08: Proceedings of the 15th ACM conference on Computer and communications security*, pages 279–288, New York, NY, USA, 2008. ACM. ISBN 978-1-59593-810-7. doi: 10.1145/1455770.1455806. URL http://dx.doi.org/10.1145/1455770.1455806.

[14] Kasperskey Lab. First SMS Trojan detected for smartphones running Android. http://www.kaspersky.com/news?id=207576158, August 2010.

[15] James C. King. Symbolic execution and program testing. *Commun. ACM*, 19(7):385–394, July 1976. ISSN 0001-0782. doi: 10.1145/360248.360252. URL http://dx.doi.org/10.1145/360248.360252.

[16] Lookout. Update: Security Alert: DroidDream Malware Found in Official Android Market. http://blog.mylookout.com/blog/2011/03/01/security-alert-malware-found-%in-official-android-market-droiddream/.

[17] A. M. Memon, M. E. Pollack, and M. L. Soffa. Hierarchical GUI test case generation using automated planning. *IEEE Transactions on Software Engineering*, 27(2):144–155, February 2001. ISSN 00985589. doi: 10.1109/32.908959. URL http://dx.doi.org/10.1109/32.908959.

[18] A.M. Memon. An event-flow model of gui-based applications for testing. *Software Testing, Verification and Reliability*, 17(3):137–157, 2007.

[19] Atif Memon, Ishan Banerjee, and Adithya Nagarajan. GUI Ripping: Reverse Engineering of Graphical User Interfaces for Testing. *Reverse Engineering, Working Conference on*, pages 260+, 2003. ISSN 1095-1350. doi: 10.1109/WCRE.2003.1287256. URL http://dx.doi.org/10.1109/WCRE.2003.1287256.

[20] Jon Oberheide. Dissecting android's bouncer, June 2012. https://blog.duosecurity.com/2012/06/dissecting-androids-bouncer/.

[21] A. Pretschner, O. Slotosch, E. Aiglstorfer, and S. Kriebel. Model-based testing for real. *International Journal on Software Tools for Technology Transfer (STTT)*, 5(2):140–157, March 2004. ISSN 1433-2779. doi: 10.1007/s10009-003-0128-3. URL http://dx.doi.org/10.1007/s10009-003-0128-3.

[22] T. Raffetseder, C. Kruegel, and E. Kirda. Detecting system emulators. *Information Security*, pages 1–18, 2007.

[23] S. Raghavan and H. Garcia-Molina. Crawling the hidden web. In *Proceedings of the International Conference on Very Large Data Bases*, pages 129–138, 2001.

[24] Robotium. http://code.google.com/p/robotium/.

[25] P. Saxena, D. Akhawe, S. Hanna, F. Mao, S. McCamant, and D. Song. A symbolic execution framework for javascript. In *Security and Privacy (SP), 2010 IEEE Symposium on*, pages 513–528. IEEE, 2010.

[26] Koushik Sen, Darko Marinov, and Gul Agha. CUTE: a concolic unit testing engine for C. *SIGSOFT Softw. Eng. Notes*, 30(5):263–272, September 2005. doi: 10.1145/1095430.1081750. URL http://dx.doi.org/10.1145/1095430.1081750.

[27] Yi-Min Wang, Doug Beck, Xuxian Jiang, and Roussi Roussev. Automated Web Patrol with Strider HoneyMonkeys: Finding Web Sites that Exploit Browser Vulnerabilities. In *IN NDSS*, 2006. URL http://citeseerx.ist.psu.edu/viewdoc/summary?doi=10.1.1.100.224.

[28] Ryan Whitwam. Circumventing google's bouncer, android's anti-malware system, June 2012. http://www.extremetech.com/computing/130424-circumventing-googles-bounc%er-androids-anti-malware-system.

[29] Carsten Willems, Thorsten Holz, and Felix Freiling. Toward Automated Dynamic Malware Analysis Using CWSandbox. *IEEE Security and Privacy*, 5(2):32–39, March 2007. ISSN 1540-7993. doi: 10.1109/MSP.2007.45. URL http://dx.doi.org/10.1109/MSP.2007.45.

[30] L-K Yan and H Yin. DroidScope: Seamlessly Reconstructing the OS and Dalvik. In *Proceedings of USENIX Security Symposium*. USENIX Association, 2012. URL http://portal.acm.org/citation.cfm?id=1558977.1558997.

[31] C. Zheng, S. Zhu, S. Dai, G. Gu, X. Gong, X. Han, and W. Zou. Smartdroid: an automatic system for revealing ui-based trigger conditions in android applications. In *Proceedings of the second ACM workshop on Security and privacy in smartphones and mobile devices*, pages 93–104. ACM, 2012.

[32] Yajin Zhou and Xuxian Jiang. Dissecting android malware: Characterization and evolution. *Security and Privacy, IEEE Symposium on*, 2012.

AppProfiler: A Flexible Method of Exposing Privacy-Related Behavior in Android Applications to End Users

Sanae Rosen
University of Michigan
Ann Arbor, MI
sanae@umich.edu

Zhiyun Qian
University of Michigan
Ann Arbor, MI
zhiyunq@umich.edu

Z. Morley Mao
University of Michigan
Ann Arbor, MI
zmao@umich.edu

ABSTRACT

Although Android's permission system is intended to allow users to make informed decisions about their privacy, it is often ineffective at conveying meaningful, useful information on how a user's privacy might be impacted by using an application. We present an alternate approach to providing users the knowledge needed to make informed decisions about the applications they install. First, we create a *knowledge base* of mappings between API calls and fine-grained privacy-related behaviors. We then use this knowledge base to produce, through static analysis, high-level *behavior profiles* of application behavior. We have analyzed almost 80,000 applications to date and have made the resulting behavior profiles available both through an Android application and online. Nearly 1500 users have used this application to date. Based on 2782 pieces of application-specific feedback, we analyze users' opinions about how applications affect their privacy and demonstrate that these profiles have had a substantial impact on their understanding of those applications. We also show the benefit of these profiles in understanding large-scale trends in how applications behave and the implications for user privacy.

Categories and Subject Descriptors

D.4.6 [**Security and Protection**]: Access controls

General Terms

Security

Keywords

android; smartphones; permissions; privacy

1. INTRODUCTION

The rise of mobile devices has lead to new concerns regarding application privacy and security. Not only are these devices now nearly as powerful and functional as personal computers, but they also carry detailed information about users' personal lives, such as their location, phone calls, and SMS messages. Much attention has been given to the threat of malware targeting these systems. Furthermore, these new capabilities mean that otherwise legitimate applications can become a significant privacy concern as well. Recent events, such as the outcry surrounding Carrier IQ [6] and concern over the Facebook application's behavior [14] suggest that the general public would appreciate being better informed about how the software on their phones impacts privacy. Furthermore, different users may have different expectations and needs with regards to privacy. Merely filtering out malicious applications is no longer sufficient; users also need to better understand the behavior of legitimate applications. Our goal is to produce a system that allows users to understand the privacy implications of applications they install by providing profiles of privacy-related application behavior.

The Android permission system is an important step towards addressing this problem, allowing users to make informed decisions by requiring that applications declare which capabilities they intend to use at install time. However, as we discuss in §2.1, this system has significant limitations. As the permission system is tightly integrated into Android, any substantial changes would require rewriting existing applications, meaning it lacks the flexibility needed to adapt to the rapidly changing world of application privacy. Furthermore, as it also serves as a capability enforcement mechanism, the descriptions it provides of applications are excessively broad, in order to meet the needs of developers. Because of these limitations, we argue permissions are the wrong abstraction to use in helping end users understand application behavior. We propose instead analyzing applications offline to create *behavior profiles*, separating the problem of understanding application behavior from that of capability enforcement.

To do this, it is necessary to automatically extract information about application behavior from applications. In traditional operating systems, work has been done on observing application behavior at a low level, e.g., by monitoring system calls [23]. This level of abstraction provides detailed and accurate information, but is hard to translate to something meaningful to users. The permission system provides very high-level information about application behavior, but is not specific enough to be useful, as we discuss in §2.1. In between the two, in API-driven systems such as mobile systems, applications access most sensitive information and functionality through API calls. In order to make use of these API calls, we start by building a *knowledge base* which consists of a series of *rules* translating API calls to application behaviors. We have identified 221 distinct application behaviors for which we have created rules. For example, we have identified four specific API calls that compare the user's distance to a given location. The mapping of these API calls to this behavior category is an example of a rule.

Given such a knowledge base, we create behavior profiles that provide more insightful information than the existing permission system. For example, consider an application requesting permission to access the GPS. The associated profile would indicate that the application is additionally concerned with the user's proximity to a location, and requests GPS updates at a rapid rate. An excerpt from a behavior profile, compared with the equivalent permission, is shown in Table 1, §4.2. To provide these profiles we use a second mapping, from matched rules to profile entries.

This two-step translation approach has significant advantages over the permission system as well. It gives a great deal of flexibility in how we present information. We can provide high-level profiles to non-technical users, but just as easily we can provide detailed technical information to security experts, using the same information extracted using the knowledge base.

We give users access to these profiles through an Android application and a web page. We do not address the problem of determining if an application's behavior is acceptable, leaving it to the user to make that judgment based upon their own requirements. For this paper, we have focused on Android, but in principle this approach would work for any system relying on API calls for access to important functionality.

Our work has the following novel contributions:

- A method of creating a *knowledge base* mapping API calls to application descriptions, and then using this knowledge base to create *profiles* of application behavior.

- An efficient application of this method to the large-scale, automated analysis of applications in Google Play. We currently analyze an average of 500 applications per day on a single server, and our approach is completely parallelizable. So far we have analyzed almost 80,000 applications.

- A large-scale survey of the privacy- and security-relevant behavior of a significant cross-section of Google Play, as well as user perceptions of these behaviors. Some of our findings include determining users are concerned about behavior which is most prevalent in ad libraries, and determining that many applications are less intrusive than they appear from the permissions they request.

- We identify a number of ways in which permissions do not provide information that users care about (e.g., user-triggered SMS messages vs. those occurring in the background) and offer suggestions to improve the permission system.

The paper is organized as follows. §2 summarizes related work in this area. We provide an overview of our approach and threat model in §3. In §4 we discuss how to create and use the knowledge base, how to make this analysis scalable and automatic, and how we make the results available to the public. In §5, we examine how well our system performs against a variety of application types, examine a number of prominent applications in depth, look at large-scale trends in application behavior, and examine how users of our AppProfiles application make use of our profiles.

2. BACKGROUND AND RELATED WORK

We first give some background on the Android permission system followed by a summary of related work.

2.1 Android Permission System and its Limitations

In the permission system, applications declare the capabilities, or "permissions", they intend to use at install time. Permissions cover broad classes of functionality, like "Internet" or "Read Phone State", and they must have been declared for an application to access that functionality. There are several issues with this approach.

1. Some permissions are so prevalent that users are likely to ignore them, such as the Internet permission [4, 17].

2. Permissions generally cover broad, vague categories of functionality and give insufficiently detailed information for users to make meaningful decisions [15]. For example, Read Phone State covers everything from reading the phone number to reading the OS software version [15].

3. Applications often request permissions they don't use, so permissions don't necessarily correspond to application behavior [16, 4].

4. Occasionally behavior which should be protected with a permission is not, allowing applications to bypass the permission system [26, 21].

5. If a problem is found with the permission system, it is hard to fix due to tight integration with the Android system, making problems 1, 2, and 4 hard to address. This results in a trade-off between OS stability and fine-grained permissions [3].

These issues suggest that the permission system's ability to provide useful information to end users is limited.

2.2 Related Work

Previous work has approached the problem of understanding application behavior in different ways. One much-studied area is the permission system. It has significant limitations, and many papers have explored or attempted to address these limitations. Recent work by Grace et al. [22] detects mechanisms by which permissions granted to one application can be leaked to another, either inadvertently or deliberately through collusion. The Apex system [30] proposed by Nauman et al. illustrates that the permission system may be too broad to be useful, and implements a more sophisticated permission system that allows users to limit the scope of key permissions. Roesner et al. [32] present a permission system where users directly grant permissions to applications at runtime in a non-intrusive manner by integrating permission granting with existing UI elements. Extensive misuse of the permission system by developers has been identified by Barrera et al. [4]. Kirin [12] detects potentially dangerous applications at install-time based on combinations of permissions and intent strings. TISSA [36] gives users more control over how applications with permissions access their data. However, any change to the permission system would require fundamental changes to Android, which may limit how likely these solutions are to be implemented.

Other work seeks to understand applications at the system level. The use of low-level features like system calls to detect anomalous behavior is a technique that has been used in traditional operating systems [23], but it has also been successful for Android. Crowdroid [5] detects malicious applications masquerading as other applications using Linux-level system calls to detect anomalous behavior among applications with the same name and version number. Information gleaned at this level is more accurate and fine-grained than at the permission level, but it is likely not of direct use to the average user in understanding application behavior.

The limitations of these two approaches — permissions and system-level information — suggest that it is worth looking elsewhere for a solution. The Android Framework API has the benefit of providing extensive and accurate information, like the system layer. We show that it can also be used to accurately and flexibly emulate the kind of high-level profiling the permission system attempts to do. We leverage results from several papers to accomplish this. Work by Felt et al. [16], and PScout, by Au et al. [3] maps API calls to permissions and allows developers to determine what permissions they should use. We have made extensive use of their data set as a starting point to understanding the Android API. Unlike them, however, we address the problem that permissions may not provide sufficient information to users. Our work also builds upon a paper by Enck et al. [11], which demonstrates the feasibility of using existing static analysis tools for Java to detect malicious behavior in Android applications. Similarly, Lu et al. [29] have constructed a system to statically detect certain Android-specific security vulnerabilities. Unlike these papers, we take the approach of creating a comprehensive picture of privacy-relevant application behavior rather than identifying specific instances of malicious or vulnerable behavior.

Several other studies have developed complementary mechanisms to improve user and developer control of applications. For example, AppFence [24] introduces innocuous *shadow data* to replace sensitive data and introduces new privacy controls for existing applications. Quire [9] provides a framework to allow applications to determine the call chain of requests made, allowing applications to protect themselves from other malicious applications. A recent study by Szydlowski [34] explores the feasibility of detecting malicious behavior dynamically in iOS applications. Finally, TaintDroid, by Enck et al., [10] modifies the operating system to track the flow of sensitive data to detect when this data is exfiltrated. All of these have goals orthogonal to ours, however.

3. OVERVIEW

In AppProfiles, we create descriptions of security- and privacy-relevant behavior which enable users to make informed decisions about what applications to allow on their phones. As the Android API imposes a structure on how applications access sensitive information or functionality, we leverage it to detect behaviors of interest using static analysis (with a few limitations, as described in §5.1). This approach is complementary to the permission system and does not attempt to replace existing malware detection tools such as antivirus software. We do not seek to constrain application behavior, the way the permission system does, or to detect malicious applications that attempt to subvert the constraints imposed by the Android API.

In order to do this, we start by creating a *knowledge base* of mappings between API calls and application behavior types. Such a mapping necessarily involves some degree of manual effort, but there are several tools and techniques we use to minimize the effort involved. We start with a list of key security- and privacy-relevant API calls, which we map to behavior descriptions. Existing research [16, 3] allows this mapping to be constructed easily and automatically. Next, we identify API calls which benefit from having more specific entries in our knowledge base associated with them. For example, it may be valuable to detect if certain arguments are passed to a given API call. We describe in § 4.1 how to refine our rules more systematically. Borrowing from the terminology used by our static analysis tool, we call each entry in the knowledge base a *rule*.

Next, this knowledge base is used to create *application behavior profiles*. We use an existing static analysis tool to detect the code patterns in our knowledge base. We translate this data into profiles using a second mapping between rule matchings and higher-level descriptions, which are intended to be accessible to end users. This mapping to high-level descriptions also allows behavior to be inferred from combinations of rules triggered. For example,

consider an application where a rule involving taking a photograph has been triggered, but a rule for showing the user a preview of the image has not been triggered. The corresponding behavior profile entry would indicate to the user that the application is capable of taking photographs without displaying anything on the screen.

There are two major concerns in producing our knowledge base: accuracy, and completeness. As there is no ground truth to compare against, these are hard to evaluate. However, as we use permissions as a starting point and then add a significant amount of additional data, it is necessarily more complete than the permission system. Furthermore, the feedback we have collected indicates that users have found the new information gathered to be substantial and useful (see §5.4). We have also added rules based on security threats from known malware, as anti-viruses do (for example, sending SMS messages without user input), but unlike them we can cover behavior that is not explicitly malicious and which requires human judgment to evaluate (for example, collecting different types of location data.) As new privacy threats become apparent we can easily add new rules. We evaluate the overall accuracy of the entire system in §5.1.

An important feature of this approach is that we have separated the collection of data (using our knowledge base) from the interpretation of this data (as profiles). This allows for a wide range of different types of profile information to be created without modifying the data collection method. We only provide information to ordinary users which is designed to be comprehensible and of relevance in trying to determine whether to use an application. However, advanced users might want to have access to more technical details. These advanced profiles also allow us, and potentially other researchers, to perform further analysis. We give some examples of the types of analysis enabled by these profiles in §5.2 and §5.3.

The final step is to use these profiles to evaluate whether this application is appropriate to run on a given device. This will vary with the needs of the user, so we allow users to make that decision based on their needs. As we have been collecting feedback from users regarding their views on application behavior, future work could include making an application privacy rating available to users based on the profiles as well as user feedback.

We emphasize that our focus is on allowing users to make informed decisions about legitimate applications, not on detecting malware. We do not attempt to deal with native code or applications that take extraordinary steps to prevent analysis — we are focused on detecting how the Android API is used and anything that is external to this API, or that attempts to subvert its protections, is outside the scope of this work. We also do not attempt to determine what is an unacceptable privacy violation. Much of the behavior we discover may, in context, be harmless. For example, an app that covertly tracks a phone in case it is stolen is indistinguishable from spyware. Others may differ from user to user. For example, not all users may be concerned with applications that track their location. The goal of AppProfiler is to give users the ability to make informed decisions about the applications they install, something which we believe cannot currently adequately be done.

4. DESIGN AND IMPLEMENTATION

There are four significant aspects to the design of the system. First, we describe how we create our knowledge base. Second, we explain how this knowledge base is used to generate behavior profiles. Third, we discuss how to develop a scalable system to produce such profiles for the available applications in Google Play. Finally, we discuss how we make these profiles readily available to end users.

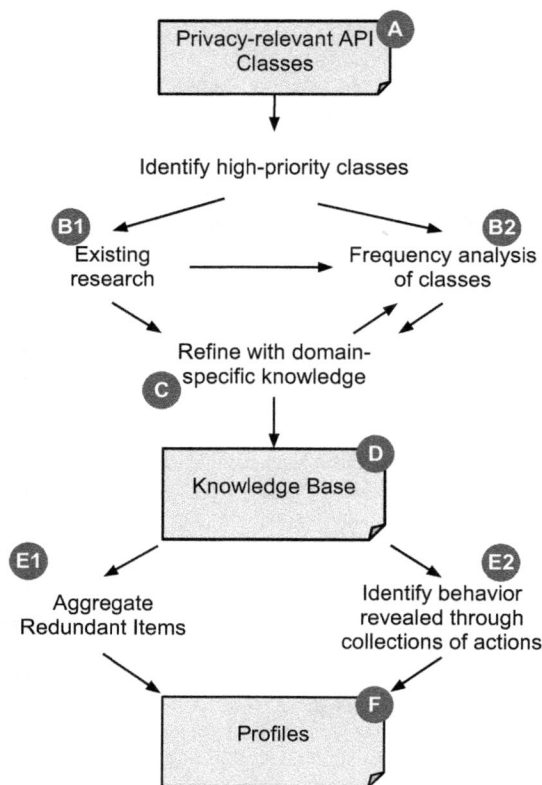

Figure 1: Conceptual overview of profile creation process.

4.1 Creating a Knowledge Base

We wish to identify a set of privacy-relevant API calls and map them to appropriate behavior types which summarize the privacy implications of those calls. For example, if the API call "android.telephony.SmsManager.sendTextMessage" is detected and its first argument is a constant, we wish to map this to the behavior, "sends text messages to a fixed phone number". As the range of these possible mappings is very large, a method is needed to systematically create rules and determine which API calls to detect. We use the Android permission system to do some of the work, taking advantage of research [16, 3] on automatically mapping permissions to function calls. While this is sufficient for our system to function, substantially more detailed information can be provided by a deeper examination of the Android API.

Our approach to enhancing the knowledge base in this manner is summarized in Figure 1. We start by creating a list of rules that match very broad types of behavior, mostly at the level of classes (step A in the figure), based on existing API-to-permission mappings, as well as through manual effort. As the API classes are well-documented and clearly-named, manually identifying which additional classes are of interest required little effort. We then increase the quantity and specificity of the information we provide. This also requires some manual effort, but this can be significantly reduced by first determining which parts of the API would benefit from more detailed analysis, then covering the remaining, less interesting, parts of the API with more general rules.

To do so, we first refer again to previous research to identify key areas of the API (step B1). For example, previous work [15, 4] suggests that the Location, Internet and Phone State permissions are among the most commonly used, as well as highly privacy-sensitive. Therefore, adding more detail in these areas would allow users to better understand a wide range of applications.

We also ran additional tests to identify and confirm which classes are significant (step B2). We ran a preliminary version of our profiler on a selection of applications, including popular and randomly selected applications from several markets, as well as a selection of malware [7]. By doing so we confirmed the results of existing research and identified other areas in which more detail would be helpful, focusing on more common or dangerous behavior.

Once we narrow down a number of classes of interest in this manner, we manually examine the methods of each class and determine which are of potential significance to users (Step C). For example, detecting the API call that reads the phone number of a device, or reads device-specific IDs, is likely to be of interest to users. Detecting the API call that specifies a format for the name of the network operator, prior to retrieving that name, likely is not. For large, complex parts of the API we iterate over steps B2 and C to further refine our knowledge base.

Most of our rules deal with short, specific API patterns, such as function calls and their arguments, or combinations of function calls, as it makes it easier to build up complex profiles from this information later.

To make this process more concrete, here is an example of how two sets of rules get developed.

1. Using an existing mapping of permissions to API calls (step A), we identify which classes use the "Location" permission. We spend more effort here because previous research suggests location data is important to users (step B1). We create a preliminary set of *rules* that match any use of the Location classes.

2. After running these rules on a preliminary set of applications, we determine that the LocationManager and Address classes, among others, are widely used (Step B2).

3. We examine the methods of these classes. We identify those that look interesting: these include a series of methods in "LocationManager" concerned with how often location updates are given. In "Address", there are a series of methods concerned with various types of address data, ranging from the user's country to their street address. We create a new set of rules that match with each of these API calls (Step C).

4. We use the results of the rule matchings to decide where more detail is needed.

   - We determine that many of the specific functions from the Address class are rarely used, so for our final set of rules we combine similar functions. For example, we place all those related to human-readable, fine-grained addresses together (e.g. getAddressLine, getThoroughfare), and we place all those pertaining to the user's country together (e.g. getCountryCode, getCountryName). We are now done with creating the set of rules for "Address." (step D)

   - Conversely, many of the specific API calls in LocationManager are very common. Therefore, it is worthwhile to expend more effort in creating more specific rules to describe these, and so we iterate again over step B and C. For example, we notice "requestLocationUpdates" is very common. It takes arguments determining how often these updates happen, which may be of interest to users, as the frequency of updates impacts their battery life. We create rules for different update frequencies and again run these rules on our set of applications.

5. Finally, we notice a lot of applications retrieve location data at the maximum possible rate. We manually examine a few,

and determine that what is actually happening is they request repeated updates, but stop the request as soon as they have adequate data. Older versions of the API did not allow a single location update to be requested. We treat this pattern separately so as to not claim that applications which do this are wasting battery. We now can add these rules to our knowledge base (step D).

As a result of this process, we have now identified twelve rules for our knowledge base. One, associated with LocationManager, identifies if the method "requestLocationUpdates" has been used at all. Seven more narrow down the frequency of these updates. Four are associated with "Address": one checks if the application requests information about the user's country, another about the user's state, another about the user's postal code, and the last about the user's street address. Several more rules are associated with these classes: the full knowledge base can be seen at http://appprofiles.eecs.umich.edu/tech.html. We give an example of the knowledge base entry for checking the user's state below:

```
Category:
Location - Type
Subcategory:  Regional data - State

FunctionCall call:
call.function.enclosingClass.name startsWith
"android.location.Address"
and call.function.name == "getAdminArea"
FunctionCall call:
call.function.enclosingClass.name startsWith
"android.location.Address"
and call.function.name == "getSubAdminArea"
```

4.2 Developing Profiles

This knowledge base is then applied to better understanding application behavior. We start by extracting the API calls in our knowledge base from the application source code. In order to do this, we use a tool called the Fortify Static Code Analyzer [18], which is able to use the rules in our knowledge base to identify code in each application that matches our rules.

Once we have a complete list of which rules in our knowledge base have been triggered for a given application, we process this data in order to produce an easily understandable final product. We combine redundant rules (E1) and detect behavior inferred from the total set of rules (E2). Some forms of analysis are best done by inferring results from several rules. For example, we wish to know if a SMS message was sent in the context of a background service. We have one rule for detecting SMS messages being sent, and another for detecting classes that run as background services. By looking at where the former rule was triggered, if it occurs in a class that runs as a background service, we know it happened in the background. In fact, we can then determine if any rule is triggered in the background in the same way.

To make this approach more concrete, here is an example of how this process occurs.

1. We run the rules against the application, which reveals which rules are triggered and in which classes they occur. Rules are triggered which indicate:

   - The application asks for the fine-grained or coarse-grained location, whichever is most recent.

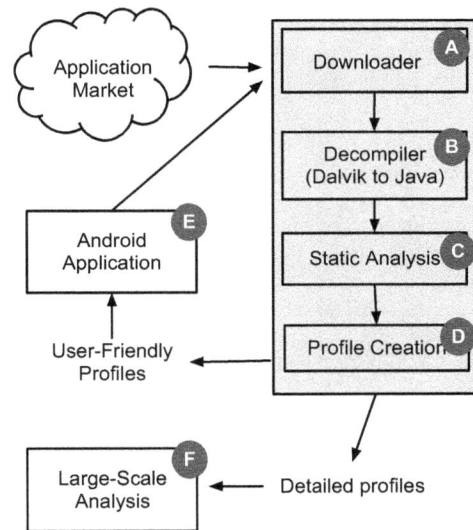

Figure 2: Overview of the application analysis system

   - Location updates are requested every five minutes in one location; every ten minutes in another.
   - The application requests that the distance to a fixed location be calculated.
   - The phone's IMEI is requested.
   - We also identify, where possible, which classes are run in the foreground and which run as background services. Looking at which methods are called by classes in other files sometimes does not work reliably.

2. We organize the results of these rule matches, incorporating data on whether classes run into the foreground or background, as well as data on which classes belong to which ad library (Step E2). Of the two rules indicating how often the application requests updates, we only report the worst-behaving one (Step E1).

   - The application selects the best of the fine-grained or coarse-grained location; this happens in the background.
   - The application requests updates every 5 minutes (this being the worst-case).
   - The application cares about proximity to a location; this occurs in the foreground.
   - A unique, personally-identifiable ID is requested by Google's ad library. We cannot determine if this happens in the foreground or background.

Additionally, we adjust our profiles based on our audience. A technical user might be interested in knowing which phone-specific IDs are being tracked, for example, whereas a more casual user might only care that they are being tracked. As our profiles are created by a script that maps combinations of triggered rules to higher-level descriptions, it is straightforward to create different types of profiles by changing this mapping. Essentially, we separated data collection from processing, analyzing, and displaying the data to gain flexibility in the amount and nature of data that we present to various audiences. This also made it easy to add functionality as needed. For example, we added the ability to determine if behavior originates from third-party libraries without requiring substantial changes to our system.

Table 1: Comparison of feedback types with the associated permission in a sample app. We use the following notation: <text> indicates the context in the application in which the rule is triggered, such as in an activity (i.e., the foreground). [text] indicates an associated major ad library.

Permissions	Our User Summaries	Our Technical Summaries
• fine (GPS) location - Access fine location sources such as the Global Positioning System on the phone, where available. Malicious apps may use this to determine where you are, and may consume additional battery power.	• Gathers fairly precise location data (e.g. GPS) • Reads your latitude or longitude • Uses more of your phone's resources than recommended by Google to retrieve your location data. • Concerned with your proximity to a given location (for example, may be alerted if you are near a particular store.)	• Can use GPS OR network <context unknown> • Latitude/Longitude <broadcast> [googleads] • Updates every 1s or less <activity> [jumptap.adtag] • Asks for periodic updates <activity> • Proximity to location <on click> <activity>

We currently produce two forms of output (see Table 1). One is more technical and detailed, and primarily for the benefit of researchers and security professionals. We used this to perform analysis on trends in application behavior, such as comparing the behavior of third-party code with application-specific code. We plan to make it available in the near future. The second is simpler, and is aimed at security-conscious but non-technical end users. We have made these profiles available through an application in Google Play which to date has seen almost 1500 downloads.

4.3 Large-Scale Application Analysis

Next, we demonstrate that these profiles can be used, in the long term, to analyze all the available (i.e., free) applications in Google Play.

We start with an existing list of all applications in the market [27], containing 276,016 apps, around 45% of which appear to be no longer be accessible. Building off of the Unofficial Android Market API [1], a script downloads these applications. (This is step A in Figure 2).

For the next stage (step B in Figure 2) we use ded [11] to decompile each application. Once we produce the source code, we analyze it using Fortify (step C) and the rules we derived as described above. We pass the resulting data to another set of scripts, which uses the set of rules triggered to create higher-level descriptions of application behavior (Step D).

We processed over 33,000 applications in 67 days on one server, a time period which included a number of interruptions as we tweaked our system. We analyzed on average about 500 applications per day. An additional 27,000 applications were queried but unreachable. We investigated a number of cases to confirm that there was no application with that package name currently active in the market, and that likely the application had been removed. Using a few servers of various speeds, we have already processed 65% of our app list. Furthermore, the system could be further optimized. For example, a system using a custom static analysis tool operating on disassembled Dalvik bytecode would be able to eliminate the time spent decompiling applications, which we found accounted for over 90% of the time spent.

There are a number of technical limitations due to artifacts of how we implemented the system. The decompilation process is not perfect [11]. We examine some randomly selected applications in §5.1.1 to better understand the impact of these errors. Alternately, the application could be disassembled using a tool like baksmali [33], although in that case a custom analyzer would also need to be built.

We make results available through an android application, *AppProfiles* (Step E in Figure 2). It allows users to select an application to look up from a list of applications installed. We give users a less technical version of the profiles (see Figure 1 for a brief example.) We also allow users to submit feedback on application behavior. They can toggle actions they don't like and indicate whether the application behaves as expected overall. Since we download applications from Google Play and not the user's phone we are limited to free applications. We additionally made the profiles viewable on our website using a similar interface, at http://appprofiles.eecs.umich.edu.

5. RESULTS AND ANALYSIS

We present several types of analysis below. First, we measure the accuracy of our system and identify any limitations that may impact its accuracy. Second, we examine three applications in depth to better understand these limitations, as well as demonstrate the sort of information our profiles make available. Third, we look at how our profiles can be used to quickly and easily gain an understanding of the market as a whole. We compare trends in library-specific and application-specific code and look at how popular applications differ from other applications. Finally, we examine feedback that users have given us about our profiles and what they indicate about the applications they run.

5.1 Testing Profile Accuracy

In order to evaluate the accuracy of our profiles, we first examine a set of popular applications and of one of randomly selected applications, which we examine manually to determine what our profiles should detect. We also examine a set of malware that has well-studied behavior as a worst-case analysis of the accuracy of our system.

5.1.1 Confirmation through dynamic analysis

In order to measure how often the behaviors we detect occur in practice, we created a dynamic analysis testing framework based on TaintDroid [10], with the added ability to detect behavior corresponding to that found in our profiles. This testing framework is somewhat limited, as certain types of functionality cannot be detected by this dynamic testing system. For example, the technical version of our profiles distinguishes between applications using

HTTP libraries and those using TCP libraries, but the former results in the latter being called at runtime. Nevertheless, it helps illustrate the limitations of our system.

We analyzed a selection of two types of applications: popular applications and randomly chosen ones. For the latter, we excluded two that would not run at all, and two where language barriers prevented us from understanding the application's behavior and thus prevented us from thoroughly exercising the application. We compared against our more technical profiles, but when accounting for the accuracy of these profiles, we combined similar rules regarding Internet use, as these are very common, often appear together and are usually correctly detected — they would tend to artificially inflate the accuracy of our profiles.

We selected 10 popular applications from the front page of Google Play. They cover a range of different application types and publishers. Overall we found that applications that make extensive use of third-party libraries may have higher rates of false positives. For example, one application uses a debugging library whose behavior is not triggered at runtime but whose source code is included in the APK. This is an inherent problem with static analysis — however, using static analysis allowed us to cover far more applications. Conversely, errors in decompilation can result in behavior not being detected in our rules. Given the limitations of our testing framework, any values on accuracy should be taken with a grain of salt. However, an average of 10% of behavior triggered dynamically did not appear in our profiles; we had a 23% false positive rate.

We selected 15 applications at random, discarding four for the reasons described above. We had a 16% false positive rate and 15% false negative rate; most false negatives were caused by a single application which failed to decompile correctly. The lower false positive rate may be due to these applications being much simpler and easier to exercise thoroughly. For both application sets, there was no clear pattern in the behaviors we missed, as these appear to be due to decompilation errors or the use of native code.

5.1.2 Testing Malware With Known Behavior

We would like to reiterate that the goal of this project is not to detect malicious software, and in particular not to detect malicious software that takes extraordinary steps to hide its behavior from researchers. Nevertheless, examining the behavior of known malware is useful for several reasons. First, many malicious applications have been well-studied and analyzed by a third party, which means that a ground truth for their expected behavior exists. The same is not true of most legitimate applications. Furthermore, as many of them take extensive steps to obfuscate their behavior, they allow us to do a worst-case evaluation and determine the limitations of our system. We downloaded the entire Contagio mobile malware sample on January 7, 2011, and randomly selected a number of applications to analyze in detail (see Table 2). We could find a description of 28 of these randomly selected applications from a security researcher or organization [28, 25, 19, 35]. Overall, our profiles detected an average of 59% of the expected behavior.

SMS-related behavior was one of the most common and serious behavior types we detected, and we were able to detect this in applications that rely on root exploits or native code. We also frequently detected these applications collecting location data and unique phone IDs, and using the Internet, although legitimate applications do this as well. Frequently, suspicious behavior occurs in the background (i.e., in Services or broadcast receivers). Our highest rate of failure was in detecting applications that download additional binaries, likely because malware does not generally use the provided API for doing so.

Table 2: Accuracy of our profiles for 28 malware samples. The last row applies to apps that exhibit suspicious behavior in a background application component. The false positive rate is likely an overestimate as security researchers may have felt some behavior is not worth listing.

Behavior Categories	Detected correctly	False Negatives	False Positives
Suspicious SMS	9	1	1
Normal SMS	0	0	0
Phone calls	1	1	2
Interacts with other apps	1	1	4
Downloads/installs apps	1	11	0
Collects list of apps	1	1	1
Runs Linux commands/root	4	2	1
Collects location data	8	0	4
Collects phone IDs	16	1	2
Adds bookmarks	0	1	0
Uses the Internet	16	0	2
Behavior occurs in background	17	N/A	N/A

We may also have detected some previously unknown behavior in some of the malware samples. In a few cases, the detected behavior was entirely different from the behavior we expected based on the behavior profiles written by security experts. Not only did we fail to detect the expected malicious behavior, but we also detected previously unknown malicious behavior. We manually verified, by examining the application source code, that our profiles in these cases matched the malware's actual behavior. A likely explanation is that these applications were mislabeled.

Overall, while the accuracy of our profiles is somewhat limited when it comes to malware, and we specifically did not aim to be able to detect malware with this system, we were nevertheless successful more often than not, and we have furthermore been able to detect previously overlooked behavior in malicious applications.

5.2 Case Studies

We have chosen three popular applications to analyze in depth in order to demonstrate the behavior these profiles can reveal. Two were found by our users to have a great deal of concerning behavior, and one was overwhelmingly rated as harmless.

5.2.1 Facebook [13]

As many of our users were concerned about the behavior of the Facebook application, we selected it for detailed examination. In our profile, we predict it can exhibit intrusive location behavior. It asks for the user's latitude and longitude and proximity to other locations. It also accesses video functionality as well as information about the carrier and the phone number. Based on our survey results, users seemed especially concerned about its ability to access their phone number and location, including the fact that it appears to query their location very frequently. On the other hand, they were not concerned about its use of the Internet.

Our technical profile suggests that the location related actions and those related to the user's phone number happen in an "Activity", i.e., a component the users interact with directly, whereas much of the Internet-related functionality happens in a background process with which users do not interact. Our profiles did not detect certain behavior for which permissions are requested; in particular, we detected nothing related to SMS messages. We used our dynamic testing tool to determine that our profiles were correct, at the time of analysis, and the application is over-requesting permissions.

Although its permissions and our user-friendly profiles paint the application as being overly aggressive in its use of privacy-sensitive functionality, it is less intrusive than it might seem, as much of its controversial behavior is only triggered by the explicit actions of the user. Nevertheless, our profiles are more accurate than the permissions in determining its behavior. This suggests determining the context of privacy-affecting behavior may be worth including in our more user-friendly profiles — we may need to expand this part of our analysis to be able to determine this context in every case.

5.2.2 Angry Birds [2]

This is another application which is both popular among Android users in general and distrusted among users of our application. As with Facebook, users seem particularly concerned about its location-related behavior; they also object to the use of cookies and personally identifiable phone identifiers. Unlike Facebook, this application appears to make use of native code, which we cannot analyze. Nevertheless, we were able to detect much behavior of concern.

Our profiles predict that the application itself is not very intrusive. However, like many free applications it contains ad libraries (we detected code from five) and these ads are responsible for much of the privacy-intrusive behavior. Dynamic testing confirmed this trend. It also determined that a great deal of of information is written to the debug log, including personal IDs and information about the carrier. The only discrepancy between our profiles and our testing is that the latter did not detect any use of the telephony manager or the sensor manager, behaviors which were in our profiles.

This example indicates two important features of our analysis. First of all, false positives will always be an issue in static analysis, as code may be present but never triggered. Secondly, our results confirm that a significant amount of concerning behavior occurs in ad libraries. This is a strong reminder that ad-supported applications might have a hidden cost in terms of privacy.

5.2.3 Reddit is Fun [31]

We chose this application as it was the most frequently ranked as having acceptable behavior by users and we wish to determine how a positively ranked application might differ from a negatively ranked one. The permissions, and the author's writeup, indicate that it should access the Internet, store data on the SD card, access the network connectivity state and start automatically on boot. Our profiles suggest that it can additionally update the user's browser history, process phone numbers in some manner, and use cookies. It accesses the Internet using both Webviews (a library to present information to users) and direct HTTP connections. All the behavior in our profiles was confirmed to exist through our dynamic verification framework.

The biggest difference between this application and the above ones is that this one does not collect location data, which as we discuss later seems to generally be of great concern to users. Furthermore, the developers explain in detail in the market writeup what the application does, which may make users feel more comfortable with its behavior.

Table 3: A comparison of types of behavior seen in the top 9 most common third-party libraries.

Behavior type	Google Ads	Google Analytics	Facebook	Admob	Millenialmedia (ads)	Flurry (ad/analytics)	Twitter4j	Phonegap (app platform)	Mobclix (ad/analytics)
Internet	*	*	*	*	*	*	*	*	*
Internet - webview	*		*	*	*	*		*	*
Location - passive	*	*		*				*	*
Location - active								*	*
Audio manager	*			*				*	
Hardware sensors					*			*	
Cookies		*							*
Camera								*	
Unique ids								*	
Phone number								*	
Bookmarks									*
Detect other tasks									*

5.3 Large-scale Analysis of App Behavior

5.3.1 Third-Party Library Use

Given that many applications make extensive use of third-party libraries, and prior research suggests that ad libraries are often quite intrusive in terms of privacy [20], we examine these more closely. First, we used a simple heuristic to identify these libraries. We counted the occurrence of every class name and its associated package name, keeping track of duplicates. As a common code obfuscation tool seems to also produce identical class names and package names across applications (e.g., a.b.java) we excluded class names fitting such a pattern. We then created a list of frequently repeated classes, using 100 unique instances across distinct applications as a cutoff. While this might exclude some minor libraries, it should cover any of significance. We then reran our behavior aggregation script, only this time dividing behavior into that unique to the application and that originating from a third-party library.

The behavior of the top 9 are summarized in Table 3. The overall trends — the widespread use of location data and personally identifiable information — is consistent with existing research [20]. There is a lot of variation in the behavior of these libraries, but in general those that merely integrate with an existing service (like Facebook and Twitter) are fairly non-intrusive, whereas ad libraries tend to be more intrusive. However, many of the top ad libraries are less intrusive than those seen in our case studies. This suggests it may be possible for ad libraries to meet user privacy expectations while still remaining commercially viable. Phonegap is an unusual case. Since it is a platform for assisting in creating applications it exhibits a wide range of behavior.

We also compared the behavior common in our total set of third-party libraries with that which is common in regular applications. We have show the most common behaviors from both cases in Figure 3. Sometimes, their behavior is quite similar — both use webviews a great deal (the standard API for rendering a webpage from a URL) and Internet-related behavior in general is common for both. In other cases, they behave quite differently. Third-party

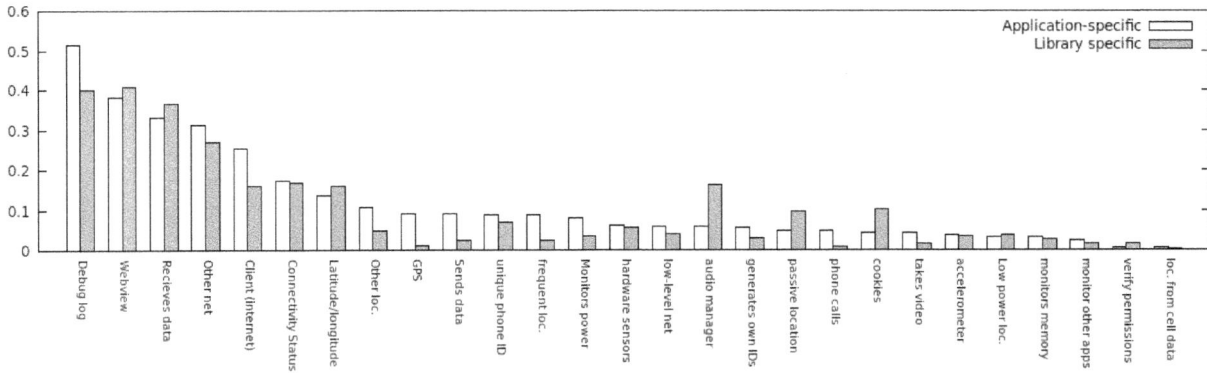

Figure 3: Comparison of the most common behavior in application-specific code versus that in third-party library code.

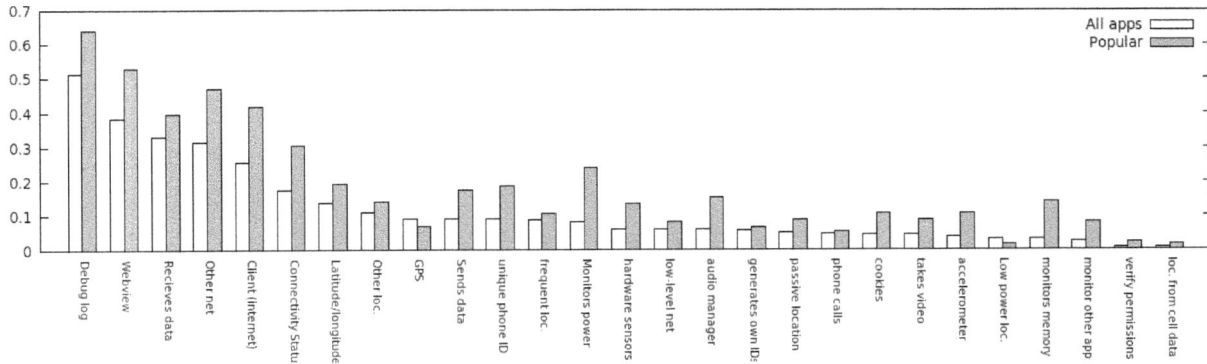

Figure 4: Comparison of the most common behavior for all apps versus that in 170 popular apps (application-specific code only).

libraries make greater use of cookies, for example. It is common for either to access a user's location, but there are some fundamental differences in how they do it. Third-party libraries are more likely to ask for a cached location, and applications are more likely to specify that they need to use the GPS exclusively. Overall, our results are consistent with existing research [20].

5.3.2 *Popular Applications*

It is also interesting to observe how the most popular applications compare with all other applications. A comparison can be seen in Figure 4, which shows application-specific code only— library-specific code exhibits the same trends. Of our total set of apps, at least one rule has been triggered in application-specific code for 66% of applications, and in third-party library code for 55% of applications (note that not all apps use third-party libraries). Of the popular applications, 74% have relevant behavior in application-specific code, and 79% in third-party code. This trend is reflected in Figure 4, where it can be seen that more popular applications exhibit all but two types of behavior more commonly than average. This difference is more pronounced in behaviors related to monitoring the system status; popular applications are more likely to monitor memory usage, power state, connectivity state, and the status of other applications. These differences suggest that research focusing only on the most popular applications may not reflect behavior in the market as a whole.

One other interesting fact is that the most common behavior detected in all cases is to print to the debug log, something which Google recommends that developers turn off in published applications [8]. This could leak important information, such as a user's private information, as we found in our case studies.

5.4 User Feedback from AppProfiles

The release of our application has demonstrated that there is interest in better understanding what smartphone applications do. Within the first week, we had 833 downloads, and a total of 1482 at the time of writing. Feedback has been positive, with an average rating of 4.1. Users have indicated that they feel such an app is much-needed.

We gave users the option of anonymously submitting feedback on the applications they use (see Figure 5). These results are not representative of the entire population of smart phone users, as the findings are likely to be skewed towards those who are interested in security and privacy issues. However, as the use of this application is entirely voluntary and only useful to the privacy-conscious, this is arguably the demographic whose responses are most relevant.

We surveyed the feedback submitted roughly a week after uploading our application. At the time, we had 1839 distinct items of anonymous feedback covering a total of 456 unique applications. 63% of those applications were ranked as acceptable by at least one user, 28% as exhibiting surprising but acceptable behavior, and 43% as exhibiting unacceptable behavior.

The most commonly rated applications are summarized in Table 4. Ad-driven popular games and social media applications seem to be particularly controversial, likely for the reasons discussed in §5.2. It was also fairly uncommon for an application to exhibit unexpected behavior without users also considering that behavior objectionable. The least controversial applications tend to be work-oriented or provide some basic utility, such as Dropbox, Google Docs or Flash Player. The "reddit is fun" application is an exception, perhaps because it is not ad-oriented.

Table 4: Top most common applications in each category by number of ratings; percent of feedback items in that category also shown for each app.

Acceptable		Surprising		Not Acceptable	
com.andrewshu.android.reddit	56 (90%)	com.facebook.katana	13 (14%)	com.facebook.katana	53 (58%)
com.dropbox.android	40 (83%)	com.pandora.android	6 (26%)	com.zynga.words	31 (86%)
com.alensw.PicFolder	27 (90%)	com.amazon.kindle	6 (22%)	com.rovio.angrybirds	29 (91%)
com.bigtincan.android.adfree	22 (88%)	com.devuni.flashlight	5 (13%)	org.zwanoo.android.speedtest	19 (68%)
com.adobe.flashplayer	21 (95%)	org.zwanoo.android.speedtest	5 (18%)	com.imdb.mobile	13 (76%)
com.google.android.apps.docs	19 (100%)	com.evernote	4 (23%)	com.amazon.kindle	14 (63%)
com.google...chromephone	17 (81%)	com.game.CeramicDestroyer	4 (50%)	mobi.mgeek.TunnyBrowser	14 (78%)
org.connectbot	17 (100%)	com.google...googlevoice	4 (28%)	com.skype.raider	12 (50%)
com.facebook.katana	16 (18%)	com.linkedin.android	4 (40%)	com.farproc.wifi.analyzer	12 (60%)
com.agi.android.augmentedreality	14 (15%)	com.skype.raider	4 (17%)	com.weather.Weather	9 (53%)

Table 5: Variability of user opinions on behavior within major permission types. Each percentage indicates how often users flag it as objectionable in applications where it occurs. "Location" includes only API calls that can be performed with both location permissions.

Permission	Average	standard deviation	notes
camera	27%	30%	66% photo without preview; video 37%; preview, no photo 2.6%
read phone state	24%	13%	detecting phone calls 40%, IMEI 26%
location (either)	16%	9%	heavy resource usage 29%.
read sms	7%	7%	reading message contents 13%
internet	6%	7%	cookies 23%
write sms	5%	5%	

Users also had the option of indicating if they object to specific behaviors. Interestingly, the behaviors users object to do not overlap significantly with those exhibited by malware (see Table 6). For example, users seem most concerned with applications accessing their location, and less concerned about SMS behavior, even accounting for the fact that location behavior is more common. The fact that there is a marked difference between the set of unpopular behavior and the set associated with malware, in addition to the fact that there are many popular applications from well-established companies which are criticized heavily by users, suggests that there is a segment of users which are strongly concerned about privacy in general. Simply focusing on overtly malicious applications is not sufficient as there is a demand for transparency in the behavior of *all* applications.

Additionally, user opinions on different behavior types covered by the same permission varied greatly. This strongly suggests that permissions are providing information at the wrong granularity. On average, wherever any given behavior appears in an application profile, it is flagged as objectionable 11% of the time (standard deviation of 14%). Behavior falling under the Internet permission, for example, was flagged as objectionable 5.8% of the time on average, but the use of cookies specifically was flagged as objectionable 23% of the time. Some more data on common behaviors can be seen in Table 5.

Most notably, users only care about certain types of behavior covered by the "read phone state" permission. In particular, they object to anything that could be used to track them, or detect when they're making phone calls. For location, users care first about high resource usage, then about how fine-grained the data on their location is. Additionally, for an application to determine the user's distance to a given location, or to determine the direction in which they are traveling, is viewed as objectionably as using fine-grained location data. For camera-related behavior, users' opinions varied

considerably between the four associated rules. In particular, using the camera to show a preview only was viewed as far less objectionable than the other behavior, which involved actually taking a picture. However, we have very few data points for some camera-related behavior. Finally, users are not particularly concerned about SMS messages, but they are slightly more concerned about SMS messages being read than messages being sent. The former has privacy implications, whereas the latter could cost them money and is common in malware. Perhaps privacy issues are viewed as a bigger threat than malware.

Additionally, there are 19 behavior types which correspond to none of the currently existing permissions. Of these, 6 never actually occur in any application we were given feedback on. These six all involve using obscure sensors. Users flagged the remainder as objectionable, on average, 5.5% of the time. Some, such as writing to the debug log or looking at phone orientation data, were never flagged as objectionable at all, and so perhaps not being covered by a permission makes sense in those cases. Being alerted when packages are installed, and using the accelerometer, however, were highly unpopular, both being flagged 9.5% of the time.

We later created a second feedback form with additional questions asking whether the users intend to uninstall the application, and whether the profiles had an impact on their view of the application. 71% of feedback items indicated that the profiles had changed the users' opinions, and 8.8% indicated that they would uninstall the application as a result of our profiles.

5.5 Lessons Learned

We have demonstrated that users find these profiles to be useful and informative, and that extracting this kind of data allows us to better understand behavior trends in the application market as a whole. We have also learned a great deal about user expectations of application behavior and the limitations of the permission system

Table 6: Comparison of the top ten most frequent behaviors observed in malware versus behaviors rated as objectionable by users.

Indicative of malware	disliked by users
SMS	**Location**
Send Text Message	Reads latitude or longitude
Copy SMS object	High resource use
Deprecated SMS manager	Misc. location use
Read contents of SMS	Use cached location
Privacy	**Privacy**
Get a unique id	Uses cookies
Get phone number	Get a unique id
Get carrier info	Detects phone calls
Internet	**Internet**
Send HTTP post	Check connection status
Miscellaneous	**Miscellaneous**
Use telephony manager	Take video
Triggered on boot completed	Uses the audio manager

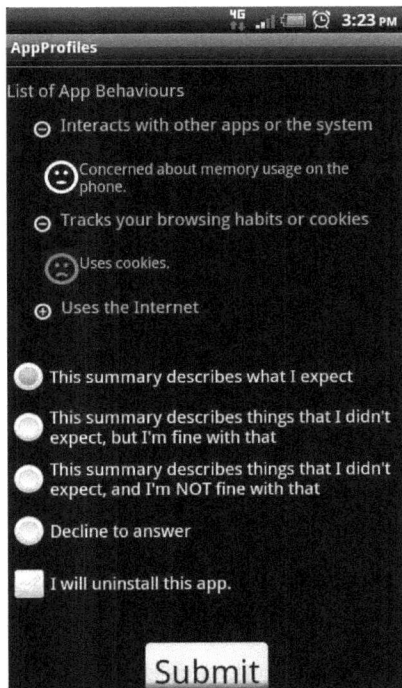

Figure 5: Example of feedback form

as it currently stands, and so we offer a few suggestions as to how a permission system should be designed.

The permission system does not seem to be fine-grained enough to meet the needs of users. For example, the "Internet" permission may be too broad — for example, users care a great deal about the use of cookies, but not all kinds of network use. They care more about some types of location data than others, and care about reading phone IDs and phone numbers but not other aspects of the phone state. However, many of these distinctions cannot be made with the current permission system; permissions should be fine-grained enough to allow users to make these distinctions.

Furthermore, it seems valuable to differentiate between actions performed by users and actions performed in the background. For example, malware frequently sends SMS messages without the input of the user. It would be valuable to differentiate user-triggered actions from other actions in some cases and require different permissions accordingly, as has been suggested in previous work [32].

Finally, it seems that there are significant differences between third-party library code (such as that used by advertisements) and code written as part of a specific application. If users are greatly concerned about privacy, then they may be more concerned about libraries which might monitor them across applications, than an individual application. Differentiating between permissions unique to an application and those used by third-party libraries may be useful.

6. CONCLUSION

We have described a method for systematically detecting privacy-related application behavior in mobile systems where the most significant aspects of application behavior are mediated through a well-defined application framework. This method has two components; creating a knowledge base of API calls with privacy-relevant behavior, and using this knowledge base to produce behavior profiles for applications. We have demonstrated that it is a highly effective method of allowing both end users and researchers to better understand how applications behave. Finally, we have demonstrated that it is possible to create such profiles efficiently, given the almost 80,000 applications we have analyzed to date.

7. ACKNOWLEDGMENTS

This work is partly funded by NSF grants CNS-1059372, CNS-0964545, CNS-1050157, CNS-1039657 and Navy grant N00014-09-1-0705. We would like to thank Felt et. al., for making the Stowaway data set available, Enck. et al., for making ded available, and HP for providing us with a copy of HP Fortify SCA. We would like to thank Alex Halderman and Eric Wustrow for their valuable comments on the paper. We would also like to thank the anonymous reviewers whose comments helped improve the final version.

8. REFERENCES

[1] android-market-api — Android Market for all Developers! http://code.google.com/p/android-market-api/.

[2] Angry birds. https://play.google.com/store/apps/details?id=com.rovio.angrybirds.

[3] K. W. Y. Au, Y. F. Zho, Z. Huang, and D. Lie. PScout: Analyzing the Android Permission Specification. In *Proc. ACM Computer and Communications Security*, October 2012.

[4] D. Barrera, H. G. Kayacik, P. C. van Oorschot, and A. Somayaji. A Methodology for Empirical Analysis of Permission-Based Security Models and its Application to Android. In *Proc. ACM Computer and Communications Security*, October 2010.

[5] I. Burguera, U. Zurutuza, and S. Nadjm-Tehrani. Crowdroid: Behavior-Based Malware Detection System for Android. In *Proc. ACM SPSM*, 2011.

[6] Carrier IQ Drama Continues. http://yro.slashdot.org/story/11/12/03/2112220/carrier-iq-drama-continues.

[7] Contagio Mobile. http://contagiominidump.blogspot.com/.

[8] A. Developers. Preparing for release. http://developer.android.com/tools/publishing/preparing.html.

[9] M. Dietz, S. Shekhar, Y. Pisetsky, A. Shu, and D. S. Wallach. Quire: Lightweight Provenance for Smart Phone Operating Systems. In *Proc. of USENIX Security Symposium*, August 2011.

[10] W. Enck, P. Gilbert, B.-G. Chun, L. P. Cox, R. Jung, P. McDaniel, and A. N. Sheth. TaintDroid: An Information-Flow Tracking System for Realtime Privacy Monitoring on Smartphones. In *Proc. Operating Systems Design and Implementation*, October 2010.

[11] W. Enck, D. Octeau, P. McDaniel, and S. Chaudhuri. A Study of Android Application Security. In *Proc. of USENIX Security Symposium*, August 2011.

[12] W. Enck, M. Ongtang, and P. McDaniel. On Lightweight Mobile Phone Application Certification. In *Proc. ACM Computer and Communications Security*, 2009.

[13] Facebook for android. https://play.google.com/store/apps/details?id=com.facebook.katana.

[14] Facebook Spies on Phone Users' Text Messages, Report Says. http://www.news.com.au/breaking-news/facebook-spies-on-phone-users-text-messages-report-says/story-e6frfku0-1226282017490.

[15] A. Felt, K. Greenwood, and D. Wagner. The Effectivenes of Application Permissions. In *Proc. USENIX Web Application Development*, 2011.

[16] A. P. Felt, E. Chin, S. Hanna, D. Song, and D. Wagner. Android Permissions Demystified. In *Proc. ACM Computer and Communications Security*, 2011.

[17] A. P. Felt, E. Ha, S. Egelman, A. Haney, E. Chin, and D. Wagner. Android Permissions: User Attention, Comprehension, and Behavior. In *Proc. SOUPS*, 2012.

[18] Hp fortify. https://www.fortify.com/.

[19] FortiGuard Threat Research and Response. http://www.fortiguard.com/.

[20] M. Grace, W. Zhou, X. Jiang, and A.-R. Sadeghi. Unsafe Exposure Analysis of Mobile In-App Advertisements. In *WiSec*, April 2012.

[21] M. Grace, Y. Zhou, Z. Wang, and X. Jiang. Systematic Detection of Capability Leaks in Stock Android Smartphones. In *Proc. Network and Distributed System Security Symposium*, 2012.

[22] M. Grace, Y. Zhou, Z. Wang, and X. Jiang. Systematic Detection of Capability Leaks in Stock Android Smartphones. In *Proc. Network and Distributed System Security Symposium*, February 2012.

[23] S. A. Hofmeyr, S. Forrest, and A. Somayaji. Intrusion Detection Using Sequences of System Calls. *J. Comput. Secur.*, 6(3):151–180, August 1998.

[24] P. Hornyaick, S. Han, J. Jung, S. Schechter, and D. Wetherall. These Aren't the Droids You're Looking For: Retrofitting Android to Protect Data from Imperious Applications. In *Proc. ACM Computer and Communications Security*, October 2011.

[25] X. Jiang. Mobile Security Alerts. http://www.csc.ncsu.edu/faculty/jiang/.

[26] Zero-Permission Android Applications. http://leviathansecurity.com/blog/archives/17-Zero-Permission-Android-Applications.html.

[27] List of Android Applications. http://nocrappyapps.com/media/app_ratings/androidappratings-current.csv.

[28] The Lookout Blog. http://blog.mylookout.com/.

[29] L. Lu, Z. Li, Z. Wu, W. Lee, and G. Jiang. CHEX: Statically Vetting Android Apps for Component Hijacking Vulnerabilities. In *Proc. ACM Computer and Communications Security*, October 2012.

[30] M. Nauman, S. Khan, and X. Zhang. Apex: Extending Android Permission Model and Enforcement with User-defined Runtime Constraints. In *ASIACCS*, 2010.

[31] Reddit is fun. https://play.google.com/store/apps/details?id=com.andrewshu.android.reddit.

[32] F. Roesner, T. Kohno, A. Moshchuk, B. Parno, H. J. Wang, and C. Cowan. User-Driven Access Control: Rethinking Permission Granting in Modern Operating Systems. In *Proc. IEEE Symposium on Security and Privacy* May 2012.

[33] smali/baksmali. http://code.google.com/p/smali/.

[34] M. Szydlowski, M. Egele, C. Kruegel, and G. Vigna. Challenges for Dynamic Analysis of iOS Applications. In *iNetSec*, 2012.

[35] virustotal. https://www.virustotal.com/.

[36] Y. Zhou, X. Zhang, X. Jiang, and V. W. Freeh. Taming Information-Stealing Smartphone Applications (on Android). In *Proc. Trust and Trustworthy Computing*, June 2011.

Smart Keys for Cyber-Cars: Secure Smartphone-based NFC-enabled Car Immobilizer

Christoph Busold,
Ahmad-Reza Sadeghi,
Christian Wachsmann

Intel CRI-SC, TU Darmstadt,
Germany

christoph.busold@cased.de,
ahmad.sadeghi@cased.de,
christian.wachsmann@cased.de

Alexandra Dmitrienko

Fraunhofer SIT, Darmstadt,
Germany

alexandra.dmitrienko@cased.de

Hervé Seudié,
Majid Sobhani,
Ahmed Taha

TU Darmstadt, Germany

herve.seudie@cased.de, majid.
sobhani@cased.de, ahmed.
taha@cased.de

ABSTRACT

Smartphones have become very popular and versatile devices. An emerging trend is the integration of smartphones into automotive systems and applications, particularly access control systems to unlock cars (doors and immobilizers). Smartphone-based automotive solutions promise to greatly enhance the user's experience by providing advanced features far beyond the conventional dedicated tokens/transponders.

We present the first *open* security framework for secure smartphone-based immobilizers. Our generic security architecture protects the electronic access tokens on the smartphone and provides advanced features such as context-aware access policies, remote issuing and revocation of access rights and their delegation to other users. We discuss various approaches to instantiate our security architecture based on different hardware-based trusted execution environments, and elaborate on their security properties. We implemented our immobilizer system based on the latest Android-based smartphone and a microSD smartcard. Further, we support the algorithmic proofs of the security of the underlying protocols with automated formal verification tools.

Categories and Subject Descriptors

D.4.6 [**Security and Protection**]: Access controls; K.6.5 [**Security and Protection**]: Authentication

General Terms

Security, Design

Keywords

Immobilizer; Mobile Security; Access Control; Delegation

1. INTRODUCTION

Today, smartphones are high performance platforms providing a wide range of features and have become an integral part of our daily life. The increasing computing and storage capabilities, the vast number and variety of apps available on app stores and new communication interfaces, such as Near Field Communication (NFC), provide many deployment possibilities for smartphones, including electronic ticketing [1], payment [27] and access control [46, 22]. In this context, an emerging trend is the integration of smartphones into modern automotive systems and applications such as access control to unlock, configure and start vehicles [41, 39, 47]. In particular, the NFC interface is well-suited for such applications due to its short nominal communication range (of a few centimeters) providing basic assurance of the user's physical proximity.

In this paper, we focus on smartphone-based NFC-enabled immobilizer systems. An electronic vehicle immobilizer is an anti-theft device that prevents starting the vehicle's engine unless the corresponding access token is (physically) present and authenticated. Currently, this access token is a transponder (i.e., an RFID chip) embedded into the mechanical car key or a contactless smartcard.

Smartphone-based immobilizer systems promise to enhance the user experience by providing a variety of appealing new features and enabling flexible applications beyond what is provided today by conventional transponder-based immobilizer systems. They do not require users to obtain a physical transponder but allow them to use their smartphone to remotely obtain electronic car keys (or access rights for the immobilizer). Moreover, access rights can be delegated to other users, revoked or bound to specific policies. In particular, automotive applications with a highly dynamic or large set of users, such as car sharing and fleet management, can highly benefit from smartphone-based immobilizers.

Despite the mentioned advantages for users, the core challenge concerns the security aspects of smartphone-based immobilizer systems. Smartphones are complex devices and appealing targets of attacks (e.g., by malware), especially when they are used in security-critical applications.

The traditional immobilizers used in practice are closed and proprietary systems and suffer from various security vulnerabilities, as recent attacks show [31, 33, 24, 50]. The reasons are conceptual protocol design flaws as well as the deployment of insecure or weak cryptographic schemes. On the other hand, several prototypes of commercial smartphone-based and NFC-enabled immobilizer systems have been introduced recently [41, 39, 47], but without providing technical details or information on their security properties.

Our goal and contribution. We present an *open* smartphone-based immobilizer system architecture and the underlying security framework, which provides enhanced functional and security features and overcomes the security issues of the conventional immobilizer systems. In particular, our contribution is as follows:

Framework for smartphone-based immobilizer systems. Our framework considers the functional and security requirements on the protocols and the system architecture of a smartphone-based solution under realistic adversary models.

Evaluation of existing security hardware. We evaluate and discuss various instantiations of our security architecture using different approaches to establish trusted execution environments on smartphones. We discuss which security guarantees can be provided by these instantiations, under which assumptions, and how some of these assumptions can be fulfilled by leveraging the features of security hardware currently available on recent smartphones.

Formal tool-based protocol analysis. Our protocols design is based on the protocols in [22], which we adapt to the immobilizer system. Additionally, we analyze the security of these protocols using the automated verification tool ProVerif [15], which is complementary to the cryptographic security analysis in [22].

Implementation. We present an implementation of our immobilizer system on Android using the latest smartphone hardware and a secure microSD smartcard. We show that it is feasible to implement a secure NFC-enabled and smartphone-based immobilizer system. In particular, we discuss the conditions for the secure integration of enhanced features such as delegation under a strong but realistic adversary model, where the adversary has full control over the software on the smartphone platform. Hereby, we take the technical limitations of currently available security hardware for smartphones into account.

Outline. We present our framework for smartphone-based immobilizer systems and the requirement analysis in Section 2. We describe the platform security architecture in Section 3 and discuss the available secure hardware in Section 4. We present the implementation and evaluation of our solution in Section 5 and analyze its security in Section 6. Finally, we give an overview of related work in Section 7 and conclude in Section 8.

2. REQUIREMENT ANALYSIS

We first introduce the system and adversary model, our assumptions and present our objectives and requirements.

2.1 System Model

Our system model is depicted in Figure 1 and involves a car manufacturer M, a car C, a car owner O and a car user U. The manufacturer M produces cars equipped with immobilizers, which are electronic control units that prevent unauthorized users from starting the car engine. Moreover,

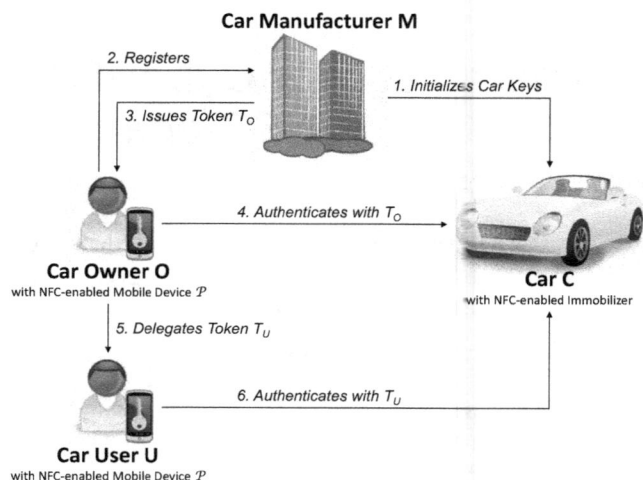

Figure 1: System model

M also represents car dealers and service stations authorized by the car manufacturer. The car owner O is a private person or a company that has purchased the car and received an electronic access control token T_O from M. The token is securely deployed and stored on the mobile platform $\mathcal{P}$ of O. The car user U is a person who is authorized by O to use the car. This can be a friend or a family member of the car owner, or an employee of the company owning the car. The authorization is given by means of issuing a delegated access control token T_U which grants U access to C.

2.2 Adversary Model

Communication channels. The adversary $\mathcal{A}$ has full control over all communication channels except the channel between the car manufacturer M and the car C, which we assume to be secure.[1] Specifically, $\mathcal{A}$ can eavesdrop, inject, replay and modify all messages transmitted over the channels between O and M, O and U, O and C, and U and C.[2]

Smartphone platform. We assume that each mobile platform $\mathcal{P}$ consists of an untrusted host $\mathcal{H}$ and a trusted execution environment (TrEE) $\mathcal{S}$. $\mathcal{A}$ can perform software attacks against the untrusted host $\mathcal{H}$ and install, modify or compromise all software components installed on $\mathcal{P}$. However, we exclude hardware attacks and assume that $\mathcal{A}$ cannot compromise $\mathcal{S}$. We provide a detailed discussion on instantiations of TrEE on top of different security hardware available for mobile platforms in Section 4.

Immobilizer. We assume that the immobilizer C is trusted as in conventional (non-NFC-based) immobilizer systems. Specifically, we assume that an adversary who compromises the immobilizer can start the car without attacking the mo-

---

[1] A secure communication channel between the car C and the manufacturer M can be established using standard protocols such as SSL.

[2] Note, that we exclude relay attacks since the focus of this paper is a secure immobilizer system architecture for NFC-enabled smartphones. One possible solution to reduce the risk of relay attacks are distance bounding techniques, which can be combined with our scheme.

bile platform. Hence, we exclude attacks against the immobilizer component.

2.3 Objectives

As in traditional immobilizer systems, our main objective is to prevent unauthorized access to the immobilizer:

O1: Access control. Only authorized entities, namely O authorized by M and U authorized by O, should be able to unlock the immobilizer C.

Further, the performance, i.e., the time needed for authentication is a significant usability aspect, which is essential for a positive user experience:

O2: Performance. Authentication of O or U to C should be performed within an unnoticeable time interval [37, 8].

Moreover, the compatibility to existing smartphones is important to ensure the applicability of the solution in practice:

O3: Compatibility. An important requirement is the compatibility to commodity mobile platforms. The immobilizer system should be compatible with existing hardware and require no or only minor changes to the mobile operating system.

A smartphone-based immobilizer system should enable new appealing features, such as the remote issuing and revocation of electronic tokens, remote replacement of electronic keys in case of loss or theft of the mobile device, or provide mechanisms to ensure access revocation of former car owners in case of car re-sell. Hence, our additional objectives are as follows:

O4: Remote issuing. The car manufacturer M should be able to *remotely* (e.g., via the Internet) issue and deploy the electronic access token T_O to the car owner O.

O5: Remote revocation. M should be able to *remotely* revoke access tokens T_O issued t O. Moreover, revocation of T_O by M should automatically revoke all delegated tokens T_U issued by O.

Some other desirable enhanced features include token delegation and support for context-aware access policies:

O6: Delegation. A car owner O should be able to securely delegate her access rights to a third party U.

O7: Policy-based access control. A car owner O should be able to restrict access of delegated users to the car based on contextual information such as time and location.

As we discuss later in Section 6, off-the-shelf smartphone platforms and security hardware can be used to achieve objectives (O1) to (O5). However, due to the technical constraints of available security hardware and the limitations posed by some security hardware manufacturers, objectives (O6) and (O7) cannot be realized with the currently available commodity hardware.

2.4 Security Requirements

Protocol-specific requirements.

The main security objective of an immobilizer system is the secure authentication of the car owner O (or the delegated user U) to the immobilizer C.

Platform-specific requirements.

Mobile platforms typically host a mobile operating system that can potentially be compromised and expose all secrets stored on the platform. Hence, to achieve objective (O1), the security-sensitive data used in the underlying protocols must be protected against untrusted code. Therefore, we define the following security requirements on the underlying mobile platform:

SR1: Secure storage. Security-sensitive data should not be accessible by untrusted software components while stored on the platform.

SR2: Isolation. The system components operating on security-sensitive data must be trusted and isolated from the untrusted components.

Further, it has to be ensured that the security sensitive operations, such as authentication and delegation, are triggered by the user rather than by malware. Moreover, advanced use cases, such as delegation and policy-based access control, rely on security-critical user inputs, such as passwords and user-defined access-control policies. Hence, for these use cases we need an additional security requirement:

SR3: Secure user interface. The user (the car owner O or the car user U) should be able to securely communicate with the trusted components.

Discussion. To achieve isolation on the platform, one could apply virtualization-based approaches or use a hardened operating system that provides isolation properties (such as proposed in [22]). However, this requires changes to the underlying operating system and may be hard to achieve in practice (O3). Hence, our primary goal is to leverage the general purpose secure hardware available for commodity mobile platforms to establish a hardware-isolated trusted execution environment (TrEE). Although the technology to achieve the objectives (SR1) to (SR3) is partially available, it is not widespread. In particular, a secure user interface (SR3) can be realized only with certain types of secure hardware. We provide an overview of available secure hardware and discuss its features in more details in Section 4.

3. SYSTEM DESIGN

In this section, we present a secure NFC-based immobilizer system. The solution includes cryptographic protocols for the secure interaction between the involved entities and a mobile security architecture to protect security-sensitive data, such as the cryptographic secrets used in the protocols, when they are processed and stored on the mobile platform.

3.1 Mobile Platform Security Architecture

Our security architecture is depicted in Figure 2. The execution environment of the mobile platform is divided into two independent worlds: An untrusted host $\mathcal{H}$ and a trusted execution environment $\mathcal{S}$. The host runs on the general purpose processor of the mobile device, while the TrEE is established on top of secure hardware. Such secure hardware can be either embedded into the smartphone or attached to the mobile device via the standard communication interfaces, which does not require any changes to commodity platforms.

Depending on the type of the secure hardware used, the TrEE can either have a direct (secure) connection to the

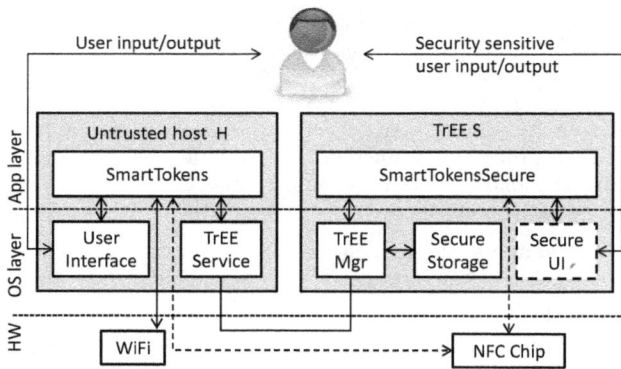

Figure 2: Mobile platform security architecture. Dashed boxes indicate optional components that are not available on current security hardware. Further, the NFC chip can be either controlled by the smartphone OS or have a direct connection to the TrEE, indicated by dashed lines.

NFC chip or must rely on the untrusted operating system to handle the NFC (illustrated as a dashed line in Figure 2). In contrast, the WiFi or the mobile network interface that is used for the communication with, e.g., the car manufacturer M, is always managed by the operating system.

The functionality of our system is realized within the SmartTokens app and the SmartTokensSecure component residing at the application level. The SmartTokens app manages the access control tokens and handles different protocols (such as registration, delegation and authentication), while the SmartTokensSecure component is only invoked to perform the computations involving security-critical data, such as the cryptographic secrets used in the protocols. All security-sensitive data is handled by the SmartTokensSecure component. This data never leaves the TrEE in cleartext and is securely stored in the SecureStorage component of S.

The SmartTokens and SmartTokensSecure apps communicate via a channel established between both execution environments. The channel is handled by the TrEEService and TrEEMgr components residing at the operating system level. These components are responsible for multiplexing the communication between the different applications running on the phone. TrEEMgr additionally manages the access of different TrEE applications to the SecureStorage component, so that other applications, possibly residing within the TrEE, cannot access the cryptographic parameters of the SmartTokensSecure app.

The user input is handled by two components in the system: The user interface UI provided by the operating system residing within H and a secure user interface SecureUI based on the TrEE. UI is used for the ordinary interaction with the user, while all security-sensitive data, such as passwords and access control policies are handled by the SecureUI component. SecureUI is customized with a background picture or a unique paraphrase only known to the user and the TrEE, allowing the user to distinguish between SecureUI and UI.

Note, that SecureUI based on the TrEE can be provided only by certain types of secure hardware, as we discuss later in Section 4. Thus, this component is optional in our system architecture (indicated by a dashed box in Figure 2). The

architecture instantiation without the SecureUI can achieve the basic objectives in Section 2.3, while the advanced objectives are achievable only in a relaxed adversary model, where the adversary cannot compromise the UI.

3.2 Protocol Design

Our protocol design is along the lines of the token-based access control system by Dmitrienko et al. [22]. This scheme consists of six protocols for initialization, user registration, token issuing, token delegation and the authentication protocol for registered and delegated users, respectively. In the following, we briefly describe these protocols.

Initialization of TrEE. The manufacturer of the trusted execution environment S installs the SmartTokensSecure app in S and initializes the SecureStorage of S with a unique decryption/encryption key pair $(sk_\mathcal{P}, pk_\mathcal{P})$ and a platform certificate $cert_\mathcal{P}$, which attests that S is a genuine trusted execution environment and that only S knows the secret decryption key $sk_\mathcal{P}$ that corresponds to the public encryption key $pk_\mathcal{P}$.

Immobilizer initialization. The car manufacturer M initializes the immobilizer C with an authentication secret $K_{\mathrm{Auth}}^{\mathsf{C}}$ and an encryption key $K_{\mathrm{Enc}}^{\mathsf{C}}$, which are both used in the authentication protocol.

Owner registration. Before purchasing a car, the car owner O registers her platform $\mathcal{P}$ with the car manufacturer M. In this process, M verifies the platform certificate $cert_\mathcal{P}$ of $\mathcal{P}$ and generates an authentication secret $K_{\mathrm{Auth}}^{\mathsf{O,M}}$ and decryption key $K_{\mathrm{Enc}}^{\mathsf{O,M}}$ for O, which are used later in the token issuing protocol. Further, M encrypts both keys with $pk_\mathcal{P}$ and sends the ciphertext back to S, where the SmartTokensSecure app decrypts both keys and stores them in SecureStorage.

Token issuing. In this protocol, M generates an authentication key $K_{\mathrm{Auth}}^{\mathsf{O}}$, which is used in the authentication protocol to unlock the immobilizer C, and a delegation key $K_{\mathrm{Del}}^{\mathsf{O}}$ that is used in the delegation protocol to create delegated tokens. Both keys and the identity ID_O of O are authenticated with the immobilizer authentication secret $K_{\mathrm{Auth}}^{\mathsf{C}}$ and encrypted under the immobilizer encryption key $K_{\mathrm{Enc}}^{\mathsf{C}}$, i.e.,

$$\sigma_\mathsf{M} := \mathrm{MAC}\left(K_{\mathrm{Auth}}^{\mathsf{C}}; ID_\mathsf{O}, K_{\mathrm{Auth}}^{\mathsf{O}}, K_{\mathrm{Del}}^{\mathsf{O}}\right)$$

$$T_\mathsf{O} := \mathrm{Enc}\left(K_{\mathrm{Enc}}^{\mathsf{C}}; ID_\mathsf{O}, K_{\mathrm{Auth}}^{\mathsf{O}}, K_{\mathrm{Del}}^{\mathsf{C}}, \sigma_\mathsf{M}\right)$$

T_O is the *access token* of O for C and used later in the authentication protocol. Furthermore, M and the SmartTokensSecure app in S establish a secure channel based on $K_{\mathrm{Auth}}^{\mathsf{O,M}}$ and $K_{\mathrm{Enc}}^{\mathsf{O,M}}$, which is used to send T_O from M to SmartTokensSecure. Finally, SmartTokensSecure stores $K_{\mathrm{Auth}}^{\mathsf{O}}, K_{\mathrm{Del}}^{\mathsf{O}}$ and T_O in the SecureStorage of S.

Car owner authentication. The authentication protocol is depicted in Figure 3: O uses the SmartTokens app to initiate an authentication request sent from O's mobile platform $\mathcal{P}$ to the immobilizer C. Then C sends its identifier ID_C and a random N (the bit-length μ of N is a security-critical parameter [22]) to SmartTokensSecure on $\mathcal{P}$, which replies with σ_O to the SmartTokens app in H that eventually sends $(\sigma_\mathsf{O}, T_\mathsf{O})$ to C. Next, C decrypts T_O with $K_{\mathrm{Enc}}^{\mathsf{C}}$ to obtain $K_{\mathrm{Auth}}^{\mathsf{O}}$, verifies σ_M and σ_O using $K_{\mathrm{Auth}}^{\mathsf{C}}$ and $K_{\mathrm{Auth}}^{\mathsf{O}}$, respec-

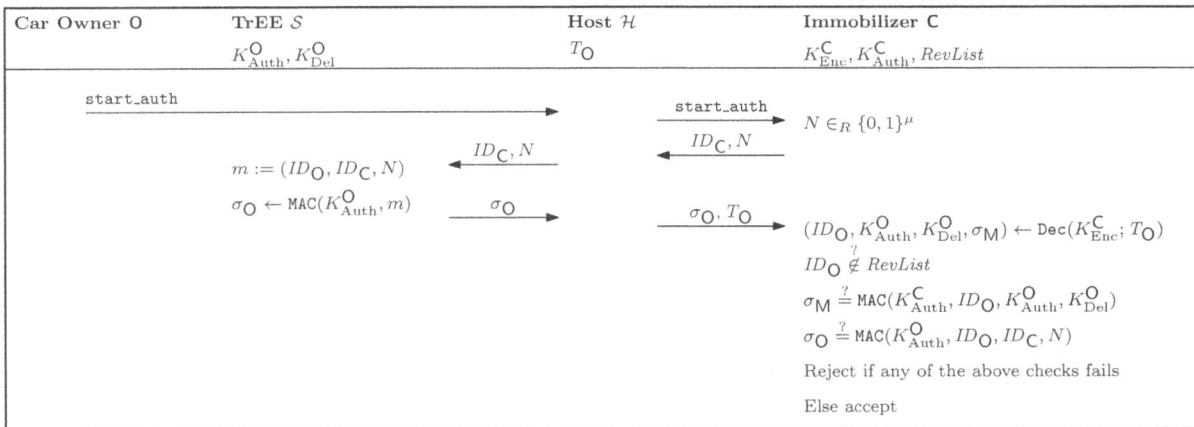

Car Owner O	TrEE $\mathcal{S}$	Host $\mathcal{H}$	Immobilizer C
$K_{\mathrm{Auth}}^O, K_{\mathrm{Del}}^O$		T_O	$K_{\mathrm{Enc}}^C, K_{\mathrm{Auth}}^C, RevList$

start_auth $\longrightarrow$ start_auth $\longrightarrow$ $N \in_R \{0,1\}^\mu$

$\xleftarrow{\quad ID_C, N \quad}$ $\xleftarrow{\quad ID_C, N \quad}$

$m := (ID_O, ID_C, N)$

$\sigma_O \leftarrow \mathrm{MAC}(K_{\mathrm{Auth}}^O, m)$ $\xrightarrow{\quad \sigma_O \quad}$ $\xrightarrow{\quad \sigma_O, T_O \quad}$

$(ID_O, K_{\mathrm{Auth}}^O, K_{\mathrm{Del}}^O, \sigma_M) \leftarrow \mathrm{Dec}(K_{\mathrm{Enc}}^C; T_O)$

$ID_O \overset{?}{\notin} RevList$

$\sigma_M \overset{?}{=} \mathrm{MAC}(K_{\mathrm{Auth}}^C, ID_O, K_{\mathrm{Auth}}^O, K_{\mathrm{Del}}^O)$

$\sigma_O \overset{?}{=} \mathrm{MAC}(K_{\mathrm{Auth}}^O, ID_O, ID_C, N)$

Reject if any of the above checks fails

Else accept

Figure 3: Authentication protocol

tively, and accepts only if both verifications are successful. Otherwise, C rejects.

Token delegation. The car owner O delegates her access rights to another car user U by creating a delegated token T_U. Specifically, SmartTokensSecure in the TrEE of O's platform creates an authentication secret K_{Auth}^U for U, authenticates it along with the identifier ID_U of U using K_{Auth}^O and encrypts all data under the delegation key K_{Del}^O:

$$\sigma_O := \mathrm{MAC}\left(K_{\mathrm{Auth}}^O; ID_U, K_{\mathrm{Auth}}^U\right)$$

$$T_U := \mathrm{Enc}\left(K_{\mathrm{Del}}^O; ID_U, K_{\mathrm{Auth}}^U, \sigma_O\right)$$

Furthermore, O and U establish a secure channel based on the platform key of U's TrEE, which is used to transfer T_U to SmartTokensSecure in the TrEE of U's device.

Car user authentication. For the authentication of a delegated car user U, U's TrEE sends to the immobilizer C two tokens, T_O and T_U. C first decrypts T_O to obtain K_{Del}^O, which is then used to decrypt K_{Auth}^U from T_U. The rest of the authentication protocol is the same as in Figure 3. Note that T_U is linked to T_O since T_U is a ciphertext that can be decrypted only with the delegation key K_{Del}^O of O, which is included in T_O.

Remote revocation. The remote revocation of tokens is realized in a form of revocation lists deployed by M to the car immobilizer C. Revocation of T_O by M automatically revokes all delegated tokens T_U issued by O, since T_O is involved in the authentication of each delegated user U.

Secure user input. The token delegation protocol requires a secure input from the car owner O to the SmartTokensSecure app. Specifically, the car user O must approve the delegation of her access rights and specify the corresponding access control policy for the car user U.

4. SECURE HARDWARE

In the following, we analyze the features of the available security hardware for smartphones and discuss which of them are most appropriate for the realization of a secure smartphone-based immobilizer system.

Most known security hardware available for modern smartphones includes ARM TrustZone [4], MShield [11], smartcards, SIM-cards and secure microSD cards [26]. A comparison of the corresponding features is depicted in Table 1. Note that all considered security hardware provides secure storage (SR1) and isolation (SR2).

ARM TrustZone. ARM TrustZone [4] allows for establishment of a trusted execution environment (TrEE) that could provide a secure user interface (SR3), eventually fulfilling all of our platform-related security requirements. However, TrustZone is available only on a few platforms, such as Apple's iPhone. Further, it is usually deactivated or locked by the phone manufacturer and cannot be used by third party applications running on the phone. Although the TrustZone API is public and software emulators are available, only selected third party developers get access to TrustZone development boards.

MShield. MShield is a closed TrEE that can be used by third party developers with the help of the on-board credentials (ObC) security framework [11, 34]. However, MShield is hardly available in practice and can only be found in a few high-end Nokia smartphones.

SIM-cards. SIM-cards are the most widespread TrEEs and available on every phone. However, SIM-cards are typically closed systems controlled by the network operators. Hence, a solution based on SIM-cards would be available only to customers of the particular network operator controlling the SIM-card.

Embedded secure elements. Embedded secure elements are available on some recent NFC-enabled Android phones, such as the Samsung Nexus S and the Samsung Galaxy Nexus. However, they are locked and can only be used with the Google Wallet payment system [28].

Combining the secure element and the NFC interface into one chip allows them to operate passively, i.e., without the power supply of the smartphone platform. In this mode, the secure element and NFC chips use the RF field generated by the NFC reader as power supply, a feature NFC inherited from contactless smartcards. Provided that the NFC chip in the phone supports this mode, it could be used to run the authentication protocol (Figure 3) even when the battery of the phone is depleted. On the protocol side, only a minor

Table 1: Comparison of current secure smartphone hardware

Security hardware	Secure storage (SR1)	Isolation (SR2)	Secure user interface (SR3)	Open to 3rd parties	Availability
ARM TrustZone [4]	+	+	+	-	some phones, e.g., iPhone (not activated)
TI MShield [11]	+	+	-	with ObC [34]	some phones, e.g., Nokia
SIM-card	+	+	-	-	every phone
Embedded SE	+	+	-	-	some phones, e.g., Samsung Nexus S and Galaxy Nexus
Secure microSD card [26]	+	+	-	+	any phone with microSD slot
Secure microSD card with NFC [49]	+	+	-	+	any phone with microSD slot & NFC antenna

modification would be required: The tokens must be stored in the secure element to make them available to the TrEE when the host is powered down.

Secure microSD cards. A promising approach is using secure microSD cards, which are microSD memory cards that include a secure element. They can be used in every smartphone with a microSD card slot. Some of these cards include an NFC chip that uses an NFC antenna integrated in the microSD card or can be connected to an external NFC antenna built into the phone [49]. Such microSD cards enable solutions that reach a large number of users because they can even be used on phones without an integrated NFC interface. However, microSD cards with integrated NFC are hardly available and most stock phones are not equipped with NFC antennas.

ARM TrustZone seems to be the most suitable TrEE for our architecture, since it satisfies all platform-related security requirements, while all other TrEE types do not provide a secure user interface. However, developments for TrustZone are currently limited to development boards, thus we have to consider other types of TrEEs for our prototype.

Our implementation of the smartphone-based immobilizer system uses an NFC-enabled smartphone with a secure microSD card, which seems to be the most applicable configuration in practice. Due to unavailability of a secure user interface when using only a microSD card, our prototype implementation achieves only the objectives (O1) - (O5), while achieving objectives (O6) - (O7) requires either a more enhanced TrEE or a weaker adversary model. We provide an evaluation and detailed discussion of this aspect in Section 6.

5. IMPLEMENTATION AND EVALUATION

We now describe our implementation and present the performance measurements for the authentication protocols. Figure 4 shows the hardware setup we used.

Smartphone. We implemented the immobilizer application on Android using an NFC-enabled Samsung Galaxy S3 smartphone. The NFC hardware of the Galaxy S3 comes with a built-in secure element used for the Google Wallet electronic payment system [28]. However, this secure element is locked and cannot be used for custom applications such as our immobilizer system. Therefore, we use a Giesecke & Devrient Mobile Security Card 1.0, which is a microSD smart card that allows installation of custom applications. The underlying smart card operating system complies to the JavaCard 2.2.2 and GlobalPlatform 2.2.1 specifications and provides all primitives required by the protocols: Public-key encryption (RSA), symmetric encryption (AES in CBC mode), a cryptographic hash function (SHA1) and a cryptographic random number generator

The UI component of our architecture is represented by the keyboard and display drivers already present in the Android OS. The TrEEService implementation is based on the smart card API provided by the Seek-for-Android project [44]. It enables access to smartcards via APDUs as defined in ISO7816. The Galaxy S3 stock firmware already contains this smart card API for the built-in secure element, however, it is not enabled for the Mobile Security Card. Therefore, we had to replace the firmware of the phone with a custom build of CyanogenMod9 [20] based on Android 4.0.3 where we included the smart card API patches (version 2.3.2). However, Seek-for-Android plans to release a plugin-in terminal for the Mobile Security Card, which can be used with the existing API and thus would not require a custom firmware.

Our implementation of the communication protocols and the SmartTokens application are based on [22]. However, they implemented the TrEE in software as an operating system service on top of a hardened Android OS. Our system in contrast does not require a hardened OS but utilizes a hardware isolated TrEE. The functionality of the SmartTokensSecure component in our architecture (Section 3.2) is implemented in a JavaCard applet that uses the secure storage of the smart card. Moreover, we implemented an interface to the smart card that is compatible to the existing SmartTokens application.

Immobilizer. The immobilizer implementation uses a setup similar to commercially available immobilizer systems [40, 7]. Specifically, we use an Arduino Uno [5], which is a commercial development board based on a 8 bit Atmel AVR microcontroller with 32 KB memory clocked at 16 MHz. The Arduino is connected via a Serial Peripheral Interface (SPI) to an NFC interface [38] based on the PN532 controller [42].

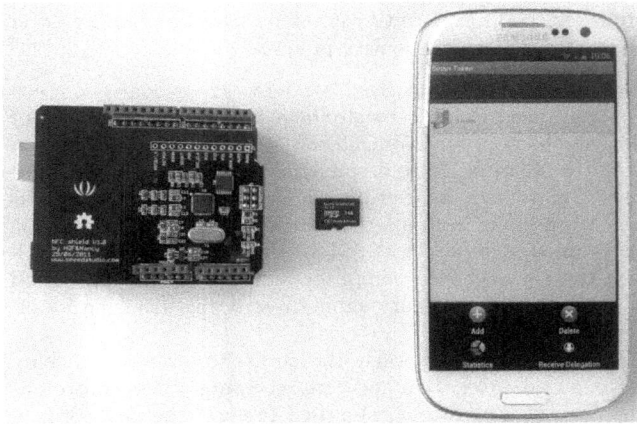

Figure 4: Prototype setup consisting of an Arduino Uno board with NFC shield, a secure microSD smart card and a Samsung Galaxy S3 smartphone (left to right).

Table 2: Performance measurements

User Type	Challenge Time (ms)	Response Time (ms)	Verification Time (ms)	Session Time (ms)
Owner	72.05	384.90	24.00	480.95
User	72.20	544.85	41.65	658.70

The implementation of the immobilizer uses the cryptographic primitives provided by the AVR-Crypto-Lib [10], which is an open source library optimized for AVR microcontrollers. Furthermore, we adapted the NFC library provided with the PN532 NFC controller so that the NFC hardware emulates a contactless smartcard according to the NFC Forum type 4 and ISO14443-4 specifications [32, 2].

Performance Evaluation. We evaluated the performance of our implementation of the authentication protocol running between the smartphone and the immobilizer. For this purpose, we made the following measurements: (1) the time required to start the authentication mechanism and to get the challenge from the immobilizer after the NFC connection has been established, (2) the time required by the phone to send the response to the immobilizer, (3) the time required by the immobilizer to verify the phone's response, and (4) the time required for the complete authentication protocol. The results of our measurements averaged over 20 protocol runs are shown in Table 2. Our solution requires 480.95 ms ($\pm$26.95 ms) for the whole authentication process of the car owner and 658.70 ms ($\pm$74.30 ms) for the authentication of the car user, which is sufficient to provide positive user experience [37].

6. SECURITY CONSIDERATIONS

In this section we discuss our security architecture with respect to the security objectives outlined in Section 2.4.

6.1 Protocol Analysis

As mentioned in Section 3.2 our protocols are adapted from [22]. While security proofs of the protocols in crypto-graphic models are shown in [22], we additionally analyze the security of the protocols using automated verification tools. In this context prominent verification tools are ProVerif [15], Scyther [17] and Avispa [6]. We use ProVerif since it provides the largest feature set compared to other tools [18, 19, 21]. In contrast to other verification tools, ProVerif allows modeling of any known cryptographic function using the applied pi calculus specification language [3]. The corresponding protocol specifications were successfully verified by ProVerif, additionally supporting the cryptographic proofs and providing the confidence in fulfillment of the security objectives.

Formal Verification using ProVerif.
ProVerif takes as input a formal description of the protocols, the adversary model and the security objectives based on the applied pi calculus specification language and proves or disproves the claimed security properties. This formal specification includes the following components:

Agents. Agents represent the protocol participants (car manufacturer M, car owner O, car user U and immobilizer C), which have different *roles* such as being the sender/receiver of a protocol message.

Events. Events model the actions performed by the agents, such as computations and sending/receiving messages.

Communication channels. The communication channels are used to transfer messages between the agents.

Security properties. The security properties specify the confidentiality and authentication objectives of the protocols (Section 2.4). We use the common ProVerif specification of authentication based on the correspondence property [16], which states that every successful execution of a protocol step implies that the involved entities were honest and followed the protocol specification.

Adversary. The adversary and its capabilities are modeled as an agent that aims to violate the security objectives. Note that ProVerif uses the Dolev-Yao adversary model [23] by default, which corresponds to the adversary model in Section 2.2. Further, we assume that the car manufacturer M, the immobilizer C and the trusted execution environments S of all mobile platforms are trusted while all other agents are untrusted.

Based on the formal specification, ProVerif proves or disproves the security properties. Specifically, the confidentiality property is checked by searching for protocol states where the adversary learns at least one of the cryptographic secrets. The authentication goal is checked by searching for protocol states where a message originating from the adversary is accepted by the immobilizer even though the adversary does not know the underlying authentication secrets.

The detailed formal specification, proof and result of the formal verification of the protocols using ProVerif can be found in the full version of this paper.

6.2 Analysis of the Security Architecture

Our security architecture leverages the underlying security hardware to satisfy the requirements (SR1) and (SR2). Particularly, it relies on a separate processor providing an isolated execution environment and a dedicated secure memory. Further, to satisfy (SR2), we ensure that the security-sensitive data is never available in plain text to untrusted code (as detailed in Section 3.2). Therefore, the code running on the untrusted host cannot access any secrets which are stored and processed inside the trusted execution environment (required by the protocols to achieve objective (O1), as we showed in Section 6.1.).

6.3 Advanced Security Features

Advanced objectives such as secure delegation (O6) and policy-based access control (O7) require a secure user interface to handle security-sensitive user input (as discussed in Section 3.2). Particularly, token delegation relies on a password-based authentication of the delegated user U against the car owner O before the delegated token is issued. Without a secure user interface, the password can be intercepted by malware and redirected to a malicious device that can impersonate U and receive the delegated token T_U. Further, context-aware access control requires the car owner O to define access control policies during the delegation process. When entered via an untrusted user interface, the access policy can be manipulated by a malware without consent of the car owner.

As we discussed in Section 4, among the currently available secure hardware ARM TrustZone seems to be capable of providing a secure user interface. However, currently it is not freely programmable. Thus, in the following, we discuss possible alternatives to a secure user interface on the phone that can provide a reasonable trade-off between the available technologies and the desired security features.

NFC proximity. NFC proximity provides a means to input a single bit of information directly into the TrEE. Particularly, a user can authorize or invoke a security sensitive operation such as token delegation or authentication by tapping his phone to the NFC reader. However, the following aspects have to be considered when using NFC proximity to authorize security sensitive operations: First, in case the NFC interface is handled by the operating system, the malware can emulate the proximity to the NFC reader by pretending to receive data from the NFC interface. Thus, NFC-based proximity can be reliably provided only by TrEEs that feature a direct connection to the NFC chip so that the untrusted operating system cannot spoof the communication. Examples of such secure hardware are SIM-cards, embedded secure elements and secure microSD cards with an integrated NFC chip. Moreover, a powerful adversary with specialized equipment may extend the nominal NFC range of 10–20 cm up to 1–10 meters [29] and trigger NFC without consent of the user. Furthermore, NFC-based proximity may potentially be subject to relay attacks [25]. In this case it can be applied only in a weaker adversary model that excludes these kinds of attacks.

NFC proximity enables secure delegation over the NFC interface. Particularly, the car owner O can authenticate the user U based on a visual contact, while both platforms can use a secure channel based on a key established via NFC[3].

---

[3]Note that the NFC link is commonly assumed not being

However, NFC proximity cannot be used to securely enter context-aware access control policies.

Car on-board computer. Modern car on-board computers (e.g., head units) typically have large displays and input devices that can be leveraged as user interface. Moreover, it might be reasonable to assume that the car on-board computer (and hence its user interface) is trusted, since attacks on car on-board computers are much less common than attacks on mobile devices[4]. Moreover, the attacker controlling the car on-board computer most likely will have good chances to start the car engine directly by attacking its internal infrastructure.

The system that leverages the car user interface can achieve both, secure delegation and context-aware access control, as the car user interface can be used to enter the password required for the delegation, as well as to define context-aware security policies in a secure way.

7. RELATED WORK

In this section, we discuss existing immobilizer systems in practice and in literature. Further, we give an overview on related work regarding access control with smartphones.

NFC-based Immobilizers.

NXP Semiconductors presented the prototype of an NFC-based immobilizer system [41]. The security of this approach relies on the secure element of the smartphone. However, it is unclear how this secure element is instantiated and whether this approach requires new phones with special security hardware. Furthermore, in contrast to our approach, this system does not consider delegation and may not be usable in advanced use cases such as car sharing applications.

NFC-based immobilizer systems supporting car sharing were proposed independently by the automotive component suppliers Valeo [39] and Continental [47]. They collaborated with network operators (Orange and Deutsche Telecom, respectively) and used SIM-cards as secure execution environments for the protection of their electronic car keys. While SIM-cards are available on each mobile platform, they are controlled by different network operators. Hence the solutions by Valeo and Continental would probably be available only to the customers of those network providers. Furthermore, there is no public information on the security mechanisms used in these solutions.

Transponder-based Immobilizers.

Lemke et al. [35] present a system model and requirement analysis for electronic immobilizer systems that use dedicated hardware tokens. The proposed model does not capture advanced use cases such as delegation and thus cannot be applied to our system. Moreover, their model is concerned with the security aspects of the immobilizer, while we focus on the security of the user's mobile device and the protection of the authentication secrets from the untrusted mobile OS.

The first open specification of a security protocol stack for

---

susceptible to man-in-the-middle attacks [29]. Hence, when combined with visual authentication, it can be used for secure authenticated key establishment.

[4]More than 25,000 new malicious Android apps have been discovered in Q1 and Q2 of 2012 [51], while attacks on on-board computers are not widespread and very involved [43]

transponder-based immobilizer systems has been published by Atmel [9, 36]. Tillich et al. [48] uncovered several vulnerabilities in this stack and proposed fixes. This demonstrates the advantages of open approach to security design, which we also follow.

The first attempt of using public-key cryptography in immobilizer systems has been made by Heyszl et al. [30]. They showed that it is feasible to implement lightweight elliptic curve cryptography on resource-constrained transponders. However, since the amount of data to be transferred in their authentication protocol exceeds the constrained bandwidth of the NFC interface, their scheme is not appropriate for NFC-based immobilizer systems.

Delegable Access Control With Smartphones.

Our work is along the lines of the SmartToken system by Dmitrienko et al. [22], which enables NFC-enabled smartphones to maintain electronic access control tokens that can be delegated to other users. Specifically, we adapt the protocols of the SmartToken scheme to the immobilizer use case and provide a tool-based security verification of these protocols. Further, we introduce a new platform security architecture that, in contrast to the architecture of the SmartToken system, does not rely on trusted operating system components and can be built on top of commodity mobile operating systems.

Another smartphone-based access control system supporting delegation of access rights has been presented by Bauer et al. [14, 12, 13]. The system uses Bluetooth instead of NFC and is based on public-key cryptography. Delegation is expressed in form of a digitally signed certificate, while our delegable access control tokens carrying policies are based on symmetric cryptography to minimize the communication overhead and to meet the bandwidth constrains of NFC[5]. Further, we consider the mobile platform security aspects of protecting authentication secrets, while the work by Bauer et al. considers more complicated (particularly, role-based) access control policies and usability issues.

8. CONCLUSION

We presented the first open security framework and instantiation for smartphone-based NFC-enabled immobilizers. Unlike the conventional, closed and proprietary immobilizer systems that suffer from various vulnerabilities, our open approach allows the independent evaluation of our solution by the research community. Our framework consists of a set of secure protocols (adapted from [22]) and a security architecture for the mobile platform. We analyze the security of the underlying protocols using automated formal verification tools. Moreover, we analyze the security of our architecture and discuss which objectives can be achieved using off-the-shelf secure hardware for mobile platforms. We show that available hardware allows remote issuing and remote revocation of electronic tokens, which cannot be achieved with classical (transponder-based) immobilizer systems. Further, we outline approaches to achieve more advanced security features, such as secure delegation and context-aware access control.

---

[5]While the nominal NFC transmission rate is 106 kpbs, the bandwidth usable in practice is only about 10 kbps [45].

9. REFERENCES

[1] MIFARE4Mobile.org. http://mifare4mobile.org/files/1213/3283/4766/12-03-20_NFC_Ticketing_Europe_2012.pdf, 2012.

[2] Near Field Communication Forum. http://www.nfc-forum.org/home/.

[3] M. Abadi and C. Fournet. Mobile values, new names, and secure communication. In *28th ACM SIGPLAN-SIGACT Symposium on Principles of Programming Languages (POPL'01)*. ACM, 2001.

[4] T. Alves and D. Felton. TrustZone: Integrated hardware and software security. *Information Quaterly*, 3(4), 2004.

[5] Arduino. http://www.arduino.cc/.

[6] A. Armando, D. Basin, Y. Boichut, Y. Chevalier, L. Compagna, J. Cuellar, P. Hankes Drielsma, P.-C. Heám, J. Mantovani, S. Mödersheim, D. von Oheimb, M. Rusinowitch, J. Santiago, M. Turuani, L. Viganò, and L. Vigneron. The AVISPA tool for the automated validation of internet security protocols and applications. In *17th International Conference on Computer Aided Verification (CAV'05)*. Springer, 2005.

[7] Atmel. Car access. http://www.atmel.com/applications/automotive/car_access/default.aspx.

[8] ATMEL. Automotive Compilation Volume 7 December 2010. http://www.atmel.com/Images/atmel_autocompilation_vol7_dec2010.pdf, 2010.

[9] Atmel. Open source immobilizer protocol stack. http://www.atmel.com/dyn/products/tools_card.asp?tool_id=17197, 2010. registration required.

[10] AVR cryptographic library. Set of cryptographic primitives for Atmel AVR microcontrollers. https://www.das-labor.org/wiki/AVR-Crypto-Lib.

[11] J. Azema and G. Fayad. M-Shield mobile security technology: Making wireless secure. Texas Instruments white paper, 2008. http://focus.ti.com/pdfs/wtbu/ti_mshield_whitepaper.pdf.

[12] L. Bauer, L. Cranor, R. W. Reeder, M. K. Reiter, and K. Vaniea. Comparing access-control technologies: A study of keys and smartphones. Technical report, 2007.

[13] L. Bauer, L. F. Cranor, M. K. Reiter, and K. Vaniea. Lessons learned from the deployment of a smartphone-based access-control system. In *3rd symposium on Usable privacy and security (SOUPS'07)*. ACM, 2007.

[14] L. Bauer, S. Garriss, J. M. McCune, M. K. Reiter, J. Rouse, and P. Rutenbar. Device-enabled authorization in the Grey system. In *8th International Conference on Information Security (ISC'05)*. Springer-Verlag, 2005.

[15] B. Blanchet. An efficient cryptographic protocol verifier based on Prolog rules. In *14th IEEE Computer Security Foundations Workshop (CSFW'01)*. IEEE Computer Society, 2001.

[16] B. Blanchet. From secrecy to authenticity in security protocols. In *9th International Static Analysis Symposium (SAS'02)*. Springer Verlag, 2002.

[17] C. Cremers. *Scyther - Semantics and Verification of Security Protocols*. Ph.D. dissertation, Eindhoven University of Technology, 2006.

[18] C. Cremers. Unbounded verification, falsification, and characterization of security protocols by pattern refinement. In *15th ACM conference on Computer and communications security (CCS'08)*. ACM, 2008.

[19] C. Cremers, P. Lafourcade, and P. Nadeau. Comparing state spaces in automatic protocol analysis. In *Formal to Practical Security*. Springer Berlin Heidelberg, 2009.

[20] CyanogenMod. http://www.cyanogenmod.com/.

[21] N. Dalal, J. Shah, K. Hisaria, and D. Jinwala. A comparative analysis of tools for verification of security protocols. *IJCNS*, 3(10):779–787, 2010.

[22] A. Dmitrienko, A.-R. Sadeghi, S. Tamrakar, and C. Wachsmann. SmartTokens: Delegable access control with NFC-enabled smartphones. In *5th International Conference on Trust & Trustworthy Computing (TRUST'12)*, 2012.

[23] D. Dolev and A. Yao. On the security of public key protocols. *IEEE Transactions on Information Theory*, 29(2):198–207, 1983.

[24] A. Francillon, B. Danev, and S. Čapkun. Relay attacks on passive keyless entry and start systems in modern cars. In *Network and Distributed System Security Symposium (NDSS)*, 2011.

[25] L. Francis, G. Hancke, K. Mayes, and K. Markantonakis. Practical NFC peer-to-peer relay attack using mobile phones. In *6th International Conference on Radio Frequency Identification: Security and Privacy Issues (RFIDSec'10)*. Springer-Verlag, 2010.

[26] Giesecke & Devrient Secure Flash Solutions. The Mobile Security Card SE 1.0 offers increased security. http://www.gd-sfs.com/the-mobile-security-card/mobile-security-card-se-1-0/.

[27] Google. http://www.google.com/wallet/.

[28] Google Wallet. http://www.google.com/wallet/, 2012.

[29] E. Haselsteiner and K. Breitfuß. Security in Near Field Communication (NFC). Strengths and weaknesses. In *Workshop on RFID Security*, 2006.

[30] J. Heyszl and F. Stumpf. Asymmetric cryptography in automotive access and immobilizer systems. 9th Embedded Security in Cars Conference, 2011.

[31] S. Indesteege, N. Keller, O. Dunkelman, E. Biham, and B. Preneel. A practical attack on KeeLoq. In *27th Annual International Conference on the Theory and Applications of Cryptographic Techniques (EUROCRYPT'08)*. Springer-Verlag, 2008.

[32] International Organization for Standardization. *International Standard ISO/IEC 14443-4. Identification cards – Contactless integrated circuit cards – Proximity cards.*

[33] M. Kasper, T. Kasper, A. Moradi, and C. Paar. Breaking KeeLoq in a flash: On extracting keys at lightning speed. In *2nd International Conference on Cryptology in Africa (AFRICACRYPT'09)*. Springer, 2009.

[34] K. Kostiainen, J.-E. Ekberg, N. Asokan, and A. Rantala. On-board credentials with open provisioning. In *4th ACM Symposium on Information, Computer, and Communications Security (ASIACCS'09)*. ACM, 2009.

[35] K. Lemke, A.-R. Sadeghi, and C. Stüble. An open approach for designing secure electronic immobilizers. In *Information Security Practice and Experience (ISPEC'05)*, 2005.

[36] P. Lepek. Configurable, secure, open immobilizer implementation. In *Embedded Security in Cars*, 2010.

[37] R. Näätänen, O. Syssoeva, and R. Takegata. Automatic time perception in the human brain for intervals ranging from milliseconds to seconds. *Psychophysiology*, 41(4):660–663, 2004.

[38] NFC Shield. Near Field Communication interface for Arduino. http://www.seeedstudio.com/wiki/NFC_Shield.

[39] NFC World. Orange and Valeo demonstrate NFC car key concept, 2010. http://www.nfcworld.com/2010/10/07/34592/orange-and-valeo-demonstrate-nfc-car-key-concept/.

[40] NXP. Car access and immobilizers. http://www.nxp.com/products/automotive/car_access_immobilizers/.

[41] NXP. NXP and Continental demonstrate the world's first concept car embedding NFC at Mobile World Congress, 2011. http://www.nxp.com/news/press-releases/2011/02/nxp-and-continental-demonstrate-the-world-s-first-concept-car-embedding-nfc-at-mobile-world-congress.html.

[42] PN532 Near Field Communication (NFC) controller. NXP Semiconductors. http://www.nxp.com/products/identification_and_security/reader_ics/nfc_devices/series/PN532.html.

[43] Scientific American. Hack My Ride: Cyber Attack Risk on Car Computers , 2011. http://www.scientificamerican.com/article.cfm?id=hack-my-ride.

[44] Secure Element Evaluation Kit for the Android platform. http://code.google.com/p/seek-for-android/.

[45] S. Tamrakar, J.-E. Ekberg, and N. Asokan. Identity verification schemes for public transport ticketing with NFC phones. In *ACM workshop on Scalable Trusted Computing (STC'11)*. ACM, 2011.

[46] Telcred. secure offline access control with NFC. http://www.telcred.com/, 2012.

[47] Telecom. Deutsche Telekom and automotive supplier Continental demonstrated car keys, 2011. http://www.telekom.com/innovation/connectedcar/81840.

[48] S. Tillich and M. Wójcik. Security analysis of an open car immobilizer protocol stack. 10th International Conference on Applied Cryptograpy and Network Security (ACNS'12), 2012.

[49] Tyfone. Tyfone to license SideTap MicroSD NFC and Secure Element Card technologies to AboMem, 2011. http://tyfone.com/newsroom/?p=541.

[50] R. Verdult, F. Garcia, and J. Balasch. Gone in 360 seconds: Hijacking with Hitag2. In *21st USENIX Security Symposium*, 2012.

[51] ZDNet. Android malware numbers explode to 25,000 in June 2012. http://www.zdnet.com/android-malware-numbers-explode-to-25000-in-june-2012-7000001046/, 2012.

FENCE: Continuous Access Control Enforcement in Dynamic Data Stream Environments

Rimma V. Nehme[1†], Hyo-Sang Lim[2,3], Elisa Bertino[3]

[1]Microsoft Jim Gray Systems Lab, USA
[2]Computer and Telecommunications Engineering Division, Yonsei University, South Korea
[3]Department of Computer Science and Cyber Center, Purdue University, USA
rimman@microsoft.com, hyosang@yonsei.ac.kr, bertino@cs.purdue.edu

ABSTRACT

In this paper, we address the problem of *continuous access control enforcement* in dynamic data stream environments, where *both* data and query security restrictions may potentially change in real-time. We present *FENCE* framework that effectively addresses this problem. The distinguishing characteristics of *FENCE* include: (1) the *stream-centric* approach to security, (2) the *symmetric* model for security settings of both continuous queries and streaming data, and (3) two alternative *security-aware query processing* approaches that can optimize query execution based on regular and security-related selectivities. In *FENCE*, both data and query security restrictions are modeled *symmetrically* in the form of security meta-data, called *"security punctuations"* embedded inside data streams. We distinguish between two types of security punctuations, namely, the *data security punctuations* (or short, *dsps*) which represent the access control policies of the streaming data, and the *query security punctuations* (or short, *qsps*) which describe the access authorizations of the continuous queries. We also present our encoding method to support XACML(eXtensible Access Control Markup Language) standard. We have implemented *FENCE* in a prototype DSMS and present our performance evaluation. The results of our experimental study show that *FENCE*'s approach has low overhead and can give great performance benefits compared to the alternative security solutions for streaming environments.

Categories and Subject Descriptors

H.2 [**Database Management**]: General—*security, integrity, and protection*

Keywords

Access Control; Data Stream; XACML

1. INTRODUCTION

1.1 Security in Dynamic Environments

Due to recent developments in pervasive and ubiquitous computing, many enterprises begin to provide high-quality services based on real-time data, e.g., patient monitoring, location-based services, ubiquitous social networking [1, 2, 3]. The information in such applications arrives in the form of infinite data streams to a Data Stream Management System (DSMS) where continuous queries are evaluated.

One of the biggest challenges in such dynamic environments is *access control enforcement* – the ability to permit or deny a request to perform an operation (e.g., a read operation). Given the *long-running* nature of continuous queries, the content of the streaming data and along with it its "sensitivity" may change frequently over the lifetime of query execution. Furthermore, queries themselves may also experience frequent changes in their access control privileges, while they are being executed. Such changes in security may be due to mobility and varying context of the users receiving the results of continuous queries, e.g., results may be accessed via mobile phones, PDAs or iPhones from any place and at any time. Clearly, the users streaming their data can be rightly concerned about a possible unauthorized access to their real-time information and a potential violation of their privacy. In short, security settings of *both* data and queries can be concurrently very dynamic.

1.2 Motivating Examples

Example 1: *Ubiquitous healthcare system.* Healthcare systems support real-time monitoring and access to vital signs data of patients by doctors and nurses. Consider a physician executing a query Q that monitors the health state of his patients, e.g., heart rate, blood pressure, etc. Over time, while Q is being executed, the physician may continuously acquire different role(s)[1], which implicitly translates into different access privileges. The patients, transmitting their data should have the ability to control in which role their doctor can access their real-time health information.

Example 2: *Location-Based Services.* Recent improvements in location-based technologies have spurred a new wave of mobile services, such as location-based applications and geo-social networking [5]. Such applications naturally raise privacy concerns. It is essential to provide support for users to be able to frequently change their access control policies based on their preferences, to restrict who can "see" their real-time whereabouts (e.g., where they are, whom they are with, or what they are doing).

Based on the real-life examples above, we can observe that dynamic changes in security are natural in streaming environments. We can also observe that changes in security may come not only from (i) the dynamic preferences of the users sending their data (i.e., the *data providers*) but also from (ii) the dynamic privileges of the users receiving the results of continuous queries running on DSMS (i.e., the *query specifiers*).

---

† Rimma V. Nehme did this work when she was at Purdue University.

---

[1]Here, we assume the system is using a role-based access control(RBAC) model [4].

1.3 Challenges

Fast data arrival rate. A common characteristic of data streams is a high data volume and a rapid arrival rate [2]. It is not feasible to store all data from all streams and take random accesses to it as it is done in traditional databases. Therefore, ideally, security processing must be done on-the-fly and the speed of processing must be faster than the data incoming rate.

Dynamic changes in security. As we have discussed in Section 1.1, frequent changes in security settings of data and queries are expected to be the norm. Thus, an access control enforcement mechanism must be extremely adaptive to runtime changes in security (and its statistics).

Correctness of enforcement. The foremost challenge is the prevention of any information leaks that may occur when access is no longer authorized. At any time, only the data elements that satisfy both the query and the data security policies at the same time must be outputted as query results.

Low overhead. The results in streaming environments are expected to be produced in near-real-time. Since access control enforcement is nothing but an added "overhead" compared to regular continuous query processing, its cost must be as low as possible not to decrease the utility of DSMSs.

Support for Standards. As the XACML (eXtensible Access Control Markup Language) standard [6] is increasingly being adopted in applications requiring high interoperability such as e-business and large enterprise systems [7], it is crucial that the access control system be able to specification and enforcement of XACML policies [8].

1.4 Our Contributions: FENCE Framework

To address the above-mentioned challenges, in our previous work [9], we have proposed *Security Punctuation* model that supports online enforcement of access control in data stream environments. In the subsequent work [10], we have proposed the initial version of *FENCE* framework (short for *Continuous Access Control Enforcement in Dynamic Data Stream Environments*) that addresses the limitation of *Security Punctuation* model that focuses only on security restrictions associated with data. In this paper, we provide the full descriptions of *FENCE* framework and extend the framework to enable a much richer security semantics for various applications' needs. The new extensions introduce new technical difficulties for which we present our solutions in this paper. Our major contributions can be summarized as follows:

- We present *FENCE*, which models *both* data-side and query-side dynamic security restrictions *symmetrically* using streaming "security punctuations"[2]. *FENCE* distinguishes between two types of *sps*, namely, the *data security punctuations* (*dsps*) and the *query security punctuations* (*qsps*).

- *FENCE* supports security-aware continuous query processing by combining *dsps* and *qsps*. *FENCE* is equipped with two adaptive methods, namely: (1) the *Security Filter Approach* (*SFA*), and (2) the *Query Rewrite Approach* (*QRA*). We discuss their advantages and the limitations and describe how they can adapt to both data as well as security-related selectivities.

- Since access control policies may change in the middle of query execution, *FENCE* distinguishes between two types of

---

[2]Similar to [9], in this paper, we chose to name the security metadata – "security punctuations", because by introducing *dsps* and *qsps* into data streams, we subdivide (i.e., punctuate) infinite data streams into finite partitions with associated security restrictions.

---

security policy enforcement semantics, namely the *deferred* and the *immediate* enforcements. In the deferred enforcement, the access control policies are enforced on only the data tuples that arrive *after* the policy change. In the immediate enforcement, a policy is enforced *instantly* including the tuples that have arrived *before* the new policy and are not yet outputted as query results.

- *FENCE* supports XACML for specification of access control policies that are conveyed by security punctuations. Since XACML is too verbose and heavy for use in data stream environments, as part of *FENCE*, we have implemented an efficient method for encoding XACML policies into security punctuations. Compared to use plain XACML policies, the encoding method allows us to greatly reduce the size of the security punctuations, which is crucial in order to reduce the access control overhead.

- We have implemented *FENCE* in a prototype DSMS [11]. Our experimental study shows that *FENCE* efficiently supports access control enforcement with frequent data and query security changes and the overhead is low relative to regular continuous query processing.

2. PROBLEM FORMULATION

We first give the definition of *Continuous Query Processing* (or CQP for short). In traditional CQP, queries are registered in DSMS, and only the data tuples that satisfy the predicates of the queries are produced as results. We call these predicates – *query predicates* – and formally define CQP as follows:

DEFINITION 2.1. (*CQP*) *Suppose that a data element $d=(v_1, v_2, ..., v_n)$ from a data stream has n attributes and a query predicate $\varphi_Q(attr_1, attr_2, ..., attr_n)$ on d represents the condition of a given continuous query Q. Then, whenever d arrives, continuous query processing mechanism produces d as a result of Q if and only if $\varphi_Q(v_1, v_2, ..., v_n)$ is true.*

In *Security-Aware Continuous Query Processing* (SA-CQP), we introduce a new type of predicates called *security predicates*, which determine whether a query may access arriving data tuples based on the current security restrictions. We distinguish between two types of security predicates, namely: (1) the *data-side security predicates*, which represent the data provider's security policies on the streaming data and (2) the *query-side security predicates*, which describe the query specifier's current access authorizations. SA-CQP enforces access control on data streams by only producing the results that satisfy *both* the query predicates and the security predicates. SA-CQP can be formally described as follows:

DEFINITION 2.2. (*SA-CQP*) *Suppose that a data element $d = (v_1, v_2, ..., v_n)$ from a data stream has n attributes, a query predicate $\varphi_Q(attr_1, attr_2, ..., attr_n)$ on d represents the condition of a given continuous query Q, and a security predicate $\varphi_S(attr_1, attr_2, ..., attr_n)$ on d represents a security policy S. Then, whenever d arrives, security-aware continuous query processing outputs d as a result of Q if and only if $\varphi_Q(v_1, v_2, ..., v_r) \wedge \varphi_S(v_1, v_2, ..., v_n)$ are both true.*

Figure 1 visually depicts the SA-CQP concept. Query predicates are denoted by φ_Q, and security predicates φ_S are composed of two types of security predicates, namely the *data-side security predicates* and the *query-side security predicates* denoted by φ_{ds} and φ_{qs}, respectively. We focus on dynamic security in data stream environments (specifically, changes in access control), while continuous queries are being executed.

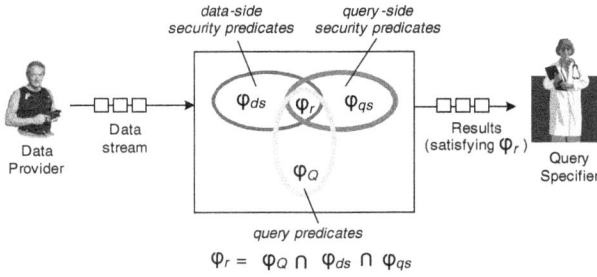

$$\varphi_r = \varphi_Q \cap \varphi_{ds} \cap \varphi_{qs}$$

Figure 1: Conceptual idea of SA-CQP.

3. OVERVIEW OF FENCE FRAMEWORK

To model dynamic security, *FENCE* extends the concept of security punctuations introduced in [9]. *Security punctuations* (or short, *sp*s) are metadata embedded inside data streams that describe the following aspects: (i) who has access rights, (ii) to which streaming data objects, and (iii) when. By processing embedded inside streams *sp*s, a DSMS can easily support *online* flexible, dynamic, and fast access control enforcement over streaming data, while queries are being evaluated.

Figure 2 shows a high level overview of *FENCE* architecture which involves three types of users: (1) a data provider – a user continuously sending his or her streaming data with the interleaved *dsp*s, that describe the real-time security preferences on his or her streaming data; (2) a query specifier – a user who registers a continuous query on the server to be evaluated on the incoming streaming data. As can be seen from Figure 2, a query specifier also streams his or her real-time context (via a data stream), based on which *qsp*s that describe the real-time access privileges of the continuous query are generated; (3) a DSMS administrator – a user responsible for specifying policies that guarantee that correct authorizations are given to the queries based on the context of the query specifiers.

The *Security Analyzer* component in Figure 2 is responsible for generating *qsp*s according to the organization's security policy registered by the DSMS administrator. Both data and query-side security are symmetrically modeled by security punctuations. This *symmetry* facilitates a simpler model and similar processing for both data and query security metadata inside DSMS. When *sp*s arrive, the query processor interprets *sp*s as security predicates by processing the data-side and the query-side *sp*s alike, and then, produces results that satisfy both the query predicates as well as the security predicates.

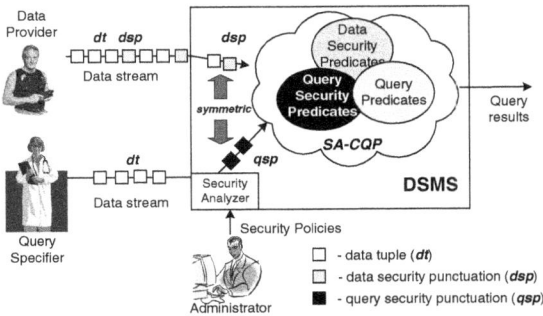

Figure 2: Overview of *FENCE* architecture.

FENCE is a general framework and is not restricted to any particular data or access control model. But to make our discussion concrete here, we first consider a *Role-Based Access Control* (*RBAC*) model [4, 12], and show how it can be implemented in *FENCE*. We

then show in Section 5 how we can support a more general access control model, that is, XACML.

4. MODELING DYNAMIC SECURITY

In this section, we present the schema and the semantics of the security punctuations in *FENCE*. We provide examples of various *sp*s and describe the scenarios of *sp* generation.

4.1 Security Punctuation Schema

In *FENCE*, we employ security punctuations to model symmetrically both the data and the query-side dynamic security restrictions. Such symmetric model makes SA-CQP simpler and allows security-related code re-use in DSMS. We call the *sp*s representing data provider's preferences for security – the *data security punctuations* (*dsp*s) and the *sp*s representing the query specifiers' access privileges – the *query security punctuations* (*qsp*s). Figure 3 shows a general *sp* schema applicable to both *dsp*s and *qsp*s. We discuss each field in the *sp* schema next.

- *Punctuation Type* (*pt*): describes whether the punctuation is a data or a query security punctuation.
- *Data Description Part* (*ddp*): specifies which object(s) the access control policy applies to, e.g., which stream(s), tuple(s), or tuple attribute(s) [9].
- *Security Restriction Part* (*srp*): denotes both the access control model type and the subjects authorized by the policy. For example, if RBAC is used (see Section 3), the *srp* specifies RBAC as the model type and a set of role(s) that are authorized by the *sp*.
- *Sign*: indicates whether the authorization represented by the *sp* is positive(i.e., allow) or negative(i.e., deny) (see [13] for more details).
- *Timestamp* (*ts*): is the time when the *sp* was generated.
- *Enforcement* (*et*): indicates the security policy enforcement setting. We distinguish between two types of enforcement, namely the *Deferred* (*D*) enforcement and the *Immediate* (*I*) enforcement, the semantics of which is described in Section 4.2.

Type (*pt*)	Data Description Part (*ddp*)	Security Restriction Part (*srp*)	*sign*	Time-stamp (*ts*)	Enforce-ment (*et*)
dsp/ *qsp*	Stream(s), Tuple(s), Attribute(s) ...	Access Control Model Type & Value	+/-	🕐	I/D

Figure 3: General security punctuation schema.

4.2 Semantics of Security Punctuations

A security policy may be expressed by one or more *sp*s and may apply to zero or more tuples. A set of consecutive *dsp*s or *qsp*s form a "*batch*" of *sp*s which is interpreted as a single access control policy or a complex authorization. All *sp*s of the same policy (or authorization) have the same timestamp *ts* – the time when the policy was created and the *sp*s were generated. If there is no *sp* authorizing access to an object, "denial-by-default" is enforced, i.e., an access to a streaming object is denied unless explicitly allowed.

The security predicate of a security punctuation *sp* (denoted as φ_{sp}) is generated from *ddp*, *srp*, and *sign* of *sp* as follows.

If *sp.sign* is positive(i.e., '+'),
$\varphi_{sp} = (\text{data\_value} \in sp.ddp) \wedge (\text{current\_user} \in sp.srp)$.

If *sp.sign* is negative(i.e., '-'),
$\varphi_{sp} = \neg ((\text{data\_value} \in sp.ddp) \wedge (\text{current\_user} \in sp.srp))$.

For a batch of *sps* consisting of k *sps* (denoted as a set of k *sps*, $\{sp_1, sp_2, ..., sp_k\}$), the security predicate of the batch is generated as follows[3].

$$\varphi_{\{sp_1, sp_2, ..., sp_k\}} = \bigwedge_{i=1}^{k} \varphi_{sp_i}$$

Since we assume "denial-by-default", if there is no positive *sp* in the batch, $\varphi_{\{sp_1, sp_2, ..., sp_k\}} = 0$.

Another important semantic attribute is the access control policy's *enforcement* setting. In traditional DBMSs, the enforcement semantics of security policies is clear – a policy applies to *all* data (i.e., the entire dataset) stored in the system. Furthermore, the policies do *not* change in the middle of query execution, and even if they do, they are not reflected on the results until the query is executed over again. In contrast, In DSMSs, the semantics is not quite so clear. Since data streams are infinite and queries are continuously being evaluated, whenever a new *sps* (with a new policy) arrives, there may be data tuples (that have arrived before the *sp*) and are in the pipelines of the continuous query execution plan, that according to the *sp* are no longer accessible (the reverse may also be true, the previously unaccessible tuples may not be accessed by the query). To properly reflect the users' security preferences in the system, we introduce two ways of policy enforcement, namely the *deferred* and the *immediate* enforcements, specified in the *et* attribute of an *sp*. In the case of the deferred enforcement, a policy represented by an *sp* applies only to the data that arrives *after* the *sp*, i.e., the tuples whose timestamps are greater than that of the *sp*. For example, if a user carrying a cell phone device enters a casino, he or she may want to instantly prevent others from knowing his or her precise whereabouts. Thus, an *sp* with the deferred enforcement will be injected into his stream transmitting the user's real-time location updates. With the immediate enforcement setting, the new policy affects both the (near past) data that has arrived to the DSMS *before* the current *sp* as well as to the future data that follows *after* it. Hence, the policy here may apply to both the "historic" and the "future" data. For example, in some applications, e.g., health monitoring, or financial applications, users cannot afford to wait for the arrival of new streaming data after a policy changes. In a healthcare application, this could be a matter of saving a patient's life.

Figure 4 visually illustrates the difference between the immediate and deferred enforcement semantics. Consider sp_7, where 7 is the timestamp of the *sp*. Tuples denoted by the integers 1 through 6 represent the data tuples that have arrived before the sp_7, and tuples 8 through 11 after the sp_7. With the immediate enforcement, sp_7's policy will apply to tuples 1 through 11. With the deferred enforcement, sp_7's policy will only apply to tuples 8 through 11. To support the immediate security enforcement, we only consider the streaming data that is inside DSMS (Figure 4). A recent past data window can be further customized based on the application needs, e.g., last 1 hour of data only. To enable the immediate security policy enforcement, we maintain a global window W_G of the streaming data in DSMS , and W_G periodically slides purging the data tuples that will no longer be needed.

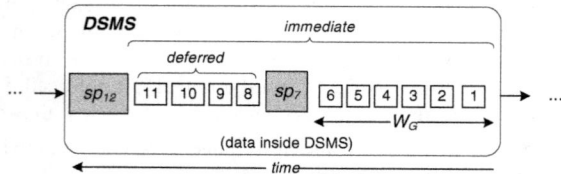

Figure 4: *sp* immediate and deferred enforcement.

---

[3] Here, for simplicity, we assume that *sps* of a batch are combined in conjunction. However, it can be adopted to other operations such as disjunction, intersect, and override.

4.3 Examples of Security Punctuations

Consider the following data streams: S_1 – a heart data stream, S_2 – a blood pressure data stream and S_3 – a respiration data stream. Let $R = \{D_1, D_2, D_3, D_4, D_5\}$ be the set of roles in DSMS[4]. The following *dsps* and *qsps* may specified[5]:

Data Security Punctuations

dsp_1: <dsp|S_1,*,*|D_2|+|12:00:00PM|D>
only queries registered by a cardiologist (role D_2) can query the stream S_1 (heart rate) after this punctuation arrives due to deferred semantics (i.e., $dsp_1.et = D$). This is an example of a *stream level policy*.

dsp_2: <dsp|*,[30,120],*|D_4|+|12:00:00PM|D>
only queries registered by a general physician (role D_4) can access data tuples (from any data stream) of patients with ids between 30 and 120, after this punctuation arrives ($dsp_2.et = D$). This is an example of a *tuple level policy*.

dsp_3: <dsp|$\{S_1, S_2\}$,*,$\{HeartBeat\}$|$\{D_2, D_5\}$|+|12:00:00PM|I>
only a cardiologist (D_2) or a nurse-on-duty (D_5) can query the heart beat from streams S_1 and S_2. This is an example of an *attribute level policy*.

Query Security Punctuations

qsp_1: <qsp|null|D_1|+|12:00:00PM|D>
query acquires a role of a dermatologist (D_1) with deferred enforcement, i.e., the role applies to the query after the arrival of qsp_1 and will pertain to the data tuples with the timestamp greater than $qsp_1.ts$.

qsp_2: <qsp|S_1,*,*|D_4|+|12:00:00PM|D>
query acquires a general physician (D_4) role and the current authorization of role D_4 is the permission to only access stream S_1 (heart data stream). The enforcement is deferred.

qsp_3: <qsp|null|$\{D_2, D_5\}$|null|12:00:00PM|I>
query now acquires roles D_2 and D_5 with an immediate enforcement.

Combination of DSPs and QSPs

To determine which data tuples, the query currently has access to, the intersection of the data and the query security punctuations is evaluated [9, 15]. Only if the intersection between the policies of *dsps* and the authorizations of *qsps* is non-empty, the access to the streaming data elements is granted.

5. SUPPORTING XACML POLICIES

In this section we show how our security punctuation approach can support a complex access control policy language, like XACML.

5.1 A Brief Introduction to XACML

An XACML policy consists of one or more rules. A rule specifies an atomic authorization constraint, that is, which access request can be authorized or denied under which conditions. A rule thus consists of three major components:

- Effect: it specifies the rule decision. It can take two values: "Permit" to authorize the access request; "Deny" to refuse the access request.

- Target: it specifies the set of access requests the rule is intended to restrict.

- Condition: it is a Boolean combination of predicates specifying when the rule applies to a request.

---

[4] The roles can be as follows: D_1 = dermatologist, D_2 = cardiologist, D_3 = hospital employee, D_4 = general physician, and D_5 = nurse-on-duty.

[5] The different fields in an *sp* are separated by a vertical bar "|".

The target, in turn, consists of three components:

- Subject: it specifies a set of subjects, requesting accesses to the protected resources.

- Resource: it specifies the protected resources, such as data, system components or services.

- Action: it specifies a requested operation on the protected resources.

As a policy can include more than one rule and rules may specify different effects (e.g. permit and deny), conflicts may arise among the rules applicable to a given request. To resolve this conflict, XACML provides several combination algorithms such as Deny Override, and Permit Override. The specific combination algorithm to use is also indicated in the policy. In addition to these components, XACML has many additional features to specify general access control policies. However, in the current version of *FENCE*, we only support a basic form of XACML policies. In particular, we assume that policies have no conflicting rules.

Figure 5 shows an example XACML policy; this policy expresses the RBAC authorization encoded by the security punctuation dsp_2 introduced in Section 4.3.[6] The example policy has a single rule with a "permit" effect; therefore this rule gives access. In addition to the effect, the rule has two other elements: $<$Target$>$ and $<$Condition$>$. The target specifies that the access requests to which the rule applies are read requests for the S1 stream by role D4. The condition specifies that specifies that the rule applies to the requests only when the id of the data is between 30 and 120.

5.2 Encoding XACML Policies into Security Punctuations

As the example in Figure 5 shows, even the specification of a simple policy consisting of only a rule requires quite a verbose statement. We have thus developed an approach by which the essential policy information is extracted and used for constructing the components of the security punctuations, that is: the Data Description Part (i.e., object), the Security Restriction Part (i.e., subject), and the Sign (i.e., allow or deny). The Type and Enforcement components are obtained from the context of the policy, whereas the Time-stamp is set to the current time. The resulting security punctuation is then encoded according to a bitmap representation in order to further reduce the size.

Fields in Punctuations	Corresponding XACML parts
data description part	
- stream level	//Policy/Rule/Target/Resource/ResourceMatch/AttributeValue
- tuple level	//Policy/Rule/Condition
- attribute level	//Policy/Rule/Target/Subjects/Subject/SubjectMatch/AttributeValue
security restriction part	//Policy/Rule/Target/Subjects/Subject/SubjectMatch/AttributeValue
sign	if (//Policy/Rule/@Effect == "Permit") then '+' else '-'
type	derived from where the policy comes from
enforcement	derived from the context of the policy
time-stamp	current time

Table 1: Mapping between security punctuations and XACML policies with XPATH expressions.

Table 1 shows the mapping between the security punctuations and XACML policies which use XPATH expressions for denoting the protected objects. If a policy consists of more than one rule, each rule is represented as an individual security punctuation. The policy thus is represented by a batch of consecutive security punctuations as discussed in Section 4.2.

---

[6] Note that XACML is able to represent all policies that can be expressed in RBAC, as XACML is a more general model than RBAC. We refer the reader to [14] for details about modeling RBAC with XACML. As a result, in *FENCE* one can encode RBAC policies by using the native format provided by *FENCE* or in XACML.

Figure 5: An Example of XACML Access Control Policy.

In order to reduce the size of the security punctuations we encode them using a bitmap representation as illustrated in Figure 6(a). Our bitmap representation directly maps the security punctuation schema into a compact form of bitstring. Figure 6(b) shows an example of the bitmap representation which encodes the data security punctuation dsp_2 introduced in Section 4.3. The field for a binary selection such as *type*, *sign*, and *et* is represented as a single bit. In the example, *type* = 0 (means dsp), *sign* = 1 (means positive), and *et* = 1 (means differed enforcement). *ddp* is represented by three different parts of the bitstring which specify the stream level(s), the tuple level(t_1 and t_2), and the attribute level(a), respectively. *ddp.s* represents an ID of a data stream which will be affected by the policy. As in the example, 0 means any data stream. *ddp.t_1* and *ddp.t_2* are used to represents a condition of tuples which should be satisfied for enforcing the policy. In our representation, the condition is described as a range from the minimum value *ddp.t_1* to the maximum value *ddp.t_2*. By default, the attribute of the range is the ID of the data provider. For other attributes, the attribute ID is described in *ddp.a*. Consider the policy in Figure 5; this policy is enforced for all the tuples whose provider ID is between 30 and 120. *ddp.a* represents the ID of a data stream attribute. In the example, 0 means any attribute. *srp* represents the ID of a role identifying the subject to whom the policy applies. In the example, role 4 (i.e., a general physician) can access data. *ts* represents the time (in ms.) when the *sp* is generated.

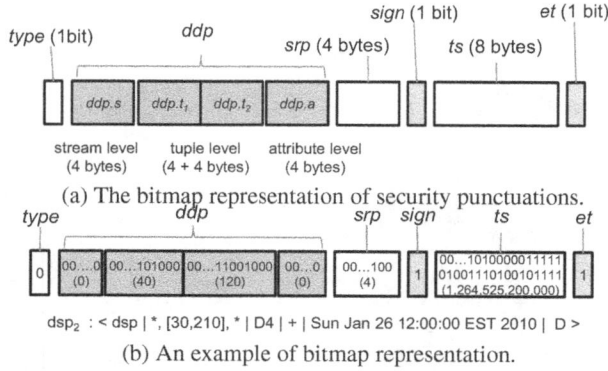

(a) The bitmap representation of security punctuations.

dsp_2 : < dsp | *, [30,210], * | D4 | + | Sun Jan 26 12:00:00 EST 2010 | D >

(b) An example of bitmap representation.

Figure 6: The bitmap representation of security punctuations and an example of the encoding.

Here, we assume that IDs and attributes of data streams are integer (i.e., 4 bytes). In this bitmap representation, a security punctuation encoding the XACML policy in Figure 5 only requires 227 bits, whereas when expressed in XML requires 2,686 bytes.

With respect to the time required for translating the policies from the XML format into our bitmap representation, we note that such translation is executed only when the data providers introduce some new policies. In most cases, the data providers will have available a repository of XACML policies, already encoded as bitmaps, from which to select the policies to use for certain data or based on certain context. Under our approach, each time a new policy is introduced, the system will translate it into the corresponding bitmap representation and store it into the policy repository for future re-use. As such the time required for the mapping of a policy is amortized over multiple embeddings of the same policy.

6. QUERY PROCESSING IN FENCE

In order to support efficient SA-CQP, the following key issues must be addressed: (1) how should the query predicates and the security predicates be evaluated together, (2) how should the security predicates be adapted, whenever a new *dsp* or a *qsp* arrives, and (3) how should the immediate and the deferred enforcement semantics be efficiently and correctly executed. In this section, we address the above issues by presenting the two alternative query processing methods. To motivate our proposed solutions, we begin with a naive method.

6.1 Naive Approach

A naive method for query processing with dynamic security takes a very simple approach, it completely separates the access control processing from regular CQP. Such strategy evaluates security predicates at a designated point – either before or after query execution plan. The former and the latter strategies are also known as *pre-filtering* and *post-filtering*, respectively [9]. Figure 7 illustrates the naive approach along with *FENCE* approach which integrates access control processing with query processing. Here, $A,...Z$ represent the input data streams with the embedded in them *dsp*s from data providers, and C represents a stream transmitting *qsp*s.

In naive pre-filtering method, a security filter, which discards data elements that do not satisfy the security predicates is placed *before* the query execution plan. Therefore, only the data tuples that the query has the access rights to can enter the query plan, e.g., [16, 17]. The post-filtering method is the reverse of the pre-filtering: the query predicates are evaluated first, and then the results get filtered *post-mortem* based on the access control policy of the data and the access rights of the query. In both the pre- and

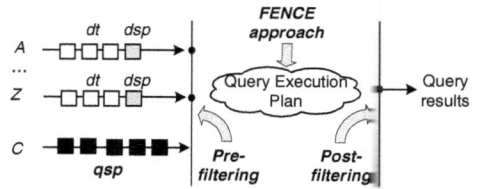

Figure 7: Query processing with *sps*.

the post-filtering methods, the fixed placement of the access control filters may add significant processing overheads and considerably limit query performance. If the access control policies are "loose", but the query predicates are very selective, the pre-filtering method may result in a heavy security-related processing overhead prior the query execution plan. This may be unnecessary, if the query predicates end up discarding the majority of the tuples anyways. In contrast, the post-filtering method may introduce the unnecessary processing overhead when very expensive query predicates (e.g., joins, groups by) are evaluated first, only for the tuples to be discarded later by the security predicates, due to query not having the access rights to them.

In the following sections, to overcome the limitations of the naive method, we propose two efficient SA-CQP methods employed in *FENCE*, namely the *Security Filter Approach* (*SFA*) and the *Query Rewrite Approach* (*QRA*). Both *SFA* and *QRA* have a key advantage – they *integrate* security processing together with traditional query processing and can adapt to not only data-related but also security-related selectivities. Such deep integration with traditional continuous query processing can help reduce the waste of resources, when few subjects have access rights to data.

6.2 Security Filter Approach (SFA)

The main idea of *SFA* is to introduce a special physical operator that performs access control-based filtering into the query execution plan. We call this new operator a *Security Shield Plus* (SS^+) operator[7], and it is handled just like any other traditional query operator in query processing and query optimization. SS^+ operator can be viewed as a "select operator" that filters input data tuples based on the security predicates determined based on the arrived *dsp*s and *qsp*s. The filtering condition of SS^+ changes dynamically whenever a new *dsp* or a *qsp* arrives. Figure 8 shows how the *SFA*-based SA-CQP works with SS^+ operators. The triangle-shaped operators in the figure are the SS^+ operators filtering data based on the security predicates of the query. Just like for an ordinary select operator, the location of SS^+ in the query plan is determined by the query optimizer according to the selectivities of the security predicates. If the selectivity is high, the SS^+ operator is pushed down in the query plan to come before the operators with lower selectivity (similar to "selection pushdown"). Contrary to traditional select operator, however, SS^+ is a stateful operator: it stores the most recently arrived *dsp*s and *qsp*s in its buffers: $Buffer_{dsp}$ and $Buffer_{qsp}$, respectively[8], and computes their intersection to determine the current security predicates to for filtering data. We describe the detailed algorithms for SFA in Appendix A.

By encapsulating all security processing inside SS^+ operators, *SFA*-based SA-CQP can interleave security predicates with traditional query predicates. *SFA*, however, may require substantial modifications to the codebases of the current DSMSs (see Section

---

[7] SS^+ is similar in spirit to the initially proposed *Security Shield* (SS) operator in [9], however, its semantics is more sophisticated, providing support for both *dsp*s and *qsp*s with richer semantics.

[8] As mentioned in Section 4.1, all *sps* that belong to the same policy have the same timestamp *ts*. Therefore, $Buffer_{dsp}$ and $Buffer_{qsp}$ store the *sp*s for data and queries respectively, that have arrived most recently and have the same *ts*.

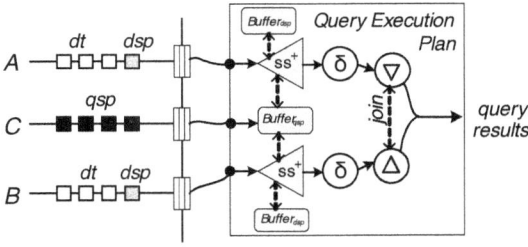

Figure 8: *SFA*-based SA-CQP.

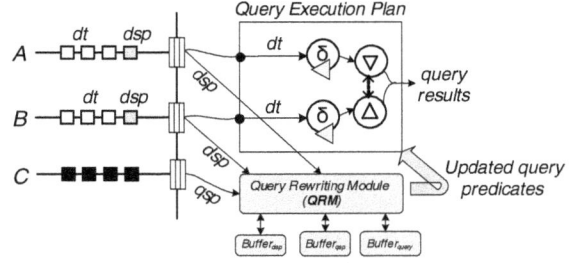

Figure 9: *QRA*-based SA-CQP.

6.4). In the next section, we propose another SA-CQP approach that minimizes the need to change existing DSMSs and largely reuses them as they are.

6.3 Query Rewrite Approach (QRA)

The main idea behind the *QRA*-based SA-CQP comes from the observation that dynamic enforcement of security policies can be seen as a "dynamic rewriting of queries"[9]. According to the SA-CQP definition (in Section 2), we consider a query registered in DSMS that consists of query predicates and security predicates, where security predicates are updated whenever a new *sp* arrives. A DSMS can support dynamic security changes in SA-CQP by creating a "new" query with the integrated in it latest security predicates and replacing with it the current query. Table 2 shows the example of the query rewriting method. Here, the original query predicate $(R.a = S.a) \wedge (0 < R.b < 100) \wedge (0 < S.c < 100)$ is rewritten into $(R.a = S.a) \wedge (0 < R.b < 50) \wedge (50 < S.c < 100)$ to reflect the access control policies described by the dsp_1 and the qsp_1.

Table 2: Example of query rewriting.

Original Predicates	Rewritten Predicates
$Q.p_1 \rightarrow (R.a = S.a)$	$Q.p_1' \rightarrow R.a = S.a$
$Q.p_2 \rightarrow (0 < R.b < 100)$	$Q.p_2' \rightarrow 0 < R.b < 50 \quad //Q.p_2 + dsp_1$
$Q.p_3 \rightarrow (0 < S.c < 100)$	$Q.p_3' \rightarrow 50 < S.c < 100 \quad //Q.p_3 + qsp_1$
$dsp_1 \rightarrow (0 < R.b < 50)$	
$qsp_1 \rightarrow (50 < S.c < 100)$	

Figure 9 gives an overview of the *QRA*-based SA-CQP. Compared to *SFA*, where SS^+ operators process *sps* in the query plan, the *QRA* uses a centralized module, called the *Query Rewriting Module* (*QRM*), to process *sps*. QRM consumes *dsps* and *qsps* immediately upon their arrival to the system and stores them in the global $Buffer_{dsp}$ and the $Buffer_{qsp}$, respectively. QRM also stores traditional query predicates in the $Buffer_{query}$. Whenever new *sps* arrive, QRM rewrites the corresponding query using the information stored in these buffers. Regular data stream tuples are processed by the query processor in the same way as in traditional DSMSs. We note that *sps* are not sent into the query execution plan, but rather consumed by the *QRM* module to generate a new query. In that regard, the query operators do not need to be "security punctuation-aware" as in the *SFA*. We describe the detailed algorithms for QRA in Appendix B.

QRA has the advantage of minimizing the need for modification of the existing DSMS components, e.g., query algebra, optimization rules, and the executor. Since the approach produces a new (rewritten) form of the same query to adapt to dynamic security policies, the existing query processor and the optimizer can be largely re-used (as they are) to implement the SA-CQP. In the next section, we discuss the pros and the cons of the *SFA* and the *QRA* in more detail.

6.4 Pros and Cons of QRA and SFA

The major difference between the *QRA* and the *SFA* is the abstraction level of the security predicates. In the *QRA*, security predicates are represented as logical conditions of a query. In contrast, in the *SFA*, security predicates are encapsulated in separate physical (SS^+) operators in the query execution plan. This difference contributes to both the pros and the cons of the approaches.

The main advantage of the *QRA* is that the existing query processor infrastructure can be largely re-used as it is, since the *sps* are not propagated into the query execution plan. Here, a query plan consist of only "traditional" query operators and the dynamic changes in the access control are implemented by the *Query Rewriting Module* (*QRM*). The QRM is nearly all that needs to be added to the system in this case. Conceptually, the *QRA* treats the existing query optimizer as a "black box" and invokes it as a sub-routine, with a query specification that integrates both the query and the security predicates. Such approach is faithful to the goal of minimizing code changes in existing systems, but may result in a blow-up in optimization time by a factor equal to the number of sub-routine invocations. In the worst case, this may happen every time a new *dsp* or a *qsp* arrives to the system. Clearly, the main disadvantage here is that this approach is not very robust to dynamic changes in security. Potentially, every new *dsp* and *qsp* may lead to the query plan rewriting, the optimizer re-invocation and the physical query plan migration, thus consuming the precious resources from producing continuous query results.

The main advantages of the *SFA* include its high performance and robustness to dynamic changes in security. Whenever a new *qsp* or *dsp* arrives, only the SS^+ operators are affected to reflect the changes in security policy, and the rest of the query plan does not need to be modified. The *SFA* approach is also more amenable to shared query processing in the case of multiple queries. If queries have the same query predicates (even if their authorizations are different), the processing can be shared with the proper security filters installed before and after the shared sub-part in the execution plan. Introducing new operators into the query algebra and making the existing query operators security-aware, however, brings its disadvantages. The query optimizer must now become aware of these new operators, their semantics and must also adjust the cost model to reflect the streaming *sps* statistics and the cost of their processing. In summary, the codebase of DSMS may need to undergo significant changes to accommodate the security-awareness inside the query processor.

7. EXPERIMENTAL STUDY

In this section, we report the results of our experimental evaluation of *FENCE* to answer the following questions:

- How effective is security punctuation mechanism (with embedded into streams *dsps* and *qsps*) compared to alternatives? (Section 7.2)

---

[9]Query rewriting is generally used to compose queries or manage views. In this paper, we exploit the query rewriting concept for the purpose of combining security and query predicates to adapt to dynamic changes in access control.

- How do the *SFA* and the *QRA* methods compare against each other, and against the naive approach in terms of query performance? (Section 7.3)

- How big is the overhead of access control enforcement relative to the cost of continuous query execution? (Section 7.4)

- How much can we reduce the size of the XACML policies with our encoding method? How large is the overhead of the encoding method? (Section 7.5)

7.1 Experimental Setup

We have implemented *FENCE* in a prototype DSMS called *CAPE* [11]. All our experiments are run on a machine with Java 1.6.0.0 runtime, Windows Vista with Intel(R) Core(TM) Duo CPU @1.86 GHz processor and 2GB of RAM. We use an XML DOM parser for encoding XACML policies into security punctuations. For the experiments, we consider a geo-social networking application scenario described in Section 1. For data, we use the *Network-based Moving Objects Generator* [18] to generate data streams with total of 110K moving objects (e.g., people driving in cars with GPS devices, pedestrians walking on the streets with mobile phones) in the city of Worcester, MA USA. We have instrumented the generated data streams with two additional attributes, namely the "age" and the "interests". The values for the "age" attribute follow a normal distribution with mean $\mu = 20$, and the values for the "interests" attribute are randomly generated out of 10 possible choices, e.g., `dating`, `friendship`, `movies`, etc. Each data tuple also contains a timestamp.

In our setup, we've considered a scenario, where *dsp*s are generated by data providers on their physical devices, and the streaming data arrives to the DSMS with already interleaved *dsp*s. The *dsp*s in the data streams describe the *tuple-granularity* access control policies, i.e., a security policy applies to an entire tuple, and thus, implicitly to all of its attributes. All tuple policies are described by a *single dsp* or a *single qsp*. We decided to represent policies using a single *sp* as this, in our belief, is likely to represent the most frequent case. Only occasionally, more complex security policies may require multiple *sp*s to represent it. Roles in our experimental setup, $R_1, R_2 \ldots R_n$ represent various *real-life* "roles" of subjects encountered in a geo-social networking application, e.g., R_1 may represent a "`family member`", R_2 a "`friend`", R_3 a "`stranger`", R_4 a "`co-worker`"..

When determining a query for our experiments, we envisioned a query that allows people to "connect" to each other based on similar interests, age and current geographic location (for example, to spontaneously meet at a nearby coffee shop). We thus use the following query in our experiments:

```
SELECT * FROM S1, S2, CoffeeShops AS CS
  WHERE distance(S1.loc, S2.Loc) < 5 AND
  maxdistance(S2.loc, S3.Loc, CS) < 5 AND
  intersect(S1.interests, S2.interests) AND
  difference(S1.age, S2.age) < 10
```

This query may be executed by a user in a geo-social networking application, where one stream ($S1$) represents his or her data stream and another data stream ($S2$) of other users.

To simulate dynamic *query-side* security policies, we insert a new *qsp* periodically into the stream transmitting *qsp*s. *qsp*s are generated using random role assignments from $R_1 \ldots R_{30}$. The default *dsp* to tuple ratio is 1:10, which means there is one *dsp* per 10 tuples. The average policy size in *dsp*s is 5 roles. The *qsp* to data ratio is 1:100, which means that for every 100 data stream elements (data tuples + *dsp*s), a new *qsp* is generated. The *qsp*s depict only role changes. For simplicity, we've omitted the changes in the

privileges of roles that could be specified in *qsp*s (e.g., by organizations). Unless mentioned otherwise, the default parameters and their values used in the experiments are as specified in Table 3.

Table 3: Default experimental parameters.

Parameter	Value	Description
dsp/t	1:10	Average *dsp* to tuple ratio
qsp/(dsp/t)	1:100	Average *qsp* to (*dsp* + tuple ratio)
φ_{ds}	5 roles	Average size (in # of roles) of *dsp*s
φ_{qs}	10 roles	Average size (in # of roles) of *qsp*s
P_{ds}	*tuple-level*	Data-side policy applicability (i.e., policy level)
P_{qs}	*role-change*	Query-side authorization
et	Deferred	Default enforcement semantics
$|W_G|$	1000 tuples	Size of W_G window

To simulate dynamic changes in security policies, we imitate different possible real-life scenarios. The generation of security policies with changing characteristics is managed as follows: we start with an initial set of parameters, and over time the parameter values are varied, e.g., for frequency variation, the transition: $(1/1) \rightarrow (1/10) \rightarrow (1/30) \rightarrow (1/50) \rightarrow (1/100)$ (illustrated in Table 4), means that initially *sp* to tuple ratio was 1 to 1 (i.e., every tuple has a unique policy), after some time it was changed to 1 to 10, and then to 1 to 30 and so on. Other kinds of transitions in security policies are depicted in Table 4.

Table 4: Security dynamicity characteristics.

Frequency variation: $(1/1) \rightarrow (1/10) \rightarrow (1/30) \rightarrow (1/50) \rightarrow (1/100)$
Scope variation: $(|R| = 1) \rightarrow (|R| = 10) \rightarrow (|R| = 50) \rightarrow (|R| = 100)$
Intersection variation: $(\varphi_{ds \cap qs} = 0) \rightarrow (\varphi_{ds \cap qs} = 0.5) \rightarrow (\varphi_{ds \cap qs} = 1)$

7.2 Effectiveness of Security Punctuations

Our first set of experiments compares the performance of the three alternative access control mechanisms on streaming data: (1) non-streaming, (2) tuple-embedded, and (3) security punctuation-based (see Figure 10(a) and 10(b)). We refer to them in the charts as *non-streaming*, *tuple* and *sp*, respectively. In the case of non-streaming method, the tuple policies arrive to the system separately from the data. We assume that in the non-streaming case, users specify their policies using SQL, and send them separately over the network. When SQL-based access control policies are received, the non-streaming method parses them and stores them in a global policy hash table. For each arriving data stream tuple, the non-streaming method checks this policy table to retrieve all relevant security policies. In tuple-embedded approach, tuples' schema is extended by adding an additional attribute to store the access control policies. Thus, each individual tuple carries its access control policy, i.e., all authorized roles that are allowed to access it. In the *sp* approach, *dsp*s are interleaved with the streaming data. For the query-side dynamic policy changes, we use a stream of *qsp*s to simulate the changes in the roles of the executing query (in all three cases).

Figure 10(a) compares the average output rates for the three alternatives. As can be seen, the average output rate using the *sp* approach is significantly higher than for the alternative methods(ranging from 30%-55% compared to the non-streaming approach and 8% to almost 70% to the tuple-based approach). Obviously, the lower the *sp* to tuple ratio, i.e., more policies are shared by data tuples, the more advantageous the *sp* approach becomes. We note that, in *sp* model, sharing of policies is easy, and since they are already interleaved with the data, a lot of processing overhead is minimized (e.g., determining which policies are applicable to which data tuples), since *sp*s always precede their associated data.

Figure 10(b) shows the average execution cost for the three alternatives, which follows a similar pattern as described above for

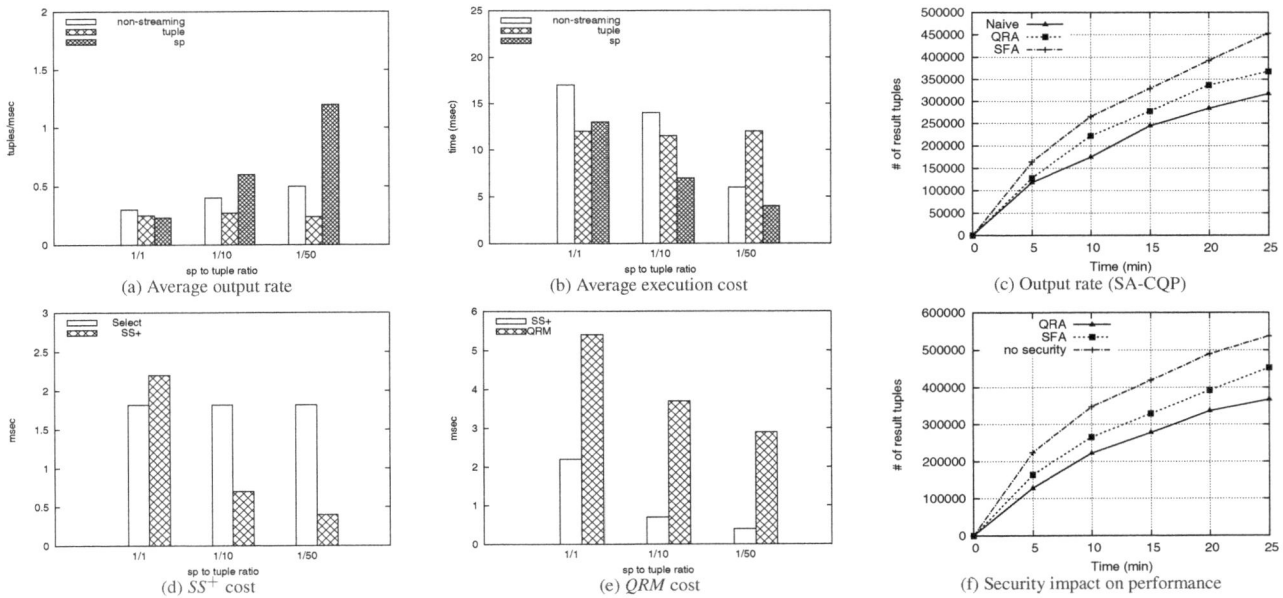

Figure 10: Experimental results in query processing.

the average output rate. The *sp* approach has a slightly higher cost for the 1/1 case, as there is a distinct *dsp* for each tuple, consuming more space, and requiring more processing. However, if policies are shared, which is the most likely scenario in a typical application, the *sp* approach significantly outperforms the other methods.

7.3 Comparison of SA-CQP Methods

In this experiment, we've compared the performance of the security-aware query processing alternatives (described in Section 6), specifically the naive approach, the security filter approach (*SFA*) and the query rewriting approach (*QRA*). In the naive approach, we've used the post-filtering method. We ran the query for 25 minutes several times, each time varying the dynamic security characteristics as depicted in Table 4. Figure 10(c) shows the total number of result tuples produced over time when using these different query processing strategies. As a general trend, we have observed that, the *SFA* has about 14 to 22% higher output rate than the *QRA* and 24 to 37% higher than the *Naive* approach. Clearly, we can see that the fixed placement of security processing, often can limit query performance in the case where the security conditions are largely dynamic.

7.4 Overhead of Security Enforcement

In this experiment, we evaluate the "overhead" of continuous access control enforcement on continuous query performance. We begin by first measuring the processing costs specific to the *SFA* and the *QRA*. Then, we compare the output rate of "security-free" continuous query execution (as a base case) to the output rates of the SA-CQP methods. Lastly, we present the overall overhead of these SA-CQP methods relative to the total query execution cost.

As can be seen from Figure 10(d), for the 1/1 *sp* to tuple ratio, the SS^+ cost is close to the cost of select operator. There is an additional overhead in SS^+ to compute a filtering predicate based on the arriving *dsp*s and *qsp*s, that is not present in the regular selection and accounts for the disparity in the 1/1 case. However, as one can observe, the more tuples share the same security policies, the smaller the overhead of the SS^+ operator becomes compared to selection.

In Figure 10(e), we present our comparison of the security pro-

cessing cost in the *QRA* method, specifically, the average execution cost of the query rewriting module (*QRM*). Here, we only measure the cost of the query plan rewriting. As can be seen, the *QRM* execution has a higher overhead compared to SS^+ execution (in some cases, by as much as 80%). The reason for such big cost discrepancy is that in SS^+, only a policy intersection with the opposite buffer needs to be performed (which in most cases consists of only a single *sp*). Whereas, the *QRM* module has to scan through all query predicates in the query to determine if the security predicates from the newly arrived *sp* can be combined with any of the existing query predicates.

To evaluate the impact of continuous access control enforcement on query performance, we ran the query with and without security-awareness enabled. Figure 10(f) shows the total number of tuples produced over time for both methods compared to traditional continuous query execution as a baseline. We have abstracted the total security overhead in each method and illustrate it in Figure 11. As can be seen, query rewriting approach, on average, results in 21% overhead compared to the query execution cost, whereas query filter approach in only 7%. The more frequently *sp*s arrive (i.e., the more dynamic the policies are), the larger is the *QRM*'s overhead.

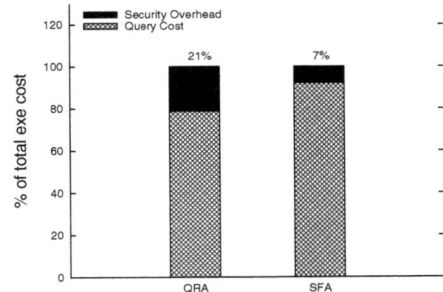

Figure 11: Security enforcement overheads.

7.5 Efficiency of the XACML Encoding Method

We now focus on the security punctuation mechanism in order to assess the efficiency of our approach for the encoding of XACML policies. In these experiments, we use the following four sets of XACML policies:

- Set 1: it is a set consisting of policies which have the same structure of the policy in Figure 5.

- Set 2: a set of policies which have one more element compared to the policies in Set 1 (i.e., there are two roles affected by the policies).

- Set 3: a set of policies which have one more <CONDITION> element compared to the policies in Set 1 (i.e., the condition of the policies consists of two predicates connected with conjunction).

- Set 4: a set of policies which have one more <SUBJECT> and <CONDITION> elements compared to the policies in Set 1 (i.e., two roles in the subject and two predicates in the condition).

Figure 12(a) reports the result of the comparison between the size of the XACML policies and size of the encoded security punctuations. The results show that our encoding method reduces the size from 98.04% (for the policies in Set 1) to 97.61% (for the policies in Set 4). Notice that, even though the size of XACML policies are not quite different, the policies in the each test sets require a different number of punctuations for their representation; for example, the policies in Set 1 are represented by one sp, whereas the policies in set Set 2 and Set 3 require two sps, and the policies in Set 4 three sps.

Figure 12(b) reports the encoding time for the various policy sets. From the results, we can see that the processing time is proportional to the size of XACML policies (and not to the number of encoded punctuations). The reason is that the most expensive part of the encoding is the parsing of the XACML policies. Almost 83% of the encoding time (in Set 1) is due to the XML parsing which conducted only once for an XACML policy.

The results in Figure 12(c) show the advantage of an approach whereby policies are pre-encoded and stored in a policy repository in their encoded format. The results show that the advantage increases as the ratio of re-used policies increases. As we already mentioned in Section 5, we think the situation in which the same policies are re-used is likely to be very common since the access control policies are routinely applied according to the context of users or systems.

8. RELATED WORK

Streaming Databases. In the past few years, streaming databases became a hot topic [19]. The notion of *punctuations* has been first presented in [20] as a delimiter to partition infinite streams into finite sub-streams. Punctuation as an unblocking mechanism for blocking operators (e.g., sort) to purge the state has been proposed in [21, 22, 23]. [9] proposed to implement security on data streams via punctuations. However, the work has only considered the changes in the data-side security policies, overlooking the problem of dynamic security for continuous queries. We fill this gap in this paper and extend the security punctuation model to support dynamic security for both data and queries.

Security and Privacy Preservation. Agrawal et al coined the concept of Hippocratic databases [24] to incorporate the privacy protection within RDBMS. Hippocratic databases use privacy metadata to represent the data owner's privacy preferences and the the data collector's privacy policies. The data is outputted only when the policies meet the preferences. The work focuses on relational databases only and does not address the challenges present in the streaming context.

The notion of continuous access control has been introduced by Sandhu et al. as part of the *UCON* model [25, 26]. To the best of our knowledge, apart from the initial theoretical paper, our work is the first real instance of the *UCON* model. One of the reasons for the lack of real systems is that it is difficult to implement in practice [25]. Our work is the first to do so. [27] proposed a data stream access control framework based on rewriting queries. Compare to the work, *FENCE* focuses on the dynamic changes of access control policies. The problem of access control in dynamic environments has raised significant interests in research community [28, 29, 30]. [31] extends RBAC model to Temporal-RBAC, which supports periodic role enabling and disabling and temporal dependencies among permissions. GEO-RBAC [32] is an RBAC with spatial awareness. For most of these access control models, however, the changes in policies do not get reflected on the results until the query is re-executed after the change.

Context-aware access control. Another area of related work is the context-awareness in access control. The main idea here is to employ contextual parameters as inputs to the access control model (e.g., a context-sensitive RBAC model 33]). In our paper, we accommodate the requirements of context-aware access control by providing support for: (1) generation of security punctuations based on the real-time context data streams, and (2) support for the immediate enforcement of security policies.

XACML. Recently, XACML is widely used in distributed information systems and serviced oriented systems [34]. However, even though service deployments and requests are dynamic in these systems, adopting access control policies still tend to be static just like in traditional information systems. In our work, we exploit the XACML to represent dynamic changes of access control policies in data streams. There are several compression techniques developed to save the network bandwidth. The comparison and analysis among these techniques can be found in [35]. XACML compression also have been studied by Qing [8]. The work exploits popular compression techniques such as GZip and wbXML for efficient communication in mobile environments. In [36], XACML policies are converted into compact representations to build a high-speed XACML enforcement engine. In our work, instead of compressing XML documents, we provide an encoding method to overcome the verbose nature of XML.

9. CONCLUSION AND FUTURE WORK

In this paper, we address the problem of continuous access control enforcement in streaming environments, where both data and query security restrictions may change while queries are being executed. We have proposed *FENCE* framework, where data and query access control policies are modeled symmetrically using *dsps* and *qsps*. We have implemented our approach in a prototype DSMS. Our experimental results show that *FENCE* has low overheads and is suitable for data stream environments where security is dynamic. We also have provided an encoding method which transforms XACML access control policies into small-sized security punctuations. We have shown that the overhead of the encoding is low. We believe our work makes an important contribution to both fields of databases and security in that it is the first to propose and implement a practical approach for online continuous access control enforcement.

In the future, we plan to explore the sp mechanism even further. One possible direction is to extend the sp model to support streaming data integrity to provide assurance that the streaming data is not altered during the transmission.

10. ACKNOWLEDGEMENTS

The work reported in this paper has been partially supported by NSF under grants CNS-1111512 and CNS-0964294. Hyo-Sang

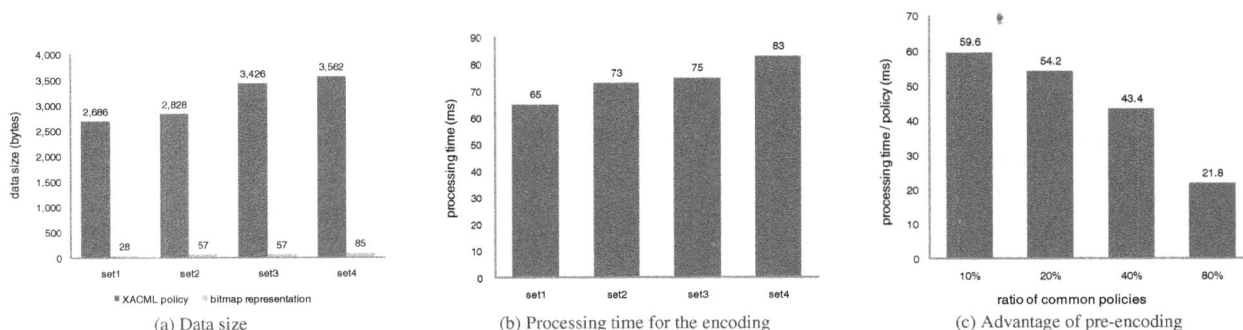

Figure 12: Experimental results in the XACML support.

(a) Data size   (b) Processing time for the encoding   (c) Advantage of pre-encoding

Lim has been supported by Basic Science Research Program through the National Research Foundation of Korea(NRF) funded by the Ministry of Education, Science and Technology (NRF-2012R1A1 A1042875).

11. REFERENCES

[1] E. Wu et al., "High-performance complex event processing over streams," in *SIGMOD*, 2006, pp. 407–418.

[2] L. Golab and M. T. Ozsu, "Issues in data stream management," *SIGMOD Rec.*, vol. 32, no. 2, pp. 5–14, 2003.

[3] M. Ali et al., "Nile-PDT: a phenomenon detection and tracking framework for dsmss," in *VLDB*, 2005, pp. 1295–1298.

[4] R. Sandhu et al., "Role-based access control models," *IEEE Computer*, vol. 29, no. 2, pp. 38–47, 1996. [Online]. Available: citeseer.ist.psu.edu/sandhu96rolebased.html

[5] The Carbon Project, "http://www.thecarbonproject.com/."

[6] XACML and O. S. S. T. Committee, "Extensible access control markup language (xacml) committee specification 2.0," 2005.

[7] E. Bertino and A. Squicciarini, "A flexible access control model for web services," in *Proceedings of the 6th International Conference On Flexible Query Answering Systems*, 2004, pp. 13–16.

[8] R. Qing and C. Adams, "A comparison of compression techniques for xml-based security policies in mobile computing environments," in *Proceedings of the Workshop on New Challenges for Access Control (NCAC)*, April 27, 2005, pp. 209–232.

[9] R. Nehme et al., "Security punctuation framework for enforcing access control on streaming data," in *ICDE*, 2008.

[10] R. Nehme et al., "FENCE: Continuous Access Control Enforcement in Dynamic Data Stream Environments," in *ICDE*, 2010.

[11] E. Rundensteiner et al., "Cape: Continuous query engine with heterogeneous-grained adaptivity," in *VLDB*, 2004.

[12] D. Ferraiolo et al., "Proposed NIST standard for role-based access control," *ACM Trans. Inf. Syst. Secur.*, vol. 4, no. 3, pp. 224–274, 2001.

[13] E. Bertino et al., "An extended authorization model for relational databases," *TKDE*, vol. 9, no. 1, pp. 85–101, 1997.

[14] R. Ferrini and E. Bertino, "Supporting RBAC with XACML+OWL," 14th ACM Symposium on Access Control Models and Technologies(SACMAT 2009), Stresa, Italy, June 3-5, 2009.

[15] D. Wijesekera and S. Jajodia, "A propositional policy algebra for access control," *ACM TISSEC*, vol. 6, no. 2, pp. 286–325, 2003.

[16] W. Fan, C. Chan, and M. Garofalakis, "Secure XML querying with security views," in *SIGMOD*, 2004, pp. 587–598.

[17] S. Rizvi et al., "Extending query rewriting techniques for fine-grained access control," in *SIGMOD*, 2004, pp. 551–562.

[18] T. Brinkhoff, "Generating network-based moving objects," in *SSDBM*, 2000, p. 253.

[19] M. Hammad et. al., "Efficient execution of sliding-window queries over streams." Purdue University, Tech. Rep., 2003.

[20] P.Tucker et al., "Applying punctuation schemes to queries over data streams." *IEEE Data Eng. Bull.*, vol. 26, no. 1, 2003.

[21] L. Ding, N. Mehta, E. A. Rundensteiner, and G. T. Heineman, "Joining punctuated streams," in *EDBT*, 2004, pp. 587–604.

[22] L. Ding and E. A. Rundensteiner, "Evaluating window joins over punctuated streams," in *CIKM*, 2004, pp. 98–107.

[23] H. Li et al., "Safety guarantee of continuous join queries over punctuated data streams," in *VLDB*, 2006, pp. 19–30.

[24] R. Agrawal, J. Kiernan, R. Srikant, and Y. Xu, "Hippocratic databases," in *VLDB*, 2002, pp. 143–154.

[25] J. Park and R. Sandhu, "Towards usage control models: beyond traditional access control," in *SACMAT*, 2002, pp. 57–64.

[26] J. Park et al., "The UCON-ABC usage control model," *ACM Trans. Inf. Syst. Secur.*, vol. 7, no. 1, pp. 128–174, 2004.

[27] B. Carminati et al., "A framework to enforce access control over data streams," *ACM Trans. Inf. Syst. Secur.*, vol. 13, no. 3, 2010.

[28] C. Ribeiro et al., "Spl: An access control language for security policies with complex constraints," in *NDSSS*, 2001.

[29] P. Bonatti et al., "An algebra for composing access control policies," *ACM TISSEC*, vol. 5, no. 1, pp. 1–35, 2002.

[30] M. Backes et al., "An algebra for composing enterprise privacy policies," in *Res. Report 3557, IBM Research*, 2004.

[31] E.Bertino et al., "TRBAC: A temporal role-based access control model," *ACM Trans. Inf. Syst. Secur.*, vol. 4, no. 3, pp. 191–233, 2001.

[32] M. Damiani et al., "GEO-RBAC: A spatially aware RBAC," *ACM TISSEC*, vol. 10, no. 1, 2007.

[33] A. Kumar, N. Karnik, and G. Chafle, "Context sensitivity in role-based access control," *SIGOPS Oper. Syst. Rev.*, vol. 36, no. 3, pp. 53–66, 2002.

[34] Y. Demchenko et al., "Policy based access control in dynamic grid-based collaborative environment," in *Proc. The 2006 International Symposium on Collaborative Technologies and Systems*, 2006, pp. 14–18.

[35] C. Augeri et al., "An analysis of xml compression efficiency," in *Proceedings of the 2007 workshop on Experimental computer science*, 2007.

[36] A. X. Liu et al., "Xengine: a fast and scalable XACML policy evaluation engine," in *SIGMETRICS*, 2008.

APPENDIX

A. DETAILED ALGORITHMS FOR SFA

Since the rest of processing is similar to traditional CQP, we only explain the execution of SS^+ operator[10]. Figure 13 shows the pseudocode for SS^+ execution. If the input to SS^+ is a security punctuation (*dsp* or *qsp*), the *security_predicates* variable that represents the current intersection of the data and the query security policies gets updated to reflect the changes in policies (Step 3). If the input is a data tuple, it is propagated to the next operator in the pipeline

---

[10]To preserve the correct security semantics during execution, traditional query operators in *SFA* need to be modified to become "security punctuation-aware", as described in [9].

if and only if the data tuple's security policy satisfies the *security_predicates* condition, otherwise, the tuple is discarded (Step 8).

Algorithm **SSPlusExecution**(*o* – streaming object)
1: **if** (*o.type* == "security punctuation") **then**
2:     *sp* ← *o*
3:     *security_predicates* ← **ProcessSp**(*sp*)
4:     **if** (*sp.et* == "immediate") **then**
5:         **ProcessImmediateSp**(*sp*)
6:     **end if**
7: **else if** (*o.type* == "data tuple") **then**
8:     **if** (*o* does not satisfy *security_predicates*), discard *o*
        else propagate *o*
9: **end if**

Figure 13: SS^+ execution in *SFA*.

Figure 14 shows the algorithm for computing the *security_predicates* in SS^+ operator. Every newly arrived *sp* is intersected with the security buffer storing the opposite type of *sps*, e.g., $qsp \cap Buffer_{dsp}$ (Step 2) and $dsp \cap Buffer_{qsp}$ (Step 5). This intersection is stored in the *security_predicates* variable, which represents the current filtering condition.

Algorithm **ProcessSp**(*sp* – security punctuation)
1: **if** (*sp.pt* == "qsp") **then**
2:     *security_predicates* ← Intersect(*sp*, $Buffer_{dsp}$)
3:     update $Buffer_{qsp}$ with *sp*
4: **else if** (*sp.pt* == "dsp") **then**
5:     *security_predicates* ← Intersect(*sp*, $Buffer_{qsp}$)
6:     update $Buffer_{dsp}$ with *sp*
7: **end if**
8: **return** *security_predicates*

Figure 14: Processing of *sp* in SS^+ .

If an *sp* has an immediate enforcement setting (Step 4 in Figure 13), in addition to the change in the *security_predicates* variable (to be reflected on the future data), the historic data in the W_G window (which has arrived earlier than the *sp*) must be re-processed to be affected by the changes in the policy. To efficiently handle the immediate enforcement, we introduce a notion of the "narrowing intersection scope" for security policies. Informally, the narrowing means that the updated *security_predicates* (representing access control filtering condition) is more selective than prior to the change. Definition A.1 formally describes the narrowing scope.

DEFINITION A.1. *Let φ_i be the security predicate at time ts_i and φ_j at time ts_j ($ts_i < ts_j$). If the security predicate has changed between time ts_i and ts_j (i.e., $\varphi_i \neq \varphi_j$), and if $\exists$ any data tuple d that makes $\varphi_j(d)$ = false but makes $\varphi_i(d)$ = true, the policy scope is said to be narrowing.*

Figure 15 shows the algorithm for processing the immediate *sps* using the notion of narrowing for optimizing the immediate enforcement execution. If the scope is narrowing, it means that there may be tuples in the query pipeline that might have already passed through the SS^+ (based on the earlier security policies), but now are no longer accessible (because of the narrowed intersection of policies). Therefore, to enforce the access control in such case immediately, it is enough to consider only the data tuples that have already passed the SS^+ in the query plan. To prevent that data from being outputted as results, the new SS^+ operator is activated at the root of the execution plan until all of the pipelined data (that has arrived prior to the *sp*) is processed (Step 3). Otherwise, if the policy is *not* narrowing, the tuples stored in the W_G must be re-processed using the plan to immediately see the results (otherwise, possibly not produced) thus reflecting the new security policy (Step 5 and 6).

This can be done by clearing the data tuples from all of the query operators' queues, and then, feeding the data tuples from W_G into the query plan.

Algorithm **ProcessImmediateSp**(*sp* – sec. punctuation)
1:   *scope* ← *DeterminePolicyScope*(*sp*)
2:   **if** (*scope* == "narrowing") **then**
3:     *ActivatePostFiltering*(*sp*)
4:   **else**
5:     discard all data tuples in the query plan
6:     start query processing with W_G
7:   **end if**

Figure 15: Processing of "immediate *sps*"

B. DETAILED ALGORITHMS FOR QRA

Figure 16 shows the pseudocode for the *QRA*-based SA-CQP algorithm. Compared to the *SFA* which implements SA-CQP using SS^+ operators, *QRA* realizes SA-CQP by executing the *QRM*, which may rewrite the entire query execution plan in an effort to combine the security predicates with the query predicates. In the algorithm in Figure 16, if the input is an *sp*, the *QRM* rewrites the continuous query plan to integrate the new security predicates into the execution plan (Step 3). The processing for the immediate enforcement is the same as in the *SFA*-based algorithm. If the input is a regular data tuple, the query processor evaluates it as in the regular continuous query processing (Step 8). We note that, in the context of *QRA*, the *QRM* is a separate module from the query processor module, thus, largely not requiring any modifications to the DSMS optimizer and executor.

Algorithm **QRA_SA-CQP**(*o* – streaming object)
1: **if** (*o.type* == "security punctuation") **then**
2:     *sp* ← *o*
3:     **RewritingQuery**(*sp*)
4:     **if** (*sp.et* == "immediate") **then**
5:         **ProcessImmediateSp**(*sp*)
6:     **end if**
7: **else if** (*o.type* == "data tuple") **then**
8:     do continuous query processing with *o*
9: **end if**

Figure 16: SA-CQP using *QRA*.

Figure 17 shows the query rewriting algorithm used by the *QRM*. Just like in the *SFA* algorithm, the *dsps* and the *qsps* are intersected to produce the updated security predicates (Step 2 and 5). In addition to this intersection, *QRA* also intersects the security predicates with the query predicates to produce the predicates to be used in the query execution (equivalent to φ_r in Figure 1) (Step 9). The rewritten continuous query is optimized by the optimizer, and the new plan replaces the previously used execution plan (Steps 10-11).

Algorithm **RewritingQuery**(*sp* – security punctuation)
1: **if** (*sp.pt* == "qsp") **then**
2:     *security_predicates* ← Intersect(*sp*, $Buffer_{dsp}$)
3:     update $Buffer_{qsp}$ with *sp*
4: **else if** (*sp.pt* == "dsp") **then**
5:     *security_predicates* ← Intersect(*sp*, $Buffer_{qsp}$)
6:     update $Buffer_{dsp}$ with *sp*
7: **end if**
8: *query_predicates* ← Find($Buffer_{query}$, current query)
9: *new_Q* ← Intersect(*security_predicates*, *query_predicates*)
10: *new_qp* ← Optimize(*new_Q*)
11: replace current query plan with *new_qp*

Figure 17: Algorithm for query rewriting.

Mining Parameterized Role-Based Policies

Zhongyuan Xu
Department of Computer Science
Stony Brook University, USA
zhoxu@cs.stonybrook.edu

Scott D. Stoller
Department of Computer Science
Stony Brook University, USA
stoller@cs.stonybrook.edu

ABSTRACT

Role-based access control (RBAC) offers significant advantages over lower-level access control policy representations, such as access control lists (ACLs). However, the effort required for a large organization to migrate from ACLs to RBAC can be a significant obstacle to adoption of RBAC. Role mining algorithms partially automate the construction of an RBAC policy from an ACL policy and possibly other information. These algorithms can significantly reduce the cost of migration to RBAC.

This paper defines a parameterized RBAC (PRBAC) framework in which users and permissions have attributes that are implicit parameters of roles and can be used in role definitions. Parameterization significantly enhances the scalability of RBAC, by allowing much more concise policies. This paper presents algorithms for mining such policies and reports the results of evaluating the algorithms on case studies. To the best of our knowledge, these are the first policy mining algorithms for a PRBAC framework. An evaluation on three small but non-trivial case studies demonstrates the effectiveness of our algorithms.

Categories and Subject Descriptors: D.4.6 [**Operating Systems**]: Security and Protection—*Access Controls*; H.2.8 [**Database Management**]: Database Applications—*Data Mining*

Keywords: role mining; role-based access control

1. INTRODUCTION

Role-based access control (RBAC) offers significant advantages over lower-level access control policy representations, such as access control lists (ACLs). However, the effort required for a large organization to migrate from ACLs to RBAC can be a significant obstacle to adoption of RBAC. Role mining algorithms partially automate the construction of an RBAC policy from an ACL policy and possibly other information, such as user attributes. These algorithms can significantly reduce the cost of migration to RBAC.

Several versions of the role mining problem have been proposed. The most widely studied versions involve finding a minimum-size RBAC policy consistent with (i.e., equivalent to) given ACLs. Another important version of the problem arises when user attribute information is available. In this case, it is also desirable to maximize interpretability (also called "semantic meaning") of role membership with respect to the attribute information—in other words, to find roles whose membership can be characterized well using the attributes—and to minimize as policy size. Similarly, if permissions have attributes, interpretability of the set of permissions granted to each role can also be taken into account in an overall policy quality metric.

Allowing roles to have parameters significantly enhances the scalability of RBAC, by allowing much more concise policies. Parameterization is especially useful for expressing application-layer security policies. For example, consider a policy for a university. To grant different permissions to users (*e.g.*, faculty or students) in different classes or departments, in an RBAC model without parameters, we would need to create a separate role and corresponding permission assignment rules for each course or department, leading to a large and unwieldy policy. In a parameterized RBAC model, this policy can be expressed using a few policy statements parameterized by the class identifier or department name.

This paper defines an expressive parameterized RBAC (PRBAC) framework that supports a simple form of attribute-based access control (ABAC). In our framework, (1) users and permissions have attributes that are implicit parameters of roles, (2) the set of users assigned to a role is specified by an expression over user attributes, and (3) the set of permissions granted to a role is specified by an expression over permission attributes. We make role parameters implicit, rather than explicit, because it makes the framework and algorithms slightly simpler; our approach can easily be adapted to handle roles with explicit parameters. Every user and permission has an "id" attribute containing a unique name, so specifying the users and permissions associated with a role by enumeration, as in traditional RBAC, is a simple case of (2) and (3), respectively.

The main contribution of this paper is two algorithms for mining PRBAC policies from ACLs, user attributes, and permission attributes. To the best of our knowledge, it is the first policy mining algorithm for any parameterized RBAC framework or ABAC framework. At a high level, both algorithms work as follows. First, a conventional role mining algorithm is used to generate a set of candidate roles; attributes and parameterization are not considered in this step. For a policy like the above example, this step would produce a separate role granting appropriate permissions to the chair of each department. Second, the algorithm attempts to form parameterized roles by merging sets of candidate roles from the first step; the resulting parameterized roles are added to the set of candidate roles. Containing the example, this step would form a parameterized role from the set of roles containing the chair role for each department. Third, the algorithm decides which of the candidate roles generated in the first two steps to include in the final policy. Inspired by [13], we consider two strategies for this. The *elimination* strategy repeatedly removes low-quality roles from the set of candidate roles, until no more roles can be removed without losing some of the permissions granted in the given ACL policy. The *selection* strategy repeatedly selects the highest-quality candidate role for inclusion in the PRBAC policy, until all permissions granted in the given ACL policy are granted by the PRBAC policy. For each of these two algorithms, we first present a simpler version that does not consider role hierarchy, and then present a version that generates hierarchical policies.

To evaluate whether these algorithms can successfully generate meaningful parameterized roles, we wrote three small but non-trivial PRBAC policies, generated ACL policies and attribute data from them, ran our algorithms on the resulting ACL policies and attribute data, and compared the mined PRBAC policies with the original policies. One of our algorithms successfully reconstructed the original PRBAC policies for all three case studies.

There are several directions for future work: applying the algorithms to more and larger case studies and developing better insight into when the algorithms succeed at producing intuitively desirable policies; adapting the algorithms to support a more conventional form of PRBAC in which role parameters are explicit; exploring algorithms for updating existing PRBAC policies, like StateMiner does for RBAC policies [10]; and exploring algorithms for mining ABAC policies. Our PRBAC framework already supports a simple form of ABAC. More thorough support for ABAC requires extending attribute expressions to allow membership tests for set-valued attributes, linear constraints for numerical attributes, etc., and then extending the policy mining algorithms to handle these features.

Section 2 defines our PRBAC framework. Section 3 defines the PRBAC mining problem. Section 4 presents our algorithms. Section 6 evaluates the algorithms on case studies. Section 7 discusses related work.

2. PARAMETERIZED RBAC (PRBAC)

PRBAC policies refer to attributes of users and permissions. User-attribute data is represented as a tuple $\langle U, A_U, f_U \rangle$, where U is a set of users, A_U is a set of user attributes, and f_U is a function such that $f_U(u, a)$ is the value of attribute a for user u. There is a special user attribute called uid that has a unique value for each user. This allows traditional identity-based roles to be represented in the same way as other roles. Similarly, permission-attribute data is represented as a tuple $\langle P, A_P, f_P \rangle$, where P is a set of permissions, A_P is a set of permission attributes, and f_P is a function such that $f_P(p, a)$ is the value of attribute a for permission p. Informally, a permission may be regarded as involving a resource and an operation, and a permission attribute may be an attribute of the resource or an attribute (i.e., argument) of the operation. There is a special permis-

sion attribute called pid that has a unique value for each permission. Let AttrVal be the set of all legal attribute values. We assume AttrVal includes a special value "$\perp$" that indicates that the value of an attribute is unknown.

Attribute expressions are used to express the sets of users and permissions associated with roles. A *conjunctive user-attribute expression* e_c is a function from user attributes A_U to $\mathrm{Set}(\mathrm{AttrVal} \setminus \{\perp\}) \cup \{\top\}$. The symbol $\top$ denotes the set of all legal values for an attribute. We say that expression e_c *uses* an attribute a if $e_c(a) \neq \top$. We refer to the set $e_c(a)$ as the conjunct for attribute a. A user u satisfies expression e_c, denoted $u \models e_c$, iff $(\forall a \in A_U : f_U(u, a) \in e_c(a))$. For example, if $A_U = \{\mathrm{dept}, \mathrm{level}\}$, the function e_c with $e_c(\mathrm{dept}) = \{\mathrm{CS}\}$ and $e_c(\mathrm{level}) = \{\mathrm{undergrad}, \mathrm{grad}\}$ is a conjunctive user-attribute expression, which we write with syntactic sugar as $\mathrm{dept} = \mathrm{CS} \wedge \mathrm{level} \in \{\mathrm{undergrad}, \mathrm{grad}\}$ (note that, when $e_c(a)$ is a singleton set $\{v\}$, we may write the conjunct as $a \in \{v\}$ or $a = v$). An *user-attribute expression* is a set, representing a disjunction, of conjunctive user-attribute expressions. A user u satisfies a user-attribute expression e, denoted $u \models e$, iff $(\exists e_c \in e : u \models e_c)$. The meaning of a user-attribute expression e, denoted $[\![e]\!]_U$ is the set of users that satisfy it: $[\![e]\!]_U = \{u \in U \mid u \models e\}$. We say that a user-attribute expression e *characterizes* $[\![e]\!]_U$. We say that e *uses* an attribute a if some conjunctive user-attribute expression in e uses a. The definitions of *conjunctive permission-attribute expression* and *permission-attribute expression* are similar, except using the set A_P of permission attributes instead of the set A_U of user attributes. The meaning of a permission-attribute expression e, denoted $[\![e]\!]_P$ is the set of permissions that satisfy it: $[\![e]\!]_P = \{p \in P \mid p \models e\}$.

Constraints are used to express parameterization. Traditional PRBAC frameworks use explicit role parameters to indirectly express equalities between user attributes and permissions attributes; in our framework, such equalities are expressed directly, as constraints. For example, consider the policy that the chair of a department can update the course schedule for the department. This can be expressed using explicit role parameters by introducing a role chair(dept) and using a permission assignment rule such as PA(chair(dept), $\langle$write, courseSchedule(dept)$\rangle$). In our framework, we would define a chair role with the chairs of all departments as members, with permissions to write all course schedules, and with the constraint that the user's department equals the permission's department. The constraint ensures that each member of the role gets only the appropriate permissions. Informally, attributes used in the constraint act as role parameters.

A *constraint* is a set of equalities of the form $a_u = a_p$, where a_u is a user attribute and a_p is a permission attribute. User u and permission p satisfy constraint c, denoted $u, p \models c$, if for each equality $a_u = a_p$ in c, $f_U(u, a_u) = f_P(p, a_p)$.

A *core PRBAC policy* is a tuple $\langle U, P, R \rangle$ where U is a set of users, P is a set of permissions, and R is a set of roles, each represented as a tuple $\langle e_u, e_p, c \rangle$, where e_u is a user-attribute expression, e_p is a permission-attribute expression, and c is a constraint. For a role $r = \langle e_u, e_p, c \rangle$, let $\mathrm{uae}(r) = e_u$, $\mathrm{pae}(r) = e_p$, and $\mathrm{con}(r) = c$.

For example, the role $\langle$uid $= \{\mathrm{Alice}, \mathrm{Bob}\}, \mathrm{operation} = \mathrm{write} \wedge \mathrm{resource} = \mathrm{courseSchedule}, \mathrm{dept} = \mathrm{dept}\rangle$ has members Alice and Bob, has permissions to write course schedules for all departments (because the department attribute of the course schedule is not restricted by the permission-attribute expression), and has constraint dept = dept. If

$f_U(\text{Alice}, \text{dept}) = \text{CS}$ and $f_U(\text{Bob}, \text{dept}) = \text{EE}$, the constraint ensures that Alice only gets permission to write the CS course schedule, and Bob only gets permission to write the EE course schedule.

The user-permission assignment $\text{UPA}(\pi)$ induced by a policy π is defined by

$$\text{asgndU}(r, U) = \{u \in U \mid u \models \text{uae}(r)\}$$
$$\text{asgndP}(r, P) = \{p \in P \mid p \models \text{pae}(r)\}$$
$$\text{asgndUP}(r, U, P) = \{\langle u, p \rangle \in \text{asgndU}(r, U) \times \text{asgndP}(r, P) \mid u, p \models \text{con}(r)\}$$
$$\text{UPA}(\langle U, P, R \rangle) = \bigcup_{r \in R} \text{asgndUP}(r, U, P)$$

A *hierarchical PRBAC policy* is a tuple $\pi = \langle U, P, R, RH \rangle$, where U, P, and R are the same as in a core PRBAC policy, and the role hierarchy RH is an acyclic transitive binary relation on roles. A tuple $\langle r, r' \rangle$ in RH means that r is junior to r' (or, equivalently, r' is senior to r). This means that r inherits members from r', and r' inherits permissions from r. This is captured in the equations

$$\text{ancestors}(r, R, RH) = \{r' \in R \mid \langle r, r' \rangle \in RH\}$$
$$\text{descendants}(r, R, RH) = \{r' \in R \mid \langle r', r \rangle \in RH\}$$
$$\text{authU}(r, U, R, RH) = \text{asgndU}(r, U) \cup \bigcup_{r' \in \text{ancestors}(r, R, RH)} \text{asgndU}(r', U)$$
$$\text{authP}(r, P, R, RH) = \text{asgndP}(r, P) \cup \bigcup_{r' \in \text{descendants}(r, R, RH)} \text{asgndP}(r', P)$$

The user-permission assignment $\text{UPA}(\pi)$ induced by a hierarchical PRBAC policy π is defined by:

$$\text{authUP}(r, U, P, R, RH) = \{\langle u, p \rangle \in \text{authU}(r, U, R, RH) \times \text{authP}(r, P, R, RH) \mid u, p \models \text{con}(r)\}$$
$$\text{UPA}(\langle U, P, R, RH \rangle) = \bigcup_{r \in R} \text{authUP}(r, U, P, R, RH)$$

In the definition of $\text{authUP}(r, U, P)$, all authorized users and permissions of r, including the inherited ones, are subject to the constraint associated with r. However, constraints are not "inherited"; in particular, the constraint associated with a role r affects only r's contribution to the user-permission relation induced by the policy.

3. THE PROBLEM

A core PRBAC policy $\pi = \langle U, P, R \rangle$ is *consistent* with an ACL policy $\pi' = \langle U', P', UP' \rangle$ if $U = U'$, $P = P'$, and $\text{UPA}(\pi) = UP'$. A hierarchical PRBAC policy $\pi = \langle U, P, R, RH \rangle$ is *consistent* with an ACL policy $\pi' = \langle U', P', UP' \rangle$ if $U = U'$, $P = P'$, and $\text{UPA}(\pi) = UP'$.

A *policy quality metric* is a function from PRBAC policies to a totally-ordered set, such as the natural numbers. The ordering is chosen so that small values indicate high quality; this might seem counter-intuitive at first glance but is natural for metrics based on policy size.

The *core PRBAC policy mining problem* is: given an ACL policy π' and policy quality metric Q_{pol}, find a core PRBAC policy π that is consistent with π' and has the best quality, according to Q_{pol}, among policies consistent with π'. The *hierarchical PRBAC policy mining problem* is the same except that π is a hierarchical PRBAC policy.

Our algorithms aim to optimize the policy's *weighted structural complexity* (WSC), which is a generalization of policy size [8]. The weighted structural complexity of a core PRBAC policy is defined by

$$\text{WSC}(e_c) = \sum_{a \in \text{domain}(e_c)} e_c(a) = \top \,?\, 0 : |e_c(a)|$$
$$\text{WSC}(c) = |c|$$
$$\text{WSC}(\langle e_u, e_p, c \rangle) = w_1 \sum_{e_c \in e_u} \text{WSC}(e_c) + w_2 \sum_{e_c \in e_p} \text{WSC}(e_c) + w_3 \text{WSC}(c)$$
$$\text{WSC}(\langle U, P, R \rangle) = \sum_{r \in R} \text{WSC}(r),$$

where $|s|$ is the cardinality of set s, and the w_i are user-specified weights. The weighted structural complexity WSC_H of a hierarchical PRBAC policy is defined in the same way, except with an additional term $w_4 |RH|$, where the size of the role hierarchy RH is the number of tuples in it.

4. ALGORITHMS

This section presents our algorithms for the problems defined in Section 3.

4.1 Mining Core PRBAC Policies: Elimination Algorithm

Step 1: Generate Candidate Roles.

This step uses a traditional role mining algorithm to generate a set R_{can} of un-parameterized candidate roles without role hierarchy. Each role r in R_{can} is associated with a set $\text{asgndU}(r)$ of assigned users and a set $\text{asgndP}(r)$ of assigned permissions. We use CompleteMiner [11, 12] to generate candidate roles. Briefly, CompleteMiner generates a candidate role for every set of permissions that can be obtained by intersecting the sets of permissions granted to some users by the ACL policy. Note that CompleteMiner's goal is to include every reasonable candidate role in its output; CompleteMiner does not attempt to produce a minimum-sized policy.

We assume that no two candidate roles have exactly the same set of assigned users, and that no two candidate roles have exactly the same set of assigned permissions. This is true for the result of CompleteMiner and other standard role mining algorithms, because two roles with the same set of users or permissions can easily be merged into a single role.

Step 2: Generate Attribute Expressions for Candidate Roles.

This step computes minimum-sized attribute expressions that characterize the assigned users and assigned permissions of each candidate role, with preference given to (1) attribute expressions that do not use uid or pid, since attribute-based policies are generally preferable to identity-based policies, even when they have higher WSC, because attribute-based generalize better, and (2) conjunctive attribute expressions, because they are simpler than attribute expressions that use disjunction (in addition to conjunction).

Given a set s of users and the set U of all users, let $\text{minExpU}(s, U)$ be a minimum-sized user-attribute expression that characterizes s, subject to the preferences described above. Given a set s of permissions and the set P of all permissions, let $\text{minExpP}(s, P)$ be a minimum-sized permission-attribute expression that characterizes s, subject to the preferences described above. In both cases, at least one such attribute expression exists, because attributes uid and pid are present and have a unique value for each user or permission, respectively. For each $r \in R_{can}$, this step sets $\text{uae}(r) = \text{minExpU}(\text{asgndU}(r), U)$ and $\text{pae}(r) = \text{minExpP}(\text{asgndP}(r), P)$.

Our algorithm to compute $\text{minExpU}(s, U)$ appears in Figure 1; the algorithm for minExpP is the same, except that A_U and f_U are replaced with A_P and f_P, respectively. The pseudocode for minExpU simply embodies the preferences described above. It uses an auxiliary function $\text{simplifyExp}(e)$ that simplifies an attribute expression e by repeatedly looking for pairs of conjunctions c_1 and c_2 in e that differ in the value of a single attribute a and replacing c_1 and c_2 with a single conjunction c that agrees with c_1 and c_2 for all attributes except a and that maps a to $c_1(a) \cup c_2(a)$.

The pseudocode for minExpU also uses an auxiliary function minConjExpU that computes a minimum-sized conjunctive user-attribute expression that characterizes s, with preference given to attribute expressions that do not use uid. The first for-loop computes a conjunctive user-attribute expression e that attempts to characterize s without using uid. If this fails, then uid is needed to characterize s, and the algorithm returns a user-attribute expression that uses only uid. Otherwise, the algorithm uses e as a starting point for computation of a minimum-sized user-attribute expression for s that does not use uid. How could a smaller user-attribute expression e' for s differ from e? It cannot be that some conjunct of e' is a strict subset of the corresponding conjunct of e, because then some user in s will not satisfy that conjunct. The only way that e' could differ from e is by replacement of some conjuncts with $\top$. The second for-loop considers all expressions that differ from e in this way.

Step 3: Generate Constraints for Candidate Roles.

We take $\text{con}(r)$ to contain every equality that holds between every assigned user and every assigned permission of r. In other words, for each attribute a_u in A_U and each attribute a_p in A_P, we add the equality $a_u = a_p$ to $\text{con}(r)$ iff $\forall u \in \text{asgndU}(r). \forall p \in \text{asgndP}(r). u, p \models a_u = a_p$. This is the strictest constraint that can be associated with r, because any stricter constraint would incorrectly eliminate some user-permission pairs in $\text{asgndUP}(r, U, P)$. Using the strictest constraint for each role facilitates merging of roles in the next step.

Step 4: Merge Candidate Roles.

This step creates additional candidate roles by merging sets of candidate roles. A set s of roles is *mergeable* if there exists a role r' with the same assigned users, same assigned permissions, and same or larger user-permission assignment as the roles in s collectively, and $\text{asgndUP}(r', U, P) \subseteq UP'$, i.e., if there exists r' such that $\text{asgndU}(r') = \bigcup_{r \in s} \text{asgndU}(r)$ and $\text{asgndP}(r') = \bigcup_{r \in s} \text{asgndP}(r)$ and $\bigcup_{r \in s} \text{asgndUP}(r, U, P) \subseteq \text{asgndUP}(r', U, P) \subseteq UP'$. Assuming that all roles have distinct sets of assigned users and permissions (as mentioned in Step 1), s is mergeable only if there exists a constraint that can be associated with r' that prevents users assigned to one of the roles in s from incorrectly gaining permissions assigned to one of the other roles in s. Thus, to

```
function minExpU(s, U):
    // compute conjunctive and disjunctive user-attribute
    // expressions for s, and then compare them.
1:  e_c = {minConjExpU(s, U)}
2:  e_d = simplifyExp(⋃_{u∈s} minConjExpU(u, U))
3:  if e_c does not use uid and e_d uses uid
4:      return e_c
5:  end if
6:  if e_d does not use uid and e_c uses uid
7:      return e_d
8:  end if
9:  if WSC(e_c) ≤ WSC(e_d)
10:     return e_c
11: else
12:     return e_d
13: end if

function minConjExpU(s, U):
    // check whether uid is needed to characterize s
    // in a conjunctive user-attribute expression.
14: for a in A_U \ {uid}
15:     e(a) = ⋃_{u∈s} f_U(u, a)
16:     if ⊥ ∈ e(a)
17:         e(a) = ⊤
18:     end if
19: end for
20: e(uid) = ⊤
21: if [[e]]_U ≠ s
        // uid is necessary (and sufficient) to characterize s
        // in a conjunctive user-attribute expression.
22:     return f_∅[uid ↦ ⋃_{u∈s} f_U(u, uid)]
23: end if
    // e characterizes s. check if there's a smaller conjunc-
    // tive user-attribute expression that characterizes s.
24: for each non-empty subset A of A_U \ {uid}
25:     e' = e[a ↦ ⊤ for a in A]
26:     if [[e']]_U = s
27:         if WSC(e') < WSC(e)
28:             e = e'
29:         end if
30:     end if
31: end for
32: return e
```

Figure 1: Algorithm to compute $\text{minExpU}(s)$, where s is a set of users, and U is the set of all users. $f[x \mapsto y]$ denotes (a copy of) function f modified so that $f(x) = y$. $f_\emptyset$ denotes the empty function, i.e., the function whose domain is the empty set.

maximize the chance of a successful merge, we identify the strictest constraint that can be associated with r' and then check whether it prevents such gaining of permissions. The constraint associated with r' must not eliminate any user-permission assignment associated with any role in s. From Step 3, for each role r, $\text{con}(r)$ is the strictest constraint that does not eliminate any user-permission assignment associated with r, so $\text{con}(r')$ must be weaker (i.e., less strict) than or equal to $\text{con}(r)$ for each r in s, so the strictest constraint that can be associated with r' is $\text{con}(r') = \bigcap_{r \in s} \text{con}(r)$. If the role r' with the assigned users, assigned permissions, and constraint specified above satisfies $\text{asgndUP}(r', U, P) \subseteq$

```
1:   R' = R_can
     // R_mrg contains roles produced by merging.
2:   R_mrg = {}
     // for each r in R', remove r from R', then attempt to
     // merge r' with each remaining role in R' and each role
     // in R_mrg.
3:   for each r in R'
4:       R' = R' \ {r}
5:       for each r' in R' ∪ R_mrg
6:           r'' = merge({r, r'})
7:           if UPA(r'') ⊆ UP'
8:               R_mrg = R_mrg ∪ {r''}
9:           end if
10:      end for
11:  end for
12:  R_can = R_can ∪ R_mrg
```

Figure 2: Step 4 (Merge Candidate Roles) of elimination algorithm for core PRBAC policy mining.

UP' (note that $\bigcup_{r \in s}$ asgndUP$(r, U, P) \subseteq$ asgndUP(r', U, P) holds by construction), then s is mergeable, and we set uae$(r') = $ minExpU(asgndU$(r'), U)$ and pae$(r') = $ minExpP(asgndP$(r'), P)$ and then add r' to R_{can} (note that we leave the roles in s in R_{can}); if not, s is not mergeable. Let merge(s) denote the role r' defined above.

A simple algorithm for this step attempts to merge every subset s of R_{can}. We optimize the algorithm by exploiting a monotonicity property of merge, namely: $s \subseteq s'$ implies asgndUP(merge$(s), U, P) \subseteq$ UPA(merge$(s'), U, P)$. Thus, if UPA(merge$(s)) \not\subseteq UP'$, the algorithm does not attempt to merge supersets s' of s, because UPA(merge$(s')) \not\subseteq UP'$ holds and hence s' is not mergeable. The algorithm also exploits the property merge$(s \cup \{r\}) = $ merge$(\{$merge$(s), r\})$, which implies that arbitrary merges can be realized by merging in one role at a time. Pseudo-code for this step appears in Figure 2. The general structure of the code is similar to CompleteMiner [11, 12]. Our implementation incorporates another optimization, not shown in Figure 2. The order in which roles are merged does not affect the result, so we extend the algorithm to avoid merging the same roles in different orders. We define an arbitrary total order on roles. For each role r produced by merging, let maxMerge(r) be the largest role used in the merges that produced r. In line 6, if r' was produced by merging, r is merged with r' only if $r > $ maxMerge(r').

Step 5 (Optional): Eliminate Unnecessary Constraints.

For a role r, an equality in con(r) is *unnecessary* if removing it from con(r) leaves asgndUP(r) unchanged. This optional step removes each unnecessary equality from the constraint of each role in R_{can}.

Informally, one cannot tell from the given input whether to include unnecessary constraints in the PRBAC policy, because they do not affect consistency with the given ACL policy. Note that these "unnecessary" constraints may have been useful during merging, because they may help to prevent user-permission assignments from growing when roles are merged, but they provide no benefit after merging. The argument in favor of removing them (after merging) is to reduce policy size and hence increase policy quality. The argument in favor of keeping them is to be more conservative from the security perspective, specifically, to minimize the risk that the policy grants to a new user a permission that the new user should not have. This is related to how well the policy generalizes.

We consider this step as optional; in other words, the user decides whether unnecessary constraints should be removed.

Step 6: Eliminate Low-Quality Removable Candidate Roles.

This step eliminates low-quality removable candidate roles; the remaining roles form the generated PRBAC policy.

A *role quality metric* is a function $Q(r, U, P, R)$, where r is a new role whose quality is returned, U and P are the sets of users and permissions, respectively, R is the set of existing roles, and the range is a totally-ordered set. The ordering is chosen so that large values indicate high quality (note: this is opposite to the interpretation of the ordering for policy quality metrics).

Based on our goal of minimizing the generated policy's WSC, we define a role quality metric that assigns higher quality to roles with smaller WSC that cover more uncovered user-permission pairs; "uncovered" means that the user-permission pairs are not covered by roles in R. We capture this notion of quality using the ratio $\frac{|\text{uncovUP}(r, U, P, R)|}{\text{WSC}(r)}$ as the first component of the role quality metric, where uncovUP(r, U, P, R) is the set of user-permission pairs covered by r and not covered by roles in R. Among roles with the same value of this ratio, we assign higher quality to roles that cover more user-permission pairs. We capture this by using $|\text{uncovUP}(r, U, P, R)|$ as the second component of the role quality metric, and ordering values of the role quality metric lexicographically. In summary, the role quality metric Q is defined as follows.

$$\text{uncovUP}(r, U, P, R) = \text{asgndUP}(r, U, P) \setminus \bigcup_{r' \in R} \text{asgndUP}(r', U, P)$$

$$Q(r, U, P, R) = \langle \frac{|\text{uncovUP}(r, U, P, R)|}{\text{WSC}(r)}, |\text{uncovUP}(r, U, P, R)| \rangle$$

A role r is *removable*, denoted removable(r, U, P, R), if every user-permission pair covered by r is also covered by another role in R. Formally,

$$\text{removable}(r, U, P, R) = \text{asgndUP}(r, U, P) \subseteq \bigcup_{r' \in R \setminus \{r\}} \text{asgndUP}(r', U, P)$$

Pseudo-code for step 6 appears in Figure 3. In each iteration, R contains roles currently known to be in the result policy, and R_{can} contains roles that might later get added to the result policy. The algorithm evaluates removability of a role with respect to $R_{can} \cup R$ (instead of R), in order to minimize the set of roles considered unremovable; this leaves more roles in R_{can}, eligible for removal, and therefore leads to better policy quality. The algorithm evaluates role quality with respect to R, because this provides a better estimate of the role's quality in the final policy.

4.2 Mining Core PRBAC Policies: Selection Algorithm

Steps 1–5 of the selection algorithm for mining core PRBAC policies are the same as in the elimination algorithm for mining core PRBAC policies in Section 4.1. Step 6 is as follows.

```
1:   R = ∅
2:   while UPA(⟨U, P, R⟩) ≠ UP
         // move unremovable roles from candidates R_can
         // to result R.
3:      R_unrm = {r ∈ R_can | ¬removable(r, U, P, R_can ∪ R)}
4:      R_can = R_can \ R_unrm
5:      R = R ∪ R_unrm
         // discard the lowest-quality candidate role
6:      if ¬empty(R_can)
7:         r_min = a role in R_can with minimal quality, i.e.,
8:              ∀r ∈ R_can. Q(r_min, U, P, R) ≤ Q(r, U, P, R).
9:         R_can = R_can \ {r_min}
10:     end if
11:  end while
12:  return ⟨U, P, R⟩
```

Figure 3: Step 6 (Eliminate Low-Quality Removable Candidate Roles) of elimination algorithm for core PRBAC policy mining.

Step 6: Select Roles.

This step selects candidate roles for inclusion in the generated policy. It selects roles from highest quality to lowest, until every pair in the user-permission relation in the given ACL policy is covered. It uses the same role quality metric as Step 6 of the elimination algorithm in Section 4.1. Pseudo-code for this step is as follows.

```
1: R = ∅
2: while UPA(⟨U, P, R⟩) ≠ UP
3:    r_max = a role in R_can with maximal quality, i.e.,
4:         ∀r ∈ R_can. Q(r_max, U, P, R) ≥ Q(r, U, P, R).
5:    R = R ∪ {r_max}
6:    R_can = R_can \ {r_max}
7: end while
8: return ⟨U, P, R⟩
```

4.3 Mining Hierarchical PRBAC Policies: Elimination Algorithm

Steps 1–5 of this algorithm are the same as in the core PRBAC policy mining algorithm in Section 4.1. The remaining steps are as follows.

Step 6: Compute Role Hierarchy.

This step computes all possible role hierarchy relations between candidate roles. Let $r_1 \prec r_2$ if $r_1 \neq r_2 \wedge \text{asgndP}(r_1) \subseteq \text{asgndP}(r_2) \wedge \text{asgndU}(r_1) \supseteq \text{asgndU}(r_2)$. Let RH_{all} be the transitive reduction of $\prec$.

Step 7: Generate Result Policy.

This step starts by storing some current information about each candidate role in auxiliary data structures. Specifically, let $\text{authU}_0(r) = \text{asgndU}(r)$ and $\text{authP}_0(r) = \text{asgndP}(r)$ and $\text{authUP}_0(r) = \text{asgndUP}(r)$. Note that the assigned users and permissions might change as we generate the hierarchical policy, because some assigned users and permissions might become inherited instead. In contrast, the authorized users and permissions of each role r never change, always remaining equal to $\text{authU}_0(r)$ and $\text{authP}_0(r)$, respectively. Similarly, $\text{asgndUP}(r)$ might change, but $\text{authUP}(r)$ always remains equal to $\text{authUP}_0(r)$.

Our algorithm always generates policies with full inheri-

tance [13]. This implies that a role hierarchy edge in RH_{all} is included in the result policy whenever the roles that it connects are included in the policy. Therefore, we associate with each candidate role the cost (WSC) of the edges that will be added to the policy if that role is added. We define a size metric on roles that reflects this: for a role r in R_{can}, and a set R of roles that have already been selected to be in the result policy,

$$\text{sizeof}(r, R, RH_{\text{all}}) =$$
$$\text{WSC}(r) + \tfrac{w_4}{2}|\{r' \in R \mid \langle r, r'\rangle \in RH_{\text{all}} \vee \langle r', r\rangle \in RH_{\text{all}}\}|$$

The coefficient $\frac{w_4}{2}$ (recall that w_4 is introduced in Section 3) reflects that half of the cost of each inheritance relationship is attributed to each of the involved roles.

We define a role quality metric $Q_H(r, R, RH)$ similar to the metric in the non-hierarchical case, except using sizeof instead of WSC and using $\text{authUP}_0(r)$ instead of $\text{asgndUP}(r)$.

$$\text{uncovUP}_H(r, R) = \text{authUP}_0(r) \setminus \bigcup_{r' \in R} \text{authUP}_0(r')$$

$$Q_H(r, R, RH) = \frac{|\text{uncovUP}_H(r, R)|}{\text{sizeof}(r, RH)}$$

We define a function removable similar to the one in the non-hierarchical case, except using $\text{authUP}_0(r)$ instead of $\text{asgndUP}(r)$.

$$\text{removable}_H(r, R) = \text{authUP}_0(r) \subseteq \bigcup_{r' \in R \setminus \{r\}} \text{authUP}_0(r')$$

Pseudo-code for this step appears in Figure 5. It is similar to the pseudo-code in Figure 3 for Step 6 of the elimination algorithm for mining core PRBAC policies. The main difference is that this algorithm calls minExpU and minExpP to update uae(r) and pae(r), respectively, after roles have been added to the set R of roles that will be included in the generated policy. This reflects the fact that, in the presence of role hierarchy, we are free to choose $\text{asgndU}(r)$ in a way that minimizes the WSC of the policy, provided authU(r, U, R, RH) remains equal to $\text{authU}_0(r)$, and similarly for $\text{asgndP}(r)$.

$\text{minExpU}_H(r, U, R, RH)$ returns a minimum-sized user attribute expression for r that excludes users that can be inherited from other roles in R along edges in RH if excluding those users reduces WSC(uae(r)); this is legitimate, because the sets of users assigned to and inherited by a role may overlap. Let inheritedU(r, R, RH) denote the set of users that r inherits, i.e.,

$$\text{inheritedU}(r, R, RH) = \bigcup_{r' \in \text{ancestors}(r, R, RH)} \text{authU}_0(r').$$

Ideally, $\text{minExpU}_H(r, U, R, RH)$ would find a subset s of inheritedU(r) that minimizes WSC(minExpU(authU$_0(r) \setminus s$)) and return minExpU(authU$_0(r) \setminus s$). In practice, trying all subsets s of inheritedU(r, R, RH) would be too slow. An obvious heuristic approximation is to try only the extrema— in other words, only $s = \emptyset$ and $s = \text{inheritedU}(r, R, RH)$. We adopt a heuristic approximation, shown in Figure 4 that is somewhat more thorough and correspondingly more expensive: it is exponential in the number of attributes, but polynomial in the number of users. Similar to our algorithm for minExpU in Figure 1, it starts by constructing an upper-bound expression e (for authU$_0(r)$) without using uid and then considers the expressions obtained setting to ⊤ the conjuncts of e corresponding to each subset of the attributes.

function $\text{minExpU}_{\text{H}}(r, U, R, RH)$:
   // try to construct an expression representing a set
   // in the required range, without using uid
1: for a in $A_U \setminus \{\text{uid}\}$
2:    $e(a) = \bigcup_{u \in \text{authU}_0(r)} f_U(u, a)$
3:    if $\perp \in e(a)$
4:      $e(a) = \top$
5:    end if
6: end for
7: $e(\text{uid}) = \top$
8: for each non-empty subset A of A_U
9:    $e' = e[a \mapsto \top$ for a in $A]$
10:   // try to remove values from conjuncts of e'
11:   for a in $A_U \setminus A$
12:     for v in $e(a)$
13:       $e'' = e'[a \mapsto e'(a) \setminus \{v\}]$
14:       if $\text{isInRange}(e'', r, R, RH)$
15:         $e' = e''$
16:       end if
17:     end for
18:   end for
19:   if $\text{isInRange}(e', r, R, RH) \wedge \text{WSC}(e') < \text{WSC}(e)$
20:    $e = e'$
21:   end if
22: end for
23: if $\text{isInRange}(e, r, R, RH)$
24:    return e
25: end if
   // uid is need to represent a set in the required range.
   // choose the smallest set in that range, to get the
   // smallest expression.
26: return $f_\emptyset[\text{uid} \mapsto \bigcup_{u \in \text{authU}_0(r) \setminus \text{inheritedU}(r, R, RH)} f_U(u, \text{uid})]$

   // check whether $[\![e]\!]_U$ is in the required range
   function $\text{isInRange}(e, r, R, RH)$:
27: return $\text{authU}_0(r) \setminus \text{inheritedU}(r, R, RH) \subseteq [\![e]\!]_U$
28:      $\wedge \; [\![e]\!]_U \subseteq \text{authU}_0(r)$

Figure 4: Algorithm for $\text{minExpU}_{\text{H}}(r, U, R, RH)$.

1: $R = \emptyset$
2: while $\text{UPA}(\langle U, P, R, RH \rangle) \neq UP$
    // move unremovable roles from candidates R_{can}
    // to result R.
3:    $R_{unrm} = \{r \in R_{can} \mid \neg\text{removable}_{\text{H}}(r, R_{can} \cup R)\}$
4:    $R_{can} = R_{can} \setminus R_{unrm}$
5:    $R = R \cup R_{unrm}$
    // update uae and pae of candidate roles,
    // based on updated R
6:    for r in R_{can}
7:      $\text{uae}(r) = \text{minExpU}_{\text{H}}(r, R, RH_{\text{all}})$
8:      $\text{pae}(r) = \text{minExpP}_{\text{H}}(r, R, RH_{\text{all}})$
9:    end for
    // discard the lowest-quality candidate role
10:   if $\neg\text{empty}(R_{can})$
11:    $r_{\min} = $ a role in R_{can} with minimal quality, $i.e.,$
12:        $\forall r \in R_{can}. \; Q_{\text{H}}(r_{\min}, R, RH) \leq Q_{\text{H}}(r, R, RH)$.
13:    $R_{can} = R_{can} \setminus \{r_{\min}\}$
14:    remove tuples containing $r_{\min}$ from RH_{all}
15:   end if
16: end while
17: $\text{finalizePolicy}(R, RH_{\text{all}})$

   procedure $\text{finalizePolicy}(R, RH_{\text{all}})$:
   // adjust uae and pae of roles in policy, based on final
   // role hierarchy, to reduce WSC.
18: for r in R
19:    $\text{uae}(r) = \text{minExpU}_{\text{H}}(r, R, RH_{\text{all}})$
20:    $\text{pae}(r) = \text{minExpP}_{\text{H}}(r, R, RH_{\text{all}})$
21: end for
22: $RH = \{\langle r, r' \rangle \in RH_{\text{all}} \mid r \in R \wedge r' \in R\}$
23: return $\langle U, P, R, RH \rangle$

Figure 5: Step 6 (Eliminate Low-Quality Removable Candidate Roles) of elimination algorithm for hierarchical PRBAC policy mining.

However, instead of simply checking whether the resulting expression now denotes a larger set or still denotes the same set (namely, $\text{authU}_0(r)$) as in Fig 1, it exploits the flexibility that the expression may characterize any set between $\text{authU}_0(r) \setminus \text{inheritedU}(r)$ and $\text{authU}_0(r)$, by removing values from conjuncts of e (in order to make the denoted set smaller, partially counteracting the effect of setting some conjuncts to $\top$), provided the resulting expression still represents a superset of $\text{authU}_0(r) \setminus \text{inheritedU}(r)$, and then checks whether the resulting expression characterizes a set in the required range. If this fails to produce an expression representing a set in the required range, then an expression using uid is constructed.

$\text{minExpP}_{\text{H}}(r, P, R, RH)$ is defined similarly, except using $\text{inheritedP}(r, R, RH)$ instead of $\text{inheritedU}(r, R, RH)$, where $\text{inheritedP}(r, R, RH) = \bigcup_{r' \in \text{descendants}(r, R, RH)} \text{authP}_0(r')$.

Because we minimize $\text{WSC}(\text{uae}(r))$ and $\text{WSC}(\text{pae}(r))$ instead of $\text{asgndU}(r)$ and $\text{asgndP}(r)$, some inheritance relationships might become useless, if the users and permissions inherited by a role r through those relationships are also in $\text{asgndU}(r)$ and $\text{asgndP}(r)$, respectively. Such inheritance relationships could be eliminated without changing $\text{authUP}(r)$. We leave such relationships in the policy, because we want to generate policies with complete inheritance, as mentioned above. To illustrate the benefits of this approach, consider a problem instance in which there are user attributes indicating which users are employees (e.g., isEmployee = true) and which users are faculty (e.g., position = faculty), and that all faculty are employees. Suppose role mining produces roles corresponding to employee and faculty. If the assigned users of the employee role are characterized by isEmployee = true, then users in the faculty role are assigned users of the employee role, so an inheritance relationship between these roles is useless and could be eliminated, but this inheritance relationship is semantically meaningful and natural, so it is better to keep it in the policy.

4.4 Mining Hierarchical PRBAC Policies: Selection Algorithm

Steps 1–5 of this algorithm are the same as in the elimination algorithm for mining hierarchical PRBAC policies in Section 4.3. Step 6 is as follows.

```
1:  R = ∅
2:  while UPA(⟨U, P, R, RH⟩) ≠ UP
        // select the highest quality candidate role
3:      r_max = a role in R_can with maximal quality, i.e.,
4:          ∀r ∈ R_can. Q_H(r_max, R, RH_all) ≥ Q_H(r, R, RH_all).
5:      R = R ∪ {r_max}
6:      R_can = R_can \ {r_max}
        // update uae and pae of candidate roles,
        // based on updated R
7:      for r in R_can
8:          uae(r) = minExpU_H(r, U, R, RH_all)
9:          pae(r) = minExpP_H(r, U, R, RH_all)
10:     end for
11: end while
12: finalizePolicy(R, RH_all)
```

Figure 6: Step 6 (Select Roles) of selection algorithm for hierarchical PRBAC policy mining.

Step 6: Select Roles.

Pseudo-code for this step appears in Figure 6. It is similar to the pseudocode for Step 6 of the selection algorithm for mining core PRBAC policies in Section 4.2. The main differences are the addition of the for-loop to adjust the user-attribute expressions and permission-attribute expressions of previously selected roles when another role is selected, and the addition of the call to finalizePolicy at the end.

4.5 Complexity Analysis

This complexity analysis applies to all four of the above algorithms. The running time of CompleteMiner in Step 1 is worst-case exponential in $|P|$ but acceptable in practice, based on our experience applying it to small inputs in this work and larger inputs in previous work [13]. Let $R_{can}(i)$ denote the value of R_{can} after Step i; note that $|R_{can}(i)|$ is worst-case exponential in the size of the input policy. The running time of Step 2 is $O(|R_{can}(1)| \times (2^{|A_U|} + 2^{|A_P|}))$. The running time of Step 3 is $O(|R_{can}(2)| \times |A_U| \times |A_P|)$. The running time of Step 4 is $O(2^{|R_{can}(3)|})$, since every subset of $R_{can}(3)$ is explored in the worst case; however, the optimizations in Step 4 greatly reduce the number of explored subsets in our case studies. Steps 5, 6, and 7 are polynomial in $|R_{can}(4)|$, $|R_{can}(5)|$, and $|R_{can}(6)|$, respectively.

5. CASE STUDIES

This section describes the PRBAC policies we developed as case studies to illustrate our policy language and evaluate our algorithms.

The policies are written in a concrete syntax with the following kinds of statements. $uae(r, e)$ associates conjunctive user-attribute expression e with role r. $pae(r, e)$ associates conjunctive permission-attribute expression e with role r. The overall user attribute expression associated with role r is the disjunction of the expressions in the uae statements for r; similarly for the permission-attribute expression. $con(r, c)$ associates constraint c with role r. $rh(r, r')$ means that r is junior to r'. $userAttrib(u, a_1 = v_1, a_2 = v_2, \ldots)$ means that, for user u, attribute a_1 has value v_1, attribute a_2 has value v_2, etc.; $uid = u$ is implicit. $permAttrib(p, a_1 = v_1, a_2 = v_2, \ldots)$ is the analogous statement for permissions.

In each policy, we included only a few users in each "role instance", e.g., two or three users in each department. This provides sufficient data for the algorithm to discover the patterns, i.e., the parameterization. Increasing the number of users in each role instance only helps the algorithm, by providing stronger evidence for each pattern.

These case studies are small in size but non-trivial in structure. They includes roles with membership specified using uid, roles with membership specified using other attributes, roles with overlapping membership, roles with disjoint membership, roles with multiple pae statements, roles with constraints with multiple conjuncts, linear role hierarchy, diamond-shaped role hierarchy, etc.

University Case Study.

Our university case study controls access to gradebooks and course schedules. The policy appears in Figure 7, except that most of the userAttrib and permAttrib statements are omitted, to save space. For convenience, we give users names such as csStu1 and eeStu1, instead of Alice and Bob. User attributes include: position (student, faculty, or staff), dept (the user's academic or administrative department), crsTaken (course number of course being taken by a student; to keep the example small, we assume the student is taking at most one course, and it is in the student's department), crsTaught (course number of course taught by a faculty or TA; same assumptions as for crsTaken). Permission attributes include: resource (resource to which the operation is applied), operation (requested operation), dept (department to which the resource belongs), crsNum (number of the course that the resource is for), and student (student whose scores are read, for operation=readScoreStudent). The conjunct crsTaken=crsNum in the constraint for the Student role ensures that students can apply the readScoreStudent operation only to courses the student is taking. This is not essential, but it is natural and is advisable according to the defense-in-depth principle.

Healthcare Case Study.

Our healthcare case study controls access to items in electronic health records. The policy appears in Figure 8, except that most of the userAttrib and permAttrib statements are omitted, to save space. User attributes include: position (doctor or nurse; for other users, this attribute equals ⊥); ward (the ward a patient or nurse is in), specialty (the medical specialty of a doctor), team (the medical team a doctor is in), and agentFor (the patient for which a user is an agent). Permissions for access to a health record have resource=HR ("HR" is short for "health record"). Other attributes of permissions for health records include: operation (the requested operation), patient (the patient that the HR is for), topic (the medical specialty to which the HR item is related), treatingTeam (the team of doctors treating the patient the HR is for), and ward (the ward housing the patient that the HR is for).

Engineering Department Case Study.

Our engineering department case study controls access to project-related documents. It is based on the running example in [9]. The policy appears in Figure 9, except that most of the userAttrib and permAttrib statements are omitted, to save space. The role hierarchy is a lattice: it has a diamond shape. User attributes include: dept (the user's department), project (the project the user is involved in; to keep the example small, we assume the user is involved in

// Student Role
uae(Student, position=student)
// Student can read his own scores in gradebook for course
// he is taking.
pae(Student, operation=readScoreStudent
            and resource=gradebook)
con(Student, dept=dept and crsTaken=crsNum
            and uid=student)

// Teaching Assistant (TA) Role
uae(TA, uid in {csStu2, eeStu2, csStu3, eeStu3})
// TA can add and read scores for any student in
// gradebook for course he/she is teaching.
pae(TA, operation in {addScore, readScore}
        and resource=gradebook)
con(TA, dept=dept and crsTaught=crsNum)

// Instructor Role
uae(Instructor, uid in {csFac1, csFac2, eeFac1, eeFac2})
// Instructor can change a score and assign a course grade
// in gradebook for course he/she is teaching.
pae(Instructor, operation in {changeScore, assignGrade}
                and resource=gradebook)
con(Instructor, dept=dept and crsTaught=crsNum)
rh(TA, Instructor)

// Department Chair Role
uae(Chair, uid in {csChair, eeChair})
// Chair can read and write course schedule for
// his/her department.
pae(Chair, operation in {read, write}
            and resource=courseSchedule)
// Chair can assign grades for courses in his/her
// department.
pae(Chair, operation=assignGrade and resource=gradebook)
con(Chair, dept=dept)

// Registrar Role
uae(Registrar, dept=registrar)
// Staff in registrar's office can modify course schedules
// for all departments.
pae(Registrar, operation=write and resource=courseSchedule)

// User Attribute Data. The userAttrib statement for one
// user is shown here; the full policy contains 19 users.
userAttrib(csStu1, position=student, dept=cs, crsTaken=101)

// Permission Attribute Data. The permAttrib statement
// for one permission is shown here; the full policy
// contains 26 permissions.
permAttrib(cs101addScore, dept=cs, crsNum=101,
    operation=addScore, resource=gradebook)

Figure 7: University case study

at most one project, and it is in the user's department), and
specialty (the user's specialty, e.g., testing). Permission attributes include: resource (resource to which the operation
is applied), operation (requested operation), dept (department to which the resource belongs), and project (project
to which the resource belongs).

// Nurse Role
uae(Nurse, position=nurse)
// Nurse can read and add HR items with topic=general
// for patients in his/her ward.
pae(Nurse, resource=HR and operation in {readItem, addItem}
            and topic=general)
con(Nurse, ward=ward)

// Doctor Role
uae(Doctor, position=doctor)
// Doctor can read and add HR items related to his specialty
// for patients being treated by his/her team.
pae(Doctor, resource=HR
            and operation in {readItem, addItem})
con(Doctor, team=treatingTeam and specialty=topic)

// Patient Role
uae(Patient, uid in {oncPat1, oncPat2, carPat1, carPat2})
// A patient can read and add items with topic=patientNote
// in his/her HR.
pae(Patient, resource=HR
            and operation in {readItem, addItem}
            and topic=patientNote)
con(Patient, uid=patient)

// Agent Role
uae(Agent, uid in {agent1, agent2})
// Agent can add an item with topic=agentNote in HR
// for patient whose agent he/she is.
pae(Agent, resource=HR and operation=addItem
        and topic=agentNote)
// Agent can read an item with topic patientNote or
// agentNote in HR for patient whose agent he/she is.
pae(Agent, resource=HR and operation=readItem
        and topic in {patientNote, agentNote})
con(Agent, agentFor=patient)

// User Attribute Data. The userAttrib statement for one
// user is shown here; the full policy contains 14 users.
userAttrib(oncNurse1, position=nurse, ward=oncWard)

// Permission Attribute Data. The permAttrib statement
// for one permission is shown here; the full policy
// contains 24 permissions.
permAttrib(rdOncItemOncPat1, resource=HR,
    operation=readItem, patient=oncPat1, topic=oncology,
    treatingTeam=oncTeam1, ward=oncWard)

Figure 8: Healthcare case study

6. EVALUATION

This section describes an evaluation of the effectiveness
of our algorithms, based on the case studies in Section 5.
For each case study, we generated an equivalent ACL policy
and an attribute data file from the PRBAC policy, ran our
hierarchical PRBAC policy mining algorithms on the resulting ACL policy and attribute data, and then compared the
generated PRBAC policy to the original PRBAC policy.

The same methodology could be applied starting with synthetic (i.e., pseudo-randomly generated) PRBAC policies.
We did not do this, for two reasons. First, it is difficult to

// Engineer Role
// In this example, all users are engineers.
uae(Engineer, true)
// Engineer can read the project plan and test plan
// for the project he/she is working on.
pae(Engineer, operation=read
                and resource in {projectPlan, testPlan})
con(Engineer, dept=dept and project=project)

// ProductionEngineer Role
uae(ProductionEngineer, specialty=production)
// Production Engineer can write the project plan
// for the project he/she is working on.
pae(ProductionEngineer, operation=write
                and resource=projectPlan)
con(ProductionEngineer, dept=dept and project=project)
rh(Engineer, ProductionEngineer)

// QualityEngineer Role
uae(QualityEngineer, specialty=testing)
// Quality Engineer can write the test plan for the
// project he/she is working on.
pae(QualityEngineer, operation=write and
                resource=testPlan)
con(QualityEngineer, dept=dept and project=project)
rh(Engineer, QualityEngineer)

// ProjectLead Role
uae(ProjectLead, specialty=management)
// Project Lead can create a budget for the project
// he/she is leading.
pae(ProjectLead, operation=create and resource=budget)
con(ProjectLead, dept=dept and project=project)
rh(ProductionEngineer, ProjectLead)
rh(QualityEngineer, ProjectLead)

// User Attribute Data. The userAttrib statement for one
// user is shown here; the full policy contains 14 users.
userAttrib(qe1, dept=ads, project=alpha, specialty=testing)

// Permission Attribute Data. The permAttrib statement
// for one permission is shown here; the full policy
// contains 10 permissions.
permAttrib(rpa1, dept=ads, project=alpha, operation=read,
    resource=projectPlan)

Figure 9: Engineering department case study

generate "realistic" synthetic policies, so effectiveness of our algorithm on synthetic policies might not be representative of its effectiveness on real policies. Second, it is difficult to evaluate the effectiveness of our algorithms on synthetic policies: in case of differences between the synthetic policy and the mined policy, there would be no basis for determining which one is better (for example, the synthetic policy might be unnecessarily complicated, and the mined policy might be better). We could determine which policy has lower WSC, but minimizing WSC is just a heuristic aimed at helping the algorithm discover high-level structure, and we do not know what the best high-level structure is for synthetic policies. Ideally, we would evaluate the algorithms on access control policies in actual use, but we do not know of any publicly

Case Study	$|U|$	$|P|$	$|UP|$	$|A_U|$	$|A_P|$	$|R_{can}|$	$|R|$	Time
university	19	26	42	4	5	203	5	2.1 1.2
healthcare	14	24	42	5	6	42	4	.55 .43
eng. dept.	14	10	42	3	4	24	4	.21 .19

Figure 10: Running times and size metrics for case studies.

available deployed access control policies with accompanying attribute data.

In summary, for all three case studies the selection algorithm for mining hierarchical PRBAC policies, without optional Step 5 (Eliminate Unnecessary Constraints), successfully reconstructs the original PRBAC policy from the ACLs and attribute data.

We implemented the algorithms in Java and ran them on a laptop with an Intel Core i3 2.13 GHz CPU. In our experiments, all weights w_i in the definition of WSC are equal to 1. Table 10 shows, for each case study, several size metrics and the running times of both algorithms. The "$|R_{can}|$" column contains the size of R_{can} after Step 4. The "Time" column contains the running times (in seconds) for the elimination and selection algorithms, respectively, for mining hierarchical PRBAC policies and including the optional Step 5. We also measured the running time of each step. In all cases except one, Step 4 is the most expensive step; the one exception is the elimination algorithm on the university case study, for which Step 7 is the most expensive step.

Results of university case study.

We ran the elimination and selection algorithms on ACLs and attribute data generated from the university case study. Without Step 5 (Eliminate Unnecessary Constraints), the selection algorithm reconstructs the original PRBAC policy. The elimination algorithm does slightly worse, producing two roles, corresponding to TAs for CS101 and CS601, instead of a single parameterized TA role. With Step 5 (Eliminate Unnecessary Constraints), the output of the elimination algorithm stays the same, and the output of the selection algorithm becomes the same as the output of the elimination algorithm.

Results of healthcare case study.

We ran the elimination and selection algorithms on ACLs and attribute data generated from the healthcare case study. Without Step 5 (Eliminate Unnecessary Constraints), both algorithms reconstruct the original PRBAC policy. With Step 5 (Eliminate Unnecessary Constraints), the elimination algorithm still reconstructs the original PRBAC policy, but the selection algorithm does slightly worse, producing two roles, corresponding to cardiologists and oncologists, instead of a single parameterized Doctor role.

Results of engineering department case study.

We ran the elimination and selection algorithms on ACLs and attribute data generated from the engineering department case study. The selection algorithm reconstructs the original PRBAC policy. The elimination algorithm reconstructs the ProductionEngineer and ProjectLead roles, but each of the other two roles in the resulting policy contain some general engineers and some quality engineers. For both algorithms, the results are unaffected by Step 5 (Eliminate Unnecessary Constraints).

Limitations.

Our algorithm does not reconstruct the original policy for some variants of the health care case study, because CompleteMiner does not generate the candidate roles that need to be merged to produce the original roles. For example, suppose we modify the policy so that a patient's agent has all permissions of that patient, plus some agent-specific permissions. As a result, the agent's permissions are a superset of the patient's permissions, and the roles generated by CompleteMiner all have the property that, if the role contains the patient, then it also contains the agent. This prevents subsequent steps of the algorithm from discovering a parameterized patient role, because different constraints are needed for patients and agents, as one can see from the patient and Agent roles in Figure 8. To overcome this limitation, Step 1 should be extended to take attribute information into account when generating candidate roles.

7. RELATED WORK

As mentioned in Section 1, we are not aware of any prior work on policy mining for PRBAC or ABAC. Our policy mining algorithms build on two pieces of prior work on role mining for RBAC: Vaidya, Atluri, and Warner's CompleteMiner algorithm for generating candidate roles [11, 12], and Xu and Stoller's elimination and selection algorithms for deciding which candidate roles to include in the final policy [13]. The novel part of our algorithms are the middle steps, in which constraint generation and role merging are used to discover parameterization.

Xu and Stoller's elimination algorithm is partly inspired by Molloy et al.'s Hierarchical Miner algorithm for mining roles with semantic meaning based on user-attribute data [8]. Colantonio et al. developed a different method for taking user-attribute data into account during role mining; their method partitions the set of users based on the values of selected attributes, and then performs role mining separately for each of the resulting sets of users [2].

We use role quality and policy quality metrics based on weighted structural complexity [8]. Other role quality and policy quality metrics have been proposed. Colantonio et al. proposed metrics that measure how well roles fit the hierarchical structures of an organization and its business processes [1]. These metrics could be incorporated in our algorithm. Qi al. proposed a metric for optimality of role hierarchies and an efficient heuristic algorithm for mining role hierarchies based on that metric [5]. Their work could be extended to accommodate parameters and combined with our approach to discovering parameterized roles.

Several access control frameworks that support some form of parameterized roles have been proposed. The earliest ones are by Giuri and Iglio [4] and Lupu and Sloman [7]; the role templates and policy templates, respectively, in these frameworks support parameterized roles. More recently, Ge and Osborn [3] and Li and Mao [6] proposed RBAC frameworks with parameterized roles. The most visible difference between parameterization in these frameworks and ours is that role parameters are explicit in these frameworks but implicit in ours. However, this difference is more superficial than significant: our approach to PRBAC policy mining can be adapted to PRBAC frameworks with explicit parameters.

8. ACKNOWLEDGEMENTS

This material is based upon work supported by ONR under Grant N00014-07-1-0928, NSF under Grant CNS-0831298, and AFOSR under Grant FA0550-09-1-0481.

9. REFERENCES

[1] A. Colantonio, R. Di Pietro, A. Ocello, and N. V. Verde. A formal framework to elicit roles with business meaning in RBAC systems. In *Proc. 14th ACM Symposium on Access Control Models and Technologies (SACMAT)*, pages 85–94, 2009.

[2] A. Colantonio, R. Di Pietro, and N. V. Verde. A business-driven decomposition methodology for role mining. *Computers & Security*, 2012.

[3] M. Ge and S. L. Osborn. A design for parameterized roles. In *Research Directions in Data and Applications Security XVIII, IFIP TC11/WG 11.3 Eighteenth Annual Conference on Data and Applications Security*, pages 251–264. Kluwer, 2004.

[4] L. Giuri and P. Iglio. Role templates for content-based access control. In *Proc. 2nd ACM Workshop on Role Based Access Control (RBAC'97)*, pages 153–159, November 1997.

[5] Q. Guo, J. Vaidya, and V. Atluri. The role hierarchy mining problem: Discovery of optimal role hierarchies. In *Proc. 2008 Annual Computer Security Applications Conference (ACSAC)*, pages 237–246. IEEE Computer Society, 2008.

[6] N. Li and Z. Mao. Administration in role based access control. In *Proc. ACM Symposium on InformAtion, Computer and Communications Security (ASIACCS)*, pages 127–138. ACM Press, Mar. 2007.

[7] E. Lupu and M. Sloman. Reconciling role based management and role based access control. In *Proc. 2nd ACM Workshop on Role Based Access Control (RBAC'97)*, pages 135–141, November 1997.

[8] I. Molloy, H. Chen, T. Li, Q. Wang, N. Li, E. Bertino, S. B. Calo, and J. Lobo. Mining roles with multiple objectives. *ACM Trans. Inf. Syst. Secur.*, 13(4), 2010.

[9] R. S. Sandhu, V. Bhamidipati, and Q. Munawer. The ARBAC97 model for role-based administration of roles. *ACM Trans. Inf. Syst. Secur.*, 2(1):105–135, 1999.

[10] H. Takabi and J. B. D. Joshi. StateMiner: an efficient similarity-based approach for optimal mining of role hierarchy. In *Proc. 15th ACM Symposium on Access Control Models and Technologies (SACMAT)*, pages 55–64, 2010.

[11] J. Vaidya, V. Atluri, and J. Warner. RoleMiner: Mining roles using subset enumeration. In *Proc. 13th ACM Conference on Computer and Communications Security (CCS)*, pages 144–153, 2006.

[12] J. Vaidya, V. Atluri, J. Warner, and Q. Guo. Role engineering via prioritized subset enumeration. *IEEE Trans. Dependable Secur. Comput.*, 7(3):300–314, 2010.

[13] Z. Xu and S. D. Stoller. Algorithms for mining meaningful roles. In *Proc. 17th ACM Symposium on Access Control Models and Technologies (SACMAT)*, pages 57–66, 2012.

I See We Still Like C

Ronnie L. Killough
Southwest Research Institute®
San Antonio, Texas
rkillough@swri.org

ABSTRACT

The latest rankings of computer language popularity once again list C as the most popular programming language[1]. As a computer scientist that has written a lot of C code over the years, I must admit that makes me smile. While I don't write code much anymore, I like writing code, and I like writing it in C. Apparently so do a lot of other people. However, C was also the most popular programming language 25 years ago which is one indication that, in the field of software development, not much has changed. Are software developers unwilling to accept new paradigms or are the new paradigms proposed to-date simply unacceptable? This talk discusses what has and hasn't changed in the area of software development, how change (or the lack of it) relates to application security, and concludes with some thoughts on possible directions for the future.

Categories and Subject Descriptors

D.2.3 [**Software Engineering**]: Coding Tools and Techniques – *Standards.*

Keywords

Software development; application security; software security policies

Ronnie Killough is a director of research & development at Southwest Research Institute (SwRI). In his twenty-two years at SwRI, Ronnie has developed software for applications such as cruise missile simulators, space shuttle control center systems, and unmanned spacecraft. In his role as Director of the Communications and Embedded Systems department, he is responsible for the oversight of several areas of technology, including network-centric systems, tactical communications, cyber security, smart energy systems, and high-reliability software. Ronnie is currently serving as software systems lead for the NASA-funded Cyclone Global Navigation Satellite System (CYGNSS) mission, and has previously served on NASA Independent Review Teams (IRTs) for various missions. In addition to his passion for space, Ronnie has served as an investigator on software and security research projects funded by agencies such as DHS, DARPA, and AFRL.

REFERENCES

[1] http://www.tiobe.com/index.php/content/paperinfo/tpci/index.html. Viewed 12/19/2012.

A New Approach for Delegation in Usage Control

Xiao Liang Hu
Department of Computer Science
The University of Western Ontario
London, ON, Canada, N6A 5B7
xhu84@uwo.ca

Sylvia L. Osborn
Department of Computer Science
The University of Western Ontario
London, ON, Canada, N6A 5B7
sylvia@csd.uwo.ca

ABSTRACT

UCON (Usage Control), a recent access control model, allows temporal control of the usage of permissions according to three criteria: Authorizations, oBligations and Conditions. In this paper, we investigate delegation in UCON and propose a new approach to achieve user-user total and partial delegations with the enforcement of constraints by taking advantage of UCON's existing components: Authorizations, oBligations and Conditions. The approach we propose can be modified and extended, without much effort, to other access control models accommodated by UCON and to a distributed environment.

Categories and Subject Descriptors

D.4.6 [**Operating Systems**]: Security and Protection—*Access controls*; K.6 [**MANAGEMENT OF COMPUTING AND INFORMATION SYSTEMS**]: Security and ProtectionUnauthorized access (e.g., hacking, phreaking)

Keywords

Delegation, Usage Control, UCON, RBAC

1. INTRODUCTION

UCON (Usage Control), introduced by Park and Sandhu [7] in 2002, is designed to be flexible and adaptable in today's distributed and open computing environments. This model has features to ensure the continuity of access decisions and the mutability of attributes throughout the whole usage process. For example, consider a user making an international call with a calling card: the carrier's system should first verify the user's ID (pre-authorization), and then keep checking and updating the balance periodically (on-going authorization). The authorization and updating of the balance before and during the usage embody UCON's continuity and mutability. In addition to authorization (A), obligations (B) and conditions (C) are two other criteria of UCON.

RBAC (Role Based Access Control) is a widely-used access control model. There are several RBAC models, such as Sandhu et al.'s RBAC model family [12], Nyanchama and Osborn's RGM (Role Graph Model) [5] and the NIST model [11]. All have 5 components: users, roles, permissions, user-role assignments and permission-role assignments. The partially ordered role hierarchy of RBAC, called the role graph in the RGM, is a flexible and convenient means to organize and manage permissions.

Delegation is an auxiliary but integral function in information systems, used for the purpose of emergency backup, work-load sharing, and collaboration [1]. In a delegation, a *delegator* is the user who originates and transfers permissions to others, and a *delegatee* is the receiver who assumes the delegated duties [15]. There are many security-related issues concerning delegations in access control, such as cascading/transitive delegations, constraints imposed on delegations, and revocation[15]. Although UCON has been discussed for several years, the delegation issue in UCON has not yet been systematically investigated, particularly issues such as constraints, totality of delegations and cascading delegations. This paper focuses on some basic facets of delegations in UCON.

The paper is organized as follows: Section 2 gives background on RBAC, the UCON model, its compatibility with RBAC, delegations in RBAC and its constraints and some related work on delegation in UCON . Section 3 investigates the authorization of delegated permissions, maps constraints into UCON's oBligations and Conditions and proposes enhanced models to support delegations in UCON. This is supported by two extensive examples. The final Section contains conclusions and future work.

2. BACKGROUND

2.1 RGM and ARGM

The discussions which follow assume the RGM is being used to describe an RBAC model. In the RGM, a role is a container of privileges (called permissions in other models). Edges in the role graph indicate that the privileges of a junior role are inherited by its senior role(s). Furthermore, the RGM defines the privileges which are directly assigned to the role, not inherited from juniors, as *direct privileges*, and combines direct and inherited privileges as *effective privileges* [5]. The RGM also has a group graph which shows subset relationships among groups of users.

The RGM has been extended with an administrative model (the ARGM), where administrative roles govern administrative domains, such that users assigned to these administrative roles can alter the role graph within an administrative domain [13]. Since delegation temporarily alters user-role assignment, the delegation model for the ARGM requires that any user who is to be a delegator be assigned to a delegator role which is a special administrative role. Partial delegations (of a role) are handled by having the delegator create a delegation role; others, like user-user delegations, are handled in the group graph [15].

2.2 The UCON$_{ABC}$ Model

In 2004, Park and Sandhu[7] presented UCON$_{ABC}$ with three components, A (*Authorizations*), B (*oBligations*) and C (*Conditions*), which are enforced temporally to satisfy the continuity and mutability requirements throughout the process of a usage.

Authorizations: *Authorizations* are predicates to be evaluated for subjects' access requests; the predicates consider subject attributes, object attributes, requested rights and a set of authorization rules [8]. Based on the temporal sequence of usage, authorization can be further divided into pre-Authorization (*pre*A) and ongoing-Authorization (*on*A) as shown in the first two rows of Table 1. *pre*A means authorization is conducted before the usage, while *on*A means authorization will continue during the process of usage, e.g. the balance checking and deduction during a long distance call (onA2), which represents UCON's continuity. By enumerating atomic scenarios, all feasible combinations of attribute updates, namely mutability, and authorization in UCON are indicated with "Y" in Table 1, where a blank means attributes are *immutable* during a usage and "Y" means attributes are updated before a usage. The 0 in the table header means attributes are immutable during a usage, 1 means attributes are updated before a usage, namely pre-update, etc.

	0 immutable	1 pre-update	2 on-update	3 post-update
preA	Y	Y		Y
onA	Y	Y	Y	Y
preB	Y	Y		Y
onB	Y	Y	Y	Y
preC	Y			
onC	Y			

Table 1: 16 Basic UCON Models[8]

Obligations: *Obligations* represent requirements to be satisfied before, during or after a usage. For example, *pre*B could be parents' prior consent to a child's access to a film, and *on*B can be the existence of an advertising bar in a browser during usage. The subject and object of an obligation, *OBS*(Obligation Subject) and *OBO*(Obligation Object), can be the same as the subject and object of the usage, or not. In the first example of *pre*B, the children are the subject of the usage but the parents are the object, *OBS*. In the second example, the user is *OBS*, but *OBO* is the advertising bar, not the target object. An obligation can be triggered by the subject and object's attributes, and the obligation can require the updating of *OBS* or *OBO*'s attributes as well. All feasible combinations of obligations with attribute updates are in the middle two rows of Table 1.

Conditions: *Conditions* are things like system load, IP location, business hours, etc., which are independent of any

subject or object in a usage. Since conditions are objective, the only feasible atomic models of conditions are immutable *pre*C0 and *on*C0, as shown in Table 1.

The above three components are decisive factors in UCON; the 16 atomic models in Table 1 can be further combined and applied to practical access scenarios and accommodate access control models such as MAC, DAC, RBAC, etc. E.g., a doctor can prescribe a certain medication only if the patient agrees on a consent form and another backup doctor is present [6]. This policy is a UCON$_{preA0preB0onB0}$ scenario, in which doctor is the subject. As for *pre*B, OBS and OBO are the patient and consent form respectively; the presence of the backup doctor is an on-going obligation, *on*B0.

Usage's State Transitions: The state transition of an access process is driven by the change or mutability of attribute values. A typical access process has seven possible states, {*initial, requesting, denied, accessing, on-going checking, revoked, end*} [16]. Figure 1 illustrates an access process's state transition throughout its lifetime. Attributes can be updated *before usage, during (on-going) usage* and *after usage*. Usage control actions are usually preformed by the system or subjects. In an access process, the updating of attributes can be conducted simultaneously but give a single state transition. *Obligation actions* are different from usage control actions in that obligations are mandatory requirements to be fulfilled for an access itself rather than an authorization of an access request. During a usage, once an attribute is updated, the system will trigger the state transition to *ongoingcheck*. Based on the new status of attributes after the update, *on*A, *on*B, *on*C or any combination of them will be re-evaluated for further access, and the system may either revoke the usage or go on to allow the access[4].

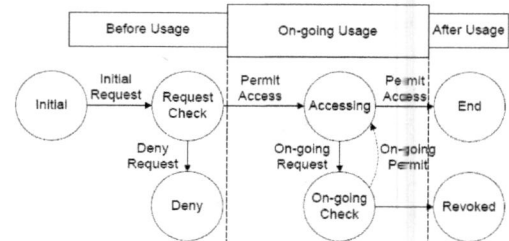

Figure 1: UCON's access state transition [4]

2.3 Partial and Total Delegations in RBAC and Constraints

Delegations can be divided into partial and total delegations, and in [14], delegations are further divided into user-user total delegations, and permission-user (partial) delegations. In a partial delegation, only a subset of the delegator's permissions are delegated, while in a total delegation all of the user or role's permissions are delegated. In the RGM's user-user total delegation, delegators with delegation permissions will assign delegatees directly to their groups with time and delegation constraints to finish the delegation. In a partial delegation, the delegator creates a delegation role in the role graph with partial permissions and the delegatee is assigned to the delegation role to obtain the permissions.

Constraints are an inevitable means to enforce original access control policies, circumscribe the delegator's behavior and prevent potential hazards in delegations. The RGM [14] defines 10 delegation constraints, and actually there could be even more depending on system requirements. For instance, the *Max. Privilege Set constraint* prevents delegatees from collecting too many permissions in a system. The *SOD (Separation of Duty) constraint* ensures that mutually exclusive permissions will not be activated simultaneously.

2.4 UCON's Compatibility with RBAC

Park and Sandhu [8] proposed that RBAC can be accommodated by UCON's authorization process, namely as $UCON_{preA0}$, in which RBAC's user-role assignment is mapped to subject attributes and permission-role assignment is regarded as attributes of objects and rights in UCON. They exemplify that $RBAC_1$[1] with activation can be supported by $UCON_{preA0}$ as follows[8]:[2]

$RBAC_1$ with activation $UCON_{preA0}$:

$ROLE$ is a partially ordered role set with dominance $\geq$

$P = \{(o, r)\}$

$actRole : S \to 2^{ROLE}$

$Prole : P \to 2^{ROLE}$

$ATT(S) = \{\}$

$ATT(O) = \{Prole\}$

$allowed(s, o, r) \Rightarrow \exists role \in actRole(s),$
$\qquad \exists role' \in Prole(o, r), role \geq role'$

$P = \{(o, r)\}$ means a permission is an approved right to access an object. $ROLE$ is a partially-ordered role graph, in which each role has some permissions. $actRole$ is a function to retrieve a subject's active roles. Similarly, function $Prole$ returns a set of roles that carry permissions to access a given object. $\{actRole\}$ is a role set, which is one of the subject's attributes and indicates the active role set assumed by the subject. The object, O, has a similar attribute, $\{Prole\}$, which consists of the roles having permissions to access this object. Therefore, if any of the requester's roles, $actRole(s)$, dominates any of the permission roles, $Prole(o, r)$, in the role hierarchy, the request is allowed.

2.5 Related Work

Zhang et al.'s $UCON_D$ [17] is the first model for delegations in UCON. They formally define the entities in their model such as permission, usage decision and delegation context, and they discussed the process of cascading delegation and revocation in both client-based and server-based architectures. However, in the model they do not refer to the basic features of delegation like total delegation and partial delegation and miss some critical delegation constraints such as Separation of Duty and Maximum Privilege Set.

Jin et al.[3] proposed an improved architecture for delegations between collaborative UCON domains. They introduced seven more atomic models for delegations in UCON, and the assumption is that delegation is a separate component, D, in UCON. Actually, the verification of delegation itself is still an authorization, A, and the relevant attributes, actions and constraints can be accommodated by the original UCON models' three criteria, A, B, and C, as we will show in the next section.

Farzad et al.[9] introduced an administrative model for UCON, in which they discussed the manipulation and management of attributes in UCON and the transfer and implication of these capabilities. The delegation in question is orthogonal to the one we discuss in this paper. Our approach

focuses on the delegations of permissions to access objects in information systems, not the management of attributes.

3. A NEW APPROACH FOR DELEGATION IN UCON

The main idea of our approach is to take the validation of delegated permissions as Authorization, A, and to map (most of) delegation constraints as oBligations, B, and Conditions, C. We will use RBAC's user-user total delegation and partial delegation to exemplify our approach. Because user-user total delegations and partial delegations are general for most access control models and (as just shown) RBAC can be accommodated by UCON, this approach can be extended and applied to other access control models accommodated by UCON as well. The discussion of our new approach is within the Policy layer of the PEI framework [10], namely "what" security should be enforced.

3.1 Authorization of Delegated Permissions

When a delegated permission is requested by a delegatee, the authorization of the delegated permission, namely the existence and validation of the delegation, is evaluated as a preA0. The checking of the delegation's requirements, e.g. pre-oBligations and pre-Conditions, follows the preA0. The constraints of the delegation are usually the last ones to be checked in each criterion. For example, a permission of preA0onA2 scenario is delegated with a Maximum Privilege Set constraint, so the overall evaluation of this delegated permission can be interpreted as $preA0_D preC0_D onA2_D$. The subscript D means the evaluation of a delegated permission. $preA0_D$ and $onA2_D$ replaces preA0 and onA2, for the delegatee is the subject of the usage, not the delegator. $preC0_D$ is the Maximum Privilege Set constraint following $preA0_D$. If this permission originally has another condition, this constraint, $preC0_D$, will follow it. Constraints will be discuss further in the next subsection.

3.2 Delegation Constraints in UCON

Constraints tethered on delegations is a mechanism to circumscribe delegators' behavior and prevent potential hazards. In [15], there are ten types of constraints defined for delegations in RBAC. Most of these constraints can be mapped into UCON's B(oBligations) and C(Conditions) during the *pre* or *on-going* stage to confine delegations. In a real system, some constraints can be designated by the delegator when the delegation is issued, while others may be designed by the SSO(System Security Officer) at system design time and be unknown to the delegator. Resolution of conflicting permissions and constraints will not be discussed in this paper. Here, we assume that constraints should be enforced before or during the execution of delegations.

Maximum Privilege Set: The *Maximum Privilege Set* constraint can be mapped as *preC0* in UCON, namely an immutable condition before the usage of delegation. Before a delegated permission is activated, the cardinality of the delegatee's current permission set should be checked.

Separation of Duty: The *Separation of Duty* constraint can be further divided into DSOD (Dynamic Separation of Duty) and SSOD (Static Separation of Duty). SSOD indicates that two permissions are defined to conflict - the user, here the delegatee, cannot be assigned these two mutually exclusive permissions [15]. Because SSOD is enforced be-

---

[1]$RBAC_1$ is an sub-model of RBAC96 with role hierarchy without constraints and administrative roles.

[2]The notation used here and later is adapted from [8]

fore the designation of delegations, it will not be mapped to UCON here. On the other hand, DSOD is checked during the execution of the delegation and prevents delegatees from activating mutually exclusive permissions at the same time, so it can be mapped to UCON's $preC0$.

Absence: The *Absence* constraint confines a delegatee's usage of delegated permissions with the delegator's work status. For example, only if the delegator is not at work, can the delegatee execute the delegated permissions, which can be taken as UCON's $preB1$. Specifically, the delegator should update her status in the system before the usage of delegated permissions. Here, this obligation's OBS is the delegator, and the OBO is the delegator's status. OBA is the delegator's updating action. Actually, in a real system the delegator's status could be retrieved by a system process.

Time Interval: *Time interval* is defined as the parameter of a delegation edge drawn from a delegator to a delegatee in the ARGM, which indicates the expiration time of the delegation. But the *time constraint* here is regarded as a constraint on delegations, which limits the time frame when the privileges can be activated, e.g. daily from 9 a.m. to 5 p.m. Therefore, the time constraint can be mapped as both $preC0$ and $onC0$.

Location: The *Location* constraint defines where a delegatee can execute delegated permissions, like IP address, the user's physical location, etc., which can be taken as $preC0$ and $onC0$, to be checked before and during a delegation.

Constraints	UCON's Sub-models
Maximum Privilege Set	$preC0$
SSOD	-
DSOD	$preC0$
Absence	$preB1$
Location, Time	$preC0$, $onC0$

Table 2: Summary of Constraint's Mappings to UCON$_{ABC}$

Table 2 is a summary of the mapping of the above constraints to oBligations and Conditions. In a real information system, there could be even more diverse and individual constraints depending on system and user requirements.

3.3 Enhanced Delegation Models in UCON

As discussed above, we take the validation of delegated permissions as Authorizations, and map most constraints to oBligations and Conditions. Although it is taken as an authorization, a delegation's validation includes the delegator, the delegatee and the delegated permissions, which is different from the authorization's original definition in UCON. Therefore, we will define the authorization of a delegation with immutable attributes as $preA0_D$, the one with attributes being pre-updated as $preA1_D$, the one with attributes having on-going updating as $onA2_D$, etc. Similarly, mapping constraints to obligations and conditions is denoted as $preB1_D$, $preC0_D$, $onC0_D$, etc. Furthermore, the validity of a delegation needs to be checked regularly during usage of delegated permissions, namely $onA0_D$, in case the delegation is revoked half way through. In this way, we finely divide the examination of requests for delegated permissions, and further combine it with the evaluation of delegated permissions themselves.

Figure 2 shows a delegation example for a preA0onA2 scenario with a Maximum Privilege Set constraint, which can be interpreted as $preA0_DpreC0_DonA0_DonA2_D$. The origi-

nal authorization is transformed to the authorization of the delegation, $preA0_D$, and the original on-going authorization includes the updating of the delegatee's attributes rather than the subject's (the delegator's). The Maximum Privilege Set constraint is appended as a condition, $preC0_D$, and the ongoing regular checking of the delegation is $onA0_D$. This example will be formally described in Section 3.6.

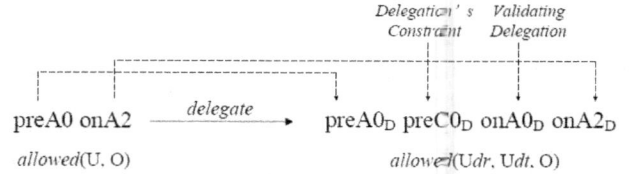

Figure 2: the Delegation of preA0onA2

Considering the mutability of delegators, delegatees and objects' attributes before, during and after the usage of delegated permissions, several enhanced models for the authorization, obligation and condition requirements are indicated in Table 3 with "Y". The obligational and conditional models correspond to the constraints' mappings in Table 2. The formal expression of these models follows UCON$_{ABC}$'s notation system and conventions, and some symbolic expression for delegations in the ARGM [15] are adopted as well. We will formally define the models that are pertinent to the example scenarios discussed here, indicated by an underscored "Y". The definitions of enhanced models will be modified and made in the light of Park and Sandhu's work[8].

	0 immutable	1 pre-update	2 on-update	3 post-update
$preA_D$	Y	Y		Y
onA_D	Y	Y	Y	Y
$preB_D$	Y	Y		
onB_D	Y			
$preC_D$	Y			
onC_D	Y			

Table 3: Enhanced Models for Authorization of Delegations in UCON

3.4 Definitions of Enhanced Models

3.4.1 The Model preA0$_D$

Definition 1. $preA0_D$ has the following components:
— $U_{dr}, U_{dt}, O, P, ATT(U_{dr}), ATT(U_{dt}), ATT(O)$
and $preA_D$;
— $allowed(u_{dr}, u_{dt}, o, p_{dt}) \Rightarrow$
$\quad preA_D(ATT(u_{dr}), ATT(u_{dt}), o, p_{dt})$.

UCON$_{preA0_D}$ consists of delegator users (U_{dr}), delegatee users (U_{dt}), objects (O), permissions (P), delegators' attributes ($ATT(U_{dr})$), delegatees' attributes ($ATT(U_{dt})$), objects' attributes ($ATT(O)$) and a $preA_D$. $preA_D$ is a functional predicate to validate the delegation by $ATT(U_{dr})$, $ATT(U_{dt})$ and P, and the request of activating a delegated permission is examined using these three components, e.g. the delegator's id, the delegatee's id and the requested permission's id. If a delegation relation does exist and is valid, the request is preliminarily allowed, which is indicated by

272

$allowed(u_{dr}, u_{dt}, o, p_{dt})$, though the delegation's constraints is checked later. Note that p_{dt} represents delegated permissions, and $allowed$'s notation is slightly different from UCON's original definition in Section 2.4, where we semantically replace rights, r, with two separate components, objects and permissions, namely o and p.

$UCON_{ABC}$[8] uses "imply" connectives, $\Rightarrow$, rather than "if" to formulate the UCON models, which means the right-hand side of the connective is not sufficient to allow the usage but is necessary. This enables the decision process to make a finer and richer control by including other necessary rules [8]. Therefore, preA0$_D$ and the rest of the model definitions conform to this convention.

3.4.2 The Model preA1$_D$

Definition 2. preA1$_D$ has the following components:
— $U_{dr}, U_{dt}, O, P, ATT(U_{dr}), ATT(U_{dt}), ATT(O)$ and preA$_D$;
— $allowed(u_{dr}, u_{dt}, o, p_{dt}) \Rightarrow$
    $preA_D(ATT(u_{dr}), ATT(u_{dt}), o, p_{dt})$;
— $preUpdate(ATT(u_{dr})), preUpdate(ATT(u_{dt})),$
$preUpdate(ATT(o))$.

Based on preA0$_D$'s definition, the model preA1$_D$ defines three more procedures, $preUpdate(ATT(u_{dr}))$, $preUpdate(ATT(u_{dt}))$ and $preUpdate(ATT(o))$, which are applied to update delegators, delegatees and objects' attributes before the usage, respectively.

3.4.3 The Model onA0$_D$

Definition 3. onA0$_D$ has the following components:
— $U_{dr}, U_{dt}, O, P, ATT(U_{dr}), ATT(U_{dt}), ATT(O)$ are not changed from preA0$_D$;
— onA_D (ongoing-Authorization);
— $allowed(u_{dr}, u_{dt}, o, p_{dt}) \Rightarrow true$;
— $stopped(u_{dr}, u_{dt}, o, p_{dt}) \Leftarrow$
    $\neg onA_D(ATT(u_{dr}), ATT(u_{dt}), ATT(o), p_{dt})$;

The seven basic elements' definitions are not changed from preA0$_D$. onA$_D$ is an ongoing authorization process, which repeatedly checks the attributes during the usage. Usually, the ongoing examination is activated by timers or events in real systems. The preliminary request, preA$_D$, is assumed always allowed, which is indicated by $allowed(u_{dr}, u_{dt}, o, p_{dt}) \Rightarrow true$. If any of the attributes does not satisfy the requirements of a usage any more, the onA$_D$ executes the *stopped* procedure to revoke the usage, denoted as $stopped(u_{dr}, u_{dt}, o, p_{dt}) \Leftarrow \neg onA_D(ATT(u_{dr}), ATT(u_{dt}), ATT(o), p_{dt})$.

3.4.4 The Model onA2$_D$

Definition 4. onA2$_D$ has the following components:
— $U_{dr}, U_{dt}, O, P, ATT(U_{dr}), ATT(U_{dt}), ATT(O)$ are not changed from preA0$_D$;
— onA_D (ongoing-Authorization);
— $allowed(u_{dr}, u_{dt}, o, p_{dt}) \Rightarrow true$;
— $stopped(u_{dr}, u_{dt}, o, p_{dt}) \Leftarrow$
    $\neg onA_D(ATT(u_{dr}), ATT(u_{dt}), ATT(o), p_{dt})$;
— $onUpdate(ATT(u_{dr})), onUpdate(ATT(u_{dt})),$
$onUpdate(ATT(o))$.

On the basis of onA0$_D$'s definition, the model onA2$_D$ defines three more procedures, $onUpdate(ATT(u_{dr}))$, $onUpdate$

$(ATT(u_{dt}))$ and $onUpdate(ATT(o))$. They are procedures to update delegators, delegatees, and objects' attributes during a delegation's usage.

3.4.5 The Model preB0$_D$

Both the preB0$_D$ and onB0$_D$ definitions are based on those of preB0 and onB0 in [8]. The definitions of $OBS, OBO, OBA, preOBL, getPreOBL$ and $preFulfilled$ do not change from $UCON_{ABC}$'s preB0. The difference is that subjects are delegatee users, U_{dt}, rather than delegator users, U_{dr}, in the enhanced models. Even if a delegator designates a delegation with a constraint, which can be interpreted as an obligation, the constraint is still a preB$_D$ or onB$_D$ appended by the delegation, not initially belonging to the delegated permission. In this case, the delegator or a designated third-party can be the OBS in the obligation. The following definition formalizes the preB0$_D$ model.

Definition 5. preB0$_D$ has the following components:
— $U_{dr}, U_{dt}, O, P, ATT(U_{dr}), ATT(U_{dt}), ATT(O)$ are not changed from preA0$_D$;
— OBS, OBO and OBA, (obligation subjects, obligation objects and obligation actions);
— $preB_D$, (pre-obligation predicates);
— $preOBL$, (a set of pre-obligation requirements to be satisfied);
— $preOBL \subseteq OBS \times OBO \times OBA$;
— $preFulfilled : OBS \times OBO \times OBA \rightarrow \{true, false\}$;
— $getPreOBL : U_{dr} \times U_{dt} \times O \times P \rightarrow 2^{preOBL}$;
— $preB_D(u_{dr}, u_{dt}, o, p_{dt}) =$
$\bigwedge_{(obs_i, obo_i, oba_i) \in getPreOBL(u_{dr}, o, p_{dt})} preFulfilled(obs_i, obo_i, oba_i)$;
— $preB_D(u_{dr}, u_{dt}, o, p_{dt}) = true \Leftarrow$
    $getPreOBL(u_{dr}, u_{dt}, o, p_{dt}) = \varnothing$;
— $allowed(u_{dr}, u_{dt}, o, p_{dt}) \Rightarrow preB_D(u_{dr}, u_{dt}, o, p_{dt})$.

$preB_D$ is a pre-obligation predicate for the request of a delegated permission. $preOBL$ is a set of pre-defined obligational requirements to be satisfied before the usage. A pre-obligation consists of obs, obo and oba, and the execution result of an obligation, $preFulfilled$, is either $true$ or $false$. In UCON, the selection of obligations for a usage, $getPreOBL$, is based on subjects, objects, and permissions, but the subjects here include both delegatee users and delegator users. Only if every pre-obligation is satisfied, namely, each $preFullfilled(obs_i, obo_i, oba_i)$ is true, is the request of the delegated permission allowed. If no pre-obligations are selected, the $preB_D(u_{dr}, u_{dt}, o, p_{dt})$ is $true$ by default.

3.4.6 The Model onB0$_D$

Definition 6. onB0$_D$ has the following components:
— $U_{dr}, U_{dt}, O, P, ATT(U_{dr}), ATT(U_{dt}), ATT(O), OBS, OBO$ and OBA are not changed from preB0$_D$;
— T, a series of timestamps for checking onB0;
— onB_D, (ongoing obligation predicates);
— $onOBL$, (a set of ongoing obligation requirements to be satisfied);
— $onOBL \subseteq OBS \times OBO \times OBA \times T$;
— $onFulfilled : OBS \times OBO \times OBA \times T \rightarrow \{true, false\}$;
— $getOnOBL : U_{dr} \times U_{dt} \times O \times P \rightarrow 2^{onOBL}$;
— $onB_D(u_{dr}, u_{dt}, o, p_{dt}) =$
$\bigwedge_{(obs_i, obo_i, oba_i, t_i) \in getOnOBL(u_{dr}, u_{dt}, o, p_{dt})} onFulfilled(obs_i, obo_i, oba_i, t_i)$;

— $onB_D(u_{dr}, u_{dt}, o, p_{dt}) = true \Leftarrow$
$\quad getOnOBL(u_{dr}, u_{dt}, o, p_{dt}) = \varnothing$;
— $allowed(u_{dr}, u_{dt}, o, p_{dt}) \Rightarrow true$;
— $stopped(u_{dr}, u_{dt}, o, p_{dt}) \Leftarrow \neg onB_D(u_{dr}, u_{dt}, o, p_{dt})$.

T is a series of time stamps for periodical ongoing examination, and onB_D is an ongoing obligation predicate. $onOBL$ is a set of ongoing obligational requirements to be satisfied during the usage. An ongoing obligation consists of obs, obo, oba and timestamp, t. The checking result of an ongoing obligation, $onFulfilled$, is either $true$ or $false$. The selection of ongoing obligations, $getOnOBL$, is based on U_{dr}, U_{dt}, O, and P. The continuity of a usage, $allowed(u_{dr}, u_{dt}, o, p_{dt})$, is decided by the fulfillment of all ongoing obligations, namely, only if each $onFulfilled(obs_i, obo_i, oba_i, t_i)$ is $true$. If any ongoing obligation is not fulfilled, the onB_D executes the $stopped$ procedure to terminate the usage. Like preB0$_D$, if no ongoing obligation is selected, the result is $true$ by default. Like onA0$_D$ and onA2$_D$, the preliminary authorization is always assumed $allowed$ by default.

3.4.7 The Model preC0$_D$

Definition 7. preC0$_D$ has the following components:
— $U_{dr}, U_{dt}, O, P, ATT(U_{dr}), ATT(U_{dt}), ATT(O)$ are not changed from preA0$_D$;
— $preC_D$, (pre-condition predicates);
— $preCON$, (a set of pre-conditions available);
— $getPreCON : U_{dr} \times U_{dt} \times O \times P \to 2^{preCON}$;
— $preConChecked : preCon \to \{true, false\}$;
— $preC_D(u_{dr}, u_{dt}, o, p_{dt}) =$
$\quad \bigwedge_{preCon_i \in getPreCON(u_{dr}, u_{dt}, o, p_{dt})} pre-$
$\quad ConChecked(preCon_i)$;
— $allowed(u_{dr}, u_{dt}, o, p_{dt}) \Rightarrow preC_D(u_{dr}, u_{dt}, o, p_{dt})$.

The Seven basic components' definitions are not changed from preA0$_D$. $preCON$ is a set of pre-conditions for a request's evaluation. $getPreCON$ is a function to select the conditions applicable to a request from the $preCON$ set. The selecting process is determined by delegators(U_{dr}), delegatees(U_{dt}), Objects(O) and Permissions(P). $preConChecked$, namely the result of a condition's checking, is either $true$ or $false$. Finally, if a request is allowed, namely $allowed(u_{dr}, u_{dt}, o, p_{dt})$, each pre-condition's checking result, $preConChecked(preCon_i)$, should be $true$.

3.5 Delegation's preA0$_D$ in RBAC

Since we take RBAC's user-user total delegation and partial delegation to exemplify the delegations in UCON, in this section we will formally describe delegation's preA0$_D$ in RBAC by taking advantage of UCON's compatibility with RBAC$_1$. This definition conforms to RBAC$_1$'s representation in UCON [8].

Definition 8. Delegation's preA0$_D$ in RBAC$_1$:
$P = \{(o, p_{dt})\}$
DR is a set of delegators.
DT is a set of delegatees.
$ROLE$ is a partially role graph
$actRole_{dr} : U_{dr} \to 2^{ROLE}$
$actRole_{dt} : U_{dt} \to 2^{ROLE}$
$Prole : P \to 2^{ROLE}$
$ATT(U_{dr}) = \{dr, actRole_{dr}\}$
$ATT(U_{dt}) = \{dt, actRole_{dt}\}$

$ATT(O) = \{Prole\}$
R_{dt} is the set of delegated roles carrying the permissions to be delegated
$allowed(u_{dr}, u_{dt}, o, p_{dt}) \Rightarrow \exists r_{delegator} \in actRole_{dr}(u_{dr})$
$allowed(u_{dr}, u_{dt}, o, p_{dt}) \Rightarrow$
$\quad \exists role \in actRole_{dr}(u_{dr}), \exists role'' \in Prole(o, p_{dt}),$
$\quad role \geq role''$

$P = \{(o, p_{dt})\}$ shows that a permission consists of an approved right to access an object, and p_{dt} is a permission to be delegated. $ROLE$ is a partially-ordered role graph, in which each role has some permissions. $actRole_{dr}$ is a function to retrieve a delegator user's active roles in the role hierarchy. Similarly, the function $actRole_{ct}$ returns a delegatee user's active roles in $ROLE$. Function $Prole$ returns a set of roles that carry permissions to access a given object. $\{actRole_{dr}\}$ represents a role set assumed by the delegator, which is treated as one of a delegator's attributes. Accordingly, a delegatee's attribute, $ATT(U_{dt})$, includes their active roles set, $\{actRole_{dt}\}$. dr and dt are delegators and delegatees from DR and DT, taken as the delegators' and delegatees' membership attributes, respectively. $\{Prole\}$ is an object's attribute including the roles which have permissions to access this object. R_{dt} represents delegated roles. In a user-user total delegation, R_{dt} is the delegator's active role set, while in a partial delegation it is the delegation role created by the delegator in the role graph. R_{dt}'s effective privilege set is the set of privileges to be delegated, P_{dt}.

In this definition, there are two necessary conditions for the establishment of a delegation:
• In the ARGM, a delegator should be first assigned to the administrative role, $r_{delegator}$.
• If any of the delegator's active roles, $actRole_{dr}(u_{dr})$, dominates any of the object's permission role set, $Prole(o, p_{dt})$, in the role hierarchy, the delegatee's request is allowed.

The above example is just the validation of a delegation relationship, and the usage of the delegated privilege itself and the enforcement of constraints are not included yet.

3.6 Example 1: The Scenario of preA0$_D$preC0$_D$onA0$_D$onA2$_D$

The first example is motivated by the scenario where an authorized user is allowed to read an on-line document within one minute. Only after the delegation is activated, can the delegatee request to read the document. This is a example of a delegation scenario of a privilege of type preA0onA2. We also add a constraint, a Maximum Privilege Set constraint, preC0$_D$, to the delegation.

Example 1. The scenario of preA0$_D$preC0$_D$onA0$_D$onA2$_D$:
T is a user's usage time to access an object
N is a non-negative integer for a user's current privilege set
$ROLE$ is a partially ordered role graph
DR is a set of delegators.
DT is a set of delegatees.
$P = \{(o, p_{dt})\}$
$actRole_{dr} : U_{dr} \to 2^{ROLE}$
$actRole_{dt} : U_{dt} \to 2^{ROLE}$
$Prole : P \to 2^{ROLE}$
$ATT(U_{dr}) = \{dr, actRole_{dr}\}$
$ATT(U_{dt}) = \{dt, actRole_{dt}\}$
$ATT(O) = \{Prole\}$
R_{dt} is the set of delegated roles to carry the privileges to

be delegated

O is the web page to be visited in this example

$tCounter : S \times O \to 2^T$ ($tCounter$ is a time counter for a user's access to an object.)

$ATT(U_{dt}, O) = \{tCounter\}$

$MaxPrivSET$ is a constant for the Maximum Privilege Set constraint

$curPrivSet : U_{dt} \to 2^N$

$preCon_D : \{(curPrivSet(u_{dt}) < MaxPrivSET)\}$

$getPreCON(u_{dr}, u_{dt}, o, p_{dt}) =$
$$\begin{cases} true, & if\ curPrivSet(u_{dt}) < maxPrivSET; \\ false, & if\ curPrivSet(u_{dt}) \geq maxPrivSET. \end{cases}$$

$allowed(u_{dr}, u_{dt}, o, p_{dt}) \Rightarrow \exists r_{delegator} \in actRole_{dr}(u_{dr})$

$allowed(u_{dr}, u_{dt}, o, p_{dt}) \Rightarrow$
$\quad \exists role \in actRole_{dr}(u_{dr}), \exists role'' \in Prole(o, p_{dt}),$
$\quad role \geq role''$

$allowed(u_{dr}, u_{dt}, o, p_{dt}) \Rightarrow tCounter(u_{dt}, o) > 0$

$allowed(u_{dr}, u_{dt}, o, p_{dt}) \Rightarrow$
$\quad preConChecked(getPreCON(u_{dr}, u_{dt}, o, p_{dt}))$

$stopped(u_{dr}, u_{dt}, o, p_{dt}) \Leftarrow u_{dt} \notin DT \vee u_{dr} \notin DR$

$stopped(u_{dr}, u_{dt}, o, p_{dt}) \Leftarrow tCounter(u_{dt}, o) \leq 0$

$onUpdate(tCounter(u_{dt}, o))$, repeatedly deducting the time counter.

The definitions of $P, actRole_{dr}, actRole_{dt}, Prole, ATT(U_{dr})$, $ATT(U_{dt}), ATT(O)$ and R_{dt} are not changed from Section 3.5. O is the web page to be visited in this example. $tCounter$ is a function to retrieve the usage time of a user's access to an object, which is one of the access's attributes. $MaxPrivSET$ is the Maximum Privilege Set constraint defined as a constant. The cardinality of a delegatee user's current permission set is returned by function $curPrivSet$. This example has only one pre-condition requirement, in which the cardinality of the requester's current privilege set should be less than MaxPrivSET. If satisfied, the result of $getPreCON$'s is $true$, otherwise, $false$.

Several necessary conditions for this example are explained as follows, and the first two necessary conditions are the same as in Section 3.5 for the preliminary authorization of this delegation:

- An additional pre-authorization is that the time counter of a usage should be greater than zero, which is a preA0$_D$, because the usage can be suspended and reactivated later.
- The only pre-condition, preC0$_D$, to be satisfied is that the cardinality of the delegatee's current permission set should be less than MaxPrivSET.
- During the usage, if the delegation is revoked by the delegator, namely $u_{dt} \notin DT$, or the delegator's permission to originate delegations is revoked by SSO, namely $u_{dr} \notin DR$, the usage should be stopped. This is a onA0$_D$.
- If the usage time exceeds the duration, namely $tCounter(u_{dt}, o) \leq 0$, the usage is revoked.

$onUpdate(tCounter(u_{dt}, o))$, onA2$_D$, is an ongoing update to regularly deduct from the timing counter during the delegatee's usage.

3.7 Example 2: The Scenario of preA0$_D$preA1$_D$preB0$_D$preC0$_D$onA0$_D$onB0$_D$

Example 2 shows a scenario where a privilege of type preA0preA1preB0onB0 is to be delegated. The example is motivated by a situation in which an authorized user is allowed to edit an on-line document no more than 3 times with the endorsement of an agreement beforehand while be-

ing monitored by another user during the editing. In this delegation, we append a DSOD constraint, namely, the editor cannot be the monitor at the same time. Therefore, after the delegation, preA0preA1preB0onB0 is translated into preA0$_D$preA1$_D$preB0$_D$preC0$_D$onA0$_D$onB0$_D$, and the constraint is checked before the usage to prevent the delegatee from executing the monitoring and editing privileges simultaneously. Note that in a practical system, monitoring and editing could be two different privileges.

Example 2. The scenario of preA0$_D$preA1$_D$preB0$_D$preC0$_D$onA0$_D$onB0$_D$:

N is a non-negative integer for the usage counter, initially 3, in this example

$uCounter : U_{dt} \to N$;

$P = \{(o, p_{dt})\}$

$ROLE$ is a partially ordered role graph

DR is a set of delegators.

DT is a set of delegatees.

$actRole_{dr} : U_{dr} \to 2^{ROLE}$

$actRole_{dt} : U_{dt} \to 2^{ROLE}$

$Prole : P \to 2^{ROLE}$

$ATT(U_{dr}) = \{dr, actRole_{dr}\}$

$ATT(U_{dt}) = \{dt, uCounter, actRole_{dt}\}$

$ATT(O) = \{Prole\}$

R_{dt} is the set of delegated roles to carry the privileges to be delegated

O is the web pages to be visited in this example

$preOBS = U_{dt}$

$preOBO = \{license\_agreement\}$

$preOBA = \{agree\}$

$getPreOBL(u_{dr}, u_{dt}, o, p_{dt}) =$
$\quad \{(u_{dt}, license\_agreement, agree)\}$

$curPrivSet : U_{dt} \to 2^P$

$preCon_D : \{(priv4 \leftrightarrow priv3)\}$

$getPreCON(u_{dr}, u_{dt}, o, p_{dt}) =$
$$\begin{cases} true, & if\ priv4 \notin curPrivSet(u_{dt}); \\ false, & if\ priv4 \in curPrivSet(u_{dt}). \end{cases}$$

$onOBS = U_{monitor}$

$onOBO = \{monitor\_page\}$

$onOBA = \{monitor\}$

$T = \{always\}$

$getOnOBL(u_{dr}, u_{dt}, o, p_{dt}) =$
$\quad \{(u_{monitor}, monitor\_page, monitor, always)\}$

$allowed(u_{dr}, u_{dt}, o, p_{dt}) \Rightarrow \exists r_{delegator} \in actRole_{dr}(u_{dr})$

$allowed(u_{dr}, u_{dt}, o, p_{dt}) \Rightarrow$
$\quad \exists role \in actRole_{dr}(u_{dr}), \exists role'' \in Prole(o, p_{dt}),$
$\quad role \geq role''$

$allowed(u_{dr}, u_{dt}, o, p_{dt}) \Rightarrow uCounter(u_{dt}) > 0$

$allowed(u_{dr}, u_{dt}, o, p_{dt}) \Rightarrow$
$\quad preFulfilled(u_{dt}, license\_agreement, agree)$

$allowed(u_{dr}, u_{dt}, o, p_{dt}) \Rightarrow$
$\quad preConChecked(getPreCON(u_{dr}, u_{dt}, o, p_{dt}))$

$stopped(u_{dr}, u_{dt}, o, p_{dt}) \Leftarrow u_{dt} \notin DT \vee u_{dr} \notin DR$

$stopped(u_{dr}, u_{dt}, o, p_{dt}) \Leftarrow$
$\quad \neg onFulfilled(u_{monitor}, monitor\_page, monitor, always)$

$preUpdate(uCounter(u_{dt})) : uCounter(u_{dt}) =$
$\quad uCounter(u_{dt}) - 1$.

The definitions of $P, actRole_{dr}, actRole_{dt}, Prole, ATT(U_{dr})$, $ATT(U_{dt}), ATT(O)$ and R_{dt} are not changed from Section 3.6. $uCounter$ is a usage counter to be deducted by one before the usage and after each successful request, which is one of U_{dt}'s attributes. $preOBS, preOBO$ and $preOBA$ are three elements in the $preB0_D$. In this example, $getPreOBL$ needs the delegatee to endorse an agreement before the usage. $curPrivSet$ is a function to get a user's current permission set. $preC0_D$ has only one conditional requirement, which is the mutual exclusivity of $priv4$ and $priv3$. Since $priv3$ is delegated, if the delegatee has the $priv4$ at the same time, the $getPreCON$'s result is $false$, otherwise, $true$. $onOBS, onOBO$ and $onOBA$ are three elements in the $onB0_D$, which requests a monitor to be online and monitoring during the execution of the delegated privilege.

Several necessary conditions for this example are explained as follows, and the first two necessary conditions are the same as in Section 3.5 for the preliminary authorization of this delegation:

- Only if the requester's usage counter is greater than zero, is the request allowed. Note that this is another $preA0_D$, in addition to the authorization of the delegation relationship.
- Before the usage, the delegatee should sign an agreement, namely, $preB0_D$.
- The pre-condition, $preC0_D$, is that the delegatee should not hold a privilege conflicting with the delegated privilege.
- During the usage, if the delegator or delegatee's membership of DR or DT is removed, the usage is stopped, namely, $onA0_D$.
- During the usage, if the monitoring user is off-line, the editing is suspended immediately. This is $onB0_D$.

$preUpdate(uCounter(u_{dt}))$ means the delegatee's attribute, the usage counter, should be decremented by one before the usage.

4. CONCLUSIONS AND FUTURE WORK

We have discussed the delegations in UCON, proposed a new approach to implement delegations in UCON, and formally defined several enhanced models for the authorization of delegations and their constraints. The existing features of UCON have been used to accomplish this. User-user total delegation and partial delegation are two primary types of delegations. This work has just finished some fundamental work for delegations in UCON within closed systems, and our discussion mainly focuses in the policy layer under the PEI framework. We have tried to be as general as possible; we can easily modify and apply the approach to distributed systems and other access control models which can be accommodated by UCON.

We have implemented a prototype to demonstrate the ideas presented here [2]; space did not permit us to include details of the prototype.

Future work includes the definition of unfinished enhanced models of authorization, obligation and conditions and dynamic delegations. We would like to investigate issues other than partial and total delegations, such as cascading/transitive delegation, delegation's revocation, etc. The updating of attributes after the usage of a delegated permissions will also be considered.

5. ACKNOWLEDGMENTS

The financial support of the Natural Sciences and Engineering Research Council of Canada is gratefully acknowledged.

6. REFERENCES

[1] Ezedin Barka and Ravi Sandhu. Framework for Role-based delegation models. In *ACSAC '00*, pages 168–176, 2000.

[2] Xiao Liang Hu. A new approach for delegations in usage control. Master's thesis, The University of Western Ontario, 2012.

[3] Yongming Jin, Jinqiang Ren, Jinqiang Huiping Sun, Suming Li, and Zhong Chen. An improved scheme for delegation based on usage control. In *Proceedings of the 2008 Int. Conf. on Future Generation Communication and Networking*, pages 74–78. IEEE Computer Society, 2008.

[4] Basel Katt, Xinwen Zhang, Ruth Breu, Michael Hafner, and Jean-Pierre Seifert. A general obligation model and continuity: enhanced policy enforcement engine for usage control. In *Proc. .13th ACM SACMAT*, pages 123–132, 2008.

[5] Matunda Nyanchama and Sylvia L. Osborn. The role graph model and conflict of interest. *ACM TISSEC*, 2(1):p3–33, Feb. 1999.

[6] Jaehong Park. *Usage Control: A Unified Framework for Next Generation Access Control*. PhD thesis, George Mason University, 2003.

[7] Jaehong Park and Ravi Sandhu. Towards usage control models: beyond traditional access control. In *Proceedings of 7th ACM SACMAT*, pages 57–64, 2002.

[8] Jaehong Park and Ravi Sandhu. The UCONABC usage control model. *ACM TISSEC*, 7(1):128–174, February 2004.

[9] Farzad Salim, Jason Reid, and Ed Dawson. An administrative model for UCONABC In *Proc. 8th Australasian Conf. on Inf. Security - Volume 105*, pages 32–38, 2010.

[10] Ravi Sandhu. The PEI Framework for Application-Centric Security. In *1st Int. Workshop on Security and Comm. Networks (IWSCN)*, pages 1–5, 2009.

[11] Ravi Sandhu, David Ferraiolo, and Richard Kuhn. The NIST model for role-based access control: towards a unified standard. In *Proc. 5th ACM RBAC workshop*, pages 47–63, 2000.

[12] Ravi Sandhu, Edward J. Coyne, Hal L. Feinstein, and Charles E. Youman. Role-based access control models. *Computer*, 29(2):p38–47, Feb. 1996.

[13] He Wang and Sylvia L. Osborn. An administrative model for role graphs. In *DBSec*, pages 302–315, 2003.

[14] He Wang and Sylvia L. Osborn. Delegation in the role graph model. In *Proc. 11th ACM SACMAT*, pages 91–100, 2006.

[15] He Wang and Sylvia L. Osborn. Static and dynamic delegation in the role graph model. *IEEE Trans. on Knowl. Data Eng.*, 23:1569–1582, Oct. 2011.

[16] Xinwen Zhang. *Formal Model and Analysis of Usage Control*. PhD thesis, George Mason University, 2006.

[17] Zhiyong Zhang, Lin Yang, Qingqi Pei, and Jianfeng Ma. Research on usage control model with delegation characteristics based on OM-AM methodology. In *Proc. 2007 IFIP Int. Conf. on Network and Parallel Computing Workshops*, pages 238–243, 2007.

Towards Secure Provenance-Based Access Control in Cloud Environments

Adam Bates, Ben Mood, Masoud Valafar, and Kevin Butler
Department of Computer and Information Science
University of Oregon, Eugene, OR
{amb,bmood,valafar,butler}@cs.uoregon.edu

ABSTRACT

As organizations become increasingly reliant on cloud computing for servicing their data storage requirements, the need to govern access control at finer granularities becomes particularly important. This challenge is increased by the lack of policy supporting data migration across geographic boundaries and through organizations with divergent regulatory policies. In this paper, we present an architecture for secure and distributed management of provenance, enabling its use in security-critical applications. *Provenance*, a metadata history detailing the derivation of an object, contains information that allows for expressive, policy-independent access control decisions. We consider how to manage and validate the metadata of a provenance-aware cloud system, and introduce protocols that allow for secure transfer of provenance metadata between end hosts and cloud authorities. Using these protocols, we develop a provenance-based access control mechanism for Cumulus cloud storage, capable of processing thousands of operations per second on a single deployment. Through the introduction of replicated components, we achieve overhead costs of just 14%, demonstrating that provenance-based access control is a practical and scalable solution for the cloud.

Categories and Subject Descriptors

C.2.0. [**Computer-Communication Networks**]: General — *Security and protection*; H.3.4. [**Information Systems**]: Information Storage and Retrieval — *Systems and Software*

General Terms

Security, Storage

Keywords

Provenance, Access Control, Secure Storage

1. INTRODUCTION

Cloud computing has become a fundamental part of the modern computing landscape. Organizations are moving computing to cloud environments for a number of reasons, from easy management of resources to leveraging the elasticity implicit in the cloud model. Along with this comes an increased reliance on outsourced cloud services, and thus concern over data security and management. These concerns are well-founded based on widely-publicized instances where cloud services have not provided stated security guarantees, or have been used as the launching point for attacks on other services [11].

For the cloud customer, a necessary step for managing data is access control. Today, cloud storage services provide explicit access control lists (ACL) for sharing or protecting data. Managing access control in this manner is time-consuming even on a single machine, and scales poorly in the cloud due to the presence of data migration. When crossing organizational boundaries, data may be subject to a new set of access policies that require the explicit creation of new access rules. To avoid the need for constant policy editing, it would be desirable if data carried with it the necessary information to make accurate access control decisions.

Another largely unaddressed concern is the attribution of data as it enters the cloud and moves around within this environment. This is an issue that many organizations have not faced to this point, and it addresses a characteristic inherent to the cloud: data can be replicated transparently and stored in multiple locations. Amazon, for example, has data centers not only in the eastern and western United States, but also in Europe, all representing the same cloud abstraction. This can be useful since data is now closer to more users and widespread redundancy is assured. However, issues such as compliance can be in conflict with this migration. For example, US regulations governing the protection of data differ from those laid out by the European Union's Directive 95/46/EC [27]. As a result, data created in the US may risk being out of compliance if it is silently transferred to European data centers. As another example, companies subject to US International Traffic in Arms Regulations (ITAR) must follow strict export restrictions such as preventing data from physically leaving the United States. While Amazon's GovCloud service is designed with these compliance issues in mind [2] customers not only pay more for the service but do not benefit from geographic redundancy within the US, since GovCloud is deployed separately from the rest of the Amazon cloud service and only within one data center. Because of these and associated concerns regarding the jurisdiction of cloud data [19, 12], users of general-purpose clouds must be careful about uploading data since support for data migration, as well as other forms of controlling access and movement, is not provided, an issue that Peterseon et al. call data sovereignty [24].

This paper proposes that *data provenance* provides the necessary support to address these challenges. With provenance, information is kept about the origin and pedigree of data through documenting the initial conditions and variables under which data was created, and the conditions under which any modifications were made. It thus allows for more robust access decisions: by using the lineage of data, rather than its ephemeral present condition, we can change the *stateless* access control decision into a *stateful* decision.

While proposals exist to support provenance in the cloud [21], the issue of securing provenance in such environments has been left unaddressed. Providing this security is challenging for a variety of reasons. Securely generating and collecting provenance is difficult, as is transmitting it in a secure and trustworthy fashion. We propose additions to the cloud infrastructure that support the secure management of provenance for use in access decisions. *Policy enforcement points* (PEPs) collect provenance from hosts and act as the arbiters of whether to allow reading or writing to cloud storage. *Policy decision points* (PDPs) are system components responsible for ensuring provenance validity and policy compliance of data prior to allowing it into cloud storage. Finally, *provenance databases* store provenance for querying by PDP. Our implementation of the system is deployed in a real cloud environment. Our focus is the management and mediation of data and its provenance as it travels to and beyond organizational boundaries.

Our contributions can thus be summarized as follows:

- We design a system and associated protocols for securing and managing provenance in distributed cloud environments. This is the first system we are aware of that contains this functionality.

- We present an access control scheme based on the use of provenance attributes for policy decisions, and mechanisms for evaluating and optimizing these decisions in cloud environments.

- We evaluate our prototype implementation using the Cumulus cloud storage environment on the University of Oregon's ACISS science cloud, and show that provenance-based access controls can support thousands of operations per second on a single deployment with an imposed overhead cost as low as 14%.

Section 2 provides further background about data provenance and the Nimbus and Cumulus cloud systems. Section 3 describes the design of our system, including details on operation. Section 4 describes our prototype implementation, while in Section 5 we evaluate our design through intensive testing of overhead and scalability. Section 6 describes related work, and we conclude in Section 7.

2. BACKGROUND

2.1 Cloud Storage

Organizations use cloud storage systems to outsource their storage needs. Once the storage is leased, organizations can delegate read and write access to users. Based on granted permissions, users download files, process them on some host, and then upload the data back to the cloud. Nimbus is an open-source project for converting clusters of computers into an infrastructure-as-a-service cloud. Nimbus provides a storage system, Cumulus, which includes an authentication module that provides discretionary access control and a back-end that allows cloud providers to connect Cumulus to various storage devices. Cumulus is compatible with Amazon S3 REST API [1], exposing a set of commands for uploading, reading and updating files on the storage system.

Discretionary access control schemes in existing cloud storage systems suffer from many challenges. Once permissions are granted, cloud storage operations happen anonymously. Thus, organizations cannot keep track of who accesses their data. Moreover, organizations cannot track what happens to data after it exits the cloud boundary. They cannot answer questions such as: *Which application processed the data? What other datasets were used to generate current data? What were the host system conditions, such as security level and geographic location, when this data was processed?*

This lack of monitoring complicates the enforcement of data access. Organizations may wish to prevent access by hosts outside of their institutional boundaries, block hosts in certain geographical regions due to legal restrictions, or ensure that hosts accessing their data can provide certain integrity assurances.

2.2 Provenance

Provenance provides information on the actions taken on data from its genesis onwards. More specifically, provenance information describes the sources and the processing the data has undergone to get to its current state. Provenance information can be used to answer questions such as: *Which programs, applications, and datasets helped produce the data? In what environment was the data produced?*

Provenance information has a wide range of critical applications. In some cases, the value of data depends on its sources. Data provenance can identify the trusted or knowledgeable sources, making it useful as a mechanism for ensuring regulatory purposes. However, provenance information cannot be trusted unless its integrity is assured. Moreover, provenance must be protected differently than regular data. Recent work has explored scenarios where provenance requires different security than the data it describes [6]. Knowledge of a file's provenance may reveal secret details about company processes and environments, and may sometimes be more sensitive than the data itself. Unlike typical data, which can be created, modified or deleted, provenance metadata is immutable and append-only, requiring an efficient management infrastructure as it grows over time.

To address the challenge of collecting provenance from the host, we leverage the PASS system [20]. PASS overlays its own file system on top of raw storage and intercepts system calls in the kernel to generate provenance information. Whereas PASS provides a mechanism for collecting provenance on host systems, our purpose is to develop an infrastructure for securely sharing and applying provenance in distributed environments.

3. SYSTEM DESIGN

This work sets out to address the challenge of securely managing provenance metadata in the cloud. To this end,

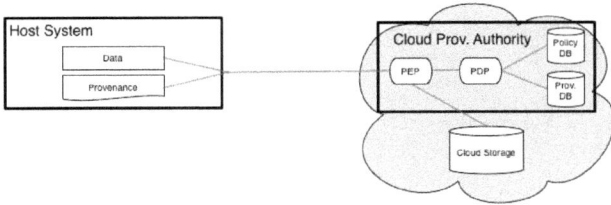

Figure 1: Cloud Provenance Authority system overview.

1. $C \rightarrow PA :$ $n_c, Guid_c, oid$

2. $PA \rightarrow C :$ $n_{pa}, PC_{oid,t-1}, Sign[K_{pa}^-, PC_{oid,t-1}||n_c]$

3. $C \rightarrow PA :$ $Sign[K_c^-, PC_{oid,t}||n_{pa}], PC_{oid,t}, Object$

4. $PA \rightarrow C :$ $Sign[K_{pa}^-, PC_{oid,t}]$

Table 1: Commitment protocol for write operation between Clients (C) and the Cloud Provenance Authority (PA).

$n_i :$	nonce issued by i
$K_i^+, K_i^- :$	i's private key and public key
$Hash(m) :$	digest of message m
$Sign[k, m] :$	signature of message m using key k
$Guid_i :$	global user identifier for user i
$oid :$	object identifier
$a||b :$	concatenation of two strings, a and b
$Object :$	data object
$PC_t :$	t-th chain in provenance chain
$PI_t :$	provenance information of t-th version of the file

Figure 2: Summary of notations.

we assume that end hosts reliably generate complete and accurate provenance records, employing a trusted mechanism that collects and transmits provenance to the cloud. This challenge is orthogonal to our work and has previously been explored elsewhere. Most notably, the Hi-Fi system introduces a provenance reference monitor by leveraging the Linux security module framework [17, 25].

Our work considers an actively malicious adversary, in contrast to the benign environment considered in previous cloud provenance work [22, 21]. This attacker will attempt to manipulate provenance inputs to a security-critical cloud function such as access control or integrity verification. The attacker may attempt to alter the secrecy or integrity levels of an object by modifying its provenance chain, or discover hidden processing information by inspecting an object's ancestry. The attack surface considered in this work is the components comprising our Cloud Provenance Authority.

A further consideration in our work is protecting existing data from being tainted by untrusted hosts or organizations. This is a special case of integrity enforcement that is of major concern in the cloud environment. Shifts in organizational trust may occur often, causing frequent changes to our access control policy. For this reason, we wish for our system to be able to adapt to changes in policy quickly. We will soon show that provenance can be used in policy generation to quickly infer access control labels.

With this in mind, our system sets out to achieve the following goals:

- *Secure Distributed Provenance.* Previous work on secure provenance has focused on individual hosts [14, 13], while literature on managing provenance in distributed environments has left security unaddressed [21].

- *Fast Evaluation.* Many provenance use cases focus on infrequent, offline costs [22] or on data objects with limited ancestry [9]. Our architecture must provide efficient evaluation of remote data objects, even when they possess extensive ancestries.

- *Provenance-based Access Control.* We pursue an access control mechanism that accepts provenance as input in addition to subjects, objects and actions.

Due to space concerns, we have omitted a complete threat model and security analysis. Our design draws its security from previous work on signed provenance chains [14]. In this work, we present a scalable and efficient methodology for extending these constructions to distributed environments.

3.1 Design Overview

Our *Cloud Provenance Authority* architecture, shown in Figure 1, is a set of distributed components responsible for mediating access to cloud storage while collecting and managing provenance metadata. This architecture forms an overlay for existing cloud services, and thus does not require any modifications to cloud infrastructure. This system is data agnostic, allowing it to be applied to any level of cloud abstraction with only minor modification.

The core components of the Cloud Provenance Authority are the *Policy Enforcement Point (PEP)*, *Policy Decision Point (PDP)*, *Provenance Database*, and *Policy Database*. The PEP checks integrity of user requests and enforces access control on data according to an organization's policy. The PDP keeps organization policies and evaluates requests against the policies. The Provenance and Policy Databases store provenance information and security policies, respectively. The system operations are as follows:

- A user requests to store data on the cloud storage. The PEP then receives the request, approves it through the PDP, and stores the data on cloud storage.

- A user requests data stored on the cloud. The PEP receives the request, approves it through the PDP, and sends data to user.

- A user requests provenance from the Cloud Provenance Authority. The PEP receives the request and approves it through the PDP, which shares the provenance information for the PEP to return to the user.

3.2 System Operation

3.2.1 Writing Data to Cloud Storage

When a user tries to write a file to cloud storage, a query consisting of the data and its provenance is sent to the Cloud

Provenance Authority. The PEP component receives the query and acts as a transparent proxy for all cloud storage operations. It checks the integrity of the request and sends it to the PDP, which evaluates it against a set of pre-defined policies. The PDP then informs the PEP of the outcome. If the operation is allowed, the PEP updates data in cloud storage on behalf of the user, transmits the provenance of the data to the PDP's provenance database, and sends an acknowledgement to the user.

To transmit the new chain to the cloud authority and provide mutual non-repudiability, the client follows a provenance commitment protocol. The protocol is described in Table 1 and uses the list of notations explained in Figure 2. In the first two steps of this protocol, the client and the cloud authority exchange initialization information. At step 3, the client sends provenance information with the write request to the Cloud Provenance Authority. The cloud sends back the signed operation to the client at step 4. This ensures mutual non-repudiability. The dialog between the cloud provenance authority and the client is mediated through the PEP.

Provenance integrity assurance is a critical component of our system design. Each time a write is committed to cloud storage, a new data version must be accounted for in the associated provenance records. Since we want to make sure that we can track the provenance information at each version of the data, we use a secure provenance chain introduced by Hasan et al. [14]. Equation 1 summarizes how the provenance chain is created at each step:

$$PC_t = Sign[K_u^-, hash(PI_t || PC_{t-1})] \qquad (1)$$

Provenance chains prevent a variety of tampering attacks by tracking writes and securing the associated provenance. The provenance chain, signed by the user, connects the provenance information of a newly modified file to previous versions. Creating a chain of signed provenance commitments ensures that links are not removed, added, or altered.

3.2.2 Reading Data from Cloud Storage

The read operation from cloud storage is very similar to the write operation. When the PEP receives the query, it queries the PDP for an access control decision. The PDP retrieves the latest provenance information from the database and checks the information against the security policy. If the query is compatible with the policies, the PEP sends the file to the user.

In order to avoid losing track of the ancestry of a given file, each file has a reference back to the cloud. This reference consists of the cloud identification, file identification (used by the cloud storage) and the version of the file in the cloud. This information can inform an auditor where to find a file's provenance. The main advantage of such a reference is to address the problem of provenance growth [5].

3.2.3 Provenance Management and Retrieval

In order to create a scalable architecture for cloud provenance, a necessary first step is detaching provenance from the its associated data. There are two disadvantages for a system that stores the data and provenance in tandem. The first disadvantage of such a system is it makes provenance information visible to everyone who has access to data. On occasion, provenance can require different security than the data it describes [6].The second disadvantage is that provenance information can grow arbitrarily large as a result of

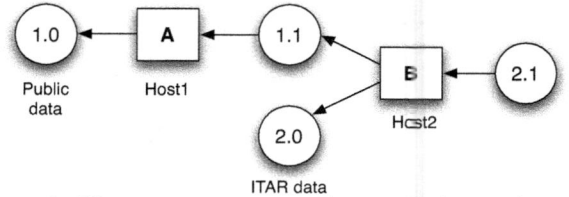

Figure 3: The provenance causality graph for artifact 2.1. Ancestors have been annotated with data labels.

the processing that occurs to data on a single host, hampering performance and scalability. Thus, in our architecture we do not transmit provenance with every file access. Instead, we entrust provenance storage to PDP components.

In turn, this leads to another design question regarding entities with multiple storage servers: *If data retrieved from storage unit A is then stored on storage unit B, is the provenance information on A duplicated to B?* Our answer to this question is *no*. Instead, the provenance information remains in storage unit A, which permits B to access portions of provenance on demand.

This protocol works as follows: upon requesting provenance information, the user provides a chain of certificates. The first certificate is signed by the organization that owns the data, O_0. This certificate contains the delegation rights to another organization, O_1. The next chain contains the delegation rights to O_2, issued by O_1. The sequence of chains continues until one organization grants access to a user, U, as shown in Equation 2:

$$Sign[K_{O_0}^-, Delegation, O_1]$$
$$Sign[K_{O_1}^-, Delegation, O_2] \qquad (2)$$
$$Sign[K_{O_2}^-, read, U]$$

In this manner, cloud provenance authorities can cooperate with each other to track data. For environments that require end user's to inspect provenance information, the query interface can be exposed to clients outside the cloud.

3.3 Provenance-Based Access Control

The Cloud Provenance Authority can be leveraged to perform security-critical functions, such as access control, in a manner that benefits from the rich contextual information that provenance provides. As described by Rosenthal et al. [26], attribute-based access control is superior to role-based access control for provenance due to improved scalability, flexibility, and the ability to modularize policy concerns (i.e., only one attribute needs to be inspected if a change in policy occurs). Attributes of data can be extracted and used to create labels for use in access control decisions. To extract all the attributes of the data, two properties should be assured: (1) the availability of complete data ancestry from original sources to its current form, and (2) the availability of all the necessary attributes of the sources. Our access control language is a simplified model of the provenance-based access control scheme presented by Cadenhead et al. [8].

Provenance-based labeling possesses two appealing characteristics: (1) the ability to dynamically adapt to sudden changes in policy, and (2) the ability to express access decisions based on a variety of attributes and levels of granularity. Consider the example shown in Figure 3. In this case, artifact 2.1 has been generated from the results of two

280

data sets, one of which is public data, and one of which is technical data related to defense and hence subject to ITAR regulations. In order to comply with ITAR, cloud nodes have the following simplified policy rule:

```
<Rule>
  <Operation>migrate-foreign</Operation>
   <Object>
    <Attribute Name="ITAR">
   </Object>
   <Result>deny</Result>
</Rule>
```

This rule states that migration of data to a cloud server outside of the US will be denied if the data contains the ITAR attribute. In Figure 3, we see that as host B combines artifacts 1.1 and 2.0, the corresponding provenance record will have the following entry:

```
<record>
  <record-type>INPUT</record-type>
  <record-data>
    <xref pnode="B" version="2.0" />
  </record-data>
  <record-type>INPUT</record-type>
  <record-data>
    <xref pnode="A" version="1.1" />
  </record-data>
</record>
```

and following the XREF to artifact 2.0 will uncover the ITAR attribute. As a result, the new record will not be allowed to migrate to foreign cloud centers. Host2 is now the provenance authority for artifact 2.1, but another party accessing the object can check the chain of records, which now includes artifact 2.1, artifact 2.0, and artifacts 1.1 and 1.0 hosted by Host1. This is a simplification of the operations, which would involve read and write restrictions based on location of the requesting party and rules defining the semantics of the migrate-foreign operation, but is meant to show that label inference is possible over a provenance attribute set. Policy can similarly be defined that conforms to Bell-LaPadula MLS confidentiality model [3], Biba integrity models [4], or supporting Chinese Wall policy [7] based on attributes of the provenance artifacts.

More formally, let us consider the provenance system as a state machine with subjects $S = \{s_1, s_2, \ldots\}$, objects $O = \{o_1, o_2, \ldots\}$, attributes $A = \{a_1, a_2, \ldots\}$, actions $T = \{t_1, t_2, \ldots\}$, values $V = \{v_1, v_2, \ldots\}$, and states $\Sigma = \{\sigma_1, \sigma_2, \ldots\}$. An access decision in the system will be based on the evaluation of $O \times A \times T \times \Sigma \to V$ where Σ represents the current state of the Cloud Provenance Authority as defined by the policy in place by the organization. Access control decisions are defined with the set $V = \{\text{allow}, \text{deny}\}$. Subjects and objects can be identified in terms of their attributes such that when subject s_1 with attribute set a_1 acts on object o_2 created by subject s_2 with attributes a_2, a new object o_3 is created with attributes $a_3 = a_1 || a_2$. The access decision is contingent on the evaluation of the attributes associated with object o_3 so that when the access policy is evaluated, the result is $o_3 \times a_1 || a_2 \times T \times \sigma_n \to \{\text{allow}, \text{deny}\}$. Note that the provenance record for o_3 will be a secure provenance chain as defined by Hasan and each object o_i and attribute

set a_i is signed by its associated subject s_j (note that subjects can clearly sign arbitrary numbers of objects and attribute sets as they are created and modified). The attribute set a_3 is thus equivalent to $Sign[K_{s_1}^-, a_1] || Sign[K_{s_2}^-, a_2]$, ensuring that the attributes cannot be tampered with. Thus in our above example with the migration policy as dictated giving system state σ_i and action $t_j = \text{migrate-foreign}$, even if $o_1 \times a_1 \times t_j \times \sigma_i \to \{\text{allow}\}$, the newly created object will cause a policy decision $o_1 \times a_3 \times t_j \times \sigma_i \to \{\text{deny}\}$ due to a_3 receiving the ITAR tag from a_2.

Because we can reconstruct the complete ancestry of existing objects, we are free to make arbitrary modifications to our policy without loss of accuracy. A change in policy only requires the one-time cost of re-evaluating the provenance chains of existing artifacts. Unlike traditional labeling mechanisms, the history of modifications is kept as the provenance, making it clear by examining the metadata how the current label has been derived.

4. IMPLEMENTATION

We implemented the architecture described in Section 3 to run on separate virtual machines on an OpenStack KVM cloud service running on the University of Oregon's ACISS high performance cluster. Each component was provisioned with 2 vCPUs and 4GB memory. Each physical host was connected to a 1:1 provisioned Voltaire 8700 switch with fiber channel. The switch had 2 10 GbE trunks to a Cisco router that connected to the university network. Our client scripts connected to the Cloud Provenance Authority components over the campus network. They ran on a commodity PC containing an Intel 3.00GHz dual-core and running the Linux 2.6.38 kernel. The Cloud Provenance Authority was an overlay to a Cumulus storage server. The REST API of Cumulus is consistent with other cloud storage system APIs such as Amazon S3. Accordingly, our system can be implemented on any other compatible cloud storage systems.

The PEP, implemented in Python, acted as a transparent proxy to a Cumulus cloud store. The PEP was responsible for facilitating communication between with the client and PDP using the protocol outlined in Table 1. The PEP authenticated the client, verified provenance chain signatures, and mediated requests by checking policies with the PDP via remote procedure calls. The PEP was stateless, querying the PDP for user information and access decisions.

The PDP server, also implemented in Python, connected locally to a sqlite3 database that stored policy, provenance, and client session information. The PDP reconstructed provenance chains by storing tuples of chain sequence numbers and file handle references for the provenance metadata. To evaluate our system we implemented three different access control mechanisms for the PDP: a basic whitelist-by-hostname policy, an MLS policy that evaluated provenance chains and labeled each object after the highest secrecy level in its history, and an optimized MLS mechanism that cached decisions in order to avoid repetitive parsing of object ancestry.

A final component, a client host, submitted requests to the PEP to get and put data in the cloud store. These operations were either allowed or disallowed by the PDP based on the active policy. The client used PASS as the host provenance system. Provenance information was queried using Path Query Language (PQL) [15]. For the MLS mechanisms, attributes from the PASS provenance metadata were

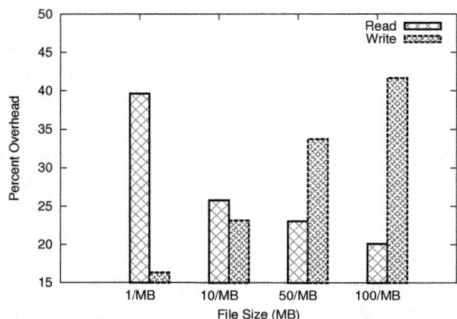

(a) End-to-end system overhead.

Request	Step	1M	10M	50M	100M
Put Obj.	From User: Parse Req.	0.012	0.035	0.185	0.418
Put Obj.	To PDP: Get User Info	0.003	0.003	0.003	0.003
Put Obj.	To PDP: Check policy	0.004	0.004	0.004	0.005
Put Obj.	To Storage: Write Data	0.109	0.153	0.384	0.603
Put Obj.	To PDP: Append Prov.	0.004	0.004	0.004	0.005
Get Obj.	From User: Parse Req.	0.001	0.001	0.001	0.001
Get Obj.	To PDP: Check Policy	0.003	0.003	0.003	0.003
Get Obj.	To Storage: Read Data	0.015	0.089	0.385	0.757
Get Obj.	To User: Send Data	0.007	0.028	0.113	0.187

(b) Microbenchmarks for Policy Enforcement Point.

Figure 4: Performance cost of Cloud Provenance Authority architecture.

mapped to secrecy levels, and then submitted to the cloud authority in order to trigger access control decisions.

5. EVALUATION

5.1 System Overhead

Remote storage already has an associated delay, so our infrastructure needs to maintain a minimal performance footprint. We begin by investigating the overhead imposed by our system on write and read operations compared to basic cloud storage use. For this trial, a client host issued write and read requests of increasing size to a single PEP. The requests were checked against a simple whitelist policy at a single PDP, then processed. Figure 4a shows the percent overhead of our system relative to the raw cost of the Cumulus read and write operations. The overhead imposed decreases with the size of read operations, as low as 20%. Overhead increases with the size of write operations, with a low of 17.4% on small writes.

To better understand these costs, we recorded microbenchmarks for the various operations at the PEP. These results are displayed in Table 4b, with size-dependent fields highlighted. Because the PEP acts as a proxy to the storage, twice as much data transmission is required over raw storage access. The overhead of write operations increases with file size due to disproportionate growth in the time required to parse write requests. Without these transmission costs, the performance footprint is extremely small. Because the PDP is not involved in transmission of the actual object, it is underutilized for both the read and write operations.

Configuration	Avg. Speed (s)	Overhead
Direct Read	0.0928	0.0%
1 PEP Proxy	0.9512	90.2%
2 PEP Proxies	0.4901	81.1%
3 PEP Proxies	0.3551	73.0%
4 PEP Proxies	0.2643	64.8%
5 PEP Proxies	0.2205	14.0%

Table 2: Read speeds with additional PEP components.

5.2 Distributed Enforcement Points

While the performance cost imposed by redundant transmission is considerable, it was necessary to our overlay design to avoid requiring special changes to PASS or the Ama-

zon API. Fortunately, overhead cost can be easily decreased by using a distributed set of PEPs to process user requests. As noted in Section 5.1, a single PDP is underutilized in a deployment featuring a single PEP, allowing for the distributing of PEP tasks until either cloud storage or the PDP form a new system bottleneck. In a new trial, a single client executed batches of 100 reads of a 10/MB file with up to 5 PEPs running as separate instances within a university cloud service. Table 2 shows the results of this trial. As the system becomes more distributed, the per-request cost of the batch operations decreases by a factor of 4, resulting in an overhead as low as 14%.

5.3 Provenance Size

Another factor contributing to the duration of write transactions is the size of the provenance information that is attempting to be committed. A provenance chain's immutable nature can lead to unwieldy growth in the number of records, leading to considerable overhead on write transactions if large amounts of provenance has been stored locally or if new provenance is being migrated into storage. This cost is entirely separate from the size of the actual data. To analyze the impact of provenance growth on system performance, we repeated the previous trial for a single object with increasingly large provenance chains. Under three different access control mechanisms, we measured the speed with which the PDP arrived at an access decision. Figure 5a depicts the results. The unoptimized MLS policy, which re-parses the entire object ancestry with each request, became prohibitively expensive at large provenance sizes. In contrast, the whitelist and memoized MLS policies need only parse the newly appended provenance records.

5.4 Extreme Workload

To assess our infrastructure's ability to handle real-world workloads, we tested each of our access control mechanisms against the 1998 World Soccer Cup website trace. Envisioning a frequent-read-infrequent-write scenario, we mapped 99.8% of the HTTP requests in the trace to GET requests for our file, and the other remaining 0.2% to PUT requests. We selected a 10 minute window of 606,060 requests for analysis. Using the 5 PEP deployment from Section 5.2, we played the trace through one second at a time and observed the utilization level required for our infrastructure to handle the load in real time. To better isolate our system's performance, the PEPs transmitted empty acknowledgement messages to the user instead of communicating with Cumulus storage. All of

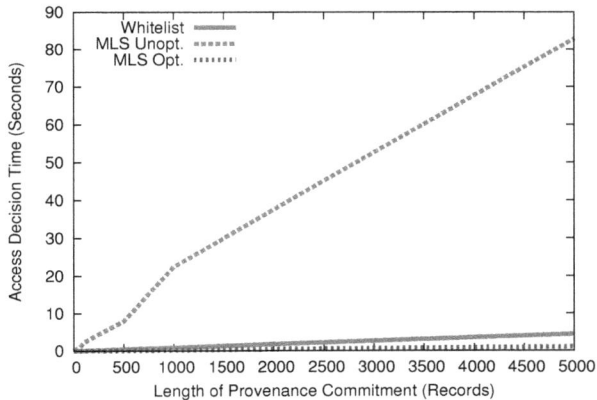

(a) Provenance chain size effect on PDP response times.   (b) Utilization during 1998 World Cup trace web requests.

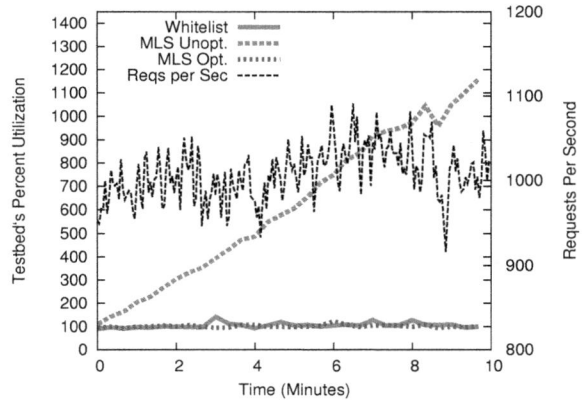

Figure 5: Performance of provenance-based access control mechanisms.

the other system functions, including provenance migration and evaluation, were active for the experiment.

The performance of each mechanism is pictured in Figure 5b. The system load under the different access controls appears on the primary y-axis, while the trace workload in requests per second appear on the secondary y-axis. The performance of the unoptimized MLS mechanism, which is dependent on length of the object's ancestry, degrades over time. The optimized MLS mechanism was nearly able to handle the entire workload in real time, averaging 100.2% utilization over the course of the trial (i.e. 12 seconds of total delay were observed). Even on a modest deployment using a single centralized provenance database, our infrastructure handles thousands of access decisions per second.

6. RELATED WORK

Provenance systems have been well studied and surveyed in scientific contexts [28, 10, 18]. Provenance information can be recorded at various levels of abstraction. Application-level provenance systems collect provenance at the semantic level of the applications [30], while provenance systems for workflow engines record provenance at the level of workflow stages [29]. Provenance systems can also be implemented at the kernel level by intercepting system calls and recording them as provenance information. The provenance-aware storage system (PASS) [20] that we integrate into our system leverages the kernel-level approach. Muniswamy-Reddy et al. [22, 21] were the first to consider the challenges of adopting provenance to the cloud. They leveraged Amazon's S3 data storage to extend their host level provenance collector (PASS) [20] to the cloud environment. We extend this work by developing a distributed provenance management infrastructure under a malicious threat model.

During the past few years, several studies have recognized the importance of securing provenance [19, 13, 17]. Braun et al. [6] discuss that provenance requires its own security model that differs from regular data. Hasan et al. [14] consider a scheme for securely collecting and auditing provenance records with a focus on preventing undetected rewriting of provenance history. We use their approach to provide integrity for provenance information in the cloud. Rosenthal et al. [26] discuss an attribute-based access control scheme for provenance information. Their emphasis is on determin-

ing access based on provenance attributes. In our work, the permission to access provenance information is granted by the organization that owns the data. Another line of work by Ni et al. [23] modifies the provenance records to enable finer-grained policies for accessing provenance information. Given the significantly different features of cloud environment, our main target in this paper is scalability.

Ensuring that provenance metadata is properly collected and securely communicated makes certain demands of host systems. McDaniel et al. [17, 25] propose addressing the challenge of provenance mediation through *provenance monitors*. Their scheme exhibits reference monitor guarantees by preventing circumvention of provenance recording mechanisms, assuring the trustworthiness of collected information. Trusted computing, particularly trusted platform modules (TPMs) and attested boot mechanisms, provide a means of supporting this bottom-up trust model [16]. However, implementing such systems in the cloud requires support (e.g., remote attestation) from cloud providers. The secure provenance system that we propose in this paper can work on normal services offered by cloud providers.

7. CONCLUSION

This paper has introduced an architecture for managing provenance metadata in the cloud and provides a means for using provenance as the basis for an attribute-based access control system suitable for enforcing organizational security policies. Through the use of provenance to enforce access control, we effectively shift the access control paradigm from a stateless decision made strictly on the current state of data, to a stateful decision based on the data's origin and lineage. Our prototype implementation shows that such a system is also practical, supporting thousands of operation per second on a modestly specified deployment. These investigations are a preliminary exploration into the myriad challenges faced when securing provenance at scale across organizational boundaries and within the cloud.

Acknowledgemnts

We thank the members of the OSIRIS Lab at the University of Oregon for their helpful comments and suggestions, and Chris Hoge and the ACISS staff for their assistance and support. This work is supported by NSF grant CNS-1118046.

8. REFERENCES

[1] Amazon. Amazon Simple Storage Service (S3), 2011.

[2] Amazon. Amazon Web Services: Risk and Compliance. http://media.amazonwebservices.com/AWS_Risk_and_Compliance_Whitepaper.pdf, 2012.

[3] D. Bell and L. LaPadula. Secure Computer Systems: Mathematical Foundations and Model. Technical Report M74-244, MITRE Corporation, Bedford, MA, 1973.

[4] K. J. Biba. Integrity Considerations for Secure Computer Systems. *Proceedings of the 4th Annual Symposium on Computer Architecture*, 5(7):135–140, 1977.

[5] U. Braun, S. Garfinkel, D. A. Holland, K. Muniswamy-Reddy, and M. Seltzer. Issues in Automatic Provenance Collection. In *Proceedings of the 2006 International Provenance and Annotation Workshop*, Chicago, Illinois, May 2006.

[6] U. Braun, A. Shinnar, and M. Seltzer. Securing Provenance. In *Proceedings of the USENIX Workshop on Hot Topics in Security (HotSec)*, San Jose, CA, 2008.

[7] D. F. C. Brewer and M. J. Nash. The Chinese Wall Security Policy. In *Proceedings of the 10th IEEE Symposium on Security and Privacy*, Oakland, CA, USA, 1989.

[8] T. Cadenhead, V. Khadilkar, M. Kantarcioglu, and B. Thuraisingham. A Language for Provenance Access Control. In *CODASPY '11: Proceedings of the first ACM Conference on Data and Application Security and Privacy*, pages 133–144, San Antonio, TX, USA, 2011. ACM Press.

[9] M. Dietz, S. Shekhar, Y. Pisetsky, A. Shu, and D. S. Wallach. QUIRE: Lightweight Provenance for Smart Phone Operating Systems. In *Proceedings of the 20th USENIX Security Symposium*, 2011.

[10] J. Freire, D. Koop, E. Santos, and C. T. Silva. Provenance for Computational Tasks: A Survey. *Computing in Science and Engineering*, 10(3):11–21, 2008.

[11] J. Galante, O. Karif, and P. Alpeyav. Sony's Network Breach Shows Amazon Cloud's Appeal for Hackers. *Bloomberg News*, 16 May 2011.

[12] R. Gellman. Privacy in the Clouds: Risks to Privacy and Confidentiality from Cloud Computing. *World Privacy Forum*, pages 1–26, 2009.

[13] R. Hasan, R. Sion, and M. Winslett. Introducing Secure Provenance: Problems and Challenges. In *Proceedings of the 2007 ACM Workshop on Storage Security and Survivability*, StorageSS '07, pages 13–18, New York, NY, USA, 2007. ACM.

[14] R. Hasan, R. Sion, and M. Winslett. The Case of the Fake Picasso: Preventing History Forgery with Secure Provenance. In *FAST '09: Proceedings of the 7th USENIX Conference on File and Storage Technologies*, 2009.

[15] D. A. Holland and M. Seltzer. PQL - Path Query Language. http://www.eecs.harvard.edu/syrah/pql/, 2011.

[16] J. Lyle and A. Martin. Trusted Computing and Provenance: Better Together. In *TaPP '10: Proceedings of the 2nd USENIX Workshop on the Theory and Practice of Provenance*, Berkeley, CA, USA, 2010.

[17] P. McDaniel, K. Butler, S. McLaughlin, R. Sion, E. Zadok, and M. Winslett. Towards a Secure and Efficient System for End-to-End Provenance. In *TaPP '10: Proceedings of the 2nd USENIX Workshop on the Theory and Practice of Provenance*, 2010.

[18] L. Moreau, B. Ludäscher, I. Altintas. et al. Special Issue: The First Provenance Challenge. *Concurrency and Computation: Practice and Experience*, 20(5):409–418, 2008.

[19] M. Mowbray. The Fog over the Grimpen Mire: Cloud Computing and the Law. *Scripted Journal of Law, Technology and Society*, 6(1), Apr. 2009.

[20] K. Muniswamy-Reddy, D. A. Holland, U. Braun, and M. Seltzer. Provenance-Aware Storage Systems. In *Proceedings of the 2006 USENIX Annual Technical Conference*, 2006.

[21] K. Muniswamy-Reddy, P. Macko, and M. I. Seltzer. Provenance for the Cloud. In *FAST '10: Proceedings of the 8th USENIX Conference on File and Storage Technologies*, 2010.

[22] K. Muniswamy-Reddy and M. Seltzer. Provenance as First-Class Cloud Data. In *Proceedings of the ACM ACM SIGOPS International Workshop on Large Scale Distributed Systems and Middleware (LADIS)*, 2009.

[23] Q. Ni, S. Xu, E. Bertino, R. Sandhu, and W. Han. An Access Control Language for a General Provenance Model. In *Secure Data Management*, Aug. 2009.

[24] Z. N. J. Peterson, M. Gondree, and R. Beverly. A Position Paper on Data Sovereignty: The Importance of Geolocating Data in the Cloud. In *HotCloud'11: Proceedings of the 3rd USENIX Workshop on Hot Topics in Cloud Computing*, June 2011.

[25] D. Pohly, S. McLaughlin, P. McDaniel, and K. Butler. Hi-Fi: Collecting High-Fidelity Whole-System Provenance. In *Proceedings of the 2012 Annual Computer Security Applications Conference*, ACSAC '12, Orlando, FL, USA, 2012.

[26] A. Rosenthal, L. Seligman, A. Chapman, and B. Blaustein. Scalable Access Controls for Lineage. In *TaPP '09: Proceedings of the 1st USENIX Workshop on the Theory and Practice of Provenance*, San Francisco, CA, USA, 2009.

[27] G. Shaffer. Globalization and Social Protection: The Impact of EU and International Rules in the Ratcheting Up of US Data Privacy Standards. *Yale Journal of International Law*, 25:1–88, 2000.

[28] Y. Simmhan, B. Plale, and D. Gannon. A Survey of Data Provenance in e-Science. *ACM SIGMOD Record*, 34(3):31–36, 2005.

[29] M. Szomszor and L. Moreau. Recording and Reasoning over Data Provenance in Web and Grid Services. In *International Conference on Ontologies, Databases and Applications of SEmantics (ODBASE'03)*, volume 2888, pages 603–620, 2003.

[30] J. Widom. Trio: A System for Integrated Management of Data, Accuracy, and Lineage. Technical Report 2004-40, Stanford InfoLab, Aug. 2004.

Engineering Access Control Policies for Provenance-aware Systems *

Lianshan Sun
Dept. of Computer Science
Shaanxi Univ. of Sci. & Tech.
Xi'an, Shaanxi, China.
sunlianshan@gmail.com

Jaehong Park
Insitute for Cyber Security
Univ. of Texas at San Antonio
San Antonio, TX, USA
jae.park@utsa.edu

Ravi Sandhu
Insitute for Cyber Security
Univ. of Texas at San Antonio
San Antonio, TX, USA
ravi.sandhu@utsa.edu

ABSTRACT

Provenance is meta-data about how data items become what they are. A variety of provenance-aware access control models and policy languages have been recently discussed in the literature. However, the issue of eliciting access control requirements related to provenance and of elaborating them as provenance-aware access control policies (ACPs) has received much less attention. This paper explores the approach to engineering provenance-aware ACPs since the beginning of software development. Specifically, this paper introduces a typed provenance model (TPM) to abstract complex provenance graph and presents a TPM-centric process for identification, specification, and refinement of provenance-aware ACPs. We illustrate this process by means of a homework grading system.

Categories and Subject Descriptors

D.2.10 [**Software Engineering**]: Design—*Representation, Methodologies*; D.4.6 [**Security and Protection**]: Access Controls

Keywords

Provenance; typed provenance model; provenance-aware access control policy; PAC; PBAC; TPM; OPM

1. INTRODUCTION

Provenance captures the origins and processes by which a data item became what it is [3]. In the last decade we have seen the emergence of provenance-aware systems (PAS), which generate, store, process, and disseminate provenance to improve trustworthiness of data items in domains such as scientific workflow, intelligence, and healthcare systems [7].

Provenance itself must be securely protected when it is used to verify trustworthiness and integrity of data items in

*This work is partially supported by NSF (No. CNS-1111925), NSF of China (No. 61202019), and SUST Foundation (No. BJ09-13).

PAS [9]. However, provenance differs from traditional data items and meta-data in that it is an immutable directed graph incrementally captured at run-time. We refer to the provenance in a PAS as a provenance graph. It includes nodes for artifacts (data objects), processes, or agents involved in producing a piece of data and edges for causality dependencies (provenance dependencies) among nodes [12]. Note that a sub-graph of a provenance graph as a unit may show meaningful provenance semantic and could be treated as sensitive resources or be used to adjudicate access requests [4, 15]. Traditional access control models, policy languages, policy authoring tools, enforcement infrastructures, as well as methodologies for engineering access control policies can not be straightforwardly adopted for provenance-aware access control [2, 9].

Researchers have recently proposed a variety of provenance-aware access control models [1, 2, 9, 15] and corresponding policy languages [4, 14]. Provenance could affect access control in at least two ways. The first is the so-called provenance access control or PAC, where provenance itself could be sensitive and should be properly protected [1]. Note that data items with provenance do not have to be sensitive when their provenance is sensitive. For example, provenance of an insensitive report, such as which agent had authored a report and how, could be sensitive. The second is the provenance-based access control or PBAC [15], where provenance as the immutable history about data items can be used to adjudicate access requests on the data items. For example, in a homework grading system, a professor can grade homework of her students if and only if the homework was not graded before and has been reviewed at least two times.

However, provenance-aware access control policies (ACPs), including PAC policies and PBAC policies, could be very complex due to the complexity of provenance. Even with the availability of provenance-aware access control models and policy languages, several practical issues need to be further examined and corresponding solutions need to be developed for engineering provenance-aware ACPs.

First, provenance is usually very complex and hard to be understood in a semantically meaningful way. Also, while existing policy languages [4, 15] assume the availability of some form of provenance graphs [12], the provenance graph is usually not available when eliciting security requirements and defining provenance-aware ACPs at the beginning of PAS development [13, 15]. Therefore, we suggest provenance should be modeled in abstractions, which are meaningful enough and readily available for policy authors to efficiently define provenance-aware ACPs. Recently, Park et al propose to construct provenance-aware ACPs from the named abstract dependency path patterns of a provenance graph, called dependency names [13, 15]. However, the nature of abstracted dependency names, relationships among them, and the manner of modeling and using them to construct provenance-aware ACPs should be further studied.

Second, some access control requirements that can be implemented as provenance-aware ACPs are originally functional requirements in a traditional provenance-unaware system and were implemented inside functional modules. For example, in workflow systems, one common constraint is that an activity A can start only after another activity B is finished. Such constraints are typically implemented as hard-coded logic in a provenance-unaware system. However, as shown in the rest of this paper, these constraints can be implemented as PBAC policies. That means, from the beginning of PAS development, developers need to decide what parts of general user requirements can be and should be captured as access control requirements that will be implemented as provenance-aware ACPs.

Inspired by the idea of security engineering[1] [6, 21], this paper explores the issues of engineering provenance-aware ACPs, specifically the issues of identifying access control requirements out of user requirements that can be implemented as provenance-aware ACPs, modeling provenance in abstraction for efficient specification of ACPs, and engineering provenance-aware ACPs in a systematic manner. Specifically, this paper introduces a typed provenance model (TPM) to abstract complex provenance graph at design level. A TPM captures semantically meaningful provenance abstractions which can be used to efficiently define and manage provenance-aware ACPs. These ACPs can then be evaluated according to the provenance graph. Furthermore, this paper presents a TPM-centric policy development process for identification, specification, and refinement of provenance-aware ACPs from the beginning of PAS development. We illustrate the concept of TPM and the process by a homework grading system.

We organize the rest of this paper as follows. Section 2 introduces preliminaries used in the rest of this paper. Section 3 presents the typed provenance model. Section 4 introduces a TPM centric process for engineering ACPs and applies it in a homework grading system. Section 5 discusses related work and section 6 concludes the paper.

2. PROVENANCE-AWARE SYSTEMS

This section introduces the Open Provenance Model, the general form of provenance-aware ACPs, and a homework grading system used as an example in the rest of the paper.

2.1 Provenance Data Model

A provenance data model defines the scheme of the provenance to be captured. Recently, a community-developed provenance data model, called Open Provenance Model (OPM), has been crafted, refined, and formally defined following a series of challenge workshops. OPM has gained attention as it provides a foundation for the causality dependencies of provenance and enables inter-operability of provenance

across systems [12]. As shown in Figure 1 OPM organizes provenance as a directed acyclic graph, which includes three types of entities, three types of direct dependencies (shown in solid line) and two types of indirect dependencies (shown in dashed line). A provenance graph conforming to OPM is referred as an OPM graph in the rest of this paper.

Entities include artifacts, processes, and agents. In PAS, artifacts are data objects; processes are modules which take some artifacts as inputs, generate some artifacts as outputs; and agents are users who control the processes. Direct dependencies are dependencies directly related to a process and consist of *used, wasGeneratedBy*, and *wasControlledBy*, which are abbreviated as u, g, and c respectively. Figure 1 shows that a process $p2$ used an artifact $a2$ which was generated by a process $p1$. Process $p1$ used another artifact $a1$ and was controlled by an agent Ag.

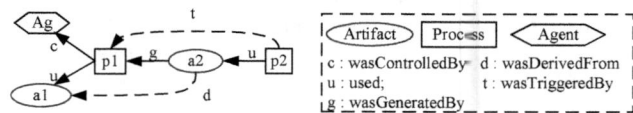

Figure 1: OPM Causality Dependencies.

OPM also defines indirect dependencies, such as *wasDerivedFrom* and *wasTriggeredBy*. The edge $d(a2, a1)$ in Figure 1 denotes that $a2$ was derived from $a1$ and $t(p2, p1)$ denotes that $p2$ was triggered by $p1$. The semantic of an indirect dependency could to some extent be characterized by a path in the OPM graph. For example, $d(a2, a1)$ could be mapped to the path $g(a2, p1) \cdot u(p1, a1)$, where '·' operator concatenates two adjacent edges. This paper assumes only direct dependencies will be captured in an OPM graph. Indirect dependencies can be derived from the direct ones.

2.2 Provenance-aware Access Control Policies

Access control is the process of mediating each access request and evaluating it against some access control policies according to given facts to grant or deny the access request [17, 18]. An access control policy is generally a set of predicates and can be defined as a first-order formula [8]:

$$\forall x_1 \cdots x_m (f \Rightarrow \mathbf{P}(s, a, o)), \qquad (1)$$

where f is a first-order formula, x_i ($i=1,\ldots m$) is a variable used in formula f, the predicate $\mathbf{P}(s, a, o)$ being true means the subject s is allowed to perform action a on an object o and the vector (s, a, o) forms an access request, '$\Rightarrow$' denotes that f is sufficient in granting an access request.

A provenance-aware access control policy is a policy defined with regard to provenance data. Policy architects need to define ACPs by utilizing some meaningful control units of provenance, which are often not the individual nodes or edges of a provenance graph but the entire subgraphs of a provenance graph. It is necessary to apply some grouping strategies on a provenance graph to identify these control units. One strategy is to define regular expression of path patterns on a provenance graph [4]. Park et al further named the regular expressions by literally meaningful dependency names to improve the efficiency of specifying PBAC Policies [13, 15]. Each dependency name can be seen as a short name of a provenance question against a particular starting node v to compute all nodes which caused v in a provenance graph. For example, *OwnedBy* is a short name of the provenance question "who are the owners of a document?".

---

[1]Security engineering believes that access control models and policy languages regulate what kind of ACPs can be specified. However, it is sometimes necessary or at least helpful to identify, specify, and verify ACPs from the beginning of software development.

In PAC, the access request (s, a, o) in the policy equation 1 could be extended to include some provenance questions. An access request in PAS can be defined as a 3-tuple as follows $(s, a, [q](o))$. Here $[q](o)$ denotes provenance answers of a set of optional provenance questions against the object o. $[q]$ denotes that provenance questions are optional.

In PBAC, the formula f in the policy equation 1 could be defined using provenance, which is the answer of some special provenance questions for the purpose of access control. That is, f could include a sub-formula $f' = p_1$ ($\wedge|\vee$) p_2 $\cdots$ ($\wedge|\vee$) p_n, where each access condition p_i is an expression of applying set operations, common logical operations, and basic mathematical operations on the answers of provenance questions against either s or o. Similar to the formula 1, a provenance-aware access control policy can be formally specified in a form:

$$\forall x_1 \cdots x_m (f' \Leftarrow \mathbf{P}(s, a, [q](o))), \qquad (2)$$

where f' and $(s, a, [q](o))$ has semantics as explained above. Note that the left arrow '$\Leftarrow$' means that the provenance assertions are conditions necessary but not sufficient for granting an access request because PAC and PBAC usually do not work alone but together with other traditional access control models, such as role-based ones.

For example, consider a policy that says a user u can see who is the owner of a homework h if u is the grader of the homework. This policy can be formulated as follows

$$\forall h \forall u (u \in GradedBy(h) \Leftarrow \mathbf{P}(u, query, OwnedBy(h)),$$

where $OwnedBy$ and $GradedBy$ are two provenance questions which query who owned and graded the homework h.

2.3 A Homework Grading System

A homework grading subsystem (HGS) is a running example in the rest of this paper. We assume that HGS has deployed a simple role-based subsystem, which can authenticates a user as either a *Student* or a *Professor*.

R_1. A student can upload, replace and submit her own homework. A homework can be submitted only once but can be replaced many times before final submission.

R_2. A student or a professor can review a submitted homework if she was neither the owner nor one of existing reviewers of the homework, and the homework has been reviewed less than three times and not been graded.

R_3. A professor can grade a homework by appending some existing reviews of the homework if the homework has been reviewed at least two times.

R_4. A student can see how many times her homework has been reviewed or graded.

R_5. A reviewer can see whether her review on a homework was appended to a grade or not.

R_6. A professor who grades a homework can see who are the author and reviewers of the homework, and whether a homework was reviewed with conflict of interests (i.e. a homework was reviewed by its owner).

3. PROVENANCE IN ABSTRACTION

A PAS needs to answer various provenance questions. Most of them are proposed by domain users without enough technical knowledge. For example, a professor may ask who owned a homework and whether and when a homework was submitted. Domain users usually do not understand the complex provenance graph, not to mention how to use it to answer the obscure provenance questions in natural language [4, 10]. Because a provenance graph can only be captured at run-time, what developers can perceive at design time are only elements of conceptual software models, such as use cases, scenarios, or classes. An intuitive idea is to allow developers to design application specific types of possible provenance dependencies among different conceptual entities such as classes, actors, and business operations.

This section introduces an abstract model of a provenance graph, the typed provenance model (TPM). TPM is about application-specific conceptual provenance types while OPM is about the application-independent scheme of representing provenance instances. TPM captures entity types, provenance dependency types among entity types, as well as relationships and constraints among dependency types.

3.1 Entity types and dependency types

Each entity type in a TPM is a class which can be instantiated into nodes in an OPM graph. In the provenance graph of the HGS, an artifact node could be instantiated from a class in design model, for example *Homework*. A process node could be instantiated from a business operation in requirements model or a method of a class in design model, for example *upload* and *submit*. An agent could be instantiated from an actor of the target system, for example organizational roles the *Student* and *Professor*.

Dependency type is the core concept of a TPM. It has roots in the notion of "dependency name" [13, 15] and is actually a classifier of similar semantics of multiple dependency paths in an OPM graph. We formally define a dependency type T as a composition of its literal name (N), an effect entity type E, and a cause entity type C as follows.

$$T := N(E, C). \qquad (3)$$

Note that N is a unique name of T and literally shows semantics of T. We will use the symbolic identifier T or the literal name N interchangeably to refer to a dependency type in the rest of this paper. A dependency type can be instantiated into a provenance dependency instance by instantiating both the effect node type and cause node type. For example, a dependency type $ReviewedBy(Homework, User)$ can be instantiated into $ReviewedBy(hw_1, u_1)$ to denote that a homework instance hw_1 was reviewed by a user u_1. If we view each dependency type as a mapping from the effect node to its cause nodes, $ReviewedBy(hw_1)$ returns the set of users who reviewed the homework hw_1, and we have $ReviewedBy(hw_1, u_1) \equiv u_1 \in ReviewedBy(hw_1)$.

TPM includes two kinds of dependency types, the primitive ones, which can be instantiated into individual edges of an OPM graph, and the complex ones, which cannot be instantiated into individual edges rather into subgraphs of an OPM graph. Each complex type needs to be mapped to a composition of primitive types to make itself interpretable according to an OPM graph.

3.2 Primitive dependency types

Each primitive dependency type abstracts the semantics of a set of edges in a provenance graph and could be from a process type to either an artifact type or an agent type, or from an artifact type to a process type. Primitive dependency types related to the same process type can be grouped together to form a process-centered directed graph of provenance in abstraction, called provenance type graph.

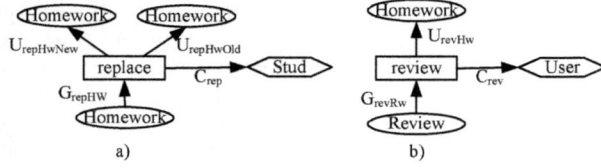

Figure 2: Primitive dependency types.

Figure 2-a is a provenance type graph centered at the *replace* process in the HGS. It shows that a process *replace* (*rep*) will take two homework as inputs. One is the old version of a homework *(hw)* to be replaced and the other is the new homework that is used to replace the old one. The process *replace* is controlled by students (*stud*) and generates a new version of homework as its output. Figure 2-a defines four primitive dependency types T_1 to T_4 as follows. Note that we assume that data is never overwritten or updated in place. Any modification to a data object will create a uniquely new instance of it in a provenance graph.

$$T_1 := U_{repHwOld}(rep, Hw), \quad T_2 := U_{repHwNew}(rep, Hw),$$
$$T_3 := G_{repHW}(Hw, rep), \quad T_4 := C_{rep}(rep, Stud).$$

Here, $U_{repHwOld}$, $U_{repHwNew}$, G_{repHW}, and C_{rep} are unique type names, which literally expose the application specific semantics of dependency types. U, G, and C indicates that the type is an application specific subtype of *Used, wasGeneratedBy*, and *wasControlledBy* dependencies in OPM respectively. For example, $U_{repHwOld}$ means a process *replace* used an *old* version of *homework* as its input. Figure 2-b is a provenance type graph centered at the *review* process.

Each process type that can be finally instantiated into processes at run-time is a method in software design model or a business operation that can be refined into a set of methods. Each method signature could leads to a provenance type graph as shown in Figure 2.

3.3 Complex dependency types

TPM also includes the so-called complex dependency types to encapsulate the complex semantics which cannot be captured by individual primitive dependency types. Each complex dependency type can be defined as a composition of primitive dependency types.

First, the most basic complex dependency type is the concatenation of two primitive dependency types with the operator '·'. To put formally, a complex dependency type $T := T_i \cdot T_j$ means that the effect node type and the cause node type of T are the effect node type of T_i and the cause node type of T_j respectively, and the cause node type of T_i is same as the effect node type of T_j. For example, T_7 below captures the semantics that a homework (Hw) was uploaded (*up*) by a student (*Stud*).

$$T_5 := G_{upHw}(Hw, up); \quad T_6 := C_{up}(up, Stud)$$
$$T_7 := UploadedBy(Hw, Stud) := T_5 \cdot T_6,$$

where G_{upHw} and C_{up} mean that an upload process generates homework and is controlled by students respectively.

Second, each edge of a provenance graph is directional. Its tail node is the cause that its head node became what it

is. However, users could ask which are the effect nodes of a given cause node. We can formally denote the inversion of a dependency type T as $T^{-1} = N^{-1}(C, E)$. It means that a cause node of type C caused one or more effect nodes of type E in the sense of N. For example, T_{12} below computes the set of reviews related to a specific homework. $T_8 - T_{10}$ are primitive dependency types in Figure 2-b.

$$T_8 := G_{revRw}(Rw, rev), T_9 := U_{revHw}(rev, Hw),$$
$$T_{10} := C_{rev}(rev, User), T_{11} := ReviewOn(Rw, Hw) := T_8 \cdot T_9,$$
$$T_{12} := T_{11}^{-1} := ReviewOn^{-1}(Hw, Rw) := T_9^{-1} \cdot T_8^{-1}.$$

Third, some semantics of provenance dependency can be denoted by paths with arbitrary lengths in OPM graph. We can apply regular expression operators over existing dependency types to concisely compose dependency types modeling these semantics. They are the operator "*" for 0 or more of the preceding element, the operator "+" for 1 or more of the preceding element, and the operator "?" for 0 or one of the preceding element. For example, an uploaded homework can be replaced many times before final submission by its author. T_{15} captures the provenance dependency between the submitted homework and its history versions.

$$T_{13} := G_{subHw}(Hw, sub), T_{14} := U_{subHw} sub, Hw),$$
$$T_{15} := SubmisionOn(Hw, Hw) := T_{13} \cdot T_{14} \cdot (T_3 \cdot T_1) * .$$

Fourth, some semantics can be validated by several paths in a provenance graph either disjunctively or conjunctively. To this end, we introduce two operators to reason about the provenance. The conjunctive and disjunctive operator $\wedge$ and $\vee$ enable the refinement of a dependency type into multiple conjunctive or disjunctive sub-types. Note that a dependency type can be composed with another via the operator $\vee$ or $\wedge$ if and only if they have the same cause node type and effect node type. In the HGS, only the owner of a homework can upload, replace, and submit it and a homework reviewed by its owner is involved in conflict of interests. T_{18} and T_{20} below capture semantics between *Homework* and *Student*.

$$T_{16} := ReplacedBy(Hw, Stud) := ((T_3 \cdot T_1)*) \cdot T_3 \cdot T_4;$$
$$T_{17} := SubmittedBy(Hw, Stud) := T_{13} \cdot C_{sub}(sub, Stud);$$
$$T_{18} := OwnedBy(Hw, Stud)$$
$$:= T_{17} \vee (T_{15}? \cdot T_{16}) \vee (T_{15}? \cdot (T_3 \cdot T_1 * \cdot T_7);$$
$$T_{19} := ReviewedBy(Hw, User) := T_9^{-1} \cdot T_{10};$$
$$T_{20} := ReviewedCOI(Hw, User) := T_{18} \wedge T_{19},$$

where T_{18} is defined as three disjunctive sub-types. In T_{18}, T_{17} says that the user who submitted the homework is its owner; $(T_{15}? \cdot T_{16})$ says that the user who replaced it is its owner; $(T_{15}? \cdot (T_3 \cdot T_1) * \cdot T_7)$ says that the user who uploaded it is its owner. Notice that *Stud* is a subclass of *User*.

Note that developers have to ensure that complex dependency types are correctly composed to ensure the correctness of the ACPs specified with them. Various constraints may exist among dependency types. For example one dependency type can be combined with another via the operator $\vee$ or $\wedge$ provided they have the same cause node type and effect node type. Another typical constraint would be that one dependency type cannot be preceded by another one. In the HGS, suppose a dependency type T_r denotes a homework is the new replacement of another homework and T_s denotes a homework is a submitted version of another homework.

$T_s \cdot T_r$ is semantically right while $T_r \cdot T_s$ is wrong because the *replace* process on a homework cannot be activated after the *submit* process on the same homework happened. Note that we do not explore the formalization and verification of various syntactical and semantical constraints in this paper but leave them as our future work.

The set of composition operators introduced in this section is complete in a sense that the concatenation operator '·' and the inversion operator '$^{-1}$' provide sufficient expressiveness of our TPM in terms of abstracting any paths of a provenance graph which carry meaningful provenance dependencies among two nodes. However, new operators can still be added because developers can define their own reasoning rules on provenance types and formulate the rules as new operators of composing complex dependency types for convenience. By introducing complex dependency types and their mapping to compositions of primitive dependency types, a TPM enables the developers to efficiently define ACPs for PAS even when the provenance graph is not available, and ensures that the ACPs defined using dependency types can be evaluated according to the provenance graph captured at run-time.

4. ENGINEERING ACPS BASED ON TPM

This section first describes a TPM-centric process for engineering provenance-aware ACPs, then applies it in the HGS.

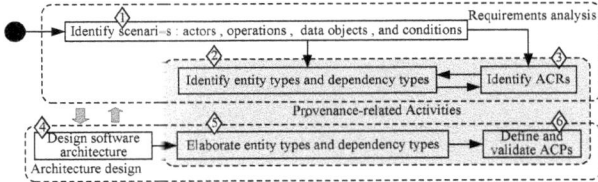

Figure 3: A TPM-centric process.

4.1 Process Overview

The process for engineering ACPs is embedded in the overall process of PAS development. As shown in Figure 3, rectangles in solid lines are activities and arrows are control flows between two activities. Two white rounded rectangles in dashed lines are containers for requirements analysis activities and architecture design activities. As the dark area shows, the activities for defining ACPs over typed provenance model spread across at least requirements analysis and architecture design phases. We introduce these activities and the related artifacts as follows.

1. *Identify scenarios: actors, operations, data objects, and conditions.* Identify scenarios of the target system by general requirements analysis methods. Each scenario is a short story of how a user interacts with the system to accomplish her task in a specific circumstance. In particular some provenance questions may be identified as special scenarios [11], which are the sources of identifying data objects with provenance. Each scenario usually describes who can perform what operations on what objects under what conditions.

   A set of tuples (*actor, operation, object, conditions*) can be identified from each scenario. Each user appears only as a general actor, for example organizational roles *Student* and *Professor* in the HGS. Some

conditions could be identified as access control requirements guarding business operations against data objects. For provenance questions, the operations are mainly various queries on provenance of data objects and conditions defined using provenance.

2. *Identify entity types and dependency types.* Analyzing each provenance question, identify a set of data objects whose provenance is needed to answer the provenance question, as well as actors and operations related to these data objects and define them as entity types in typed provenance model. Identify dependency types that are necessary for answering provenance questions. Choose appropriate and unique type names to carry the semantics of provenance dependencies.

3. *Identify access control requirements (ACRs).* After activities 1 and 2 are done, developers can start identifying ACRs related to provenance. On one hand, some provenance dependencies denoted by provenance types are sensitive and corresponding ACRs should be defined to protect them. On the other hand, some conditions guarding the operations against data objects identified in step 1 can be recognized as ACRs related to provenance, which could have not been identified as dependency types in step 2. So an iteration exists between activities 2 and 3.

4. *Design software architecture (SA).* Designing a software architecture entails allocating requirements into different components and defining connections among them. Each component provides a set of interfaces consumed by other components. Each interface includes a set of method signatures. In our opinion, the method is the minimal unit out of which primitive dependency types can be derived. For example, a *replace* method may lead to primitive dependency types of T_1 to T_4. A software architecture often includes multiple views. This paper only shows the role of the class diagram in deriving the primitive dependency types. Other views, such as state diagram, might also affects the way of modeling provenance types.

5. *Elaborate entity types and dependency types.* Refine both process types (the business operations) and artifact types (the classes at requirements level) into method signatures and classes in the software architecture. Derive necessary primitive dependency types out of the software architecture model. Map each complex dependency type to a composition of primitive dependency types, which is the key to refine ACRs identified in step 3 as ACPs that can be evaluated against the OPM graph.

6. *Define and validate ACPs.* Formally specify ACPs corresponding to the ACRs identified in step 3 according to the refined entity types and dependency types. Validate consistency among the ACPs and ACRs.

This process emphasizes the role of typed provenance model in specifying provenance-aware ACPs in the overall PAS development process. Note that the process itself is intuitive and does not promise to produce a good enough set of ACPs, which heavily depends on the experiences of policy architects. Several issues including the automatic derivation of primitive dependency types out of software architecture and the formalization and automatic verification of the correctness of a TPM model should be solved in the future.

Table 1: A list of scenarios of the HGS.

No.	actor	operation	data objects	conditions
1.1	Student	upload	a **homework**	C0: Any student in the HGS
1.2	Student	replace/submit	a **homework** to get a new or submitted **homework**	C1: Owner of homework C2: Homework was non-submitted.
2	Student or Professor	review	a **homework** to produce a **review**	C3: (Not C1) Not Owner of the homework C4: (Not C2) The homework was submitted C5: Not reviewed the homework before C6: The homework was not graded C7: Number of reviews of the homework < 3
3	Professor	grade	a **homework** to produce a **grade**	C8: Number of reviews of the homework ≥ 2
4	Student	query-prov-of	a **homework** on its reviewed times and graded state	C9: (C1) Owner of the homework
5	Student or Professor	query-prov-of	a **review** as part of a grade	C10: Owner of the review
6	Professor	query-prov-of	a **homework** on its author, reviewers, and whether it is reviewed by a user involved in conflict of interests.	C11: Any professor in the HGS

4.2 Process in Action

In this section, we further articulate the provenance-related activities shown in Figure 3 by applying them in the HGS.

4.2.1 Step 1: Identify and specify scenarios

Identifying scenarios is a common task in primary software development methodologies. We do not discuss in detail but just present the resulted scenarios in table 1, which are elicited from the requirements of the HGS in section 2.3. Scenarios 1.1-1.2 are from the requirement R_1. Scenarios 2-6 are from the requirements R_2-R_6 respectively. Note that scenarios 4-6 are provenance questions.

4.2.2 Step 2: Define entity and dependency types

Based on provenance questions 4-6 in Table 1, we can easily identify the data classes whose provenance should be captured. They are *Homework*, *Review* and *Grade*. We can further identify actors (UT) and operations (PT) related to these data classes (AT) as shown in Table 2. Most operations are literally comprehensible while *query-prov-of* is an operation to query provenance of either a homework, a review, or a grade.

Table 2: Entity types of the HGS.

ET	:=	$UT \mid AT \mid PT.$
UT	:=	$User \mid Stud \mid Prof.$
AT	:=	$Homework \mid Review \mid Grade.$
PT	:=	$upload \mid replace \mid submit$
		$\mid review \mid grade \mid query\text{-}prov\text{-}of.$

We identify dependency types as shown in Table 3 that are necessary to answer provenance questions (scenarios 4-6) in Table 1. Most of them have been introduced in section 3 except for the second and third types, which denote that a homework (Hw) or a review (Rw) is used by a *grade (grd)* process. Table 3 also shows the provenance questions that can be answered using a specific dependency type.

Table 3: Dependency types from prov. questions.

No	Dependency types	Question (type description)
1	$U_{revHw}(rev, Hw)$	4 (review used Hw)
2	$U_{grdHw}(grd, Hw)$	4 (grade used Hw)
3	$U_{grdRw}(grd, Rw)$	5 (grade used Rw)
4	$ReviewedBy(Hw, User)$	6 (Hw was ReviewedBy user)
5	$OwnedBy(Hw, Stud)$	6 (Hw was OwnedBy stud)
6	$ReviewCOI(Hw, User)$	6 (Hw was Reviewedby owner)

The dependency types listed in Table 3 include both primitive types (1-3) and complex types (4-6) but are not exhaustive. Dependencies types could be identified and further specified among any two entity types in ET. In addition, both the entity types and dependency types may need to be refined while designing a software architecture.

4.2.3 Step 3: Identify Provenance-aware ACRs

Based on proper access control models, developers can decide which conditions in Table 1 can be and should be ACRs. This paper focuses on identifying ACRs that can be implemented as provenance-aware ACPs under the guidance of both PAC model [1, 2, 9], where provenance is sensitive resources to be protected, and PBAC model [15], where provenance is used to adjudicate access requests.

In the HGS, we first identify PAC requirements from provenance questions (scenarios 4-6) in Table 1. Second, we identify access conditions that can be defined using provenance, i.e. identifying PBAC requirements. Note that all scenarios with conditions C1-C10 in Table 1 can be defined as PBAC requirements except for those only related to roles, such as C0 and C11. These PBAC requirements introduce new dependency types (such as 2, 5, 6 in Table 4) that were not identified in Table 3.

Table 4: Dependency types from ACRs.

No	Dependency types used to specify	conditions in Table 1
1	$OwnedBy(Hw, Stud)$	C1, C3, C9
2	$G_{subHw}(Hw, sub)$	C2, C4
3	$ReviewedBy(Hw, User)$	C5
4	$U_{grdHW}(grd, Hw)$	C6
5	$ReviewOn(Rw, Hw)$	C7, C8
6	$ReviewOf(Rw, User)$	C10

Finally, we need to identify new PAC requirements for the newly identified dependency types. For simplicity, we assume that provenance is not accessible to users if it is not explicitly permitted by provenance questions in table 1.

4.2.4 Step 4: Design software architecture

Based on the scenarios in Table 1, we define the software architecture of the HGS as a class diagram. Figure 4 defines a class hierarchy of various documents, including *Document*, *Homework*, *Review*, and *Grade*, and a class hierarchy of organizational roles which include *User*, *Stud*, and *Prof*. These classes except for the super class *Document* have been introduced as entity types in table 2. In Figure 4, each descendant class of *Document* overloads its methods to implement different business operations in Table 2. For example, the method $Hw.create(...)$ is a refinement of the business operation *upload* while $Rw.create(...)$ is a refinement of *review*. For simplicity, we omit the details of the

290

signature of each method. The class diagram is an important source for identifying primitive dependency types.

4.2.5 Step 5: Elaborate entity and dependency types

With software architecture models, we can elaborate some entity types, especially the process types and artifact types, define primitive dependency types according to method signatures implementing business operations in requirements model, and elaborate complex dependency types in Table 3 and 4 into compositions of primitive dependency types.

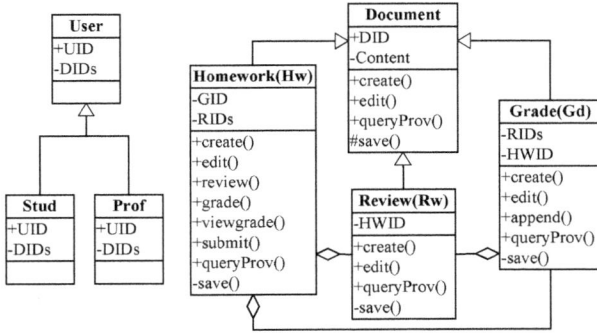

Figure 4: The class diagram of the HGS.

Some business operations identified as process types should be elaborated into method signatures according to software architecture. For example, $Hw.create(\cdots)$ is a process type elaborated from the process type *upload* given in table 2 while $Rw.create(\cdots)$ is elaborated from the process type *review* given in table 2. According to the elaborated process types, we can define primitive dependency types. For example, the method $Hw.create(\cdots)$ takes the homework content which is a string with arbitrary length as its input and produces a homework object as its output. So we can define corresponding primitive dependency types to capture provenance dependencies related to the process type $Hw.create(\cdots)$ as follows. T_{22} is the more accurate form of T_5 introduced in section 3.3, and T_{23} for T_6.

$$T_{21} := U_{upHw}(Hw.create, String),$$
$$T_{22} := G_{upHW}(Hw.create, Hw), T_{23} := C_{up}(Hw.create, Stud).$$

If one business operation is implemented as a chain of methods concatenated via method invocations in software architecture, the corresponding process type could be elaborated into multiple process types and the primitive dependency types related to the original process type should then become complex dependency types.

Complex dependency types in Table 3, 4 can be elaborated into compositions of available dependency types. For example, the dependency type $OwnedBy$ captures the provenance dependency between a homework and its owner. However, designers have to clearly define how the owning relationship was established, such as from the successful execution of the methods $create$, $edit$, and $submit$ of the $Homework$ class. We have defined the $OwnedBy$ dependency type as T_{18} in section 3.3, where T_1, T_3, T_4, T_6, and T_7 need to be redefined because the process types (the business operations, *upload* and *replace*) they relied on have been refined as $Hw.create$ and $Hw.edit$ in software architecture. In this way, we can map all complex dependency types in Table 3, 4 into com-

positions of available dependency types along with the refinement of software architecture.

4.2.6 Step 6: Define and validate ACPs

Using dependency types in Table 3 and 4 and their inversions, we can formally define ACPs in Table 5 to implement access conditions in Table 1. We formalize ACPs as a first-order formula given in equation 2. In Table 5, the letters 'u', 'h', 'g', and 'r' denotes an instance of *User*, *Homework*, *Grade*, and *Review* respectively. Each dependency type serves as a mapping from the effect node to its cause nodes. For example, $ReviewedBy(h)$ returns a set of users who have reviewed the homework h.

Note that ACPs in table 5 are defined on business operations so that we can easily validate them against access control requirements (access conditions) in table 1. However, each business operation may be implemented as a series of methods of architectural components in real settings. Developers need to further refine the ACPs given in Table 5 to get ACPs defined over architectural methods and validate them against access control requirements. Sun et al have discussed this issue in role-based access control systems built on component middleware [20, 22]. We will conduct the similar research on provenance-aware access control systems in the future.

5. RELATED WORK AND DISCUSSION

Provenance differs from traditional data and meta-data in that it is immutable and in a form of directed graph [2]. Not only individual nodes and edges but paths with arbitrary length among nodes in a provenance graph will be treated as a whole unit when it is protected or used to adjudicate access requests. Traditional security models and policy languages are not appropriate for PAS [1, 2]. Correspondingly, policy authoring tools that worked well for traditional access control policies would not work well in the PAS [16].

Policy languages for provenance-aware ACPs have employed regular expressions to dynamically identify protected resources as a control unit [4, 14]. Park et al further introduced the dependency names that envelops a path pattern specified in regular expressions to improve the efficient specification of PBAC policies [13, 15]. The dependency names inspired us to introduce the typed provenance model, which explicitly differentiate the provenance types and their instances, and serves as the basis of efficiently specifying provenance-aware ACPs. As far as we know, no research has previously modeled provenance as we do in this paper.

Provenance-aware security models like PAC [1, 2, 9, 15] and PBAC [13, 15] often do not work alone in real systems. They need to integrate with other access control models, such as RBAC [17, 18]. This paper emphasized on specification of ACPs over provenance in a similar way that is found in role engineering [19] on RBAC policies over roles. Issues of co-design of provenance-aware and other provenance-unaware ACPs are beyond the scope of this paper though we believe our approach is somewhat analogous with role-engineering and it is possible to integrate them together.

This work is the first step of our efforts in realizing idea of security engineering [5, 6, 19, 21] in provenance-aware access control systems. As far as we know, No similar work has been done on engineering provenance-aware ACPs with considerations of the special characteristics of provenance in contrast to general data and meta data. Similar to a

Table 5: Access Control Policies of HGS.

No.	Policies
1.2	$\forall u \forall h \; (u \in OwnedBy(h) \; \wedge \; Submittedby(h) = \phi\;) \Leftarrow \mathbf{P}(u, replace/submit, h)$
2	$\forall u \forall h \begin{pmatrix} u \in OwnedBy(h) \; \wedge \; G_{subHW}(h) \neq \phi \wedge u \notin ReviewedBy(h) \wedge \\ U_{grdHw}^{-1}(h) = \phi \wedge |ReviewOn^{-1}(h)| < 3 \end{pmatrix} \Leftarrow \mathbf{P}(u, review, h)$
3	$\forall u \forall h \; (|ReviewOn^{-1}(h)| \geq 2) \Leftarrow \mathbf{P}(u, grade, h)$
4	$\forall u \forall h \; (u \in OwnedBy(h)) \Leftarrow \mathbf{P}\left(u, query\text{-}prov\text{-}of, \{|U_{revHw}^{-1}(h)|, U_{grdHw}^{-1}(h)\}\right)$
5	$\forall u \forall r \; (u \in ReviewOf(r)) \Leftarrow \mathbf{P}(u, query\text{-}prov\text{-}of, U_{grdRw}^{-1}(r))$
6	$\forall u \forall h \; (u \in Prof \Leftarrow \mathbf{P}(u, query\text{-}prov\text{-}of, \{OwnedBy(h), ReviewedBy(h), ReviewedCOI(h)\}))$

general security engineering solution, our method should be integrated with the overall software development process. So fat there exists only one development methodology specific for PAS, called PrIMe [11]. PrIMe instructs developers to identify provenance questions and then to adapt the target system to collect provenance for answering provenance questions [11]. However, PrIMe did not identify and model provenance at an abstract enough level for efficient specification and management of ACPs.

6. CONCLUSION AND FUTURE WORK

In provenance-aware systems, developers need to identify some original functional requirements as access control requirements that can be implemented as provenance-aware ACPs. They also need some kinds of provenance in abstractions to efficiently define the provenance-aware ACPs before a real provenance graph is captured at run-time. To solve these issues of developing provenance-aware ACPs, this paper argues that it is necessary to engineer provenance-aware ACPs from the beginning of PAS development. We introduce a typed provenance model (TPM) to abstract complex provenance graph. TPM forms a solid basis for efficient definition of provenance-aware ACPs. Furthermore, we present a TPM-centric process embedded in the overall software development process to guide the identification, specification, and refinement of provenance-aware ACPs from the very beginning of PAS development. In the future, we will apply our approach in additional systems to empirically evaluate its practicality of working together with the overall PAS development methodology, such as PrIMe [11], and other security engineering methodology, such as role-engineering [19]. We will also try to define a formal modeling language for TPM to automatically validate its consistency.

7. REFERENCES

[1] U. Braun and A. Shinnar. A security model for provenance. Technical Report TR-04-06, Harvard University Computer Science, Jan 2006.

[2] U. Braun, A. Shinnar, and M. Seltzer. Secure provenance. In *The 3rd USENIX Workshop on Hot Topics in Sec.*, pages 1–5, Berkeley, CA, USA, 2008.

[3] P. Buneman, S. Khanna, and W. C. Tan. Data provenance: Some basic issues. FST TCS 2000, pages 87–93, 2000.

[4] T. Cadenhead, V. Khadilkar, and et al. A language for provenance access control. CODASPY '11, pages 133–144, 2011.

[5] R. Crook, D. Ince, and B. Nuseibeh. On modelling access policies: relating roles to their organisational context. RE'05, pages 157–166, 2005.

[6] B. Fabian, S. Gürses, and et al. A comparison of security requirements engineering methods. *Requir. Eng.*, 15(1):7–40, Mar. 2010.

[7] P. Groth, S. Jiang, and et al. An architecture for provenance systems. Technical report, University of Southampton, February 2006.

[8] J. Y. Halpern and V. Weissman. Using first-order logic to reason about policies. *ACM Trans. Inf. Syst. Secur.*, 11(4):21:1–21:41, July 2008.

[9] R. Hasan, R. Sion, and M. Winslett. Introducing secure provenance: problems and challenges. StorageSS '07, pages 13–18, 2007.

[10] C. Lim, S. Lu, A. Chebotko, and F. Fotouhi. Opql: A first OPM-level query language for scientific workflow provenance. SCC '11, pages 136–143, 2011.

[11] S. Miles, P. Groth, and et al. Prime: A methodology for developing provenance-aware applications. *ACM Trans. Softw. Eng. Methodol.*, 20(3):8:1–8:42, 2011.

[12] L. Moreau, B. Clifford, and et al. The open provenance model — core specification (v1.1). *Future Generation Computer Systems*, December 2009.

[13] D. Nguyen, J. Park, and R. Sandhu. Dependency path patterns as the foundation of access control in provenance-aware systems. Tapp '2012, 2012.

[14] Q. Ni, S. Xu, E. Bertino, R. Sandhu, and W. Han. An access control language for a general provenance model. SDM '09, pages 68–88, 2009.

[15] J. Park, D. Nguyen, and R. Sandhu. A provenance-based access control model. In *10th Annual Conf. on Privacy, Security and Trust*, 2012.

[16] R. W. Reeder, L. Bauer, and et al. Expandable grids for visualizing and authoring computer security policies. CHI '08, pages 1473–1482, 2008.

[17] P. Samarati and S. D. C. d. Vimercati. Access control: Policies, models, and mechanisms. FOSAD '00, pages 137–196, London, UK, 2001. Springer-Verlag.

[18] R. Sandhu and P. Samarati. Access control: principle and practice. *Communications Magazine, IEEE*, 32(9):40 –48, sept. 1994.

[19] M. Strembeck. Scenario-driven role engineering. *IEEE Security and Privacy*, 8:28–35, 2010.

[20] L. Sun and G. Huang. Towards accuracy of role-based access control configurations in component-based systems. *J. Syst. Archit.*, 57(3):314–326, Mar. 2011.

[21] L. Sun, G. Huang, and et al. An approach for generation of J2EE access control configurations from requirements specification. QSIC '08, pages 87–96. IEEE Computer Society, 2008.

[22] L. Sun, G. Huang, and H. Mei. Validating access control configurations in J2EE applications. CBSE '08, pages 64–79, 2008.

Linking Anonymous Location Traces Through Driving Characteristics

Bin Zan
WINLAB, Rutgers University
671 Route 1 South
North Brunswick, NJ
08902-3390
zanb@winlab.rutgers.edu

Zhanbo Sun
Rensselaer Polytechnic
Institute
110 8th St
Troy, NY 12180-3590
sunz2@rpi.edu

Marco Gruteser
WINLAB, Rutgers University
671 Route 1 South
North Brunswick, NJ
08902-3390
gruteser@winlab.rutgers.edu

Xuegang Ban
Rensselaer Polytechnic
Institute
110 8th St
Troy, NY 12180-3590
banx@rpi.edu

ABSTRACT

Efforts to anonymize collections of location traces have often sought to reduce re-identification risks by dividing longer traces into multiple shorter, unlinkable segments. To ensure unlinkability, these algorithms delete parts from each location trace in areas where multiple traces converge, so that it is difficult to predict the movements of any one subject within this area and identify which follow-on trace segments belongs to the same subject. In this paper, we ask whether it is sufficient to base the definition of unlinkability on movement prediction models or whether the revealed trace segments themselves contain a fingerprint of the data subject that can be used to link segments and ultimately recover private information. To this end, we study a large set of vehicle locations traces collected through the Next Generation Simulation program. We first show that using vehicle moving characteristics related features, it is possible to identify outliers such as trucks or motorcycles from general passenger automobiles. We then show that even in a dataset containing similar passenger automobiles only, it is possible to use outlier driving behaviors to link a fraction of the vehicle trips. These results show that the definition of unlinkability may have to be extended for very precise location traces.

Categories and Subject Descriptors

K.4.1 [**COMPUTERS AND SOCIETY**]: Public Policy Issues—*Privacy*

Keywords

privacy, mix-zone, anonymity, outlier, ROC curve

1. INTRODUCTION

The broad adoption of location-based services has led to an increasing number of services and applications that monitor and record time-series location traces of peoples movements [16, 19, 18, 22]. While some applications require knowledge of the user, a number of applications can enhance privacy by working with anonymous location records. Traffic engineering-related applications that monitor traffic states and other performance measures are one example of such applications.

As in other contexts, achieving strong anonymity in a dataset of location records requires more effort than just deleting identifiers such as user ids, login names, cell phone IDs, or IP addresses [7, 17, 4]. For this reason, a frequently proposed technique to enhance the anonymity of location records is to delete portions of the location traces themselves. This includes trip starting/ending points, which might point to a sensitive location where a user does not want to be seen or a particularly identifying location such as a home, which would make it easier to re-identify a location trace [11, 3].

Since it is difficult, however, to scrub all such locations from traces, a frequently proposed concept is to also delete portions of the data within trips, so that longer trips are divided into shorter unlinkable segments. This will limit the privacy leakage to the information within one short segment, if a re-identification at one location were to occur. Variations of this concept are known under the names of mix-zones [5, 9] or path cloaking [13, 23], and have been the subject of many follow-up studies (e.g., [6, 20, 15, 10, 21]). These approaches do have in common that they define and evaluate unlinkability primarily through the use of movement prediction models. Informally, two trip segments are unlinkable if it is difficult to predict the missing portion of the path with sufficient precision to determine that these two segments are indeed recorded from the same user.

In this paper, we test whether this assumption remains sufficient as the time-series location traces become more precise. For example, typical GPS receivers in vehicles can provide location samples at an updating rate of 1 Hz and with an error of less than 3 m in most cases. Given such precise movement traces, are there other unique patterns embedded in the traces, which would allow linking of two location trace segments without using the prediction models?

One form of such unique patterns are outliers in vehicle moving characteristics. We studied a large set of vehicle traces and tried to identify such outliers. In particular, we considered an outlier as a vehicle which exhibits higher speed, higher acceleration, or a larger number of lane changes compared to the other nearby vehicles, which are grouped inside the same anonymity group. Here, an anonymity group can be considered as a number of close-by vehicles whose trace data are available to the adversary without direct associated information to their real IDs.

The reasons a vehicle may have very distinguishable moving characteristics comparing to others can be classified into two categories: intrinsic and extrinsic. Intrinsic reasons are due to the physical nature of a vehicle, for example a large and heavy delivery truck usually has smaller mean acceleration than a small passenger automobile. Extrinsic reasons are the result of the driver's driving propensity/behavior or other external conditions. For example, many of us tend to drive faster when we are pressed by time. The intrinsic and extrinsic causes are not absolutely disconnected from each other. Many times they are related and both contribute to distinguishable moving characteristics.

The rest of the paper is organized as follows. In section 2, we briefly describe the adversary model. In section 3, we discuss our motivation with a set of data analysis results. Section 4, we study several possible learning models an adversary can use to attack existing mix-zone models. In section 5, we evaluate the proposed learning models and the impacts on the mix-zone model. Section 6 concludes our work.

2. ADVERSARY MODEL

We consider a scenario where an adversary, perhaps an insider, has gained access to a database with the location trace information from drivers. A location trace is defined by a sequence of times-tamped location records with approximately meter-level precision at a time resolution of about one second. We assume that mix zone privacy techniques have been applied: all identifiers such as vehicle license plates associated with the traces have been removed. To distinguish different traces in this dataset, they have been replaced with pseudo identifiers. Furthermore, a long trace is split into several short segments with different pseudo-IDs in order to reduce the possible information leakage due to long term tracking [3]. The mix-zone model [5] is assumed to be used in which all the location traces are discarded inside mix-zones, leaving only segments outside that area. Based on all the available trace segments (which may belong to different users but are all mixed together), an adversary's task is to identify which segments were generated by the same user. In other words, the adversary tries to link segments after the mix zone to a segment before the mix zone (which the adversary may have already correctly associated with the target).

3. FEASIBILITY OF LOCATION TRACE OUTLIER DETECTION

So far the analysis on privacy preserving models has been purely based on predicting and matching the reemergence of vehicles out of the mix-zone. That is, the adversary can link two trace segments if he/she can correctly predict where or when a vehicle will appear. The privacy results of such an analysis are based on the hidden assumption that no other way of linking vehicle traces exists. In this section, we will explore the feasibility of linking trace segments based on characteristics of their movement.

3.1 The Rise of an Outlier

Consider the example shown in Fig. 1 where one vehicle tends to drive significantly faster than other nearby vehicles.

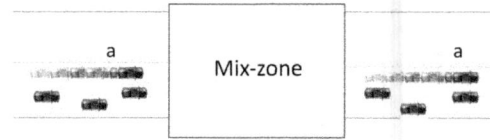

Figure 1: A fast car appears as an outlier.

Let us assume that all the vehicle traces outside the mix-zone are available to the adversary since vehicle a has very different movement characteristics (higher speed) both before the mix-zone and after, the adversary could assume that these two trace segments were generated by the same vehicle and link them into a single trace. In practice, the success of such heuristics will depend on actual speed distributions as well as their tendency to maintain speed long enough to traverse a mix-zone. We refer to vehicle a an outlier because its movement pattern is very different from the others. The above example actually indicates that outliers could destroy the mix-zone mechanism for the easy linkability between the traces.

In [12], Grubbs defined an outlier as: "one that appears to deviate markedly from other members of the sample in which it occurs." When considering all trace segments of a group of vehicles as samples, an outlier segment must appear to deviate markedly from the others. As discussed above, special movement characteristics could lead to an outlier. The cause of such special characteristics can be considered from two sides: intrinsic and extrinsic. The difference between a typical delivery truck and a typical passenger automobile is intrinsic (similarly between a motorcycle and an automobile). On the other hand, a particular driver's speed as mentioned in the above example is an extrinsic cause of being an outlier. Our work will focus on intrinsic reasons first and then move to the extrinsic causes.

According to the US Bureau of Transportation Statistics [1], there were 8,212,267 motorcycles, 10,770,054 trucks and 230,444,440 passenger automobiles in the US in 2010. Therefore, we will see only one truck for every 25 vehicles observed on average (Note that the ratio of trucks and motorcycles is only 4.4% and 3.3% of the total number of vehicles, respectively). From everyday observation, trucks and motorcycles have different movement patterns from passenger automobiles. An adversary can exploit this knowledge to help him/her to identify a truck (or a motorcycle) target from a group of automobiles and to link the trace segments of the truck (or motorcycle) before and after mix-zones. Considering the ratio of trucks and motorcycles to the total number of vehicles on the road, such a scenario will stand out and be easily observed.

3.2 The Observation of Real World Driving Characteristics

In this subsection, we use a set of results to illustrate the feasibility of outlier detection based on vehicle movement characteristics. Since extrinsic cases are based more on individual behavior, we will focus first on discussing cases that are based on intrinsic reasons. The following results are based on NGSIM [2] data which consists of detailed vehicle trajectories, wide-area detectors, and supporting data from researching driver behavior. The vehicle trajectory data was collected using digital video cameras to record the precise location of each vehicle on a 0.5- to 1.0-kilometer section of roadway every one-tenth of a second. The portion of data we use covers the southbound direction of highway US 101 (Hollywood Freeway) in Los Angeles, California. The video cameras were mounted on a 36-story building, 10 Universal City Plaza, which is located adjacent to the U.S. Highway 101 and Lankershim Boulevard interchange in the Universal City neighborhood.

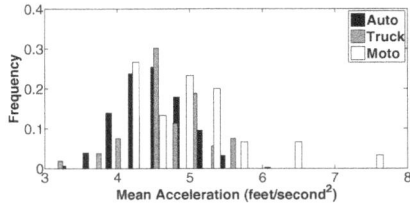

Figure 2: Histogram of mean acceleration for trucks, autos and motos.

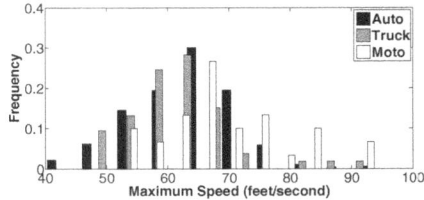

Figure 3: Histogram of maximum speed for trucks, autos and motos.

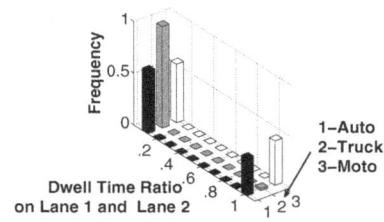

Figure 4: Histogram of dwell time ratios on left most lanes for trucks, autos and motos.

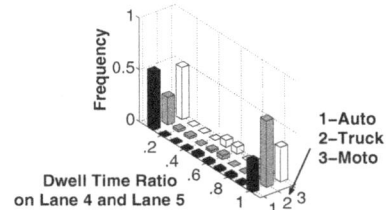

Figure 5: Histogram of dwell time ratios on right most lanes for trucks, autos and motos.

The vehicle trajectory data was transcribed from the video data using a customized software application developed for NGSIM. The total length of the road segment is about 2100 feet and there are five main lanes throughout the section. Lane numbers start from the left-most lane. The total time spans from 7:50am to 8:05am on June 15, 2005. There are 2086 passenger automobiles (autos), 53 trucks and 30 motorcycles (motos) traces in the dataset. Note, the distribution of vehicle types in this dataset is similar to the US Bureau of Transportation Statistics [1].

First, we show a histogram plot of mean acceleration for motos, trucks and autos in Fig. 2. As can be seen, motorcycles tend to have a larger mean acceleration compared to automobiles and trucks (e.g., most of the motorcycles show a mean acceleration higher than 4.2 ft/s^2). The acceleration of trucks tends to be smaller compared to other vehicle types. As shown in the figure, the minimum mean acceleration belongs to trucks. Under certain circumstances (e.g., the target is the only typical motorcycle among a group of automobiles), an adversary could easily identify the target solely based on the difference in the mean acceleration between these two types of vehicles. This ability to distinguish between vehicles increases the linkability of vehicle traces before and after mix-zones.

Similar observations can also be seen in other vehicle movement characteristics. Fig. 3 shows the histogram plots of the maximum speed for trucks, automobiles and motorcycles. As with the mean acceleration, most motorcycles tend to have larger values of maximum speed while automobiles have both larger and smaller values than trucks. The former is quite consistent with our intuition while the latter is not. To explain why automobiles have both larger and smaller maximum speeds, we note that the drivers of automobiles cover a large range of the population, so some of them tend to drive fast while many others tend to drive slowly (e.g., seniors). On the other hand, the people who drive trucks are mostly professional drivers that are either young or in their middle ages. Thus, it is also reasonable to see that the use of automobiles covers a larger range in terms of the maximum speed. However, from the figure, we can conclude again that under certain circumstances, it is easy for an adversary to identify a target vehicle if he/she can exploit the maximum speed information (e.g., when the target is a typical

motorcycle and the other vehicles are all common automobiles or trucks).

The above two examples do not have a clear way to distinguish a truck from other types of vehicles based on one particular movement characteristic. However, some trends can at least be observed. For example, trucks generally have a relatively small mean acceleration and maximum speed. Our proposed adversary model does not require a strong difference in one particular movement characteristic, instead, small differences in multiple characteristics can allow for a way to distinguish target types of vehicles from the groups of vehicles.

In the next subsection, we will illustrate more possible movement characteristics that can be used for intrinsic cause outlier detection.

3.3 Exploiting Other Features

There are a few movement characteristics that may be useful for intrinsic cause outlier detection. In this subsection, we illustrate two other characteristics that are useful for identifying trucks from other vehicles.

3.3.1 Lane Changing

As more and more detailed and accurate location information becomes available, some movement characteristics (patterns) that were not available before, are easier to obtained. For example, when the GPS or other location devices become accurate enough, recognizing the lane a vehicle is moving on becomes feasible. For example, in the NGSIM [2] dataset all vehicle traces are recorded with lane information. As another example, High Accuracy Nationwide Differential GPS (HA-NDGPS) system which is currently under development can provide 10-15 centimeter accuracy.

In Fig. 4, we show the histogram of dwll time ratios on left most lanes for trucks, automobiles and motorcycles. The question of which lanes to stay may appear as a driver's preference or an extrinsic reason at the first glance. However, if the special movement

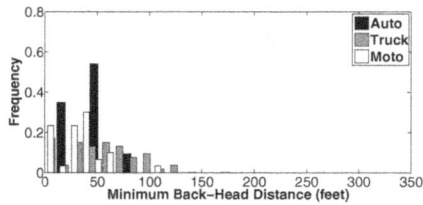

Figure 6: Histogram of minimum back-headway distance for trucks, autos and motos.

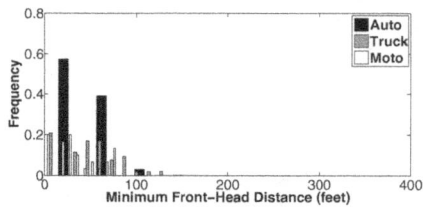

Figure 7: Histogram of minimum front-headway distance for trucks, autos and motos.

pattern appears in most trucks, we may presume that this is the result from intrinsic or mixed of the intrinsic and extrinsic reasons. In fact, it is reasonable to assume truck drivers tend to drive on the outer (right most) lanes instead of inner (left most) lanes because trucks can not move as flexible as small automobiles generally. Inner lanes are usually reserved for fast moving vehicles, slow in lane changing and speed changing discourage truck drivers to stay in the inner lanes. The result in Fig. 5 complement what is shown in Fig. 4. Trucks do not stay on the inner lanes most times, instead they tend to appear in the outer lanes. Above plots indicate the possibility for an adversary to detect a truck outlier out of automobiles and other type of vehicles.

3.3.2 Headway Distance

Some features or characteristics may not be always available or only available for some vehicles. However, once available, they may increase an adversary's ability to detect certain types of vehicles or a special kind of target. One example is the headway information. Headway is defined as the head-to-head distance between a vehicle and its immediate frontward vehicle (front-headway) or the vehicle immediate afterward (back-headway). The maximum headway distance does not help the adversary much since the values can be very large when there is no vehicle nearby. Intuitively, headway distance (especially front-headway) can be useful for distinguishing trucks and small automobiles, because trucks tend to leave more space in front of them. However, the effectiveness of using headway distance is strongly related to the penetration rate. If an adversary has obtained all vehicles' location traces, then it can compute the accurate headway distance for each one, otherwise, the value may not be correct. Consider a scenario, where vehicle a is immediately followed by vehicle 'b'. The location trace of a is not known by the adversary, then the front-headway distance of vehicle 'b' can't be computed. Therefore, the usage of headway distance is limited.

As shown in Fig. 6 and Fig. 7, trucks have the largest front-headway distance and back-headway distance compared to automobiles, while motorcycles have the smallest values. Although, this is not true for all the cases, the characteristic over large amount of samples will be useful when adding such knowledge into a ma-

chine learning classification model. As we will show in the next section, one characteristic alone may not be able to differentiate all trucks or motorcycles from automobiles, however it can be very helpful when combined with other movement characteristics.

4. TRACE OUTLIER DETECTION ALGORITHMS

The previous section shows the feasibility of location trace outlier detection. In this section, we provide detailed methods for such detection.

4.1 Intrinsic Outlier Detection

Recall that intrinsic outlier movements are caused by less common types of vehicle. In particular, we consider the case where an adversary knows a priori that the vehicle of interest is a less common vehicle (e.g., a truck or motorcycle) when trying to track the vehicle. This task would become significantly easier, if the adversary can first filter out the traces from all other vehicle types because this would result in a smaller anonymity set and less probability of linking error.

To realize this type of vehicle filtering, we use machine learning classification approaches. An adversary uses historical data to train the classification model, and then uses the model to classify and filter vehicles crossing a mix-zone. Compared to the extrinsic techniques we will discuss later, a key advantage of this method is that the training dataset is not limited to traces from the target vehicle but can also use traces from other vehicles of the same type. This results in a larger sample pool and can build a better model for outlier detection. However, the adversary must know the intrinsic nature of the target vehicle (e.g., vehicle type) and the characteristic must belong to a less common vehicle. If the confidence level is low, an adversary still has to resort to more general outlier detection strategies, to be discussed later.

In particular, we studied three classic machine learning models, and compared their performance. To be more specific, we studied Linear Discriminant Analysis (LDA), Quadratic Discriminant Analysis (QDA) and Naive Bayes Models. LDA generates linear boundaries, QDA and NB can both generate quadratic boundaries. For more details about these learning models, the interested reader could consult [14].

The input of each machine learning model are the road segment traces obtained from NGSIM data [2]. Available information includes vehicle ID, global time, local X, local Y, vehicle length, vehicle width, vehicle velocity, vehicle acceleration, lane identification, preceding vehicle, following vehicle, space-headway and vehicle class, etc. Local X and Y is the distance from the front center of the vehicle to the left most edge of the road segment and to the entry edge of the segment respectively. The space headway information only covers the front-headway distance, however, with the preceding vehicle and following vehicle information, back-headway distance can be computed and used in the adversary model. For more detailed information regarding the NGSIM data, please refer to [2].

Based on above dataset, we further extract the following sample based movement characteristics:

1. speed (5 features): maximum speed, minimum speed, average speed, median speed, standard deviation of speed.
2. acceleration (8 features): maximum acceleration, maximum deceleration, average acceleration, average deceleration, median acceleration, median deceleration, standard deviation of acceleration, standard deviation of deceleration.
3. proportion (4 features): acceleration greater than 5 ft/s^2, de-

celeration greater than 5 ft/s^2, speed greater than 60 ft/s, speed less than 20 ft/s.

4. lane position (6 features): frequency on visiting lane 1, 2, 3, 4, 5, total number of lane switching.

5. headway (4 features): minimum distance to the vehicle in front, average distance to the vehicle in front, minimum distance to the vehicle after, average distance to the vehicle after.

Before illustrating our proposed adversary models in the next subsection, we go through several initial observations from studying.

- Some movement characteristics may help an adversary more than others with building the outlier detection models. For example, in the 1927 data samples collected from US101 highway between 7:50am and 8:05am (including both automobiles and trucks), the residual error of a QDA model on maximum speed is only 0.34. While with minimum speed, the error rate is 0.56 which is much larger.

- A movement characteristic itself may not be good enough to differentiate vehicles. However, a combination of such characteristics can be useful. For example, using LDA to distinguish three types of vehicles (trucks, automobiles and motorcycles) from the same dataset with average acceleration, the (residual) error rate is 0.41. If based on the combination of multiple dimensions: maximum speed, average acceleration, proportion of deceleration, the ratio of frequency of visiting lane 4 and 5, and the number of lane changes, the error rate reduce to 0.11.

- Increasing the total number of movement characteristics to be used may not always lead to better performance.

- To find a set of boundaries for classifying trucks, automobiles and motorcycles through one learning model is not easy. Instead, we choose to train a set of models each of which can distinguish a pair of vehicle types.

4.2 Feature Selection or Dimension Reduction

For building proper learning models, it is necessary to filter some characteristics (or features) which cause more noise than they contribute to the outlier detection. Therefore, we studied two methods to improve the performance.

4.2.1 Manual Feature Selection

The first strategy is to select a number of features which performs well individually. Multiple selected features are combined together to form learning models in high dimensions. For example, assume we extract a total of n features from the vehicle trace dataset, then for each feature, a learning model is built. All features are then ordered based on the performance in training dataset. Next, the top m features are selected to form the best combination. This method has several advantages. First, the resulted model is easier to be understood. Each feature corresponds to a movement characteristic which has clear definition. Second, the performance can be estimated. Since all the features have real physical meaning, it is relative easy to estimate the performance based on user's daily observation. One disadvantage is that such a method is slow. For every pair of features, the adversary needs to generate a learning model, and sort the results based on performance. Another disadvantage is that the result may not be optimal. Some features may have correlation, thus putting them together may not contribute more information for a learning model.

As part of our evaluation results, the basic features we manually selected are maximum speed, average acceleration, proportion of

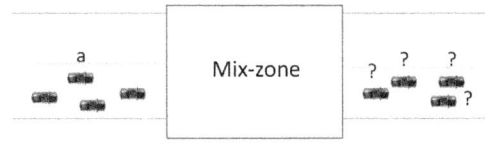

Figure 8: A general outlier detection scenario

deceleration greater than 5 ft/s^2, frequency on visiting lane 4 and 5.

4.2.2 Principle Component Analysis Based Dimension Reduction

The second strategy is to use a dimension reduction method. In our study, we use Principle Component Analysis (PCA) to project all the features onto m best dimensions and then train the learning model based on these m dimensions. The advantage of this method is that it is fully automatic and it can achieve better performance than the previous method. That is because if two features are strongly correlated, it will only appear as one dimension after projection in PCA. One disadvantage of such a method is the selected dimensions in the end may not have clear physical meaning, thus the results cannot be always interpreted easily.

4.3 General Outlier Detection: Extrinsic

In the extrinsic case, it is not clear that we can build a learning model based on historical data from different drivers and different trips. For example, the special movement characteristics of a driver during a trip (e.g., due to time pressure) may not appear in his/her previous trip two days ago. And there is no training dataset available from general location trace data to indicate if a driver is under time pressure or not. Comparing to intrinsic, extrinsic is more unstable and more case dependent and/or time dependent. Therefore, the machine learning model for outlier detection must be built on the fly and in real time. Assume that before a mix-zone, the trajectory of a target vehicle a is known as shown in Fig. 8, the challenge for an adversary is now to identify the same target vehicle after the mix-zone. Since there is no historical data that can be used, the size of the training dataset relies on the length of the road segment before the mix-zone. While we still can use machine learning models, we need assume the target vehicle itself is a class. There are two strategies available for the adversary:

4.3.1 One-to-One

In this method, the trace from the target vehicle forms a class, and all the other traces from the remaining vehicles of the anonymity set form the second class. The learning model detects the target based on binary classification result for the dataset after the mix-zone. This method is easy to implement, however due to the small number of data samples available in the first class compared to the second class, the classification model may not be able to generate a good boundary for a binary classification model.

4.3.2 One-to-Many

In this method, not only the trace from the target vehicle forms a class, but also all other vehicles form classes independently. The adversary builds multiple binary classification learning models for the target with all the other vehicles. To detect the outlier, the adversary runs all learning models for each trace segment collected after mix-zone to determine if a trace looks more like the target or one of the others.

5. EVALUATION

In this section, we study the proposed outlier detection techniques with the NGSIM [2] dataset. The True Positive Rate (TPR) and the False Positive Rate (FPR) are used as measures to characterize the ability of an adversary to track a vehicle through a mix-zone. The same dataset which has been studied in the section 3.2 is used. Here we give a brief introduction of the dataset again. All the location traces are collected from the US101 highway. The dataset covers the traffic data between 7:50am and 8:05am. It includes a total of 1875 automobiles, 52 trucks and 25 motorcycles, all of which have trajectories longer than 2000 feet. To date, we have focused more on intrinsic factors, since there is a relative large training dataset available. A small number of vehicle traces are removed. These are those which 1) were less than 2000 feet long; 2) never had any vehicle driving in front; 3) never had any vehicle following behind. The first condition is to reduce the possible impact from factors other than the vehicle movement characteristics, the second and third conditions are to make sure we can use the same dataset when comparing the performance of different outlier detection algorithms (with and without headway information).

The results presented here focus on showing the Receiver Operating Characteristic (ROC) curves of different learning models. An ROC graph is a technique for visualizing, organizing and selecting classifiers based on their performance. It is not only a generally useful performance graphing method, but also very useful for domains with skewed class distribution and unequal classification error cost [8]. The data source input into the outlier detection algorithm mostly follows skewed class distributions. Thus, it is beneficial to use the ROC curves for comparing the performance of different learning models. On the other hand, through the ROC curves, the tradeoff between quantity of attacks and quality of attacks (in terms of confidence level) can be easily observed.

5.1 Outlier Detection: Intrinsic

First, we show the results based on manual feature selection. The performance of the three different machine learning models LDA, QDA and Naive Bayes for truck detection are shown in Fig. 9. The main point is that by properly selecting a learning model an adversary can identify a truck or a motorcycle from common automobiles. This means that additional information leaks from the traces that could be used to compromise mix-zone protection. The features we manually selected are maximum speed, average acceleration, proportion of deceleration greater than 5 ft/s^2, frequency of visiting lane 4 and 5. As shown in the ROC graphs, in general, to improve the confidence of tracking a target, an adversary has to sacrifice the quantity of the overall attacks. As the confidence level increases, the number of vehicles that can be tracked decreases. Nonetheless, even an adversary who can claim a very high confidence in tracking a target just occasionally may be unacceptable.

Fig. 9(a), Fig. 9(b) and Fig. 9(c) show results (for the LDA, QDA and Naive Bayes models) from the training dataset and results of 10-fold cross validation on the QDA as well as Naive Bayes model, respectively. As can be noticed from Fig. 9(a), all the three learning models generate better ROC curves than randomly guessing (the diagonal line in the figure) in training. This indicates that with machine learning classification models an adversary is able to identify trucks from automobiles under certain circumstances. To be more specific, the ROC curve of the QDA model crossing the point at FPR=0.2 and TPR=0.7 indicates that an adversary can identify a truck with 70% success rate if it is indeed a truck. 20% of the time, the adversary will mis-identify an automobile as a truck. The 10-fold cross validation as shown in Fig. 9(b) and Fig. 9(c) evaluates the learning model by rotating training and testing data (in 9:1 ra-

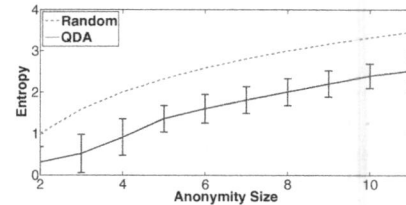

Figure 11: Entropy reduction due to outlier detection.

tio) 10 times. Although the Naive Bayes model does not perform very well, as can be inferred from Fig. 9(b), using QDA, an adversary can achieve higher success rate (about 96%) when he/she only focuses on tracking 40% of the trucks which show the most evidence of being a truck. This is a considerable improvement of the tracking ability of an adversary. For instance, in a group of ten vehicles containing one truck and nine automobiles passing through a mix-zone, an adversary only has about a 30% failure rate to mis-classify one of the nine automobiles as a truck while the real truck is able to be identified in 40% of cases. This dramatically reduces the protection of a mix-zone for such outlier vehicles, since the mix-zone model predicts a 90% failure rate. The QDA learning model can also help an adversary when there are multiple trucks in the anonymity group. For example, if there are two trucks in ten vehicles, an adversary only has a 28% failure rate to mis-classify one out of the eight automobiles as a truck while it has a 40% success rate to identify the real trucks. With an overall success rate of more than 30%, he/she can identify the right trace of the target truck.

Fig. 9(d), Fig. 9(e) and Fig. 9(f) show the results when the headway information (which has been discussed in section 3.3.2) is available. Both training and testing results show that with headway information, an adversary will have a better chance to detect a truck under all three models. For example, as shown in Fig. 9(e), an adversary can achieve roughly 1% FPR under 35% TPR. This means that in a group of ten vehicles, one of which is a truck, passing through a mix-zone, the adversary only has a 8.6% chance to mis-classify one automobile as a truck while he/she is able to identify the real truck at a rate of 35%. This compares to a 90% failure rate with random guessing and shows that the protection of the mix-zone has deteriorated.

In Fig. 10, we assume that an adversary will perform a principal component analysis on the dataset. This operation projects all the characteristics (features) onto the 10 most important dimensions. The boundary is then generated only based on the 10 dimensions. Compared to Fig. 9, the performance is slightly better in both the training dataset and the testing dataset. This indicates that an adversary can achieve better results if he/she has a better learning model or data mining method. The better an adversary can do, the worse the current mix-zone model will be. In additional to all of the above observations, we also note that among all these three models, QDA performs the best and the headway information improves the performance of every learning model. We interpret this as evidence that further improvement is possible on outlier detection techniques if the adversary has better learning models or data mining algorithms.

In our study, we also evaluated the outlier detection techniques on motorcycle identification. Similar results were observed. However due to space limitations, the results are omitted from this paper.

Since entropy is one of the most important factors in evaluating

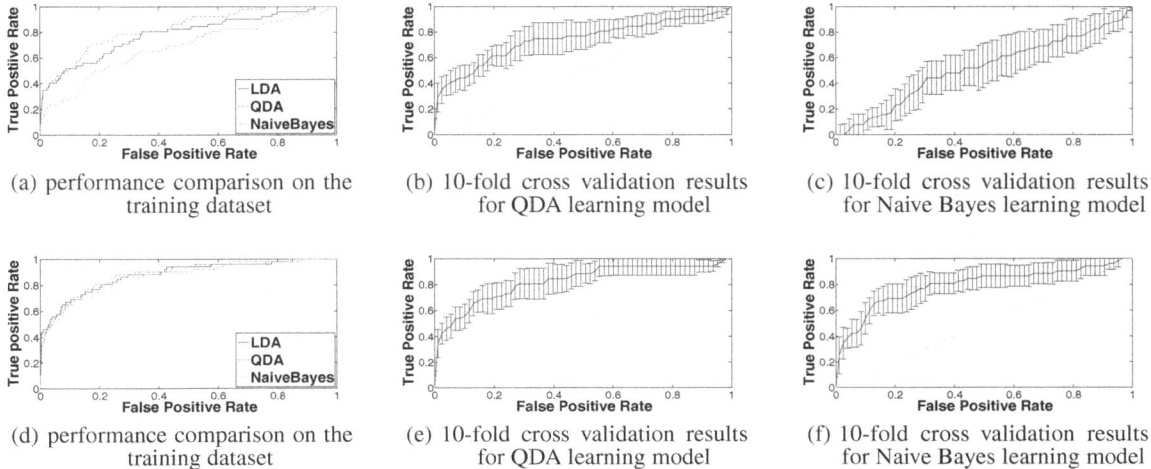

(a) performance comparison on the training dataset

(b) 10-fold cross validation results for QDA learning model

(c) 10-fold cross validation results for Naive Bayes learning model

(d) performance comparison on the training dataset

(e) 10-fold cross validation results for QDA learning model

(f) 10-fold cross validation results for Naive Bayes learning model

Figure 9: Detecting truck from automobiles with manual feature selection

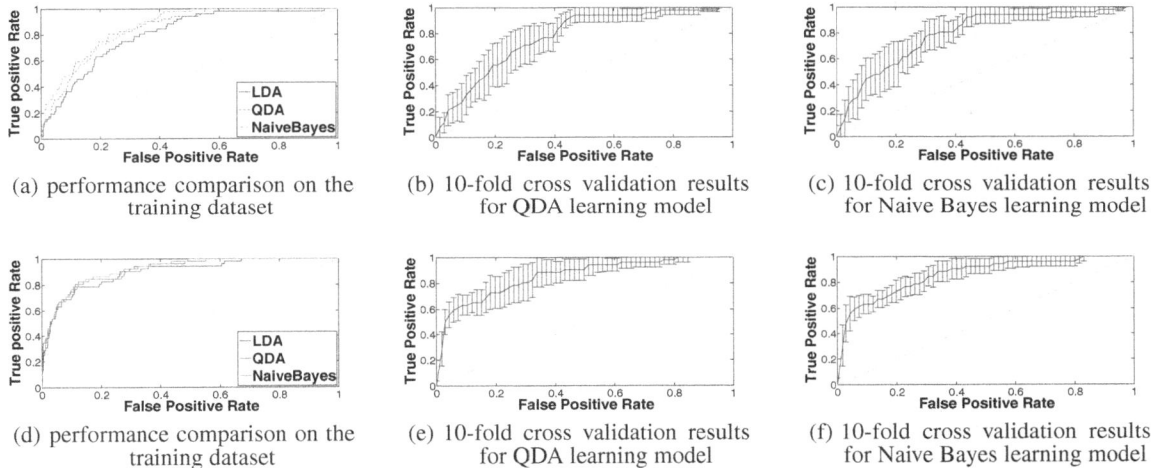

(a) performance comparison on the training dataset

(b) 10-fold cross validation results for QDA learning model

(c) 10-fold cross validation results for Naive Bayes learning model

(d) performance comparison on the training dataset

(e) 10-fold cross validation results for QDA learning model

(f) 10-fold cross validation results for Naive Bayes learning model

Figure 10: Detecting trucks from automobiles using PCA projection on the first 10 dimensions.

a mix-zone model, in Fig. 11, we compare the original system entropy of a mix-zone with the one after the QDA learning model is used. As can be seen from the figure, while varying the size of the anonymity set, the QDA learning model always reduces the system entropy by at least 1. This reduction helps the adversary significantly, considering that entropy is a logarithmic value.

Finally, in another set of experiments, we create 55 groups of ten vehicles. Each group has one truck and the remaining are all automobiles which are moving closest to the truck. With the QDA model, an adversary can successfully identify and track trucks in the 22 of the 55 groups.

5.2 More General Outlier Detection: Extrinsic

Last, in this subsection, we show preliminary results on more general outlier detection: extrinsic and/or mixed cases. In this experiment, all 2000 feet long trace segments are further divided into three portions. The vehicle trace dataset from first and third por-

tions are assumed to be available by the adversary. All trace dataset from the second portion of the road are removed in order to simulate a mix-zone model. Assume there is no intrinsic knowledge available such as vehicle type. The dataset from the first segment are used as training data. The adversary tries to link all the pairs of the traces belonging to the same vehicle. The learning model used is QDA. Different from previous work, in this part we assume the target can be any vehicle.

As shown in Fig. 12, the tracking rate, which is defined as the success rate at which an adversary can identify a particular target from a group of vehicles is largely increasing with the learning model compared to random guessing. For instance, in a ten vehicle anonymity set, the learning model has a 28% tracking rate, which is a good improvement for an adversary who originally had only a 10% tracking rate. As mentioned before, we define the anonymity set size as the number of nearby vehicles whose trace data are available to the adversary.

This figure has shown the tracking rate for any randomly picked

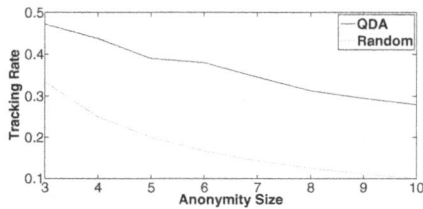

Figure 12: With the proposed generic outlier detection method, tracking rate is increased.

vehicle from the dataset. This indicates that there are a large number of cases in which the target may not have special movement characteristics compared to other vehicles. In practice, however, the adversary can ignore those cases and concentrate on outlier vehicles that can be tracked with high confidence.

6. CONCLUSION

In this paper, we have studied whether existing models to measure the degree of privacy in anonymized location traces hold as location traces continue to become more precise. Using data captured from vehicles we have shown that fine-grained location traces reveal speed distribution and acceleration patterns that can be used to distinguish traces from different vehicle types (e.g., trucks and cars). Our analysis on NGSIM location trace shows that an adversary can identify 40% trucks from cars with success rate of 96%. We have also shown that it is possible to identify outlier driving patterns such as higher speed, which could be used to link anonymous segments of location traces and eventually recover complete trips. Our preliminary results show that the general outlier detection technique can improve an adversary's ability to identify a trace segment of any user from an average tracking rate of 10% to 28%. While this rate is still relatively small, and would be smaller still if a vehicle trip passes over multiple mix zones, these findings show that movement characteristics reveal information. An immediate countermeasure is to revert back to coarser location traces but a full solution to this issue remains an open problem. We believe that further research is warranted to refine the definition of unlinkability for very fine-grained location traces.

7. REFERENCES

[1] National transportation statistics 2012. online, accessed Sept. 14, 2012.

[2] Next generation simulation (ngsim). online, accessed Sept. 14, 2012.

[3] H. X. Baik Hoh, Macro Gruteser and A. Alrabady. Achieving guaranteed anonymity in gps traces via uncertainty-aware path cloaking. In *IEEE Transactions on Mobile Computing 9 (8)*, 2010.

[4] H. X. Baik Hoh, Marco Gruteser and A. Alrabady. Enhancing security and privacy in traffic-monitoring systems. *Pervasive Computing, IEEE*, 5(4):38 –46, 2006.

[5] A. R. Beresford and F. Stajano. Mix zones: User privacy in location-aware services. In *In Proc. of the 2nd IEEE Annual Conference on Pervasive Computing and Communications Workshops (PERCOMW04)*, pages 127–131, 2004.

[6] L. Buttyan, T. Holczer, and I. Vajda. On the effectiveness of changing pseudonyms to provide location privacy in vanets. In *Proceedings of Workshop on Security and Privacy in Ad hoc and Sensor Networks*, 2007.

[7] D. Chaum, C. O. T. Acm, R. Rivest, and D. L. Chaum. Untraceable electronic mail, return addresses, and digital pseudonyms. *Communications of the ACM*, 24:84–88, 1981.

[8] T. Fawcett. Roc graphs: Notes and practical considerations for researchers. Technical report, HP Laboratories, 2004.

[9] J. Freudiger, M. Raya, M. Fĺelegyhĺczi, P. Papadimitratos, and J.-P. Hubaux. Mix-Zones for Location Privacy in Vehicular Networks. In *ACM Workshop on Wireless Networking for Intelligent Transportation Systems (WiN-ITS)*, Vancouver, 2007.

[10] B. Gedik and L. Liu. Location privacy in mobile systems: A personalized anonymization model. In *Distributed Computing Systems, 2005. ICDCS 2005. Proceedings. 25th IEEE International Conference on*, pages 620 –629, 2005.

[11] P. Golle and K. Partridge. On the anonymity of home/work location pairs. In *Proceedings of the 7th International Conference on Pervasive Computing*, Pervasive '09, pages 390–397, Berlin, Heidelberg, 2009. Springer-Verlag.

[12] F. E. Grubbs. *Procedures for Detecting Outlying Observations in Samples*. Defense Technical Information Center, 1974.

[13] M. Gruteser and D. Grunwald. Anonymous usage of location-based services through spatial and temporal cloaking. In *ACM MobiSys*, pages 31–42, 2003.

[14] T. Hastie, R. Tibshirani, and J. Friedman. *The elements of statistical learning: data mining, inference and prediction*. Springer, 2 edition, 2009.

[15] B. Hoh and M. Gruteser. Preserving privacy in gps traces via uncertainty-aware path cloaking. In *Proceedings of ACM CCS*, 2007.

[16] B. Hull, V. Bychkovsky, Y. Zhang, K. Chen, M. Goraczko, A. K. Miu, E. Shih, H. Balakrishnan, and S. Madden. Cartel: A distributed mobile sensor computing system. In *4th ACM SenSys*, Boulder, CO, November 2006.

[17] J. Krumm. Inference attacks on location tracks. In *Proceedings of the Fifth International Conference on Pervasive Computing (Pervasive), volume 4480 of LNCS*, pages 127–143. Springer-Verlag, 2007.

[18] U. Lee, E. Magistretti, M. Gerla, P. Bellavista, and A. Corradi. Opportunistic dissemination and harvesting of urban monitoring information in vehicular sensor networks. In *UCLA, Tech. Rep*, 2007.

[19] U. Lee, B. Zhou, M. Gerla, E. Magistretti, P. Bellavista, and A. Corradi. Mobeyes: smart mobs for urban monitoring with a vehicular sensor network. *Wireless Communications, IEEE*, 13(5):52 –57, 2006.

[20] M. Li, K. Sampigethaya, L. Huang, and R. Poovendran. Swing & swap: user-centric approaches towards maximizing location privacy. In *Proceedings of the 5th ACM WPES' 06*.

[21] M. F. Mokbel, C. yin Chow, and W. G. Aref. The new casper: Query processing for location services without compromising privacy. In *In VLDB*, pages 763–774, 2006.

[22] T. Nadeem, S. Dashtinezhad, C. Liao, and L. Iftode. Trafficview: Traffic data dissemination using car-to-car communication. *ACM SIGMOBILE Mobile Computing and Communications Review*, 8, 2004.

[23] B. Zan, P. Hao, M. Gruteser, and X. Ban. Vtl zone-based path cloaking algorithms. In *Proceedings of the 2011 IEEE 14th International Conference on Intelligent Transportation Systems (ITSC 2011)*, 2011.

Insured Access: An Approach to Ad-hoc Information Sharing for Virtual Organizations

Naoki Tanaka[†,‡,*], Marianne Winslett[†,*], Adam J. Lee[◦], David K. Y. Yau[◇,*], Feng Bao[‡]
† Department of Computer Science, University of Illinois at Urbana-Champaign
‡ Cryptography & Security Department, Institute for Infocomm Research
* Advanced Digital Sciences Center
◦ Department of Computer Science, University of Pittsburgh
◇ Department of Computer Science, Purdue University

ABSTRACT

A virtual organization (VO) is a group of organizations that have banded together to achieve a common goal. Often a VO could function more effectively if its members were willing to share certain information. However, a typical VO member will not want to share its own information because the member will not benefit directly from the information's reuse, yet will be blamed if the reuse turns out badly.

In this paper, we present *insured access*, the first economically sustainable system for encouraging appropriate information sharing in VOs. Before accessing information, a VO member must purchase a liability policy from the insurance arm of the VO. Insured access uses actuarial principles to set up and run the VO's insurance arm, and provides the following benefits: VO members who share their information are compensated if the information is misused, and can expect a *positive* benefit from sharing; members who use information well are rewarded and those who misuse it are penalized appropriately; and the level of risk-taking in the system is capped at a certain level. We demonstrate the sustainability of insured sharing through simulations of a map-sharing scenario.

Categories and Subject Descriptors: H.4 [Information Systems Applications]: Miscellaneous; D.4.6 [Operating Systems]: Security and Protection—Access controls

Keywords: Insured Access; Risk-Aware Authorization; Risk-Based Access Control; Actuarial Science

1. INTRODUCTION

A shared goal binds VO members together, such as when a consortium responds to a business opportunity, or agencies work together to respond to a flood and nuclear disaster. Any sufficiently large organization operates as a VO, because its internal divisions have their own vested interests that do not always align with the VO's best interests.

Often, to be successful in achieving the shared goal, VO members need to share information with each other. Information sharing usually requires a VO member to take information that it collected for its own internal purposes, and release it to another for a different purpose. Since the first member – the information *producer* – has set the access control policy to match its original internal use for the information, sharing requires policy changes. Further, the producer will usually be blamed if another member – the information *consumer*[1] – misuses the information, and will not directly benefit if the consumer makes good use of it. Thus, producers are often reluctant to share.

The misaligned incentives for sharing stem from traditional approaches to authorization, which try to *eliminate* risk for individual VO members, rather than *maximize VO productivity while bounding risk*. To fix this, researchers have proposed approaches where a VO allocates "risk tokens" to its members, which they can use to "pay" for risky accesses to information that would not otherwise be allowed. However, it is not clear why producers would want to participate in a risk-token-based economy, or whether the VO would really benefit. Token-based economies also face problems like hoarding and shortages.

In recent decades, the business community has benefited from the use of actuarial methods to manage many kinds of business risks, but information sharing has not been among them. In this paper, we address this gap by introducing *insured access*, an insurance-based approach to incentivize information providers to allow risky accesses that are likely to benefit the VO. Our contributions:

- We propose *sustainable* methods for a VO to determine the price of a particular information access and decide whether to grant a particular access request, given a bound ε on the risk that the VO is willing to tolerate.

- We show that information providers can expect to benefit from sharing and providers will have recourse when information sharing turns out badly for the provider.

- We demonstrate the use of insured access in a simulation, and show that the system behaves as predicted.

The rest of the paper is organized as follows. Section 2 discusses related work, and Section 3 presents the details of insured access. Section 4 presents experimental results, and Section 5 concludes the paper.

---

[1] A member may both produce and consume information.

2. RELATED WORK

To address the problem of encouraging appropriate sharing of sensitive defense-related information in a VO, the MITRE JASON report [1] proposed a *risk-based access control* approach. In their approach, principals use *risk tokens* to purchase access rights to data. The access price is the expected value of damages due to this access. The VO decides how much risk it can handle during the next fiscal period, creates that many tokens, and allocates them to its members. Risk-based access control does not effectively control the worst-case aggregate damages, and does not distinguish between good and bad risk-takers.

The JASON report inspired follow-on papers addressing specific aspects of a risk-based approach, such as how to integrate trust and risk into RBAC [4], consider relative security risks in RBAC [13], balance the risks and benefits [17], combine risk-based access control with fuzzy logic [3], and allocate risk tokens to VO members [12]. But none of these schemes provides reasons for a rational, self-interested VO member to volunteer to provide information. In addition, none of these schemes provides a clear bound on the worst-case damages, or ensures that members who use information badly are treated differently from those who use it well. With no incentive for consumers to try to use information well, they may expose the VO to unnecessary risk.

Token-based approaches face other challenges as well. VO members may hoard tokens in anticipation of future shortages, spend leftover tokens carelessly at the end of a fiscal period, or be unable to obtain tokens when they truly need them. A cash-based scheme will lessen these problems, assuming that VO members behave rationally.

Cash can be coupled with decision theory to decide how much an access might benefit an information consumer or the VO [11]. Decision theory could show whether the likely rewards associated with a particular access exceed its potential risks. In practice, though, a consumer may be unwilling to share detailed information about its planned use of the information, making it hard to do decision-theoretic analysis of risks and rewards at the VO level.

Recent work proposes ways to price access to personal data, such as online behavior and demographic characteristics, using differential privacy and auction mechanisms [7, 14]. Like insured access, these works propose pricing schemes for sensitive information. However, these works assume that upfront payments are sufficient to entice providers to participate. This is appropriate for the low-risk settings these works target, where an individual's aggregate income from sharing will almost surely exceed their aggregate damages. In contrast, insurance is appropriate for situations where there is a very small chance of very high damage.

Conversely, insured access could use auction-based data pricing to bring providers higher profits than the fee-for-service and profit-sharing schemes we propose. However, to reach a fair price, auctions need multiple potential bidders. Insured access is aimed at ad-hoc, non-routine information needs that are too atypical to be institutionalized into a VO's role-based access control system. Single-expected-bid auctions will default to the minimum allowed bid, which is a fee-for-service model. If multiple potential bidders are likely, then the information need is sufficiently routine for the VO to adopt lighter-weight methods than insured access.

Finally, insured access can benefit from ways to reduce the sensitivity of shared information. For example, if a con-

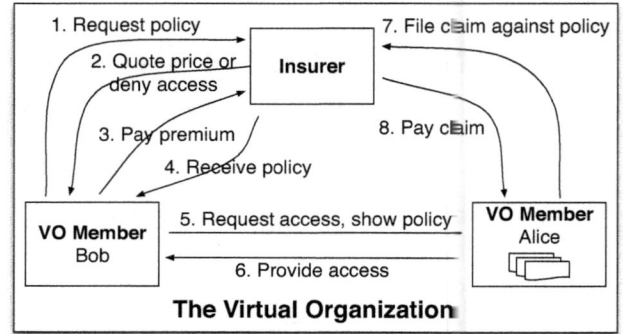

Figure 1: System Model for Insured Access

sumer needs only part of a sensitive map, then removing the other parts may greatly reduce the expected damages and hence the price of insurance. A second technique is to generalize the shared information, e.g., releasing the approximate location of a gas pipeline rather than its exact location. Differential privacy is a third technique, but it is practical only when the consumer needs the result of a statistical analysis over many data items. Differential privacy is not effective when the consumer needs the data items themselves, such as a set of maps or phone numbers.

Hoo [9] indicates the potential of using actuarial methods to manage computer security risk, but no concrete scheme for access control was ever proposed. Insured access is the first complete, economically sustainable system for encouraging appropriate information sharing in VOs.

3. INSURED ACCESS

The VO can either use an external insurer or self-insure, but we consider only the case of self-insurance because the VO will have to expose very sensitive information to the insurer. We begin with a quick overview of insured access, then provide additional detail in the subsections that follow.

Before insured accesses begin, the VO members set up an internal VO insurance group (the *insurer*), agree on what kinds of information to share, and decide how much risk the insurer can assume. The VO members who become information consumers supply the startup capital for the insurer.

In Figure 1, a producer Alice has information that can be shared with others. To obtain access, consumer Bob asks the insurer for a policy covering the specific information he wants to access (1). The policy will insure Alice against damages she might incur because she shared that information with Bob. If the insurer is willing to issue the policy, it gives Bob a price (2), which Bob can choose to pay (3). We assume *consumers are rational, self-interested, and risk-adverse*, so Bob will only buy the policy if its price is less than the benefit he expects to gain from accessing the information. With the policy in hand (4), Bob asks Alice for access (5). Alice examines the policy and can give Bob the information (6). If Bob misuses the information and Alice suffers damages as a result, Alice can submit a claim to the insurer (7) and be reimbursed for her suffering (8). The policy can specify conditions of use, such as secure handling precautions or limits on the purpose of use. If Bob may have violated those rules, then the insurer can request reimbursement from Bob of the amount paid to Alice.

302

Insurance-based access control is a new idea in the security world and differs from the usual liability insurance, under which asset owners (i.e., providers) buy policies to protect themselves. With insured access, consumers pay for policies that protect providers. This means that consumers must consider potential damages when deciding whether to access information, as well as benefits; and providers need not consider damages when deciding whether to share. Because of this difference, existing actuarial methods cannot be directly applied to purchase decisions in insured access, and we propose appropriate formulas for this task.

The price Bob pays for the policy is called the *premium*, which depends on how risk-averse the insurer is, what information Bob wants to access, the history of past claims for that information, and the insurer's *premium principle* (pricing methodology). Based on Bob's track record, the insurer can reward Bob with lower premiums if Bob's other policies have no recent claims, and penalize him otherwise. The insurer can refuse to issue a policy to Bob because of his track record, or because the insurer needs to limit the risk associated with its current portfolio of policies.

If the VO members are very unlucky or the data used to set prices is insufficient, then the insurer might run out of funds to pay claims and be ruined. The insurer guarantees that at the moment it issues a policy, the new policy does not make the chance of eventual ruin cross a threshold ε agreed upon in advance by VO members. To estimate likely claim amounts for rare events that it has never seen, i.e., *tail events*, the insurer can use *extreme value theory*. The insurer can also use stop-loss policies and reinsurance to limit its exposure to tail risk, as discussed later.

If the insurer's chance of eventual ruin ever exceeds ε in spite of these precautions, the VO members have several options. They may choose to supply additional capital reserves. They may choose to take no action, so that the insurer runs out of money if its luck remains poor, necessitating internal loans, unpaid claims, or delayed claim payments. The insurer may raise premiums to increase capital. Or it may transfer some of its risk to a reinsurer.

Each VO member, and the VO as a whole, can expect to benefit from insured access. A consumer expects a net benefit from each insured access, as otherwise it would not buy the policy. Providers' losses attributable to sharing are reimbursed by the insurer's payments on their claims. So that providers directly benefit from sharing, an additional fee that goes directly to the provider can be included in each premium, to cover the provider's additional costs attributable to sharing, plus a profit. A second, complementary, and more conservative option is for the premium to include a fee retained by the insurer and intended as *future profit* for the provider. Then at the end of each fiscal period, the insurer's excess capital reserves can be shared with providers. If desired, the same two fee-based approaches can be used to cover the costs of running the insurer, or give it an expected profit; in this paper, we assume that the insurer is non-profit and cost-free. We also assume that the benefits and damages attributable to sharing accrue only to the provider and consumer, without impact on other VO members, though insured access can also be used in more complex situations with potential collateral benefits and damages. Finally, as discussed later, the VO must set up the system so that each act of sharing is expected to benefit the VO

as a whole, i.e., the shared purpose that binds its members together.

3.1 Pricing

Consider a particular insured access. The insurer does not know in advance what the total size of all claims on that policy will be, but it can represent this quantity by a random variable X representing the *risk* associated with a particular consumer accessing a particular piece of information owned by a particular producer. More precisely, X represents the total amount of claims that will eventually be paid to the producer under that policy. For now, let us assume that the insurer knows the probability distribution for X, and discuss how this information can be used to set the price.

The most widely adopted approach to pricing risk in general is the *Principle of Equivalent Utility*, in which the premium P is calculated by solving the following equation (p. 4):[2]

$$E[u_I(w_I + P - X)] = u_I(w_I). \qquad (1)$$

Here u_I is the utility function of the insurer I, and w_I is its current capital. This principle says that the premium P should be set to the amount at which the insurer is equally happy whether or not the policy is issued, i.e., indifferent.

The exact formula to calculate P depends on the utility function $u(z)$. Given $u(z)$, we can derive the *risk aversion index* $r(z) = -\frac{u''(z)}{u'(z)}$ of a principal. More risk averse principals have more concave utility functions.

With a linear utility function, $u(z) = z$ and $r(z) = 0$, meaning the principal is risk-neutral. Let π denote a premium pricing principle. If we use a linear utility function in the Principle of Equivalent Utility in Formula 1, we get $\pi[X] = E[X]$, which is called the *Net Premium*. With the Net Premium, the insurer sells a policy for the expected amount of its claims. In the long run, an insurer could break even with the Net Principle. However, in practice insurers usually prefer to set prices higher than the Net Premium, because it requires high capital reserves to avoid ruin.

With an exponential utility function $u(z) = 1 - e^{-\alpha z}$, for $\alpha > 0$, the risk aversion index $r(z) = \alpha$, and we derive the *Exponential Principle* from Formula 1:

$$\pi[X] = \frac{1}{\alpha} \log(m_X(\alpha)), \qquad (2)$$

where $m_X(\alpha) = E[e^{\alpha X}]$ is the moment generating function of X around α, and X represents the risk (total claims) associated with a policy. We could add an additional fee to $\pi[X]$ to support the provider or insurer, as discussed previously.

Although there are pros and cons for each principle, the Exponential Principle is particularly widely used in actuarial literature [16]. Among its favorable properties, the following two are especially important:

Additivity for independent risks. $\pi[X + Y] = \pi[X] + \pi[Y]$, where X and Y are independent.

Superadditivity for positively correlated risks. $\pi[X + Y] \geq \pi[X] + \pi[Y]$, where X and Y are positively correlated.

For independent risks from separate acts of sharing, the additivity means that the price for one policy covering all of them is the same as the total price for separate policies for each. Thus, an insurer can price a new policy without having to analyze its aggregate risk across all its policies.

---

[2]All mentions of page numbers in this paper refer to [10].

Superadditivity for positively correlated risks is important because allowing several instances of information sharing can introduce a much larger risk than just the sum of each risk, if they are positively correlated. For example, military phone books are often classified, even if each number in them is unclassified. The Exponential Principle also enjoys subadditivity for negatively correlated risks, i.e., it reflects the fact that diversification can reduce overall risk. Because of these favorable properties, we use the Exponential Principle in the remainder of this paper.

To summarize, given an access request (risk) X, the insurer uses Formula 2 to compute a premium, tacking on a fee to go directly to the provider if desired.

3.2 Tail Events, Ruin, & Reinsurance

The insurer groups similar risks into a *class*, as discussed in detail later, such that all risks X in the class follow the same probability distribution, and assigns the same premium to all risks in the class. The previous section assumes that the insurer knows this distribution, but the insurer may only know its own history for the class, consisting of the details of every policy it issued and every claim it received. From this data, the insurer can produce an approximation to X's distribution. Often, X is known to belong to a particular family of distributions. In that case, the claims history can be used to estimate the parameters of the distributions, using maximum-likelihood estimation [2]. With a long enough history, one might expect a very good approximation.

In the real world, however, damage-causing events have an extremely long-tailed distribution, where the tail includes many highly unlikely catastrophic events. A claims history is a finite random sample from this long-tailed distribution. Thus, if an insurer prices premiums solely based on the history and without considering the unseen long tail, the insurer eventually face ruin (pp. 87-111). *Extreme value theory* can help by providing a basis for statistical modeling of unseen tail events [8]. Still, it only approximates the true risk distribution.

To handle the risk of high-damage events it has never observed, an insurer can buy a stop-loss insurance policy (pp. 8-13) from a reinsurer. The insurer pays claims as usual until the total payout exceeds a threshold d specified in the policy; the reinsurer pays subsequent claims. The stop-loss policy transfers tail risks to the reinsurer and lowers the variance of the insurer's portfolio. Stop-loss is provably optimal for reducing the variance of the insurer's claims (Theorem 1.4.3, p. 11), when the reinsurer uses the Net Principle.

Once the VO members have set a bound ε for their insurer's chance of eventual ruin and decided how risk-averse (α) the insurer is, then *ruin theory* (pp. 87-111) specifies the minimum capital the insurer needs to keep the chance of ruin below ε. The classical ruin model assumes that independent, identically distributed (iid) claims arrive according to a Poisson process and that the insurer's income from premiums holds steady at each time step. Under the Exponential Principle, we have:

$$\alpha = \frac{1}{w_I} |\log \varepsilon|, \text{ i.e., } \varepsilon = e^{-\alpha w_I}, \tag{3}$$

where α is the insurer's risk aversion index, w_I is its initial capital, and ε is the upper bound on ruin probability. Even if the insurer does not experience tail events, the chance of ruin may approach ε due to bad luck. Given its current capital and α, an insurer can apply Formula 3 periodically to determine whether the current upper bound ε' on the chance of ruin is still below ε, and work to increase capital if not. For correlated risks or unsteady premium income, the insurer will need to perform lengthy simulations to determine the chance of ruin, as discussed later.

3.3 Defining Classes of Risks

If the insurer does not know the probability distribution of a new risk X, it cannot use Formula 2 to set the premium. If risks are correlated, then Formula 3 no longer applies, so issuing the policy might push the chance of ruin above ε. To ensure that this does not happen, the insurer can run simulations to compute the probability of ruin, but this is a very lengthy process. Preanalysis offers a solution to these problems. The VO members can identify all the classes of insured access requests that they might like to allow in the future. Similar to traditional access control, each class might identify a type of information, a group of VO members allowed to access this data, and constraints on the context under which such accesses are to be permitted.

The insurer must subdivide classes until all risks (i.e., expected total policy claims) in the same class fit the same probability distribution, and then use that distribution to determine the (identical) premium for all policies to be issued in that class. Subdividing a class can be approached as a mixture model problem [5], where subclasses all belong to the same family of distributions, but with different parameters. Expectation maximization is popular for creating mixture models. Real-world claim sizes for many kinds of policies are exponentially distributed, so subdivision is not as daunting as it might sound. The classes must not become so small that the claims history for a class is too small for statistical significance of tests of goodness of fit, i.e., there is not enough data to compute its distribution's parameters within a desired error bound.

The insurer must periodically check that recent claims history is consistent with what it expected, by rebuilding its probability distribution for historical claims data for a class, and looking for changes and trends that may suggest premium changes. To help with this task, the insurer can employ *actuarial credibility theory* (pp. 203-227), which helps a model-builder extrapolate from a small sample that is highly relevant (recent history), by exploiting a large set of data that is not quite so relevant (the rest of history).

Preanalysis also helps the insurer with the problem of ensuring that its chance of ruin will not exceed ε once it issues a new policy. With correlated risks, computing the chance of ruin requires lengthy simulations. Positively correlated risks can significantly increase the overall risk, while the aggregate risk of policies with negatively correlated claim sizes can be lower than the sum of their individual risks. Thus the insurer can use portfolio management theory from the financial engineering community to reduce its overall risk by diversifying the types of risk assumed. The insurer can analyze historical data to estimate the correlations between risks of different classes in advance, run simulations to estimate the chance of ruin given particular numbers of policies in each class, and use the simulation results to cap the number of policies sold in each class.

3.4 Purchase Decisions

A consumer can use decision theory to determine its expected financial benefit from accessing a piece of information. Then the consumer must decide whether the benefit is worth the price of the policy. Because the consumer's benefit is uncertain and the consumer is risk-averse, it is too simplistic to buy the policy as long as the expected benefit exceeds the premium. Instead, consider the following inequality, similar to the Principle of Equivalent Utility:

$$E[u(w + Y - P)] \geq u(w), \qquad (4)$$

where u is the consumer's utility function, w is its capital (or wealth) that it can use, and Y is a random variable representing the consumer's expected additional value (or revenue) from accessing the information. Let the consumer have an exponential utility function with parameter α_c. Then from Formula 4, we can derive the maximum premium P^+ the consumer is willing to pay:

$$P^+ = -\frac{1}{\alpha_c} \log(m_Y(-\alpha_c)), \qquad (5)$$

where $m_Y(-\alpha_c) = E[e^{-\alpha_c Y}]$ is the moment generating function of Y around $-\alpha_c$. Thus, the consumer buys the policy if the premium is no more than P^+, reflecting the expected benefit and the chance that he might be worse off after using the information. As noted earlier, traditional actuarial methods do not provide this sort of decision theoretic formula to compare policy prices with possible benefits.

3.5 Rewarding Good Risk-takers

In the discussion so far, the insurer sets premiums based solely on the class of risk, i.e., the type of consumer, information, and circumstances of access. The VO can benefit by encouraging good risk-takers, i.e., consumers who do not result in claims, by giving them lower premiums. This is called a *bonus-malus system* (pp. 135-146), a branch of credibility theory. Though much more sophisticated methods are available, we adopt the simple and effective Dutch system (pp. 136-138), still used for auto insurance in the Netherlands.

The system has 14 steps, each with its own weight, which is a discount factor to be multiplied with the policy price obtained by a premium principle. These steps are updated at policy renewal. Consumers with no claims in the previous period ascend one step and get lower premiums, but those with claims filed against their policies descend several steps, resulting in higher prices.

3.6 Bootstrapping the Insurer

In deciding what types of sharing will be allowed, VO members must be careful to align members' individual incentives with the VO's shared purpose so that a consumer's benefit is also a benefit for the VO. If incentives are aligned, then every act of sharing has an expected net positive benefit for the VO. To help align incentives, the VO can offer an incentive scheme that rewards consumers with *wages* when their use of shared information benefits the VO as a whole. Molloy et al. [12] present an abstract model of a VO member's wage as a function of her own profit and the profit of all members, plus a base salary. The key for this scheme is how to choose the function so that making optimal decisions for the VO as a whole is in the member's best interest. With the right function, rational members will try to request insured accesses whose expected outcomes are aligned with the common goal of the VO.

The benefits directly attributable to insured access must be weighed against the opportunity cost to the members who contributed the insurer's capital reserves. However, if insured access is as popular and beneficial among VO members as they expected it to be when they set up the insurer, then the opportunity costs of capital reserves for consumers will be offset by their realized gains due to sharing.

At startup, an insurer may have no historical claim information of its own. It may be able to use historical data from other organizations. If some relevant data is available for modeling a risk, but not enough for statistical significance, the insurer can use actuarial credibility theory to extrapolate from the relevant data plus a large set of slightly related data, to provide better risk estimates. With regard to rare events, the insurer can also use extreme value theory to obtain better estimates of the tail parts of risk distributions from available data. Even without historical data, actuaries manage to estimate future claim amounts for new classes of risks, including such exotic risks as alien abduction and damage to the legs of Heidi Klum, Michael Flatley, and Mariah Carey. Thus we can assume that actuaries will be able to get the system off the ground.

The insurer must determine the fees and/or profit-sharing scheme for the producers at startup. Perhaps the simplest profit-sharing approach is to wait until the end of a fiscal period, calculate the level of capital that the insurer must retain for probability of ruin ε, and distribute the excess capital among the producers. More sophisticated methods distribute the insurer's funds in excess of the *optimal dividend barrier*, which maximizes the total expected present value of the distributions (dividends) before ruin; there is a simple closed-form formula for the optimal dividend barrier under the common assumption that claim sizes follow an exponential distribution [6]. Once the barrier is set, VO members must decide whether to distribute the profit evenly or according to each producer's amount of sharing, risk assumed, benefit derived by consumers, or any other factor.

4. EXPERIMENTS

In this section, we use discrete event simulations to confirm that the theory presented in the previous section correctly predicts the likely outcome of insured access in an example scenario, and to understand the effect of different parameters on the outcome. Our simulator is written in C++, and uses the Boost C++ Libraries and their Math Toolkit. Our results show that on average, the expected capital of each VO member, the insurer, and the VO as a whole does grow over time. We also examine the insurer's probability of ruin as a function of its degree of risk aversion. Testing the techniques for estimation of distributions from claims data is beyond the scope of this paper, as real claims data is not available to us.

For the reasons discussed earlier, we price policies using the Exponential Principle, and use Formula 5 for consumers' policy purchase decisions. We consider a range of values for the Exponential Principle's parameter α, which is the insurer's degree of risk aversion. Figure 2 shows the upper bound ε on the probability of eventual ruin from Formula 3, with a range of risk aversion indexes for the insurer and a fixed initial capital, with and without a log scale. This figure is intended to help the reader visualize the impact of risk aversion on the chance of ruin; note, however, that Formula 3's assumptions do not quite hold in our simulations,

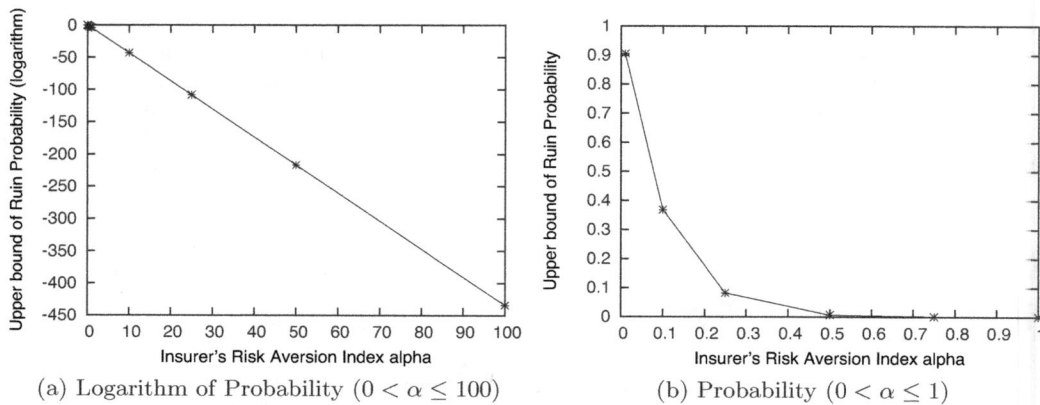

(a) Logarithm of Probability $(0 < \alpha \leq 100)$ (b) Probability $(0 < \alpha \leq 1)$

Figure 2: Upper Bounds on Ruin Probabilities

as the insurer's income from premiums will not be constant at each unit of time and the insured accesses will not all have identical claim size distributions.

The simulations model a scenario where the VO is partitioned into producers and consumers. Each producer produces one unique map. Some maps are more sensitive than others, depending on who the consumer is. This sensitivity is reflected in the parameters of their distributions of claim sizes, and thus in their premiums. We model each insured access as an independent (uncorrelated) risk. We model the arrival of requests for insured access using a separate Poisson process for each consumer. For purchased policies, we model the arrival of claims using one Poisson process for each issued policy. The process starts only after the policy is issued, and we limit it to at most one claim per policy.

For each potential insured access, the consumer expects a certain benefit, modeled as a random variable, against which the premium must be weighed. The consumer's *profit* is its actual benefit minus the premium it paid. The exponential family of distributions is widely used in many disciplines for modeling outcomes of various kinds of transactions. Among the many members of the exponential family, normal distributions are common and easy to visualize, so we use normally distributed benefits. We model the receipt of benefit from insured accesses with a separate Poisson process for each access. The benefit's process starts only after the policy is issued, and the benefit arrives at most once per policy. For any Poisson process, the time between each pair of consecutive events is exponentially distributed.

For total claim sizes, which we refer to simply as *claims*, we adopt two distributions from the exponential family, which is widely used for modeling claims. The first is a normal distribution. However, a normal distribution can overestimate the total claims on a policy, because if one waits long enough when using a Poisson process for claim arrival, a claim will eventually arrive for any given policy. In contrast, in real life many policies never have any claims at all. The zero-adjusted gamma distribution (ZAGA) [15] is very effective at modeling this situation, because it explicitly models the chance of there being no claim at all. Thus when a claim arrives under the Poisson process, the ZAGA distribution explicitly models the chance that the "claim" is $0. The ZAGA distributions we used have fatter tails than the normal distributions, thus illustrating the impact of rarer events.

When a consumer requests an insured access, we choose its producer uniformly at random from the producers it has not purchased from previously.

When a consumer requests a policy, the insurer uses the Exponential Principle to set the premium for the policy. The consumer computes its expected benefit from the insured access, then uses Formula 5 to determine the maximum premium it is willing to pay. If this is less than the quoted premium, the consumer buys the policy. Each consumer has its own parameter α_c for risk aversion, chosen uniformly at random from $[.1, 10]$, and hence its own maximum premium for a particular map.

The simulation has to use concrete numbers for the benefit of maps and for claim sizes. For each map, we choose an average benefit uniformly at random in $[1.0, 1.5]$, with its average claims drawn uniformly at random from $[.5, 1]$ for the normal distribution. For the normal distributions, the range of possible means of claims and benefits is narrow and relatively close, as otherwise the outcome of the simulation will be dominated by the larger values. For the normal distributions, standard deviations are set so that three standard deviations from the mean (a reasonable threshold for tail events) is at most twice the mean, so that the tail starts by 3 for benefits and by 2 for claims. The ZAGA distributions are chosen so ZAGA claims have the same average amount as normally distributed claims. This means that when there is a non-zero ZAGA claim with probability 0.1 on average, its average amount is ten times higher than the average value under the normal distributions. To avoid dull simulations where the quoted premiums are usually larger than the maximum premium the consumer will pay, the mean of the distributions for benefits is generally larger than that for claims. The average claim size is equal to the premium under the Net Principle, which in turn is less than the premium under the Exponential Principle, which governs what the consumer will pay. In the simulation, premiums do not include a fee for the insurer or producer, and we do not share profits, so producers break even. We simulate the behavior of 10 consumers and 10 providers and track the wealth (capital) of each consumer plus the insurer, each of whom has an initial capital of 10 for sharing. The benefit from sharing comes from outside the VO, i.e., it is not taken from other VO members' capital. The insurer's ini-

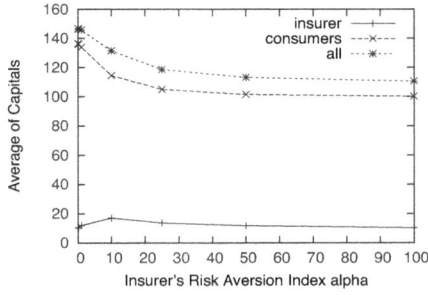

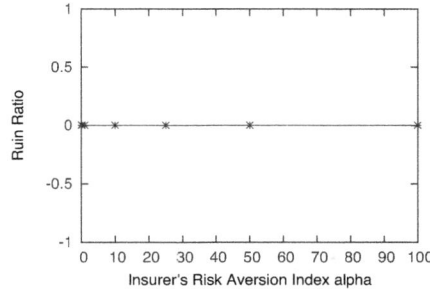

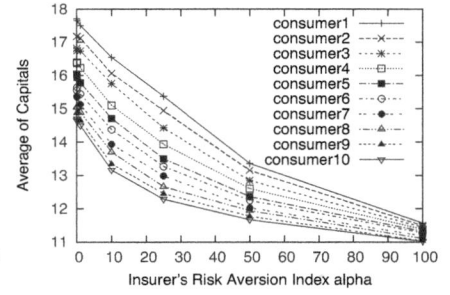

(a) Average Capital (Normal Claim Dis-tribution)

(b) Ruin Ratio (Normal Claim Distribu-tion)

(c) Average Capital with Bonus-Malus (Normal Claim Distribution)

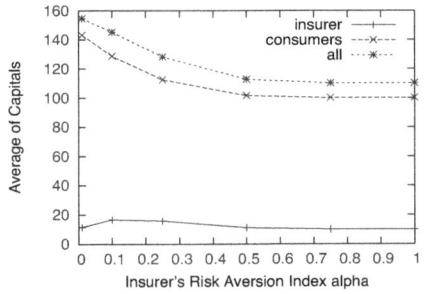

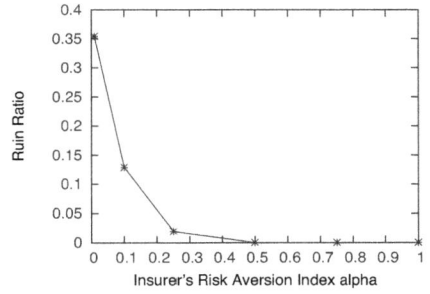

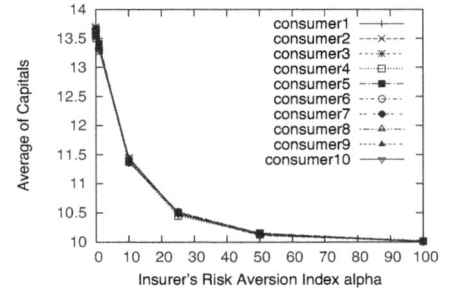

(d) Average Capital (ZAGA Claim Dis-tribution)

(e) Ruin Ratio (ZAGA Claim Distribu-tion)

(f) Average Capital without Bonus-Malus (Normal Claim Distribution)

Figure 3: Simulation Results

tial capital is rather low, a deliberate choice to allow us to investigate ruin empirically.

The simulation needs concrete λ parameters for the Poisson processes' exponentially-distributed inter-arrival times. We choose the λ parameters randomly from a normal distribution, with the means of the distributions chosen so that benefits typically arrive before claims, and consumers usually make their next insured access request after the previous request's benefits and claims are known. That translates to an average of five time steps between requests from the same consumer, two time steps for the claims on a new policy to arrive, and one time step to learn the benefits of an insured access. We run the simulation 100 time steps, which is about twice as much time as consumers usually need to get a chance to buy all 10 maps, with this range of Poisson parameters. We repeat the simulation 1,000 times and report the averages across all simulations. We computed the standard error for each reported average, as the standard deviation divided by the square root of the number of runs. The resulting error bars were too small to be observed, so we do not include them in the figures.

In addition to the capital of the insurer and the VO consumers, we present the *ruin ratio*, which gives the chance of insurer insolvency for a given level of insurer risk aversion. The ruin ratio is the fraction of runs where the insurer' capital became negative. In runs where ruin occurs, we assume that the VO loans the insurer enough funds to continue to pay claims until it is back in the black. Thus the simulation continues even after ruin, on borrowed funds.

Figures 3a and 3d present the average capital at the end of the simulation. The three lines in these graphs give the

average capital of the insurer, the average sum of capital across all consumers, and the average sum of the capital of the insurer and the consumers. Figures 3b and 3e present the ruin ratio, which is rather large when the risk aversion index α is small and claims follow ZAGA distributions, even though the ruin ratio is always 0 when claims follow normal distributions. This is because claim sizes can be quite large under a ZAGA distribution, even though the average claim is generally smaller than the average benefit. More concretely, if we ignore the chance of a \$0 claim with ZAGA and instead assume that claims are always positive, then for ZAGA's parent family of gamma distributions, the average claim size is $k\theta = (5 + 10)/2 \times 0.99 \simeq 7.5$, while the mean claim size once \$0 claims are taken into account as in ZAGA is just $(0 + 0.2)/2 \times 7.5 = 0.75$. In contrast, the average claim size when claims follow a normal distribution is always $(0.5 + 1.0)/2 = 0.75$.

These figures show that the more risk averse insurer (i.e., larger α) has less capital but a lower ruin ratio, because the number of insured accesses decreases as α gets larger. Although the upper bounds on ruin probability in Figure 2 rely on assumptions not satisfied by our experiments, Figure 3e shows that these upper bounds are actually very good approximations. The ruin ratio for ZAGA claim distributions is rather large, due to the insurer's low initial capital and the high \$7.5 average claim size. In practice, as discussed earlier, the VO must start with sufficient capital for its planned portfolio size and take corrective action if the ruin probability approaches the VO's cap.

We evaluated how bonus-malus systems affect the capital of principals, using the Dutch system explained earlier. The

307

steps of consumers are updated every five time units according to the transition table, based on their number of claims in the previous period. To differentiate between good and bad risk takers, we set the probability of the ith consumer causing a claim to $i/10$.

Figures 3c and 3f show the results with normal claim distributions, with and without a bonus-malus system. These figures show the average capital of each consumer at the end of the run. These graphs show that consumers who cause fewer claims (i.e., those who have smaller ID numbers) have more capital when the bonus-malus system is enforced[3]. Without bonus-malus, there are no such differences among consumers. These results confirm that the bonus-malus system can reward good risk takers and punish bad ones.

5. CONCLUSION

We have presented *insured access*, the first demonstrably sustainable system for encouraging appropriate information sharing in a VO. Before insured sharing starts, VO members agree on the VO's degree α of risk aversion and its maximum tolerable level of risk, i.e., the chance ε that eventually the VO might not be able to compensate an information provider for damages attributable to sharing. The VO finds or sets up an insurer whose actions are governed by α and ε. To obtain access to a piece of information owned by VO member Alice, VO member Bob must purchase a liability policy from the insurer. The insurer will not issue the policy if the VO would be exposed to more than its maximum tolerable aggregate level of risk as a result. Otherwise, the price of the policy is determined by the type of information, the insurer's current capital reserves, Bob's track record, the insurer's bonus-malus scheme, and the insurer's premium pricing principle. If Bob misuses Alice's information and Alice suffers damages as a result, then Alice can submit a claim and be reimbursed for her suffering.

We showed how to estimate the risk associated with an insured access, i.e., the probability distribution of future damages to the provider. We showed how reinsurance can cap the risk associated with rare events, and provided two schemes to ensure that information providers directly benefit from sharing. Our simulations of a map-sharing scenario showed that each participating VO member, and the VO as a whole, can expect to benefit from insured access, while the risk of failure of the system is limited by ε.

Acknowledgements: This work was supported in part by National Science Foundation awards CNS-0963943, CNS-0964295 and CNS-0963715.

6. REFERENCES

[1] Anonymous. Horizontal Integration: Broader Access Models for Realizing Information Dominance. Technical Report JSR-04-132, MITRE Corporation JASON Program Office, December 2004.

[2] L. L. Cam. Maximum Likelihood: An Introduction. *International Statistical Review / Revue Internationale de Statistique*, 58(2):153–171, Aug. 1990.

[3] P.-C. Cheng, P. Rohatgi, C. Keser, P. A. Karger, G. M. Wagner, and A. S. Reninger. Fuzzy Multi-Level Security: An Experiment on Quantified Risk-Adaptive Access Control. In *Proceedings of the IEEE Symposium on Security and Privacy*, pages 222–230, May 2007.

[4] N. Dimmock, A. Belokosztolszki, D. Eyers, J. Bacon, and K. Moody. Using trust and risk in role-based access control policies. In *Proceedings of the Symposium on Access Control Models and Technologies*, pages 156–162, 2004.

[5] I. Dinov. Expectation maximization and mixture modeling tutorial. *Statistics Online Computational Resource*, 2008.

[6] H. U. Gerber, E. S. W. Shiu, and N. Smith. Methods for estimating the optimal dividend barrier and the probability of ruin. *Insurance: Mathematics and Economics*, 42(1):243–254, Feb 2008.

[7] A. Ghosh and A. Roth. Selling Privacy at Auction. In *Proceedings of the 12th ACM Conference on Electronic Commerce*, pages 199–208, 2011.

[8] M. Gilli and E. Këllezi. An Application of Extreme Value Theory for Measuring Financial Risk. *Computational Economics*, 27(2-3):207–228, May 2006.

[9] K. Hoo. How much is enough? A risk-management approach to computer security. Working paper, Center for International Security and Cooperation, June 2000.

[10] R. Kaas, M. Goovaerts, J. Dhaene, and M. Denuit. *Modern Actuarial Risk Theory Using R*. Springer, second edition, 2008.

[11] G. Lebanon, M. Scannapieco, M. Fouad, and E. Bertino. Beyond k-Anonymity: A Decision Theoretic Framework for Assessing Privacy Risk. In *Privacy in Statistical Databases*, volume 4302 of *Lecture Notes in Computer Science*, pages 217–232. Springer Berlin / Heidelberg, 2006.

[12] I. Molloy, P.-C. Cheng, and P. Rohatgi. Trading in risk: using markets to improve access control. In *Proceedings of the 15th New Security Paradigms Workshop*, pages 107–125, 2008.

[13] N. Nissanke. Risk based security analysis of permissions in RBAC. In *Proceedings of the 2nd International Workshop on Security in Information Systems*, pages 332–341, 2004.

[14] C. Riederer, V. Erramilli, and A. Chaintreau. For Sale : Your Data By : You. In *Proceedings of the 10th ACM Workshop on Hot Topics in Networks*, pages 1–6, 2011.

[15] E. Tong, C. Mues, and L. Thomas. A zero-adjusted gamma model for estimating loss given default on residential mortgage loans. In *Proceedings of the Credit Scoring and Credit Control XII Conference*, pages 24–26, Aug. 2011.

[16] A. Tsanakas and E. Desli. Measurement and Pricing of Risk in Insurance Markets. *Risk Analysis*, 25(6):1653–1668, 2005.

[17] L. Zhang, A. Brodsky, and S. Jajodia. Toward information sharing: benefit and risk access control (BARAC). In *Proceedings of the 7th IEEE International Workshop on Policies for Distributed Systems and Networks*, pages 9–53, 2006.

---

[3]When we did the same experiment with ZAGA claim distributions, bonus-malus did not significantly impact capital, as ZAGA distributions already model the probability of filing claims.

Mediums: Visual Integrity Preserving Framework*

Tongbo Luo, Xing Jin, and Wenliang Du

Dept. of Electrical Engineering & Computer Science, Syracuse University
Syracuse, New York, USA

ABSTRACT

The UI redressing attack and its variations have spread across several platforms, from web browsers to mobile systems. We study the fundamental problem underneath such attacks, and formulate a generic model called the *container threat model*. We believe that the attacks are caused by the system's failure to preserve visual integrity. From this angle, we study the existing countermeasures and propose a generic approach, Mediums framework, to develop a *Trusted Display Base* (TDB) to address this type of problems. We use the side channel to convey the lost visual information to users. From the access control perspective, we use the dynamic binding policy model to allow the server to enforce different restrictions based on different client-side scenarios.

Categories and Subject Descriptors

Security and Privacy [**Systems security**]: [Browser Security]

Keywords

Visual Integrity, Touchjacking, Web Container Model

1. INTRODUCTION

On May 31 2010, hundreds of thousands of Facebook users have fallen for a social-engineering trick which allowed a clickjacking worm to spread quickly over Facebook during that holiday weekend. The trick, which uses a clickjacking exploit, means that visiting users are tricked into "LIKING" a page without necessarily realizing that they are recommending it to all of their Facebook friends.

The phenomenon of such a proliferation of attacks without proper protections is hard to understand. Since the first bug report on the negative usage of iframe by [16], Clickjacking attacks with various forms have been proposed. They take advantage of transparent iframes. The similar technique has also been extended to the mobile platforms [11]. Although many countermeasures have been proposed to deal with this type of problems [1, 4, 8], we are more interested in knowing what fundamental flaw has caused such attacks, so we can develop countermeasures that directly address the fundamental flaw.

We believe that all the attacks discussed above are caused by the system's failure to preserve visual integrity, i.e., to ensure what users perceive is the same as what the system "see", so users' actions are based on the correct interpretation of the information presented to them. Based on this understanding, we further believe that an ideal solution is to preserve the visual integrity. This can be done using the techniques related to visualization. We will discuss this approach in the paper. However, we also point out that this ideal solution is not completely feasible, due to the limitation of the current technologies related to visualization. Therefore, it is essential for the system to identify whether the visual integrity is in danger; if it is, the system should restrict the access.

This is basically an access control problem. Namely, a system should adopt a good access control model to deal with the visual integrity problem. Much of the existing work selects an ad hoc access control to address a particular attack, making them inapplicable to the other variations. We believe that a generic approach should be adopted, so we can develop access control systems that can address the attacks at the fundamental level. Although we may not be able to develop one access control system that fits all the protection needs, the approach that we take should be applicable to all the variations of the visual integrity attacks.

The contribution of our work is the following:

1. Our paper is the first work to fomulate the container threat model, and try to deal with this attack vector on mobile device.

2. Our work is the first to use side channels to convey the lost visual information to users on mobile device. We have also developed a novel dynamic binding policy model to defeat the attacks on visual integrity on mobile device.

3. We have implemented our solutions in Android on WebView container, and our evaluation results are quite encouraging.

*The project was supported by the Google Research Award and the NSF Award No. 1017771.

2. MOTIVATION

In this section, we briefly review an attack vector called *Visual-hijacking* which is caused by the compromise of visual integrity. Visual-hijacking is a set of attacks that uses various visual techniques to trick users into unwittingly clicking on disguised user-interface (UI) elements on the screen, usually resulting in damage to the victim. We formulate the visual integrity problem into a common attack model named *Container-based Visual Attack Model*. We treat all the variations of the visual-hijacking attacks equally in this paper when we explain our solutions.

2.1 Existing Attacks Using Iframe

The most famous attack caused by the compromise of visual integrity was introduced by Robert Hansen and Jeremiah Grossman in 2008. The technique is called **Clickjacking** [3], which takes advantage of the CSS design specification "opacity". The attack uses multiple transparent or opaque layers to trick a user into clicking on a button or link in a page, while the user's actual intention is to click on a different page. Using a similar technique, keystrokes can also be hijacked. With a carefully crafted combination of stylesheets, iframes, and text boxes, a user can be led to believe that they are typing in the password field on the pages associated with their email or bank accounts, but instead, they are typing in an invisible frame controlled by the attacker.

However, it is not always necessary to make elements invisible to compromise the visual integrity of a page. The **UI redressing** [15] attack is an example. The main idea of the UI redressing attack is to seamlessly merge two or more webpages, making them look like one, tricking users into perform an action that is different from the users' intentions. This user interface (UI) redressing method is especially useful when there are buttons with nonspecific text like "Download", "Click here" or "Exit". Another variant of clickjacking is to use JavaScript to make a small transparent iframe to follow the mouse cursor. For this attack, it is not important where a user moves his mouse, the click will always occur in the invisible iframe.

Many proof-of-concept attacks based on the clickjacking techniques have also been published. *Facebook Likejacking* [19] uses visible Facebook Like buttons to redress the contents, and thus tricks users of a website into posting a Facebook status update for a site that they did not necessarily like. *Twitter Tweetbomb* [12] uses the same technique to attack the Twitter network. Combining the invisible element technique with HTML5 File API, *Filejacking* [7] uses the invisible technique to get the user's uploaded private files. Flash Settings are also another victim to Clickjacking.

2.2 Existing Attacks on WebView

Similar attacks have been extended to the mobile platforms. Using iframes, the attacks on the mobile platforms are similar to those on the desktop platforms. However, on the mobile platform, similar attacks can be launched without iframes. **TapJacking** [18] is an example, and it occurs when a malicious application displays a fake user interface (via an Android component called Toast), to hide the real interface underneath. When users interact with this interface, the interaction events actually go to the real interface underneath (e.g. a phone dialer). Using this technique, an attacker can potentially trick a user into making purchases,

making expensive phone calls, clicking on ads, granting permissions, or even deleting data from the phone.

Confused deputy attacks can also be applied to another type of web container, the **WebView**. The WebView technology packages the basic functionalities of browsers into a class. Similar to iframe, which allows one web application to be embedded in another potentially untrusted web application, WebView allows a web application to be embedded in a potentially untrusted Android application. For most cases, the owner of the Android application is not the same as the owner of the web application inside WebView. Technologies similar to WebView are adopted by various mobile platforms, including iOS and Windows Phone, although the corresponding classes are called different names. For the sake of simplicity, we only use the term WebView throughout this paper.

Attack the **Touchjacking** [11], which can be launched successfully to redirect user's touch-screen event to the target WebView, triggering actions on the web page inside the targeted WebView. Similar to clickjacking attacks, the attacker can develop a malicious Android application with multiple WebView instances embedded. The attacker puts a visible or invisible WebView instance above another instance to redress the webpage inside WebView, and redirects user's touch screen events. The attack works on all popular mobile platforms, including iOS, Android, and Windows Phone.

2.3 Miscellaneous Attacks

According to the security blogger [6], a new technique called **Cursorjacking** was demonstrated. It deceives users by using a custom cursor image, where the pointer was displayed with an offset, so the displayed cursor was shifted to the right from the actual mouse position. With clever positioning of page elements, attackers can direct user's clicks to the desired elements. Since our work only focuses on the mobile devices, Cursorjacking is not in our scope.

3. CONTAINER THREAT MODEL

We use a generic model called the *web container threat model* to model the attacks on visual integrity across different platforms. All the attacks described in the previous section take place under a similar scenario: The victim application is embedded in another application via the components provided by the system. These components are the essential part that makes the attack successful. We use the term **Container** to refer to these components in this paper. The application that holds the container is called *host* application, and the application loaded into the container is called *guest* application. For example, in the `iframe` container case, the main page is the host, and the pages loaded into the iframes are the guest. In the Android `WebView` container case, the Android application is the host, and the web page inside WebView is the guest.

It should be noted that for the iframe and WebView containers, even though the attacker has all the privileges of the host app [5], the integrity of the data in the containers is still preserved, because of the sandbox access control mechanisms provided by these system components. The users' credentials of the guest webpage will be stored inside the container, which is a part of the system (browser or mobile system). Namely, the host application cannot directly tamper with the contents in their containers. Although WebView does provide mechanisms in its current design to allow the host to tamper with the data in the container [10], those channels will soon be secured in future versions. The attacker only has the access to the UI-based APIs of the container for the layout purpose. Those APIs are designed for the general view-based UI objects in the system.

3.1 Weaken of Trusted Display Base

As we all know, security in any system must be built upon a solid Trusted Computing Base (TCB), and web security is no exception. Web applications rely on several TCB components to achieve security. In the container threat model, a secure container must serve as the TCB to allow web pages to be embedded in a untrusted host without compromising the data integrity. To achieve this goal, a well-designed container needs to enforce access control on exposed APIs that allow the host to interact with the container.

However, there is no access control enforced on the UI-based APIs exposed by the container. Through these APIs, the malicious host app can manipulate the display properties of the container and its inside contents. For example, the host application can set the position and size of the container; the alpha value of the contents in the container can also be decided by the host. Without access control on these UI-based APIs, there is no trusted computing base to ensure visual security. We call this kind of trusted computing base the **Trusted Display Base**(TDB). We will discuss why the weaken of TDB can lead to the compromise of visual integrity, and eventually lead to security breaches. We will explain how our Midiums framework rebuild solid TDB on container as well.

4. REBUILD TRUSTED DISPLAY BASE

As we discussed in the previous section, the weaken of Trusted Display Base (TDB) is due to the lack of access control on the UI-based APIs exposed by the container. As the result, visual information is lost and the visual integrity is compromised.

4.1 The Mediums Framework

In order to rebuild TDB, we propose a generic solution, the Mediums framework, to defend against the attacks on visual integrity. The Mediums framework consists of two solutions. In the first solution, we use side channels to convey the lost visual information to users. In the second solution, we know that sometimes the lost visual information cannot be completely conveyed to users, so we developed an enhanced access control model to complement the side channel solution.

Three key components in the design of Mediums framework are: Environment Monitor, Side-Channel Notifier and Dynamic Binding Engine. `Environment Monitor` is the module to intercept each UI event performed by the user before it reaches the rendering engine. This monitor analyzes the potential visual information lost at the place the UI event happened and returns the level of dangerous to the framework. Once Mediums framework receives the signal from Environment Monitor, it triggers `Side-Channel Notifier` and `Dynamic Binding Engine` to minimize the impact by notifying user the dangerous of visual integrity compromise through side-channels or dynamically binding the access control policy defined by the server. We will explain why these two approaches can successfully rebuild TDB later.

It is important to notice that Mediums focuses on attacks

under Web Container Threat Model. Mediums does not target on any specific container but is a more generic solution to deal with how to rebuild TDB to preserve the visual integrity of the webpage in the container. Only `EnvironmentMonitor` depends on the UI architecture of the platform (i.e. Android UI module in WebView case and browser rendering engine in iframe case). However, the design of `Side-ChannelNotifier` and `DynamicBindingEngine` is platform independent. Therefore, although we only implement and evaluate Medium framework for WebView case, it can also be applied to iframe case without changing the design.

4.2 Visualization Enhancement

As we just said, the fundamental problem that causes the compromise of visual integrity is the loss of visual information when the system conveys its information to the user. Therefore, the best solution is to enhance the communication channel to reduce the information loss, so what users learn is identical to what the system knows and Mediums framework builds the TDB.

Several solutions were proposed to permanently or temporarily disable the visualization features to prevent the information loss. For example, the *X-Frame-Option* HTTP header allows the guest web app to prevent the container from being invisible. However, those solutions solve the problem at the cost of user experience. Instead of banning these features, we propose to use side channels to make up for the lost information. We will describe some of the side channels that are suitable for this goal.

4.2.1 Mobile Device Sensors

Some side channels used by desktops/laptops may not be available for mobile devices. For example, there is no cursor on the screen for most mobile systems. However, most mobile devices have embedded sensors, such as accelerometer or vibrator; they can be used as side channels. In our implementation, we have chosen the **vibrator**, **speaker** and **flashlight** as our side changes. For example, when the user touches a display area that has overlapping WebViews, the system will vibrate the device; if the user touches on a transparent overlaid area, the device will beep. Those three types of sensors are only for the proof-of-concept purposes, and they can be extended to other types of sensors.

4.2.2 System UI

We can use the unique display features of mobile system as side channels. **Toast** mechanism in Android can be used: a toast notification is a message that pops up on the surface of the window; it only fills the amount of space required for the message and the user's current activity remains visible and interactive. The notification automatically fades in and out, and does not accept interaction events. If the Mediums framework detects that the user's current touch event is in an area with potential information loss, a toast message shown in Figure 1(a) will pop up. The status bar is another choice for side channels. An application can add an icon (with an optional message) to the system's **status bar**, which is normally located at the top of the screen. The color and content of the icon will alert users about a potential visual information lost. Users can read more details about the lost visual information by clicking on the status bar. Compared to the toast and sensor approach, the notification message is more persistent and stays there much longer (see Figure 1(b)). It is also important to notice that those system UIs are triggered by the Mediums framework so that it is impossible for the attackers to block this side-channel.

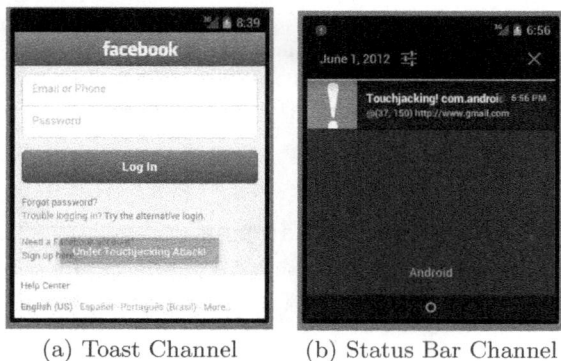

(a) Toast Channel   (b) Status Bar Channel

Figure 1: Side Channel on Mobile Devices

4.2.3   Security Concerns

There are several attacks that can be launched against our Mediums framework. First, attacker can intercept user's events before the Mediums framework gets the event. Malicious host applications can intercept the user events through the hook APIs exposed by the container. For example, by invoking the method *setOnKeyListener* of WebView, Android applications can register an event handler callback function, which will be triggered when a key is pressed in this WebView. To defeat this attack, we enforce the access control before the event hits the hook, guaranteeing that the monitor cannot be bypassed.

Moreover, to minimize the impact of unintended UI event, Mediums framework records whether users have performed click on each WebView instance or not. If framework detects that it is the first time for the user to click on the WebView instance with potential visual information lost, Mediums will discard this UI event and trigger the side-channel notifier to alert user. Users do not have to confirm that they indeed want to complete the action. If user believes the visual information lost is by design and wants to perform click on it, they just need to repeat the same action on the WebView isntance again. Mediums framework would not trigger the side-channel notifier since it has already saved user's choice on this WebView instance.

Second, attackers can attempt to block our side channels. Mediums framework will detect whether current side-channel is disabled by user or attacker, and automatically switch to other side-channel to notify user. For example, if the users turn off the speaker or ringtone, the framework needs to switch to the toast or status bar as the side channel which cannot be blocked by the attacker.

4.3   Dynamic Binding Framework

Even if we can use side channels to convey the lost dimension, users may still ignore them, as they are indeed different from an actual dimension. In these cases, a good system should be more intelligent in deciding whether it should allow users to conduct certain actions or not. Although a number of solutions have been proposed [8, 13], they seem to depend on ad hoc policies that can solve one type of problems, but it is difficult to be applied to other similar problems. The reason is that these solutions were not developed from the *access control angle*. Our framework allows us to treat the visual integrity problem as an access control problem, and can thus lead to a more generic solution.

Policy models decide when a click or touch action should be allowed or denied. Ideally, if the visual integrity is more likely to be compromised, the control on the access should be more restricted. There are two types of policy models: static binding model and dynamic binding model.

4.3.1   Static Binding Policy Model

In the static binding policy model, the access control policy is set when server constructs the webpage. The policy can be set and enforced by the client side or the server side, but they both suffer from the reliability and accuracy issues.

In the `client only` model, the client side sets and enforces the access control policy. Several work took this approach [13]. From the policy's reliability perspective, since the enforcer is at the client side, which is the place where all the access actions take place, by gathering all the environment information at the moment when the action happens, the enforcer can effectively enforce the access control policy. However, from the accuracy perspective, when the client sets the policy without the support from the server, they cannot take the contents in the container into consideration. This may lead to the granularity problem and affect the accuracy of the policies.

In the `server only` model, the policy is set and enforced by the web server. The widely adopted solution Framebuster [8] took this approach. Two major barriers make this access control policy either inaccurate or unreliable. Due to the lack of real-time environment information at the client side, when the server sets the policy, it is hard to predict the visualization environment when the user's action takes place. For the reliability issue, since the action happens at the client side, without the support from the specifically designed client framework, the servers do not have sufficient information to set the correct policy; this will reduce the reliability [17].

4.3.2   Dynamic Binding Policy Model

We propose to use a dynamic binding policy framework to solve the above problems. In this model, the server sets different access control policies for different client-side conditions. Although none of the existing works formally defined this policy model, some of the existing solutions, such as *X-Frame-Options* [14], take this approach. With the support of the browser that recognizes this new HTTP header, the web server can decide whether its pages can be loaded into the iframe or not. The recent project [4] proposed to allow the web application to use Sensitive-UI to mark the objects that do not want to be overlapped.

The limitations of those solutions are the following: The X-Frame-Options solution only deals with one situation, i.e., whether the page is loaded in the container or not. The Sensitive-UI solution only supports one action no matter what the client-side situation was. Moreover, the client-side environment can be dynamically changed. It is highly possible that the container does not overlap with others when the page was first loaded, but it overlaps with others when user performs click actions later. Since the server cannot predict the client-side situation when the access takes place, this framework should allow the web developers to define policies that depend on the runtime conditions on the client side. Therefore, to support more accurate finer-grained access control policy in this model, we propose to use the *dynamic binding* framework.

Dynamic binding framework pre-defined several client-side scenarios that may cause visual information loss, and for each scenario, it sets actions to alleviate the loss. The web developers can associate the policy to the whole webpage or certain DOM objects based on the contents of the webpage. For example we can integrate the Contego [9] model to Mediums framework to enable the web developers to assign subset of privileges to specific DOM element of the webpage.

```
if (Senarios #1)       Allow Privilege Subset 1
else if (Senarios #2)  Allow Privilege Subset 2
else if (Senarios #3)  Allow no Privilege
if (Senarios #4)       Deny Privilege Subset 4
```

In WebView case, a concrete sample case is given in the following:

```
if (not in a WebView)
    Allow {Clickable, Attach-Cookie}
else if (embedded in a overlapping WebView)
    Allow {Clickable}
else if (embedded in an invisible WebView)
    Allow {}
```

5. IMPLEMENTATION

We have implementd the visualization enhancement using the side channel solution and the dynamic binding solution for the Android system (version 4.0.3). Figure 2 demonstrates the high-level architecture of our implementation.

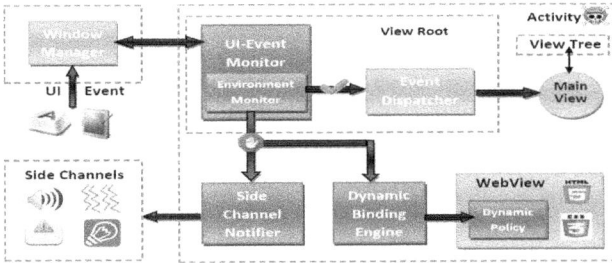

Figure 2: Mediums Framework Overview

The `UI-Event Monitor` located in the `RootView` object of each application intercepts every touch action performed by users, and invokes the `Environment Monitor`, which traverses the view tree of the application to detect whether there is a potential visual information loss or not. If there is a potential danger at the place where the touch action occurs, and the user has not been notified enough times, the framework will discard the event and trigger the protection mechanism to notify the users through side channels. Otherwise, the event will be dispatched to the target UI object.

5.1 UI-Event Monitor

The primary goal of the UI-event monitor is to intercept each UI event in the system and check the potential visual information loss before the event affects the application. To achieve this goal, The UI-event monitor needs to be placed in the event dispatching path, before the event reaches the application. Due to the page limitation, details of how the Android event handling mechanism works are not included in this paper; they can be found in the extended version of the paper.

5.2 Environment Monitor

The Environment Monitor is a module in the ViewRoot class to measure the danger level for the possible visual information loss. The module needs to extract the coordinate of the touch event from the event object, and traverses the view tree to find out all the views that contain this coordinate. Based on the predefined danger standard, the Environment Monitor will return the alert level. In our current implementation, we define the safe situation as the alert level 0; when a visible WebView instance overlaps with another UI object, the alert level is 1; when an invisible WebView instance is present but without overlapping with others, the alert level is 2; when an invisible WebView instance overlaps with others, the alert level is 3. The higher the alert level is, the more dangerous it is when the visual information is lost.

5.3 Side Channel Notifier

Once the UI-event monitor detects the potential visual information loss, it will check whether the user has been notified for a pre-defined number of times. If so, i.e., the user has been informed enough times, the notifier will not be triggered and the event will be dispatched. This means that the user has decided to accept the potential risk, and there is no need to continue "anonying" the user. Otherwise, side channel notification will be triggered. In our prototype, the alert level 1 will trigger the Vibrator; the alert level 2 will trigger the Vibrator and a Toast message; and the alert level 3 will trigger the Vibrator, a Toast message, and System Alert Bar.

5.4 Dynamic Binding Engine

The Dynamic Binding Engine will be triggered to dynamically bind the access control policy defined by the web application inside WebView. To use the Mediums prototype, web developers embed the dynamic policy in the HTTP headers and send to the WebView along with the webpage contents. In order to recognize the new dynamic binding policy header (i.e. the *DBPolicy* field), we need to modify the parser module to extract the value of DBPolicy field, and return the policy information to the WebView instance. WebView uses the WebKit rendering engine to parse and display web pages, and it is implemented as a native C++ library (*WebCore.so*). The class *WebUrlLoaderClient* in the WebKit library will fetch the response from the network driver; it then invokes the hook *didReceiveResponse*, and the code registered to the hook will begin parse the whole response. The Dynamic Binding Engine implements the code in this hook to retrieve the policy in the DBPolicy field.

Since policies are retrieved by WebKit, we need to find a way to return it to the WebView which is a Java class. The WebView Java package uses *BrowserFrame* class to represent a frame of a page, and WebKit library uses *WebFrame* class to represent the same concept. These two classes are binded togather through the JNI mechanism in Android. Therefore, the WebKit library can invoke the callback functions implemented in the C++ class *WebCoreFrameBridge* to return values from the native library to the Java framework. We add a new callback function called *jniSetPolicy* for the WebKit library to return the policy to the BrowserFrame instance. BrowserFrame will invoke the setPolicy function exposed by WebView class through the *WebViewCore* or *CallbackProxy*. Figure 3 shows the process.

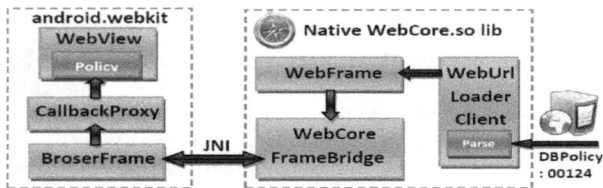

Figure 3: Dynamic Binding Engine

The dynamic policy should be stored at a secure place where cannot be tampered by malicious apps. We add a private field *policy* in the WebView class to store the dynamic policy set by the webpage. We also add a new *protected* methods *setPolicy* to allow the WebKit to set the dynamic policy. It is important to note that the setPolicy method is only accessible from the code within the android.webkit package in the Java framework. Therefore, malicious Android applications cannot invoke this method or directly change the value of private field *policy* in WebView class.

6. EVALUATION

We evaluated the Mediums framwork on the Android platform to demonstrate how our solution can effectively alleviate the visual hijacking attacks without sacrificing much user experience. The evaluation environment is Samsung Nexus S phone with Samsung Exynos 3110 processor, 512 MB Mobile DDR RAM and 4.0-inch screen.

6.1 Attack Scenarios

For our evaluation purpose, we wrote an Android application with various kinds of Touchjacking in it. To users, the main purpose of this application is to to conduct surveys, but behind the scene, the application tries to attack the user's online web account. We use two particular attacks, Keystroke Hijacking attack and Invisible WebView Touchjacking attack in our experiments.

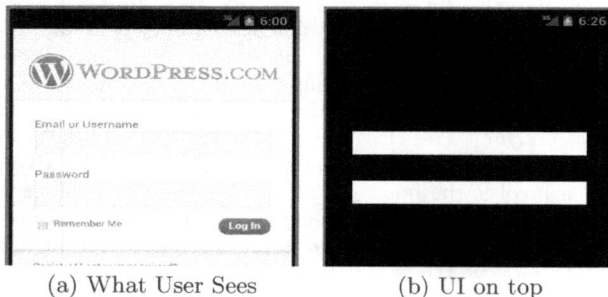

(a) What User Sees   (b) UI on top

Figure 4: WebView overlapped with UI component

Figure 4 shows how was Keystroke Hijacking attack set up. In our app, we use a WebView to load the WordPress login page, and on top of it, we put two text input fields (native Android UI objects), each covering one text field on the web page. Therefore, the users see what is shown in Figure 4(a), but when they type the username and password, they actually type the information in those native UI objects (Figure 4(b)), which belong to the host Android application.

Figure 5 demonstrates how the Invisible WebView Touchjacking attack works. The WebView (Figure 5(a)) that loads

a survey webpage is put underneath another transparent WebView. Figure 5(b) shows the transparent WebView (we intentionally make the picture non-transparant so readers can see it). What the users sees on the screen is a survey (Figure 5(a)), but when they select their choices, they actually click the "Write a Post" link on the transparent WordPress webpage.

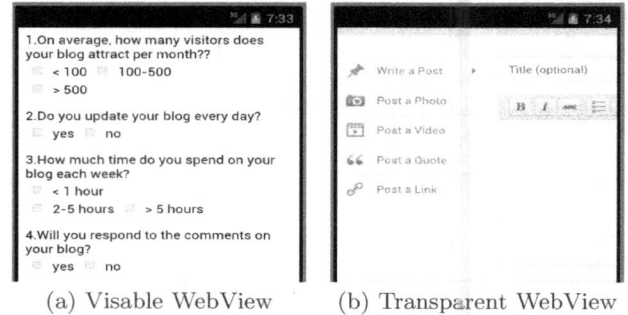

(a) Visable WebView   (b) Transparent WebView

Figure 5: Transparent WebView Overlapping

6.2 Evaluation of Visual Enhancement

6.2.1 Experiment Setup

We used two Samsung Nexus S phones to do user experience study. We installed the original system (Android 4.0.3) on one phone, and on the other phone, we installed the modified Android that has our Mediums framework. We designed two similar Android apps and both of them used the WebView component to load a survey web app in the WebView component. The topics and questions in the survey are different but share the similar layout. At certain pages in both survey apps, we overlapped both transparent WebView and visible native UI component to achieve the Touchjacking attack scenarios described above.

We randomly choose the 86 participants in different places such as library, street, restaurant and etc. The age of the participants ranges from 19 to 30. We also asked how much they knew about mobile security before the test and the results shows in the following subsections. We used survey app to distract participants' attention from our goal to test the side channel visualization. Before the test, we told participants that when they found something abnormal they can ask us, we would give some suggestions, since we did not want them to behave in a more (or less) trusting manner. Every participant was asked to finish the survey on both smartphones, and we collected participants' basic information such as sex, age, education level and major, etc. Even if the attacks were launched successfully during the evaluation, they would not cause real damage to the participant's account. We observe whether our framework can help users prevent the attacks or not.

Three major aspects can directly reflect the effectiveness of the side channel visualization solution, and we will design experiments to evaluate them. These aspects are formulated as the following questions:

- Can participants get the side channel signals generated by the Mediums Framework?

- Do participants have proper reactions to side channel signals?

Side Channel Usage	Receive Signal	Get Meaning	Perform Click	Attack Succeed
-	0	0	78	90.7%
T only	64	62	24	27.9%
V only	70	49	37	57.0%
V + T	77	75	11	12.8%
V + T + N	81	80	6	6.97%

V = Vibration Side Channel; T = Toast Side Channel;
N = Notification Bar Side Channel

Table 1: Survey Results Among 86 Participants

- Does the solution affect user experience?

6.2.2 User's Information Acquistion

In our evaluation, we used three side channels to convey the lost visual information: Vibration, Toast and Notification Bar. Among the 86 participants(Table 1), 81% participants noticed the vibration and 74% were aware of the toast. When we combined them together, 90% got the side channel signal. When we used the vibration, toast and alert bar together, the number becomes 94%. We also records the the reason why more participants miss the side-channel signals. This is because the viberation and toast only last for short period of time.

6.2.3 User's Reaction to Information

Another important factor that directly affects the success of our solution is whether the users is aware of the danger after they receive the side channel signals. The users' reactions to the signals may vary depending on their knowledge about the mobile security. After finishing two survey apps, we asked how much they knew about mobile security, such as the clickjacking and touchjacking attacks. On a scale of 1 to 5, 1 means knowing nothing and 5 means knowing much. Our results showed that the average rating was 1.76, which means most of participants know nothing or little about the clickjacking and touchjacking attacks. This way, we can test the effectiveness of our secure mechanism for people even without any knowledge. Table 1 shows the results we obtained. In the normal WebView without any Mediums framework, 8 participants chose not to click, because most of them know a lot about clickjacking and touchjacking, they thought it was not secure to perform actions on these apps, so they gave up on the survey. Among the 70 participants who noticed the vibration, only 49 (70%) chose not to click. Participants didn't connect the vibration to the potential danger because normal apps can vibrate too. Similarly, the toast approach has a lower success rate 27.9%, which is better than vibration, but some participants said that without vibration they did not notice the toast message. However, using vibration, toast and alert bar together is the most reliable way to alert users, which significantly dropped the touchjacking attack's success rate to 6.97%.

6.2.4 Usability of Solution

We also need to evaluate how the side channel signals affect user experience We also collected feedback on how annoyed the participants were when using apps in our framework. On a scale of 1 to 5, being 1 means "not at all" and being 5 means "very annoying". The average rating was 1.65, which is the acceptable level.

The overhead introduced by our framework to monitor each UI event and check environment is another factor that may affect user experience. We measured the overhead using 100 applications from the Android Market, the range of the overhead per touch event was from 0 to 6 milliseconds. The time basically comes from the view tree transversal, more precisely, it depends on the number of nodes in the view tree. The number of view objects in the applications that we tested ranges from 10 to 89.

6.3 Evaluation of Dynamic Binding

We tested the performance on the smartphones for four web applications (phpBB3, Collabtive, WordPress, and phpCalander) and shows the overhead introduced by Mediums in Figure 6. In this section, we evaluate the defense to the attacks mentioned in 6.1 by enforcing dynamic binding.

Place	Client-side Scenarios	Action Index	Actions
1st	not in WebView	0	Do Nothing
2nd	loaded in WebView	1	Remove From Screen
3rd	loaded in an overlapping WebView	2	Unclickable WebView
4th	loaded in an invisible WebView	3	Visible WebView
5th	loaded in an overlapping invisible WebView	4	Visible & Unclickable

Table 2: Mediums Scenarios and Action Definations

In order to prevent the Touchjacking, web developers set the policy header as **header("DBPolicy: 00124")** in the php file (Only 1 line of code need to be added). Each number of the DBPolicy value corresponds to one client-side situation defined by the Mediums framework. The value of each digit represents the action that needs to be taken if the client side satisfies the scenario. We use the definition in Table 2 to convert the policy to the following readable form:

```
if (not in a WebView)
    Do Nothing                               --> Take Action 0
else if (loaded in a WebView)
    Do Nothing                               --> Take Action 0
else if (loaded in an overlapping WebView)
    Set WebView Visibility to 'Gone'         --> Take Action 1
else if (loaded in an invisible WebView)
    Set WebView as Unclickable               --> Take Action 2
else if (loaded in an overlapping invisible WebView)
    Set WebView as Unclickable and Visible   --> Take Action 4
```

To defend against the keystroke hijacking attack (see Figure 4), WordPress developers can take the action to remove the WebView instance from the screen. Therefore, the 3rd digit of the DBPolicy value is set to 1. As results, if the webpage is subject to the keystroke hijacking attack, the dynamic binding engine detects the situation and enforces the dynamic policy. The WebView instance is removed from the screen, leaving only the overlapped UI objects depicted in Figure 4(b). Therefore, user can clearly know that they are under the attack and can stop.

To defend against the Invisible WebView Touchjacking attack depicted in Figure 5, developers set the 5th number of the DBPolicy value to 4. This policy defines that if the WebView is transparent and is overlapping with other objects, WebView instance should be made unclickable and visible. Therefore, when the attack is launched, the screen will look like that in Figure 5(b), clearly showing the attack intent.

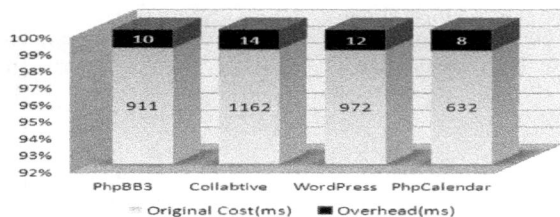

Figure 6: Dynamic Binding Performance Overhead

7. RELATED WORK

Section 2 has already described the work that is related to the attacks on visual integrity. We will not repeat them. We focus on discussing the existing solutions. We divide them into three categories.

Client-Side Solution: Some solutions purely depend on the client-side framework such as web browser. For example, by banning some particular features of the container, such as the transparent feature, web browser can alleviate the risk of the attacks. Some well-known projects include the ClearClick component in the NoScript [13] Firefox plug-in and Anti-Clickjacking component in the GuardedID project. All these solutions enhance the security by either temporarily or permanently banning features of container.

Server-Side Solution: Several solutions were proposed to modify the server-side code to defeat the attacks on visual integrity. No change to the client side is needed. One solution is to prevent web pages from being loaded into the container, and thus thwart the attacks. By embedding a piece of javascript code at the very beginning of the webpage, the webpage using Framebuster [8] can bust out from the iframe. However, this approach is not very reliable [17]. Another solution is to add unguessable secret to the URL of each web page, so the navigation can only start from certain trusted pages [2]. A third solution is to ask users to take additional actions, such as requiring the user to mark a checkbox, type in password, or solve a CAPTCHA, before clicking on the important button. These actions make it harder for clickjackers, as they now have to trick users into taking those actions. The last two solutions require significant changes on the server-side code.

Hybrid Solution: A hybrid solution is to let the server side set the policy on visual integrity, and depend on the browser to enforce the policy. Our dynamic binding approach takes a similar approach, but provides a finer granularity. We have already distinguished our work with some well-known projects in section 4.3.2.

8. SUMMARY

In this paper, we systematically study a class of UI redressing attacks, and we point out that the fundamental flaw of these attacks are the system's failure to preserve visual integrity. Based on this observation, we propose two solutions, a visualization method and a dynamic binding model.

We implement our solutions in Android 4.0.3 system and our evaluation demonstrates encouraging results.

9. REFERENCES

[1] A. Chaitrali, S. Kapil, V. Arunabh, and P. Traynor. On the disparity of display security in mobile and traditional web browsers. In *SCS Technical Report*.

[2] T. Close. The confused deputy rides again! http://waterken.sourceforge.net/clickjacking/.

[3] R. Hansen. Clickjacking. http://ha.ckers.org/blog/20080915/clickjacking/.

[4] L. Huang, A., H. Wang, S. Schechter and C. Jackson. Clickjacking: Attacks and defenses. In *USENIX Security Symposium*, 2012.

[5] C. Jackson. *Improving browser security policies*. PhD thesis, Stanford, CA, USA, 2009. AAI3382749.

[6] K. Kotowicz. Cursorjacking. http://blog.kotowicz.net/2012/01/cursorjacking-again.html.

[7] K. Kotowicz. Filejacking: How to make a file server from your browser (with html5 of course), 2011.

[8] E. Lawrence. Ie8 security part vii: Clickjacking defenses. http://blogs.msdn.com/b/ie/archive/2009/01/27/ie8-security-part-vii-clickjacking-cefenses.aspx.

[9] T. Luo and W. Du. Contego: capability-based access control for web browsers. In *Proceedings of the 4th international conference on Trust and trustworthy computing (TRUST 2011)*.

[10] T. Luo, H. Hao, W. Du, Y. Wang, and H. Yin. Attacks on webview in the android system. In *Proceedings of the 27th Annual Computer Security Applications Conference*, ACSAC 11.

[11] T. Luo, X. Jin, A. Ajai, and W. Du. Touchjacking attacks on web in android, ios, and windows phone. In *Proceedings of 5TH International Symposium on Foundations & Practice of Security (FPS 2012)*.

[12] M. Mahemoff. Explaining the "don't click" clickjacking tweetbomb. 2009.

[13] G. Maone. Hello clearclick, goodbye clickjacking! http://hackademix.net/2008/10/08/hello-clearclick-goodbye-clickjacking/

[14] Mozilla Developer Network. The x-frame-options response header.

[15] M. Niemietz. Ui redressing: Attacks and countermeasures revisited. In *in CONFidence 2011*.

[16] J. Ruderman. Bug 154957 - iframe content background defaults to transparent., 2002.

[17] G. Rydstedt, E. Bursztein, D. Boneh, and C. Jackson. Busting frame busting: a study of clickjacking vulnerabilities at popular sites. In *in IEEE Oakland Web 2.0 Security and Privacy (W2SF 2010)*.

[18] G. Rydstedt, E.e Bursztein, and D. Boneh. Framing attacks on smart phones and dumb routers: Tap-jacking and geo-localization. In *in Usenix Workshop on Offensive Technologies (wOOt 2010)*.

[19] SophosLabs. Facebook worm - likejacking. 2010.

Effect of Grammar on Security of Long Passwords

Ashwini Rao
Carnegie Mellon University
arao@cmu.edu

Birendra Jha
Massachusetts Institute of
Technology
bjha@mit.edu

Gananand Kini
Carnegie Mellon University
ganu@cmu.edu

ABSTRACT

Use of long sentence-like or phrase-like passwords such as "abiggerbetterpassword" and "thecommunistfairy" is increasing. In this paper, we study the role of grammatical structures underlying such passwords in diminishing the security of passwords. We show that the results of the study have direct bearing on the design of secure password policies, and on password crackers used for enforcing password security. Using an analytical model based on Parts-of-Speech tagging we show that the decrease in search space due to the presence of grammatical structures can be more than 50%. A significant result of our work is that the strength of long passwords does not increase uniformly with length. We show that using a better dictionary e.g. Google Web Corpus, we can crack more long passwords than previously shown (20.5% vs. 6%). We develop a proof-of-concept grammar-aware cracking algorithm to improve the cracking efficiency of long passwords. In a performance evaluation on a long password dataset, 10% of the total dataset was exclusively cracked by our algorithm and not by state-of-the-art password crackers.

Categories and Subject Descriptors: D.4.6 [**Operating Systems**]: Security and Protection–*Authentication*

General Terms: Security, Algorithms, Performance

Keywords: Password; Passphrase; Cracking; Grammar; Policy

1. INTRODUCTION

Text-based password authentication is a widely deployed user authentication mechanism. Use of text-based passwords involves a trade-off between usability and security. System assigned passwords and user-selected passwords subject to complex constraints (e.g. including mixed-case, symbols and digits) are harder to guess, but less usable[22]. Conversely, simple, memorable user-selected passwords offer poor resilience to guessing.

To obtain a good compromise between security and usability, researchers and organizations are recommending the use of longer user-selected passwords with simpler composition

requirements, e.g. minimum 16 character passwords[21] and sentence-like or phrase-like passphrases[6, 11, 3, 12, 27]. In the minimum 16 character password policy, the only restriction is that passwords cannot contain spaces. An example of a passphrase policy is "choose a password that contains at least 15 characters and at least four words with spaces between the words"[6]. The increase in the length of the password supposedly makes the password difficult to guess.

To memorize longer passwords users may rely on memory aids such as rules of English language grammar. Users may use memory aids voluntarily or due to policy recommendations. Our analysis of a set of 1434 passwords of 16 characters or more from a published study[21] shows that more than 18% of users voluntarily chose passwords that contain grammatical structures. Each of these passwords contains a sequence of two or more dictionary words. An example is "abiggerbetterpassword" that contains the grammatical structure "Determiner Adjective Adjective Noun". Table 1 provides more examples. In addition to grammatical structures we also found other types of structures such as postal addresses, email addresses and URLs. Given the evidence of use of structural patterns in long passwords, we are motivated to investigate its effect on password security. Studies on password security so far have focused only on structural dependencies at the character level[35, 33, 21].

Main Contributions: (1) We propose an analytical framework to estimate the decrease in search space due to the presence of grammatical structures in long passwords. We use a simple natural language processing technique, Parts-of-Speech (POS) tagging, to model the grammatical structures. (2) We show that the strength of a long password does not necessarily increase with the number of characters or words in the password. Due to the presence of structures, two passwords of similar length may differ in strength by orders of magnitude. (3) We develop a novel cracking algorithm to increase the cracking efficiency of long passwords. Our cracking algorithm automatically combines multiple words using our POS tagging framework to generate password guesses. (4) We show that it is necessary to analyze the distribution of grammatical structures underlying password values in addition to the distribution of password values themselves to quantify the decrease in guessing effort.

2. BACKGROUND AND RELATED WORK

Parts-of-Speech Tagging: It is the process of assigning a part of speech to each word in a sentence[25]. In English language, parts of speech are noun, verb, adjective etc. For example, the parts of speech for a sentence

Table 1: Examples of phrases in long password dataset

Category	Password Example	Phrase	Total
Simple	abiggerbetterpassword	a bigger better password	178
Substitution	thereisnomored0ts	there is no more dots	20
Extra Symbol	longestpasswordever8	longest password ever	70
	Total out of 1434		268

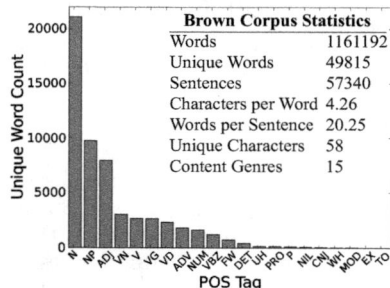

Brown Corpus Statistics

Words	1161192
Unique Words	49815
Sentences	57340
Characters per Word	4.26
Words per Sentence	20.25
Unique Characters	58
Content Genres	15

Figure 1: **Brown Corpus statistics and count of unique words (*Unique Word Count*) for top 21 Parts-of-Speech tags (*POS Tag*) in the Brown Corpus. *N, NP, ADJ,...* correspond to *Noun, Noun Proper, Adjective,...* The uneven distribution of word counts among POS tags has important implications on password search space and guessing effort.**

"She runs fast" are "Pronoun Verb Adverb". Given a sequence of words ($word_1\, word_2\, \ldots\, word_n$), a POS tagger such as CLAWS[19] can output a sequence of tags, one tag per word (($word_1, tag_1$) ($word_2, tag_2$) $\ldots$ ($word_n, tag_n$)).

Natural Language Corpora: The field of natural language processing commonly uses collection of real data samples or corpus to train and test tools[25]. Two examples are the Google Web Corpus[17] and the Brown Corpus[23]. The Google Web Corpus is a corpus of 1 trillion word tokens of English text collected from web pages and it contains 1 to 5 word n-grams and their frequency counts. The Brown Corpus is a corpus of printed English language of more than 1 million words. It contains articles from 15 genres such as fiction, government, news, and user reviews. Because of the presence of multiple genres, the Brown Corpus is considered a balanced corpus that well represents the entire printed English language. Sentences in the Brown Corpus are POS tagged. The Simple Brown POS tag set consists of 30 tag types. Fig. 1 contains the statistics of the Brown Corpus and the unique word counts for popular tag types.

Password Security: Current password security primarily focuses on the relationships at character level. In[33] the authors estimate the password search space using Shannon entropy[32] at the character level. Password crackers that enumerate password search space use zeroth or higher order Markov models trained on character probability distribution[7, 26]. In[26] authors assume that for memorability, user models a password as a sequence of characters whose distribution is similar to the distribution of characters in her native language. In[16] authors studied the linguistic properties of Amazon Payphrase[1] dataset where majority of the Payphrases are a sequence of two words. Authors investigate whether users choose their Payphrases as a sequence of words which occurs as-is in an existing natural language corpus. Further, they conjecture about guessing effort of

passphrases if the distribution of passphrases are identical to the distribution of phrases in a natural language corpus such as Google Web Corpus. In this work, we assume that users model their password as a sequence of words following the rules of grammar such as "Determiner Adjective Noun". The sequence need not occur as-is in a natural language corpus. An example of such password is "the communist fairy" that occurs in the long-password dataset presented in Table 1 but not in the Google Web Corpus. By making a relaxed assumption we model a more powerful adversary who can attack defenses such as use of nonsensical phrases[27].

3. SEARCH SPACE ANALYSIS

The password search space is the set of all possible unique password values. In this section we investigate how the presence of grammatical structures modifies the password search space. One can consider a password value as a sequence of characters, a sequence of words, or a sequence of words generated using the rules of grammar. We propose an analytical framework to estimate the size of the password search space under each of the three assumptions. By comparing the three estimated sizes we can understand the level of reduction in the size of the password search space when grammar structures are present. Via numerical evaluation, we show that the reduction in search space could be 50% or more.

3.1 Computing Search Space Size

Consider a password that contains up to n words. If the words are from a dictionary $D=\{$the, sun, king, handsome,...$\}$ that contains $numw$ unique words, the size of the password search space of all possible word sequences is

$$\mathcal{G}(\text{word}) = \sum_{i=1}^{n} numw^i \qquad (1)$$

Consider a word as any sequence of characters, for example "llmmnn", and not only the elements in a standard dictionary. Now, the password search space is bigger than $\mathcal{G}(\text{word})$. Let $numc$ be the number of unique characters possible and $avgc$ be the average number of characters per word. We can approximate the size of the password search space of all possible character sequences as

$$\mathcal{G}(\text{char}) = \sum_{i=1}^{n} numc^{avgc \times i} \qquad (2)$$

Let us now consider a password as a sequence of words created using grammatical rules. For example, a user may pick "thehandsomeking" based on the grammatical rule "Determiner Adjective Noun". To estimate the search space under this assumption, we need to define the set of valid grammatical rules. Modeling rules of natural language grammar is a difficult problem[25]. English language parsers and generators use Context Free Grammar (CFG) or more powerful Context Sensitive Grammar (CSG) to approximately model the rules of grammar. A CFG or CSG can recursively generate infinitely long sentences. For long passwords,

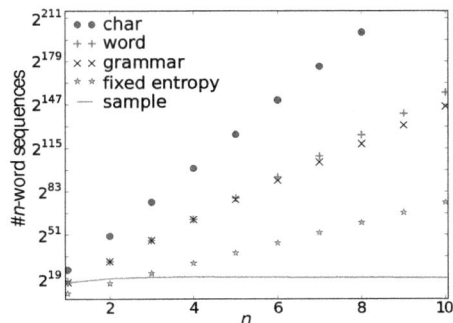

Figure 2: Comparison of the size of password search space treating password as a sequence of characters (*char*), a sequence of words (*word*), and a sequence of words generated using grammatical structures (*grammar*). Numbers are based on the Brown Corpus statistics. n is the number of words in the password. The difference between *word* and *grammar* widens as n increases. We also plot search space estimation using 1.75 bits per character of Shannon entropy (*fixed entropy*) and the actual number of unique n-word sequences in the Brown Corpus (*sample*). We explain their significance in Section 6.3.

it is unlikely that we will need to generate infinitely long sentences. For finite length sentences, a Regular Language is sufficient and it reduces computational complexity from $O(n^3)$ to $O(n)$. Parts-Of-Speech (POS) tagging technique described in Section 2 is equivalent to using a Regular Language, and we use it to model the rules of grammar.

We consider each grammatical rule as a sequence of POS tags. We extract POS tag sequences from a POS-tagged corpus that is representative of a long password dataset. This approach of generating grammatical rules is similar to expanding the CFG rewrite rules up to a finite length sans the complexity of the CFG rewrite rules. We can modify the grammar by including or excluding POS tag sequences.

Consider the set of all POS tags {Noun, Verb, Adjective, Determiner,...}. Each POS tag is associated with a dictionary of words e.g. dictionary of "Noun" is {king, queen,...}. Examples of POS tag sequences include "Determiner Adjective Noun" and "Determiner Determiner Noun". We consider a POS tag sequence as grammatical if it is observed in a corpus. We refer to a grammatical tag sequence as a *tag-rule*. "Determiner Adjective Noun" is a tag-rule because it is present in the Brown Corpus. However, "Determiner Determiner Noun" is not a tag-rule because it is not present in the corpus. The search space of a tag-rule is the set of word sequences it generates. For example, the tag-rule "Determiner Adjective Noun" generates the set of word sequences {"the handsome king", "the beautiful queen",...}. The size of the search space of a tag-rule is equal to the product of the size of dictionaries of individual tags in the sequence. The size of the grammatical password search space, $\mathcal{G}$(grammar), is equal to the sum of the sizes of search space of the tag-rules. For precise equations, refer to [30].

3.2 Numerical Evaluation

We need a corpus to numerically evaluate the password search space model proposed in Section 3.1. We use the Brown Corpus, a balanced corpus that contains representa-

Table 2: *grammar* password search space as a percentage of *word* password search space (from Fig. 2). Note the significant decrease in password search space due to the presence of grammatical structures.

#words	1	2	3	4	5
$\frac{grammar}{word}$ %	100	99.92	96.90	80.66	46.95

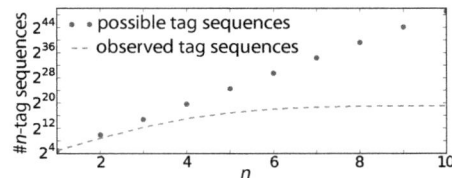

Figure 3: Comparison of the number of tag sequences observed in the Brown Corpus with the number of tag sequences possible with 30 POS tags. The *observed tag sequences*, which are a small fraction of the *possible tag sequences*, generate the *grammar* password search space in Fig. 2.

tive grammatical structures (tag-rules) for English language. We believe users will model their long passwords using tag-rules similar to the tag-rules in the Brown Corpus; we find that 84% of the long passwords from "Simple" category in Table 1 were generated using tag-rules from the Brown Corpus. Using the Brown Corpus should provide useful insights into the effect of structure on the password search space.

To evaluate the size of password search space of character sequences, $\mathcal{G}$(char) in (2), and word sequences, $\mathcal{G}$(word) in (1), we use the character and word statistics from Fig. 1. The number of unique characters $numc$=58, number of unique words in the dictionary $numw$=49815, and average number of characters in a word $avgc$=4.26. In Fig. 2 we plot the size of the password search space $char=58^{4.26 \times i}$ and $word=49815^i$ as a function of number of words i in the password.

To evaluate the password search space of word sequences generated by tag-rules, $\mathcal{G}$(grammar), we need a set of POS tags, a dictionary for each POS tag, and the set of tag-rules. We use the Simple Brown Corpus POS tag set with 30 tags. We get the dictionary for each tag from the Brown Corpus (Fig. 1). We extract the tag-rules from the Brown Corpus as explained in[30]. In Fig. 3, we plot the number of observed tag sequences (tag-rules) and possible tag sequences. Number of observed tag sequences is much less than the number of possible tag sequences, and the difference increases with length. Observed tag sequences and possible tag sequences generate the *grammar* and *word* search spaces in Fig. 2.

From Fig. 2 we can compare the password search space sizes of *char*, *word*, and *grammar*. Note that *char* $\gg$ *word* $>$ *grammar*. To emphasize the decrease in password search space due to the presence of grammar, we tabulate the ratio of *grammar* to *word* in Table 2. Observe that for a password of length 5 words, the decrease is more than 50%.

4. DISTRIBUTION ANALYSIS

When password values have underlying grammatical structures, it is important to understand the role of these structures in decreasing the guessing effort. Guessing effort can be defined as the number of values an attacker has to enumerate to guess a password. Guessing effort is a function of (a) size of the password search space, which is the set of all possible unique password values and (b) distribution of password values, which depends on how users choose password values from the password search space. So far, research involving analysis of password distributions[16, 15, 31] has not considered the effect of underlying grammatical structures.

In Section 3 we showed that the grammatical structures reduce the password search space, which implies reduced guessing effort. This is because the maximum number of values an attacker has to enumerate is equal to the size of the search space. In this section we show that the distribution of grammatical structures can also reduce the guessing effort. This reduction is in addition to the reduction due to the distribution of the password values themselves.

4.1 Reduction in Guessing Effort

A uniform distribution maximizes the guessing effort[28]. Conversely, a non-uniform distribution reduces the guessing effort. Usually, user-chosen password distributions are not uniform[15]. Given a set of user chosen passwords such as {mypassword, mypassword, iloveu}, non-uniformity is evident as password values are not unique. In the past, research has associated uniformity solely with uniqueness of password values. For example, [31] ensures that password values do not repeat often and [15] computes the distribution by counting the repetition of password values. However, for passwords generated using grammatical structures, underlying structure may cause non-uniformity even if the password values are unique. For example, the values in the set {"tangy food", "pretty cat", "naughty kid"} are unique, but all values are generated using "Adjective Noun". Hence, uniqueness of password values is a necessary, but not sufficient condition to ensure uniformity.

Grammatical structures, or tag-rules, split the password search space unevenly; the size of the search space of individual tag-rules are different e.g. the size of "Noun Noun" is greater than the size of "Adjective Noun". Recall from Section 3 that the search space of a tag-rule is the number of word sequences it generates. The effort required to guess a password generated by a tag-rule is a function of the size of its search space. Given a set of user chosen passwords, we can analyze how the underlying tag-rules are distributed. If users are using certain rules more often than the others, an attacker can use this information to reduce her guessing effort. For example, if the password set contains only the tag-rule "Adjective Noun" then the attacker need not enumerate other tag-rules. Specifically, if the users are choosing weaker tag-rules more often than the stronger tag-rules, reduction in guessing effort can be higher. In Fig. 4 we group the tag-rules from the Brown Corpus by their search space size expressed in bits or $\log_2$. Observe that some tag-rules have small search spaces e.g. for tag-rules of length 3 (*3-gram*), 8.9% of the rules have 10-19 bits of strength. Further, our analysis of unique 2-word and 3-word sequences from the Brown Corpus shows that weaker tag-rules occur more often than stronger tag-rules. More details about this analysis is available in[30].

To ensure uniform distribution over a set of password values (a) password values have to be unique, and (b) each tag-rule should have *proportional representation*. Intuitively, proportional representation implies that a tag-rule with a larger search space should generate more password values in the set. Unless these conditions are satisfied, the distribution is not uniform, and the guessing effort decreases.

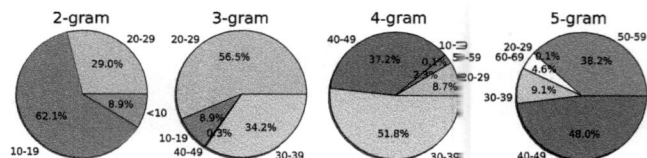

Figure 4: Tag-rules of length 2 to 5 grouped by the size of their search space (in bits or $\log_2$). Numbers outside indicate the range of bits, and numbers inside indicate the percentage of tag-rules with those many bits. Tag-rules divide the password search space unevenly, and many tag-rules have low strength. For example, 8.9% of *3-gram* tag-rules have 10-19 bits of strength.

Table 3: Data set ExSet

Password	Phrase
Ihave3cats	I have 3 cats
Ihave4dogs	I have 4 dogs
Ihave5fish	I have 5 fish
Ihad1cat.	I had 1 cat.
Ihad1goat	I had 1 goat

We prove this in[30] by posing the problem of computing an attacker's guessing effort as an optimization problem.

5. PASSWORD CRACKERS

We investigate whether state-of-the-art cracking tools such as John the Ripper (JTR)[7], Hashcat[5] and Weir Algorithm[35] can crack long passwords efficiently. This is important because crackers are used in auditing user passwords and estimating the strength of password policies[21]. We discuss the shortcomings of these crackers in cracking long passwords. We show ways to improve cracking efficiency for both long passwords in general and long passwords generated using grammatical structures. We propose a novel algorithm to improve cracking efficiency. Our cracking algorithm uses the POS tag framework introduced in Section 3.

5.1 Shortcomings of Current Crackers

A password cracker tries to recover a plain text value of a password hash value. The cracker generates candidate password guesses, hashes them, and compares them with the available hashes until a match is found. A heuristic dictionary-based cracker[7, 5, 35] uses a dictionary of values to generate candidate passwords. A dictionary may contain leaked passwords[21], words from many languages[10], common quotes, music lyrics, movie titles[24] etc. Cracker may use the dictionary values as-is or transform them by applying mangling rules. An example of a mangling rule is "capitalize first alphabet", which transforms a dictionary value "password" to "Password". Alternatively, an intelligent brute-force cracker, eventually, enumerates the entire password search space[7]. Below we explain the main shortcomings of current crackers in cracking long passwords using the example data set, ExSet in Table 3 and a dictionary, ExD={I, have, had, cats, dogs, fish, cat, goat}.

JTR in Wordlist mode and Hashcat are dictionary-based crackers. Their mangling rules can combine a single dictionary value in different ways, for example "catscats" or "catsstac" from "cats". They can append, prefix or insert specific strings to a dictionary value, and delete parts of the dictionary value. However, JTR can not combine multiple values from the dictionary to form longer passwords. To crack passwords such as "Ihave3cats" from ExSet using dictionary ExD, user has to (1) write multiple mangling rules for example "prefix I", "append had" or "prefix Ihave" or (2) explicitly add the value "Ihave3cats" to the dictionary ExD. To add longer values to the dictionary, user has to generate the values himself or collect them from existing sources such as books, Web etc. Hashcat can combine up to two values from the input dictionary, but for more values it has issues similar to JTR.

Weir Algorithm is another dictionary based technique. It improves cracking efficiency by improving the order in which mangling rules are applied to the values in the dictionary. Weir Algorithm generates a set of base structures from a training corpus. A base structure in Weir Algorithm is a sequence of "L", "D", and "S" that denote "Letter", "Digit", and "Special Symbol". Each base structure is assigned a probability. Weir Algorithm learns the digits and special symbols to insert into "D" and "S" from the training corpus. For letter sequences in a base structure, Weir Algorithm tries to fit values from the dictionary whose length exactly matches the length of the letter sequence. For example, for "LLLL" in a base structure "LLLLDLLLS", it tries to fit values {have, cats, dogs, fish, goat} from dictionary ExD. It cannot combine shorter values such as "I" and "had" to form a longer value "Ihad" that fits the sequence "LLLL". This shortcoming is similar to that of JTR and Hashcat. Although trained on passwords in dataset ExSet, Weir Algorithm cannot crack any password from dataset ExSet using the dictionary ExD; it cannot create "Ihave" and "Ihad" from "I", "have" and "had".

To force Weir Algorithm to generate longer values, we can train it with passwords containing words separated by a single space. Weir Algorithm treats space as a special symbol. We have to remove spaces from the generated password guesses. If we train Weir Algorithm on phrases listed in the dataset ExSet, it generates a base structure "LSLLLSD-SLLLL". Now, it can crack passwords such as "Ihad3cats" using dictionary ExD. However, this approach generates guesses such as {Ihad1had, Ifish5have, Icats3fish ...} that may be in the search space of all word sequences, $\mathcal{G}(\text{word})$, but not in the search space of word sequences generated using grammatical structures, $\mathcal{G}(\text{grammar})$. From Section 3, $\mathcal{G}(\text{word})$ can exceed $\mathcal{G}(\text{grammar})$ by more than 50% for 5-word length.

JTR Incremental mode, an intelligent brute-force cracker, uses a Markov model trained on 3-gram letter frequency distribution to generate password guesses. Based on our experiments, letter frequencies are effective for conventional short passwords consisting of sequence of characters but not for longer passwords with multiple words.

5.2 Evaluation on Long Password Dataset

We evaluate the cracking efficiency of JTR, Hashcat and Weir Algorithm with experiments on a published long password dataset[21]. We introduce this dataset in Section 1. It contains 1434 passwords of minimum length 16 characters, and was collected as part of a field study. Subjects could create their passwords using any character except the space character. To test the cracking efficiency on long passwords, we use the complete long password dataset, henceforth referred to as P16. To test the cracking efficiency on long passwords with underlying grammatical structures, we use a subset from P16 containing simple phrases, hence-

Table 4: Dictionaries used for evaluating crackers. Dictionary "L" is a large dictionary combining the datasets Myspace, Rockyou, Brown, 1gram, Dic-0294, Basic Full, Basic Alphabetic, Free Full, Free Alphabetic, Paid, Alphabetic, Paid Lowercase. In column *Name* "-x" indicates minimum length of the words in the dictionary.

Name	#Words	Description
L-8	35267653	Minimum length 8 values from L
LASCII	39251222	All length ASCII values from L
GW25-8	3625636435	Google Web Corpus 2-5 grams
B210	5942441	Brown 2-10 gram word sequences

Table 5: Performance of crackers on long passwords (P16) and long passwords with underlying grammatical structures (P16S). *Experiment* is the name of the experiment. *NM* indicates no mangling. *%P16 Cracked* is % of passwords cracked out of 1434 passwords in P16. *%P16S Cracked* is % of passwords cracked out of 144 passwords in P16S. *Guesses* is the total number of password guesses. *SC?* indicates if experimental session completed after *Guesses*.

Experiment	%Cracked		Total	SC?
	P16	P16S	Guesses	
JTR L-8	13.6	6.9	2.31E10	Yes
JTR L-8 NM	8.5	4.8	3.42E7	Yes
JTR GW25-8	20.5	34.7	2.48E12	Yes
JTR GW25-8 NM	11.08	27.7	3.4E9	Yes
Weir LASCII	12	4.8	1.07E12	No
Weir Space LASCII	7.6	3.4	1.26E12	No
JTR Incremental	0	0	2.48E12	No

forth, P16S. We are not aware of datasets that exclusively contain user-selected long passwords with underlying grammatical structures. P16S contains 144 passwords. To create P16S, we manually examine each password in P16 using tools such as the Microsoft Word Breaker[34], and identify passwords with multiple words. We initially include all passwords with two or more words (e.g. "compromisedemail", "thereisnomored0ts") except those that contain repetitions of a single word (e.g. "elephantelephant"). We further categorize the passwords into three groups: simple phrase, phrase with symbol substitution and phrase with extra symbols. Table 1 shows example for each category. For our experiments, we use passwords with simple phrases containing 2 to 5 words. One of our experiments uses the Google Web Corpus that contains n-grams of length up to 5. Hence, testing on passwords with more than 5 words will not permit fair comparison. Table 4 describes our dictionaries;"L" contains publicly available datasets, "GW" has data from the Google Web Corpus and "B" has data from the Brown Corpus.

We tabulate our experimental results in Table 5. We allow all experiments to make up to 2.5E12 guesses; we indicate if an experiment terminated earlier in the "SC?" column. We terminated two experiments before 2.5E12 guesses due to their excessive memory consumption. For brevity, we omit the less significant experimental results from Table 5. In our experiments, we try to overcome the main shortcoming of current crackers: They do not generate longer values automatically; user has to generate and add longer values to the dictionary. Specifically, we do the following:

Use a better dictionary of long values: given the evidence that, for longer passwords, users choose word sequences, we hypothesize that a corpus of word sequences is a better dictionary. Experiments on long password datasets until now have not tested this hypothesis. We test the hypothesis using word-grams in the Google Web Corpus and the Brown Corpus, but other corpora may also be explored. Using the Google Web Corpus as dictionary, we crack 20.5% of long passwords from dataset P16 ("JTR GW25-8"). For the same number of guesses, published experiments, using publicly available datasets similar to dictionary "L", crack 6% from P16[21]. Using the Brown Corpus, we crack only 0.3% from P16 ("JTR B210").

Use workarounds to generate longer values automatically: we use the workaround for Weir Algorithm explained in Section 5.1. From experiment "Weir Space LASCII", we find that this approach generates large number of guesses and fails to improve cracking efficiency of long passwords.

JTR L-8, JTR L-8 NM, JTR GW25-8, JTR GW25-8 NM: we run JTR in word mode using dictionaries L-8 and GW25-8. We run JTR with and without mangling rules. Dictionary values have minimum 8 characters as mangling rules can concatenate them to form 16-character length guesses. JTR GW25-8 outperforms other experiments. Using 2.48E12 guesses it cracks 20.5% passwords from P16 and 34.7% passwords from P16S. Even with lower number of guesses it outperforms other experiments.

Weir LASCII: we train the Weir Algorithm using minimum 16-character passwords from the Myspace and Rockyou, and run it using the dictionary LASCII. We terminated this experiment before 2.5E12 guesses as the memory consumption became unwieldy. Weir LASCII does not match the performance of JTR GW25-8.

Weir Space LASCII: we train Weir Algorithm on sequences of 1 to 10 words from the Brown Corpus and run it using the dictionary LASCII. The words were separated with a single space. We strip spaces from the generated guesses and check if they crack any passwords. Weir Space LASCII does not match the performance of JTR GW25-8.

JTR Incremental: we train JTR Incremental mode on minimum 16-character passwords from Myspace and Rockyou datasets. We configure it to generate passwords between 16 and 23 characters in length inclusive. JTR Incremental mode experiment fails to crack any passwords.

Experimental results show that using a good dictionary of long password values can improve cracking efficiency. However, relying only on existing sources to build dictionaries may not be ideal. Existing sources contain values that people use often and by relying on them we may fail to crack passwords that contain uncommon and nonsensical phrases e.g. "the communist fairy" in P16S. Building a Markov model based on word gram frequencies as opposed to letter gram frequencies may be useful. However, training these word gram models on existing sources can run into similar issues. We explore a novel technique to automatically generate longer password values.

5.3 Grammar Aware Cracking

A cracker should ideally emulate user behavior to generate password candidates; if passwords contain grammatical structures, crackers should use grammatical structures. We develop proof-of-concept of such a cracker using the POS tag framework in Section 3. It automatically combines words into longer password values using sequences of POS tags. Main challenges in our approach are (1) identify a set of POS

Table 6: Performance of grammar-aware cracker on long passwords with underlying grammatical structures (P16S). *%Cracked BWeb* is % of P16S cracked using dictionary BWeb. *%Cracked with BWeb90* is % of P16S cracked with dictionary BWeb90. *%Exclusive* is % of P16S cracked by grammar-aware cracker, but not by other crackers in Table 5.

Guesses	%Cracked with BWeb	%Cracked with BWeb90	%Exclusive
5E10	9.7	18.7	4.8
1E12	14.5	25	9
2.5E12	15.2	27	10.4
10E12	20.1	29.1	11.8
40E12	25.6	35.4	13.8

tag sequences that are grammatical (tag-rules). It is possible to identify tag-rules from existing corpus e.g. the Brown Corpus or long password datasets and (2) build a dictionary for individual POS tags. The level of difficulty in building tag dictionaries depends on the type of POS tag. Closed tags such as "Determiner" and "Conjunction" (e.g. *the, and*) contain small number of values that do not change much with time. Open tags such as "Noun" and "Noun Proper" have large dictionaries and also grow with time.

Our main goal is to evaluate the value of a grammar aware cracking approach. Will a grammar-aware cracker allow an attacker to crack passwords that can not otherwise be cracked? We assume that an attacker has access to a good set of tag-rules. We believe that assuming otherwise leads to a security-through-obscurity model. As use of long passwords increases, it is likely that long password data sets will become public, and attackers can use tag-rules from these datasets. To simulate a scenario that provides maximum advantage to an attacker, we extract tag-rules from P16S long password dataset used in Section 5.2. We tag the passwords in P16S using the CLAWS[19] POS tagger.

First, we build a dictionary for each POS tag using the Brown Corpus and a small web text corpus[9]. We include the web text corpus because the Brown Corpus, compiled in year 1961, does not contain Internet related words. We use all words, including repetitions, from the Brown Corpus and all words that occurred at least 10 times in the web text corpus (373 words). Words in the Brown Corpus are tagged. We tag the words in the web text corpus using CLAWS. If a word has a noun tag, we assign it to the noun dictionary and so on. We refer to this first set of tag dictionaries as BWeb. Next, we build an alternate set of tag dictionaries from BWeb. To reduce the size of a tag dictionary, we compute the cumulative probability distribution of word frequencies within the dictionary and discard words that do not meet the 0.9 cumulative probability cutoff. We apply this reduction process to all POS tags except "Noun", "Proper Noun", "Adjective", and "Cardinal Number". We call this alternate set BWeb90. Intuition for BWeb90 is that users use few popular words for closed tags, but not for open tags.

The inputs to the grammar aware cracker are a set of tag-rules, a set of tag dictionaries, and the maximum number of guesses it can make. The cracker computes the size of each tag-rule (Section 3), sorts the tag-rules by their size, and selects the subset of smallest tag-rules whose sizes add up to the number of guesses. The cracker generates word sequences from identified tag-rules using the tag dictionaries, and outputs them as password candidates.

Table 7: Comparison of passphrase strength; strength is not a direct function of length. *Tag-Rule* **lists the tag-rule that can generate the passphrase.** *Guesses* **is based on the size of the search space of** *Tag-Rule* **and effort required to mangle the phrase.** *Time* **estimates the time required to guess a given passphrase.**

Passphrase	Tag-Rule	Guesses	Time
Th3r3 can only b3 #1!	EX MOD V DET PRO	1.3E12	22 min
Hammered asinine requirements.	VD ADJ N	12.6E12	3.5 h
Superman is $uper str0ng!	NP V ADJ ADV	12.3E15	142 d
My passw0rd is $uper str0ng!	PRO NP V ADJ ADV	1.7E18	56 yr

Table 6 details the performance of our grammar-aware cracker. The columns "%Cracked with BWeb" and "%Cracked with BWeb90" list percentage of dataset P16S cracked using dictionaries BWeb and BWeb90 respectively. The "Exclusive" column lists the percentage of P16S that was exclusively cracked by grammar-aware cracker, but not by other crackers in Table 5. For 5E10 guesses, grammar-aware cracker cracked 18.7% of passwords, which is better than "Weir Algorithm" (4.8%) and "JTR Incremental" (0%). Although not listed in Table 6, it performs better than "JTR L-8" for 2.3E10 guesses. At 2.5E12 guesses it cracks 27% passwords, but that is not better than the performance of "JTR GW25-8" (34.7%). However, grammar-aware cracker cracks 10% new passwords from P16S dataset. This 10% was not cracked by "JTR GW25-8" or other experiments. Grammar-aware cracker consumes <10MB of storage versus >50GB for "JTR GW25-8". It is scalable as number of guesses increases, easier for operations such as network transfer and dictionary sorting, and provides flexibility in targeting different user groups e.g. use different "Proper Noun" dictionary for users from North America and Asia. From initial results, we believe that grammar-aware approach has potential to improve cracking efficiency of long passwords.

6. POLICY IMPLICATIONS

In this section, we highlight the need for policy makers to understand the impact of grammatical structures on security of long passwords. We examine some of the implicit assumptions within passphrase policies in light of the results on search space and guessing from Sections 3, 4 and 5. Many policies consider a passphrase as a long sequence of characters or words[8, 2, 3, 6] and estimate security metrics such as size of search space and guessing effort accordingly[6, 14]. However, when users choose sentence-like or phrase-like passphrases, due to grammatical structures the search space and guessing effort will decrease. Further, because of structure, the strength of the passphrase does not increase uniformly with the length i.e. a longer passphrase is not necessarily stronger than a shorter passphrase.

6.1 Passphrase Strength and Length Relation

Consider the passphrase examples in Table 7. The examples "Th3r3 can only b3 #1!", "Superman is $uper str0ng!" and "My passw0rd is $uper str0ng!" are from technology and academic websites[4, 12, 3]. The example "Hammered asinine requirements." is a synthetic example based on a recommendation to use nonsensical phrase[27]. The tag-rule column lists one of the grammatical structures that can generate the passphrase. The number of guesses is an estimate of the total number of passphrases the tag-rule can generate. It considers the size of the tag-rule search space and a fixed number of additional guesses required to mangle the phrase. The time column estimates the time required to

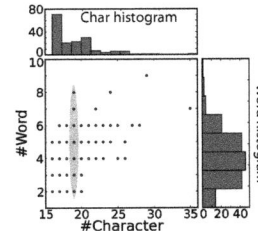

Figure 5: User behavior on long passwords containing simple phrases. Total number of characters in the passwords tends to remain the same as the number of words increases (shaded oval). Users seem to meet the policy requirement of minimum 16 characters with fewer long words ("compromisedemail") or more short words ("thosedamnhackers").

guess passphrases generated by the tag-rule using a guessing rate of 1 billion guesses per second. This rate is realistic considering that current state-of-the-art GPU accelerated machines achieve up to 33 billion comparisons per second and can be built with less than USD 3000[13]. From the guessing effort and time estimates, we see that passphrase strength is not a direct function of the number of words or characters in the passphrase. The passphrase "Th3r3 can only b3 #1!" has more words than "Hammered asinine requirements.", but is one order of magnitude weaker. Similarly, "Hammered asinine requirements." has more characters than "Superman is $uper str0ng!", but is one order of magnitude weaker. Underlying structures and not just the number of characters or words determine the strength of a passphrase. Passphrase policies that do not consider this[3] may unwittingly allow passphrases such as "Th3r3 can only be #1!" and "My passw0rd is $uper str0ng!" that differ in strength by three orders of magnitude.

6.2 User Behavior and Passphrase Policy

While studying the long password data set[21], we observed that users tend to choose fewer long words or more short words to generate a password that meets the policy requirement of minimum 16 characters. For example, the passwords "compromisedemail" and "thosedamnhackers" contain 16 characters, but two and three words respectively. Fig. 5 plots the word and character statistics for long passwords in simple category from Table 1. All passwords in the shaded oval have 19 characters (x-axis) and between two to eight words (y-axis). Observe similar behavior for passwords with 16, 17, etc. characters. We found some explanation for this behavior in the field of cognitive psychology. Jahnke and Nowaczyk say regarding experiments on word-length and short-term memory[20, Chap. 4], "Strings of short words (e.g. *cup, war*) given in tests of immediate memory are much more likely to be recalled correctly than are equally long strings of equally familiar long words (e.g. *opportunity*, *university*). Stated alternatively, subjects can remember for immediate recall about as many words as they can say in 2 s, and obviously they can say more short than long words in that time." From Section 6.1, we know that two passwords of equal length (same number of characters), but different number of words may vary in strength by orders of magnitude. Hence, passphrase policies such as "choose a password that contains at least 15 characters and at least 4 words with spaces between the words"[6] may allow weaker passphrases unless they consider user behavior and effect of structure.

6.3 Passphrase Entropy

To determine size of passphrase search space, subsequently passphrase security, some evaluations[29] use fixed entropy estimate of the English language[32]. We explain below, why this approach may be incorrect. Informally, entropy measures how much the values emitted by a source can be compressed. When values repeat more often, compression is higher and entropy is lower. Since search space of a source is the set of unique value it emits, we can use entropy to estimate size of the search space. However, an accurate estimate of entropy is necessary to do so. It is incorrect to use estimation derived from one source (e.g. English language) for another (e.g. long passwords) as they can have different distribution of values. To illustrate this point, in Fig. 2, we plot the search space estimate using the equation $2^{1.75 \times 4.26 \times i}$ where i is the number of words in the password. We use fixed entropy estimate of 1.75 bits per character for printed English from[18], which derived the estimate using a 3-word gram language model trained on large amounts of printed English sources and tested on the Brown Corpus. We use 4.26 average word length statistic from the Brown Corpus (Fig. 1). We observe from Fig. 2 that the estimation for 3-word phrases closely matches the true number of unique 3-word phrases in the Brown Corpus. For other lengths, there is varying degrees of inaccuracy.

7. CONCLUSIONS

Long passwords is a promising user authentication mechanism. However, to achieve the level of security and usability envisioned with long passwords, we have to understand the effect of structures present in them. Further, we have to make policies and enforcement tools cognizant of the effect of structures. As a first step, we developed some techniques to achieve these goals. We studied grammatical structures, but other types of structures such as postal addresses, email addresses and URLs present within long passwords may have similar impact on security. More research is necessary to fully understand the effect of structures on long passwords.

8. REFERENCES

[1] Amazon payphrase. www.amazon.com/payphrase, 2011.
[2] Bitcoin passphrase policy. https://en.bitcoin.it/wiki/Securing_your_wallet#Password_Strength, 2012.
[3] Carnegie Mellon University passphrase policy and FAQ. http://www.cmu.edu/iso/governance/guidelines/password-management.html;http://www.cmu.edu/computing/doc/accounts/passwords/faq.html#8, 2012.
[4] Cheap GPUs rendering strong passwords useless. http://it.slashdot.org/story/11/06/05/2028256/cheap-gpus-rendering-strong-passwords-useless, 2012.
[5] Hashcat advanced password recovery. http://hashcat.net/oclhashcat-plus/, 2012.
[6] Indiana University passphrase policy and strength estimation. http://kb.iu.edu/data/acpu.html#atiu;http://protect.iu.edu/cybersecurity/safeonline/passphrases, 2012.
[7] John The Ripper password cracker. http://www.openwall.com/john/, 2012.
[8] Massachusetts Institute of Technology passphrase policy. http://ist.mit.edu/security/passwords, 2012
[9] NLTK Web Text Corpus. http://nltk.googlecode.com/svn/trunk/nltk_data/index.xml, 2012.
[10] Openwall wordlists collection. http://www.openwall.com/wordlists/, 2012.
[11] University of Maryland passphrase policy. http://www.security.umd.edu/protection/passwords.html, 2012.
[12] University of Minnesota passphrase policy. http://www.oit.umn.edu/security/topics/choose-password/index.htm, 2012.
[13] Whitepixel GPU Hash Auditing. http://whitepixel.zorinaq.com/, 2012.
[14] T. Baekdal. Passphrase usability and strength estimation. http://www.baekdal.com/insights/password-security-usability, 2012.
[15] J. Bonneau. The science of guessing: analyzing an anonymized corpus of 70 million passwords. In *Proceedings of the IEEE Symposium on Security and Privacy*, pages 538–552, 2012.
[16] J. Bonneau and E. Shutova. Linguistic properties of multi-word passphrases. In *Workshop on Usable Security*, pages 1–13, 2012.
[17] T. Brants and A. Franz. *Web 1T 5-gram Version 1*. Linguistic Data Consortium. Philadelphia, PA, 2006.
[18] P. F. Brown, V. J. D. Pietra, R. L. Mercer, S. A. D. Pietra, and J. C. Lai. An estimate of an upper bound for the entropy of English. *Comput. Linguist.*, 18(1):31–40, 1992.
[19] CLAWS. Part-Of-Speech tagger for English. http://ucrel.lancs.ac.uk/claws/, 2012.
[20] J. C. Jahnke and R. H. Nowaczyk. *Cognition*. Prentice-Hall, Inc., Upper Saddle River, New Jersey, USA, 1998.
[21] P. G. Kelley et al. Guess again (and again and again): Measuring password strength by simulating password-cracking algorithms. In *Proceedings of the IEEE Symposium on Security and Privacy*, 2012.
[22] S. Komanduri et al. Of passwords and people: Measuring the effect of password-composition policies. In *Proceedings of the Annual Conference on Human factors in Computing Systems*, pages 2595–2604. ACM, 2011.
[23] H. Kucera and W. N. Francis. *Computational analysis of present-day American English*. Brown University Press, Providence, RI, 1967.
[24] C. Kuo, S. Romanosky, and L. F. Cranor. Human selection of mnemonic phrase-based passwords. In *Proceedings of the Symposium on Usable Privacy and Security*, pages 67–78. ACM, 2006.
[25] C. D. Manning and H. Schütze. *Foundations of Statistical Natural Language Processing*. MIT Press, Cambridge, MA, USA, 1999.
[26] A. Narayanan and V. Shmatikov. Fast dictionary attacks on passwords using time-space tradeoff. In *Proceedings of the ACM Conference on Computer and Communications Security*, pages 364–372, 2005.
[27] PGP. FAQ: How do I choose a good password or phrase? http://www.unix-ag.uni-kl.de/~conrad/krypto/passphrase-faq.html, 2012.
[28] J. O. Pliam. On the incomparability of entropy and marginal guesswork in brute-force attacks. In *Proceedings of the International Conference on Progress in Cryptology*, pages 67–79. Springer-Verlag, 2000.
[29] S. N. Porter. A password extension for improved human factors. *Computers & Security*, 1(1):54–56, 1982.
[30] A. Rao, B. Jha, and G. Kini. Effect of Grammar on Security of Long Passwords. Technical Report CMU-ISR-12-113, ISR Carnegie Mellon University, 2012.
[31] S. Schechter, C. Herley, and M. Mitzenmacher. Popularity is everything: A new approach to protecting passwords from statistical-guessing attacks. In *Proceedings of the USENIX conference on Hot topics in Security*, pages 1–8, 2010.
[32] C. E. Shannon. Prediction and entropy of printed English. *Bell Systems Technical Journal*, 30:50–64, 1951.
[33] R. Shay et al. Encountering stronger password requirements: User attitudes and behaviors. In *Proceedings of the Symposium on Usable Privacy and Security*, pages 1–20. ACM, 2010.
[34] K. Wang, C. Thrasher, and B.-J. P. Hsu. Web scale NLP: A case study on url word breaking. In *Proceedings of the International Conference on World Wide Web*, pages 357–366. ACM, 2011.
[35] M. Weir, S. Aggarwal, B. de Medeiros, and B. Glodek. Password cracking using probabilistic context-free grammars. In *Proceedings of the IEEE Symposium on Security and Privacy*, pages 391–405, 2009.

Accepting the Inevitable: Factoring the User into Home Computer Security

Malgorzata Urbanska[†]   Mark Roberts[†]   Indrajit Ray[†]   Adele Howe[†]

Zinta Byrne[‡]

[†]Department of Computer Science & [‡]Department of Psychology
Colorado State University Fort Collins, CO 80523

ABSTRACT

Home computer users present unique challenges to computer security. A user's actions frequently affect security without the user understanding how. Moreover, whereas some home users are quite adept at protecting their machines from security threats, a vast majority are not. Current generation security tools, unfortunately, do not tailor security to the home user's needs and actions. In this work, we propose Personalized Attack Graphs (PAG) as a formal technique to model the security risks for the home computer informed by a profile of the user attributes such as preferences, threat perceptions and activities. A PAG also models the interplay between user activities and preferences, attacker strategies, and system activities within the system risk model. We develop a formal model of a user profile to personalize a single, monolithic PAG to different users, and show how to use the user profile to predict user actions.

Categories and Subject Descriptors

K.6.5 [**Management of Computing and Information Systems**]: Security and Protection—*Invasive software, Unauthorized access*

General Terms

Human Factors, Security

Keywords

security risk modeling, attack graphs, system security, attacks and defenses, security personalization

1. SECURITY ANALYSIS FOR THE HOME USER

Effective prevention, protection and mitigation of security threats on home computers requires an understanding of the user. Different user activities can impact different vulnerabilities within the home computer system in a variety of ways. How a user uses the computer and the Internet, what types of online activities that the user typically participates in, how a user perceives security risks, even how much risk a user is willing to accept to obtain online benefits – these are some factors that need to be evaluated to tailor security measures for the home computer system. (We use the term "home computer system" to refer to both the computer and the user.) These together constitute the profile for the home computer system.

We make three contributions in this work. First, we model the security threats in a home computer as they adapt to the user of the system. We refine and extend the notion of *attack graphs* to the *Personalized Attack Graph* (PAG) for this purpose. A PAG explicitly encodes, in terms of pre- and post- conditions, the dependencies between vulnerabilities existing in a *standalone system*, the system configuration (including those influenced by user preferences), and the user activities, system actions and attacker actions. Traditional attack graph/attack tree models rely solely on network connectivity between different hosts as the enabler of related vulnerability exploitation. In other words, if and only if a vulnerability exists in a host that is connected to another host, traditional models identify a related vulnerability in the second host as exploitable. A PAG, on the other hand, works on standalone systems to identify attack scenarios; network connectivity is a non-issue.

Second, we develop a formal model of the home computer user and apply this model to "prune" and personalize a single monolithic PAG to different users. (For clarity, we will use the term "*instantiated* PAG" as opposed to a "*monolithic* PAG" when a PAG is personalized). Similar systems (that is, machines having the same architecture, running the same OS with the same configuration and same set of applications) have identical monolithic PAGs to begin with. However, depending on how the user uses a system and what the user's security related characteristics are, a PAG becomes more personalized. The instantiated PAG better reflects the true security risk of the particular system.

Finally, we show how a user profile can be modeled in Bayesian Networks to predict activities that a user undertakes on the home computer. These probability values are used in the PAG to estimate probability of occurrence of different threats to the system. We run experiments on synthetic data to demonstrate, as a proof-of-concept, how the PAG model can be used to personalize security.

2. RELATED WORK

Attack trees [8, 24] have been proposed as a systematic way to model a networked system's risk to malicious attacks. They help to organize and analyze intrusion and/or misuse scenarios in a network (also called "attack scenarios") by enumerating known vulnerabilities or weak spots in the system, and capturing the cause-consequence relationships between system configuration and these vulnerabilities in the form of an And-Or tree. Attack graphs [1, 13, 25, 29] are similar data structures that have been widely used to determine if a certain goal state can be reached by an attacker who is trying to compromise a system, starting from an initial state. An exploit dependency graph [20] is an extension of the attack graph that explicitly captures the different conjunctive and disjunctive relationships between the nodes. The notion of multiple-prerequisite graphs with three different types of nodes – state nodes, prerequisite nodes, and vulnerability instance nodes – have also been adopted for security modeling [15]. Bayesian Networks, which are probabilistic graphical models (see [14] for more information), have often been used to model the states of the attack graph and encode the probabilities of the network vulnerabilities [10, 16, 22].

While each of these representations elegantly captures all possible ways by which an attacker can compromise a specific system resource, none of them are specifically geared towards the home computer system. Network connectivity between hosts is a major model element in these models. This is, however, irrelevant in a single, standalone home computer. In addition, none of these models factor in the effect of the user's actions on security. Our notion of Personalized Attack Graphs is specifically geared towards a single, standalone system, and explicitly models the interplay between user attributes, attacker strategies, and system activities within the system risk model.

3. THE PERSONALIZED ATTACK GRAPH

A PAG is a built around a set of *exploit trees*. The terminal nodes of the PAG collect together known exploits and represent different possible security compromised states for the home computer system. To help illustrate a PAG, Figure 1 shows an example of an instantiated PAG with two possible exploit trees resulting in a compromised system. We call this graph *instantiated* because it is actually a subgraph of a larger, more generic graph with nodes included only if they capture the state of a specific home computer system. We constructed the example PAG from the vulnerabilities that were identified on an actual machine running Microsoft Windows XP Professional SP3 with common configurations. Before collecting our data, the system was secured and updated. Subsequently, the machine was disconnected from the Internet, and automatic updates were disabled. After three months, the machine was plugged into the Internet and scanned using NeXpose from Rapid7 LLC [23]. NeXpose found 216 vulnerabilities during this scan. Of these, 133 were critical, 74 severe, and 9 moderate.

For this example, the PAG includes not only possible states of the system but also states resulting from user actions that can lead to information leakage. Layers in the graph indicate preconditions, but across the graph the layers are otherwise insignificant. Nodes in the graph include system states and vulnerabilities (shown as white boxes in the figure), execution state of attack actions (gray boxes),

and execution states of user actions (dashed boxes). An arc in the graph is used to represent a state transition that contributes to a system compromise. The simplest transition is between two nodes (as in the box labeled E2). Conjunctive (AND) nodes (as in the box labeled E1) require all preconditions to be met for a state transition; they are indicated by multiple arcs that are incident on the node. Disjunctive (OR) branches (as in the box labeled E3) have a small circle for the choices and require only a single branch to be true. Each node has an associated probability; probabilities are presented as integers out of 100 within the node. Nodes that represent the execution of user actions are associated with a *user profile* (see Section 4 for details).

3.1 A Formal Model of the PAG

Our model of PAG is based on the formal model of attack trees presented in [8]. We propose to "personalize" attack graphs by explicitly capturing user, attacker and system actions, and tailoring the representation to specific home computer systems through pruning and analyzing the graphs. We build up a set of definitions that are increasingly inclusive to present the formal model of a PAG. We will refer to Figure 1 to exemplify each definition.

DEFINITION 1. *A System Attribute Template (SAT) is a generic property of a system that can contribute towards a system compromise. It can include, but is not limited to the following:*

- *system vulnerabilities as reported in different vulnerability databases,*
- *system configuration, e.g., data availability, use of security tools, open ports, un-patched software,*
- *access privileges, e.g., root account, guest account.*

In the bottom left of Figure 1, the "VBScript MsgBox()" is an instance of a system configuration SAT, while its parent "VBScript MsgBox() CVE-2010-0483" is an instance of a system vulnerability SAT, and "User is Reading Email" is an instance of an access privilege SAT (user has privilege to read email).

Only some instances of SATs are relevant for a specific system. A successful security compromise depends on which relevant instances of SATs are present or absent (that is true or false). Instantiating an attribute template with truth values on the specific instances allows us to implicitly capture the susceptibility of the system. We define a *System Attribute* with such a concept in mind.

DEFINITION 2. *A System Attribute, s_i, is a Bernoulli random variable representing the state of an instance of a System Attribute Template. It is associated with a state – True / 1 or False / 0 – and a probability value, $Pr(s_i)$, indicating the probability of the state being True / 1.*

For example, for the system in Figure 1, s_1 = "VBScript MsgBox() CVE-2010-0483" is a system attribute when associated with a truth value, signifying whether the specific vulnerability exists or not. $Pr(s_1)$ is the probability of the attribute being in state *True*.

DEFINITION 3. *A User Attribute Template (UAT) is a generic property of a user that helps describe the influence of the user to home computer security. It is specified in terms of parameters that include but are not limited to:*

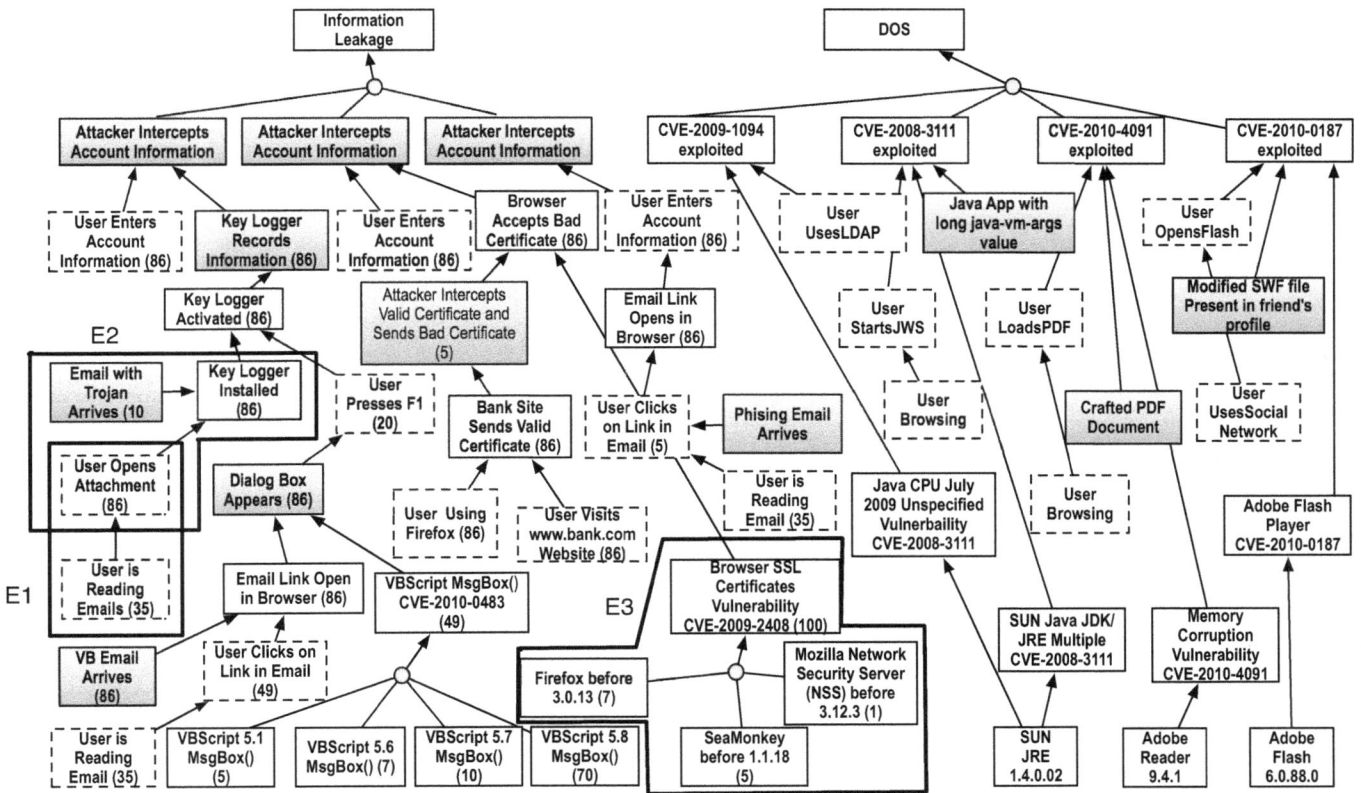

Figure 1: An example of a Personalized Attack Graph representing two exploits.

- *user system configuration choices, e.g., use of specific browser,*
- *user habits or activities, e.g., checking email at specific intervals, clicking indiscriminately on links,*
- *a user's sensitive information (assets) that need to be protected.*

The User Attribute Template helps capture a user's impact on security much the same way as SAT helps capture the system characteristics. Thus, the UAT contains only those parameters that are relevant for securing the home system. For example, Figure 1 shows that the bank account can be compromised by the user using the browser Firefox before version 3.0.13. Using such a browser, consequently, is an instance of the user preference UAT.

DEFINITION 4. *A User Attribute, u_i, is a Bernoulli random variable representing the state of an instance of a User Attribute Template. It is associated with a state – True / 1 or False / 0 – and a probability value, $Pr(u_i)$, indicating the probability of the state being True.*

The notion of User Profile that we define later on (see Section 4) is different from UAT although some of the parameters of UAT can be parameters of User Profile. The difference is that the user profile concerns characteristic features of human beings that directly affect user attributes that are of type habits and activities. To illustrate, the education level of a user can be considered a parameter of user profile but is not an user attribute as defined in Definition 4.

DEFINITION 5. *An Attack Attribute Template (AAT) is a generic representation of the conditions set up by an attacker (in terms of actions that the attacker can/has taken) that lead to exploitation of a vulnerability and enable a successful attack. It includes, but is not limited to*

- *performing scanning of a system*
- *installing malicious software*
- *delivering specially crafted messages*

Referring to box E1 in Figure 1, "Key Logger Installed" is an instance of installing malicious software AAT.

DEFINITION 6. *An Attack Attribute, a_i, is a Bernoulli random variable representing the state of an instance of an Attack Attribute Template. It is associated with a state – True / 1 or False / 0 – and a probability value, $Pr(a_i)$, indicating the probability of the state being True.*

To analyze a system for potential compromise, we make a closed-world assumption for attacks. For a successful attack to take place, the corresponding attributes should have the value of true. If corresponding values are false (or are rendered false), an attack will not be successful. Consider, for example, the attacker attribute "Phishing Email Arrives" (extreme right side of PAG in Figure 1). If we expect that the attacker cannot ever successfully deliver a phishing email, this attribute will be false. Thus, we can be assured that the exploit described by this scenario will never occur. Modeling these attributes as Bernoulli random variables allows us to compute the probability of a system being compromised.

DEFINITION 7. *Atomic Exploit: Let S be a set of system attributes, U be a set of user attributes, and A be a set of attacker attributes. Let $X = S \cup U \cup A$. Let $s_j \in S, u_k \in U, a_l \in A$ and $x_i = (s_j, u_k, a_l) \in X$. Let $\mathcal{F}$, a conditional dependency between a pair of attributes in X, be defined as $\mathcal{F} : X \times X \to [0, 1]$. Let $x_{pre}, x_{post} \in X$ be two attributes. Then $AtmExp : x_{pre} \to x_{post}$ is called an atomic exploit iff*

1. *$x_{pre} \neq x_{post}$, and*
2. *if $x_{post} = True$ with probability $\mathcal{F}(x_{pre}, x_{post}) > 0$, then $x_{pre} = True$*

The attribute x_{pre} is the pre-condition of the exploit denoted as $pre(AtmExp)$ and x_{post} the post condition denoted as $post(AtmExp)$.

An atomic exploit allows an attribute x_{post} to be transformed from x_{pre} with a some probability $\mathcal{F}(x_{pre}, x_{post})$. It is the simplest state transition that potentially leads to some security breach in the system. It can be visualized as a graph with two nodes x_{pre} and x_{post} with an arc from x_{pre} to x_{post} (rectangle E2 in Figure 1).

DEFINITION 8. *Branch-Decomposed Exploit In order to build more complex exploits, let $BranchExp = \{x_{pre_1}, \ldots, x_{pre_k}, x_{post}\} \subseteq X$ be a set of attributes such that if $x_{post} = True$ with some non-zero probability,*

1. *$\forall i, x_{pre_i} = True$, or*
2. *$\exists i, x_{pre_i} = True$*

then $BranchExp$ is called a Branch-Decomposed Exploit. *Case (1) is called an* and-decomposition *and has the precondition: $pre(BranchExp) = \{x_{pre_1}, \ldots, x_{pre_k}\}$. Case (2) is called an* or-decomposition *and has the precondition: $pre(BranchExp) = x_{pre_i}, \forall i = 1, \ldots k$. The postcondition of both cases is: $post(BranchExp) = x_{post}$.*

A branch-decomposed exploit that is an and-decomposition is visually represented as a set of nodes $x_{pre_1}, \ldots, x_{pre_k}, x_{post}$ with arcs from x_{pre_i} to x_{post}. For an or-decomposition, the arcs from the x_{pre_i}'s are incident to a small circle from which an arc is incident on x_{post}. In Figure 1, an example of an or-decomposed branch exploit is the set of attributes enclosed by E3, while an and-decomposed exploit is the set of attributes enclosed by E1. We will call a set E of attributes an exploit, if either E is an atomic exploit or a branch-decomposed exploit.

DEFINITION 9. *Exploit Tree – Let X be a set of attributes and E be either an atomic exploit or a branch-decomposed exploit. An* Exploit Tree *is a tuple $ET = \langle \epsilon_{root}, \mathcal{E}, \mathcal{P} \rangle$, where:*

1. *$\mathcal{E} = \{E_1, E_2, \ldots, E_n\}$ is a set of exploits defined over the set of attributes X.*
   - *$x \in X \leftrightarrow \exists E_i \mid x \in E_i$*
   - *If $x \in E_i, x \neq \epsilon_{root} \mid x = post(E_i)$ then $\exists E_j, j \neq i \mid x \in pre(E_j) \wedge \nexists E_k, k \neq j \neq i \mid x \in pre(E_k)$*
2. *$\epsilon_{root} \in X$ is a goal attribute that the attacker wants to be true such that $\nexists E_i \in \mathcal{E} \mid epsilon_{root} \in pre(E_i)$*
3. *$\mathcal{P}$ is a set of estimated probability distributions. The elements of $\mathcal{P}$ are all the $Pr(x)$'s associated with attributes x's in ET.*

By the above definition, any proper subtree of an exploit tree is also an exploit tree. An exploit tree is characterized more by the goal attribute, ϵ_{root}, that the attacker wants to be true (as perceived by a security analyst), rather than the other attributes and the associated state transitions.

A home computer system may have only one exploit tree. However, more often than not, several goal attributes will be "of interest" to the attacker, requiring several exploit trees. Moreover, these exploit trees can be related to one another in the sense that rendering a goal attribute to be true in one tree leads to an attribute in another tree being true. To model this scenario we introduce the notion of Personalized Attack Graph.

DEFINITION 10. *A Personalized Attack Graph is a set of related exploit trees. It is represented by a tuple $PAG = \langle \mathcal{G}_1, \mathcal{G}_2, \mathcal{V}_1, \mathcal{V}_2 \rangle$, where:*

1. *$\mathcal{G}_1 = \mathcal{E}_p, \ldots, \mathcal{E}_q$ and $\mathcal{G}_2 = \mathcal{E}_m, \ldots, \mathcal{E}_r$ are disjoint sets of exploit trees such that $\mathcal{E}_i \in \mathcal{G}_1 \leftrightarrow \mathcal{E}_i \notin \mathcal{G}_2$.*
2. *Let $\mathcal{V}_1$ be the set of goal attributes of exploit trees in $\mathcal{G}_1$ and $\mathcal{V}_2$ the set of goal attributes in $\mathcal{G}_2$ such that $\mathcal{V}_1 \cup \mathcal{V}_2 = \mathcal{V}$, the set of all attributes in $\mathcal{G}_1$ and $\mathcal{G}_2$ and $\mathcal{V}_1 \cap \mathcal{V}_2 = \phi$. A goal attribute $v_i \in \mathcal{V}_1$ iff $\nexists x_k \in \mathcal{E}_d \in \mathcal{G}_2 \mid pre(x_k) = v_i$. A goal attribute $v_j \in \mathcal{V}_2$ iff $\exists x_l \in \mathcal{E}_b \in \mathcal{G}_1 \mid pre(x_l) = v_j$.*

Essentially, a PAG is a graph constructed out of the exploit trees, E_i's, present in a home system. The set of exploit trees is partitioned into two sets $\mathcal{G}_1$ and $\mathcal{G}_2$. The set $\mathcal{G}_1$ consists of all those exploit trees that have those goal attributes which are goals in themselves and do not lead to different attributes in other exploit trees being set to true; these goal attributes are not pre-conditions of any attribute of any exploit tree. These goal attributes are the terminal nodes of the PAG. The set $\mathcal{G}_2$, on the other hand, consists of all those exploit trees that have goal attributes that, if set to true, can lead further to attributes in other exploit trees to be set to true as well; these goal attributes are pre-conditions of some other attributes. To prevent cycles, we explicitly forbid the goal attributes in $\mathcal{V}_2$ to be pre-conditions of attributes of exploit trees in $\mathcal{G}_2$. A cycle in a PAG (if it was allowed to exist) would contain a sequence of goal attributes of the form $v_1, v_2, \ldots, v_n, v_1$ such that $v_1 \in pre(x_a) \in pre(x_b), \ldots, \in pre(v_2), \in pre(x_k) \ldots \in pre(v_3) \ldots \in pre(v_n) \ldots \in pre(v_1)$. By following this sequence the attacker sets to true what has already been set to true, and is essentially of no value to further risk analysis; this follows from the monotonicity property [1].

4. MODELING THE HOME USER

The most important characteristic of the PAG that differentiates it from other threat modeling paradigms is its ability to capture the contribution of the human user to system security. What activities a user performs on their computer, how they perceive the risks and what benefits they think accrue from their activities impacts the security threat to the home computer. Thus, the PAG requires several types of information about the user and leverages that information to identify the vulnerabilities that are most severe or likely for a specific home computer system.

User information is represented as User Attributes in the PAG. User attributes include user actions, preferences, and assets. At this time, user actions, user preferences and assets are manually incorporated into a general version of the PAG. For example, Figure 1 includes "User is Reading Emails" and "User Opens Attachment" as user actions, "Firefox before 3.0.13" and "SUN JRE 1.4.0.02" as user preferences and "User Enters Account Information" as assets. The user actions and assets are identified from the vulnerability descriptions.

User preferences are represented as the probabilities associated with the User Attributes. These probabilities are critical to determining what poses the strongest threats to a home computer system. To compute these probabilities, we develop a model, represented as a Bayesian Network, that relates characteristics of home computer users to preferences and behavioral tendencies.

Our Bayesian network model has been significantly influenced by two prior models of human behavior in computer security: Ng, Kankanhalli and Xu's [19] and Claar's [6]. Ng et al. adapts the Health Belief Model (HBM) [27, 26], to predict computer security behavior. Their model includes six primary factors and one moderating factor that can predict a person's decisions about security. We use these primary factors and the moderating factor in our model. The moderating factor is the output node of the Bayesian Network and called the *target node*. The six primary factors we use are:

- *Perceived severity* captures a user's belief in the seriousness of a possible security violation from a specific activity.
- *Perceived benefits* captures a user's perception of effectiveness or benefit of adopting an action or a specific preference.
- *Perceived barriers* describes a user's perception of cost or disadvantages associated with specific actions or preferences.
- *Risk tolerance* describes an individual's ability to handle or undertake different degrees of potentially harmful activities. (It is intended to account for the result of studies that have shown that users are willing to accept risk if the potential benefit is viewed as more important [21, 12]. Ng et al. [19] calls this factor as *Perceived susceptibilty* while Claar [6] terms this as *Perceived vulnerability*. We believe that the term Risk Tolerance is more appropriate, keeping the nature of the factor in mind.)
- *Self-efficacy* captures a user's belief that he or she is capable of taking specific action. (It has been observed to be an important factor in several home user studies [2, 3, 18].)
- *Cues to action* captures the user's motivation to cause a change in behavior. (Some studies [11, 30, 2] have shown importance of cues to action that encourage users to undertake certain activities.)

Several studies [31, 4, 11] have also shown that a user's *prior knowledge* and *prior experience* with computers and security may affect how the user perceives and acts on security threats. We include this as two other factors that can predict a user's decisions about security.

As in Claar's work [6], our model includes demographic factors (*gender, age, socio-economic,* and *education*) as predictors of user's decisions about security. Inclusion of these demographic factors is further supported by other studies:

Friedman et al.[9] (user community), Szewczyk et al.[30] (socio-economic factors) [9, 4, 18, 11] (age and gender).

4.1 Predicting user actions

The user attribute probabilities for a specific user is calculated from the values for the 12 factors italicized above. The user will be led through a series of questions and answers that results in specific values (in the range [0,1]) for a given user. The demographic factors, prior knowledge and prior experience are straightforward characteristics of the user and are easy to evaluate. The six factors – risk tolerance, perceived severity, perceived benefits, perceived barriers, self efficacy, and cues to action – on the other hand, are more difficult to assess; we expect to determine how best to do so from the human subject studies that we are currently pursuing that relate the users' perceptions to their actions in security settings.

To predict user actions we use the values of these factors as inputs to Bayesian Networks. For every user attribute (see Definition 4) that is relevant for a given user, we build a Bayesian Network. This collection of BNs is called a *Bayesian User Profile* (BUP). Each of the networks (or subnets) in the BUP provides the posterior probability value for a specific user attribute in an instantiated PAG when the subnet is populated with evidence values corresponding to the specific user. To estimate the prior probabilities we rely on the previously mentioned user studies (such as [30]).

The dependent variable of the Bayesian Network gives the probability for a given user attribute. We call this output the *target node* of the subnet.

To make concrete how users can lead to different BUP target values, we present three hypothetical user profiles and set the value of the independent variables for those users in the corresponding BUPs. UserA is a retired person who was recently given a Windows XP machine that runs Internet explorer (IE). UserA is familiar with the inventory computer system from a recent job but is a new user of the Internet and email. UserB is a 20-year-old college student with a portable laptop running Windows7. UserB has used computers since kindergarten, is very confident when using them, and insists on browsing the Internet with Firefox. UserB automatically accepts any dialog that the browser displays. UserC is a 22-year-old college student who happens to be a computer science major. UserC is aware of security concerns and is diligent about installing updates and being observant of what her computer downloads. As an example, Table 1a shows the calculated values from the BUP for the three users and a set of the user attributes from the right side of the PAG in Figure 1.

Let us consider the example configuration for UserA more specifically. According to the description given above, we can assume that UserA is unlikely to use any social network or read PDF files. However, there is still a nonzero probability that user can take these actions. For this reason, we assigned probability equal to 0.015 to these attributes. For this example, let us further assume that UserA is a highly educated female at age 60 with very good socioeconomic standing, but she has very low experience in Internet. The example question can be: what is the likelihood of her opening a flash file (attribute "OpensFlash")? She has a harm avoidance personality (Risk Tolerance on low level) and she perceives lower severity for taking this action because she does not know much about security concerns in Internet.

Table 1: Results of experiments to determine which system attributes are most relevant for DOS exploit

(a) User attribute probabilities of engaging in specific activities.

User Attribute	UserA	UserB	UserC
UsesSocialNetwork	0.015	0.974	0.961
OpensFlash	0.914	0.972	0.959
UsesLDAP	0.015	0.949	0.015
Browsing	0.922	0.974	0.971
StartsJWS	0.929	0.966	0.015
LoadsPDF	0.015	0.974	0.963

(b) Probability estimates of vulnerabilities from CVSS scores.

Vulnerability	CVSS		p(e)
	AC	Base	
CVE-2009-1094	0.71	10	0.99968
CVE-2010-4091	0.61	9.3	0.85888
CVE-2010-0187	0.61	4.3	0.85888
CVE-2008-3111	0.71	10	0.99968

(c) How individual vulnerability probabilities change w.r.t. user profiles.

Exploit Name	User Profile		
	UserA	UserB	UserC
DOS Exploit	0.121	0.542	0.169
CVE-2009-1094	0.007	0.474	0.007
CVE-2010-0187	0.001	0.075	0.073
CVE-2008-3111	0.12	0.132	0.002
CVE-2010-4091	0.002	0.106	0.105

This flash file also contains interesting information about upcoming political event; therefore the perceived benefit is at a medium level. But because she does not know much about the Internet, she is not sure how to find and run this file (Perceived Barriers). In addition, she does not feel comfortable and is afraid to take this action (Self Efficacy is at a low level). Nevertheless, because her good friend recommended that she open the file, the Cues to Action are at a medium level.

For each of the user attributes, similar scenarios are considered and appropriate subnet configuration is assigned. The effect of these characteristics is translated to probability values for the user attributes by the corresponding Bayesian networks for the other values presented in Table 1a.

Note that, since there can be multiple occurrences of the same user attribute in an *instantiated* PAG, there can be a one-to-many relationship between a target node of a subnet and user attributes in the instantiated PAG. Additionally, not all subnets in an instantiated BUP will be relevant to an instantiated PAG. For example, if we are interested in determining the probability of the user logging into a social network portal in the PAG in Figure 1, then we will be interested in determining the probability of the user attribute "UsesSocialNetwork"; we will not be interested in the user attribute "UsesEmail."

5. USER-CENTRIC SECURITY ANALYSIS

Our goal in this work is to develop a methodology for personalizing security by matching home computer security to each user. To achieve this, we instantiate a PAG and use the BUP to update probabilities within the PAG. Owing to the dynamic nature of the threat model, it appears appropriate to use a Bayesian Network to calculate the changing probability values in the PAG. We thus implement a PAG as a Bayesian Network for analysis purposes. To avoid confusion, we would like to re-iterate that Bayesian Networks are used in two different contexts in this work – one to model the likelihood that the user engages in specific activities (a value we read from the target nodes of each subnet of the BUP) and the other to facilitate automated analysis of the PAG (that we discuss next).

In the experiments below, we focus on the Denial of Service (DOS) exploit tree of the PAG presented in Figure 1 (see the right most exploit tree, starting under node "DOS"). We choose this subgraph because it contains sufficient numbers of system, user, and attacker attributes to support our analysis: four CVE vulnerabilities, six user actions, and three system attributes that rely on the system configuration. We assess the impact that the user profile has on system compromise probability estimates in the PAG.

We implemented both the BUP and the DOS subtree of the PAG with the Bayesian Network package called SMILE [7]. Each system, user, or attack attribute (see Definitions 2, 4 and 6) is a node in the Bayesian Network with arcs connecting to its preconditions and/or postconditions.

Each node has single prior probability, p, associated with it (see Section 3.1). Leaf nodes have a probability of existence. All other nodes have a probability of being exploited. The probability of vulnerability nodes (beginning with CVE in Figure 1) are calculated from equations in [22], which apply values from the Common Vulnerability Scoring System (CVSS) [17]. Table 1b presents the set of vulnerabilities we use in this paper with associated vectors from the Base Metric Group of CVSS. The columns include the Access Vector (AV), the Access Complexity (AC), the Authentication Score (AU), and the Base Score from CVSS and the corresponding calculated probabilities. For all vulnerabilities, the AV score was 1 and the AU score was 0.704. The attack attribute nodes of the PAG have probabilities estimated from expert knowledge. Similarly, expert knowledge is used to compute probability values for system attributes that are not vulnerabilities.

User attributes in the PAG that are connected with target nodes from a BUP retrieve their probabilities from those targets. Each relevant subnet of a BUP provides a probability value for a target node that attaches to a user attribute node in the PAG (see Definition 4). Each of the user attribute nodes in a PAG is connected to some target node in the user profile (see Section 4.1), as it is an execution state that is directed by user activity.

We begin by examining which system attributes (see Definition 2) are most relevant to the DOS exploit. To perform the experiment, we apply the three user profiles and observe the probabilities of the four CVE vulnerability related systems attributes in the DOS exploit (the Or-decompositions of the DOS exploit in Figure 1). In this experiment, we do not adjust any evidence related to system or attack attributes, nor do we set specific evidence. So our results are based only on the estimated probabilities that came from the original PAG for system and attack nodes.

As can be seen in Table 1c, the probabilities of the vulnerabilities do change based on the user profile. In this case, CVE-2008-3111 (a Java vulnerability) is more likely for UserA, CVE-2009-1094 (a LDAP vulnerability) is more likely for UserB, and CVE-2010-4091 (an Acrobat Reader vulnerability) is more likely for UserC.

We next examine how changes in the presence of evidence impact the final probability of the DOS exploit. We manually set the evidence of specific nodes to *NotExists* or *Exists* as appropriate, which effectively sets the values to 0.05 and

0.95 respectively. We then update the BN and read the value of the exploit node.

Table 2 shows the probability of the DOS exploit before any changes are made (the baseline) and after a set of user action changes are applied. There is little change to the DOS exploit occurring if the user is using (or likely to use) Social Media, Starts a Java Web Start Application, or just Browsing the Internet. However, it is also clear that the probability of exploit increases greatly for UserA and UserC if a LDAP connection is started. Conversely, if UserB were to get rid of the LDAP connection, then the probability of exploit drops dramatically. These results suggest that the DOS exploit is sensitive to the user's actions, and the probability can jump dramatically if the user takes the worst-case action. The results also suggest that understanding the user's current actions or likely actions can contribute to selecting which action(s) are important to observe.

6. SUMMARY AND FUTURE WORK

Studies have repeatedly shown that routine computer activities such as checking emails, web browsing, and filling out on-line forms, deliver the vast majority of security threats to the home computer [5, 28]. This happens most of the time because many users do not fully understand how their activities impact security. To design effective security tools for the home user, we need to determine which user actions might impact security. Towards this end, we investigate the problem of personalizing security risk analysis and matching home computer security to each user's needs. We extend the classical attack graph model for security risk analysis to include the different actions that a user can take and the implications of those actions on home computer security. We call this model the Personalized Attack Graph model. A PAG captures the interplay between user actions, attacker strategies, and system activities. We demonstrate how a PAG can be instantiated as a Bayesian Network to rank potential security risks. This, in turn, allows us to propose suitable interventions for activities that can be potential risks. Toward generalization to different users, we formalize a model of a user and apply this model to personalize a single, monolithic graph to different users.

Our long term goal is to develop a semi-autonomous, intelligent and personalized approach to computer security that leverages psychological studies of what users want/need, what security and privacy risks are imminent based on the status of the system and the user's actions, and what interventions will be most effective. The PAG is the core model for capturing the relationships between different user actions, system states and vulnerabilities. The PAG will be the core representation for an on-line security agent that will monitor user actions deemed to be critical to security and suggest actions that will keep the system safe.

However, the PAG does not enumerate the details needed to either analyze what can happen or identify intervention plans to protect the user. As the next step, we plan to use AI planning techniques to determine what activities need to be monitored and what actions can be taken to prevent security breaches while taking into account the user's desired level of security risk and utility for performing a specific action.

One of the components of the PAG model is estimated probability values for different attributes. While we have a sound basis for estimating probability values for system attributes and we have discussed how probability values for user attributes can be determined via the creation of user profiles, we are still in the process of determining a good way to estimate attack attribute probabilities. Currently, we are basing this on expert opinion. Future work includes subject studies to assess perceptions of risk and investigating more informed ways of estimating these probability values.

7. ACKNOWLEDGMENT

This material is based upon work supported by the National Science Foundation under Grant No. 0905232. Any opinions, findings, and conclusions or recommendations expressed in this material are those of the authors and do not necessarily reflect the views of the National Science Foundation.

8. REFERENCES

[1] AMMANN, P., WIJESEKERA, D., AND KAUSHIK, S. Scalable, graph-based network vulnerability analysis. In *Proc. of the 9th ACM Conference on Computer and Communications Security* (Washington, DC, 2002).

[2] AYTES, K., AND CONNOLLY, T. Computer security and risky computing practices: A rational choice perspective. *Journal of Organizational and End User Computing 16*, 3 (July-Sept 2004), 22–40.

[3] BRYANT, P., FURNELL, S., AND PHIPPEN, A. Improving protection and security awareness amongst home users. In *Advances in Networks, Computing and Communications 4*, P. S. Dowland and S. M. Furnell, Eds. University of Plymouth, April 2008.

[4] BYRNE, Z., WEIDERT, J., LIFF, J., HORVATH, M., SMITH, C., HOWE, A., AND RAY, I. Perceptions of internet threats: Behavioral intent to click again. In *Proc. of the Society for Industrial and Organizational Psychology Conference* (San Diego, CA, April 2012).

[5] CERT COORDINATION CENTER, SOFTWARE ENGINEERING INSTITUTE. Home computer security. Available at `http://www.cert.org/homeusers/HomeComputerSecurity/`, 2008.

[6] CLAAR, C. L. *The Adoption of Computer Security: An Analysis of Home Personal Computer User Behavior Using the Health Belief Model*. PhD thesis, Utah State University, 2011.

[7] DECISION SYSTEMS LABRATORY, UNIVERSITY OF PITTSBURGH. GeNIe and SMILE Homepage. Available from `http://genie.sis.pitt.edu/`.

[8] DEWRI, R., POOLSAPPASIT, N., RAY, I., AND WHITLEY, D. Optimal security hardening using multi-objective optimization on attack tree models of networks. In *Proc. of the 14th ACM Conference on Computer and Communications Security* (Alexandria, VA, 2007).

[9] FRIEDMAN, B., HURLEY, D., HOWE, D., NISSENBAUM, H., AND FELTEN, E. Users' conceptions of risks and harms on the web: A comparative study. In *Extended Abstracts of the Conference on Human Factors in Computing Systems* (Minneapolis, MN, USA, 2002).

[10] FRIGAULT, M., AND WANG, L. Measuring network security using bayesian network-based attack graphs. In *Proc. of the 32nd Annual IEEE International*

Table 2: Results showing how evidence set at specific user nodes (top) and user/system/attack nodes (bottom) impacts the DOS Exploit probability.

Nodes Existence	UserA		UserB		UserB	
	DOS	Change	DOS	Change	DOS	Change
Baseline	0.121		0.542		0.169	
¬ UsesSocialNetwork	0.120	-0.001	0.509	-0.033	0.107	-0.062
UsesSocialNetwork	0.181	0.059	0.543	0.001	0.172	0.003
OpensFlash + UsesSocialNetwork	0.186	0.065	0.544	0.002	0.174	0.005
¬ UsesLDAP	0.116	-0.005	0.268	**-0.275**	0.163	-0.006
UsesLDAP	0.476	**0.354**	0.557	0.015	0.555	**0.386**
¬ Browsing	0.008	-0.113	0.488	-0.054	0.076	-0.093
Browsing	0.131	0.010	0.544	0.001	0.172	0.003
¬ LoadsPDF	0.120	-0.001	0.491	-0.051	0.077	-0.092
LoadsPDF	0.221	0.100	0.545	0.003	0.175	0.006
Browsing + LoadsPDF	0.221	0.100	0.545	0.003	0.175	0.006

Computer Software and Applications Conference (Washington, DC, 2008).

[11] FURNELL, S., BRYANT, P., AND PHIPPEN, A. Assessing the security perceptions of personal internet users. *Computers & Security 26*, 5 (August 2007), 410–417.

[12] GOOD, N., DHAMIJA, R., GROSSKLAGS, J., THAW, D., ARONOWITZ, S., MULLIGAN, D., AND KONSTAN, J. Stopping spyware at the gate: A user study of privacy, notice and spyware. In *Proc. of the 2005 symposium on Usable privacy and security* (Pittsburgh, PA, USA, 2005).

[13] JHA, S., SHEYNER, O., AND WING, J. M. Two formal analysis of attack graphs. In *Proc. of the 15th IEEE Computer Security Foundations Workshop* (Cape Breton, Nova Scotia, Canada, 2002).

[14] KORB, K. B., AND NICHOLSON, A. E. *Bayesian artificial intelligence*. CRC Press, Boca Raton, FL, 2011.

[15] LIPPMAN, R., INGOLS, K., SCOTT, C., PIWOWARSKI, K., KRATKIEWICZ, K., AND CUNNINGHAM, R. Validating and restoring defense in depth using attack graphs. In *Proc. of the Military Communications Conference* (Washington DC, 2006).

[16] LIU, Y., AND MAN, H. Network vulnerability assessment using Bayesian networks. In *Proc. of the SPIE – Data Mining, Intrusion Detection, Information Assurance, and Data Networks Security* (Orlando, FL, USA, 2005).

[17] MELL, P., SCARFONE, K., AND ROMANOSKY, S. *CVSS – A Complete Guide to the Common Vulnerability Scoring System Version 2.0*. FIRST - Forum of Incident Response and Security Teams, June 2007.

[18] MILNE, G. R., LABRECQUE, L. I., AND CROMER, C. Toward an understanding of the online consumer's risky behavior and protection practices. *Journal of Consumer Affairs 43*, 3 (Fall 2009), 449–473.

[19] NG, B.-Y., KANKANHALLI, A., AND XU, Y. Studying users' computer security behavior: A health belief perspective. *Decision Support Systems 46*, 4 (March 2009), 815–825.

[20] NOEL, S., JAJODIA, S., O'BERRY, B., AND JACOBS, M. Efficient minimum-cost network hardening via exploit dependency graphs. In *Proc. of the 19th*

Annual Computer Security Applications Conference (Las Vegas, NV, 2003).

[21] PEW INTERNET. What internet users do online | Pew research center's internet & american life project. http://www.pewinternet.org/Static-Pages/Trend-Data/Online-Activites-Total.aspx, October 2011.

[22] POOLSAPPASIT, N., DEWRI, R., AND RAY, I. Dynamic security risk management using bayesian attack graphs. *IEEE Transactions on Dependable and Secure Computing 9*, 1 (January–February 2012), 61–74.

[23] RAPID7. Nexpose Community Edition. Available from http://www.rapid7.com/products/nexpose-community-edition.jsp.

[24] RAY, I., AND POOLSAPPASIT, N. Using attack trees to identify malicious attacks from authorized insiders. In *Proc. of the 10th European Symposium on Research in Computer Security* (Milan, Italy, 2005).

[25] RITCHEY, R., AND AMMANN, P. Using model checking to analyze network vulnerabilities. In *Proc. of the IEEE Symposium on Security and Privacy* (Oakland, CA, 2000).

[26] ROSENSTOCK, I., STRECHER, V., AND BECKER, M. Social learning theory and the health belief model. *Health Education Quarterly 15*, 2 (Summer 1988), 175–183.

[27] ROSENSTOCK, I. M. Why people use health services. *Milbank Memorial Fund Quarterly 44*, 3 (1966), 94–127.

[28] SANS INSTITUTE. SANS top-20 2007 security risks (2007 annual update). Available at http://www.sans.org/top20/2007/top20.pdf, October 2008.

[29] SHEYNER, O., HAINES, J., JHA, S., LIPPMANN, R., AND WING, J. M. Automated generation and analysis of attack graphs. In *Proc. of the IEEE Symposium on Security and Privacy* (Oakland, CA, USA, 2002).

[30] SZEWCZYK, P., AND FURNELL, S. Assessing the online security awareness of Australian Internet users. In *Proc. of the 8th Annual Security Conference: Discourses in Security Assurance & Privacy* (Las Vegas, NV, USA, 2009).

[31] WASH, R. Folk models of home computer security. In *Proc. of the Sixth Symposium on Usable Privacy and Security* (Redmond, WA, USA, 2010).

All Your Browser-saved Passwords Could Belong to Us: a Security Analysis and a Cloud-based New Design

Rui Zhao
University of Colorado Colorado Springs
Department of Computer Science
Colorado Springs, CO 80918, USA
rzhao@uccs.edu

Chuan Yue
University of Colorado Colorado Springs
Department of Computer Science
Colorado Springs, CO 80918, USA
cyue@uccs.edu

ABSTRACT

Web users are confronted with the daunting challenges of creating, remembering, and using more and more strong passwords than ever before in order to protect their valuable assets on different websites. Password manager is one of the most popular approaches designed to address these challenges by saving users' passwords and later automatically filling the login forms on behalf of users. Fortunately, all the five most popular Web browsers have provided password managers as a useful built-in feature. Unfortunately, the designs of all those Browser-based Password Managers (BPMs) have severe security vulnerabilities. In this paper, we uncover the vulnerabilities of existing BPMs and analyze how they can be exploited by attackers to crack users' saved passwords. Moreover, we propose a novel Cloud-based Storage-Free BPM (CSF-BPM) design to achieve a high level of security with the desired confidentiality, integrity, and availability properties. We have implemented a CSF-BPM system into Firefox and evaluated its correctness and performance. We believe CSF-BPM is a rational design that can also be integrated into other popular Web browsers.

Categories and Subject Descriptors

D.4.6 [**Software**]: Operating Systems—*Security and Protection.*; H.4.3 [**Information Systems**]: Communications Applications—*Information browsers*; K.4.4 [**Computing Milieux**]: Electronic Commerce—*Security.*

Keywords

Web browser, password manager, security, phishing, cloud

1. INTRODUCTION

Text-based passwords still occupy the dominant position in online user authentication [7, 16, 17]. They protect online accounts with valuable assets, and thus have been continuously targeted by various cracking and harvesting attacks.

Password security heavily depends on creating strong passwords and protecting them from being stolen. However, researchers have demonstrated that strong passwords that are sufficiently long, random, and hard to crack by attackers are often difficult to remember by users [5, 12, 22, 24, 36]. Meanwhile, no matter how strong they are, online passwords are also vulnerable to harvesting attacks such as phishing [19, 27, 39, 40]. These hard problems have been further aggravated by the fact that Web users have more online accounts than before and are forced to create and remember more and more usernames and passwords probably using insecure practices such as sharing passwords across websites [13, 30].

Password manager, particularly Browser-based Password Manager (BPM) is one of the most popular approaches that can potentially best address the online user authentication and password management problems. Browser integration enables BPMs to easily save users' login information including usernames and passwords into a database, and later automatically fill the login forms on behalf of users. Therefore, users do not need to remember a large number of strong passwords; meanwhile, BPMs will only fill the passwords on the login forms of the corresponding websites and thus can potentially protect against phishing attacks.

Fortunately, all the five most popular browsers Internet Explorer, Firefox, Google Chrome, Safari, and Opera have provided password managers as a useful built-in feature. Unfortunately, the designs of all those BPMs have severe security vulnerabilities. In essence, our key observation is that the encrypted passwords stored by those BPMs are very weakly protected – they can be trivially decrypted by attackers for logging into victims' accounts on the corresponding websites. We have developed tools to demonstrate that once stolen, the encrypted website login information saved by the five browsers (without using a master password in Firefox and Opera) can all be easily decrypted by attackers. When a master password is used in Firefox or Opera, even though decrypting a user's login information becomes harder, brute force attacks and phishing attacks against the master password are still quite possible.

In this paper, we uncover the vulnerabilities of existing BPMs and analyze how they can be exploited by attackers to crack users' saved passwords. Moreover, we propose a novel Cloud-based Storage-Free BPM (CSF-BPM) design to achieve a high level of security with the desired confidentiality, integrity, and availability properties. CSF-BPM is cloud-based storage-free in the sense that the protected data will be completely stored in the cloud – nothing needs to be stored on a user's computer. We want to move the storage into the cloud for two main reasons. One is that in the long run trustworthy storage services in the cloud [8, 25] can better protect a regular user's data than a local computer. The other is that the stored data can be easily accessible to the user across different OS accounts and different computers.

We have followed standard responsible disclosure practices and reported those vulnerabilities to the respective browser vendors. We have implemented a CSF-BPM system and seamlessly integrated it into Firefox. We have evaluated the correctness and performance of this system. We believe CSF-BPM is a rational design that can also be integrated into other popular browsers to make the online experience of Web users more secure, convenient, and enjoyable.

2. RELATED WORK AND BACKGROUND

In this section, we review the related work and the background information of BPMs in the five most popular browsers.

2.1 Related Work

Researchers pointed out long ago that weak passwords suffer from brute-force and dictionary attacks [12, 24]. However, strong passwords that are sufficiently long, random, and hard to crack by attackers are often difficult to remember by users due to human memory limitations [5, 36]. Recently, Florêncio and Herley performed a large-scale study of Web password habits and demonstrated the severity of the security problems such as sharing passwords across websites and using weak passwords [13]. A large-scale user study recently performed by Komanduri et al. demonstrated that many Web users write down or otherwise store their passwords, especially those higher-entropy passwords [22].

To help users better manage their online accounts and enhance their password security, researchers have proposed many solutions such as password managers [34], single sign-on systems [23, 31], graphical passwords [11, 32], and password hashing systems [15, 28, 38]. As analyzed in Section 1, password managers especially BPMs have the great potential to best address the challenges of using many strong passwords and protecting against phishing attacks. Web Wallet [34] is an anti-phishing solution and is also a password manager that can help users fill login forms using stored information; but as pointed out by the authors, users have a strong tendency to use traditional Web forms for typing sensitive information instead of using a special browser sidebar user interface. The security concerns of single sign-on systems are analyzed in [23], and the business model limitations are analyzed in [31]. Security limitations of graphical passwords are analyzed in [11, 32]. Security and usability limitations of password hashing systems are analyzed in [10, 15]. We do not advocate against any of these other approaches. We simply focus on the BPM security in this paper.

2.2 Password Manager Feature of Browsers

Table 1 lists the basic information on the BPM feature of the recent versions of the five most popular Web browsers. We can see that the BPM feature configuration locations are very different among browsers. Indeed, the feature configuration interfaces shown on those locations are also very different among browsers in terms of the configuration options and functions. The BPM feature is enabled by default in four browsers but not in Safari. Only Firefox and Opera employ a master password mechanism, which is, however, not enabled by default so users may not be aware of its

importance. Only Firefox and Google Chrome provide a password synchronization mechanism that can allow users to access the saved passwords across different computers.

Table 1: Basic information of BPMs in five browsers.

Browser	Configuration Location	Enabled by Default	Master Password	Password Sync.
Internet Explorer (9.0)	Internet options → Content → AutoComplete Settings → User names and passwords on forms	Yes	No	No
Firefox (15.0)	Options → Security → Passwords	Yes	Yes	Yes
Google Chrome (21.0)	Settings → Show advanced settings... → Passwords and forms	Yes	No	Yes
Safari (5.1)	Preferences → AutoFill → User names and passwords	No	No	No
Opera (12.02)	Settings → Preferences → Forms → Password Manager	Yes	Yes	No

In terms of the dynamic behavior, the interfaces for triggering the remembering and autofill of passwords are inconsistent among browsers. For example, all the browsers display a dialog box to ask a user whether the entered password for the current website should be saved. Only the dialog boxes displayed by Firefox, Google Chrome, and Opera are associated with the address bar, thus technically hard to be spoofed. For another example, Internet Explorer, Firefox, and Opera require a user action before auto-filling the password value on a website; however, Google Chrome and Safari autofill the username and password values once a user visits a login webpage, providing more opportunities for malicious JavaScript to manipulate the login form and information.

3. VULNERABILITY ANALYSIS

In this section, we define the threat model and assumptions, use an analogy to justify the essential problem of existing BPMs, and provide a detailed vulnerability analysis.

3.1 Threat Model and Assumptions

"Where a threat intersects with a vulnerability, risk is present [3]." For BPMs, the threat sources are attackers who want to steal the stored sensitive login information. Our basic threat model is that attackers can temporarily install malware such as Trojan horses and bots on a user's computer using attacks such as drive-by downloads [26, 33]. The installed malware can then steal the login information stored by BPMs. For example, Stone-Gross et al. inferred that 38% of the credentials stolen by the Torpig bot were obtained from the password managers of browsers, rather than by intercepting actual login sessions [30]. Indeed, if the occurrences of such threats are rare or do not have high impacts, BPMs would not bother to encrypt their stored passwords in the first place. Therefore, we do not intend to further identify threat sources, but focus on investigating the vulnerabilities of BPMs that could be exploited by potential threat sources to easily decrypt the stored passwords.

We assume that the installed malware cannot further compromise the operating system to directly identify cryptographic keys from a computer's memory [14] because this identification often requires elevated privilege and is prone to false positives. We assume that the installed malware can be removed from the system in a timely manner, so that even though sensitive login information stored by BPMs can be stolen within a short period of time, attackers cannot use tools such as keyloggers to further intercept users' passwords for a long period of time. This assumption is reasonable. One typical example is that anti-malware programs such as Microsoft Forefront Endpoint Protection may detect the infection, report the suspicious file transmission, and finally remove the malware and infected files. Another typical example is that solutions such as the Back to the Future framework [18] can restore the system to a prior good state and preserve system integrity. We also assume (as assumed in all the BPMs) that domain name systems are secure and reliable, and we do not specifically consider pharming attacks.

3.2   The Essential Problem and An Analogy

The essential problem is that the encrypted passwords stored by BPMs of the five most popular browsers are very weakly protected. In our investigation, we found without the protection of a master password mechanism, the encrypted passwords stored by the five BPMs (Table 1) can be trivially decrypted by attackers for logging into victims' accounts on the corresponding websites. We have developed tools and verified this severe vulnerability of the latest versions of the five BPMs on Windows 7. This vulnerability is common to all these browsers because the keys used by these browsers for encrypting/decrypting a user's login information can be easily extracted or generated by attackers. The decrypted login information can be easily sent out to attackers and the entire attack could be finished in one second. In the cases when a master password is used by a user in Firefox or Opera (Table 1), even though decrypting a user's login information becomes harder, brute force attacks and phishing attacks against the master password are still quite possible.

Before taking readers into the details of the vulnerabilities in the next two subsections, we want to use an analogy to justify the problem. Suppose we use a safe to store valuables in a home. There is no guarantee that burglars cannot enter the home, but should we allow burglars to easily figure out the combination to open the safe? If the answer is "Yes", why should we bother to use a safe in the first place? A computer (or its OS) is similar to a home, a BPM is similar to a safe because it stores valuable online account information, and a master password is similar to the combination to the safe. Similarly, there is no guarantee that attackers cannot remotely break into the computer [26, 30, 33], but should we allow attackers to easily decrypt the passwords saved by a BPM? If the answer is "Yes", why should a BPM bother to encrypt the saved passwords in the first place?

The current reality is that the "safe" of Google Chrome, Internet Explorer, and Safari does not allow a user to set a "combination" at all. Our decryption tools can easily and accurately open the "safe". Firefox and Opera allow a user to set a "combination", but they do not make it mandatory. Our decryption tools can also easily and accurately open the "safe" of Firefox and Opera if a "combination" was not set. For example, using drive-by downloads, an attacker can deliver our decryption tools to a user's computer and trigger their execution. In one second, all the passwords and usernames saved by BPMs can be completely decrypted and sent back to the attacker's website or email account. The malware detector installed on the user's computer may report suspicious activities, and the user may immediately take actions to disable the Internet connection. But it could

be too late! With a successful drive-by download, attackers can perform many types of malicious activities. However, similar to burglars, if attackers know they can easily open the "safe", they would like to first steal the most valuable items from the "safe" within a short period of time.

3.3   Without a Master Password Mechanism

Through source code analysis, binary file analysis, and experiments, we found both Firefox and Opera use the three-key Triple-DES algorithm to encrypt a user's passwords for different websites. *Firefox* saves each encrypted username, encrypted password, and plaintext login webpage URL address into the *login* table of an SQLite database file named *signons.sqlite*. The Triple-DES keys are generated once by Firefox and then saved into a binary file named *key3.db* starting from the byte offset location 0x2F90. Although the keys generated on different computers are different, they are not bound to a particular computer or protected by other mechanisms. Therefore, as verified by our tools, an attacker can simply steal both the *signons.sqlite* file and the *key3.db* file and then accurately decrypt every username and password pair on any computer.

Opera encrypts each username and password pair together with the login webpage URL address, and then saves both the ciphertext and Triple-DES keys into a binary file named *wand.dat*. Therefore, this file is self-contained; an attacker can simply steal it and then decrypt every username and password pair on any computer. We have reverse engineered *wand.dat* and developed a tool that can accurately perform such attacks. In more details, this tool identifies special block structures starting from the byte offset location 0x24 in the file, constructs the triple-DES keys saved in each block structure, and finally decrypts the ciphertext saved in each block structure.

In their latest Window 7 versions, all the other three browsers Internet Explorer, Google Chrome, and Safari use the Windows API functions *CryptProtectData* and *CryptUnprotectData* to perform encryption and decryption, respectively. The key benefit of using these two functions is that typically, the encrypted data can only be decrypted under the same Windows user account. To use these two API functions, an application (e.g., a browser) does not generate or provide encryption/decryption keys because the symmetric keys will be deterministically generated in these two functions based (by default) on the profile of the current Windows user. An application can use the *dwFlags* input parameter to specify that the keys should be simply associated with the current computer; it can also use the *pOptionalEntropy* input parameter to provide additional entropy to the two functions.

We found *Google Chrome* saves each plaintext username, encrypted password, and plaintext login webpage URL address into the *logins* table of an SQLite database file named *Login Data*. Google Chrome does not provide additional entropy to the two API functions. *Safari* saves each plaintext username, encrypted password, and plaintext login webpage URL address into a special property list file named *keychain.plist*. Safari provides a static 144-byte salt as the additional entropy to the two API functions. *Internet Explorer* encrypts each username and password pair and saves the ciphertext as a *value data* under the Windows registry entry: "HKEY_CURRENT_USER\Software\Microsoft\ Internet Explorer\IntelliForms\Storage2\". Each saved *value* data can be indexed by a *value name*, which is calculated by hashing the login webpage URL address. Internet Explorer also provides the login webpage URL address as the additional entropy to the two API functions.

We found all these three browsers set the *dwFlags* input parameter value as the default value zero, which means that the symmetric keys are associated with each individual Windows 7 user. Therefore, it is not very easy for attackers to decrypt the stolen ciphertexts on another computer or using another Windows account. However, attackers can simply decrypt the stolen ciphertexts on the victim's machine when the victim is logged into the Windows; then, the decrypted login information can be directly sent back to attackers. We have developed tools that can decrypt the ciphertexts stored by all these three browsers. In more details, for Google Chrome, our tool selects each record from the *logins* table of the *Login Data* SQLite database, converts the encrypted password from the SQLite BLOB type to a string type, and supplies the encrypted password to the *CryptUnprotectData* function. For Safari, our tool converts the *keychain.plist* property list file to an XML document, parses the XML document to obtain each encrypted password, and supplies the encrypted password and that static 144-byte salt to the *CryptUnprotectData* function. For Internet Explorer, our tool hashes the popular login webpage URL addresses contained in a dictionary, queries the Windows registry using each hashed URL address to identify a matched *value name*, and supplies the associated *value data* and the corresponding login webpage URL address (as the additional entropy) to the *CryptUnprotectData* function.

3.4 With a Master Password Mechanism

The BPMs of Firefox and Opera allow a user to set a master password (Table 1) to further protect the encryption keys or encrypted passwords. In **Firefox**, the master password and a global 160-bit salt will be hashed using a SHA-1 algorithm to generate a master key. This master key is used to encrypt those three Triple-DES keys before saving them to the *key3.db* file. Firefox also uses this master key to encrypt a hard-coded string "password-check" and saves the ciphertext to the *key3.db* file; later, Firefox will decrypt this ciphertext to authenticate a user before further decrypting the three Triple-DES keys. In **Opera**, a master key is generated based on the master password and a 128-bit salt. The salt itself is encrypted using the master password and saved to a specific file named *Opcert6.data*. The master key and Triple-DES keys will be used to double-encrypt each website password. Finally, the ciphertext including the encrypted login webpage URL address, encrypted username, and double-encrypted password will be saved to the *wand.dat* file.

Using a master password can better protect the stored passwords in both browsers. However, the master password mechanism should be carefully designed to maximize security. One main security concern is the brute force attacks against the master password. For one example, if the computation time for verifying a master password is very small as in Firefox and Opera (both of them reject an invalid master password in milliseconds), it is still possible to effectively perform brute force attacks against a user's master password. For another example, encrypting the hard-coded "password-check" string in Firefox for user authentication does not increase security and may actually decrease security in the case when both the *signons.sqlite* file and the

key3.db file are stolen. Although decrypting the Triple-DES keys is still very difficult if the master password is unknown, an attacker can simply bypass this user authentication step using an instrumented Firefox. Moreover, this hard-coded plaintext and its ciphertext encrypted by the master key can also be used by an attacker to verify the correctness of dictionary or brute-force attacks against the master password.

Another main security concern is the phishing attacks against the master password. For example, attackers can use the JavaScript *prompt()* function to create fake master password entry dialog boxes, which can be displayed by any webpage on all the five browsers without being blocked by browsers' "block pop-up windows" options because they are not in a separate HTML document. We speculate that even such a simple spoofing technique can effectively obtain master passwords from vulnerable users. Indeed, a malicious webpage can also use JavaScript and CSS (Cascading Style Sheets) to create sophisticated dialog boxes that are more similar to genuine master password entry dialog boxes.

4. CSF-BPM DESIGN

We now present the design of CSF-BPM. It is cloud-based storage-free in the sense that the protected data will be completely stored in the cloud – nothing needs to be stored on a user's computer. We want to move the storage into the cloud for two key reasons. One is that in the long run trustworthy storage services in the cloud [8, 25] can better protect a regular user's data than a local computer. The other is that the stored data can be easily accessible to the user across different OS accounts on the same computer and across computers at different locations. This design differs from the BPM designs of all the five most popular browsers. Based on the threat model and assumptions defined in the last section, we design CSF-BPM to synthesize the desired security properties such as confidentiality, integrity, and availability.

4.1 High-level Architecture

Figure 1 illustrates the high-level architecture of CSF-BPM. The BPM of the browser simply consists of a User Interface (UI) component, a Record Management (RM) component, a Record Generation (RG) component, a Record Decryption (RD) component, and a record synchronization (Sync) component. The UI component will provide configuration and management interfaces accessible at a single location. The BPM itself does not include any persistent storage component such as a file or database; instead, it will generate Encrypted Login Information Records (ELIRs), save *protected ELIRs* to a Secure and Reliable Storage (SRS) service in the cloud, and retrieve protected ELIRs in real-time whenever needed. Such a generic BPM design can be seamlessly integrated into different browsers.

An SRS service simply needs to support user authentication (e.g., over HTTPS) and per-user storage so that its deployment in the cloud can be easily achieved. For example, the synchronization service associated with Firefox or Google Chrome (Table 1) could be directly used as an SRS service without making any modification. The SRS service will store a Per-User Protected ELIRs (PUPE) data object (to be illustrated in Figure 2) for each SRS user. The communication protocol between the BPM and SRS is also very simple: after a user is authenticated to SRS, the Sync component of BPM will transparently send HTTPS requests to SRS to *retrieve* or *save* the protected ELIRs of the user. An

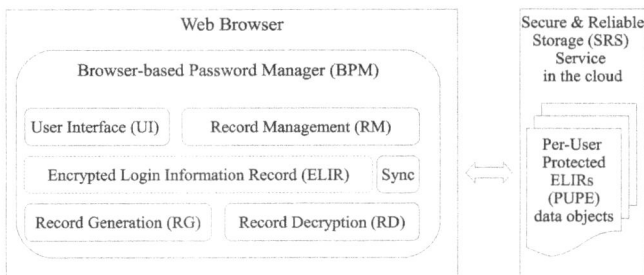

Figure 1: High-level architecture of the Cloud-based Storage-Free BPM (CSF-BPM).

SRS service should be highly reliable and available. However, to further increase reliability and availability, the BPM can store protected ELIRs to multiple independent SRS services. One of them is used as the primary SRS service; others will be used as secondary SRS services. The Sync component of BPM will transparently synchronize protected ELIRs from the primary SRS service to secondary SRS services.

4.2 Design Details

To use CSF-BPM, a user needs to remember a Single Strong Master Password (SSMP) with the strength [4] assured by a proactive password checker and certain length requirement [6, 21, 37]. The user also needs to set up an account (srsUsername, srsPassword) on an SRS service and configure this service once through the UI component of BPM. At the beginning of each browsing session, the user needs to authenticate to the SRS service and provide the SSMP to BPM. After that, BPM will take care of everything else such as triggering the remembering of website passwords, encrypting and decrypting ELIRs, and triggering the autofill of passwords. Both the srsUsername and srsPassword pair and SSMP need be provided only once in a session through the UI component of BPM, and users will be explicitly informed of such a usage requirement. These design choices could be helpful in protecting SSMP against phishing attacks.

The basic format of an ELIR record is shown in Table 2. Here, recordSalt is a large and sufficiently random per-record salt generated by BPM. It is used to calculate the symmetric record key (denoted recordKey) for encrypting a user's plaintext password (denoted sitePassword) for an account (denoted siteUsername) on a website (with siteURL as the login webpage URL address). The recordKey can be deterministically generated by using a password-based key derivation function such as PBKDF2 specified in the PKCS5 specification version 2.0 [20]. The basic format of an ELIR record can also include the IDs (or names) of the username and password fields in the login webpage, and it can be further extended if necessary.

Table 2: The basic format of an ELIR record.

siteURL	siteUsername	encryptedSitePassword	recordSalt	...

Using PBKDF2 [20], our SSMP-based key derivation and password encryption process consists of five steps illustrated in Formulas 1, 2, 3, 4, and 5. The input parameters mainSalt and aeSalt in Formulas 1 and 2 are large and sufficiently random per-user salts generated by BPM at the first time when a user authenticates to the SRS service through the UI component of BPM. In Formulas 1, 2, and 3, the input parameters c1, c2, and c3 represent iteration counts for key stretching; the input parameters dkLen1, dkLen2, and dkLen3 represent lengths of the derived keys, and they are related to the underlying pseudorandom function used in the PBKDF2 implementation.

$$mainKey = PBKDF2(SSMP, mainSalt, c1, dkLen1) \quad (1)$$

$$aeKey = PBKDF2(mainKey, aeSalt, c2, dkLen2) \quad (2)$$

$$recordKey = PBKDF2(mainKey, recordSalt, c3, dkLen3) \quad (3)$$

$$encryptedSitePassword = E(recordKey, sitePassword) \quad (4)$$

$$protectedELIRs = AE(aeKey, concatenatedELIRs) \quad (5)$$

The salts and iteration counts in PBKDF2 are used to secure against dictionary and brute-force attacks, and they need not be kept secret [20]. The strength of SSMP also helps secure against these two types of attacks. In Formula 1, a mainKey is calculated and will be used in each browsing session. SSMP is typed only once and will be erased from memory after mainKey is calculated. In Formula 3, a unique recordKey is generated (using the per-record recordSalt) for each website account of the user. In Formula 4, a NIST-approved symmetric encryption algorithm E such as AES [1] (together with a block cipher mode of operation if the sitePassword is long) can be used to encrypt the sitePassword. In Formula 5, a NIST-approved Authenticated Encryption block cipher mode AE such as CCM (Counter with CBC-MAC) [2] can be used to simultaneously protect confidentially and authenticity (integrity) of the concatenatedELIRs of an SRS user.

The iteration count c1 used in Formula 1 should be large so that the mainKey calculation will take a few seconds; therefore, brute force attacks against SSMP become computationally infeasible. But c1 should not be too large to make a user wait for a long period of time at the beginning of a session. Iteration counts c2 and c3 should not be too large so that generating aeKey and recordKey would not cause a user to perceive any delay. The mainKey is kept in memory in the whole browsing session, while aeKey and recordKey are scrubbed immediately after use. We assumed in Section 3 that attackers cannot identify cryptographic keys from memory. Countermeasures [14] can be taken to further protect this single mainKey in memory. Although Formula 5 will simultaneously protect confidentially and authenticity (integrity) of the concatenatedELIRs of an SRS user, encrypting each sitePassword in Formula 4 is still important. This is because the concatenatedELIRs is also kept in memory in the whole browsing session. In comparison with the mainKey which is basically a random-looking value, the structure of ELIR records and concatenatedELIRs can be easily identified from memory. Therefore, assuming an attacker cannot identify the mainKey but can identify ELIR records from memory, it is still computationally infeasible for the attacker to crack each individual recordKey and decrypt the corresponding sitePassword.

Overall, all the computations including salt generation, key derivation, encryption, and decryption etc. are performed on BPM. Neither the SSMP nor any derived cryptographic key will be revealed to an SRS service or a third

mainSalt	aeSalt	PBKDF-id	PBKDF-params
E-id	E-params	AE-id	AE-params
protectedELIRs		.....	

Figure 2: The Per-User Protected ELIRs (PUPE) data object saved for each SRS user.

party. An SRS service does not need to provide any special computational support to BPM; it simply needs to save a PUPE data object for each SRS user.

As illustrated in Figure 2, each PUPE object contains the protectedELIRs (Formula 5) of an SRS user and all the algorithm related information. Here, PBKDF-id specifies the identifier for the PBKDF2 key derivation function [20]; PBKDF-params specify the PBKDF2 parameters such as c1, c2, c3, dkLen1, dkLen2, and dkLen3 used in Formulas 1, 2, and 3. E-id and E-params specify the identifier and parameters, respectively, for the symmetric encryption algorithm (and the mode of operation) used in Formula 4. AE-id and AE-params specify the identifier and parameters, respectively, for the authenticated encryption block cipher mode used in Formula 5. For example, if AE-id specifies the CCM authenticated encryption block cipher mode [2], then AE-params will contain the Nonce and the Associated Data input parameters used by CCM. Each PUPE data object can be simply saved as a binary or encoded string object for an SRS user because its structure does not need to be known or taken care of by any SRS service. Such a PUPE data object design makes the selection of algorithms and the selection of SRS services very flexible.

The iteration counts c1, c2, and c3 can be flexibility adjusted by BPM with or without user intervention to maximize security while minimizing inconvenience to users [9]. In our current design, CSF-BPM adaptively computes the maximum values of iteration counts based on the specified computation times for Formulas 1, 2, and 3, respectively. For example, if a 10-second computation time is specified for deriving the mainKey, CSF-BPM will run Formula 1 for 10 seconds to derive the mainKey and meanwhile finalize the corresponding c1 value. Such a scheme allows CSF-BPM to easily maximize the security strength of key derivation within a specified delay limit on each individual computer.

To decrypt the saved website passwords for autofill, BPM will perform five steps: (1) retrieve the PUPE data object saved for the SRS user; (2) generate the mainKey and aeKey using Formulas 1 and 2; (3) decrypt and verify the protectedELIRs using the reverse process of Formula 5 such as the CCM Decryption-Verification process [2]; (4) obtain the recordSalt of each ELIR and generate the recordKey using Formula 3; (5) finally, decrypt the encryptedSitePassword using the reverse process of Formula 4. Note that at step (3), both the integrity of the protectedELIRs and the authenticity of the BPM user are verified because the success of this step relies on using the correct SSMP. Also at this step, siteURL and siteUsername of all the ELIRs can be obtained by BPM to determine whether this user has previously saved login information for the currently visited website. Normally, the first three steps will be performed once for the entire browsing session, and the last two steps will be performed once for each currently visited website that the user has previously saved login information for it.

Because all the salts are randomly generated by BPM, the protectedELIRs saved to different SRS accounts or dif-

ferent SRS services will be different. BPM can transparently change mainSalt, aeSalt, and every recordSalt whenever necessary. A user also has the flexibility to change SSMP and any sitePassword whenever necessary. In these cases, all what need to be done by BPM is to update the new PUPE data object and ELIRs to each corresponding SRS service account. A user can also flexibly change any srsPassword, which is completely independent of SSMP.

4.3 Design Rationales and Security Analysis

In terms of the confidentiality, first, by having a unique cloud-based storage-free architecture, CSF-BPM can in the long run effectively reduce the opportunities for attackers to steal and further crack regular users' saved passwords. Second, even if attackers (including insiders of an SRS service) can steal the saved data, it is computationally infeasible for attackers to decrypt the stolen data to obtain users' login information for different websites. CSF-BPM provides this security guarantee by mandating a strong SSMP that satisfies certain strength requirements [6, 21, 37], by using the PBKDF2 key derivation function [20] with randomly generated salts and adaptively computed large iteration counts, and by following NIST-approved symmetric encryption [1] and authenticated encryption [2] algorithms. Basically, even if attackers can steal the saved data, they have to guess a user's strong SSMP in a very large space (determined mainly by the length and character set requirements of SSMP) with each try taking seconds of computation time.

In terms of the integrity, the NIST-approved CCM authenticated encryption algorithm [2] enables CSF-BPM to accurately detect both any invalid SSMP try and any modification to a saved PUPE data object. Moreover, this detection is securely performed in the sense that attackers cannot take advantage of it to effectively conduct brute force attacks against the SSMP.

In terms of the availability, an SRS simply needs to be a storage service in the cloud and it does not need to provide any special computational support. Such a design decision makes it very easy to either use an existing storage service in the cloud as an SRS service or deploy a new SRS service by an organization. CSF-BPM supports multiple SRS services and it uses a simple HTTPS-based communication protocol; these design decisions also further enhance the availability.

CSF-BPM offers a better security in comparison with the BPMs of Firefox and Opera that also provide a master password mechanism. Firefox and Opera save the encrypted data locally on a user's computer and they do not use strong key derivation functions (Section 3.4); thus their confidentiality assurance is weak in consideration of brute force attacks. Both Firefox and Opera can detect an invalid master password try, but the detection mechanism is not secure (Section 3.4). Both browsers do not detect any modification to the saved data; the modified data will still be decrypted into incorrect and often non-displayable values, but no information is provided to a user. Opera does not provide a password synchronization mechanism, while the Sync mechanism of Firefox is tightly bound to Mozilla's own server [41]; thus, the availability of the saved data is not well assured by these two BPMs.

Other cloud-based password system design alternatives also exist, but they often have different design objectives and limitations. For example, Passpet [38] can help a user generate passwords for different websites based on a master password. Similar to Password Multiplier [15], Passpet is essentially a password generator instead of a password manager because it uses password hashing techniques to deterministically generate website passwords instead of remembering users' original passwords. Requiring users to migrate their original passwords to hashed passwords is a biggest limitation of hashing-based password generation solutions as acknowledged in the Password Multiplier paper [15]. In addition, Passpet imposes very special requirements on its remote storage server: the SRP authentication protocol [35] must be used and some specific commands must be supported. These requirements limit the deployability of Passpet.

5. IMPLEMENTATION AND EVALUATION

CSF-BPM is designed in a generic way so that it is implementable in different Web browsers and meanwhile it can easily use different SRS services. We have implemented a CSF-BPM system using JavaScript and seamlessly integrated it into the Firefox Web browser. This system can directly use the Firefox Sync server operated by Mozilla [41] as an SRS service without making any modification to this server; thus, a free SRS service is directly available to users. Note that in our implementation, the interfaces for triggering the remembering and autofill of passwords in Firefox (Section 2.2) are not changed; only the operations happen behind the scenes are changed. Currently, we used the PBKDF2 [20], CCM [2], and AES [1] implementations provided in the Stanford JavaScript Crypto Library [29].

We made some modifications to the Sync module in Firefox. In the original Sync module, a 26-character Sync key is generated when a user creates a Sync account. This Sync key is not shared with the Firefox Sync server, and is mainly used to protect other cryptographic keys that are stored on the Firefox Sync server for a user. A user must save this Sync key and provide it to Firefox on different computers together with the Sync account username and password whenever the Sync mechanism needs to be used. This requirement limits the usability of the Sync mechanism. The Sync key is not needed at all in the CSF-BPM design. Therefore, in our implementation, one main modification to the Sync module is removing the dependence of using Firefox Sync server on Sync key for the password manager feature. As a result, a user does not need to save and provide the Sync key at all if he or she uses CSF-BPM and uses the Firefox Sync server as the SRS service. The other main modification is that we use a Weave Basic Object (WBO) [41] assigned to the default Mozilla *passwords collection* to store the PUPE object in the Firefox Sync server. Both modifications are specific to using the Firefox Sync server as the SRS service.

We have built the Firefox version CSF-BPM on a Ubuntu Linux system. We have evaluated the correctness of our implementation and its integration with Firefox. We selected 30 popular or our frequently used websites to perform the evaluation. On each website, we (1) opened Firefox and typed an SRS account (i.e., a Firefox Sync account) and SSMP; (2) logged into the website and confirmed to save the website password; (3) logged out the website and logged into it again with the auto-filled password; and (4) finally closed Firefox, re-opened Firefox, typed the SRS account and SSMP, and logged into the website again with the auto-filled password. By performing those steps, we verified that our implementation works precisely as designed; meanwhile,

it integrates smoothly with Firefox and does not cause any logic or runtime error.

We have conducted both micro-benchmark experiments and macro-benchmark experiments to evaluate the performance of CSF-BPM. In those experiments, we ran CSF-BPM on a desktop computer with 2.33GHz CPU, 3.2 GB memory, and 100Mbps network card. In our experiments, we evaluated the performance of key derivation, password encryption and decryption, concatenatedELIRs encryption and decryption, and PUPE upload and retrieval. Overall, all those operations were efficiently performed, and we did not observe any noticeable delay.

6. DISCUSSION

We analyzed in Section 4 that CSF-BPM provides a high level of security. We now further discuss the usability and limitations of CSF-BPM. To be fair, we compare the usability of our Firefox version CSF-BPM with that of the combined Firefox master password mechanism and Sync mechanism. As mentioned in Section 5, our implemented CSF-BPM only changes the operations happening behind the scenes; therefore, its overall usability is comparable to that of the combined Firefox master password mechanism and Sync mechanism. Moreover, our implemented CSF-BPM has one obvious usability improvement because it uses the Firefox Sync server as an SRS service but does not require a user to save and provide the 26-character Sync key generated by Firefox. In CSF-BPM, the PUPE object is already protected, thus the Sync key is no longer needed at all.

In terms of limitations, first, our current CSF-BPM is implemented in JavaScript. The security and performance of CSF-BPM can be further improved if those cryptographic algorithms are implemented in C++. Currently, we are working on implementing those cryptographic algorithms into a Firefox XPCOM (Cross Platform Component Object Model) component using C++. Second, if a CSF-BPM user forgets the SSMP, all the passwords saved on SRS services cannot be correctly decrypted. Therefore, remembering the SSMP becomes very important for CSF-BPM users. However, remembering an SSMP should be much easier than remembering many strong passwords for different websites. Third, at the beginning of a Web browsing session, a user must wait for a few seconds so that CSF-BPM can complete the mainKey derivation. However, once the mainKey is derived, password remembering and autofill operations can be smoothly performed by users as usual.

7. CONCLUSION

In this paper, we uncovered the vulnerabilities of existing BPMs and analyzed how they can be exploited by attackers to crack users' saved passwords. Moreover, we proposed a novel Cloud-based Storage-Free BPM (CSF-BPM) design to achieve a high level of security with the desired confidentiality, integrity, and availability properties. We implemented a CSF-BPM system and seamlessly integrated it into the Firefox Web browser. We evaluated the correctness and performance of this system. Our evaluation results demonstrate that CSF-BPM can be efficiently used to manage online passwords. We believe CSF-BPM is a rational design that can also be integrated into other popular Web browsers to make the online experience of Web users more secure, convenient, and enjoyable.

8. REFERENCES

[1] Advanced Encryption Standard (AES). In *NIST FIPS 197*, 2001.

[2] The CCM Mode for Authentication and Confidentiality. In *NIST SP 800-38C*, 2004.

[3] Information Security Handbook: A Guide for Managers. In *NIST SP 800-100*, 2007.

[4] Electronic Authentication Guideline. In *NIST SP 800-63-1*, 2011.

[5] A. Adams and M. A. Sasse. Users are not the enemy. *Commun. ACM*, 42(12):40–46, 1999.

[6] M. Bishop and D. V. Klein. Improving system security via proactive password checking. *Computers & Security*, 14(3):233–249, 1995.

[7] J. Bonneau, C. Herley, P. C. van Oorschot, and F. Stajano. The quest to replace passwords: A framework for comparative evaluation of web authentication schemes. In *Proc. of IEEE S&P*, 2012.

[8] K. D. Bowers, A. Juels, and A. Oprea. Hail: a high-availability and integrity layer for cloud storage. In *Proc. of CCS*, 2009.

[9] X. Boyen. Halting password puzzles: hard-to-break encryption from human-memorable keys. In *Proc. of USENIX Security Symposium*, 2007.

[10] S. Chiasson, P. C. van Oorschot, and R. Biddle. A usability study and critique of two password managers. In *Proc. of USENIX Security Symposium*, 2006.

[11] D. Davis, F. Monrose, and M. K. Reiter. On user choice in graphical password schemes. In *Proc. of USENIX Security Symposium*, 2004.

[12] D. C. Feldmeier and P. R. Karn. Unix password security – ten years later. In *Proc. of CRYPTO*, 1989.

[13] D. Florêncio and C. Herley. A large-scale study of web password habits. In *Proc. of WWW*, 2007.

[14] J. A. Halderman, S. D. Schoen, N. Heninger, W. Clarkson, W. Paul, J. A. Calandrino, A. J. Feldman, J. Appelbaum, and E. W. Felten. Lest we remember: Cold boot attacks on encryption keys. In *Proc. of USENIX Security Symposium*, 2008.

[15] J. A. Halderman, B. Waters, and E. W. Felten. A convenient method for securely managing passwords. In *Proc. of WWW*, 2005.

[16] C. Herley and P. C. van Oorschot. A research agenda acknowledging the persistence of passwords. *IEEE Security & Privacy*, 10(1):28–36, 2012.

[17] C. Herley, P. C. van Oorschot, and A. S. Patrick. Passwords: If we're so smart, why are we still using them? In *Proc. of FC*, 2009.

[18] F. Hsu, H. Chen, T. Ristenpart, J. Li, and Z. Su. Back to the future: A framework for automatic malware removal and system repair. In *Proc. of ACSAC*, 2006.

[19] M. Jakobsson and S. Myers. *Phishing and Countermeasures: Understanding the Increasing Problem of Electronic Identity Theft*. Wiley-Interscience, ISBN 0-471-78245-9, 2006.

[20] B. Kaliski. RFC 2898, PKCS5: Password-Based Cryptography Specification Version 2.0, 1999.

[21] P. G. Kelley, S. Komanduri, M. L. Mazurek, R. Shay, T. Vidas, L. Bauer, N. Christin, L. F. Cranor, and J. Lopez. Guess again (and again and again): Measuring password strength by simulating password-cracking algorithms. In *Proc. of IEEE S&P*, 2012.

[22] S. Komanduri, R. Shay, P. G. Kelley, M. L. Mazurek, L. Bauer, N. Christin, L. F. Cranor, and S. Egelman. Of passwords and people: Measuring the effect of password-composition policies. In *Proc. of CHI*, 2011.

[23] D. P. Kormann and A. D. Rubin. Risks of the passport single signon protocol. *Comput. Networks*, 33(1-6):51–58, 2000.

[24] R. Morris and K. Thompson. Password security: a case history. *Commun. ACM*, 22(11):594–597, 1979.

[25] R. A. Popa, J. Lorch, D. Molnar, H. J. Wang, and L. Zhuang. Enabling security in cloud storage slas with cloudproof. In *Proc. of USENIX ATC*, 2011.

[26] N. Provos, P. Mavrommatis, M. A. Rajab, and F. Monrose. All your iframes point to us. In *Proc. of USENIX Security Symposium*, 2008.

[27] Rachna Dhamija and J.D.Tygar and Marti Hearst. Why phishing works. In *Proc. of CHI*, 2006.

[28] B. Ross, C. Jackson, N. Miyake, D. Boneh, and J. C. Mitchell. Stronger password authentication using browser extensions. In *Proc. of USENIX Security Symposium*, 2005.

[29] E. Stark, M. Hamburg, and D. Boneh. Symmetric cryptography in javascript. In *Proc. of ACSAC*, 2009.

[30] B. Stone-Gross, M. Cova, L. Cavallaro, B. Gilbert, M. Szydlowski, R. A. Kemmerer, C. Kruegel, and G. Vigna. Your botnet is my botnet: analysis of a botnet takeover. In *Proc. of CCS*, 2009.

[31] S.-T. Sun, Y. Boshmaf, K. Hawkey, and K. Beznosov. A billion keys, but few locks: the crisis of web single sign-on. In *Proc. of NSPW*, pages 61–72, 2010.

[32] J. Thorpe and P. van Oorschot. Human-seeded attacks and exploiting hot-spots in graphical passwords. In *Proc. of USENIX Security Symposium*, 2007.

[33] Y.-M. Wang, D. Beck, X. Jiang, R. Roussev, C. Verbowski, S. Chen, and S. T. King. Automated web patrol with strider honeymonkeys: Finding web sites that exploit browser vulnerabilities. In *Proc. of NDSS*, 2006.

[34] M. Wu, R. C. Miller, and G. Little. Web wallet: preventing phishing attacks by revealing user intentions. In *Proc. of SOUPS*, pages 102–113, 2006.

[35] T. Wu. The secure remote password protocol. In *Proc. of NDSS*, 1998.

[36] J. Yan, A. Blackwell, R. Anderson, and A. Grant. Password memorability and security: Empirical results. *IEEE Security and Privacy*, 2(5):25–31, 2004.

[37] J. J. Yan. A note on proactive password checking. In *Proc. of NSPW*, pages 127–135, 2001.

[38] K.-P. Yee and K. Sitaker. Passpet: convenient password management and phishing protection. In *Proc. of SOUPS*, pages 32–43, 2006.

[39] C. Yue. Preventing the Revealing of Online Passwords to Inappropriate Websites with LoginInspector. In *Proc. of USENIX LISA*, 2012.

[40] C. Yue and H. Wang. BogusBiter: A Transparent Protection Against Phishing Attacks. *ACM Transactions on Internet Technology*, 10(2):1–31, 2010.

[41] Firefox Sync Service. https://wiki.mozilla.org/Services/Sync.

iBigTable: Practical Data Integrity for BigTable in Public Cloud

Wei Wei
North Carolina State
University
890 Oval Drive
Raleigh, North Carolina,
United States
wwei5@ncsu.edu

Ting Yu
North Carolina State
University
890 Oval Drive
Raleigh, North Carolina,
United States
yu@csc.ncsu.edu

Rui Xue
State Key Lab. of Information
Security
Institute of Information
Engineering
Chinese Academy of
Sciences, China
xuerui@iie.ac.cn

ABSTRACT

BigTable is a distributed storage system that is designed to manage large-scale structured data. Deploying BigTable in a public cloud is an economic storage solution to small businesses and researchers who need to deal with data processing tasks over large amount of data but often lack capabilities to obtain their own powerful clusters. As one may not always trust the public cloud provider, one important security issue is to ensure the integrity of data managed by BigTable running at the cloud. In this paper, we present iBigTable, an enhancement of BigTable that provides scalable data integrity assurance. We explore the practicality of different authenticated data structure designs for BigTable, and design a set of security protocols to efficiently and flexibly verify the integrity of data returned by BigTable. More importantly, iBigtable preserves the simplicity, applicability and scalability of BigTable, so that existing applications over BigTable can interact with iBigTable seamlessly with minimum or no change of code (depending on the mode of iBigTable). We implement a prototype of iBigTable based on HBase, an open source BigTable implementation. Our experimental results show that iBigTable imposes reasonable performance overhead while providing integrity assurance.

Categories and Subject Descriptors

H.2 [Database Management]: Security, integrity, and protection

General Terms

Security, Design, Algorithms

Keywords

Data Integrity; Cloud Storage; Big Data

1. INTRODUCTION

BigTable [10] is a distributed data storage system designed to scale into the petabyte range across hundreds or even thousands of commodity machines. It has been widely used in several products at Google such as Google Maps, Google Analytics and Gmail. Moreover, in recent years many organizations have adopted the data model of BigTable, and developed their own implementations of BigTable such as HBase [4] and Cassandra [2]. HBase is used to power the messages infrastructure at Facebook [7], and also used as a data storage for Hadoop [3] and MapReduce [11] to facilitate large-scale data processing. Cassandra is used in companies such as Twitter, Cisco and Netflix as a reliable and scalable storage infrastructure.

Running BigTable in a cloud managed by a third party is an economic storage solution to small businesses and researchers who need to deal with data processing tasks over large amount of data but often lack capabilities to obtain their own powerful clusters. However, it introduces several security issues. In particular, if we do not fully trust the cloud provider, we have to protect the integrity of one's data. Specifically, when we retrieve data from BigTable, there should be a way to verify that the returned data from the cloud are indeed what we want, i.e., no data are improperly modified by the cloud, and it has returned exactly the data we request, nothing less, nothing more.

This problem shares a lot of similarities with integrity protection in outsourced databases. Indeed, many techniques have been proposed in the literature to address data integrity issues, including correctness, completeness and freshness. Many of these techniques are based on cryptographic authenticated data structures, which require a database system to be modified [12, 16, 18]. Some others are probabilistic approaches, which do not require to modify existing systems but may inject some fake data into outsourced databases [20, 24, 25]. It seems that we can directly apply existing techniques for database outsourcing to BigTable in the cloud. However, though the two systems share many similarities (e.g., they both host data at an untrusted third party, and support data retrieval), and the principle ideas of integrity verification can be applied, the actual design and deployment of authentication schemes are significantly different, due to several fundamental differences between DBMSs and BigTable. In fact, such differences bring both challenges and opportunities to assure the integrity of BigTable.

For instance, on the one hand, BigTable by design distributes data among large number of nodes. As BigTable horizontally partitions data into tablets across multiple nodes, it is common to merge or split the data of multiple nodes from time to time for load balancing or to accommodate new data. How to handle authenticated data structures during data merging or splitting is not considered in past work on database outsourcing, as it is commonly assumed that data are hosted by a single database. Also, because of the distributed nature of BigTable, it is impractical to store authenticated structures for data residing in different machines into a single node, due to the limited storage capacity of a single node. It also brings scalability issues if we adopt a centralized integrity verification scheme at a single point (e.g., at a trusted third-party). On the other hand, the data model of BigTable is significantly simpler than that of traditional DMBSs. In particular, its query model (or the interface to retrieve data) is extremely simple. For example, it does not support join and other complex query operators as in DBMSs. This may allow us to design much simpler and efficient authenticated structures and protocols to verify data integrity.

Besides integrity verification and efficiency, another important consideration is to preserve the interface of BigTable as much as possible so that existing applications running over BigTable do not need to be re-implemented or modified significantly. Ideally, it should only involve minor change (or no change at all) at the application to enjoy integrity guarantee from BigTable.

In this paper, we present iBigTable, an enhancement to BigTable with the addition of scalable data integrity assurance while preserving its simplicity and query execution efficiency in the cloud. To be scalable, iBigTable decentralizes integrity verification processes among different distributed nodes that participate in data retrieval. It also includes efficient schemes to merge and split authenticated data structures among multiple nodes, which is a must to preserve the scalability and efficiency of BigTable. iBigTable tries to utilize the unique properties of BigTable to reduce the cost of integrity verification and preserve its interface to applications as much as possible. Such properties include its column oriented data model, parallel data processing, and its cache mechanism. Our major contributions are summarized as follows:

- We explore different authenticated data structure designs, and propose a *Two-Level Merkle B+ Tree*, which utilizes the column-oriented data model and achieves efficient integrity verification for projected range queries.

- We design efficient mechanisms to handle authenticated data structure changes for efficient batch update, and tablet split and merge by introducing a *Partial Tree Verification Object*.

- We build a prototype of iBigTable based on HBase [4], an open source implementation of BigTable. The prototype shows that the security components in iBigTable can be easily integrated into existing BigTable implementations.

- We analyze the security and practicability of iBigTable, and conduct experimental evaluation. Our analysis and experimental results show that iBigTable can ensure data integrity while imposing reasonable performance overhead.

Though our discussion in the rest of the paper is for BigTable, the proposed authenticated data structures and integrity verification mechanisms can be similarly applied to distributed storage systems modelled after BigTable.

The rest of the paper is organized as follows. We introduce BigTable in Section 2. In Section 3, we describe the data outsourcing model we target, state assumptions and attack models. Section 4 explains the major design choices of iBigTable, and section 5 illustrate how the data integrity is guaranteed for different data operations. Section 6 discusses the security and practicability of iBigTable and provides the experimental evaluation results. Section 7 compares our work with related work. Finally, the paper concludes in Section 8.

2. BACKGROUND

Bigtable is a distributed storage system for managing structured data. A table in BigTable is a sparse distributed, persistent, multidimensional sorted map [10]. Columns in BigTable is grouped together to form a column family. Each value in BigTable is associated with a row key, a column family, a column and a timestamp, which are combined to uniquely identify the value. The row key, column family name, column name and value can be arbitrary strings. A key-value pair is called a cell in BigTable. A row consists of a group of cells with the same row key. A tablet is a group of rows within a row range specified by a start row key and an end row key and is the basic unit for load balancing in BigTable. In BigTable, clients can insert or delete rows, retrieve a row based on a row key, iterate a set of rows similar to range queries, or only retrieve specific column families or columns over a set of rows similar to projected range queries in databases.

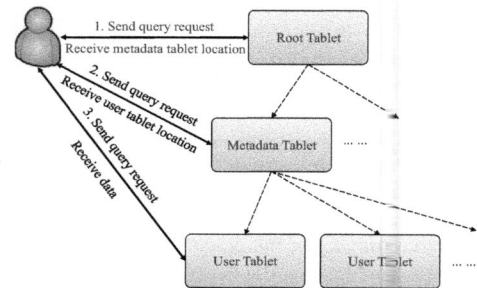

Figure 1: BigTable: Tablet Location Hierarchy.

BigTable consists of a master and multiple tablet servers. It horizontally partitions data into tablets across tablet servers, which achieves scalability. The master is mainly responsible for assigning tablets to tablet servers. Each tablet server manages a set of tablets. Tablet servers handle read and write requests to the tablets that they serve. There are three types of tablets: root tablet, metadata tablet and user tablet. All three types of tablets share the same data structure. There is only one root tablet. The root tablet contains the locations of all metadata tablets. Each metadata tablet contains the locations of a set of user tablets. All user data are stored in user tablets. The root tablet is never split to ensure that the tablet location hierarchy has no more than three levels. Figure 1 shows the tablet location hierarchy and how a query is executed by traversing the tablet location hierarchy, which usually requires three network round-trips (find metadata tablet through the root table, find user tablet through a metadata tablet, and retrieve data from a user tablet) if tablet locations are not found in client-side cache.

3. SYSTEM MODEL

3.1 BigTable in Cloud

BigTable can be deployed in either a private cloud (e.g., a large private cluster), or a public cloud, for example Amazon EC2 [1]. In a private cloud, all entities belong to a single trusted domain, and all data processing steps are executed within this domain. There is no interaction with other domains at all. Thus, security is not taken into consideration for BigTable in a private cloud. However, in a public cloud, there are three types of entities from different domains: cloud providers, data owners, and clients. Cloud providers provide public cloud services. Data owners store and manage their data in BigTable deployed in public cloud. Clients retrieve data owners' data for analysis or further processing. This data processing model presents two significant differences:

- Cloud providers are not completely trusted by the public - data owners and clients. Furthermore, could providers may be malicious or compromised by attackers due to different vulnerabilities such as software bugs, and careless administration.

- The communications and data transmitted between the public and cloud providers are through public networks. It is possible that the communications are eavesdropped, or even tampered to launch different attacks.

Therefore, before BigTable can be safely deployed and operated in a public cloud, several security issues need to be addressed, including confidentiality, integrity, and availability. In this paper, we focus on protecting data integrity of BigTable deployed in a public cloud, which includes three aspects: correctness, completeness and freshness.

Correctness: it verifies if all rows in a query result are generated from the original data set without being tampered. It is generally achieved by verifying signatures or hashes that authenticate the authenticity of the query result.

Completeness: it verifies if all rows in a query result are generated from the original data set without being tampered. It is generally achieved by verifying signatures or hashes that authenticate the authenticity of the query result.

Freshness: it verifies if queries are executed over the up-to-date data. It is challenging to provide freshness guarantees because old data is still valid data at some past time point.

3.2 Assumptions and Attack Models

First, we assume that cloud providers are not necessarily trusted by data owners and clients. Second, we assume that a data owner has a public/private key pair, its public key is known to all, and it is the only party who can manage its data, including data updates and tablet split and merge. Third, we assume that all communications go through a secure channel (e.g., through SSL) between the cloud and clients. Any tampered communication can be detected by both the cloud and clients at each end immediately.

Based on the above assumptions, we concentrate on the analysis of malicious behavior from the public cloud. We do not limit the types of malicious actions a cloud provider may take. Instead, they may behave arbitrarily to compromise data integrity at its side. For example, the cloud can maliciously modify the data or return an incorrect result to users by removing or tampering some data in the result. Moreover, it could just report that certain data does not exist to save its computation and minimize the cost even if the data does exist in the cloud. Additionally, it may initiate replay attacks by returning some old data instead of using the latest data updated by the data owner.

4. SYSTEM DESIGN

In this section, we illustrate the major design of iBigTable, and explain the design choices we make to provide scalable integrity assurance for BigTable. One straightforward way to provide integrity assurance is to build a centralized authenticated data structure. However, data in BigTable is stored across multiple nodes, and may go up to the scale of petabytes. The authentication data could also go up to a very large size. Thus, it is impractical to store authentication data in a single node. Moreover, the single node will become a bottleneck for data integrity verification. To ensure performance and scalability, we propose to build a Merkle

Hash Tree (MHT) based authenticated data structure for each tablet in BigTable, and implement a decentralized integrity verification scheme across multiple tablet servers to ensure data integrity of BigTable. Note that we assume that readers have certain knowledge of MHT. If readers are not familiar with MHT, please refer to Appendix A for details.

4.1 Distributed Authenticated Data Structure

BigTable horizontally partitions data into tablets across tablet servers. A natural solution is to utilize BigTable's distributed nature to distribute authenticated data across tablets. Figure 2(a) shows a distributed authenticated data structure design. First, it builds a MHT-based authenticated data structure for each tablet in BigTable, including the root tablet, metadata tablets, and user tablets. Second, it stores the root hash of the authenticated data structure of a tablet along with the tablet location record in its corresponding higher level tablet (either the root tablet or a metadata tablet), as shown in Figure 2(a). Third, the root hash of the root tablet is stored at the data owner so that clients can always retrieve the latest root hash from the data owner for integrity verification. To improve performance, clients may not only cache the location data of tablets, but also their root hashes for efficient integrity verification.

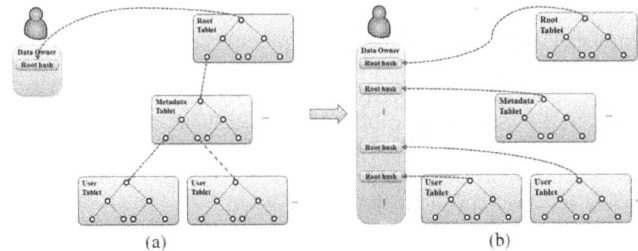

Figure 2: Distributed Authenticated Data Structure Design.

This design distributes authenticated data across tablets, which are served by different tablet servers. To guarantee integrity, it only requires the data owner to store a single hash for the whole data set in BigTable. However, any data update requires authenticated data structure update to be propagated from a user tablet to a metadata tablet and from the metadata tablet to the root tablet. The update propagation process requires either the data owner or tablet servers get involved, either of which complicates the existing data update process in BigTable and downgrades the update performance. Moreover, as the root hash of the root tablet is updated, the root hashes of other tablets cached in clients to improve performance are not valid any more. Thus, clients have to retrieve the latest root hash of the root tablet, and contact tablet servers to retrieve the latest root hashes of other tablets for their requests even if the location data of the tablets stored in metadata tablets or the root tablet is not changed, which hurts read performance.

To address the above issues, we propose a different distributed MHT-based design, which is shown in Figure 2(b). This design also distributes authenticated data across tablets like what the previous design does. But it makes two major design changes. First, it removes the dependency between the authenticated data structures of tablets so that there is no need to propagate an authenticated data update across multiple tablets. In this way, the authenticated data update process is greatly simplified since it does not require either the data owner or tablet servers to propagate any update, which preserve the existing data update protocols in BigTable and minimize communication cost. Second, instead of storing one hash in the data owner, it stores the root hash of each tablet in the data owner, which requires more storage compared with the previous design. However, note that the root hash that the data owner stores for each tablet is only of a few bytes (e.g., 15 bytes for MD5 and 20 bytes for SHA1), while the data stored in a tablet is usually from several hundred megabytes to a few gigabytes [10]. Therefore, even for BigTable with data of petabyte scale, the root hashes of all tablets can be easily maintained by the data owner with moderate storage. Our discussion in the rest of the paper is based on this design.

4.2 Decentralized Integrity Verification

As the authenticated data is distributed into tablets across tablet servers, the integrity verification process is naturally distributed across tablet servers, shown in Figure 3. Like a query execution in BigTable, the query execution with integrity assurance in iBigTable also requires three roundtrip communications between a client and tablet servers in order to locate the right metadata and user tablet, and retrieve data. However, for each round-trip, the client needs a way to verify the data sent by a tablet server. To achieve that, first a tablet server generates a Verification Object (VO) for the data sent to the client, which usually contains a set of hashes. Since the authenticated data for a tablet is completely stored in the tablet server, the tablet server is able to generate the VO without communicating with anyone else, which greatly simplifies the VO generation process and adds no communication cost. Second, the tablet server sends the VO along with the data to the client. Third, when the client receives the data and the corresponding VO, the client runs a verification algorithm to verify the integrity of the received data. One step that is not shown in Figure 3 is that in order to guarantee the freshness of the data, the client needs to retrieve the root hash of the tablet from the data owner on demand or update the cached root hash of the tablet from time to time. How often the client makes such updates depends on the freshness requirement of specific applications, which is a tradeoff between freshness and performance. With the cached root hashes and locations of tablets, the query execution may only require one round-trip between a client and a tablet server, which is exactly the same as that in the original BigTable. This is important as iBigTable strives to preserve the original BigTable communication protocol so that its adoption requires minimum modification to existing BigTable deployment.

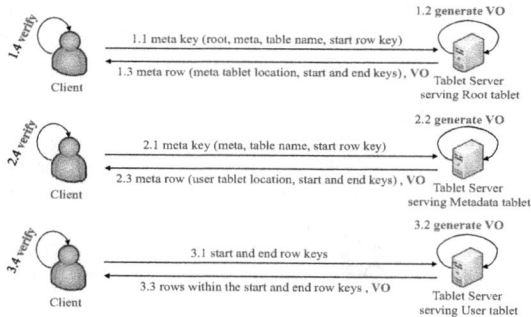

Figure 3: Decentralize Integrity Verification.

As can be seen from Figure 3, the major performance overhead in iBigTable comes from three parts: the computation cost at tablet servers for VO generation, the communication cost between clients and tablet servers for VO transmission, and the computation cost at clients for VO verification. We will evaluate and analyze the performance overhead added by the three parts in section 6.3.

Note that although in our design we assume that the data owner as a trusted party stores the root hashes and handles the root hash retrieval requests to guarantee that clients can always get the latest root hashes for freshness verification, many approaches that have been studied extensively in the field of certificate validation and revocation for ensuring the freshness of signed messages can be directly applied to our design, which do not requires that the data owner be online to handle the root hash retrieval requests [16, 17, 25]. For example, the data owner can sign the root hashes with an expiration time and publish those signatures at a place that can be accessed by clients, and reissues the signatures after they are expired. In the rest of the paper, for simplicity, we still assume that the data owner stores the root hashes and handles the root hash retrieval requests.

4.3 Tablet-based Authenticated Data Structure

In BigTable, since all three types of tablets share the same data structure, we propose to design an authenticated data structure based on the tablet structure, and use it for all tables in BigTable. We compare different authenticated data structure by analyzing how well they can support the major operations provided in BigTable. Authenticated data structure based approaches are mainly divided into two categories, signature aggregation based approaches [16, 18] and Merkle Hash Tree(MHT) based approaches [12, 16]. Although both of them can guarantee correctness and completeness, it is unknown how to efficiently guarantee freshness using signature aggregation based approaches [16]. Moreover, techniques based on signature aggregation incur significant computation cost in client side and much larger storage cost in server side compared with MHT-based approaches [16]. Thus, we focus on exploring MHT-based authenticated data structures in the following.

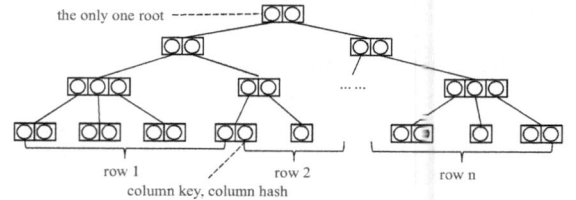

Figure 4: SL-MBT: Single-Level Merkle B+ Tree.

SL-MBT: A single-level Merkle B+ tree. BigTable is column-oriented data storage. Each column value is stored with a key as a key value pair $(key_c, value_c)$, where key_c includes row key and column key specified by column family name and column name. It is straightforward to build a Merkle B+ tree based on all key value pairs in a tablet, which is called SL-MBT shown in Figure 4. In a SL-MBT, all leaves are the hashes of key value pairs. In this way, it is simple to generate a VO for a single column value. Now that all column values are strictly sorted based on row key and column key, the hashes of the key value pairs belonging to a row are adjacent to each other among the leaves of the tree. Thus, it is also straightforward and efficient to generate a VO for a single row query. The same logic can be applied to row-based range queries.

Suppose the fan-out of SL-MBT is f, there are n_r rows in a tablet, each row r_i has n_{cf} column families, and each column family has n_c columns. Then, the height of SL-MBT in the tablet is equal to $h_t = \log_f(n_r \cdot n_{cf} \cdot n_c)$. Say we run a range query with n_q rows returned, where n_q is greater than 0. The height of the partial tree built based on all key value pairs returned equals to $h_p = \log_f(n_q \cdot n_{cf} \cdot n_c)$. The number of hashes H_r returned in the VO is:

$$H_r = (f - 1) \cdot (h_t - h_p)$$
$$= (f - 1) \cdot \log_f(n_r/n_q) \tag{1}$$

344

The number of hashes H_c that need to be computed at the client side includes: 1) the number of hashes in the partial tree built based on all received key value pairs; 2) the number of hashes for computing the root hash using hashes in the VO, computed as follows:

$$H_c = \sum_{i=0}^{\log_f(n_q \cdot n_{cf} \cdot n_c)} f^i + \log_f(n_r/n_q) \quad (2)$$

If the range query is projected only to one column, it means that the server only needs to return the column values for n_q rows. To verify those column values, one way we can do is to verify each column value separately. In this case, both H_r and H_c are linear to n_q, which are computed as follows:

$$H_r = n_q \cdot (f - 1) \cdot h_t \quad (3)$$
$$H_c = n_q \cdot (1 + h_t) \quad (4)$$

Based on SL-MBT, it is expensive to generate and verify VOs for projected range queries.

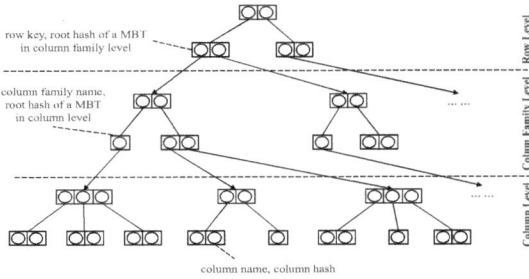

Figure 5: ML-MBT: Multi-Level Merkle B+ Tree.

ML-MBT: A multi-level Merkle B+ tree. Different from SL-MBT, ML-MBT builds multiple Merkle B+ trees in three different levels shown in Figure 5:

1. Column Level: we build a Merkle B+ tree based on all column key value pairs within a column family for a specific row, called Column Tree. Each leaf is the hash of a column key value pair. We have one column tree per column family within a row.

2. Column Family Level: we build a Merkle B+ tree, based on all column family values within a row, called Column Family Tree. Each leaf is the root hash of the column tree of a column family. We have one column family tree per row.

3. Row Level: we build a Merkle B+ tree based on all row values within a tablet, called Row Tree. Each leaf is the root hash of the column family tree of a row. We only have one row tree in a tablet.

Given the same range query mentioned above, the H_r in ML-MBT is the same as that returned in SL-MBT. However, H_c in ML-MBT is much smaller than that in SL-MBT, computed as follows:

$$H_c = \sum_{i=0}^{\log_f n_q} f^i + \log_f(n_r/n_q) \quad (5)$$

The partial tree built at the client side for ML-MBT is based on all received rows instead of all received key value pairs. Thus, the number of hashes in the partial tree is much smaller than that

for SL-MBT. Compared with SL-MBT, another advantage of ML-MBT is that the client is able to cache the root hashes for trees in different levels to improve the performance of some queries. For example, by caching a root hash of a column family tree, for projected queries within the row, we only need to return hashes from trees under the column family level. Although ML-MBT presents some advantages over SL-MBT, it shares the same disadvantage with SL-MBT for projected range queries.

TL-MBT: A two-level Merkle B+ tree. Considering the unique properties of column-oriented data storage, where a column may not have values for many rows, it seems reasonable to build a column tree based on all values of a specific column over all rows. Due to missing column values in rows, the height of different column trees may be different. Based on this observation, we can also build a column family tree based on all values of a specific column family over all rows. To facilitate row-based queries, we can also build a row tree based on all rows in a tablet. In this way, we may build a Merkle B+ tree for rows, for each column family, and for each column respectively. We call them Data trees. Further, we build another Merkle B+ tree based on all root hashes of Data trees in the tablet, which is called an Index tree. Figure 6 shows the structure of such a two-level Merkle B+ tree. The top level is the Index level where the Index tree is, and the bottom level is the Data level where all Data trees are. Each leaf of Index tree points to a Data tree. Its key is a special value for row tree, the column family name for a column family tree, or the column name for a column tree, and its hash is the root hash of its corresponding Data tree.

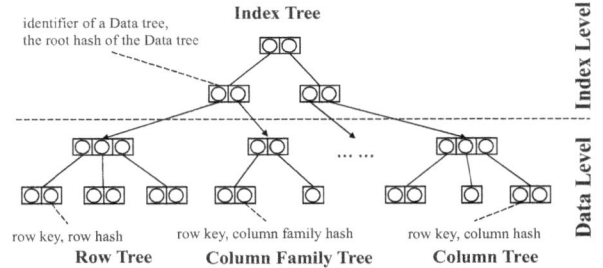

Figure 6: TL-MBT: Two-Level Merkle B+ Tree.

To generate a VO based on TL-MBT, we first need to find all necessary Data trees of a query through the Index tree, which can be done by checking what column families or columns are returned or if the whole row is returned. Second, based on the Index tree and the related Data trees, we use a standard Merkle B+ tree VO generation process to construct a VO for the query. For instance, for row-based range queries, servers only need to find the row tree through the Index tree and use both the Index tree and the row tree to generate a VO, and clients can verify data integrity using the VO efficiently. We argue that although the Index tree increases the total height of the authenticated data structure, its height is relative small since the number of table columns is much less than the number of rows, and the Index tree could be completely cached in both the server side and the client side, which can reduce the communication cost and verification cost. Thus, the performance of TL-MBT is comparable to ML-MBT for row-based queries.

However, it is much more efficient than SL-MBT and ML-MBT for single column projection. Considering the aforementioned range query with single column projection, H_r and H_c in TL-MBT are:

$$H_r = (f - 1) \cdot (h_m + \log_f(n_r/n_q)) \quad (6)$$

$$H_c = \sum_{i=0}^{\log_f n_q} f^i + \log_f(n_r/n_q) + h_m \qquad (7)$$

In Equation 6 and 7, h_m is the height of the Index tree. Neither of H_r and H_c is linear to n_q. For a projection on multiple columns, we need to verify results for each column separately. In this case, the cost is linear to the number of columns projected in the query. However, compared with SL-MBT and ML-MBT, the update cost may increase by about 3 times since we need to update column tree, column family tree and row tree, which may have the same height, plus the Index tree. We argue that TL-MBT provides a flexible data structure for clients to specify how they want to build such a TL-MBT based on their own needs. For example, if they will never run queries with column-level projection, then it is not necessary to build column trees. In this case, we may only have row tree and column family trees in Data level.

Based on the above analysis, we choose to use TL-MBT as the authenticated data structure for the design of iBigTable.

5. DATA OPERATIONS

Based on TL-MBT, we describe how clients ensure the integrity of the major data operations of BigTable. We address several challenges, including range query across multiple tablets, efficient batch updates, tablet merge and split. In our design, the data owner stores the root hash of each tablet, and any client can request the latest root hash of any tablet from the data owner for integrity verification. Without loss of generality, we assume that clients always have the latest root hashes of tablets for integrity verification.

5.1 Data Access

We start our discussion from range queries[1]. In Section 4.2, we illustrate a general process to run query with integrity protection in iBigTable. The execution of range queries within a tablet follows exactly the same process shown in Figure 3. However, we need to handle range queries across multiple tablets differently. Figure 7 shows a running example for data query and updates. Initially, we have 10 rows with keys from 0 to 90 in a tablet. Figure 7(a) and 7(b) show the initial MB+ tree for the tablet and the result returned for a range query from 15 to 45 including data and VO. We will explain in detail of major operations based on the running example.

Range Queries Across Tablets. To provide integrity assurance for range queries across tablets, it is necessary to retrieve authenticated data from different tablets since the authenticated data structure built for a tablet is only used to verify integrity of data within the tablet. We observe that to handle a range query across tablets, the range query is usually split into multiple sub-queries, each of which retrieves rows from one tablet. More importantly, the query ranges of the sub queries are continuous since the query split is based on the row range that each tablet serves, which is stored along with the tablet location in a meta row as shown in Figure 3. Suppose that there are two tablets, one serves rows from 1 to 10 and the other serves rows from 11 to 20, and a range query is to retrieves rows from 5 to 15 across the two tablets. In this case, the query is splits into two sub queries with query ranges from 5 to 10 and from 11 to 15. In this way, we can apply the same process of range query answering within a tablet to guarantee integrity for each sub query.

However, the completeness of the original range query across tablets may not be guaranteed since a tablet server may return a wrong row range for a user tablet, which results in an incomplete result set returned to clients. Thus, we want to make sure that the

---

[1] A single row query as a special case of range query can be handled in the same way that a range query is executed.

row range of the user tablet is correctly returned. During the query verification process, it is guaranteed by the verification of meta row performed by clients because the row range of a user tablet is part of the data of the meta row, which has been authenticated. It is also why we not only need to guarantee integrity of data stored in user tablets, but also data stored in the root and metadata tablets.

Single Row Update. In iBigTable, we support integrity protection for dynamic updates such as insertion, modification and deletion. Due to the space limit, we focus on discussing how to insert a new row into the data storage, which covers most of aspects of how modification and deletion are handled. Insertion shares the same process to find the user tablet where the new row should be inserted based on the key of the new row. Here we do not reiterate this process again. The rest of the steps to insert a row into the user tablet are shown in Figure 8.

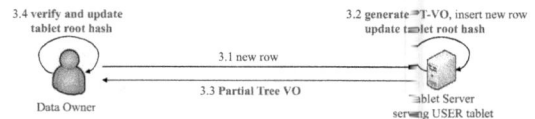

Figure 8: Single Row Insert with Integrity Protection.

Here, we introduce a new type of VO called *Partial Tree Verification Object* (PT-VO). The difference between a VO and a PT-VO is that a PT-VO contains keys along with hashes, while a VO does not. With those keys, a PT-VO allows us to insert new data within the partial tree range directly. Thus, when the data owner receives a PT-VO from the tablet server, it can directly update the PT-VO locally to compute the new root hash of the original authenticated data structure. Figure 7(c) shows the PT-VO returned for an insertion at key 45. As can be seen from Figure 8, an insertion with integrity protection is completed without additional round-trip, and its integrity is guaranteed since the verification and the root hash update are done directly by the data owner.

Efficient Batch Update. In iBigTable, we can execute a range query to retrieve a set of rows at one time and only run verification once. Motivated by this observation, we think about how we can do a batch update, for example inserting multiple rows without doing verification each time a new row is inserted. We observe the fact from single row update that the data owner is able to compute the new root hash based on a PT-VO. Based on this observation, we propose two simple yet effective schemes to improve the efficiency of insertions for two different cases.

In the first case where we assume that the data owner knows within which range new rows falls, the data owner can require servers to return a PT-VO for the range before any insertion really happens. Any new row falling into the range can be inserted directly without requiring the server to return a VO again because the data owner is able to compute the new root hash of the tablet with the PT-VO and the new row. Thus, even if 1000 rows are inserted within this range, no additional VO needs to be returned for them. But both the data owner and tablet servers have to update the root hash locally, which is inevitable in any case.

In the second case where we assume that a PT-VO for a range is already cached in the data owner side, the data owner does not need to request it. As long as we have the PT-VO for a range, we do not need any VO from servers if we insert rows within the range. For example, Figure 7(b) and 7(d) show such an example. First, the data owner runs a range query from 15 to 45 with a request for a PT-VO instead of a VO without keys. Then, the data owner inserts a row with key 45. In this case, there is no need requiring any VO from the tablet server for the insertion.

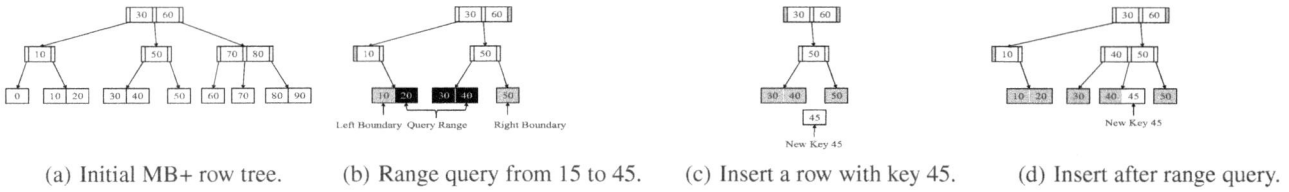

(a) Initial MB+ row tree. (b) Range query from 15 to 45. (c) Insert a row with key 45. (d) Insert after range query.

Figure 7: A running example.

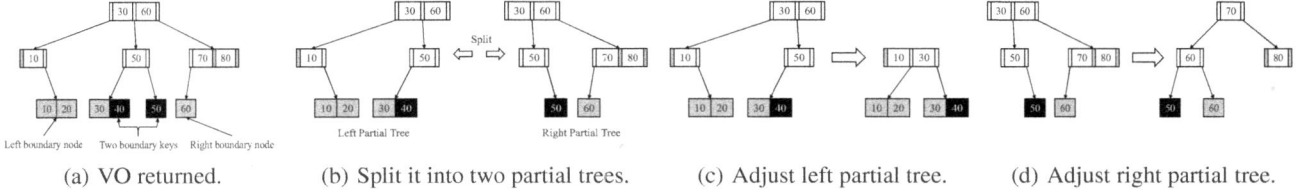

(a) VO returned. (b) Split it into two partial trees. (c) Adjust left partial tree. (d) Adjust right partial tree.

Figure 9: Split the tablet at key 45.

5.2 Tablet Changes

As the size of a tablet changes, the data owner may want to split a tablet or merge two tablets for load balancing. For both tablet split and merge, we need to rebuild an authenticated data structure and update the root hashes for newly created tablets. One straightforward way is to retrieve all data hashes in tablets involved and compute new root hashes for newly created tablets in the data owner side. However, this incurs high communication and computation overhead in both the data owner side and tablet servers. In the following, we explain how we can efficiently compute the root hashes for newly created tablets when tablet split or merge happens. For simplicity, we assume that there is only one Data tree and no Index tree in tablets when we discuss tablet split or merge, since the Index tree of TL-MBT in a tablet can be rebuilt based on Data trees. Further, all Data trees are split or merged in the same way.

Tablet Split. Regarding tablet split, a straightforward way is to split the root of each tree and form two new roots using its children. For example, given the current root we can split it in the middle, and use the left part as the root of one tablet and the right part as the root of the other tablet. In this way, to split a Data tree and compute new root hashes for newly created tablets, the data owner only needs to retrieve the hashes of children in the root of the Data tree from an appropriate tablet server.

The main advantage of the above approach is its simplicity. It can be easily implemented. However, splitting at the middle of the root (or any pre-fixed splitting point) prevents us from doing flexible load balancing dynamically based on data access patterns and work loads. Here, we propose a simple yet effective approach to allow the data owner to specify an arbitrary split point for a tablet (instead of always along one child of the root), which can be any key within the range served by the tablet. The approach works as follows: 1) The data owner sends a tablet split request with a key as the split point to the appropriate tablet server. For example, the data owner splits the previous tablet at key 45; 2) The server returns a VO for the split request to the data owner shown in Figure 9(a). The VO for split not only contains all data in a PT-VO, but also includes keys and hashes of the left and right neighbors of each left-most or right-most node in the PT-VO; 3) When the data owner receives the VO, the data owner splits it into two partial trees shown in Figure 9(b). The left tree contains all keys less than the split key, and the right tree contains all keys larger than or equal to the split key; 4)

Algorithm 1 Adjust left partial tree VO

Require: T_l {the left partial tree}
Ensure: T_a {the adjusted left partial tree}
1: $p \leftarrow GetRoot(T_l)$
2: **while** $p \neq null$ **do**
3:     remove any key without right child in p
4:     $p_{rm} \leftarrow$ the rightmost child of p
5:     **if** IsValidNode(p) is false **then**
6:         $p_{ls} \leftarrow$ the left sibling of p
7:         **if** CanMergeNodes(p, p_{ls}) **then**
8:             merge p and p_{ls}
9:         **else**
10:             shift keys from p_{ls} to p through their parent
11:         **end if**
12:     **end if**
13:     $p \leftarrow p_{rm}$
14: **end while**
15: **return** $T_a \leftarrow T_l$

The data owner adjusts both trees using two similar processes and computes the root hashes for the two new tablets. The adjusted trees are shown in both Figure 9(c) and 9(d). Due to the similarity of adjustments for both trees and space limit, we only describe the process for left tree in Algorithm 1.

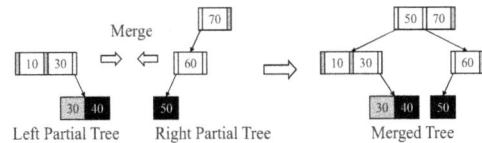

Figure 10: Tablet Merge.

Tablet Merge. Tablet merge is a reverse process of table split. It tries to merge two continuous tablets into a new one. As two tablets merge, we need to merge the authenticated data structures. Motivated by the tablet split approach and the Partial Tree VO, we describe an efficient tablet merge approach as follows: 1) The data owner sends a tablet merge request to the appropriate tablet servers serving two continuous tablets to be merged; 2) The server serving the tablet with smaller keys returns a VO for its largest key, and the server serving the tablet with larger keys returns a VO for its smallest key, which are shown in Figure 10; 3) When the data owner receives two VOs for the two tablets, it directly merges them into one using the process described in Algorithm 2. Then, the data owner computes the root hash for the new tablet based on the merged VO.

Our discussion focus on the tablet-based authenticated data structure split and merge at the data owner side. The same process can be applied at the server side.

Algorithm 2 Merge two partial tree VOs

Require: T_l and T_r {represent two partial trees separately}
Ensure: T_m {the merged partial tree}
1: $k \leftarrow$ the least key in T_r
2: $h_l \leftarrow GetHeight(T_l)$
3: $h_r \leftarrow GetHeight(T_r)$
4: $h_{min} \leftarrow GetMin(h_l, h_r)$
5: **if** $h_l \leq h_r$ **then**
6:     $p_{lm} \leftarrow$ the leftmost node in T_r at h_{min}
7:     add k to p_{lm}
8:     $p_{merged} \leftarrow$ merge the root of T_l and p_{lm}
9:     **if** IsValidNode(p_{merged}) is false **then**
10:         run a node split process for p_{merged}
11:     **end if**
12:     **return** $T_m \leftarrow T_r$
13: **else**
14:     $p_{rm} \leftarrow$ the rightmost node in T_l at h_{min}
15:     add k to p_{rm}
16:     $p_{merged} \leftarrow$ merge the root of T_r and p_{rm}
17:     **if** IsValidNode(p_{merged}) is false **then**
18:         run a standard node split process for p_{merged}
19:     **end if**
20:     **return** $T_m \leftarrow T_l$
21: **end if**

---

6. ANALYSIS AND EVALUATION

6.1 Security Analysis

We analyze in the following how iBigTable achieves the three aspects of data integrity protection.

Correctness. In iBigTable, the Merkle tree based authenticated data structure is built for each tablet, and the root hash of the authenticated data structure is stored in the data owner. For each client request to a tablet, a tablet server serving the tablet returns a VO along with the data to the client. The client is able to compute a root hash of the tablet using the VO and the data received. To guarantee the integrity of the data received, the client needs to retrieve the root hash of the tablet from the data owner, and then compare the root hash received from the data owner and the computed root hash. The comparison result indicates if the data has been tampered. Thus, the correctness of iBigTable is guaranteed. Any malicious modification can be detected by the verification process.

Completeness. The completeness of range queries within a tablet is guaranteed by the MHT-based authenticated data structure built for each tablet. For range queries across tablets, each of them is divided into several sub-range queries with continuous range based on the original query range and data range served by tablets so that each sub-range query only queries data within a tablet. Thus, the completeness of range queries across tablets is guaranteed by two

points: 1) the sub-range queries are continuous without any gap; 2) the completeness of each sub-range query is guaranteed by the authenticated data structure of its corresponding tablet.

Freshness. In iBigTable, the data owner is able to compute the new root hash of the authenticated data structure for a tablet when any data in the tablet is updated. Thus, clients can always get the latest root hash of a tablet from the data owner to verify the authenticity of data in the tablet. Even though there is no data update to any tablet, tablet split or merge may happen since a tablet may become a bottleneck because of too much load or for better tablet organization to improve performance. In this case, iBigTable also enables the data owner to compute the new root hashes for new tablets created during the split or merge process to guarantee the freshness of tablet root hashes, which is the key for freshness verification.

6.2 Practicability Analysis

We argue that iBigTable achieves simplicity, flexibility and efficiency, which makes it practical as a scalable storage with integrity protection.

Simplicity. First, we add new interfaces and change part of existing implementation to achieve integrity protection while keeping existing BigTable interface, which enables existing applications to run on iBigTable without any change. Second, iBigTable preserves BigTable existing communication protocols while providing integrity verification, which minimizes modification to existing BigTable deployment for its adoption.

Flexibility. We provide different ways to specify how and when clients want to enable integrity protection. Existing client applications can enable or disable integrity protection by configuring a few options without any code change, and new client applications may use new interfaces to design a flexible integrity protection scheme based on specific requirements. There is no need to change any configuration of iBigTable servers when integrity protection is enabled or disabled at the client side.

Efficiency. We implement iBigTable without changing existing query execution process, but only attach VOs along with data for integrity verification. We make the best use of cache mechanisms to reduce communication cost. We introduce the *Partial Tree Verification Object* to design a set of mechanisms for efficient batch updates, and for efficient and flexible tablet split and merge.

Note that though iBigTable only allows the data owner to modify data, most applications running on top of BigTable do not involve frequent date updates. So it is unlikely that the data owner becomes a performance bottleneck.

6.3 Experimental Evaluation

System Implementation. We have implemented a prototype of iBigTable based on HBase [4], an open source implementation of BigTable. Although HBase stores data in a certain format and builds indexes to facilitate the data retrieval, we implement the authenticated data structure as a separated component loosely coupled with existing components in HBase, which not only simplifies the implementation but also minimize the influence on the existing mechanisms of HBase. We add new interfaces so that clients can specify integrity options in a flexible way when doing queries or updates. We also enable them to configure such options in a configuration file in the client side without changing their application code. Besides, we add new interfaces to facilitate the integrity protection and efficient data operations. For example, for efficient batch updates a client may want to pre-fetch a PT-VO directly based on a range without returning actual data. Finally, iBigTable automatically reports any violation against data integrity to the client.

Experiment Setup. We deploy HBase with iBigTable extension across multiple hosts deployed in Virtual Computing Lab (VCL), a distributed computing system with hundreds of hosts connected through campus networks [8]. All hosts used have similar hardware and software configuration (Intel(R) Xeon(TM) CPU 3.00GHz, 8G Memory, Red Hat Enterprise Linux Server release 5.1, Sun JDK 6, Hadoop-0.20.2 and HBase-0.90.4). One of the hosts is used for the master of HBase and the NameNode of HDFS. Other hosts are running as tablet servers and data nodes. We consider our university cloud as a public cloud, which provides the HBase service, and run experiments from a client through a home network with 30Mbps download and 4Mbps upload. To evaluate the performance overhead of iBigTable and the efficiency of the proposed mechanisms, we design a set of experiments using synthetic data sets we build based on some typical settings in BigTable [10]. We use MD5 [6] to generate hashes.

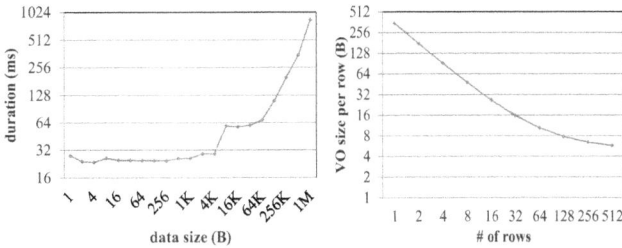

Figure 11: Time to Receive Data from Server. Figure 12: VO Size Per Row vs Number of Rows.

Baseline Experiment. Before we evaluate the performance of write and read operations in iBigTable, we run a simple data transmission through the targeting network because the result is going to be helpful to understand the performance result later. In the experiment, the client sends a request to a server for a certain amount of data. The server generates the amount of random data and sends the data back to the client. Figure 11 shows the time to receive a certain amount of data from a server using logarithmic scale. The result shows that it almost takes the same time to transmit data less than 4KB, where the network connection initialization may dominate the communication time. The time is doubled from 4KB to 8KB till around 64KB. After 64KB, the time linearly increases, which is probably because the network is saturated.

To understand how the VO size changes for range queries, we run an experiment to quantify the VO size for different ranges based on a data set with about 256MB data, which is the base data set for later update and read experiments. Figure 12 shows the VO size per row for different sizes of range queries. For a range with more than 64 rows, the VO size per row is around 10 bytes. Although the total VO size increases as the size of range queries increases, the VO size per row actually decreases, shown in Figure 12 with logarithmic scale.

Write Performance. Regarding different data operations, we first conduct experiments to evaluate the write performance overhead caused by iBigTable, where we sequentially writes 8K rows into an empty table with different write buffer sizes. The data size of each row is about 1KB. Figure 13 shows the number of rows written per second by varying the write buffer size for HBase, iBigTable and iBigTable with Efficient Update (EU). The result shows the performance overhead caused by iBigTable ranges from 10% to 50%, but iBigTable with EU only causes a performance overhead about 1.5%, and the write performance increases as the write buffer size increases. Figure 14 shows the breakdown of

performance overhead introduced by iBigTable, which shows the client computation overhead, the server computation overhead and the communication overhead between client and server. As can be seen from the figure, the major performance overhead comes from transmitting the VOs. The computation overhead from both client and server ranges from 2% to 5%.

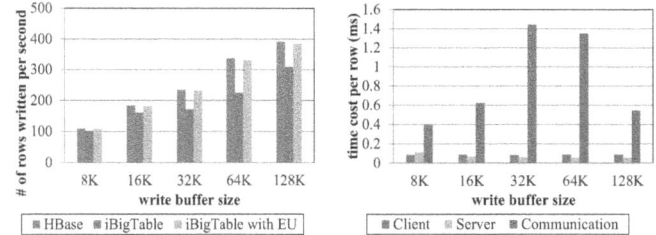

Figure 13: Write Performance Comparison between HBase and iBigTable. Figure 14: The Breakdown of iBigTable Write Overhead.

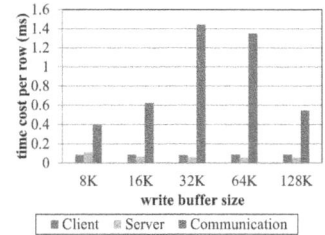

Based on our observation, the large variation of performance overhead is caused by the network transmission of VOs generated by iBigTable for data integrity protection. Although the total size of VOs generated for different write buffer sizes is the same, the number of data with VOs transmitted in each remote request is different in different cases. Different sizes of data may cause a different delay of network transmission, but it may not be always a case, which is shown in Figure 11. iBigTable with EU shows a great performance improvement since there is at most one time VO transmission in this case, and the major overhead of iBigTable with EU is the client-side computation overhead of computing the new root hash for newly inserting data, which is very small, compared with iBigTable.

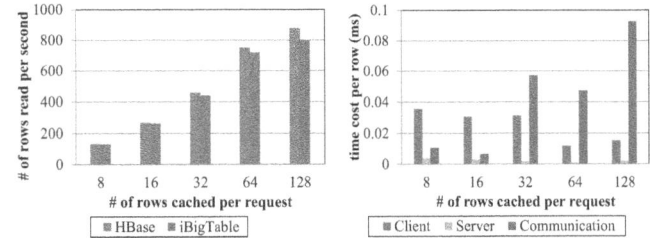

Figure 15: Read Performance Comparison between HBase and iBigTable. Figure 16: The Breakdown of iBigTable Read Overhead.

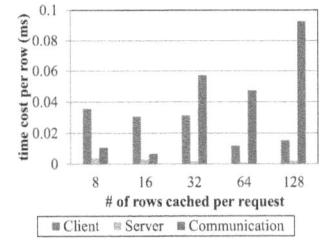

Read Performance. We also run experiments to evaluate the read performance overhead of iBigTable. Figure 15 shows how the number of rows read per second changes based on different number of rows cached per request for a scan. The result shows that the read performance overhead ranges from 1% to 8%. Figure 16 shows the breakdown of iBigTable read overhead. The communication overhead can be explained by the result shown in Figure 11 because the total amount of data transmitted for the first two cases ranges from 8KB to 32KB. In the rest of cases, the size of data is about or larger than 64KB, which results in a large network delay for data transmission. In this case, as the VO size increases, the communication overhead becomes more visible. Based on our observation from experiments, the computation overhead of both the client and servers is about 1%. Still, the major part of performance downgrade is caused by the variation of data transmission between the client and servers.

TL-MBT Performance. To illustrate how TL-MBT affects the performance, we execute a single column update of 16K rows on an existing table with about 30GB data across all tablets, each of which has 256MB data or so. The experiments run against different authenticated data structure configurations of TL-MBT: Row Level, Column Family Level and Column Level, which decides what data trees we build for a tablet. For example, regarding Column Level, we build trees for rows, each column family and each column. It means that for a single column update, we need to update four authenticated trees, which are row tree, column family tree, column tree and Index tree. Due to the small size of Index tree, the VO size of Column Level is roughly tripled compared with those of Row Level, and the client-side computation and server-side computation overhead are about triple too. Figure 17 shows the number of rows updated per second versus the write buffer size for three different configurations of TL-MBT. The result indicates that as the number of trees that need to be updated increases, the performance decreases dramatically in some cases. The major reason for the performance downgrade is still caused by the additional data transmitted for data verification.

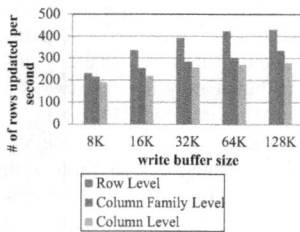

Figure 17: TL-MBT Update Performance in iBigTable.

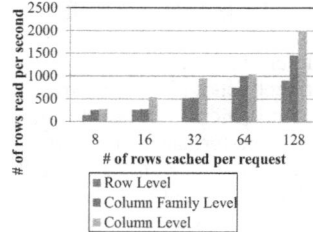

Figure 18: Projection Query with TL-MBT Support in iBigTable.

We also evaluate the read performance for projected queries in iBigTable with TL-MBT by executing a single column scan for 16K rows. For TL-MBT with Row Level, even though we only need a single column value, we still need to retrieve the whole row for data verification in the client side. Similarly, we need to retrieve the whole column family for TL-MBT with Column Family Level. Thus, the TL-MBT with Column Level minimizes the communication overhead since there is no need to transmit additional data for data verification for column projection. Although its computation cost is the lowest one among three different configurations, the major difference is the size of data transmitted between the client and servers. Figure 18 shows how much the TL-MBT can improve the read efficiency for projected queries. Due to the network delay for different data sizes, we see the large performance variation for different cases in the figure.

Overall, the computation overhead in both client and servers for different cases ranges from 1% to 5%. However, the generated VOs for data verification may affect the performance to a large extent for different cases, which depends on how much data is transmitted between the client and servers in a request. Due to the space limit, we do not analyze the performance overhead for tablet split and merge. In general, since the performance overhead for tablet split and merge only involves several hashes transmission and computation, it is negligible compared with the time needed to complete

tablet split and merge, which involves a certain amount of data movement across tablet servers.

7. RELATED WORK

Several open-source, distributed data storages have been implemented modelled after BigTable, for example HBase [4] and Hypertable [5], which are widely used for both academia research and commercial companies. Carstoiu et al. [9] focused on the performance evaluation of HBase. You et al. [27] proposed a solution called HDW, based on Google's BigTable, to build and manage a large scale distributed data warehouse for high performance OLAP analysis. Few work pays attention to the data integrity issue of BigTable in a public cloud. Although Ko et al. [21] mentioned the integrity issues of BigTable in a hybrid cloud, no further discussion on a practical solution was elaborated.

Data integrity issues have been studied for years in the field of outsourcing database [12–14, 18, 19, 24]. Different from traditional database, BigTable is a distributed data storage system involving multi-entity communication and computation, which presents challenges to directly adopt any of existing authenticated data structure. Xie et al. [24] proposed a probabilistic approach by inserting a small amount of fake records into outsourced database so that the integrity of the system can be effectively audited by analyzing the inserted records in the query results. Yang et al. [26] discussed different approaches to handling some types of join queries for outsourced database, which is not relevant to the query model of BigTable. Xie et al. [25] analyzed the different approaches to provide freshness guarantee over different integrity protection schemes, which is complementary to our work for BigTable.

Additionally, Lee et al. [15] proposed algorithms to attach branch to or remove branch from B+ tree for self-tuning data placement in parallel database system, but the branch attaching algorithm is only for two branches that have the same height, and the branch removal algorithm is not flexible because no split point can be specified. Sun et al. [22] designed algorithm to merge B+ tree covering the same key range, which is different from our problem since the row range in each tablet is non-overlapping. Zhou et al. [23] discussed data integrity verification in the cloud, and proposed an approach called partitioned MHT (P-MHT) that may be applied to data partitions. But it may not be scalable since when an update happens to one data partition, the update has to be propagated across all data partitions to update the P-MHT, which renders it as an impractical solution for BigTable. To the best of our knowledge, iBigTable is the first work to propose a practical solution to address the unique challenges and ensure the data integrity for running BigTable in a public cloud.

8. CONCLUSION AND FUTURE WORK

In this paper, we have presented iBigTable, which enhances BigTable with scalable data integrity assurance while preserving its simplicity and query execution efficiency in public cloud. We have explored the practicality of different authenticated data structure designs for BigTable, designed a scalable and distributed integrity verification scheme, implemented a prototype of iBigTable based on HBase [4], evaluated the performance impact resulted from the proposed scheme, and tested it across multiple hosts deployed in our university cloud. Our initial experimental results show that the proposed scheme can ensure data integrity while imposing reasonable performance overhead.

As a storage system, BigTable is often used in conjunction with MapReduce [11] for big data processing. In future, we plan to investigate on the integrity protection of MapReduce with iBigTable for secure big data processing.

9. ACKNOWLEDGMENTS

The authors would like to thank the anonymous reviewers for their helpful suggestions. This work is partially supported by the U.S. Army Research Office under grant W911NF-08-1-0105 managed by NCSU Secure Open Systems Initiative (SOSI), by the NSF under grants CNS-0747247 and CCF-0914946, by NSFC under Grants No. 61170280, and SPRPCAS under Grant No. XDA06010701, and by K.C. Wong Education Foundation. The contents of this paper do not necessarily reflect the position or the policies of the U.S. Government.

10. REFERENCES

[1] Amazon Elastic Compute Cloud. *http://aws.amazon.com/ec2/*.

[2] Cassandra. *http://cassandra.apache.org/*.

[3] Hadoop Tutorial. *http://public.yahoo.com/gogate/hadoop-tutorial/start-tutorial.html*.

[4] Hbase. *http://hbase.apache.org/*.

[5] Hypertable. *http://hypertable.org/*.

[6] MD5. *http://en.wikipedia.org/wiki/MD5*.

[7] The Underlying Technology of Messages. http://www.facebook.com/notes/facebook-engineering/the-underlying-technology-of-messages/454991608919.

[8] Virtual Computing Lab. http://vcl.ncsu.edu/.

[9] D. Carstoiu, A. Cernian, and A. Olteanu. Hadoop hbase-0.20.2 performance evaluation. In *New Trends in Information Science and Service Science (NISS), 2010 4th International Conference on*, pages 84 –87, may 2010.

[10] F. Chang, J. Dean, S. Ghemawat, W. C. Hsieh, D. A. Wallach, M. Burrows, T. Chandra, A. Fikes, and R. E. Gruber. Bigtable: A distributed storage system for structured data. *ACM Trans. Comput. Syst.*, 26:4:1–4:26, June 2008.

[11] J. Dean and S. Ghemawat. Mapreduce: simplified data processing on large clusters. In *OSDI'04: Proceedings of the 6th conference on Symposium on Opearting Systems Design & Implementation*, pages 10–10, Berkeley, CA, USA, 2004. USENIX Association.

[12] P. Devanbu, M. Gertz, C. Martel, and S. G. Stubblebine. Authentic data publication over the internet. *J. Comput. Secur.*, 11:291–314, April 2003.

[13] M. T. Goodrich and R. Tamassia. Efficient authenticated dictionaries with skip lists and commutative hashing. Technical report, TECH. REP., JOHNS HOPKINS INFORMATION SECURITY INSTITUTE, 2001.

[14] H. Hacigümüş, B. Iyer, C. Li, and S. Mehrotra. Executing sql over encrypted data in the database-service-provider model. In *Proceedings of the 2002 ACM SIGMOD international conference on Management of data*, SIGMOD '02, pages 216–227, New York, NY, USA, 2002. ACM.

[15] M. L. Lee, M. Kitsuregawa, B. C. Ooi, K.-L. Tan, and A. Mondal. Towards self-tuning data placement in parallel database systems. In *Proceedings of the 2000 ACM SIGMOD international conference on Management of data*, SIGMOD '00, pages 225–236, New York, NY, USA, 2000. ACM.

[16] F. Li, M. Hadjieleftheriou, G. Kollios, and L. Reyzin. Dynamic authenticated index structures for outsourced databases. In *Proceedings of the 2006 ACM SIGMOD international conference on Management of data*, SIGMOD '06, pages 121–132, New York, NY, USA, 2006. ACM.

[17] S. Micali. Efficient certificate revocation. Technical report, Cambridge, MA, USA, 1996.

[18] H. Pang, A. Jain, K. Ramamritham, and K.-L. Tan. Verifying completeness of relational query results in data publishing. In *Proceedings of the 2005 ACM SIGMOD international conference on Management of data*, SIGMOD '05, pages 407–418, New York, NY, USA, 2005. ACM.

[19] W. Pugh. Skip lists: a probabilistic alternative to balanced trees. *Commun. ACM*, 33:668–676, June 1990.

[20] R. Sion. Query execution assurance for outsourced databases. In *Proceedings of the 31st international conference on Very large data bases*, VLDB '05, pages 601–612. VLDB Endowment, 2005.

[21] K. J. Steven Y. Ko and R. Morales. The hybrex model for confdentiality and privacy in cloud computing. 2011.

[22] X. Sun, R. Wang, B. Salzberg, and C. Zou. Online b-tree merging. In *Proceedings of the 2005 ACM SIGMOD international conference on Management of data*, SIGMOD '05, pages 335–346, New York, NY, USA, 2005. ACM.

[23] Z. Wenchao, M. William R., T. Tao, Z. Zhuoyao, S. Micah, T. L. Boon, and L. Insup. Towards secure cloud data management. *University of Pennsylvania Department of Computer and Information Science Technical Report No. MS-CIS-10-10.*, Feb 2010.

[24] M. Xie, H. Wang, J. Yin, and X. Meng. Integrity auditing of outsourced data. In *Proceedings of the 33rd international conference on Very large data bases*, VLDB '07, pages 782–793. VLDB Endowment, 2007.

[25] M. Xie, H. Wang, J. Yin, and X. Meng. Providing freshness guarantees for outsourced databases. In *Proceedings of the 11th international conference on Extending database technology: Advances in database technology*, EDBT '08, pages 323–332, New York, NY, USA, 2008. ACM.

[26] Y. Yang, D. Papadias, S. Papadopoulos, and P. Kalnis. Authenticated join processing in outsourced databases. In *Proceedings of the 35th SIGMOD international conference on Management of data*, SIGMOD '09, pages 5–18, New York, NY, USA, 2009. ACM.

[27] J. You, J. Xi, C. Zhang, and G. Guo. Hdw: A high performance large scale data warehouse. In *Proceedings of the 2008 International Multi-symposiums on Computer and Computational Sciences*, pages 200–202, Washington, DC, USA, 2008. IEEE Computer Society.

APPENDIX

A. MERKLE HASH TREE

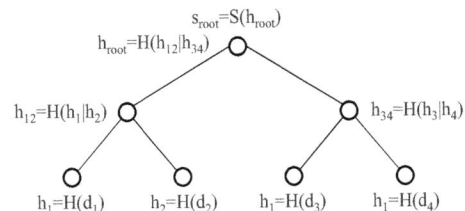

Figure 19: A Merkle Hash Tree Example.

A Merkle Hash Tree (MHT) is a type of data structure, which contains hash values representing a summary information about a large piece of data, and is used to verify the authenticity of the original data. Figure 19 shows an example of a Merkle Hash Tree. Each leaf node is assigned a digest $H(d)$, where H is a one-way hash function. The value of each inner node is derived from its child nodes, e.g. $h_i = H(h_l|h_r)$ where $|$ denotes concatenation. The value of the root node is signed, usually by the data owner. The tree can be used to authenticate any subset of the data by generating a verification object (VO). For example, to authenticate d_1, the VO contains h_2, h_{34} and the root signature s_{root}. The recipient first computes $h_1 = H(d_1)$ and $H(H(h_1|h_2)|h_{34})$, then checks if the latter is the same with the signature s_{root}. If so, d_1 is accepted; otherwise, it indicates that d_1 has been altered.

Multi-user Dynamic Proofs of Data Possession using Trusted Hardware

Stephen R. Tate
Dept. of Computer Science
UNC Greensboro
srtate@uncg.edu

Roopa Vishwanathan
Dept. of Computer Science
UNC Greensboro
r_vishwa@uncg.edu

Lance Everhart
Dept. of Computer Science
UNC Greensboro
lmeverh2@uncg.edu

ABSTRACT

In storage outsourcing services, clients store their data on a potentially untrusted server, which has more computational power and storage capacity than the individual clients. In this model, security properties such as integrity, authenticity, and freshness of stored data ought to be provided, while minimizing computational costs at the client, and communication costs between the client and the server. Using trusted computing technology on the server's side, we propose practical constructions in the provable data possession model that provide *integrity* and *freshness* in a dynamic, multi-user setting, where groups of users can update their shared files on the remote, untrusted server. Unlike previous solutions based on a single-user, single-device model, we consider a multi-user, multi-device model. Using trusted hardware on the server helps us to eliminate some of the previously known challenges with this model, such as *forking* and *rollback* attacks by the server. We logically separate bulk storage and data authentication issues to different untrusted remote services, which can be implemented either on the same or different physical servers. With only minor modifications to existing services, the bulk storage component can be provided by large-scale storage providers such as Google, CloudDrive, DropBox, and a smaller specialized server equipped with a trusted hardware chip can be used for providing data authentication. Our constructions eliminate client-side storage costs (clients do not need to maintain persistent state), and are suitable for situations in which multiple clients work collaboratively on remotely stored, outsourced data.

Categories and Subject Descriptors

H.4 [**Information Systems Applications**]: Miscellaneous; H.3.2 [**Software**]: Security and Protection—*authentication, verification, cryptographic controls*

Keywords

Cloud storage; data outsourcing; trusted hardware

1. INTRODUCTION

In this paper, we devise and present natural and important extensions of the Dynamic Provable Data Possession (DPDP) work of Erway *et al.* [8]. In DPDP, a client maintains a dataset on a remote untrusted server, and the system needs to support data access and modification requests, including data additions, modifications, and deletions. The DPDP protocol provides a proof of integrity when data is accessed, so that the client is assured that neither the untrusted server nor another malicious party has tampered with the data. The solution of Erway *et al.* relies on techniques from authenticated data structures, and in particular maintains an authenticated skip list over data blocks. All operations on the skip list are $O(\log n)$ expected time, and the proof of integrity consists of a sequence of hashes from the leaf or leaves corresponding to the data being accessed up to the root of the skip list, so the time and space required for such a proof is also $O(\log n)$. The client keeps a copy of the root hash value locally, and that is all that is required to authenticate any data access from the server.

The DPDP solution just described assumes a model in which there is a single client using a single client-side device, which does not allow for one of the main advantages of remote storage: the ability of users to access their data from anywhere, on a wide variety of devices, some of which may have only sporadic network access. Furthermore, we would like to support not only multiple client-side devices, but also multiple users, so that any authorized user can update the remotely stored data from any device, but unauthorized users (including a malicious server) cannot make any changes that will be presented as valid on subsequent accesses. Moving from a single-user, single-device client model to a multiple-user, multiple-device client model introduces some obvious problems, as well as some subtle ones, as we describe next.

Allowing multiple client-side devices in the DPDP model of Erway et al. [8] means that each device must have access to the root hash, so there is no single local storage area for root hashes. Considering a user with a desktop system and a mobile device, if the root hash is stored and updated on the desktop computer, and the user later accesses his data from a mobile device, that device may not have the most current root hash for verification. A naïve solution would be to store root hashes remotely with the data, signed by an authorized user's key for integrity — since the key would change far less often than the data hash, keys could be kept on devices in protected local storage. Alternatively, private signing keys could even be stored remotely, encrypted by a key that is derived from a passphrase that can be entered locally on any device, similar to the way "Firefox Sync" stores passwords — this technique can be relatively secure, particularly if combined with some other method of access control.

The problem with the naïve solution is one of **freshness** [33]: If we store root hashes on a remote server, signed or not, when we retrieve them we have no way of knowing that the server is returning our most recent value. This is similar in concept to the well-known notion of a replay attack, and in the context of remote storage is sometimes called a "roll back attack" [10] or a "forking attack" [19, 32]. The notion of forking comes from the following scenario: consider what would happen if the server made a snapshot of the current data, including the root hash, and then accepted a change from the user's desktop system. The user (or perhaps even a different authorized user) then accesses the data from a mobile device, and is given the old copy from the snapshot. These two versions could then be associated with these two different client machines, and could evolve separately, forking the stored data contents into two (or more) histories of changes that form a consistent view for that device. If there is no authentic communication between the devices, there is no way to detect that they are working with different versions of the data. In the distributed computing community, it is accepted that this is impossible to avoid without either a trusted server or communication between different clients, and a notion of "fork consistency" has been defined for this: a solution has fork consistency if the view of any client device is internally consistent, even if globally there are multiple histories. Examples of work in the distributed computing community that explores this notion include the SUNDR networked file server [16] and the SPORC group collaboration system [9].

Since client devices may only occasionally be online, we cannot rely on direct device-to-device communication to detect forked storage state, so some form of trusted server must be used. Our focus in this paper is to minimize the amount of trust needed to create a system that avoids problems with forking, while maintaining integrity and freshness of data. In particular, we don't want to trust the parties running the server, nor do we want to trust an open computing system, regardless of who is running the system. Our solution utilizes lightweight trusted hardware, similar to the Trusted Platform Modules (TPMs) [31] that are being included in many current systems. While our technique could be implemented using current TPM standards, the resulting solution would be inefficient, so we instead consider TPM extensions proposed by Sarmenta *et al.* for efficient "virtual monotonic counters" (counters which can never repeat values, even across machine reboots) [25]. These extensions are consistent with existing TPM capabilities, but allow for better and more efficient support for applications that rely on monotonic counters. While not providing the same level of assurance as a purely-hardware based solution, one could also implement our technique using other forms of small-size trusted computing models such as TrustVisor [21], or its predecessor Flicker [22].

In addition to considering a server that maintains a single data store, we extend this to consider a hierarchy of stored objects like a standard tree-based filesystem. Our solution for this model avoids keeping a signed root hash for each stored object, but rather relies on the hierarchical structure to define "control points" which have associated signed values. These control points correspond to places in the hierarchy in which access control changes, and so are significantly less numerous than the number of objects. This both reduces the number of trusted values that must be managed through our trusted hardware-based solution and reduces the number of public key operations that must be performed to verify signatures when data is accessed. Control points also give a convenient way to increase throughput for a complete remote storage solution, by distributing management of different control points across separate servers. While certain aspects of our solution, such as the bulk storage server, can be further distributed for load balancing or resilience, properties of the authentication server create significant challenges for distributing further, and we leave these challenges open for future work.

Contributions: In summary, the work described in this paper provides the following contributions:

- We extend the DPDP model to allow for data updates from multiple devices as well as multiple users in an authorized group, and provide a solution that avoids client-to-client communication by using a small TPM-like trusted hardware component. Supporting this solution, we provide two specific implementations that have slightly different properties (one of which provides anonymity to users within a group).

- We develop a new, efficient way of validating many virtual monotonic counters at once, layered on top of the TPM extensions proposed by Sarmenta *et al.* [25]. This solution is several orders of magnitude faster than the straightforward solution, allowing the processing of requests at realistic server speeds.

- We extend the single data object model to support a hierarchical filesystem in which updates for different parts of the hierarchy are restricted to users or groups of users, and we provide a general framework for efficiently supporting this model.

- We provide some preliminary experimental results that explore the feasibility of these techniques, and how well they scale to multiple active users.

1.1 Paper Outline

In Section 2, we briefly review and compare relevant related work. In Section 3, we describe the multi-user DPDP scheme using trusted hardware, and describe two possible implementations of it that use either group signatures or user certificates. In Section 4, we extend our multi-user DPDP scheme to multiple objects in a hierarchical filesystem. In Section 5, we provide security definitions and analysis. In Section 6, we present some preliminary experimental results, and in Section 7, we conclude the paper.

2. RELATED WORK

Security issues in outsourced storage systems have led to the development of two main solution models: proofs of data possession (PDP) which offer tamper-evidence, and proofs of retrievability (PoR) which offer tamper-tolerance. Our work is designed to fit into the PDP model.

The concept of PDP was introduced by Ateniese *et al.* who presented an efficient protocol for static (read-only) data stores [1], and in later work designed a protocol for a somewhat limited dynamic setting [3]. Subsequently, Erway *et al.* presented a fully dynamic PDP protocol [8]. Our paper is most closely aligned with this line of work, in an extended model with multiple users and multiple client devices, while maintaining the $O(\log n)$ efficiency of the best previous fully dynamic single-user, single-device solution due to Erway *et al.* [8]. Specific challenges in this extension were described in the Introduction.

Iris [28] offers practical solutions to most major security issues such as integrity, freshness, scalability, and retrievability, but requires a trusted third party that can perform involved computations and store fairly large quantities of cached data. Proofs of retrievability (PoRs) [13, 26, 35, 28] are a related concept in which the client is assured of data retrievability, in addition to just data integrity and freshness verification (we do not deal with retrievability). In recent work in secure storage, Xiong *et al.* [34] and Goodrich *et al.* [11] have independently proposed ways to securely store, share and distribute data through a public, untrusted cloud. These works tackle a different issue: they focus on providing *confidentiality* of data stored on the server, whereas we focus on providing *integrity* and *freshness* of data. Confidentiality is an orthogonal issue for us, and can be layered on top of our protocols (by using encryption, access control policies, private communication channels, etc.).

Although our work is in the PDP model, which has a different flavor than the distributed computing community's idea of remote file storage, there are some distributed computing works that are worth mentioning. One of the early influential works in secure remote file storage was SUNDR [16, 20] which is a network file system stored on an untrusted, possibly remote, server. SUNDR introduced the notion of "fork consistency" that gives any two clients the ability to detect inconsistencies in their views of data, only if the clients can communicate with each other (and also maintain local meta-data). It was widely accepted that fork consistency is the best notion of data consistency one can achieve in the presence of an untrusted server and non-communicating clients, and SUNDR's forking semantics were used by others to implement remote storage protocols [6, 17, 5]. Our contribution relative to SUNDR and related work is a solution in the DPDP model in which clients do not communicate with each other and in which the only trusted server component is an embedded TPM.

Other works that provide integrity and consistency guarantees include SPORC [9], Venus [27] (requires a core group of trusted clients to be always online), Depot [18], and works that use a trusted component such as A2M [7]. TrInc [15] proposes the use of monotonic counter-based attestation in a peer-to-peer distributed system. We consider monotonic counters in the context of remote untrusted storage, and analyze the issues that come up therein (e.g., concurrency, consistency). Also, as we discuss in Section 6, a direct application of monotonic counter-based attestation to remote storage would result in a system with an unacceptably slow throughput of between 1 and 3 requests per second, which is insufficient for practical applications.

All of these distributed computing works are robust, have many desirable properties, and are interesting in their own ways. But by and large, they require clients to store some form of local meta-data for verification purposes. Our use-case consists of multiple clients that access the server from non-communicating devices that can have sporadic and/or untrusted network connections. To avoid the need for all clients to keep all of their devices always up-to-date with the latest local meta-data, one of our main motivating goals is to eliminate client-side meta-data storage.

To increase attestation throughput, we introduce a novel technique for batching TPM counter attestations. A similar problem was addressed by Moyer *et al.* for the purpose of providing attestations for a general web server, and their solution shares some properties with ours including the use of Merkle hash trees [24]. However, while they also answer multiple client requests with a single TPM attestation operation, their solution relies on an external, trusted time server. By using a time server, Moyer *et al.* can provide attestations for static content using a cached recent attestation, which reduces latency for static requests; however, handling dynamic requests re-introduces a small latency, resulting in similar performance to our technique, while still requiring the trusted time server.

3. MULTI-USER DPDP SOLUTION

In this section, we provide a threat model for our work, and extend the single-user, single-device DPDP model to the multi-user, multi-device model.

3.1 Threat Model

Assets and Goals: In the most basic model, the asset we are concerned with is a data object that is stored on a remote, network-accessible resource, and associated metadata that is maintained to support the security requirements. The goal is to preserve *integrity* (including authentication of updates) and *freshness* of the data object as seen by remote clients. In particular, users accessing the data object should be able to tell if the data that they received is the latest data that was stored by an authorized user (see "parties" below). For the purposes of this paper, we do not consider other goals such as confidentiality and availability, both of which can be addressed independently (e.g., [34, 11, 4, 18]). Extensions to multiple objects with more involved group-oriented access control policies are considered in Section 4.

Parties: The main parties actively involved in the system are clients and the service providers. The service providers are the Storage Server (**SS**) and the Authentication Server (**AS**), the latter of which is equipped with a Trusted Platform Module (TPM) chip whose properties are described in Definition 1. Both can potentially be corrupt, could collaborate, and can collude with outside parties. Clients and other parties are divided into authorized and unauthorized users, and only authorized clients are allowed to modify the data object in a way that will be accepted by users on subsequent accesses. Other non-participating, peripheral parties include the TPM manufacturer and a Privacy CA that certifies public keys belonging to the TPM.

Definition 1. The *Trusted Platform Security Assumption* is the assumption that TPMs are built by a honest manufacturer according to an open specification, and satisfy the following properties:

1. *Tamper-resistant hardware:* It is infeasible to extract or modify secret data or keys that are stored in protected locations in the TPM, except through well-defined interfaces given in the TPM specification.

2. *Secure Encryption:* The asymmetric encryption algorithm used by the TPM is CCA-secure.

3. *Secure Signatures:* The digital signature algorithm used by the TPM is existentially unforgeable under adaptive chosen message attacks.

4. *One-way Functions:* For generating hash digests, the TPM uses strongly collision-resistant one-way functions.

5. *Trustworthy PrivacyCA:* Only valid TPM-bound keys are certified by a trusted PrivacyCA.

Note that we do not rely on system-level attestation properties used in a lot of trusted computing applications, but only on properties of the TPM chip.

Threat Vectors: Attackers can consist of any collusion between servers and non-authorized clients, who can intercept and tamper with communication in arbitrary ways. Beyond this, we do not enumerate specific attacks, but rather take the approach that is common in cryptography: we model all colluding attackers as a single computational adversary, and any attack that can be performed by this adversary in polynomial time is fair game. The specific sequence of actions followed by the adversary, and how it chooses to use its resources, are non-deterministic in nature. The formal security properties of our constructions are sketched in the longer version of this paper [30], and are addressed more fully in ongoing work.

3.2 DPDP Definitions

The intuition behind DPDP is simple: A server stores a data object, which can be read from or updated. While the intuition is simple, a full definition of the precise model was one of the contributions of Erway *et al.*, who provided careful definitions of core operations and required communication. In the simple data model of Erway *et al.*, there is a single data object with multiple blocks, and blocks can be read, modified, inserted, or deleted [8]. While page limitations do not allow for a full repetition of the DPDP model here, we provide a brief overview, and refer the reader to the original paper for full details.

The system is initialized using a KeyGen operation which establishes cryptographic keys. Information is stored on a server, while the client retains a small amount of verification information called the metadata. Authenticated retrievals work by the client evaluating a Challenge function to create a retrieval challenge message to send to the server, who executes a Prove procedure which produces the data being retrieved along with a proof P of its authenticity, which is sent back to the user. The user then uses a Verify procedure to check the proof against a local copy of the data store's current metadata M_c. Updates also involve three functions, where the client starts by executing a PrepareUpdate function to create messages to send to the server. The server executes a PerformUpdate function, which updates the data it is storing, calculates new metadata $M_{c'}$, and creates a proof P that the update was performed correctly. Upon receiving $M_{c'}$ and P, the client executes a VerifyUpdate function with the proof and its copy of current metadata M_c to verify that the update was performed correctly.

Since we are considering multiple users, we refer to the group of one or more users that is authorized to modify this data object as the "authorized modifiers." In Section 4 we will show how this can be extended to a hierarchical filesystem of objects, supporting different access control lists for different objects. As explained in the Introduction, the key

to supporting access from multiple devices is the ability to store the authenticating metadata on a shared but potentially untrusted server, and this causes problems with freshness and forking attacks. Sarmenta *et al.* sketched a solution to a similar problem using trusted hardware to support monotonic counters [25], but assumed a single user making updates with access control on the server to enforce this. We use Sarmenta *et al.*'s work as a starting point, and devise a solution that allows us to deal effectively with groups of authorized modifiers, and we also provide significant efficiency improvements when compared with the original techniques.

3.3 Virtual Monotonic Counters

Sarmenta *et al.* consider the issue of freshness for remote storage [25], and propose the use of a TPM as a solution. Among other capabilities, a standard TPM contains monotonic counters, which are hardware-based counters that can only be incremented, and will never repeat a value, even over a reboot. Additionally, TPMs work with Attestation Identity Keys (AIKs), which are digital signature keypairs whose secret key is only usable inside the TPM and is only used for signing (attesting) values that come from inside the TPM. A local or remote user can obtain the current counter value with a high level of assurance by having the TPM sign the counter value along with a user-supplied nonce.

Many interesting applications can be designed using dedicated monotonic counters, but unfortunately TPMs support only a very limited number of monotonic counters in hardware, and have just one counter active in any boot cycle. The main contribution of Sarmenta *et al.* was the idea of "virtual monotonic counters," leveraging the limited protected hardware to support a very large number of independent monotonic counters, along with two implementations of this general idea. One solution, called the log-based scheme, can be implemented using current TPMs, but can be very inefficient in some situations. The other solution, the hash tree-based scheme, provides much better performance but requires small and practical extensions to TPMs.

In the context of a digital wallet application, Tate and Vishwanathan performed a thorough experimental comparison of the log-based scheme and the hash tree-based scheme under a variety of workloads [29]. A representative result from that paper showed that when maintaining 1024 virtual counters, the hash tree-based scheme performed around 900 times faster than the log-based scheme for round-robin counter requests. On realistic non-uniform distributions, the average gain decreased to around 15 times faster for the hash-tree based scheme, but the worst case has an amazing speed difference of over 2000 times. While our remote storage solution could in fact use either of these virtual monotonic counter implementations, due to these substantial speed improvements we focus on the hash tree-based scheme. We next give a quick review of virtual monotonic counters and the hash tree-based scheme, and then explain our technique for "batching" attestation requests that allows the server to attest counter values at a rate that is a couple of orders magnitude higher than straightforward application of prior techniques.

3.3.1 Basic Techniques

Hash trees are a well-known tool for authenticating large data sets [23], where some part of the data set can be authenticated without knowing or processing the rest of the data set (contrasted with, for example, hashing the entire data set, requiring re-hashing and processing all data in order to very authenticity). Hash trees work by providing an *authenticating path* for any data in a leaf of the tree, along with a hash value from the root of the tree that can be compared against a known-good hash value.

Sarmenta *et al.* show how to support many virtual monotonic counters by using a hash tree of counter values with the root hash protected by trusted hardware (an enhanced TPM). While protecting a large number of virtual monotonic counters, the only value that must be closely protected is the root hash, which is well within the capability of even limited devices like TPMs. By carefully defining operations that update the root hash (which require the user to provide authenticating path information to the TPM), the necessary security properties of virtual monotonic counters can be assured. While not used by Sarmenta *et al.* for remote storage applications, they do allow for data to be associated with each counter at a hash tree leaf, and that data is tightly bound to the counter since it must be provided as leaf-data in any authentication operation. We make use of this associated data in a non-obvious way, to support access control in our multi-user DPDP solution. We briefly list operations defined by Sarmenta *et al.* on virtual monotonic counters — note that the result of all operations is provided in the form of an "execution certificate", which contains the user-supplied nonce and is signed by a TPM-bound AIK:

- CreateCounter($pos, data, nonce$) → id: Creates a new counter in hash tree position *pos*, with a random component of the *id* assigned by the TPM (this is so that hashtree positions can be reused for new counters, with negligible probability of reusing an actual *id* that would "reset" that counter). *data* is the data associated with the counter.

- ReadCounter($id, nonce$) → ($count, data$): Returns the current count value and associated data for counter *id*.

- IncrementCounter($id, data, nonce$) → $count$: Increments counter *id* and associates new *data* with the new count value, returning the incremented counter value.

To these operations we make a simple addition to provide an attested copy of the root hash — note that we could do this by simply reading any counter, but providing a direct command simplifies our applications:

- AttestRoot($nonce$) → $root\_hash$: Returns an attested copy of the root hash.

3.3.2 Batching Attestations

While virtual monotonic counters provide the functionality needed for our remote storage solution, the performance of the basic solutions from Sarmenta *et al.* would only be sufficient for low-volume applications. Every data read operation will require retrieving an attested counter value, which means the TPM must perform a digital signature operation for this attestation. Tests timing signature speed of a variety of version 1.2 TPMs found that digital signature speed varied from around 300ms to around 760ms [12], and so the fastest of these TPMs would only be able to make about three signatures per second. Since every attestation must include a user-supplied nonce in the signed counter value, it is not clear how we could satisfy client requests any faster than this three-per-second baseline; however, we next show

how we can batch requests to greatly improve the rate at which counter verifications can be provided.

We once again rely on hash trees as a tool to enable the solution to our problem. Counter attestation requests are of the form ReadCounter($id, nonce$), as described in the previous section, so consider a sequence of n such requests given as $(id_1, nonce_1), (id_2, nonce_2), \ldots, (id_n, nonce_n)$. To answer these requests efficiently, we create a hash tree with the request nonces at the leaves, and call the root hash of this tree $TPMnonce$. We issue the TPM command AttestRoot($TPMnonce$), getting a signed copy of an execution certificate containing both the TPM-managed counter hashtree root and $TPMnonce$.

The server then assembles responses to attestation requests as follows: For request $(id_i, nonce_i)$, it sends out the authenticating path from the virtual monotonic counter hash tree for counter id_i (which includes the counter value and the root hash), the authenticating path from the nonce hash tree for $nonce_i$ (which includes $TPMnonce$), and the signed attestation that links the counter root hash with $TPMnonce$. We argue that this is secure, based on the following reasoning (which we formalize in the full version of this paper): $TPMnonce$ must have been computed after the server received $nonce_i$, since $nonce_i$ went into the computation of $TPMnonce$ through a secure hash function for which it is infeasible to find collisions. Furthermore, the TPM attestation must have taken place after $TPMnonce$ was computed, since that is included in the signed TPM response. These two facts taken together ensure that the counter root hash, which the TPM guarantees was current when the attestation was made, is no older than the time that $nonce_i$ was received by the server. Finally, since the counter hash tree guarantees that the reported value of counter id_i was current when the attestation was made, then that virtual monotonic counter value is no older than the time that $nonce_i$ was received — this is precisely the freshness guarantee that we are seeking.

The technique just described gives a way to answer multiple attestation requests with a single TPM attestation operation. Since the TPM operation is the bottleneck in responding to rapid attestation requests, this can give significant increases in the rate at which attestation requests can be answers. When responding to a stream of requests, we overlap request batching with TPM operations, as shown in this diagram:

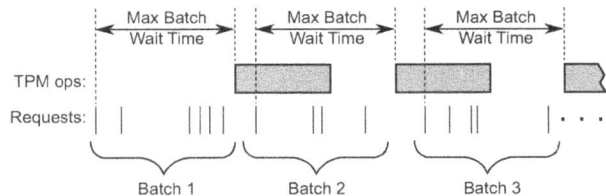

Requests are denoted by vertical bars, and TPM operations are denoted by the boxes. At all times the server is either in an `idle` state, meaning no attestation requests are outstanding, or a `batching` state. We define a parameter called the "Max Batch Wait Time" to be amount of time the system waits after receiving an attestation request until it starts a TPM operation. If the server is `idle` and it receives a request, it sets a timer for "Max Batch Wait Time" and enters the `batching` state. When the timer runs out, the server sends attestation command to the TPM (using

$TPMnonce$), and re-enters the `idle` state. When the TPM command completes, the server constructs attestation responses, which it sends to clients. Selecting the "Max Batch Wait Time" is a trade-off between the rate at which requests can be serviced (the higher the wait time, the larger the batches, so the more efficient the service), and the maximum latency of a request.

It is important to note that the client interface for getting an attested counter value is almost identical to before: the client provides the counter id and a nonce, and receives a response that includes a TPM-signed attestation that depends in a strong way on the nonce that the client provided. Verification on the client side must add a verification of the nonce hash tree path, but that is the only difference from the straightforward use of virtual monotonic counters. As we will see in the Experiments section, this batching technique significantly increases the rate at which counter attestations can be produced.

3.4   Multi-User DPDP

To define multi-user DPDP, we first introduce notation for users and groups, as well as generic notation for testing group membership. We use U to denote the entire universe of users, both those with access to the data object and those without, and there is a designated group $G \subseteq U$ of users that are authorized to modify the data object. A special user, known as the group manager and denoted GM, is authorized to create the data object with the remote storage service and can designate which users are members of G. We assume a generic digital signature based service which can be used to authenticate whether a message was created by a member of G. In particular, there is a public key PK_G associated with the group, and each user u has an individual signing key $SK_{G,u}$ associated with this group. Two basic operations are supported:

- $GSign(SK_{G,u}, m) \rightarrow \sigma$: Used by user u to create a signature σ on message m.

- $GVerify(PK_G, m, \sigma) \rightarrow$ true/false: Verifies whether σ is a valid signature on m for group G (using G's public key PK_G).

We assume that any such signature scheme satisfies basic unforgeability properties, and in Section 3.6 we describe two different schemes to implement this service.

The key problem with extending earlier DPDP results, such as the work of Erway *et al.* [8], involves maintaining authentication metadata in a centrally accessible location so that clients have assurance that metadata that they retrieve from this central location is authentic and fresh. Our solution logically separates the problems of maintaining metadata from the problem of bulk storage into two servers, the "Authentication Server" (denoted **AS**) and the "Storage Server" (denoted **SS**), respectively. This is a logical separation, and the two servers could in fact be hosted on the same physical server, although the requirements are different. **AS** requires a TPM, but has low storage and throughput requirements, whereas **SS** has high storage and throughput requirements but does not need a TPM to authenticate operations. The two servers only interact with client devices, and never directly with each other, so could in fact be provided by two entirely separate entities.

3.4.1   **AS**: *The Authentication Server*

In this section we describe the authentication server **AS**. This server is a means for storing metadata associated with the stored data in such a way that the client can be sure that it is authentic and fresh. Metadata is stored in a pair $m = (vno, M_c)$ that ties it to a version number, and **AS** also stores a signature σ over m that can be verified as a signature from an authorized modifier (i.e., $GVerify(PK_G, m, \sigma)$ accepts the signature as coming from a member of the group G). When queried, **AS** can provide both m and the matching σ, and can also use its TPM to attest to the fact that the version number in m is the current version number. In the notation below, $auth\_vno$ refers to this TPM attestation on the version number: specifically, $auth\_vno$ will be produced as the result of an interactive protocol in which the client sends a random $nonce$ to the server, which executes the TPM command $\mathsf{ReadCounter}(id, nonce)$ — $auth\_vno$ is the resulting execution certificate that includes the version number and nonce signed by a TPM-bound AIK.

- $\mathsf{Init}(PK_G, nonce) \rightarrow id$: Access control on **AS** only allows the group manager to execute this command, which initializes **AS** to set up a new data store. **AS** assigns an id number to the new data store, and executes the TPM command $\mathsf{CreateCounter}(pos, PK_G, nonce)$. Note that the second argument to $\mathsf{CreateCounter}$ is the data that is bound by the TPM to this new counter, and by setting this to be the group G's verification key PK_G, we bind that verification key to the counter in a strong, TPM-enforced way.

- $\mathsf{GetVersion}(id, nonce) \rightarrow (auth\_vno, m, \sigma)$: This command provides the current version number and data identified by id, in a way that can be authenticated as authorized and fresh. In particular, σ is a valid signature on m (i.e., $GVerify(PK_G, m, \sigma)$ accepts), and the version number in m is attested to by the TPM as current by executing TPM command $\mathsf{ReadCounter}(id, nonce)$ and returning the AIK-signed execution certificate as $auth\_vno$ (along with m and σ).

- $\mathsf{GetCurrNextVersion}(id, nonce) \rightarrow (auth\_vno, m, \sigma, nv)$: This is the similar to $\mathsf{GetVersion}$, but sets an exclusive lock for this client for id (if some other client holds a lock on id, this operation fails), and returns the next available version number nv in addition to the attested current version number.

- $\mathsf{ReleaseLock}(id)$: This releases the lock that this client holds on id, and is used when the protocol must be aborted (e.g., due to a failure with **SS**).

- $\mathsf{UpdateVersion}(id, m, \sigma, nonce) \rightarrow auth\_vno$: First, **AS** first checks to make sure that this client holds the update lock for this id, with the same "new version number" that is in m, and then retrieves the data associated with counter id (which was set in Init to be the verification key PK_G, and retained as this value on all subsequent operations). **AS** then runs $GVerify(PK_G, m, \sigma)$ to verify that this update is coming from an authorized group member. If these tests succeed, **AS** executes TPM command $\mathsf{IncrementCounter}(id, PK_G, nonce)$ and returns the AIK-signed execution certificate showing the new version number. Whether successful or not, in any case, **AS** invalidates the update lock held by this client for id.

There are a few important things to note about the services provided by **AS**. First, since GM initializes the system by associating PK_G with the virtual monotonic counter id, and the only change to this counter is through UpdateVersion which keeps the same data PK_G, this binds the authorized group strongly to this counter, and only updates which are accompanied by a signature that verifies with this key are accepted.[1] Note that the clients do not have to trust **AS** on this point, since the counter-associated data PK_G is part of the signed execution certificate ($auth\_vno$) that accompanies all responses to client requests — clients could immediately tell if this public verification key were changed by a malicious **AS**. Another important thing to notice is the use of the exclusive update lock: This allows the full update, including interaction with **SS**, to be atomic and sequenced with other requests from other concurrent clients. This lock should have some timeout value so that a client that fails before completing the update operation would not lock up the system (if a slow client responds after the timeout, the only consequence would be that the UpdateVersion operation fails).

3.4.2 SS: *The Storage Server*

The storage server **SS** is primarily an implementation of a basic single-client DPDP scheme, with the addition of version numbers and locks to handle concurrency and consistency issues. Due to page limitations we do not go into details here, but will instead focus on how **SS** is modified to address problems that are unique to the multi-client setting. Our two significant changes include the use of version numbers and the addition of an update lock.

Version numbers form a monotonically increasing sequence of values, and each time the data is updated a new version number is assigned. The server retains old versions for some amount of time, but may only update the most recent version, similar to partially persistent data structures [14]. Every client request to **SS** must contain a version number, but otherwise looks like a standard DPDP request. While the source of the version numbers is not relevant for the functioning of **SS**, we note here that our full protocol retrieves version numbers from **AS**, which in turn gets them from virtual monotonic counters managed by its TPM.

Since the requests to **SS** are coming through a single monotonic source, the requests should, for the most part, be monotonically sequenced. It is still possible for **SS** to receive out-of-sequence requests due to some clients being slower than others, and we keep old versions for some time so that slow clients are not indefinitely delayed due to failed requests. We discuss more fully how concurrency and consistency issues are resolved in Section 3.5, after the full protocol is defined. As far as **SS** is concerned, its behavior is controlled by the system parameter $accom\_time$ (or "accommodation time"), which could be mutually agreed upon when the group manager sets up service with **SS**. Version numbers are managed by keeping track of the highest version number seen so far in a request ($curr\_vno$) and a set old_vno_deaths that stores, for each old version number, a "time of death" after which requests for that version will no longer be answered. To update these values, when the server receives the first request for a new version number, beyond $curr\_vno$, it puts $curr\_vno$ in the old_vno_deaths sets with a "time of death" set to the current time plus $accom\_time$, and then $curr\_vno$ is updated with the newly-received version number. Therefore, slow clients have the amount of time specified by $accom\_time$ to get read requests in before the old version dies. Note that $curr\_vno$ is *not* updated when the DPDP operation PerformUpdate is performed — rather it is the next request from a client that contains the new version number that triggers the update. This is an important point which will be explained more fully in Section 3.5.

SS is also enhanced from a single-client DPDP server by the inclusion of update locking. When a data object is initially created on **SS**, the public key of the authorized modifier group is stored on the server, and lock requests must be signed to show that they came from an authorized user. In particular, at the beginning of an update the client requests an exclusive update lock using both the current version number and the next version number. Each lock request must be signed by the client identifying it as a member of an authorized group. If the signature verifies, **SS** allows the client to proceed with the update. Unlike read requests, there is no accommodation time for update requests, so the version number must match $curr\_vno$ and there must be no other client locking that version in order for the request to succeed. To protect against clients that fail, a system parameter $lock\_timeout$ determines how long the lock will be held before the lock is released and the overdue PerformUpdate request will not be accepted.

3.4.3 *Complete Multi-User DPDP Protocol*

In this section we describe how the client works with **AS** and **SS** in the complete multi-user DPDP protocol. First we present the protocol for authenticated data retrieval.

Retrieve protocol for user u:

1. **Get Version Number:** u generates a random *nonce* and executes GetVersion(id, *nonce*) with **AS** to get the current, fresh version number vno of the data object, and signature σ over a tuple $m = (vno, M_c)$, where M_c is in the form of metadata from the underlying DPDP system. u verifies the TPM-based freshness attestation on vno, checks that the version number in the freshness attestation matches the version number in the signed tuple, and computes $GVerify(PK_G, m, \sigma)$ to verify that M_c was authenticated by an authorized modifier (i.e., member of G).

2. **Get Data:** u and **SS** execute Challenge and Prove using version number vno, and u verifies the result using Verify and metadata M_c from the previous step. If all verifications succeed, u is assured that it has retrieved authentic data.

Next, we give the protocol for a user to update part or all of the stored data.

Update protocol for user u:

1. **Get Version Numbers:** u picks a random *nonce* and executes GetCurrNextVersion(id, *nonce*) with **AS** to get current version number vno and next version number nv, and an exclusive update lock registered with **AS**. If u fails to receive the lock from **AS**, it delays based on some backoff strategy and tries again. A successful execution of GetCurrNextVersion provides a signed tu-

---

[1] For key management purposes, it might be good to have a "change key" command that GM could execute, but this is a simple extension that we leave out of our current discussion.

ple $m = (cvno, M_c)$ containing current metadata M_c, and is verified as it was in the retrieve protocol.

2. **Perform Update:** This is an interactive protocol run between C and **SS**. u sends $GSign(SK_{G,u}(cvno, nvno))$ to **SS** to obtain an update lock. **SS** verifies the signature with PK_G, and if verification is successful, grants an update lock to u. Once the lock is obtained, u can perform whatever data retrievals are necessary to prepare its update using $cvno$,[2] and then use Prepare-Update to make the update request that u sends to **SS**. **SS** then executes PerformUpdate to produce updated metadata M'_c and proof $P_{M'_c}$ which it sends back to u. Finally, u uses the VerifyUpdate procedure from the DPDP scheme to check the information **SS** provided — if the update information is not accepted, then u should contact **AS** to release its update lock, and then follow error-handling procedures to decide whether to retry the update or just report an error to the user.

3. **Update Version Number:** If the update transaction with **SS** was accepted in the previous step, then we finish the transaction by updating the metadata storage on **AS**: First, u constructs the pair $m = (nvno, M'_c)$ and computes $\sigma = GSign(SK_{G,u}, m)$. Then u executes UpdateVersion$(id, m, \sigma, nonce)$ with **AS**. If this succeeds, **AS** will complete the operation, which includes releasing its update lock for this transaction.

3.5 Concurrency, Consistency, and Freshness

In this section we address issues of concurrent updates, and show how multiple devices and users each get a consistent view of the data with strong freshness guarantees. We use the term "client" to refer to a user/device pair, so different clients could in fact represent the same user accessing the service from different devices. The following example shows the different possibilities for timing of requests from multiple clients, where **AS** interaction is shown on the left of the time-line (which goes down), and **SS** interaction is shown on the right. Clients are identified as c1, c2, and so on, and requests are abbreviated for compactness (e.g., GCV is for GetCurrentVersion, UpV is for UpdateVersion, etc.).

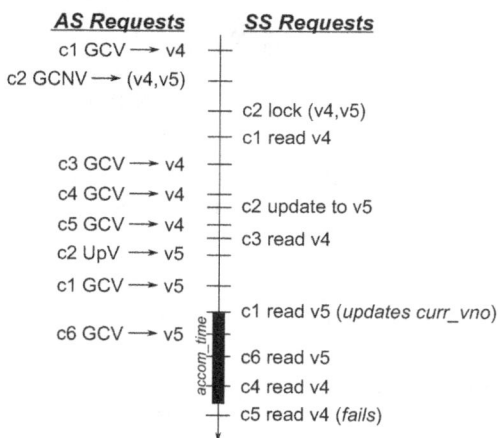

We consider a few interesting scenarios below that could potentially involve race conditions when there is an overlap

---

[2]Note that the authenticated version number provides a reliable way of validating data cached for added efficiency.

between clients who try to read/update the data store at the same time. We do not consider clients whose read-only requests overlap with each other, or clients whose update requests do not overlap with other requests, since those are straightforward cases. In the diagram, client c2 is updating the data store, while all other clients are reading data.

Overlapping read/update requests: Client c1 places a request which starts before any c2 operations, and so will complete its operation with the version that was current when c1 made its request to **AS** (assuming it does so in time — see "slow clients" below for the alternative). c3 and c4 both start read requests by getting the initial version number (v4) from **AS**, and succeed with this version number despite the fact that c2 performs the update operation on **SS** before they issue the read request to **SS**. In our protocol, the current version number tracked by **SS** is not updated until a read request comes in with a new version number. The point of this is to guarantee that the version number on **AS** has been updated, without requiring any interaction between **SS** and **AS**. Therefore when c3's read request is made to **SS**, it proceeds as if there had been no update operation on **SS**. For c4, there is indeed a new version on **SS**, but the previous version is returned because the read request comes before the accommodation time for old versions expires.

Overlapping update requests: Update locks on **SS** and **AS** are granted exclusively to an authorized, requesting client for up until a maximum time limit (to prevent starvation), so it is not possible for two or more legitimate updates that correctly follow our protocol to overlap. Since lock requests are signed, it is impossible for an unauthorized user to be granted a lock and start an update sequence, so overlapping with unauthorized users is also not a possibility.

Slow clients: When c1's read request comes through for version v5, $curr\_vno$ is updated on **SS** and the accommodation time clock is started. At that point we have two clients who have not completed their read requests, with c5 being a particularly slow client that does not complete its read request until after the accommodation time expires. Therefore, c5's request fails, which is the only possible action in a system that enforces freshness. A slow client performing an update proceeds analogously, with the requirement that it must complete its update before the locks time out. While this isn't strictly necessary to enforce freshness, some form of lock timeout is necessary to recover from client failures. If handling slow client updates becomes a problem, either the lock timeout can be increased or the client could be allowed to complete its update operation if no other client has requested and captured the update lock.

3.6 Group Implementations

In this section we describe two ways of implementing the digital signature group membership verification service, with slightly different properties.

Using a Group Signatures Scheme: Group signature schemes are ideally suited to the system we have described. We consider the group signature scheme due to Ateniese *et al.* [2] — due to the tight correspondence between group signature operations and our required operations of $GSign$ and $GVerify$, we do not provide extensive details here. For readers unfamiliar with group signature schemes, we refer them to the Ateniese *et al.* paper for further information.

When a group signature scheme is set up by a group manager, the manager receives both a secret group manager key SK_{GM} and a group public key PK_G, and can use these values to admit individual users to the group through a Join operation. On admission, each member u receives a secret signing key $SK_{G,u}$. This maps quite directly to the definitions of $GSign$ and $GVerify$ that we require, so a group signature scheme is a natural fit for our protocol.

A group signature scheme provides several additional properties that are not necessary in the way we have defined our multi-user DPDP scheme, but might be useful in some situations. In particular, group signature schemes are designed so that signatures from different members of a group are indistinguishable without knowledge of a special secret or trapdoor. In our setting, this means that the data store could be updated so that anyone can verify that the update was made by a legitimate group member, but without additional information it would be infeasible to tell which group member made the update. Signature schemes provide various methods to Open a signature and determine who created a particular signature, but typically only the group manager or some other specially-designated user can do that. This property might be useful in situations where sensitive data is stored on a shared storage server, and tracking that information back to an individual user is undesirable.

Using a Standard Signatures Scheme and Certificates: Standard digital signature schemes such as RSA have been studied far more extensively than group signature schemes, so it might be desirable to rely on standard signatures when the stronger group anonymity properties of group signatures are not needed. In this case, the group manager serves as a certification authority (CA) and issues group-membership certificates to individual users to link their individual public verification keys to the group.

Mapping to our requirements, every signature σ produced by $GSign$ will include not only the user-produced RSA signature, but also a copy of the signing party's group membership certificate. The group public key PK_G is simply the verification key for certificates issued by the group manager, and the $GVerify$ operation checks the validity of the group membership certificate and the RSA signature, both of which are present in signature σ. This is a straightforward scheme the satisfies the requirements of our protocols, albeit without any additional anonymity properties.

4. HIERARCHICAL STORAGE

In this section, we extend the single-object DPDP protocol of Section 3 to a multi-object protocol, where the users update shared objects stored in a filesystem hierarchy. We could, of course, directly use the solution of the previous section where we treat each filesystem object (both files and directories) as a separate, protected data store, each with its own virtual monotonic counter and metadata, but that does not take advantage of savings that are possible due to the hierarchical structure of the filesystem.

Let client groups create files/directories (henceforth referred to as *objects*) on **SS**, and set permission levels for those objects by assigning each object a *label* ℓ, indicating whether the object has the same set of authorized modifiers as its parent. In typical filesystems, most objects will inherit the set of authorized modifiers from its parent, and in that case ℓ is set to "inherit"; otherwise, ℓ is set to "control point",

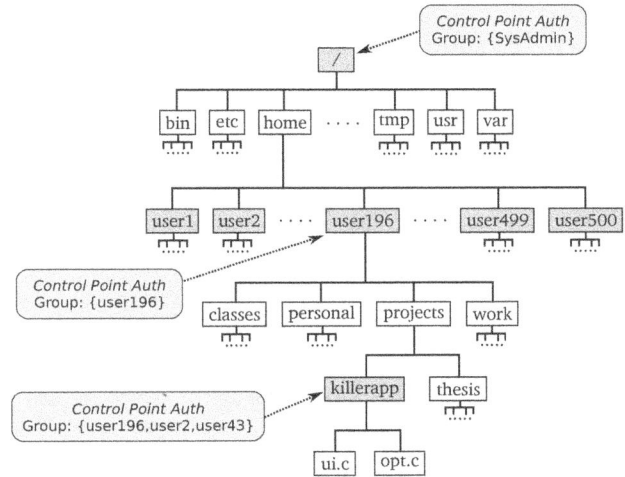

Figure 1: Sample file hierarchy with control points shaded grey, and three control points

and the object is designated as a control point. Authentication data is either signed or propagated up through "inherit" links to a signed directory, where we minimize the use of expensive signatures through inherit labels. An example of such a structure is illustrated in Figure 1.

In Figure 1, the system root directory is designated as a control point, users' home directories are designated as control points as well, since they are exclusively controlled by each user. The contents of each user's home directory is under the exclusive control of that user, but a user can assign read/write privileges selectively to other users if they so wish. In our example, user196 can allow a workgroup permission to modify a collaborative project directory, such as killerapp/ in the figure. Since killerapp/ does not inherit the exclusive permissions of its parent directory, it is designated as a control point.

We now describe protocols for retrieving (reading) an object and updating (writing) to an object.

Protocols for user u:

- **Retrieve:** To retrieve an object from the filesystem, the user performs an authenticated read of that object from the multi-user DPDP data store, which provides the proof and metadata for that retrieve. The user verifies the proof, and checks to see if the object is a control point. If the object is a control point, the user contacts **AS** to verify that the metadata is valid (i.e., has a valid group signature) and fresh. Otherwise, the verification continues recursively up the tree. The final result of a retrieve operation is either verified data or the special response reject indicating that the operation failed.

- **Update:** Update is similar to retrieve, in that the user first accesses and updates the object that she is interested in — if that object is a control point, she signs the metadata and sends it to **AS** to update the current version number. If the object is not a control point, then the user recursively updates the parent object with the new metadata (which continues until a control point is reached).

Referring to Figure 1 for an example, if a user196 is retrieving a file /home/user196/classes/exam.txt, then she will need to do an authenticated read of the file exam.txt, which produces metadata M_{c1} for that file. Since exam.txt is not a control point, there is no verification for M_{c1} on **AS**, but M_{c1} should be embedded in the classes directory object, so we do an authenticated read of that directory information which returns a proof and metadata for the classes directory, which we will call M_{c2}. However, since classes is also not a control point, we cannot verify M_{c2} directly, so do an authenticated retrieve of the metadata M_{c2} from the user196 home directory, which returns the home directory metadata M_{c3}. This *is* a control point, so we verify that M_{c3} is the current value for user196 control point using **AS**, and verification of this metadata authenticates all of the accesses below it, inductively authenticating the file exam.txt.

An update to exam.txt would work similarly to this, but performing updates along the path to the control point rather than just verifications.

The main difference between our hierarchical data storage solution and our original multi-user DPDP solution is in the use of control points. To make this more precise, we provide the following formal definitions of operations on control points.

Definition 2. Hierarchical Storage

1. retrieveControlPoint$((c_i, object), \alpha, P_\alpha) \to \eta$;
   $\eta \in$ ("accept","reject"): This is an interactive protocol run between the client, **AS**, and **SS**, where the client wishes to retrieve a control point stored on **SS**, and verify its integrity and freshness. The client first contacts **AS** to get and verify the current version number and metadata associated with this control point, and then challenges **SS** to prove possession of the control point. The client then verifies the proof given by **SS** using the meta-data obtained from **AS**. If the verification succeeds, the client is assured that it received authentic and fresh data.

2. updateControlPoint$((c_i, \text{object}), (c_i, \text{newObject}),$
   $Sign_{PK_G}(c_i, \text{newObject}), \alpha) \to ((c_i, \text{newObject}), \alpha')$:
   This is an interactive protocol run between the client, **AS** and **SS**, in which the client wishes to update a current control point (c_i, object) with $(c_i, \text{newObject})$. The client first gets the current version number of the control point, and the signature over the control point from **AS**, via the GetVersionNumber protocol, and verifies them. If the verification succeeds, the client executes PerformUpdate with **SS**, where **SS** will prove that it performed the update correctly. If the client accepts the proof, it will update the version information meta-data on **AS** by executing the UpdateVersion protocol.

5. SECURITY PROPERTIES

In this section we discuss the formal security properties of our scheme. We first give some intuition, and then move to a few technical details, with the complete details left to the full version of this paper [30]. Security requirements are defined using a game between an adversary and an oracle that plays the part of honest parties executing the protocol under question. The standard DPDP security model, as developed by Erway *et al.* [8], defines an "Adaptive Chosen File" (or ACF) attack on the system. We use this game as a starting point, adopting certain aspects of the POR security game defined by Juels and Kaliski [13] and extending to explicitly handle multiple objects and groups of users.

All colluding dishonest parties are modeled as a single adversarial entity, $\mathcal{A}$, which is only restricted by requiring that attacks run in polynomial time. Since $\mathcal{A}$ subsumes the functionality of the potentially corrupt **AS**, it has access to **AS**'s TPM, restricted by the Trusted Platform Security Assumption (so $\mathcal{A}$ has no access to any protected data such as secret keys managed by the TPM). On the other side of this game, we model all honest authorized modifiers as a "verifier" party $\mathcal{V}$, since these parties are verifying that the changes that they make are reflected by the servers (i.e., by $\mathcal{A}$). $\mathcal{V}$ operates as an oracle that $\mathcal{A}$ interacts with, maintaining secrets for authorized users such as group signing keys, and exposing an interface that includes oracle functions $\mathcal{O}^{update}$ and $\mathcal{O}^{retrieve}$ that provide ways for $\mathcal{A}$ to request that standard DPDP operations be initiated by $\mathcal{V}$. Keeping this high-level notation simple necessitates an unusual feature in our model: a client performing a retrieve or update operation performs several steps to prepare a request, perform the request by interacting with the servers, and verify the server responses. However, the servers are under control of the adversary, so $\mathcal{A}$ must provide a "callback" interface for the oracle to interact with the adversarially controlled servers.

The ACF game starts in a *setup phase*, where $\mathcal{A}$ interacts with the oracle to create arbitrary files, access and modify them, all while monitoring what $\mathcal{V}$ and **AS**'s TPM do for these requests. At the end of the setup phase, $\mathcal{A}$ returns a file identifier *id* for which it will try to fool the clients into accepting a bogus version. At this point we need to define the "good" version of file *id*; we use an intuitive description here, since a more rigorous treatment (which is in the full version of this paper) requires establishing non-trivial notation. The basic idea is straightforward: if we take the sequence of updates performed during the setup phase, and extract just the update operations made by users who can legitimately affect file *id*, then an honest execution of these update operations produces the "good" version of the file, which we denote as F_{id}.

So finally, the adversary wins this game if it can convince $\mathcal{O}^{retrieve}$ to accept anything other than F_{id}. More rigorously, in the game we execute the following experiment for adversary $\mathcal{A}$ and multi-user DPDP scheme MDPDP, where λ is a security parameter that determines lengths of keys and other cryptographic properties:

$$\text{Experiment } \mathbf{Exp}^{setup}_{\mathcal{A}, MDPDP}(\lambda)$$
$$id \leftarrow \mathcal{A}^{\mathcal{O}}(1^\lambda)$$
$$f \leftarrow \mathcal{O}^{retrieve}(id)$$
$$\text{output "win" if } f \neq \text{reject and } f \neq F_{id}$$

Our final security definition follows directly from this experiment, saying that no polynomial time adversary can win this game with better than negligible probability.

Definition 3. Scheme MDPDP is a secure multi-user DPDP scheme for hierarchical storage if, for any polynomial time adversary $\mathcal{A}$ and any $c \geq 1$, there exists a $\lambda_0 > 0$ so that for all $\lambda \geq \lambda_0$,

$$Prob\left[\mathbf{Exp}^{setup}_{\mathcal{A}, MDPDP}(\lambda) = \text{"win"}\right] < \frac{1}{\lambda^c} .$$

The full theoretical analysis of the MDPDP scheme presented in this paper is beyond the scope of this conference paper. Details are provided in the full paper showing that our scheme is a secure multi-user DPDP scheme under this definition.

6. EXPERIMENTS

In this section, we present preliminary results of experiments into the practicality of the system we have described in this paper. The experiments in this paper are not intended to be an extensive performance evaluation, but are meant as a preliminary exploration of the feasibility of our approach. As mentioned earlier, prior work has provided extensive comparisons of the log-based and the hash tree-based virtual monotonic counter schemes [29], so we concentrate here on the more efficient hash tree-based scheme.

The storage server **SS** is a modified DPDP server, and performance is consistent with the experiments performed by Erway *et al.* [8] so we do not report those results here. Instead, we focus on our main innovation, the TPM-based authentication server **AS**, which is also the main bottleneck of the system due to speed limitations of the TPM.

Since our system requires modest extensions of a standard TPM, we could not perform our tests on TPM hardware, but instead use the timing-accurate TPM simulator of Gunupudi and Tate [12]. We use a timing profile of an Infineon TPM, which provides the fastest RSA signature time (308.88ms) of any TPM model, and perform tests on a server with an Intel Xeon X3353 processor and CPU-based computations written in Java and run under the IcedTea6 1.6 JVM. The TPM simulator supports plugins for TPM extensions, and we created a hashtree plugin to provide virtual monotonic counters using the techniques described in Section 3.

In this test setting, doing a single isolated virtual monotonic counter attestation, complete with server processing and setting up the authenticated command, takes 425ms; therefore, the maximum request throughput that could be achieved by directly applying the techniques of Sarmenta *et al.* [25] is approximately 2.35 requests per second.

Using our technique of batched attestation (described in Section 3.3.2), we achieve dramatically higher throughput rates, suitable for many practical applications. We tested multiple batch sizes, starting at 400 requests and going up to 2800 requests in steps of 400, running 50 tests at each size and computing the average time, giving the results below.

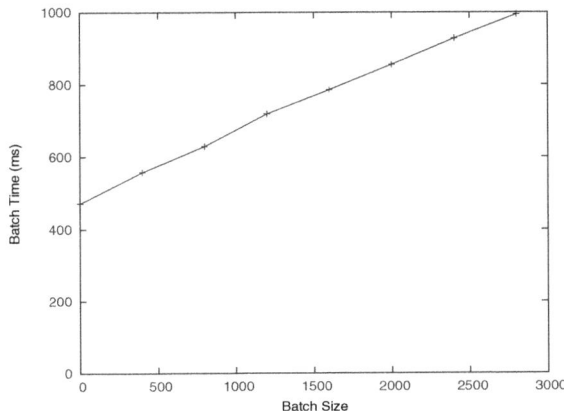

The times were very consistent, varying by at most 10%

around the average over the 50 runs. The batch times show a linear increase as the batch size increases, which is expected since building the nonce hash tree and creating attestation responses are both linear time operations in the batch size.

To optimize our use of resources, we balance time of CPU time with the TPM time, as that keeps both computational resources at full utilization. Specifically, while a TPM request is outstanding, we are using the CPU to post-process the results of the previous TPM operation and construct the nonce tree for the next TPM request. If these times are balanced, we complete construction of the nonce tree at the same time the previous TPM request finishes, so we are immediately ready to issue the next command to the TPM. The TPM time is a constant 425ms regardless of batch size, and so TPM and CPU time are balanced when the total time is twice this, or 850ms. Zooming in on our graph, we see that this happens with a batch size of approximately 1975 requests. At that size, we process 1975 requests every 425 ms, giving *an optimized throughput of 4647 requests per second*. This is a dramatic improvement, with a throughput around 2000 times greater than the base rate of 2.35 requests per second. This is fast enough to satisfy even some very demanding applications.

7. CONCLUSION AND FUTURE WORK

Using lightweight trusted hardware on a remote storage server, we extend previous work in the area of dynamic provable data possession (DPDP) and construct DPDP protocols for the setting where multiple collaborative users work on remotely stored shared data. Our constructions provide proofs of integrity, freshness, and when used to implement a hierarchical filesystem they authenticate both the data itself and its place in the filesystem. A new method of batching attestations provides throughput for multiple attestations that is several orders of magnitude greater than the straightforward solution, bringing this well into the range of practical application.

In ongoing work, we are further developing the theoretical security model and performing more extensive performance evaluation. A practically relevant direction for future work would be to explore the idea of load-balancing across multiple servers. With respect to our model, it should be straightforward to distribute the storage server across multiple machines for load-balancing client requests, but it is harder to distribute the authentication server tasks since our current protocols depend on the the TPM and virtual monotonic counter being globally unique for each control point. One possible solution is to distribute control points to different **AS**es; however, it's not clear how to duplicate resources for an individual control point, and so distributing in this manner simply creates multiple points of failure when validating a path in the filesystem, making the system more brittle. We leave the search for a better solution as an open problem.

8. ACKNOWLEDGMENTS

The work reported in this paper is supported by the National Science Foundation under Grant No. 0915735. The authors would like to thank Adam Lee and the anonymous reviewers for their helpful comments.

9. REFERENCES

[1] G. Ateniese, R. C. Burns, R. Curtmola, J. Herring, L. Kissner, Z. N. J. Peterson, and D. X. Song. Provable data possession at untrusted stores. In *ACM CCS*, pages 598–609, 2007.

[2] G. Ateniese, J. Camenisch, M. Joye, and G. Tsudik. A practical and provably secure coalition resistant group signature scheme. In *CRYPTO*, pages 255–270, 2000.

[3] G. Ateniese, R. D. Pietro, L. V. Mancini, and G. Tsudik. Scalable and efficient provable data possession. In *SecureComm*, 2008. Article 9.

[4] K. D. Bowers, A. Juels, and A. Oprea. Hail: a high-availability and integrity layer for cloud storage. In *ACM CCS*, pages 187–198, 2009.

[5] C. Cachin. Integrity and consistency for untrusted services. In *SOFSEM*, pages 1–14, 2011.

[6] C. Cachin, I. Keidar, and A. Shraer. Fail-aware untrusted storage. In *DSN*, pages 494–503, 2009.

[7] B.-G. Chun, P. Maniatis, S. Shenker, and J. Kubiatowicz. Attested append-only memory: making adversaries stick to their word. In *SOSP*, pages 189–204, 2007.

[8] C. C. Erway, A. Küpçü, C. Papamanthou, and R. Tamassia. Dynamic provable data possession. In *ACM CCS*, pages 213–222, 2009.

[9] A. J. Feldman, W. P. Zeller, M. J. Freedman, and E. W. Felten. SPORC: Group collaboration using untrusted cloud resources. In *OSDI*, pages 337–350, 2010.

[10] J. Feng, Y. Chen, D. Summerville, W.-S. Ku, and Z. Su. Enhancing cloud storage security against roll-back attacks with a new fair multi-party non-repudiation protocol. In *Proc. IEEE Consumer Communications and Networking Conference (CCNC)*, pages 521–522, 2011.

[11] M. T. Goodrich, M. Mitzenmacher, O. Ohrimenko, and R. Tamassia. Practical oblivious storage. In *ACM CODASPY*, pages 13–24, 2012.

[12] V. Gunupudi and S. R. Tate. Timing-accurate TPM simulation for what-if explorations in trusted computing. In *Proceedings of the International Symposium on Performance Evaluation of Computer and Telecommunicatoin Systems (SPECTS)*, pages 171–178, 2010.

[13] A. Juels and B. S. Kaliski, Jr. PORs: Proofs of retrievability for large files. In *ACM CCS*, pages 584–597, 2007.

[14] H. Kaplan. Persistent data structures. In *Handbook on Data Structures and Applications*. CRC Press, 2001.

[15] D. Levin, J. R. Douceur, J. R. Lorch, and T. Moscibroda. TrInc: Small trusted hardware for large distributed systems. In *NSDI*, pages 1–14, 2009.

[16] J. Li, M. N. Krohn, D. Mazières, and D. Shasha. Secure untrusted data repository (SUNDR). In *OSDI*, pages 121–136, 2004.

[17] J. Li and D. Mazières. Beyond one-third faulty replicas in Byzantine fault tolerant systems. In *NSDI*, 2007.

[18] P. Mahajan, S. T. V. Setty, S. Lee, A. Clement, L. Alvisi, M. Dahlin, and M. Walfish. Depot: Cloud storage with minimal trust. In *OSDI*, pages 307–322, 2010.

[19] D. Mazieres and D. Shasha. Don't trust your file server. In *Workshop on Hot Topics in Operating Systems*, pages 113–118, 2001.

[20] D. Mazières and D. Shasha. Building secure file systems out of Byzantine storage. In *ACM PODC*, pages 108–117, 2002.

[21] J. M. McCune, Y. Li, N. Qu, Z. Zhou, A. Datta, V. D. Gligor, and A. Perrig. TrustVisor: Efficient TCB reduction and attestation. In *IEEE Symposium on Security and Privacy*, pages 143–158, 2010.

[22] J. M. McCune, B. Parno, A. Perrig, M. K. Reiter, and H. Isozaki. Flicker: An execution infrastructure for TCB minimization. In *EuroSys*, pages 315–328, 2008.

[23] R. C. Merkle. A digital signature based on a conventional encryption function. In *CRYPTO*, pages 369–378, 1987.

[24] T. Moyer, K. Butler, J. Schiffman, P. McDaniel, and T. Jaeger. Scalable web content attestation. In *ACSAC*, pages 95–104, 2009.

[25] L. F. G. Sarmenta, M. v. Dijk, C. W. O'Donnell, J. Rhodes, and S. Devadas. Virtual monotonic counters and count-limited objects using a TPM without a trusted OS. In *Proceedings of the First ACM Workshop on Scalable Trusted Computing*, pages 27–42, 2006.

[26] H. Shacham and B. Waters. Compact proofs of retrievability. In *ASIACRYPT*, pages 90–107, 2008.

[27] A. Shraer, C. Cachin, A. Cidon, I. Keidar, Y. Michalevsky, and D. Shaket. Venus: verification for untrusted cloud storage. In *CCSW*, pages 19–30, 2010.

[28] E. Stefanov, M. van Dijk, A. Oprea, and A. Juels. Iris: A scalable cloud file system with efficient integrity checks. *IACR Cryptology ePrint Archive*, 2011, 2011.

[29] S. R. Tate and R. Vishwanathan. Performance evaluation of TPM-based digital wallets. In *International Symposium on Performance Evaluation of Computer and Telecommunication Systems*, pages 179–186, 2010.

[30] S. R. Tate, R. Vishwanathan, and L. Everhart. Multi-user dynamic proofs of data possession using trusted hardware – expanded version. Available at http://span.uncg.edu/pubs, 2012.

[31] Trusted Computing Group. Trusted Platform Module Specifications – Parts 1–3. Available at https://www.trustedcomputinggroup.org/specs/TPM/.

[32] M. van Dijk, J. Rhodes, L. F. G. Sarmenta, and S. Devadas. Offline untrusted storage with immediate detection of forking and replay attacks. In *Workshop on Scalable Trusted Computing*, pages 41–48, 2007.

[33] M. van Dijk, L. Sarmenta, C. O'Donnell, and S. Devadas. Proof of freshness: How to efficiently use an online single secure clock to secure shared untrusted memory. Technical Report CSG Memo 496, MIT, 2006.

[34] H. Xiong, X. Zhang, D. Yao, X. Wu, and Y. Wen. Towards end-to-end secure content storage and delivery with public cloud. In *ACM CODASPY*, pages 257–266, 2012.

[35] Q. Zheng and S. Xu. Fair and dynamic proofs of retrievability. In *ACM CODASPY*, pages 237–248, 2011.

Adaptive Data Protection in Distributed Systems

Anna Cinzia Squicciarini
College of Information
Sciences and Technology
Pennsylvania State
University
University Park, PA
16802

Giuseppe Petracca
College of Information
Sciences and Technology
Pennsylvania State
University
University Park, PA
16802

Elisa Bertino
Computer Science
Department
Purdue University
West Lafayette, IN
47906

ABSTRACT

Security is an important barrier to wide adoption of distributed systems for sensitive data storage and management. In particular, one unsolved problem is to ensure that customers data protection policies are honored, regardless of where the data is physically stored and how often it is accessed, modified, and duplicated. This issue calls for two requirements to be satisfied. First, data should be managed in accordance to both owners' preferences and to the local regulations that may apply. Second, although multiple copies may exist, a consistent view across copies should be maintained. Toward addressing these issues, in this work we propose innovative policy enforcement techniques for adaptive sharing of users' outsourced data. We introduce the notion of autonomous self-controlling objects (SCO), that by means of object-oriented programming techniques, encapsulate sensitive resources and assure their protection by means of adaptive security policies of various granularity, and synchronization protocols. Through extensive evaluation, we show that our approach is effective and efficiently manages multiple data copies.

Categories and Subject Descriptors

C.2 [**COMPUTER-COMMUNICATION NETWORKS**
]: Security and protection (e.g., firewalls)

Keywords

Security, Distributed Systems

1. INTRODUCTION

A distributed system is by definition a collection of independent computers that appear to the users of the system as a single coherent system. With the advances of distributed technologies, including cloud computing, wireless networks, grid computing, distributed systems are nowadays proliferating. Data stored in these systems may often encode sensitive information, and if distributed across regions or nations it should be protected as mandated by organizational policies and legal regulations.

Ensuring that policies associated with data distributed across domain (regardless of where the data is physically stored and how often it is accessed, modified, and duplicated) are honored is an important challenge. Depending on the degree of distribution, and the size of the data consumers' base, users' data may be stored in multiple locations, based on providers internal scheduling and management processes. Therefore, as data travels across sites and is modified by multiple parties, it may be replicated and accessed from remote locations. In these cases, access restrictions have to apply not only to changes by the content originators (or content owners) but also to privacy and auditing regulations that are in place in the location where data is stored and managed.

We notice that data replication in distributed systems is the norm. In newer environments, such as cloud computing, data replication is anticipated to gain even more importance, as the reliability requirements of customers increase. It has been envisioned that replication technologies will become part of the storage foundation. Cloud providers are to leverage this technology to meet existing as well as evolving customer requirements. Replication will not only enable data recovery in the cloud, but server recovery in the cloud as well [4,9].

Toward addressing these issues, in this work we propose innovative policy enforcement techniques for adaptive sharing of users' outsourced data. In particular, we introduce the notion of *self-controlling objects* (SCOs), that encapsulate sensitive resources and assure their protection through the provision of adaptive security policies.

SCO are movable data containers, generated by end users through automated wizards. A given SCO may be distributed across domains if the originator wishes, and content recipients may consume the encapsulated resource at any time. Access privileges will be verified at the time of consumption, based on both the recipient credentials and the context wherein access takes place. Accordingly, the content will be decrypted and accessed on the fly. No centralized policy enforcement engine or decision point is required in order to enforce the security requirements, since the core security modules belong to the object itself.

SCOs provide strong security guarantees, even in presence of multiple copies of the same SCO disseminated across the cloud, and adapt to local compliance requirements. SCOs support a synchronization and update protocol that relies on a subset of the SCO themselves. As part of our solution, we also show how SCOs can either use locally pre-loaded policies or securely accept new policies from trusted authorities.

To effectively accomplish adaptive data protection our design satisfies the following unique properties: strong binding between security policies and data, interoperability, portability, and object security. Protection of encapsulated data is achieved by provisioning owner-specified security policies that are tightly bound with the content, and executable within the SCO. To ensure interoperability, our SCOs are self-contained, and do not require any dedicated software to execute, other than the Java running environment. Self-containment ensures portability, in that SCOs may be moved and replicated without the need of installing dedicated software. To guarantee adaptivity, the policies embedded in the SCO are sensitive to the location and other contextual dimensions that may affect the enforcement process. Finally, object security is guaranteed by advanced cryptographic primitives, such as Ciphertext-Policy Attribute-Based Encryption [2] and Oblivious Hashing for program tracing [14], combined with extended and advanced object-oriented coding techniques. We have implemented a running prototype of the proposed architecture and protocols using Java^{TM}-based technologies [11, 21] along with advanced cryptographic protocols and cross-checking techniques to guarantee acceptable trustworthiness of the SCOs. In the paper, we discuss the results of our experiments on a distributed system testbed which includes several physical and virtual nodes installed. Our results demonstrate the resiliency of our architecture even in case of multiple SCO nodes faults.

The rest of the paper is organized as follows. Next section provides background notions. Next, in Section 3, we provide an overview of the notion of SCO. Section 4 discusses the security policies. Section 5 introduces our synchronization algorithms. Section 6 discusses the most important properties achieved by our solution, whereas Section 7 discusses implementation and security of our solution. Section 8 reports experimental results. Section 9 discusses related work and Section 10 concludes the paper.

2. CIPHERTEXT-POLICY ATTRIBUTE- BASED ENCRYPTION

In this section, we briefly discuss the basic cryptographic protocol underlying our solution. The Ciphertext-Policy Attribute-Based Encryption (CP-ABE) [2] is a type of public-key encryption scheme. In the CP-ABE scheme, there exists a trusted party that generates a public key which can be used by any entity to encrypt a message irrespective of its recipients. The message sender encrypts the message using the public key. A trusted party computes the private key. Only entities satisfying the rules are able to compute the private key. The schema includes four phases:

- *Setup*: The trusted third party takes as input implicit security parameters and outputs the public key PK_{ABE} of ABE protocol and a master key MK. The master key is only known to the trusted party who generated it.

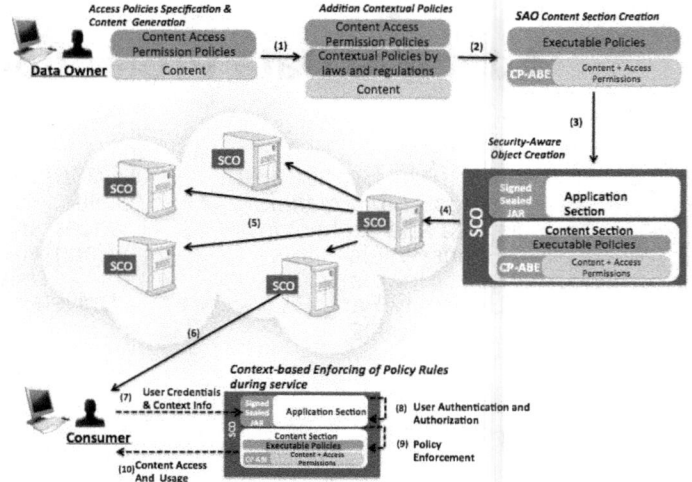

Figure 1: Overall Approach

- *Encrypt(PK, M, A)*: The encryption algorithm takes as input the public key PK, a message M, and an access structure A over the universe of desired attributes. The algorithm encrypts M and produces a ciphertext M' which implicitly contains the access structure A. M' can only be decrypted by the entity which possesses a set of attributes that satisfy the access structure.

- *KeyGen(MK,S)*: The private key generation algorithm is carried out by the trusted entity. The algorithm takes as input the master key MK and a set of attribute values, S on which access control would be achieved. The outcome of $KeyGen(MK, S)$ is a private key SK_S.

- *Decrypt(M', SK)*: The decryption algorithm takes as input the ciphertext M', and the private key SK_S. The output is the original message M.

3. THE SCO-BASED SOLUTION

We illustrate the functionality offered by our policy-protection framework through a use-case (see Figure 1). We particularly focus on a cloud computing domain, wherein data is replicated to facilitate users' access across location. A SCO is generated by a content originator subscribed to a cloud provider. The content originator triggers the SCO generation process as he places sensitive content (e.g. text, video or image file) on the Cloud Service Provider he is subscribed to. SCOs may protect files of different kind, including images, text, and media content.

The originator indicates the file to protect as well as its security policies (step 1), which are encoded and embedded in the SCO. Notice that the security policies can include constructs to specify access control, authentication and usage controls. Furthermore, they are enforced according to contextual criteria defined by the content owners, to ensure, for example, compliance with location-specific regulations and policies. In addition to the content owner's rules, prior to being signed and sealed, the SCO is loaded with rules whose enforcement guarantees compliance with security and data disclosure regulations (e.g. auditing requirements), as shown in step 3 and 4. The SCO is then stored at a single service provider (SP), and possibly duplicated for greater dependability and availability. The content stored in each SCO may be accessed at time by authorized users, SPs for processing and analysis, and auditors, to meet compliance requirements. Each time access to the SCO protected content is attempted, its policy is evaluated according to the requestor's credential and location (step 5). If permitted by the policy, the content is then rendered according to the granted privilege.

Notice that as SCO instances are accessed, replicated and moved across different locations, two requirements must be always addressed: (1) The policy enforced by the SCO must comply with the legal regulations of the SCO storage location. For example, the SCO is stored in a EU server, and therefore, data disclosure laws apply. (2) Modifications to the SCO content file must be propagated to all SCO copies, for obvious consistency reasons. To address the first requirement, the policy in the SCO is organized in rules of varying priority, and may include specific applicability requirements, defined in terms of pre-defined context-specific rules. New high-priority rules may be added to the SCO, using a third-party invocation protocol.To address the second requirement, the SCO applies a quick synchronization protocol to all the available copies. The update process entails a coordinated cooperative protocol among one or multiple copies of the same SCO and ensures that the most up to date content version is rendered to the SCO being accessed.

4. POLICIES

We now introduce a simple representation of the security policies supported by our protection mechanism and their enforcement process. Our representation allows to enforce simple access control and usage requirements. The design of both the language and the resolution algorithm is partly inspired by the XACML language, which represents the de-facto standard in terms of access control.

4.1 Policy Specification

We define a security policy as a collection of rules, i.e. $p = \{r_1, \ldots, r_n\}, n \geq 1$. Each rule controls access and usage of a given content by a certain user (or collection of users). It may either target a single content item f (e.g. file) stored within the SCO, or if the SCO stores multiple content elements (i.e. files), it may refer to all the files in the SCO. For simplicity, we assume that the policy rules within a same SCO are atomic, do not overlap, and do not conflict among one another.

DEFINITION 4.1 (POLICY RULE). *A policy rule r is a tuple* $\langle \mathtt{s}, \mathtt{o}, \mathtt{effect}{:}\mathtt{act}, \mathtt{cond}\|\mathtt{Cont} \rangle$, *where:*

- s *is the subject element. It can be the name of a user, or of any collection of users, e.g. subscriber or Amazon SP2, or a special user collection anyuser representing all users.*
- o *is a content item or a set of content items.*
- effect:act *denotes the effect of the rule in case of truthful evaluation and impacts the selection of the rule when multiple rules exist in the same policy. The* effect *takes one of the following values:* AbsolutePermit, AbsoluteDeny, FinalPermit. act *denotes the privilege applied to the content, in terms of its access and consumption. It is left null in case of* AbsoluteDeny *effect.*

- cond *is an optional element that further refines the applicability of the rule to the subject in the rule through the specification of predicates on the subject attributes (combined with anyuser) and/or the object attributes.*
- cont *is a set of boolean conjunctive conditions defined against a set of pre-defined contextual variables.*

The context component of our rule model is the key to support adaptive SCO, as this component specifies the contextual conditions controlling the activation of rules in the security policy. In the current version of the language, we support two types of contexts: the *Environment* context, that depends on the characteristics of the host system, and the *Location* context that depends on the subject location. Each context type consists of a set of pre-defined variables. Examples include *IP address* for location conditions, and *OS* or *System Version* for the environment conditions.

4.2 Rules Enforcement Process

The rules enforcement process consists two steps. The first step identifies a set of applicable rules, as not all rules are always applicable to all contexts. The second step enforces the highest priority rule among the set of applicable rules identified by the first step.

Rules Applicability A rule r in a SCO policy is applicable to an access request if and only if: (a) the user meets the subject specification in (r.s); and (b) the user's and objects attributes verify true the condition set r.cond, and (c) the context conditions r.Cont, if present.

To verify the applicability of a given rule, at the time of an access request, the policy enforcement engine at the SCO obtains the user credential and verifies its validity. It further verifies whether the user attributes satisfy the access conditions. Next, the SCO collects information required in order to establish if the context definitions are satisfied. To achieve this, various actions are undertaken, depending upon the specific context conditions to be verified. Context primitives deployed within the SCO have direct access to the host system (e.g. a global clock to check temporal conditions in the Environment context) or they use metadata carried by the actions. For example, the location of the SP can be determined using the IP address. The SCO performs an IP lookup and uses the range of the IP address to find the most probable location of the SP, so as to match it against the location defined in the condition constraint.

Notice that we assume that each SCO copy is always able to gather the location information (i.e. the IP address and a free port number) of the machine on which it is running. This information is needed also to ensure the capability for a SCO copy to communicate with other copies. Even in an environment where the applications execution is controlled, these two pieces of information must always be available. For this purpose, protected APIs can be used (see Section 7.1), to ensure the correct use of such sensitive information solely for the purpose of of communications among SCOs. If other contextual information is necessary for the evaluation of policy rules is not available to the SCO, the policy rules will be defined as indeterminate. This will block the use of the SCO copy for security reasons.

Rule Selection Upon determining the set of applicable rules, the rule-selection algorithm is executed (see Appendix A for a detailed flow). By definition, each rule can only have one of three effects: AbsolutePermit, AbsoluteDeny, FinalPermit.

1. An applicable rule whose effect is `AbsolutePermit` has the highest priority, that is, access is granted regardless of the effects of other applicable rules. The motivation for the `AbsolutePermit` rule is that access requests required by law enforcement institutions or national security agencies should always be able to circumvent the access restrictions specified by the owner and organizational policies. We assume that `AbsolutePermit` rules are always pre-loaded within the SCO, and defined to meet the regulatory requirements imposed by countries and jurisdictional locations where the content may move to. Additional `AbsolutePermit` rules may also be dynamically added to the SCO, as it moves in unforeseen locations. In such case, rules are obtained from a third party (see Section 7.1). The presence of context in rules with an `AbsolutePermit` effect has the ability to confine the geographic locations under which a given regulation is enforced. For example, the rule $\langle$`anyuser,f`$_1$`, AbsolutePermit : read, subject.CountryOfOrigin =`$'$`France'`, `role = Auditor`$||$ `location = France`$\rangle$ specifies that any French auditor can read file f_1 when the file in located in France.

2. If no `AbsolutePermit` rule is applicable, the `AbsoluteDeny` rules are considered. If one `AbsoluteDeny` is applicable, access is denied. For example, a rule may specify that accesses must blocked from certain geographical areas, considered unsafe or legally prohibited (e.g. for copyright agreements). An example of rule with such effect is as follows: $\langle$`anyuser,f`$_1$`, AbsoluteDeny: read,subject.location = China`$||$`location = China`$\rangle$.

3. If neither `AbsolutePermit` rules or `AbsoluteDeny` rules are applicable, the most specific applicable rule with a `FinalPermit` is evaluated. The effect of such rules is to represent criteria that are preferred by content owner and that are to be met in order to obtain access. These rules may also include context conditions.

4. Finally, if no applicable rule exists, access is denied; the "deny takes precedence" principle is adopted.

Upon a positive access control decision (i.e. an `AbsolutePermit` or an `FinalPermit` decision) by a rule r, the access is granted according to the specified action set in **r.act**. The action set can vary according to the specific content type hosted within the SCO. For example, for image files, allowed actions are *view, edit, download*.

Architecturally, rules are translated into executable Java policy files and access structures for encryption (see Section 7.1), according to the cryptographic protocol used for content protection and access. Possibly applicable rules are pre-loaded in each SCO as it is created, based on the specific SP's servers' locations and anticipated location access. We assume that rules with a `FinalPermit` effect entered by the content originator do not change, but additional `AbsolutePermit` and `AbsoluteDeny` rules may need to be added to the SCO as it is accessed from unknown locations whereby `AbsolutePermit` and `AbsoluteDeny` rules are applicable.

5. SYNCHRONIZATION AND VERSIONING

SCOs may be replicated for a number of reasons, including workload distribution, disaster recovery, efficiency. Given the unique nature of SCOs, as SCO copies are generated, it is crucial to guarantee that the same policies and usage conditions apply for the object replica.

By replicating a SCO, a network of SCOs is inherently created (referred to as SCON), whereby nodes are SCO copies and edges their connections. To ensure consistency and proper policy enforcement, a distributed synchronization mechanism is to be deployed. The synchronization mechanism should be scalable, and incur in a low-traffic network overhead. A simple coverage algorithm can synchronize the content of all the SCON nodes upon change. However, if the number of nodes in the SCON increases drastically, the synchronization may incur in poor performance. Conversely, a fully centralized system may not scale effectively, if SCOs are spread across different locations. Therefore, we need an efficient structure to guarantee full synchronization of the SCO copies while at the same time reducing the number of messages exchanged among copies. Our solution lies in the notion of *SCON View*, representing an elastic view V of nodes in the SCON. Nodes in V are SCOs, and are referred to as *Master* nodes, in that they are always synchronized. The remaining nodes in the network are *Slave* nodes and are instead synchronized only after contacting a Master node.

5.1 SCO Network Creation

Starting from the generic SCON of identical copies, we build a network's view as the basis for our synchronization protocol. First, notice that SCOs keep track of how many copies exist in the SCON, by maintaining a shared counter of the known SCO copies in a local and encrypted registry *Network Management Information (NMI)*, which is updated each time a new copy is created and later synchronized. To build the network, we apply the following procedure. As mentioned, each SCO can either be a Slave node or a Master node. At the time of creation of the SCO, the first α of its identical SCO copies are by default Master nodes. Starting from the $\alpha + 1$th copy, the subsequently generated copies will be Slave nodes up until the $\omega\alpha$ threshold is reached. For example, let α be equal to 5, and assume that 6 copies of the same SCO exist. Let ω be equal to 2. Regardless of the actual synchronization mechanism, copies from 1 to 5 are synchronized at each change, as they are Master copies, while the copy number 6 in order to be synchronized must communicate with one of the Master copies. As the number of SCO copies grows we continue to maintain an acceptable ratio between overall SCO copies and Master copies, in order to ensure good performance of the synchronization system. Suppose that we need α Master copies every $\omega\alpha$ SCO copies. Let n be the current total number of SCO copies. Let the nodes be sorted by the time of creation, by means of a timestamp. Upon creating a new instance of the SCO, the following *node-ratio rule* applies:

$$\begin{cases} k(\omega\alpha) \leq n \leq k(\omega\alpha) + \alpha & n_{th} \text{ node is Master} \\ k(\omega\alpha) + \alpha < n < k(\omega\alpha) + \omega\alpha & n_{th} \text{ node is Slave} \end{cases}$$

(1)

k represents the Master/Slave ratio according to the nodes' number. It is incremented each time $n = k(\omega\alpha) + \omega\alpha$. Upon generating a SCO instance, its connection to existing SCOs are to be established. SCO Masters and Slaves each maintain information about some of the nodes in the SCON. Precisely, each time a Master is generated, it stores its current local position (IP and port number) and uses the originally available position and port number to connect with its original version. As the new copy informs its parent node, the SCO updates its NMI registry by adding a new record, up until a set threshold of known copies, discussed next. It then propagates the information to the Master nodes merging the list with the new records stored at each Master. Until there are less than $\omega\alpha$ Master nodes in the SCON, all nodes are completely connected. From the $\alpha + 1$ Master, each node, whether Master or Slave, must be connected to Master nodes with a degree γ.

DEFINITION 5.1 (NODES CONNECTIVITY). *Let N be the set of copies of a same SCO, distributed across multiple SPs. Let M be the set of Master nodes such that $M \subseteq N$ and $e = (n, n')$ be a connection between two nodes. For each node $n \in N$ the following rule applies:*

$$\begin{cases} \exists e = (n, n_i) \forall n, n_i \in N & |N| \leq \alpha \\ \exists e_1, \ldots, e_\gamma, e_i = (n, n_i) \wedge n_i \in M, \forall i \in [1, \gamma] & |N| > \alpha \end{cases}$$

By satisfying this simple rule, our system is robust against $\gamma - 1$ simultaneous faults of Master nodes. In other words, if we set $\gamma = 3$ and two simultaneous Master nodes faults occur during synchronization, no Master node will be isolated in the SCON. Further, any Slave node will still be able to synchronize by querying the surviving Master node. If a Master is determined to be faulty, the other Master nodes will update their connections in order to meet again the connectivity rule. If the failed Master node recovers, it is then treated like a new node, and it will be a Master or a Slave following the rule of Eq. 1.

EXAMPLE 5.1. *Assume: $\omega = 2, \alpha = 5, \gamma = 3$. An example of SCON with $n = 8$ is shown in Figure 2 (top). By deleting any $\gamma - 1$ nodes together with their connections, all the remaining nodes in the graph SCON are still connected, satisfying the connectivity rule. Hence, erasing 2 Master nodes (or two connections) leaves the network connected.*

Each connection also has a communication cost ϕ, estimated by the SCOs by computing the distance with the other connected SCO (through IP lookup). The actual value of γ, as well as α and ω can be set empirically. As we show in our experimental evaluation, changes in these parameters only slightly affect the performance of the overall system.
We are now ready to define the SCON. The algorithm for the SCON construction is reported in Appendix A.

DEFINITION 5.2 (SCO NETWORK). *$G = (N, E, W)$ is called SCO network (SCON), with N the set of nodes and E the set of arcs, such that the elements of E are pairs of elements of N ($|E| \subseteq |N|^2$); and $W : E \times \Phi \to w \in \Re^+$ is the edge labeling function. W maps the communication cost ϕ to an edge weight w. Each node $n \in V$ is an instance of a SCO, which is abstracted by a tuple of $n = < n_{ID}, m, NMI, l, CS >$. Where n_{ID} is the id, $m \in \{M, S\}$ indicates where the node is a Slave or a Master, NMI is the information needed for network management. Finally, l is the current location (IP, port) of the node, and CS represents the SCO content, i.e. the protected content and policies included in the SCO. G satisfies the following properties:*

- *The CS component is identical upon synchronization across all nodes in N.*
- *$\forall n \in N$, $m = M$ (n is a Master) or $m = S$ (n is a slave), according to the node-ratio rule of Equation (1)*

- *$\forall n \in N$ satisfies the connectivity rule of Def. 5.1.*
- *$\forall e_{ij}, \in E$ exists a corresponding weight w_{ij} according to the weight function W.*

We denote the components of nodes using the dot notation.
The cost of traversing the $SCON$ is $\Theta(SCON) = \sum_{i=0}^{|E|} W(e_i, \Phi_i) = \sum_{i=0}^{|E|} w_i$. For example, W may assign weights according to the following mapping. Let $e_{i,j} = (n_i, n_j)$ be the edge linking n_i, n_j. Let $l.IP$ denote the machine's IP address.

$$w_{ij} = \begin{cases} 0 & n_i.m = S \wedge n_j.m = M \\ 1 & n_i.m, n_j.m = M \wedge n_j.l.IP = n_i.l.IP \\ 2 & n_i.m, n_j.m = M \wedge n_j.l.IP \neq n_i.l.IP \end{cases} \quad (2)$$

As we discuss next, the weight of each edge is used by the synchronization algorithm for optimization purposes.

5.2 Synchronization Algorithms

The synchronization process varies depending on whether the node to be synchronized is a Master or a Slave. It entails a collaborative protocol among Master nodes while it is a 2-party protocol for SCO slaves.
Master Synchronization: The Master node synchronization process is triggered upon receiving an update to the content or to the policy rules of one of its SCOs, or when new network management information is to be exchanged (e.g. a new Master is added). The update is a collaborative process that maps to the problem of finding the minimum spanning tree (MST) of the SCON View. For this purpose, we adopt a parallel search algorithm [7]. The nodes obey the same algorithm and exchange *update* messages with neighbors until the MST is constructed, traversing low-cost connections first. The algorithm determines fragments of the MST and connects them progressively, until one MST if found. At the end of the algorithm execution, each node knows its precedent and successor in the MST, and therefore it is able to pass updates along. The algorithm reaches the optimal solution with a complexity of $O(\sqrt{N} \log^* N)$, where N is the number of nodes.

EXAMPLE 5.2. *In our example, assume that the updated Master node is the node with number 5 and that the weights of the arcs are assigned according to the rule of Equation 2. Figure 2 shows one possible construction of the MST.*

Slave Node Synchronization: Synchronization can occur in two directions: from a Slave node to a Master node and vice versa. In the first case, the Slave node contacts the Master node to communicate the changes occurred at the Slave's content or its policy rules (by an authorized user), so as to allow the Master node to propagate the update among the nodes of the view V. In the second case, a Slave node needs to check for updates within the view V of Master nodes to update its local Content Section. This second type of synchronization can occur either periodically, or at each access, to ensure a tighter control. When synchronization is requested, the Slave node connects to any of the Master nodes among the set of adjacent-known Master nodes. The choice of such Master node is random, so as to ensure a fair distribution of workload on Master nodes. We now elaborate on the synchronization processes for the two directions.
Slave Update: As a Slave obtains an access request from a third party it may contact a Master node to check for

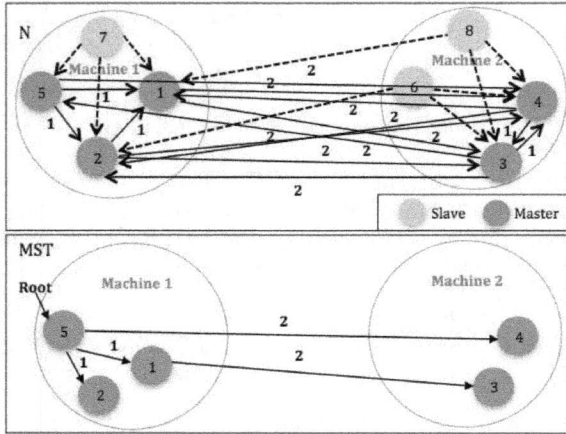

Figure 2: The two steps of synchronization: MST construction and updates.

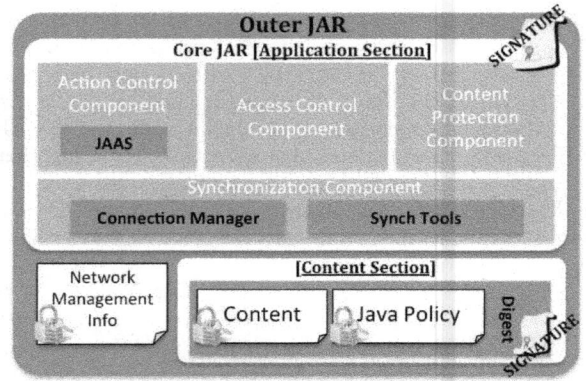

Figure 3: SCO Architecture

updates in the SCON. Upon opening a secure connection, the Slave sends the digest of its current CS, so as to allow the Master to check if the received digest matches the current digest within its CS. If the two digests are the same, the update will not be necessary. Otherwise, the SCO Slave obtains the new CS and NMI. The redeployment aspects of the SCO are discussed in Sec. 7.1.

Master Update: When a Slave node contacts a Master to send an updated version of the managed content, the Slave node sends to the Master the SCO updated content or network information (denoted as CS and NMI respectively in Def. 5.2). We notice that this case presents an interesting transaction aspect: if two content files on SCO instances were updated simultaneously, multiple inconsistent versions of the same SCO may exist. To address this issue, two alternative solutions are possible. The Master node may apply one of the following two strategies (according to its configuration): (1) If one of the SCO instances was modified under an `AbsolutePermit` rule, it is used for propagation. Other conflicting copies are detached, that is they are handled as independent SCO objects, unrelated from the SCON. (2) Locking mechanisms may be enforced [15], which block multiple accesses in write mode at the same time.

6. PROPERTIES

We briefly discuss relevant properties of our solution, related to correctness, robustness, and consistency.

PROPERTY 6.1 (ENFORCEMENT CORRECTNESS). *Given a SCO, if a rule with* `AbsolutePermit` *or* `AbsoluteDeny` *is applicable to a request q, it is always enforced.*

This property is guaranteed by the combined effect of the enforcement algorithm and of the synchronization process. The enforcement algorithm guarantees that rules with `AbsolutePermit` and `AbsoluteDeny` effects are given highest priority. If the rule is not local to the SCO, the synchronization process guarantees that the applicable rule is passed along to the SCO.

Robustness here refers to the ability of the SCO to withstand crashes of one or multiple machines hosting SCOs.

PROPERTY 6.2 (ROBUSTNESS). *The SCON is resilient to up to $\gamma - 1$ multiple Master nodes failure.*

This property is the result of the connectivity rule (see Definition 3). Each node, whether Master or Slave, will always be connected to at least γ Masters, and therefore resistant to up to $\gamma - 1$ simultaneous failures. Consistency of SCON is defined as follows.

DEFINITION 6.1 (SCON CONSISTENCY). *Let SCON be the SCO Network constructed according to Definition 5.2. The set of SCON is in a consistent state if and only if: 1) each Master node carries the most up to date content and policy version; 2) upon an access request q, each Slave node enforces the highest priority policies rule that applies to q.*

PROPERTY 6.3 (CONSISTENCY). *The SCON satisfies the consistency definition.*

This property can be demonstrated by analyzing the SCON, and the guarantees provided by the synchronization algorithms. Precisely, the requirement (a) of Def. 6.1 is satisfied by construction of the SCON. The SCON defines a set of connected masters (see Algorithm in Appendix A), whereas the synchronization process ensures that each Master is timely informed about the latest version of the SCO's content. Condition (b) is a consequence of the enforcement correctness property (Property 1): every SCO applies the policy enforcement algorithm, which selects the highest priority rule.

7. ARCHITECTURE

We now present the implementation details of the SCO architecture, along with a discussion on the SCO security.

7.1 Implementation of SCO

Each SCO is constructed and accessed using several cryptographic keys. One key set is used for encryption and decryption of sensitive content using the Cyphertext-Policy Based Attribute scheme (CP-ABE) [2], whereas the second key pair is associated with the owners' identity, and is used for signature purposes. Further, some of the low sensitive information, such as the SCON information uses a SCO specific key shared among the SCO copies.

Core Components: Architecturally, the SCO includes two components and the Network Management Information (NMI), all wrapped into an external JAR (see Figure 6). The first component, referred to as *Application Section*, is a set of unmodifiable software modules, signed and sealed to ensure integrity of the application. The Application Section is itself deployed in a nested JAR. The second component, referred to as *Content Section*, stores the protected content items, the Java policy file that records the policies implementing the security rules. This section and the NMI represent the dynamic part of the SCO and is modified upon updates. Since the Content Section stores confidential data, a signed digest of the content and of the Java policy file is added at each update, using the key of the user committing the update. The NMI, instead, stores the shared counter and the address known neighbors. NMI is also encrypted using the SCO specific key. The Application Section is further organized into four components: Authentication and Access Control Component (AAC), Action Control Component (ACC), Content Protection Component (CPC), and Synchronization Component (SYC). The AAC implements the authentication and authorization mechanisms, by exploiting the services offered by Java Authentication and Authorization Services (JAAS) [11] and Security Manager. By means of JAAS primitives, the SCO accepts X.509 certificates[1]. The ACC implements mechanisms for managing access to protected content, according to the outcome of the authentication and authorization process. This component accesses the Java policy file, which dictates what portions of the code to execute upon verification of identities and of authorization. The ACC also deals with the NMI. The CPC manages the protected content stored in the Content Section, as well as the protocols to re-deploy the new Content Section upon updates. Content encryption and access control enforcement are integrated by the use of the CP-ABE scheme [2].

Policies Implementation: The security policies are translated into Java policies (stored into the Java policy file) and access structures that are the input for CP-ABE encryption. CP-ABE supports the notion of attribute-based policies as a criteria for encryption and it is complementary to the Java policy. The access structures are embedded as part of the encrypted content, as by the CP-ABE construction, and therefore not separately stored. These keys are known to the owners and the certification authorities only, and always extracted by valid certificates used for authentication. Conversely, the Java policy file is stored in the Content Section. Each Java Policy specifies which party can access a specific resource (code, file) and how, while which subject is entitled to decrypt -and therefore view- the protected content is addressed by means of the CP-ABE boolean access structure entries. Content is encrypted using the $Encrypt(PK, T, f)$ primitive, where T is the access structure representing the attribute-based conditions (in terms of conjunctions and disjunctions) and f is the file being encrypted, while PK is the encryption key of the owner. We assume that CP-ABE keys are managed by the certificate authorities issuing the attribute certificates used for attributes verification.

Copy management: Copy management and communication protocols are managed by the SYC component. The SYC handles secure communication protocols and traces the copies, to support secure versioning. It is organized into two sub-components: the Connection Manager and the Synch Tools. The Connection Manager handles all processes for

creating a connection to another SCO copy or accepting a connection request sent by another SCO copy, besides implementing the Challenge-Handshake Authentication Protocol. The Synch Tools implement all the mechanisms for synchronization between copies, whether Masters or Slaves. Both components ensure secure connections through SSL.

Context Retrieval for policy evaluation Every time the SCO moves in a new location (geographical or cyber), contextual information is used in order to verify if new secure policy rules apply to the specific location of consumption. To guarantee this high level of adaptivity, the system must be able to retrieve, at any single access attempt, all the information needed to define the current context, both in term of time and physical and/or cyber space. Geographical information is generated by the GeoIP service [8] that uses as input only the IP address of the machine hosting the SCO. Temporal information (i.e. 10:11 AM Tuesday, March 06, 2012, Eastern Standard Time (EST) -05.00 UTC) is generated by using the WorldTimeServer service [8] that uses as input the current geographical location of the SCO.

Depending on where and how the SCO is accessed, obtaining this information may require different approaches. For example, data stored on cloud service providers can be accessed in two different ways, as simple documents stored in a virtual drive (for example by using Amazon Cloud Drive, Dropbox, or Windows Live Sky Drive), or as application data accessible by applications built and hosted on the SP (for example data stored in Amazon S3 used by application hosted in Amazon EC2). These two ways of data consumption are substantially different. In the case of virtual drives, a copy of the SCO is downloaded from the virtual space on the user's machine. The context information is retrieved directly by the SCO that wraps the content, running on the local machine, by exploiting the Global Services [8].

In case an application accesses data stored by the provider (e.g. an application built on Amazon EC2 accesses data stored on Amazon S3), the context information must be provided by the provider hosting the data and the application. The SP generates and makes available a context file, using the provider's APIs. The context file includes the current time and geographical location of consumption, and an identifier of the **Cyber Location** (e.g., Windows Azure Domain) where the information was captured. If the SCO is located on a public domain or on a public network, location and temporal information are retrieved by the SCO through the context information file. We provide a concrete example in the context of Amazon Web Services APIs in the code snippet below.

```
AmazonS3 s3 = new AmazonS3Client(new PropertiesCre-
dentials(S3Sample.class.getResourceAsStream
("AwsCredentials.properties")));
s3.createBucket(bucketName);
s3.putObject(new PutObjectRequest(bucketName, key, SCO));
S3Object object = s3.getObject(new
GetObjectRequest(bucketName, key));
AmazonEC2 ec2 = new AmazonEC2Client(credentials);
AllocateAddressResult aar = ec2.allocateAddress();
aar.getPublicIP();
```

The example shows how to store the SCO in the AmazonS3 storage service, and retrieve the content from the SCO using Amazon EC2. The AmazonEC2 instance can retrieve the information needed to create the current context of data consumption and create the context file. The

---

[1] The SCO may be configured to interpret any other authentication token - such as XACML, SAML, X.509.

actual location is defined by the public IP address (retrieved by the `allocateAddress()` function), where the AmazonEC2 instance is actually running. The same approach could be adopted by other Cloud providers, like Windows Azure or Rackspace.

If it is not possible to retrieve all the information needed to define the current context, the context will be defined as indeterminate. This will render the SCO not accessible.

Adaptiveness: If the policy enforcement mechanism determines the lack of a rule applicable to the current context, the SCO before enforcing the `FinalPermit` rules forwards a policy request to retrieve high-priority rules applicable to the current context, if any. We assume that a trusted authority (CA) managed by the SP is responsible collecting contextual policies that implement local laws or regulations. Thus, the SP updates the SCO policy rules, whenever the SCO is in an unknown and unexpected context. The execution flow is as follows. The SCO sends a request to the CA, through an encrypted channel requesting for high priority rules. The CA after having verified the request's authenticity, determines whether any policy rules applicable to the context specified by the SCO exist. If some policy rules are found, the CA executes the policies translation and redefines a new Content Section with a new encrypted content and a Java policy (without modifying the location information). The CA calculates the new digest and signs it with its private key, to ensure integrity. Once the new content section is ready, the CA sends it to the SCO that replaces its current content section and activates the synchronization process, to disseminate the newly acquired rules. If no policy rule referred to the specified context is found by the CA in its policy rules set, the CA returns no output, and the `FinalPermit` rule is applied.

7.2 Security Features

We discuss possible attacks to our SCO-based framework. We assume that a content originator does not release sensitive information to unauthorized parties, and secret keys used for signature generation and content encryption are kept secret. Conversely, an attacker may try to access information directly from the SCO that is disseminated in the network or try to disassemble the SCO to gain access to the protected content. We only consider attacks to the SCOs. Attacks attempting to exploit the communication between SCO are prevented by means of encrypted authenticated sessions and use of challenge response protocols.

Disassembling and Reverse Engineering: By disassembling the SCO outer JAR, an attacker will be able to get the internal elements of a SCO. The disassembled Core JAR will show the attacker all .class files. The class files once extracted can easily be decompiled into the original source code using Java decompiler tools. To mitigate this risk, we adopt Java-specific obfuscation techniques, which leverage polymorphism and exception mechanism to drastically reduce the precision of points-to-point analysis of the programs [17]. Regarding the Application Section, the attacker cannot change the content after disassembling the Section, nor can he reassemble it with modified classes, files, or packages, because of the protection offered by the JAR seal and signature techniques. As a result of the disassembling, no sensitive information can be obtained from reverse engineering since this information is not within the code but is retrieved by the originator's certificate, at the SCO execution time. The attributes and keys used for decrypting the content under the CP-ABE scheme are never stored, but retrieved when needed. Instead, in the Content Section the Java Policy file is encrypted using the RSA encryption algorithm with the owner's secret key of 2048 bits, and therefore resistant against brute force attacks. Even if the attacker obtains the decryption key used to read the Java Policy file, it will never be able to alter the content, if the CP-ABE key used for content encryption remains secret. CP-ABE is by construction resistant to collusion and chosen plaintext attacks. The only possibly useful information stored in the Application Section is the key encrypting the NMI. Since we rely on advanced obfuscation techniques and store the key in randomized fashion, it is hard to retrieve it. Even in case the key is obtained, the attacker only learns the connections of the SCO and the size of the SCON.

Security Policy modification: A malicious user might attempt to tamper with the SCO in order to change the security policy and gain access to protected content. Our architecture leverages the properties of the CP-ABE encryption schema rendering this attack not feasible. In the CP-ABE the access permission policy is directly and implicitly contained within the protected content. There is no actual policy file that an attacker can modify to change the access decision. Even if the attacker decrypts and reads the Java Policy file, the file does not provide information about the actual authorization and privileges in terms of content access. A user will be able to decrypt the protected content only if her attributes satisfy the attribute-based policy used for content encryption. A malicious user could overcome this control by trying to build a set of attributes to satisfy the access structure for the encrypted content. Such attack would fail during the authentication phase, in that the attacker would need to provide a valid certificate with those attributes, for which he would need the CP-ABE master key stored at the authority.

Unauthorized copy of protected content: A malicious user with right to access the encrypted protected content can generate another possible attack. Once the user is granted access to the protected content, the user attempts to copy it, and save it in a decrypted form in order to allow unauthorized users to read the content. We mitigate this attack by decrypting the content always on the fly and transferring it directly to the content rendering application, therefore preventing the attacker from intercepting temporary files. The content rendering application (such as the Java application window) is then in charge of securely rendering the content.

Bypassing Authentication: An attacker could try to bypass the authentication process and try to directly access the protected content. A way for the attacker to do so is to modify the code within the Application Section. This approach would not work since both the digital signature and the sealing guarantee the JAR file integrity. This ensures that the code within classes and packages cannot be changed. Alternatively, the attacker may try to change the behavior of our application. The attacker can try to exploit malicious external code, able to communicate with our internal code, thus altering the proper functioning of the application. For example, an attacker could insert malicious code and bypass the authentication step so to jump directly to a different point of the execution. To solve this problem, we exploit program tracing techniques [14], by inserting in the application code a set of checkpoints. Each checkpoint controls the current

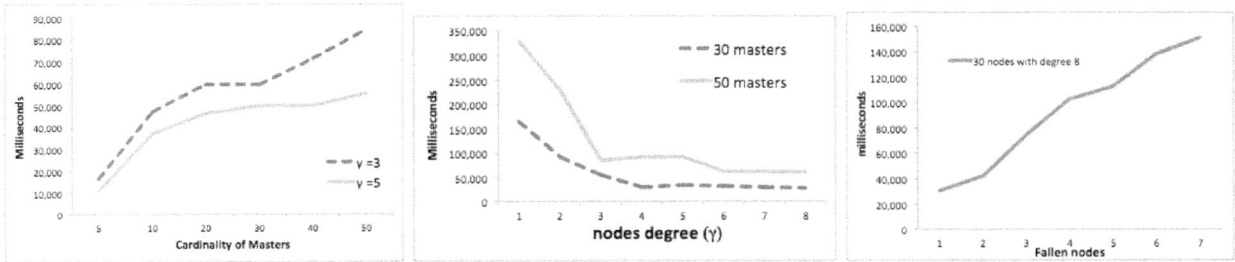

Figure 4: (a) Synchronization for networks of increasing size and γ, (b) Synchronization for networks of same size and different γ (c) Robustness of SCON

value of a set of global oblivious hash variables whose value is continuously changed during the application execution using the oblivious hash technique. During the execution each checkpoint controls the value contained in these hash variables. If the value of a hash variable is different from what it would be obtained from a proper code execution, the checkpoint fails and the application is forced to end. This technique allows us to force a particular sequence of instruction execution within methods, and a certain sequence of method calls within a class or between classes. An attacker cannot eliminate the checkpoints used for program tracing because these checkpoints are directly inserted in the signed code. Any such change would be detected by the verification of the code signature.

Java Corruption: Undoubtedly, the most challenging attack to our architecture is corruption through compromised Java environments. With a corrupted Java Running Environment (JRE) the attacker may overcome all the Java-based security controls (signature, sealing, authentication). Hence, the attacker may authenticate, read and modify the JAR. However, unless the attacker has a valid cryptographic key, the attacker cannot access the content or the policy. Henceforth, while the synchronization mechanism may fail, the confidentiality and integrity of the content are guaranteed, since the keys are never stored in the application. To quickly detect a corrupted JRE we tie together various control mechanisms, and continually do crosschecks and stop any execution as soon as any crosscheck fails. These checks include integrity checks on the system environment, validating manifest of sensitive directories, validating the runtime JAR, and checking that the extended Policy Manager is operating. These system integrity checks are repeated more times during the execution of the application, before critical points. Examples of critical points are: permission check, policy enforcement, protected content encryption/decryption, and creation of secure connections between SCOs. A stronger solution consists of deploying a Java Security Extension for the JRE, that provides assurance of correct system operation and integrity even in presence of successful attacks on the underlying operating system. The primary objective of this security extension is improving the level of the operational integrity of the Java application. This approach, originally proposed by Wheeler [24] consists of extensions to the Java 2 security system. The JRE extended components can be directly contained in our SCO, and ready to be loaded at each execution. The SCO will run only if all the extended components are properly loaded, to

ensure proper functioning of all the Java security services. More details are reported in the Appendix.

8. EXPERIMENTAL EVALUATION

We tested our framework on the Emulab testbed. The test environment consists of several OpenSSL-enabled servers: one head node which is the certificate authority, and several computing nodes. Each of the servers is installed with the Eucalyptus middleware [6]. We used Linux-based servers running Fedora5 OS. Each server has a a 64-bit Intel Quad Core Xeon E5530 processor, 4 GB RAM, and a 500 GB Hard Drive, and is equipped to run the JRE 6. We conducted several tests to evaluate the performance of the two key operations supported by our framework: (1) node synchronization; (2) Content Section update.

Concerning the synchronization algorithms, we tested the overall time required to complete synchronization processes. We considered networks of Master nodes only. As shown in Figure 4(a), we varied the number of Master nodes from 5 to 50. We run two tests, with SCON of γ equal to 3 and 5, respectively. With a higher connectivity ($\gamma = 5$) the synchronization is consistently faster, for every SCON size. We notice that even if the synchronization times for 50 Master nodes appear relatively high, this synchronization may help to quickly update several hundreds nodes. For example, we estimated that 50 Master nodes with $\gamma = 3$ may tolerate about 400 Slave nodes. To obtain such estimate, in a separate test we measured the time for synchronizing a Slave node by obtaining the Content Section from a Master node. The overall synchronization time consists of: (1) the connection and authentication time; and (2) the Content Section update time. Using a file of average size 20Mb, and a connection with a speed of 100Mb/sec the overall synchronization time is 240 ms. This implies that even in absence of parallelization, a Slave node may have to wait up to 240ms to be updated. Within 2 seconds, each Master node can serve 8 Slave nodes for a total of 400 Slave nodes.

Next, to better investigate how to reduce the synchronization time, we tested the effect of the Master nodes degree, γ. We tested the synchronization times for values of γ ranging from 1 to 10. We repeated these tests for different network sizes. As reported in Figure 4 (b), the overall trend is the same: the times for synchronization drop drastically after a certain value of γ. For values higher than such optimal value, the times remain seemingly constant. The optimal value appears to be approximately at $\gamma = \frac{|M|}{10}$, where $|M|$ is the Masters' cardinality. Based on these two experiments, we conclude that efficient synchronizations can be achieved with acceptable tolerance without requiring highly connected networks. Additionally, we tested the synchronization time in case of failed nodes. The results are reported in Figure 4 (c). The test considers a SCON with 30 Master nodes, and $\gamma = 8$. Each test considers an increasing number of failed nodes from 1 to all but one (7). Clearly, the times increase significantly, due to the time spent by a node waiting for the response. Yet, the synchronization can be completed within 150 sec.

To evaluate content update times, we tracked the time required for constructing a new Content Section (see Sect. 7). For a file of size equal to 1.2 MB, the overall update time is equal to 850ms. Most of the update time is due to the cryptographic operations. Encryption time under CP-ABE is proportional to the complexity of the policy. For this experiment, we considered an access tree with 20 leaves, resulting in a content encryption time of 640ms. Our experiments with files of different size reflect the complexity of the original CP-ABE protocol [2]. The other operations required to complete the update, i.e. content replacement, digest creation signature are in the order of few milliseconds, with the exception of the digest creation time, which takes 160ms.

Finally, we tested the overall size of the SCO. The Application Section is fixed, and it has a size of 350 KB. The Content Section includes one Java Policy file, which is about 5 KB and the content. This Policy file size changes slightly depending upon the number of grant and deny in the Java policy. The NMI is also small, $< 20KB$ and its size depends on γ (# of known Master nodes). The size of the protected content file is to be added also. With the encryption, the NMI and Content Section files increase of a few bytes.

9. RELATED WORK

Access control [22, 25] and data management outsourcing techniques targeting the cloud have been recently proposed [1, 13, 18]. Further, cloud-specific cryptographic-based approaches for ensuring remote data integrity have been developed [23]. Ateniese et al. [1] proposed the Provable Data Possession model for ensuring possession of files on untrusted storages, as well as a publicly verifiable version, which allows anyone to challenge the server for data possession [5]. These schemes are effective with static data, but are not suitable for dynamic scenarios where data may change and be used within and outside the cloud domain. Subsequently, Wang and et al. [23] proposed a data outsourcing protocol specific to the cloud. Wang's work is focused on auditing of stored data from trusted parties, and does not deal with access policies, nor does it provide aspects of data management.

The notion of SCO is corroborated by previous projects [10, 16] and our own results [20]. Our approaches are closely related to self-defending objects (SDO) [10] and self-protecting objects. SDOs are Java-based solutions for persistent protection to certain objects. SPOs are software components hosted in federated databases. The objective of SDOs is to ensure that all the policies related to any given object are enforced irrespective of which distributed database the object has been migrated to. SDOs depend on a Trusted Common Core for authentication and authorization, and therefore are not applicable in distributed systems. In fact, the realm of application of both SDOs and SPOs is restricted to centrally controlled systems that support trusted cores and federations. As a result, adaptiveness, synchronization and versioning issues are not considered. Related to the idea of self-protecting data is also the work on sticky polices [16] that focuses on portability of disclosure policies by means of declarative policies tightly coupled to sensitive data by means of cryptographic algorithms. However, these policies are designed for federated organizations, and therefore lack adaptiveness to the domain of application.

Furthermore, enterprise Java Beans (EJB), Microsoft's Component Object Model (COM), and the Common Object Request Broker Architecture (CORBA) are all object-oriented frameworks for building three-tiered applications. While they differ in design and exact functionality, all are based on distributed objects, location transparency, declarative transaction processing, and integrated security. They share SCO's goals of offering object-oriented technologies to facilitate distributed transactions and programming in distributed systems, but target trusted enterprises. Similarly, Orleans [3] offers a software framework focusing on synchronization of distributed programming objects and recovery on the cloud. Despite these similarities it fundamentally differs from our approach in that it focuses on programming environments and does not involve any protection of the objects, nor it is concerned about controlling accesses or usage.

Distributed synchronization protocols have also been widely investigated in the past [15]. However, these protocols are based on the use of software agents external to the objects (e.g. a lock manager), whereas in our case the SCO encapsulates all the software needed for an update and only the availability of a Java environment is required. Also those protocols do not include any protection mechanism for the object, nor do they support policies based on contexts or other properties of the access requestor. Yet, implementing a locking mechanism for our SCO-based architecture is part of our future work.

Other well-known cryptographic primitives have been developed not only to protect remote data from attacks to confidentiality and integrity, but also to support condition evaluation on encrypted data [12,19]. These approaches may be suitable for secure content rendering from the SCO, but are complementary to our architecture, in that they address confidentiality, rather than distributed management.

10. CONCLUSION

We presented an approach for secure and distributed data management. The idea behind our solution is to protect the data by means of wrappers applied to the targeted content file(s) which protect the content as it travels across domains by locally enforcing security policies. The policies may be dynamic, and adapt to the location and other contextual dimensions. We plan to further develop the policy language and support more articulated contexts. We will also investigate how to support distributed locking systems.

11. ACKNOWLEDGEMENT

Portion of the work from Dr. Squicciarini was funded by the National Science Foundation under Award #1250319 "Collaborative Research: Brokerage Services for the Next Generation Cloud". Portions of the work from Dr. Bertino was funded by National Science Foundation under Award # 1111512 "Privacy-Enhanced Secure Data Provenance".

12. REFERENCES

[1] G. Ateniese, R. Burns, R. Curtmola, J. Herring, L. Kissner, Z. Peterson, and D. Song. Provable data possession at untrusted stores. In *ACM conference on Computer and Communications Security*, pages 598–609, 2007.

[2] J. Bethencourt, A. Sahai, and B. Waters. Ciphertext-policy attribute-based encryption. In *2007 IEEE Symposium on Security and Privacy*, SP '07, pages 321–334, Washington, DC, USA, 2007.

[3] S. Bykov, A. Geller, G. Kliot, J. R. Larus, R. Pandya, and J. Thelin. Orleans: cloud computing for everyone. In *Proceedings of the 2nd ACM Symposium on Cloud Computing*, SOCC '11, pages 16:1–16:14, New York, NY, USA, 2011. ACM.

[4] R. Crozer. Mr rental trials azure as telstra cloud redundancy. http://www.itnews.com.au/News/306871,mr-rental-trials-azure-as-telstra-cloud-redundancy.aspx.

[5] R. Curtmola, O. Khan, R. Burns, and G. Ateniese. MR-PDP: Multiple-replica provable data possession. In *The 28th International Conference on Distributed Computing Systems*, pages 411 –420, June 2008.

[6] Eucalyptus Systems. http://www.eucalyptus.com/.

[7] R. G. Gallager, P. A. Humblet, and P. M. Spira. A distributed algorithm for minimum-weight spanning trees. *ACM Trans. Program. Lang. Syst.*, 5:66–77, January 1983.

[8] GeoIP Web Service. http://www.webservicex.net/geoipservice.asmx.

[9] Gordon's Notes. Reliability and the cloud - redundancy required. http://notes.kateva.org/2011/05/reliability-and-cloud-redundancy.html.

[10] J. W. Holford, W. J. Caelli, and A. W. Rhodes. Using self-defending objects to develop security aware applications in java. In *27th Australasian conference on Computer science - Volume 26*, ACSC '04, pages 341–349, Darlinghurst, Australia, Australia, 2004.

[11] Java Authentication and Authorization Services. http://java.sun.com/products/archive/jaas/.

[12] J. Katz, A. Sahai, and B. Waters. Predicate encryption supporting disjunctions, polynomial equations, and inner products. In *27th annual international conference on Advances in cryptology*, pages 146–162, Berlin, Heidelberg, 2008. Springer-Verlag.

[13] M. Lillibridge, S. Elnikety, A. Birrell, M. Burrows, and M. Isard. A cooperative internet backup scheme. In *USENIX Annual Technical Conference*, pages 29–41, 2003.

[14] D. Liu and S. Xu. MuTT: A Multi-Threaded Tracer for Java Programs. In *8th IEEE/ACIS International Conference on Computer and Information Science*, pages 949–954, 2009.

[15] M. T. Ozsu and P. Valduriez. *Principles of Distributed Database Systems, 2/E*. Prentice Hall, 1999.

[16] H. C. Pöhls. Verifiable and revocable expression of consent to processing of aggregated personal data. In *International Conference on Information and Communications Security (ICICS)*, pages 279–293, 2008.

[17] Y. Sakabe, M. Soshi, and A. Miyaji. Java obfuscation with a theoretical basis for building secure mobile agents. In A. Lioy and D. Mazzocchi, editors, *Communications and Multimedia Security. Advanced Techniques for Network and Data Protection*, volume 2828 of *Lecture Notes in Computer Science*, pages 89–103. 2003.

[18] T. J. E. Schwarz and E. L. Miller. Store, forget, and check: Using algebraic signatures to check remotely administered storage. In *IEEE International Conference on Distributed Systems*, page 12, 2006.

[19] N. Smart and F. Vercauteren. Fully Homomorphic Encryption with Relatively Small Key and Ciphertext Sizes. In *Public Key Cryptography â PKC 2010*, volume 6056 of *Lecture Notes in Computer Science*, pages 420–443. 2010.

[20] A. Squicciarini, G. Petracca, and E. Bertino. Adaptive data management for self-protecting objects in cloud computing systems. In *The International Conference on Network and Service Management (CNSM)*, 2012.

[21] Sun. Lesson: Packaging programs in jar files. http://java.sun.com/docs/books/tutorial/deployment/jar/.

[22] Q. Wang and H. Jin. Data leakage mitigation for discretionary access control in collaboration clouds. In *16th ACM symposium on Access control models and technologies*, SACMAT '11, pages 103–112, New York, NY, USA, 2011. ACM.

[23] Q. Wang, C. Wang, J. Li, K. Ren, and W. Lou. Enabling public verifiability and data dynamics for storage security in cloud computing. In *ESORICS*, pages 355–370, 2009.

[24] D. M. Wheeler, A. Conyers, J. Luo, and A. Xiong. Java security extensions for a java server in a hostile environment. In *ACSAC*, pages 64–73, 2001.

[25] S. Yu, C. Wang, K. Ren, and W. Lou. Achieving secure, scalable, and fine-grained data access control in cloud computing. In *Proceedings IEEE INFOCOM*, pages 1–9, 2010.

APPENDIX

A: Algorithms

In this appendix we provide the main algorithms presented in the paper. First, we present the operational flow of the policy enforcement algorithm. The algorithm is displayed in Figure 5. Algorithm 1 reports the node creation process.

Algorithm 1: SCO Network node addition

Require: ω Ratio
$\alpha \geq 5$ nodes ratio
$\gamma \geq 2$ Redundancy Threshold
$SelectedMs$ Set of Masters to be contacted during synchronization
NMI Network Management Information
$selectRandomM(SelectedMs)$ Selects a new Master from NMI that it is not in SelectMs set

---

Begin
t = NMI.getNumCopies()
SelectedMs = {}
if $(t = k(\omega\alpha) + \omega\alpha)$ **then**
  k++
end if
if $(k(\omega\alpha) \leq t \leq k(\omega\alpha) + \alpha)$ **then**
  %Master
  if $(t \leq 2)$ **then**
    for (count := t; count > 1; count –) **do**
      SelectedMs := NMI.selectRandomM(SelectedM)
    end for
  else
    if $\gamma > t - 1$ **then**
      count:= $t - 1$
    else
      count:= γ
    end if
    while count$\neq$ 0 **do**
      SelectedMs$\leq$ NMI.selectRandomM(SelectedM)
      count−−
    end while
  end if
  PORT := n.getFreePort()
  NMI.addNewMaster(IP,PORT)
  NMI.incNumCopies() startSynch(NMI)
else
  %Slave
  count := γ
  while (count $\neq$ 0) **do**
    SelectedMs $\leq$ NMI.selectRandomM(SelectedM)
    count−−
  end while
  NMI.incNumCopies()
  startSynch(NMI)
end if
End

B: Security Extensions

The Java-based security extensions proposed in Section 7.2 provide assurance of correct system operation and integrity even in presence of successful attacks on the underlying operating system. The primary objective of this security extension is improving the level of the operational integrity of the Java application. The idea, originally proposed by Wheeler [24] relies on extensions to the Java 2 security system, including the Security Manager, the Class Loader and the Policy Manager. The JRE extended components can be

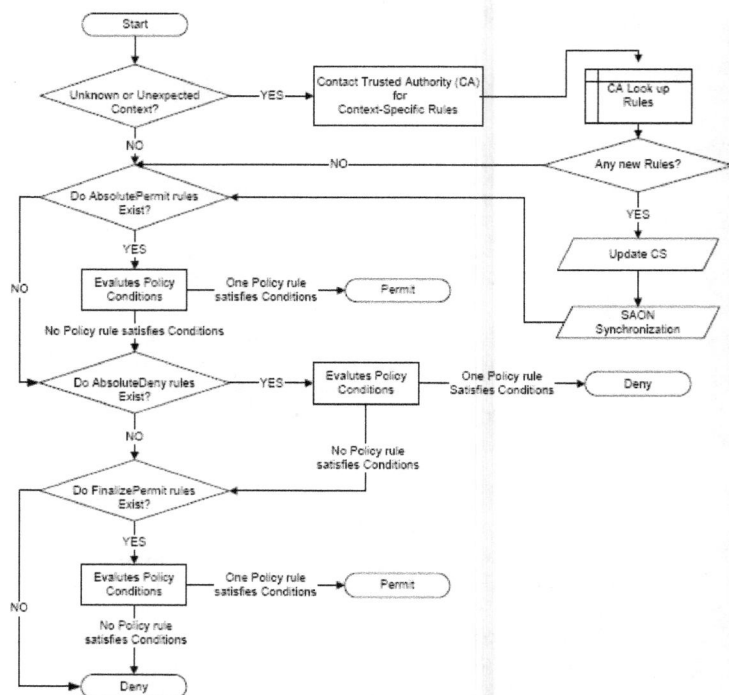

Figure 5: Policy Evaluation and Enforcement

directly contained in our SCO, and ready to be loaded at each execution. The extensions create a strong dependency between these components. For example, the Class Loader will not operate without the extended Security Manager. The extended Security Manager performs system integrity checks during startup and during normal permission checks. These checks include integrity checks on the system environment, validating manifest of sensitive directories, validating the run-time Jar (rt.Jar), and checking that the extended Policy Manager is operating.

These system integrity checks are repeated during the execution of the application, before critical points. Examples of critical points of the execution are: permission check, policy enforcement, protected content encryption/decryption, and creation of secure connections between SPCs and Synchronization Managers. The extended policy manager checks that the system's configuration (.policy and .conf files) are not modified, by verifying theirs digital signature. Before the Class Loader loads any classes, its loads the extended Security Manager, which checks the system and validates that the extended Policy Manager is loaded. If any of the integrity checks fails, each extended component notifies the other components of the failure, and attempts to shut down the system operation. Furthermore, to prevent any sensitive operation from being performed for newly loaded classes, the extended Policy Manager denies access to all services and resources by returning a null permission in response to any query.

Towards Self-Repairing Replication-Based Storage Systems Using Untrusted Clouds

Bo Chen, Reza Curtmola
Department of Computer Science
New Jersey Institute of Technology
{bc47,crix}@njit.edu

ABSTRACT

Distributed storage systems store data redundantly at multiple servers which are geographically spread throughout the world. This basic approach would be sufficient in handling server failure due to natural faults, because when one server fails, data from healthy servers can be used to restore the desired redundancy level. However, in a setting where servers are untrusted and can behave maliciously, data redundancy must be used in tandem with Remote Data Checking (RDC) to ensure that the redundancy level of the storage systems is maintained over time.

All previous RDC schemes for distributed systems impose a heavy burden on the data owner (client) during data maintenance: To repair data at a faulty server, the data owner needs to first download a large amount of data, re-generate the data to be stored at a new server, and then upload this data at a new healthy server. We propose RDC − SR, a novel RDC scheme for replication-based distributed storage systems. RDC − SR enables Server-side Repair (thus taking advantage of the premium connections available between a CSP's data centers) and places a minimal load on the data owner who only has to act as a *repair coordinator*. The main insight behind RDC − SR is that the replicas are differentiated based on a controllable amount of masking, which offers RDC − SR flexibility in handling different adversarial strengths. Also, replica generation must be time consuming in order to avoid certain colluding attacks from malicious servers. Our prototype for RDC − SR built on Amazon AWS validates the practicality of this new approach.

Categories and Subject Descriptors

H.3.2 [**Information Storage and Retrieval**]: Information Storage

General Terms

Security, Design, Performance

Keywords

Cloud storage, remote data integrity checking, server-side repair, replicate on the fly, Amazon AWS

1. Introduction

The recent proliferation of cloud services has made it easier than ever to build distributed storage systems based on Cloud Storage Providers (CSPs). Traditionally, a distributed storage system stores data redundantly at multiple servers which are geographically spread throughout the world. In a benign setting where the storage servers always behave in a non-adversarial manner, this basic approach would be sufficient in order to deal with server failure due to natural faults. In this paper however, we consider a setting in which the storage servers are untrusted and may act maliciously. In this setting, Remote Data Checking (RDC) [3, 4, 15, 21] can be used to ensure that the data remains recoverable over time even if the storage servers are untrusted.

When a distributed storage system is used in tandem with remote data checking, we can distinguish several phases throughout the lifetime of the storage system: Setup, Challenge, and Repair. To outsource a file F, the data owner creates multiple replicas of the file during Setup and stores them at multiple storage servers (one replica per server). During the Challenge phase, the data owner can ask periodically each server to provide a proof that the server's replica has remained intact. If a replica is found corrupt during the Challenge phase, the data owner can take actions to Repair the corrupted replica using data from the healthy replicas, thus restoring the desired redundancy level in the system. The Challenge and Repair phases will alternate over the lifetime of the system.

In cloud storage outsourcing, a data owner stores data in a distributed storage system that consists of multiple cloud storage servers. The storage servers may belong to the same CSP (*e.g.,* Amazon has multiple data centers in different locations), or to different CSPs. The ultimate goal of the data owner is that the data will be retrievable at any point of time in the future. Conforming to this notion of storage outsourcing, the data owner would like to outsource *both the storage and the management* of the data. In other words, after the Setup phase, the data owner should only have to store a small, constant, amount of data and should be involved as little as possible in the maintenance of the data. In previous work, the data owner can have minimal involvement in the Challenge phase when using an RDC scheme that has public verifiability (*i.e.,* the task of verifying that data remains retrievable can be delegated to a third party auditor). However, in all previous work [12, 7], the Repair phase imposes a significant burden on the data owner, who needs to expend a significant amount of computation and communication. For example, to repair data at a failed server, the data owner needs to first download an amount of data equal to the file size, re-generate the data to be stored at a new server, and then upload this data at a new healthy server ([12, 7]). Archival storage deals with large amounts of data (Terabytes or Petabytes) and thus maintaining the health of the data imposes a heavy burden on the data owner.

In this work, we ask the question: Is it possible to design an RDC scheme which can repair corrupted data with the least data owner intervention? We answer this question in the positive by exploring a model which minimizes the data owner's involvement in the Repair phase, thus fully realizing the vision of outsourcing both the storage and management of data. During Repair, the data owner simply acts as a *repair coordinator*, which allows the data owner to manage data using a lightweight device. This is in contrast with previous work, which imposes a heavy burden on the data owner during Repair. The main challenge is how to ensure that the untrusted servers manage the data properly over time (*i.e.*, take necessary actions to maintain the desired level of redundancy when some of the replicas have failed).

Main objective: Informally, our main objective is to design an RDC scheme for a replication-based distributed storage system which has the following properties:

– the system stores t replicas of the data owner's original file
– the system imposes a small load on the verifier during the Challenge phase.
– the system imposes a small management load on the data owner (by minimizing the involvement of the data owner during the Repair phase).

The first two properties alone can be achieved based on techniques proposed in previous work ([12] provides multiple replica guarantees, whereas RDC based on spot-checking [3, 15, 21] supports a lightweight verification mechanism in the Challenge phase). The challenge is to achieve the third property without giving up any of the first two properties. We meet these objectives by proposing a new model and by re-designing the three phases of a traditional RDC protocol.

1.1 Solution overview

Two insights motivate the design of our solution:

Insight 1. Replica differentiation: The storage servers should be required to store t different replicas. Otherwise, if all replicas are identical, an economically motivated set of colluding servers could attempt to save storage by simply storing only one replica and redirect all client's challenges to the one server storing the replica.

Previous work [6, 17] proposed to store identical replicas at storage servers which are in different locations. To check that each server stores a replica, they require servers to respond fast, thus relying on the network delay and bandwidth properties. While storing identical replicas has the advantage of simplicity, in Sec. 2.1 we show that this approach has major limitations. Moreover, we show that for real-world CSPs, one of the assumptions made by [6] does not hold.

Insight 2. Server-side repair: We can minimize the load on the data owner during the Repair phase by relying on the servers to collaborate in order to generate a new replica whenever a replica has failed. This is advantageous because of two reasons:

(a) the servers are usually connected through premium network connections (high bandwidth), as opposed to the

data owner's connection which may have limited download/upload bandwidth. Our experiments in Table 2 (Appendix A) show that Amazon AWS has premium Internet connection of up to tens of MB/s between its data centers.

(b) the computational burden during the Repair phase is shifted to the servers, allowing data owners to remain lightweight.

Previous RDC schemes for replication-based distributed storage systems ([12]) do not give the storage servers access to the original data owner's file. Each replica is a masked/encrypted version of the original file. As a result, the Repair phase imposes a high burden on the data owner: The communication and computation cost to create a new replica is linear with the size of the replica because the data owner needs to download a replica, unmask/decrypt it, create a new replica and upload the new replica. If the servers do not have access to the original file, this intense level of data owner involvement during Repair is unavoidable.

In this paper, we propose to use a different paradigm, in which the data owner gives the servers both access to the original file and the means to generate new replicas. This will allow the servers to generate a new replica by collaborating between themselves during Repair.

A Basic Approach and Its Limitations. A straightforward approach would be for the data owner to create *different* replicas by using masking/encryption of the original file. The data owner would reveal to the servers the key material used to create the masked/encrypted replicas. During Repair, the servers themselves could recover the original file from a healthy replica and restore the corrupted replica, reducing the burden on the data owner.

This basic approach is vulnerable to a potential attack, the *replicate on the fly (ROTF) attack*: During Repair, a malicious set of servers could claim they generate a new replica whenever an existing replica has failed, but in reality they do not create the replica (using this strategy, an economically motivated set of servers tries to use less storage than their contractual obligation). When the client checks the newly generated replica during the Challenge phase, the set of malicious servers can collaborate to generate the replica *on the fly* and pass the verification successfully (this replica is then immediately deleted after passing the challenge in order to save storage). This will hurt the reliability of the storage system, because in time the system will end up storing much fewer than t replicas, unbeknownst to the client.

Overcoming the ROTF attack. The new paradigm we introduce in this paper, which allows the servers to generate a new replica by collaborating between themselves during Repair, has the important advantage of minimizing the load on the data owner during data maintenance. However, this comes at the cost of allowing a new attack avenue for servers, the ROTF attack.

To overcome the ROTF attack, we *make replica creation to be time consuming*. In this way, malicious servers cannot generate replicas on the fly during Challenge without being detected.

Contributions. In this paper, we propose RDC − SR, a novel RDC scheme for replication-based distributed storage systems, which enables Server-side Repair. Compared to all the previous distributed RDC schemes, which impose a high load on the data owner in the Repair phase, our RDC − SR scheme imposes a small load on both the verifier in the Challenge phase and the data owner in the Repair phase. To the best of our knowledge, we are the first to propose the server-side repair strategy and an RDC scheme that implements it in the context of a real-world CSP. Specifically, our paper makes the following contributions:

- We point out limitations of a previous network delay-based model for establishing data geolocation and revise this model to suit our approach. Based on experiments on the Amazon cloud platform, we show that one of the assumptions made in the network delay-based model does not hold in practice. We further show that an RDC scheme built on such a model can only provide a very low data possession assurance.

- We revise this model to include replica differentiation and time-consuming replica generation, in order to limit the ability of economically-motivated adversaries to cheat. In this new model, in which servers are allowed to generate new replicas, the burden during the Repair phase is shifted to the server side, allowing lightweight clients to perform data maintenance. We observe that this new paradigm enables a new attack, the *replicate on the fly (ROTF)* attack, which requires us to consider a new adversarial model, the α-cheating adversary that seeks to cheat by only storing an α fraction of its contractual storage obligations.

- All previous distributed RDC schemes place a heavy burden on the client during repair. We propose RDC − SR, a novel RDC scheme for replication-based distributed storage systems. RDC − SR enables Server-side Repair (thus taking advantage of the premium connections available between a CSP's data centers) and places a minimal load on the client who only has to act as a *repair coordinator*. To integrate our new model into RDC − SR, we devise a novel technique by which replicas are differentiated based on a controllable amount of masking; this offers RDC − SR flexibility in handling different adversarial strengths. We prove that RDC − SR can mitigate the ROTF attack.

- We provide guidelines on how to choose the parameters for RDC − SR in a practical setting and build a prototype for RDC − SR on Amazon AWS. The experimental results show that: (a) RDC − SR imposes only a small load on the verifier in the Challenge phase and a small management load on the data owner in the Repair phase; (b) RDC − SR can easily differentiate benign and adversarial CSP behavior when relying on a time threshold, as 95% of the benign cases are under the threshold, while 100% of the adversarial cases are over the threshold.

2. Models for Checking Replica Storage

In this section, we first review a previously proposed theoretical framework that relies purely on network delay to establish the geolocation of files at cloud providers, and point out several limitations of this model when used with a basic RDC protocol on the Amazon cloud service provider. The main limitation is that one of its assumptions does not hold in a practical setting, and thus a protocol that relies only on the network delay to detect server misbehavior can only offer

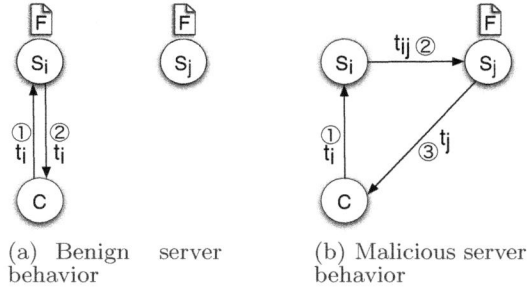

(a) Benign server behavior   (b) Malicious server behavior

Figure 1: Auditing protocol: Client C checks if server s_i has a file copy F.

a very low data possession guarantee. We then augment this model to include time-consuming replica generation in order to make RDC usable for geolocation of files in the context of a real-world cloud storage provider such as Amazon.

2.1 A Network Delay-based Model and Its Limitations

Benson, Dowsley and Shacham proposed a theoretical model for verifying that copies of a client's data are stored at different geographic locations [6] (we refer to it as the "BDS model"). This model allows to derive a condition which can be used to detect if a server at some location does not have a copy of the data. The idea behind the condition is that an auditor which challenges a storage server must receive an answer within a certain time, otherwise the server is considered malicious. The time is chosen such that a server that does not have the challenged data cannot provide an answer by using data from a server at a different geolocation.

The BDS model [6]. The customer (client) makes a contract with the CSP to store one copy of the client's file in each of the CSP's k data centers. For simplicity, if we assume that $k = 2$, then a file copy should be stored at s_i and another file copy at s_j. The goal is to build an audit protocol that tests if the cloud provider is really storing one copy of the file in each of the two data centers s_i and s_j. Several assumptions need to be made:

(Assumption 1) The locations of all data centers of the cloud provider are known.

(Assumption 2) The cloud provider does not have any exclusive Internet connection between the data centers.

(Assumption 3) For each datacenter s, it is possible to have access to a machine that is located very close to s (*i.e.*, very small network latency), such as in the same data center.

Consider the case when the client wants to check if s_i is storing a copy of the file. As shown in Figure 1(b), s_i and s_j may be colluding malicious servers who only store one copy of the file at s_j; when s_i is challenged by the client to prove data possession, it redirects the challenge to s_j, who answers directly to the client. To prevent such an attack, the client imposes a certain time limit for receiving the answer.

Let T_i be the upper bound on the execution time of some auditing protocol by a datacenter s_i, t_i be the network delay between the client and s_i, and t_{ij} be the network delay between data centers s_i and s_j. For a network delay time t, we use the notation $max(t)$ to denote the upper bound on t and $min(t)$ to denote the lower bound on t.

If the data center s_i is honest, the client accepts the audit protocol execution as valid if the elapsed time for receiving the answer is $T_i + 2 * max(t_i)$, because that is the time needed to receive the answer in the worst case scenario. On the other hand, if the answer is received after $min(t_i) + min(t_{ij}) + min(t_j)$, the client should consider the audit protocol execution invalid, since s_i may be dishonest and may be using data from another data center. Thus $T_i + 2 * max(t_i) \leq min(t_i) + min(t_{ij}) + min(t_j)$, or

$$T_i \leq min(t_i) + min(t_{ij}) + min(t_j) - 2 * max(t_i) \quad (1)$$

Limitations of the basic PoR protocol based on BDS model. Based on the condition derived from the BDS model, [6] proposed a basic Proof of Retrievability (PoR) protocol which seeks to ensure that a set of storage servers not only store n copies of the client's data, but also that these copies are stored at specific geographic locations known to the client. In the PoR protocol, the client stores identical copies of a file at multiple storage servers, and for each copy, it also stores authentication tags (one tag for each file block). To check that a server has a copy of the file, the auditor asks the server to provide several randomly chosen file blocks and their corresponding MAC tags. If the auditor receives the answer within a certain time, the auditor checks if the MAC tags are valid tags for the file blocks. In this protocol, the auditor challenges as many random blocks as it is possible for s_i to access in time T_i.

Based on Assumption 3 in the BDS model, the auditor can be located very close to s_i, which means that $min(t_i)$ and $max(t_i)$ will be small compared to t_{ij} and t_j. Thus, the value of T_i will be mainly determined by $min(t_{ij})$ and $min(t_j)$, which is determined by the quality (bandwidth) of the Internet connection between s_i and s_j and by the distance between s_i and s_j. Low bandwidth Internet connection and large distance between s_i and s_j will result in larger values of $min(t_{ij})$ and $min(t_j)$, thus resulting in a larger T_i. A larger T_i means the auditor can challenge more blocks while still being able to differentiate a benign server from a malicious server (the auditor should be able to challenge a large enough number of randomly chosen blocks in order to gain a reasonable confidence that the entire file is stored by the server).

To ensure that T_i is large enough (and thus the protocol has practical value), the BDS model relies explicitly on the assumption that there is no exclusive Internet connection between data centers (Assumption 2). The BDS model also relies on the implicit assumption that the data centers should be far away from each other. However, our measurements with the Amazon CSP show that these assumptions do not hold (see Tables 2 and 3 in Appendix A). In general, the network delay is the sum between propagation delay (the time it takes the signal to travel from sender to the receiver) and the transmission delay (the time required to push all the data bits into the wire). From Table 2, we can see that the download bandwidth between different S3 data centers varies between 11-36 MB/s, which is significantly higher than the bandwidth between a point outside the data centers and the data centers (less than 1 MB/s between our institution and different S3 data centers). We also notice that inside a data center the download bandwidth is very high (between 32-52 MB/s) and the propagation delay is very small (between 0.2-0.7 milliseconds). Finally, we notice from Table 3 that the propagation delay between certain

S3 data centers is quite small (*e.g.*, 11 milliseconds between N. California and Oregon).

Using the numbers in Tables 2 and 3, with s_i and s_j being the Virginia and the N. California data centers respectively, and assuming that the auditor is located within s_i and challenges k 4KB random file blocks from s_i, Equation (1) for the basic PoR protocol becomes $x \cdot k \leq 80 + 0.3k$, where x is the time to access one random file block. According to our experiments on Amazon S3, $x \approx 30$ milliseconds (refer to Appendix C), thus $k \leq 2.66$. This means the basic PoR protocol applied in the setting of the Amazon CSP allows the auditor to challenge at most two random file blocks in each protocol execution. This provides a very low data possession assurance (comparatively, to achieve 99% confidence that misbehavior will be detected when the server corrupts 1% of the file, the auditor should challenge 460 randomly chosen file blocks [3]).

2.2 A New Model to Enable Server-side Repair

The main problem with the basic PoR protocol based on the BDS model (cf. Sec. 2.1) is that all the file copies are identical and the auditor relies solely on the network delay to detect malicious server behavior. As a result, the protocol must assume that there is no exclusive Internet connection between the data centers (Assumption 2 in the BDS model). Having established in Section 2.1 that this assumption does not hold in a practical setting, we augment the BDS model to make it usable in a practical setting. Namely, we require that the file replicas stored at each server must be different and personalized for each server. Upon being challenged, each server must produce an answer that is dependent on its own replica. As a result, a server cannot answer a challenge by using another server's replica. An economically-motivated server who does not possess its assigned replica may try to cheat by using another server's replica. But to do this, the cheating server must first generate its own replica in order to successfully answer a challenge. As a result, our model does not rely purely on network delay to differentiate benign behavior from malicious behavior, but also on the time it takes to generate a file replica. This allows us to eliminate Assumption 2 from the BDS model, because we require that *replica generation be time consuming*.

We propose a model in which the client creates t different file replicas and stores them at t data centers owned by the same CSP (one replica at each data center). To illustrate the model for $t = 2$, the data owner generates file replicas $\mathbf{F}_i$ and $\mathbf{F}_j$; server s_i stores $\mathbf{F}_i$ and s_j stores $\mathbf{F}_j$. Even when replicas are different, malicious servers may execute the ROTF attack, in which a server that does not possess its assigned replica may try to cheat by using replicas from other servers to generate its assigned replica on the fly during the Challenge phase. Using the same notation as in the BDS model in Section 2.1, an audit protocol execution should be considered invalid if the answer is received after $min(t_i) + min(t_{ij}) + min(t_j) + min(t_R)$, where t_R denotes the time required to generate replica $\mathbf{F}_i$ (more precisely, the time required to generate the portion of $\mathbf{F}_i$ that is necessary to construct a correct answer). Thus, the condition used to differentiate benign from malicious behavior becomes:

$$T_i + 2 * max(t_i) \leq min(t_i) + min(t_{ij}) + min(t_j) + min(t_R) \quad (2)$$

We only need to make the following two assumptions (note

that we do not assume there is no exclusive Internet connection between the data centers like in the BDS model):

(Assumption 1) The locations of all datacenters of the cloud provider are known.

(Assumption 2) For each datacenter s, it is possible to have access to a machine that is located very close to s (*i.e.*, very small network latency), such as in the same data center.

3. System and Adversarial Model

3.1 System Model

The client wants to outsource the storage of a file $\mathbf{F}$. To ensure high reliability and fault tolerance of the data, the client creates t *distinct* replicas and outsources them to t data centers (storage servers) owned by a CSP (one replica at each data center). To ensure that the t replicas remain healthy over time, the client challenges each of the t servers periodically. Upon finding a corrupted replica, the client acts as a *repair coordinator* who oversees the repair of the corrupted replica (the CSP, who has premium network connection between its data centers, uses the healthy replicas to repair the corrupted replica; the client should have minimal involvement in the repair process).

We note that, given an individual file replica, say $\mathbf{F}_i$, the CSP can generate any another replica, say $\mathbf{F}_j$, in two steps: first recover the original file $\mathbf{F}$ from $\mathbf{F}_i$, and then generate $\mathbf{F}_j$.

3.2 Adversarial model

We assume that the CSP is rational and economically motivated. The CSP will try to cheat only if cheating cannot be detected and if it achieves some economic benefit, such as using less storage than required by contract. An economically motivated adversary captures many practical settings in which malicious servers will not cheat and risk their reputation, unless they can achieve a clear financial gain. We also note that when the adversary is fully malicious, *i.e.*, it tries to corrupt the client's data without regard to its own resource consumption, there is no solution to the problem of building a reliable system with t replicas [7, 12].

The ROTF attack. We are particularly concerned with the following *replicate on the fly (ROTF) attack*: During Repair, a set of colluding servers could claim they generate a new replica whenever an existing replica has failed, but in reality they do not create and store the replica. When the client checks the newly generated replica during the Challenge phase, the set of malicious servers can collaborate to generate the replica on the fly and pass the verification successfully. Immediately after the check, the servers delete the newly generated replica, only to re-generate it on the fly when the client initiates the next check. This will hurt the reliability of the storage system, because in time the system will end up storing much fewer than t replicas, unbeknownst to the client.

To illustrate the ROTF attack, consider the setting in Figure 1(b), where s_i and s_j should to store replicas $\mathbf{F}_i$ and $\mathbf{F}_j$, respectively, but only s_j stores $\mathbf{F}_j$. When s_i is being challenged to prove possession of $\mathbf{F}_i$, s_i can retrieve $\mathbf{F}_j$ from s_j, and generate $\mathbf{F}_i$ on the fly in order to pass the challenge. Or, it can forward the challenge to s_j, who uses $\mathbf{F}_j$ to generate on the fly $\mathbf{F}_i$ and then uses $\mathbf{F}_i$ to construct a valid response to the challenge. Immediately after the challenge, $\mathbf{F}_i$ is deleted.

The α-cheating adversary. A CSP is obligated by contract to store t file replicas, which requires a total of $t|\mathbf{F}|$ storage. However, a dishonest CSP may try to use less than $t|\mathbf{F}|$ storage space and hope that this will go undetected (*e.g.*, executes the ROTF attack). We use the following definition to denote a CSP that is using only an α fraction of its contractual storage obligation:

Definition 3.1. *An α-cheating adversary is an economically-motivated adversary that can successfully pass a challenge by only using $\alpha t|\mathbf{F}|$ storage (where $\frac{1}{t} \le \alpha \le 1$).*

Note that if $\alpha < \frac{1}{t}$, then the CSP stores less than $|\mathbf{F}|$, which means that any single-replica RDC scheme [3, 15] would be enough to detect the CSP's dishonest behavior. Thus, we do not consider the case when $\alpha < \frac{1}{t}$.

Adversarial Strategies. Replica generation in our model is time consuming. A dishonest CSP trying to cheat by storing less replicas and executing the ROTF attack is always better off by keeping a copy of the original file $\mathbf{F}$. While this strategy requires some additional storage, it increases considerably the CSP's chances to cheat undetectably because the CSP can generate any individual replica from $\mathbf{F}$ in one step. Otherwise, cheating would require a two-step process: To generate a particular replica that is being challenged and which is not in its possession, say $\mathbf{F}_i$, the CSP would need to first recover $\mathbf{F}$ from an existing replica, say $\mathbf{F}_j$, and then generate $\mathbf{F}_i$ from $\mathbf{F}$. Since replica generation is a time consuming operation (and similarly recovering $\mathbf{F}$ from one of its replicas is also time-consuming), this two-step process would considerably increase the client's chances of detecting the CSP's dishonest behavior. Thus, we assume a dishonest CSP always stores a copy of the original file $\mathbf{F}$.

Also, recall that most RDC schemes ensure efficiency by using spot checking [3, 15, 21]: The client challenges the server to prove possession of a randomly chosen subset of c blocks out of all the n file blocks. This can provide a high likelihood that the server is storing the entire file.

An α-cheating adversary can adopt several strategies to distribute its $\alpha t|\mathbf{F}|$ storage among the t servers, which will influence its ability to remain undetected. A *basic strategy* is when the adversary chooses to store on one of the servers the original file $\mathbf{F}$, and to store on each of $\lfloor \alpha t \rfloor - 1$ servers a particular different replica. Thus, no data is stored on the remaining $t - \lfloor \alpha t \rfloor$ servers. In this case, when one of the $t - \lfloor \alpha t \rfloor$ servers is challenged, it can always generate the c challenged blocks on the fly and then construct the answer to the challenge. Let σ be the time required to generate the c challenged blocks for one replica.

It turns out that the *best data distribution strategy for cheating* is when the adversary stores in each of the t servers an α fraction of the blocks from the corresponding replica for that server. Thus, the adversary will still only use $\alpha t|\mathbf{F}|$ storage space in total[1]. When any of the t servers is challenged, this server will already possess, on average, an α fraction of the c blocks that are being challenged. Thus, on average, it only needs to generate on the fly a $(1-\alpha)$ fraction of the c challenged blocks, which it can do in time $(1-\alpha)\sigma$. Since, $(1-\alpha)\sigma < \sigma$, this strategy is always better than the previously presented basic strategy.

---

[1]Recall that we have assumed that the adversary always stores one original file copy $\mathbf{F}$, thus the total storage is $(\alpha t + 1)|\mathbf{F}|$; when t is large, this can be approximated by $\alpha t|\mathbf{F}|$.

4. An RDC Scheme with Server-side Repair

In this section, we propose RDC − SR, the first replication-based Remote Data Checking scheme that supports Server-side Repair.

The original file F has n blocks, $F = \{b_1, \ldots, b_n\}$, and each contains s symbols in $GF(p)$, where p is a large prime (at least 80 bits). We use j to denote the index of a block within a file / replica (i.e., $j \in \{1 \ldots n\}$), and k to denote the index of a symbol in a block (i.e., $k \in \{1 \ldots s\}$). Let κ be a security parameter. We make use of two pseudo-random functions (PRFs) h and γ with the following parameters:

$- h : \{0,1\}^{\kappa} \times \{0,1\}^{*} \rightarrow \{0,1\}^{\log p}$

$- \gamma : \{0,1\}^{\kappa} \times \{0,1\}^{*} \rightarrow \{0,1\}^{\log p}$

RDC − SR overview. Like any RDC system for a multiple-server setting [12, 7, 24, 11], RDC − SR consists of three phases: Setup, Challenge and Repair. During the Setup phase, the client first preprocesses the original file and generates t distinct replicas. We use i to denote the index of the replica (i.e., $i \in \{1 \ldots t\}$). To differentiate the replicas, we adopt a masking strategy similar as in [12], in which every symbol of the original file is masked individually by adding a random value modulo p. We introduce a new parameter η, which denotes the number of masking operations imposed on each symbol when generating a distinct replica. η can help control the computational load caused by the masking, e.g., we can choose a larger η if we try to make the masking more expensive for a block. This has the advantage that we can adjust the load for masking to defend against different adversarial strenghts (see Sec. 3.2). The client then generates verification tags for every replica, one tag per file block. Each verification tag is computed similarly as in [21], namely as a message authentication code by combining universal hashing with a PRF [16, 20, 22, 27]. After having generated t distinct replicas and the corresponding verification tags, the client sends those replicas to t different data centers of the CSP (one replica per server), and the set of all verification tags to each data center. The client also makes public the key used for generating the distinct replicas, so that the servers can use it during Repair to generate new replicas on their own.

During the Challenge phase the client acting as the verifier uses spot checking to check the replica at each server s_i, in which it randomly samples a small subset of blocks from a replica and checks their validity based on the the server s_i's response. Such a technique can detect replica corruption with high probability [3], and has the advantage of only imposing a small overhead on both the client and the server. We use a threshold τ for our new model (see Sec.2.2): If the response from a server is not received within time τ, then that replica will be considered corrupted.

The Repair phase is activated when the verifier has detected a corrupted replica during Challenge. The client acts as the repair coordinator, i.e., it coordinates the CSP's servers to repair the corruption. We take advantage of the fact that a CSP usually has premium bandwidth between its data centers (refer to Table 2) and permit the servers to collaborate among themselves to restore the corrupted replica (the key for generating distinct replicas is known to the CSP). Thus, the system only imposes a small management load on the client (data owner).

A detailed description of RDC − SR is provided in Fig-

We construct RDC − SR in three phases, Setup, Challenge, and Repair. All arithmetic operations are in $GF(p)$, unless noted otherwise explicitly.

Setup: The client runs $(K_1, K_2) \leftarrow$ KeyGen(1^{κ}), and picks s random numbers $\delta_1, \ldots, \delta_s \xleftarrow{R} GF(p)$. The client also chooses α and determines the values η and τ, and then executes: For $1 \leq i \leq t$:

1. Run $(t_{i1}, \ldots, t_{in}, F_i) \leftarrow$ GenReplicaAndMetadata$(K_1, K_2, F, i, \delta_1, \ldots, \delta_s, \eta)$

2. Send F_i to server S_i for storage (each S_i is located in a different data center of the CSP) and send the verification tags $t_{i1}, \ldots, t_{in}$ to each server .

The client may now delete the file F and stores only a small, constant, amount of data: $K_1, \delta_1, \ldots, \delta_s, \eta$, and τ. K_2 is made public.

Challenge: Client C uses spot checking to check possession of each replica F_i stored at server S_i. In this process, each server uses its stored replica and the corresponding verification tags to prove data possession. Suppose C challenges server S_i. Let query Q be the c-element set $\{(j, v_j)\}$, in which j denotes the index of the block to be challenged, and v_j is a randomly chosen value from $GF(p)$.

1. C generates Q and sends Q to server S_i

2. S_i runs $(\rho_1, \ldots, \rho_s, t) \leftarrow$ GenProof$(Q, F_i, t_{i1}, \ldots, t_{in})$

3. S_i sends to C the proof of possession $(\rho_1, \ldots, \rho_s, t)$

4. C checks whether the response time is larger than τ. If yes, C declares S_i as faulty. Otherwise, C checks the validity of the proof $(\rho_1, \ldots, \rho_s, t)$ by running CheckProof$(K_1, \delta_1, \ldots, \delta_s, Q, \rho_1, \ldots, \rho_s, t, i)$

Repair: Assume that in the Challenge phase C has identified a faulty server whose index is y (i.e., the corresponding replica has been corrupted). C acts as the repair coordinator. It communicates with the CSP, asks for a new server from the same data center to replace the corrupted server, and co-ordinates from where the new server can retrieve a healthy replica to restore the corrupted replica. Suppose S_i is selected to provide the healthy replica. The new server will reuse the index of the faulty server, namely, y.

1. Server S_y retrieves the replica $F_i = \{m_{i1}, \ldots, m_{in}\}$ and all the verification tags from server S_i

2. Server S_y generates its own replica:
   For $1 \leq j \leq n$:
   - For $1 \leq k \leq s$: $m_{yjk} = m_{ijk} - \sum_{l=1}^{\eta} \gamma_{K_2}(i||j||k||l) + \sum_{l=1}^{\eta} \gamma_{K_2}(y||j||k||l)$

Figure 2: RDC − SR: a replication-based RDC system with Server-side Repair

---

ures 2 and 3, together with the following explanation of the three phases.

The Setup phase. The client first generates keys K_1 and K_2. K_1 will be used to compute the verification tags and K_2 will be used in generating distinct replicas. It then picks s random numbers, η, and threshold τ (refer to Sec. 5 − Parameterization and Guidelines on how to exactly determine η and τ). The client then calls GenReplicaAndMetadata t times in order to generate t distinct replicas and the corresponding verification tags. Each replica will be sent to a server located in a different data center of the CSP. The entire set of verification tags will be sent to each server. The client may then delete the original file and only keep a small amount of key material.

KeyGen(1^κ): Randomly choose two keys: $K_1, K_2 \xleftarrow{R} \{0,1\}^\kappa$.
Return (K_1, K_2)

GenReplicaAndMetadata($K_1, K_2, F, i, \delta_1, \ldots, \delta_s, \eta$):

1. Parse F as $\{b_1, \ldots, b_n\}$

2. Generate the i-th replica:
   For $1 \leq j \leq n$:
   - Mask block b_j at the symbol level and get m_{ij}:
     For $1 \leq k \leq s$: $m_{ijk} = b_{jk} + \sum_{l=1}^{\eta} \gamma_{K_2}(i\|j\|k\|l)$

3. Compute verification tags:
   For $1 \leq j \leq n$: $t_{ij} = h_{K_1}(i\|j) + \sum_{k=1}^{s} \delta_k m_{ijk}$

4. Return $(t_{i1}, \ldots, t_{in}, F_i = \{m_{i1}, \ldots, m_{in}\})$

GenProof($Q, F_i, t_{i1}, \ldots, t_{in}$):

1. Parse Q as a set of c pairs (j, v_j). Parse F_i as $\{m_{i1}, \ldots, m_{in}\}$.

2. Compute ρ and t:
   - For $1 \leq k \leq s$: $\rho_k = \sum_{(j, v_j) \in Q} v_j m_{ijk} \mod p$
   - $t = \sum_{(j, v_j) \in Q} v_j t_{ij} \mod p$

3. Return $(\rho_1, \ldots, \rho_s, t)$

CheckProof($K_1, \delta_1, \ldots, \delta_s, Q, \rho_1, \ldots, \rho_s, t, i$):

1. Parse Q as a set of c pairs (j, v_j).

2. If $t = \sum_{(j, v_j) \in Q} v_j h_{K_1}(i\|j) + \sum_{k=1}^{s} \delta_k \rho_k \mod p$, return "success". Otherwise return "failure".

Figure 3: Components of RDC − SR

In GenReplicaAndMetadata, the client masks the original file at the symbol level, applying η masking operations to each symbol. Each masking operation consists of adding a pseudo-random value to the symbol; this pseudo-random value is the output of a PRF applied over the concatenation of the replica index, the block index, the symbol index, and an integer l ($l \in \{1 \ldots \eta\}$).

The Challenge phase. For this phase, we integrate spot checking [3, 15, 21] with our new model introduced in Sec. 2.2. The client (verifier) sends a challenge request to each of the t servers. For each challenge, the client selects c random replica blocks for checking. The challenged server parses the request, calls GenProof to generate the proof, and sends back the proof. If the client does not receive the proof within time τ, it marks that particular server as faulty and its replica as corrupt. Otherwise, the client checks the validity of the proof by calling CheckProof.

The Repair phase. During the Repair phase, the client acts as the repair coordinator; our approach here is novel compared to previous work, in which the client itself repairs the data by downloading the entire file to regenerate a corrupt replica [12, 7, 11]. The client contacts the CSP, reports the corruption, and coordinates the CSP's servers to repair the corruption. The server which is found faulty in the Challenge phase should be replaced by a new server from the same data center. The new server contacts one of the healthy servers, retrieves a replica, un-masks it to restore the original file, and masks the original file to regenerate the corrupted replica. The new server directly retrieves the entire set of verification tags from this healthy server (recall that the entire set of verification tags is stored at every server). Note that the size of the set of all verification tags is always small compared to the data.

5. Guidelines for using RDC − SR

In order to setup the system, the data owner must initially decide the type of adversary it wants to protect the data against. Concretely, by picking a value for α, the data owner seeks to protect its data against a CSP that is modeled as an α-cheating adversary. For example, by picking a small α, the data owner achieves protection against a CSP that will try to cheat by corrupting a large amount of the data. This type of corruption is easier to detect and, as a result, the data owner can afford to use a smaller masking factor. On the other hand, by picking a large α, the data owner seeks protection against a more stealthy CSP that only corrupts a small fraction of the data. As a result, the data owner needs to use a larger masking factor.

Once the data owner fixes α, it can derive the two parameters: η (the masking factor) and τ (the time threshold used to validate the audit protocol).

Estimating η. From Sec. 3, we have $T_i \leq min(t_i) + min(t_{ij}) + min(t_j) + min(t_R) - 2 * max(t_i)$, which can be further simplified as $T_i \leq t_{ij} + t_j - t_i + t_R$ (Let x be the time each of the c challenged file blocks contributes to the generation of the proof by the server. Since T_i is the upper bound on the execution time of the auditing protocol (as defined in Sec. 2.1), we have $c \cdot x \leq T_i$. Based on the triangle inequality, we always have $t_{ij} + t_j - t_i \geq 0$. To have a coarse evaluation of η, we neglect $t_{ij} + t_j - t_i$, which is always small compared to t_R (milliseconds compared to seconds, as shown in Table 4 of Appendix B which contains some typical values based on our experiments for Amazon S3). Thus, we get $c \cdot x \leq t_R$.

Let t_{prf} denote the time required to compute one PRF (specifically, one computation of the function γ used to mask a symbol in RDC − SR). Then, for a challenge that checks c blocks, assuming that the adversary adopts the best attack strategy (see Sec. 3.2), we have $t_R = (1 - \alpha) \cdot c \cdot s \cdot \eta \cdot t_{prf}$. We thus get $c \cdot x \leq t_R = (1 - \alpha) \cdot c \cdot s \cdot \eta \cdot t_{prf}$, which means that $\eta \geq \frac{x}{(1-\alpha) \cdot s \cdot t_{prf}}$ (recall that s is the number of symbols in a file block). The client should choose η as the smallest integer which satisfies this condition.

Estimating τ. The time threshold τ can be computed as $c \cdot x + 2 \cdot t_i$. As defined earlier in this section, x denotes the time each of the c challenged file blocks contributes to the generation of the proof by the server, which should include the time for accessing one block and computing the proof for one block. t_i denotes the network delay between the challenged server and the client.

It turns out it is not trivial to estimate x for the Amazon CSP. In our experiments, the value x exhibits some variation due to the fact that sampling a random block in Amazon S3 can be very large in some rare cases (in those cases it will be difficult to differentiate between benign and malicious CSP behavior). However, based on our experiments we observed that, out of 240 protocol executions, 95% of the values for x are within the range [0.025 sec, 0.034 sec] for the AWS Oregon region. Thus, the data owner should use the top value in this range (0.034 sec) to estimate x in the formula for τ if the data is stored in the Oregon S3 region. We propose three ways in which the data owner can acquire x: First of all, data owners can estimate x themselves by measuring it directly in the target data centers; Secondly, the CSP could determine such a range and publish it; Thirdly, it can be estimated by a trusted third party. Note that if x is estimated by data owners or trusted third parties, the CSP should not be able to differentiate the events of "estimating x" and "regular data access", thus it cannot affect the effectiveness of verification by artificially manipulating the value of x.

6. Security Analysis for RDC − SR

Our RDC − SR scheme is an RDC scheme and it can be easily shown that, in the context of each individual server that holds a replica, RDC − SR provides the data owner with a guarantee of data possession of that replica by using an efficient spot checking mechanism [3, 15]. Note that confidentiality of the data from the CSP is an orthogonal problem to RDC (although our RDC − SR scheme could easily achieve confidentiality by encrypting the original file and then storing masked replicas of the encrypted file).

As opposed to previous work on RDC, the paradigm we introduce in this paper allows the servers themselves to generate new replicas for repair purposes. This opens the door to a new attack, the *replicate on the fly (ROTF) attack*, in which the economically-motivated servers claim to store t replicas, but in reality they store less than $t|\mathbf{F}|$ data and generate the missing data on the fly upon being challenged by the client. The following theorem shows that RDC − SR can mitigate the ROTF attack executed by an α-cheating adversary (defined in Sec. 3.2):

THEOREM 6.1. *In* RDC − SR, *an α-cheating adversary can successfully execute the ROTF attack without being detected with a probability of at most $\alpha^c c(1-\alpha)$, where c is the number of file blocks checked by the client in a challenge.*

For fixed values of α, we can always choose c such that the probability that a server is cheating successfully without being detected becomes negligibly small. For example, if a server is storing only 90% of the data (*i.e.*, $\alpha = 0.9$), challenging $c = 400$ random blocks, ensures that the upper bound on the probability of server cheating is $1.99 * 10^{-17}$.

PROOF. Per Definition 3.1, an α-cheating adversary is an economically-motivated adversary that only uses $\alpha t|\mathbf{F}|$ storage (where $1/t \leq \alpha \leq 1$). We have established in Sec. 3.2 that the best data distribution strategy for cheating is when each malicious server stores only an α fraction of the blocks from the replica it is supposed to store. Thus each malicious server is missing an $(1-\alpha)$ fraction of the file blocks.

As described in Sec. 5, the time threshold τ in RDC − SR is computed based on the assumption that every time the client randomly checks c blocks from a file stored in one of the t servers, at least $(1-\alpha)c$ blocks are from the missing $(1-\alpha)$ fraction of the file, and thus the server has to compute $(1-\alpha)c$ blocks on the fly. However, if the number of checked blocks from the $(1-\alpha)$ missing fraction is less than $(1-\alpha)c$, then the cheating server will be able to successfully pass the check because it has to generate less than $(1-\alpha)c$ blocks on the fly and can provide a reply in a time less than τ.

When a server is missing an $(1-\alpha)$ fraction of the file blocks and the client randomly challenges c blocks, let P be the probability that less than $(1-\alpha)c$ blocks will be challenged among the missing file blocks. This is the probability that the cheating server is able to cheat successfully without being detected. We evaluate P next.

Evaluating P is equivalent to evaluating the probability that the number of challenged blocks that are among the non-missing α fraction of blocks is at least $c\alpha + 1$. The number of possible cases that more than $c\alpha + 1$ challenged

blocks are from the non-missing α fraction of the file is: $\binom{n\alpha}{c} + \binom{n\alpha}{c-1} + ... + \binom{n\alpha}{c-c(1-\alpha)+1}$, where n is the total number of file blocks.

Thus, $P = \frac{\binom{n\alpha}{c} + \binom{n\alpha}{c-1} + ... + \binom{n\alpha}{c-c(1-\alpha)+1}}{\binom{n}{c}}$. Considering that $\binom{n\alpha}{x-1} \leq \binom{n\alpha}{x}$ whenever $2 \leq x \leq \frac{n\alpha+1}{2}$, and that $c \leq \frac{n\alpha+1}{2}$ always holds in practice because c is a small constant in the RDC literature (*e.g.*, $c = 400$) compared to n, we have:
$$P \leq \frac{\binom{n\alpha}{c}c(1-\alpha)}{\binom{n}{c}} = \frac{\binom{n\alpha}{c}}{\binom{n}{c}}c(1-\alpha) = \frac{n\alpha(n\alpha-1)...(n\alpha-c+1)}{n(n-1)...(n-c+1)}c(1-$$
$$\alpha) = \frac{n\alpha}{n}\frac{n\alpha-1}{n-1}...\frac{n\alpha-c+1}{n-c+1}c(1-\alpha) = \alpha\frac{n}{n}\alpha\frac{n-\frac{1}{\alpha}}{n-1}...\alpha\frac{n-\frac{c-1}{\alpha}}{n-(c-1)}c(1-$$
$$\alpha) \leq \alpha^c c(1-\alpha).$$
Thus, $P \leq \alpha^c c(1-\alpha)$. $\square$

7. Implementation and Experiments

7.1 Background on Amazon's Cloud Services (AWS)

We provide some background for Amazon's cloud services within the United States, called Amazon Web Services (AWS). EC2 is Amazon's cloud computing service and S3 is Amazon's cloud storage service. In the United States, Amazon has three EC2 regions (US East - Virginia, US West - North California, and US West - Oregon) and three S3 regions (US Standard, US West - North California, and US West - Oregon). Based on our measurements in Table 2 and 3 of Appendix A, the following EC2 and S3 regions are located extremely close to each other and have very high network connection between them, thus we consider them in the same region: Virginia (EC2 US East - Virginia and S3 US Standard), N. California (EC2 US West - North California and S3 US West - North California), and Oregon (EC2 US West - Oregon and S3 US West - Oregon).

7.2 Experimental Setup

We build and test our prototype for RDC − SR on Amazon Web Services (AWS). Each server is run on an EC2 large instance (4 ECUs, 2 Cores, and 7.5GB Memory, created from Amazon Linux AMI 64-bit image). The client is run on a machine located in our institute, equipped with Intel Core 2 Duo system with two CPUs (each running at 3.0GHz, with a 6144KB cache), 333GHz frontside bus, 4GB RAM and a Hitachi HDP725032GLA360 360GB hard disk with ext4 file system. In the following, our EC2 instances and S3 data are located in the Oregon region, unless noted otherwise. The prototype for RDC − SR has been implemented in C and uses OpenSSL version 1.0.0e [1] for cryptographic operations. From Sec. 5, we have $\eta \geq \frac{x}{(1-\alpha)\cdot s \cdot t_{prf}}$ and we also choose $x = 0.034$ sec. We estimate $t_{prf} = 4.3$ μsec for an EC2 large instance (EC2 Oregon). We choose 40 KB for the file block size and 80-bit prime number p, thus s is 4000.

We use the following values for (α, η) in our experiments: $(0.6, 5), (0.7, 7), (0.8, 10)$ (recall from Sec. 5 that once α is fixed, η can be computed). We use these values for α to reflect an economically-motivated CSP (such a CSP would not likely be interested in saving a small amount of storage, so we don't consider cases when $\alpha > 0.8$). The experimental results are averaged over 20 runs, unless noted otherwise.

Preprocess. The file to be outsourced is preprocessed by an EC2 large instance, generating 3 different replicas and the corresponding verification tags. The replicas are then stored at 3 different S3 regions, one replica per region. All the verification tags are stored at every S3 region. In our

α	η	operation	throughput (MB/s)
0.6	5	masking	0.44
		verification tag	5.2
		total	0.41
0.7	7	masking	0.32
		verification tag	5.2
		total	0.3
0.8	10	masking	0.22
		verification tag	5.2
		total	0.21

Table 1: Preprocessing throughput

experiments, we adopt a slightly different strategy from the scheme described in Sec. 4: One of the 3 different replicas is the actual original file. This strategy speeds up the repairing of a corrupted replica, because the replica can be computed directly from the original file (a similar approach was proposed in [13, 19]).

We measure the time for masking, verification tag generation and total preprocessing for one masked replica under three sets of (α, η) parameters. We repeat the experiments for four different file sizes (20MB, 50MB, 80MB, and 100MB). Table 1 shows the throughput for total preprocessing and its different components.

We have several observations for Table 1: First, the throughput of masking operation decreases when α increases. This is expected because a larger α means that it is more difficult to detect the adversarial behavior, thus, we need a larger η, hence more computations are required for masking. Secondly, the throughput of verification tag computation is independent of α, due to the fact that the verification tags are computed over the masked replica, which is independent of η, hence independent of α. Thirdly, the throughput of total preprocessing, which includes masking and verification tag computation, is always close to but a little smaller than the throughput of masking, since the verification tag computation is very efficient (can generate verification tags for more than 5MB data in one second) and only has a small impact to the total preprocessing time.

Challenge. The client issues a challenge to the server (run in an EC2 large instance). The server samples blocks from S3 in the same region, and computes and sends back the proof. The client then checks the proof. For simplicity, we only challenge the server running in EC2 Oregon which is responsible for the replica stored in S3 Oregon. The number of blocks to be challenged is $c = 400$, which provides a high guarantee to detect data corruption by the server [3]. For the chosen values of α (Table 1) and c, the probability that a server performs the ROTF attack without being detected is less than $1.38 * 10^{-37}$ (cf. Sec. 6). Amazon S3 offers a REST API to access data, which is based on the HTTP/1.0 protocol. Although HTTP supports operations on multiple ranges of the target object in one request, Amazon S3 only supports one range. This means that in order to sample 400 random blocks, we must send 400 different requests for a one-block range. This explains partially the large variation we observe in block access time for S3 (Figures 4(b) and 5(b)), thus we average the block access time over 100 runs. We examine two cases:

- *Benign case:* The CSP is honest, *i.e.*, it strictly stores the replicas in the corresponding regions according to the con-

tract. Upon challenge, the server uses the data from the same region to pass the challenge. In this case, the total server computation includes sampling challenged blocks from S3 of the same region and computing the proof.

- *Adversarial case:* The CSP is cheating by not storing all replicas in their entirety according to the contract. The malicious CSP adopts the best attack strategy described in Sec. 3.2. Because the server will only have an α fraction of the challenged blocks, it retrieves the other $(1 - \alpha)$ fraction from another region and recreates the missing blocks on the fly. The total server computation for this case includes sampling challenged blocks from S3 of the same region, generating a $1 - \alpha$ fraction of the challenged blocks (by masking the original file blocks), and computing the proof.

We repeat the experiments for different sets of (α, η) parameters and for different file sizes. Figure 4 and 5 show the server computation and client computation for both cases.

For the benign case, we observe from Fig. 4 that the total server computation and its various components as well as the client (verifier) computation are independent of file size and of α. This is expected because: First of all, we rely on spot checking [3] which always randomly samples a fixed number of blocks from the masked replica, thus can maintain constant server/client computation. Secondly, during a challenge, the operations on both server and client are over the masked replica, which is independent of η, hence independent of α. Figure 4(d) shows that the time for the client to check the proof is less than 7 *msec*, which justifies our claim that the system imposes a small load on the verifier during the challenge phase.

For the adversarial case, we observe from Fig. 5 that the total server computation and its various components are independent of filesize. The reason has been explained in the benign case. For Figure 5(c), we expected to see that the masking time is independent of α, because: The malicious server always stores only an α fraction of the corresponding data, and generates the $1 - \alpha$ fraction of challenged blocks on the fly (by masking). Larger α means that the malicious server has to generate less challenged blocks but generating one challenged block will be more expensive, thus, the masking time for the $1 - \alpha$ fraction of challenged blocks should be almost constant. However, Figure 5(c) shows that for the case of $\alpha = 0.7$, the masking time is larger than those of other two cases. This discrepancy can be explained because we must always choose η as an integer number. The server masking time is $400(1-\alpha) \cdot s \cdot \eta \cdot t_{prf}$, which is determined by the multiplication of $1-\alpha$ and η. For the case of $\alpha = 0.7$, the minimum integer for η is 7, thus, $(1 - \alpha) \cdot \eta = 2.1$. For both cases $\alpha = 0.6$ and $\alpha = 0.8$, $(1-\alpha) \cdot \eta = 2 < 2.1$. This explains where such a discrepancy comes from. However, note that there is a lower bound on the server masking time, because $400(1-\alpha) \cdot s \cdot \eta \cdot t_{prf} \geq 400(1-\alpha) \cdot s \cdot t_{prf} \cdot \frac{x}{(1-\alpha) \cdot s \cdot t_{prf}} = 400x = 13.6$ *sec*. We observe that most of the points in Figure 5(c) are over this lower bound, except the point in 20MB filesize when $\alpha = 0.6$, but we still consider this point as valid since it is only 1% smaller. The existence of the lower bound for the server masking time guarantees that even if the malicious server has the magic power to access the data and compute the proof instantly (*i.e.*, the times shown in Figure 5(b) and Figure 5(d) are 0), it still cannot cheat successfully, since the time for generating the $1 - \alpha$ fraction of challenged blocks

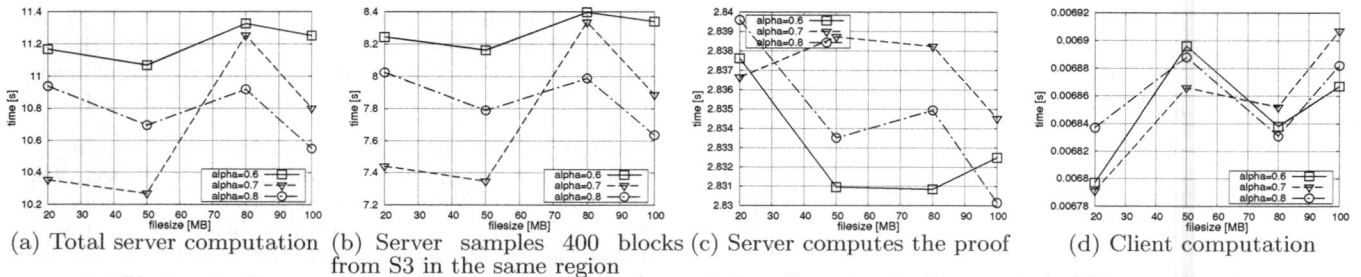

(a) Total server computation (b) Server samples 400 blocks from S3 in the same region (c) Server computes the proof (d) Client computation

Figure 4: Computational cost for the server and the client in challenge phase (benign case).

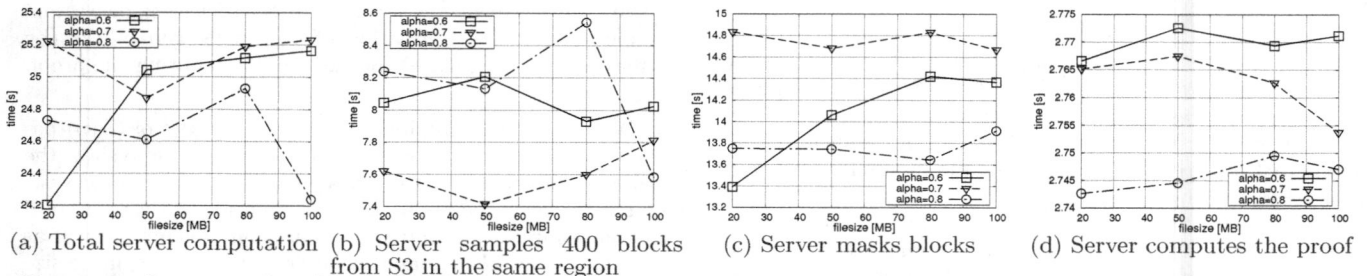

(a) Total server computation (b) Server samples 400 blocks from S3 in the same region (c) Server masks blocks (d) Server computes the proof

Figure 5: Computational cost for the server and its various components in challenge phase (adversarial case).

will be always larger than $400x$, which is the total server computation for the benign case.

Figure 5(d) shows that the time for the server to compute the proof varies with α. However, we can still conclude that this time is independent of α given that the variance is quite small (around 1%).

According to the guidelines for establishing the time threshold τ in Sec. 5, τ should be 13.7 sec (c=400, $x = 0.034$ sec, $t_i = 0.045$ sec based on our experiments). We see that 95% of the individual runs for Figure 4(a) are below this threshold, and 100% of the individual runs for Figure 5(a) are above this threshold. This confirms the practical value of using a time threshold to establish if the CSP is malicious.

Repair. We assume that the replica stored in S3 Oregon has been found corrupted, and the replica stored in S3 California is retrieved to repair the corruption. The repair server runs in a large instance from EC2 Oregon. The server downloads the replica from S3 California and masks it to generate the replica for S3 Oregon. The server also downloads all the verification tags from another S3 region (this time is negligible in our experiment). The results are shown in Figure 6 (this includes time for masking to generate a new replica, as described Table 1). We observe from Figure 6(a) that, for repairing one replica, total server computation increases with α. This is because, as shown in Preprocessing, larger α will result in larger masking computation, and the masking computation dominates the total repair computation.

One significant advantage in the repair phase is that the client can be kept lightweight, e.g., the client only needs to exchange a few messages to coordinate the repair procedure. This justifies our claim that the system imposes a small management load on the data owner during repair.

8. Related Work

RDC for the single-server setting. Early RDC schemes have focused on ensuring the integrity of outsourced data in the static setting. Such schemes include Provable Data

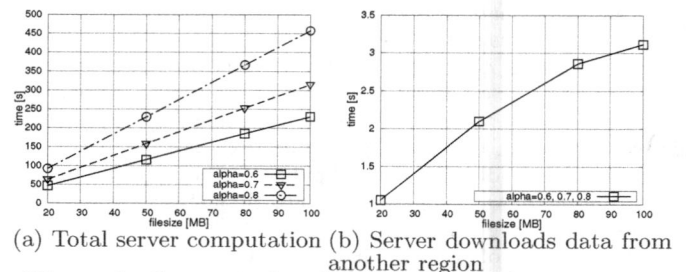

(a) Total server computation (b) Server downloads data from another region

Figure 6: Computational cost for repairing a replica.

Possession (PDP) [3] and Proofs of Retrievability (PoR) [15, 21]. Later RDC schemes investigated models that can provide strong integrity guarantees while supporting dynamic operations on the outsourced data [5, 14, 25, 23, 28, 10, 9].

RDCs for the multiple-server setting. RDC has been extended to the multiple-server setting (distributed RDC). Curtmola et al. proposed MR-PDP [12], an efficient RDC scheme for replication-based distributed storage systems, which differentiates the replicas by random masking. We adapt this technique in our work. Bowers et al. [7] and Wang et al. [24] built RDC schemes for erasure coding-based distributed storage systems. Chen et al. [11] proposed an RDC scheme for network coding-based distributed storage systems. All the aforementioned distributed RDCs adopt client-side repair, in which the client is intensively involved in the repair procedure, i.e., the client will retrieve the data, generate and upload the new data to repair the corruption. Our work proposes server-side repair, a novel strategy which is different from all the previous distributed RDCs.

A new direction for RDC. All the previous RDC schemes are cryptography-based, i.e., the security of the proposed schemes are inherited from the security of the cryptographic primitives. Bowers et al. [8] propose RAFT, a new time-based RDC scheme which can enable a client to obtain a proof that a given file is distributed across an expected number of physical storage devices in a single datacenter.

Although RAFT and our work share the idea of using a time-based mechanism to detect malicious behavior, they are fundamentally different in their basic approach and goals, and in the system and adversarial models. *First*, while in RDC − SR the replicas are differentiated based on controllable masking to mitigate the ROTF attack, RAFT mainly relies on the I/O bottleneck of a single hard drive, specifically, on the fact that the time required for two parallel reads from two different drives is clearly less that the time required for two sequential reads from a single drive. *Second*, in RDC − SR the file is replicated t times and the t replicas are stored in t different data centers (which may belong to the same CSP or to different CSPs). Within one data center, RDC − SR does not impose requirements on how exactly should the replica be stored. The data owner seeks to enable the self-repairing functionality while ensuring that a certain number of replicas are stored in the cloud at all times, so that the desired level of reliability is maintained. In RAFT, the file is encoded and is stored by the cloud server using the desired number of hard drives. The data owner wants to ensure that the server stores the file so that it can tolerate a certain number of hard drive failures. *Third*, in RDC − SR we introduce the α-cheating adversary, in which the cloud servers collude with each other to cheat by only storing an α fraction of the contractual storage, and there are no requirements for how exactly the adversary stores the data on the hard drives. In RAFT, a cheap-and-lazy adversary tries to cut corners by storing less redundant data on a smaller number of disks or by mapping file blocks unevenly across hard drives.

Benson et al. [6] propose another time-based model (BDS model) to guarantee that multiple replicas are distributed to different data centers of the CSP. Our work adapts this model to enable the server-side repair.

Watson et al. [26] propose LoSt, which formalizes the concept of Proofs of Location (PoL). A PoL relies on a geolocation scheme [6] and a Proof of Retrievability (PoR) scheme. We summarize the differences between RDC − SR and LoSt. *First*, the goals are different. RDC − SR aims at enabling self-repair, a novel functionality for replication-based distributed storage systems that, when combined with periodic integrity checks provides an efficient mechanism to ensure long-term data reliability. In particular, RDC − SR does not try to enforce specific locations of the data. LoSt aims at ensuring that the outsourced file copies are stored within the specified region and requires a landmark infrastructure to verify the location of the data. *Second*, the system model is different. RDC − SR has two entities, namely, the client and the storage servers (CSP), in which the client is always trusted and the storage servers are untrusted and may collude. In LoSt there are three entities, the client, the CSP, and the data centers, and the model assumes that theres is no collusion between the CSP and the data centers. *Third*, the basic idea for the solution is different. RDC − SR relies on the differentiation of the replicas based on controllable masking to defend against the ROTF (replicate on the fly) attack. Instead, LoSt relies on "recoding" to efficiently differentiate (done at the CSP with CSP's private key) the file tags for each server, while each server will keep the same file copy.

Other work. Similar with the work of Reiter at al. [18],

our scheme relies on the idea that only a prover which has the data can respond quickly enough to pass a challenge. Unlike our work however, their work is set in the context of P2P networks and the verifier (client) needs to keep the data for the verification purpose.

9. Acknowledgements

This research was sponsored by the US National Science Foundation CAREER grant 1054754-CNS.

10. References

[1] OpenSSL. http://www.openssl.org/.

[2] Wget. http://www.gnu.org/software/wget/.

[3] G. Ateniese, R. Burns, R. Curtmola, J. Herring, O. Khan, L. Kissner, Z. Peterson, and D. Song. Remote data checking using provable data possession. *ACM Trans. Inf. Syst. Secur.*, 14, June 2011.

[4] G. Ateniese, R. Burns, R. Curtmola, J. Herring, L. Kissner, Z. Peterson, and D. Song. Provable data possession at untrusted stores. In *Proc. of ACM Conference on Computer and Communications Security (CCS '07)*, 2007.

[5] G. Ateniese, R. D. Pietro, L. V. Mancini, and G. Tsudik. Scalable and efficient provable data possession. In *Proc. of International ICST Conference on Security and Privacy in Communication Networks (SecureComm '08)*, 2008.

[6] K. Benson, R. Dowsley, and H. Shacham. Do you know where your cloud files are? In *Proc. of ACM Cloud Computing Security Workshop (CCSW '11)*, 2011.

[7] K. Bowers, A. Oprea, and A. Juels. HAIL: A high-availability and integrity layer for cloud storage. In *Proc. of ACM Conference on Computer and Communications Security (CCS '09)*, 2009.

[8] K. D. Bowers, M. V. Dijk, A. Juels, A. Oprea, and R. L. Rivest. How to tell if your cloud files are vulnerable to drive crashes. In *Proc. of ACM Conference on Computer and Communications Security (CCS '11)*, 2011.

[9] B. Chen and R. Curtmola. Poster: Robust dynamic remote data checking for public clouds. In *Proc. of ACM Conference on Computer and Communications Security (CCS '12)*, 2012.

[10] B. Chen and R. Curtmola. Robust dynamic provable data possession. In *Proc. of International Conference on Security and Privacy in Cloud Computing (ICDCS-SPCC '12)*, 2012.

[11] B. Chen, R. Curtmola, G. Ateniese, and R. Burns. Remote data checking for network coding-based distributed storage systems. In *Proc. of ACM Cloud Computing Security Workshop (CCSW '10)*, 2010.

[12] R. Curtmola, O. Khan, R. Burns, and G. Ateniese. MR-PDP: Multiple-replica provable data possession. In *Proc. of International Conference on Distributed Computing Systems (ICDCS '08)*, 2008.

[13] A. G. Dimakis, P. B. Godfrey, Y. Wu, M. O. Wainwright, and K. Ramchandran. Network coding for distributed storage systems. *IEEE Trans. on Inf. Theory*, 56, Sept. 2010.

[14] C. Erway, A. Kupcu, C. Papamanthou, and R. Tamassia. Dynamic provable data possession. In

Proc. of ACM Conference on Computer and Communications Security (CCS '09), 2009.

[15] A. Juels and B. S. Kaliski. PORs: Proofs of retrievability for large files. In *Proc. of ACM Conference on Computer and Communications Security (CCS '07)*, 2007.

[16] H. Krawczyk. LFSR-based hashing and authentication. In *Proc. of Annual International Cryptology Conference (CRYPTO '94)*, 1994.

[17] Z. N. J. Peterson, M. Gondree, and R. Beverly. A position paper on data sovereignty: the importance of geolocating data in the cloud. In *Proc. of USENIX Workshop on Hot Topics in Cloud Computing (HotCloud '11)*, 2011.

[18] M. K. Reiter, V. Sekar, C. Spensky, and Z. Zhang. Making peer-assisted content distribution robust to collusion using bandwidth puzzles. *Information Systems Security*, pages 132–147, 2009.

[19] R. Rodrigues and B. Liskov. High availability in dhts: Erasure coding vs. replication. In *Proc. of International workshop on Peer-To-Peer Systems (IPTPS '05)*, 2005.

[20] P. Rogaway. Bucket hashing and its application to fast message authentication. In *Proc. of Annual International Cryptology Conference (CRYPTO '95)*, 1995.

[21] H. Shacham and B. Waters. Compact proofs of retrievability. In *Proc. of Annual International Conference on the Theory and Application of Cryptology and Information Security (ASIACRYPT '08)*, 2008.

[22] V. Shoup. On fast and provably secure message authentication based on universal hashing. In *Proc. of Annual International Cryptology Conference (CRYPTO '96)*, 1996.

[23] E. Stefanov, M. van Dijk, A. Oprea, and A. Juels. Iris: A scalable cloud file system with efficient integrity checks. In *Proc. of Annual Computer Security Applications Conference (ACSAC '12)*, 2012.

[24] C. Wang, Q. Wang, K. Ren, and W. Lou. Ensuring data storage security in cloud computing. In *Proc. of IEEE International Workshop on Quality of Service (IWQoS '09)*, 2009.

[25] Q. Wang, C. Wang, K. Ren, W. Lou, and J. Li. Enabling public auditability and data dynamics for storage security in cloud computing. *IEEE Trans. on Parallel and Distributed Syst.*, 22(5), May 2011.

[26] G. J. Watson, R. Safavi-Naini, M. Alimomeni, M. E. Locasto, and S. Narayan. Lost: location based storage. In *Proc. of ACM Cloud Computing Security Workshop (CCSW '12)*, 2012.

[27] M. N. Wegman and J. L. Carter. New hash functions and their use in authentication and set equality. *Journal of Computer and System Sciences*, 22(3):265 – 279, 1981.

[28] Q. Zheng and S. Xu. Fair and dynamic proofs of retrievability. In *Proc. of ACM Conference on Data and Application Security and Privacy (CODASPY '11)*, 2011.

APPENDIX

A. Measurements for the Amazon CSP

Tables 2 and 3 show the bandwidth and the propagation delay between Amazon S3 data centers (regions) and between our institution and different S3 data centers (regions). For measurements, we used an EC2 instance within the corresponding Amazon data centers. To measure bandwidth, we used Wget [2] to download a large file. To measure the propagation delay, we adopt the method introduced in [6] that is, we measure the time between sending a SYN packet and receiving a SYN-ACK packet of a TCP connection, half of which is considered as the propagation delay. All the results in Tables 2 and 3 are averaged over 20 runs.

	Virginia	N. California	Oregon
Virginia	32.7	11.62	12.59
N. California	11.95	48.03	36.05
Oregon	14.07	26.43	52.18
Our institution	0.816	0.456	0.439

Table 2: Download bandwidth (in MB/s): (rows 1-3) between S3 data centers (regions); (row 4) between our institution and different S3 data centers.

	Virginia	N. California	Oregon
Virginia	0.579	40	49
N. California	40	0.705	11
Oregon	49	11	0.212
Our institution	4	40	45

Table 3: Propagation delay (in milliseconds): (rows 1-3) between S3 data centers (regions); (row 4) between our institution and different S3 data centers.

B. Network Delays for Amazon CSP

Table 4 shows the values of $t_{ij} + t_j - t_i$ for Amazon AWS, which are used in Sec. 5.

i	j	$t_{ij} + t_j - t_i$ (in seconds)
Virginia	N. California	0.08
Virginia	Oregon	0.098
N. California	Virginia	0.08
N. California	Oregon	0.022
Oregon	Virginia	0.098
Oregon	N. California	0.022

Table 4: Values of $t_{ij} + t_j - t_i$ if the client is located within a data region of AWS S3

C. Sampling Blocks from Amazon S3

We wrote a program running in an EC2 instance (Amazon Virginia region) to randomly sample 4KB blocks from S3 Virginia region. We collect the time in Table 5. All the results are averaged over 20 runs.

# of blocks	1	10	40	400
time (sec.)	0.026062	0.260492	1.024863	10.191946

Table 5: The time for randomly sampling 4KB blocks from Amazon S3 Virginia region

Author Index

www.ingramcontent.com/pod-product-compliance
Lightning Source LLC
Chambersburg PA
CBHW080703220326
41598CB00033B/5288